Artificial Intelligence

A Modern Approach

Third Edition

Stuart Russell

Peter Norvig

PEARSON

Authorized adaptation from the United States edition, entitled *Artificial Intelligence: A Modern Approach, Third Edition,* ISBN 9780136042594, by Stuart Russell and Peter Norvig, published by Pearson Education Inc.© 2010, Pearson Education Inc.

Indian Subcontinent Version

ISBN: 978-93-325-1869-8

First Impression

This edition is authorized for sale only in India, Bangladesh, Bhutan, Pakistan, Nepal, Sri Lanka and the Maldives. Circulation of this edition outside of these territories is UNAUTHORIZED.

Published by Dorling Kindersley (India) Pvt. Ltd., licensees of Pearson Education in South Asia.

Head Office: 7th Floor, Knowledge Boulevard, A-8(A), Sector 62, Noida 201 309, UP, India.
Registered Office: 11 Community Centre, Panchsheel Park, New Delhi 110 017, India.

Printed in India by Repro India Ltd.

Table of Contents

INTRODUCTION

In which we try to explain why we consider artificial intelligence to be a subject most worthy of study, and in which we try to decide what exactly it is, this being a good thing to decide before embarking.

INTELLIGENCE We call ourselves *Homo sapiens*—man the wise—because our **intelligence** is so important to us. For thousands of years, we have tried to understand *how we think*; that is, how a mere handful of matter can perceive, understand, predict, and manipulate a world far larger and more complicated than itself. The field of **artificial intelligence**, or AI, goes further still: it attempts not just to understand but also to *build* intelligent entities.

ARTIFICIAL INTELLIGENCE

AI is one of the newest fields in science and engineering. Work started in earnest soon after World War II, and the name itself was coined in 1956. Along with molecular biology, AI is regularly cited as the "field I would most like to be in" by scientists in other disciplines. A student in physics might reasonably feel that all the good ideas have already been taken by Galileo, Newton, Einstein, and the rest. AI, on the other hand, still has openings for several full-time Einsteins and Edisons.

AI currently encompasses a huge variety of subfields, ranging from the general (learning and perception) to the specific, such as playing chess, proving mathematical theorems, writing poetry, driving a car on a crowded street, and diagnosing diseases. AI is relevant to any intellectual task; it is truly a universal field.

1 WHAT IS AI?

We have claimed that AI is exciting, but we have not said what it *is*. In Figure 1 we see eight definitions of AI, laid out along two dimensions. The definitions on top are concerned with *thought processes* and *reasoning*, whereas the ones on the bottom address *behavior*. The definitions on the left measure success in terms of fidelity to *human* performance, whereas the ones on the right measure against an *ideal* performance measure, called **rationality**. A system is rational if it does the "right thing," given what it knows.

RATIONALITY

Historically, all four approaches to AI have been followed, each by different people with different methods. A human-centered approach must be in part an empirical science, in-

From Chapter 1 of *Artificial Intelligence: A Modern Approach*, Third Edition. Stuart Russell and Peter Norvig.

Thinking Humanly	Thinking Rationally
"The exciting new effort to make computers think ... *machines with minds*, in the full and literal sense." (Haugeland, 1985)	"The study of mental faculties through the use of computational models." (Charniak and McDermott, 1985)
"[The automation of] activities that we associate with human thinking, activities such as decision-making, problem solving, learning ..." (Bellman, 1978)	"The study of the computations that make it possible to perceive, reason, and act." (Winston, 1992)
Acting Humanly	**Acting Rationally**
"The art of creating machines that perform functions that require intelligence when performed by people." (Kurzweil, 1990)	"Computational Intelligence is the study of the design of intelligent agents." (Poole *et al.*, 1998)
"The study of how to make computers do things at which, at the moment, people are better." (Rich and Knight, 1991)	"AI ... is concerned with intelligent behavior in artifacts." (Nilsson, 1998)

Figure 1 Some definitions of artificial intelligence, organized into four categories.

volving observations and hypotheses about human behavior. A rationalist[1] approach involves a combination of mathematics and engineering. The various group have both disparaged and helped each other. Let us look at the four approaches in more detail.

1.1 Acting humanly: The Turing Test approach

TURING TEST

The **Turing Test**, proposed by Alan Turing (1950), was designed to provide a satisfactory operational definition of intelligence. A computer passes the test if a human interrogator, after posing some written questions, cannot tell whether the written responses come from a person or from a computer. Programming a computer to pass a rigorously applied test provides plenty to work on. The computer would need to possess the following capabilities:

NATURAL LANGUAGE PROCESSING

KNOWLEDGE REPRESENTATION

AUTOMATED REASONING

MACHINE LEARNING

- **natural language processing** to enable it to communicate successfully in English;
- **knowledge representation** to store what it knows or hears;
- **automated reasoning** to use the stored information to answer questions and to draw new conclusions;
- **machine learning** to adapt to new circumstances and to detect and extrapolate patterns.

[1] By distinguishing between *human* and *rational* behavior, we are not suggesting that humans are necessarily "irrational" in the sense of "emotionally unstable" or "insane." One merely need note that we are not perfect: not all chess players are grandmasters; and, unfortunately, not everyone gets an A on the exam. Some systematic errors in human reasoning are cataloged by Kahneman *et al.* (1982).

Turing's test deliberately avoided direct physical interaction between the interrogator and the computer, because *physical* simulation of a person is unnecessary for intelligence. However, the so-called **total Turing Test** includes a video signal so that the interrogator can test the subject's perceptual abilities, as well as the opportunity for the interrogator to pass physical objects "through the hatch." To pass the total Turing Test, the computer will need

TOTAL TURING TEST

- **computer vision** to perceive objects, and
- **robotics** to manipulate objects and move about.

COMPUTER VISION

ROBOTICS

These six disciplines compose most of AI, and Turing deserves credit for designing a test that remains relevant 60 years later. Yet AI researchers have devoted little effort to passing the Turing Test, believing that it is more important to study the underlying principles of intelligence than to duplicate an exemplar. The quest for "artificial flight" succeeded when the Wright brothers and others stopped imitating birds and started using wind tunnels and learning about aerodynamics. Aeronautical engineering texts do not define the goal of their field as making "machines that fly so exactly like pigeons that they can fool even other pigeons."

1.2 Thinking humanly: The cognitive modeling approach

If we are going to say that a given program thinks like a human, we must have some way of determining how humans think. We need to get *inside* the actual workings of human minds. There are three ways to do this: through introspection—trying to catch our own thoughts as they go by; through psychological experiments—observing a person in action; and through brain imaging—observing the brain in action. Once we have a sufficiently precise theory of the mind, it becomes possible to express the theory as a computer program. If the program's input–output behavior matches corresponding human behavior, that is evidence that some of the program's mechanisms could also be operating in humans. For example, Allen Newell and Herbert Simon, who developed GPS, the "General Problem Solver" (Newell and Simon, 1961), were not content merely to have their program solve problems correctly. They were more concerned with comparing the trace of its reasoning steps to traces of human subjects solving the same problems. The interdisciplinary field of **cognitive science** brings together computer models from AI and experimental techniques from psychology to construct precise and testable theories of the human mind.

COGNITIVE SCIENCE

Cognitive science is a fascinating field in itself, worthy of several textbooks and at least one encyclopedia (Wilson and Keil, 1999). We will occasionally comment on similarities or differences between AI techniques and human cognition. Real cognitive science, however, is necessarily based on experimental investigation of actual humans or animals. We will leave that for other texts, as we assume the reader has only a computer for experimentation.

In the early days of AI there was often confusion between the approaches: an author would argue that an algorithm performs well on a task and that it is *therefore* a good model of human performance, or vice versa. Modern authors separate the two kinds of claims; this distinction has allowed both AI and cognitive science to develop more rapidly. The two fields continue to fertilize each other, most notably in computer vision, which incorporates neurophysiological evidence into computational models.

1.3 Thinking rationally: The "laws of thought" approach

SYLLOGISM

The Greek philosopher Aristotle was one of the first to attempt to codify "right thinking," that is, irrefutable reasoning processes. His **syllogisms** provided patterns for argument structures that always yielded correct conclusions when given correct premises—for example, "Socrates is a man; all men are mortal; therefore, Socrates is mortal." These laws of thought were supposed to govern the operation of the mind; their study initiated the field called **logic**.

LOGIC

Logicians in the 19th century developed a precise notation for statements about all kinds of objects in the world and the relations among them. (Contrast this with ordinary arithmetic notation, which provides only for statements about *numbers*.) By 1965, programs existed that could, in principle, solve *any* solvable problem described in logical notation. (Although if no solution exists, the program might loop forever.) The so-called **logicist** tradition within artificial intelligence hopes to build on such programs to create intelligent systems.

LOGICIST

There are two main obstacles to this approach. First, it is not easy to take informal knowledge and state it in the formal terms required by logical notation, particularly when the knowledge is less than 100% certain. Second, there is a big difference between solving a problem "in principle" and solving it in practice. Even problems with just a few hundred facts can exhaust the computational resources of any computer unless it has some guidance as to which reasoning steps to try first. Although both of these obstacles apply to *any* attempt to build computational reasoning systems, they appeared first in the logicist tradition.

1.4 Acting rationally: The rational agent approach

AGENT

An **agent** is just something that acts (*agent* comes from the Latin *agere*, to do). Of course, all computer programs do something, but computer agents are expected to do more: operate autonomously, perceive their environment, persist over a prolonged time period, adapt to change, and create and pursue goals. A **rational agent** is one that acts so as to achieve the best outcome or, when there is uncertainty, the best expected outcome.

RATIONAL AGENT

In the "laws of thought" approach to AI, the emphasis was on correct inferences. Making correct inferences is sometimes *part* of being a rational agent, because one way to act rationally is to reason logically to the conclusion that a given action will achieve one's goals and then to act on that conclusion. On the other hand, correct inference is not *all* of rationality; in some situations, there is no provably correct thing to do, but something must still be done. There are also ways of acting rationally that cannot be said to involve inference. For example, recoiling from a hot stove is a reflex action that is usually more successful than a slower action taken after careful deliberation.

All the skills needed for the Turing Test also allow an agent to act rationally. Knowledge representation and reasoning enable agents to reach good decisions. We need to be able to generate comprehensible sentences in natural language to get by in a complex society. We need learning not only for erudition, but also because it improves our ability to generate effective behavior.

The rational-agent approach has two advantages over the other approaches. First, it is more general than the "laws of thought" approach because correct inference is just one of several possible mechanisms for achieving rationality. Second, it is more amenable to scientific development than are approaches based on human behavior or human thought. The standard of rationality is mathematically well defined and completely general, and can be "unpacked" to generate agent designs that provably achieve it. Human behavior, on the other hand, is well adapted for one specific environment and is defined by, well, the sum total of all the things that humans do. *This text concentrates on general principles of rational agents and on components for constructing them.* Despite the apparent simplicity with which the problem can be stated, an enormous variety of issues come up when we try to solve it.

One important point to keep in mind: Achieving perfect rationality—always doing the right thing—is not feasible in complicated environments. The computational demands are just too high. We will adopt the working hypothesis that perfect rationality is a good starting point for analysis. It simplifies the problem and provides the appropriate setting for most of the foundational material in the field. **Limited rationality** means acting appropriately when there is not enough time to do all the computations one might like.

LIMITED RATIONALITY

2 THE FOUNDATIONS OF ARTIFICIAL INTELLIGENCE

In this section, we provide a brief history of the disciplines that contributed ideas, viewpoints, and techniques to AI. Like any history, this one is forced to concentrate on a small number of people, events, and ideas and to ignore others that also were important. We organize the history around a series of questions. We certainly would not wish to give the impression that these questions are the only ones the disciplines address or that the disciplines have all been working toward AI as their ultimate fruition.

2.1 Philosophy

- Can formal rules be used to draw valid conclusions?
- How does the mind arise from a physical brain?
- Where does knowledge come from?
- How does knowledge lead to action?

Aristotle (384–322 B.C.) was the first to formulate a precise set of laws governing the rational part of the mind. He developed an informal system of syllogisms for proper reasoning, which in principle allowed one to generate conclusions mechanically, given initial premises. Much later, Ramon Lull (d. 1315) had the idea that useful reasoning could actually be carried out by a mechanical artifact. Thomas Hobbes (1588–1679) proposed that reasoning was like numerical computation, that "we add and subtract in our silent thoughts." The automation of computation itself was already well under way. Around 1500, Leonardo da Vinci (1452–1519) designed but did not build a mechanical calculator; recent reconstructions have shown the design to be functional. The first known calculating machine was constructed around 1623 by the German scientist Wilhelm Schickard (1592–1635), although the Pascaline, built in 1642 by Blaise Pascal (1623–1662), is more famous. Pascal wrote that "the arithmetical machine produces effects which appear nearer to thought than all the actions of animals." Gottfried Wilhelm Leibniz (1646–1716) built a mechanical device intended to carry out operations on concepts rather than numbers, but its scope was rather limited. Leibniz did surpass Pascal by building a calculator that could add, subtract, multiply, and take roots, whereas the Pascaline could only add and subtract. Some speculated that machines might not just do calculations but actually be able to think and act on their own. In his 1651 book *Leviathan*, Thomas Hobbes suggested the idea of an "artificial animal," arguing "For what is the heart but a spring; and the nerves, but so many strings; and the joints, but so many wheels."

It's one thing to say that the mind operates, at least in part, according to logical rules, and to build physical systems that emulate some of those rules; it's another to say that the mind itself *is* such a physical system. René Descartes (1596–1650) gave the first clear discussion of the distinction between mind and matter and of the problems that arise. One problem with a purely physical conception of the mind is that it seems to leave little room for free will: if the mind is governed entirely by physical laws, then it has no more free will than a rock "deciding" to fall toward the center of the earth. Descartes was a strong advocate of the power of reasoning in understanding the world, a philosophy now called **rationalism**, and one that counts Aristotle and Leibnitz as members. But Descartes was also a proponent of **dualism**. He held that there is a part of the human mind (or soul or spirit) that is outside of nature, exempt from physical laws. Animals, on the other hand, did not possess this dual quality; they could be treated as machines. An alternative to dualism is **materialism**, which holds that the brain's operation according to the laws of physics *constitutes* the mind. Free will is simply the way that the perception of available choices appears to the choosing entity.

RATIONALISM

DUALISM

MATERIALISM

Given a physical mind that manipulates knowledge, the next problem is to establish the source of knowledge. The **empiricism** movement, starting with Francis Bacon's (1561–1626) *Novum Organum*,[2] is characterized by a dictum of John Locke (1632–1704): "Nothing is in the understanding, which was not first in the senses." David Hume's (1711–1776) *A Treatise of Human Nature* (Hume, 1739) proposed what is now known as the principle of **induction**: that general rules are acquired by exposure to repeated associations between their elements. Building on the work of Ludwig Wittgenstein (1889–1951) and Bertrand Russell (1872–1970), the famous Vienna Circle, led by Rudolf Carnap (1891–1970), developed the doctrine of **logical positivism**. This doctrine holds that all knowledge can be characterized by logical theories connected, ultimately, to **observation sentences** that correspond to sensory inputs; thus logical positivism combines rationalism and empiricism.[3] The **confirmation theory** of Carnap and Carl Hempel (1905–1997) attempted to analyze the acquisition of knowledge from experience. Carnap's book *The Logical Structure of the World* (1928) defined an explicit computational procedure for extracting knowledge from elementary experiences. It was probably the first theory of mind as a computational process.

EMPIRICISM

INDUCTION

LOGICAL POSITIVISM

OBSERVATION SENTENCES

CONFIRMATION THEORY

[2] The *Novum Organum* is an update of Aristotle's *Organon*, or instrument of thought. Thus Aristotle can be seen as both an empiricist and a rationalist.

[3] In this picture, all meaningful statements can be verified or falsified either by experimentation or by analysis of the meaning of the words. Because this rules out most of metaphysics, as was the intention, logical positivism was unpopular in some circles.

The final element in the philosophical picture of the mind is the connection between knowledge and action. This question is vital to AI because intelligence requires action as well as reasoning. Moreover, only by understanding how actions are justified can we understand how to build an agent whose actions are justifiable (or rational). Aristotle argued (in *De Motu Animalium*) that actions are justified by a logical connection between goals and knowledge of the action's outcome:

> But how does it happen that thinking is sometimes accompanied by action and sometimes not, sometimes by motion, and sometimes not? It looks as if almost the same thing happens as in the case of reasoning and making inferences about unchanging objects. But in that case the end is a speculative proposition ... whereas here the conclusion which results from the two premises is an action. ... I need covering; a cloak is a covering. I need a cloak. What I need, I have to make; I need a cloak. I have to make a cloak. And the conclusion, the "I have to make a cloak," is an action.

In the *Nicomachean Ethics* (Book III. 3, 1112b), Aristotle further elaborates on this topic, suggesting an algorithm:

> We deliberate not about ends, but about means. For a doctor does not deliberate whether he shall heal, nor an orator whether he shall persuade, ... They assume the end and consider how and by what means it is attained, and if it seems easily and best produced thereby; while if it is achieved by one means only they consider *how* it will be achieved by this and by what means *this* will be achieved, till they come to the first cause, ... and what is last in the order of analysis seems to be first in the order of becoming. And if we come on an impossibility, we give up the search, e.g., if we need money and this cannot be got; but if a thing appears possible we try to do it.

Aristotle's algorithm was implemented 2300 years later by Newell and Simon in their GPS program. We would now call it a regression planning system.

Goal-based analysis is useful, but does not say what to do when several actions will achieve the goal or when no action will achieve it completely. Antoine Arnauld (1612–1694) correctly described a quantitative formula for deciding what action to take in cases like this. John Stuart Mill's (1806–1873) book *Utilitarianism* (Mill, 1863) promoted the idea of rational decision criteria in all spheres of human activity. The more formal theory of decisions is discussed in the following section.

2.2 Mathematics

- What are the formal rules to draw valid conclusions?
- What can be computed?
- How do we reason with uncertain information?

Philosophers staked out some of the fundamental ideas of AI, but the leap to a formal science required a level of mathematical formalization in three fundamental areas: logic, computation, and probability.

The idea of formal logic can be traced back to the philosophers of ancient Greece, but its mathematical development really began with the work of George Boole (1815–1864), who worked out the details of propositional, or Boolean, logic (Boole, 1847). In 1879, Gottlob Frege (1848–1925) extended Boole's logic to include objects and relations, creating the first-order logic that is used today.[4] Alfred Tarski (1902–1983) introduced a theory of reference that shows how to relate the objects in a logic to objects in the real world.

ALGORITHM

The next step was to determine the limits of what could be done with logic and computation. The first nontrivial **algorithm** is thought to be Euclid's algorithm for computing greatest common divisors. The word *algorithm* (and the idea of studying them) comes from al-Khowarazmi, a Persian mathematician of the 9th century, whose writings also introduced Arabic numerals and algebra to Europe. Boole and others discussed algorithms for logical deduction, and, by the late 19th century, efforts were under way to formalize general mathematical reasoning as logical deduction. In 1930, Kurt Gödel (1906–1978) showed that there exists an effective procedure to prove any true statement in the first-order logic of Frege and Russell, but that first-order logic could not capture the principle of mathematical induction needed to characterize the natural numbers. In 1931, Gödel showed that limits on deduction do exist. His **incompleteness theorem** showed that in any formal theory as strong as Peano arithmetic (the elementary theory of natural numbers), there are true statements that are undecidable in the sense that they have no proof within the theory.

INCOMPLETENESS THEOREM

COMPUTABLE

This fundamental result can also be interpreted as showing that some functions on the integers cannot be represented by an algorithm—that is, they cannot be computed. This motivated Alan Turing (1912–1954) to try to characterize exactly which functions *are* **computable**—capable of being computed. This notion is actually slightly problematic because the notion of a computation or effective procedure really cannot be given a formal definition. However, the Church–Turing thesis, which states that the Turing machine (Turing, 1936) is capable of computing any computable function, is generally accepted as providing a sufficient definition. Turing also showed that there were some functions that no Turing machine can compute. For example, no machine can tell *in general* whether a given program will return an answer on a given input or run forever.

TRACTABILITY

Although decidability and computability are important to an understanding of computation, the notion of **tractability** has had an even greater impact. Roughly speaking, a problem is called intractable if the time required to solve instances of the problem grows exponentially with the size of the instances. The distinction between polynomial and exponential growth in complexity was first emphasized in the mid-1960s (Cobham, 1964; Edmonds, 1965). It is important because exponential growth means that even moderately large instances cannot be solved in any reasonable time. Therefore, one should strive to divide the overall problem of generating intelligent behavior into tractable subproblems rather than intractable ones.

NP-COMPLETENESS

How can one recognize an intractable problem? The theory of **NP-completeness**, pioneered by Steven Cook (1971) and Richard Karp (1972), provides a method. Cook and Karp showed the existence of large classes of canonical combinatorial search and reasoning problems that are NP-complete. Any problem class to which the class of NP-complete problems can be reduced is likely to be intractable. (Although it has not been proved that NP-complete

[4] Frege's proposed notation for first-order logic—an arcane combination of textual and geometric features—never became popular.

problems are necessarily intractable, most theoreticians believe it.) These results contrast with the optimism with which the popular press greeted the first computers—"Electronic Super-Brains" that were "Faster than Einstein!" Despite the increasing speed of computers, careful use of resources will characterize intelligent systems. Put crudely, the world is an *extremely* large problem instance! Work in AI has helped explain why some instances of NP-complete problems are hard, yet others are easy (Cheeseman *et al.*, 1991).

PROBABILITY

Besides logic and computation, the third great contribution of mathematics to AI is the theory of **probability**. The Italian Gerolamo Cardano (1501–1576) first framed the idea of probability, describing it in terms of the possible outcomes of gambling events. In 1654, Blaise Pascal (1623–1662), in a letter to Pierre Fermat (1601–1665), showed how to predict the future of an unfinished gambling game and assign average payoffs to the gamblers. Probability quickly became an invaluable part of all the quantitative sciences, helping to deal with uncertain measurements and incomplete theories. James Bernoulli (1654–1705), Pierre Laplace (1749–1827), and others advanced the theory and introduced new statistical methods. Thomas Bayes (1702–1761), who appears on the front cover of this book, proposed a rule for updating probabilities in the light of new evidence. Bayes' rule underlies most modern approaches to uncertain reasoning in AI systems.

1.2.3 Economics

- How should we make decisions so as to maximize payoff?
- How should we do this when others may not go along?
- How should we do this when the payoff may be far in the future?

UTILITY

The science of economics got its start in 1776, when Scottish philosopher Adam Smith (1723–1790) published *An Inquiry into the Nature and Causes of the Wealth of Nations*. While the ancient Greeks and others had made contributions to economic thought, Smith was the first to treat it as a science, using the idea that economies can be thought of as consisting of individual agents maximizing their own economic well-being. Most people think of economics as being about money, but economists will say that they are really studying how people make choices that lead to preferred outcomes. When McDonald's offers a hamburger for a dollar, they are asserting that they would prefer the dollar and hoping that customers will prefer the hamburger. The mathematical treatment of "preferred outcomes" or **utility** was first formalized by Léon Walras (pronounced "Valrasse") (1834-1910) and was improved by Frank Ramsey (1931) and later by John von Neumann and Oskar Morgenstern in their book *The Theory of Games and Economic Behavior* (1944).

DECISION THEORY

GAME THEORY

Decision theory, which combines probability theory with utility theory, provides a formal and complete framework for decisions (economic or otherwise) made under uncertainty—that is, in cases where probabilistic descriptions appropriately capture the decision maker's environment. This is suitable for "large" economies where each agent need pay no attention to the actions of other agents as individuals. For "small" economies, the situation is much more like a **game**: the actions of one player can significantly affect the utility of another (either positively or negatively). Von Neumann and Morgenstern's development of **game theory** (see also Luce and Raiffa, 1957) included the surprising result that, for some games, a rational agent should adopt policies that are (or least appear to be) randomized. Unlike decision theory, game theory does not offer an unambiguous prescription for selecting actions.

For the most part, economists did not address the third question listed above, namely, how to make rational decisions when payoffs from actions are not immediate but instead result from several actions taken *in sequence*. This topic was pursued in the field of **operations research**, which emerged in World War II from efforts in Britain to optimize radar installations, and later found civilian applications in complex management decisions. The work of Richard Bellman (1957) formalized a class of sequential decision problems called **Markov decision processes.**

OPERATIONS RESEARCH

Work in economics and operations research has contributed much to our notion of rational agents, yet for many years AI research developed along entirely separate paths. One reason was the apparent complexity of making rational decisions. The pioneering AI researcher Herbert Simon (1916–2001) won the Nobel Prize in economics in 1978 for his early work showing that models based on **satisficing**—making decisions that are "good enough," rather than laboriously calculating an optimal decision—gave a better description of actual human behavior (Simon, 1947). Since the 1990s, there has been a resurgence of interest in decision-theoretic techniques for agent systems (Wellman, 1995).

SATISFICING

2.4 Neuroscience

- How do brains process information?

NEUROSCIENCE

Neuroscience is the study of the nervous system, particularly the brain. Although the exact way in which the brain enables thought is one of the great mysteries of science, the fact that it *does* enable thought has been appreciated for thousands of years because of the evidence that strong blows to the head can lead to mental incapacitation. It has also long been known that human brains are somehow different; in about 335 B.C. Aristotle wrote, "Of all the animals, man has the largest brain in proportion to his size."[5] Still, it was not until the middle of the 18th century that the brain was widely recognized as the seat of consciousness. Before then, candidate locations included the heart and the spleen.

Paul Broca's (1824–1880) study of aphasia (speech deficit) in brain-damaged patients in 1861 demonstrated the existence of localized areas of the brain responsible for specific cognitive functions. In particular, he showed that speech production was localized to the portion of the left hemisphere now called Broca's area.[6] By that time, it was known that the brain consisted of nerve cells, or **neurons**, but it was not until 1873 that Camillo Golgi (1843–1926) developed a staining technique allowing the observation of individual neurons in the brain (see Figure 2). This technique was used by Santiago Ramon y Cajal (1852–1934) in his pioneering studies of the brain's neuronal structures.[7] Nicolas Rashevsky (1936, 1938) was the first to apply mathematical models to the study of the nervous sytem.

NEURON

[5] Since then, it has been discovered that the tree shrew (*Scandentia*) has a higher ratio of brain to body mass.

[6] Many cite Alexander Hood (1824) as a possible prior source.

[7] Golgi persisted in his belief that the brain's functions were carried out primarily in a continuous medium in which neurons were embedded, whereas Cajal propounded the "neuronal doctrine." The two shared the Nobel prize in 1906 but gave mutually antagonistic acceptance speeches.

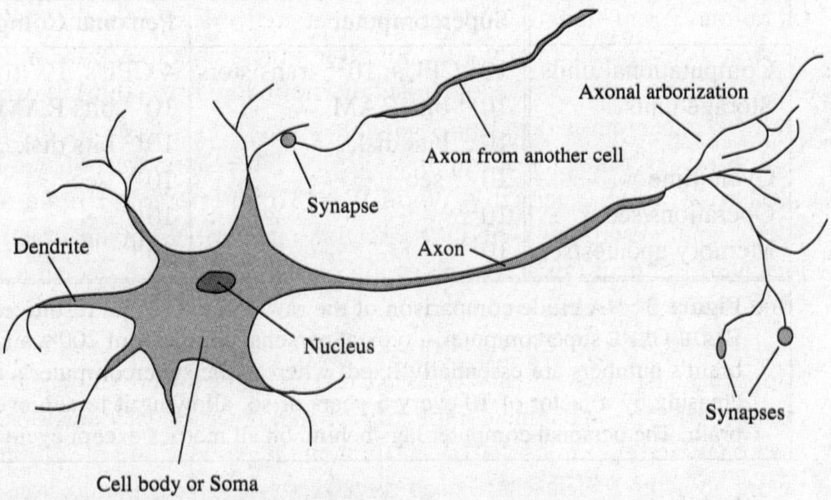

Figure 2 The parts of a nerve cell or neuron. Each neuron consists of a cell body, or soma, that contains a cell nucleus. Branching out from the cell body are a number of fibers called dendrites and a single long fiber called the axon. The axon stretches out for a long distance, much longer than the scale in this diagram indicates. Typically, an axon is 1 cm long (100 times the diameter of the cell body), but can reach up to 1 meter. A neuron makes connections with 10 to 100,000 other neurons at junctions called synapses. Signals are propagated from neuron to neuron by a complicated electrochemical reaction. The signals control brain activity in the short term and also enable long-term changes in the connectivity of neurons. These mechanisms are thought to form the basis for learning in the brain. Most information processing goes on in the cerebral cortex, the outer layer of the brain. The basic organizational unit appears to be a column of tissue about 0.5 mm in diameter, containing about 20,000 neurons and extending the full depth of the cortex about 4 mm in humans).

We now have some data on the mapping between areas of the brain and the parts of the body that they control or from which they receive sensory input. Such mappings are able to change radically over the course of a few weeks, and some animals seem to have multiple maps. Moreover, we do not fully understand how other areas can take over functions when one area is damaged. There is almost no theory on how an individual memory is stored.

The measurement of intact brain activity began in 1929 with the invention by Hans Berger of the electroencephalograph (EEG). The recent development of functional magnetic resonance imaging (fMRI) (Ogawa *et al.*, 1990; Cabeza and Nyberg, 2001) is giving neuroscientists unprecedentedly detailed images of brain activity, enabling measurements that correspond in interesting ways to ongoing cognitive processes. These are augmented by advances in single-cell recording of neuron activity. Individual neurons can be stimulated electrically, chemically, or even optically (Han and Boyden, 2007), allowing neuronal input–output relationships to be mapped. Despite these advances, we are still a long way from understanding how cognitive processes actually work.

The truly amazing conclusion is that *a collection of simple cells can lead to thought, action, and consciousness* or, in the pithy words of John Searle (1992), *brains cause minds.*

	Supercomputer	Personal Computer	Human Brain
Computational units	10^4 CPUs, 10^{12} transistors	4 CPUs, 10^9 transistors	10^{11} neurons
Storage units	10^{14} bits RAM	10^{11} bits RAM	10^{11} neurons
	10^{15} bits disk	10^{13} bits disk	10^{14} synapses
Cycle time	10^{-9} sec	10^{-9} sec	10^{-3} sec
Operations/sec	10^{15}	10^{10}	10^{17}
Memory updates/sec	10^{14}	10^{10}	10^{14}

Figure 3 A crude comparison of the raw computational resources available to the IBM BLUE GENE supercomputer, a typical personal computer of 2008, and the human brain. The brain's numbers are essentially fixed, whereas the supercomputer's numbers have been increasing by a factor of 10 every 5 years or so, allowing it to achieve rough parity with the brain. The personal computer lags behind on all metrics except cycle time.

The only real alternative theory is mysticism: that minds operate in some mystical realm that is beyond physical science.

Brains and digital computers have somewhat different properties. Figure 3 shows that computers have a cycle time that is a million times faster than a brain. The brain makes up for that with far more storage and interconnection than even a high-end personal computer, although the largest supercomputers have a capacity that is similar to the brain's. (It should be noted, however, that the brain does not seem to use all of its neurons simultaneously.) Futurists make much of these numbers, pointing to an approaching **singularity** at which computers reach a superhuman level of performance (Vinge, 1993; Kurzweil, 2005), but the raw comparisons are not especially informative. Even with a computer of virtually unlimited capacity, we still would not know how to achieve the brain's level of intelligence.

SINGULARITY

2.5 Psychology

- How do humans and animals think and act?

The origins of scientific psychology are usually traced to the work of the German physicist Hermann von Helmholtz (1821–1894) and his student Wilhelm Wundt (1832–1920). Helmholtz applied the scientific method to the study of human vision, and his *Handbook of Physiological Optics* is even now described as "the single most important treatise on the physics and physiology of human vision" (Nalwa, 1993, p.15). In 1879, Wundt opened the first laboratory of experimental psychology, at the University of Leipzig. Wundt insisted on carefully controlled experiments in which his workers would perform a perceptual or associative task while introspecting on their thought processes. The careful controls went a long way toward making psychology a science, but the subjective nature of the data made it unlikely that an experimenter would ever disconfirm his or her own theories. Biologists studying animal behavior, on the other hand, lacked introspective data and developed an objective methodology, as described by H. S. Jennings (1906) in his influential work *Behavior of the Lower Organisms*. Applying this viewpoint to humans, the **behaviorism** movement, led by John Watson (1878–1958), rejected *any* theory involving mental processes on the grounds

BEHAVIORISM

that introspection could not provide reliable evidence. Behaviorists insisted on studying only objective measures of the percepts (or *stimulus*) given to an animal and its resulting actions (or *response*). Behaviorism discovered a lot about rats and pigeons but had less success at understanding humans.

COGNITIVE PSYCHOLOGY

Cognitive psychology, which views the brain as an information-processing device, can be traced back at least to the works of William James (1842–1910). Helmholtz also insisted that perception involved a form of unconscious logical inference. The cognitive viewpoint was largely eclipsed by behaviorism in the United States, but at Cambridge's Applied Psychology Unit, directed by Frederic Bartlett (1886–1969), cognitive modeling was able to flourish. *The Nature of Explanation*, by Bartlett's student and successor Kenneth Craik (1943), forcefully reestablished the legitimacy of such "mental" terms as beliefs and goals, arguing that they are just as scientific as, say, using pressure and temperature to talk about gases, despite their being made of molecules that have neither. Craik specified the three key steps of a knowledge-based agent: (1) the stimulus must be translated into an internal representation, (2) the representation is manipulated by cognitive processes to derive new internal representations, and (3) these are in turn retranslated back into action. He clearly explained why this was a good design for an agent:

> If the organism carries a "small-scale model" of external reality and of its own possible actions within its head, it is able to try out various alternatives, conclude which is the best of them, react to future situations before they arise, utilize the knowledge of past events in dealing with the present and future, and in every way to react in a much fuller, safer, and more competent manner to the emergencies which face it. (Craik, 1943)

After Craik's death in a bicycle accident in 1945, his work was continued by Donald Broadbent, whose book *Perception and Communication* (1958) was one of the first works to model psychological phenomena as information processing. Meanwhile, in the United States, the development of computer modeling led to the creation of the field of **cognitive science**. The field can be said to have started at a workshop in September 1956 at MIT. (This is just two months after the conference at which AI itself was "born.") At the workshop, George Miller presented *The Magic Number Seven*, Noam Chomsky presented *Three Models of Language*, and Allen Newell and Herbert Simon presented *The Logic Theory Machine*. These three infiuential papers showed how computer models could be used to address the psychology of memory, language, and logical thinking, respectively. It is now a common (although far from universal) view among psychologists that "a cognitive theory should be like a computer program" (Anderson, 1980); that is, it should describe a detailed information-processing mechanism whereby some cognitive function might be implemented.

2.6 Computer engineering

- How can we build an efficient computer?

For artificial intelligence to succeed, we need two things: intelligence and an artifact. The computer has been the artifact of choice. The modern digital electronic computer was invented independently and almost simultaneously by scientists in three countries embattled in

World War II. The first *operational* computer was the electromechanical Heath Robinson,[8] built in 1940 by Alan Turing's team for a single purpose: deciphering German messages. In 1943, the same group developed the Colossus, a powerful general-purpose machine based on vacuum tubes.[9] The first operational *programmable* computer was the Z-3, the invention of Konrad Zuse in Germany in 1941. Zuse also invented floating-point numbers and the first high-level programming language, Plankalkül. The first *electronic* computer, the ABC, was assembled by John Atanasoff and his student Clifford Berry between 1940 and 1942 at Iowa State University. Atanasoff's research received little support or recognition; it was the ENIAC, developed as part of a secret military project at the University of Pennsylvania by a team including John Mauchly and John Eckert, that proved to be the most influential forerunner of modern computers.

Since that time, each generation of computer hardware has brought an increase in speed and capacity and a decrease in price. Performance doubled every 18 months or so until around 2005, when power dissipation problems led manufacturers to start multiplying the number of CPU cores rather than the clock speed. Current expectations are that future increases in power will come from massive parallelism—a curious convergence with the properties of the brain.

Of course, there were calculating devices before the electronic computer. The earliest automated machines, dating from the 17th century, were discussed in Section 2.1 of this chapter. The first *programmable* machine was a loom, devised in 1805 by Joseph Marie Jacquard (1752–1834), that used punched cards to store instructions for the pattern to be woven. In the mid-19th century, Charles Babbage (1792–1871) designed two machines, neither of which he completed. The Difference Engine was intended to compute mathematical tables for engineering and scientific projects. It was finally built and shown to work in 1991 at the Science Museum in London (Swade, 2000). Babbage's Analytical Engine was far more ambitious: it included addressable memory, stored programs, and conditional jumps and was the first artifact capable of universal computation. Babbage's colleague Ada Lovelace, daughter of the poet Lord Byron, was perhaps the world's first programmer. (The programming language Ada is named after her.) She wrote programs for the unfinished Analytical Engine and even speculated that the machine could play chess or compose music.

AI also owes a debt to the software side of computer science, which has supplied the operating systems, programming languages, and tools needed to write modern programs (and papers about them). But this is one area where the debt has been repaid: work in AI has pioneered many ideas that have made their way back to mainstream computer science, including time sharing, interactive interpreters, personal computers with windows and mice, rapid development environments, the linked list data type, automatic storage management, and key concepts of symbolic, functional, declarative, and object-oriented programming.

---

[8] Heath Robinson was a cartoonist famous for his depictions of whimsical and absurdly complicated contraptions for everyday tasks such as buttering toast.

[9] In the postwar period, Turing wanted to use these computers for AI research—for example, one of the first chess programs (Turing *et al.*, 1953). His efforts were blocked by the British government.

2.7 Control theory and cybernetics

- How can artifacts operate under their own control?

Ktesibios of Alexandria (c. 250 B.C.) built the first self-controlling machine: a water clock with a regulator that maintained a constant flow rate. This invention changed the definition of what an artifact could do. Previously, only living things could modify their behavior in response to changes in the environment. Other examples of self-regulating feedback control systems include the steam engine governor, created by James Watt (1736–1819), and the thermostat, invented by Cornelis Drebbel (1572–1633), who also invented the submarine. The mathematical theory of stable feedback systems was developed in the 19th century.

CONTROL THEORY

The central figure in the creation of what is now called **control theory** was Norbert Wiener (1894–1964). Wiener was a brilliant mathematician who worked with Bertrand Russell, among others, before developing an interest in biological and mechanical control systems and their connection to cognition. Like Craik (who also used control systems as psychological models), Wiener and his colleagues Arturo Rosenblueth and Julian Bigelow challenged the behaviorist orthodoxy (Rosenblueth *et al.*, 1943). They viewed purposive behavior as arising from a regulatory mechanism trying to minimize "error"—the difference between current state and goal state. In the late 1940s, Wiener, along with Warren McCulloch, Walter Pitts, and John von Neumann, organized a series of influential conferences that explored the new mathematical and computational models of cognition. Wiener's book *Cybernetics* (1948) became a bestseller and awoke the public to the possibility of artificially intelligent machines. Meanwhile, in Britain, W. Ross Ashby (Ashby, 1940) pioneered similar ideas. Ashby, Alan Turing, Grey Walter, and others formed the Ratio Club for "those who had Wiener's ideas before Wiener's book appeared." Ashby's *Design for a Brain* (1948, 1952) elaborated on his idea that intelligence could be created by the use of **homeostatic** devices containing appropriate feedback loops to achieve stable adaptive behavior.

CYBERNETICS

HOMEOSTATIC

OBJECTIVE FUNCTION

Modern control theory, especially the branch known as stochastic optimal control, has as its goal the design of systems that maximize an **objective function** over time. This roughly matches our view of AI: designing systems that behave optimally. Why, then, are AI and control theory two different fields, despite the close connections among their founders? The answer lies in the close coupling between the mathematical techniques that were familiar to the participants and the corresponding sets of problems that were encompassed in each world view. Calculus and matrix algebra, the tools of control theory, lend themselves to systems that are describable by fixed sets of continuous variables, whereas AI was founded in part as a way to escape from the these perceived limitations. The tools of logical inference and computation allowed AI researchers to consider problems such as language, vision, and planning that fell completely outside the control theorist's purview.

2.8 Linguistics

- How does language relate to thought?

In 1957, B. F. Skinner published *Verbal Behavior*. This was a comprehensive, detailed account of the behaviorist approach to language learning, written by the foremost expert in the field. But curiously, a review of the book became as well known as the book itself, and served to almost kill off interest in behaviorism. The author of the review was the linguist Noam Chomsky, who had just published a book on his own theory, *Syntactic Structures*. Chomsky pointed out that the behaviorist theory did not address the notion of creativity in language—it did not explain how a child could understand and make up sentences that he or she had never heard before. Chomsky's theory—based on syntactic models going back to the Indian linguist Panini (c. 350 B.C.)—could explain this, and unlike previous theories, it was formal enough that it could in principle be programmed.

COMPUTATIONAL LINGUISTICS

Modern linguistics and AI, then, were "born" at about the same time, and grew up together, intersecting in a hybrid field called **computational linguistics** or **natural language processing**. The problem of understanding language soon turned out to be considerably more complex than it seemed in 1957. Understanding language requires an understanding of the subject matter and context, not just an understanding of the structure of sentences. This might seem obvious, but it was not widely appreciated until the 1960s. Much of the early work in **knowledge representation** (the study of how to put knowledge into a form that a computer can reason with) was tied to language and informed by research in linguistics, which was connected in turn to decades of work on the philosophical analysis of language.

3 THE HISTORY OF ARTIFICIAL INTELLIGENCE

With the background material behind us, we are ready to cover the development of AI itself.

3.1 The gestation of artificial intelligence (1943–1955)

The first work that is now generally recognized as AI was done by Warren McCulloch and Walter Pitts (1943). They drew on three sources: knowledge of the basic physiology and function of neurons in the brain; a formal analysis of propositional logic due to Russell and Whitehead; and Turing's theory of computation. They proposed a model of artificial neurons in which each neuron is characterized as being "on" or "off," with a switch to "on" occurring in response to stimulation by a sufficient number of neighboring neurons. The state of a neuron was conceived of as "factually equivalent to a proposition which proposed its adequate stimulus." They showed, for example, that any computable function could be computed by some network of connected neurons, and that all the logical connectives (and, or, not, etc.) could be implemented by simple net structures. McCulloch and Pitts also suggested that suitably defined networks could learn. Donald Hebb (1949) demonstrated a simple updating rule for modifying the connection strengths between neurons. His rule, now called **Hebbian learning**, remains an influential model to this day.

HEBBIAN LEARNING

Two undergraduate students at Harvard, Marvin Minsky and Dean Edmonds, built the first neural network computer in 1950. The SNARC, as it was called, used 3000 vacuum tubes and a surplus automatic pilot mechanism from a B-24 bomber to simulate a network of 40 neurons. Later, at Princeton, Minsky studied universal computation in neural networks. His Ph.D. committee was skeptical about whether this kind of work should be considered mathematics, but von Neumann reportedly said, "If it isn't now, it will be someday." Minsky was later to prove influential theorems showing the limitations of neural network research.

There were a number of early examples of work that can be characterized as AI, but Alan Turing's vision was perhaps the most influential. He gave lectures on the topic as early as 1947 at the London Mathematical Society and articulated a persuasive agenda in his 1950 article "Computing Machinery and Intelligence." Therein, he introduced the Turing Test, machine learning, genetic algorithms, and reinforcement learning. He proposed the *Child Programme* idea, explaining "Instead of trying to produce a programme to simulate the adult mind, why not rather try to produce one which simulated the child's?"

3.2 The birth of artificial intelligence (1956)

Princeton was home to another influential figure in AI, John McCarthy. After receiving his PhD there in 1951 and working for two years as an instructor, McCarthy moved to Stanford and then to Dartmouth College, which was to become the official birthplace of the field. McCarthy convinced Minsky, Claude Shannon, and Nathaniel Rochester to help him bring together U.S. researchers interested in automata theory, neural nets, and the study of intelligence. They organized a two-month workshop at Dartmouth in the summer of 1956. The proposal states:[10]

> We propose that a 2 month, 10 man study of artificial intelligence be carried out during the summer of 1956 at Dartmouth College in Hanover, New Hampshire. The study is to proceed on the basis of the conjecture that every aspect of learning or any other feature of intelligence can in principle be so precisely described that a machine can be made to simulate it. An attempt will be made to find how to make machines use language, form abstractions and concepts, solve kinds of problems now reserved for humans, and improve themselves. We think that a significant advance can be made in one or more of these problems if a carefully selected group of scientists work on it together for a summer.

There were 10 attendees in all, including Trenchard More from Princeton, Arthur Samuel from IBM, and Ray Solomonoff and Oliver Selfridge from MIT.

Two researchers from Carnegie Tech,[11] Allen Newell and Herbert Simon, rather stole the show. Although the others had ideas and in some cases programs for particular applications such as checkers, Newell and Simon already had a reasoning program, the Logic Theorist (LT), about which Simon claimed, "We have invented a computer program capable of thinking non-numerically, and thereby solved the venerable mind–body problem."[12] Soon after the workshop, the program was able to prove most of the theorems in Chapter 2 of Russell

[10] This was the first official usage of McCarthy's term *artificial intelligence*. Perhaps "computational rationality" would have been more precise and less threatening, but "AI" has stuck. At the 50th anniversary of the Dartmouth conference, McCarthy stated that he resisted the terms "computer" or "computational" in deference to Norbert Weiner, who was promoting analog cybernetic devices rather than digital computers.

[11] Now Carnegie Mellon University (CMU).

[12] Newell and Simon also invented a list-processing language, IPL, to write LT. They had no compiler and translated it into machine code by hand. To avoid errors, they worked in parallel, calling out binary numbers to each other as they wrote each instruction to make sure they agreed.

and Whitehead's *Principia Mathematica*. Russell was reportedly delighted when Simon showed him that the program had come up with a proof for one theorem that was shorter than the one in *Principia*. The editors of the *Journal of Symbolic Logic* were less impressed; they rejected a paper coauthored by Newell, Simon, and Logic Theorist.

The Dartmouth workshop did not lead to any new breakthroughs, but it did introduce all the major figures to each other. For the next 20 years, the field would be dominated by these people and their students and colleagues at MIT, CMU, Stanford, and IBM.

Looking at the proposal for the Dartmouth workshop (McCarthy *et al.*, 1955), we can see why it was necessary for AI to become a separate field. Why couldn't all the work done in AI have taken place under the name of control theory or operations research or decision theory, which, after all, have objectives similar to those of AI? Or why isn't AI a branch of mathematics? The first answer is that AI from the start embraced the idea of duplicating human faculties such as creativity, self-improvement, and language use. None of the other fields were addressing these issues. The second answer is methodology. AI is the only one of these fields that is clearly a branch of computer science (although operations research does share an emphasis on computer simulations), and AI is the only field to attempt to build machines that will function autonomously in complex, changing environments.

3.3 Early enthusiasm, great expectations (1952–1969)

The early years of AI were full of successes—in a limited way. Given the primitive computers and programming tools of the time and the fact that only a few years earlier computers were seen as things that could do arithmetic and no more, it was astonishing whenever a computer did anything remotely clever. The intellectual establishment, by and large, preferred to believe that "a machine can never do *X*." AI researchers naturally responded by demonstrating one *X* after another. John McCarthy referred to this period as the "Look, Ma, no hands!" era.

Newell and Simon's early success was followed up with the General Problem Solver, or GPS. Unlike Logic Theorist, this program was designed from the start to imitate human problem-solving protocols. Within the limited class of puzzles it could handle, it turned out that the order in which the program considered subgoals and possible actions was similar to that in which humans approached the same problems. Thus, GPS was probably the first program to embody the "thinking humanly" approach. The success of GPS and subsequent programs as models of cognition led Newell and Simon (1976) to formulate the famous **physical symbol system** hypothesis, which states that "a physical symbol system has the necessary and sufficient means for general intelligent action." What they meant is that any system (human or machine) exhibiting intelligence must operate by manipulating data structures composed of symbols. We will see later that this hypothesis has been challenged from many directions.

PHYSICAL SYMBOL SYSTEM

At IBM, Nathaniel Rochester and his colleagues produced some of the first AI programs. Herbert Gelernter (1959) constructed the Geometry Theorem Prover, which was able to prove theorems that many students of mathematics would find quite tricky. Starting in 1952, Arthur Samuel wrote a series of programs for checkers (draughts) that eventually learned to play at a strong amateur level. Along the way, he disproved the idea that computers can do only what they are told to: his program quickly learned to play a better game than its creator. The program was demonstrated on television in February 1956, creating a strong impression. Like Turing, Samuel had trouble finding computer time. Working at night, he used machines that were still on the testing floor at IBM's manufacturing plant.

John McCarthy moved from Dartmouth to MIT and there made three crucial contributions in one historic year: 1958. In MIT AI Lab Memo No. 1, McCarthy defined the high-level

LISP

language **Lisp**, which was to become the dominant AI programming language for the next 30 years. With Lisp, McCarthy had the tool he needed, but access to scarce and expensive computing resources was also a serious problem. In response, he and others at MIT invented time sharing. Also in 1958, McCarthy published a paper entitled *Programs with Common Sense*, in which he described the Advice Taker, a hypothetical program that can be seen as the first complete AI system. Like the Logic Theorist and Geometry Theorem Prover, McCarthy's program was designed to use knowledge to search for solutions to problems. But unlike the others, it was to embody general knowledge of the world. For example, he showed how some simple axioms would enable the program to generate a plan to drive to the airport. The program was also designed to accept new axioms in the normal course of operation, thereby allowing it to achieve competence in new areas *without being reprogrammed*. The Advice Taker thus embodied the central principles of knowledge representation and reasoning: that it is useful to have a formal, explicit representation of the world and its workings and to be able to manipulate that representation with deductive processes. It is remarkable how much of the 1958 paper remains relevant today.

1958 also marked the year that Marvin Minsky moved to MIT. His initial collaboration with McCarthy did not last, however. McCarthy stressed representation and reasoning in formal logic, whereas Minsky was more interested in getting programs to work and eventually developed an anti-logic outlook. In 1963, McCarthy started the AI lab at Stanford. His plan to use logic to build the ultimate Advice Taker was advanced by J. A. Robinson's discovery in 1965 of the resolution method (a complete theorem-proving algorithm for first-order logic). Work at Stanford emphasized general-purpose methods for logical reasoning. Applications of logic included Cordell Green's question-answering and planning systems (Green, 1969b) and the Shakey robotics project at the Stanford Research Institute (SRI). The latter project was the first to demonstrate the complete integration of logical reasoning and physical activity.

Minsky supervised a series of students who chose limited problems that appeared to

MICROWORLD

require intelligence to solve. These limited domains became known as **microworlds**. James Slagle's SAINT program (1963) was able to solve closed-form calculus integration problems typical of first-year college courses. Tom Evans's ANALOGY program (1968) solved geometric analogy problems that appear in IQ tests. Daniel Bobrow's STUDENT program (1967) solved algebra story problems, such as the following:

> If the number of customers Tom gets is twice the square of 20 percent of the number of advertisements he runs, and the number of advertisements he runs is 45, what is the number of customers Tom gets?

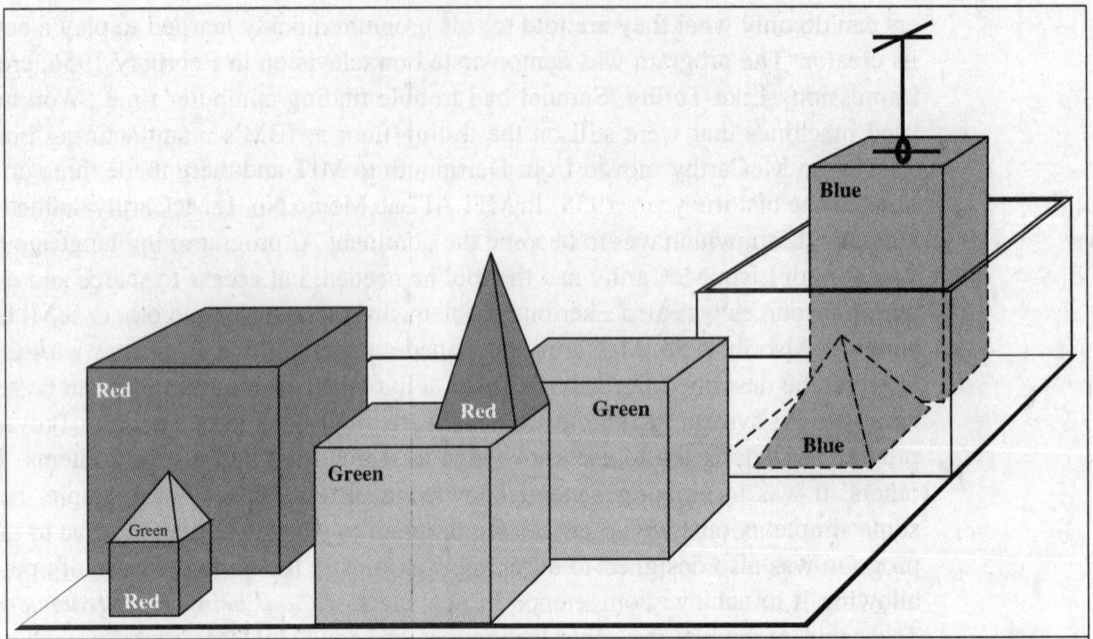

Figure 4 A scene from the blocks world. SHRDLU (Winograd, 1972) has just completed the command "Find a block which is taller than the one you are holding and put it in the box."

The most famous microworld was the blocks world, which consists of a set of solid blocks placed on a tabletop (or more often, a simulation of a tabletop), as shown in Figure 4. A typical task in this world is to rearrange the blocks in a certain way, using a robot hand that can pick up one block at a time. The blocks world was home to the vision project of David Huffman (1971), the vision and constraint-propagation work of David Waltz (1975), the learning theory of Patrick Winston (1970), the natural-language-understanding program of Terry Winograd (1972), and the planner of Scott Fahlman (1974).

Early work building on the neural networks of McCulloch and Pitts also flourished. The work of Winograd and Cowan (1963) showed how a large number of elements could collectively represent an individual concept, with a corresponding increase in robustness and parallelism. Hebb's learning methods were enhanced by Bernie Widrow (Widrow and Hoff, 1960; Widrow, 1962), who called his networks **adalines**, and by Frank Rosenblatt (1962) with his **perceptrons**. The **perceptron convergence theorem** (Block *et al.*, 1962) says that the learning algorithm can adjust the connection strengths of a perceptron to match any input data, provided such a match exists.

3.4 A dose of reality (1966–1973)

From the beginning, AI researchers were not shy about making predictions of their coming successes. The following statement by Herbert Simon in 1957 is often quoted:

> It is not my aim to surprise or shock you—but the simplest way I can summarize is to say that there are now in the world machines that think, that learn and that create. Moreover,

> their ability to do these things is going to increase rapidly until—in a visible future—the range of problems they can handle will be coextensive with the range to which the human mind has been applied.

Terms such as "visible future" can be interpreted in various ways, but Simon also made more concrete predictions: that within 10 years a computer would be chess champion, and a significant mathematical theorem would be proved by machine. These predictions came true (or approximately true) within 40 years rather than 10. Simon's overconfidence was due to the promising performance of early AI systems on simple examples. In almost all cases, however, these early systems turned out to fail miserably when tried out on wider selections of problems and on more difficult problems.

The first kind of difficulty arose because most early programs knew nothing of their subject matter; they succeeded by means of simple syntactic manipulations. A typical story occurred in early machine translation efforts, which were generously funded by the U.S. National Research Council in an attempt to speed up the translation of Russian scientific papers in the wake of the Sputnik launch in 1957. It was thought initially that simple syntactic transformations based on the grammars of Russian and English, and word replacement from an electronic dictionary, would suffice to preserve the exact meanings of sentences. The fact is that accurate translation requires background knowledge in order to resolve ambiguity and establish the content of the sentence. The famous retranslation of "the spirit is willing but the flesh is weak" as "the vodka is good but the meat is rotten" illustrates the difficulties encountered. In 1966, a report by an advisory committee found that "there has been no machine translation of general scientific text, and none is in immediate prospect." All U.S. government funding for academic translation projects was canceled. Today, machine translation is an imperfect but widely used tool for technical, commercial, government, and Internet documents.

The second kind of difficulty was the intractability of many of the problems that AI was attempting to solve. Most of the early AI programs solved problems by trying out different combinations of steps until the solution was found. This strategy worked initially because microworlds contained very few objects and hence very few possible actions and very short solution sequences. Before the theory of computational complexity was developed, it was widely thought that "scaling up" to larger problems was simply a matter of faster hardware and larger memories. The optimism that accompanied the development of resolution theorem proving, for example, was soon dampened when researchers failed to prove theorems involving more than a few dozen facts. *The fact that a program can find a solution in principle does not mean that the program contains any of the mechanisms needed to find it in practice.*

MACHINE EVOLUTION

GENETIC ALGORITHM

The illusion of unlimited computational power was not confined to problem-solving programs. Early experiments in **machine evolution** (now called **genetic algorithms**) (Friedberg, 1958; Friedberg *et al.*, 1959) were based on the undoubtedly correct belief that by making an appropriate series of small mutations to a machine-code program, one can generate a program with good performance for any particular task. The idea, then, was to try random mutations with a selection process to preserve mutations that seemed useful. Despite thousands of hours of CPU time, almost no progress was demonstrated. Modern genetic algorithms use better representations and have shown more success.

Failure to come to grips with the "combinatorial explosion" was one of the main criticisms of AI contained in the Lighthill report (Lighthill, 1973), which formed the basis for the decision by the British government to end support for AI research in all but two universities. (Oral tradition paints a somewhat different and more colorful picture, with political ambitions and personal animosities whose description is beside the point.)

A third difficulty arose because of some fundamental limitations on the basic structures being used to generate intelligent behavior. For example, Minsky and Papert's book *Perceptrons* (1969) proved that, although perceptrons (a simple form of neural network) could be shown to learn anything they were capable of representing, they could represent very little. In particular, a two-input perceptron (restricted to be simpler than the form Rosenblatt originally studied) could not be trained to recognize when its two inputs were different. Although their results did not apply to more complex, multilayer networks, research funding for neural-net research soon dwindled to almost nothing. Ironically, the new back-propagation learning algorithms for multilayer networks that were to cause an enormous resurgence in neural-net research in the late 1980s were actually discovered first in 1969 (Bryson and Ho, 1969).

3.5 Knowledge-based systems: The key to power? (1969–1979)

The picture of problem solving that had arisen during the first decade of AI research was of a general-purpose search mechanism trying to string together elementary reasoning steps to find complete solutions. Such approaches have been called **weak methods** because, although general, they do not scale up to large or difficult problem instances. The alternative to weak methods is to use more powerful, domain-specific knowledge that allows larger reasoning steps and can more easily handle typically occurring cases in narrow areas of expertise. One might say that to solve a hard problem, you have to almost know the answer already.

WEAK METHOD

The DENDRAL program (Buchanan *et al.*, 1969) was an early example of this approach. It was developed at Stanford, where Ed Feigenbaum (a former student of Herbert Simon), Bruce Buchanan (a philosopher turned computer scientist), and Joshua Lederberg (a Nobel laureate geneticist) teamed up to solve the problem of inferring molecular structure from the information provided by a mass spectrometer. The input to the program consists of the elementary formula of the molecule (e.g., $C_6H_{13}NO_2$) and the mass spectrum giving the masses of the various fragments of the molecule generated when it is bombarded by an electron beam. For example, the mass spectrum might contain a peak at $m = 15$, corresponding to the mass of a methyl (CH_3) fragment.

The naive version of the program generated all possible structures consistent with the formula, and then predicted what mass spectrum would be observed for each, comparing this with the actual spectrum. As one might expect, this is intractable for even moderate-sized molecules. The DENDRAL researchers consulted analytical chemists and found that they worked by looking for well-known patterns of peaks in the spectrum that suggested common substructures in the molecule. For example, the following rule is used to recognize a ketone (C=O) subgroup (which weighs 28):

if there are two peaks at x_1 and x_2 such that
(a) $x_1 + x_2 = M + 28$ (M is the mass of the whole molecule);

(b) $x_1 - 28$ is a high peak;
(c) $x_2 - 28$ is a high peak;
(d) At least one of x_1 and x_2 is high.
then there is a ketone subgroup

Recognizing that the molecule contains a particular substructure reduces the number of possible candidates enormously. DENDRAL was powerful because

> All the relevant theoretical knowledge to solve these problems has been mapped over from its general form in the [spectrum prediction component] ("first principles") to efficient special forms ("cookbook recipes"). (Feigenbaum *et al.*, 1971)

The significance of DENDRAL was that it was the first successful *knowledge-intensive* system: its expertise derived from large numbers of special-purpose rules. Later systems also incorporated the main theme of McCarthy's Advice Taker approach—the clean separation of the knowledge (in the form of rules) from the reasoning component.

With this lesson in mind, Feigenbaum and others at Stanford began the Heuristic Programming Project (HPP) to investigate the extent to which the new methodology of **expert systems** could be applied to other areas of human expertise. The next major effort was in the area of medical diagnosis. Feigenbaum, Buchanan, and Dr. Edward Shortliffe developed MYCIN to diagnose blood infections. With about 450 rules, MYCIN was able to perform as well as some experts, and considerably better than junior doctors. It also contained two major differences from DENDRAL. First, unlike the DENDRAL rules, no general theoretical model existed from which the MYCIN rules could be deduced. They had to be acquired from extensive interviewing of experts, who in turn acquired them from textbooks, other experts, and direct experience of cases. Second, the rules had to reflect the uncertainty associated with medical knowledge. MYCIN incorporated a calculus of uncertainty called **certainty factors**, which seemed (at the time) to fit well with how doctors assessed the impact of evidence on the diagnosis.

EXPERT SYSTEMS

CERTAINTY FACTOR

The importance of domain knowledge was also apparent in the area of understanding natural language. Although Winograd's SHRDLU system for understanding natural language had engendered a good deal of excitement, its dependence on syntactic analysis caused some of the same problems as occurred in the early machine translation work. It was able to overcome ambiguity and understand pronoun references, but this was mainly because it was designed specifically for one area—the blocks world. Several researchers, including Eugene Charniak, a fellow graduate student of Winograd's at MIT, suggested that robust language understanding would require general knowledge about the world and a general method for using that knowledge.

At Yale, linguist-turned-AI-researcher Roger Schank emphasized this point, claiming, "There is no such thing as syntax," which upset a lot of linguists but did serve to start a useful discussion. Schank and his students built a series of programs (Schank and Abelson, 1977; Wilensky, 1978; Schank and Riesbeck, 1981; Dyer, 1983) that all had the task of understanding natural language. The emphasis, however, was less on language *per se* and more on the problems of representing and reasoning with the knowledge required for language understanding. The problems included representing stereotypical situations (Cullingford, 1981), describing human memory organization (Rieger, 1976; Kolodner, 1983), and understanding plans and goals (Wilensky, 1983).

The widespread growth of applications to real-world problems caused a concurrent increase in the demands for workable knowledge representation schemes. A large number of different representation and reasoning languages were developed. Some were based on logic—for example, the Prolog language became popular in Europe, and the PLANNER family in the United States. Others, following Minsky's idea of **frames** (1975), adopted a more structured approach, assembling facts about particular object and event types and arranging the types into a large taxonomic hierarchy analogous to a biological taxonomy.

FRAMES

3.6 AI becomes an industry (1980–present)

The first successful commercial expert system, R1, began operation at the Digital Equipment Corporation (McDermott, 1982). The program helped configure orders for new computer systems; by 1986, it was saving the company an estimated $40 million a year. By 1988, DEC's AI group had 40 expert systems deployed, with more on the way. DuPont had 100 in use and 500 in development, saving an estimated $10 million a year. Nearly every major U.S. corporation had its own AI group and was either using or investigating expert systems.

In 1981, the Japanese announced the "Fifth Generation" project, a 10-year plan to build intelligent computers running Prolog. In response, the United States formed the Microelectronics and Computer Technology Corporation (MCC) as a research consortium designed to assure national competitiveness. In both cases, AI was part of a broad effort, including chip design and human-interface research. In Britain, the Alvey report reinstated the funding that was cut by the Lighthill report.[13] In all three countries, however, the projects never met their ambitious goals.

Overall, the AI industry boomed from a few million dollars in 1980 to billions of dollars in 1988, including hundreds of companies building expert systems, vision systems, robots, and software and hardware specialized for these purposes. Soon after that came a period called the "AI Winter," in which many companies fell by the wayside as they failed to deliver on extravagant promises.

3.7 The return of neural networks (1986–present)

BACK-PROPAGATION

In the mid-1980s at least four different groups reinvented the **back-propagation** learning algorithm first found in 1969 by Bryson and Ho. The algorithm was applied to many learning problems in computer science and psychology, and the widespread dissemination of the results in the collection *Parallel Distributed Processing* (Rumelhart and McClelland, 1986) caused great excitement.

CONNECTIONIST

These so-called **connectionist** models of intelligent systems were seen by some as direct competitors both to the symbolic models promoted by Newell and Simon and to the logicist approach of McCarthy and others (Smolensky, 1988). It might seem obvious that at some level humans manipulate symbols—in fact, Terrence Deacon's book *The Symbolic*

[13] To save embarrassment, a new field called IKBS (Intelligent Knowledge-Based Systems) was invented because Artificial Intelligence had been officially canceled.

Species (1997) suggests that this is the *defining characteristic* of humans—but the most ardent connectionists questioned whether symbol manipulation had any real explanatory role in detailed models of cognition. This question remains unanswered, but the current view is that connectionist and symbolic approaches are complementary, not competing. As occurred with the separation of AI and cognitive science, modern neural network research has bifurcated into two fields, one concerned with creating effective network architectures and algorithms and understanding their mathematical properties, the other concerned with careful modeling of the empirical properties of actual neurons and ensembles of neurons.

3.8 AI adopts the scientific method (1987–present)

Recent years have seen a revolution in both the content and the methodology of work in artificial intelligence.[14] It is now more common to build on existing theories than to propose brand-new ones, to base claims on rigorous theorems or hard experimental evidence rather than on intuition, and to show relevance to real-world applications rather than toy examples.

AI was founded in part as a rebellion against the limitations of existing fields like control theory and statistics, but now it is embracing those fields. As David McAllester (1998) put it:

> In the early period of AI it seemed plausible that new forms of symbolic computation, e.g., frames and semantic networks, made much of classical theory obsolete. This led to a form of isolationism in which AI became largely separated from the rest of computer science. This isolationism is currently being abandoned. There is a recognition that machine learning should not be isolated from information theory, that uncertain reasoning should not be isolated from stochastic modeling, that search should not be isolated from classical optimization and control, and that automated reasoning should not be isolated from formal methods and static analysis.

In terms of methodology, AI has finally come firmly under the scientific method. To be accepted, hypotheses must be subjected to rigorous empirical experiments, and the results must be analyzed statistically for their importance (Cohen, 1995). It is now possible to replicate experiments by using shared repositories of test data and code.

The field of speech recognition illustrates the pattern. In the 1970s, a wide variety of different architectures and approaches were tried. Many of these were rather *ad hoc* and fragile, and were demonstrated on only a few specially selected examples. In recent years, approaches based on **hidden Markov models** (HMMs) have come to dominate the area. Two aspects of HMMs are relevant. First, they are based on a rigorous mathematical theory. This has allowed speech researchers to build on several decades of mathematical results developed in other fields. Second, they are generated by a process of training on a large corpus of real speech data. This ensures that the performance is robust, and in rigorous blind tests the HMMs have been improving their scores steadily. Speech technology and the related field of handwritten character recognition are already making the transition to widespread industrial

HIDDEN MARKOV MODELS

[14] Some have characterized this change as a victory of the **neats**—those who think that AI theories should be grounded in mathematical rigor—over the **scruffies**—those who would rather try out lots of ideas, write some programs, and then assess what seems to be working. Both approaches are important. A shift toward neatness implies that the field has reached a level of stability and maturity. Whether that stability will be disrupted by a new scruffy idea is another question.

and consumer applications. Note that there is no scientific claim that humans use HMMs to recognize speech; rather, HMMs provide a mathematical framework for understanding the problem and support the engineering claim that they work well in practice.

Machine translation follows the same course as speech recognition. In the 1950s there was initial enthusiasm for an approach based on sequences of words, with models learned according to the principles of information theory. That approach fell out of favor in the 1960s, but returned in the late 1990s and now dominates the field.

Neural networks also fit this trend. Much of the work on neural nets in the 1980s was done in an attempt to scope out what could be done and to learn how neural nets differ from "traditional" techniques. Using improved methodology and theoretical frameworks, the field arrived at an understanding in which neural nets can now be compared with corresponding techniques from statistics, pattern recognition, and machine learning, and the most promising technique can be applied to each application. As a result of these developments, so-called **data mining** technology has spawned a vigorous new industry.

DATA MINING

Judea Pearl's (1988) *Probabilistic Reasoning in Intelligent Systems* led to a new acceptance of probability and decision theory in AI, following a resurgence of interest epitomized by Peter Cheeseman's (1985) article "In Defense of Probability." The **Bayesian network** formalism was invented to allow efficient representation of, and rigorous reasoning with, uncertain knowledge. This approach largely overcomes many problems of the probabilistic reasoning systems of the 1960s and 1970s; it now dominates AI research on uncertain reasoning and expert systems. The approach allows for learning from experience, and it combines the best of classical AI and neural nets. Work by Judea Pearl (1982a) and by Eric Horvitz and David Heckerman (Horvitz and Heckerman, 1986; Horvitz *et al.*, 1986) promoted the idea of *normative* expert systems: ones that act rationally according to the laws of decision theory and do not try to imitate the thought steps of human experts. The Windows™ operating system includes several normative diagnostic expert systems for correcting problems.

BAYESIAN NETWORK

Similar gentle revolutions have occurred in robotics, computer vision, and knowledge representation. A better understanding of the problems and their complexity properties, combined with increased mathematical sophistication, has led to workable research agendas and robust methods. Although increased formalization and specialization led fields such as vision and robotics to become somewhat isolated from "mainstream" AI in the 1990s, this trend has reversed in recent years as tools from machine learning in particular have proved effective for many problems. The process of reintegration is already yielding significant benefits.

3.9 The emergence of intelligent agents (1995–present)

Perhaps encouraged by the progress in solving the subproblems of AI, researchers have also started to look at the "whole agent" problem again. The work of Allen Newell, John Laird, and Paul Rosenbloom on SOAR (Newell, 1990; Laird *et al.*, 1987) is the best-known example of a complete agent architecture. One of the most important environments for intelligent agents is the Internet. AI systems have become so common in Web-based applications that the "-bot" suffix has entered everyday language. Moreover, AI technologies underlie many

Internet tools, such as search engines, recommender systems, and Web site aggregators.

One consequence of trying to build complete agents is the realization that the previously isolated subfields of AI might need to be reorganized somewhat when their results are to be tied together. In particular, it is now widely appreciated that sensory systems (vision, sonar, speech recognition, etc.) cannot deliver perfectly reliable information about the environment. Hence, reasoning and planning systems must be able to handle uncertainty. A second major consequence of the agent perspective is that AI has been drawn into much closer contact with other fields, such as control theory and economics, that also deal with agents. Recent progress in the control of robotic cars has derived from a mixture of approaches ranging from better sensors, control-theoretic integration of sensing, localization and mapping, as well as a degree of high-level planning.

Despite these successes, some influential founders of AI, including John McCarthy (2007), Marvin Minsky (2007), Nils Nilsson (1995, 2005) and Patrick Winston (Beal and Winston, 2009), have expressed discontent with the progress of AI. They think that AI should put less emphasis on creating ever-improved versions of applications that are good at a specific task, such as driving a car, playing chess, or recognizing speech. Instead, they believe AI should return to its roots of striving for, in Simon's words, "machines that think, that learn and that create." They call the effort **human-level AI** or HLAI; their first symposium was in 2004 (Minsky *et al.*, 2004). The effort will require very large knowledge bases; Hendler *et al.* (1995) discuss where these knowledge bases might come from.

HUMAN-LEVEL AI

ARTIFICIAL GENERAL INTELLIGENCE

A related idea is the subfield of **Artificial General Intelligence** or AGI (Goertzel and Pennachin, 2007), which held its first conference and organized the *Journal of Artificial General Intelligence* in 2008. AGI looks for a universal algorithm for learning and acting in any environment, and has its roots in the work of Ray Solomonoff (1964), one of the attendees of the original 1956 Dartmouth conference. Guaranteeing that what we create is really **Friendly AI** is also a concern (Yudkowsky, 2008; Omohundro, 2008).

FRIENDLY AI

3.10 The availability of very large data sets (2001–present)

Throughout the 60-year history of computer science, the emphasis has been on the *algorithm* as the main subject of study. But some recent work in AI suggests that for many problems, it makes more sense to worry about the *data* and be less picky about what algorithm to apply. This is true because of the increasing availability of very large data sources: for example, trillions of words of English and billions of images from the Web (Kilgarriff and Grefenstette, 2006); or billions of base pairs of genomic sequences (Collins *et al.*, 2003).

One influential paper in this line was Yarowsky's (1995) work on word-sense disambiguation: given the use of the word "plant" in a sentence, does that refer to flora or factory? Previous approaches to the problem had relied on human-labeled examples combined with machine learning algorithms. Yarowsky showed that the task can be done, with accuracy above 96%, with no labeled examples at all. Instead, given a very large corpus of unannotated text and just the dictionary definitions of the two senses—"works, industrial plant" and "flora, plant life"—one can label examples in the corpus, and from there **bootstrap** to learn new patterns that help label new examples. Banko and Brill (2001) show that techniques like this perform even better as the amount of available text goes from a million words to a billion and that the increase in performance from using more data exceeds any difference in algorithm choice; a mediocre algorithm with 100 million words of unlabeled training data outperforms the best known algorithm with 1 million words.

As another example, Hays and Efros (2007) discuss the problem of filling in holes in a photograph. Suppose you use Photoshop to mask out an ex-friend from a group photo, but now you need to fill in the masked area with something that matches the background. Hays and Efros defined an algorithm that searches through a collection of photos to find something that will match. They found the performance of their algorithm was poor when they used a collection of only ten thousand photos, but crossed a threshold into excellent performance when they grew the collection to two million photos.

Work like this suggests that the "knowledge bottleneck" in AI—the problem of how to express all the knowledge that a system needs—may be solved in many applications by learning methods rather than hand-coded knowledge engineering, provided the learning algorithms have enough data to go on (Halevy *et al.*, 2009). Reporters have noticed the surge of new applications and have written that "AI Winter" may be yielding to a new Spring (Havenstein, 2005). As Kurzweil (2005) writes, "today, many thousands of AI applications are deeply embedded in the infrastructure of every industry."

4 THE STATE OF THE ART

What can AI do today? A concise answer is difficult because there are so many activities in so many subfields. Here we sample a few applications.

Robotic vehicles: A driverless robotic car named STANLEY sped through the rough terrain of the Mojave dessert at 22 mph, finishing the 132-mile course first to win the 2005 DARPA Grand Challenge. STANLEY is a Volkswagen Touareg outfitted with cameras, radar, and laser rangefinders to sense the environment and onboard software to command the steering, braking, and acceleration (Thrun, 2006). The following year CMU's BOSS won the Urban Challenge, safely driving in traffic through the streets of a closed Air Force base, obeying traffic rules and avoiding pedestrians and other vehicles.

Speech recognition: A traveler calling United Airlines to book a flight can have the entire conversation guided by an automated speech recognition and dialog management system.

Autonomous planning and scheduling: A hundred million miles from Earth, NASA's Remote Agent program became the first on-board autonomous planning program to control the scheduling of operations for a spacecraft (Jonsson *et al.*, 2000). REMOTE AGENT generated plans from high-level goals specified from the ground and monitored the execution of those plans—detecting, diagnosing, and recovering from problems as they occurred. Successor program MAPGEN (Al-Chang *et al.*, 2004) plans the daily operations for NASA's Mars Exploration Rovers, and MEXAR2 (Cesta *et al.*, 2007) did mission planning—both logistics and science planning—for the European Space Agency's Mars Express mission in 2008.

Game playing: IBM's DEEP BLUE became the first computer program to defeat the world champion in a chess match when it bested Garry Kasparov by a score of 3.5 to 2.5 in an exhibition match (Goodman and Keene, 1997). Kasparov said that he felt a "new kind of intelligence" across the board from him. *Newsweek* magazine described the match as "The brain's last stand." The value of IBM's stock increased by $18 billion. Human champions studied Kasparov's loss and were able to draw a few matches in subsequent years, but the most recent human-computer matches have been won convincingly by the computer.

Spam fighting: Each day, learning algorithms classify over a billion messages as spam, saving the recipient from having to waste time deleting what, for many users, could comprise 80% or 90% of all messages, if not classified away by algorithms. Because the spammers are continually updating their tactics, it is difficult for a static programmed approach to keep up, and learning algorithms work best (Sahami *et al.*, 1998; Goodman and Heckerman, 2004).

Logistics planning: During the Persian Gulf crisis of 1991, U.S. forces deployed a Dynamic Analysis and Replanning Tool, DART (Cross and Walker, 1994), to do automated logistics planning and scheduling for transportation. This involved up to 50,000 vehicles, cargo, and people at a time, and had to account for starting points, destinations, routes, and conflict resolution among all parameters. The AI planning techniques generated in hours a plan that would have taken weeks with older methods. The Defense Advanced Research Project Agency (DARPA) stated that this single application more than paid back DARPA's 30-year investment in AI.

Robotics: The iRobot Corporation has sold over two million Roomba robotic vacuum cleaners for home use. The company also deploys the more rugged PackBot to Iraq and Afghanistan, where it is used to handle hazardous materials, clear explosives, and identify the location of snipers.

Machine Translation: A computer program automatically translates from Arabic to English, allowing an English speaker to see the headline "Ardogan Confirms That Turkey Would Not Accept Any Pressure, Urging Them to Recognize Cyprus." The program uses a statistical model built from examples of Arabic-to-English translations and from examples of English text totaling two trillion words (Brants *et al.*, 2007). None of the computer scientists on the team speak Arabic, but they do understand statistics and machine learning algorithms.

These are just a few examples of artificial intelligence systems that exist today. Not magic or science fiction—but rather science, engineering, and mathematics, to which this book provides an introduction.

5 SUMMARY

This chapter defines AI and establishes the cultural background against which it has developed. Some of the important points are as follows:

- Different people approach AI with different goals in mind. Two important questions to ask are: Are you concerned with thinking or behavior? Do you want to model humans or work from an ideal standard?

- We adopt the view that intelligence is concerned mainly with **rational action**. Ideally, an **intelligent agent** takes the best possible action in a situation. We study the problem of building agents that are intelligent in this sense.
- Philosophers (going back to 400 B.C.) made AI conceivable by considering the ideas that the mind is in some ways like a machine, that it operates on knowledge encoded in some internal language, and that thought can be used to choose what actions to take.
- Mathematicians provided the tools to manipulate statements of logical certainty as well as uncertain, probabilistic statements. They also set the groundwork for understanding computation and reasoning about algorithms.
- Economists formalized the problem of making decisions that maximize the expected outcome to the decision maker.
- Neuroscientists discovered some facts about how the brain works and the ways in which it is similar to and different from computers.
- Psychologists adopted the idea that humans and animals can be considered information-processing machines. Linguists showed that language use fits into this model.
- Computer engineers provided the ever-more-powerful machines that make AI applications possible.
- Control theory deals with designing devices that act optimally on the basis of feedback from the environment. Initially, the mathematical tools of control theory were quite different from AI, but the fields are coming closer together.
- The history of AI has had cycles of success, misplaced optimism, and resulting cutbacks in enthusiasm and funding. There have also been cycles of introducing new creative approaches and systematically refining the best ones.
- AI has advanced more rapidly in the past decade because of greater use of the scientific method in experimenting with and comparing approaches.
- Recent progress in understanding the theoretical basis for intelligence has gone hand in hand with improvements in the capabilities of real systems. The subfields of AI have become more integrated, and AI has found common ground with other disciplines.

BIBLIOGRAPHICAL AND HISTORICAL NOTES

The methodological status of artificial intelligence is investigated in *The Sciences of the Artificial*, by Herb Simon (1981), which discusses research areas concerned with complex artifacts. It explains how AI can be viewed as both science and mathematics. Cohen (1995) gives an overview of experimental methodology within AI.

The Turing Test (Turing, 1950) is discussed by Shieber (1994), who severely criticizes the usefulness of its instantiation in the Loebner Prize competition, and by Ford and Hayes (1995), who argue that the test itself is not helpful for AI. Bringsjord (2008) gives advice for a Turing Test judge. Shieber (2004) and Epstein *et al.* (2008) collect a number of essays on the Turing Test. *Artificial Intelligence: The Very Idea*, by John Haugeland (1985), gives a readable account of the philosophical and practical problems of AI. Significant early papers in AI are anthologized in the collections by Webber and Nilsson (1981) and by Luger (1995). The *Encyclopedia of AI* (Shapiro, 1992) contains survey articles on almost every topic in AI, as does Wikipedia. These articles usually provide a good entry point into the research literature on each topic. An insightful and comprehensive history of AI is given by Nils Nillson (2009), one of the early pioneers of the field.

The most recent work appears in the proceedings of the major AI conferences: the biennial International Joint Conference on AI (IJCAI), the annual European Conference on AI (ECAI), and the National Conference on AI, more often known as AAAI, after its sponsoring organization. The major journals for general AI are *Artificial Intelligence*, *Computational Intelligence*, the *IEEE Transactions on Pattern Analysis and Machine Intelligence*, *IEEE Intelligent Systems*, and the electronic *Journal of Artificial Intelligence Research*. There are also many conferences and journals devoted to specific areas. The main professional societies for AI are the American Association for Artificial Intelligence (AAAI), the ACM Special Interest Group in Artificial Intelligence (SIGART), and the Society for Artificial Intelligence and Simulation of Behaviour (AISB). AAAI's *AI Magazine* contains many topical and tutorial articles, and its Web site, aaai.org, contains news, tutorials, and its Web site, `aaai.org`, contains news, tutorials, and background information.

EXERCISES

These exercises are intended to stimulate discussion, and some might be set as term projects.

1 Define in your own words: (a) intelligence, (b) artificial intelligence, (c) agent, (d) rationality, (e) logical reasoning.

2 Read Turing's original paper on AI (Turing, 1950). In the paper, he discusses several objections to his proposed enterprise and his test for intelligence. Which objections still carry weight? Are his refutations valid? Can you think of new objections arising from developments since he wrote the paper? In the paper, he predicts that, by the year 2000, a computer will have a 30% chance of passing a five-minute Turing Test with an unskilled interrogator. What chance do you think a computer would have today? In another 50 years?

3 Are reflex actions (such as flinching from a hot stove) rational? Are they intelligent?

4 Suppose we extend Evans's ANALOGY program so that it can score 200 on a standard IQ test. Would we then have a program more intelligent than a human? Explain.

5 The neural structure of the sea slug *Aplysia* has been widely studied (first by Nobel Laureate Eric Kandel) because it has only about 20,000 neurons, most of them large and easily manipulated. Assuming that the cycle time for an *Aplysia* neuron is roughly the same as for a human neuron, how does the computational power, in terms of memory updates per second, compare with the high-end computer described in Figure 3?

6 How could introspection—reporting on one's inner thoughts—be inaccurate? Could I be wrong about what I'm thinking? Discuss.

7 To what extent are the following computer systems instances of artificial intelligence:

- Supermarket bar code scanners.
- Web search engines.
- Voice-activated telephone menus.
- Internet routing algorithms that respond dynamically to the state of the network.

8 Many of the computational models of cognitive activities that have been proposed involve quite complex mathematical operations, such as convolving an image with a Gaussian or finding a minimum of the entropy function. Most humans (and certainly all animals) never learn this kind of mathematics at all, almost no one learns it before college, and almost no one can compute the convolution of a function with a Gaussian in their head. What sense does it make to say that the "vision system" is doing this kind of mathematics, whereas the actual person has no idea how to do it?

9 Why would evolution tend to result in systems that act rationally? What goals are such systems designed to achieve?

10 Is AI a science, or is it engineering? Or neither or both? Explain.

11 "Surely computers cannot be intelligent—they can do only what their programmers tell them." Is the latter statement true, and does it imply the former?

12 "Surely animals cannot be intelligent—they can do only what their genes tell them." Is the latter statement true, and does it imply the former?

13 "Surely animals, humans, and computers cannot be intelligent—they can do only what their constituent atoms are told to do by the laws of physics." Is the latter statement true, and does it imply the former?

14 Examine the AI literature to discover whether the following tasks can currently be solved by computers:

a. Playing a decent game of table tennis (Ping-Pong).
b. Driving in the center of Cairo, Egypt.
c. Driving in Victorville, California.
d. Buying a week's worth of groceries at the market.
e. Buying a week's worth of groceries on the Web.
f. Playing a decent game of bridge at a competitive level.
g. Discovering and proving new mathematical theorems.
h. Writing an intentionally funny story.
i. Giving competent legal advice in a specialized area of law.
j. Translating spoken English into spoken Swedish in real time.
k. Performing a complex surgical operation.

For the currently infeasible tasks, try to find out what the difficulties are and predict when, if ever, they will be overcome.

15 Various subfields of AI have held contests by defining a standard task and inviting researchers to do their best. Examples include the DARPA Grand Challenge for robotic cars, The International Planning Competition, the Robocup robotic soccer league, the TREC information retrieval event, and contests in machine translation, speech recognition. Investigate five of these contests, and describe the progress made over the years. To what degree have the contests advanced toe state of the art in AI? Do what degree do they hurt the field by drawing energy away from new ideas?

INTELLIGENT AGENTS

From Chapter 2 of *Artificial Intelligence: A Modern Approach*, Third Edition. Stuart Russell and Peter Norvig.

INTELLIGENT AGENTS

In which we discuss the nature of agents, perfect or otherwise, the diversity of environments, and the resulting menagerie of agent types.

The concept of **rational agents** is central to our approach to artificial intelligence. In this chapter, we make this notion more concrete. We will see that the concept of rationality can be applied to a wide variety of agents operating in any imaginable environment. This concept can be used to develop a small set of design principles for building successful agents—systems that can reasonably be called **intelligent**.

We begin by examining agents, environments, and the coupling between them. The observation that some agents behave better than others leads naturally to the idea of a rational agent—one that behaves as well as possible. How well an agent can behave depends on the nature of the environment; some environments are more difficult than others. We give a crude categorization of environments and show how properties of an environment influence the design of suitable agents for that environment. We describe a number of basic "skeleton" agent designs.

1 AGENTS AND ENVIRONMENTS

ENVIRONMENT
SENSOR
ACTUATOR

An **agent** is anything that can be viewed as perceiving its **environment** through **sensors** and acting upon that environment through **actuators**. This simple idea is illustrated in Figure 1. A human agent has eyes, ears, and other organs for sensors and hands, legs, vocal tract, and so on for actuators. A robotic agent might have cameras and infrared range finders for sensors and various motors for actuators. A software agent receives keystrokes, file contents, and network packets as sensory inputs and acts on the environment by displaying on the screen, writing files, and sending network packets.

PERCEPT
PERCEPT SEQUENCE

We use the term **percept** to refer to the agent's perceptual inputs at any given instant. An agent's **percept sequence** is the complete history of everything the agent has ever perceived. In general, *an agent's choice of action at any given instant can depend on the entire percept sequence observed to date, but not on anything it hasn't perceived.* By specifying the agent's choice of action for every possible percept sequence, we have said more or less everything

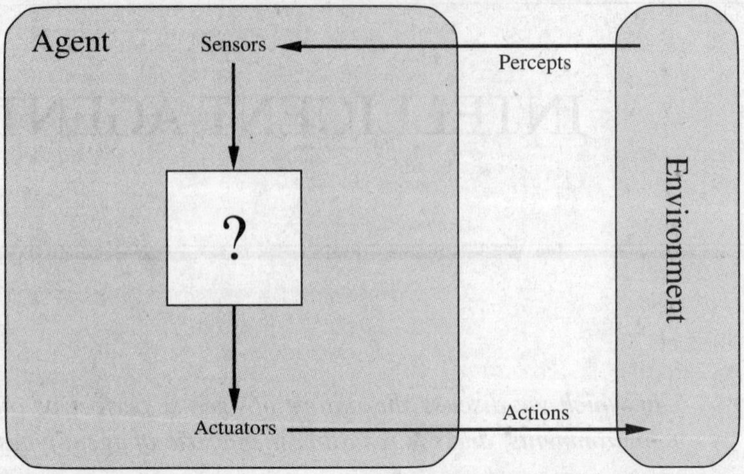

Figure 1 Agents interact with environments through sensors and actuators.

there is to say about the agent. Mathematically speaking, we say that an agent's behavior is described by the **agent function** that maps any given percept sequence to an action.

AGENT FUNCTION

We can imagine *tabulating* the agent function that describes any given agent; for most agents, this would be a very large table—infinite, in fact, unless we place a bound on the length of percept sequences we want to consider. Given an agent to experiment with, we can, in principle, construct this table by trying out all possible percept sequences and recording which actions the agent does in response.[1] The table is, of course, an *external* characterization of the agent. *Internally*, the agent function for an artificial agent will be implemented by an **agent program**. It is important to keep these two ideas distinct. The agent function is an abstract mathematical description; the agent program is a concrete implementation, running within some physical system.

AGENT PROGRAM

To illustrate these ideas, we use a very simple example—the vacuum-cleaner world shown in Figure 2. This world is so simple that we can describe everything that happens; it's also a made-up world, so we can invent many variations. This particular world has just two locations: squares A and B. The vacuum agent perceives which square it is in and whether there is dirt in the square. It can choose to move left, move right, suck up the dirt, or do nothing. One very simple agent function is the following: if the current square is dirty, then suck; otherwise, move to the other square. A partial tabulation of this agent function is shown in Figure 3 and an agent program that implements it appears in Figure 8.

Looking at Figure 3, we see that various vacuum-world agents can be defined simply by filling in the right-hand column in various ways. The obvious question, then, is this: *What is the right way to fill out the table?* In other words, what makes an agent good or bad, intelligent or stupid? We answer these questions in the next section.

1 If the agent uses some randomization to choose its actions, then we would have to try each sequence many times to identify the probability of each action. One might imagine that acting randomly is rather silly, but we show later in this chapter that it can be very intelligent.

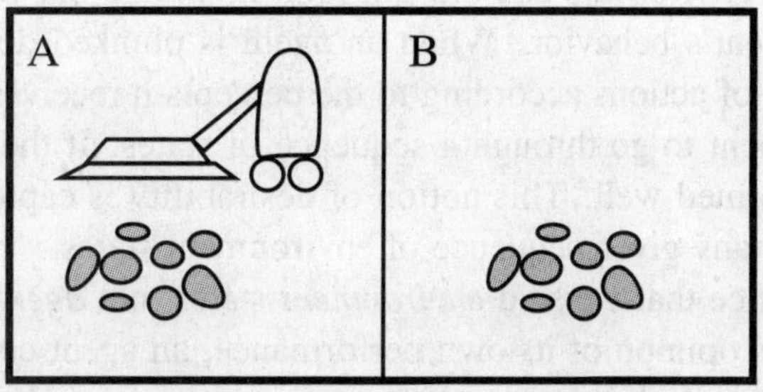

Figure 2 A vacuum-cleaner world with just two locations.

Percept sequence	Action
$[A, Clean]$	*Right*
$[A, Dirty]$	*Suck*
$[B, Clean]$	*Left*
$[B, Dirty]$	*Suck*
$[A, Clean], [A, Clean]$	*Right*
$[A, Clean], [A, Dirty]$	*Suck*
⋮	⋮
$[A, Clean], [A, Clean], [A, Clean]$	*Right*
$[A, Clean], [A, Clean], [A, Dirty]$	*Suck*
⋮	⋮

Figure 3 Partial tabulation of a simple agent function for the vacuum-cleaner world shown in Figure 2.

Before closing this section, we should emphasize that the notion of an agent is meant to be a tool for analyzing systems, not an absolute characterization that divides the world into agents and non-agents. One could view a hand-held calculator as an agent that chooses the action of displaying "4" when given the percept sequence "2 + 2 =," but such an analysis would hardly aid our understanding of the calculator. In a sense, all areas of engineering can be seen as designing artifacts that interact with the world; AI operates at (what the authors consider to be) the most interesting end of the spectrum, where the artifacts have significant computational resources and the task environment requires nontrivial decision making.

2 Good Behavior: The Concept of Rationality

RATIONAL AGENT

A **rational agent** is one that does the right thing—conceptually speaking, every entry in the table for the agent function is filled out correctly. Obviously, doing the right thing is better than doing the wrong thing, but what does it mean to do the right thing?

We answer this age-old question in an age-old way: by considering the *consequences* of the agent's behavior. When an agent is plunked down in an environment, it generates a sequence of actions according to the percepts it receives. This sequence of actions causes the environment to go through a sequence of states. If the sequence is desirable, then the agent has performed well. This notion of desirability is captured by a **performance measure** that evaluates any given sequence of environment states.

PERFORMANCE MEASURE

Notice that we said *environment* states, not *agent* states. If we define success in terms of agent's opinion of its own performance, an agent could achieve perfect rationality simply by deluding itself that its performance was perfect. Human agents in particular are notorious for "sour grapes"—believing they did not really want something (e.g., a Nobel Prize) after not getting it.

Obviously, there is not one fixed performance measure for all tasks and agents; typically, a designer will devise one appropriate to the circumstances. This is not as easy as it sounds. Consider, for example, the vacuum-cleaner agent from the preceding section. We might propose to measure performance by the amount of dirt cleaned up in a single eight-hour shift. With a rational agent, of course, what you ask for is what you get. A rational agent can maximize this performance measure by cleaning up the dirt, then dumping it all on the floor, then cleaning it up again, and so on. A more suitable performance measure would reward the agent for having a clean floor. For example, one point could be awarded for each clean square at each time step (perhaps with a penalty for electricity consumed and noise generated). *As a general rule, it is better to design performance measures according to what one actually wants in the environment, rather than according to how one thinks the agent should behave.*

Even when the obvious pitfalls are avoided, there remain some knotty issues to untangle. For example, the notion of "clean floor" in the preceding paragraph is based on average cleanliness over time. Yet the same average cleanliness can be achieved by two different agents, one of which does a mediocre job all the time while the other cleans energetically but takes long breaks. Which is preferable might seem to be a fine point of janitorial science, but in fact it is a deep philosophical question with far-reaching implications. Which is better—a reckless life of highs and lows, or a safe but humdrum existence? Which is better—an economy where everyone lives in moderate poverty, or one in which some live in plenty while others are very poor? We leave these questions as an exercise for the diligent reader.

2.1 Rationality

What is rational at any given time depends on four things:

- The performance measure that defines the criterion of success.
- The agent's prior knowledge of the environment.
- The actions that the agent can perform.
- The agent's percept sequence to date.

DEFINITION OF A RATIONAL AGENT

This leads to a **definition of a rational agent**:

> *For each possible percept sequence, a rational agent should select an action that is expected to maximize its performance measure, given the evidence provided by the percept sequence and whatever built-in knowledge the agent has.*

Consider the simple vacuum-cleaner agent that cleans a square if it is dirty and moves to the other square if not; this is the agent function tabulated in Figure 3. Is this a rational agent? That depends! First, we need to say what the performance measure is, what is known about the environment, and what sensors and actuators the agent has. Let us assume the following:

- The performance measure awards one point for each clean square at each time step, over a "lifetime" of 1000 time steps.
- The "geography" of the environment is known *a priori* (Figure 2) but the dirt distribution and the initial location of the agent are not. Clean squares stay clean and sucking cleans the current square. The *Left* and *Right* actions move the agent left and right except when this would take the agent outside the environment, in which case the agent remains where it is.
- The only available actions are *Left*, *Right*, and *Suck*.
- The agent correctly perceives its location and whether that location contains dirt.

We claim that *under these circumstances* the agent is indeed rational; its expected performance is at least as high as any other agent's. Exercise 2 asks you to prove this.

One can see easily that the same agent would be irrational under different circumstances. For example, once all the dirt is cleaned up, the agent will oscillate needlessly back and forth; if the performance measure includes a penalty of one point for each movement left or right, the agent will fare poorly. A better agent for this case would do nothing once it is sure that all the squares are clean. If clean squares can become dirty again, the agent should occasionally check and re-clean them if needed. If the geography of the environment is unknown, the agent will need to explore it rather than stick to squares A and B. Exercise 2 asks you to design agents for these cases.

2.2 Omniscience, learning, and autonomy

OMNISCIENCE

We need to be careful to distinguish between rationality and **omniscience**. An omniscient agent knows the *actual* outcome of its actions and can act accordingly; but omniscience is impossible in reality. Consider the following example: I am walking along the Champs Elysées one day and I see an old friend across the street. There is no traffic nearby and I'm not otherwise engaged, so, being rational, I start to cross the street. Meanwhile, at 33,000 feet, a cargo door falls off a passing airliner,[2] and before I make it to the other side of the street I am flattened. Was I irrational to cross the street? It is unlikely that my obituary would read "Idiot attempts to cross street."

This example shows that rationality is not the same as perfection. Rationality maximizes *expected* performance, while perfection maximizes *actual* performance. Retreating from a requirement of perfection is not just a question of being fair to agents. The point is that if we expect an agent to do what turns out to be the best action after the fact, it will be impossible to design an agent to fulfill this specification—unless we improve the performance of crystal balls or time machines.

[2] See N. Henderson, "New door latches urged for Boeing 747 jumbo jets," *Washington Post*, August 24, 1989.

Our definition of rationality does not require omniscience, then, because the rational choice depends only on the percept sequence *to date*. We must also ensure that we haven't inadvertently allowed the agent to engage in decidedly underintelligent activities. For example, if an agent does not look both ways before crossing a busy road, then its percept sequence will not tell it that there is a large truck approaching at high speed. Does our definition of rationality say that it's now OK to cross the road? Far from it! First, it would not be rational to cross the road given this uninformative percept sequence: the risk of accident from crossing without looking is too great. Second, a rational agent should choose the "looking" action before stepping into the street, because looking helps maximize the expected performance. Doing actions *in order to modify future percepts*—sometimes called **information gathering**—is an important part of rationality. A second example of information gathering is provided by the **exploration** that must be undertaken by a vacuum-cleaning agent in an initially unknown environment.

INFORMATION GATHERING

EXPLORATION

LEARNING

Our definition requires a rational agent not only to gather information but also to **learn** as much as possible from what it perceives. The agent's initial configuration could reflect some prior knowledge of the environment, but as the agent gains experience this may be modified and augmented. There are extreme cases in which the environment is completely known *a priori*. In such cases, the agent need not perceive or learn; it simply acts correctly. Of course, such agents are fragile. Consider the lowly dung beetle. After digging its nest and laying its eggs, it fetches a ball of dung from a nearby heap to plug the entrance. If the ball of dung is removed from its grasp *en route*, the beetle continues its task and pantomimes plugging the nest with the nonexistent dung ball, never noticing that it is missing. Evolution has built an assumption into the beetle's behavior, and when it is violated, unsuccessful behavior results. Slightly more intelligent is the sphex wasp. The female sphex will dig a burrow, go out and sting a caterpillar and drag it to the burrow, enter the burrow again to check all is well, drag the caterpillar inside, and lay its eggs. The caterpillar serves as a food source when the eggs hatch. So far so good, but if an entomologist moves the caterpillar a few inches away while the sphex is doing the check, it will revert to the "drag" step of its plan and will continue the plan without modification, even after dozens of caterpillar-moving interventions. The sphex is unable to learn that its innate plan is failing, and thus will not change it.

AUTONOMY

To the extent that an agent relies on the prior knowledge of its designer rather than on its own percepts, we say that the agent lacks **autonomy**. A rational agent should be autonomous—it should learn what it can to compensate for partial or incorrect prior knowledge. For example, a vacuum-cleaning agent that learns to foresee where and when additional dirt will appear will do better than one that does not. As a practical matter, one seldom requires complete autonomy from the start: when the agent has had little or no experience, it would have to act randomly unless the designer gave some assistance. So, just as evolution provides animals with enough built-in reflexes to survive long enough to learn for themselves, it would be reasonable to provide an artificial intelligent agent with some initial knowledge as well as an ability to learn. After sufficient experience of its environment, the behavior of a rational agent can become effectively *independent* of its prior knowledge. Hence, the incorporation of learning allows one to design a single rational agent that will succeed in a vast variety of environments.

3 THE NATURE OF ENVIRONMENTS

TASK ENVIRONMENT

Now that we have a definition of rationality, we are almost ready to think about building rational agents. First, however, we must think about **task environments**, which are essentially the "problems" to which rational agents are the "solutions." We begin by showing how to specify a task environment, illustrating the process with a number of examples. We then show that task environments come in a variety of flavors. The flavor of the task environment directly affects the appropriate design for the agent program.

3.1 Specifying the task environment

PEAS

In our discussion of the rationality of the simple vacuum-cleaner agent, we had to specify the performance measure, the environment, and the agent's actuators and sensors. We group all these under the heading of the **task environment**. For the acronymically minded, we call this the **PEAS** (**P**erformance, **E**nvironment, **A**ctuators, **S**ensors) description. In designing an agent, the first step must always be to specify the task environment as fully as possible.

The vacuum world was a simple example; let us consider a more complex problem: an automated taxi driver. We should point out, before the reader becomes alarmed, that a fully automated taxi is currently somewhat beyond the capabilities of existing technology. The full driving task is extremely *open-ended*. There is no limit to the novel combinations of circumstances that can arise—another reason we chose it as a focus for discussion. Figure 4 summarizes the PEAS description for the taxi's task environment. We discuss each element in more detail in the following paragraphs.

Agent Type	Performance Measure	Environment	Actuators	Sensors
Taxi driver	Safe, fast, legal, comfortable trip, maximize profits	Roads, other traffic, pedestrians, customers	Steering, accelerator, brake, signal, horn, display	Cameras, sonar, speedometer, GPS, odometer, accelerometer, engine sensors, keyboard

Figure 4 PEAS description of the task environment for an automated taxi.

First, what is the **performance measure** to which we would like our automated driver to aspire? Desirable qualities include getting to the correct destination; minimizing fuel consumption and wear and tear; minimizing the trip time or cost; minimizing violations of traffic laws and disturbances to other drivers; maximizing safety and passenger comfort; maximizing profits. Obviously, some of these goals conflict, so tradeoffs will be required.

Next, what is the driving **environment** that the taxi will face? Any taxi driver must deal with a variety of roads, ranging from rural lanes and urban alleys to 12-lane freeways. The roads contain other traffic, pedestrians, stray animals, road works, police cars, puddles, and potholes. The taxi must also interact with potential and actual passengers. There are also some optional choices. The taxi might need to operate in Southern California, where snow is seldom a problem, or in Alaska, where it seldom is not. It could always be driving on the right, or we might want it to be flexible enough to drive on the left when in Britain or Japan. Obviously, the more restricted the environment, the easier the design problem.

The **actuators** for an automated taxi include those available to a human driver: control over the engine through the accelerator and control over steering and braking. In addition, it will need output to a display screen or voice synthesizer to talk back to the passengers, and perhaps some way to communicate with other vehicles, politely or otherwise.

The basic **sensors** for the taxi will include one or more controllable video cameras so that it can see the road; it might augment these with infrared or sonar sensors to detect distances to other cars and obstacles. To avoid speeding tickets, the taxi should have a speedometer, and to control the vehicle properly, especially on curves, it should have an accelerometer. To determine the mechanical state of the vehicle, it will need the usual array of engine, fuel, and electrical system sensors. Like many human drivers, it might want a global positioning system (GPS) so that it doesn't get lost. Finally, it will need a keyboard or microphone for the passenger to request a destination.

In Figure 5, we have sketched the basic PEAS elements for a number of additional agent types. Further examples appear in Exercise 4. It may come as a surprise to some readers that our list of agent types includes some programs that operate in the entirely artificial environment defined by keyboard input and character output on a screen. "Surely," one might say, "this is not a real environment, is it?" In fact, what matters is not the distinction between "real" and "artificial" environments, but the complexity of the relationship among the behavior of the agent, the percept sequence generated by the environment, and the performance measure. Some "real" environments are actually quite simple. For example, a robot designed to inspect parts as they come by on a conveyor belt can make use of a number of simplifying assumptions: that the lighting is always just so, that the only thing on the conveyor belt will be parts of a kind that it knows about, and that only two actions (accept or reject) are possible.

SOFTWARE AGENT
SOFTBOT

In contrast, some **software agents** (or software robots or **softbots**) exist in rich, unlimited domains. Imagine a softbot Web site operator designed to scan Internet news sources and show the interesting items to its users, while selling advertising space to generate revenue. To do well, that operator will need some natural language processing abilities, it will need to learn what each user and advertiser is interested in, and it will need to change its plans dynamically—for example, when the connection for one news source goes down or when a new one comes online. The Internet is an environment whose complexity rivals that of the physical world and whose inhabitants include many artificial and human agents.

3.2 Properties of task environments

The range of task environments that might arise in AI is obviously vast. We can, however, identify a fairly small number of dimensions along which task environments can be categorized. These dimensions determine, to a large extent, the appropriate agent design and the applicability of each of the principal families of techniques for agent implementation. First,

Agent Type	Performance Measure	Environment	Actuators	Sensors
Medical diagnosis system	Healthy patient, reduced costs	Patient, hospital, staff	Display of questions, tests, diagnoses, treatments, referrals	Keyboard entry of symptoms, findings, patient's answers
Satellite image analysis system	Correct image categorization	Downlink from orbiting satellite	Display of scene categorization	Color pixel arrays
Part-picking robot	Percentage of parts in correct bins	Conveyor belt with parts; bins	Jointed arm and hand	Camera, joint angle sensors
Refinery controller	Purity, yield, safety	Refinery, operators	Valves, pumps, heaters, displays	Temperature, pressure, chemical sensors
Interactive English tutor	Student's score on test	Set of students, testing agency	Display of exercises, suggestions, corrections	Keyboard entry

Figure 5 Examples of agent types and their PEAS descriptions.

we list the dimensions, then we analyze several task environments to illustrate the ideas. The definitions here are informal.

FULLY OBSERVABLE
PARTIALLY OBSERVABLE

Fully observable vs. **partially observable**: If an agent's sensors give it access to the complete state of the environment at each point in time, then we say that the task environment is fully observable. A task environment is effectively fully observable if the sensors detect all aspects that are *relevant* to the choice of action; relevance, in turn, depends on the performance measure. Fully observable environments are convenient because the agent need not maintain any internal state to keep track of the world. An environment might be partially observable because of noisy and inaccurate sensors or because parts of the state are simply missing from the sensor data—for example, a vacuum agent with only a local dirt sensor cannot tell whether there is dirt in other squares, and an automated taxi cannot see what other drivers are thinking. If the agent has no sensors at all then the environment is **unobservable**. One might think that in such cases the agent's plight is hopeless, but the agent's goals may still be achievable, sometimes with certainty.

UNOBSERVABLE

SINGLE AGENT
MULTIAGENT

Single agent vs. **multiagent**: The distinction between single-agent and multiagent environments may seem simple enough. For example, an agent solving a crossword puzzle by itself is clearly in a single-agent environment, whereas an agent playing chess is in a two-agent environment. There are, however, some subtle issues. First, we have described how an entity *may* be viewed as an agent, but we have not explained which entities *must* be viewed as agents. Does an agent A (the taxi driver for example) have to treat an object B (another vehicle) as an agent, or can it be treated merely as an object behaving according to the laws of physics, analogous to waves at the beach or leaves blowing in the wind? The key distinction is whether B's behavior is best described as maximizing a performance measure whose value depends on agent A's behavior. For example, in chess, the opponent entity B is trying to maximize its performance measure, which, by the rules of chess, minimizes agent A's performance measure. Thus, chess is a **competitive** multiagent environment. In the taxi-driving environment, on the other hand, avoiding collisions maximizes the performance measure of all agents, so it is a partially **cooperative** multiagent environment. It is also partially competitive because, for example, only one car can occupy a parking space. The agent-design problems in multiagent environments are often quite different from those in single-agent environments; for example, **communication** often emerges as a rational behavior in multiagent environments; in some competitive environments, **randomized behavior** is rational because it avoids the pitfalls of predictability.

COMPETITIVE

COOPERATIVE

DETERMINISTIC

STOCHASTIC

Deterministic vs. **stochastic**. If the next state of the environment is completely determined by the current state and the action executed by the agent, then we say the environment is deterministic; otherwise, it is stochastic. In principle, an agent need not worry about uncertainty in a fully observable, deterministic environment. (In our definition, we ignore uncertainty that arises purely from the actions of other agents in a multiagent environment; thus, a game can be deterministic even though each agent may be unable to predict the actions of the others.) If the environment is partially observable, however, then it could *appear* to be stochastic. Most real situations are so complex that it is impossible to keep track of all the unobserved aspects; for practical purposes, they must be treated as stochastic. Taxi driving is clearly stochastic in this sense, because one can never predict the behavior of traffic exactly; moreover, one's tires blow out and one's engine seizes up without warning. The vacuum world as we described it is deterministic, but variations can include stochastic elements such as randomly appearing dirt and an unreliable suction mechanism (Exercise 13). We say an environment is **uncertain** if it is not fully observable or not deterministic. One final note: our use of the word "stochastic" generally implies that uncertainty about outcomes is quantified in terms of probabilities; a **nondeterministic** environment is one in which actions are characterized by their *possible* outcomes, but no probabilities are attached to them. Nondeterministic environment descriptions are usually associated with performance measures that require the agent to succeed for *all possible* outcomes of its actions.

UNCERTAIN

NONDETERMINISTIC

EPISODIC

SEQUENTIAL

Episodic vs. **sequential**: In an episodic task environment, the agent's experience is divided into atomic episodes. In each episode the agent receives a percept and then performs a single action. Crucially, the next episode does not depend on the actions taken in previous episodes. Many classification tasks are episodic. For example, an agent that has to spot defective parts on an assembly line bases each decision on the current part, regardless of previous decisions; moreover, the current decision doesn't affect whether the next part is defective. In sequential environments, on the other hand, the current decision could affect all future decisions.[3] Chess and taxi driving are sequential: in both cases, short-term actions can have long-term consequences. Episodic environments are much simpler than sequential environments because the agent does not need to think ahead.

STATIC
DYNAMIC

Static vs. **dynamic**: If the environment can change while an agent is deliberating, then we say the environment is dynamic for that agent; otherwise, it is static. Static environments are easy to deal with because the agent need not keep looking at the world while it is deciding on an action, nor need it worry about the passage of time. Dynamic environments, on the other hand, are continuously asking the agent what it wants to do; if it hasn't decided yet, that counts as deciding to do nothing. If the environment itself does not change with the passage of time but the agent's performance score does, then we say the environment is **semidynamic**. Taxi driving is clearly dynamic: the other cars and the taxi itself keep moving while the driving algorithm dithers about what to do next. Chess, when played with a clock, is semidynamic. Crossword puzzles are static.

SEMIDYNAMIC

DISCRETE
CONTINUOUS

Discrete vs. **continuous**: The discrete/continuous distinction applies to the *state* of the environment, to the way *time* is handled, and to the *percepts* and *actions* of the agent. For example, the chess environment has a finite number of distinct states (excluding the clock). Chess also has a discrete set of percepts and actions. Taxi driving is a continuous-state and continuous-time problem: the speed and location of the taxi and of the other vehicles sweep through a range of continuous values and do so smoothly over time. Taxi-driving actions are also continuous (steering angles, etc.). Input from digital cameras is discrete, strictly speaking, but is typically treated as representing continuously varying intensities and locations.

KNOWN
UNKNOWN

Known vs. **unknown**: Strictly speaking, this distinction refers not to the environment itself but to the agent's (or designer's) state of knowledge about the "laws of physics" of the environment. In a known environment, the outcomes (or outcome probabilities if the environment is stochastic) for all actions are given. Obviously, if the environment is unknown, the agent will have to learn how it works in order to make good decisions. Note that the distinction between known and unknown environments is not the same as the one between fully and partially observable environments. It is quite possible for a *known* environment to be *partially* observable—for example, in solitaire card games, I know the rules but am still unable to see the cards that have not yet been turned over. Conversely, an *unknown* environment can be *fully* observable—in a new video game, the screen may show the entire game state but I still don't know what the buttons do until I try them.

As one might expect, the hardest case is *partially observable*, *multiagent*, *stochastic*, *sequential*, *dynamic*, *continuous*, and *unknown*. Taxi driving is hard in all these senses, except that for the most part the driver's environment is known. Driving a rented car in a new country with unfamiliar geography and traffic laws is a lot more exciting.

Figure 6 lists the properties of a number of familiar environments. Note that the answers are not always cut and dried. For example, we describe the part-picking robot as episodic, because it normally considers each part in isolation. But if one day there is a large

---

3 The word "sequential" is also used in computer science as the antonym of "parallel." The two meanings are largely unrelated.

Task Environment	Observable	Agents	Deterministic	Episodic	Static	Discrete
Crossword puzzle	Fully	Single	Deterministic	Sequential	Static	Discrete
Chess with a clock	Fully	Multi	Deterministic	Sequential	Semi	Discrete
Poker	Partially	Multi	Stochastic	Sequential	Static	Discrete
Backgammon	Fully	Multi	Stochastic	Sequential	Static	Discrete
Taxi driving	Partially	Multi	Stochastic	Sequential	Dynamic	Continuous
Medical diagnosis	Partially	Single	Stochastic	Sequential	Dynamic	Continuous
Image analysis	Fully	Single	Deterministic	Episodic	Semi	Continuous
Part-picking robot	Partially	Single	Stochastic	Episodic	Dynamic	Continuous
Refinery controller	Partially	Single	Stochastic	Sequential	Dynamic	Continuous
Interactive English tutor	Partially	Multi	Stochastic	Sequential	Dynamic	Discrete

Figure 6 Examples of task environments and their characteristics.

batch of defective parts, the robot should learn from several observations that the distribution of defects has changed, and should modify its behavior for subsequent parts. We have not included a "known/unknown" column because, as explained earlier, this is not strictly a property of the environment. For some environments, such as chess and poker, it is quite easy to supply the agent with full knowledge of the rules, but it is nonetheless interesting to consider how an agent might learn to play these games without such knowledge.

Several of the answers in the table depend on how the task environment is defined. We have listed the medical-diagnosis task as single-agent because the disease process in a patient is not profitably modeled as an agent; but a medical-diagnosis system might also have to deal with recalcitrant patients and skeptical staff, so the environment could have a multiagent aspect. Furthermore, medical diagnosis is episodic if one conceives of the task as selecting a diagnosis given a list of symptoms; the problem is sequential if the task can include proposing a series of tests, evaluating progress over the course of treatment, and so on. Also, many environments are episodic at higher levels than the agent's individual actions. For example, a chess tournament consists of a sequence of games; each game is an episode because (by and large) the contribution of the moves in one game to the agent's overall performance is not affected by the moves in its previous game. On the other hand, decision making within a single game is certainly sequential.

The code repository associated with this text (aima.cs.berkeley.edu) includes implementations of a number of environments, together with a general-purpose environment simulator that places one or more agents in a simulated environment, observes their behavior over time, and evaluates them according to a given performance measure. Such experiments are often carried out not for a single environment but for many environments drawn from an **environment class**. For example, to evaluate a taxi driver in simulated traffic, we would want to run many simulations with different traffic, lighting, and weather conditions. If we designed the agent for a single scenario, we might be able to take advantage of specific properties of the particular case but might not identify a good design for driving in general. For this

ENVIRONMENT CLASS

ENVIRONMENT GENERATOR

reason, the code repository also includes an **environment generator** for each environment class that selects particular environments (with certain likelihoods) in which to run the agent. For example, the vacuum environment generator initializes the dirt pattern and agent location randomly. We are then interested in the agent's average performance over the environment class. A rational agent for a given environment class maximizes this average performance. Exercises 8 to 13 take you through the process of developing an environment class and evaluating various agents therein.

4 THE STRUCTURE OF AGENTS

So far we have talked about agents by describing *behavior*—the action that is performed after any given sequence of percepts. Now we must bite the bullet and talk about how the insides work. The job of AI is to design an **agent program** that implements the agent function—the mapping from percepts to actions. We assume this program will run on some sort of computing device with physical sensors and actuators—we call this the **architecture**:

AGENT PROGRAM

ARCHITECTURE

$$agent = architecture + program\ .$$

Obviously, the program we choose has to be one that is appropriate for the architecture. If the program is going to recommend actions like *Walk*, the architecture had better have legs. The architecture might be just an ordinary PC, or it might be a robotic car with several onboard computers, cameras, and other sensors. In general, the architecture makes the percepts from the sensors available to the program, runs the program, and feeds the program's action choices to the actuators as they are generated.

4.1 Agent programs

Many agent programs have the same skeleton: they take thecurrent percept as input from the sensors and return an action to the actuators.[4] Notice thedifference between the agent program, which takes the current percept as input, and the agentfunction, which takes the entire percept history. The agent program takes just the currentpercept as input because nothing more is available from the environment; if the agent's actionsneed to depend on the entire percept sequence, the agent will have to remember the percepts.

We describe the agent programs in simple pseudocode language. (The online code repository contains implementations in real programminglanguages.) For example, Figure 7 shows a rather trivial agent program that keeps track ofthe percept sequence and then uses it to index into a table of actions to decide what to do.The table—an example of which is given for the vacuum world in Figure 3—representsexplicitly the agent function that the agent program embodies. To build a rational agent in this way, we as designers must construct a table that contains the appropriate action for every possible percept sequence.

[4] There are other choices for the agent program skeleton; for example, we could have the agent programs be **coroutines** that run asynchronously with the environment. Each such coroutine has an input and output port and consists of a loop that reads the input port for percepts and writes actions to the output port.

```
function TABLE-DRIVEN-AGENT(percept) returns an action
  persistent: percepts, a sequence, initially empty
              table, a table of actions, indexed by percept sequences, initially fully specified

  append percept to the end of percepts
  action ← LOOKUP(percepts, table)
  return action
```

Figure 7 The TABLE-DRIVEN-AGENT program is invoked for each new percept and returns an action each time. It retains the complete percept sequence in memory.

It is instructive to consider why the table-driven approach to agent construction is doomed to failure. Let $\mathcal{P}$ be the set of possible percepts and let T be the lifetime of the agent (the total number of percepts it will receive). The lookup table will contain $\sum_{t=1}^{T} |\mathcal{P}|^t$ entries. Consider the automated taxi: the visual input from a single camera comes in at the rate of roughly 27 megabytes per second (30 frames per second, 640×480 pixels with 24 bits of color information). This gives a lookup table with over $10^{250,000,000,000}$ entries for an hour's driving. Even the lookup table for chess—a tiny, well-behaved fragment of the real world—would have at least 10^{150} entries. The daunting size of these tables (the number of atoms in the observable universe is less than 10^{80}) means that (a) no physical agent in this universe will have the space to store the table, (b) the designer would not have time to create the table, (c) no agent could ever learn all the right table entries from its experience, and (d) even if the environment is simple enough to yield a feasible table size, the designer still has no guidance about how to fill in the table entries.

Despite all this, TABLE-DRIVEN-AGENT *does* do what we want: it implements the desired agent function. The key challenge for AI is to find out how to write programs that, to the extent possible, produce rational behavior from a smallish program rather than from a vast table. We have many examples showing that this can be done successfully in other areas: for example, the huge tables of square roots used by engineers and schoolchildren prior to the 1970s have now been replaced by a five-line program for Newton's method running on electronic calculators. The question is, can AI do for general intelligent behavior what Newton did for square roots? We believe the answer is yes.

In the remainder of this section, we outline four basic kinds of agent programs that embody the principles underlying almost all intelligent systems:

- Simple reflex agents;
- Model-based reflex agents;
- Goal-based agents; and
- Utility-based agents.

Each kind of agent program combines particular components in particular ways to generate actions. Section 4.6 explains in general terms how to convert all these agents into *learning*

```
function REFLEX-VACUUM-AGENT([location,status]) returns an action
    if status = Dirty then return Suck
    else if location = A then return Right
    else if location = B then return Left
```

Figure 8 The agent program for a simple reflex agent in the two-state vacuum environment. This program implements the agent function tabulated in Figure 3.

agents that can improve the performance of their components so as to generate better actions. Finally, Section 4.7 describes the variety of ways in which the components themselves can be represented within the agent. This variety provides a major organizing principle for the field and for the book itself.

4.2 Simple reflex agents

SIMPLE REFLEX AGENT

The simplest kind of agent is the **simple reflex agent**. These agents select actions on the basis of the *current* percept, ignoring the rest of the percept history. For example, the vacuum agent whose agent function is tabulated in Figure 3 is a simple reflex agent, because its decision is based only on the current location and on whether that location contains dirt. An agent program for this agent is shown in Figure 8.

Notice that the vacuum agent program is very small indeed compared to the corresponding table. The most obvious reduction comes from ignoring the percept history, which cuts down the number of possibilities from 4^T to just 4. A further, small reduction comes from the fact that when the current square is dirty, the action does not depend on the location.

Simple reflex behaviors occur even in more complex environments. Imagine yourself as the driver of the automated taxi. If the car in front brakes and its brake lights come on, then you should notice this and initiate braking. In other words, some processing is done on the visual input to establish the condition we call "The car in front is braking." Then, this triggers some established connection in the agent program to the action "initiate braking." We call such a connection a **condition–action rule**,[5] written as

CONDITION–ACTION RULE

if *car-in-front-is-braking* **then** *initiate-braking*.

Humans also have many such connections, some of which are learned responses (as for driving) and some of which are innate reflexes (such as blinking when something approaches the eye). There are several different ways in which such connections can be learned and implemented.

The program in Figure 8 is specific to one particular vacuum environment. A more general and flexible approach is first to build a general-purpose interpreter for condition–action rules and then to create rule sets for specific task environments. Figure 9 gives the structure of this general program in schematic form, showing how the condition–action rules allow the agent to make the connection from percept to action. (Do not worry if this seems

[5] Also called **situation–action rules, productions,** or **if–then rules**.

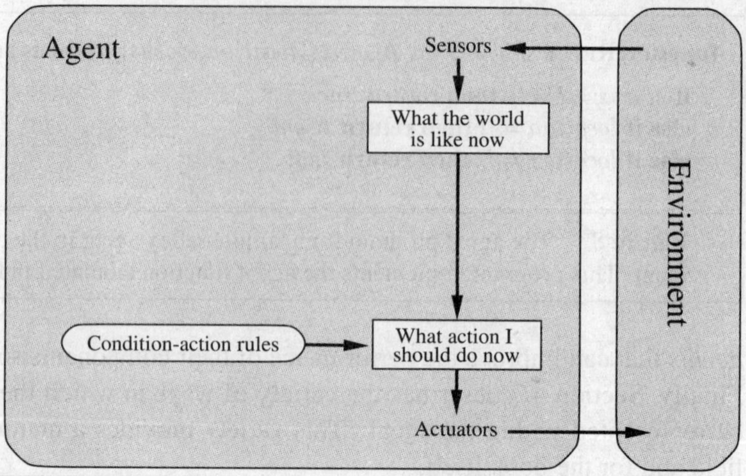

Figure 9 Schematic diagram of a simple reflex agent.

```
function SIMPLE-REFLEX-AGENT(percept) returns an action
  persistent: rules, a set of condition–action rules

  state ← INTERPRET-INPUT(percept)
  rule ← RULE-MATCH(state, rules)
  action ← rule.ACTION
  return action
```

Figure 10 A simple reflex agent. It acts according to a rule whose condition matches the current state, as defined by the percept.

trivial; it gets more interesting shortly.) We use rectangles to denote the current internal state of the agent's decision process, and ovals to represent the background information used in the process. The agent program, which is also very simple, is shown in Figure 10. The INTERPRET-INPUT function generates an abstracted description of the current state from the percept, and the RULE-MATCH function returns the first rule in the set of rules that matches the given state description. Note that the description in terms of "rules" and "matching" is purely conceptual; actual implementations can be as simple as a collection of logic gates implementing a Boolean circuit.

Simple reflex agents have the admirable property of being simple, but they turn out to be of limited intelligence. The agent in Figure 10 will work *only if the correct decision can be made on the basis of only the current percept—that is, only if the environment is fully observable.* Even a little bit of unobservability can cause serious trouble. For example, the braking rule given earlier assumes that the condition *car-in-front-is-braking* can be determined from the current percept—a single frame of video. This works if the car in front has a centrally mounted brake light. Unfortunately, older models have different configurations of taillights, brake lights, and turn-signal lights, and it is not always possible to tell from a single image whether the car is braking. A simple reflex agent driving behind such a car would either brake continuously and unnecessarily, or, worse, never brake at all.

We can see a similar problem arising in the vacuum world. Suppose that a simple reflex vacuum agent is deprived of its location sensor and has only a dirt sensor. Such an agent has just two possible percepts: $[Dirty]$ and $[Clean]$. It can *Suck* in response to $[Dirty]$; what should it do in response to $[Clean]$? Moving *Left* fails (forever) if it happens to start in square A, and moving *Right* fails (forever) if it happens to start in square B. Infinite loops are often unavoidable for simple reflex agents operating in partially observable environments.

RANDOMIZATION

Escape from infinite loops is possible if the agent can **randomize** its actions. For example, if the vacuum agent perceives $[Clean]$, it might flip a coin to choose between *Left* and *Right*. It is easy to show that the agent will reach the other square in an average of two steps. Then, if that square is dirty, the agent will clean it and the task will be complete. Hence, a randomized simple reflex agent might outperform a deterministic simple reflex agent.

We mentioned in Section 3 that randomized behavior of the right kind can be rational in some multiagent environments. In single-agent environments, randomization is usually *not* rational. It is a useful trick that helps a simple reflex agent in some situations, but in most cases we can do much better with more sophisticated deterministic agents.

4.3 Model-based reflex agents

The most effective way to handle partial observability is for the agent to *keep track of the part of the world it can't see now*. That is, the agent should maintain some sort of **internal state** that depends on the percept history and thereby reflects at least some of the unobserved aspects of the current state. For the braking problem, the internal state is not too extensive—just the previous frame from the camera, allowing the agent to detect when two red lights at the edge of the vehicle go on or off simultaneously. For other driving tasks such as changing lanes, the agent needs to keep track of where the other cars are if it can't see them all at once. And for any driving to be possible at all, the agent needs to keep track of where its keys are.

INTERNAL STATE

Updating this internal state information as time goes by requires two kinds of knowledge to be encoded in the agent program. First, we need some information about how the world evolves independently of the agent—for example, that an overtaking car generally will be closer behind than it was a moment ago. Second, we need some information about how the agent's own actions affect the world—for example, that when the agent turns the steering wheel clockwise, the car turns to the right, or that after driving for five minutes northbound on the freeway, one is usually about five miles north of where one was five minutes ago. This knowledge about "how the world works"—whether implemented in simple Boolean circuits or in complete scientific theories—is called a **model** of the world. An agent that uses such a model is called a **model-based agent**.

MODEL-BASED AGENT

Figure 11 gives the structure of the model-based reflex agent with internal state, showing how the current percept is combined with the old internal state to generate the updated description of the current state, based on the agent's model of how the world works. The agent program is shown in Figure 12. The interesting part is the function UPDATE-STATE, which

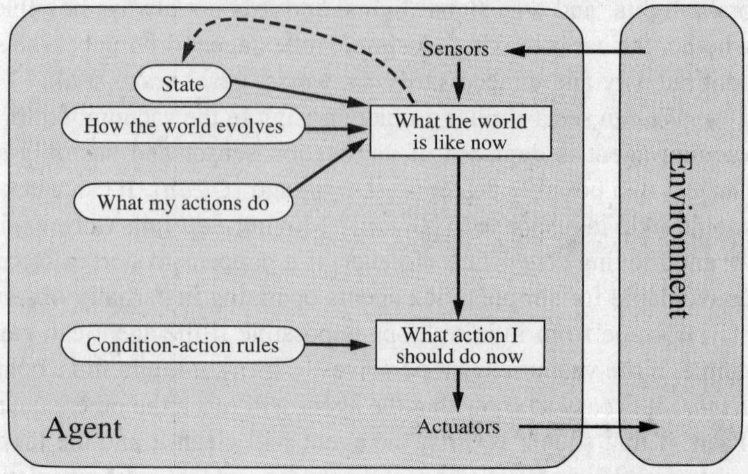

Figure 11 A model-based reflex agent.

```
function MODEL-BASED-REFLEX-AGENT(percept) returns an action
  persistent: state, the agent's current conception of the world state
              model, a description of how the next state depends on current state and action
              rules, a set of condition–action rules
              action, the most recent action, initially none

  state ← UPDATE-STATE(state, action, percept, model)
  rule ← RULE-MATCH(state, rules)
  action ← rule.ACTION
  return action
```

Figure 12 A model-based reflex agent. It keeps track of the current state of the world, using an internal model. It then chooses an action in the same way as the reflex agent.

is responsible for creating the new internal state description. The details of how models and states are represented vary widely depending on the type of environment and the particular technology used in the agent design.

Regardless of the kind of representation used, it is seldom possible for the agent to determine the current state of a partially observable environment *exactly*. Instead, the box labeled "what the world is like now" (Figure 11) represents the agent's "best guess" (or sometimes best guesses). For example, an automated taxi may not be able to see around the large truck that has stopped in front of it and can only guess about what may be causing the hold-up. Thus, uncertainty about the current state may be unavoidable, but the agent still has to make a decision.

A perhaps less obvious point about the internal "state" maintained by a model-based agent is that it does not have to describe "what the world is like now" in a literal sense. For

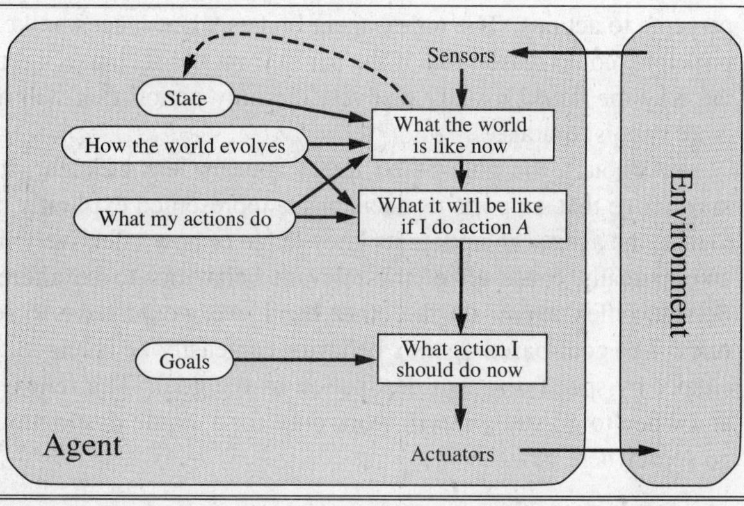

Figure 13 A model-based, goal-based agent. It keeps track of the world state as well as a set of goals it is trying to achieve, and chooses an action that will (eventually) lead to the achievement of its goals.

example, the taxi may be driving back home, and it may have a rule telling it to fill up with gas on the way home unless it has at least half a tank. Although "driving back home" may *seem* to an aspect of the world state, the fact of the taxi's *destination* is actually an aspect of the agent's internal state. If you find this puzzling, consider that the taxi could be in exactly the same place at the same time, but intending to reach a different destination.

4.4 Goal-based agents

Knowing something about the current state of the environment is not always enough to decide what to do. For example, at a road junction, the taxi can turn left, turn right, or go straight on. The correct decision depends on where the taxi is trying to get to. In other words, as well as a current state description, the agent needs some sort of **goal** information that describes situations that are desirable—for example, being at the passenger's destination. The agent program can combine this with the model (the same information as was used in the model-based reflex agent) to choose actions that achieve the goal. Figure 13 shows the goal-based agent's structure.

GOAL

Sometimes goal-based action selection is straightforward—for example, when goal satisfaction results immediately from a single action. Sometimes it will be more tricky—for example, when the agent has to consider long sequences of twists and turns in order to find a way to achieve the goal. **Search** and **planning** are the subfields of AI devoted to finding action sequences that achieve the agent's goals.

Notice that decision making of this kind is fundamentally different from the condition–action rules described earlier, in that it involves consideration of the future—both "What will happen if I do such-and-such?" and "Will that make me happy?" In the reflex agent designs, this information is not explicitly represented, because the built-in rules map directly from percepts to actions. The reflex agent brakes when it sees brake lights. A goal-based agent, in principle, could reason that if the car in front has its brake lights on, it will slow down. Given the way the world usually evolves, the only action that will achieve the goal of not hitting other cars is to brake.

Although the goal-based agent appears less efficient, it is more flexible because the knowledge that supports its decisions is represented explicitly and can be modified. If it starts to rain, the agent can update its knowledge of how effectively its brakes will operate; this will automatically cause all of the relevant behaviors to be altered to suit the new conditions. For the reflex agent, on the other hand, we would have to rewrite many condition–action rules. The goal-based agent's behavior can easily be changed to go to a different destination, simply by specifying that destination as the goal. The reflex agent's rules for when to turn and when to go straight will work only for a single destination; they must all be replaced to go somewhere new.

4.5 Utility-based agents

Goals alone are not enough to generate high-quality behavior in most environments. For example, many action sequences will get the taxi to its destination (thereby achieving the goal) but some are quicker, safer, more reliable, or cheaper than others. Goals just provide a crude binary distinction between "happy" and "unhappy" states. A more general performance measure should allow a comparison of different world states according to exactly how happy they would make the agent. Because "happy" does not sound very scientific, economists and

UTILITY computer scientists use the term **utility** instead.[6]

We have already seen that a performance measure assigns a score to any given sequence of environment states, so it can easily distinguish between more and less desirable ways of

UTILITY FUNCTION getting to the taxi's destination. An agent's **utility function** is essentially an internalization of the performance measure. If the internal utility function and the external performance measure are in agreement, then an agent that chooses actions to maximize its utility will be rational according to the external performance measure.

Let us emphasize again that this is not the *only* way to be rational—we have already seen a rational agent program for the vacuum world (Figure 8) that has no idea what its utility function is—but, like goal-based agents, a utility-based agent has many advantages in terms of flexibility and learning. Furthermore, in two kinds of cases, goals are inadequate but a utility-based agent can still make rational decisions. First, when there are conflicting goals, only some of which can be achieved (for example, speed and safety), the utility function specifies the appropriate tradeoff. Second, when there are several goals that the agent can aim for, none of which can be achieved with certainty, utility provides a way in which the likelihood of success can be weighed against the importance of the goals.

Partial observability and stochasticity are ubiquitous in the real world, and so, therefore, is decision making under uncertainty. Technically speaking, a rational utility-based agent

EXPECTED UTILITY chooses the action that maximizes the **expected utility** of the action outcomes—that is, the utility the agent expects to derive, on average, given the probabilities and utilities of each

[6] The word "utility" here refers to "the quality of being useful," not to the electric company or waterworks.

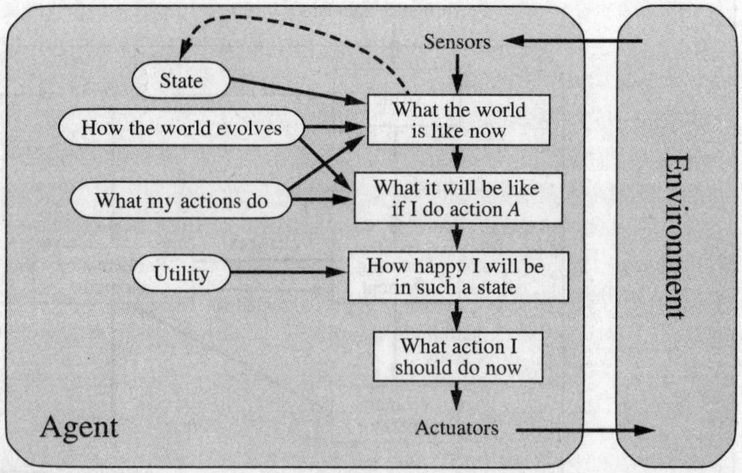

Figure 14 A model-based, utility-based agent. It uses a model of the world, along with a utility function that measures its preferences among states of the world. Then it chooses the action that leads to the best expected utility, where expected utility is computed by averaging over all possible outcome states, weighted by the probability of the outcome.

outcome. Any rational agent must behave as *if* it possesses a utility function whose expected value it tries to maximize. An agent that possesses an *explicit* utility function can make rational decisions with a general-purpose algorithm that does not depend on the specific utility function being maximized. In this way, the "global" definition of rationality—designating as rational those agent functions that have the highest performance—is turned into a "local" constraint on rational-agent designs that can be expressed in a simple program.

The utility-based agent structure appears in Figure 14. Utility-based agent programs appear in Part IV, where we design decision-making agents that must handle the uncertainty inherent in stochastic or partially observable environments.

At this point, the reader may be wondering, "Is it that simple? We just build agents that maximize expected utility, and we're done?" It's true that such agents would be intelligent, but it's not simple. A utility-based agent has to model and keep track of its environment, tasks that have involved a great deal of research on perception, representation, reasoning, and learning. Choosing the utility-maximizing course of action is also a difficult task, requiring ingenious algorithms. Even with these algorithms, perfect rationality is usually unachievable in practice because of computational complexity.

4.6 Learning agents

We have described agent programs with various methods for selecting actions. We have not, so far, explained how the agent programs *come into being*. In his famous early paper, Turing (1950) considers the idea of actually programming his intelligent machines by hand.

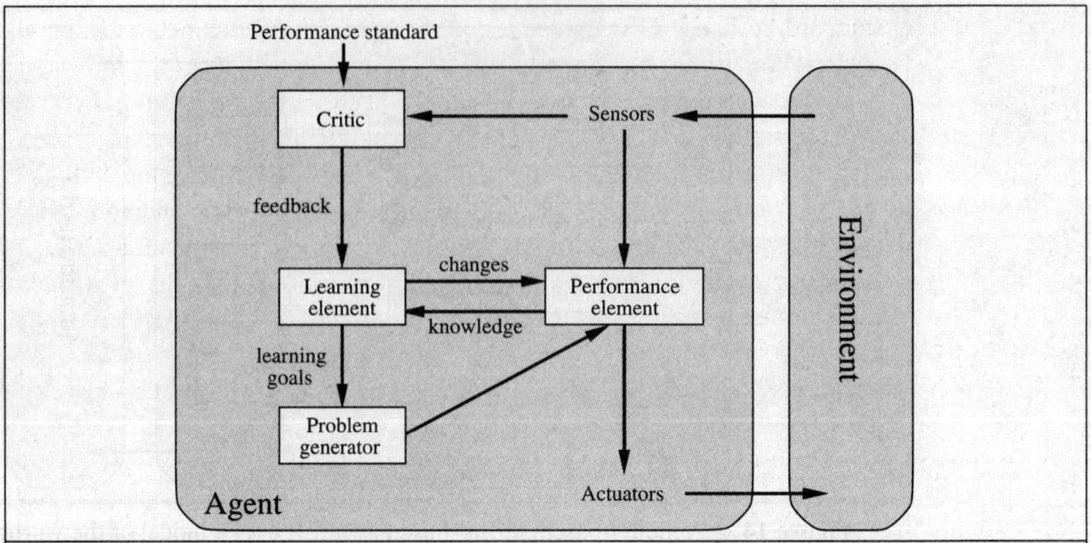

Figure 15 A general learning agent.

He estimates how much work this might take and concludes "Some more expeditious method seems desirable." The method he proposes is to build learning machines and then to teach them. In many areas of AI, this is now the preferred method for creating state-of-the-art systems. Learning has another advantage, as we noted earlier: it allows the agent to operate in initially unknown environments and to become more competent than its initial knowledge alone might allow. In this section, we briefly introduce the main ideas of learning agents.

LEARNING ELEMENT

PERFORMANCE ELEMENT

A learning agent can be divided into four conceptual components, as shown in Figure 15. The most important distinction is between the **learning element**, which is responsible for making improvements, and the **performance element**, which is responsible for selecting external actions. The performance element is what we have previously considered to be the entire agent: it takes in percepts and decides on actions. The learning element uses feedback from the **critic** on how the agent is doing and determines how the performance element should be modified to do better in the future.

CRITIC

The design of the learning element depends very much on the design of the performance element. When trying to design an agent that learns a certain capability, the first question is not "How am I going to get it to learn this?" but "What kind of performance element will my agent need to do this once it has learned how?" Given an agent design, learning mechanisms can be constructed to improve every part of the agent.

The critic tells the learning element how well the agent is doing with respect to a fixed performance standard. The critic is necessary because the percepts themselves provide no indication of the agent's success. For example, a chess program could receive a percept indicating that it has checkmated its opponent, but it needs a performance standard to know that this is a good thing; the percept itself does not say so. It is important that the performance standard be fixed. Conceptually, one should think of it as being outside the agent altogether because the agent must not modify it to fit its own behavior.

PROBLEM GENERATOR

The last component of the learning agent is the **problem generator**. It is responsible for suggesting actions that will lead to new and informative experiences. The point is that if the performance element had its way, it would keep doing the actions that are best, given what it knows. But if the agent is willing to explore a little and do some perhaps suboptimal actions in the short run, it might discover much better actions for the long run. The problem generator's job is to suggest these exploratory actions. This is what scientists do when they carry out experiments. Galileo did not think that dropping rocks from the top of a tower in Pisa was valuable in itself. He was not trying to break the rocks or to modify the brains of unfortunate passers-by. His aim was to modify his own brain by identifying a better theory of the motion of objects.

To make the overall design more concrete, let us return to the automated taxi example. The performance element consists of whatever collection of knowledge and procedures the taxi has for selecting its driving actions. The taxi goes out on the road and drives, using this performance element. The critic observes the world and passes information along to the learning element. For example, after the taxi makes a quick left turn across three lanes of traffic, the critic observes the shocking language used by other drivers. From this experience, the learning element is able to formulate a rule saying this was a bad action, and the performance element is modified by installation of the new rule. The problem generator might identify certain areas of behavior in need of improvement and suggest experiments, such as trying out the brakes on different road surfaces under different conditions.

The learning element can make changes to any of the "knowledge" components shown in the agent diagrams (Figures 9, 11, 13, and 14). The simplest cases involve learning directly from the percept sequence. Observation of pairs of successive states of the environment can allow the agent to learn "How the world evolves," and observation of the results of its actions can allow the agent to learn "What my actions do." For example, if the taxi exerts a certain braking pressure when driving on a wet road, then it will soon find out how much deceleration is actually achieved. Clearly, these two learning tasks are more difficult if the environment is only partially observable.

The forms of learning in the preceding paragraph do not need to access the external performance standard—in a sense, the standard is the universal one of making predictions that agree with experiment. The situation is slightly more complex for a utility-based agent that wishes to learn utility information. For example, suppose the taxi-driving agent receives no tips from passengers who have been thoroughly shaken up during the trip. The external performance standard must inform the agent that the loss of tips is a negative contribution to its overall performance; then the agent might be able to learn that violent maneuvers do not contribute to its own utility. In a sense, the performance standard distinguishes part of the incoming percept as a **reward** (or **penalty**) that provides direct feedback on the quality of the agent's behavior. Hard-wired performance standards such as pain and hunger in animals can be understood in this way.

In summary, agents have a variety of components, and those components can be represented in many ways within the agent program, so there appears to be great variety among learning methods. There is, however, a single unifying theme. Learning in intelligent agents can be summarized as a process of modification of each component of the agent to bring the components into closer agreement with the available feedback information, thereby improving the overall performance of the agent.

4.7 How the components of agent programs work

We have described agent programs (in very high-level terms) as consisting of various components, whose function it is to answer questions such as: "What is the world like now?" "What action should I do now?" "What do my actions do?" The next question for a student of AI is, "How on earth do these components work?" It takes about a thousand pages to begin to answer that question properly, but here we want to draw the reader's attention to some basic distinctions among the various ways that the components can represent the environment that the agent inhabits.

Roughly speaking, we can place the representations along an axis of increasing complexity and expressive power—**atomic**, **factored**, and **structured**. To illustrate these ideas, it helps to consider a particular agent component, such as the one that deals with "What my actions do." This component describes the changes that might occur in the environment as the result of taking an action, and Figure 16 provides schematic depictions of how those transitions might be represented.

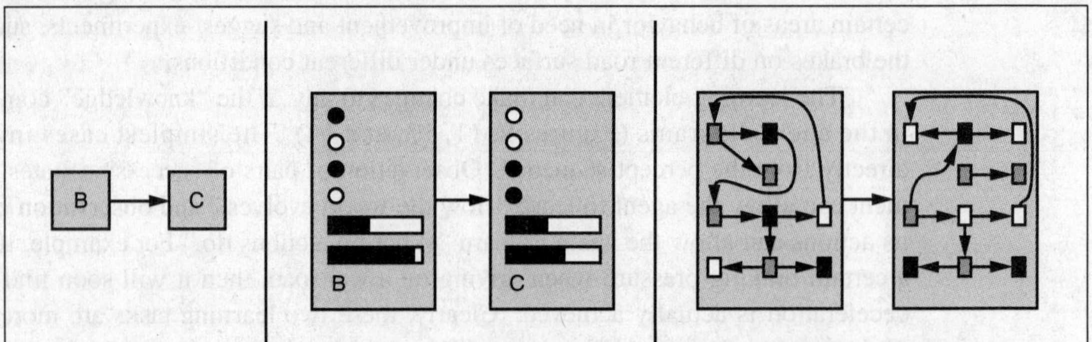

(a) Atomic (b) Factored (b) Structured

Figure 16 Three ways to represent states and the transitions between them. (a) Atomic representation: a state (such as B or C) is a black box with no internal structure; (b) Factored representation: a state consists of a vector of attribute values; values can be Boolean, real-valued, or one of a fixed set of symbols. (c) Structured representation: a state includes objects, each of which may have attributes of its own as well as relationships to other objects.

ATOMIC REPRESENTATION

In an **atomic representation** each state of the world is indivisible—it has no internal structure. Consider the problem of finding a driving route from one end of a country to the other via some sequence of cities. For the purposes of solving this problem, it may suffice to reduce the state of world to just the name of the city we are in—a single atom of knowledge; a "black box" whose only discernible property is that of being identical to or different from another black box. The algorithms underlying **search** and **game-playing**, **Hidden Markov**

models, and **Markov decision processes** all work with atomic representations—or, at least, they treat representations *as if* they were atomic.

FACTORED REPRESENTATION

VARIABLE

ATTRIBUTE

VALUE

Now consider a higher-fidelity description for the same problem, where we need to be concerned with more than just atomic location in one city or another; we might need to pay attention to how much gas is in the tank, our current GPS coordinates, whether or not the oil warning light is working, how much spare change we have for toll crossings, what station is on the radio, and so on. A **factored representation** splits up each state into a fixed set of **variables** or **attributes**, each of which can have a **value**. While two different atomic states have nothing in common—they are just different black boxes—two different factored states can share some attributes (such as being at some particular GPS location) and not others (such as having lots of gas or having no gas); this makes it much easier to work out how to turn one state into another. With factored representations, we can also represent *uncertainty*—for example, ignorance about the amount of gas in the tank can be represented by leaving that attribute blank. Many important areas of AI are based on factored representations, including **constraint satisfaction** algorithms, **propositional logic**, **planning**, **Bayesian networks**, and **machine learning** algorithms.

STRUCTURED REPRESENTATION

For many purposes, we need to understand the world as having *things* in it that are *related* to each other, not just variables with values. For example, we might notice that a large truck ahead of us is reversing into the driveway of a dairy farm but a cow has got loose and is blocking the truck's path. A factored representation is unlikely to be pre-equipped with the attribute $TruckAheadBackingIntoDairyFarmDrivewayBlockedByLooseCow$ with value $true$ or $false$. Instead, we would need a **structured representation**, in which objects such as cows and trucks and their various and varying relationships can be described explicitly. (See Figure 16(c).) Structured representations underlie **relational databases** and **first-order logic**, **first-order probability models**, **knowledge-based learning** and much of **natural language understanding**. In fact, almost everything that humans express in natural language concerns objects and their relationships.

EXPRESSIVENESS

As we mentioned earlier, the axis along which atomic, factored, and structured representations lie is the axis of increasing **expressiveness**. Roughly speaking, a more expressive representation can capture, at least as concisely, everything a less expressive one can capture, plus some more. Often, the more expressive language is *much* more concise; for example, the rules of chess can be written in a page or two of a structured-representation language such as first-order logic but require thousands of pages when written in a factored-representation language such as propositional logic. On the other hand, reasoning and learning become more complex as the expressive power of the representation increases. To gain the benefits of expressive representations while avoiding their drawbacks, intelligent systems for the real world may need to operate at all points along the axis simultaneously.

5 SUMMARY

This chapter has been something of a whirlwind tour of AI, which we have conceived of as the science of agent design. The major points to recall are as follows:

- An **agent** is something that perceives and acts in an environment. The **agent function** for an agent specifies the action taken by the agent in response to any percept sequence.
- The **performance measure** evaluates the behavior of the agent in an environment. A **rational agent** acts so as to maximize the expected value of the performance measure, given the percept sequence it has seen so far.
- A **task environment** specification includes the performance measure, the external environment, the actuators, and the sensors. In designing an agent, the first step must always be to specify the task environment as fully as possible.
- Task environments vary along several significant dimensions. They can be fully or partially observable, single-agent or multiagent, deterministic or stochastic, episodic or sequential, static or dynamic, discrete or continuous, and known or unknown.
- The **agent program** implements the agent function. There exists a variety of basic agent-program designs reflecting the kind of information made explicit and used in the decision process. The designs vary in efficiency, compactness, and flexibility. The appropriate design of the agent program depends on the nature of the environment.
- **Simple reflex agents** respond directly to percepts, whereas **model-based reflex agents** maintain internal state to track aspects of the world that are not evident in the current percept. **Goal-based agents** act to achieve their goals, and **utility-based agents** try to maximize their own expected "happiness."
- All agents can improve their performance through **learning**.

BIBLIOGRAPHICAL AND HISTORICAL NOTES

The central role of action in intelligence—the notion of practical reasoning—goes back at least as far as Aristotle's *Nicomachean Ethics*. Practical reasoning was also the subject of McCarthy's (1958) influential paper "Programs with Common Sense." The fields of robotics and control theory are, by their very nature, concerned principally with physical agents. The concept of a **controller** in control theory is identical to that of an agent in AI. Perhaps surprisingly, AI has concentrated for most of its history on isolated components of agents—question-answering systems, theorem-provers, vision systems, and so on—rather than on whole agents. The discussion of agents in the text by Genesereth and Nilsson (1987) was an influential exception. The whole-agent view is now widely accepted and is a central theme in recent texts (Poole *et al.*, 1998; Nilsson, 1998; Padgham and Winikoff, 2004; Jones, 2007).

CONTROLLER

The roots of the concept of rationality lie in philosophy and economics. In AI, the concept was of peripheral interest until the mid-1980s, when it began to suffuse many discussions about the proper technical foundations of the field. A paper by Jon Doyle (1983) predicted that rational agent design would come to be seen as the core mission of AI, while other popular topics would spin off to form new disciplines.

Careful attention to the properties of the environment and their consequences for rational agent design is most apparent in the control theory tradition—for example, classical control systems (Dorf and Bishop, 2004; Kirk, 2004) handle fully observable, deterministic environments; stochastic optimal control (Kumar and Varaiya, 1986; Bertsekas and Shreve, 2007) handles partially observable, stochastic environments; and hybrid control (Henzinger and Sastry, 1998; Cassandras and Lygeros, 2006) deals with environments containing both discrete and continuous elements. The distinction between fully and partially observable environments is also central in the **dynamic programming** literature developed in the field of operations research (Puterman, 1994).

Reflex agents were the primary model for psychological behaviorists such as Skinner (1953), who attempted to reduce the psychology of organisms strictly to input/output or stimulus/response mappings. The advance from behaviorism to functionalism in psychology, which was at least partly driven by the application of the computer metaphor to agents (Putnam, 1960; Lewis, 1966), introduced the internal state of the agent into the picture. Most work in AI views the idea of pure reflex agents with state as too simple to provide much leverage, but work by Rosenschein (1985) and Brooks (1986) questioned this assumption. In recent years, a great deal of work has gone into finding efficient algorithms for keeping track of complex environments (Hamscher *et al.*, 1992; Simon, 2006). The Remote Agent program that controlled the Deep Space One spacecraft is a particularly impressive example (Muscettola *et al.*, 1998; Jonsson *et al.*, 2000).

Goal-based agents are presupposed in everything from Aristotle's view of practical reasoning to McCarthy's early papers on logical AI. Shakey the Robot (Fikes and Nilsson, 1971; Nilsson, 1984) was the first robotic embodiment of a logical, goal-based agent. A full logical analysis of goal-based agents appeared in Genesereth and Nilsson (1987), and a goal-based programming methodology called agent-oriented programming was developed by Shoham (1993). The agent-based approach is now extremely popular in software engineering (Ciancarini and Wooldridge, 2001). It has also infiltrated the area of operating systems, where **autonomic computing** refers to computer systems and networks that monitor and control themselves with a perceive–act loop and machine learning methods (Kephart and Chess, 2003). Noting that a collection of agent programs designed to work well together in a true multiagent environment necessarily exhibits modularity—the programs share no internal state and communicate with each other only through the environment—it is common within the field of **multiagent systems** to design the agent program of a single agent as a collection of autonomous sub-agents. In some cases, one can even prove that the resulting system gives the same optimal solutions as a monolithic design.

AUTONOMIC COMPUTING

MULTIAGENT SYSTEMS

The goal-based view of agents also dominates the cognitive psychology tradition in the area of problem solving, beginning with the enormously influential *Human Problem Solving* (Newell and Simon, 1972) and running through all of Newell's later work (Newell, 1990). Goals, further analyzed as *desires* (general) and *intentions* (currently pursued), are central to the theory of agents developed by Bratman (1987). This theory has been influential both in natural language understanding and multiagent systems.

Horvitz *et al.* (1988) specifically suggest the use of rationality conceived as the maximization of expected utility as a basis for AI. The text by Pearl (1988) was the first in AI to cover probability and utility theory in depth; its exposition of practical methods for reasoning and decision making under uncertainty was probably the single biggest factor in the rapid shift towards utility-based agents in the 1990s.

The general design for learning agents portrayed in Figure 15 is classic in the machine learning literature (Buchanan *et al.*, 1978; Mitchell, 1997). Examples of the design, as embodied in programs, go back at least as far as Arthur Samuel's (1959, 1967) learning program for playing checkers.

Interest in agents and in agent design has risen rapidly in recent years, partly because of the growth of the Internet and the perceived need for automated and mobile **softbot** (Etzioni and Weld, 1994). Relevant papers are collected in *Readings in Agents* (Huhns and Singh, 1998) and *Foundations of Rational Agency* (Wooldridge and Rao, 1999). Texts on multiagent systems usually provide a good introduction to many aspects of agent design (Weiss, 2000a; Wooldridge, 2002). Several conference series devoted to agents began in the 1990s, including the International Workshop on Agent Theories, Architectures, and Languages (ATAL), the International Conference on Autonomous Agents (AGENTS), and the International Conference on Multi-Agent Systems (ICMAS). In 2002, these three merged to form the International Joint Conference on Autonomous Agents and Multi-Agent Systems (AAMAS). The journal *Autonomous Agents and Multi-Agent Systems* was founded in 1998. Finally, *Dung Beetle Ecology* (Hanski and Cambefort, 1991) provides a wealth of interesting information on the behavior of dung beetles. YouTube features inspiring video recordings of their activities.

EXERCISES

1 Suppose that the performance measure is concerned with just the first T time steps of the environment and ignores everything thereafter. Show that a rational agent's action may depend not just on the state of the environment but also on the time step it has reached.

2 Let us examine the rationality of various vacuum-cleaner agent functions.

a. Show that the simple vacuum-cleaner agent function described in Figure 3 is indeed rational under the assumptions listed in Section 2.1.

b. Describe a rational agent function for the case in which each movement costs one point. Does the corresponding agent program require internal state?

c. Discuss possible agent designs for the cases in which clean squares can become dirty and the geography of the environment is unknown. Does it make sense for the agent to learn from its experience in these cases? If so, what should it learn? If not, why not?

3 For each of the following assertions, say whether it is true or false and support your answer with examples or counterexamples where appropriate.

a. An agent that senses only partial information about the state cannot be perfectly rational.

b. There exist task environments in which no pure reflex agent can behave rationally.

c. There exists a task environment in which every agent is rational.

d. The input to an agent program is the same as the input to the agent function.

e. Every agent function is implementable by some program/machine combination.

f. Suppose an agent selects its action uniformly at random from the set of possible actions. There exists a deterministic task environment in which this agent is rational.

g. It is possible for a given agent to be perfectly rational in two distinct task environments.

h. Every agent is rational in an unobservable environment.

i. A perfectly rational poker-playing agent never loses.

4 For each of the following activities, give a PEAS description of the task environment and characterize it in terms of the properties listed in Section 3.2.

- Playing soccer.
- Exploring the subsurface oceans of Titan.
- Shopping for used AI books on the Internet.
- Playing a tennis match.
- Practicing tennis against a wall.
- Performing a high jump.
- Knitting a sweater.
- Bidding on an item at an auction.

5 Define in your own words the following terms: agent, agent function, agent program, rationality, autonomy, reflex agent, model-based agent, goal-based agent, utility-based agent, learning agent.

6 This exercise explores the differences between agent functions and agent programs.

a. Can there be more than one agent program that implements a given agent function? Give an example, or show why one is not possible.

b. Are there agent functions that cannot be implemented by any agent program?

c. Given a fixed machine architecture, does each agent program implement exactly one agent function?

d. Given an architecture with n bits of storage, how many different possible agent programs are there?

e. Suppose we keep the agent program fixed but speed up the machine by a factor of two. Does that change the agent function?

7 Write pseudocode agent programs for the goal-based and utility-based agents.

The following exercises all concern the implementation of environments and agents for the vacuum-cleaner world.

8 Implement a performance-measuring environment simulator for the vacuum-cleaner world depicted in Figure 2 and specified in section 2.1. Your implementation should be modular so that the sensors, actuators, and environment characteristics (size, shape, dirt placement, etc.) can be changed easily. (*Note:* for some choices of programming language and operating system there are already implementations in the online code repository.)

9 Implement a simple reflex agent for the vacuum environment in Exercise 8. Run the environment with this agent for all possible initial dirt configurations and agent locations. Record the performance score for each configuration and the overall average score.

10 Consider a modified version of the vacuum environment in Exercise 8, in which the agent is penalized one point for each movement.

a. Can a simple reflex agent be perfectly rational for this environment? Explain.

b. What about a reflex agent with state? Design such an agent.

c. How do your answers to **a** and **b** change if the agent's percepts give it the clean/dirty status of every square in the environment?

11 Consider a modified version of the vacuum environment in Exercise 8, in which the geography of the environment—its extent, boundaries, and obstacles—is unknown, as is the initial dirt configuration. (The agent can go *Up* and *Down* as well as *Left* and *Right*.)

a. Can a simple reflex agent be perfectly rational for this environment? Explain.

b. Can a simple reflex agent with a *randomized* agent function outperform a simple reflex agent? Design such an agent and measure its performance on several environments.

c. Can you design an environment in which your randomized agent will perform poorly? Show your results.

d. Can a reflex agent with state outperform a simple reflex agent? Design such an agent and measure its performance on several environments. Can you design a rational agent of this type?

12 Repeat Exercise 11 for the case in which the location sensor is replaced with a "bump" sensor that detects the agent's attempts to move into an obstacle or to cross the boundaries of the environment. Suppose the bump sensor stops working; how should the agent behave?

13 The vacuum environments in the preceding exercises have all been deterministic. Discuss possible agent programs for each of the following stochastic versions:

a. Murphy's law: twenty-five percent of the time, the *Suck* action fails to clean the floor if it is dirty and deposits dirt onto the floor if the floor is clean. How is your agent program affected if the dirt sensor gives the wrong answer 10% of the time?

b. Small children: At each time step, each clean square has a 10% chance of becoming dirty. Can you come up with a rational agent design for this case?

SOLVING PROBLEMS BY SEARCHING

SOLVING PROBLEMS BY SEARCHING

In which we see how an agent can find a sequence of actions that achieves its goals when no single action will do.

Reflex agents base their actions on a direct mapping from states to actions. Such agents cannot operate well in environments for which this mapping would be too large to store and would take too long to learn. Goal-based agents, on the other hand, consider future actions and the desirability of their outcomes.

PROBLEM-SOLVING AGENT

This chapter describes one kind of goal-based agent called a **problem—solving agent**. Problem-solving agents use **atomic** representations–that is, states of the world are considered as wholes, with no internal structure visible to the problem-solving algorithms. Goal-based agents that use more advanced **factored** or **structured** representations are usually called **planning agents.**

Our discussion of problem solving begins with precise definitions of **problems** and their **solutions** and give several examples to illustrate these definitions. We then describe several general-purpose search algorithms that can be used to solve these problems. We will see several **uninformed** search algorithms—algorithms that are given no information about the problem other than its definition. Although some of these algorithms can solve any solvable problem, none of them can do so efficiently. **Informed** search algorithms, on the other hand, can do quite well given some guidance on where to look for solutions.

In this chapter, we limit ourselves to the simplest kind of task environment, for which the solution to a problem is always a *fixed sequence* of actions.

This chapter uses the concepts of asymptotic complexity (that is, $O()$ notation) and NP-completeness. Readers unfamiliar with these concepts should consult Appendix: Mathematical Background.

1 PROBLEM-SOLVING AGENTS

Intelligent agents are supposed to maximize their performance measure. Achieving this is sometimes simplified if the agent can adopt a **goal** and aim at satisfying it. Let us first look at why and how an agent might do this.

Imagine an agent in the city of Arad, Romania, enjoying a touring holiday. The agent's performance measure contains many factors: it wants to improve its suntan, improve its Romanian, take in the sights, enjoy the nightlife (such as it is), avoid hangovers, and so on. The decision problem is a complex one involving many tradeoffs and careful reading of guidebooks. Now, suppose the agent has a nonrefundable ticket to fly out of Bucharest the following day. In that case, it makes sense for the agent to adopt the **goal** of getting to Bucharest. Courses of action that don't reach Bucharest on time can be rejected without further consideration and the agent's decision problem is greatly simplified. Goals help organize behavior by limiting the objectives that the agent is trying to achieve and hence the actions it needs to consider. **Goal formulation**, based on the current situation and the agent's performance measure, is the first step in problem solving.

GOAL FORMULATION

We will consider a goal to be a set of world states—exactly those states in which the goal is satisfied. The agent's task is to find out how to act, now and in the future, so that it reaches a goal state. Before it can do this, it needs to decide (or we need to decide on its behalf) what sorts of actions and states it should consider. If it were to consider actions at the level of "move the left foot forward an inch" or "turn the steering wheel one degree left," the agent would probably never find its way out of the parking lot, let alone to Bucharest, because at that level of detail there is too much uncertainty in the world and there would be too many steps in a solution. **Problem formulation** is the process of deciding what actions and states to consider, given a goal. We discuss this process in more detail later. For now, let us assume that the agent will consider actions at the level of driving from one major town to another. Each state therefore corresponds to being in a particular town.

PROBLEM FORMULATION

Our agent has now adopted the goal of driving to Bucharest and is considering where to go from Arad. Three roads lead out of Arad, one toward Sibiu, one to Timisoara, and one to Zerind. None of these achieves the goal, so unless the agent is familiar with the geography of Romania, it will not know which road to follow.[1] In other words, the agent will not know which of its possible actions is best, because it does not yet know enough about the state that results from taking each action. If the agent has no additional information, then it is has no choice but to try one of the actions at random.

But suppose the agent has a map of Romania. The point of a map is to provide the agent with information about the states it might get itself into and the actions it can take. The agent can use this information to consider *subsequent* stages of a hypothetical journey via each of the three towns, trying to find a journey that eventually gets to Bucharest. Once it has found a path on the map from Arad to Bucharest, it can achieve its goal by carrying out the driving actions that correspond to the legs of the journey. In general, *an agent with several immediate options of unknown value can decide what to do by first examining* future *actions that eventually lead to states of known value.*

To be more specific about what we mean by "examining future actions," we have to be more specific about properties of the environment. For now, we assume that the environment

[1] We are assuming that most readers are in the same position and can easily imagine themselves to be as clueless as our agent. We apologize to Romanian readers who are unable to take advantage of this pedagogical device.

is **observable**, so the agent always knows the current state. For the agent driving in Romania, it's reasonable to suppose that each city on the map has a sign indicating its presence to arriving drivers. We also assume the environment is **discrete**, so at any given state there are only finitely many actions to choose from. This is true for navigating in Romania because each city is connected to a small number of other cities. We will assume the environment is **known**, so the agent knows which states are reached by each action. (Having an accurate map suffices to meet this condition for navigation problems.) Finally, we assume that the environment is **deterministic**, so each action has exactly one outcome. Under ideal conditions, this is true for the agent in Romania—it means that if it chooses to drive from Arad to Sibiu, it does end up in Sibiu. Of course, conditions are not always ideal.

Under these assumptions, the solution to any problem is a fixed sequence of actions. "Of course!" one might say, "What else could it be?" Well, in general it could be a branching strategy that recommends different actions in the future depending on what percepts arrive. For example, under less than ideal conditions, the agent might plan to drive from Arad to Sibiu and then to Rimnicu Vilcea but may also need to have a contingency plan in case it arrives by accident in Zerind instead of Sibiu. Fortunately, if the agent knows the initial state and the environment is known and deterministic, it knows exactly where it will be after the first action and what it will perceive. Since only one percept is possible after the first action, the solution can specify only one possible second action, and so on.

SEARCH
SOLUTION
EXECUTION

The process of looking for a sequence of actions that reaches the goal is called **search**. A search algorithm takes a problem as input and returns a **solution** in the form of an action sequence. Once a solution is found, the actions it recommends can be carried out. This is called the **execution** phase. Thus, we have a simple "formulate, search, execute" design for the agent, as shown in Figure 1. After formulating a goal and a problem to solve, the agent calls a search procedure to solve it. It then uses the solution to guide its actions, doing whatever the solution recommends as the next thing to do—typically, the first action of the sequence—and then removing that step from the sequence. Once the solution has been executed, the agent will formulate a new goal.

OPEN-LOOP

Notice that while the agent is executing the solution sequence it *ignores its percepts* when choosing an action because it knows in advance what they will be. An agent that carries out its plans with its eyes closed, so to speak, must be quite certain of what is going on. Control theorists call this an **open-loop** system, because ignoring the percepts breaks the loop between agent and environment.

We first describe the process of problem formulation, and then devote the bulk of the chapter to various algorithms for the SEARCH function. We do not discuss the workings of the UPDATE-STATE and FORMULATE-GOAL functions further in this chapter.

1.1 Well-defined problems and solutions

PROBLEM

A **problem** can be defined formally by five components:

INITIAL STATE

- The **initial state** that the agent starts in. For example, the initial state for our agent in Romania might be described as $In(Arad)$.

```
function SIMPLE-PROBLEM-SOLVING-AGENT(percept) returns an action
  persistent: seq, an action sequence, initially empty
              state, some description of the current world state
              goal, a goal, initially null
              problem, a problem formulation

  state ← UPDATE-STATE(state, percept)
  if seq is empty then
      goal ← FORMULATE-GOAL(state)
      problem ← FORMULATE-PROBLEM(state, goal)
      seq ← SEARCH(problem)
      if seq = failure then return a null action
  action ← FIRST(seq)
  seq ← REST(seq)
  return action
```

Figure 1 A simple problem-solving agent. It first formulates a goal and a problem, searches for a sequence of actions that would solve the problem, and then executes the actions one at a time. When this is complete, it formulates another goal and starts over.

ACTIONS

APPLICABLE

- A description of the possible **actions** available to the agent. Given a particular state s, ACTIONS(s) returns the set of actions that can be executed in s. We say that each of these actions is **applicable** in s. For example, from the state $In(Arad)$, the applicable actions are $\{Go(Sibiu), Go(Timisoara), Go(Zerind)\}$.

TRANSITION MODEL

SUCCESSOR

- A description of what each action does; the formal name for this is the **transition model**, specified by a function RESULT(s, a) that returns the state that results from doing action a in state s. We also use the term **successor** to refer to any state reachable from a given state by a single action.[2] For example, we have

$$\text{RESULT}(In(Arad), Go(Zerind)) = In(Zerind)\,.$$

STATE SPACE

GRAPH

PATH

Together, the initial state, actions, and transition model implicitly define the **state space** of the problem—the set of all states reachable from the initial state by any sequence of actions. The state space forms a directed network or **graph** in which the nodes are states and the links between nodes are actions. (The map of Romania shown in Figure 2 can be interpreted as a state-space graph if we view each road as standing for two driving actions, one in each direction.) A **path** in the state space is a sequence of states connected by a sequence of actions.

GOAL TEST

- The **goal test**, which determines whether a given state is a goal state. Sometimes there is an explicit set of possible goal states, and the test simply checks whether the given state is one of them. The agent's goal in Romania is the singleton set $\{In(Bucharest)\}$.

[2] Many treatments of problem solving, including previous editions of this text, use a **successor function**, which returns the set of all successors, instead of separate ACTIONS and RESULT functions. The successor function makes it difficult to describe an agent that knows what actions it can try but not what they achieve. Also, note some author use RESULT(a, s) instead of RESULT(s, a), and some use DO instead of RESULT.

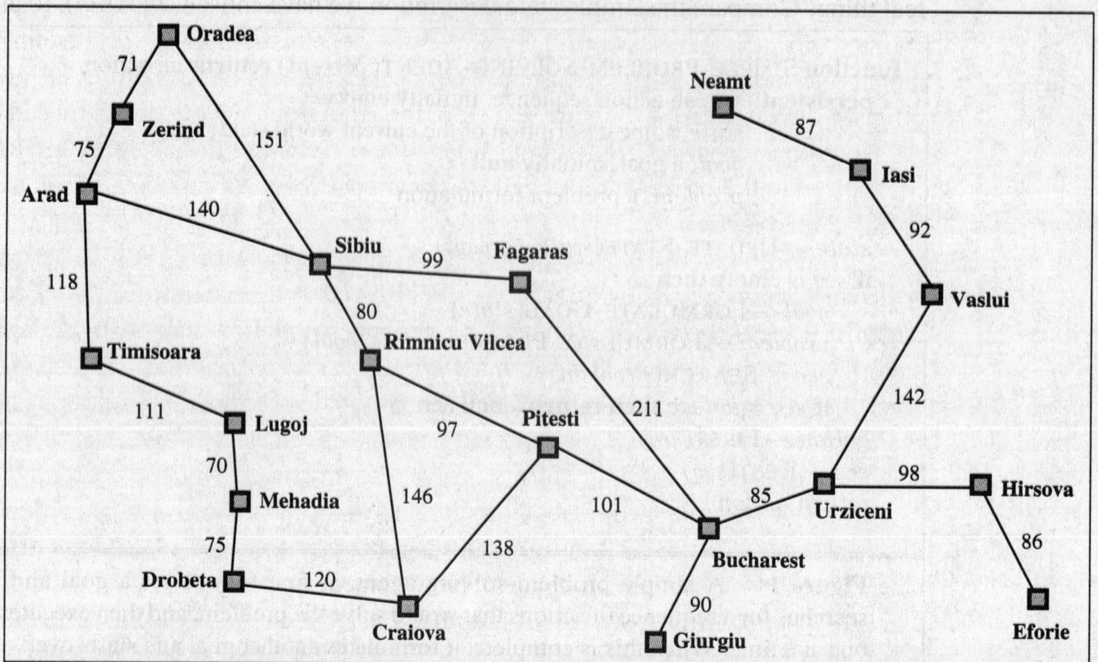

Figure 2 A simplified road map of part of Romania.

Sometimes the goal is specified by an abstract property rather than an explicitly enumerated set of states. For example, in chess, the goal is to reach a state called "checkmate," where the opponent's king is under attack and can't escape.

PATH COST

- A **path cost** function that assigns a numeric cost to each path. The problem-solving agent chooses a cost function that reflects its own performance measure. For the agent trying to get to Bucharest, time is of the essence, so the cost of a path might be its length in kilometers. In this chapter, we assume that the cost of a path can be described as the *sum* of the costs of the individual actions along the path.[3] The **step cost** of taking action a in state s to reach state s' is denoted by $c(s, a, s')$. The step costs for Romania are shown in Figure 2 as route distances. We assume that step costs are nonnegative. [4]

STEP COST

The preceding elements define a problem and can be gathered into a single data structure that is given as input to a problem-solving algorithm. A **solution** to a problem is an action sequence that leads from the initial state to a goal state. Solution quality is measured by the path cost function, and an **optimal solution** has the lowest path cost among all solutions.

OPTIMAL SOLUTION

1.2 Formulating problems

In the preceding section we proposed a formulation of the problem of getting to Bucharest in terms of the initial state, actions, transition model, goal test, and path cost. This formulation seems reasonable, but it is still a *model*—an abstract mathematical description—and not the

[3] This assumption is algorithmically convenient but also theoretically justifiable.

[4] The implications of negative costs are explored in Exercise 8.

real thing. Compare the simple state description we have chosen, *In(Arad)*, to an actual cross-country trip, where the state of the world includes so many things: the traveling companions, the current radio program, the scenery out of the window, the proximity of law enforcement officers, the distance to the next rest stop, the condition of the road, the weather, and so on. All these considerations are left out of our state descriptions because they are irrelevant to the problem of finding a route to Bucharest. The process of removing detail from a representation is called **abstraction**.

ABSTRACTION

In addition to abstracting the state description, we must abstract the actions themselves. A driving action has many effects. Besides changing the location of the vehicle and its occupants, it takes up time, consumes fuel, generates pollution, and changes the agent (as they say, travel is broadening). Our formulation takes into account only the change in location. Also, there are many actions that we omit altogether: turning on the radio, looking out of the window, slowing down for law enforcement officers, and so on. And of course, we don't specify actions at the level of "turn steering wheel to the left by one degree."

Can we be more precise about defining the appropriate level of abstraction? Think of the abstract states and actions we have chosen as corresponding to large sets of detailed world states and detailed action sequences. Now consider a solution to the abstract problem: for example, the path from Arad to Sibiu to Rimnicu Vilcea to Pitesti to Bucharest. This abstract solution corresponds to a large number of more detailed paths. For example, we could drive with the radio on between Sibiu and Rimnicu Vilcea, and then switch it off for the rest of the trip. The abstraction is *valid* if we can expand any abstract solution into a solution in the more detailed world; a sufficient condition is that for every detailed state that is "in Arad," there is a detailed path to some state that is "in Sibiu," and so on. The abstraction is *useful* if carrying out each of the actions in the solution is easier than the original problem; in this case they are easy enough that they can be carried out without further search or planning by an average driving agent. The choice of a good abstraction thus involves removing as much detail as possible while retaining validity and ensuring that the abstract actions are easy to carry out. Were it not for the ability to construct useful abstractions, intelligent agents would be completely swamped by the real world.

2 EXAMPLE PROBLEMS

The problem-solving approach has been applied to a vast array of task environments. We list some of the best known here, distinguishing between *toy* and *real-world* problems. A **toy problem** is intended to illustrate or exercise various problem-solving methods. It can be given a concise, exact description and hence is usable by different researchers to compare the performance of algorithms. A **real-world problem** is one whose solutions people actually care about. Such problems tend not to have a single agreed-upon description, but we can give the general flavor of their formulations.

TOY PROBLEM

REAL-WORLD PROBLEM

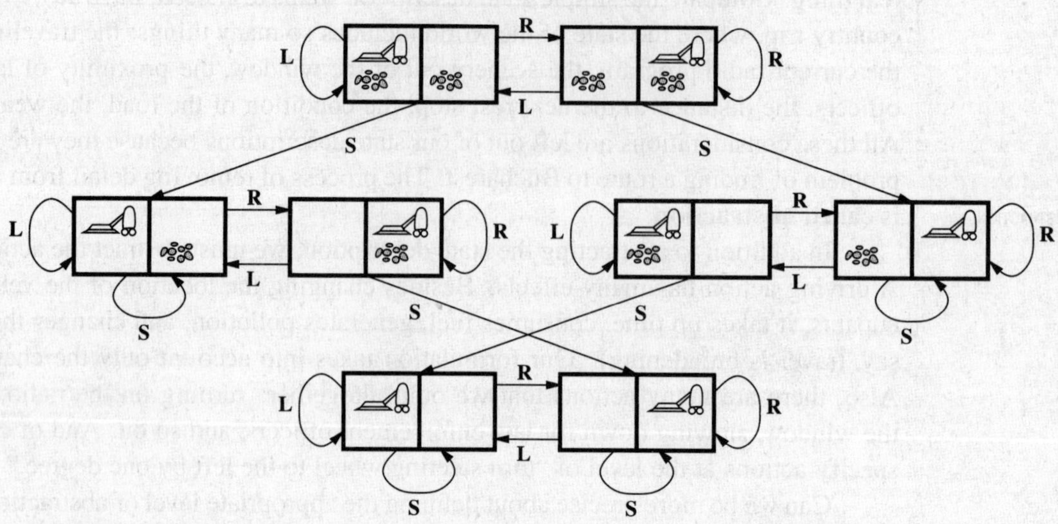

Figure 3 The state space for the vacuum world. Links denote actions: L = *Left*, R = *Right*, S = *Suck*.

2.1 Toy problems

The first example we examine is the **vacuum world**. This can be formulated as a problem as follows:

- **States**: The state is determined by both the agent location and the dirt locations. The agent is in one of two locations, each of which might or might not contain dirt. Thus, there are $2 \times 2^2 = 8$ possible world states. A larger environment with n locations has $n \cdot 2^n$ states.
- **Initial state**: Any state can be designated as the initial state.
- **Actions**: In this simple environment, each state has just three actions: *Left*, *Right*, and *Suck*. Larger environments might also include *Up* and *Down*.
- **Transition model**: The actions have their expected effects, except that moving *Left* in the leftmost square, moving *Right* in the rightmost square, and *Suck*ing in a clean square have no effect. The complete state space is shown in Figure 3.
- **Goal test**: This checks whether all the squares are clean.
- **Path cost**: Each step costs 1, so the path cost is the number of steps in the path.

Compared with the real world, this toy problem has discrete locations, discrete dirt, reliable cleaning, and it never gets any dirtier.

8-PUZZLE

The **8-puzzle**, an instance of which is shown in Figure 4, consists of a 3×3 board with eight numbered tiles and a blank space. A tile adjacent to the blank space can slide into the space. The object is to reach a specified goal state, such as the one shown on the right of the figure. The standard formulation is as follows:

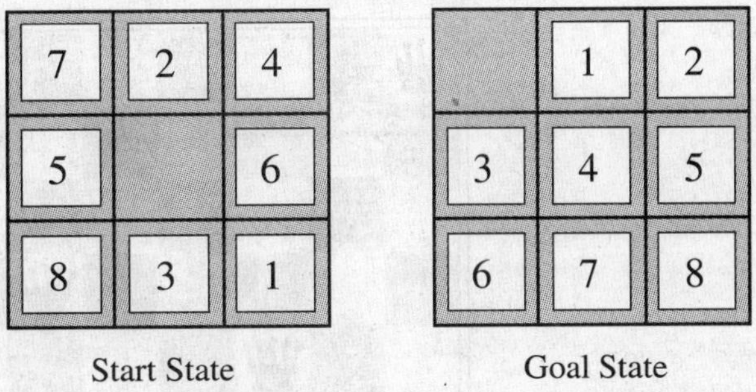

Figure 4 A typical instance of the 8-puzzle.

- **States**: A state description specifies the location of each of the eight tiles and the blank in one of the nine squares.
- **Initial state**: Any state can be designated as the initial state. Note that any given goal can be reached from exactly half of the possible initial states (Exercise 4).
- **Actions**: The simplest formulation defines the actions as movements of the blank space *Left*, *Right*, *Up*, or *Down*. Different subsets of these are possible depending on where the blank is.
- **Transition model**: Given a state and action, this returns the resulting state; for example, if we apply *Left* to the start state in Figure 4, the resulting state has the 5 and the blank switched.
- **Goal test**: This checks whether the state matches the goal configuration shown in Figure 4. (Other goal configurations are possible.)
- **Path cost**: Each step costs 1, so the path cost is the number of steps in the path.

What abstractions have we included here? The actions are abstracted to their beginning and final states, ignoring the intermediate locations where the block is sliding. We have abstracted away actions such as shaking the board when pieces get stuck and ruled out extracting the pieces with a knife and putting them back again. We are left with a description of the rules of the puzzle, avoiding all the details of physical manipulations.

SLIDING-BLOCK PUZZLES

The 8-puzzle belongs to the family of **sliding-block puzzles**, which are often used as test problems for new search algorithms in AI. This family is known to be NP-complete, so one does not expect to find methods significantly better in the worst case than the search algorithms described in this chapter and the next. The 8-puzzle has $9!/2 = 181,440$ reachable states and is easily solved. The 15-puzzle (on a 4×4 board) has around 1.3 trillion states, and random instances can be solved optimally in a few milliseconds by the best search algorithms. The 24-puzzle (on a 5×5 board) has around 10^{25} states, and random instances take several hours to solve optimally.

8-QUEENS PROBLEM

The goal of the **8-queens problem** is to place eight queens on a chessboard such that no queen attacks any other. (A queen attacks any piece in the same row, column or diagonal.) Figure 5 shows an attempted solution that fails: the queen in the rightmost column is attacked by the queen at the top left.

Figure 5 Almost a solution to the 8-queens problem. (Solution is left as an exercise.)

Although efficient special-purpose algorithms exist for this problem and for the whole n-queens family, it remains a useful test problem for search algorithms. There are two main kinds of formulation. An **incremental formulation** involves operators that *augment* the state description, starting with an empty state; for the 8-queens problem, this means that each action adds a queen to the state. A **complete-state formulation** starts with all 8 queens on the board and moves them around. In either case, the path cost is of no interest because only the final state counts. The first incremental formulation one might try is the following:

INCREMENTAL FORMULATION

COMPLETE-STATE FORMULATION

- **States**: Any arrangement of 0 to 8 queens on the board is a state.
- **Initial state**: No queens on the board.
- **Actions**: Add a queen to any empty square.
- **Transition model**: Returns the board with a queen added to the specified square.
- **Goal test**: 8 queens are on the board, none attacked.

In this formulation, we have $64 \cdot 63 \cdots 57 \approx 1.8 \times 10^{14}$ possible sequences to investigate. A better formulation would prohibit placing a queen in any square that is already attacked:

- **States**: All possible arrangements of n queens ($0 \leq n \leq 8$), one per column in the leftmost n columns, with no queen attacking another.
- **Actions**: Add a queen to any square in the leftmost empty column such that it is not attacked by any other queen.

This formulation reduces the 8-queens state space from 1.8×10^{14} to just 2,057, and solutions are easy to find. On the other hand, for 100 queens the reduction is from roughly 10^{400} states to about 10^{52} states (Exercise 5)—a big improvement, but not enough to make the problem tractable.

Our final toy problem was devised by Donald Knuth (1964) and illustrates how infinite state spaces can arise. Knuth conjectured that, starting with the number 4, a sequence of factorial, square root, and floor operations will reach any desired positive integer. For example, we can reach 5 from 4 as follows:

$$\left\lfloor \sqrt{\sqrt{\sqrt{\sqrt{\sqrt{(4!)!}}}}} \right\rfloor = 5 .$$

The problem definition is very simple:

- **States**: Positive numbers.
- **Initial state**: 4.
- **Actions**: Apply factorial, square root, or floor operation (factorial for integers only).
- **Transition model**: As given by the mathematical definitions of the operations.
- **Goal test**: State is the desired positive integer.

To our knowledge there is no bound on how large a number might be constructed in the process of reaching a given target—for example, the number 620,448,401,733,239,439,360,000 is generated in the expression for 5—so the state space for this problem is infinite. Such state spaces arise frequently in tasks involving the generation of mathematical expressions, circuits, proofs, programs, and other recursively defined objects.

2.2 Real-world problems

ROUTE-FINDING PROBLEM

We have already seen how the **route-finding problem** is defined in terms of specified locations and transitions along links between them. Route-finding algorithms are used in a variety of applications. Some, such as Web sites and in-car systems that provide driving directions, are relatively straightforward extensions of the Romania example. Others, such as routing video streams in computer networks, military operations planning, and airline travel-planning systems, involve much more complex specifications. Consider the airline travel problems that must be solved by a travel-planning Web site:

- **States**: Each state obviously includes a location (e.g., an airport) and the current time. Furthermore, because the cost of an action (a flight segment) may depend on previous segments, their fare bases, and their status as domestic or international, the state must record extra information about these "historical" aspects.
- **Initial state**: This is specified by the user's query.
- **Actions**: Take any flight from the current location, in any seat class, leaving after the current time, leaving enough time for within-airport transfer if needed.
- **Transition model**: The state resulting from taking a flight will have the flight's destination as the current location and the flight's arrival time as the current time.
- **Goal test**: Are we at the final destination specified by the user?
- **Path cost**: This depends on monetary cost, waiting time, flight time, customs and immigration procedures, seat quality, time of day, type of airplane, frequent-flyer mileage awards, and so on.

Commercial travel advice systems use a problem formulation of this kind, with many additional complications to handle the byzantine fare structures that airlines impose. Any seasoned traveler knows, however, that not all air travel goes according to plan. A really good system should include contingency plans—such as backup reservations on alternate flights—to the extent that these are justified by the cost and likelihood of failure of the original plan.

TOURING PROBLEM

Touring problems are closely related to route-finding problems, but with an important difference. Consider, for example, the problem "Visit every city in Figure 2 at least once, starting and ending in Bucharest." As with route finding, the actions correspond to trips between adjacent cities. The state space, however, is quite different. Each state must include not just the current location but also the *set of cities the agent has visited*. So the initial state would be $In(Bucharest)$, $Visited(\{Bucharest\})$, a typical intermediate state would be $In(Vaslui)$, $Visited(\{Bucharest, Urziceni, Vaslui\})$, and the goal test would check whether the agent is in Bucharest and all 20 cities have been visited.

TRAVELING SALESPERSON PROBLEM

The **traveling salesperson problem** (TSP) is a touring problem in which each city must be visited exactly once. The aim is to find the *shortest* tour. The problem is known to be NP-hard, but an enormous amount of effort has been expended to improve the capabilities of TSP algorithms. In addition to planning trips for traveling salespersons, these algorithms have been used for tasks such as planning movements of automatic circuit-board drills and of stocking machines on shop floors.

VLSI LAYOUT

A **VLSI layout** problem requires positioning millions of components and connections on a chip to minimize area, minimize circuit delays, minimize stray capacitances, and maximize manufacturing yield. The layout problem comes after the logical design phase and is usually split into two parts: **cell layout** and **channel routing**. In cell layout, the primitive components of the circuit are grouped into cells, each of which performs some recognized function. Each cell has a fixed footprint (size and shape) and requires a certain number of connections to each of the other cells. The aim is to place the cells on the chip so that they do not overlap and so that there is room for the connecting wires to be placed between the cells. Channel routing finds a specific route for each wire through the gaps between the cells. These search problems are extremely complex, but definitely worth solving. Later in this chapter, we present some algorithms capable of solving them.

ROBOT NAVIGATION

Robot navigation is a generalization of the route-finding problem described earlier. Rather than following a discrete set of routes, a robot can move in a continuous space with (in principle) an infinite set of possible actions and states. For a circular robot moving on a flat surface, the space is essentially two-dimensional. When the robot has arms and legs or wheels that must also be controlled, the search space becomes many-dimensional. Advanced techniques are required just to make the search space finite. In addition to the complexity of the problem, real robots must also deal with errors in their sensor readings and motor controls.

AUTOMATIC ASSEMBLY SEQUENCING

Automatic assembly sequencing of complex objects by a robot was first demonstrated by FREDDY (Michie, 1972). Progress since then has been slow but sure, to the point where the assembly of intricate objects such as electric motors is economically feasible. In assembly problems, the aim is to find an order in which to assemble the parts of some object. If the wrong order is chosen, there will be no way to add some part later in the sequence without undoing some of the work already done. Checking a step in the sequence for feasibility is a difficult geometrical search problem closely related to robot navigation. Thus, the generation of legal actions is the expensive part of assembly sequencing. Any practical algorithm must avoid exploring all but a tiny fraction of the state space. Another important assembly problem is **protein design**, in which the goal is to find a sequence of amino acids that will fold into a three-dimensional protein with the right properties to cure some disease.

PROTEIN DESIGN

3 SEARCHING FOR SOLUTIONS

Having formulated some problems, we now need to solve them. A solution is an action sequence, so search algorithms work by considering various possible action sequences. The possible action sequences starting at the initial state form a **search tree** with the initial state at the root; the branches are actions and the **nodes** correspond to states in the state space of the problem. Figure 6 shows the first few steps in growing the search tree for finding a route from Arad to Bucharest. The root node of the tree corresponds to the initial state, *In(Arad)*. The first step is to test whether this is a goal state. (Clearly it is not, but it is important to check so that we can solve trick problems like "starting in Arad, get to Arad.") Then we need to consider taking various actions. We do this by **expanding** the current state; that is, applying each legal action to the current state, thereby **generating** a new set of states. In this case, we add three branches from the **parent node** *In(Arad)* leading to three new **child nodes**: *In(Sibiu), In(Timisoara),* and *In(Zerind)*. Now we must choose which of these three possibilities to consider further.

SEARCH TREE

NODE

EXPANDING

GENERATING

PARENT NODE

CHILD NODE

This is the essence of search—following up one option now and putting the others aside for later, in case the first choice does not lead to a solution. Suppose we choose Sibiu first. We check to see whether it is a goal state (it is not) and then expand it to get *In(Arad)*, *In(Fagaras)*, *In(Oradea)*, and *In(RimnicuVilcea)*. We can then choose any of these four or go back and choose Timisoara or Zerind. Each of these six nodes is a **leaf node**, that is, a node with no children in the tree. The set of all leaf nodes available for expansion at any given point is called the **frontier**. (Many authors call it the **open list**, which is both geographically less evocative and less accurate, because other data structures are better suited than a list.) In Figure 6, the frontier of each tree consists of those nodes with bold outlines.

LEAF NODE

FRONTIER

OPEN LIST

The process of expanding nodes on the frontier continues until either a solution is found or there are no more states to expand. The general TREE-SEARCH algorithm is shown informally in Figure 7. Search algorithms all share this basic structure; they vary primarily according to how they choose which state to expand next—the so-called **search strategy**.

SEARCH STRATEGY

The eagle-eyed reader will notice one peculiar thing about the search tree shown in Figure 6: it includes the path from Arad to Sibiu and back to Arad again! We say that *In(Arad)* is a **repeated state** in the search tree, generated in this case by a **loopy path**. Considering such loopy paths means that the complete search tree for Romania is *infinite* because there is no limit to how often one can traverse a loop. On the other hand, the state space—the map shown in Figure 2—has only 20 states. As we discuss in Section 4, loops can cause

REPEATED STATE

LOOPY PATH

certain algorithms to fail, making otherwise solvable problems unsolvable. Fortunately, there is no need to consider loopy paths. We can rely on more than intuition for this: because path costs are additive and step costs are nonnegative, a loopy path to any given state is never better than the same path with the loop removed.

REDUNDANT PATH

Loopy paths are a special case of the more general concept of **redundant paths**, which exist whenever there is more than one way to get from one state to another. Consider the paths Arad–Sibiu (140 km long) and Arad–Zerind–Oradea–Sibiu (297 km long). Obviously, the second path is redundant—it's just a worse way to get to the same state. If you are concerned about reaching the goal, there's never any reason to keep more than one path to any given state, because any goal state that is reachable by extending one path is also reachable by extending the other.

In some cases, it is possible to define the problem itself so as to eliminate redundant paths. For example, if we formulate the 8-queens problem so that a queen can be placed in any column, then each state with n queens can be reached by $n!$different paths; but if we reformulate the problem so that each new queen is placed in the leftmost empty column, then each state can be reached only through one path.

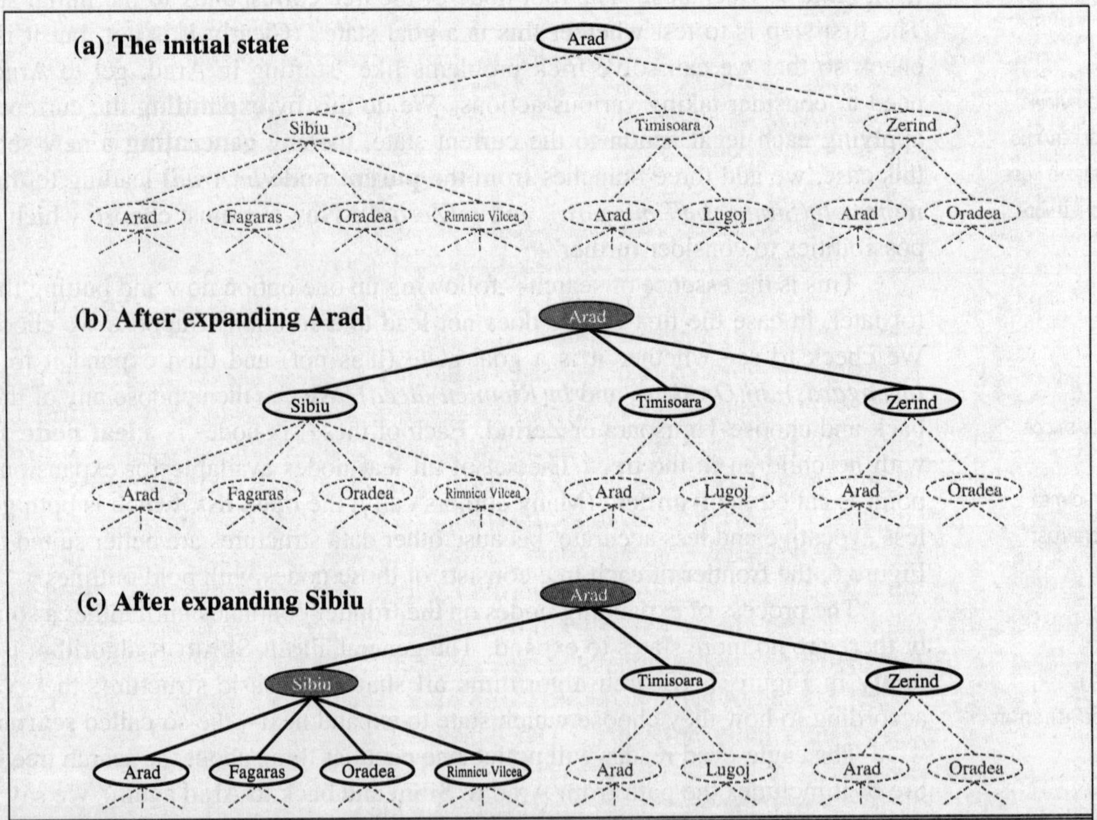

Figure 6 Partial search trees for finding a route from Arad to Bucharest. Nodes that have been expanded are shaded; nodes that have been generated but not yet expanded are outlined in bold; nodes that have not yet been generated are shown in faint dashed lines.

function TREE-SEARCH(*problem*) **returns** a solution, or failure
  initialize the frontier using the initial state of *problem*
  loop do
    if the frontier is empty **then return** failure
    choose a leaf node and remove it from the frontier
    if the node contains a goal state **then return** the corresponding solution
    expand the chosen node, adding the resulting nodes to the frontier

function GRAPH-SEARCH(*problem*) **returns** a solution, or failure
  initialize the frontier using the initial state of *problem*
  initialize the explored set to be empty
  loop do
    if the frontier is empty **then return** failure
    choose a leaf node and remove it from the frontier
    if the node contains a goal state **then return** the corresponding solution
    add the node to the explored set
    expand the chosen node, adding the resulting nodes to the frontier
      only if not in the frontier or explored set

Figure 7 An informal description of the general tree-search and graph-search algorithms. The parts of GRAPH-SEARCH marked in bold italic are the additions needed to handle repeated states.

In other cases, redundant paths are unavoidable. This includes all problems where the actions are reversible, such as route-finding problems and sliding-block puzzles. Route-finding on a **rectangular grid** (like the one used later for Figure 9) is a particularly important example in computer games. In such a grid, each state has four successors, so a search tree of depth d that includes repeated states has 4^d leaves; but there are only about $2d^2$ distinct states within d steps of any given state. For $d = 20$, this means about a trillion nodes but only about 800 distinct states. Thus, following redundant paths can cause a tractable problem to become intractable. This is true even for algorithms that know how to avoid infinite loops.

RECTANGULAR GRID

As the saying goes, *algorithms that forget their history are doomed to repeat it.* The way to avoid exploring redundant paths is to remember where one has been. To do this, we augment the TREE-SEARCH algorithm with a data structure called the **explored set** (also known as the **closed list**), which remembers every expanded node. Newly generated nodes that match previously generated nodes—ones in the explored set or the frontier—can be discarded instead of being added to the frontier. The new algorithm, called GRAPH-SEARCH, is shown informally in Figure 7. The specific algorithms in this chapter draw on this general design.

EXPLORED SET

CLOSED LIST

Clearly, the search tree constructed by the GRAPH-SEARCH algorithm contains at most one copy of each state, so we can think of it as growing a tree directly on the state-space graph, as shown in Figure 8. The algorithm has another nice property: the frontier **separates** the state-space graph into the explored region and the unexplored region, so that every path from

SEPARATOR

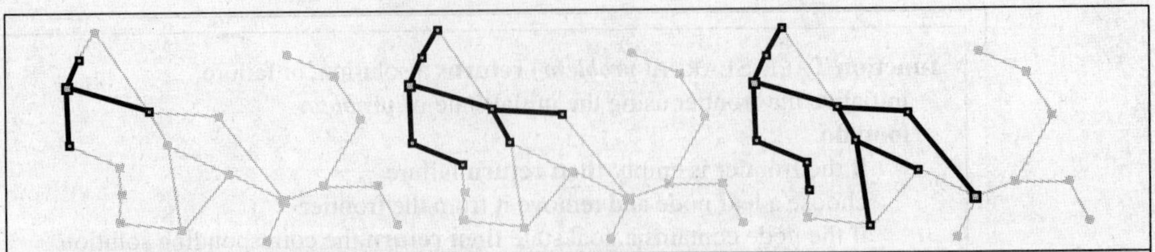

Figure 8 A sequence of search trees generated by a graph search on the Romania problem of Figure 2. At each stage, we have extended each path by one step. Notice that at the third stage, the northernmost city (Oradea) has become a dead end: both of its successors are already explored via other paths.

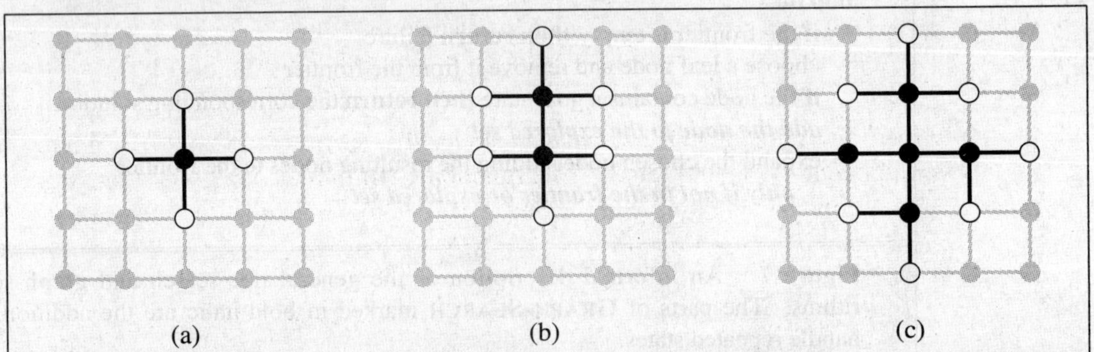

Figure 9 The separation property of GRAPH-SEARCH, illustrated on a rectangular-grid problem. The frontier (white nodes) always separates the explored region of the state space (black nodes) from the unexplored region (gray nodes). In (a), just the root has been expanded. In (b), one leaf node has been expanded. In (c), the remaining successors of the root have been expanded in clockwise order.

the initial state to an unexplored state has to pass through a state in the frontier. (If this seems completely obvious, try Exercise 13 now.) This property is illustrated in Figure 9. As every step moves a state from the frontier into the explored region while moving some states from the unexplored region into the frontier, we see that the algorithm is *systematically* examining the states in the state space, one by one, until it finds a solution.

3.1 Infrastructure for search algorithms

Search algorithms require a data structure to keep track of the search tree that is being constructed. For each node n of the tree, we have a structure that contains four components:

- n.STATE: the state in the state space to which the node corresponds;
- n.PARENT: the node in the search tree that generated this node;
- n.ACTION: the action that was applied to the parent to generate the node;
- n.PATH-COST: the cost, traditionally denoted by $g(n)$, of the path from the initial state to the node, as indicated by the parent pointers.

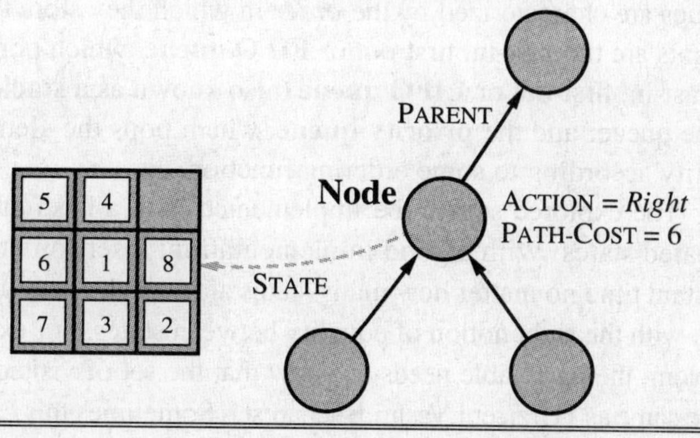

Figure 10 Nodes are the data structures from which the search tree is constructed. Each has a parent, a state, and various bookkeeping fields. Arrows point from child to parent.

Given the components for a parent node, it is easy to see how to compute the necessary components for a child node. The function CHILD-NODE takes a parent node and an action and returns the resulting child node:

```
function CHILD-NODE(problem, parent, action) returns a node
  return a node with
      STATE = problem.RESULT(parent.STATE, action),
      PARENT = parent, ACTION = action,
      PATH-COST = parent.PATH-COST + problem.STEP-COST(parent.STATE, action)
```

The node data structure is depicted in Figure 10. Notice how the PARENT pointers string the nodes together into a tree structure. These pointers also allow the solution path to be extracted when a goal node is found; we use the SOLUTION function to return the sequence of actions obtained by following parent pointers back to the root.

Up to now, we have not been very careful to distinguish between nodes and states, but in writing detailed algorithms it's important to make that distinction. A node is a bookkeeping data structure used to represent the search tree. A state corresponds to a configuration of the world. Thus, nodes are on particular paths, as defined by PARENT pointers, whereas states are not. Furthermore, two different nodes can contain the same world state if that state is generated via two different search paths.

Now that we have nodes, we need somewhere to put them. The frontier needs to be stored in such a way that the search algorithm can easily choose the next node to expand according to its preferred strategy. The appropriate data structure for this is a **queue**. The operations on a queue are as follows:

QUEUE

- EMPTY?(*queue*) returns true only if there are no more elements in the queue.
- POP(*queue*) removes the first element of the queue and returns it.
- INSERT(*element*, *queue*) inserts an element and returns the resulting queue.

Queues are characterized by the *order* in which they store the inserted nodes. Three common variants are the first-in, first-out or **FIFO queue**, which pops the *oldest* element of the queue; the last-in, first-out or **LIFO queue** (also known as a **stack**), which pops the *newest* element of the queue; and the **priority queue**, which pops the element of the queue with the highest priority according to some ordering function.

FIFO QUEUE
LIFO QUEUE
PRIORITY QUEUE

The explored set can be implemented with a hash table to allow efficient checking for repeated states. With a good implementation, insertion and lookup can be done in roughly constant time no matter how many states are stored. One must take care to implement the hash table with the right notion of equality between states. For example, in the traveling salesperson problem, the hash table needs to know that the set of visited cities {Bucharest,Urziceni,Vaslui} is the same as {Urziceni,Vaslui,Bucharest}. Sometimes this can be achieved most easily by insisting that the data structures for states be in some **canonical form**; that is, logically equivalent states should map to the same data structure. In the case of states described by sets, for example, a bit-vector representation or a sorted list without repetition would be canonical, whereas an unsorted list would not.

CANONICAL FORM

3.2 Measuring problem-solving performance

Before we get into the design of specific search algorithms, we need to consider the criteria that might be used to choose among them. We can evaluate an algorithm's performance in four ways:

- **Completeness**: Is the algorithm guaranteed to find a solution when there is one?
- **Optimality**: Does the strategy find the optimal solution, as defined in section 1.1?
- **Time complexity**: How long does it take to find a solution?
- **Space complexity**: How much memory is needed to perform the search?

COMPLETENESS
OPTIMALITY
TIME COMPLEXITY
SPACE COMPLEXITY

Time and space complexity are always considered with respect to some measure of the problem difficulty. In theoretical computer science, the typical measure is the size of the state space graph, $|V| + |E|$, where V is the set of vertices (nodes) of the graph and E is the set of edges (links). This is appropriate when the graph is an explicit data structure that is input to the search program. (The map of Romania is an example of this.) In AI, the graph is often represented *implicitly* by the initial state, actions, and transition model and is frequently infinite. For these reasons, complexity is expressed in terms of three quantities: b, the **branching factor** or maximum number of successors of any node; d, the **depth** of the shallowest goal node (i.e., the number of steps along the path from the root); and m, the maximum length of any path in the state space. Time is often measured in terms of the number of nodes generated during the search, and space in terms of the maximum number of nodes stored in memory. For the most part, we describe time and space complexity for search on a tree; for a graph, the answer depends on how "redundant" the paths in the state space are.

BRANCHING FACTOR
DEPTH

To assess the effectiveness of a search algorithm, we can consider just the **search cost**—which typically depends on the time complexity but can also include a term for memory usage—or we can use the **total cost**, which combines the search cost and the path cost of the solution found. For the problem of finding a route from Arad to Bucharest, the search cost is the amount of time taken by the search and the solution cost is the total length of the path

SEARCH COST
TOTAL COST

in kilometers. Thus, to compute the total cost, we have to add milliseconds and kilometers. There is no "official exchange rate" between the two, but it might be reasonable in this case to convert kilometers into milliseconds by using an estimate of the car's average speed (because time is what the agent cares about). This enables the agent to find an optimal tradeoff point at which further computation to find a shorter path becomes counterproductive.

4 UNINFORMED SEARCH STRATEGIES

UNINFORMED SEARCH

BLIND SEARCH

This section covers several search strategies that come under the heading of **uninformed search** (also called **blind search**). The term means that the strategies have no additional information about states beyond that provided in the problem definition. All they can do is generate successors and distinguish a goal state from a non-goal state. All search strategies are distinguished by the *order* in which nodes are expanded. Strategies that know whether one non-goal state is "more promising" than another are called **informed search** or **heuristic search** strategies; they are covered in Section 5.

INFORMED SEARCH

HEURISTIC SEARCH

4.1 Breadth-first search

BREADTH-FIRST SEARCH

Breadth-first search is a simple strategy in which the root node is expanded first, then all the successors of the root node are expanded next, then *their* successors, and so on. In general, all the nodes are expanded at a given depth in the search tree before any nodes at the next level are expanded.

Breadth-first search is an instance of the general graph-search algorithm (Figure 7) in which the *shallowest* unexpanded node is chosen for expansion. This is achieved very simply by using a FIFO queue for the frontier. Thus, new nodes (which are always deeper than their parents) go to the back of the queue, and old nodes, which are shallower than the new nodes, get expanded first. There is one slight tweak on the general graph-search algorithm, which is that the goal test is applied to each node when it is *generated* rather than when it is selected for expansion. This decision is explained below, where we discuss time complexity. Note also that the algorithm, following the general template for graph search, discards any new path to a state already in the frontier or explored set; it is easy to see that any such path must be at least as deep as the one already found. Thus, breadth-first search always has the shallowest path to every node on the frontier.

Pseudocode is given in Figure 11. Figure 12 shows the progress of the search on a simple binary tree.

How does breadth-first search rate according to the four criteria from the previous section? We can easily see that it is *complete*—if the shallowest goal node is at some finite depth d, breadth-first search will eventually find it after generating all shallower nodes (provided the branching factor b is finite). Note that as soon as a goal node is generated, we know it is the shallowest goal node because all shallower nodes must have been generated already and failed the goal test. Now, the *shallowest* goal node is not necessarily the *optimal* one;

```
function BREADTH-FIRST-SEARCH(problem) returns a solution, or failure
  node ← a node with STATE = problem.INITIAL-STATE, PATH-COST = 0
  if problem.GOAL-TEST(node.STATE) then return SOLUTION(node)
  frontier ← a FIFO queue with node as the only element
  explored ← an empty set
  loop do
     if EMPTY?(frontier) then return failure
     node ← POP(frontier)  /* chooses the shallowest node in frontier */
     add node.STATE to explored
     for each action in problem.ACTIONS(node.STATE) do
        child ← CHILD-NODE(problem, node, action)
        if child.STATE is not in explored or frontier then
           if problem.GOAL-TEST(child.STATE) then return SOLUTION(child)
           frontier ← INSERT(child, frontier)
```

Figure 11 Breadth-first search on a graph.

technically, breadth-first search is optimal if the path cost is a nondecreasing function of the depth of the node. The most common such scenario is that all actions have the same cost.

So far, the news about breadth-first search has been good. The news about time and space is not so good. Imagine searching a uniform tree where every state has b successors. The root of the search tree generates b nodes at the first level, each of which generates b more nodes, for a total of b^2 at the second level. Each of *these* generates b more nodes, yielding b^3 nodes at the third level, and so on. Now suppose that the solution is at depth d. In the worst case, it is the last node generated at that level. Then the total number of nodes generated is

$$b + b^2 + b^3 + \cdots + b^d = O(b^d) .$$

(If the algorithm were to apply the goal test to nodes when selected for expansion, rather than when generated, the whole layer of nodes at depth d would be expanded before the goal was detected and the time complexity would be $O(b^{d+1})$.)

As for space complexity: for any kind of graph search, which stores every expanded node in the *explored* set, the space complexity is always within a factor of b of the time complexity. For breadth-first graph search in particular, every node generated remains in memory. There will be $O(b^{d-1})$ nodes in the *explored* set and $O(b^d)$ nodes in the frontier,

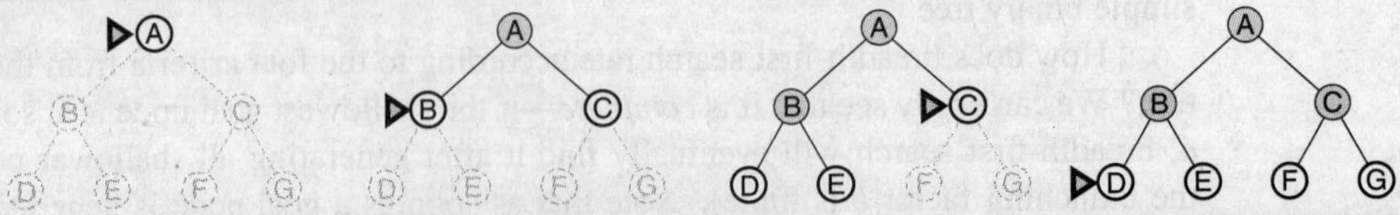

Figure 12 Breadth-first search on a simple binary tree. At each stage, the node to be expanded next is indicated by a marker.

so the space complexity is $O(b^d)$, i.e., it is dominated by the size of the frontier. Switching to a tree search would not save much space, and in a state space with many redundant paths, switching could cost a great deal of time.

An exponential complexity bound such as $O(b^d)$ is scary. Figure 13 shows why. It lists, for various values of the solution depth d, the time and memory required for a breadth-first search with branching factor $b = 10$. The table assumes that 1 million nodes can be generated per second and that a node requires 1000 bytes of storage. Many search problems fit roughly within these assumptions (give or take a factor of 100) when run on a modern personal computer.

Depth	Nodes	Time	Memory
2	110	.11 milliseconds	107 kilobytes
4	11,110	11 milliseconds	10.6 megabytes
6	10^6	1.1 seconds	1 gigabyte
8	10^8	2 minutes	103 gigabytes
10	10^{10}	3 hours	10 terabytes
12	10^{12}	13 days	1 petabyte
14	10^{14}	3.5 years	99 petabytes
16	10^{16}	350 years	10 exabytes

Figure 13 Time and memory requirements for breadth-first search. The numbers shown assume branching factor $b = 10$; 1 million nodes/second; 1000 bytes/node.

Two lessons can be learned from Figure 13. First, *the memory requirements are a bigger problem for breadth-first search than is the execution time.* One might wait 13 days for the solution to an important problem with search depth 12, but no personal computer has the petabyte of memory it would take. Fortunately, other strategies require less memory.

The second lesson is that time is still a major factor. If your problem has a solution at depth 16, then (given our assumptions) it will take about 350 years for breadth-first search (or indeed any uninformed search) to find it. In general, *exponential-complexity search problems cannot be solved by uninformed methods for any but the smallest instances.*

4.2 Uniform-cost search

When all step costs are equal, breadth-first search is optimal because it always expands the *shallowest* unexpanded node. By a simple extension, we can find an algorithm that is optimal with any step-cost function. Instead of expanding the shallowest node, **uniform-cost search** expands the node n with the *lowest path cost* $g(n)$. This is done by storing the frontier as a priority queue ordered by g. The algorithm is shown in Figure 14.

UNIFORM-COST SEARCH

In addition to the ordering of the queue by path cost, there are two other significant differences from breadth-first search. The first is that the goal test is applied to a node when it is *selected for expansion* (as in the generic graph-search algorithm shown in Figure 7) rather than when it is first generated. The reason is that the first goal node that is *generated*

```
function UNIFORM-COST-SEARCH(problem) returns a solution, or failure
  node ← a node with STATE = problem.INITIAL-STATE, PATH-COST = 0
  frontier ← a priority queue ordered by PATH-COST, with node as the only element
  explored ← an empty set
  loop do
     if EMPTY?(frontier) then return failure
     node ← POP(frontier)  /* chooses the lowest-cost node in frontier */
     if problem.GOAL-TEST(node.STATE) then return SOLUTION(node)
     add node.STATE to explored
     for each action in problem.ACTIONS(node.STATE) do
        child ← CHILD-NODE(problem, node, action)
        if child.STATE is not in explored or frontier then
           frontier ← INSERT(child, frontier)
        else if child.STATE is in frontier with higher PATH-COST then
           replace that frontier node with child
```

Figure 14 Uniform-cost search on a graph. The algorithm is identical to the general graph search algorithm in Figure 7, except for the use of a priority queue and the addition of an extra check in case a shorter path to a frontier state is discovered. The data structure for *frontier* needs to support efficient membership testing, so it should combine the capabilities of a priority queue and a hash table.

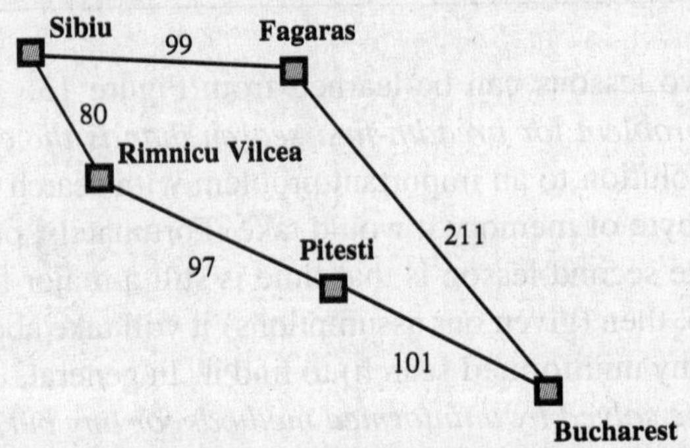

Figure 15 Part of the Romania state space, selected to illustrate uniform-cost search.

may be on a suboptimal path. The second difference is that a test is added in case a better path is found to a node currently on the frontier.

Both of these modifications come into play in the example shown in Figure 15, where the problem is to get from Sibiu to Bucharest. The successors of Sibiu are Rimnicu Vilcea and Fagaras, with costs 80 and 99, respectively. The least-cost node, Rimnicu Vilcea, is expanded next, adding Pitesti with cost $80 + 97 = 177$. The least-cost node is now Fagaras, so it is expanded, adding Bucharest with cost $99 + 211 = 310$. Now a goal node has been generated, but uniform-cost search keeps going, choosing Pitesti for expansion and adding a second path to Bucharest with cost $80+97+101=278$. Now the algorithm checks to see if this new path is better than the old one; it is, so the old one is discarded. Bucharest, now with g-cost 278, is selected for expansion and the solution is returned.

It is easy to see that uniform-cost search is optimal in general. First, we observe that whenever uniform-cost search selects a node n for expansion, the optimal path to that node has been found. (Were this not the case, there would have to be another frontier node n' on the optimal path from the start node to n, by the graph separation property of Figure 9; by definition, n' would have lower g-cost than n and would have been selected first.) Then, because step costs are nonnegative, paths never get shorter as nodes are added. These two facts together imply that *uniform-cost search expands nodes in order of their optimal path cost.* Hence, the first goal node selected for expansion must be the optimal solution.

Uniform-cost search does not care about the *number* of steps a path has, but only about their total cost. Therefore, it will get stuck in an infinite loop if there is a path with an infinite sequence of zero-cost actions—for example, a sequence of *NoOp* actions.[5] Completeness is guaranteed provided the cost of every step exceeds some small positive constant ϵ.

Uniform-cost search is guided by path costs rather than depths, so its complexity is not easily characterized in terms of b and d. Instead, let C^* be the cost of the optimal solution,[6] and assume that every action costs at least ϵ. Then the algorithm's worst-case time and space complexity is $O(b^{1+\lfloor C^*/\epsilon \rfloor})$, which can be much greater than b^d. This is because uniform-cost search can explore large trees of small steps before exploring paths involving large and perhaps useful steps. When all step costs are equal, $b^{1+\lfloor C^*/\epsilon \rfloor}$ is just b^{d+1}. When all step costs are the same, uniform-cost search is similar to breadth-first search, except that the latter stops as soon as it generates a goal, whereas uniform-cost search examines all the nodes at the goal's depth to see if one has a lower cost; thus uniform-cost search does strictly more work by expanding nodes at depth d unnecessarily.

4.3 Depth-first search

DEPTH-FIRST SEARCH

Depth-first search always expands the *deepest* node in the current frontier of the search tree. The progress of the search is illustrated in Figure 16. The search proceeds immediately to the deepest level of the search tree, where the nodes have no successors. As those nodes are expanded, they are dropped from the frontier, so then the search "backs up" to the next deepest node that still has unexplored successors.

The depth-first search algorithm is an instance of the graph-search algorithm in Figure 7; whereas breadth-first-search uses a FIFO queue, depth-first search uses a LIFO queue. A LIFO queue means that the most recently generated node is chosen for expansion. This must be the deepest unexpanded node because it is one deeper than its parent—which, in turn, was the deepest unexpanded node when it was selected.

As an alternative to the GRAPH-SEARCH-style implementation, it is common to implement depth-first search with a recursive function that calls itself on each of its children in turn. (A recursive depth-first algorithm incorporating a depth limit is shown in Figure 17.)

---

[5] *NoOp*, or "no operation," is the name of an assembly language instruction that does nothing.

[6] Here the "star" in C^* means an optimal value for C.

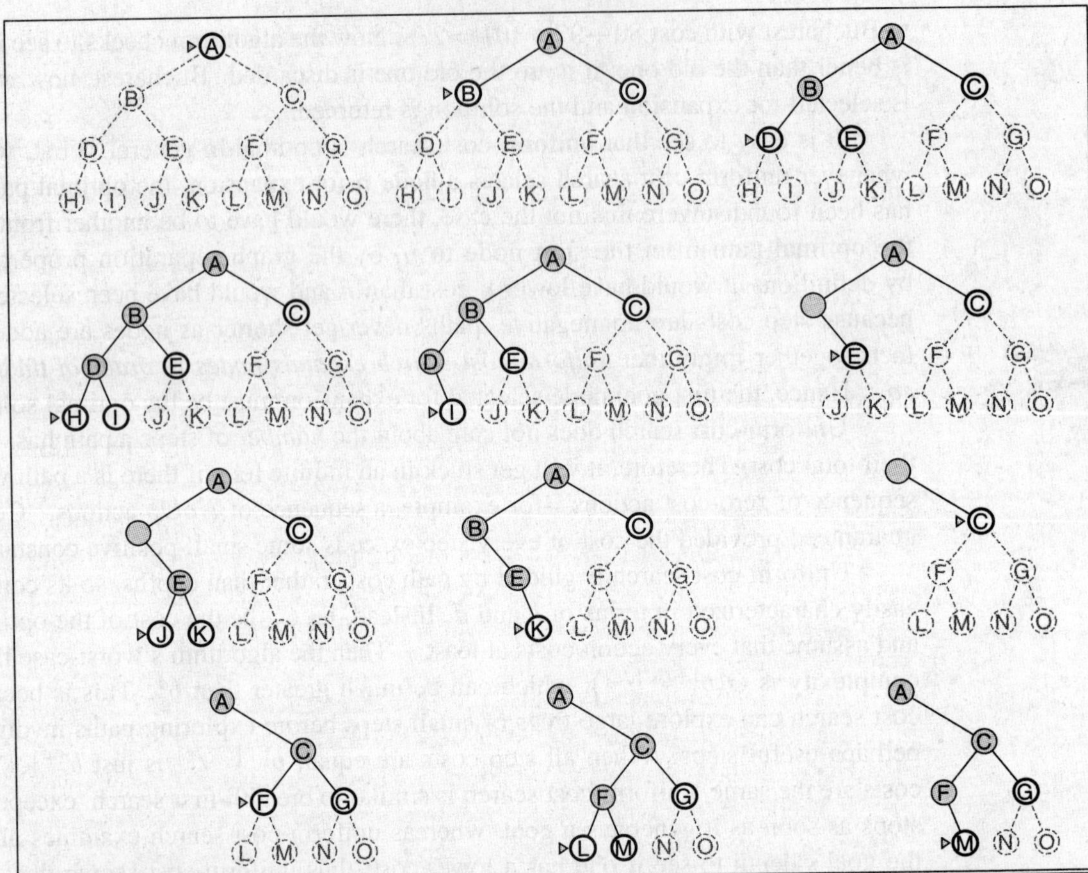

Figure 16 Depth-first search on a binary tree. The unexplored region is shown in light gray. Explored nodes with no descendants in the frontier are removed from memory. Nodes at depth 3 have no successors and M is the only goal node.

The properties of depth-first search depend strongly on whether the graph-search or tree-search version is used. The graph-search version, which avoids repeated states and redundant paths, is complete in finite state spaces because it will eventually expand every node. The tree-search version, on the other hand, is *not* complete—for example, in Figure 6 the algorithm will follow the Arad–Sibiu–Arad–Sibiu loop forever. Depth-first tree search can be modified at no extra memory cost so that it checks new states against those on the path from the root to the current node; this avoids infinite loops in finite state spaces but does not avoid the proliferation of redundant paths. In infinite state spaces, both versions fail if an infinite non-goal path is encountered. For example, in Knuth's 4 problem, depth-first search would keep applying the factorial operator forever.

For similar reasons, both versions are nonoptimal. For example, in Figure 16, depth-first search will explore the entire left subtree even if node C is a goal node. If node J were also a goal node, then depth-first search would return it as a solution instead of C, which would be a better solution; hence, depth-first search is not optimal.

The time complexity of depth-first graph search is bounded by the size of the state space (which may be infinite, of course). A depth-first tree search, on the other hand, may generate all of the $O(b^m)$ nodes in the search tree, where m is the maximum depth of any node; this can be much greater than the size of the state space. Note that m itself can be much larger than d (the depth of the shallowest solution) and is infinite if the tree is unbounded.

So far, depth-first search seems to have no clear advantage over breadth-first search, so why do we include it? The reason is the space complexity. For a graph search, there is no advantage, but a depth-first tree search needs to store only a single path from the root to a leaf node, along with the remaining unexpanded sibling nodes for each node on the path. Once a node has been expanded, it can be removed from memory as soon as all its descendants have been fully explored. (See Figure 16.) For a state space with branching factor b and maximum depth m, depth-first search requires storage of only O(bm)nodes. Using the same assumptions as for Figure 13 and assuming that nodes at the same depth as the goal node have no successors, we find that depth-first search would require 156 kilobytes instead of 10 exabytes at depth d = 16, a factor of 7 trillion times less space. This has led to the adoption of depth-first tree search as the basic workhorse of many areas of AI, including constraint satisfaction, propositional satisfiability, and logic programming. For the remainder of this section, we focus primarily on the tree-search version of depth-first search.

BACKTRACKING SEARCH

A variant of depth-first search called **backtracking search** uses still less memory. In backtracking, only one successor is generated at a time rather than all successors; each partially expanded node remembers which successor to generate next. In this way, only *O*(m) memory is needed rather than *O*(*bm*). Backtracking search facilitates yet another memory-saving (and time-saving) trick: the idea of generating a successor by *modifying* the current state description directly rather than copying it first. This reduces the memory requirements to just one state description and *O*(*m*)actions. For this to work, we must be able to undo each modification when we go back to generate the next successor. For problems with large state descriptions, such as robotic assembly, these techniques are critical to success.

4.4 Depth-limited search

DEPTH-LIMITED SEARCH

The embarrassing failure of depth-first search in infinite state spaces can be alleviated by supplying depth-first search with a predetermined depth limit ℓ. That is, nodes at depth ℓ are treated as if they have no successors. This approach is called **depth-limited search**. The depth limit solves the infinite-path problem. Unfortunately, it also introduces an additional source of incompleteness if we choose $\ell < d$, that is, the shallowest goal is beyond the depth limit. (This is likely when d is unknown.) Depth-limited search will also be nonoptimal if we choose $\ell > d$. Its time complexity is $O(b^\ell)$ and its space complexity is $O(b\ell)$. Depth-first search can be viewed as a special case of depth-limited search with $\ell = \infty$.

Sometimes, depth limits can be based on knowledge of the problem. For example, on the map of Romania there are 20 cities. Therefore, we know that if there is a solution, it must be of length 19 at the longest, so $\ell = 19$ is a possible choice. But in fact if we studied the

```
function DEPTH-LIMITED-SEARCH(problem, limit) returns a solution, or failure/cutoff
  return RECURSIVE-DLS(MAKE-NODE(problem.INITIAL-STATE), problem, limit)

function RECURSIVE-DLS(node, problem, limit) returns a solution, or failure/cutoff
  if problem.GOAL-TEST(node.STATE) then return SOLUTION(node)
  else if limit = 0 then return cutoff
  else
      cutoff_occurred? ← false
      for each action in problem.ACTIONS(node.STATE) do
          child ← CHILD-NODE(problem, node, action)
          result ← RECURSIVE-DLS(child, problem, limit − 1)
          if result = cutoff then cutoff_occurred? ← true
          else if result ≠ failure then return result
      if cutoff_occurred? then return cutoff else return failure
```

Figure 17 A recursive implementation of depth-limited tree search.

map carefully, we would discover that any city can be reached from any other city in at most 9 steps. This number, known as the **diameter** of the state space, gives us a better depth limit, which leads to a more efficient depth-limited search. For most problems, however, we will not know a good depth limit until we have solved the problem.

DIAMETER

Depth-limited search can be implemented as a simple modification to the general tree- or graph-search algorithm. Alternatively, it can be implemented as a simple recursive algorithm as shown in Figure 17. Notice that depth-limited search can terminate with two kinds of failure: the standard *failure* value indicates no solution; the *cutoff* value indicates no solution within the depth limit.

4.5 Iterative deepening depth-first search

ITERATIVE DEEPENING SEARCH

Iterative deepening search (or iterative deepening depth-first search) is a general strategy, often used in combination with depth-first tree search, that finds the best depth limit. It does this by gradually increasing the limit—first 0, then 1, then 2, and so on—until a goal is found. This will occur when the depth limit reaches d, the depth of the shallowest goal node. The algorithm is shown in Figure 18. Iterative deepening combines the benefits of depth-first and breadth-first search. Like depth-first search, its memory requirements are modest: $O(bd)$ to be precise. Like breadth-first search, it is complete when the branching factor is finite and optimal when the path cost is a nondecreasing function of the depth of the node. Figure 19 shows four iterations of ITERATIVE-DEEPENING-SEARCH on a binary search tree, where the solution is found on the fourth iteration.

Iterative deepening search may seem wasteful because states are generated multiple times. It turns out this is not too costly. The reason is that in a search tree with the same (or nearly the same) branching factor at each level, most of the nodes are in the bottom level, so it does not matter much that the upper levels are generated multiple times. In an iterative deepening search, the nodes on the bottom level (depth d) are generated once, those on the

```
function ITERATIVE-DEEPENING-SEARCH(problem) returns a solution, or failure
  for depth = 0 to ∞ do
    result ← DEPTH-LIMITED-SEARCH(problem, depth)
    if result ≠ cutoff then return result
```

Figure 18 The iterative deepening search algorithm, which repeatedly applies depth-limited search with increasing limits. It terminates when a solution is found or if the depth-limited search returns *failure*, meaning that no solution exists.

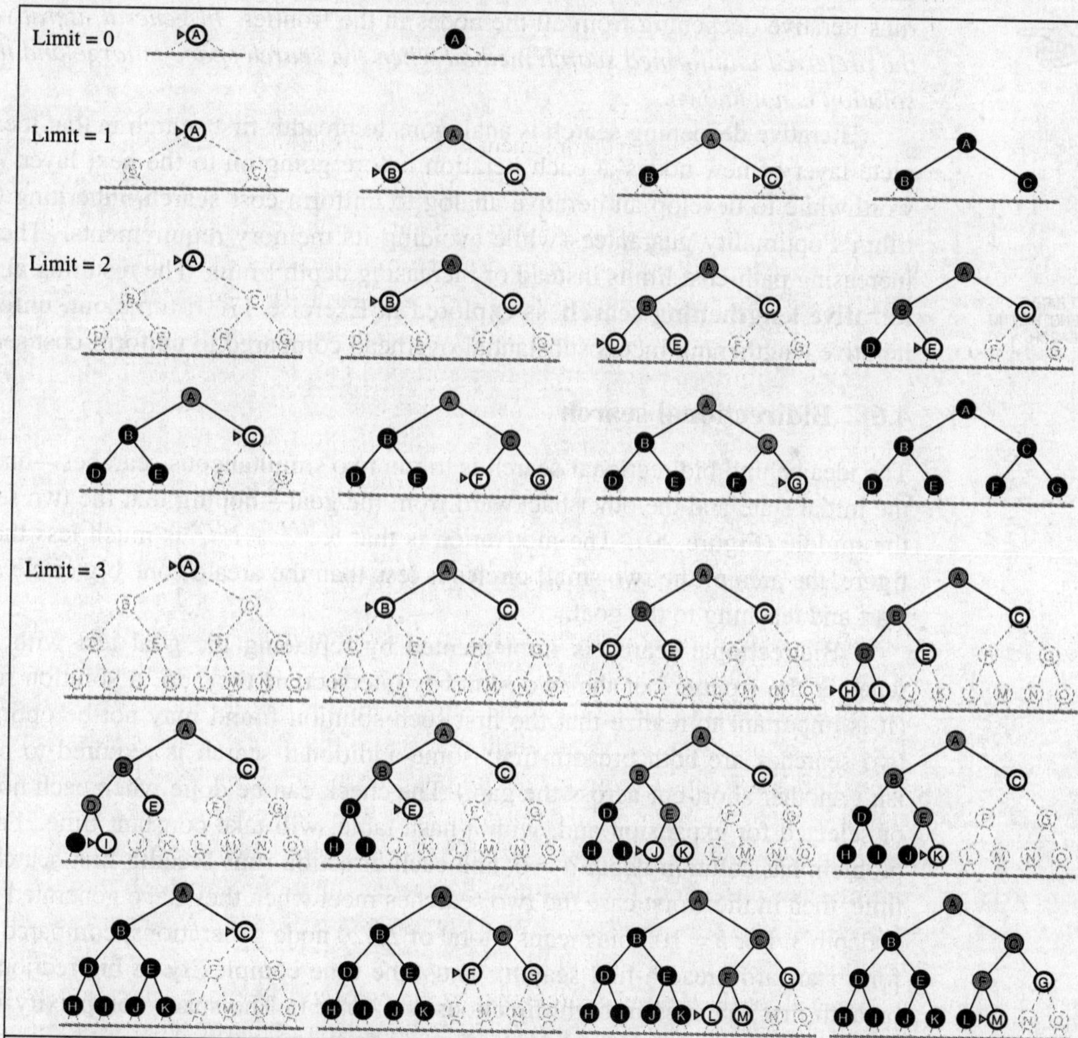

Figure 19 Four iterations of iterative deepening search on a binary tree.

next-to-bottom level are generated twice, and so on, up to the children of the root, which are generated d times. So the total number of nodes generated in the worst case is

$$N(\text{IDS}) = (d)b + (d-1)b^2 + \cdots + (1)b^d ,$$

which gives a time complexity of $O(b^d)$—asymptotically the same as breadth-first search. There is some extra cost for generating the upper levels multiple times, but it is not large. For example, if $b = 10$ and $d = 5$, the numbers are

$$\begin{aligned} N(\text{IDS}) &= 50 + 400 + 3,000 + 20,000 + 100,000 = 123,450 \\ N(\text{BFS}) &= 10 + 100 + 1,000 + 10,000 + 100,000 = 111,110 . \end{aligned}$$

If you are really concerned about repeating the repetition, you can use a hybrid approach that runs breadth-first search until almost all the available memory is consumed, and then runs iterative deepening from all the nodes in the frontier. *In general, iterative deepening is the preferred uninformed search method when the search space is large and the depth of the solution is not known.*

Iterative deepening search is analogous to breadth-first search in that it explores a complete layer of new nodes at each iteration before going on to the next layer. It would seem worthwhile to develop an iterative analog to uniform-cost search, inheriting the latter algorithm's optimality guarantees while avoiding its memory requirements. The idea is to use increasing path-cost limits instead of increasing depth limits. The resulting algorithm, called

ITERATIVE LENGTHENING SEARCH

iterative lengthening search, is explored in Exercise 17. It turns out, unfortunately, that iterative lengthening incurs substantial overhead compared to uniform-cost search.

4.6 Bidirectional search

The idea behind bidirectional search is to run two simultaneous searches—one forward from the initial state and the other backward from the goal—hoping that the two searches meet in the middle (Figure 20). The motivation is that $b^{d/2} + b^{d/2}$ is much less than b^d, or in the figure, the area of the two small circles is less than the area of one big circle centered on the start and reaching to the goal.

Bidirectional search is implemented by replacing the goal test with a check to see whether the frontiers of the two searches intersect; if they do, a solution has been found. (It is important to realize that the first such solution found may not be optimal, even if the two searches are both breadth-first; some additional search is required to make sure there isn't another short-cut across the gap.) The check can be done when each node is generated or selected for expansion and, with a hash table, will take constant time. For example, if a problem has solution depth $d = 6$, and each direction runs breadth-first search one node at a time, then in the worst case the two searches meet when they have generated all of the nodes at depth 3. For $b = 10$, this means a total of 2,220 node generations, compared with 1,111,110 for a standard breadth-first search. Thus, the time complexity of bidirectional search using breadth-first searches in both directions is $O(b^{d/2})$. The space complexity is also $O(b^{d/2})$. We can reduce this by roughly half if one of the two searches is done by iterative deepening, but at least one of the frontiers must be kept in memory so that the intersection check can be done. This space requirement is the most significant weakness of bidirectional search.

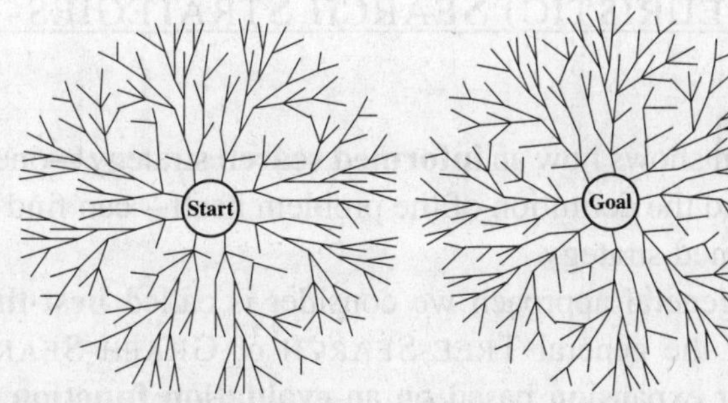

Figure 20 A schematic view of a bidirectional search that is about to succeed when a branch from the start node meets a branch from the goal node.

The reduction in time complexity makes bidirectional search attractive, but how do we search backward? This is not as easy as it sounds. Let the **predecessors** of a state x be all those states that have x as a successor. Bidirectional search requires a method for computing predecessors. When all the actions in the state space are reversible, the predecessors of x are just its successors. Other cases may require substantial ingenuity.

PREDECESSOR

Consider the question of what we mean by "the goal" in searching "backward from the goal." For the 8-puzzle and for finding a route in Romania, there is just one goal state, so the backward search is very much like the forward search. If there are several *explicitly listed* goal states—for example, the two dirt-free goal states in Figure 3—then we can construct a new dummy goal state whose immediate predecessors are all the actual goal states. But if the goal is an abstract description, such as the goal that "no queen attacks another queen" in the n-queens problem, then bidirectional search is difficult to use.

4.7 Comparing uninformed search strategies

Figure 21 compares search strategies in terms of the four evaluation criteria set forth in Section 3.2. This comparison is for tree-search versions. For graph searches, the main differences are that depth-first search is complete for finite state spaces and that the space and time complexities are bounded by the size of the state space.

Criterion	Breadth-First	Uniform-Cost	Depth-First	Depth-Limited	Iterative Deepening	Bidirectional (if applicable)
Complete?	Yes^a	Yes^{a,b}	No	No	Yes^a	Yes^{a,d}
Time	$O(b^d)$	$O(b^{1+\lfloor C^*/\epsilon \rfloor})$	$O(b^m)$	$O(b^\ell)$	$O(b^d)$	$O(b^{d/2})$
Space	$O(b^d)$	$O(b^{1+\lfloor C^*/\epsilon \rfloor})$	$O(bm)$	$O(b\ell)$	$O(bd)$	$O(b^{d/2})$
Optimal?	Yes^c	Yes	No	No	Yes^c	Yes^{c,d}

Figure 21 Evaluation of tree-search strategies. b is the branching factor; d is the depth of the shallowest solution; m is the maximum depth of the search tree; l is the depth limit. Superscript caveats are as follows: ^{a} complete if b is finite; ^{b} complete if step costs $\geq \epsilon$ for positive ϵ; ^{c} optimal if step costs are all identical; ^{d} if both directions use breadth-first search.

5 INFORMED (HEURISTIC) SEARCH STRATEGIES

INFORMED SEARCH

This section shows how an **informed search** strategy—one that uses problem-specific knowledge beyond the definition of the problem itself—can find solutions more efficiently than can an uninformed strategy.

BEST-FIRST SEARCH

EVALUATION FUNCTION

The general approach we consider is called **best-first search**. Best-first search is an instance of the general TREE-SEARCH or GRAPH-SEARCH algorithm in which a node is selected for expansion based on an **evaluation function**, $f(n)$. The evaluation function is construed as a cost estimate, so the node with the *lowest* evaluation is expanded first. The implementation of best-first graph search is identical to that for uniform-cost search (Figure 14), except for the use of f instead of g to order the priority queue.

HEURISTIC FUNCTION

The choice of f determines the search strategy. (For example, as Exercise 21 shows, best-first tree search includes depth-first search as a special case.) Most best-first algorithms include as a component of f a **heuristic function**, denoted $h(n)$:

$$h(n) = \text{ estimated cost of the cheapest path from the state at node } n \text{ to a goal state.}$$

(Notice that $h(n)$ takes a *node* as input, but, unlike $g(n)$, it depends only on the *state* at that node.) For example, in Romania, one might estimate the cost of the cheapest path from Arad to Bucharest via the straight-line distance from Arad to Bucharest.

Heuristic functions are the most common form in which additional knowledge of the problem is imparted to the search algorithm. We study heuristics in more depth in Section 6. For now, we consider them to be arbitrary, nonnegative, problem-specific functions, with one constraint: if n is a goal node, then $h(n) = 0$. The remainder of this section covers two ways to use heuristic information to guide search.

5.1 Greedy best-first search

GREEDY BEST-FIRST SEARCH

Greedy best-first search[7] tries to expand the node that is closest to the goal, on the grounds that this is likely to lead to a solution quickly. Thus, it evaluates nodes by using just the heuristic function; that is, $f(n) = h(n)$.

STRAIGHT-LINE DISTANCE

Let us see how this works for route-finding problems in Romania; we use the **straight-line distance** heuristic, which we will call h_{SLD}. If the goal is Bucharest, we need to know the straight-line distances to Bucharest, which are shown in Figure 22. For example, $h_{SLD}(In(Arad)) = 366$. Notice that the values of h_{SLD} cannot be computed from the problem description itself. Moreover, it takes a certain amount of experience to know that h_{SLD} is correlated with actual road distances and is, therefore, a useful heuristic.

Figure 23 shows the progress of a greedy best-first search using h_{SLD} to find a path from Arad to Bucharest. The first node to be expanded from Arad will be Sibiu because it is closer to Bucharest than either Zerind or Timisoara. The next node to be expanded will be Fagaras because it is closest. Fagaras in turn generates Bucharest, which is the goal. For this particular problem, greedy best-first search using h_{SLD} finds a solution without ever

[7] The first edition of *Artificial Intelligence: A Modern Approach* calls this **greedy search**; other authors have called it **best-first search**. Our more general usage of the latter term follows Pearl (1984).

Arad	366	**Mehadia**	241
Bucharest	0	**Neamt**	234
Craiova	160	**Oradea**	380
Drobeta	242	**Pitesti**	100
Eforie	161	**Rimnicu Vilcea**	193
Fagaras	176	**Sibiu**	253
Giurgiu	77	**Timisoara**	329
Hirsova	151	**Urziceni**	80
Iasi	226	**Vaslui**	199
Lugoj	244	**Zerind**	374

Figure 22 Values of h_{SLD}—straight-line distances to Bucharest.

expanding a node that is not on the solution path; hence, its search cost is minimal. It is not optimal, however: the path via Sibiu and Fagaras to Bucharest is 32 kilometers longer than the path through Rimnicu Vilcea and Pitesti. This shows why the algorithm is called "greedy"—at each step it tries to get as close to the goal as it can.

Greedy best-first tree search is also incomplete even in a finite state space, much like depth-first search. Consider the problem of getting from Iasi to Fagaras. The heuristic suggests that Neamt be expanded first because it is closest to Fagaras, but it is a dead end. The solution is to go first to Vaslui—a step that is actually farther from the goal according to the heuristic—and then to continue to Urziceni, Bucharest, and Fagaras. The algorithm will never find this solution, however, because expanding Neamt puts Iasi back into the frontier, Iasi is closer to Fagaras than Vaslui is, and so Iasi will be expanded again, leading to an infinite loop. (The graph search version *is* complete in finite spaces, but not in infinite ones.) The worst-case time and space complexity for the tree version is $O(b^m)$, where m is the maximum depth of the search space. With a good heuristic function, however, the complexity can be reduced substantially. The amount of the reduction depends on the particular problem and on the quality of the heuristic.

5.2 A* search: Minimizing the total estimated solution cost

A* SEARCH

The most widely known form of best-first search is called **A* search** (pronounced "A-star search"). It evaluates nodes by combining $g(n)$, the cost to reach the node, and $h(n)$, the cost to get from the node to the goal:

$$f(n) = g(n) + h(n) .$$

Since $g(n)$ gives the path cost from the start node to node n, and $h(n)$ is the estimated cost of the cheapest path from n to the goal, we have

$$f(n) = \text{ estimated cost of the cheapest solution through } n .$$

Thus, if we are trying to find the cheapest solution, a reasonable thing to try first is the node with the lowest value of $g(n) + h(n)$. It turns out that this strategy is more than just reasonable: provided that the heuristic function $h(n)$ satisfies certain conditions, A* search is both complete and optimal. The algorithm is identical to UNIFORM-COST-SEARCH except that A* uses $g + h$ instead of g.

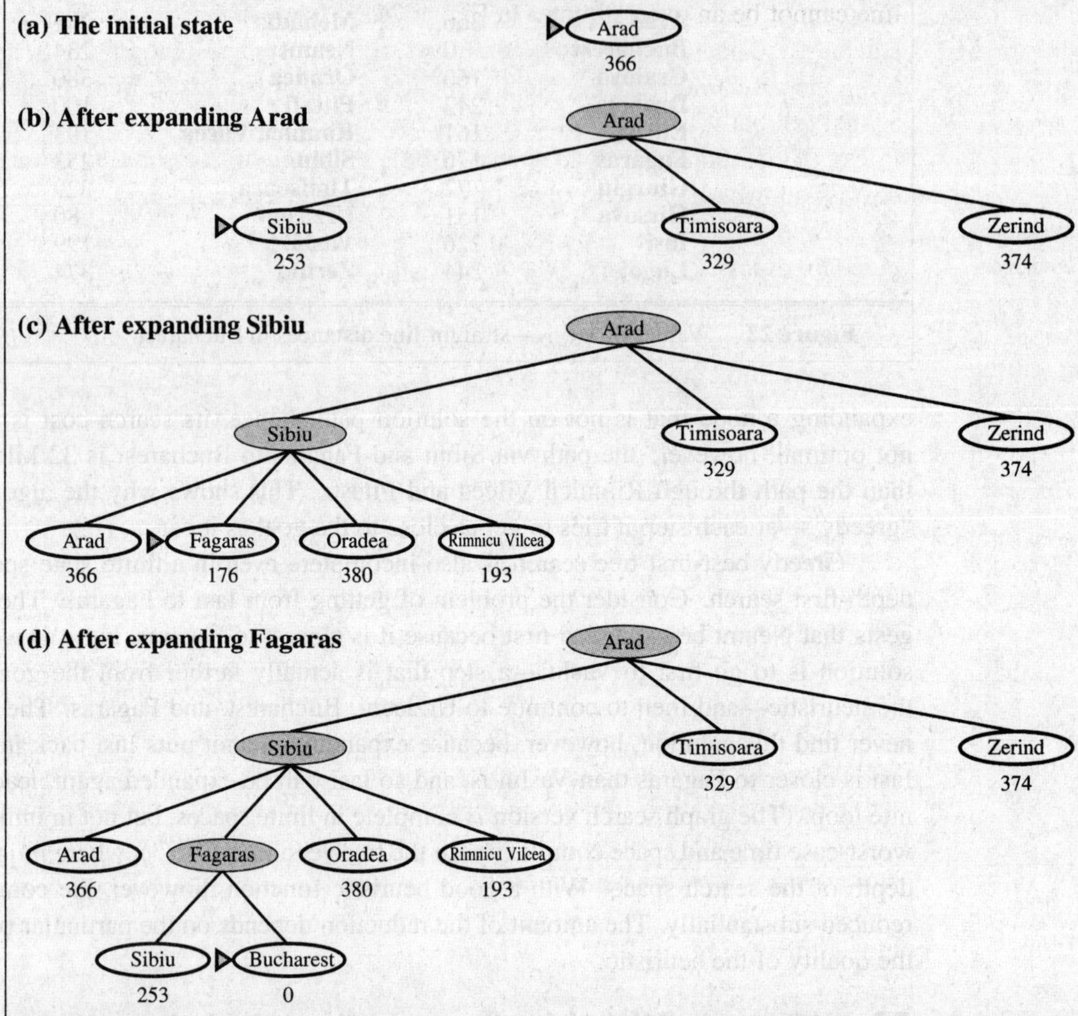

Figure 23 Stages in a greedy best-first tree search for Bucharest with the straight-line distance heuristic h_{SLD}. Nodes are labeled with their h-values.

Conditions for optimality: Admissibility and consistency

ADMISSIBLE HEURISTIC

The first condition we require for optimality is that $h(n)$ be an **admissible heuristic**. An admissible heuristic is one that *never overestimates* the cost to reach the goal. Because $g(n)$ is the actual cost to reach n along the current path, and $f(n) = g(n) + h(n)$, we have as an immediate consequence that $f(n)$ never overestimates the true cost of a solution along the current path through n.

Admissible heuristics are by nature optimistic because they think the cost of solving the problem is less than it actually is. An obvious example of an admissible heuristic is the straight-line distance h_{SLD} that we used in getting to Bucharest. Straight-line distance is admissible because the shortest path between any two points is a straight line, so the straight line cannot be an overestimate. In Figure 24, we show the progress of an A* tree search for Bucharest. The values of g are computed from the step costs in Figure 2, and the values of h_{SLD} are given in Figure 22. Notice in particular that Bucharest first appears on the frontier at step (e), but it is not selected for expansion because its f-cost (450) is higher than that of Pitesti (417). Another way to say this is that there *might* be a solution through Pitesti whose cost is as low as 417, so the algorithm will not settle for a solution that costs 450.

CONSISTENCY
MONOTONICITY

A second, slightly stronger condition called **consistency** (or sometimes **monotonicity**) is required only for applications of A* to graph search.[8] A heuristic $h(n)$ is consistent if, for every node n and every successor n' of n generated by any action a, the estimated cost of reaching the goal from n is no greater than the step cost of getting to n' plus the estimated cost of reaching the goal from n':

$$h(n) \leq c(n, a, n') + h(n') .$$

TRIANGLE INEQUALITY

This is a form of the general **triangle inequality**, which stipulates that each side of a triangle cannot be longer than the sum of the other two sides. Here, the triangle is formed by n, n', and the goal G_n closest to n. For an admissible heuristic, the inequality makes perfect sense: if there were a route from n to G_n via n' that was cheaper than $h(n)$, that would violate the property that $h(n)$ is a lower bound on the cost to reach G_n.

It is fairly easy to show (Exercise 29) that every consistent heuristic is also admissible. Consistency is therefore a stricter requirement than admissibility, but one has to work quite hard to concoct heuristics that are admissible but not consistent. All the admissible heuristics we discuss in this chapter are also consistent. Consider, for example, h_{SLD}. We know that the general triangle inequality is satisfied when each side is measured by the straight-line distance and that the straight-line distance between n and n' is no greater than $c(n, a, n')$. Hence, h_{SLD} is a consistent heuristic.

Optimality of A*

As we mentioned earlier, A* has the following properties: *the tree-search version of A* is optimal if $h(n)$ is admissible, while the graph-search version is optimal if $h(n)$ is consistent.*

We show the second of these two claims since it is more useful. The argument essentially mirrors the argument for the optimality of uniform-cost search, with g replaced by f—just as in the A* algorithm itself.

The first step is to establish the following: *if $h(n)$ is consistent, then the values of $f(n)$ along any path are nondecreasing.* The proof follows directly from the definition of consistency. Suppose n' is a successor of n; then $g(n') = g(n) + c(n, a, n')$ for some action a, and we have

$$f(n') = g(n') + h(n') = g(n) + c(n, a, n') + h(n') \geq g(n) + h(n) = f(n) .$$

The next step is to prove that *whenever A* selects a node n for expansion, the optimal path to that node has been found.* Were this not the case, there would have to be another frontier node n' on the optimal path from the start node to n, by the graph separation property of

[8] With an admissible but inconsistent heuristic, A* requires some extra bookkeeping to ensure optimality.

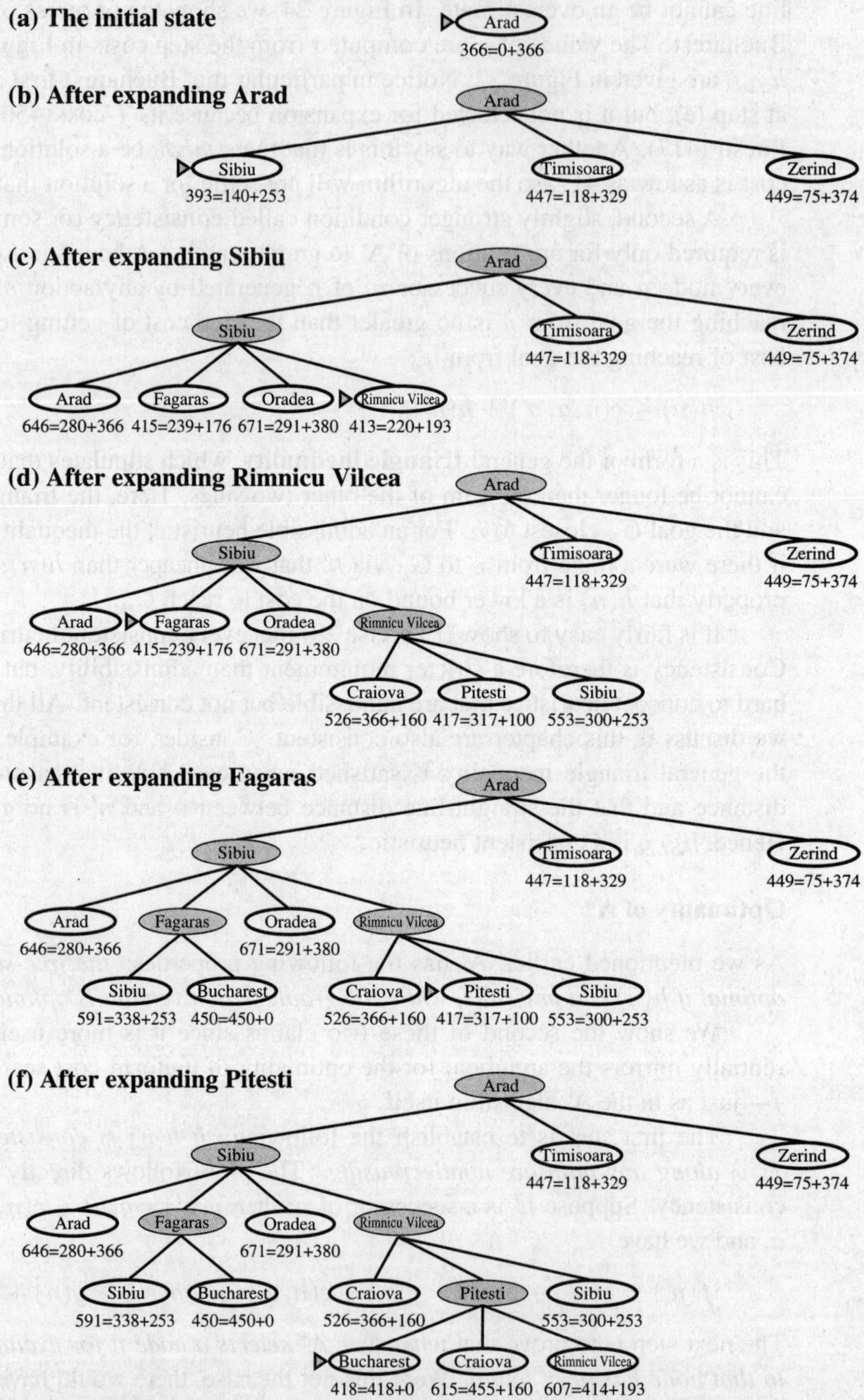

Figure 24 Stages in an A* search for Bucharest. Nodes are labeled with $f = g + h$. The h values are the straight-line distances to Bucharest taken from Figure 22.

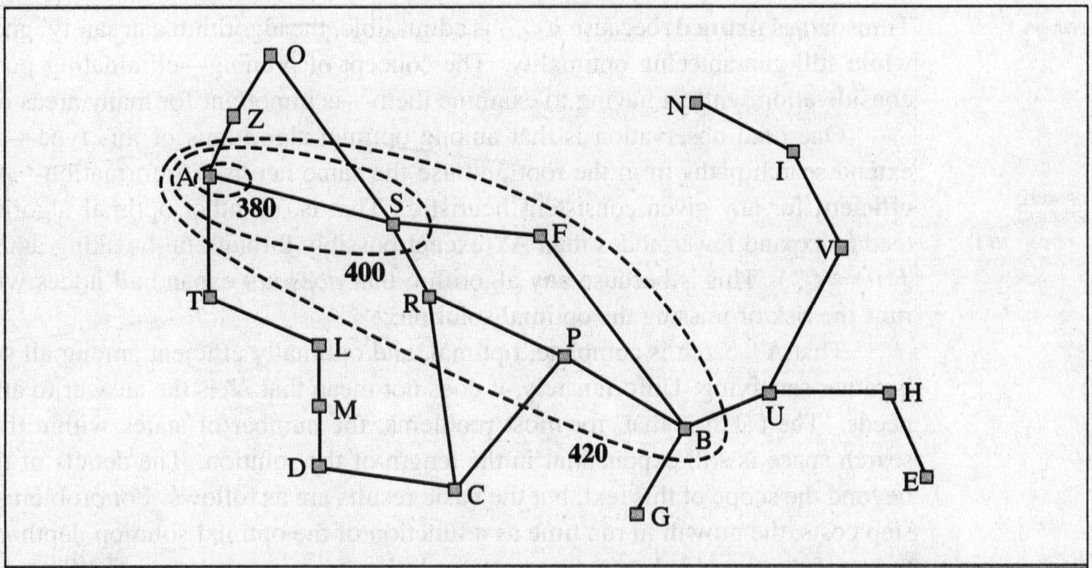

Figure 25 Map of Romania showing contours at $f = 380$, $f = 400$, and $f = 420$, with Arad as the start state. Nodes inside a given contour have f-costs less than or equal to the contour value.

Figure 9; because f is nondecreasing along any path, n' would have lower f-cost than n and would have been selected first.

From the two preceding observations, it follows that the sequence of nodes expanded by A* using GRAPH-SEARCH is in nondecreasing order of $f(n)$. Hence, the first goal node selected for expansion must be an optimal solution because f is the true cost for goal nodes (which have $h = 0$) and all later goal nodes will be at least as expensive.

CONTOUR

The fact that f-costs are nondecreasing along any path also means that we can draw **contours** in the state space, just like the contours in a topographic map. Figure 25 shows an example. Inside the contour labeled 400, all nodes have $f(n)$ less than or equal to 400, and so on. Then, because A* expands the frontier node of lowest f-cost, we can see that an A* search fans out from the start node, adding nodes in concentric bands of increasing f-cost.

With uniform-cost search (A* search using $h(n) = 0$), the bands will be "circular" around the start state. With more accurate heuristics, the bands will stretch toward the goal state and become more narrowly focused around the optimal path. If C^* is the cost of the optimal solution path, then we can say the following:

- A* expands all nodes with $f(n) < C^*$.
- A* might then expand some of the nodes right on the "goal contour" (where $f(n) = C^*$) before selecting a goal node.

Completeness requires that there be only finitely many nodes with cost less than or equal to C^*, a condition that is true if all step costs exceed some finite ϵ and if b is finite.

Notice that A* expands no nodes with $f(n) > C^*$—for example, Timisoara is not expanded in Figure 24 even though it is a child of the root. We say that the subtree below

PRUNING

Timisoara is **pruned**; because h_{SLD} is admissible, the algorithm can safely ignore this subtree while still guaranteeing optimality. The concept of pruning—eliminating possibilities from consideration without having to examine them—is important for many areas of AI.

OPTIMALLY EFFICIENT

One final observation is that among optimal algorithms of this type—algorithms that extend search paths from the root and use the same heuristic information—A* is **optimally efficient** for any given consistent heuristic. That is, no other optimal algorithm is guaranteed to expand fewer nodes than A* (except possibly through tie-breaking among nodes with $f(n) = C^*$). This is because any algorithm that *does not* expand all nodes with $f(n) < C^*$ runs the risk of missing the optimal solution.

That A* search is complete, optimal, and optimally efficient among all such algorithms is rather satisfying. Unfortunately, it does not mean that A* is the answer to all our searching needs. The catch is that, for most problems, the number of states within the goal contour search space is still exponential in the length of the solution. The details of the analysis are beyond the scope of this text, but the basic results are as follows. For problems with constant step costs, the growth in run time as a function of the optimal solution depth d is analyzed in terms of the the **absolute error** or the **relative error** of the heuristic. The absolute error is defined as $\Delta \equiv h^* - h$, where h^* is the actual cost of getting from the root to the goal, and the relative error is defined as $\epsilon \equiv (h^* - h)/h^*$.

ABSOLUTE ERROR

RELATIVE ERROR

The complexity results depend very strongly on the assumptions made about the state space. The simplest model studied is a state space that has a single goal and is essentially a tree with reversible actions. (The 8-puzzle satisfies the first and third of these assumptions.) In this case, the time complexity of A* is exponential in the maximum absolute error, that is, $O(b^{\Delta})$. For constant step costs, we can write this as $O(b^{\epsilon d})$, where d is the solution depth. For almost all heuristics in practical use, the absolute error is at least proportional to the path cost h^*, so ϵ is constant or growing and the time complexity is exponential in d. We can also see the effect of a more accurate heuristic: $O(b^{\epsilon d}) = O((b^{\epsilon})^d)$, so the effective branching factor (defined more formally in the next section) is b^{ϵ}.

When the state space has many goal states—particularly *near-optimal* goal states—the search process can be led astray from the optimal path and there is an extra cost proportional to the number of goals whose cost is within a factor ϵ of the optimal cost. Finally, in the general case of a graph, the situation is even worse. There can be exponentially many states with $f(n) < C^*$ even if the absolute error is bounded by a constant. For example, consider a version of the vacuum world where the agent can clean up any square for unit cost without even having to visit it: in that case, squares can be cleaned in any order. With N initially dirty squares, there are 2^N states where some subset has been cleaned and all of them are on an optimal solution path—and hence satisfy $f(n) < C^*$—even if the heuristic has an error of 1.

The complexity of A* often makes it impractical to insist on finding an optimal solution. One can use variants of A* that find suboptimal solutions quickly, or one can sometimes design heuristics that are more accurate but not strictly admissible. In any case, the use of a good heuristic still provides enormous savings compared to the use of an uninformed search. In Section 6, we look at the question of designing good heuristics.

Computation time is not, however, A*'s main drawback. Because it keeps all generated nodes in memory (as do all GRAPH-SEARCH algorithms), A* usually runs out of space long

```
function RECURSIVE-BEST-FIRST-SEARCH(problem) returns a solution, or failure
  return RBFS(problem, MAKE-NODE(problem.INITIAL-STATE), ∞)

function RBFS(problem, node, f_limit) returns a solution, or failure and a new f-cost limit
  if problem.GOAL-TEST(node.STATE) then return SOLUTION(node)
  successors ← [ ]
  for each action in problem.ACTIONS(node.STATE) do
      add CHILD-NODE(problem, node, action) into successors
  if successors is empty then return failure, ∞
  for each s in successors do  /* update f with value from previous search, if any */
      s.f ← max(s.g + s.h, node.f))
  loop do
      best ← the lowest f-value node in successors
      if best.f > f_limit then return failure, best.f
      alternative ← the second-lowest f-value among successors
      result, best.f ← RBFS(problem, best, min(f_limit, alternative))
      if result ≠ failure then return result
```

Figure 26 The algorithm for recursive best-first search.

before it runs out of time. For this reason, A* is not practical for many large-scale problems. There are, however, algorithms that overcome the space problem without sacrificing optimality or completeness, at a small cost in execution time. We discuss these next.

5.3 Memory-bounded heuristic search

ITERATIVE-DEEPENING A*

The simplest way to reduce memory requirements for A* is to adapt the idea of iterative deepening to the heuristic search context, resulting in the **iterative-deepening A*** (IDA*) algorithm. The main difference between IDA* and standard iterative deepening is that the cutoff used is the f-cost $(g+h)$ rather than the depth; at each iteration, the cutoff value is the smallest f-cost of any node that exceeded the cutoff on the previous iteration. IDA* is practical for many problems with unit step costs and avoids the substantial overhead associated with keeping a sorted queue of nodes. Unfortunately, it suffers from the same difficulties with real-valued costs as does the iterative version of uniform-cost search described in Exercise 17. This section briefly examines two other memory-bounded algorithms, called RBFS and MA*.

RECURSIVE BEST-FIRST SEARCH

Recursive best-first search (RBFS) is a simple recursive algorithm that attempts to mimic the operation of standard best-first search, but using only linear space. The algorithm is shown in Figure 26. Its structure is similar to that of a recursive depth-first search, but rather than continuing indefinitely down the current path, it uses the *f_limit* variable to keep track of the f-value of the best *alternative* path available from any ancestor of the current node. If the current node exceeds this limit, the recursion unwinds back to the alternative path. As the recursion unwinds, RBFS replaces the f-value of each node along the path with a **backed-up value**—the best f-value of its children. In this way, RBFS remembers the f-value of the best leaf in the forgotten subtree and can therefore decide whether it's worth

BACKED-UP VALUE

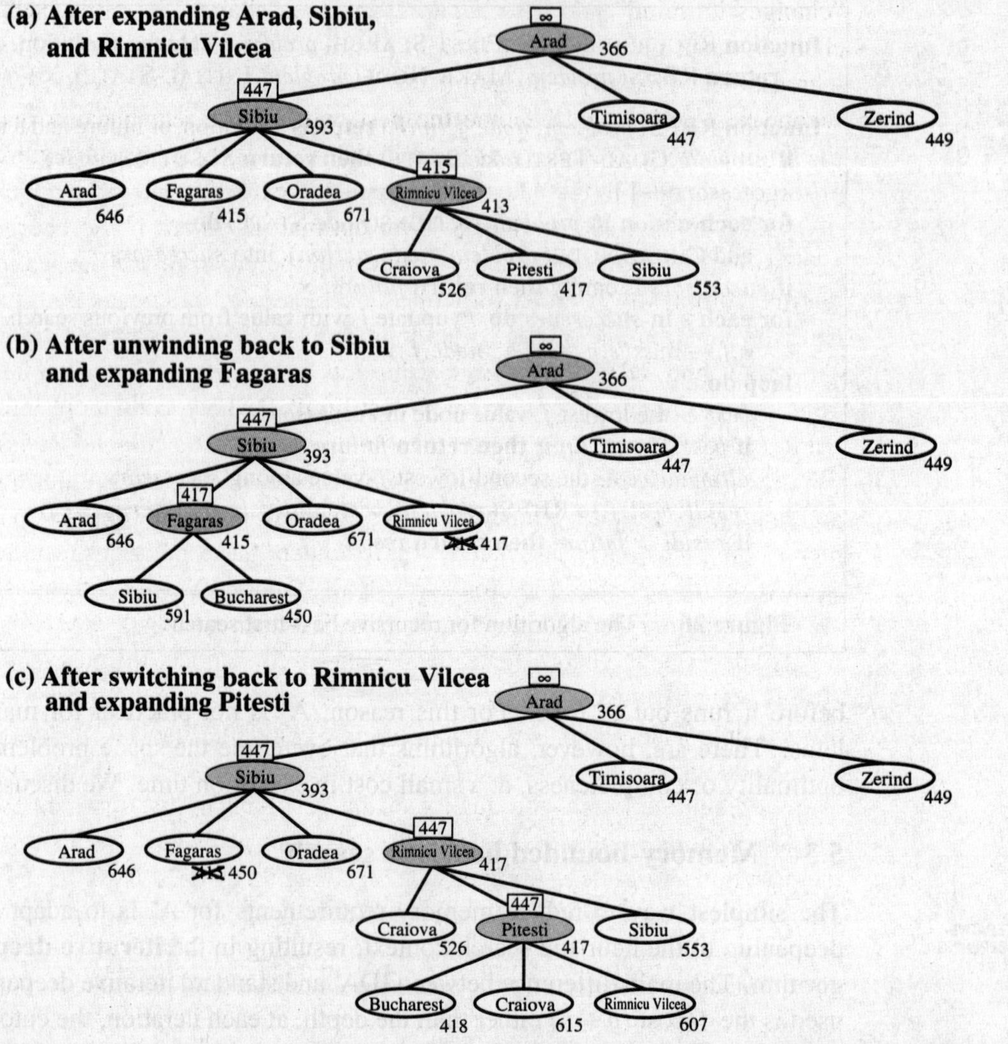

Figure 27 Stages in an RBFS search for the shortest route to Bucharest. The f-limit value for each recursive call is shown on top of each current node, and every node is labeled with its f-cost. (a) The path via Rimnicu Vilcea is followed until the current best leaf (Pitesti) has a value that is worse than the best alternative path (Fagaras). (b) The recursion unwinds and the best leaf value of the forgotten subtree (417) is backed up to Rimnicu Vilcea; then Fagaras is expanded, revealing a best leaf value of 450. (c) The recursion unwinds and the best leaf value of the forgotten subtree (450) is backed up to Fagaras; then Rimnicu Vilcea is expanded. This time, because the best alternative path (through Timisoara) costs at least 447, the expansion continues to Bucharest.

reexpanding the subtree at some later time. Figure 27 shows how RBFS reaches Bucharest.

RBFS is somewhat more efficient than IDA*, but still suffers from excessive node regeneration. In the example in Figure 27, RBFS follows the path via Rimnicu Vilcea, then "changes its mind" and tries Fagaras, and then changes its mind back again. These mind changes occur because every time the current best path is extended, its f-value is likely to increase—h is usually less optimistic for nodes closer to the goal. When this happens, the second-best path might become the best path, so the search has to backtrack to follow it. Each mind change corresponds to an iteration of IDA* and could require many reexpansions of forgotten nodes to recreate the best path and extend it one more node.

Like A* tree search, RBFS is an optimal algorithm if the heuristic function $h(n)$ is admissible. Its space complexity is linear in the depth of the deepest optimal solution, but its time complexity is rather difficult to characterize: it depends both on the accuracy of the heuristic function and on how often the best path changes as nodes are expanded.

IDA* and RBFS suffer from using *too little* memory. Between iterations, IDA* retains only a single number: the current f-cost limit. RBFS retains more information in memory, but it uses only linear space: even if more memory were available, RBFS has no way to make use of it. Because they forget most of what they have done, both algorithms may end up reexpanding the same states many times over. Furthermore, they suffer the potentially exponential increase in complexity associated with redundant paths in graphs (see Section 3).

MA*
SMA*

It seems sensible, therefore, to use all available memory. Two algorithms that do this are **MA*** (memory-bounded A*) and **SMA*** (simplified MA*). SMA* is—well—simpler, so we will describe it. SMA* proceeds just like A*, expanding the best leaf until memory is full. At this point, it cannot add a new node to the search tree without dropping an old one. SMA* always drops the *worst* leaf node—the one with the highest f-value. Like RBFS, SMA* then backs up the value of the forgotten node to its parent. In this way, the ancestor of a forgotten subtree knows the quality of the best path in that subtree. With this information, SMA* regenerates the subtree only when all other paths have been shown to look worse than the path it has forgotten. Another way of saying this is that, if all the descendants of a node n are forgotten, then we will not know which way to go from n, but we will still have an idea of how worthwhile it is to go anywhere from n.

The complete algorithm is too complicated to reproduce here,[9] but there is one subtlety worth mentioning. We said that SMA* expands the best leaf and deletes the worst leaf. What if *all* the leaf nodes have the same f-value? To avoid selecting the same node for deletion and expansion, SMA* expands the *newest* best leaf and deletes the *oldest* worst leaf. These coincide when there is only one leaf, but in that case, the current search tree must be a single path from root to leaf that fills all of memory. If the leaf is not a goal node, then *even if it is on an optimal solution path*, that solution is not reachable with the available memory. Therefore, the node can be discarded exactly as if it had no successors.

SMA* is complete if there is any reachable solution—that is, if d, the depth of the shallowest goal node, is less than the memory size (expressed in nodes). It is optimal if any optimal solution is reachable; otherwise, it returns the best reachable solution. In practical terms, SMA* is a fairly robust choice for finding optimal solutions, particularly when the state space is a graph, step costs are not uniform, and node generation is expensive compared to the overhead of maintaining the frontier and the explored set.

[9] A rough sketch appeared in the first edition of *Artificial Intelligence: A Modern Approach.*

THRASHING

On very hard problems, however, it will often be the case that SMA* is forced to switch back and forth continually among many candidate solution paths, only a small subset of which can fit in memory. (This resembles the problem of **thrashing** in disk paging systems.) Then the extra time required for repeated regeneration of the same nodes means that problems that would be practically solvable by A*, given unlimited memory, become intractable for SMA*. That is to say, *memory limitations can make a problem intractable from the point of view of computation time.* Although no current theory explains the tradeoff between time and memory, it seems that this is an inescapable problem. The only way out is to drop the optimality requirement.

5.4 Learning to search better

METALEVEL STATE SPACE

OBJECT-LEVEL STATE SPACE

We have presented several fixed strategies—breadth-first, greedy best-first, and so on—that have been designed by computer scientists. Could an agent *learn* how to search better? The answer is yes, and the method rests on an important concept called the **metalevel state space**. Each state in a metalevel state space captures the internal (computational) state of a program that is searching in an **object-level state space** such as Romania. For example, the internal state of the A* algorithm consists of the current search tree. Each action in the metalevel state space is a computation step that alters the internal state; for example, each computation step in A* expands a leaf node and adds its successors to the tree. Thus, Figure 24, which shows a sequence of larger and larger search trees, can be seen as depicting a path in the metalevel state space where each state on the path is an object-level search tree.

METALEVEL LEARNING

Now, the path in Figure 24 has five steps, including one step, the expansion of Fagaras, that is not especially helpful. For harder problems, there will be many such missteps,and a **metalevel learning** algorithm can learn from these experiences to avoid exploring unpromising subtrees. The goal of learning is to minimize the **total cost** of problem solving, trading off computational expense and path cost.

6 HEURISTIC FUNCTIONS

In this section, we look at heuristics for the 8-puzzle, in order to shed light on the nature of heuristics in general.

The 8-puzzle was one of the earliest heuristic search problems. As mentioned in Section 2, the object of the puzzle is to slide the tiles horizontally or vertically into the empty space until the configuration matches the goal configuration (Figure 28).

The average solution cost for a randomly generated 8-puzzle instance is about 22 steps. The branching factor is about 3. (When the empty tile is in the middle, four moves are possible; when it is in a corner, two; and when it is along an edge, three.) This means that an exhaustive tree search to depth 22 would look at about $3^{22} \approx 3.1 \times 10^{10}$ states. A graph search would cut this down by a factor of about 170,000 because only $9!/2 = 181,440$ distinct states are reachable. (See Exercise 4.) This is a manageable number, but

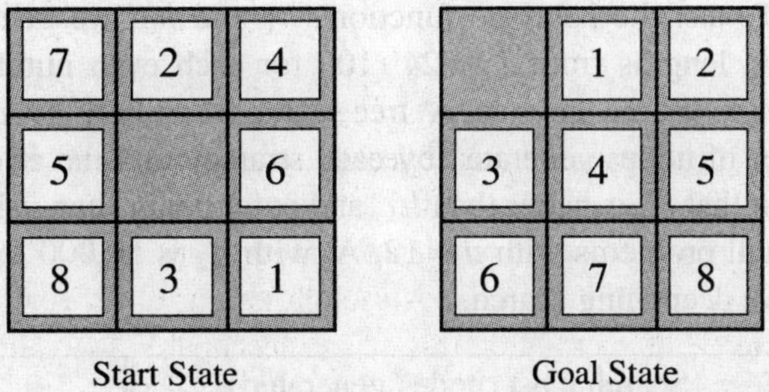

Figure 28 A typical instance of the 8-puzzle. The solution is 26 steps long.

the corresponding number for the 15-puzzle is roughly 10^{13}, so the next order of business is to find a good heuristic function. If we want to find the shortest solutions by using A*, we need a heuristic function that never overestimates the number of steps to the goal. There is a long history of such heuristics for the 15-puzzle; here are two commonly used candidates:

- h_1 = the number of misplaced tiles. For Figure 28, all of the eight tiles are out of position, so the start state would have $h_1 = 8$. h_1 is an admissible heuristic because it is clear that any tile that is out of place must be moved at least once.
- h_2 = the sum of the distances of the tiles from their goal positions. Because tiles cannot move along diagonals, the distance we will count is the sum of the horizontal and vertical distances. This is sometimes called the **city block distance** or **Manhattan distance**. h_2 is also admissible because all any move can do is move one tile one step closer to the goal. Tiles 1 to 8 in the start state give a Manhattan distance of

MANHATTAN DISTANCE

$$h_2 = 3 + 1 + 2 + 2 + 2 + 3 + 3 + 2 = 18 .$$

As expected, neither of these overestimates the true solution cost, which is 26.

6.1 The effect of heuristic accuracy on performance

EFFECTIVE BRANCHING FACTOR

One way to characterize the quality of a heuristic is the **effective branching factor** b^*. If the total number of nodes generated by A* for a particular problem is N and the solution depth is d, then b^* is the branching factor that a uniform tree of depth d would have to have in order to contain $N + 1$ nodes. Thus,

$$N + 1 = 1 + b^* + (b^*)^2 + \cdots + (b^*)^d .$$

For example, if A* finds a solution at depth 5 using 52 nodes, then the effective branching factor is 1.92. The effective branching factor can vary across problem instances, but usually it is fairly constant for sufficiently hard problems. (The existence of an effective branching factor follows from the result, mentioned earlier, that the number of nodes expanded by A* grows exponentially with solution depth.) Therefore, experimental measurements of b^* on a small set of problems can provide a good guide to the heuristic's overall usefulness. A well-designed heuristic would have a value of b^* close to 1, allowing fairly large problems to be solved at reasonable computational cost.

To test the heuristic functions h_1 and h_2, we generated 1200 random problems with solution lengths from 2 to 24 (100 for each even number) and solved them with iterative deepening search and with A* tree search using both h_1 and h_2. Figure 29 gives the average number of nodes generated by each strategy and the effective branching factor. The results suggest that h_2 is better than h_1, and is far better than using iterative deepening search. Even for small problems with $d = 12$, A* with h_2 is 50,000 times more efficient than uninformed iterative deepening search.

	Search Cost (nodes generated)			Effective Branching Factor		
d	IDS	A*(h_1)	A*(h_2)	IDS	A*(h_1)	A*(h_2)
2	10	6	6	2.45	1.79	1.79
4	112	13	12	2.87	1.48	1.45
6	680	20	18	2.73	1.34	1.30
8	6384	39	25	2.80	1.33	1.24
10	47127	93	39	2.79	1.38	1.22
12	3644035	227	73	2.78	1.42	1.24
14	–	539	113	–	1.44	1.23
16	–	1301	211	–	1.45	1.25
18	–	3056	363	–	1.46	1.26
20	–	7276	676	–	1.47	1.27
22	–	18094	1219	–	1.48	1.28
24	–	39135	1641	–	1.48	1.26

Figure 29 Comparison of the search costs and effective branching factors for the ITERATIVE-DEEPENING-SEARCH and A* algorithms with h_1, h_2. Data are averaged over 100 instances of the 8-puzzle for each of various solution lengths d.

One might ask whether $h2$ is *always* better than $h1$. The answer is "Essentially, yes." It is easy to see from the definitions of the two heuristics that, for any node n, $h2(n) > h_1(n)$. We

DOMINATION

thus say that h_2 **dominates** h_1. Domination translates directly into ef?ciency: A^* using h_2 will never expand more nodes than A* using h_1 (except possibly for some nodes with $f(n) = C^*$). The argument is simple. Recall the observation that every node with $f(n) < C^*$ will surely be expanded. This is the same as saying that every node with $h(n) < C^* - g(n)$ will surely be expanded. But because h_2 is at least as big as h_1 for all nodes, every node that is surely expanded by A^* search with h_2 will also surely be expanded with h_1, and h_1 might cause other nodes to be expanded as well. Hence, it is generally better to use a heuristic function with higher values, provided it is consistent and that the computation time for the heuristic is not too long.

6.2 Generating admissible heuristics from relaxed problems

We have seen that both h_1 (misplaced tiles) and h_2 (Manhattan distance) are fairly good heuristics for the 8-puzzle and that h_2 is better. How might one have come up with h_2? Is it possible for a computer to invent such a heuristic mechanically?

h_1 and h_2 are estimates of the remaining path length for the 8-puzzle, but they are also perfectly accurate path lengths for *simplified* versions of the puzzle. If the rules of the puzzle were changed so that a tile could move anywhere instead of just to the adjacent empty square, then h_1 would give the exact number of steps in the shortest solution. Similarly, if a tile could move one square in any direction, even onto an occupied square, then h_2 would give the exact number of steps in the shortest solution. A problem with fewer restrictions on the actions is RELAXED PROBLEM called a **relaxed problem**. The state-space graph of the relaxed problem is a *supergraph* of the original state space because the removal of restrictions creates added edges in the graph.

Because the relaxed problem adds edges to the state space, any optimal solution in the original problem is, by definition, also a solution in the relaxed problem; but the relaxed problem may have *better* solutions if the added edges provide short cuts. Hence, *the cost of an optimal solution to a relaxed problem is an admissible heuristic for the original problem.* Furthermore, because the derived heuristic is an exact cost for the relaxed problem, it must obey the triangle inequality and is therefore **consistent**.

If a problem definition is written down in a formal language, it is possible to construct relaxed problems automatically.[10] For example, if the 8-puzzle actions are described as

> A tile can move from square A to square B if
> A is horizontally or vertically adjacent to B **and** B is blank,

we can generate three relaxed problems by removing one or both of the conditions:

(a) A tile can move from square A to square B if A is adjacent to B.
(b) A tile can move from square A to square B if B is blank.
(c) A tile can move from square A to square B.

From (a), we can derive h_2 (Manhattan distance). The reasoning is that h_2 would be the proper score if we moved each tile in turn to its destination. The heuristic derived from (b) is discussed in Exercise 31. From (c), we can derive h_1 (misplaced tiles) because it would be the proper score if tiles could move to their intended destination in one step. Notice that it is crucial that the relaxed problems generated by this technique can be solved essentially *without search*, because the relaxed rules allow the problem to be decomposed into eight independent subproblems. If the relaxed problem is hard to solve, then the values of the corresponding heuristic will be expensive to obtain.[11]

A program called ABSOLVER can generate heuristics automatically from problem definitions, using the "relaxed problem" method and various other techniques (Prieditis, 1993). ABSOLVER generated a new heuristic for the 8-puzzle that was better than any preexisting heuristic and found the first useful heuristic for the famous Rubik's Cube puzzle.

One problem with generating new heuristic functions is that one often fails to get a single "clearly best" heuristic. If a collection of admissible heuristics $h_1 \ldots h_m$ is available for a problem and none of them dominates any of the others, which should we choose? As it turns out, we need not make a choice. We can have the best of all worlds, by defining

$$h(n) = \max\{h_1(n), \ldots, h_m(n)\} .$$

[10] There exist formal languages suitable for this task; with formal descriptions that can be manipulated, the construction of relaxed problems can be automated. For now, we use English.

[11] Note that a perfect heuristic can be obtained simply by allowing h to run a full breadth-first search "on the sly." Thus, there is a tradeoff between accuracy and computation time for heuristic functions.

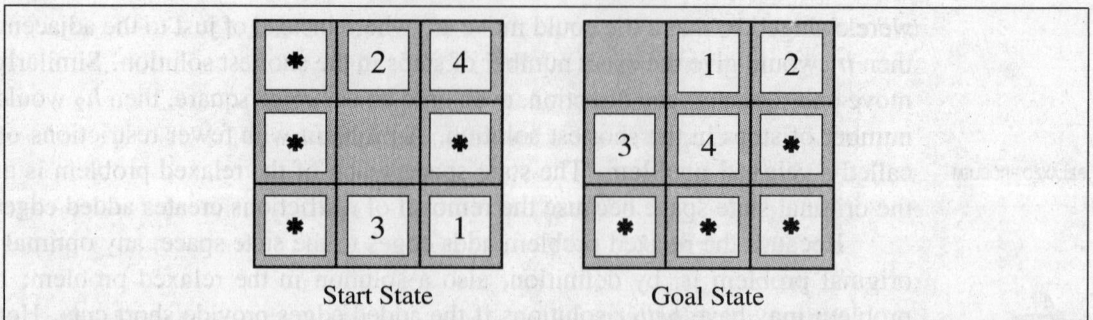

Figure 30 A subproblem of the 8-puzzle instance given in Figure 28. The task is to get tiles 1, 2, 3, and 4 into their correct positions, without worrying about what happens to the other tiles.

This composite heuristic uses whichever function is most accurate on the node in question. Because the component heuristics are admissible, h is admissible; it is also easy to prove that h is consistent. Furthermore, h dominates all of its component heuristics.

6.3 Generating admissible heuristics from subproblems: Pattern databases

SUBPROBLEM

Admissible heuristics can also be derived from the solution cost of a **subproblem** of a given problem. For example, Figure 30 shows a subproblem of the 8-puzzle instance in Figure 28. The subproblem involves getting tiles 1, 2, 3, 4 into their correct positions. Clearly, the cost of the optimal solution of this subproblem is a lower bound on the cost of the complete problem. It turns out to be more accurate than Manhattan distance in some cases.

PATTERN DATABASE

The idea behind **pattern databases** is to store these exact solution costs for every possible subproblem instance—in our example, every possible configuration of the four tiles and the blank. (The locations of the other four tiles are irrelevant for the purposes of solving the subproblem, but moves of those tiles do count toward the cost.) Then we compute an admissible heuristic h_{DB} for each complete state encountered during a search simply by looking up the corresponding subproblem configuration in the database. The database itself is constructed by searching back[12] from the goal and recording the cost of each new pattern encountered; the expense of this search is amortized over many subsequent problem instances.

The choice of 1-2-3-4 is fairly arbitrary; we could also construct databases for 5-6-7-8, for 2-4-6-8, and so on. Each database yields an admissible heuristic, and these heuristics can be combined, as explained earlier, by taking the maximum value. A combined heuristic of this kind is much more accurate than the Manhattan distance; the number of nodes generated when solving random 15-puzzles can be reduced by a factor of 1000.

One might wonder whether the heuristics obtained from the 1-2-3-4 database and the 5-6-7-8 could be *added*, since the two subproblems seem not to overlap. Would this still give an admissible heuristic? The answer is no, because the solutions of the 1-2-3-4 subproblem and the 5-6-7-8 subproblem for a given state will almost certainly share some moves—it is

[12] By working backward from the goal, the exact solution cost of every instance encountered is immediately available. This is an example of **dynamic programming**.

unlikely that 1-2-3-4 can be moved into place without touching 5-6-7-8, and vice versa. But what if we don't count those moves? That is, we record not the total cost of solving the 1-2-3-4 subproblem, but just the number of moves involving 1-2-3-4. Then it is easy to see that the sum of the two costs is still a lower bound on the cost of solving the entire problem. This is the idea behind **disjoint pattern databases**. With such databases, it is possible to solve random 15-puzzles in a few milliseconds—the number of nodes generated is reduced by a factor of 10,000 compared with the use of Manhattan distance. For 24-puzzles, a speedup of roughly a factor of a million can be obtained.

DISJOINT PATTERN DATABASES

Disjoint pattern databases work for sliding-tile puzzles because the problem can be divided up in such a way that each move affects only one subproblem—because only one tile is moved at a time. For a problem such as Rubik's Cube, this kind of subdivision is difficult because each move affects 8 or 9 of the 26 cubies. More general ways of defining additive, admissible heuristics have been proposed that do apply to Rubik's cube (Yang *et al.*, 2008), but they have not yielded a heuristic better than the best nonadditive heuristic for the problem.

6.4 Learning heuristics from experience

A heuristic function $h(n)$ is supposed to estimate the cost of a solution beginning from the state at node n. How could an agent construct such a function? One solution was given in the preceding sections—namely, to devise relaxed problems for which an optimal solution can be found easily. Another solution is to learn from experience. "Experience" here means solving lots of 8-puzzles, for instance. Each optimal solution to an 8-puzzle problem provides examples from which $h(n)$ can be learned. Each example consists of a state from the solution path and the actual cost of the solution from that point. From these examples, a learning algorithm can be used to construct a function $h(n)$ that can (with luck) predict solution costs for other states that arise during search.

FEATURE

Inductive learning methods work best when supplied with **features** of a state that are relevant to predicting the state's value, rather than with just the raw state description. For example, the feature "number of misplaced tiles" might be helpful in predicting the actual distance of a state from the goal. Let's call this feature $x_1(n)$. We could take 100 randomly generated 8-puzzle configurations and gather statistics on their actual solution costs. We might find that when $x_1(n)$ is 5, the average solution cost is around 14, and so on. Given these data, the value of x_1 can be used to predict $h(n)$. Of course, we can use several features. A second feature $x_2(n)$ might be "number of pairs of adjacent tiles that are not adjacent in the goal state." How should $x_1(n)$ and $x_2(n)$ be combined to predict $h(n)$? A common approach is to use a linear combination:

$$h(n) = c_1x_1(n) + c_2x_2(n)\ .$$

The constants c_1 and c_2 are adjusted to give the best fit to the actual data on solution costs. One expects both c_1 and c_2 to be positive because misplaced tiles and incorrect adjacent pairs make the problem harder to solve. Notice that this heuristic does satisfy the condition that $h(n) = 0$ for goal states, but it is not necessarily admissible or consistent.

7 SUMMARY

This chapter has introduced methods that an agent can use to select actions in environments that are deterministic, observable, static, and completely known. In such cases, the agent can construct sequences of actions that achieve its goals; this process is called **search**.

- Before an agent can start searching for solutions, a **goal** must be identified and a well-defined **problem** must be formulated.
- A problem consists of five parts: the **initial state**, a set of **actions**, a **transition model** describing the results of those actions, a **goal test** function, and a **path cost** function. The environment of the problem is represented by a **state space**. A **path** through the state space from the initial state to a goal state is a **solution**.
- Search algorithms treat states and actions as **atomic**: they do not consider any internal structure they might possess.
- A general TREE-SEARCH algorithm considers all possible paths to find a solution, whereas a GRAPH-SEARCH algorithm avoids consideration of redundant paths.
- Search algorithms are judged on the basis of **completeness**, **optimality**, **time complexity**, and **space complexity**. Complexity depends on b, the branching factor in the state space, and d, the depth of the shallowest solution.
- **Uninformed search** methods have access only to the problem definition. The basic algorithms are as follows:
  - **Breadth-first search** expands the shallowest nodes first; it is complete, optimal for unit step costs, but has exponential space complexity.
  - **Uniform-cost search** expands the node with lowest path cost, $g(n)$, and is optimal for general step costs.
  - **Depth-first search** expands the deepest unexpanded node first. It is neither complete nor optimal, but has linear space complexity. **Depth-limited search** adds a depth bound.
  - **Iterative deepening search** calls depth-first search with increasing depth limits until a goal is found. It is complete, optimal for unit step costs, has time complexity comparable to breadth-first search, and has linear space complexity.
  - **Bidirectional search** can enormously reduce time complexity, but it is not always applicable and may require too much space.
- **Informed search** methods may have access to a **heuristic** function $h(n)$ that estimates the cost of a solution from n.
  - The generic **best-first search** algorithm selects a node for expansion according to an **evaluation function**.
  - **Greedy best-first search** expands nodes with minimal $h(n)$. It is not optimal but is often efficient.

- **A* search** expands nodes with minimal $f(n) = g(n) + h(n)$. A* is complete and optimal, provided that $h(n)$ is admissible (for TREE-SEARCH) or consistent (for GRAPH-SEARCH). The space complexity of A* is still prohibitive.
- **RBFS** (recursive best-first search) and **SMA*** (simplified memory-bounded A*) are robust, optimal search algorithms that use limited amounts of memory; given enough time, they can solve problems that A* cannot solve because it runs out of memory.

- The performance of heuristic search algorithms depends on the quality of the heuristic function. One can sometimes construct good heuristics by relaxing the problem definition, by storing precomputed solution costs for subproblems in a pattern database, or by learning from experience with the problem class.

BIBLIOGRAPHICAL AND HISTORICAL NOTES

The topic of state-space search originated in more or less its current form in the early years of AI. Newell and Simon's work on the Logic Theorist (1957) and GPS (1961) led to the establishment of search algorithms as the primary weapons in the armory of 1960s AI researchers and to the establishment of problem solving as the canonical AI task. Work in operations research by Richard Bellman (1957) showed the importance of additive path costs in simplifying optimization algorithms. The text on *Automated Problem Solving* by Nils Nilsson (1971) established the area on a solid theoretical footing.

Most of the state-space search problems analyzed in this chapter have a long history in the literature and are less trivial than they might seem. The missionaries and cannibals problem used in Exercise 9 was analyzed in detail by Amarel (1968). It had been considered earlier—in AI by Simon and Newell (1961) and in operations research by Bellman and Dreyfus (1962).

The 8-puzzle is a smaller cousin of the 15-puzzle, whose history is recounted at length by Slocum and Sonneveld (2006). It was widely believed to have been invented by the famous American game designer Sam Loyd, based on his claims to that effect from 1891 onward (Loyd, 1959). Actually it was invented by Noyes Chapman, a postmaster in Canastota, New York, in the mid-1870s. (Chapman was unable to patent his invention, as a generic patent covering sliding blocks with letters, numbers, or pictures was granted to Ernest Kinsey in 1878.) It quickly attracted the attention of the public and of mathematicians (Johnson and Story, 1879; Tait, 1880). The editors of the *American Journal of Mathematics* stated, "The '15' puzzle for the last few weeks has been prominently before the American public, and may safely be said to have engaged the attention of nine out of ten persons of both sexes and all ages and conditions of the community." Ratner and Warmuth (1986) showed that the general $n \times n$ version of the 15-puzzle belongs to the class of NP-complete problems.

The 8-queens problem was first published anonymously in the German chess magazine *Schach* in 1848; it was later attributed to one Max Bezzel. It was republished in 1850 and at that time drew the attention of the eminent mathematician Carl Friedrich Gauss, who attempted to enumerate all possible solutions; initially he found only 72, but eventually he found the correct answer of 92, although Nauck published all 92 solutions first, in 1850. Netto (1901) generalized the problem to n queens, and Abramson and Yung (1989) found an $O(n)$ algorithm.

Each of the real-world search problems listed in the chapter has been the subject of a good deal of research effort. Methods for selecting optimal airline flights remain proprietary for the most part, but Carl de Marcken (personal communication) has shown that airline ticket pricing and restrictions have become so convoluted that the problem of selecting an optimal flight is formally *undecidable*. The traveling-salesperson problem is a standard combinatorial problem in theoretical computer science (Lawler *et al.*, 1992). Karp (1972) proved the TSP to be NP-hard, but effective heuristic approximation methods were developed (Lin and Kernighan, 1973). Arora (1998) devised a fully polynomial approximation scheme for Euclidean TSPs. VLSI layout methods are surveyed by Shahookar and Mazumder (1991), and many layout optimization papers appear in VLSI journals.

Uninformed search algorithms for problem solving are a central topic of classical computer science (Horowitz and Sahni, 1978) and operations research (Dreyfus, 1969). Breadth-first search was formulated for solving mazes by Moore (1959). The method of **dynamic programming** (Bellman, 1957; Bellman and Dreyfus, 1962), which systematically records solutions for all subproblems of increasing lengths, can be seen as a form of breadth-first search on graphs. The two-point shortest-path algorithm of Dijkstra (1959) is the origin of uniform-cost search. These works also introduced the idea of explored and frontier sets (closed and open lists).

A version of iterative deepening designed to make efficient use of the chess clock was first used by Slate and Atkin (1977) in the CHESS 4.5 game-playing program. Martelli's algorithm B (1977) includes an iterative deepening aspect and also dominates A*'s worst-case performance with admissible but inconsistent heuristics. The iterative deepening technique came to the fore in work by Korf (1985a). Bidirectional search, which was introduced by Pohl (1971), can also be effective in some cases.

The use of heuristic information in problem solving appears in an early paper by Simon and Newell (1958), but the phrase "heuristic search" and the use of heuristic functions that estimate the distance to the goal came somewhat later (Newell and Ernst, 1965; Lin, 1965). Doran and Michie (1966) conducted extensive experimental studies of heuristic search. Although they analyzed path length and "penetrance" (the ratio of path length to the total number of nodes examined so far), they appear to have ignored the information provided by the path cost $g(n)$. The A* algorithm, incorporating the current path cost into heuristic search, was developed by Hart, Nilsson, and Raphael (1968), with some later corrections (Hart *et al.*, 1972). Dechter and Pearl (1985) demonstrated the optimal efficiency of A*.

The original A* paper introduced the consistency condition on heuristic functions. The monotone condition was introduced by Pohl (1977) as a simpler replacement, but Pearl (1984) showed that the two were equivalent.

Pohl (1977) pioneered the study of the relationship between the error in heuristic functions and the time complexity of A*. Basic results were obtained for tree search with unit step costs and a single goal node (Pohl, 1977; Gaschnig, 1979; Huyn *et al.*, 1980; Pearl, 1984) and with multiple goal nodes (Dinh *et al.*, 2007). The "effective branching factor" was proposed by Nilsson (1971) as an empirical measure of the efficiency; it is equivalent to assuming a time cost of $O((b^*)^d)$. For tree search applied to a graph, Korf *et al.* (2001) argue that the time cost is better modeled as $O(b^{d-k})$, where k depends on the heuristic accuracy; this analysis has elicited some controversy, however. For graph search, Helmert and Röger (2008) noted that several well-known problems contained exponentially many nodes on optimal solution paths, implying exponential time complexity for A* even with constant absolute error in h.

There are many variations on the A* algorithm. Pohl (1973) proposed the use of *dynamic weighting*, which uses a weighted sum $f_w(n) = w_g g(n) + w_h h(n)$ of the current path length and the heuristic function as an evaluation function, rather than the simple sum $f(n) = g(n) + h(n)$ used in A*. The weights w_g and w_h are adjusted dynamically as the search progresses. Pohl's algorithm can be shown to be ϵ-admissible—that is, guaranteed to find solutions within a factor $1 + \epsilon$ of the optimal solution, where ϵ is a parameter supplied to the algorithm. The same property is exhibited by the A^*_ϵ algorithm (Pearl, 1984), which can select any node from the frontier provided its f-cost is within a factor $1 + \epsilon$ of the lowest-f-cost frontier node. The selection can be done so as to minimize search cost.

Bidirectional versions of A* have been investigated; a combination of bidirectional A* and known landmarks was used to efficiently find driving routes for Microsoft's online map service (Goldberg *et al.*, 2006). After caching a set of paths between landmarks, the algorithm can find an optimal path between any pair of points in a 24 million point graph of the United States, searching less than 0.1% of the graph. Others approaches to bidirectional search include a breadth-first search backward from the goal up to a fixed depth, followed by a forward IDA* search (Dillenburg and Nelson, 1994; Manzini, 1995).

A* and other state-space search algorithms are closely related to the *branch-and-bound* techniques that are widely used in operations research (Lawler and Wood, 1966). The relationships between state-space search and branch-and-bound have been investigated in depth (Kumar and Kanal, 1983; Nau *et al.*, 1984; Kumar *et al.*, 1988). Martelli and Montanari (1978) demonstrate a connection between dynamic programming and certain types of state-space search. Kumar and Kanal (1988) attempt a "grand uni?cation" of heuristic search, dynamic programming, and branch-and-bound techniques under the name of CDP—the "composite decision process."

Because computers in the late 1950s and early 1960s had at most a few thousand words of main memory, memory-bounded heuristic search was an early research topic. The Graph Traverser (Doran and Michie, 1966), one of the earliest search programs, commits to an operator after searching best-first up to the memory limit. IDA* (Korf, 1985a, 1985b) was the first widely used optimal, memory-bounded heuristic search algorithm, and a large number of variants have been developed. An analysis of the efficiency of IDA* and of its difficulties with real-valued heuristics appears in Patrick *et al.* (1992).

RBFS (Korf, 1993) is actually somewhat more complicated than the algorithm shown in Figure 26, which is closer to an independently developed algorithm called **iterative expansion** (Russell, 1992). RBFS uses a lower bound as well as the upper bound; the two algorithms behave identically with admissible heuristics, but RBFS expands nodes in best-first

ITERATIVE EXPANSION

order even with an inadmissible heuristic. The idea of keeping track of the best alternative path appeared earlier in Bratko's (1986) elegant Prolog implementation of A* and in the DTA* algorithm (Russell and Wefald, 1991). The latter work also discusses metalevel state spaces and metalevel learning.

The MA* algorithm appeared in Chakrabarti *et al.* (1989). SMA*, or Simplified MA*, emerged from an attempt to implement MA* as a comparison algorithm for IE (Russell, 1992). Kaindl and Khorsand (1994) have applied SMA* to produce a bidirectional search algorithm that is substantially faster than previous algorithms. Korf and Zhang (2000) describe a divide-and-conquer approach, and Zhou and Hansen (2002) introduce memory-bounded A* graph search and a strategy for switching to breadth-first search to increase memory-efficiency (Zhou and Hansen, 2006). Korf (1995) surveys memory-bounded search techniques.

The idea that admissible heuristics can be derived by problem relaxation appears in the seminal paper by Held and Karp (1970), who used the minimum-spanning-tree heuristic to solve the TSP. (See Exercise 30.)

The automation of the relaxation process was implemented successfully by Prieditis (1993), building on earlier work with Mostow (Mostow and Prieditis, 1989). Holte and Hernadvolgyi (2001) describe more recent steps towards automating the process. The use of pattern databases to derive admissible heuristics is due to Gasser (1995) and Culberson and Schaeffer (1996, 1998); disjoint pattern databases are described by Korf and Felner (2002); a similar method using symbolic patterns is due to Edelkamp (2009). Felner *et al.* (2007) show how to compress pattern databases to save space. The probabilistic interpretation of heuristics was investigated in depth by Pearl (1984) and Hansson and Mayer (1989).

By far the most comprehensive source on heuristics and heuristic search algorithms is Pearl's (1984) *Heuristics* text. This text provides especially good coverage of the wide variety of offshoots and variations of A*, including rigorous proofs of their formal properties. Kanal and Kumar (1988) present an anthology of important articles on heuristic search, and Rayward-Smith *et al.* (1996) cover approaches from Operations Research. Papers about new search algorithms—which, remarkably, continue to be discovered—appear in journals such as *Artificial Intelligence* and *Journal of the ACM*.

PARALLEL SEARCH

The topic of **parallel search** algorithms was not covered in the chapter, partly because it requires a lengthy discussion of parallel computer architectures. Parallel search became a popular topic in the 1990s in both AI and theoretical computer science (Mahanti and Daniels, 1993; Grama and Kumar, 1995; Crauser *et al.*, 1998) and is making a comeback in the era of new multicore and cluster architectures (Ralphs *et al.*, 2004; Korf and Schultze, 2005). Also of increasing importance are search algorithms for very large graphs that require disk storage (Korf, 2008).

EXERCISES

1 Explain why problem formulation must follow goal formulation.

2 Your goal is to navigate a robot out of a maze. The robot starts in the center of the maze facing north. You can turn the robot to face north, east, south, or west. You can direct the robot to move forward a certain distance, although it will stop before hitting a wall.

a. Formulate this problem. How large is the state space?

b. In navigating a maze, the only place we need to turn is at the intersection of two or more corridors. Reformulate this problem using this observation. How large is the state space now?

c. From each point in the maze, we can move in any of the four directions until we reach a turning point, and this is the only action we need to do. Reformulate the problem using these actions. Do we need to keep track of the robot's orientation now?

d. In our initial description of the problem we already abstracted from the real world, restricting actions and removing details. List three such simplifications we made.

3 Suppose two friends live in different cities on a map, such as the Romania map shown in Figure 2. On every turn, we can simultaneously move each friend to a neighboring city on the map. The amount of time needed to move from city i to neighbor j is equal to the road distance $d(i, j)$ between the cities, but on each turn the friend that arrives first must wait until the other one arrives (and calls the first on his/her cell phone) before the next turn can begin. We want the two friends to meet as quickly as possible.

a. Write a detailed formulation for this search problem. (You will find it helpful to define some formal notation here.)

b. Let $D(i, j)$ be the straight-line distance between cities i and j. Which of the following heuristic functions are admissible? (i) $D(i, j)$; (ii) $2 \cdot D(i, j)$; (iii) $D(i, j)/2$.

c. Are there completely connected maps for which no solution exists?

d. Are there maps in which all solutions require one friend to visit the same city twice?

4 Show that the 8-puzzle states are divided into two disjoint sets, such that any state is reachable from any other state in the same set, while no state is reachable from any state in the other set. (*Hint:* See Berlekamp *et al.* (1982).) Devise a procedure to decide which set a given state is in, and explain why this is useful for generating random states.

5 Consider the n-queens problem using the "efficient" incremental formulation. Explain why the state space has at least $\sqrt[3]{n!}$ states and estimate the largest n for which exhaustive exploration is feasible. (*Hint*: Derive a lower bound on the branching factor by considering the maximum number of squares that a queen can attack in any column.)

6 Give a complete problem formulation for each of the following. Choose a formulation that is precise enough to be implemented.

a. Using only four colors, you have to color a planar map in such a way that no two adjacent regions have the same color.

b. A 3-foot-tall monkey is in a room where some bananas are suspended from the 8-foot ceiling. He would like to get the bananas. The room contains two stackable, movable, climbable 3-foot-high crates.

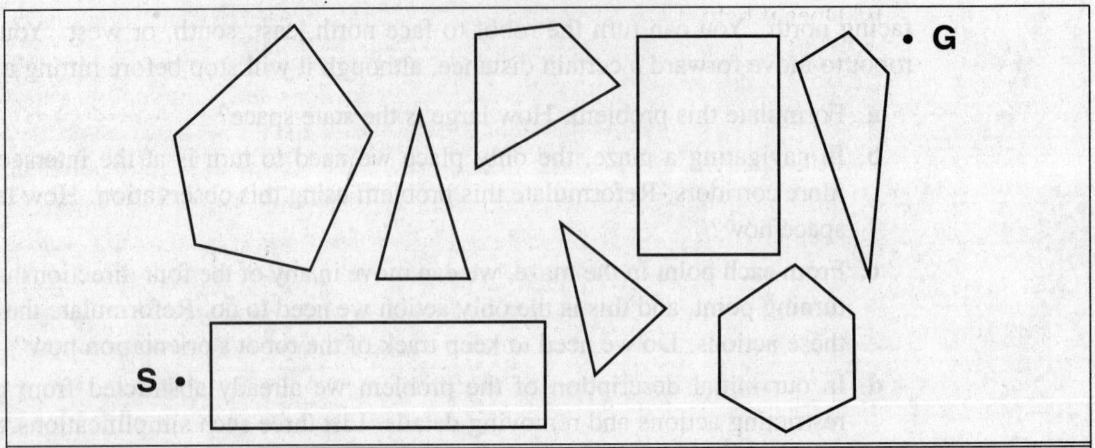

Figure 31 A scene with polygonal obstacles. S and G are the start and goal states.

c. You have a program that outputs the message "illegal input record" when fed a certain file of input records. You know that processing of each record is independent of the other records. You want to discover what record is illegal.

d. You have three jugs, measuring 12 gallons, 8 gallons, and 3 gallons, and a water faucet. You can fill the jugs up or empty them out from one to another or onto the ground. You need to measure out exactly one gallon.

7 Consider the problem of finding the shortest path between two points on a plane that has convex polygonal obstacles as shown in Figure 31. This is an idealization of the problem that a robot has to solve to navigate in a crowded environment.

a. Suppose the state space consists of all positions (x, y) in the plane. How many states are there? How many paths are there to the goal?

b. Explain briefly why the shortest path from one polygon vertex to any other in the scene must consist of straight-line segments joining some of the vertices of the polygons. Define a good state space now. How large is this state space?

c. Define the necessary functions to implement the search problem, including an ACTIONS function that takes a vertex as input and returns a set of vectors, each of which maps the current vertex to one of the vertices that can be reached in a straight line. (Do not forget the neighbors on the same polygon.) Use the straight-line distance for the heuristic function.

d. Apply one or more of the algorithms in this chapter to solve a range of problems in the domain, and comment on their performance.

8 In section 1.1 we said that we would not consider problems with negative path costs. In this exercise, we explore this decision in more depth.

a. Suppose that actions can have arbitrarily large negative costs; explain why this possibility would force any optimal algorithm to explore the entire state space.

b. Does it help if we insist that step costs must be greater than or equal to some negative constant c? Consider both trees and graphs.

c. Suppose that a set of actions forms a loop in the state space such that executing the set in some order results in no net change to the state. If all of these actions have negative cost, what does this imply about the optimal behavior for an agent in such an environment?

d. One can easily imagine actions with high negative cost, even in domains such as route finding. For example, some stretches of road might have such beautiful scenery as to far outweigh the normal costs in terms of time and fuel. Explain, in precise terms, within the context of state-space search, why humans do not drive around scenic loops indefinitely, and explain how to define the state space and actions for route finding so that artificial agents can also avoid looping.

e. Can you think of a real domain in which step costs are such as to cause looping?

9 The **missionaries and cannibals** problem is usually stated as follows. Three missionaries and three cannibals are on one side of a river, along with a boat that can hold one or two people. Find a way to get everyone to the other side without ever leaving a group of missionaries in one place outnumbered by the cannibals in that place. This problem is famous in AI because it was the subject of the first paper that approached problem formulation from an analytical viewpoint (Amarel, 1968).

a. Formulate the problem precisely, making only those distinctions necessary to ensure a valid solution. Draw a diagram of the complete state space.

b. Implement and solve the problem optimally using an appropriate search algorithm. Is it a good idea to check for repeated states?

c. Why do you think people have a hard time solving this puzzle, given that the state space is so simple?

10 Define in your own words the following terms: state, state space, search tree, search node, goal, action, transition model, and branching factor.

11 What's the difference between a world state, a state description, and a search node? Why is this distinction useful?

12 An action such as *Go(Sibiu)* really consists of a long sequence of finer-grained actions: turn on the car, release the brake, accelerate forward, etc. Having composite actions of this kind reduces the number of steps in a solution sequence, thereby reducing the search time. Suppose we take this to the logical extreme, by making super-composite actions out of every possible sequence of *Go* actions. Then every problem instance is solved by a single super-composite action, such as *Go(Sibiu)Go(Rimnicu Vilcea)Go(Pitesti)Go(Bucharest)*. Explain how search would work in this formulation. Is this a practical approach for speeding up problem solving?

13 Prove that GRAPH-SEARCH satisfies the graph separation property illustrated in Figure 9. (*Hint*: Begin by showing that the property holds at the start, then show that if it holds before an iteration of the algorithm, it holds afterwards.) Describe a search algorithm that violates the property.

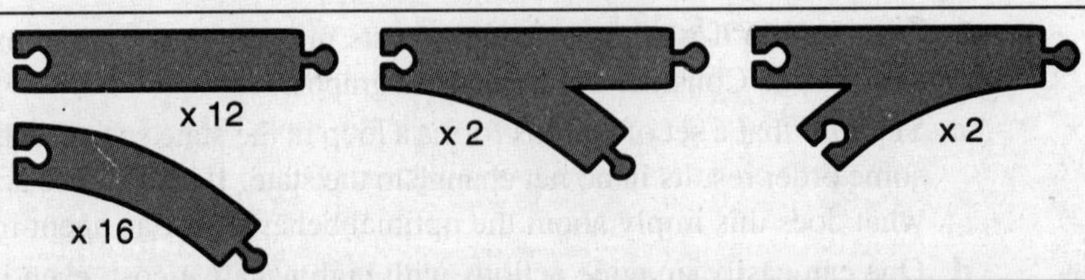

Figure 32 The track pieces in a wooden railway set; each is labeled with the number of copies in the set. Note that curved pieces and "fork" pieces ("switches" or "points") can be flipped over so they can curve in either direction. Each curve subtends 45 degrees.

14 Which of the following are true and which are false? Explain your answers.

a. Depth-first search always expands at least as many nodes as A* search with an admissible heuristic.

b. $h(n) = 0$ is an admissible heuristic for the 8-puzzle.

c. A* is of no use in robotics because percepts, states, and actions are continuous.

d. Breadth-first search is complete even if zero step costs are allowed.

e. Assume that a rook can move on a chessboard any number of squares in a straight line, vertically or horizontally, but cannot jump over other pieces. Manhattan distance is an admissible heuristic for the problem of moving the rook from square A to square B in the smallest number of moves.

15 Consider a state space where the start state is number 1 and each state k has two successors: numbers $2k$ and $2k+1$.

a. Draw the portion of the state space for states 1 to 15.

b. Suppose the goal state is 11. List the order in which nodes will be visited for breadth-first search, depth-limited search with limit 3, and iterative deepening search.

c. How well would bidirectional search work on this problem? What is the branching factor in each direction of the bidirectional search?

d. Does the answer to (c) suggest a reformulation of the problem that would allow you to solve the problem of getting from state 1 to a given goal state with almost no search?

e. Call the action going from k to $2k$ Left, and the action going to $2k+1$ Right. Can you find an algorithm that outputs the solution to this problem without any search at all?

16 A basic wooden railway set contains the pieces shown in Figure 32. The task is to connect these pieces into a railway that has no overlapping tracks and no loose ends where a train could run off onto the floor.

a. Suppose that the pieces fit together *exactly* with no slack. Give a precise formulation of the task as a search problem.

b. Identify a suitable uninformed search algorithm for this task and explain your choice.

c. Explain why removing any one of the "fork" pieces makes the problem unsolvable.

d. Give an upper bound on the total size of the state space defined by your formulation. (*Hint*: think about the maximum branching factor for the construction process and the maximum depth, ignoring the problem of overlapping pieces and loose ends. Begin by pretending that every piece is unique.)

17 **Iterative lengthening search** is an iterative analog of uniform cost search. The idea is to use increasing limits on path cost. If a node is generated whose path cost exceeds the current limit, it is immediately discarded. For each new iteration, the limit is set to the lowest path cost of any node discarded in the previous iteration.

a. Show that this algorithm is optimal for general path costs.

b. Consider a uniform tree with branching factor b, solution depth d, and unit step costs. How many iterations will iterative lengthening require?

c. Now consider step costs drawn from the continuous range $[\epsilon, 1]$, where $0 < \epsilon < 1$. How many iterations are required in the worst case?

d. Implement the algorithm and apply it to instances of the 8-puzzle and traveling salesperson problems. Compare the algorithm's performance to that of uniform-cost search, and comment on your results.

18 Describe a state space in which iterative deepening search performs much worse than depth-first search (for example, $O(n^2)$ vs. $O(n)$).

19 Write a program that will take as input two Web page URLs and find a path of links from one to the other. What is an appropriate search strategy? Is bidirectional search a good idea? Could a search engine be used to implement a predecessor function?

20 Consider the vacuum-world problem from Section 2.1.

a. Which of the algorithms defined in this chapter would be appropriate for this problem? Should the algorithm use tree search or graph search?

b. Apply your chosen algorithm to compute an optimal sequence of actions for a 3×3 world whose initial state has dirt in the three top squares and the agent in the center.

c. Construct a search agent for the vacuum world, and evaluate its performance in a set of 3×3 worlds with probability 0.2 of dirt in each square. Include the search cost as well as path cost in the performance measure, using a reasonable exchange rate.

d. Compare your best search agent with a simple randomized reflex agent that sucks if there is dirt and otherwise moves randomly.

e. Consider what would happen if the world were enlarged to $n \times n$. How does the performance of the search agent and of the reflex agent vary with n?

21 Prove each of the following statements, or give a counterexample:

a. Breadth-first search is a special case of uniform-cost search.

b. Depth-first search is a special case of best-first tree search.

c. Uniform-cost search is a special case of A* search.

22 Compare the performance of A* and RBFS on a set of randomly generated problems in the 8-puzzle (with Manhattan distance) and TSP (with MST—see Exercise 30) domains. Discuss your results. What happens to the performance of RBFS when a small random number is added to the heuristic values in the 8-puzzle domain?

23 Trace the operation of A* search applied to the problem of getting to Bucharest from Lugoj using the straight-line distance heuristic. That is, show the sequence of nodes that the algorithm will consider and the f, g, and h score for each node.

24 Devise a state space in which A* using GRAPH-SEARCH returns a suboptimal solution with an $h(n)$ function that is admissible but inconsistent.

HEURISTIC PATH ALGORITHM

25 The **heuristic path algorithm** (Pohl, 1977) is a best-first search in which the evaluation function is $f(n) = (2 - w)g(n) + wh(n)$. For what values of w is this complete? For what values is it optimal, assuming that h is admissible? What kind of search does this perform for $w = 0$, $w = 1$, and $w = 2$?

26 Consider the unbounded version of the regular 2D grid shown in Figure 9. The start state is at the origin, (0,0), and the goal state is at (x, y).

a. What is the branching factor b in this state space?

b. How many distinct states are there at depth k (for $k > 0$)?

c. What is the maximum number of nodes expanded by breadth-first tree search?

d. What is the maximum number of nodes expanded by breadth-first graph search?

e. Is $h = |u - x| + |v - y|$ an admissible heuristic for a state at (u, v)? Explain.

f. How many nodes are expanded by A* graph search using h?

g. Does h remain admissible if some links are removed?

h. Does h remain admissible if some links are added between nonadjacent states?

27 n vehicles occupy squares $(1, 1)$ through $(n, 1)$ (i.e., the bottom row) of an $n \times n$ grid. The vehicles must be moved to the top row but in reverse order; so the vehicle i that starts in $(i, 1)$ must end up in $(n - i + 1, n)$. On each time step, every one of the n vehicles can move one square up, down, left, or right, or stay put; but if a vehicle stays put, one other adjacent vehicle (but not more than one) can hop over it. Two vehicles cannot occupy the same square.

a. Calculate the size of the state space as a function of n.

b. Calculate the branching factor as a function of n.

c. Suppose that vehicle i is at (x_i, y_i); write a nontrivial admissible heuristic h_i for the number of moves it will require to get to its goal location $(n - i + 1, n)$, assuming no other vehicles are on the grid.

d. Which of the following heuristics are admissible for the problem of moving all n vehicles to their destinations? Explain.

(i) $\sum_{i=1}^{n} h_i$.
(ii) $\max\{h_1, \ldots, h_n\}$.
(iii) $\min\{h_1, \ldots, h_n\}$.

28 Invent a heuristic function for the 8-puzzle that sometimes overestimates, and show how it can lead to a suboptimal solution on a particular problem. (You can use a computer to help if you want.) Prove that if h never overestimates by more than c, A* using h returns a solution whose cost exceeds that of the optimal solution by no more than c.

29 Prove that if a heuristic is consistent, it must be admissible. Construct an admissible heuristic that is not consistent.

30 The traveling salesperson problem (TSP) can be solved with the minimum-spanning-tree (MST) heuristic, which estimates the cost of completing a tour, given that a partial tour has already been constructed. The MST cost of a set of cities is the smallest sum of the link costs of any tree that connects all the cities.

a. Show how this heuristic can be derived from a relaxed version of the TSP.

b. Show that the MST heuristic dominates straight-line distance.

c. Write a problem generator for instances of the TSP where cities are represented by random points in the unit square.

d. Find an efficient algorithm in the literature for constructing the MST, and use it with A* graph search to solve instances of the TSP.

31 In section 6.2, we defined the relaxation of the 8-puzzle in which a tile can move from square A to square B if B is blank. The exact solution of this problem defines **Gaschnig's heuristic** (Gaschnig, 1979). Explain why Gaschnig's heuristic is at least as accurate as $h1$ (misplaced tiles), and show cases where it is more accurate than both $h1$ and $h2$ (Manhattan distance). Explain how to calculate Gaschnig's heuristic efficiently.

32 We gave two simple heuristics for the 8-puzzle: Manhattan distance and misplaced tiles. Several heuristics in the literature purport to improve on this—see, for example, Nilsson (1971), Mostow and Prieditis (1989), and Hansson *et al.* (1992). Test these claims by implementing the heuristics and comparing the performance of the resulting algorithms.

BEYOND CLASSICAL SEARCH

BEYOND CLASSICAL SEARCH

In which we relax the simplifying assumptions, thereby getting closer to the real world.

You should be familiar with a certain category of problems: observable, deterministic, known environments where the solution is a sequence of actions. In this chapter, we look at what happens when these assumptions are relaxed. We begin with a fairly simple case: Sections 1 and 2 cover algorithms that perform purely **local search** in the state space, evaluating and modifying one or more current states rather than systematically exploring paths from an initial state. These algorithms are suitable for problems in which all that matters is the solution state, not the path cost to reach it. The family of local search algorithms includes methods inspired by statistical physics (**simulated annealing**) and evolutionary biology (**genetic algorithms**).

Then, in Sections 3–4, we examine what happens when we relax the assumptions of determinism and observability. The key idea is that if an agent cannot predict exactly what percept it will receive, then it will need to consider what to do under each **contingency** that its percepts may reveal. With partial observability, the agent will also need to keep track of the states it might be in.

Finally, Section 5 investigates **online search**, in which the agent is faced with a state space that is initially unknown and must be explored.

1 LOCAL SEARCH ALGORITHMS AND OPTIMIZATION PROBLEMS

The search algorithms that we have seen so far are designed to explore search spaces systematically. This systematicity is achieved by keeping one or more paths in memory and by recording which alternatives have been explored at each point along the path. When a goal is found, the *path* to that goal also constitutes a *solution* to the problem. In many problems, however, the path to the goal is irrelevant. For example, in the 8-queens problem, from the chapter "Solving Problems by Searching", what matters is the final configuration of queens, not the order in which they are added. The same general property holds for many important applications such as integrated-circuit design, factory-floor layout, job-shop scheduling, automatic programming, telecommunications network optimization, vehicle routing, and portfolio management.

LOCAL SEARCH
CURRENT NODE

If the path to the goal does not matter, we might consider a different class of algorithms, ones that do not worry about paths at all. **Local search** algorithms operate using a single **current node** (rather than multiple paths) and generally move only to neighbors of that node. Typically, the paths followed by the search are not retained. Although local search algorithms are not systematic, they have two key advantages: (1) they use very little memory—usually a constant amount; and (2) they can often find reasonable solutions in large or infinite (continuous) state spaces for which systematic algorithms are unsuitable.

OPTIMIZATION PROBLEM
OBJECTIVE FUNCTION

In addition to finding goals, local search algorithms are useful for solving pure **optimization problems**, in which the aim is to find the best state according to an **objective function**. Many optimization problems do not fit the "standard" search model. For example, nature provides an objective function—reproductive fitness—that Darwinian evolution could be seen as attempting to optimize, but there is no "goal test" and no "path cost" for this problem.

STATE-SPACE LANDSCAPE
GLOBAL MINIMUM
GLOBAL MAXIMUM

To understand local search, we find it useful to consider the **state-space landscape** (as in Figure 1). A landscape has both "location" (defined by the state) and "elevation" (defined by the value of the heuristic cost function or objective function). If elevation corresponds to cost, then the aim is to find the lowest valley—a **global minimum**; if elevation corresponds to an objective function, then the aim is to find the highest peak—a **global maximum**. (You can convert from one to the other just by inserting a minus sign.) Local search algorithms explore this landscape. A **complete** local search algorithm always finds a goal if one exists; an **optimal** algorithm always finds a global minimum/maximum.

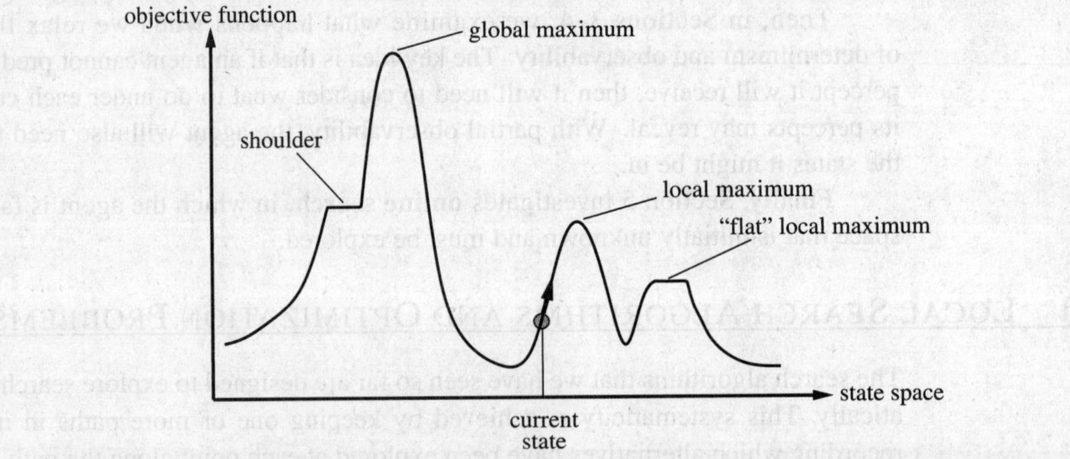

Figure 1 A one-dimensional state-space landscape in which elevation corresponds to the objective function. The aim is to find the global maximum. Hill-climbing search modifies the current state to try to improve it, as shown by the arrow. The various topographic features are defined in the text.

```
function HILL-CLIMBING(problem) returns a state that is a local maximum
  current ← MAKE-NODE(problem.INITIAL-STATE)
  loop do
     neighbor ← a highest-valued successor of current
     if neighbor.VALUE ≤ current.VALUE then return current.STATE
     current ← neighbor
```

Figure 2 The hill-climbing search algorithm, which is the most basic local search technique. At each step the current node is replaced by the best neighbor; in this version, that means the neighbor with the highest VALUE, but if a heuristic cost estimate h is used, we would find the neighbor with the lowest h.

1.1 Hill-climbing search

HILL CLIMBING

STEEPEST ASCENT

The **hill-climbing** search algorithm (**steepest-ascent** version) is shown in Figure 2. It is simply a loop that continually moves in the direction of increasing value—that is, uphill. It terminates when it reaches a "peak" where no neighbor has a higher value. The algorithm does not maintain a search tree, so the data structure for the current node need only record the state and the value of the objective function. Hill climbing does not look ahead beyond the immediate neighbors of the current state. This resembles trying to find the top of Mount Everest in a thick fog while suffering from amnesia.

To illustrate hill climbing, we will use the **8-queens problem.** Local search algorithms typically use a **complete-state formulation**, where each state has 8 queens on the board, one per column. The successors of a state are all possible states generated by moving a single queen to another square in the same column (so each state has 8 x 7=56 successors). The heuristic cost function h is the number of pairs of queens that are attacking each other, either directly or indirectly. The global minimum of this function is zero, which occurs only at perfect solutions. Figure 3(a) shows a state with h=17. The figure also shows the values of all its successors, with the best successors having h=12. Hill-climbing algorithms typically choose randomly among the set of best successors if there is more than one.

GREEDY LOCAL SEARCH

Hill climbing is sometimes called **greedy local search** because it grabs a good neighbor state without thinking ahead about where to go next. Although greed is considered one of the seven deadly sins, it turns out that greedy algorithms often perform quite well. Hill climbing often makes rapid progress toward a solution because it is usually quite easy to improve a bad state. For example, from the state in Figure 3(a), it takes just five steps to reach the state in Figure 3(b), which has $h = 1$ and is very nearly a solution. Unfortunately, hill climbing often gets stuck for the following reasons:

LOCAL MAXIMUM

- **Local maxima**: a local maximum is a peak that is higher than each of its neighboring states but lower than the global maximum. Hill-climbing algorithms that reach the vicinity of a local maximum will be drawn upward toward the peak but will then be stuck with nowhere else to go. Figure 1 illustrates the problem schematically. More

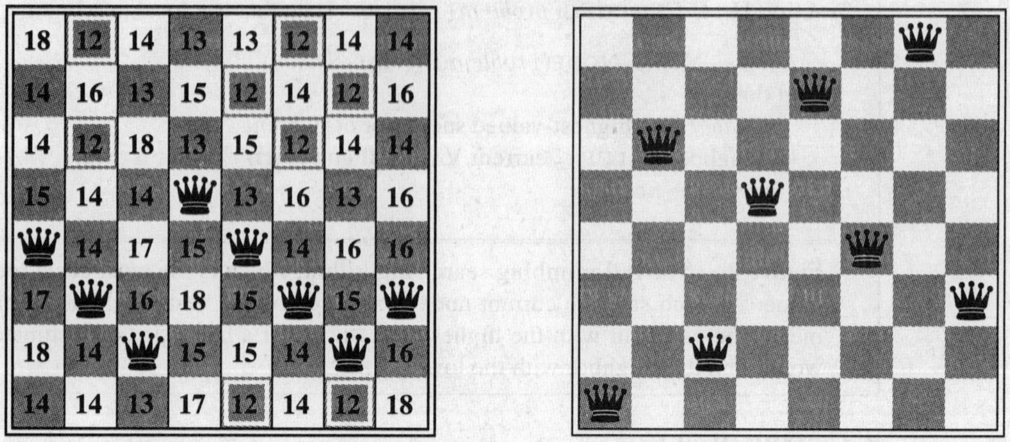

(a) (b)

Figure 3 (a) An 8-queens state with heuristic cost estimate $h = 17$, showing the value of h for each possible successor obtained by moving a queen within its column. The best moves are marked. (b) A local minimum in the 8-queens state space; the state has $h = 1$ but every successor has a higher cost.

concretely, the state in Figure 3(b) is a local maximum (i.e., a local minimum for the cost h); every move of a single queen makes the situation worse.

RIDGE

- **Ridges**: a ridge is shown in Figure 4. Ridges result in a sequence of local maxima that is very difficult for greedy algorithms to navigate.

PLATEAU

SHOULDER

- **Plateaux**: a plateau is a flat area of the state-space landscape. It can be a flat local maximum, from which no uphill exit exists, or a **shoulder**, from which progress is possible. (See Figure 1.) A hill-climbing search might get lost on the plateau.

In each case, the algorithm reaches a point at which no progress is being made. Starting from a randomly generated 8-queens state, steepest-ascent hill climbing gets stuck 86% of the time, solving only 14% of problem instances. It works quickly, taking just 4 steps on average when it succeeds and 3 when it gets stuck—not bad for a state space with $8^8 \approx 17$ million states.

SIDEWAYS MOVE

The algorithm in Figure 2 halts if it reaches a plateau where the best successor has the same value as the current state. Might it not be a good idea to keep going—to allow a **sideways move** in the hope that the plateau is really a shoulder, as shown in Figure 1? The answer is usually yes, but we must take care. If we always allow sideways moves when there are no uphill moves, an infinite loop will occur whenever the algorithm reaches a flat local maximum that is not a shoulder. One common solution is to put a limit on the number of consecutive sideways moves allowed. For example, we could allow up to, say, 100 consecutive sideways moves in the 8-queens problem. This raises the percentage of problem instances solved by hill climbing from 14% to 94%. Success comes at a cost: the algorithm averages roughly 21 steps for each successful instance and 64 for each failure.

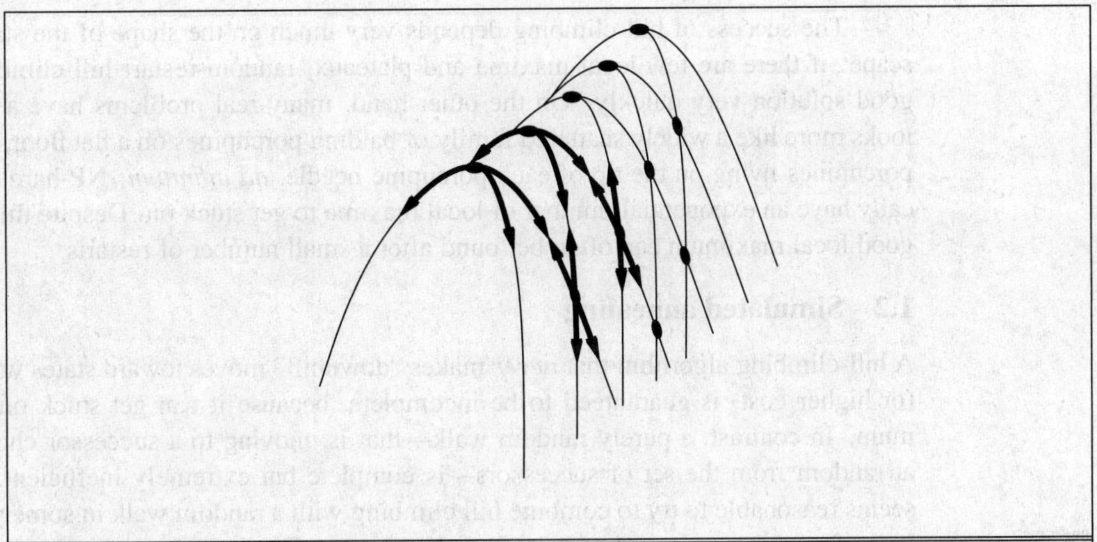

Figure 4 Illustration of why ridges cause difficulties for hill climbing. The grid of states (dark circles) is superimposed on a ridge rising from left to right, creating a sequence of local maxima that are not directly connected to each other. From each local maximum, all the available actions point downhill.

STOCHASTIC HILL CLIMBING

FIRST-CHOICE HILL CLIMBING

Many variants of hill climbing have been invented. **Stochastic hill climbing** chooses at random from among the uphill moves; the probability of selection can vary with the steepness of the uphill move. This usually converges more slowly than steepest ascent, but in some state landscapes, it finds better solutions. **First-choice hill climbing** implements stochastic hill climbing by generating successors randomly until one is generated that is better than the current state. This is a good strategy when a state has many (e.g., thousands) of successors.

RANDOM-RESTART HILL CLIMBING

The hill-climbing algorithms described so far are incomplete—they often fail to find a goal when one exists because they can get stuck on local maxima. **Random-restart hill climbing** adopts the well-known adage, "If at first you don't succeed, try, try again." It conducts a series of hill-climbing searches from randomly generated initial states,[1] until a goal is found. It is trivially complete with probability approaching 1, because it will eventually generate a goal state as the initial state. If each hill-climbing search has a probability p of success, then the expected number of restarts required is $1/p$. For 8-queens instances with no sideways moves allowed, $p \approx 0.14$, so we need roughly 7 iterations to find a goal (6 failures and 1 success). The expected number of steps is the cost of one successful iteration plus $(1-p)/p$ times the cost of failure, or roughly 22 steps in all. When we allow sideways moves, $1/0.94 \approx 1.06$ iterations are needed on average and $(1 \times 21) + (0.06/0.94) \times 64 \approx 25$ steps. For 8-queens, then, random-restart hill climbing is very effective indeed. Even for three million queens, the approach can find solutions in under a minute.[2]

[1] Generating a *random* state from an implicitly specified state space can be a hard problem in itself.

[2] Luby *et al.* (1993) prove that it is best, in some cases, to restart a randomized search algorithm after a particular, fixed amount of time and that this can be *much* more efficient than letting each search continue indefinitely. Disallowing or limiting the number of sideways moves is an example of this idea.

The success of hill climbing depends very much on the shape of the state-space landscape: if there are few local maxima and plateaux, random-restart hill climbing will find a good solution very quickly. On the other hand, many real problems have a landscape that looks more like a widely scattered family of balding porcupines on a flat floor, with miniature porcupines living on the tip of each porcupine needle, *ad infinitum*. NP-hard problems typically have an exponential number of local maxima to get stuck on. Despite this, a reasonably good local maximum can often be found after a small number of restarts.

1.2 Simulated annealing

A hill-climbing algorithm that *never* makes "downhill" moves toward states with lower value (or higher cost) is guaranteed to be incomplete, because it can get stuck on a local maximum. In contrast, a purely random walk—that is, moving to a successor chosen uniformly at random from the set of successors—is complete but extremely inefficient. Therefore, it seems reasonable to try to combine hill climbing with a random walk in some way that yields both efficiency and completeness. **Simulated annealing** is such an algorithm. In metallurgy, **annealing** is the process used to temper or harden metals and glass by heating them to a high temperature and then gradually cooling them, thus allowing the material to reach a low-energy crystalline state. To explain simulated annealing, we switch our point of view from hill climbing to **gradient descent** (i.e., minimizing cost) and imagine the task of getting a ping-pong ball into the deepest crevice in a bumpy surface. If we just let the ball roll, it will come to rest at a local minimum. If we shake the surface, we can bounce the ball out of the local minimum. The trick is to shake just hard enough to bounce the ball out of local minima but not hard enough to dislodge it from the global minimum. The simulated-annealing solution is to start by shaking hard (i.e., at a high temperature) and then gradually reduce the intensity of the shaking (i.e., lower the temperature).

SIMULATED ANNEALING

GRADIENT DESCENT

The innermost loop of the simulated-annealing algorithm (Figure 5) is quite similar to hill climbing. Instead of picking the *best* move, however, it picks a *random* move. If the move improves the situation, it is always accepted. Otherwise, the algorithm accepts the move with some probability less than 1. The probability decreases exponentially with the "badness" of the move—the amount ΔE by which the evaluation is worsened. The probability also decreases as the "temperature" T goes down: "bad" moves are more likely to be allowed at the start when T is high, and they become more unlikely as T decreases. If the *schedule* lowers T slowly enough, the algorithm will find a global optimum with probability approaching 1.

Simulated annealing was first used extensively to solve VLSI layout problems in the early 1980s. It has been applied widely to factory scheduling and other large-scale optimization tasks. In Exercise 4, you are asked to compare its performance to that of random-restart hill climbing on the 8-queens puzzle.

1.3 Local beam search

LOCAL BEAM SEARCH

Keeping just one node in memory might seem to be an extreme reaction to the problem of memory limitations. The **local beam search** algorithm[3] keeps track of k states rather than

[3] Local beam search is an adaptation of **beam search**, which is a path-based algorithm.

```
function SIMULATED-ANNEALING(problem, schedule) returns a solution state
  inputs: problem, a problem
          schedule, a mapping from time to "temperature"

  current ← MAKE-NODE(problem.INITIAL-STATE)
  for t = 1 to ∞ do
     T ← schedule(t)
     if T = 0 then return current
     next ← a randomly selected successor of current
     ΔE ← next.VALUE – current.VALUE
     if ΔE > 0 then current ← next
     else current ← next only with probability e^(ΔE/T)
```

Figure 5 The simulated annealing algorithm, a version of stochastic hill climbing where some downhill moves are allowed. Downhill moves are accepted readily early in the annealing schedule and then less often as time goes on. The *schedule* input determines the value of the temperature T as a function of time.

just one. It begins with k randomly generated states. At each step, all the successors of all k states are generated. If any one is a goal, the algorithm halts. Otherwise, it selects the k best successors from the complete list and repeats.

At first sight, a local beam search with k states might seem to be nothing more than running k random restarts in parallel instead of in sequence. In fact, the two algorithms are quite different. In a random-restart search, each search process runs independently of the others. *In a local beam search, useful information is passed among the parallel search threads.* In effect, the states that generate the best successors say to the others, "Come over here, the grass is greener!" The algorithm quickly abandons unfruitful searches and moves its resources to where the most progress is being made.

In its simplest form, local beam search can suffer from a lack of diversity among the k states—they can quickly become concentrated in a small region of the state space, making the search little more than an expensive version of hill climbing. A variant called **stochastic beam search**, analogous to stochastic hill climbing, helps alleviate this problem. Instead of choosing the best k from the the pool of candidate successors, stochastic beam search chooses k successors at random, with the probability of choosing a given successor being an increasing function of its value. Stochastic beam search bears some resemblance to the process of natural selection, whereby the "successors" (offspring) of a "state" (organism) populate the next generation according to its "value" (fitness).

STOCHASTIC BEAM SEARCH

1.4 Genetic algorithms

GENETIC ALGORITHM

A **genetic algorithm** (or **GA**) is a variant of stochastic beam search in which successor states are generated by combining *two* parent states rather than by modifying a single state. The analogy to natural selection is the same as in stochastic beam search, except that now we are dealing with sexual rather than asexual reproduction.

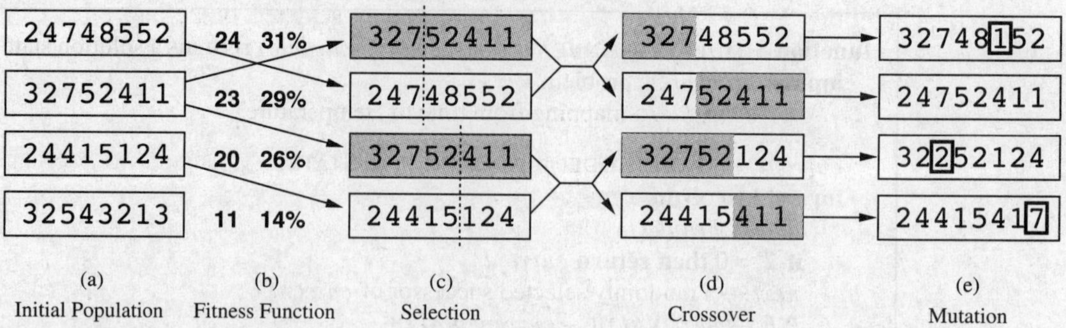

Figure 6 The genetic algorithm, illustrated for digit strings representing 8-queens states. The initial population in (a) is ranked by the fitness function in (b), resulting in pairs for mating in (c). They produce offspring in (d), which are subject to mutation in (e).

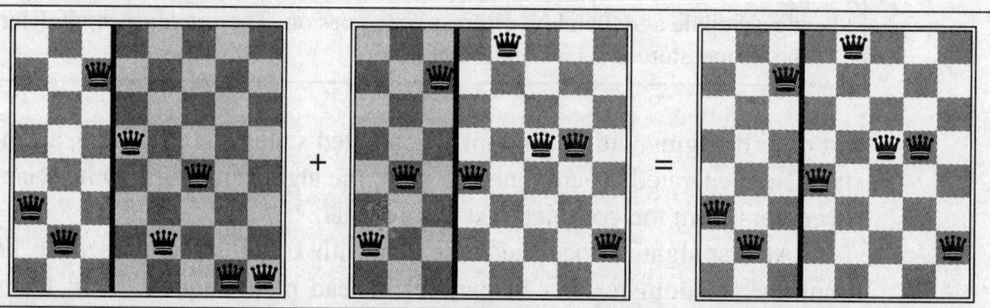

Figure 7 The 8-queens states corresponding to the first two parents in Figure 6(c) and the first offspring in Figure 6(d). The shaded columns are lost in the crossover step and the unshaded columns are retained.

Like beam searches, GAs begin with a set of k randomly generated states, called the **population**. Each state, or **individual**, is represented as a string over a finite alphabet—most commonly, a string of 0s and 1s. For example, an 8-queens state must specify the positions of 8 queens, each in a column of 8 squares, and so requires $8 \times \log_2 8 = 24$ bits. Alternatively, the state could be represented as 8 digits, each in the range from 1 to 8. (We demonstrate later that the two encodings behave differently.) Figure 6(a) shows a population of four 8-digit strings representing 8-queens states.

POPULATION
INDIVIDUAL

The production of the next generation of states is shown in Figure 6(b)–(e). In (b), each state is rated by the objective function, or (in GA terminology) the **fitness function**. A fitness function should return higher values for better states, so, for the 8-queens problem we use the number of *nonattacking* pairs of queens, which has a value of 28 for a solution. The values of the four states are 24, 23, 20, and 11. In this particular variant of the genetic algorithm, the probability of being chosen for reproducing is directly proportional to the fitness score, and the percentages are shown next to the raw scores.

FITNESS FUNCTION

In (c), two pairs are selected at random for reproduction, in accordance with the probabilities in (b). Notice that one individual is selected twice and one not at all.[4] For each pair to be mated, a **crossover** point is chosen randomly from the positions in the string. In Figure 6, the crossover points are after the third digit in the first pair and after the fifth digit in the second pair.[5]

CROSSOVER

In (d), the offspring themselves are created by crossing over the parent strings at the crossover point. For example, the first child of the first pair gets the first three digits from the first parent and the remaining digits from the second parent, whereas the second child gets the first three digits from the second parent and the rest from the first parent. The 8-queens states involved in this reproduction step are shown in Figure 7. The example shows that when two parent states are quite different, the crossover operation can produce a state that is a long way from either parent state. It is often the case that the population is quite diverse early on in the process, so crossover (like simulated annealing) frequently takes large steps in the state space early in the search process and smaller steps later on when most individuals are quite similar.

MUTATION

Finally, in (e), each location is subject to random **mutation** with a small independent probability. One digit was mutated in the first, third, and fourth offspring. In the 8-queens problem, this corresponds to choosing a queen at random and moving it to a random square in its column. Figure 8 describes an algorithm that implements all these steps.

Like stochastic beam search, genetic algorithms combine an uphill tendency with random exploration and exchange of information among parallel search threads. The primary advantage, if any, of genetic algorithms comes from the crossover operation. Yet it can be shown mathematically that, if the positions of the genetic code are permuted initially in a random order, crossover conveys no advantage. Intuitively, the advantage comes from the ability of crossover to combine large blocks of letters that have evolved independently to perform useful functions, thus raising the level of granularity at which the search operates. For example, it could be that putting the first three queens in positions 2, 4, and 6 (where they do not attack each other) constitutes a useful block that can be combined with other blocks to construct a solution.

SCHEMA

The theory of genetic algorithms explains how this works using the idea of a **schema**, which is a substring in which some of the positions can be left unspecified. For example, the schema 246***** describes all 8-queens states in which the first three queens are in positions 2, 4, and 6, respectively. Strings that match the schema (such as 24613578) are called **instances** of the schema. It can be shown that if the average fitness of the instances of a schema is above the mean, then the number of instances of the schema within the population will grow over time. Clearly, this effect is unlikely to be significant if adjacent bits are totally unrelated to each other, because then there will be few contiguous blocks that provide a consistent benefit. Genetic algorithms work best when schemata correspond to meaningful components of a solution. For example, if the string is a representation of an antenna, then the schemata may represent components of the antenna, such as reflectors and deflectors. A good

INSTANCE

[4] There are many variants of this selection rule. The method of **culling**, in which all individuals below a given threshold are discarded, can be shown to converge faster than the random version (Baum *et al.*, 1995).

[5] It is here that the encoding matters. If a 24-bit encoding is used instead of 8 digits, then the crossover point has a 2/3 chance of being in the middle of a digit, which results in an essentially arbitrary mutation of that digit.

```
function GENETIC-ALGORITHM(population, FITNESS-FN) returns an individual
  inputs: population, a set of individuals
          FITNESS-FN, a function that measures the fitness of an individual

  repeat
     new_population ← empty set
     for i = 1 to SIZE(population) do
        x ← RANDOM-SELECTION(population, FITNESS-FN)
        y ← RANDOM-SELECTION(population, FITNESS-FN)
        child ← REPRODUCE(x, y)
        if (small random probability) then child ← MUTATE(child)
        add child to new_population
     population ← new_population
  until some individual is fit enough, or enough time has elapsed
  return the best individual in population, according to FITNESS-FN

function REPRODUCE(x, y) returns an individual
  inputs: x, y, parent individuals

  n ← LENGTH(x); c ← random number from 1 to n
  return APPEND(SUBSTRING(x, 1, c), SUBSTRING(y, c + 1, n))
```

Figure 8 A genetic algorithm. The algorithm is the same as the one diagrammed in Figure 6, with one variation: in this more popular version, each mating of two parents produces only one offspring, not two.

component is likely to be good in a variety of different designs. This suggests that successful use of genetic algorithms requires careful engineering of the representation.

In practice, genetic algorithms have had a widespread impact on optimization problems, such as circuit layout and job-shop scheduling. At present, it is not clear whether the appeal of genetic algorithms arises from their performance or from their æsthetically pleasing origins in the theory of evolution. Much work remains to be done to identify the conditions under which genetic algorithms perform well.

2 Local Search in Continuous Spaces

Most real-world environments are continuous, as opposed to discrete. Yet none of the algorithms we have described (except for first-choice hill climbing and simulated annealing) can handle continuous state and action spaces, because they have infinite branching factors. This section provides a *very brief* introduction to some local search techniques for finding optimal solutions in continuous spaces. The literature on this topic is vast; many of the basic techniques

EVOLUTION AND SEARCH

The theory of **evolution** was developed in Charles Darwin's *On the Origin of Species by Means of Natural Selection* (1859) and independently by Alfred Russel Wallace (1858). The central idea is simple: variations occur in reproduction and will be preserved in successive generations approximately in proportion to their effect on reproductive fitness.

Darwin's theory was developed with no knowledge of how the traits of organisms can be inherited and modified. The probabilistic laws governing these processes were first identified by Gregor Mendel (1866), a monk who experimented with sweet peas. Much later, Watson and Crick (1953) identified the structure of the DNA molecule and its alphabet, AGTC (adenine, guanine, thymine, cytosine). In the standard model, variation occurs both by point mutations in the letter sequence and by "crossover" (in which the DNA of an offspring is generated by combining long sections of DNA from each parent).

The analogy to local search algorithms has already been described; the principal difference between stochastic beam search and evolution is the use of *sexual* reproduction, wherein successors are generated from *multiple* organisms rather than just one. The actual mechanisms of evolution are, however, far richer than most genetic algorithms allow. For example, mutations can involve reversals, duplications, and movement of large chunks of DNA; some viruses borrow DNA from one organism and insert it in another; and there are transposable genes that do nothing but copy themselves many thousands of times within the genome. There are even genes that poison cells from potential mates that do not carry the gene, thereby increasing their own chances of replication. Most important is the fact that the *genes themselves encode the mechanisms* whereby the genome is reproduced and translated into an organism. In genetic algorithms, those mechanisms are a separate program that is not represented within the strings being manipulated.

Darwinian evolution may appear inefficient, having generated blindly some 10^{45} or so organisms without improving its search heuristics one iota. Fifty years before Darwin, however, the otherwise great French naturalist Jean Lamarck (1809) proposed a theory of evolution whereby traits *acquired by adaptation during an organism's lifetime* would be passed on to its offspring. Such a process would be effective but does not seem to occur in nature. Much later, James Baldwin (1896) proposed a superficially similar theory: that behavior learned during an organism's lifetime could accelerate the rate of evolution. Unlike Lamarck's, Baldwin's theory is entirely consistent with Darwinian evolution because it relies on selection pressures operating on individuals that have found local optima among the set of possible behaviors allowed by their genetic makeup. Computer simulations confirm that the "Baldwin effect" is real, once "ordinary" evolution has created organisms whose internal performance measure correlates with actual fitness.

originated in the 17th century, after the development of calculus by Newton and Leibniz.[6] We find uses for these techniques at several places in the book, including the chapters on learning, vision, and robotics.

We begin with an example. Suppose we want to place three new airports anywhere in Romania, such that the sum of squared distances from each city on the map to its nearest airport is minimized. The state space is then defined by the coordinates of the airports: (x_1, y_1), (x_2, y_2), and (x_3, y_3). This is a *six-dimensional* space; we also say that states are defined by six **variables**. (In general, states are defined by an n-dimensional vector of variables, x.) Moving around in this space corresponds to moving one or more of the airports on the map. The objective function $f(x_1, y_1, x_2, y_2, x_3, y_3)$ is relatively easy to compute for any particular state once we compute the closest cities. Let C_i be the set of cities whose closest airport (in the current state) is airport i. Then, *in the neighborhood of the current state*, where the C_is remain constant, we have

VARIABLE

$$f(x_1, y_1, x_2, y_2, x_3, y_3) = \sum_{i=1}^{3} \sum_{c \in C_i} (x_i - x_c)^2 + (y_i - y_c)^2 . \tag{1}$$

This expression is correct *locally*, but not globally because the sets C_i are (discontinuous) functions of the state.

DISCRETIZATION

One way to avoid continuous problems is simply to **discretize** the neighborhood of each state. For example, we can move only one airport at a time in either the x or y direction by a fixed amount $\pm\delta$. With 6 variables, this gives 12 possible successors for each state. We can then apply any of the local search algorithms described previously. We could also apply stochastic hill climbing and simulated annealing directly, without discretizing the space. These algorithms choose successors randomly, which can be done by generating random vectors of length δ.

GRADIENT

Many methods attempt to use the **gradient** of the landscape to find a maximum. The gradient of the objective function is a vector ∇f that gives the magnitude and direction of the steepest slope. For our problem, we have

$$\nabla f = \left(\frac{\partial f}{\partial x_1}, \frac{\partial f}{\partial y_1}, \frac{\partial f}{\partial x_2}, \frac{\partial f}{\partial y_2}, \frac{\partial f}{\partial x_3}, \frac{\partial f}{\partial y_3} \right) .$$

In some cases, we can find a maximum by solving the equation $\nabla f = 0$. (This could be done, for example, if we were placing just one airport; the solution is the arithmetic mean of all the cities' coordinates.) In many cases, however, this equation cannot be solved in closed form. For example, with three airports, the expression for the gradient depends on what cities are closest to each airport in the current state. This means we can compute the gradient *locally* (but not *globally*); for example,

$$\frac{\partial f}{\partial x_1} = 2 \sum_{c \in C_1} (x_i - x_c) . \tag{2}$$

Given a locally correct expression for the gradient, we can perform steepest-ascent hill climb-

[6] A basic knowledge of multivariate calculus and vector arithmetic is useful for reading this section.

ing by updating the current state according to the formula

$$\mathbf{x} \leftarrow \mathbf{x} + \alpha \nabla f(\mathbf{x}) ,$$

STEP SIZE

where α is a small constant often called the **step size**. In other cases, the objective function might not be available in a differentiable form at all—for example, the value of a particular set of airport locations might be determined by running some large-scale economic simulation package. In those cases, we can calculate a so-called **empirical gradient** by evaluating the response to small increments and decrements in each coordinate. Empirical gradient search is the same as steepest-ascent hill climbing in a discretized version of the state space.

EMPIRICAL GRADIENT

Hidden beneath the phrase "α is a small constant" lies a huge variety of methods for adjusting α. The basic problem is that, if α is too small, too many steps are needed; if α is too large, the search could overshoot the maximum. The technique of **line search** tries to overcome this dilemma by extending the current gradient direction—usually by repeatedly doubling α—until f starts to decrease again. The point at which this occurs becomes the new current state. There are several schools of thought about how the new direction should be chosen at this point.

LINE SEARCH

NEWTON–RAPHSON

For many problems, the most effective algorithm is the venerable **Newton–Raphson** method. This is a general technique for finding roots of functions—that is, solving equations of the form $g(x) = 0$. It works by computing a new estimate for the root x according to Newton's formula

$$x \leftarrow x - g(x)/g'(x) .$$

To find a maximum or minimum of f, we need to find $\mathbf{x}$ such that the *gradient* is zero (i.e., $\nabla f(\mathbf{x}) = \mathbf{0}$). Thus, $g(x)$ in Newton's formula becomes $\nabla f(\mathbf{x})$, and the update equation can be written in matrix–vector form as

$$\mathbf{x} \leftarrow \mathbf{x} - \mathbf{H}_f^{-1}(\mathbf{x}) \nabla f(\mathbf{x}) ,$$

HESSIAN

where $\mathbf{H}_f(\mathbf{x})$ is the **Hessian** matrix of second derivatives, whose elements H_{ij} are given by $\partial^2 f / \partial x_i \partial x_j$. For our airport example, we can see from Equation (2) that $\mathbf{H}_f(\mathbf{x})$ is particularly simple: the off-diagonal elements are zero and the diagonal elements for airport i are just twice the number of cities in C_i. A moment's calculation shows that one step of the update moves airport i directly to the centroid of C_i, which is the minimum of the local expression for f from Equation (1).[7] For high-dimensional problems, however, computing the n^2 entries of the Hessian and inverting it may be expensive, so many approximate versions of the Newton–Raphson method have been developed.

Local search methods suffer from local maxima, ridges, and plateaux in continuous state spaces just as much as in discrete spaces. Random restarts and simulated annealing can be used and are often helpful. High-dimensional continuous spaces are, however, big places in which it is easy to get lost.

CONSTRAINED OPTIMIZATION

A final topic with which a passing acquaintance is useful is **constrained optimization**. An optimization problem is constrained if solutions must satisfy some hard constraints on the values of the variables. For example, in our airport-siting problem, we might constrain sites

[7] In general, the Newton–Raphson update can be seen as fitting a quadratic surface to f at $\mathbf{x}$ and then moving directly to the minimum of that surface—which is also the minimum of f if f is quadratic.

to be inside Romania and on dry land (rather than in the middle of lakes). The difficulty of constrained optimization problems depends on the nature of the constraints and the objective function. The best-known category is that of **linear programming** problems, in which constraints must be linear inequalities forming a **convex set** [8] and the objective function is also linear. The time complexity of linear programming is polynomial in the number of variables.

LINEAR PROGRAMMING

CONVEX SET

Linear programming is probably the most widely studied and broadly useful class of optimization problems. It is a special case of the more general problem of **convex optimization**, which allows the constraint region to be any convex region and the objective to be any function that is convex within the constraint region. Under certain conditions, convex optimization problems are also polynomially solvable and may be feasible in practice with thousands of variables. Several important problems in machine learning and control theory can be formulated as convex optimization problems.

CONVEX OPTIMIZATION

3 SEARCHING WITH NONDETERMINISTIC ACTIONS

When we assume that the environment is fully observable and deterministic and that the agent knows what the effects of each action are, the agent can calculate exactly which state results from any sequence of actions and always knows which state it is in. Its percepts provide no new information after each action, although of course they tell the agent the initial state.

When the environment is either partially observable or nondeterministic (or both), percepts become useful. In a partially observable environment, every percept helps narrow down the set of possible states the agent might be in, thus making it easier for the agent to achieve its goals. When the environment is nondeterministic, percepts tell the agent which of the possible outcomes of its actions has actually occurred. In both cases, the future percepts cannot be determined in advance and the agent's future actions will depend on those future percepts. So the solution to a problem is not a sequence but a **contingency plan** (also known as a **strategy**) that specifies what to do depending on what percepts are received. In this section, we examine the case of nondeterminism, deferring partial observability to Section 4.

CONTINGENCY PLAN

STRATEGY

3.1 The erratic vacuum world

As an example, we use the vacuum world, defined as a search problem in Section 2 of the chapter "Solving Problems by Searching". The state space has eight states, as shown in Figure 9. There are three actions—*Left*, *Right*, and *Suck*—and the goal is to clean up all the dirt (states 7 and 8). If the environment is observable, deterministic, and completely known, then the problem is trivially solvable using many different algorithms and the solution is an action sequence. For example, if the initial state is 1, then the action sequence [*Suck*,*Right*,*Suck*] will reach a goal state, 8.

[8] A set of points S is convex if the line joining any two points in S is also contained in S. A **convex function** is one for which the space "above" it forms a convex set; by definition, convex functions have no local (as opposed to global) minima.

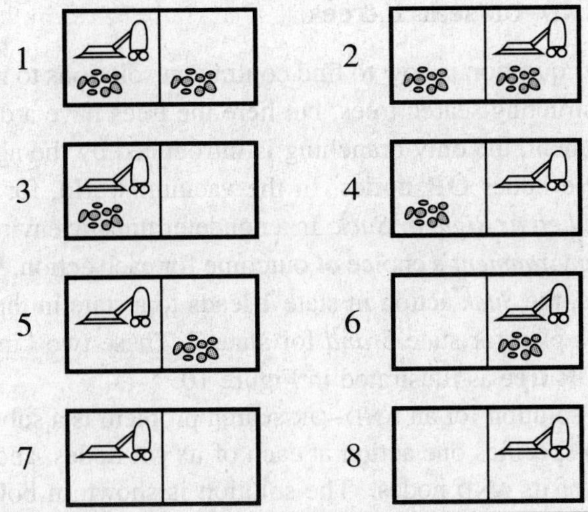

Figure 9 The eight possible states of the vacuum world; states 7 and 8 are goal states.

ERRATIC VACUUM WORLD

Now suppose that we introduce nondeterminism in the form of a powerful but erratic vacuum cleaner. In the **erratic vacuum world**, the *Suck* action works as follows:

- When applied to a dirty square the action cleans the square and sometimes cleans up dirt in an adjacent square, too.
- When applied to a clean square the action sometimes deposits dirt on the carpet.[9]

To provide a precise formulation of this problem, we need to generalize the notion of a **transition model**. Instead of defining the transition model by a RESULT function that returns a single state, we use a RESULTS function that returns a *set* of possible outcome states. For example, in the erratic vacuum world, the *Suck* action in state 1 leads to a state in the set {5,7}—the dirt in the right-hand square may or may not be vacuumed up.

We also need to generalize the notion of a **solution** to the problem. For example, if we start in state 1, there is no single *sequence* of actions that solves the problem. Instead, we need a contingency plan such as the following:

$$[Suck, \textbf{if } State = 5 \textbf{ then } [Right, Suck] \textbf{ else } [\,]] \,. \tag{3}$$

Thus, solutions for nondeterministic problems can contain nested **if–then–else** statements; this means that they are *trees* rather than sequences. This allows the selection of actions based on contingencies arising during execution. Many problems in the real, physical world are contingency problems because exact prediction is impossible. For this reason, many people keep their eyes open while walking around or driving.

9 We assume that most readers face similar problems and can sympathize with our agent. We apologize to owners of modern, efficient home appliances who cannot take advantage of this pedagogical device.

3.2 AND–OR search trees

The next question is how to find contingent solutions to nondeterministic problems. We begin by constructing search trees, but here the trees have a different character. In a deterministic environment, the only branching is introduced by the agent's own choices in each state. We call these nodes **OR nodes**. In the vacuum world, for example, at an OR node the agent chooses *Left or Right or Suck*. In a nondeterministic environment, branching is also introduced by the *environment's* choice of outcome for each action. We call these nodes **AND nodes**. For example, the *Suck* action in state 1 leads to a state in the set {5,7}, so the agent would need to find a plan for state 5 *and* for state 7. These two kinds of nodes alternate, leading to an AND–OR **tree** as illustrated in Figure 10.

OR NODE

AND NODE

AND–OR TREE

A solution for an AND–OR search problem is a subtree that (1) has a goal node at every leaf, (2) specifies one action at each of its OR nodes, and (3) includes every outcome branch at each of its AND nodes. The solution is shown in bold lines in the figure; it corresponds to the plan given in Equation (3). (The plan uses if–then–else notation to handle the AND branches, but when there are more than two branches at a node, it might be better to use a **case**

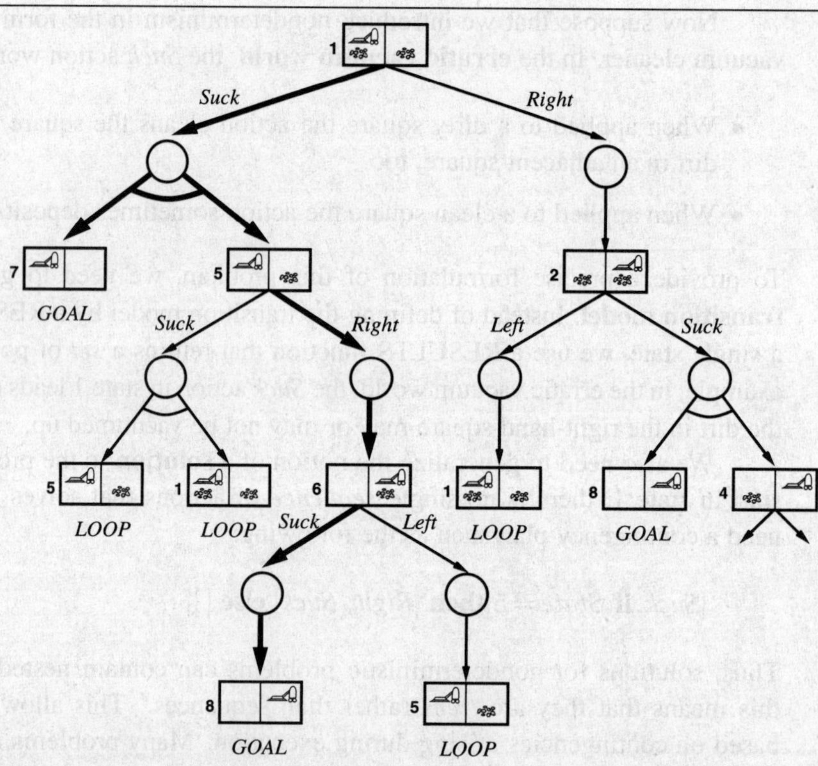

Figure 10 The first two levels of the search tree for the erratic vacuum world. State nodes are OR nodes where some action must be chosen. At the AND nodes, shown as circles, every outcome must be handled, as indicated by the arc linking the outgoing branches. The solution found is shown in bold lines.

```
function AND-OR-GRAPH-SEARCH(problem) returns a conditional plan, or failure
   OR-SEARCH(problem.INITIAL-STATE, problem, [])
---------------------------------------------------------------------------
function OR-SEARCH(state, problem, path) returns a conditional plan, or failure
   if problem.GOAL-TEST(state) then return the empty plan
   if state is on path then return failure
   for each action in problem.ACTIONS(state) do
       plan ← AND-SEARCH(RESULTS(state, action), problem, [state | path])
       if plan ≠ failure then return [action | plan]
   return failure
---------------------------------------------------------------------------
function AND-SEARCH(states, problem, path) returns a conditional plan, or failure
   for each s_i in states do
       plan_i ← OR-SEARCH(s_i, problem, path)
       if plan_i = failure then return failure
   return [if s_1 then plan_1 else if s_2 then plan_2 else ... if s_{n-1} then plan_{n-1} else plan_n]
```

Figure 11 An algorithm for searching AND–OR graphs generated by nondeterministic environments. It returns a conditional plan that reaches a goal state in all circumstances. (The notation $[x \mid l]$ refers to the list formed by adding object x to the front of list l.)

construct.) Modifying the basic problem-solving agent shown in Figure 1 to execute contingent solutions of this kind is straightforward. One may also consider a somewhat different agent design, in which the agent can act *before* it has found a guaranteed plan and deals with some contingencies only as they arise during execution. This type of **interleaving** of search and execution is also useful for exploration problems (see Section 5) and for game playing.

INTERLEAVING

Figure 11 gives a recursive, depth-first algorithm for AND–OR graph search. One key aspect of the algorithm is the way in which it deals with cycles, which often arise in nondeterministic problems (e.g., if an action sometimes has no effect or if an unintended effect can be corrected). If the current state is identical to a state on the path from the root, then it returns with failure. This doesn't mean that there is *no* solution from the current state; it simply means that if there *is* a noncyclic solution, it must be reachable from the earlier incarnation of the current state, so the new incarnation can be discarded. With this check, we ensure that the algorithm terminates in every finite state space, because every path must reach a goal, a dead end, or a repeated state. Notice that the algorithm does not check whether the current state is a repetition of a state on some *other* path from the root, which is important for efficiency. Exercise 5 investigates this issue.

AND–OR graphs can also be explored by breadth-first or best-first methods. The concept of a heuristic function must be modified to estimate the cost of a contingent solution rather than a sequence, but the notion of admissibility carries over and there is an analog of the A* algorithm for finding optimal solutions. Pointers are given in the bibliographical notes at the end of the chapter.

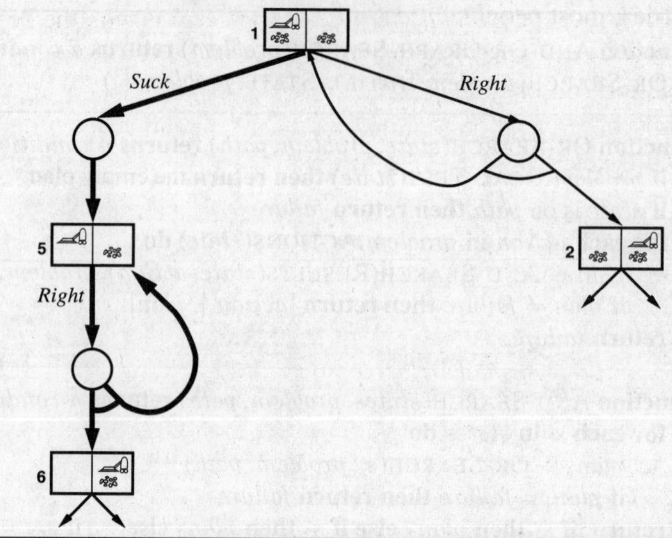

Figure 12 Part of the search graph for the slippery vacuum world, where we have shown (some) cycles explicitly. All solutions for this problem are cyclic plans because there is no way to move reliably.

3.3 Try, try again

Consider the slippery vacuum world, which is identical to the ordinary (non-erratic) vacuum world except that movement actions sometimes fail, leaving the agent in the same location. For example, moving *Right* in state 1 leads to the state set $\{1, 2\}$. Figure 12 shows part of the search graph; clearly, there are no longer any acyclic solutions from state 1, and AND-OR-GRAPH-SEARCH would return with failure. There is, however, a **cyclic solution**, which is to keep trying *Right* until it works. We can express this solution by adding a **label** to denote some portion of the plan and using that label later instead of repeating the plan itself. Thus, our cyclic solution is

CYCLIC SOLUTION

LABEL

$$[Suck, L_1 : \ Right, \textbf{if}\ State = 5\ \textbf{then}\ L_1\ \textbf{else}\ Suck]\ .$$

(A better syntax for the looping part of this plan would be "**while** $State = 5$ **do** *Right*.") In general a cyclic plan may be considered a solution provided that every leaf is a goal state and that a leaf is reachable from every point in the plan. The modifications needed to AND-OR-GRAPH-SEARCH are covered in Exercise 6. The key realization is that a loop in the state space back to a state L translates to a loop in the plan back to the point where the subplan for state L is executed.

Given the definition of a cyclic solution, an agent executing such a solution will eventually reach the goal *provided that each outcome of a nondeterministic action eventually occurs.* Is this condition reasonable? It depends on the reason for the nondeterminism. If the action rolls a die, then it's reasonable to suppose that eventually a six will be rolled. If the action is to insert a hotel card key into the door lock, but it doesn't work the first time, then perhaps it will eventually work, or perhaps one has the wrong key (or the wrong room!). After seven or eight tries, most people will assume the problem is with the key and will go back to the front desk to get a new one. One way to understand this decision is to say that the initial problem formulation (observable, nondeterministic) is abandoned in favor of a different formulation (partially observable, deterministic) where the failure is attributed to an unobservable property of the key.

4 SEARCHING WITH PARTIAL OBSERVATIONS

We now turn to the problem of partial observability, where the agent's percepts do not suffice to pin down the exact state. As noted at the beginning of the previous section, if the agent is in one of several possible states, then an action may lead to one of several possible outcomes—*even if the environment is deterministic*. The key concept required for solving partially observable problems is the **belief state**, representing the agent's current belief about the possible physical states it might be in, given the sequence of actions and percepts up to that point. We begin with the simplest scenario for studying belief states, which is when the agent has no sensors at all; then we add in partial sensing as well as nondeterministic actions.

BELIEF STATE

4.1 Searching with no observation

When the agent's percepts provide *no information at all*, we have what is called a **sensorless** problem or sometimes a **conformant** problem. At first, one might think the sensorless agent has no hope of solving a problem if it has no idea what state it's in; in fact, sensorless problems are quite often solvable. Moreover, sensorless agents can be surprisingly useful, primarily because they *don't* rely on sensors working properly. In manufacturing systems, for example, many ingenious methods have been developed for orienting parts correctly from an unknown initial position by using a sequence of actions with no sensing at all. The high cost of sensing is another reason to avoid it: for example, doctors often prescribe a broad-spectrum antibiotic rather than using the contingent plan of doing an expensive blood test, then waiting for the results to come back, and then prescribing a more specific antibiotic and perhaps hospitalization because the infection has progressed too far.

SENSORLESS

CONFORMANT

We can make a sensorless version of the vacuum world. Assume that the agent knows the geography of its world, but doesn't know its location or the distribution of dirt. In that case, its initial state could be any element of the set $\{1, 2, 3, 4, 5, 6, 7, 8\}$. Now, consider what happens if it tries the action *Right*. This will cause it to be in one of the states $\{2, 4, 6, 8\}$—the agent now has more information! Furthermore, the action sequence [*Right*,*Suck*] will always end up in one of the states $\{4, 8\}$. Finally, the sequence [*Right*,*Suck*,*Left*,*Suck*] is guaranteed to reach the goal state 7 no matter what the start state. We say that the agent can **coerce** the world into state 7.

COERCION

To solve sensorless problems, we search in the space of belief states rather than physical states.[10] Notice that in belief-state space, the problem is *fully observable* because the agent

[10] In a fully observable environment, each belief state contains one physical state.

always knows its own belief state. Furthermore, the solution (if any) is always a sequence of actions. This is because, as in many ordinary problems, the percepts received after each action are completely predictable—they're always empty! So there are no contingencies to plan for. This is true *even if the environment is nondeterminstic*.

It is instructive to see how the belief-state search problem is constructed. Suppose the underlying physical problem P is defined by ACTIONS_P, RESULT_P, GOAL-TEST_P, and STEP-COST_P. Then we can define the corresponding sensorless problem as follows:

- **Belief states**: The entire belief-state space contains every possible set of physical states. If P has N states, then the sensorless problem has up to 2^N states, although many may be unreachable from the initial state.
- **Initial state**: Typically the set of all states in P, although in some cases the agent will have more knowledge than this.
- **Actions**: This is slightly tricky. Suppose the agent is in belief state $b = \{s_1, s_2\}$, but $\text{ACTIONS}_P(s_1) \neq \text{ACTIONS}_P(s_2)$; then the agent is unsure of which actions are legal. If we assume that illegal actions have no effect on the environment, then it is safe to take the *union* of all the actions in any of the physical states in the current belief state b:

$$\text{ACTIONS}(b) = \bigcup_{s \in b} \text{ACTIONS}_P(s) .$$

On the other hand, if an illegal action might be the end of the world, it is safer to allow only the *intersection*, that is, the set of actions legal in *all* the states. For the vacuum world, every state has the same legal actions, so both methods give the same result.

- **Transition model**: The agent doesn't know which state in the belief state is the right one; so as far as it knows, it might get to any of the states resulting from applying the action to one of the physical states in the belief state. For deterministic actions, the set of states that might be reached is

$$b' = \text{RESULT}(b, a) = \{s' : s' = \text{RESULT}_P(s, a) \text{ and } s \in b\} . \tag{4}$$

With deterministic actions, b' is never larger than b. With nondeterminism, we have

$$\begin{aligned} b' = \text{RESULT}(b, a) &= \{s' : s' \in \text{RESULTS}_P(s, a) \text{ and } s \in b\} \\ &= \bigcup_{s \in b} \text{RESULTS}_P(s, a) , \end{aligned}$$

which may be larger than b, as shown in Figure 13. The process of generating the new belief state after the action is called the **prediction** step; the notation $b' = \text{PREDICT}_P(b, a)$ will come in handy.

PREDICTION

- **Goal test**: The agent wants a plan that is sure to work, which means that a belief state satisfies the goal only if *all* the physical states in it satisfy GOAL-TEST_P. The agent may *accidentally* achieve the goal earlier, but it won't *know* that it has done so.
- **Path cost**: This is also tricky. If the same action can have different costs in different states, then the cost of taking an action in a given belief state could be one of several values. (This gives rise to a new class of problems, which we explore in Exercise 9.) For now we assume that the cost of an action is the same in all states and so can be transferred directly from the underlying physical problem.

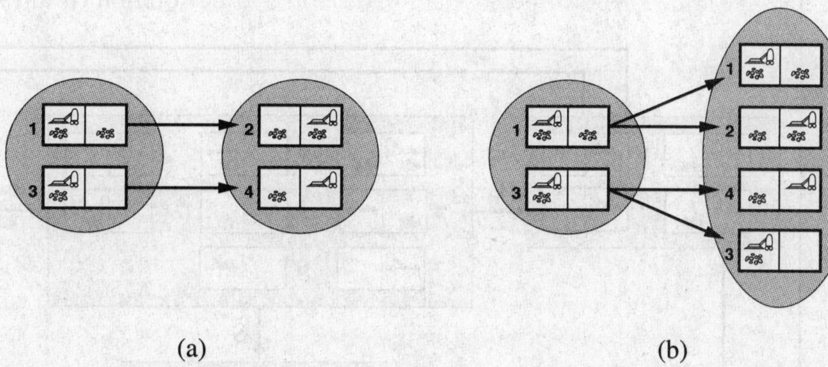

Figure 13 (a) Predicting the next belief state for the sensorless vacuum world with a deterministic action, *Right*. (b) Prediction for the same belief state and action in the slippery version of the sensorless vacuum world.

Figure 14 shows the reachable belief-state space for the deterministic, sensorless vacuum world. There are only 12 reachable belief states out of $2^8 = 256$ possible belief states.

The preceding definitions enable the automatic construction of the belief-state problem formulation from the definition of the underlying physical problem. Once this is done, we can apply many search algorithms. In fact, we can do a little bit more than that. In "ordinary" graph search, newly generated states are tested to see if they are identical to existing states. This works for belief states, too; for example, in Figure 14, the action sequence [*Suck*,*Left*,*Suck*] starting at the initial state reaches the same belief state as [*Right*,*Left*,*Suck*], namely, {5,7}. Now, consider the belief state reached by [*Left*], namely, {1,3,5,7}. Obviously, this is not identical to {5,7}, but it is a *superset*. It is easy to prove (Exercise 8) that if an action sequence is a solution for a belief state b, it is also a solution for any subset of b. Hence, we can discard a path reaching {1,3,5,7} if {5,7} has already been generated. Conversely, if {1,3,5,7} has already been generated and found to be solvable, then any *subset*, such as {5,7}, is guaranteed to be solvable. This extra level of pruning may dramatically improve the efficiency of sensorless problem solving.

Even with this improvement, however, sensorless problem-solving as we have described it is seldom feasible in practice. The difficulty is not so much the vastness of the belief-state space—even though it is exponentially larger than the underlying physical state space; in most cases the branching factor and solution length in the belief-state space and physical state space are not so different. The real difficulty lies with the size of each belief state. For example, the initial belief state for the 10×10 vacuum world contains 100×2^{100} or around 10^{32} physical states—far too many if we use the atomic representation, which is an explicit list of states.

One solution is to represent the belief state by some more compact description. In English, we could say the agent knows "Nothing" in the initial state; after moving Left, we could say, "Not in the rightmost column," and so on. Another approach is to avoid the standard search algorithms, which treat belief states as black boxes just like any other problem state. Instead, we can look inside the belief states and develop **incremental belief-state**

INCREMENTAL BELIEF-STATE SEARCH

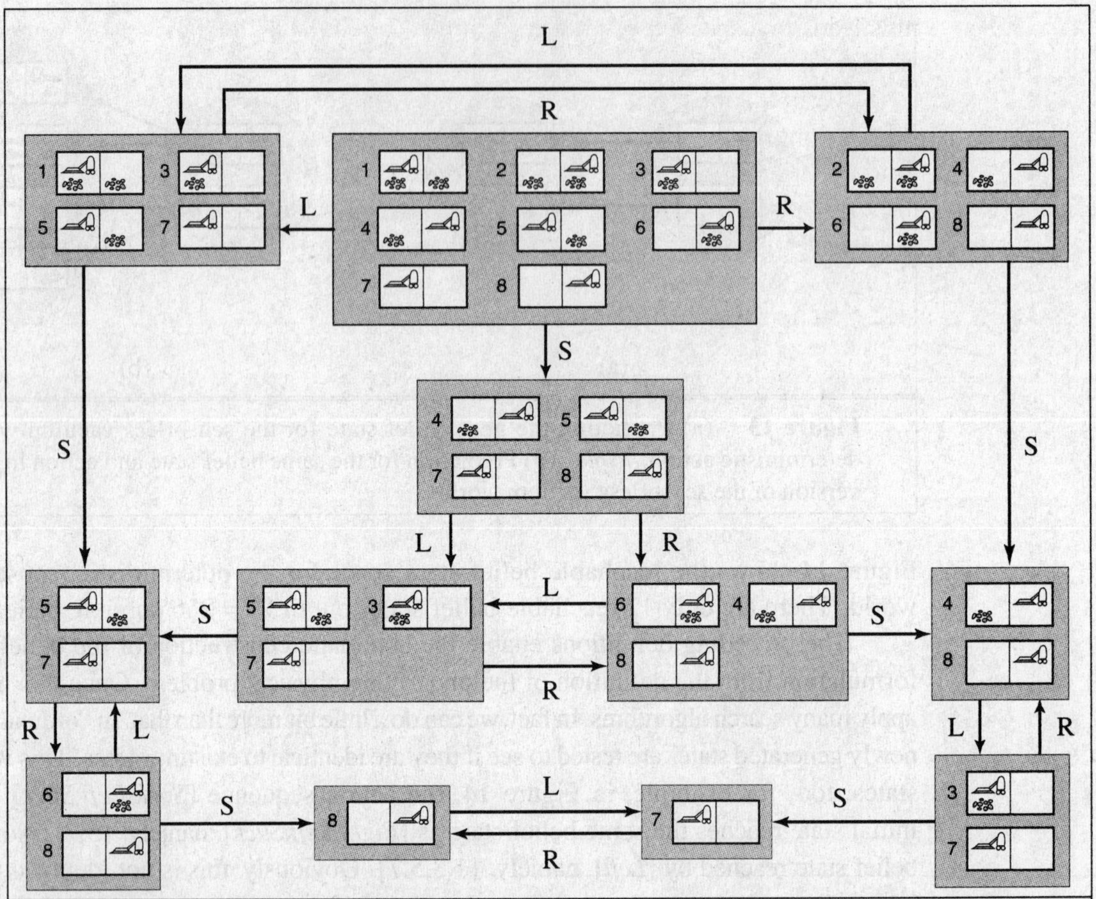

Figure 14 The reachable portion of the belief-state space for the deterministic, sensorless vacuum world. Each shaded box corresponds to a single belief state. At any given point, the agent is in a particular belief state but does not know which physical state it is in. The initial belief state (complete ignorance) is the top center box. Actions are represented by labeled links. Self-loops are omitted for clarity.

search algorithms that build up the solution one physical state at a time. For example, in the sensorless vacuum world, the initial belief state is {1,2,3,4,5,6,7,8}, and we have to find an action sequence that works in all 8 states. We can do this by first finding a solution that works for state 1; then we check if it works for state 2; if not, go back and find a different solution for state 1, and so on. Just as an AND–OR search has to find a solution for every branch at an AND node, this algorithm has to find a solution for every state in the belief state; the difference is that AND–OR search can find a different solution for each branch, whereas an incremental belief-state search has to find one solution that works for all the states.

The main advantage of the incremental approach is that it is typically able to detect failure quickly—when a belief state is unsolvable, it is usually the case that a small subset of the belief state, consisting of the first few states examined, is also unsolvable. In some cases, this leads to a speedup proportional to the size of the belief states, which may themselves be as large as the physical state space itself.

Even the most efficient solution algorithm is not of much use when no solutions exist. Many things just cannot be done without sensing. For example, the sensorless 8-puzzle is impossible. On the other hand, a little bit of sensing can go a long way. For example, every 8-puzzle instance is solvable if just one square is visible—the solution involves moving each tile in turn into the visible square and then keeping track of its location.

4.2 Searching with observations

For a general partially observable problem, we have to specify how the environment generates percepts for the agent. For example, we might define the local-sensing vacuum world to be one in which the agent has a position sensor and a local dirt sensor but has no sensor capable of detecting dirt in other squares. The formal problem specification includes a $\text{PERCEPT}(s)$ function that returns the percept received in a given state. (If sensing is nondeterministic, then we use a PERCEPTS function that returns a set of possible percepts.) For example, in the local-sensing vacuum world, the PERCEPT in state 1 is $[A, \mathit{Dirty}]$. Fully observable problems are a special case in which $\text{PERCEPT}(s) = s$ for every state s, while sensorless problems are a special case in which $\text{PERCEPT}(s) = \mathit{null}$.

When observations are partial, it will usually be the case that several states could have produced any given percept. For example, the percept $[A, \mathit{Dirty}]$ is produced by state 3 as well as by state 1. Hence, given this as the initial percept, the initial belief state for the local-sensing vacuum world will be $\{1, 3\}$. The ACTIONS, STEP-COST, and GOAL-TEST are constructed from the underlying physical problem just as for sensorless problems, but the transition model is a bit more complicated. We can think of transitions from one belief state to the next for a particular action as occurring in three stages, as shown in Figure 15:

- The **prediction** stage is the same as for sensorless problems: given the action a in belief state b, the predicted belief state is $\hat{b} = \text{PREDICT}(b, a)$.[11]
- The **observation prediction** stage determines the set of percepts o that could be observed in the predicted belief state:

$$\text{POSSIBLE-PERCEPTS}(\hat{b}) = \{o : o = \text{PERCEPT}(s) \text{ and } s \in \hat{b}\}.$$

- The **update** stage determines, for each possible percept, the belief state that would result from the percept. The new belief state b_o is just the set of states in $\hat{b}$ that could have produced the percept:

$$b_o = \text{UPDATE}(\hat{b}, o) = \{s : o = \text{PERCEPT}(s) \text{ and } s \in \hat{b}\}.$$

  Notice that each updated belief state b_o can be no larger than the predicted belief state $\hat{b}$; observations can only help reduce uncertainty compared to the sensorless case. Moreover, for deterministic sensing, the belief states for the different possible percepts will be disjoint, forming a *partition* of the original predicted belief state.

[11] Here, the "hat" in $\hat{b}$ means an estimated or predicted value for b.

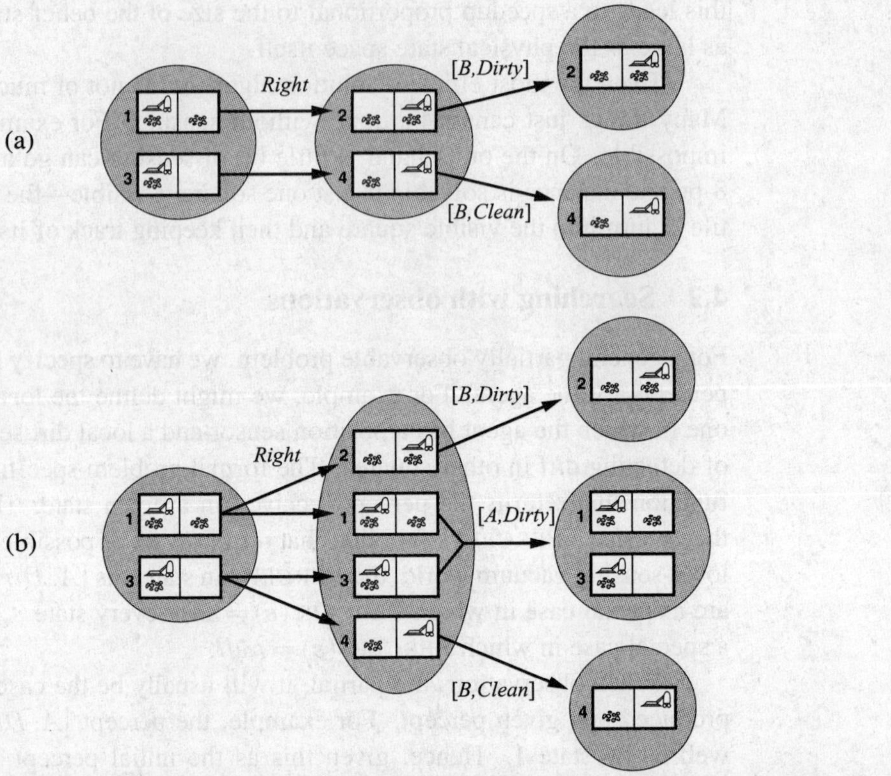

Figure 15 Two example of transitions in local-sensing vacuum worlds. (a) In the deterministic world, *Right* is applied in the initial belief state, resulting in a new belief state with two possible physical states; for those states, the possible percepts are $[B, Dirty]$ and $[B, Clean]$, leading to two belief states, each of which is a singleton. (b) In the slippery world, *Right* is applied in the initial belief state, giving a new belief state with four physical states; for those states, the possible percepts are $[A, Dirty]$, $[B, Dirty]$, and $[B, Clean]$, leading to three belief states as shown.

Putting these three stages together, we obtain the possible belief states resulting from a given action and the subsequent possible percepts:

$$\text{RESULTS}(b, a) = \{b_o : b_o = \text{UPDATE}(\text{PREDICT}(b, a), o) \text{ and } o \in \text{POSSIBLE-PERCEPTS}(\text{PREDICT}(b, a))\}\,. \tag{5}$$

Again, the nondeterminism in the partially observable problem comes from the inability to predict exactly which percept will be received after acting; underlying nondeterminism in the physical environment may *contribute* to this inability by enlarging the belief state at the prediction stage, leading to more percepts at the observation stage.

4.3 Solving partially observable problems

The preceding section showed how to derive the RESULTS function for a nondeterministic belief-state problem from an underlying physical problem and the PERCEPT function. Given

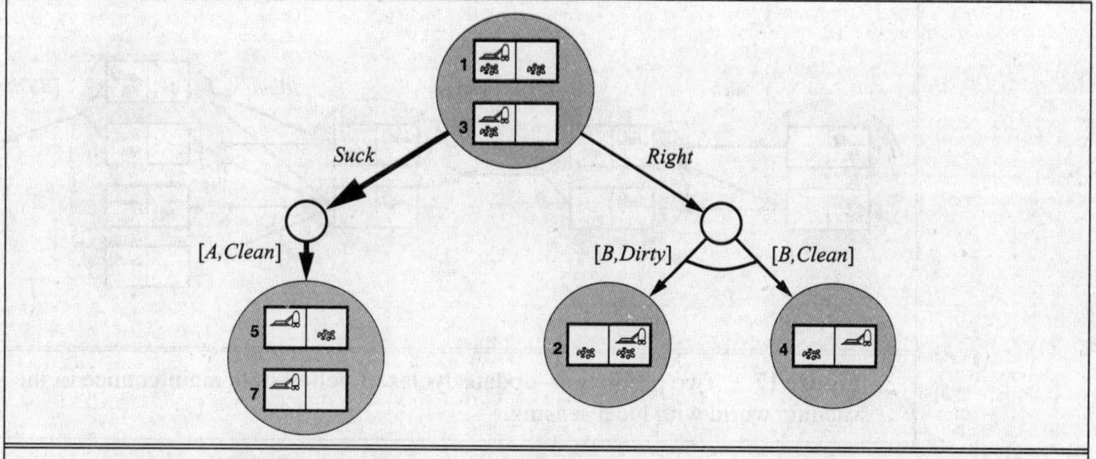

Figure 16 The first level of the AND–OR search tree for a problem in the local-sensing vacuum world; *Suck* is the first step of the solution.

such a formulation, the AND–OR search algorithm of Figure 11 can be applied directly to derive a solution. Figure 16 shows part of the search tree for the local-sensing vacuum world, assuming an initial percept $[A, Dirty]$. The solution is the conditional plan

$$[Suck, Right, \textbf{if } Bstate = \{6\} \textbf{ then } Suck \textbf{ else } []] .$$

Notice that, because we supplied a belief-state problem to the AND–OR search algorithm, it returned a conditional plan that tests the belief state rather than the actual state. This is as it should be: in a partially observable environment the agent won't be able to execute a solution that requires testing the actual state.

As in the case of standard search algorithms applied to sensorless problems, the AND–OR search algorithm treats belief states as black boxes, just like any other states. One can improve on this by checking for previously generated belief states that are subsets or supersets of the current state, just as for sensorless problems. One can also derive incremental search algorithms, analogous to those described for sensorless problems, that provide substantial speedups over the black-box approach.

4.4 An agent for partially observable environments

The design of a problem-solving agent for partially observable environments is quite similar to a simple problem-solving agent: the agent formulates a problem, calls a search algorithm (such as AND-OR-GRAPH-SEARCH) to solve it, and executes the solution. There are two main differences. First, the solution to a problem will be a conditional plan rather than a sequence; if the first step is an if–then–else expression, the agent will need to test the condition in the if-part and execute the then-part or the else-part accordingly. Second, the agent will need to maintain its belief state as it performs actions and receives percepts. This process resembles the prediction–observation–update process in Equation (5) but is actually simpler because the percept is given by the environment rather than calculated by the agent. Given an

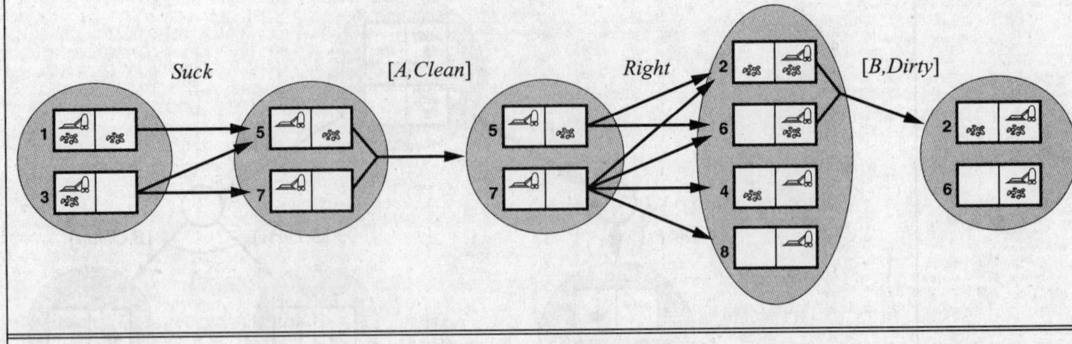

Figure 17 Two prediction–update cycles of belief-state maintenance in the kindergarten vacuum world with local sensing.

initial belief state b, an action a, and a percept o, the new belief state is:

$$b' = \text{UPDATE}(\text{PREDICT}(b, a), o) . \quad (6)$$

Figure 17 shows the belief state being maintained in the *kindergarten* vacuum world with local sensing, wherein any square may become dirty at any time unless the agent is actively cleaning it at that moment.[12]

In partially observable environments—which include the vast majority of real-world environments—maintaining one's belief state is a core function of any intelligent system. This function goes under various names, including **monitoring**, **filtering** and **state estimation**. Equation (6) is called a **recursive** state estimator because it computes the new belief state from the previous one rather than by examining the entire percept sequence. If the agent is not to "fall behind," the computation has to happen as fast as percepts are coming in. As the environment becomes more complex, the exact update computation becomes infeasible and the agent will have to compute an approximate belief state, perhaps focusing on the implications of the percept for the aspects of the environment that are of current interest. Most work on this problem has been done for stochastic, continuous-state environments with the tools of probability theory. Here we will show an example in a discrete environment with detrministic sensors and nondeterministic actions.

MONITORING
FILTERING
STATE ESTIMATION
RECURSIVE

The example concerns a robot with the task of **localization**: working out where it is, given a map of the world and a sequence of percepts and actions. Our robot is placed in the maze-like environment of Figure 18. The robot is equipped with four sonar sensors that tell whether there is an obstacle—the outer wall or a black square in the figure—in each of the four compass directions. We assume that the sensors give perfectly correct data, and that the robot has a correct map of the enviornment. But unfortunately the robot's navigational system is broken, so when it executes a *Move* action, it moves randomly to one of the adjacent squares. The robot's task is to determine its current location.

LOCALIZATION

Suppose the robot has just been switched on, so it does not know where it is. Thus its initial belief state b consists of the set of all locations. The the robot receives the percept

[12] The usual apologies to those who are unfamiliar with the effect of small children on the environment.

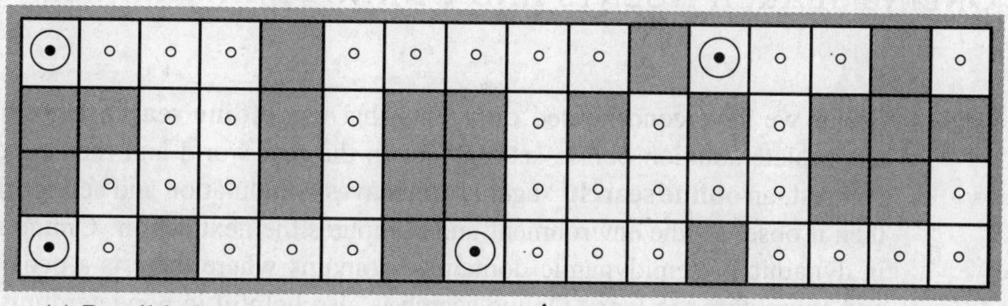

(a) Possible locations of robot after E_1 = NSW

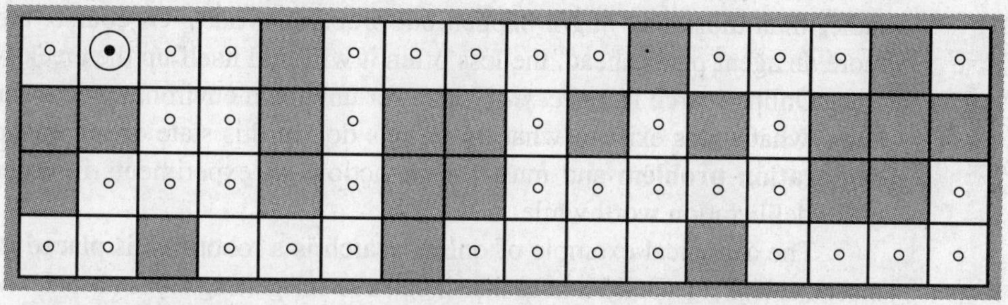

(b) Possible locations of robot After E_1 = NSW, E_2 = NS

Figure 18 Possible positions of the robot, ⊙, (a) after one observation $E_1 = NSW$ and (b) after a second observation $E_2 = NS$. When sensors are noiseless and the transition model is accurate, there are no other possible locations for the robot consistent with this sequence of two observations.

NSW, meaning there are obstacles to the north, west, and south, and does an update using the equation $b_o = \text{UPDATE}(b)$, yielding the 4 locations shown in Figure 18(a). You can inspect the maze to see that those are the only four locations that yield the percept *NWS*.

Next the robot executes a *Move* action, but the result is nondeterministic. The new belief state, $b_a = \text{PREDICT}(b_o, Move)$, contains all the locations that are one step away from the locations in b_o. When the second percept, *NS*, arrives, the robot does $\text{UPDATE}(b_a, NS)$ and finds that the belief state has collapsed down to the single location shown in Figure 18(b). That's the only location that could be the result of

$$\text{UPDATE}(\text{PREDICT}(\text{UPDATE}(b, NSW), Move), NS).$$

With nondetermnistic actions the PREDICT step grows the belief state, but the UPDATE step shrinks it back down—as long as the percepts provide some useful identifying information. Sometimes the percepts don't help much for localization: If there were one or more long east-west corridors, then a robot could receive a long sequence of *NS* percepts, but never know where in the corridor(s) it was.

5 ONLINE SEARCH AGENTS AND UNKNOWN ENVIRONMENTS

OFFLINE SEARCH

ONLINE SEARCH

So far we have concentrated on agents that use **offline search** algorithms. They compute a complete solution before setting foot in the real world and then execute the solution. In contrast, an **online search**[13] agent **interleaves** computation and action: first it takes an action, then it observes the environment and computes the next action. Online search is a good idea in dynamic or semidynamic domains—domains where there is a penalty for sitting around and computing too long. Online search is also helpful in nondeterministic domains because it allows the agent to focus its computational efforts on the contingencies that actually arise rather than those that *might* happen but probably won't. Of course, there is a tradeoff: the more an agent plans ahead, the less often it will find itself up the creek without a paddle.

EXPLORATION PROBLEM

Online search is a *necessary* idea for unknown environments, where the agent does not know what states exist or what its actions do. In this state of ignorance, the agent faces an **exploration problem** and must use its actions as experiments in order to learn enough to make deliberation worthwhile.

The canonical example of online search is a robot that is placed in a new building and must explore it to build a map that it can use for getting from A to B. Methods for escaping from labyrinths—required knowledge for aspiring heroes of antiquity—are also examples of online search algorithms. Spatial exploration is not the only form of exploration, however. Consider a newborn baby: it has many possible actions but knows the outcomes of none of them, and it has experienced only a few of the possible states that it can reach. The baby's gradual discovery of how the world works is, in part, an online search process.

5.1 Online search problems

An online search problem must be solved by an agent executing actions, rather than by pure computation. We assume a deterministic and fully observable environment, but we stipulate that the agent knows only the following:

- ACTIONS(s), which returns a list of actions allowed in state s;
- The step-cost function $c(s, a, s')$—note that this cannot be used until the agent knows that s' is the outcome; and
- GOAL-TEST(s).

Note in particular that the agent *cannot* determine RESULT(s, a) except by actually being in s and doing a. For example, in the maze problem shown in Figure 19, the agent does not know that going *Up* from (1,1) leads to (1,2); nor, having done that, does it know that going *Down* will take it back to (1,1). This degree of ignorance can be reduced in some applications—for example, a robot explorer might know how its movement actions work and be ignorant only of the locations of obstacles.

[13] The term "online" is commonly used in computer science to refer to algorithms that must process input data as they are received rather than waiting for the entire input data set to become available.

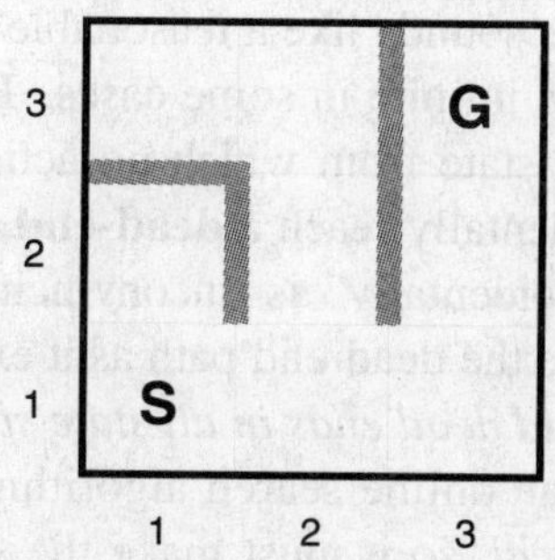

Figure 19 A simple maze problem. The agent starts at S and must reach G but knows nothing of the environment.

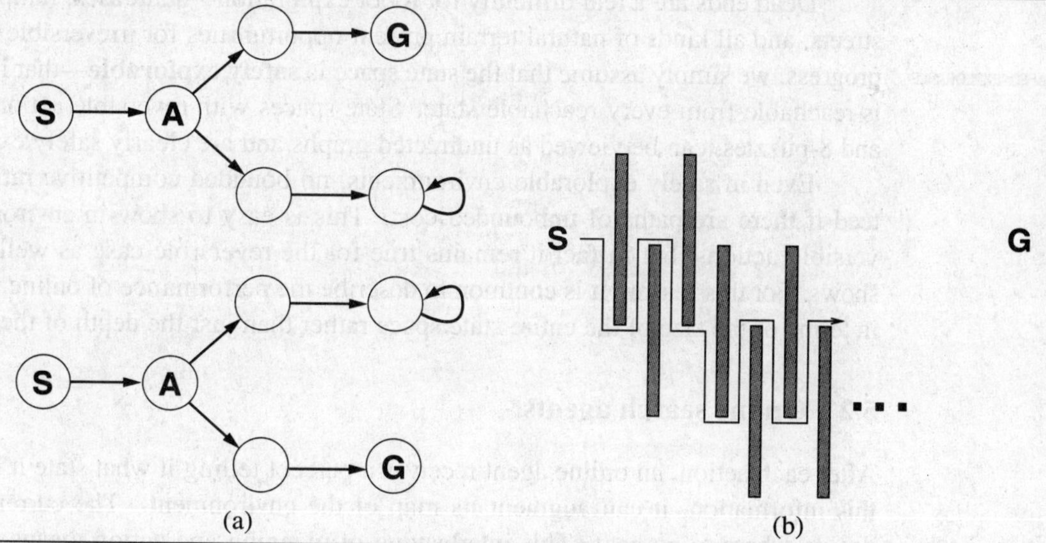

Figure 20 (a) Two state spaces that might lead an online search agent into a dead end. Any given agent will fail in at least one of these spaces. (b) A two-dimensional environment that can cause an online search agent to follow an arbitrarily inefficient route to the goal. Whichever choice the agent makes, the adversary blocks that route with another long, thin wall, so that the path followed is much longer than the best possible path.

Finally, the agent might have access to an admissible heuristic function $h(s)$ that estimates the distance from the current state to a goal state. For example, in Figure 19, the agent might know the location of the goal and be able to use the Manhattan-distance heuristic.

Typically, the agent's objective is to reach a goal state while minimizing cost. (Another possible objective is simply to explore the entire environment.) The cost is the total path cost of the path that the agent actually travels. It is common to compare this cost with the path cost of the path the agent would follow *if it knew the search space in advance*—that is, the actual shortest path (or shortest complete exploration). In the language of online algorithms, this is called the **competitive ratio**; we would like it to be as small as possible.

COMPETITIVE RATIO

IRREVERSIBLE
DEAD END
ADVERSARY ARGUMENT

Although this sounds like a reasonable request, it is easy to see that the best achievable competitive ratio is infinite in some cases. For example, if some actions are **irreversible**—i.e., they lead to a state from which no action leads back to the previous state—the online search might accidentally reach a **dead-end** state from which no goal state is reachable. Perhaps the term "accidentally" is unconvincing—after all, there might be an algorithm that happens not to take the dead-end path as it explores. Our claim, to be more precise, is that *no algorithm can avoid dead ends in all state spaces.* Consider the two dead-end state spaces in Figure 20(a). To an online search algorithm that has visited states S and A, the two state spaces look *identical*, so it must make the same decision in both. Therefore, it will fail in one of them. This is an example of an **adversary argument**—we can imagine an adversary constructing the state space while the agent explores it and putting the goals and dead ends wherever it chooses.

SAFELY EXPLORABLE

Dead ends are a real difficulty for robot exploration—staircases, ramps, cliffs, one-way streets, and all kinds of natural terrain present opportunities for irreversible actions. To make progress, we simply assume that the state space is **safely explorable**—that is, some goal state is reachable from every reachable state. State spaces with reversible actions, such as mazes and 8-puzzles, can be viewed as undirected graphs and are clearly safely explorable.

Even in safely explorable environments, no bounded competitive ratio can be guaranteed if there are paths of unbounded cost. This is easy to show in environments with irreversible actions, but in fact it remains true for the reversible case as well, as Figure 20(b) shows. For this reason, it is common to describe the performance of online search algorithms in terms of the size of the entire state space rather than just the depth of the shallowest goal.

5.2 Online search agents

After each action, an online agent receives a percept telling it what state it has reached; from this information, it can augment its map of the environment. The current map is used to decide where to go next. This interleaving of planning and action means that online search algorithms are quite different from the offline search algorithms we have seen previously. For example, offline algorithms such as A* can expand a node in one part of the space and then immediately expand a node in another part of the space, because node expansion involves simulated rather than real actions. An online algorithm, on the other hand, can discover successors only for a node that it physically occupies. To avoid traveling all the way across the tree to expand the next node, it seems better to expand nodes in a *local* order. Depth-first search has exactly this property because (except when backtracking) the next node expanded is a child of the previous node expanded.

An online depth-first search agent is shown in Figure 21. This agent stores its map in a table, RESULT$[s, a]$, that records the state resulting from executing action a in state s. Whenever an action from the current state has not been explored, the agent tries that action. The difficulty comes when the agent has tried all the actions in a state. In offline depth-first search, the state is simply dropped from the queue; in an online search, the agent has to backtrack physically. In depth-first search, this means going back to the state from which the agent most recently entered the current state. To achieve that, the algorithm keeps a table that

```
function ONLINE-DFS-AGENT(s′) returns an action
  inputs: s′, a percept that identifies the current state
  persistent: result, a table indexed by state and action, initially empty
              untried, a table that lists, for each state, the actions not yet tried
              unbacktracked, a table that lists, for each state, the backtracks not yet tried
              s, a, the previous state and action, initially null

  if GOAL-TEST(s′) then return stop
  if s′ is a new state (not in untried) then untried[s′] ← ACTIONS(s′)
  if s is not null then
      result[s, a] ← s′
      add s to the front of unbacktracked[s′]
  if untried[s′] is empty then
      if unbacktracked[s′] is empty then return stop
      else a ← an action b such that result[s′, b] = POP(unbacktracked[s′])
  else a ← POP(untried[s′])
  s ← s′
  return a
```

Figure 21 An online search agent that uses depth-first exploration. The agent is applicable only in state spaces in which every action can be "undone" by some other action.

lists, for each state, the predecessor states to which the agent has not yet backtracked. If the agent has run out of states to which it can backtrack, then its search is complete.

We recommend that the reader trace through the progress of ONLINE-DFS-AGENT when applied to the maze given in Figure 19. It is fairly easy to see that the agent will, in the worst case, end up traversing every link in the state space exactly twice. For exploration, this is optimal; for finding a goal, on the other hand, the agent's competitive ratio could be arbitrarily bad if it goes off on a long excursion when there is a goal right next to the initial state. An online variant of iterative deepening solves this problem; for an environment that is a uniform tree, the competitive ratio of such an agent is a small constant.

Because of its method of backtracking, ONLINE-DFS-AGENT works only in state spaces where the actions are reversible. There are slightly more complex algorithms that work in general state spaces, but no such algorithm has a bounded competitive ratio.

5.3 Online local search

Like depth-first search, **hill-climbing search** has the property of locality in its node expansions. In fact, because it keeps just one current state in memory, hill-climbing search is *already* an online search algorithm! Unfortunately, it is not very useful in its simplest form because it leaves the agent sitting at local maxima with nowhere to go. Moreover, random restarts cannot be used, because the agent cannot transport itself to a new state.

RANDOM WALK

Instead of random restarts, one might consider using a **random walk** to explore the environment. A random walk simply selects at random one of the available actions from the

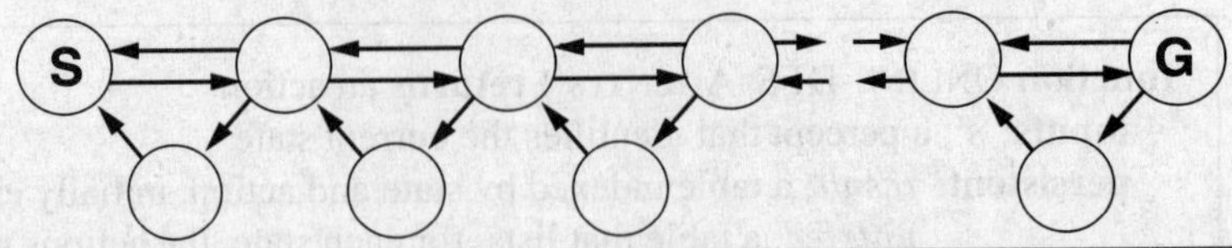

Figure 22 An environment in which a random walk will take exponentially many steps to find the goal.

current state; preference can be given to actions that have not yet been tried. It is easy to prove that a random walk will *eventually* find a goal or complete its exploration, provided that the space is finite.[14] On the other hand, the process can be very slow. Figure 22 shows an environment in which a random walk will take exponentially many steps to find the goal because, at each step, backward progress is twice as likely as forward progress. The example is contrived, of course, but there are many real-world state spaces whose topology causes these kinds of "traps" for random walks.

Augmenting hill climbing with *memory* rather than randomness turns out to be a more effective approach. The basic idea is to store a "current best estimate" $H(s)$ of the cost to reach the goal from each state that has been visited. $H(s)$ starts out being just the heuristic estimate $h(s)$ and is updated as the agent gains experience in the state space. Figure 23 shows a simple example in a one-dimensional state space. In (a), the agent seems to be stuck in a flat local minimum at the shaded state. Rather than staying where it is, the agent should follow what seems to be the best path to the goal given the current cost estimates for its neighbors. The estimated cost to reach the goal through a neighbor s' is the cost to get to s' plus the estimated cost to get to a goal from there—that is, $c(s, a, s') + H(s')$. In the example, there are two actions, with estimated costs $1+9$ and $1+2$, so it seems best to move right. Now, it is clear that the cost estimate of 2 for the shaded state was overly optimistic. Since the best move cost 1 and led to a state that is at least 2 steps from a goal, the shaded state must be at least 3 steps from a goal, so its H should be updated accordingly, as shown in Figure 23(b). Continuing this process, the agent will move back and forth twice more, updating H each time and "flattening out" the local minimum until it escapes to the right.

LRTA*

An agent implementing this scheme, which is called learning real-time A* (**LRTA***), is shown in Figure 24. Like ONLINE-DFS-AGENT, it builds a map of the environment in the *result* table. It updates the cost estimate for the state it has just left and then chooses the "apparently best" move according to its current cost estimates. One important detail is that actions that have not yet been tried in a state s are always assumed to lead immediately to the goal with the least possible cost, namely $h(s)$. This **optimism under uncertainty** encourages the agent to explore new, possibly promising paths.

OPTIMISM UNDER UNCERTAINTY

An LRTA* agent is guaranteed to find a goal in any finite, safely explorable environment. Unlike A*, however, it is not complete for infinite state spaces—there are cases where it can be led infinitely astray. It can explore an environment of n states in $O(n^2)$ steps in the worst case,

[14] Random walks are complete on infinite one-dimensional and two-dimensional grids. On a three-dimensional grid, the probability that the walk ever returns to the starting point is only about 0.3405 (Hughes, 1995).

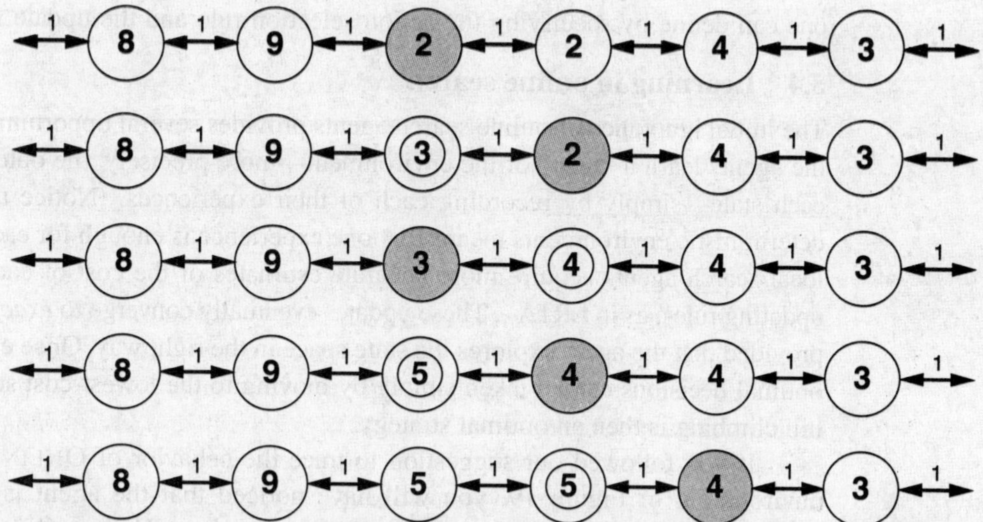

Figure 23 Five iterations of LRTA * on a one-dimensional state space. Each state is labeled with $H(s)$, the current cost estimate to reach a goal, and each link is labeled with its step cost. The shaded state marks the location of the agent, and the updated cost estimates at each iteration are circled.

```
function LRTA*-AGENT(s′) returns an action
  inputs: s′, a percept that identifies the current state
  persistent: result, a table, indexed by state and action, initially empty
              H, a table of cost estimates indexed by state, initially empty
              s, a, the previous state and action, initially null

  if GOAL-TEST(s′) then return stop
  if s′ is a new state (not in H) then H[s′] ← h(s′)
  if s is not null
      result[s, a] ← s′
      H[s] ←       min        LRTA*-COST(s, b, result[s, b], H)
              b ∈ ACTIONS(s)
  a ← an action b in ACTIONS(s′) that minimizes LRTA*-COST(s′, b, result[s′, b], H)
  s ← s′
  return a

function LRTA*-COST(s, a, s′, H) returns a cost estimate
  if s′ is undefined then return h(s)
  else return c(s, a, s′) + H[s′]
```

Figure 24 LRTA*-AGENT selects an action according to the values of neighboring states, which are updated as the agent moves about the state space.

but often does much better. The LRTA* agent is just one of a large family of online agents that one can define by specifying the action selection rule and the update rule in different ways.

5.4 Learning in online search

The initial ignorance of online search agents provides several opportunities for learning. First, the agents learn a "map" of the environment—more precisely, the outcome of each action in each state—simply by recording each of their experiences. (Notice that the assumption of deterministic environments means that one experience is enough for each action.) Second, the local search agents acquire more accurate estimates of the cost of each state by using local updating rules, as in LRTA*. These updates eventually converge to *exact* values for every state, provided that the agent explores the state space in the right way. Once exact values are known, optimal decisions can be taken simply by moving to the lowest-cost successor—that is, pure hill climbing is then an optimal strategy.

If you followed our suggestion to trace the behavior of ONLINE-DFS-AGENT in the environment of Figure 19, you will have noticed that the agent is not very bright. For example, after it has seen that the *Up* action goes from (1,1) to (1,2), the agent still has no idea that the *Down* action goes back to (1,1) or that the *Up* action also goes from (2,1) to (2,2), from (2,2) to (2,3), and so on. In general, we would like the agent to learn that *Up* increases the y-coordinate unless there is a wall in the way, that *Down* reduces it, and so on. For this to happen, we need two things. First, we need a formal and explicitly manipulable representation for these kinds of general rules; so far, we have hidden the information inside the black box called the RESULT function. Part III is devoted to this issue. Second, we need algorithms that can construct suitable general rules from the specific observations made by the agent.

6 SUMMARY

This chapter has examined search algorithms for problems beyond the "classical" case of finding the shortest path to a goal in an observable, deterministic, discrete environment.

- *Local search* methods such as **hill climbing** operate on complete-state formulations, keeping only a small number of nodes in memory. Several stochastic algorithms have been developed, including **simulated annealing**, which returns optimal solutions when given an appropriate cooling schedule.
- Many local search methods apply also to problems in continuous spaces. **Linear programming** and **convex optimization** problems obey certain restrictions on the shape of the state space and the nature of the objective function, and admit polynomial-time algorithms that are often extremely efficient in practice.
- A **genetic algorithm** is a stochastic hill-climbing search in which a large population of states is maintained. New states are generated by **mutation** and by **crossover**, which combines pairs of states from the population.

- In **nondeterministic** environments, agents can apply AND–OR search to generate **contingent** plans that reach the goal regardless of which outcomes occur during execution.
- When the environment is partially observable, the **belief state** represents the set of possible states that the agent might be in.
- Standard search algorithms can be applied directly to belief-state space to solve **sensorless problems**, and belief-state AND–OR search can solve general partially observable problems. Incremental algorithms that construct solutions state-by-state within a belief state are often more efficient.
- **Exploration problems** arise when the agent has no idea about the states and actions of its environment. For safely explorable environments, **online search** agents can build a map and find a goal if one exists. Updating heuristic estimates from experience provides an effective method to escape from local minima.

BIBLIOGRAPHICAL AND HISTORICAL NOTES

Local search techniques have a long history in mathematics and computer science. Indeed, the Newton–Raphson method (Newton, 1671; Raphson, 1690) can be seen as a very efficient local search method for continuous spaces in which gradient information is available. Brent (1973) is a classic reference for optimization algorithms that do not require such information. Beam search, which we have presented as a local search algorithm, originated as a bounded-width variant of dynamic programming for speech recognition in the HARPY system (Lowerre, 1976). A related algorithm is analyzed in depth by Pearl (1984, Ch. 5).

The topic of local search was reinvigorated in the early 1990s by surprisingly good results for large constraint-satisfaction problems such as n-queens (Minton *et al.*, 1992) and logical reasoning (Selman *et al.*, 1992) and by the incorporation of randomness, multiple simultaneous searches, and other improvements. This renaissance of what Christos Papadimitriou has called "New Age" algorithms also sparked increased interest among theoretical computer scientists (Koutsoupias and Papadimitriou, 1992; Aldous and Vazirani, 1994). In the field of operations research, a variant of hill climbing called **tabu search** has gained popularity (Glover and Laguna, 1997). This algorithm maintains a tabu list of k previously visited states that cannot be revisited; as well as improving efficiency when searching graphs, this list can allow the algorithm to escape from some local minima. Another useful improvement on hill climbing is the STAGE algorithm (Boyan and Moore, 1998). The idea is to use the local maxima found by random-restart hill climbing to get an idea of the overall shape of the landscape. The algorithm fits a smooth surface to the set of local maxima and then calculates the global maximum of that surface analytically. This becomes the new restart point. The algorithm has been shown to work in practice on hard problems. Gomes *et al.* (1998) showed that the run times of systematic backtracking algorithms often have a **heavy-tailed distribution**, which means that the probability of a very long run time is more than would be predicted if the run times were exponentially distributed. When the run time distribution is heavy-tailed, random restarts find a solution faster, on average, than a single run to completion.

TABU SEARCH

HEAVY-TAILED DISTRIBUTION

Simulated annealing was first described by Kirkpatrick *et al.* (1983), who borrowed directly from the **Metropolis algorithm** (which is used to simulate complex systems in physics (Metropolis *et al.*, 1953) and was supposedly invented at a Los Alamos dinner party). Simulated annealing is now a field in itself, with hundreds of papers published every year.

Finding optimal solutions in continuous spaces is the subject matter of several fields, including **optimization theory**, **optimal control theory**, and the **calculus of variations**. The basic techniques are explained well by Bishop (1995); Press *et al.* (2007) cover a wide range of algorithms and provide working software.

As Andrew Moore points out, researchers have taken inspiration for search and optimization algorithms from a wide variety of fields of study: metallurgy (simulated annealing), biology (genetic algorithms), economics (market-based algorithms), entomology (ant colony optimization), neurology (neural networks), animal behavior (reinforcement learning), mountaineering (hill climbing), and others.

Linear programming (LP) was first studied systematically by the Russian mathematician Leonid Kantorovich (1939). It was one of the first applications of computers; the **simplex algorithm** (Dantzig, 1949) is still used despite worst-case exponential complexity. Karmarkar (1984) developed the far more efficient family of **interior-point** methods, which was shown to have polynomial complexity for the more general class of convex optimization problems by Nesterov and Nemirovski (1994). Excellent introductions to convex optimization are provided by Ben-Tal and Nemirovski (2001) and Boyd and Vandenberghe (2004).

Work by Sewall Wright (1931) on the concept of a **fitness landscape** was an important precursor to the development of genetic algorithms. In the 1950s, several statisticians, including Box (1957) and Friedman (1959), used evolutionary techniques for optimization problems, but it wasn't until Rechenberg (1965) introduced **evolution strategies** to solve optimization problems for airfoils that the approach gained popularity. In the 1960s and 1970s, John Holland (1975) championed genetic algorithms, both as a useful tool and as a method to expand our understanding of adaptation, biological or otherwise (Holland, 1995). The **artificial life** movement (Langton, 1995) takes this idea one step further, viewing the products of genetic algorithms as *organisms* rather than solutions to problems. Work in this field by Hinton and Nowlan (1987) and Ackley and Littman (1991) has done much to clarify the implications of the Baldwin effect. For general background on evolution, we recommend Smith and Szathmáry (1999), Ridley (2004), and Carroll (2007).

EVOLUTION STRATEGY

ARTIFICIAL LIFE

Most comparisons of genetic algorithms to other approaches (especially stochastic hill climbing) have found that the genetic algorithms are slower to converge (O'Reilly and Oppacher, 1994; Mitchell *et al.*, 1996; Juels and Wattenberg, 1996; Baluja, 1997). Such findings are not universally popular within the GA community, but recent attempts within that community to understand population-based search as an approximate form of Bayesian learning might help close the gap between the field and its critics (Pelikan *et al.*, 1999). The theory of **quadratic dynamical systems** may also explain the performance of GAs (Rabani *et al.*, 1998). See Lohn *et al.* (2001) for an example of GAs applied to antenna design, and Renner and Ekart (2003) for an application to computer-aided design.

GENETIC PROGRAMMING

The field of **genetic programming** is closely related to genetic algorithms. The principal difference is that the representations that are mutated and combined are programs rather than bit strings. The programs are represented in the form of expression trees; the expressions can be in a standard language such as Lisp or can be specially designed to represent circuits, robot controllers, and so on. Crossover involves splicing together subtrees rather than substrings. This form of mutation guarantees that the offspring are well-formed expressions, which would not be the case if programs were manipulated as strings.

Interest in genetic programming was spurred by John Koza's work (Koza, 1992, 1994), but it goes back at least to early experiments with machine code by Friedberg (1958) and with finite-state automata by Fogel *et al.* (1966). As with genetic algorithms, there is debate about the effectiveness of the technique. Koza *et al.* (1999) describe experiments in the use of genetic programming to design circuit devices.

The journals *Evolutionary Computation* and *IEEE Transactions on Evolutionary Computation* cover genetic algorithms and genetic programming; articles are also found in *Complex Systems*, *Adaptive Behavior*, and *Artificial Life*. The main conference is the *Genetic and Evolutionary Computation Conference* (GECCO). Good overview texts on genetic algorithms are given by Mitchell (1996), Fogel (2000), and Langdon and Poli (2002), and by the free online book by Poli *et al.* (2008).

The unpredictability and partial observability of real environments were recognized early on in robotics projects that used planning techniques, including Shakey (Fikes *et al.*, 1972) and FREDDY (Michie, 1974). The problems received more attention after the publication of McDermott's (1978a) influential article, *Planning and Acting*.

The first work to make explicit use of AND–OR trees seems to have been Slagle's SAINT program for symbolic integration. Amarel (1967) applied the idea to propositional theorem proving, and introduced a search algorithm similar to AND-OR-GRAPH-SEARCH. The algorithm was further developed and formalized by Nilsson (1971), who also described AO*—which, as its name suggests, finds optimal solutions given an admissible heuristic. AO* was analyzed and improved by Martelli and Montanari (1973). AO* is a top-down algorithm; a bottom-up generalization of A* is A*LD, for A* Lightest Derivation (Felzenszwalb and McAllester, 2007). Interest in AND–OR search has undergone a revival in recent years, with new algorithms for finding cyclic solutions (Jimenez and Torras, 2000; Hansen and Zilberstein, 2001) and new techniques inspired by dynamic programming (Bonet and Geffner, 2005).

The idea of transforming partially observable problems into belief-state problems originated with Astrom (1965) for the much more complex case of probabilistic uncertainty. Erdmann and Mason (1988) studied the problem of robotic manipulation without sensors, using a continuous form of belief-state search. They showed that it was possible to orient a part on a table from an arbitrary initial position by a well-designed sequence of tilting actions. More practical methods, based on a series of precisely oriented diagonal barriers across a conveyor belt, use the same algorithmic insights (Wiegley *et al.*, 1996).

The belief-state approach was reinvented in the context of sensorless and partially observable search problems by Genesereth and Nourbakhsh (1993). Additional work was done on sensorless problems in the logic-based planning community (Goldman and Boddy, 1996; Smith and Weld, 1998). This work has emphasized concise representations for belief states. Bonet and Geffner (2000) introduced the first effective heuristics for belief-state search; these were refined by Bryce et al. (2006). The incremental approach to belief-state search, in which solutions are constructed incrementally for subsets of states within each belief state, was studied in the planning literature by Kurien et al. (2002); several new incremental algorithms were introduced for nondeterministic, partially observable problems by Russell and Wolfe (2005).

Algorithms for exploring unknown state spaces have been of interest for many centuries. Depth-first search in a maze can be implemented by keeping one's left hand on the wall; loops can be avoided by marking each junction. Depth-first search fails with irreversible actions; EULERIAN GRAPH the more general problem of exploring **Eulerian graphs** (i.e., graphs in which each node has equal numbers of incoming and outgoing edges) was solved by an algorithm due to Hierholzer (1873). The first thorough algorithmic study of the exploration problem for arbitrary graphs was carried out by Deng and Papadimitriou (1990), who developed a completely general algorithm but showed that no bounded competitive ratio is possible for exploring a general graph. Papadimitriou and Yannakakis (1991) examined the question of finding paths to a goal in geometric path-planning environments (where all actions are reversible). They showed that a small competitive ratio is achievable with square obstacles, but with general rectangular obstacles no bounded ratio can be achieved. (See Figure 20.)

The LRTA* algorithm was developed by Korf (1990) as part of an investigation into REAL-TIME SEARCH **real-time search** for environments in which the agent must act after searching for only a fixed amount of time (a common situation in two-player games). LRTA* is in fact a special case of reinforcement learning algorithms for stochastic environments (Barto *et al.*, 1995). Its policy of optimism under uncertainty—always head for the closest unvisited state—can result in an exploration pattern that is less efficient in the uninformed case than simple depth-first search (Koenig, 2000). Dasgupta *et al.* (1994) show that online iterative deepening search is optimally efficient for finding a goal in a uniform tree with no heuristic information. Several informed variants on the LRTA* theme have been developed with different methods for searching and updating within the known portion of the graph (Pemberton and Korf, 1992). As yet, there is no good understanding of how to find goals with optimal efficiency when using heuristic information.

EXERCISES

1 Give the name of the algorithm that results from each of the following special cases:

a. Local beam search with $k = 1$.

b. Local beam search with one initial state and no limit on the number of states retained.

c. Simulated annealing with $T = 0$ at all times (and omitting the termination test).

d. Simulated annealing with $T = \infty$ at all times.

e. Genetic algorithm with population size $N = 1$.

2 Consider the problem of building railway tracks under the assumption that pieces fit exactly with no slack. Now consider the real problem, in which pieces don't fit exactly but allow for up to 10 degrees of rotation to either side of the "proper" alignment. Explain how to formulate the problem so it could be solved by simulated annealing.

3 In this exercise, we explore the use of local search methods to solve TSPs.

a. Implement and test a hill-climbing method to solve TSPs. Compare the results with optimal solutions obtained from the A* algorithm with the MST heuristic.

b. Repeat part (a) using a genetic algorithm instead of hill climbing. You may want to consult Larrañaga *et al.* (1999) for some suggestions for representations.

4 Generate a large number of 8-puzzle and 8-queens instances and solve them (where possible) by hill climbing (steepest-ascent and first-choice variants), hill climbing with random restart, and simulated annealing. Measure the search cost and percentage of solved problems and graph these against the optimal solution cost. Comment on your results.

5 The AND-OR-GRAPH-SEARCH algorithm in Figure 11 checks for repeated states only on the path from the root to the current state. Suppose that, in addition, the algorithm were to store *every* visited state and check against that list. Determine the information that should be stored and how the algorithm should use that information when a repeated state is found. (*Hint*: You will need to distinguish at least between states for which a successful subplan was constructed previously and states for which no subplan could be found.) Explain how to use labels, as defined in Section 3.3, to avoid having multiple copies of subplans.

6 Explain precisely how to modify the AND-OR-GRAPH-SEARCH algorithm to generate a cyclic plan if no acyclic plan exists. You will need to deal with three issues: labeling the plan steps so that a cyclic plan can point back to an earlier part of the plan, modifying OR-SEARCH so that it continues to look for acyclic plans after finding a cyclic plan, and augmenting the plan representation to indicate whether a plan is cyclic. Show how your algorithm works on (a) the slippery vacuum world, and (b) the slippery, erratic vacuum world. You might wish to use a computer implementation to check your results.

7 In Section 4.1 we introduced belief states to solve sensorless search problems. A sequence of actions solves a sensorless problem if it maps every physical state in the initial belief state b to a goal state. Suppose the agent knows $h^*(s)$, the true optimal cost of solving the physical state s in the fully observable problem, for every state s in b. Find an admissible heuristic $h(b)$ for the sensorless problem in terms of these costs, and prove its admissibilty. Comment on the accuracy of this heuristic on the sensorless vacuum problem of Figure 14. How well does A* perform?

8 This exercise explores subset–superset relations between belief states in sensorless or partially observable environments.

a. Prove that if an action sequence is a solution for a belief state b, it is also a solution for any subset of b. Can anything be said about supersets of b?

b. Explain in detail how to modify graph search for sensorless problems to take advantage of your answers in (a).

c. Explain in detail how to modify AND–OR search for partially observable problems, beyond the modifications you describe in (b).

9 In section 4.1 it was assumed that a given action would have the same cost when executed in any physical state within a given belief state. (This leads to a belief-state search problem with well-defined step costs.) Now consider what happens when the assumption does not hold. Does the notion of optimality still make sense in this context, or does it require modification? Consider also various possible definitions of the "cost" of executing an action in a belief state; for example, we could use the *minimum* of the physical costs; or the *maximum*; or a cost *interval* with the lower bound being the minimum cost and the upper bound being the maximum; or just keep the set of all possible costs for that action. For each of these, explore whether A* (with modifications if necessary) can return optimal solutions.

10 Consider the sensorless version of the erratic vacuum world. Draw the belief-state space reachable from the initial belief state $\{1, 2, 3, 4, 5, 6, 7, 8\}$, and explain why the problem is unsolvable.

11 We can turn the navigation problem in Exercise 7, from the chapter "Solving Problems by Searching", into an environment as follows:

- The percept will be a list of the positions, *relative to the agent*, of the visible vertices. The percept does *not* include the position of the robot! The robot must learn its own position from the map; for now, you can assume that each location has a different "view."
- Each action will be a vector describing a straight-line path to follow. If the path is unobstructed, the action succeeds; otherwise, the robot stops at the point where its path first intersects an obstacle. If the agent returns a zero motion vector and is at the goal (which is fixed and known), then the environment teleports the agent to a *random location* (not inside an obstacle).
- The performance measure charges the agent 1 point for each unit of distance traversed and awards 1000 points each time the goal is reached.

a. Implement this environment and a problem-solving agent for it. After each teleportation, the agent will need to formulate a new problem, which will involve discovering its current location.

b. Document your agent's performance (by having the agent generate suitable commentary as it moves around) and report its performance over 100 episodes.

c. Modify the environment so that 30% of the time the agent ends up at an unintended destination (chosen randomly from the other visible vertices if any; otherwise, no move at all). This is a crude model of the motion errors of a real robot. Modify the agent so that when such an error is detected, it finds out where it is and then constructs a plan to get back to where it was and resume the old plan. Remember that sometimes getting back to where it was might also fail! Show an example of the agent successfully overcoming two successive motion errors and still reaching the goal.

d. Now try two different recovery schemes after an error: (1) head for the closest vertex on the original route; and (2) replan a route to the goal from the new location. Compare the performance of the three recovery schemes. Would the inclusion of search costs affect the comparison?

e. Now suppose that there are locations from which the view is identical. (For example, suppose the world is a grid with square obstacles.) What kind of problem does the agent now face? What do solutions look like?

12 Suppose that an agent is in a 3×3 maze environment like the one shown in Figure 19. The agent knows that its initial location is (1,1), that the goal is at (3,3), and that the actions *Up*, *Down*, *Left*, *Right* have their usual effects unless blocked by a wall. The agent does *not* know where the internal walls are. In any given state, the agent perceives the set of legal actions; it can also tell whether the state is one it has visited before.

a. Explain how this online search problem can be viewed as an offline search in belief-state space, where the initial belief state includes all possible environment configurations. How large is the initial belief state? How large is the space of belief states?

b. How many distinct percepts are possible in the initial state?

c. Describe the first few branches of a contingency plan for this problem. How large (roughly) is the complete plan?

Notice that this contingency plan is a solution for *every possible environment* fitting the given description. Therefore, interleaving of search and execution is not strictly necessary even in unknown environments.

13 In this exercise, we examine hill climbing in the context of robot navigation, using the environment in Figure 31, from the chapter "Solving Problems by Searching", as an example.

a. Repeat Exercise 11 using hill climbing. Does your agent ever get stuck in a local minimum? Is it *possible* for it to get stuck with convex obstacles?

b. Construct a nonconvex polygonal environment in which the agent gets stuck.

c. Modify the hill-climbing algorithm so that, instead of doing a depth-1 search to decide where to go next, it does a depth-k search. It should find the best k-step path and do one step along it, and then repeat the process.

d. Is there some k for which the new algorithm is guaranteed to escape from local minima?

e. Explain how LRTA* enables the agent to escape from local minima in this case.

14 Like DFS, online DFS is incomplete for reversible state spaces with infinite paths. For example, suppose that states are points on the infinite two-dimensional grid and actions are unit vectors $(1, 0)$, $(0, 1)$, $(-1, 0)$, $(0, -1)$, tried in that order. Show that online DFS starting at $(0, 0)$ will not reach $(1, -1)$. Suppose the agent can observe, in addition to its current state, all successor states and the actions that would lead to them. Write an algorithm that is complete even for bidirected state spaces with infinite paths. What states does it visit in reaching $(1, -1)$?

ADVERSARIAL SEARCH

In which we examine the problems that arise when we try to plan ahead in a world where other agents are planning against us.

1 GAMES

In **multiagent environments**, each agent needs to consider the actions of other agents and how they affect its own welfare. The unpredictability of these other agents can introduce **contingencies** into the agent's problem-solving process. In this chapter we cover **competitive** environments, in which the agents' goals are in conflict, giving rise to **adversarial search** problems—often known as **games**.

GAME

Mathematical **game theory**, a branch of economics, views any multiagent environment as a game, provided that the impact of each agent on the others is "significant," regardless of whether the agents are cooperative or competitive.[1] In AI, the most common games are of a rather specialized kind—what game theorists call deterministic, turn-taking, two-player, **zero-sum games** of **perfect information** (such as chess). In our terminology, this means deterministic, fully observable environments in which two agents act alternately and in which the utility values at the end of the game are always equal and opposite. For example, if one player wins a game of chess, the other player necessarily loses. It is this opposition between the agents' utility functions that makes the situation adversarial.

ZERO-SUM GAMES
PERFECT INFORMATION

Games have engaged the intellectual faculties of humans—sometimes to an alarming degree—for as long as civilization has existed. For AI researchers, the abstract nature of games makes them an appealing subject for study. The state of a game is easy to represent, and agents are usually restricted to a small number of actions whose outcomes are defined by precise rules. Physical games, such as croquet and ice hockey, have much more complicated descriptions, a much larger range of possible actions, and rather imprecise rules defining the legality of actions. With the exception of robot soccer, these physical games have not attracted much interest in the AI community.

[1] Environments with very many agents are often viewed as **economies** rather than games.

Games, unlike many toy problems that you may have studied, are interesting *because* they are too hard to solve. For example, chess has an average branching factor of about 35, or 10^{154} and games often go to 50 moves by each player, so the search tree has about 35^{100} nodes (although the search graph has "only" about 10^{40} distinct nodes). Games, like the real world, therefore require the ability to make *some* decision even when calculating the *optimal* decision is infeasible. Games also penalize inefficiency severely. Whereas an implementation of A* search that is half as efficient will simply take twice as long to run to completion, a chess program that is half as efficient in using its available time probably will be beaten into the ground, other things being equal. Game-playing research has therefore spawned a number of interesting ideas on how to make the best possible use of time.

PRUNING

We begin with a definition of the optimal move and an algorithm for finding it. We then look at techniques for choosing a good move when time is limited. **Pruning** allows us to ignore portions of the search tree that make no difference to the final choice, and heuristic **evaluation functions** allow us to approximate the true utility of a state without doing a complete search. Section 5 discusses games such as backgammon that include an element of chance; we also discuss bridge, which includes elements of **imperfect information** because not all cards are visible to each player. Finally, we look at how state-of-the-art game-playing programs fare against human opposition and at directions for future developments.

IMPERFECT INFORMATION

We first consider games with two players, whom we call MAX and MIN for reasons that will soon become obvious. MAX moves first, and then they take turns moving until the game is over. At the end of the game, points are awarded to the winning player and penalties are given to the loser. A game can be formally defined as a kind of search problem with the following elements:

- S_0: The **initial state**, which specifies how the game is set up at the start.
- PLAYER(s): Defines which player has the move in a state.
- ACTIONS(s): Returns the set of legal moves in a state.
- RESULT(s, a): The **transition model**, which defines the result of a move.
- TERMINAL-TEST(s): A **terminal test**, which is true when the game is over and false otherwise. States where the game has ended are called **terminal states**.
- UTILITY(s, p): A **utility function** (also called an objective function or payoff function), defines the final numeric value for a game that ends in terminal state s for a player p. In chess, the outcome is a win, loss, or draw, with values $+1$, 0, or $\frac{1}{2}$. Some games have a wider variety of possible outcomes; the payoffs in backgammon range from 0 to $+192$. A **zero-sum game** is (confusingly) defined as one where the total payoff to all players is the same for every instance of the game. Chess is zero-sum because every game has payoff of either $0 + 1$, $1 + 0$ or $\frac{1}{2} + \frac{1}{2}$. "Constant-sum" would have been a better term, but zero-sum is traditional and makes sense if you imagine each player is charged an entry fee of $\frac{1}{2}$.

TERMINAL TEST

TERMINAL STATES

GAME TREE

The initial state, ACTIONS function, and RESULT function define the **game tree** for the game—a tree where the nodes are game states and the edges are moves. Figure 1 shows part of the game tree for tic-tac-toe (noughts and crosses). From the initial state, MAX has nine possible moves. Play alternates between MAX's placing an X and MIN's placing an O until we reach leaf nodes corresponding to terminal states such that one player has three in a row or all the squares are filled. The number on each leaf node indicates the utility value of the terminal state from the point of view of MAX; high values are assumed to be good for MAX and bad for MIN (which is how the players get their names).

SEARCH TREE

For tic-tac-toe the game tree is relatively small—fewer than $9! = 362,880$ terminal nodes. But for chess there are over 10^{40} nodes, so the game tree is best thought of as a theoretical construct that we cannot realize in the physical world. But regardless of the size of the game tree, it is MAX's job to search for a good move. We use the term **search tree** for a tree that is superimposed on the full game tree, and examines enough nodes to allow a player to determine what move to make.

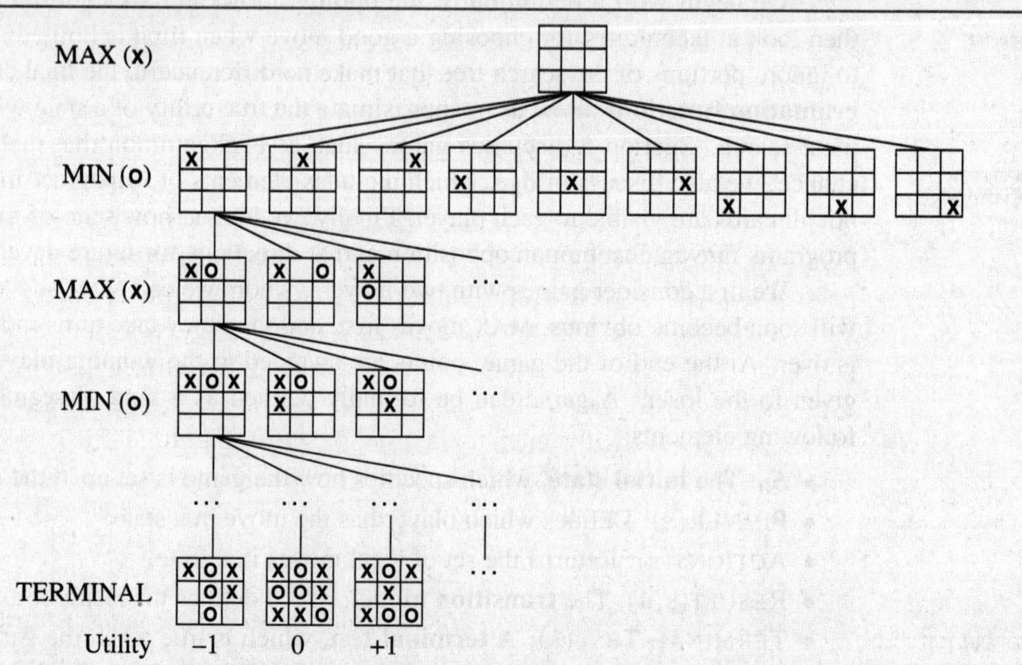

Figure 1 A (partial) game tree for the game of tic-tac-toe. The top node is the initial state, and MAX moves first, placing an X in an empty square. We show part of the tree, giving alternating moves by MIN (O) and MAX (X), until we eventually reach terminal states, which can be assigned utilities according to the rules of the game.

2 Optimal Decisions in Games

STRATEGY

In a normal search problem, the optimal solution would be a sequence of actions leading to a goal state—a terminal state that is a win. In adversarial search, MIN has something to say about it. MAX therefore must find a contingent **strategy**, which specifies MAX's move in the initial state, then MAX's moves in the states resulting from every possible response by

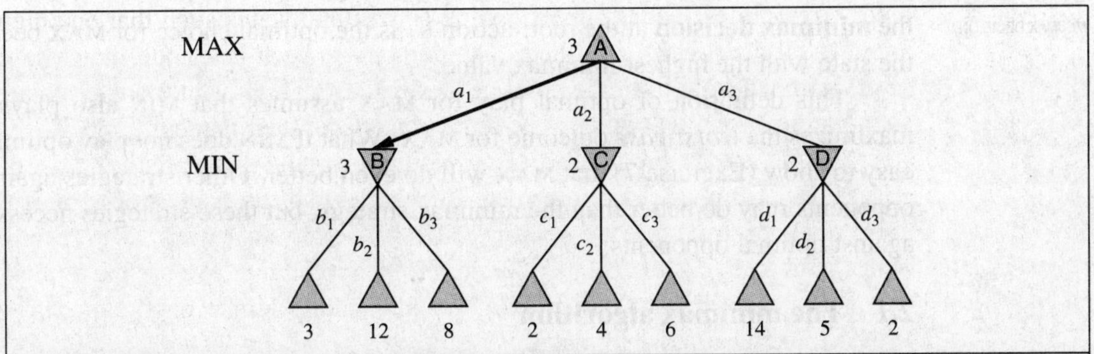

Figure 2 A two-ply game tree. The △ nodes are "MAX nodes," in which it is MAX's turn to move, and the ▽ nodes are "MIN nodes." The terminal nodes show the utility values for MAX; the other nodes are labeled with their minimax values. MAX's best move at the root is a_1, because it leads to the state with the highest minimax value, and MIN's best reply is b_1, because it leads to the state with the lowest minimax value.

MIN, then MAX's moves in the states resulting from every possible response by MIN to *those* moves, and so on. This is exactly analogous to the AND–OR search algorithm with MAX playing the role of OR and MIN equivalent to AND. Roughly speaking, an optimal strategy leads to outcomes at least as good as any other strategy when one is playing an infallible opponent. We begin by showing how to find this optimal strategy.

Even a simple game like tic-tac-toe is too complex for us to draw the entire game tree on one page, so we will switch to the trivial game in Figure 2. The possible moves for MAX at the root node are labeled a_1, a_2, and a_3. The possible replies to a_1 for MIN are b_1, b_2, b_3, and so on. This particular game ends after one move each by MAX and MIN. (In game parlance, we say that this tree is one move deep, consisting of two half-moves, each of which is called a **ply**.) The utilities of the terminal states in this game range from 2 to 14.

PLY

MINIMAX VALUE

Given a game tree, the optimal strategy can be determined from the **minimax value** of each node, which we write as MINIMAX(n). The minimax value of a node is the utility (for MAX) of being in the corresponding state, *assuming that both players play optimally* from there to the end of the game. Obviously, the minimax value of a terminal state is just its utility. Furthermore, given a choice, MAX prefers to move to a state of maximum value, whereas MIN prefers a state of minimum value. So we have the following:

$$\text{MINIMAX}(s) = \begin{cases} \text{UTILITY}(s) & \text{if TERMINAL-TEST}(s) \\ \max_{a \in Actions(s)} \text{MINIMAX}(\text{RESULT}(s,a)) & \text{if PLAYER}(s) = \text{MAX} \\ \min_{a \in Actions(s)} \text{MINIMAX}(\text{RESULT}(s,a)) & \text{if PLAYER}(s) = \text{MIN} \end{cases}$$

Let us apply these definitions to the game tree in Figure 2. The terminal nodes on the bottom level get their utility values from the game's UTILITY function. The first MIN node, labeled B, has three successor states with values 3, 12, and 8, so its minimax value is 3. Similarly, the other two MIN nodes have minimax value 2. The root node is a MAX node; its successor states have minimax values 3, 2, and 2; so it has a minimax value of 3. We can also identify

MINIMAX DECISION

the **minimax decision** at the root: action a_1 is the optimal choice for MAX because it leads to the state with the highest minimax value.

This definition of optimal play for MAX assumes that MIN also plays optimally—it maximizes the *worst-case* outcome for MAX. What if MIN does not play optimally? Then it is easy to show (Exercise 7) that MAX will do even better. Other strategies against suboptimal opponents may do better than the minimax strategy, but these strategies necessarily do worse against optimal opponents.

2.1 The minimax algorithm

MINIMAX ALGORITHM

The **minimax algorithm** (Figure 3) computes the minimax decision from the current state. It uses a simple recursive computation of the minimax values of each successor state, directly implementing the defining equations. The recursion proceeds all the way down to the leaves of the tree, and then the minimax values are **backed up** through the tree as the recursion unwinds. For example, in Figure 2, the algorithm first recurses down to the three bottom-left nodes and uses the UTILITY function on them to discover that their values are 3, 12, and 8, respectively. Then it takes the minimum of these values, 3, and returns it as the backed-up value of node B. A similar process gives the backed-up values of 2 for C and 2 for D. Finally, we take the maximum of 3, 2, and 2 to get the backed-up value of 3 for the root node.

The minimax algorithm performs a complete depth-first exploration of the game tree. If the maximum depth of the tree is m and there are b legal moves at each point, then the time complexity of the minimax algorithm is $O(b^m)$. The space complexity is $O(bm)$ for an algorithm that generates all actions at once, or $O(m)$ for an algorithm that generates actions one at a time. For real games, of course, the time cost is totally impractical, but this algorithm serves as the basis for the mathematical analysis of games and for more practical algorithms.

2.2 Optimal decisions in multiplayer games

Many popular games allow more than two players. Let us examine how to extend the minimax idea to multiplayer games. This is straightforward from the technical viewpoint, but raises some interesting new conceptual issues.

First, we need to replace the single value for each node with a *vector* of values. For example, in a three-player game with players A, B, and C, a vector $\langle v_A, v_B, v_C \rangle$ is associated with each node. For terminal states, this vector gives the utility of the state from each player's viewpoint. (In two-player, zero-sum games, the two-element vector can be reduced to a single value because the values are always opposite.) The simplest way to implement this is to have the UTILITY function return a vector of utilities.

Now we have to consider nonterminal states. Consider the node marked X in the game tree shown in Figure 4. In that state, player C chooses what to do. The two choices lead to terminal states with utility vectors $\langle v_A = 1, v_B = 2, v_C = 6 \rangle$ and $\langle v_A = 4, v_B = 2, v_C = 3 \rangle$. Since 6 is bigger than 3, C should choose the first move. This means that if state X is reached, subsequent play will lead to a terminal state with utilities $\langle v_A = 1, v_B = 2, v_C = 6 \rangle$. Hence, the backed-up value of X is this vector. The backed-up value of a node n is always the utility

```
function MINIMAX-DECISION(state) returns an action
  return arg max_{a ∈ ACTIONS(s)} MIN-VALUE(RESULT(state, a))
```

```
function MAX-VALUE(state) returns a utility value
  if TERMINAL-TEST(state) then return UTILITY(state)
  v ← −∞
  for each a in ACTIONS(state) do
     v ← MAX(v, MIN-VALUE(RESULT(s, a)))
  return v
```

```
function MIN-VALUE(state) returns a utility value
  if TERMINAL-TEST(state) then return UTILITY(state)
  v ← ∞
  for each a in ACTIONS(state) do
     v ← MIN(v, MAX-VALUE(RESULT(s, a)))
  return v
```

Figure 3 An algorithm for calculating minimax decisions. It returns the action corresponding to the best possible move, that is, the move that leads to the outcome with the best utility, under the assumption that the opponent plays to minimize utility. The functions MAX-VALUE and MIN-VALUE go through the whole game tree, all the way to the leaves, to determine the backed-up value of a state. The notation $\text{argmax}_{a \in S} f(a)$ computes the element a of set S that has the maximum value of $f(a)$.

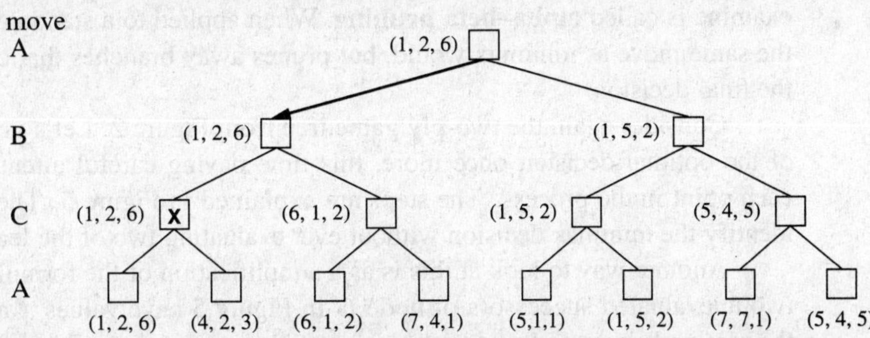

Figure 4 The first three plies of a game tree with three players (A, B, C). Each node is labeled with values from the viewpoint of each player. The best move is marked at the root.

vector of the successor state with the highest value for the player choosing at n. Anyone who plays multiplayer games, such as Diplomacy, quickly becomes aware that much more is going on than in two-player games. Multiplayer games usually involve **alliances**, whether formal or informal, among the players. Alliances are made and broken as the game proceeds. How are we to understand such behavior? Are alliances a natural consequence of optimal strategies for each player in a multiplayer game? It turns out that they can be. For example,

ALLIANCE

suppose A and B are in weak positions and C is in a stronger position. Then it is often optimal for both A and B to attack C rather than each other, lest C destroy each of them individually. In this way, collaboration emerges from purely selfish behavior. Of course, as soon as C weakens under the joint onslaught, the alliance loses its value, and either A or B could violate the agreement. In some cases, explicit alliances merely make concrete what would have happened anyway. In other cases, a social stigma attaches to breaking an alliance, so players must balance the immediate advantage of breaking an alliance against the long-term disadvantage of being perceived as untrustworthy.

If the game is not zero-sum, then collaboration can also occur with just two players. Suppose, for example, that there is a terminal state with utilities $\langle v_A = 1000, v_B = 1000 \rangle$ and that 1000 is the highest possible utility for each player. Then the optimal strategy is for both players to do everything possible to reach this state—that is, the players will automatically cooperate to achieve a mutually desirable goal.

3 ALPHA–BETA PRUNING

The problem with minimax search is that the number of game states it has to examine is exponential in the depth of the tree. Unfortunately, we can't eliminate the exponent, but it turns out we can effectively cut it in half. The trick is that it is possible to compute the correct minimax decision without looking at every node in the game tree. That is, we can use the idea of **pruning** to eliminate large parts of the tree from consideration. The particular technique we examine is called **alpha–beta pruning**. When applied to a standard minimax tree, it returns the same move as minimax would, but prunes away branches that cannot possibly influence the final decision.

ALPHA–BETA PRUNING

Consider again the two-ply game tree from Figure 2. Let's go through the calculation of the optimal decision once more, this time paying careful attention to what we know at each point in the process. The steps are explained in Figure 5. The outcome is that we can identify the minimax decision without ever evaluating two of the leaf nodes.

Another way to look at this is as a simplification of the formula for MINIMAX. Let the two unevaluated successors of node C in Figure 5 have values x and y. Then the value of the root node is given by

$$\begin{aligned} \text{MINIMAX}(root) &= \max(\min(3,12,8), \min(2,x,y), \min(14,5,2)) \\ &= \max(3, \min(2,x,y), 2) \\ &= \max(3, z, 2) \qquad \text{where } z = \min(2,x,y) \leq 2 \\ &= 3. \end{aligned}$$

In other words, the value of the root and hence the minimax decision are *independent* of the values of the pruned leaves x and y.

Alpha–beta pruning can be applied to trees of any depth, and it is often possible to prune entire subtrees rather than just leaves. The general principle is this: consider a node n

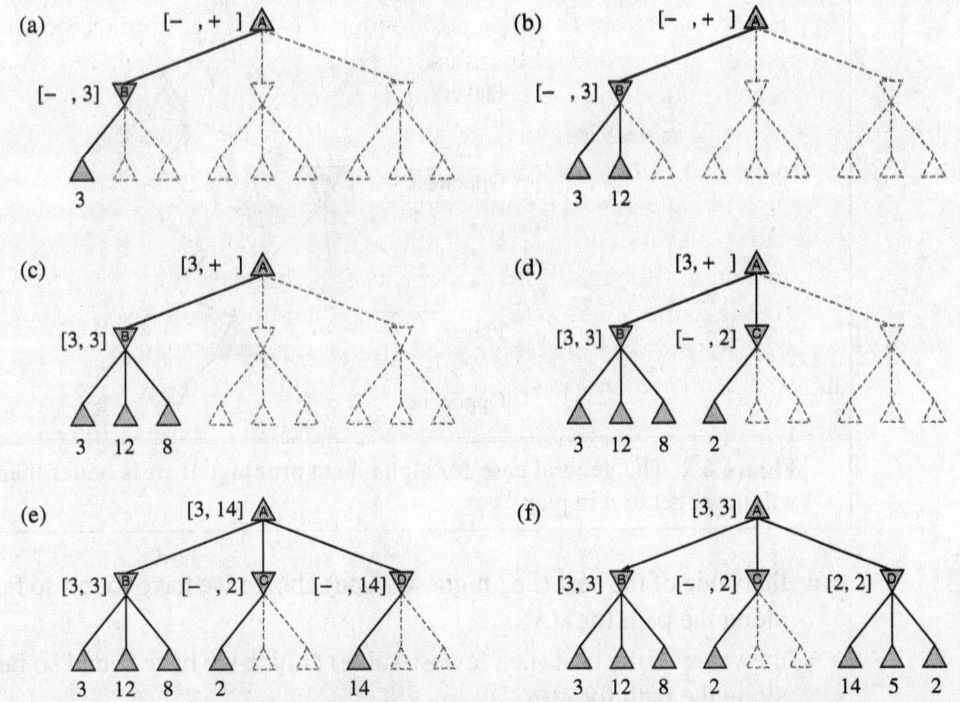

Figure 5 Stages in the calculation of the optimal decision for the game tree in Figure 2. At each point, we show the range of possible values for each node. (a) The first leaf below B has the value 3. Hence, B, which is a MIN node, has a value of *at most* 3. (b) The second leaf below B has a value of 12; MIN would avoid this move, so the value of B is still at most 3. (c) The third leaf below B has a value of 8; we have seen all B's successor states, so the value of B is exactly 3. Now, we can infer that the value of the root is *at least* 3, because MAX has a choice worth 3 at the root. (d) The first leaf below C has the value 2. Hence, C, which is a MIN node, has a value of *at most* 2. But we know that B is worth 3, so MAX would never choose C. Therefore, there is no point in looking at the other successor states of C. This is an example of alpha–beta pruning. (e) The first leaf below D has the value 14, so D is worth *at most* 14. This is still higher than MAX's best alternative (i.e., 3), so we need to keep exploring D's successor states. Notice also that we now have bounds on all of the successors of the root, so the root's value is also at most 14. (f) The second successor of D is worth 5, so again we need to keep exploring. The third successor is worth 2, so now D is worth exactly 2. MAX's decision at the root is to move to B, giving a value of 3.

somewhere in the tree (see Figure 6), such that Player has a choice of moving to that node. If Player has a better choice m either at the parent node of n or at any choice point further up, then n *will never be reached in actual play.* So once we have found out enough about n (by examining some of its descendants) to reach this conclusion, we can prune it.

Remember that minimax search is depth-first, so at any one time we just have to consider the nodes along a single path in the tree. Alpha–beta pruning gets its name from the following two parameters that describe bounds on the backed-up values that appear anywhere along the path:

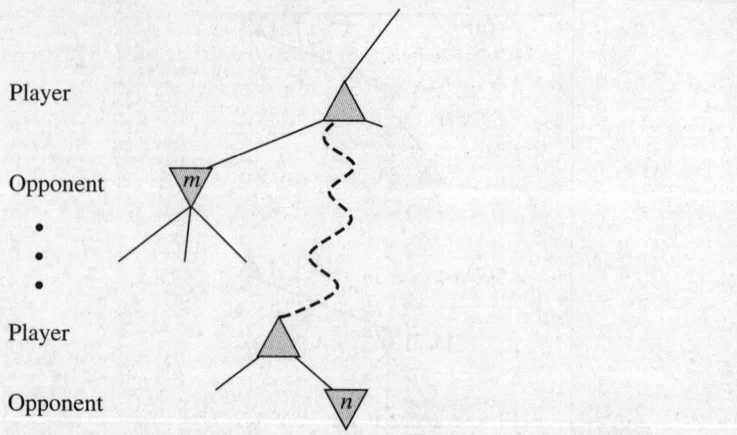

Figure 6 The general case for alpha–beta pruning. If m is better than n for Player, we will never get to n in play.

$\alpha =$ the value of the best (i.e., highest-value) choice we have found so far at any choice point along the path for MAX.

$\beta =$ the value of the best (i.e., lowest-value) choice we have found so far at any choice point along the path for MIN.

Alpha–beta search updates the values of α and β as it goes along and prunes the remaining branches at a node (i.e., terminates the recursive call) as soon as the value of the current node is known to be worse than the current α or β value for MAX or MIN, respectively. The complete algorithm is given in Figure 7. We encourage you to trace its behavior when applied to the tree in Figure 5.

3.1 Move ordering

The effectiveness of alpha–beta pruning is highly dependent on the order in which the states are examined. For example, in Figure 5(e) and (f), we could not prune any successors of D at all because the worst successors (from the point of view of MIN) were generated first. If the third successor of D had been generated first, we would have been able to prune the other two. This suggests that it might be worthwhile to try to examine first the successors that are likely to be best.

If this can be done,[2] then it turns out that alpha–beta needs to examine only $O(b^{m/2})$ nodes to pick the best move, instead of $O(b^m)$ for minimax. This means that the effective branching factor becomes $\sqrt{b}$ instead of b—for chess, about 6 instead of 35. Put another way, alpha–beta can solve a tree roughly twice as deep as minimax in the same amount of time. If successors are examined in random order rather than best-first, the total number of nodes examined will be roughly $O(b^{3m/4})$ for moderate b. For chess, a fairly simple ordering function (such as trying captures first, then threats, then forward moves, and then backward moves) gets you to within about a factor of 2 of the best-case $O(b^{m/2})$ result.

[2] Obviously, it cannot be done perfectly; otherwise, the ordering function could be used to play a perfect game!

```
function ALPHA-BETA-SEARCH(state) returns an action
  v ← MAX-VALUE(state, −∞, +∞)
  return the action in ACTIONS(state) with value v

function MAX-VALUE(state, α, β) returns a utility value
  if TERMINAL-TEST(state) then return UTILITY(state)
  v ← −∞
  for each a in ACTIONS(state) do
    v ← MAX(v, MIN-VALUE(RESULT(s,a), α, β))
    if v ≥ β then return v
    α ← MAX(α, v)
  return v

function MIN-VALUE(state, α, β) returns a utility value
  if TERMINAL-TEST(state) then return UTILITY(state)
  v ← +∞
  for each a in ACTIONS(state) do
    v ← MIN(v, MAX-VALUE(RESULT(s,a) , α, β))
    if v ≤ α then return v
    β ← MIN(β, v)
  return v
```

Figure 7 The alpha–beta search algorithm. Notice that these routines are the same as the MINIMAX functions in Figure 3, except for the two lines in each of MIN-VALUE and MAX-VALUE that maintain α and β (and the bookkeeping to pass these parameters along).

Adding dynamic move-ordering schemes, such as trying first the moves that were found to be best in the past, brings us quite close to the theoretical limit. The past could be the previous move—often the same threats remain—or it could come from previous exploration of the current move. One way to gain information from the current move is with iterative deepening search. First, search 1 ply deep and record the best path of moves. Then search 1 ply deeper, but use the recorded path to inform move ordering. Iterative deepening on an exponential game tree adds only a constant fraction to the total search time, which can be more than made up from better move ordering. The best moves are often called **Killer moves** and to try them first is called the killer move heuristic.

KILLER MOVES

Repeated states in the search tree can cause an exponential increase in search cost. In many games, repeated states occur frequently because of **transpositions**—different permutations of the move sequence that end up in the same position. For example, if White has one move, a_1, that can be answered by Black with b1 and an unrelated move a_2 on the other side of the board that can be answered by b_2, then the sequences $[a_1,b_1,a_2,b_2]$ and $[a_2,b2,a_1,b_1]$ both end up in the same position. It is worthwhile to store the evaluation of the resulting position in a hash table the first time it is encountered so that we don't have to recompute it on subsequent occurrences. The hash table of previously seen positions is traditionally called a **transposition table**. Using a transposition table can have a dramatic effect, sometimes as

TRANSPOSITION

TRANSPOSITION TABLE

much as doubling the reachable search depth in chess. On the other hand, if we are evaluating a million nodes per second, at some point it is not practical to keep all of them in the transposition table. Various strategies have been used to choose which nodes to keep and which to discard.

4 IMPERFECT REAL-TIME DECISIONS

The minimax algorithm generates the entire game search space, whereas the alpha–beta algorithm allows us to prune large parts of it. However, alpha–beta still has to search all the way to terminal states for at least a portion of the search space. This depth is usually not practical, because moves must be made in a reasonable amount of time—typically a few minutes at most. Claude Shannon's paper *Programming a Computer for Playing Chess* (1950) proposed instead that programs should cut off the search earlier and apply a heuristic **evaluation function** to states in the search, effectively turning nonterminal nodes into terminal leaves. In other words, the suggestion is to alter minimax or alpha–beta in two ways: replace the utility function by a heuristic evaluation function EVAL, which estimates the position's utility, and replace the terminal test by a **cutoff test** that decides when to apply EVAL. That gives us the following for heuristic minimax for state s and maximum depth d:

EVALUATION FUNCTION

CUTOFF TEST

$$\text{H-MINIMAX}(s,d) = \begin{cases} \text{EVAL}(s) & \text{if CUTOFF-TEST}(s,d) \\ \max_{a \in Actions(s)} \text{H-MINIMAX}(\text{RESULT}(s,a), d+1) & \text{if PLAYER}(s) = \text{MAX} \\ \min_{a \in Actions(s)} \text{H-MINIMAX}(\text{RESULT}(s,a), d+1) & \text{if PLAYER}(s) = \text{MIN}. \end{cases}$$

4.1 Evaluation functions

An evaluation function returns an *estimate* of the expected utility of the game from a given position. The idea of an estimator was not new when Shannon proposed it. For centuries, chess players (and aficionados of other games) have developed ways of judging the value of a position because humans are even more limited in the amount of search they can do than are computer programs. It should be clear that the performance of a game-playing program depends strongly on the quality of its evaluation function. An inaccurate evaluation function will guide an agent toward positions that turn out to be lost. How exactly do we design good evaluation functions?

First, the evaluation function should order the *terminal* states in the same way as the true utility function: states that are wins must evaluate better than draws, which in turn must be better than losses. Otherwise, an agent using the evaluation function might err even if it can see ahead all the way to the end of the game. Second, the computation must not take too long! (The whole point is to search faster.) Third, for nonterminal states, the evaluation function should be strongly correlated with the actual chances of winning.

One might well wonder about the phrase "chances of winning." After all, chess is not a game of chance: we know the current state with certainty, and no dice are involved. But if the search must be cut off at nonterminal states, then the algorithm will necessarily be *uncertain* about the final outcomes of those states. This type of uncertainty is induced by computational, rather than informational, limitations. Given the limited amount of computation that the evaluation function is allowed to do for a given state, the best it can do is make a guess about the final outcome.

Let us make this idea more concrete. Most evaluation functions work by calculating various **features** of the state—for example, in chess, we would have features for the number of white pawns, black pawns, white queens, black queens, and so on. The features, taken together, define various *categories* or *equivalence classes* of states: the states in each category have the same values for all the features. For example, one category contains all two-pawn vs. one-pawn endgames. Any given category, generally speaking, will contain some states that lead to wins, some that lead to draws, and some that lead to losses. The evaluation function cannot know which states are which, but it can return a single value that reflects the *proportion* of states with each outcome. For example, suppose our experience suggests that 72% of the states encountered in the two-pawns vs. one-pawn category lead to a win (utility +1); 20% to a loss (0), and 8% to a draw (1/2). Then a reasonable evaluation for states in

EXPECTED VALUE

the category is the **expected value**: $(0.72 \times +1) + (0.20 \times 0) + (0.08 \times 1/2) = 0.76$. In principle, the expected value can be determined for each category, resulting in an evaluation function that works for any state. As with terminal states, the evaluation function need not return actual expected values as long as the *ordering* of the states is the same.

In practice, this kind of analysis requires too many categories and hence too much experience to estimate all the probabilities of winning. Instead, most evaluation functions compute separate numerical contributions from each feature and then *combine* them to find

MATERIAL VALUE

the total value. For example, introductory chess books give an approximate **material value** for each piece: each pawn is worth 1, a knight or bishop is worth 3, a rook 5, and the queen 9. Other features such as "good pawn structure" and "king safety" might be worth half a pawn, say. These feature values are then simply added up to obtain the evaluation of the position.

A secure advantage equivalent to a pawn gives a substantial likelihood of winning, and a secure advantage equivalent to three pawns should give almost certain victory, as illustrated in Figure 8(a). Mathematically, this kind of evaluation function is called a **weighted linear**

WEIGHTED LINEAR FUNCTION

function because it can be expressed as

$$\text{EVAL}(s) = w_1 f_1(s) + w_2 f_2(s) + \cdots + w_n f_n(s) = \sum_{i=1}^{n} w_i f_i(s)\,,$$

where each w_i is a weight and each f_i is a feature of the position. For chess, the f_i could be the numbers of each kind of piece on the board, and the w_i could be the values of the pieces (1 for pawn, 3 for bishop, etc.).

Adding up the values of features seems like a reasonable thing to do, but in fact it involves a strong assumption: that the contribution of each feature is *independent* of the values of the other features. For example, assigning the value 3 to a bishop ignores the fact that bishops are more powerful in the endgame, when they have a lot of space to maneuver.

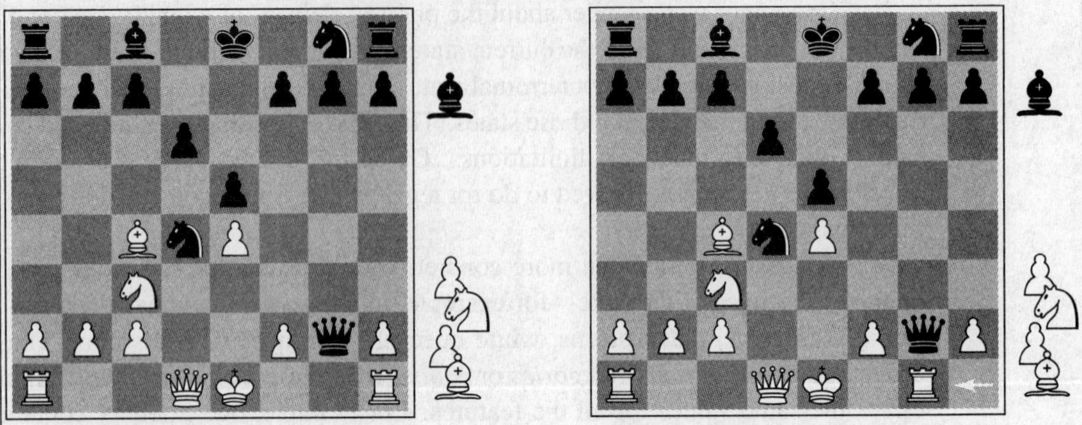

(a) White to move (b) White to move

Figure 8 Two chess positions that differ only in the position of the rook at lower right. In (a), Black has an advantage of a knight and two pawns, which should be enough to win the game. In (b), White will capture the queen, giving it an advantage that should be strong enough to win.

For this reason, current programs for chess and other games also use *nonlinear* combinations of features. For example, a pair of bishops might be worth slightly more than twice the value of a single bishop, and a bishop is worth more in the endgame (that is, when the *move number* feature is high or the *number of remaining pieces* feature is low).

The astute reader will have noticed that the features and weights are *not* part of the rules of chess! They come from centuries of human chess-playing experience. In games where this kind of experience is not available, the weights of the evaluation function can be estimated by certain machine learning techniques. Reassuringly, applying these techniques to chess has confirmed that a bishop is indeed worth about three pawns.

4.2 Cutting off search

The next step is to modify ALPHA-BETA-SEARCH so that it will call the heuristic EVAL function when it is appropriate to cut off the search. We replace the two lines in Figure 7 that mention TERMINAL-TEST with the following line:

if CUTOFF-TEST(*state*, *depth*) **then return** EVAL(*state*)

We also must arrange for some bookkeeping so that the current *depth* is incremented on each recursive call. The most straightforward approach to controlling the amount of search is to set a fixed depth limit so that CUTOFF-TEST (*state*, *depth*) returns *true* for all *depth* greater than some fixed depth d. (It must also return *true* for all terminal states, just as TERMINAL-TEST did.) The depth d is chosen so that a move is selected within the allocated time. A more robust approach is to apply iterative deepening. When time runs out, theprogram returns the move selected by the deepest completed search. As a bonus, iterative deepening also helps with move ordering.

These simple approaches can lead to errors due to the approximate nature of the evaluation function. Consider again the simple evaluation function for chess based on material advantage. Suppose the program searches to the depth limit, reaching the position in Figure 8(b), where Black is ahead by a knight and two pawns. It would report this as the heuristic value of the state, thereby declaring that the state is a probable win by Black. But White's next move captures Black's queen with no compensation. Hence, the position is really won for White, but this can be seen only by looking ahead one more ply.

QUIESCENCE

Obviously, a more sophisticated cutoff test is needed. The evaluation function should be applied only to positions that are **quiescent**—that is, unlikely to exhibit wild swings in value in the near future. In chess, for example, positions in which favorable captures can be made are not quiescent for an evaluation function that just counts material. Nonquiescent positions can be expanded further until quiescent positions are reached. This extra search is called a **quiescence search**; sometimes it is restricted to consider only certain types of moves, such as capture moves, that will quickly resolve the uncertainties in the position.

QUIESCENCE SEARCH

HORIZON EFFECT

The **horizon effect** is more difficult to eliminate. It arises when the program is facing an opponent's move that causes serious damage and is ultimately unavoidable, but can be temporarily avoided by delaying tactics. Consider the chess game in Figure 9. It is clear that there is no way for the black bishop to escape. For example, the white rook can capture it by moving to h1, then a1, then a2; a capture at depth 6 ply. But Black does have a sequence of moves that pushes the capture of the bishop "over the horizon." Suppose Black searches to depth 8 ply. Most moves by Black will lead to the eventual capture of the bishop, and thus will be marked as "bad" moves. But Black will consider checking the white king with the pawn at e4. This will lead to the king capturing the pawn. Now Black will consider checking again, with the pawn at f5, leading to another pawn capture. That takes up 4 ply, and from there the remaining 4 ply is not enough to capture the bishop. Black thinks that the line of play has saved the bishop at the price of two pawns, when actually all it has done is push the inevitable capture of the bishop beyond the horizon that Black can see.

SINGULAR EXTENSION

One strategy to mitigate the horizon effect is the **singular extension**, a move that is "clearly better" than all other moves in a given position. Once discovered anywhere in the tree in the course of a search, this singular move is remembered. When the search reaches the normal depth limit, the algorithm checks to see if the singular extension is a legal move; if it is, the algorithm allows the move to be considered. This makes the tree deeper, but because there will be few singular extensions, it does not add many total nodes to the tree.

4.3 Forward pruning

FORWARD PRUNING

So far, we have talked about cutting off search at a certain level and about doing alpha–beta pruning that provably has no effect on the result (at least with respect to the heuristic evaluation values). It is also possible to do **forward pruning**, meaning that some moves at a given node are pruned immediately without further consideration. Clearly, most humans playing chess consider only a few moves from each position (at least consciously). One approach to forward pruning is **beam search**: on each ply, consider only a "beam" of the n best moves (according to the evaluation function) rather than considering all possible moves.

BEAM SEARCH

Figure 9 The horizon effect. With Black to move, the black bishop is surely doomed. But Black can forestall that event by checking the white king with its pawns, forcing the king to capture the pawns. This pushes the inevitable loss of the bishop over the horizon, and thus the pawn sacrifices are seen by the search algorithm as good moves rather than bad ones.

Unfortunately, this approach is rather dangerous because there is no guarantee that the best move will not be pruned away.

The PROBCUT, or probabilistic cut, algorithm (Buro, 1995) is a forward-pruning version of alpha–beta search that uses statistics gained from prior experience to lessen the chance that the best move will be pruned. Alpha–beta search prunes any node that is *provably* outside the current (α, β) window. PROBCUT also prunes nodes that are *probably* outside the window. It computes this probability by doing a shallow search to compute the backed-up value v of a node and then using past experience to estimate how likely it is that a score of v at depth d in the tree would be outside (α, β). Buro applied this technique to his Othello program, LOGISTELLO, and found that a version of his program with PROBCUT beat the regular version 64% of the time, even when the regular version was given twice as much time.

Combining all the techniques described here results in a program that can play creditable chess (or other games). Let us assume we have implemented an evaluation function for chess, a reasonable cutoff test with a quiescence search, and a large transposition table. Let us also assume that, after months of tedious bit-bashing, we can generate and evaluate around a million nodes per second on the latest PC, allowing us to search roughly 200 million nodes per move under standard time controls (three minutes per move). The branching factor for chess is about 35, on average, and 35^5 is about 50 million, so if we used minimax search, we could look ahead only about five plies. Though not incompetent, such a program can be fooled easily by an average human chess player, who can occasionally plan six or eight plies ahead. With alpha–beta search we get to about 10 plies, which results in an expert level of play. Section 8 describes additional pruning techniques that can extend the effective search depth to roughly 14 plies. To reach grandmaster status we would need an extensively tuned evaluation function and a large database of optimal opening and endgame moves.

4.4 Search versus lookup

Somehow it seems like overkill for a chess program to start a game by considering a tree of a billion game states, only to conclude that it will move its pawn to e4. Books describing good play in the opening and endgame in chess have been available for about a century (Tattersall, 1911). It is not surprising, therefore, that many game-playing programs use *table lookup* rather than search for the opening and ending of games.

For the openings, the computer is mostly relying on the expertise of humans. The best advice of human experts on how to play each opening is copied from books and entered into tables for the computer's use. However, computers can also gather statistics from a database of previously played games to see which opening sequences most often lead to a win. In the early moves there are few choices, and thus much expert commentary and past games on which to draw. Usually after ten moves we end up in a rarely seen position, and the program must switch from table lookup to search.

Near the end of the game there are again fewer possible positions, and thus more chance to do lookup. But here it is the computer that has the expertise: computer analysis of endgames goes far beyond anything achieved by humans. A human can tell you the general strategy for playing a king-and-rook-versus-king (KRK) endgame: reduce the opposing king's mobility by squeezing it toward one edge of the board, using your king to prevent the opponent from escaping the squeeze. Other endings, such as king, bishop, and knight versus king (KBNK), are difficult to master and have no succinct strategy description. A computer, POLICY on the other hand, can completely *solve* the endgame by producing a **policy**, which is a mapping from every possible state to the best move in that state. Then we can just look up the best move rather than recompute it anew. How big will the KBNK lookup table be? It turns out there are 462 ways that two kings can be placed on the board without being adjacent. After the kings are placed, there are 62 empty squares for the bishop, 61 for the knight, and two possible players to move next, so there are just $462 \times 62 \times 61 \times 2 = 3,494,568$ possible RETROGRADE positions. Some of these are checkmates; mark them as such in a table. Then do a **retrograde** minimax search: reverse the rules of chess to do unmoves rather than moves. Any move by White that, no matter what move Black responds with, ends up in a position marked as a win, must also be a win. Continue this search until all 3,494,568 positions are resolved as win, loss, or draw, and you have an infallible lookup table for all KBNK endgames.

Using this technique and a *tour de force* of optimization tricks, Ken Thompson (1986, 1996) and Lewis Stiller (1992, 1996) solved all chess endgames with up to five pieces and some with six pieces, making them available on the Internet. Stiller discovered one case where a forced mate existed but required 262 moves; this caused some consternation because the rules of chess require a capture or pawn move to occur within 50 moves. Later work by Marc Bourzutschky and Yakov Konoval (Bourzutschky, 2006) solved all pawnless six-piece and some seven-piece endgames; there is a KQNKRBN endgame that with best play requires 517 moves until a capture, which then leads to a mate.

If we could extend the chess endgame tables from 6 pieces to 32, then White would know on the opening move whether it would be a win, loss, or draw. This has not happened so far for chess, but it has happened for checkers, as explained in the historical notes section.

5 STOCHASTIC GAMES

In real life, many unpredictable external events can put us into unforeseen situations. Many games mirror this unpredictability by including a random element, such as the throwing of dice. We call these **stochastic games**. Backgammon is a typical game that combines luck and skill. Dice are rolled at the beginning of a player's turn to determine the legal moves. In the backgammon position of Figure 10, for example, White has rolled a 6–5 and has four possible moves.

STOCHASTIC GAMES

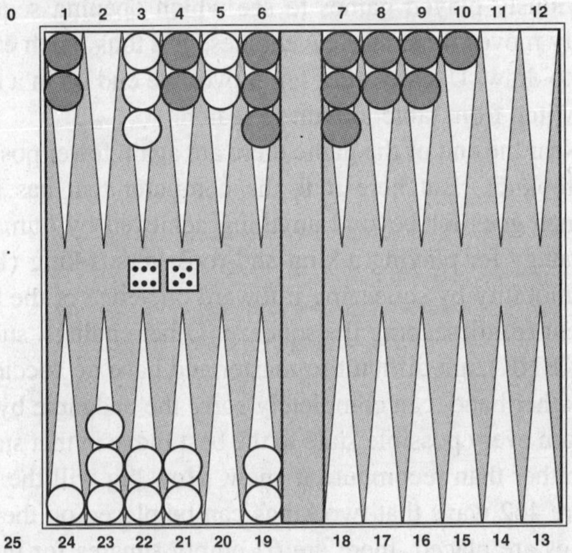

Figure 10 A typical backgammon position. The goal of the game is to move all one's pieces off the board. White moves clockwise toward 25, and Black moves counterclockwise toward 0. A piece can move to any position unless multiple opponent pieces are there; if there is one opponent, it is captured and must start over. In the position shown, White has rolled 6–5 and must choose among four legal moves: (5–10,5–11), (5–11,19–24), (5–10,10–16), and (5–11,11–16), where the notation (5–11,11–16) means move one piece from position 5 to 11, and then move a piece from 11 to 16.

Although White knows what his or her own legal moves are, White does not know what Black is going to roll and thus does not know what Black's legal moves will be. That means White cannot construct a standard game tree of the sort we saw in chess and tic-tac-toe. A game tree in backgammon must include **chance nodes** in addition to MAX and MIN nodes. Chance nodes are shown as circles in Figure 11. The branches leading from each chance node denote the possible dice rolls; each branch is labeled with the roll and its probability. There are 36 ways to roll two dice, each equally likely; but because a 6–5 is the same as a 5–6, there are only 21 distinct rolls. The six doubles (1–1 through 6–6) each have a probability of 1/36, so we say $P(1\text{–}1) = 1/36$. The other 15 distinct rolls each have a 1/18 probability.

CHANCE NODES

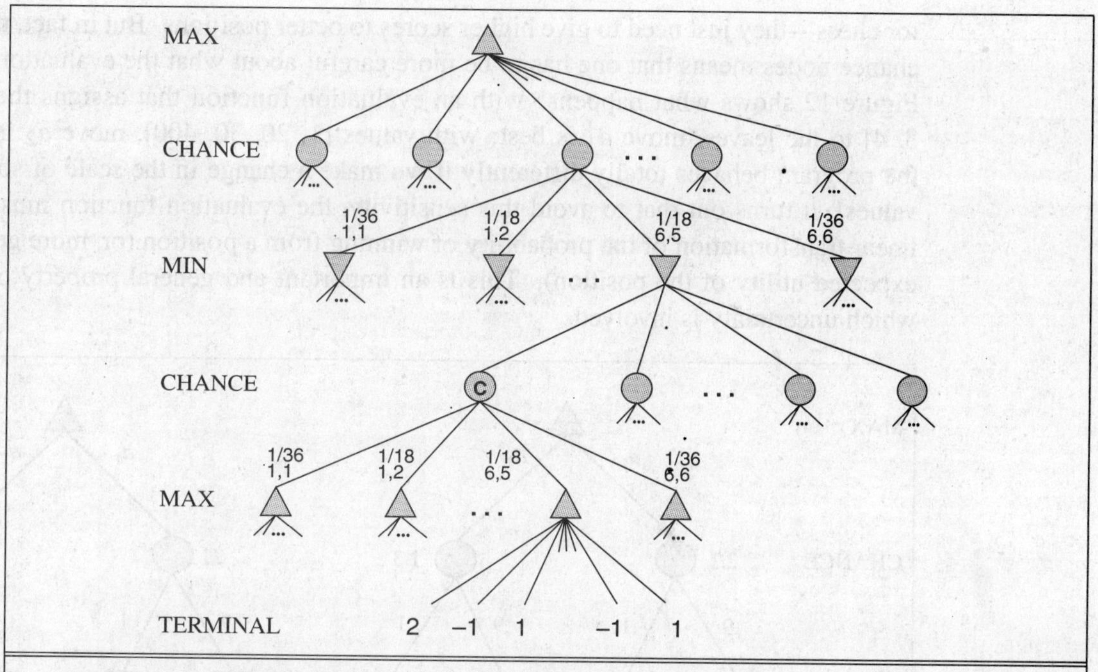

Figure 11 Schematic game tree for a backgammon position.

The next step is to understand how to make correct decisions. Obviously, we still want to pick the move that leads to the best position. However, positions do not have definite minimax values. Instead, we can only calculate the **expected value** of a position: the average over all possible outcomes of the chance nodes.

EXPECTED VALUE

This leads us to generalize the **minimax value** for deterministic games to an **expectiminimax value** for games with chance nodes. Terminal nodes and MAX and MIN nodes (for which the dice roll is known) work exactly the same way as before. For chance nodes we compute the expected value, which is the sum of the value over all outcomes, weighted by the probability of each chance action:

EXPECTIMINIMAX VALUE

$$\text{EXPECTIMINIMAX}(s) = \begin{cases} \text{UTILITY}(s) & \text{if TERMINAL-TEST}(s) \\ \max_a \text{EXPECTIMINIMAX}(\text{RESULT}(s,a)) & \text{if PLAYER}(s) = \text{MAX} \\ \min_a \text{EXPECTIMINIMAX}(\text{RESULT}(s,a)) & \text{if PLAYER}(s) = \text{MIN} \\ \sum_r P(r)\text{EXPECTIMINIMAX}(\text{RESULT}(s,r)) & \text{if PLAYER}(s) = \text{CHANCE} \end{cases}$$

where r represents a possible dice roll (or other chance event) and $\text{RESULT}(s,r)$ is the same state as s, with the additional fact that the result of the dice roll is r.

5.1 Evaluation functions for games of chance

As with minimax, the obvious approximation to make with expectiminimax is to cut the search off at some point and apply an evaluation function to each leaf. One might think that evaluation functions for games such as backgammon should be just like evaluation functions for chess—they just need to give higher scores to better positions. But in fact, the presence of chance nodes means that one has to be more careful about what the evaluation values mean. Figure 12 shows what happens: with an evaluation function that assigns the values [1, 2, 3, 4] to the leaves, move a_1 is best; with values [1, 20, 30, 400], move a_2 is best. Hence, the program behaves totally differently if we make a change in the scale of some evaluation values! It turns out that to avoid this sensitivity, the evaluation function must be a positive linear transformation of the probability of winning from a position (or, more generally, of the expected utility of the position). This is an important and general property of situations in which uncertainty is involved.

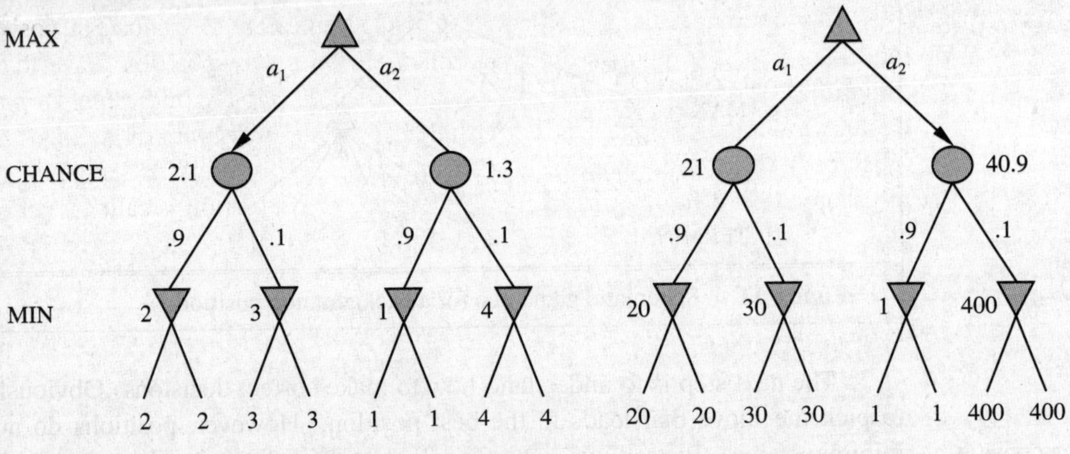

Figure 12 An order-preserving transformation on leaf values changes the best move.

If the program knew in advance all the dice rolls that would occur for the rest of the game, solving a game with dice would be just like solving a game without dice, which minimax does in $O(b^m)$ time, where b is the branching factor and m is the maximum depth of the game tree. Because expectiminimax is also considering all the possible dice-roll sequences, it will take $O(b^m n^m)$, where n is the number of distinct rolls.

Even if the search depth is limited to some small depth d, the extra cost compared with that of minimax makes it unrealistic to consider looking ahead very far in most games of chance. In backgammon n is 21 and b is usually around 20, but in some situations can be as high as 4000 for dice rolls that are doubles. Three plies is probably all we could manage.

Another way to think about the problem is this: the advantage of alpha–beta is that it ignores future developments that just are not going to happen, given best play. Thus, it concentrates on likely occurrences. In games with dice, there are *no* likely sequences of moves, because for those moves to take place, the dice would first have to come out the right way to make them legal. This is a general problem whenever uncertainty enters the picture: the possibilities are multiplied enormously, and forming detailed plans of action becomes pointless because the world probably will not play along.

It may have occurred to you that something like alpha–beta pruning could be applied to game trees with chance nodes. It turns out that it can. The analysis for MIN and MAX nodes is unchanged, but we can also prune chance nodes, using a bit of ingenuity. Consider the chance node C in Figure 11 and what happens to its value as we examine and evaluate its children. Is it possible to find an upper bound on the value of C before we have looked at all its children? (Recall that this is what alpha–beta needs in order to prune a node and its subtree.) At first sight, it might seem impossible because the value of C is the *average* of its children's values, and in order to compute the average of a set of numbers, we must look at all the numbers. But if we put bounds on the possible values of the utility function, then we can arrive at bounds for the average without looking at every number. For example, say that all utility values are between -2 and $+2$; then the value of leaf nodes is bounded, and in turn we *can* place an upper bound on the value of a chance node without looking at all its children.

MONTE CARLO SIMULATION

An alternative is to do **Monte Carlo simulation** to evaluate a position. Start with an alpha–beta (or other) search algorithm. From a start position, have the algorithm play thousands of games against itself, using random dice rolls. In the case of backgammon, the resulting win percentage has been shown to be a good approximation of the value of the position, even if the algorithm has an imperfect heuristic and is searching only a few plies (Tesauro, 1995). For games with dice, this type of simulation is called a **rollout**.

ROLLOUT

6 PARTIALLY OBSERVABLE GAMES

Chess has often been described as war in miniature, but it lacks at least one major characteristic of real wars, namely, **partial observability**. In the "fog of war," the existence and disposition of enemy units is often unknown until revealed by direct contact. As a result, warfare includes the use of scouts and spies to gather information and the use of concealment and bluff to confuse the enemy. Partially observable games share these characteristics and are thus qualitatively different from the games described in the preceding sections.

6.1 Kriegspiel: Partially observable chess

In *deterministic* partially observable games, uncertainty about the state of the board arises entirely from lack of access to the choices made by the opponent. This class includes children's games such as Battleships (where each player's ships are placed in locations hidden from the opponent but do not move) and Stratego (where piece locations are known but piece types are hidden). We will examine the game of **Kriegspiel**, a partially observable variant of chess in which pieces can move but are completely invisible to the opponent.

KRIEGSPIEL

The rules of Kriegspiel are as follows: White and Black each see a board containing only their own pieces. A referee, who can see all the pieces, adjudicates the game and periodically makes announcements that are heard by both players. On his turn, White proposes to the referee any move that would be legal if there were no black pieces. If the move is in fact not legal (because of the black pieces), the referee announces "illegal." In this case, White may keep proposing moves until a legal one is found—and learns more about the location of Black's pieces in the process. Once a legal move is proposed, the referee announces one or more of the following: "Capture on square *X*" if there is a capture, and "Check by *D*" if the black king is in check, where *D* is the direction of the check, and can be one of "Knight," "Rank," "File," "Long diagonal," or "Short diagonal." (In case of discovered check, the referee may make two "Check" announcements.) If Black is checkmated or stalemated, the referee says so; otherwise, it is Black's turn to move.

Kriegspiel may seem terrifyingly impossible, but humans manage it quite well and computer programs are beginning to catch up. It helps to recall the notion of a **belief state**—the set of all *logically possible* board states given the complete history of percepts to date. Initially, White's belief state is a singleton because Black's pieces haven't moved yet. After White makes a move and Black responds, White's belief state contains 20 positions because Black has 20 replies to any White move. Keeping track of the belief state as the game progresses is exactly the problem of **state estimation**. We can map Kriegspiel state estimation directly onto a partially observable, nondeterministic framework if we consider the opponent as the source of nondeterminism; that is, the RESULTS of White's move are composed from the (predictable) outcome of White's own move and the unpredictable outcome given by Black's reply.[3]

Given a current belief state, White may ask, "Can I win the game?" For a partially observable game, the notion of a **strategy** is altered; instead of specifying a move to make for each possible *move* the opponent might make, we need a move for every possible *percept sequence* that might be received. For Kriegspiel, a winning strategy, or **guaranteed checkmate**, is one that, for each possible percept sequence, leads to an actual checkmate for every possible board state in the current belief state, regardless of how the opponent moves. With this definition, the opponent's belief state is irrelevant—the strategy has to work even if the opponent can see all the pieces. This greatly simplifies the computation. Figure 13 shows part of a guaranteed checkmate for the KRK (king and rook against king) endgame. In this case, Black has just one piece (the king), so a belief state for White can be shown in a single board by marking each possible position of the Black king.

GUARANTEED CHECKMATE

The general AND-OR search algorithm can be applied to the belief-state space to find guaranteed checkmates. The incremental belief-state algorithm mentioned in that section often finds midgame checkmates up to depth 9—probably well beyond the abilities of human players.

In addition to guaranteed checkmates, Kriegspiel admits an entirely new concept that makes no sense in fully observable games: **probabilistic checkmate**. Such checkmates are still required to work in every board state in the belief state; they are probabilistic with respect to randomization of the winning player's moves. To get the basic idea, consider the problem of finding a lone black king using just the white king. Simply by moving randomly, the white king will *eventually* bump into the black king even if the latter tries to avoid this fate, since Black cannot keep guessing the right evasive moves indefinitely. In the terminology of probability theory, detection occurs *with probability* 1. The KBNK endgame—king, bishop

PROBABILISTIC CHECKMATE

[3] Sometimes, the belief state will become too large to represent just as a list of board states, but we will ignore this issue for now.

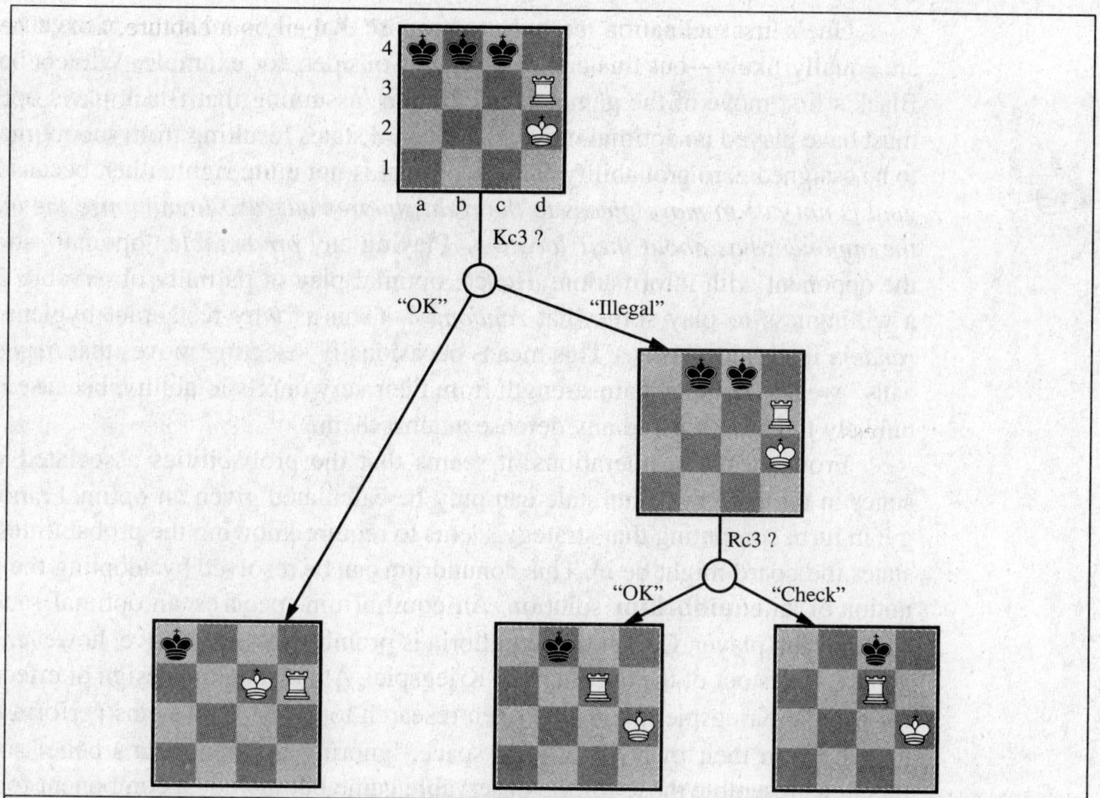

Figure 13 Part of a guaranteed checkmate in the KRK endgame, shown on a reduced board. In the initial belief state, Black's king is in one of three possible locations. By a combination of probing moves, the strategy narrows this down to one. Completion of the checkmate is left as an exercise.

and knight against king—is won in this sense; White presents Black with an infinite random sequence of choices, for one of which Black will guess incorrectly and reveal his position, leading to checkmate. The KBBK endgame, on the other hand, is won with probability $1 - \epsilon$. White can force a win only by leaving one of his bishops unprotected for one move. If Black happens to be in the right place and captures the bishop (a move that would lose if the bishops are protected), the game is drawn. White can choose to make the risky move at some randomly chosen point in the middle of a very long sequence, thus reducing ϵ to an arbitrarily small constant, but cannot reduce ϵ to zero.

It is quite rare that a guaranteed or probabilistic checkmate can be found within any reasonable depth, except in the endgame. Sometimes a checkmate strategy works for *some* of the board states in the current belief state but not others. Trying such a strategy may succeed, leading to an **accidental checkmate**—accidental in the sense that White could not *know* that it would be checkmate—if Black's pieces happen to be in the right places. (Most checkmates in games between humans are of this accidental nature.) This idea leads naturally to the question of *how likely* it is that a given strategy will win, which leads in turn to the question of *how likely* it is that each board state in the current belief state is the true board state.

ACCIDENTAL CHECKMATE

One's first inclination might be to propose that all board states in the current belief state are equally likely—but this can't be right. Consider, for example, White's belief state after Black's first move of the game. By definition (assuming that Black plays optimally), Black must have played an optimal move, so all board states resulting from suboptimal moves ought to be assigned zero probability. This argument is not quite right either, because *each player's goal is not just to move pieces to the right squares but also to minimize the information that the opponent has about their location.* Playing any *predictable* "optimal" strategy provides the opponent with information. Hence, optimal play in partially observable games requires a willingness to play somewhat *randomly*. (This is why restaurant hygiene inspectors do *random* inspection visits.) This means occasionally selecting moves that may seem "intrinsically" weak—but they gain strength from their very unpredictability, because the opponent is unlikely to have prepared any defense against them.

From these considerations, it seems that the probabilities associated with the board states in the current belief state can only be calculated given an optimal randomized strategy; in turn, computing that strategy seems to require knowing the probabilities of the various states the board might be in. This conundrum can be resolved by adopting the game-theoretic notion of an **equilibrium** solution. An equilibrium specifies an optimal randomized strategy for each player. Computing equilibria is prohibitively expensive, however, even for small games, and is out of the question for Kriegspiel. At present, the design of effective algorithms for general Kriegspiel play is an open research topic. Most systems perform bounded-depth lookahead in their own belief-state space, ignoring the opponent's belief state. Evaluation functions resemble those for the observable game but include a component for the size of the belief state—smaller is better!

6.2 Card games

Card games provide many examples of *stochastic* partial observability, where the missing information is generated randomly. For example, in many games, cards are dealt randomly at the beginning of the game, with each player receiving a hand that is not visible to the other players. Such games include bridge, whist, hearts, and some forms of poker.

At first sight, it might seem that these card games are just like dice games: the cards are dealt randomly and determine the moves available to each player, but all the "dice" are rolled at the beginning! Even though this analogy turns out to be incorrect, it suggests an effective algorithm: consider all possible deals of the invisible cards; solve each one as if it were a fully observable game; and then choose the move that has the best outcome averaged over all the deals. Suppose that each deal s occurs with probability $P(s)$; then the move we want is

$$\operatorname*{argmax}_{a} \sum_{s} P(s)\,\text{MINIMAX}(\text{RESULT}(s,a))\,. \qquad (1)$$

Here, we run exact MINIMAX if computationally feasible; otherwise, we run H-MINIMAX.

Now, in most card games, the number of possible deals is rather large. For example, in bridge play, each player sees just two of the four hands; there are two unseen hands of 13 cards each, so the number of deals is $\binom{26}{13} = 10,400,600$. Solving even one deal is quite difficult, so solving ten million is out of the question. Instead, we resort to a Monte Carlo approximation: instead of adding up *all* the deals, we take a *random sample* of N deals, where the probability of deal s appearing in the sample is proportional to $P(s)$:

$$\underset{a}{\operatorname{argmax}} \frac{1}{N} \sum_{i=1}^{N} \text{MINIMAX}(\text{RESULT}(s_i, a)) . \tag{2}$$

(Notice that $P(s)$ does not appear explicitly in the summation, because the samples are already drawn according to $P(s)$.) As N grows large, the sum over the random sample tends to the exact value, but even for fairly small N—say, 100 to 1,000—the method gives a good approximation. It can also be applied to deterministic games such as Kriegspiel, given some reasonable estimate of $P(s)$.

For games like whist and hearts, where there is no bidding or betting phase before play commences, each deal will be equally likely and so the values of $P(s)$ are all equal. For bridge, play is preceded by a bidding phase in which each team indicates how many tricks it expects to win. Since players bid based on the cards they hold, the other players learn more about the probability of each deal. Taking this into account in deciding how to play the hand is tricky, for the reasons mentioned in our description of Kriegspiel: players may bid in such a way as to minimize the information conveyed to their opponents. Even so, the approach is quite effective for bridge, as we show in Section 7.

The strategy described in Equations 1 and 2 is sometimes called *averaging over clairvoyance* because it assumes that the game will become observable to both players immediately after the first move. Despite its intuitive appeal, the strategy can lead one astray. Consider the following story:

> Day 1: Road A leads to a heap of gold; Road B leads to a fork. Take the left fork and you'll find a bigger heap of gold, but take the right fork and you'll be run over by a bus.
> Day 2: Road A leads to a heap of gold; Road B leads to a fork. Take the right fork and you'll find a bigger heap of gold, but take the left fork and you'll be run over by a bus.
> Day 3: Road A leads to a heap of gold; Road B leads to a fork. One branch of the fork leads to a bigger heap of gold, but take the wrong fork and you'll be hit by a bus. Unfortunately you don't know which fork is which.

Averaging over clairvoyance leads to the following reasoning: on Day 1, B is the right choice; on Day 2, B is the right choice; on Day 3, the situation is the same as either Day 1 or Day 2, so B must still be the right choice.

Now we can see how averaging over clairvoyance fails: it does not consider the *belief state* that the agent will be in after acting. A belief state of total ignorance is not desirable, especially when one possibility is certain death. Because it assumes that every future state will automatically be one of perfect knowledge, the approach never selects actions that *gather information* (like the first move in Figure 13); nor will it choose actions that hide information from the opponent or provide information to a partner because it assumes that they already know the information; and it will never **bluff** in poker,[4] because it assumes the opponent can see its cards.

BLUFF

[4] Bluffing—betting as if one's hand is good, even when it's not—is a core part of poker strategy.

7 State-of-the-Art Game Programs

In 1965, the Russian mathematician Alexander Kronrod called chess "the *Drosophila* of artificial intelligence." John McCarthy disagrees: whereas geneticists use fruit flies to make discoveries that apply to biology more broadly, AI has used chess to do the equivalent of breeding very fast fruit flies. Perhaps a better analogy is that chess is to AI as Grand Prix motor racing is to the car industry: state-of-the-art game programs are blindingly fast, highly optimized machines that incorporate the latest engineering advances, but they aren't much use for doing the shopping or driving off-road. Nonetheless, racing and game-playing generate excitement and a steady stream of innovations that have been adopted by the wider community. In this section we look at what it takes to come out on top in various games.

CHESS

Chess: IBM's DEEP BLUE chess program, now retired, is well known for defeating world champion Garry Kasparov in a widely publicized exhibition match. Deep Blue ran on a parallel computer with 30 IBM RS/6000 processors doing alpha–beta search. The unique part was a configuration of 480 custom VLSI chess processors that performed move generation and move ordering for the last few levels of the tree, and evaluated the leaf nodes. Deep Blue searched up to 30 billion positions per move, reaching depth 14 routinely. The key to its success seems to have been its ability to generate singular extensions beyond the depth limit for sufficiently interesting lines of forcing/forced moves. In some cases the search reached a depth of 40 plies. The evaluation function had over 8000 features, many of them describing highly specific patterns of pieces. An "opening book" of about 4000 positions was used, as well as a database of 700,000 grandmaster games from which consensus recommendations could be extracted. The system also used a large endgame database of solved positions containing all positions with five pieces and many with six pieces. This database had the effect of substantially extending the effective search depth, allowing Deep Blue to play perfectly in some cases even when it was many moves away from checkmate.

The success of DEEP BLUE reinforced the widely held belief that progress in computer game-playing has come primarily from ever-more-powerful hardware—a view encouraged by IBM. But algorithmic improvements have allowed programs running on standard PCs to win World Computer Chess Championships. A variety of pruning heuristics are used to reduce the effective branching factor to less than 3 (compared with the actual branching factor

NULL MOVE

of about 35). The most important of these is the **null move** heuristic, which generates a good lower bound on the value of a position, using a shallow search in which the opponent gets to move twice at the beginning. This lower bound often allows alpha–beta pruning without

FUTILITY PRUNING

the expense of a full-depth search. Also important is **futility pruning**, which helps decide in advance which moves will cause a beta cutoff in the successor nodes.

HYDRA can be seen as the successor to DEEP BLUE. HYDRA runs on a 64-processor cluster with 1 gigabyte per processor and with custom hardware in the form of FPGA (Field Programmable Gate Array) chips. HYDRA reaches 200 million evaluations per second, about the same as Deep Blue, but HYDRA reaches 18 plies deep rather than just 14 because of aggressive use of the null move heuristic and forward pruning.

RYBKA, winner of the 2008 and 2009 World Computer Chess Championships, is considered the strongest current computer player. It uses an off-the-shelf 8-core 3.2 GHz Intel Xeon processor, but little is known about the design of the program. RYBKA's main advantage appears to be its evaluation function, which has been tuned by its main developer, International Master Vasik Rajlich, and at least three other grandmasters.

The most recent matches suggest that the top computer chess programs have pulled ahead of all human contenders. (See the historical notes for details.)

CHECKERS

Checkers: Jonathan Schaeffer and colleagues developed CHINOOK, which runs on regular PCs and uses alpha–beta search. Chinook defeated the long-running human champion in an abbreviated match in 1990, and since 2007 CHINOOK has been able to play perfectly by using alpha–beta search combined with a database of 39 trillion endgame positions.

OTHELLO

Othello, also called Reversi, is probably more popular as a computer game than as a board game. It has a smaller search space than chess, usually 5 to 15 legal moves, but evaluation expertise had to be developed from scratch. In 1997, the LOGISTELLO program (Buro, 2002) defeated the human world champion, Takeshi Murakami, by six games to none. It is generally acknowledged that humans are no match for computers at Othello.

BACKGAMMON

Backgammon: Section 5 explained why the inclusion of uncertainty from dice rolls makes deep search an expensive luxury. Most work on backgammon has gone into improving the evaluation function. Gerry Tesauro (1992) combined reinforcement learning with neural networks to develop a remarkably accurate evaluator that is used with a search to depth 2 or 3. After playing more than a million training games against itself, Tesauro's program, TD-GAMMON, is competitive with top human players. The program's opinions on the opening moves of the game have in some cases radically altered the received wisdom.

GO

Go is the most popular board game in Asia. Because the board is 19×19 and moves are allowed into (almost) every empty square, the branching factor starts at 361, which is too daunting for regular alpha–beta search methods. In addition, it is difficult to write an evaluation function because control of territory is often very unpredictable until the endgame. Therefore the top programs, such as MOGO, avoid alpha–beta search and instead use Monte Carlo rollouts. The trick is to decide what moves to make in the course of the rollout. There is no aggressive pruning; all moves are possible. The UCT (upper confidence bounds on trees) method works by making random moves in the first few iterations, and over time guiding the sampling process to prefer moves that have led to wins in previous samples. Some tricks are added, including *knowledge-based rules* that suggest particular moves whenever a given pattern is detected and *limited local search* to decide tactical questions. Some programs also include special techniques from **combinatorial game theory** to analyze endgames. These techniques decompose a position into sub-positions that can be analyzed separately and then combined (Berlekamp and Wolfe, 1994; Müller, 2003). The optimal solutions obtained in this way have surprised many professional Go players, who thought they had been playing optimally all along. Current Go programs play at the master level on a reduced 9×9 board, but are still at advanced amateur level on a full board.

COMBINATORIAL GAME THEORY

BRIDGE

Bridge is a card game of imperfect information: a player's cards are hidden from the other players. Bridge is also a *multiplayer* game with four players instead of two, although the players are paired into two teams. As in Section 6, optimal play in partially observable games like bridge can include elements of information gathering, communication, and careful weighing of probabilities. Many of these techniques are used in the Bridge Baron program (Smith *et al.*, 1998), which won the 1997 computer bridge championship. While it does not play optimally, Bridge Baron is one of the few successful game-playing systems to use complex, hierarchical plans involving high-level ideas, such as **finessing** and **squeezing**, that are familiar to bridge players.

The GIB program (Ginsberg, 1999) won the 2000 computer bridge championship quite decisively using the Monte Carlo method. Since then, other winning programs have followed GIB's lead. GIB's major innovation is using **explanation-based generalization** to compute and cache general rules for optimal play in various standard classes of situations rather than evaluating each situation individually. For example, in a situation where one player has the cards A-K-Q-J-4-3-2 of one suit and another player has 10-9-8-7-6-5, there are $7 \times 6 = 42$ ways that the first player can lead from that suit and the second player can follow. But GIB treats these situations as just two: the first player can lead either a high card or a low card; the exact cards played don't matter. With this optimization (and a few others), GIB can solve a 52-card, fully observable deal *exactly* in about a second. GIB's tactical accuracy makes up for its inability to reason about information. It finished 12th in a field of 35 in the par contest (involving just play of the hand, not bidding) at the 1998 human world championship, far exceeding the expectations of many human experts.

EXPLANATION-BASED GENERALIZATION

There are several reasons why GIB plays at expert level with Monte Carlo simulation, whereas Kriegspiel programs do not. First, GIB's evaluation of the fully observable version of the game is exact, searching the full game tree, while Kriegspiel programs rely on inexact heuristics. But far more important is the fact that in bridge, most of the uncertainty in the partially observable information comes from the randomness of the deal, not from the adversarial play of the opponent. Monte Carlo simulation handles randomness well, but does not always handle strategy well, especially when the strategy involves the value of information.

SCRABBLE

Scrabble: Most people think the hard part about Scrabble is coming up with good words, but given the official dictionary, it turns out to be rather easy to program a move generator to find the highest-scoring move (Gordon, 1994). That doesn't mean the game is solved, however: merely taking the top-scoring move each turn results in a good but not expert player. The problem is that Scrabble is both partially observable and stochastic: you don't know what letters the other player has or what letters you will draw next. So playing Scrabble well combines the difficulties of backgammon and bridge. Nevertheless, in 2006, the QUACKLE program defeated the former world champion, David Boys, 3–2.

8 ALTERNATIVE APPROACHES

Because calculating optimal decisions in games is intractable in most cases, all algorithms must make some assumptions and approximations. The standard approach, based on minimax, evaluation functions, and alpha–beta, is just one way to do this. Probably because it has

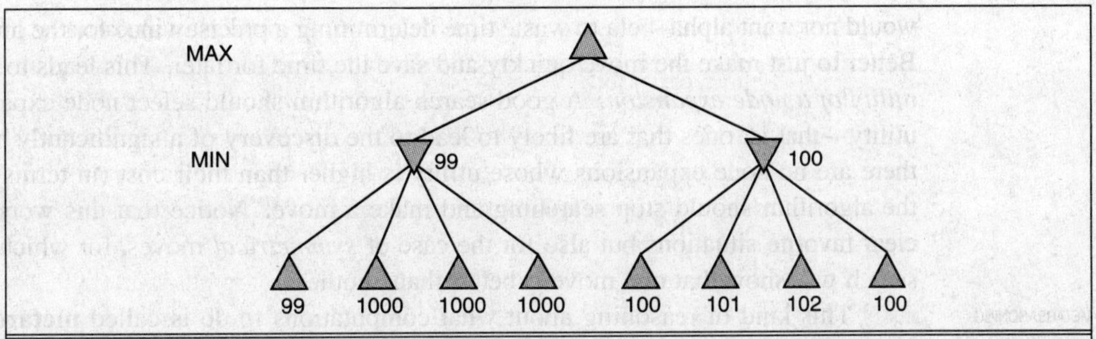

Figure 14 A two-ply game tree for which heuristic minimax may make an error.

been worked on for so long, the standard approach dominates other methods in tournament play. Some believe that this has caused game playing to become divorced from the mainstream of AI research: the standard approach no longer provides much room for new insight into general questions of decision making. In this section, we look at the alternatives.

First, let us consider heuristic minimax. It selects an optimal move in a given search tree *provided that the leaf node evaluations are exactly correct.* In reality, evaluations are usually crude estimates of the value of a position and can be considered to have large errors associated with them. Figure 14 shows a two-ply game tree for which minimax suggests taking the right-hand branch because $100 > 99$. That is the correct move if the evaluations are all correct. But of course the evaluation function is only approximate. Suppose that the evaluation of each node has an error that is independent of other nodes and is randomly distributed with mean zero and standard deviation of σ. Then when $\sigma = 5$, the left-hand branch is actually better 71% of the time, and 58% of the time when $\sigma = 2$. The intuition behind this is that the right-hand branch has four nodes that are close to 99; if an error in the evaluation of any one of the four makes the right-hand branch slip below 99, then the left-hand branch is better.

In reality, circumstances are actually worse than this because the error in the evaluation function is *not* independent. If we get one node wrong, the chances are high that nearby nodes in the tree will also be wrong. The fact that the node labeled 99 has siblings labeled 1000 suggests that in fact it might have a higher true value. We can use an evaluation function that returns a probability distribution over possible values, but it is difficult to combine these distributions properly, because we won't have a good model of the very strong dependencies that exist between the values of sibling nodes

Next, we consider the search algorithm that generates the tree. The aim of an algorithm designer is to specify a computation that runs quickly and yields a good move. The alpha–beta algorithm is designed not just to select a good move but also to calculate bounds on the values of all the legal moves. To see why this extra information is unnecessary, consider a position in which there is only one legal move. Alpha–beta search still will generate and evaluate a large search tree, telling us that the only move is the best move and assigning it a value. But since we have to make the move anyway, knowing the move's value is useless. Similarly, if there is one obviously good move and several moves that are legal but lead to a quick loss, we would not want alpha–beta to waste time determining a precise value for the lone good move. Better to just make the move quickly and save the time for later. This leads to the idea of the *utility of a node expansion*. A good search algorithm should select node expansions of high utility—that is, ones that are likely to lead to the discovery of a significantly better move. If there are no node expansions whose utility is higher than their cost (in terms of time), then the algorithm should stop searching and make a move. Notice that this works not only for clear-favorite situations but also for the case of *symmetrical* moves, for which no amount of search will show that one move is better than another.

METAREASONING This kind of reasoning about what computations to do is called **metareasoning** (reasoning about reasoning). It applies not just to game playing but to any kind of reasoning at all. All computations are done in the service of trying to reach better decisions, all have costs, and all have some likelihood of resulting in a certain improvement in decision quality. Alpha–beta incorporates the simplest kind of metareasoning, namely, a theorem to the effect that certain branches of the tree can be ignored without loss. It is possible to do much better.

Finally, let us reexamine the nature of search itself. Algorithms for heuristic search and for game playing generate sequences of concrete states, starting from the initial state and then applying an evaluation function. Clearly, this is not how humans play games. In chess, one often has a particular goal in mind—for example, trapping the opponent's queen—and can use this goal to *selectively* generate plausible plans for achieving it. This kind of goal-directed reasoning or planning sometimes eliminates combinatorial search altogether. David Wilkins' (1980) PARADISE is the only program to have used goal-directed reasoning successfully in chess: it was capable of solving some chess problems requiring an 18-move combination. As yet there is no good understanding of how to *combine* the two kinds of algorithms into a robust and efficient system, although Bridge Baron might be a step in the right direction. A fully integrated system would be a significant achievement not just for game-playing research but also for AI research in general, because it would be a good basis for a general intelligent agent.

9 SUMMARY

We have looked at a variety of games to understand what optimal play means and to understand how to play well in practice. The most important ideas are as follows:

- A game can be defined by the **initial state** (how the board is set up), the legal **actions** in each state, the **result** of each action, a **terminal test** (which says when the game is over), and a **utility function** that applies to terminal states.
- In two-player zero-sum games with **perfect information**, the **minimax** algorithm can select optimal moves by a depth-first enumeration of the game tree.
- The **alpha–beta** search algorithm computes the same optimal move as minimax, but achieves much greater efficiency by eliminating subtrees that are provably irrelevant.
- Usually, it is not feasible to consider the whole game tree (even with alpha–beta), so we

need to cut the search off at some point and apply a heuristic **evaluation function** that estimates the utility of a state.

- Many game programs precompute tables of best moves in the opening and endgame so that they can look up a move rather than search.
- Games of chance can be handled by an extension to the minimax algorithm that evaluates a **chance node** by taking the average utility of all its children, weighted by the probability of each child.
- Optimal play in games of **imperfect information**, such as Kriegspiel and bridge, requires reasoning about the current and future **belief states** of each player. A simple approximation can be obtained by averaging the value of an action over each possible configuration of missing information.
- Programs have bested even champion human players at games such as chess, checkers, and Othello. Humans retain the edge in several games of imperfect information, such as poker, bridge, and Kriegspiel, and in games with very large branching factors and little good heuristic knowledge, such as Go.

Bibliographical and Historical Notes

The early history of mechanical game playing was marred by numerous frauds. The most notorious of these was Baron Wolfgang von Kempelen's (1734–1804) "The Turk," a supposed chess-playing automaton that defeated Napoleon before being exposed as a magician's trick cabinet housing a human chess expert (see Levitt, 2000). It played from 1769 to 1854. In 1846, Charles Babbage (who had been fascinated by the Turk) appears to have contributed the first serious discussion of the feasibility of computer chess and checkers (Morrison and Morrison, 1961). He did not understand the exponential complexity of search trees, claiming "the combinations involved in the Analytical Engine enormously surpassed any required, even by the game of chess." Babbage also designed, but did not build, a special-purpose machine for playing tic-tac-toe. The first true game-playing machine was built around 1890 by the Spanish engineer Leonardo Torres y Quevedo. It specialized in the "KRK" (king and rook vs. king) chess endgame, guaranteeing a win with king and rook from any position.

The minimax algorithm is traced to a 1912 paper by Ernst Zermelo, the developer of modern set theory. The paper unfortunately contained several errors and did not describe minimax correctly. On the other hand, it did lay out the ideas of retrograde analysis and proposed (but did not prove) what became known as Zermelo's theorem: that chess is determined—White can force a win or Black can or it is a draw; we just don't know which. Zermelo says that should we eventually know, "Chess would of course lose the character of a game at all." A solid foundation for game theory was developed in the seminal work *Theory of Games and Economic Behavior* (von Neumann and Morgenstern, 1944), which included an analysis showing that some games *require* strategies that are randomized (or otherwise unpredictable).

John McCarthy conceived the idea of alpha–beta search in 1956, although he did not publish it. The NSS chess program (Newell *et al.*, 1958) used a simplified version of alpha–beta; it was the first chess program to do so. Alpha–beta pruning was described by Hart and Edwards (1961) and Hart *et al.* (1972). Alpha–beta was used by the "Kotok–McCarthy" chess program written by a student of John McCarthy (Kotok, 1962). Knuth and Moore (1975) proved the correctness of alpha–beta and analysed its time complexity. Pearl (1982b) shows alpha–beta to be asymptotically optimal among all fixed-depth game-tree search algorithms.

Several attempts have been made to overcome the problems with the "standard approach" that were outlined in Section 8. The first nonexhaustive heuristic search algorithm with some theoretical grounding was probably B* (Berliner, 1979), which attempts to maintain interval bounds on the possible value of a node in the game tree rather than giving it a single point-valued estimate. Leaf nodes are selected for expansion in an attempt to reffne the top-level bounds until one move is "clearly best." Palay (1985) extends the B* idea using probability distributions on values in place of intervals. David McAllester's (1988) conspiracy number search expands leaf nodes that, by changing their values, could cause the program to prefer a new move at the root. MGSS* (Russell and Wefald, 1989) uses decision-theoretic techniques to estimate the value of expanding each leaf in terms of the expected improvement in decision quality at the root. It outplayed an alpha–beta algorithm at Othello despite searching an order of magnitude fewer nodes. The MGSS* approach is, in principle, applicable to the control of any form of deliberation.

Alpha–beta search is in many ways the two-player analog of depth-first branch-and-bound, which is dominated by A* in the single-agent case. The SSS* algorithm (Stockman, 1979) can be viewed as a two-player A* and never expands more nodes than alpha–beta to reach the same decision. The memory requirements and computational overhead of the queue make SSS* in its original form impractical, but a linear-space version has been developed from the RBFS algorithm (Korf and Chickering, 1996). Plaat *et al.* (1996) developed a new view of SSS* as a combination of alpha–beta and transposition tables, showing how to overcome the drawbacks of the original algorithm and developing a new variant called MTD(*f*) that has been adopted by a number of top programs.

D. F. Beal (1980) and Dana Nau (1980, 1983) studied the weaknesses of minimax applied to approximate evaluations. They showed that under certain assumptions about the distribution of leaf values in the tree, minimaxing can yield values at the root that are actually *less* reliable than the direct use of the evaluation function itself. Pearl's book *Heuristics* (1984) partially explains this apparent paradox and analyzes many game-playing algorithms. Baum and Smith (1997) propose a probability-based replacement for minimax, showing that it results in better choices in certain games. The expectiminimax algorithm was proposed by Donald Michie (1966). Bruce Ballard (1983) extended alpha–beta pruning to cover trees with chance nodes and Hauk (2004) reexamines this work and provides empirical results.

Koller and Pfeffer (1997) describe a system for completely solving partially observable games. The system is quite general, handling games whose optimal strategy requires randomized moves and games that are more complex than those handled by any previous system. Still, it can't handle games as complex as poker, bridge, and Kriegspiel. Frank *et al.* (1998) describe several variants of Monte Carlo search, including one where MIN has complete information but MAX does not. Among deterministic, partially observable games, Kriegspiel has received the most attention. Ferguson demonstrated hand-derived randomized strategies for winning Kriegspiel with a bishop and knight (1992) or two bishops (1995) against a king. The first Kriegspiel programs concentrated on finding endgame checkmates and performed AND–OR search in belief-state space (Sakuta and Iida, 2002; Bolognesi and Ciancarini, 2003). Incremental belief-state algorithms enabled much more complex midgame checkmates to be found (Russell and Wolfe, 2005; Wolfe and Russell, 2007), but efficient state estimation remains the primary obstacle to effective general play (Parker *et al.*, 2005).

Chess was one of the first tasks undertaken in AI, with early efforts by many of the pioneers of computing, including Konrad Zuse in 1945, Norbert Wiener in his book *Cybernetics* (1948), and Alan Turing in 1950 (see Turing *et al.*, 1953). But it was Claude Shannon's article *Programming a Computer for Playing Chess* (1950) that had the most complete set of ideas, describing a representation for board positions, an evaluation function, quiescence search, and some ideas for selective (nonexhaustive) game-tree search. Slater (1950) and the commentators on his article also explored the possibilities for computer chess play.

D. G. Prinz (1952) completed a program that solved chess endgame problems but did not play a full game. Stan Ulam and a group at the Los Alamos National Lab produced a program that played chess on a 6×6 board with no bishops (Kister *et al.*, 1957). It could search 4 plies deep in about 12 minutes. Alex Bernstein wrote the first documented program to play a full game of standard chess (Bernstein and Roberts, 1958).[5]

The first computer chess match featured the Kotok–McCarthy program from MIT (Kotok, 1962) and the ITEP program written in the mid-1960s at Moscow's Institute of Theoretical and Experimental Physics (Adelson-Velsky *et al.*, 1970). This intercontinental match was played by telegraph. It ended with a 3–1 victory for the ITEP program in 1967. The first chess program to compete successfully with humans was MIT's MACHACK-6 (Greenblatt *et al.*, 1967). Its Elo rating of approximately 1400 was well above the novice level of 1000.

The Fredkin Prize, established in 1980, offered awards for progressive milestones in chess play. The $5,000 prize for the first program to achieve a master rating went to BELLE (Condon and Thompson, 1982), which achieved a rating of 2250. The $10,000 prize for the first program to achieve a USCF (United States Chess Federation) rating of 2500 (near the grandmaster level) was awarded to DEEP THOUGHT (Hsu *et al.*, 1990) in 1989. The grand prize, $100,000, went to DEEP BLUE (Campbell *et al.*, 2002; Hsu, 2004) for its landmark victory over world champion Garry Kasparov in a 1997 exhibition match. Kasparov wrote:

> The decisive game of the match was Game 2, which left a scar in my memory ... we saw something that went well beyond our wildest expectations of how well a computer would be able to foresee the long-term positional consequences of its decisions. The machine refused to move to a position that had a decisive short-term advantage—showing a very human sense of danger. (Kasparov, 1997)

Probably the most complete description of a modern chess program is provided by Ernst Heinz (2000), whose DARKTHOUGHT program was the highest-ranked noncommercial PC program at the 1999 world championships.

[5] A Russian program, BESM may have predated Bernstein's program.

(a) (b)

Figure 15 Pioneers in computer chess: (a) Herbert Simon and Allen Newell, developers of the NSS program (1958); (b) John McCarthy and the Kotok–McCarthy program on an IBM 7090 (1967).

In recent years, chess programs are pulling ahead of even the world's best humans. In 2004–2005 HYDRA defeated grand master Evgeny Vladimirov 3.5–0.5, world champion Ruslan Ponomariov 2–0, and seventh-ranked Michael Adams 5.5–0.5. In 2006, DEEP FRITZ beat world champion Vladimir Kramnik 4–2, and in 2007 RYBKA defeated several grand masters in games in which it gave odds (such as a pawn) to the human players. As of 2009, the highest Elo rating ever recorded was Kasparov's 2851. HYDRA (Donninger and Lorenz, 2004) is rated somewhere between 2850 and 3000, based mostly on its trouncing of Michael Adams. The RYBKA program is rated between 2900 and 3100, but this is based on a small number of games and is not considered reliable. Ross (2004) shows how human players have learned to exploit some of the weaknesses of the computer programs.

Checkers was the first of the classic games fully played by a computer. Christopher Strachey (1952) wrote the first working program for checkers. Beginning in 1952, Arthur Samuel of IBM, working in his spare time, developed a checkers program that learned its own evaluation function by playing itself thousands of times (Samuel, 1959, 1967). Samuel's program began as a novice but after only a few days' self-play had improved itself beyond Samuel's own level. In 1962 it defeated Robert Nealy, a champion at "blind checkers," through an error on his part. When one considers that Samuel's computing equipment (an IBM 704) had 10,000 words of main memory, magnetic tape for long-term storage, and a .000001 GHz processor, the win remains a great accomplishment.

The challenge started by Samuel was taken up by Jonathan Schaeffer of the University of Alberta. His CHINOOK program came in second in the 1990 U.S. Open and earned the right to challenge for the world championship. It then ran up against a problem, in the form of Marion Tinsley. Dr. Tinsley had been world champion for over 40 years, losing only three games in all that time. In the first match against CHINOOK, Tinsley suffered his fourth and fifth losses, but won the match 20.5–18.5. A rematch at the 1994 world championship ended prematurely when Tinsley had to withdraw for health reasons. CHINOOK became the official world champion. Schaeffer kept on building on his database of endgames, and in 2007 "solved" checkers (Schaeffer*et al.*, 2007; Schaeffer, 2008). This had been predicted by Richard Bellman (1965). In the paper that introduced the dynamic programming approach to retrograde analysis, he wrote, "In checkers, the number of possible moves in any given situation is so small that we confidently expect a complete digital computer solution to the problem of optimal play in this game." Bellman did not, however, fully appreciate the size of the checkers game tree. There are about 500 quadrillion positions. After 18 years of computation on a cluster of 50 or more machines, Jonathan Schaeffer's team completed an endgame table for all checkers positions with 10 or fewer pieces: over 39 trillion entries. From there, they were able to do forward alpha–beta search to derive a policy that proves that checkers is in fact a draw with best play by both sides. Note that this is an application of bidirectional search. Building an endgame table for all of checkers would be impractical: it would require a billion gigabytes of storage. Searching without any table would also be impractical: the search tree has about 8^{47} positions, and would take thousands of years to search with today's technology. Only a combination of clever search, endgame data, and a drop in the price of processors and memory could solve checkers. Thus, checkers joins Qubic (Patashnik, 1980), Connect Four (Allis, 1988), and Nine-Men's Morris (Gasser, 1998) as games that have been solved by computer analysis.

Backgammon, a game of chance, was analyzed mathematically by Gerolamo Cardano (1663), but only taken up for computer play in the late 1970s, first with the BKG program (Berliner, 1980b); it used a complex, manually constructed evaluation function and searched only to depth 1. It was the first program to defeat a human world champion at a major classic game (Berliner, 1980a). Berliner readily acknowledged that BKG was very lucky with the dice. Gerry Tesauro's (1995) TD-GAMMON played consistently at world champion level. The BGBLITZ program was the winner of the 2008 Computer Olympiad.

Go is a deterministic game, but the large branching factor makes it challeging. The key issues and early literature in computer Go are summarized by Bouzy and Cazenave (2001) and Müller (2002). Up to 1997 there were no competent Go programs. Now the best programs play *most* of their moves at the master level; the only problem is that over the course of a game they usually make at least one serious blunder that allows a strong opponent to win. Whereas alpha–beta search reigns in most games, many recent Go programs have adopted Monte Carlo methods based on the UCT (upper confidence bounds on trees) scheme (Kocsis and Szepesvari, 2006). The strongest Go program as of 2009 is Gelly and Silver's MOGO (Wang and Gelly, 2007; Gelly and Silver, 2008). In August 2008, MOGO scored a surprising win against top professional Myungwan Kim, albeit with MOGO receiving a handicap of nine stones (about the equivalent of a queen handicap in chess). Kim estimated MOGO's strength at 2–3 dan, the low end of advanced amateur. For this match, MOGO was run on an 800-processor 15 teraflop supercomputer (1000 times Deep Blue). A few weeks later, MOGO, with only a five-stone handicap, won against a 6-dan professional. In the 9×9 form of Go, MOGO is at approximately the 1-dan professional level. Rapid advances are likely as experimentation continues with new forms of Monte Carlo search. The *Computer Go*

Newsletter, published by the Computer Go Association, describes current developments.

Bridge: Smith *et al.* (1998) report on how their planning-based program won the 1998 computer bridge championship, and (Ginsberg, 2001) describes how his GIB program, based on Monte Carlo simulation, won the following computer championship and did surprisingly well against human players and standard book problem sets. From 2001–2007, the computer bridge championship was won five times by JACK and twice by WBRIDGE5. Neither has had academic articles explaining their structure, but both are rumored to use the Monte Carlo technique, which was first proposed for bridge by Levy (1989).

Scrabble: A good description of a top program, MAVEN, is given by its creator, Brian Sheppard (2002). Generating the highest-scoring move is described by Gordon (1994), and modeling opponents is covered by Richards and Amir (2007).

Soccer (Kitano *et al.*, 1997b; Visser *et al.*, 2008) and **billiards** (Lam and Greenspan, 2008; Archibald *et al.*, 2009) and other stochastic games with a continuous space of actions are beginning to attract attention in AI, both in simulation and with physical robot players.

Computer game competitions occur annually, and papers appear in a variety of venues. The rather misleadingly named conference proceedings *Heuristic Programming in Artificial Intelligence* report on the Computer Olympiads, which include a wide variety of games. The General Game Competition (Love *et al.*, 2006) tests programs that must learn to play an unknown game given only a logical description of the rules of the game. There are also several edited collections of important papers on game-playing research (Levy, 1988a, 1988b; Marsland and Schaeffer, 1990). The International Computer Chess Association (ICCA), founded in 1977, publishes the *ICGA Journal* (formerly the *ICCA Journal*). Important papers have been published in the serial anthology *Advances in Computer Chess*, starting with Clarke (1977). Volume 134 of the journal *Artificial Intelligence* (2002) contains descriptions of state-of-the-art programs for chess, Othello, Hex, shogi, Go, backgammon, poker, Scrabble, and other games. Since 1998, a biennial *Computers and Games* conference has been held.

EXERCISES

1 Suppose you have an oracle, $OM(s)$, that correctly predicts the opponent's move in any state. Using this, formulate the definition of a game as a (single-agent) search problem. Describe an algorithm for finding the optimal move.

2 Consider the problem of solving two 8-puzzles.

a. Give a complete problem formulation in the style of the chapter "Solving Problems by Searching".

b. How large is the reachable state space? Give an exact numerical expression.

c. Suppose we make the problem adversarial as follows: the two players take turns moving; a coin is flipped to determine the puzzle on which to make a move in that turn; and the winner is the first to solve one puzzle. Which algorithm can be used to choose a move in this setting?

d. Give an informal proof that someone will eventually win if both play perfectly.

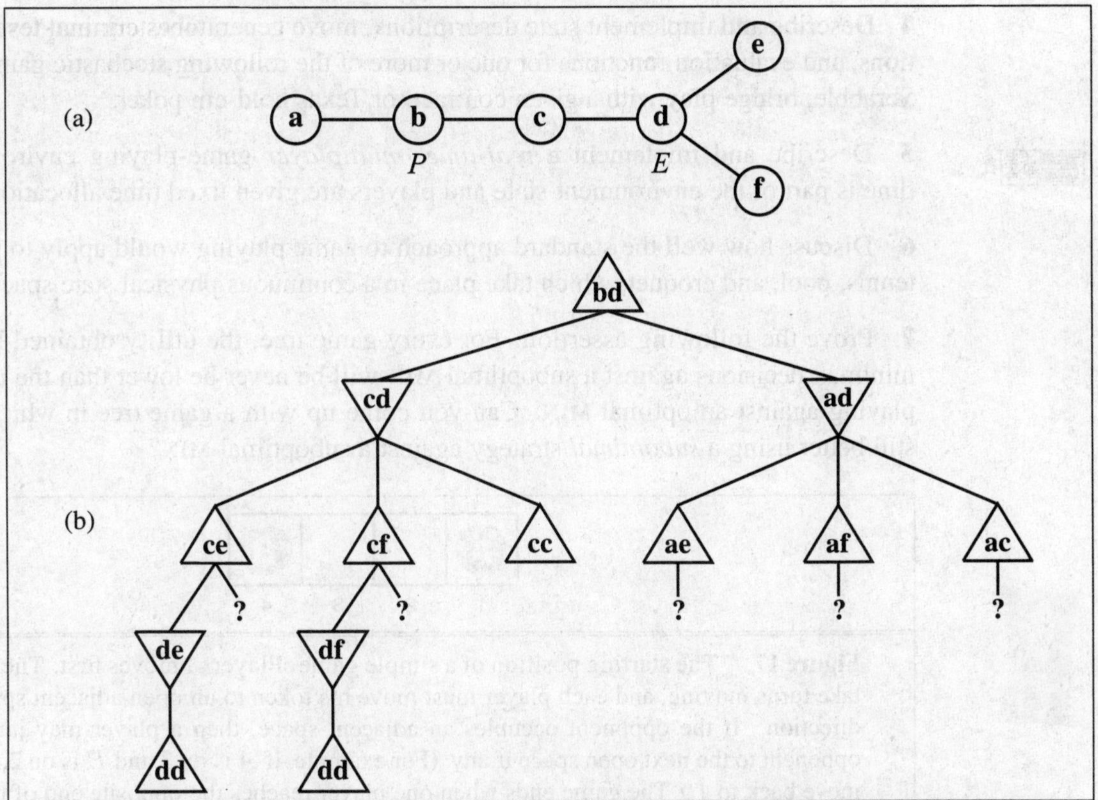

Figure 16 (a) A map where the cost of every edge is 1. Initially the pursuer P is at node **b** and the evader E is at node **d**. (b) A partial game tree for this map. Each node is labeled with the P, E positions. P moves first. Branches marked "?" have yet to be explored.

3 Imagine that, in Exercise 3 of the chapter "Solving Problems by Searching" one friend wants to avoid the other. The problem is a two-player **pursuit–evasion** game. We assume now that the players take turns moving. The game ends only when the players are on the same node; the terminal payoff to the pursuer is minus the total time taken. (The evader "wins" by never losing.) An example is shown in Figure 16.

PURSUIT–EVASION

a. Copy the game tree and mark the values of the terminal nodes.

b. Next to each internal node, write the strongest fact you can infer about its value (a number, one or more inequalities such as "≥ 14", or a "?").

c. Beneath each question mark, write the name of the node reached by that branch.

d. Explain how a bound on the value of the nodes in (c) can be derived from consideration of shortest-path lengths on the map, and derive such bounds for these nodes. Remember the cost to get to each leaf as well as the cost to solve it.

e. Now suppose that the tree as given, with the leaf bounds from (d), is evaluated from left to right. Circle those "?" nodes that would *not* need to be expanded further, given the bounds from part (d), and cross out those that need not be considered at all.

f. Can you prove anything in general about who wins the game on a map that is a tree?

4 Describe and implement state descriptions, move generators, terminal tests, utility functions, and evaluation functions for one or more of the following stochastic games: Monopoly, Scrabble, bridge play with a given contract, or Texas hold'em poker.

5 Describe and implement a *real-time*, *multiplayer* game-playing environment, where time is part of the environment state and players are given fixed time allocations.

6 Discuss how well the standard approach to game playing would apply to games such as tennis, pool, and croquet, which take place in a continuous physical state space.

7 Prove the following assertion: For every game tree, the utility obtained by MAX using minimax decisions against a suboptimal MIN will be never be lower than the utility obtained playing against an optimal MIN. Can you come up with a game tree in which MAX can do still better using a *suboptimal* strategy against a suboptimal MIN?

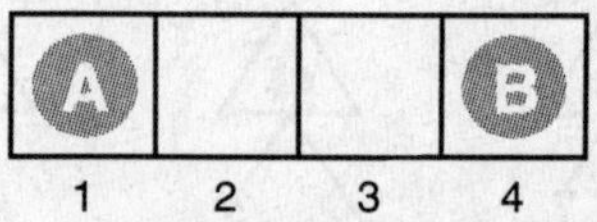

Figure 17 The starting position of a simple game. Player A moves first. The two players take turns moving, and each player must move his token to an open adjacent space in either direction. If the opponent occupies an adjacent space, then a player may jump over the opponent to the next open space if any. (For example, if A is on 3 and B is on 2, then A may move back to 1.) The game ends when one player reaches the opposite end of the board. If player A reaches space 4 first, then the value of the game to A is $+1$; if player B reaches space 1 first, then the value of the game to A is -1.

8 Consider the two-player game described in Figure 17.

a. Draw the complete game tree, using the following conventions:

- Write each state as (s_A, s_B), where s_A and s_B denote the token locations.
- Put each terminal state in a square box and write its game value in a circle.
- Put *loop states* (states that already appear on the path to the root) in double square boxes. Since their value is unclear, annotate each with a "?" in a circle.

b. Now mark each node with its backed-up minimax value (also in a circle). Explain how you handled the "?" values and why.

c. Explain why the standard minimax algorithm would fail on this game tree and briefly sketch how you might fix it, drawing on your answer to (b). Does your modified algorithm give optimal decisions for all games with loops?

d. This 4-square game can be generalized to n squares for any $n > 2$. Prove that A wins if n is even and loses if n is odd.

9 This problem exercises the basic concepts of game playing, using tic-tac-toe (noughts and crosses) as an example. We define X_n as the number of rows, columns, or diagonals with exactly n X's and no O's. Similarly, O_n is the number of rows, columns, or diagonals with just n O's. The utility function assigns $+1$ to any position with $X_3 = 1$ and -1 to any position with $O_3 = 1$. All other terminal positions have utility 0. For nonterminal positions, we use a linear evaluation function defined as $Eval(s) = 3X_2(s)+X_1(s)-(3O_2(s)+O_1(s))$.

- **a.** Approximately how many possible games of tic-tac-toe are there?
- **b.** Show the whole game tree starting from an empty board down to depth 2 (i.e., one X and one O on the board), taking symmetry into account.
- **c.** Mark on your tree the evaluations of all the positions at depth 2.
- **d.** Using the minimax algorithm, mark on your tree the backed-up values for the positions at depths 1 and 0, and use those values to choose the best starting move.
- **e.** Circle the nodes at depth 2 that would *not* be evaluated if alpha–beta pruning were applied, assuming the nodes are generated in the optimal order for alpha–beta pruning.

10 Consider the family of generalized tic-tac-toe games, defined as follows. Each particular game is specified by a set $\mathcal{S}$ of *squares* and a collection $\mathcal{W}$ of *winning positions.* Each winning position is a subset of $\mathcal{S}$. For example, in standard tic-tac-toe, $\mathcal{S}$ is a set of 9 squares and $\mathcal{W}$ is a collection of 8 subsets of $\mathcal{W}$: the three rows, the three columns, and the two diagonals. In other respects, the game is identical to standard tic-tac-toe. Starting from an empty board, players alternate placing their marks on an empty square. A player who marks every square in a winning position wins the game. It is a tie if all squares are marked and neither player has won.

- **a.** Let $N = |\mathcal{S}|$, the number of squares. Give an upper bound on the number of nodes in the complete game tree for generalized tic-tac-toe as a function of N.
- **b.** Give a lower bound on the size of the game tree for the worst case, where $\mathcal{W} = \{\}$.
- **c.** Propose a plausible evaluation function that can be used for any instance of generalized tic-tac-toe. The function may depend on $\mathcal{S}$ and $\mathcal{W}$.
- **d.** Assume that it is possible to generate a new board and check whether it is a winning position in $100N$ machine instructions and assume a 2 gigahertz processor. Ignore memory limitations. Using your estimate in (a), roughly how large a game tree can be completely solved by alpha–beta in a second of CPU time? a minute? an hour?

11 Develop a general game-playing program, capable of playing a variety of games.

- **a.** Implement move generators and evaluation functions for one or more of the following games: Kalah, Othello, checkers, and chess.
- **b.** Construct a general alpha–beta game-playing agent.
- **c.** Compare the effect of increasing search depth, improving move ordering, and improving the evaluation function. How close does your effective branching factor come to the ideal case of perfect move ordering?
- **d.** Implement a selective search algorithm, such as B* (Berliner, 1979), conspiracy number search (McAllester, 1988), or MGSS* (Russell and Wefald, 1989) and compare its performance to A*.

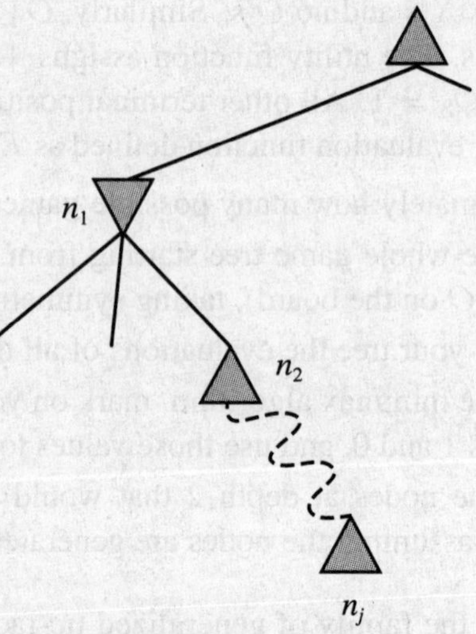

Figure 18 Situation when considering whether to prune node n_j.

12 Describe how the minimax and alpha–beta algorithms change for two-player, non-zero-sum games in which each player has a distinct utility function and both utility functions are known to both players. If there are no constraints on the two terminal utilities, is it possible for any node to be pruned by alpha–beta? What if the player's utility functions on any state differ by at most a constant k, making the game almost cooperative?

13 Develop a formal proof of correctness for alpha–beta pruning. To do this, consider the situation shown in Figure 18. The question is whether to prune node n_j, which is a max-node and a descendant of node n_1. The basic idea is to prune it if and only if the minimax value of n_1 can be shown to be independent of the value of n_j.

a. Mode n_1 takes on the minimum value among its children: $n_1 = \min(n_2, n_{21}, \ldots, n_{2b_2})$. Find a similar expression for n_2 and hence an expression for n_1 in terms of n_j.

b. Let l_i be the minimum (or maximum) value of the nodes to the *left* of node n_i at depth i, whose minimax value is already known. Similarly, let r_i be the minimum (or maximum) value of the unexplored nodes to the right of n_i at depth i. Rewrite your expression for n_1 in terms of the l_i and r_i values.

c. Now reformulate the expression to show that in order to affect n_1, n_j must not exceed a certain bound derived from the l_i values.

d. Repeat the process for the case where n_j is a min-node.

14 Prove that alpha–beta pruning takes time $O(2^{m/2})$ with optimal move ordering, where m is the maximum depth of the game tree.

15 Suppose you have a chess program that can evaluate 10 million nodes per second. Decide on a compact representation of a game state for storage in a transposition table. About how many entries can you fit in a 2-gigabyte in-memory table? Will that be enough for the

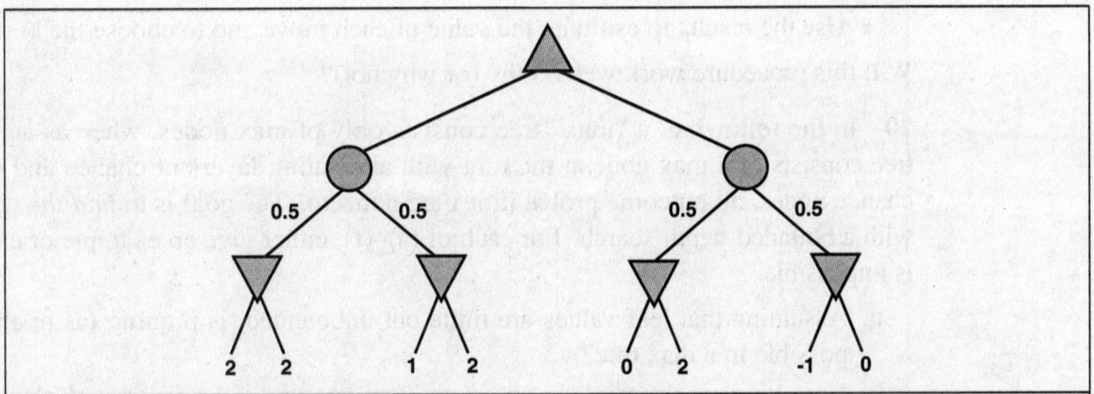

Figure 19 The complete game tree for a trivial game with chance nodes.

three minutes of search allocated for one move? How many table lookups can you do in the time it would take to do one evaluation? Now suppose the transposition table is stored on disk. About how many evaluations could you do in the time it takes to do one disk seek with standard disk hardware?

16 This question considers pruning in games with chance nodes. Figure 19 shows the complete game tree for a trivial game. Assume that the leaf nodes are to be evaluated in left-to-right order, and that before a leaf node is evaluated, we know nothing about its value—the range of possible values is $-\infty$ to ∞.

a. Copy the figure, mark the value of all the internal nodes, and indicate the best move at the root with an arrow.

b. Given the values of the first six leaves, do we need to evaluate the seventh and eighth leaves? Given the values of the first seven leaves, do we need to evaluate the eighth leaf? Explain your answers.

c. Suppose the leaf node values are known to lie between –2 and 2 inclusive. After the first two leaves are evaluated, what is the value range for the left-hand chance node?

d. Circle all the leaves that need not be evaluated under the assumption in (c).

17 Implement the expectiminimax algorithm and the *-alpha–beta algorithm, which is described by Ballard (1983), for pruning game trees with chance nodes. Try them on a game such as backgammon and measure the pruning effectiveness of *-alpha–beta.

18 Prove that with a positive linear transformation of leaf values (i.e., transforming a value x to $ax + b$ where $a > 0$), the choice of move remains unchanged in a game tree, even when there are chance nodes.

19 Consider the following procedure for choosing moves in games with chance nodes:

- Generate some dice-roll sequences (say, 50) down to a suitable depth (say, 8).
- With known dice rolls, the game tree becomes deterministic. For each dice-roll sequence, solve the resulting deterministic game tree using alpha–beta.

- Use the results to estimate the value of each move and to choose the best.

Will this procedure work well? Why (or why not)?

20 In the following, a "max" tree consists only of max nodes, whereas an "expectimax" tree consists of a max node at the root with alternating layers of chance and max nodes. At chance nodes, all outcome probabilities are nonzero. The goal is to *find the value of the root* with a bounded-depth search. For each of (a)–(f), either give an example or explain why this is impossible.

a. Assuming that leaf values are finite but unbounded, is pruning (as in alpha–beta) ever possible in a max tree?

b. Is pruning ever possible in an expectimax tree under the same conditions?

c. If leaf values are all nonnegative, is pruning ever possible in a max tree? Give an example, or explain why not.

d. If leaf values are all nonnegative, is pruning ever possible in an expectimax tree? Give an example, or explain why not.

e. If leaf values are all in the range $[0, 1]$, is pruning ever possible in a max tree? Give an example, or explain why not.

f. If leaf values are all in the range $[0, 1]$, is pruning ever possible in an expectimax tree?

g. Consider the outcomes of a chance node in an expectimax tree. Which of the following evaluation orders is most likely to yield pruning opportunities?

(i) Lowest probability first
(ii) Highest probability first
(iii) Doesn't make any difference

21 Which of the following are true and which are false? Give brief explanations.

a. In a fully observable, turn-taking, zero-sum game between two perfectly rational players, it does not help the first player to know what strategy the second player is using—that is, what move the second player will make, given the first player's move.

b. In a partially observable, turn-taking, zero-sum game between two perfectly rational players, it does not help the first player to know what move the second player will make, given the first player's move.

c. A perfectly rational backgammon agent never loses.

22 Consider carefully the interplay of chance events and partial information in each of the games in Exercise 4.

a. For which is the standard expectiminimax model appropriate? Implement the algorithm and run it in your game-playing agent, with appropriate modifications to the game-playing environment.

b. For which would the scheme described in Exercise 19 be appropriate?

c. Discuss how you might deal with the fact that in some of the games, the players do not have the same knowledge of the current state.

LOGICAL AGENTS

LOGICAL AGENTS

In which we design agents that can form representations of a complex world, use a process of inference to derive new representations about the world, and use these new representations to deduce what to do.

REASONING
REPRESENTATION
KNOWLEDGE-BASED AGENTS

Humans, it seems, know things; and what they know helps them do things. These are not empty statements. They make strong claims about how the intelligence of humans is achieved—not by purely reflex mechanisms but by processes of **reasoning** that operate on internal **representations** of knowledge. In AI, this approach to intelligence is embodied in **knowledge-based agents**.

Simple problem-solving agents know things, but only in a very limited, inflexible sense. For example, the transition model for the 8-puzzle—knowledge of what the actions do—is hidden inside the domain-specific code of the RESULT function. It can be used to predict the outcome of actions but not to deduce that two tiles cannot occupy the same space or that states with odd parity cannot be reached from states with even parity. The atomic representations used by problem-solving agents are also very limiting. In a partially observable environment, an agent's only choice for representing what it knows about the current state is to list all possible concrete states—a hopeless prospect in large environments.

LOGIC

The idea of representing states as assignments of values to variables is a step in the right direction, enabling some parts of the agent to work in a domain-independent way and allowing for more efficient algorithms. In this chapter and those that follow, we take this step to its logical conclusion, so to speak—we develop **logic** as a general class of representations to support knowledge-based agents. Such agents can combine and recombine information to suit myriad purposes. Often, this process can be quite far removed from the needs of the moment—as when a mathematician proves a theorem or an astronomer calculates the earth's life expectancy. Knowledge-based agents can accept new tasks in the form of explicitly described goals; they can achieve competence quickly by being told or learning new knowledge about the environment; and they can adapt to changes in the environment by updating the relevant knowledge.

We begin in Section 1 with the overall agent design. Section 2 introduces a simple new environment, the wumpus world, and illustrates the operation of a knowledge-based agent without going into any technical detail. Then we explain the general principles of **logic** in Section 3 and the specifics of **propositional logic** in Section 4. While less expressive than **first-order logic**, propositional logic illustrates all the basic concepts of logic; it also comes with well-developed inference technologies, which we describe in sections 5 and 6. Finally, Section 7 combines the concept of knowledge-based agents with the technology of propositional logic to build some simple agents for the wumpus world.

1 KNOWLEDGE-BASED AGENTS

KNOWLEDGE BASE
SENTENCE
KNOWLEDGE REPRESENTATION LANGUAGE
AXIOM

The central component of a knowledge-based agent is its **knowledge base**, or KB. A knowledge base is a set of **sentences**. (Here "sentence" is used as a technical term. It is related but not identical to the sentences of English and other natural languages.) Each sentence is expressed in a language called a **knowledge representation language** and represents some assertion about the world. Sometimes we dignify a sentence with the name **axiom**, when the sentence is taken as given without being derived from other sentences.

INFERENCE

There must be a way to add new sentences to the knowledge base and a way to query what is known. The standard names for these operations are TELL and ASK, respectively. Both operations may involve **inference**—that is, deriving new sentences from old. Inference must obey the requirement that when one ASKs a question of the knowledge base, the answer should follow from what has been told (or TELLed) to the knowledge base previously. Later in this chapter, we will be more precise about the crucial word "follow." For now, take it to mean that the inference process should not make things up as it goes along.

BACKGROUND KNOWLEDGE

Figure 1 shows the outline of a knowledge-based agent program. Like all our agents, it takes a percept as input and returns an action. The agent maintains a knowledge base, *KB*, which may initially contain some **background knowledge**.

Each time the agent program is called, it does three things. First, it TELLs the knowledge base what it perceives. Second, it ASKs the knowledge base what action it should perform. In the process of answering this query, extensive reasoning may be done about the current state of the world, about the outcomes of possible action sequences, and so on. Third, the agent program TELLs the knowledge base which action was chosen, and the agent executes the action.

The details of the representation language are hidden inside three functions that implement the interface between the sensors and actuators on one side and the core representation and reasoning system on the other. MAKE-PERCEPT-SENTENCE constructs a sentence asserting that the agent perceived the given percept at the given time. MAKE-ACTION-QUERY constructs a sentence that asks what action should be done at the current time. Finally, MAKE-ACTION-SENTENCE constructs a sentence asserting that the chosen action was executed. The details of the inference mechanisms are hidden inside TELL and ASK. Later sections will reveal these details.

The agent in Figure 1 appears quite similar to agents with internal state. Because of the definitions of TELL and ASK, however, the knowledge-based agent is not an arbitrary program for calculating actions. It is amenable to a description at the **knowledge level**, where

```
function KB-AGENT(percept) returns an action
  persistent: KB, a knowledge base
              t, a counter, initially 0, indicating time

  TELL(KB, MAKE-PERCEPT-SENTENCE(percept, t))
  action ← ASK(KB, MAKE-ACTION-QUERY(t))
  TELL(KB, MAKE-ACTION-SENTENCE(action, t))
  t ← t + 1
  return action
```

Figure 1 A generic knowledge-based agent. Given a percept, the agent adds the percept to its knowledge base, asks the knowledge base for the best action, and tells the knowledge base that it has in fact taken that action.

KNOWLEDGE LEVEL

we need specify only what the agent knows and what its goals are, in order to fix its behavior. For example, an automated taxi might have the goal of taking a passenger from San Francisco to Marin County and might know that the Golden Gate Bridge is the only link between the two locations. Then we can expect it to cross the Golden Gate Bridge *because it knows that that will achieve its goal*. Notice that this analysis is independent of how the taxi works at the **implementation level**. It doesn't matter whether its geographical knowledge is implemented as linked lists or pixel maps, or whether it reasons by manipulating strings of symbols stored in registers or by propagating noisy signals in a network of neurons.

IMPLEMENTATION LEVEL

A knowledge-based agent can be built simply by TELLing it what it needs to know. Starting with an empty knowledge base, the agent designer can TELL sentences one by one until the agent knows how to operate in its environment. This is called the **declarative** approach to system building. In contrast, the **procedural** approach encodes desired behaviors directly as program code. In the 1970s and 1980s, advocates of the two approaches engaged in heated debates. We now understand that a successful agent often combines both declarative and procedural elements in its design, and that declarative knowledge can often be compiled into more efficient procedural code.

DECLARATIVE

We can also provide a knowledge-based agent with mechanisms that allow it to learn for itself. These mechanisms create general knowledge about the environment from a series of percepts. A learning agent can be fully autonomous.

2 THE WUMPUS WORLD

In this section we describe an environment in which knowledge-based agents can show their worth. The **wumpus world** is a cave consisting of rooms connected by passageways. Lurking somewhere in the cave is the terrible wumpus, a beast that eats anyone who enters its room. The wumpus can be shot by an agent, but the agent has only one arrow. Some rooms contain

WUMPUS WORLD

bottomless pits that will trap anyone who wanders into these rooms (except for the wumpus, which is too big to fall in). The only mitigating feature of this bleak environment is the possibility of finding a heap of gold. Although the wumpus world is rather tame by modern computer game standards, it illustrates some important points about intelligence.

A sample wumpus world is shown in Figure 2. The precise definition of the task environment is given by the PEAS description:

- **Performance measure**: +1000 for climbing out of the cave with the gold, –1000 for falling into a pit or being eaten by the wumpus, –1 for each action taken and –10 for using up the arrow. The game ends either when the agent dies or when the agent climbs out of the cave.
- **Environment**: A 4×4 grid of rooms. The agent always starts in the square labeled [1,1], facing to the right. The locations of the gold and the wumpus are chosen randomly, with a uniform distribution, from the squares other than the start square. In addition, each square other than the start can be a pit, with probability 0.2.
- **Actuators**: The agent can move *Forward*, *TurnLeft* by 90°, or *TurnRight* by 90°. The agent dies a miserable death if it enters a square containing a pit or a live wumpus. (It is safe, albeit smelly, to enter a square with a dead wumpus.) If an agent tries to move forward and bumps into a wall, then the agent does not move. The action *Grab* can be used to pick up the gold if it is in the same square as the agent. The action *Shoot* can be used to fire an arrow in a straight line in the direction the agent is facing. The arrow continues until it either hits (and hence kills) the wumpus or hits a wall. The agent has only one arrow, so only the first *Shoot* action has any effect. Finally, the action *Climb* can be used to climb out of the cave, but only from square [1,1].
- **Sensors**: The agent has five sensors, each of which gives a single bit of information:
  - In the square containing the wumpus and in the directly (not diagonally) adjacent squares, the agent will perceive a *Stench*.
  - In the squares directly adjacent to a pit, the agent will perceive a *Breeze*.
  - In the square where the gold is, the agent will perceive a *Glitter*.
  - When an agent walks into a wall, it will perceive a *Bump*.
  - When the wumpus is killed, it emits a woeful *Scream* that can be perceived anywhere in the cave.

  The percepts will be given to the agent program in the form of a list of five symbols; for example, if there is a stench and a breeze, but no glitter, bump, or scream, the agent program will get [*Stench*, *Breeze*, *None*, *None*, *None*].

We can characterize the wumpus environment along various dimensions. Clearly, it is discrete, static, and single-agent. (The wumpus doesn't move, fortunately.) It is sequential, because rewards may come only after many actions are taken. It is partially observable, because some aspects of the state are not directly perceivable: the agent's location, the wumpus's state of health, and the availability of an arrow. As for the locations of the pits and the wumpus: we could treat them as unobserved parts of the state that happen to be immutable—in which case, the transition model for the environment is completely known; or we could say

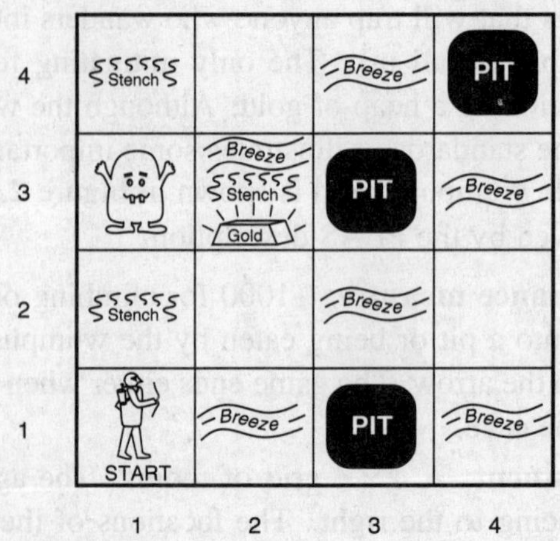

Figure 2 A typical wumpus world. The agent is in the bottom left corner, facing right.

that the transition model itself is unknown because the agent doesn't know which *Forward* actions are fatal—in which case, discovering the locations of pits and wumpus completes the agent's knowledge of the transition model.

For an agent in the environment, the main challenge is its initial ignorance of the configuration of the environment; overcoming this ignorance seems to require logical reasoning. In most instances of the wumpus world, it is possible for the agent to retrieve the gold safely. Occasionally, the agent must choose between going home empty-handed and risking death to find the gold. About 21% of the environments are utterly unfair, because the gold is in a pit or surrounded by pits.

Let us watch a knowledge-based wumpus agent exploring the environment shown in Figure 2. We use an informal knowledge representation language consisting of writing down symbols in a grid (as in Figures 3 and 4).

The agent's initial knowledge base contains the rules of the environment, as described previously; in particular, it knows that it is in [1,1] and that [1,1] is a safe square; we denote that with an "A" and "OK," respectively, in square [1,1].

The first percept is [*None*, *None*, *None*, *None*, *None*], from which the agent can conclude that its neighboring squares, [1,2] and [2,1], are free of dangers—they are OK. Figure 3(a) shows the agent's state of knowledge at this point.

A cautious agent will move only into a square that it knows to be OK. Let us suppose the agent decides to move forward to [2,1]. The agent perceives a breeze (denoted by "B") in [2,1], so there must be a pit in a neighboring square. The pit cannot be in [1,1], by the rules of the game, so there must be a pit in [2,2] or [3,1] or both. The notation "P?" in Figure 3(b) indicates a possible pit in those squares. At this point, there is only one known square that is OK and that has not yet been visited. So the prudent agent will turn around, go back to [1,1], and then proceed to [1,2].

The agent perceives a stench in [1,2], resulting in the state of knowledge shown in Figure 4(a). The stench in [1,2] means that there must be a wumpus nearby. But the

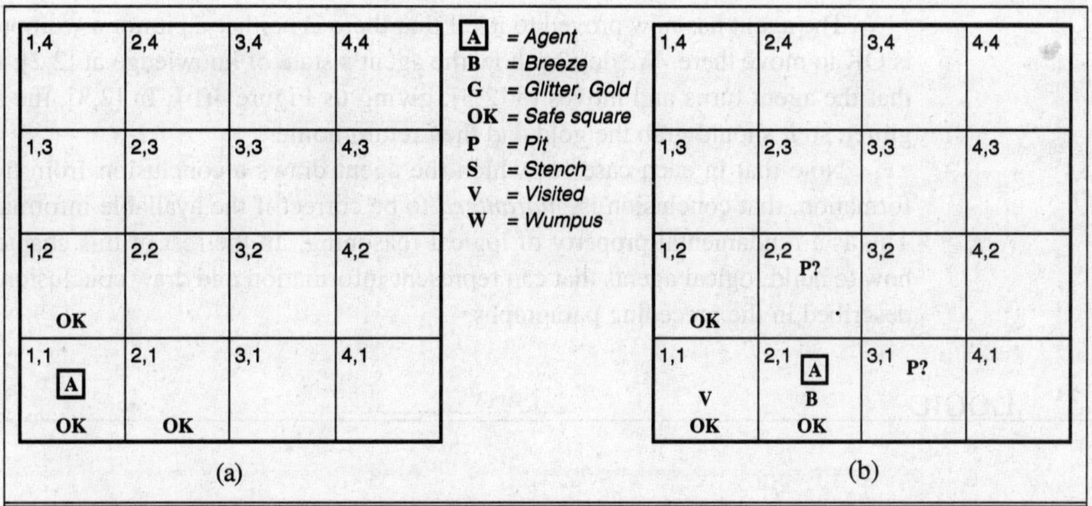

Figure 3 The first step taken by the agent in the wumpus world. (a) The initial situation, after percept [*None*, *None*, *None*, *None*, *None*]. (b) After one move, with percept [*None*, *Breeze*, *None*, *None*, *None*].

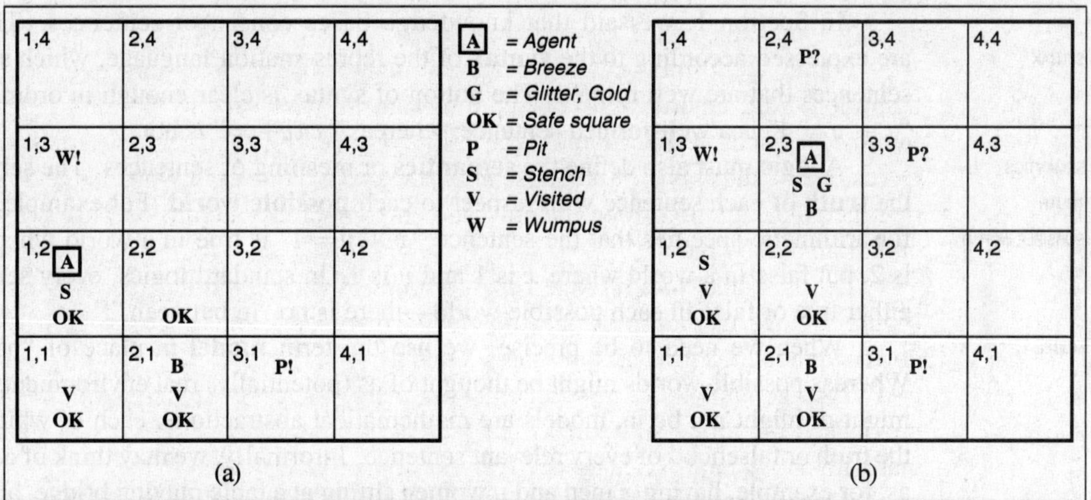

Figure 4 Two later stages in the progress of the agent. (a) After the third move, with percept [*Stench*, *None*, *None*, *None*, *None*]. (b) After the fifth move, with percept [*Stench*, *Breeze*, *Glitter*, *None*, *None*].

wumpus cannot be in [1,1], by the rules of the game, and it cannot be in [2,2] (or the agent would have detected a stench when it was in [2,1]). Therefore, the agent can infer that the wumpus is in [1,3]. The notation W! indicates this inference. Moreover, the lack of a breeze in [1,2] implies that there is no pit in [2,2]. Yet the agent has already inferred that there must be a pit in either [2,2] or [3,1], so this means it must be in [3,1]. This is a fairly difficult inference, because it combines knowledge gained at different times in different places and relies on the lack of a percept to make one crucial step.

The agent has now proved to itself that there is neither a pit nor a wumpus in [2,2], so it is OK to move there. We do not show the agent's state of knowledge at [2,2]; we just assume that the agent turns and moves to [2,3], giving us Figure 4(b). In [2,3], the agent detects a glitter, so it should grab the gold and then return home.

Note that in each case for which the agent draws a conclusion from the available information, that conclusion is *guaranteed* to be correct if the available information is correct. This is a fundamental property of logical reasoning. In the rest of this chapter, we describe how to build logical agents that can represent information and draw conclusions such as those described in the preceding paragraphs.

3 Logic

This section summarizes the fundamental concepts of logical representation and reasoning. These beautiful ideas are independent of any of logic's particular forms. We therefore postpone the technical details of those forms until the next section, using instead the familiar example of ordinary arithmetic.

In Section 1, we said that knowledge bases consist of sentences. These sentences are expressed according to the **syntax** of the representation language, which specifies all the sentences that are well formed. The notion of syntax is clear enough in ordinary arithmetic: "$x + y = 4$" is a well-formed sentence, whereas "$x4y+ =$" is not.

SYNTAX

A logic must also define the **semantics** or meaning of sentences. The semantics defines the **truth** of each sentence with respect to each **possible world**. For example, the semantics for arithmetic specifies that the sentence "$x + y = 4$" is true in a world where x is 2 and y is 2, but false in a world where x is 1 and y is 1. In standard logics, every sentence must be either true or false in each possible world—there is no "in between."[1]

SEMANTICS

TRUTH

POSSIBLE WORLD

When we need to be precise, we use the term **model** in place of "possible world." Whereas possible worlds might be thought of as (potentially) real environments that the agent might or might not be in, models are mathematical abstractions, each of which simply fixes the truth or falsehood of every relevant sentence. Informally, we may think of a possible world as, for example, having x men and y women sitting at a table playing bridge, and the sentence $x + y = 4$ is true when there are four people in total. Formally, the possible models are just all possible assignments of real numbers to the variables x and y. Each such assignment fixes the truth of any sentence of arithmetic whose variables are x and y. If a sentence α is true in model m, we say that m **satisfies** α or sometimes m **is a model of** α. We use the notation $M(\alpha)$ to mean the set of all models of α.

MODEL

SATISFACTION

Now that we have a notion of truth, we are ready to talk about logical reasoning. This involves the relation of logical **entailment** between sentences—the idea that a sentence *follows logically* from another sentence. In mathematical notation, we write

ENTAILMENT

$$\alpha \models \beta$$

[1] **Fuzzy logic** allows for degrees of truth.

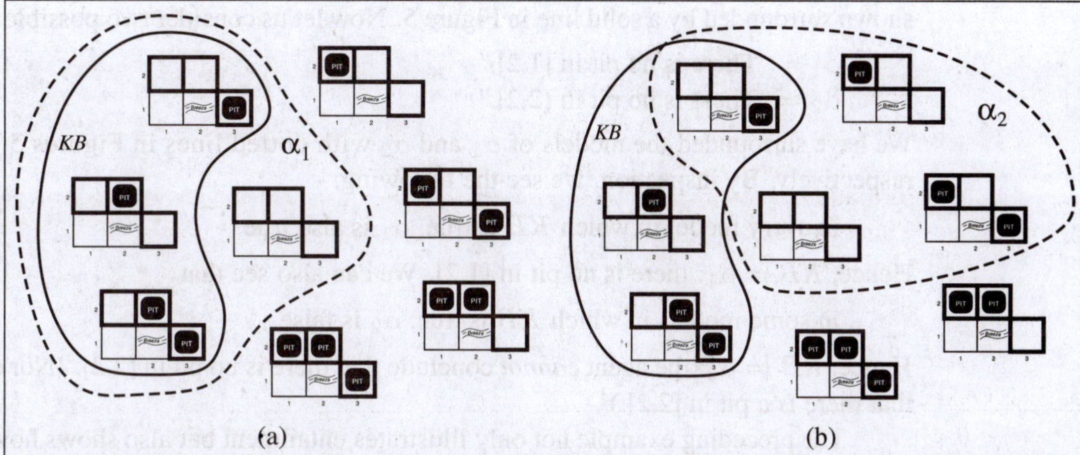

Figure 5 Possible models for the presence of pits in squares [1,2], [2,2], and [3,1]. The KB corresponding to the observations of nothing in [1,1] and a breeze in [2,1] is shown by the solid line. (a) Dotted line shows models of α_1 (no pit in [1,2]). (b) Dotted line shows models of α_2 (no pit in [2,2]).

to mean that the sentence α entails the sentence β. The formal definition of entailment is this: $\alpha \models \beta$ if and only if, in every model in which α is true, β is also true. Using the notation just introduced, we can write

$$\alpha \models \beta \text{ if and only if } M(\alpha) \subseteq M(\beta) .$$

(Note the direction of the $\subseteq$ here: if $\alpha \models \beta$, then α is a *stronger* assertion than β: it rules out *more* possible worlds.) The relation of entailment is familiar from arithmetic; we are happy with the idea that the sentence $x = 0$ entails the sentence $xy = 0$. Obviously, in any model where x is zero, it is the case that xy is zero (regardless of the value of y).

We can apply the same kind of analysis to the wumpus-world reasoning example given in the preceding section. Consider the situation in Figure 3(b): the agent has detected nothing in [1,1] and a breeze in [2,1]. These percepts, combined with the agent's knowledge of the rules of the wumpus world, constitute the KB. The agent is interested (among other things) in whether the adjacent squares [1,2], [2,2], and [3,1] contain pits. Each of the three squares might or might not contain a pit, so (for the purposes of this example) there are $2^3 = 8$ possible models. These eight models are shown in Figure 5. [2]

The KB can be thought of as a set of sentences or as a single sentence that asserts all the individual sentences. The KB is false in models that contradict what the agent knows—for example, the KB is false in any model in which [1,2] contains a pit, because there is no breeze in [1,1]. There are in fact just three models in which the KB is true, and these are

[2] Although the figure shows the models as partial wumpus worlds, they are really nothing more than assignments of *true* and *false* to the sentences "there is a pit in [1,2]" etc. Models, in the mathematical sense, do not need to have 'orrible 'airy wumpuses in them.

shown surrounded by a solid line in Figure 5. Now let us consider two possible conclusions:

α_1 = "There is no pit in [1,2]."
α_2 = "There is no pit in [2,2]."

We have surrounded the models of α_1 and α_2 with dotted lines in Figures 5(a) and 5(b), respectively. By inspection, we see the following:

in every model in which KB is true, α_1 is also true.

Hence, $KB \models \alpha_1$: there is no pit in [1,2]. We can also see that

in some models in which KB is true, α_2 is false.

Hence, $KB \not\models \alpha_2$: the agent *cannot* conclude that there is no pit in [2,2]. (Nor can it conclude that there *is* a pit in [2,2].)[3]

LOGICAL INFERENCE
MODEL CHECKING

The preceding example not only illustrates entailment but also shows how the definition of entailment can be applied to derive conclusions—that is, to carry out **logical inference**. The inference algorithm illustrated in Figure 5 is called **model checking**, because it enumerates all possible models to check that α is true in all models in which KB is true, that is, that $M(KB) \subseteq M(\alpha)$.

In understanding entailment and inference, it might help to think of the set of all consequences of KB as a haystack and of α as a needle. Entailment is like the needle being in the haystack; inference is like finding it. This distinction is embodied in some formal notation: if an inference algorithm i can derive α from KB, we write

$$KB \vdash_i \alpha\,,$$

which is pronounced "α is derived from KB by i" or "i derives α from KB."

SOUND
TRUTH-PRESERVING

An inference algorithm that derives only entailed sentences is called **sound** or **truth-preserving**. Soundness is a highly desirable property. An unsound inference procedure essentially makes things up as it goes along—it announces the discovery of nonexistent needles. It is easy to see that model checking, when it is applicable,[4] is a sound procedure.

COMPLETENESS

The property of **completeness** is also desirable: an inference algorithm is complete if it can derive any sentence that is entailed. For real haystacks, which are finite in extent, it seems obvious that a systematic examination can always decide whether the needle is in the haystack. For many knowledge bases, however, the haystack of consequences is infinite, and completeness becomes an important issue. Fortunately, there are complete inference procedures for logics that are sufficiently expressive to handle many knowledge bases.

We have described a reasoning process whose conclusions are guaranteed to be true in any world in which the premises are true; in particular, *if KB is true in the* real *world, then any sentence α derived from KB by a sound inference procedure is also true in the real world.* So, while an inference process operates on "syntax"—internal physical configurations such as bits in registers or patterns of electrical blips in brains—the process *corresponds*

[3] The agent can calculate the *probability* that there is a pit in [2,2].

[4] Model checking works if the space of models is finite—for example, in wumpus worlds of fixed size. For arithmetic, on the other hand, the space of models is infinite: even if we restrict ourselves to the integers, there are infinitely many pairs of values for x and y in the sentence $x + y = 4$.

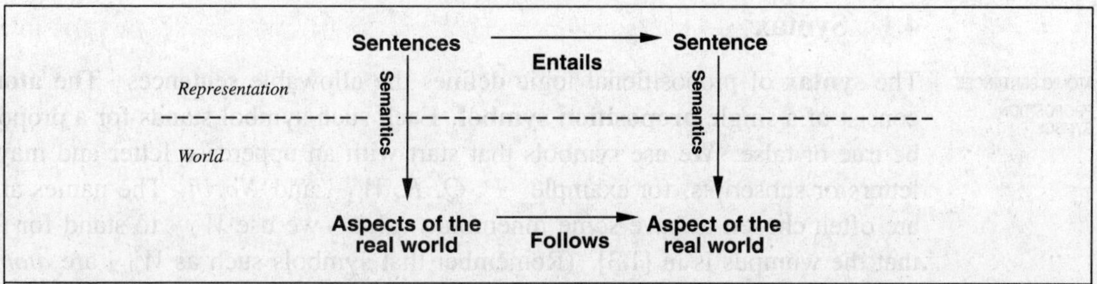

Figure 6 Sentences are physical configurations of the agent, and reasoning is a process of constructing new physical configurations from old ones. Logical reasoning should ensure that the new configurations represent aspects of the world that actually follow from the aspects that the old configurations represent.

to the real-world relationship whereby some aspect of the real world is the case[5] by virtue of other aspects of the real world being the case. This correspondence between world and representation is illustrated in Figure 6.

GROUNDING

The final issue to consider is **grounding**—the connection between logical reasoning processes and the real environment in which the agent exists. In particular, *how do we know that* KB *is true in the real world?* (After all, *KB* is just "syntax" inside the agent's head.) This is a philosophical question about which many, many books have been written. A simple answer is that the agent's sensors create the connection. For example, our wumpus-world agent has a smell sensor. The agent program creates a suitable sentence whenever there is a smell. Then, whenever that sentence is in the knowledge base, it is true in the real world. Thus, the meaning and truth of percept sentences are defined by the processes of sensing and sentence construction that produce them. What about the rest of the agent's knowledge, such as its belief that wumpuses cause smells in adjacent squares? This is not a direct representation of a single percept, but a general rule—derived, perhaps, from perceptual experience but not identical to a statement of that experience. General rules like this are produced by a sentence construction process called **learning**, which is the subject of Part V. Learning is fallible. It could be the case that wumpuses cause smells *except on February 29 in leap years*, which is when they take their baths. Thus, *KB* may not be true in the real world, but with good learning procedures, there is reason for optimism.

4 PROPOSITIONAL LOGIC: A VERY SIMPLE LOGIC

PROPOSITIONAL LOGIC

We now present a simple but powerful logic called **propositional logic**. We cover the syntax of propositional logic and its semantics—the way in which the truth of sentences is determined. Then we look at **entailment**—the relation between a sentence and another sentence that follows from it—and see how this leads to a simple algorithm for logical inference. Everything takes place, of course, in the wumpus world.

[5] As Wittgenstein (1922) put it in his famous *Tractatus*: "The world is everything that is the case."

4.1 Syntax

ATOMIC SENTENCES
PROPOSITION SYMBOL

The **syntax** of propositional logic defines the allowable sentences. The **atomic sentences** consist of a single **proposition symbol**. Each such symbol stands for a proposition that can be true or false. We use symbols that start with an uppercase letter and may contain other letters or subscripts, for example: P, Q, R, $W_{1,3}$ and $North$. The names are arbitrary but are often chosen to have some mnemonic value—we use $W_{1,3}$ to stand for the proposition that the wumpus is in [1,3]. (Remember that symbols such as $W_{1,3}$ are *atomic*, i.e., W, 1, and 3 are not meaningful parts of the symbol.) There are two proposition symbols with fixed meanings: $True$ is the always-true proposition and $False$ is the always-false proposition. **Complex sentences** are constructed from simpler sentences, using parentheses and **logical connectives**. There are five connectives in common use:

COMPLEX SENTENCES
LOGICAL CONNECTIVES

NEGATION
LITERAL

$\neg$ (not). A sentence such as $\neg W_{1,3}$ is called the **negation** of $W_{1,3}$. A **literal** is either an atomic sentence (a **positive literal**) or a negated atomic sentence (a **negative literal**).

CONJUNCTION

$\wedge$ (and). A sentence whose main connective is $\wedge$, such as $W_{1,3} \wedge P_{3,1}$, is called a **conjunction**; its parts are the **conjuncts**. (The $\wedge$ looks like an "A" for "And.")

DISJUNCTION

$\vee$ (or). A sentence using $\vee$, such as $(W_{1,3} \wedge P_{3,1}) \vee W_{2,2}$, is a **disjunction** of the **disjuncts** $(W_{1,3} \wedge P_{3,1})$ and $W_{2,2}$. (Historically, the $\vee$ comes from the Latin "vel," which means "or." For most people, it is easier to remember $\vee$ as an upside-down $\wedge$.)

IMPLICATION
PREMISE
CONCLUSION
RULES

$\Rightarrow$ (implies). A sentence such as $(W_{1,3} \wedge P_{3,1}) \Rightarrow \neg W_{2,2}$ is called an **implication** (or conditional). Its **premise** or **antecedent** is $(W_{1,3} \wedge P_{3,1})$, and its **conclusion** or **consequent** is $\neg W_{2,2}$. Implications are also known as **rules** or **if–then** statements. The implication symbol is sometimes written in other books as $\supset$ or $\rightarrow$.

BICONDITIONAL

$\Leftrightarrow$ (if and only if). The sentence $W_{1,3} \Leftrightarrow \neg W_{2,2}$ is a **biconditional**. Some other books write this as $\equiv$.

$$
\begin{array}{rcl}
Sentence & \rightarrow & AtomicSentence \mid ComplexSentence \\
AtomicSentence & \rightarrow & True \mid False \mid P \mid Q \mid R \mid \ldots \\
ComplexSentence & \rightarrow & (\ Sentence\ ) \mid [\ Sentence\ ] \\
& \mid & \neg\ Sentence \\
& \mid & Sentence \wedge Sentence \\
& \mid & Sentence \vee Sentence \\
& \mid & Sentence \Rightarrow Sentence \\
& \mid & Sentence \Leftrightarrow Sentence \\
\\
\text{OPERATOR PRECEDENCE} & : & \neg, \wedge, \vee, \Rightarrow, \Leftrightarrow
\end{array}
$$

Figure 7 A BNF (Backus–Naur Form) grammar of sentences in propositional logic, along with operator precedences, from highest to lowest.

Figure 7 gives a formal grammar of propositional logic; The BNF grammar by itself is ambiguous; a sentence with servral operators can be parsed by the grammar in multiple ways. To eliminate the ambiguity we define a precedence for each operator. The "not" operator ($\neg$) has the highest precedence, which means that in the sentence $\neg A \wedge B$ the $\neg$ binds most tightly, giving us the equivalent of $(\neg A) \wedge B$ rather than $\neg(A \wedge B)$. (The notation for ordinary arithmetic is the same: $-2+4$ is 2, not –6.) When in doubt, use parentheses to make sure of the right interpretation. Square brack-ets mean the same thing as parentheses; the choice of square brackets or parentheses is solely to make it easier for a human to read a sentence.

4.2 Semantics

Having specified the syntax of propositional logic, we now specify its semantics. The semantics defines the rules for determining the truth of a sentence with respect to a particular model. In propositional logic, a model simply fixes the **truth value**—*true* or *false*—for every proposition symbol. For example, if the sentences in the knowledge base make use of the proposition symbols $P_{1,2}$, $P_{2,2}$, and $P_{3,1}$, then one possible model is

TRUTH VALUE

$$m_1 = \{P_{1,2} = false,\ P_{2,2} = false,\ P_{3,1} = true\}\ .$$

With three proposition symbols, there are $2^3 = 8$ possible models—exactly those depicted in Figure 5. Notice, however, that the models are purely mathematical objects with no necessary connection to wumpus worlds. $P_{1,2}$ is just a symbol; it might mean "there is a pit in [1,2]" or "I'm in Paris today and tomorrow."

The semantics for propositional logic must specify how to compute the truth value of *any* sentence, given a model. This is done recursively. All sentences are constructed from atomic sentences and the five connectives; therefore, we need to specify how to compute the truth of atomic sentences and how to compute the truth of sentences formed with each of the five connectives. Atomic sentences are easy:

- *True* is true in every model and *False* is false in every model.
- The truth value of every other proposition symbol must be specified directly in the model. For example, in the model m_1 given earlier, $P_{1,2}$ is false.

For complex sentences, we have five rules, which hold for any subsentences P and Q in any model m (here "iff" means "if and only if"):

- $\neg P$ is true iff P is false in m.
- $P \wedge Q$ is true iff both P and Q are true in m.
- $P \vee Q$ is true iff either P or Q is true in m.
- $P \Rightarrow Q$ is true unless P is true and Q is false in m.
- $P \Leftrightarrow Q$ is true iff P and Q are both true or both false in m.

TRUTH TABLE

The rules can also be expressed with **truth tables** that specify the truth value of a complex sentence for each possible assignment of truth values to its components. Truth tables for the five connectives are given in Figure 8. From these tables, the truth value of any sentence s can be computed with respect to any model m by a simple recursive evaluation. For example,

P	Q	$\neg P$	$P \wedge Q$	$P \vee Q$	$P \Rightarrow Q$	$P \Leftrightarrow Q$
false	*false*	*true*	*false*	*false*	*true*	*true*
false	*true*	*true*	*false*	*true*	*true*	*false*
true	*false*	*false*	*false*	*true*	*false*	*false*
true	*true*	*false*	*true*	*true*	*true*	*true*

Figure 8 Truth tables for the five logical connectives. To use the table to compute, for example, the value of $P \vee Q$ when P is true and Q is false, first look on the left for the row where P is *true* and Q is *false* (the third row). Then look in that row under the $P \vee Q$ column to see the result: *true*.

the sentence $\neg P_{1,2} \wedge (P_{2,2} \vee P_{3,1})$, evaluated in m_1, gives $true \wedge (false \vee true) = true \wedge true = true$. Exercise 3 asks you to write the algorithm PL-TRUE?(s, m), which computes the truth value of a propositional logic sentence s in a model m.

The truth tables for "and," "or," and "not" are in close accord with our intuitions about the English words. The main point of possible confusion is that $P \vee Q$ is true when P is true or Q is true *or both.* A different connective, called "exclusive or" ("xor" for short), yields false when both disjuncts are true.[6] There is no consensus on the symbol for exclusive or; some choices are $\dot{\vee}$ or $\neq$ or $\oplus$.

The truth table for $\Rightarrow$ may not quite fit one's intuitive understanding of "P implies Q" or "if P then Q." For one thing, propositional logic does not require any relation of *causation* or *relevance* between P and Q. The sentence "5 is odd implies Tokyo is the capital of Japan" is a true sentence of propositional logic (under the normal interpretation), even though it is a decidedly odd sentence of English. Another point of confusion is that any implication is true whenever its antecedent is false. For example, "5 is even implies Sam is smart" is true, regardless of whether Sam is smart. This seems bizarre, but it makes sense if you think of "$P \Rightarrow Q$" as saying, "If P is true, then I am claiming that Q is true. Otherwise I am making no claim." The only way for this sentence to be *false* is if P is true but Q is false.

The biconditional, $P \Leftrightarrow Q$, is true whenever both $P \Rightarrow Q$ and $Q \Rightarrow P$ are true. In English, this is often written as "P if and only if Q." Many of the rules of the wumpus world are best written using $\Leftrightarrow$. For example, a square is breezy *if* a neighboring square has a pit, and a square is breezy *only if* a neighboring square has a pit. So we need a biconditional,

$$B_{1,1} \Leftrightarrow (P_{1,2} \vee P_{2,1}),$$

where $B_{1,1}$ means that there is a breeze in [1,1].

4.3 A simple knowledge base

Now that we have defined the semantics for propositional logic, we can construct a knowledge base for the wumpus world. We focus first on the *immutable* aspects of the wumpus world, leaving the mutable aspects for a later section. For now, we need the following symbols for each $[x, y]$ location:

[6] Latin has a separate word, *aut*, for exclusive or.

$P_{x,y}$ is true if there is a pit in $[x, y]$.
$W_{x,y}$ is true if there is a wumpus in $[x, y]$, dead or alive.
$B_{x,y}$ is true if the agent perceives a breeze in $[x, y]$.
$S_{x,y}$ is true if the agent perceives a stench in $[x, y]$.

The sentences we write will suffice to derive $\neg P_{1,2}$ (there is no pit in [1,2]), as was done informally in Section 3. We label each sentence R_i so that we can refer to them:

- There is no pit in [1,1]:

$$R_1 : \quad \neg P_{1,1} .$$

- A square is breezy if and only if there is a pit in a neighboring square. This has to be stated for each square; for now, we include just the relevant squares:

$$R_2 : \quad B_{1,1} \quad \Leftrightarrow \quad (P_{1,2} \lor P_{2,1}) .$$

$$R_3 : \quad B_{2,1} \quad \Leftrightarrow \quad (P_{1,1} \lor P_{2,2} \lor P_{3,1}) .$$

- The preceding sentences are true in all wumpus worlds. Now we include the breeze percepts for the first two squares visited in the specific world the agent is in, leading up to the situation in Figure 3(b).

$$R_4 : \quad \neg B_{1,1} .$$

$$R_5 : \quad B_{2,1} .$$

4.4 A simple inference procedure

Our goal now is to decide whether $KB \models \alpha$ for some sentence α. For example, is $\neg P_{1,2}$ entailed by our KB? Our first algorithm for inference is a model-checking approach that is a direct implementation of the definition of entailment: enumerate the models, and check that α is true in every model in which KB is true. Models are assignments of *true* or *false* to every proposition symbol. Returning to our wumpus-world example, the relevant proposition symbols are $B_{1,1}$, $B_{2,1}$, $P_{1,1}$, $P_{1,2}$, $P_{2,1}$, $P_{2,2}$, and $P_{3,1}$. With seven symbols, there are $2^7 = 128$ possible models; in three of these, KB is true (Figure 9). In those three models, $\neg P_{1,2}$ is true, hence there is no pit in [1,2]. On the other hand, $P_{2,2}$ is true in two of the three models and false in one, so we cannot yet tell whether there is a pit in [2,2].

Figure 9 reproduces in a more precise form the reasoning illustrated in Figure 5. A general algorithm for deciding entailment in propositional logic is shown in Figure 10. Like the BACKTRACKING-SEARCH algorithm, TT-ENTAILS? performs a recursive enumeration of a finite space of assignments to symbols. The algorithm is **sound** because it implements directly the definition of entailment, and **complete** because it works for any KB and α and always terminates—there are only finitely many models to examine.

Of course, "finitely many" is not always the same as "few." If KB and α contain n symbols in all, then there are 2^n models. Thus, the time complexity of the algorithm is $O(2^n)$. (The space complexity is only $O(n)$ because the enumeration is depth-first.) Later in this chapter we show algorithms that are much more efficient in many cases. Unfortunately, propositional entailment is co-NP-complete (i.e., probably no easier than NP-complete), so *every known inference algorithm for propositional logic has a worst-case complexity that is exponential in the size of the input.*

$B_{1,1}$	$B_{2,1}$	$P_{1,1}$	$P_{1,2}$	$P_{2,1}$	$P_{2,2}$	$P_{3,1}$	R_1	R_2	R_3	R_4	R_5	KB
false	*false*	*false*	*false*	*false*	*false*	*false*	*true*	*true*	*true*	*true*	*false*	*false*
false	*false*	*false*	*false*	*false*	*false*	*true*	*true*	*true*	*false*	*true*	*false*	*false*
⋮	⋮	⋮	⋮	⋮	⋮	⋮	⋮	⋮	⋮	⋮	⋮	⋮
false	*true*	*false*	*false*	*false*	*false*	*false*	*true*	*true*	*false*	*true*	*true*	*false*
false	*true*	*false*	*false*	*false*	*false*	*true*	*true*	*true*	*true*	*true*	*true*	<u>*true*</u>
false	*true*	*false*	*false*	*false*	*true*	*false*	*true*	*true*	*true*	*true*	*true*	<u>*true*</u>
false	*true*	*false*	*false*	*false*	*true*	*true*	*true*	*true*	*true*	*true*	*true*	<u>*true*</u>
false	*true*	*false*	*false*	*true*	*false*	*false*	*true*	*false*	*false*	*true*	*true*	*false*
⋮	⋮	⋮	⋮	⋮	⋮	⋮	⋮	⋮	⋮	⋮	⋮	⋮
true	*true*	*true*	*true*	*true*	*true*	*true*	*false*	*true*	*true*	*false*	*true*	*false*

Figure 9 A truth table constructed for the knowledge base given in the text. *KB* is true if R_1 through R_5 are true, which occurs in just 3 of the 128 rows (the ones underlined in the right-hand column). In all 3 rows, $P_{1,2}$ is false, so there is no pit in [1,2]. On the other hand, there might (or might not) be a pit in [2,2].

```
function TT-ENTAILS?(KB, α) returns true or false
  inputs: KB, the knowledge base, a sentence in propositional logic
          α, the query, a sentence in propositional logic

  symbols ← a list of the proposition symbols in KB and α
  return TT-CHECK-ALL(KB, α, symbols, { })
```

```
function TT-CHECK-ALL(KB, α, symbols, model) returns true or false
  if EMPTY?(symbols) then
      if PL-TRUE?(KB, model) then return PL-TRUE?(α, model)
      else return true // when KB is false, always return true
  else do
      P ← FIRST(symbols)
      rest ← REST(symbols)
      return (TT-CHECK-ALL(KB, α, rest, model ∪ {P = true})
              and
              TT-CHECK-ALL(KB, α, rest, model ∪ {P = false }))
```

Figure 10 A truth-table enumeration algorithm for deciding propositional entailment. (TT stands for truth table.) PL-TRUE? returns *true* if a sentence holds within a model. The variable *model* represents a partial model—an assignment to some of the symbols. The keyword **"and"** is used here as a logical operation on its two arguments, returning *true* or *false*.

$$
\begin{array}{rcll}
(\alpha \land \beta) & \equiv & (\beta \land \alpha) & \text{commutativity of } \land \\
(\alpha \lor \beta) & \equiv & (\beta \lor \alpha) & \text{commutativity of } \lor \\
((\alpha \land \beta) \land \gamma) & \equiv & (\alpha \land (\beta \land \gamma)) & \text{associativity of } \land \\
((\alpha \lor \beta) \lor \gamma) & \equiv & (\alpha \lor (\beta \lor \gamma)) & \text{associativity of } \lor \\
\neg(\neg\alpha) & \equiv & \alpha & \text{double-negation elimination} \\
(\alpha \Rightarrow \beta) & \equiv & (\neg\beta \Rightarrow \neg\alpha) & \text{contraposition} \\
(\alpha \Rightarrow \beta) & \equiv & (\neg\alpha \lor \beta) & \text{implication elimination} \\
(\alpha \Leftrightarrow \beta) & \equiv & ((\alpha \Rightarrow \beta) \land (\beta \Rightarrow \alpha)) & \text{biconditional elimination} \\
\neg(\alpha \land \beta) & \equiv & (\neg\alpha \lor \neg\beta) & \text{De Morgan} \\
\neg(\alpha \lor \beta) & \equiv & (\neg\alpha \land \neg\beta) & \text{De Morgan} \\
(\alpha \land (\beta \lor \gamma)) & \equiv & ((\alpha \land \beta) \lor (\alpha \land \gamma)) & \text{distributivity of } \land \text{ over } \lor \\
(\alpha \lor (\beta \land \gamma)) & \equiv & ((\alpha \lor \beta) \land (\alpha \lor \gamma)) & \text{distributivity of } \lor \text{ over } \land
\end{array}
$$

Figure 11 Standard logical equivalences. The symbols α, β, and γ stand for arbitrary sentences of propositional logic.

5 Propositional Theorem Proving

So far, we have shown how to determine entailment by *model checking*: enumerating models and showing that the sentence must hold in all models. In this section, we show how entailment can be done by **theorem proving**—applying rules of inference directly to the sentences in our knowledge base to construct a proof of the desired sentence without consulting models. If the number of models is large but the length of the proof is short, then theorem proving can be more efficient than model checking.

THEOREM PROVING

Before we plunge into the details of theorem-proving algorithms, we will need some additional concepts related to entailment. The first concept is **logical equivalence**: two sentences α and β are logically equivalent if they are true in the same set of models. We write this as $\alpha \equiv \beta$. For example, we can easily show (using truth tables) that $P \land Q$ and $Q \land P$ are logically equivalent; other equivalences are shown in Figure 11. These equivalences play much the same role in logic as arithmetic identities do in ordinary mathematics. An alternative definition of equivalence is as follows: any two sentences α and β are equivalent only if each of them entails the other:

LOGICAL EQUIVALENCE

$$\alpha \equiv \beta \quad \text{if and only if} \quad \alpha \models \beta \text{ and } \beta \models \alpha\,.$$

The second concept we will need is **validity**. A sentence is valid if it is true in *all* models. For example, the sentence $P \lor \neg P$ is valid. Valid sentences are also known as **tautologies**—they are *necessarily* true. Because the sentence *True* is true in all models, every valid sentence is logically equivalent to *True*. What good are valid sentences? From our definition of entailment, we can derive the **deduction theorem**, which was known to the ancient Greeks:

VALIDITY

TAUTOLOGY

DEDUCTION THEOREM

For any sentences α and β, $\alpha \models \beta$ if and only if the sentence $(\alpha \Rightarrow \beta)$ is valid.

(Exercise 5 asks for a proof.) Hence, we can decide if $\alpha \models \beta$ by checking that $(\alpha \Rightarrow \beta)$ is true in every model—which is essentially what the inference algorithm in Figure 10 does—

or by proving that $(\alpha \Rightarrow \beta)$ is equivalent to $True$. Conversely, the deduction theorem states that every valid implication sentence describes a legitimate inference.

SATISFIABILITY

The final concept we will need is **satisfiability**. A sentence is satisfiable if it is true in, or satisfied by, *some* model. For example, the knowledge base given earlier, $(R_1 \wedge R_2 \wedge R_3 \wedge R_4 \wedge R_5)$, is satisfiable because there are three models in which it is true, as shown in Figure 9. Satisfiability can be checked by enumerating the possible models until one is found that satisfies the sentence. The problem of determining the satisfiability of sentences in propositional logic—the **SAT** problem—was the first problem proved to be NP-complete. Many problems in computer science are really satisfiability problems. For example, constraint satisfaction problems that ask whether the constraints are satisfiable by some assignment.

SAT

Validity and satisfiability are of course connected: α is valid iff $\neg\alpha$ is unsatisfiable; contrapositively, α is satisfiable iff $\neg\alpha$ is not valid. We also have the following useful result:

$\alpha \models \beta$ *if and only if the sentence* $(\alpha \wedge \neg\beta)$ *is unsatisfiable.*

REDUCTIO AD ABSURDUM

REFUTATION

CONTRADICTION

Proving β from α by checking the unsatisfiability of $(\alpha \wedge \neg\beta)$ corresponds exactly to the standard mathematical proof technique of *reductio ad absurdum* (literally, "reduction to an absurd thing"). It is also called proof by **refutation** or proof by **contradiction**. One assumes a sentence β to be false and shows that this leads to a contradiction with known axioms α. This contradiction is exactly what is meant by saying that the sentence $(\alpha \wedge \neg\beta)$ is unsatisfiable.

5.1 Inference and proofs

INFERENCE RULES

PROOF

MODUS PONENS

This section covers **inference rules** that can be applied to derive a **proof**—a chain of conclusions that leads to the desired goal. The best-known rule is called **Modus Ponens** (Latin for *mode that affirms*) and is written

$$\frac{\alpha \Rightarrow \beta, \qquad \alpha}{\beta}.$$

The notation means that, whenever any sentences of the form $\alpha \Rightarrow \beta$ and α are given, then the sentence β can be inferred. For example, if $(WumpusAhead \wedge WumpusAlive) \Rightarrow Shoot$ and $(WumpusAhead \wedge WumpusAlive)$ are given, then $Shoot$ can be inferred.

AND-ELIMINATION

Another useful inference rule is **And-Elimination**, which says that, from a conjunction, any of the conjuncts can be inferred:

$$\frac{\alpha \wedge \beta}{\alpha}.$$

For example, from $(WumpusAhead \wedge WumpusAlive)$, $WumpusAlive$ can be inferred.

By considering the possible truth values of α and β, one can show easily that Modus Ponens and And-Elimination are sound once and for all. These rules can then be used in any particular instances where they apply, generating sound inferences without the need for enumerating models.

All of the logical equivalences in Figure 11 can be used as inference rules. For example, the equivalence for biconditional elimination yields the two inference rules

$$\frac{\alpha \Leftrightarrow \beta}{(\alpha \Rightarrow \beta) \wedge (\beta \Rightarrow \alpha)} \quad \text{and} \quad \frac{(\alpha \Rightarrow \beta) \wedge (\beta \Rightarrow \alpha)}{\alpha \Leftrightarrow \beta}.$$

Not all inference rules work in both directions like this. For example, we cannot run Modus Ponens in the opposite direction to obtain $\alpha \Rightarrow \beta$ and α from β.

Let us see how these inference rules and equivalences can be used in the wumpus world. We start with the knowledge base containing R_1 through R_5 and show how to prove $\neg P_{1,2}$, that is, there is no pit in [1,2]. First, we apply biconditional elimination to R_2 to obtain

$$R_6: \quad (B_{1,1} \Rightarrow (P_{1,2} \lor P_{2,1})) \land ((P_{1,2} \lor P_{2,1}) \Rightarrow B_{1,1}) .$$

Then we apply And-Elimination to R_6 to obtain

$$R_7: \quad ((P_{1,2} \lor P_{2,1}) \Rightarrow B_{1,1}) .$$

Logical equivalence for contrapositives gives

$$R_8: \quad (\neg B_{1,1} \Rightarrow \neg(P_{1,2} \lor P_{2,1})) .$$

Now we can apply Modus Ponens with R_8 and the percept R_4 (i.e., $\neg B_{1,1}$), to obtain

$$R_9: \quad \neg(P_{1,2} \lor P_{2,1}) .$$

Finally, we apply De Morgan's rule, giving the conclusion

$$R_{10}: \quad \neg P_{1,2} \land \neg P_{2,1} .$$

That is, neither [1,2] nor [2,1] contains a pit.

We found this proof by hand, but we can apply any of the search algorithms to find a sequence of steps that constitutes a proof. We just need to define a proof problem as follows:

- INITIAL STATE: the initial knowledge base.
- ACTIONS: the set of actions consists of all the inference rules applied to all the sentences that match the top half of the inference rule.
- RESULT: the result of an action is to add the sentence in the bottom half of the inference rule.
- GOAL: the goal is a state that contains the sentence we are trying to prove.

Thus, searching for proofs is an alternative to enumerating models. In many practical cases *finding a proof can be more efficient because the proof can ignore irrelevant propositions, no matter how many of them there are.* For example, the proof given earlier leading to $\neg P_{1,2} \land \neg P_{2,1}$ does not mention the propositions $B_{2,1}$, $P_{1,1}$, $P_{2,2}$, or $P_{3,1}$. They can be ignored because the goal proposition, $P_{1,2}$, appears only in sentence R_2; the other propositions in R_2 appear only in R_4 and R_2; so R_1, R_3, and R_5 have no bearing on the proof. The same would hold even if we added a million more sentences to the knowledge base; the simple truth-table algorithm, on the other hand, would be overwhelmed by the exponential explosion of models.

MONOTONICITY

One final property of logical systems is **monotonicity**, which says that the set of entailed sentences can only *increase* as information is added to the knowledge base.[7] For any sentences α and β,

$$\text{if} \quad KB \models \alpha \quad \text{then} \quad KB \land \beta \models \alpha .$$

[7] **Nonmonotonic** logics, which violate the monotonicity property, capture a common property of human reasoning: changing one's mind.

For example, suppose the knowledge base contains the additional assertion β stating that there are exactly eight pits in the world. This knowledge might help the agent draw *additional* conclusions, but it cannot invalidate any conclusion α already inferred—such as the conclusion that there is no pit in [1,2]. Monotonicity means that inference rules can be applied whenever suitable premises are found in the knowledge base—the conclusion of the rule must follow *regardless of what else is in the knowledge base*.

5.2 Proof by resolution

We have argued that the inference rules covered so far are *sound*, but we have not discussed the question of *completeness* for the inference algorithms that use them. Search algorithms such as iterative deepening search are complete in the sense that they will find any reachable goal, but if the available inference rules are inadequate, then the goal is not reachable—no proof exists that uses only those inference rules. For example, if we removed the biconditional elimination rule, the proof in the preceding section would not go through. The current section introduces a single inference rule, **resolution**, that yields a complete inference algorithm when coupled with any complete search algorithm.

We begin by using a simple version of the resolution rule in the wumpus world. Let us consider the steps leading up to Figure 4(a): the agent returns from [2,1] to [1,1] and then goes to [1,2], where it perceives a stench, but no breeze. We add the following facts to the knowledge base:

$$R_{11}: \quad \neg B_{1,2} .$$
$$R_{12}: \quad B_{1,2} \Leftrightarrow (P_{1,1} \lor P_{2,2} \lor P_{1,3}) .$$

By the same process that led to R_{10} earlier, we can now derive the absence of pits in [2,2] and [1,3] (remember that [1,1] is already known to be pitless):

$$R_{13}: \quad \neg P_{2,2} .$$
$$R_{14}: \quad \neg P_{1,3} .$$

We can also apply biconditional elimination to R_3, followed by Modus Ponens with R_5, to obtain the fact that there is a pit in [1,1], [2,2], or [3,1]:

$$R_{15}: \quad P_{1,1} \lor P_{2,2} \lor P_{3,1} .$$

Now comes the first application of the resolution rule: the literal $\neg P_{2,2}$ in R_{13} *resolves with*

RESOLVENT the literal $P_{2,2}$ in R_{15} to give the **resolvent**

$$R_{16}: \quad P_{1,1} \lor P_{3,1} .$$

In English; if there's a pit in one of [1,1], [2,2], and [3,1] and it's not in [2,2], then it's in [1,1] or [3,1]. Similarly, the literal $\neg P_{1,1}$ in R_1 resolves with the literal $P_{1,1}$ in R_{16} to give

$$R_{17}: \quad P_{3,1} .$$

In English: if there's a pit in [1,1] or [3,1] and it's not in [1,1], then it's in [3,1]. These last

UNIT RESOLUTION two inference steps are examples of the **unit resolution** inference rule,

$$\frac{\ell_1 \lor \cdots \lor \ell_k, \qquad m}{\ell_1 \lor \cdots \lor \ell_{i-1} \lor \ell_{i+1} \lor \cdots \lor \ell_k} ,$$

COMPLEMENTARY LITERALS where each ℓ is a literal and ℓ_i and m are **complementary literals** (i.e., one is the negation

CLAUSE

UNIT CLAUSE

of the other). Thus, the unit resolution rule takes a **clause**—a disjunction of literals—and a literal and produces a new clause. Note that a single literal can be viewed as a disjunction of one literal, also known as a **unit clause**.

RESOLUTION

The unit resolution rule can be generalized to the full **resolution** rule,

$$\frac{\ell_1 \vee \cdots \vee \ell_k, \qquad m_1 \vee \cdots \vee m_n}{\ell_1 \vee \cdots \vee \ell_{i-1} \vee \ell_{i+1} \vee \cdots \vee \ell_k \vee m_1 \vee \cdots \vee m_{j-1} \vee m_{j+1} \vee \cdots \vee m_n},$$

where ℓ_i and m_j are complementary literals. This says that resolution takes two clauses and produces a new clause containing all the literals of the two original clauses *except* the two complementary literals. For example, we have

$$\frac{P_{1,1} \vee P_{3,1}, \qquad \neg P_{1,1} \vee \neg P_{2,2}}{P_{3,1} \vee \neg P_{2,2}}.$$

FACTORING

There is one more technical aspect of the resolution rule: the resulting clause should contain only one copy of each literal.[8] The removal of multiple copies of literals is called **factoring**. For example, if we resolve $(A \vee B)$ with $(A \vee \neg B)$, we obtain $(A \vee A)$, which is reduced to just A.

The *soundness* of the resolution rule can be seen easily by considering the literal ℓ_i that is complementary to literal m_j in the other clause. If ℓ_i is true, then m_j is false, and hence $m_1 \vee \cdots \vee m_{j-1} \vee m_{j+1} \vee \cdots \vee m_n$ must be true, because $m_1 \vee \cdots \vee m_n$ is given. If ℓ_i is false, then $\ell_1 \vee \cdots \vee \ell_{i-1} \vee \ell_{i+1} \vee \cdots \vee \ell_k$ must be true because $\ell_1 \vee \cdots \vee \ell_k$ is given. Now ℓ_i is either true or false, so one or other of these conclusions holds—exactly as the resolution rule states.

What is more surprising about the resolution rule is that it forms the basis for a family of *complete* inference procedures. *A resolution-based theorem prover can, for any sentences α and β in propositional logic, decide whether $\alpha \models \beta$.* The next two subsections explain how resolution accomplishes this.

Conjunctive normal form

CONJUNCTIVE NORMAL FORM

The resolution rule applies only to clauses (that is, disjunctions of literals), so it would seem to be relevant only to knowledge bases and queries consisting of clauses. How, then, can it lead to a complete inference procedure for all of propositional logic? The answer is that *every sentence of propositional logic is logically equivalent to a conjunction of clauses.* A sentence expressed as a conjunction of clauses is said to be in **conjunctive normal form** or **CNF** (see Figure 14). We now describe a procedure for converting to CNF. We illustrate the procedure by converting the sentence $B_{1,1} \Leftrightarrow (P_{1,2} \vee P_{2,1})$ into CNF. The steps are as follows:

1. Eliminate $\Leftrightarrow$, replacing $\alpha \Leftrightarrow \beta$ with $(\alpha \Rightarrow \beta) \wedge (\beta \Rightarrow \alpha)$.

$$(B_{1,1} \Rightarrow (P_{1,2} \vee P_{2,1})) \wedge ((P_{1,2} \vee P_{2,1}) \Rightarrow B_{1,1}).$$

2. Eliminate $\Rightarrow$, replacing $\alpha \Rightarrow \beta$ with $\neg\alpha \vee \beta$:

$$(\neg B_{1,1} \vee P_{1,2} \vee P_{2,1}) \wedge (\neg(P_{1,2} \vee P_{2,1}) \vee B_{1,1}).$$

[8] If a clause is viewed as a *set* of literals, then this restriction is automatically respected. Using set notation for clauses makes the resolution rule much cleaner, at the cost of introducing additional notation.

3. CNF requires $\neg$ to appear only in literals, so we "move $\neg$ inwards" by repeated application of the following equivalences from Figure 11:

$$\neg(\neg\alpha) \equiv \alpha \quad \text{(double-negation elimination)}$$
$$\neg(\alpha \wedge \beta) \equiv (\neg\alpha \vee \neg\beta) \quad \text{(De Morgan)}$$
$$\neg(\alpha \vee \beta) \equiv (\neg\alpha \wedge \neg\beta) \quad \text{(De Morgan)}$$

   In the example, we require just one application of the last rule:

$$(\neg B_{1,1} \vee P_{1,2} \vee P_{2,1}) \wedge ((\neg P_{1,2} \wedge \neg P_{2,1}) \vee B_{1,1}) .$$

4. Now we have a sentence containing nested $\wedge$ and $\vee$ operators applied to literals. We apply the distributivity law from Figure 11, distributing $\vee$ over $\wedge$ wherever possible.

$$(\neg B_{1,1} \vee P_{1,2} \vee P_{2,1}) \wedge (\neg P_{1,2} \vee B_{1,1}) \wedge (\neg P_{2,1} \vee B_{1,1}) .$$

The original sentence is now in CNF, as a conjunction of three clauses. It is much harder to read, but it can be used as input to a resolution procedure.

A resolution algorithm

Inference procedures based on resolution work by using the principle of proof by contradiction introduced at the beginning of section. That is, to show that $KB \models \alpha$, we show that $(KB \wedge \neg\alpha)$ is unsatisfiable. We do this by proving a contradiction.

A resolution algorithm is shown in Figure 12. First, $(KB \wedge \neg\alpha)$ is converted into CNF. Then, the resolution rule is applied to the resulting clauses. Each pair that contains complementary literals is resolved to produce a new clause, which is added to the set if it is not already present. The process continues until one of two things happens:

- there are no new clauses that can be added, in which case KB does not entail α; or,
- two clauses resolve to yield the *empty* clause, in which case KB entails α.

The empty clause—a disjunction of no disjuncts—is equivalent to *False* because a disjunction is true only if at least one of its disjuncts is true. Another way to see that an empty clause represents a contradiction is to observe that it arises only from resolving two complementary unit clauses such as P and $\neg P$.

We can apply the resolution procedure to a very simple inference in the wumpus world. When the agent is in [1,1], there is no breeze, so there can be no pits in neighboring squares. The relevant knowledge base is

$$KB = R_2 \wedge R_4 = (B_{1,1} \Leftrightarrow (P_{1,2} \vee P_{2,1})) \wedge \neg B_{1,1}$$

and we wish to prove α which is, say, $\neg P_{1,2}$. When we convert $(KB \wedge \neg\alpha)$ into CNF, we obtain the clauses shown at the top of Figure 13. The second row of the figure shows clauses obtained by resolving pairs in the first row. Then, when $P_{1,2}$ is resolved with $\neg P_{1,2}$, we obtain the empty clause, shown as a small square. Inspection of Figure 13 reveals that many resolution steps are pointless. For example, the clause $B_{1,1} \vee \neg B_{1,1} \vee P_{1,2}$ is equivalent to $True \vee P_{1,2}$ which is equivalent to $True$. Deducing that $True$ is true is not very helpful. Therefore, any clause in which two complementary literals appear can be discarded.

```
function PL-RESOLUTION(KB, α) returns true or false
  inputs: KB, the knowledge base, a sentence in propositional logic
          α, the query, a sentence in propositional logic

  clauses ← the set of clauses in the CNF representation of KB ∧ ¬α
  new ← { }
  loop do
     for each pair of clauses Ci, Cj in clauses do
         resolvents ← PL-RESOLVE(Ci, Cj)
         if resolvents contains the empty clause then return true
         new ← new ∪ resolvents
     if new ⊆ clauses then return false
     clauses ← clauses ∪ new
```

Figure 12 A simple resolution algorithm for propositional logic. The function PL-RESOLVE returns the set of all possible clauses obtained by resolving its two inputs.

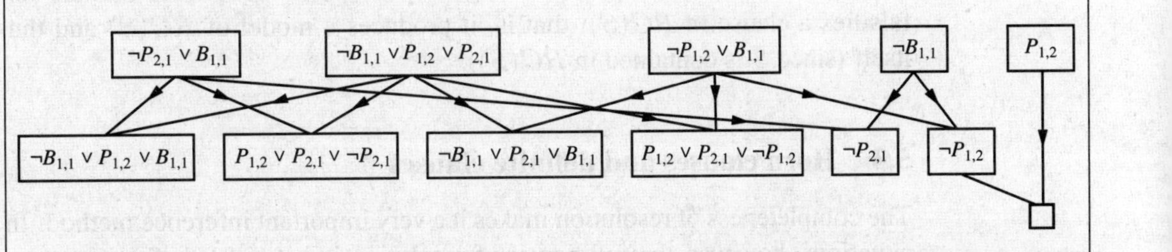

Figure 13 Partial application of PL-RESOLUTION to a simple inference in the wumpus world. $\neg P_{1,2}$ is shown to follow from the first four clauses in the top row.

Completeness of resolution

To conclude our discussion of resolution, we now show why PL-RESOLUTION is complete. RESOLUTION CLOSURE To do this, we introduce the **resolution closure** $RC(S)$ of a set of clauses S, which is the set of all clauses derivable by repeated application of the resolution rule to clauses in S or their derivatives. The resolution closure is what PL-RESOLUTION computes as the final value of the variable *clauses*. It is easy to see that $RC(S)$ must be finite, because there are only finitely many distinct clauses that can be constructed out of the symbols $P_1, \ldots, P_k$ that appear in S. (Notice that this would not be true without the factoring step that removes multiple copies of literals.) Hence, PL-RESOLUTION always terminates.

GROUND RESOLUTION THEOREM

The completeness theorem for resolution in propositional logic is called the **ground resolution theorem**:

> If a set of clauses is unsatisfiable, then the resolution closure of those clauses contains the empty clause.

This theorem is proved by demonstrating its contrapositive: if the closure $RC(S)$ does *not* contain the empty clause, then S is satisfiable. In fact, we can construct a model for S with suitable truth values for $P_1, \ldots, P_k$. The construction procedure is as follows:

For i from 1 to k,

- If a clause in $RC(S)$ contains the literal $\neg P_i$ and all its other literals are false under the assignment chosen for $P_1, \ldots, P_{i-1}$, then assign *false* to P_i.
- Otherwise, assign *true* to P_i.

This assignment to $P_1, \ldots, P_k$ is a model of S. To see this, assume the opposite—that, at some stage i in the sequence, assigning symbol P_i causes some clause C to become false. For this to happen, it must be the case that all the *other* literals in C must already have been falsified by assignments to $P_1, \ldots, P_{i-1}$. Thus, C must now look like either $(false \vee false \vee \cdots false \vee P_i)$ or like $(false \vee false \vee \cdots false \vee \neg P_i)$. If just one of these two is in $RC(S)$, then the algorithm will assign the appropriate truth value to P_i to make C true, so C can only be falsified if *both* of these clauses are in $RC(S)$. Now, since $RC(S)$ is closed under resolution, it will contain the resolvent of these two clauses, and that resolvent will have all of its literals already falsified by the assignments to $P_1, \ldots, P_{i-1}$. This contradicts our assumption that the first falsified clause appears at stage i. Hence, we have proved that the construction never falsifies a clause in $RC(S)$; that is, it produces a model of $RC(S)$ and thus a model of S itself (since S is contained in $RC(S)$).

5.3 Horn clauses and definite clauses

The completeness of resolution makes it a very important inference method. In many practical situations, however, the full power of resolution is not needed. Some real-world knowledge bases satisfy certain restrictions on the form of sentences they contain, which enables them to use a more restricted and efficient inference algorithm.

DEFINITE CLAUSE

One such restricted form is the **definite clause**, which is a disjunction of literals of which *exactly one is positive*. For example, the clause $(\neg L_{1,1} \vee \neg Breeze \vee B_{1,1})$ is a definite clause, whereas $(\neg B_{1,1} \vee P_{1,2} \vee P_{2,1})$ is not.

HORN CLAUSE

GOAL CLAUSES

Slightly more general is the **Horn clause**, which is a disjunction of literals of which *at most one is positive*. So all definite clauses are Horn clauses, as are clauses with no positive literals; these are called **goal clauses**. Horn clauses are closed under resolution: if you resolve two Horn clauses, you get back a Horn clause.

Knowledge bases containing only definite clauses are interesting for three reasons:

1. Every definite clause can be written as an implication whose premise is a conjunction of positive literals and whose conclusion is a single positive literal. (See Exercise 13.) For example, the definite clause $(\neg L_{1,1} \vee \neg Breeze \vee B_{1,1})$ can be written as the implication $(L_{1,1} \wedge Breeze) \Rightarrow B_{1,1}$. In the implication form, the sentence is easier to understand: it says that if the agent is in [1,1] and there is a breeze, then [1,1] is breezy.

   BODY

   HEAD

   FACT

   In Horn form, the premise is called the **body** and the conclusion is called the **head**. A sentence consisting of a single positive literal, such as $L_{1,1}$, is called a **fact**. It too can be written in implication form as $True \Rightarrow L_{1,1}$, but it is simpler to write just $L_{1,1}$.

$$
\begin{aligned}
\mathit{CNFSentence} &\rightarrow \mathit{Clause}_1 \wedge \cdots \wedge \mathit{Clause}_n \\
\mathit{Clause} &\rightarrow \mathit{Literal}_1 \vee \cdots \vee \mathit{Literal}_m \\
\mathit{Literal} &\rightarrow \mathit{Symbol} \mid \neg\mathit{Symbol} \\
\mathit{Symbol} &\rightarrow P \mid Q \mid R \mid \ldots \\
\mathit{HornClauseForm} &\rightarrow \mathit{DefiniteClauseForm} \mid \mathit{GoalClauseForm} \\
\mathit{DefiniteClauseForm} &\rightarrow (\mathit{Symbol}_1 \wedge \cdots \wedge \mathit{Symbol}_l) \Rightarrow \mathit{Symbol} \\
\mathit{GoalClauseForm} &\rightarrow (\mathit{Symbol}_1 \wedge \cdots \wedge \mathit{Symbol}_l) \Rightarrow \mathit{False}
\end{aligned}
$$

Figure 14 A grammar for conjunctive normal form, Horn clauses, and definite clauses. A clause such as $A \wedge B \Rightarrow C$ is still a definite clause when it is written as $\neg A \vee \neg B \vee C$, but only the former is considered the canonical form for definite clauses. One more class is the *k*-CNF sentence, which is a CNF sentence where each clause has at most *k* literals.

FORWARD-CHAINING
BACKWARD-CHAINING

2. Inference with Horn clauses can be done through the **forward-chaining** and **backward-chaining** algorithms, which we explain next. Both of these algorithms are natural, in that the inference steps are obvious and easy for humans to follow. This type of inference is the basis for **logic programming**.
3. Deciding entailment with Horn clauses can be done in time that is *linear* in the size of the knowledge base—a pleasant surprise.

5.4 Forward and backward chaining

The forward-chaining algorithm PL-FC-ENTAILS?(KB, q) determines if a single proposition symbol q—the query—is entailed by a knowledge base of definite clauses. It begins from known facts (positive literals) in the knowledge base. If all the premises of an implication are known, then its conclusion is added to the set of known facts. For example, if $L_{1,1}$ and *Breeze* are known and $(L_{1,1} \wedge \mathit{Breeze}) \Rightarrow B_{1,1}$ is in the knowledge base, then $B_{1,1}$ can be added. This process continues until the query q is added or until no further inferences can be made. The detailed algorithm is shown in Figure 15; the main point to remember is that it runs in linear time.

The best way to understand the algorithm is through an example and a picture. Figure 16(a) shows a simple knowledge base of Horn clauses with A and B as known facts. Figure 16(b) shows the same knowledge base drawn as an **AND–OR** graph. In AND–OR graphs, multiple links joined by an arc indicate a conjunction—every link must be proved—while multiple links without an arc indicate a disjunction—any link can be proved. It is easy to see how forward chaining works in the graph. The known leaves (here, A and B) are set, and inference propagates up the graph as far as possible. Wherever a conjunction appears, the propagation waits until all the conjuncts are known before proceeding. The reader is encouraged to work through the example in detail.

```
function PL-FC-ENTAILS?(KB, q) returns true or false
  inputs: KB, the knowledge base, a set of propositional definite clauses
          q, the query, a proposition symbol
  count ← a table, where count[c] is the number of symbols in c's premise
  inferred ← a table, where inferred[s] is initially false for all symbols
  agenda ← a queue of symbols, initially symbols known to be true in KB

  while agenda is not empty do
     p ← POP(agenda)
     if p = q then return true
     if inferred[p] = false then
        inferred[p] ← true
        for each clause c in KB where p is in c.PREMISE do
           decrement count[c]
           if count[c] = 0 then add c.CONCLUSION to agenda
  return false
```

Figure 15 The forward-chaining algorithm for propositional logic. The *agenda* keeps track of symbols known to be true but not yet "processed." The *count* table keeps track of how many premises of each implication are as yet unknown. Whenever a new symbol p from the agenda is processed, the count is reduced by one for each implication in whose premise p appears (easily identified in constant time with appropriate indexing.) If a count reaches zero, all the premises of the implication are known, so its conclusion can be added to the agenda. Finally, we need to keep track of which symbols have been processed; a symbol that is already in the set of inferred symbols need not be added to the agenda again. This avoids redundant work and prevents loops caused by implications such as $P \Rightarrow Q$ and $Q \Rightarrow P$.

It is easy to see that forward chaining is **sound**: every inference is essentially an application of Modus Ponens. Forward chaining is also **complete**: every entailed atomic sentence will be derived. The easiest way to see this is to consider the final state of the *inferred* table (after the algorithm reaches a **fixed point** where no new inferences are possible). The table contains *true* for each symbol inferred during the process, and *false* for all other symbols. We can view the table as a logical model; moreover, *every definite clause in the original KB is true in this model.* To see this, assume the opposite, namely that some clause $a_1 \wedge \ldots \wedge a_k \Rightarrow b$ is false in the model. Then $a_1 \wedge \ldots \wedge a_k$ must be true in the model and b must be false in the model. But this contradicts our assumption that the algorithm has reached a fixed point! We can conclude, therefore, that the set of atomic sentences inferred at the fixed point defines a model of the original KB. Furthermore, any atomic sentence q that is entailed by the KB must be true in all its models and in this model in particular. Hence, every entailed atomic sentence q must be inferred by the algorithm.

FIXED POINT

DATA-DRIVEN

Forward chaining is an example of the general concept of **data-driven** reasoning—that is, reasoning in which the focus of attention starts with the known data. It can be used within an agent to derive conclusions from incoming percepts, often without a specific query in mind. For example, the wumpus agent might TELL its percepts to the knowledge base using

$$P \Rightarrow Q$$
$$L \wedge M \Rightarrow P$$
$$B \wedge L \Rightarrow M$$
$$A \wedge P \Rightarrow L$$
$$A \wedge B \Rightarrow L$$
$$A$$
$$B$$

(a)

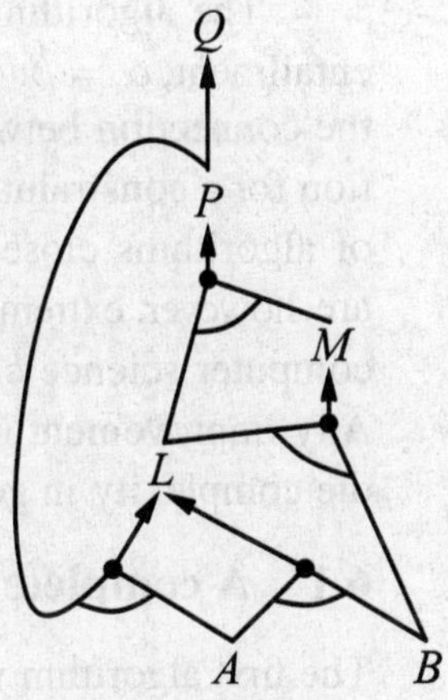

(b)

Figure 16 (a) A set of Horn clauses. (b) The corresponding AND–OR graph.

an incremental forward-chaining algorithm in which new facts can be added to the agenda to initiate new inferences. In humans, a certain amount of data-driven reasoning occurs as new information arrives. For example, if I am indoors and hear rain starting to fall, it might occur to me that the picnic will be canceled. Yet it will probably not occur to me that the seventeenth petal on the largest rose in my neighbor's garden will get wet; humans keep forward chaining under careful control, lest they be swamped with irrelevant consequences.

The backward-chaining algorithm, as its name suggests, works backward from the query. If the query q is known to be true, then no work is needed. Otherwise, the algorithm finds those implications in the knowledge base whose conclusion is q. If all the premises of one of those implications can be proved true (by backward chaining), then q is true. When applied to the query Q in Figure 16, it works back down the graph until it reaches a set of known facts, A and B, that forms the basis for a proof. As with forward chaining, an efficient implementation runs in linear time.

GOAL-DIRECTED REASONING

Backward chaining is a form of **goal-directed reasoning**. It is useful for answering specific questions such as "What shall I do now?" and "Where are my keys?" Often, the cost of backward chaining is *much less* than linear in the size of the knowledge base, because the process touches only relevant facts.

6 EFFECTIVE PROPOSITIONAL MODEL CHECKING

In this section, we describe two families of efficient algorithms for general propositional inference based on model checking: One approach based on backtracking search, and one on local hill-climbing search. These algorithms are part of the "technology" of propositional logic. This section can be skimmed on a first reading of the chapter.

The algorithms we describe are for checking satisfiability: the SAT problem. (Testing entailment, $\alpha \models \beta$, can be done by testing *un*satisfiability of $\alpha \wedge \neg\beta$.) We have already noted the connection between finding a satisfying model for a logical sentence and finding a solution for a constraint satisfaction problem, so it is perhaps not surprising that the two families of algorithms closely resemble backtracking algorithms and local search algorithms. They are, however, extremely important in their own right because so many combinatorial problems in computer science can be reduced to checking the satisfiability of a propositional sentence. Any improvement in satisfiability algorithms has huge consequences for our ability to handle complexity in general.

6.1 A complete backtracking algorithm

DAVIS–PUTNAM ALGORITHM

The first algorithm we consider is often called the **Davis–Putnam algorithm**, after the seminal paper by Martin Davis and Hilary Putnam (1960). The algorithm is in fact the version described by Davis, Logemann, and Loveland (1962), so we will call it DPLL after the initials of all four authors. DPLL takes as input a sentence in conjunctive normal form—a set of clauses. Like BACKTRACKING-SEARCH and TT-ENTAILS?, it is essentially a recursive, depth-first enumeration of possible models. It embodies three improvements over the simple scheme of TT-ENTAILS?:

- *Early termination*: The algorithm detects whether the sentence must be true or false, even with a partially completed model. A clause is true if *any* literal is true, even if the other literals do not yet have truth values; hence, the sentence as a whole could be judged true even before the model is complete. For example, the sentence $(A \vee B) \wedge (A \vee C)$ is true if A is true, regardless of the values of B and C. Similarly, a sentence is false if *any* clause is false, which occurs when each of its literals is false. Again, this can occur long before the model is complete. Early termination avoids examination of entire subtrees in the search space.

PURE SYMBOL

- *Pure symbol heuristic*: A **pure symbol** is a symbol that always appears with the same "sign" in all clauses. For example, in the three clauses $(A \vee \neg B)$, $(\neg B \vee \neg C)$, and $(C \vee A)$, the symbol A is pure because only the positive literal appears, B is pure because only the negative literal appears, and C is impure. It is easy to see that if a sentence has a model, then it has a model with the pure symbols assigned so as to make their literals *true*, because doing so can never make a clause false. Note that, in determining the purity of a symbol, the algorithm can ignore clauses that are already known to be true in the model constructed so far. For example, if the model contains $B = false$, then the clause $(\neg B \vee \neg C)$ is already true, and in the remaining clauses C appears only as a positive literal; therefore C becomes pure.
- *Unit clause heuristic*: A **unit clause** was defined earlier as a clause with just one literal. In the context of DPLL, it also means clauses in which all literals but one are already assigned *false* by the model. For example, if the model contains $B = true$, then $(\neg B \vee \neg C)$ simplifies to $\neg C$, which is a unit clause. Obviously, for this clause to be true, C must be set to *false*. The unit clause heuristic assigns all such symbols before branching on the remainder. One important consequence of the heuristic is that

```
function DPLL-SATISFIABLE?(s) returns true or false
  inputs: s, a sentence in propositional logic

  clauses ← the set of clauses in the CNF representation of s
  symbols ← a list of the proposition symbols in s
  return DPLL(clauses, symbols, { })
```

```
function DPLL(clauses, symbols, model) returns true or false
  if every clause in clauses is true in model then return true
  if some clause in clauses is false in model then return false
  P, value ← FIND-PURE-SYMBOL(symbols, clauses, model)
  if P is non-null then return DPLL(clauses, symbols – P, model ∪ {P=value})
  P, value ← FIND-UNIT-CLAUSE(clauses, model)
  if P is non-null then return DPLL(clauses, symbols – P, model ∪ {P=value})
  P ← FIRST(symbols); rest ← REST(symbols)
  return DPLL(clauses, rest, model ∪ {P=true}) or
         DPLL(clauses, rest, model ∪ {P=false}))
```

Figure 17 The DPLL algorithm for checking satisfiability of a sentence in propositional logic. The ideas behind FIND-PURE-SYMBOL and FIND-UNIT-CLAUSE are described in the text; each returns a symbol (or null) and the truth value to assign to that symbol. Like TT-ENTAILS?, DPLL operates over partial models.

any attempt to prove (by refutation) a literal that is already in the knowledge base will succeed immediately (Exercise 23). Notice also that assigning one unit clause can create another unit clause—for example, when C is set to *false*, $(C \lor A)$ becomes a unit clause, causing *true* to be assigned to A. This "cascade" of forced assignments is called **unit propagation**. It resembles the process of forward chaining with definite clauses, and indeed, if the CNF expression contains only definite clauses then DPLL essentially replicates forward chaining. (See Exercise 24.)

UNIT PROPAGATION

The DPLL algorithm is shown in Figure 17, which gives the the essential skeleton of the search process.

What Figure 17 does not show are the tricks that enable SAT solvers to scale up to large problems. It is interesting that most of these tricks are in fact rather general, and we have seen them before in other guises:

1. **Component analysis** (as seen with Tasmania in CSPs): As DPLL assigns truth values to variables, the set of clauses may become separated into disjoint subsets, called **components**, that share no unassigned variables. Given an efficient way to detect when this occurs, a solver can gain considerable speed by working on each component separately.
2. **Variable and value ordering:** Our simple implementation of DPLL uses an arbitrary variable ordering and always tries the value *true* before *false*. The **degree heuristic** suggests choosing the variable that appears most frequently over all remaining clauses.

3. **Intelligent backtracking:** Many problems that cannot be solved in hours of run time with chronological backtracking can be solved in seconds with intelligent backtracking that backs up all the way to the relevant point of conflict. All SAT solvers that do intelligent backtracking use some form of **conflict clause learning** to record conflicts so that they won't be repeated later in the search. Usually a limited-size set of conflicts is kept, and rarely used ones are dropped.
4. **Random restarts:** Sometimes a run appears not to be making progress. In this case, we can start over from the top of the search tree, rather than trying to continue. After restarting, different random choices (in variable and value selection) are made. Clauses that are learned in the first run are retained after the restart and can help prune the search space. Restarting does not guarantee that a solution will be found faster, but it does reduce the variance on the time to solution.
5. **Clever indexing** (as seen in many algorithms): The speedup methods used in DPLL itself, as well as the tricks used in modern solvers, require fast indexing of such things as "the set of clauses in which variable X_i appears as a positive literal." This task is complicated by the fact that the algorithms are interested only in the clauses that have not yet been satisfied by previous assignments to variables, so the indexing structures must be updated dynamically as the computation proceeds.

With these enhancements, modern solvers can handle problems with tens of millions of variables. They have revolutionized areas such as hardware verification and security protocol verification, which previously required laborious, hand-guided proofs.

6.2 Local search algorithms

Local search algorithms can be applied directly to satisfiability problems, provided that we choose the right evaluation function. Because the goal is to find an assignment that satisfies every clause, an evaluation function that counts the number of unsatisfied clauses will do the job. In fact, this is exactly the measure used by the MIN-CONFLICTS algorithm for CSPs. All these algorithms take steps in the space of complete assignments, flipping the truth value of one symbol at a time. The space usually contains many local minima, to escape from which various forms of randomness are required. In recent years, there has been a great deal of experimentation to find a good balance between greediness and randomness.

One of the simplest and most effective algorithms to emerge from all this work is called WALKSAT (Figure 18). On every iteration, the algorithm picks an unsatisfied clause and picks a symbol in the clause to flip. It chooses randomly between two ways to pick which symbol to flip: (1) a "min-conflicts" step that minimizes the number of unsatisfied clauses in the new state and (2) a "random walk" step that picks the symbol randomly.

When WALKSAT returns a model, the input sentence is indeed satisfiable, but when it returns *failure*, there are two possible causes: either the sentence is unsatisfiable or we need to give the algorithm more time. If we set $max\_flips = \infty$ and $p > 0$, WALKSAT will eventually return a model (if one exists), because the random-walk steps will eventually hit

```
function WALKSAT(clauses, p, max_flips) returns a satisfying model or failure
  inputs: clauses, a set of clauses in propositional logic
          p, the probability of choosing to do a "random walk" move, typically around 0.5
          max_flips, number of flips allowed before giving up

  model ← a random assignment of true/false to the symbols in clauses
  for i = 1 to max_flips do
     if model satisfies clauses then return model
     clause ← a randomly selected clause from clauses that is false in model
     with probability p flip the value in model of a randomly selected symbol from clause
     else flip whichever symbol in clause maximizes the number of satisfied clauses
  return failure
```

Figure 18 The WALKSAT algorithm for checking satisfiability by randomly flipping the values of variables. Many versions of the algorithm exist.

upon the solution. Alas, if *max_flips* is infinity and the sentence is unsatisfiable, then the algorithm never terminates!

For this reason, WALKSAT is most useful when we expect a solution to exist. On the other hand, WALKSAT cannot always detect *unsatisfiability*, which is required for deciding entailment. For example, an agent cannot *reliably* use WALKSAT to prove that a square is safe in the wumpus world. Instead, it can say, "I thought about it for an hour and couldn't come up with a possible world in which the square *isn't* safe." This may be a good empirical indicator that the square is safe, but it's certainly not a proof.

6.3 The landscape of random SAT problems

Some SAT problems are harder than others. *Easy* problems can be solved by any old algorithm, but because we know that SAT is NP-complete, at least some problem instances must require exponential run time. Some problems—thought to be quite tricky for backtracking search algorithms—are trivially easy for local search methods, such as min-conflicts. Solutions can be very densely distributed in the space of assignments, and any initial assignment is guaranteed to have a solution nearby. In these cases, the problems are easy because they are **underconstrained**.

UNDERCONSTRAINED

When we look at satisfiability problems in conjunctive normal form, an underconstrained problem is one with relatively *few* clauses constraining the variables. For example, here is a randomly generated 3-CNF sentence with five symbols and five clauses:

$$(\neg D \lor \neg B \lor C) \land (B \lor \neg A \lor \neg C) \land (\neg C \lor \neg B \lor E) \land (E \lor \neg D \lor B) \land (B \lor E \lor \neg C)\,.$$

Sixteen of the 32 possible assignments are models of this sentence, so, on average, it would take just two random guesses to find a model. This is an easy satisfiability problem, as are most such underconstrained problems. On the other hand, an *overconstrained* problem has many clauses relative to the number of variables and is likely to have no solutions.

To go beyond these basic intuitions, we must define exactly how random sentences are generated. The notation $CNF_k(m, n)$ denotes a k-CNF sentence with m clauses and n symbols, where the clauses are chosen uniformly, independently, and without replacement from among all clauses with k different literals, which are positive or negative at random. (A symbol may not appear twice in a clause, nor may a clause appear twice in a sentence.)

Given a source of random sentences, we can measure the probability of satisfiability. Figure 19(a) plots the probability for $CNF_3(m, 50)$, that is, sentences with 50 variables and 3 literals per clause, as a function of the clause/symbol ratio, m/n. As we expect, for small m/n the probability of satisfiability is close to 1, and at large m/n the probability is close to 0. The probability drops fairly sharply around $m/n = 4.3$. Empirically, we find that the "cliff" stays in roughly the same place (for $k = 3$) and gets sharper and sharper as n increases. Theoretically, the **satisfiability threshold conjecture** says that for every $k \geq 3$, there is a threshold ratio r_k such that, as n goes to infinity, the probability that $CNF_k(n, rn)$ is satisfiable becomes 1 for all values of r below the threshold, and 0 for all values above. The conjecture remains unproven.

SATISFIABILITY THRESHOLD CONJECTURE

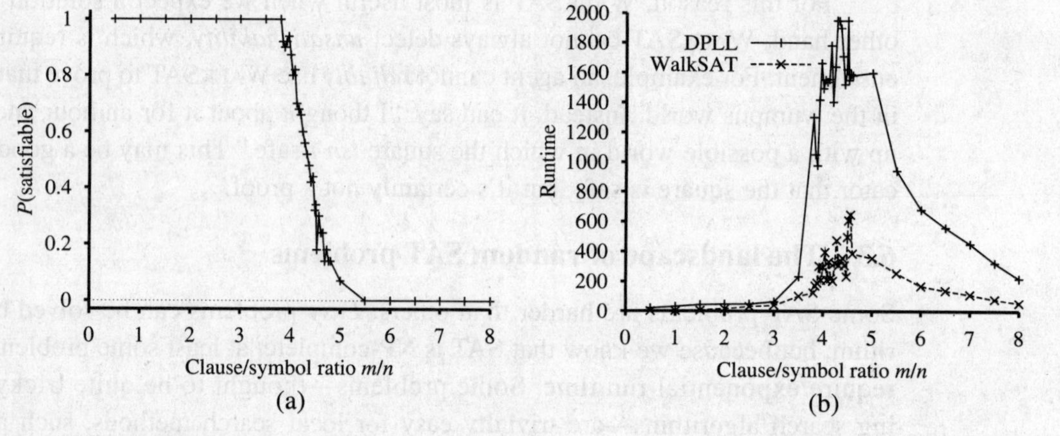

Figure 19 (a) Graph showing the probability that a random 3-CNF sentence with $n = 50$ symbols is satisfiable, as a function of the clause/symbol ratio m/n. (b) Graph of the median run time (measured in number of recursive calls to DPLL, a good proxy) on random 3-CNF sentences. The most difficult problems have a clause/symbol ratio of about 4.3.

Now that we have a good idea where the satisfiable and unsatisfiable problems are, the next question is, where are the hard problems? It turns out that they are also often at the threshold value. Figure 19(b) shows that 50-symbol problems at the threshold value of 4.3 are about 20 times more difficult to solve than those at a ratio of 3.3. The underconstrained problems are easiest to solve (because it is so easy to guess a solution); the overconstrained problems are not as easy as the underconstrained, but still are much easier than the ones right at the threshold.

7 AGENTS BASED ON PROPOSITIONAL LOGIC

In this section, we bring together what we have learned so far in order to construct wumpus world agents that use propositional logic. The first step is to enable the agent to deduce, to the extent possible, the state of the world given its percept history. This requires writing down a complete logical model of the effects of actions. We also show how the agent can keep track of the world efficiently without going back into the percept history for each inference. Finally, we show how the agent can use logical inference to construct plans that are guaranteed to achieve its goals.

7.1 The current state of the world

As stated at the beginning of the chapter, a logical agent operates by deducing what to do from a knowledge base of sentences about the world. The knowledge base is composed of axioms—general knowledge about how the world works—and percept sentences obtained from the agent's experience in a particular world. In this section, we focus on the problem of deducing the current state of the wumpus world—where am I, is that square safe, and so on.

We began collecting axioms in Section 4.3. The agent knows that the starting square contains no pit ($\neg P_{1,1}$) and no wumpus ($\neg W_{1,1}$). Furthermore, for each square, it knows that the square is breezy if and only if a neighboring square has a pit; and a square is smelly if and only if a neighboring square has a wumpus. Thus, we include a large collection of sentences of the following form:

$$
\begin{aligned}
&B_{1,1} \;\Leftrightarrow\; (P_{1,2} \lor P_{2,1}) \\
&S_{1,1} \;\Leftrightarrow\; (W_{1,2} \lor W_{2,1}) \\
&\ldots
\end{aligned}
$$

The agent also knows that there is exactly one wumpus. This is expressed in two parts. First, we have to say that there is *at least one* wumpus:

$$W_{1,1} \lor W_{1,2} \lor \cdots \lor W_{4,3} \lor W_{4,4}$$

Then, we have to say that there is *at most one* wumpus. For each pair of locations, we add a sentence saying that at least one of them must be wumpus-free:

$$
\begin{aligned}
&\neg W_{1,1} \lor \neg W_{1,2} \\
&\neg W_{1,1} \lor \neg W_{1,3} \\
&\ldots \\
&\neg W_{4,3} \lor \neg W_{4,4}\,.
\end{aligned}
$$

So far, so good. Now let's consider the agent's percepts. If there is currently a stench, one might suppose that a proposition *Stench* should be added to the knowledge base. This is not quite right, however: if there was no stench at the previous time step, then $\neg$*Stench* would already be asserted, and the new assertion would simply result in a contradiction. The problem is solved when we realize that a percept asserts something *only about the current time*. Thus, if the time step (as supplied to MAKE-PERCEPT-SENTENCE in Figure 1) is 4, then we add

$Stench^4$ to the knowledge base, rather than $Stench$—neatly avoiding any contradiction with $\neg Stench^3$. The same goes for the breeze, bump, glitter, and scream percepts.

The idea of associating propositions with time steps extends to any aspect of the world that changes over time. For example, the initial knowledge base includes $L^0_{1,1}$—the agent is in square $[1, 1]$ at time 0—as well as $FacingEast^0$, $HaveArrow^0$, and $WumpusAlive^0$. We use the word **fluent** (from the Latin *fluens*, flowing) to refer an aspect of the world that changes. Symbols associated with permanent aspects of the world do not need a time superscript and are sometimes called **atemporal variables.**

FLUENT

ATEMPORAL VARIABLE

We can connect stench and breeze percepts directly to the properties of the squares where they are experienced through the location fluent as follows.[9] For any time step t and any square $[x, y]$, we assert

$$L^t_{x,y} \Rightarrow (Breeze^t \Leftrightarrow B_{x,y})$$
$$L^t_{x,y} \Rightarrow (Stench^t \Leftrightarrow S_{x,y}) .$$

Now, of course, we need axioms that allow the agent to keep track of fluents such as $L^t_{x,y}$. These fluents change as the result of actions taken by the agent, so we need to write down the transition model of the wumpus world as a set of logical sentences.

First, we need proposition symbols for the occurrences of actions. As with percepts, these symbols are indexed by time; thus, $Forward^0$ means that the agent executes the *Forward* action at time 0. By convention, the percept for a given time step happens first, followed by the action for that time step, followed by a transition to the next time step.

EFFECT AXIOM

To describe how the world changes, we can try writing **effect axioms** that specify the outcome of an action at the next time step. For example, if the agent is at location $[1, 1]$ facing east at time 0 and goes *Forward*, the result is that the agent is in square $[2, 1]$ and no longer is in $[1, 1]$:

$$L^0_{1,1} \wedge FacingEast^0 \wedge Forward^0 \Rightarrow (L^1_{2,1} \wedge \neg L^1_{1,1}) . \quad (1)$$

We would need one such sentence for each possible time step, for each of the 16 squares, and each of the four orientations. We would also need similar sentences for the other actions: *Grab*, *Shoot*, *Climb*, *TurnLeft*, and *TurnRight*.

Let us suppose that the agent does decide to move *Forward* at time 0 and asserts this fact into its knowledge base. Given the effect axiom in Equation (1), combined with the initial assertions about the state at time 0, the agent can now deduce that it is in $[2, 1]$. That is, $\text{ASK}(KB, L^1_{2,1}) = true$. So far, so good. Unfortunately, the news elsewhere is less good: if we $\text{ASK}(KB, HaveArrow^1)$, the answer is *false*, that is, the agent cannot prove it still has the arrow; nor can it prove it *doesn't* have it! The information has been lost because the effect axiom fails to state what remains *unchanged* as the result of an action. The need to do this gives rise to the **frame problem.**[10] One possible solution to the frame problem would

FRAME PROBLEM

[9] Section 4.3 conveniently glossed over this requirement.

[10] The name "frame problem" comes from "frame of reference" in physics—the assumed stationary background with respect to which motion is measured. It also has an analogy to the frames of a movie, in which normally most of the background stays constant while changes occur in the foreground.

FRAME AXIOM

be to add **frame axioms** explicitly asserting all the propositions that remain the same. For example, for each time t we would have

$$\begin{aligned} &Forward^t \Rightarrow (HaveArrow^t \Leftrightarrow HaveArrow^{t+1}) \\ &Forward^t \Rightarrow (WumpusAlive^t \Leftrightarrow WumpusAlive^{t+1}) \\ &\ldots \end{aligned}$$

where we explicitly mention every proposition that stays unchanged from time t to time $t+1$ under the action *Forward*. Although the agent now knows that it still has the arrow after moving forward and that the wumpus hasn't died or come back to life, the proliferation of frame axioms seems remarkably inefficient. In a world with m different actions and n fluents, the set of frame axioms will be of size $O(mn)$. This specific manifestation of the frame problem is sometimes called the **representational frame problem**. Historically, the problem was a significant one for AI researchers; we explore it further in the notes at the end of the chapter.

REPRESENTATIONAL FRAME PROBLEM

The representational frame problem is significant because the real world has very many fluents, to put it mildly. Fortunately for us humans, each action typically changes no more than some small number k of those fluents—the world exhibits **locality**. Solving the representational frame problem requires defining the transition model with a set of axioms of size $O(mk)$ rather than size $O(mn)$. There is also an **inferential frame problem**: the problem of projecting forward the results of a t step plan of action in time $O(kt)$ rather than $O(nt)$.

LOCALITY

INFERENTIAL FRAME PROBLEM

The solution to the problem involves changing one's focus from writing axioms about *actions* to writing axioms about *fluents*. Thus, for each fluent F, we will have an axiom that defines the truth value of F^{t+1} in terms of fluents (including F itself) at time t and the actions that may have occurred at time t. Now, the truth value of F^{t+1} can be set in one of two ways: either the action at time t causes F to be true at $t+1$, or F was already true at time t and the action at time t does not cause it to be false. An axiom of this form is called a **successor-state axiom** and has this schema:

SUCCESSOR-STATE AXIOM

$$F^{t+1} \Leftrightarrow ActionCausesF^t \vee (F^t \wedge \neg ActionCausesNotF^t) .$$

One of the simplest successor-state axioms is the one for *HaveArrow*. Because there is no action for reloading, the $ActionCausesF^t$ part goes away and we are left with

$$HaveArrow^{t+1} \Leftrightarrow (HaveArrow^t \wedge \neg Shoot^t) . \tag{2}$$

For the agent's location, the successor-state axioms are more elaborate. For example, $L_{1,1}^{t+1}$ is true if either (a) the agent moved *Forward* from $[1,2]$ when facing south, or from $[2,1]$ when facing west; or (b) $L_{1,1}^t$ was already true and the action did not cause movement (either because the action was not *Forward* or because the action bumped into a wall). Written out in propositional logic, this becomes

$$\begin{aligned} L_{1,1}^{t+1} \Leftrightarrow\ & (L_{1,1}^t \wedge (\neg Forward^t \vee Bump^{t+1})) \\ \vee\ & (L_{1,2}^t \wedge (South^t \wedge Forward^t)) \\ \vee\ & (L_{2,1}^t \wedge (West^t \wedge Forward^t)) . \end{aligned} \tag{3}$$

Exercise 26 asks you to write out axioms for the remaining wumpus world fluents.

Given a complete set of successor-state axioms and the other axioms listed at the beginning of this section, the agent will be able to ASK and answer any answerable question about the current state of the world. For example, in Section 2 the initial sequence of percepts and actions is

$$\begin{array}{ll} \neg Stench^0 \wedge \neg Breeze^0 \wedge \neg Glitter^0 \wedge \neg Bump^0 \wedge \neg Scream^0 & ;\ Forward^0 \\ \neg Stench^1 \wedge Breeze^1 \wedge \neg Glitter^1 \wedge \neg Bump^1 \wedge \neg Scream^1 & ;\ TurnRight^1 \\ \neg Stench^2 \wedge Breeze^2 \wedge \neg Glitter^2 \wedge \neg Bump^2 \wedge \neg Scream^2 & ;\ TurnRight^2 \\ \neg Stench^3 \wedge Breeze^3 \wedge \neg Glitter^3 \wedge \neg Bump^3 \wedge \neg Scream^3 & ;\ Forward^3 \\ \neg Stench^4 \wedge \neg Breeze^4 \wedge \neg Glitter^4 \wedge \neg Bump^4 \wedge \neg Scream^4 & ;\ TurnRight^4 \\ \neg Stench^5 \wedge \neg Breeze^5 \wedge \neg Glitter^5 \wedge \neg Bump^5 \wedge \neg Scream^5 & ;\ Forward^5 \\ Stench^6 \wedge \neg Breeze^6 \wedge \neg Glitter^6 \wedge \neg Bump^6 \wedge \neg Scream^6 & \end{array}$$

At this point, we have $\text{ASK}(KB, L^6_{1,2}) = true$, so the agent knows where it is. Moreover, $\text{ASK}(KB, W_{1,3}) = true$ and $\text{ASK}(KB, P_{3,1}) = true$, so the agent has found the wumpus and one of the pits. The most important question for the agent is whether a square is OK to move into, that is, the square contains no pit nor live wumpus. It's convenient to add axioms for this, having the form

$$OK^t_{x,y} \Leftrightarrow \neg P_{x,y} \wedge \neg(W_{x,y} \wedge WumpusAlive^t)\ .$$

Finally, $\text{ASK}(KB, OK^6_{2,2}) = true$, so the square [2, 2] is OK to move into. In fact, given a sound and complete inference algorithm such as DPLL, the agent can answer any answerable question about which squares are OK—and can do so in just a few milliseconds for small-to-medium wumpus worlds.

Solving the representational and inferential frame problems is a big step forward, but a pernicious problem remains: we need to confirm that *all* the necessary preconditions of an action hold for it to have its intended effect. We said that the *Forward* action moves the agent ahead unless there is a wall in the way, but there are many other unusual exceptions that could cause the action to fail: the agent might trip and fall, be stricken with a heart attack, be carried away by giant bats, etc. Specifying all these exceptions is called the **qualification problem**. There is no complete solution within logic; system designers have to use good judgment in deciding how detailed they want to be in specifying their model, and what details they want to leave out. Probability theory allows us to summarize all the exceptions without explicitly naming them.

QUALIFICATION PROBLEM

7.2 A hybrid agent

The ability to deduce various aspects of the state of the world can be combined fairly straightforwardly with condition–action rules and with problem-solving algorithms to produce a **hybrid agent** for the wumpus world. Figure 20 shows one possible way to do this. The agent program maintains and updates a knowledge base as well as a current plan. The initial knowledge base contains the *atemporal* axioms—those that don't depend on *t*, such as the axiom relating the breeziness of squares to the presence of pits. At each time step, the new percept sentence is added along with all the axioms that depend on *t*, such as the successor-state

HYBRID AGENT

as the successor-state axioms. (The next section explains why the agent doesn't need axioms for *future* time steps.) Then, the agent uses logical inference, by ASKing questions of the knowledge base, to work out which squares are safe and which have yet to be visited.

The main body of the agent program constructs a plan based on a decreasing priority of goals. First, if there is a glitter, the program constructs a plan to grab the gold, follow a route back to the initial location, and climb out of the cave. Otherwise, if there is no current plan, the program plans a route to the closest safe square that it has not visited yet, making sure the route goes through only safe squares. Route planning is done with A* search, not with ASK. If there are no safe squares to explore, the next step—if the agent still has an arrow—is to try to make a safe square by shooting at one of the possible wumpus locations. These are determined by asking where $\text{ASK}(KB, \neg W_{x,y})$ is false—that is, where it is *not* known that there is *not* a wumpus. The function PLAN-SHOT (not shown) uses PLAN-ROUTE to plan a sequence of actions that will line up this shot. If this fails, the program looks for a square to explore that is not provably unsafe—that is, a square for which $\text{ASK}(KB, \neg OK^t_{x,y})$ returns false. If there is no such square, then the mission is impossible and the agent retreats to $[1, 1]$ and climbs out of the cave.

7.3 Logical state estimation

The agent program in Figure 20 works quite well, but it has one major weakness: as time goes by, the computational expense involved in the calls to ASK goes up and up. This happens mainly because the required inferences have to go back further and further in time and involve more and more proposition symbols. Obviously, this is unsustainable—we cannot have an agent whose time to process each percept grows in proportion to the length of its life! What we really need is a *constant* update time—that is, independent of t. The obvious answer is to save, or **cache**, the results of inference, so that the inference process at the next time step can build on the results of earlier steps instead of having to start again from scratch.

CACHING

The past history of percepts and all their ramifications can be replaced by the **belief state**—that is, some representation of the set of all possible current states of the world.[11] The process of updating the belief state as new percepts arrive is called **state estimation**. As opposed to the belief state being an explicit list of states, here we can use a logical sentence involving the proposition symbols associated with the current time step, as well as the atemporal symbols. For example, the logical sentence

$$WumpusAlive^1 \wedge L^1_{2,1} \wedge B_{2,1} \wedge (P_{3,1} \vee P_{2,2}) \qquad (4)$$

represents the set of all states at time 1 in which the wumpus is alive, the agent is at $[2, 1]$, that square is breezy, and there is a pit in $[3, 1]$ or $[2, 2]$ or both.

Maintaining an exact belief state as a logical formula turns out not to be easy. If there are n fluent symbols for time t, then there are 2^n possible states—that is, assignments of truth values to those symbols. Now, the set of belief states is the powerset (set of all subsets) of the set of physical states. There are 2^n physical states, hence 2^{2^n} belief states. Even if we used the most compact possible encoding of logical formulas, with each belief state represented

[11] We can think of the percept history itself as a representation of the belief state, but one that makes inference increasingly expensive as the history gets longer.

```
function HYBRID-WUMPUS-AGENT(percept) returns an action
  inputs: percept, a list, [stench,breeze,glitter,bump,scream]
  persistent: KB, a knowledge base, initially the atemporal "wumpus physics"
              t, a counter, initially 0, indicating time
              plan, an action sequence, initially empty

  TELL(KB, MAKE-PERCEPT-SENTENCE(percept, t))
  TELL the KB the temporal "physics" sentences for time t
  safe ← {[x, y] : ASK(KB, OK^t_{x,y}) = true}
  if ASK(KB, Glitter^t) = true then
    plan ← [Grab] + PLAN-ROUTE(current, {[1,1]}, safe) + [Climb]
  if plan is empty then
    unvisited ← {[x, y] : ASK(KB, L^{t'}_{x,y}) = false for all t' ≤ t}
    plan ← PLAN-ROUTE(current, unvisited ∩ safe, safe)
  if plan is empty and ASK(KB, HaveArrow^t) = true then
    possible_wumpus ← {[x, y] : ASK(KB, ¬ W_{x,y}) = false}
    plan ← PLAN-SHOT(current, possible_wumpus, safe)
  if plan is empty then  // no choice but to take a risk
    not_unsafe ← {[x, y] : ASK(KB, ¬ OK^t_{x,y}) = false}
    plan ← PLAN-ROUTE(current, unvisited ∩ not_unsafe, safe)
  if plan is empty then
    plan ← PLAN-ROUTE(current, {[1, 1]}, safe) + [Climb]
  action ← POP(plan)
  TELL(KB, MAKE-ACTION-SENTENCE(action, t))
  t ← t + 1
  return action

function PLAN-ROUTE(current,goals,allowed) returns an action sequence
  inputs: current, the agent's current position
          goals, a set of squares; try to plan a route to one of them
          allowed, a set of squares that can form part of the route

  problem ← ROUTE-PROBLEM(current, goals,allowed)
  return A*-GRAPH-SEARCH(problem)
```

Figure 20 A hybrid agent program for the wumpus world. It uses a propositional knowledge base to infer the state of the world, and a combination of problem-solving search and domain-specific code to decide what actions to take.

by a unique binary number, we would need numbers with $\log_2(2^{2^n}) = 2^n$ bits to label the current belief state. That is, exact state estimation may require logical formulas whose size is exponential in the number of symbols.

One very common and natural scheme for *approximate* state estimation is to represent belief states as conjunctions of literals, that is, 1-CNF formulas. To do this, the agent program simply tries to prove X^t and $\neg X^t$ for each symbol X^t (as well as each atemporal symbol whose truth value is not yet known), given the belief state at $t - 1$. The conjunction of

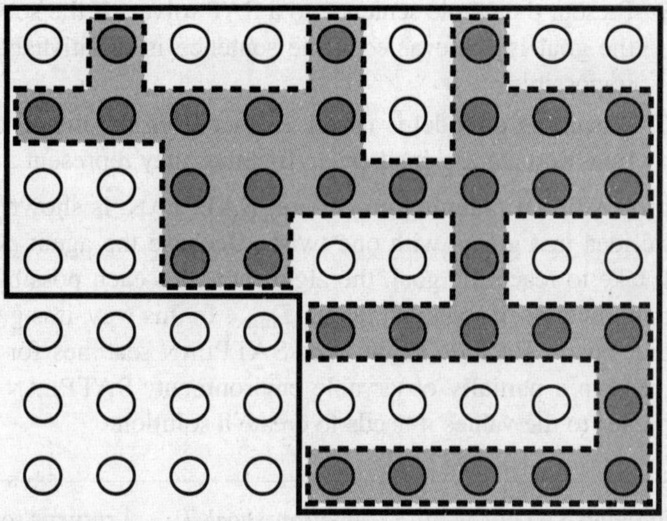

Figure 21 Depiction of a 1-CNF belief state (bold outline) as a simply representable, conservative approximation to the exact (wiggly) belief state (shaded region with dashed outline). Each possible world is shown as a circle; the shaded ones are consistent with all the percepts.

provable literals becomes the new belief state, and the previous belief state is discarded.

It is important to understand that this scheme may lose some information as time goes along. For example, if the sentence in Equation (4) were the true belief state, then neither $P_{3,1}$ nor $P_{2,2}$ would be provable individually and neither would appear in the 1-CNF belief state. (Exercise 27 explores one possible solution to this problem.) On the other hand, because every literal in the 1-CNF belief state is proved from the previous belief state, and the initial belief state is a true assertion, we know that entire 1-CNF belief state must be true. Thus, *the set of possible states represented by the 1-CNF belief state includes all states that are in fact possible given the full percept history.* As illustrated in Figure 21, the 1-CNF belief state acts as a simple outer envelope, or **conservative approximation**, around the exact belief state. We see this idea of conservative approximations to complicated sets as a recurring theme in many areas of AI.

CONSERVATIVE APPROXIMATION

7.4 Making plans by propositional inference

The agent in Figure 20 uses logical inference to determine which squares are safe, but uses A* search to make plans. In this section, we show how to make plans by logical inference. The basic idea is very simple:

1. Construct a sentence that includes
   (a) $Init^0$, a collection of assertions about the initial state;
   (b) $Transition^1, \ldots, Transition^t$, the successor-state axioms for all possible actions at each time up to some maximum time t;
   (c) the assertion that the goal is achieved at time t: $HaveGold^t \wedge ClimbedOut^t$.

2. Present the whole sentence to a SAT solver. If the solver finds a satisfying model, then the goal is achievable; if the sentence is unsatisfiable, then the planning problem is impossible.
3. Assuming a model is found, extract from the model those variables that represent actions and are assigned *true*. Together they represent a plan to achieve the goals.

A propositional planning procedure, SATPLAN, is shown in Figure 22. It implements the basic idea just given, with one twist. Because the agent does not know how many steps it will take to reach the goal, the algorithm tries each possible number of steps t, up to some maximum conceivable plan length $T_{\max}$. In this way, it is guaranteed to find the shortest plan if one exists. Because of the way SATPLAN searches for a solution, this approach cannot be used in a partially observable environment; SATPLAN would just set the unobservable variables to the values it needs to create a solution.

```
function SATPLAN(init, transition, goal, T_max) returns solution or failure
  inputs: init, transition, goal, constitute a description of the problem
          T_max, an upper limit for plan length

  for t = 0 to T_max do
     cnf ← TRANSLATE-TO-SAT(init, transition, goal, t)
     model ← SAT-SOLVER(cnf)
     if model is not null then
        return EXTRACT-SOLUTION(model)
  return failure
```

Figure 22 The SATPLAN algorithm. The planning problem is translated into a CNF sentence in which the goal is asserted to hold at a fixed time step t and axioms are included for each time step up to t. If the satisfiability algorithm finds a model, then a plan is extracted by looking at those proposition symbols that refer to actions and are assigned *true* in the model. If no model exists, then the process is repeated with the goal moved one step later.

The key step in using SATPLAN is the construction of the knowledge base. It might seem, on casual inspection, that the wumpus world axioms in Section 7.1 suffice for steps 1(a) and 1(b) above. There is, however, a significant difference between the requirements for entailment (as tested by ASK) and those for satisfiability. Consider, for example, the agent's location, initially $[1,1]$, and suppose the agent's unambitious goal is to be in $[2,1]$ at time 1. The initial knowledge base contains $L^0_{1,1}$ and the goal is $L^1_{2,1}$. Using ASK, we can prove $L^1_{2,1}$ if *Forward*^{0} is asserted, and, reassuringly, we cannot prove $L^1_{2,1}$ if, say, *Shoot*^{0} is asserted instead. Now, SATPLAN will find the plan [*Forward*^{0}]; so far, so good. Unfortunately, SATPLAN also finds the plan [*Shoot*^{0}]. How could this be? To find out, we inspect the model that SATPLAN constructs: it includes the assignment $L^0_{2,1}$, that is, the agent can be in $[2,1]$ at time 1 by being there at time 0 and shooting. One might ask, "Didn't we say the agent is in $[1,1]$ at time 0?" Yes, we did, but we didn't tell the agent that it can't be in two places at once! For entailment, $L^0_{2,1}$ is unknown and cannot, therefore, be used in a proof; for satisfiability, on the other hand, $L^0_{2,1}$ is unknown and can, therefore, be set to whatever value helps to make the goal true. For this reason, SATPLAN is a good debugging tool for knowledge bases because it reveals places where knowledge is missing. In this particular case, we can fix the knowledge base by asserting that, at each time step, the agent is in exactly one location, using a collection of sentences similar to those used to assert the existence of exactly one wumpus. Alternatively, we can assert $\neg L^0_{x,y}$ for all locations other than $[1, 1]$; the successor-state axiom for location takes care of subsequent time steps. The same fixes also work to make sure the agent has only one orientation.

SATPLAN has more surprises in store, however. The first is that it finds models with impossible actions, such as shooting with no arrow. To understand why, we need to look more carefully at what the successor-state axioms (such as Equation (3)) say about actions whose preconditions are not satisfied. The axioms *do* predict correctly that nothing will happen when such an action is executed, but they do *not* say that the action cannot be executed! To avoid generating plans with illegal actions, we must add **precondition axioms** stating that an action occurrence requires the preconditions to be satisfied.[12] For example, we need to say, for each time *t*, that

PRECONDITION AXIOMS

$$Shoot^t \Rightarrow HaveArrow^t .$$

This ensures that if a plan selects the *Shoot* action at any time, it must be the case that the agent has an arrow at that time.

SATPLAN's second surprise is the creation of plans with multiple simultaneous actions. For example, it may come up with a model in which both $Forward^0$ and $Shoot^0$ are true, which is not allowed. To eliminate this problem, we introduce **action exclusion axioms**: for every pair of actions A^t_i and A^t_j we add the axiom

ACTION EXCLUSION AXIOM

$$\neg A^t_i \lor \neg A^t_j .$$

It might be pointed out that walking forward and shooting at the same time is not so hard to do, whereas, say, shooting and grabbing at the same time is rather impractical. By imposing action exclusion axioms only on pairs of actions that really do interfere with each other, we can allow for plans that include multiple simultaneous actions—and because SATPLAN finds the shortest legal plan, we can be sure that it will take advantage of this capability.

To summarize, SATPLAN finds models for a sentence containing the initial state, the goal, the successor-state axioms, the precondition axioms, and the action exclusion axioms. It can be shown that this collection of axioms is sufficient, in the sense that there are no longer any spurious "solutions." Any model satisfying the propositional sentence will be a valid plan for the original problem. Modern SAT-solving technology makes the approach quite practical. For example, a DPLL-style solver has no difficulty in generating the 11-step solution for the wumpus world instance shown in Figure 2.

This section has described a declarative approach to agent construction: the agent works by a combination of asserting sentences in the knowledge base and performing logical inference. This approach has some weaknesses hidden in phrases such as "for each time t" and

[12] Notice that the addition of precondition axioms means that we need not include preconditions for actions in the successor-state axioms.

"for each square $[x, y]$." For any practical agent, these phrases have to be implemented by code that generates instances of the general sentence schema automatically for insertion into the knowledge base. For a wumpus world of reasonable size—one comparable to a smallish computer game—we might need a 100×100 board and 1000 time steps, leading to knowledge bases with tens or hundreds of millions of sentences. Not only does this become rather impractical, but it also illustrates a deeper problem: we know something about the wumpus world—namely, that the "physics" works the same way across all squares and all time steps—that we cannot express directly in the language of propositional logic. To solve this problem, we need a more expressive language, one in which phrases like "for each time t" and "for each square $[x, y]$" can be written in a natural way. First-order logic is such a language; in first-order logic a wumpus world of any size and duration can be described in about ten sentences rather than ten million or ten trillion.

8 Summary

We have introduced knowledge-based agents and have shown how to define a logic with which such agents can reason about the world. The main points are as follows:

- Intelligent agents need knowledge about the world in order to reach good decisions.
- Knowledge is contained in agents in the form of **sentences** in a **knowledge representation language** that are stored in a **knowledge base**.
- A knowledge-based agent is composed of a knowledge base and an inference mechanism. It operates by storing sentences about the world in its knowledge base, using the inference mechanism to infer new sentences, and using these sentences to decide what action to take.
- A representation language is defined by its **syntax**, which specifies the structure of sentences, and its **semantics**, which defines the **truth** of each sentence in each **possible world** or **model**.
- The relationship of **entailment** between sentences is crucial to our understanding of reasoning. A sentence α entails another sentence β if β is true in all worlds where α is true. Equivalent definitions include the **validity** of the sentence $\alpha \Rightarrow \beta$ and the **unsatisfiability** of the sentence $\alpha \wedge \neg\beta$.
- Inference is the process of deriving new sentences from old ones. **Sound** inference algorithms derive *only* sentences that are entailed; **complete** algorithms derive *all* sentences that are entailed.
- **Propositional logic** is a simple language consisting of **proposition symbols** and **logical connectives**. It can handle propositions that are known true, known false, or completely unknown.
- The set of possible models, given a fixed propositional vocabulary, is finite, so entailment can be checked by enumerating models. Efficient **model-checking** inference algorithms for propositional logic include backtracking and local search methods and can often solve large problems quickly.

- **Inference rules** are patterns of sound inference that can be used to find proofs. The **resolution** rule yields a complete inference algorithm for knowledge bases that are expressed in **conjunctive normal form**. **Forward chaining** and **backward chaining** are very natural reasoning algorithms for knowledge bases in **Horn form**.
- **Local search** methods such as WALKSAT can be used to find solutions. Such algorithms are sound but not complete.
- Logical **state estimation** involves maintaining a logical sentence that describes the set of possible states consistent with the observation history. Each update step requires inference using the transition model of the environment, which is built from **successor-state axioms** that specify how each **fluent** changes.
- Decisions within a logical agent can be made by SAT solving: finding possible models specifying future action sequences that reach the goal. This approach works only for fully observable or sensorless environments.
- Propositional logic does not scale to environments of unbounded size because it lacks the expressive power to deal concisely with time, space, and universal patterns of relationships among objects.

BIBLIOGRAPHICAL AND HISTORICAL NOTES

John McCarthy's paper "Programs with Common Sense" (McCarthy, 1958, 1968) promulgated the notion of agents that use logical reasoning to mediate between percepts and actions. It also raised the flag of declarativism, pointing out that telling an agent what it needs to know is an elegant way to build software. Allen Newell's (1982) article "The Knowledge Level" makes the case that rational agents can be described and analyzed at an abstract level defined by the knowledge they possess rather than the programs they run. The declarative and procedural approaches to AI are analyzed in depth by Boden (1977). The debate was revived by, among others, Brooks (1991) and Nilsson (1991), and continues to this day (Shaparau *et al.*, 2008). Meanwhile, the declarative approach has spread into other areas of computer science such as networking (Loo *et al.*, 2006).

Logic itself had its origins in ancient Greek philosophy and mathematics. Various logical principles—principles connecting the syntactic structure of sentences with their truth and falsity, with their meaning, or with the validity of arguments in which they figure—are scattered in the works of Plato. The first known systematic study of logic was carried out by Aristotle, whose work was assembled by his students after his death in 322 B.C. as a treatise called the *Organon*. Aristotle's **syllogisms** were what we would now call inference rules. Although the syllogisms included elements of both propositional and first-order logic, the system as a whole lacked the compositional properties required to handle sentences of arbitrary complexity.

SYLLOGISM

The closely related Megarian and Stoic schools (originating in the fifth century B.C. and continuing for several centuries thereafter) began the systematic study of the basic logical connectives. The use of truth tables for defining connectives is due to Philo of Megara. The

Stoics took five basic inference rules as valid without proof, including the rule we now call Modus Ponens. They derived a number of other rules from these five, using, among other principles, the deduction theorem and were much clearer about the notion of proof than proof than was Aristotle. A good account of the history of Megarian and Stoic logic is given by Benson Mates (1953).

The idea of reducing logical inference to a purely mechanical process applied to a formal language is due to Wilhelm Leibniz (1646–1716), although he had limited success in implementing the ideas. George Boole (1847) introduced the first comprehensive and workable system of formal logic in his book *The Mathematical Analysis of Logic*. Boole's logic was closely modeled on the ordinary algebra of real numbers and used substitution of logically equivalent expressions as its primary inference method. Although Boole's system still fell short of full propositional logic, it was close enough that other mathematicians could quickly fill in the gaps. Schröder (1877) described conjunctive normal form, while Horn form was introduced much later by Alfred Horn (1951). The first comprehensive exposition of modern propositional logic (and first-order logic) is found in Gottlob Frege's (1879) *Begriffschrift* ("Concept Writing" or "Conceptual Notation").

The first mechanical device to carry out logical inferences was constructed by the third Earl of Stanhope (1753–1816). The Stanhope Demonstrator could handle syllogisms and certain inferences in the theory of probability. William Stanley Jevons, one of those who improved upon and extended Boole's work, constructed his "logical piano" in 1869 to perform inferences in Boolean logic. An entertaining and instructive history of these and other early mechanical devices for reasoning is given by Martin Gardner (1968). The first published computer program for logical inference was the Logic Theorist of Newell, Shaw, and Simon (1957). This program was intended to model human thought processes. Martin Davis (1957) had actually designed a program that came up with a proof in 1954, but the Logic Theorist's results were published slightly earlier.

Truth tables as a method of testing validity or unsatisfiability in propositional logic were introduced independently by Emil Post (1921) and Ludwig Wittgenstein (1922). In the 1930s, a great deal of progress was made on inference methods for first-order logic. In particular, Gödel (1930) showed that a complete procedure for inference in first-order logic could be obtained via a reduction to propositional logic, using Herbrand's theorem (Herbrand, 1930). The important point here is that the development of efficient propositional algorithms in the 1960s was motivated largely by the interest of mathematicians in an effective theorem prover for first-order logic. The Davis–Putnam algorithm (Davis and Putnam, 1960) was the first effective algorithm for propositional resolution but was in most cases much less efficient than the DPLL backtracking algorithm introduced two years later (1962). The full resolution rule and a proof of its completeness appeared in a seminal paper by J. A. Robinson (1965), which also showed how to do first-order reasoning without resort to propositional techniques.

Stephen Cook (1971) showed that deciding satisfiability of a sentence in propositional logic (the SAT problem) is NP-complete. Since deciding entailment is equivalent to deciding unsatisfiability, it is co-NP-complete. Many subsets of propositional logic are known for which the satisfiability problem is polynomially solvable; Horn clauses are one such subset.

The linear-time forward-chaining algorithm for Horn clauses is due to Dowling and Gallier (1984), who describe their algorithm as a dataflow process similar to the propagation of signals in a circuit.

Early theoretical investigations showed that DPLL has polynomial average-case complexity for certain natural distributions of problems. This potentially exciting fact became less exciting when Franco and Paull (1983) showed that the same problems could be solved in constant time simply by guessing random assignments. The random-generation method described in the chapter produces much harder problems. Motivated by the empirical success of local search on these problems, Koutsoupias and Papadimitriou (1992) showed that a simple hill-climbing algorithm can solve *almost all* satisfiability problem instances very quickly, suggesting that hard problems are rare. Moreover, Schöning (1999) exhibited a randomized hill-climbing algorithm whose *worst-case* expected run time on 3-SAT problems (that is, satisfiability of 3-CNF sentences) is $O(1.333^n)$—still exponential, but substantially faster than previous worst-case bounds. The current record is $O(1.324^n)$ (Iwama and Tamaki, 2004). Achlioptas *et al.* (2004) and Alekhnovich *et al.* (2005) exhibit families of 3-SAT instances for which all known DPLL-like algorithms require exponential running time.

On the practical side, efficiency gains in propositional solvers have been marked. Given ten minutes of computing time, the original DPLL algorithm in 1962 could only solve problems with no more than 10 or 15 variables. By 1995 the SATZ solver (Li and Anbulagan, 1997) could handle 1,000 variables, thanks to optimized data structures for indexing variables. Two crucial contributions were the **watched literal** indexing technique of Zhang and Stickel (1996), which makes unit propagation very efficient, and the introduction of clause (i.e., constraint) learning techniques from the CSP community by Bayardo and Schrag (1997). Using these ideas, and spurred by the prospect of solving industrial-scale circuit verification problems, Moskewicz *et al.* (2001) developed the CHAFF solver, which could handle problems with millions of variables. Beginning in 2002, SAT competitions have been held regularly; most of the winning entries have either been descendants of CHAFF or have used the same general approach. RSAT (Pipatsrisawat and Darwiche, 2007), the 2007 winner, falls in the latter category. Also noteworthy is MINISAT (Een and Sörensson, 2003), an open-source implementation available at `http://minisat.se` that is designed to be easily modified and improved. The current landscape of solvers is surveyed by Gomes *et al.* (2008).

Local search algorithms for satisfiability were tried by various authors throughout the 1980s; all of the algorithms were based on the idea of minimizing the number of unsatisfied clauses (Hansen and Jaumard, 1990). A particularly effective algorithm was developed by Gu (1989) and independently by Selman *et al.* (1992), who called it GSAT and showed that it was capable of solving a wide range of very hard problems very quickly. The WALKSAT algorithm described in the chapter is due to Selman *et al.* (1996).

The "phase transition" in satisfiability of random k-SAT problems was first observed by Simon and Dubois (1989) and has given rise to a great deal of theoretical and empirical research—due, in part, to the obvious connection to phase transition phenomena in statistical physics. Cheeseman *et al.* (1991) observed phase transitions in several CSPs and conjecture that all NP-hard problems have a phase transition. Crawford and Auton (1993) located the 3-SAT transition at a clause/variable ratio of around 4.26, noting that this coincides with a sharp peak in the run time of their SAT solver. Cook and Mitchell (1997) provide an excellent summary of the early literature on the problem.

SATISFIABILITY THRESHOLD CONJECTURE

The current state of theoretical understanding is summarized by Achlioptas (2009). The **satisfiability threshold conjecture** states that, for each k, there is a sharp satisfiability threshold r_k, such that as the number of variables $n \to \infty$, instances below the threshold are *satisfiable* with probability 1, while those above the threshold are *unsatisfiable* with probability 1. The conjecture was not quite proved by Friedgut (1999): a sharp threshold exists but its location might depend on n even as $n \to \infty$. Despite significant progress in asymptotic analysis of the threshold location for large k (Achlioptas and Peres, 2004; Achlioptas *et al.*, 2007), all that can be proved for $k = 3$ is that it lies in the range [3.52,4.51]. Current theory suggests that a peak in the run time of a SAT solver is not necessarily related to the satisfiability threshold, but instead to a phase transition in the solution distribution and structure of SAT instances. Empirical results due to Coarfa *et al.* (2003) support this view. In fact, algorithms such as **survey propagation** (Parisi and Zecchina, 2002; Maneva *et al.*, 2007) take advantage of special properties of random SAT instances near the satisfiability threshold and greatly outperform general SAT solvers on such instances.

SURVEY PROPAGATION

The best sources for information on satisfiability, both theoretical and practical, are the *Handbook of Satisfiability* (Biere *et al.*, 2009) and the regular *International Conferences on Theory and Applications of Satisfiability Testing*, known as SAT.

The idea of building agents with propositional logic can be traced back to the seminal paper of McCulloch and Pitts (1943), which initiated the field of neural networks. Contrary to popular supposition, the paper was concerned with the implementation of a Boolean circuit-based agent design in the brain. Circuit-based agents, which perform computation by propagating signals in hardware circuits rather than running algorithms in general-purpose computers, have received little attention in AI, however. The most notable exception is the work of Stan Rosenschein (Rosenschein, 1985; Kaelbling and Rosenschein, 1990), who developed ways to compile circuit-based agents from declarative descriptions of the task environment. (Rosenschein's approach is described at some length in the second edition of this text.) The work of Rod Brooks (1986, 1989) demonstrates the effectiveness of circuit-based designs for controlling robots. Brooks (1991) argues that circuit-based designs are *all* that is needed for AI—that representation and reasoning are cumbersome, expensive, and unnecessary. In our view, neither approach is sufficient by itself. Williams *et al.* (2003) show how a hybrid agent design not too different from our wumpus agent has been used to control NASA spacecraft, planning sequences of actions and diagnosing and recovering from faults.

There exists a general problem of keeping track of a partially observable environment for state-based representations. Its instantiation for propositional representations was studied by Amir and Russell (2003), who identified several classes of environments that admit efficient state-estimation algorithms and showed that for several other classes the problem is intractable. The **temporal-projection** problem, which involves determining what propositions hold true after an action sequence is executed, can be seen as a special case of state estimation with empty percepts. Many authors have studied this problem because of its importance in planning; some important hardness results were established by

TEMPORAL-PROJECTION

Liberatore (1997). The idea of representing a belief state with propositions can be traced to Wittgenstein (1922).

Logical state estimation, of course, requires a logical representation of the effects of actions—a key problem in AI since the late 1950s. The dominant proposal has been the **situation calculus** formalism (McCarthy, 1963), which is couched within first-order logic. The approach taken in this chapter—using temporal indices on propositional variables—is more restrictive but has the benefit of simplicity. The general approach embodied in the SATPLAN algorithm was proposed by Kautz and Selman (1992). Later generations of SATPLAN were able to take advantage of the advances in SAT solvers, described earlier, and remain among the most effective ways of solving difficult problems (Kautz, 2006).

The **frame problem** was first recognized by McCarthy and Hayes (1969). Many researchers considered the problem unsolvable within first-order logic, and it spurred a great deal of research into nonmonotonic logics. Philosophers from Dreyfus (1972) to Crockett (1994) have cited the frame problem as one symptom of the inevitable failure of the entire AI enterprise. The solution of the frame problem with successor-state axioms is due to Ray Reiter (1991). Thielscher (1999) identifies the inferential frame problem as a separate idea and provides a solution. In retrospect, one can see that Rosenschein's (1985) agents were using circuits that implemented successor-state axioms, but Rosenschein did not notice that the frame problem was thereby largely solved. Foo (2001) explains why the discrete-event control theory models typically used by engineers do not have to explicitly deal with the frame problem: because they are dealing with prediction and control, not with explanation and reasoning about counterfactual situations.

Modern propositional solvers have wide applicability in industrial applications. The application of propositional inference in the synthesis of computer hardware is now a standard technique having many large-scale deployments (Nowick *et al.*, 1993). The SATMC satisfiability checker was used to detect a previously unknown vulnerability in a Web browser user sign-on protocol (Armando *et al.*, 2008).

The wumpus world was invented by Gregory Yob (1975). Ironically, Yob developed it because he was bored with games played on a rectangular grid: the topology of his original wumpus world was a dodecahedron, and we put it back in the boring old grid. Michael Genesereth was the first to suggest that the wumpus world be used as an agent testbed.

EXERCISES

1 Suppose the agent has progressed to the point shown in Figure 4(a), having perceived nothing in [1,1], a breeze in [2,1], and a stench in [1,2], and is now concerned with the contents of [1,3], [2,2], and [3,1]. Each of these can contain a pit, and at most one can contain a wumpus. Following the example of Figure 5, construct the set of possible worlds. (You should find 32 of them.) Mark the worlds in which the KB is true and those in which each of the following sentences is true:

α_2 = "There is no pit in [2,2]."
α_3 = "There is a wumpus in [1,3]."

Hence show that $KB \models \alpha_2$ and $KB \models \alpha_3$.

2 (Adapted from Barwise and Etchemendy (1993).) Given the following, can you prove that the unicorn is mythical? How about magical? Horned?

> If the unicorn is mythical, then it is immortal, but if it is not mythical, then it is a mortal mammal. If the unicorn is either immortal or a mammal, then it is horned. The unicorn is magical if it is horned.

3 Consider the problem of deciding whether a propositional logic sentence is true in a given model.

a. Write a recursive algorithm PL-TRUE?(s, m) that returns *true* if and only if the sentence s is true in the model m (where m assigns a truth value for every symbol in s). The algorithm should run in time linear in the size of the sentence. (Alternatively, use a version of this function from the online code repository.)

b. Give three examples of sentences that can be determined to be true or false in a *partial* model that does not specify a truth value for some of the symbols.

c. Show that the truth value (if any) of a sentence in a partial model cannot be determined efficiently in general.

d. Modify your PL-TRUE? algorithm so that it can sometimes judge truth from partial models, while retaining its recursive structure and linear run time. Give three examples of sentences whose truth in a partial model is *not* detected by your algorithm.

e. Investigate whether the modified algorithm makes TT-ENTAILS? more efficient.

4 Which of the following are correct?

a. $False \models True$.

b. $True \models False$.

c. $(A \wedge B) \models (A \Leftrightarrow B)$.

d. $A \Leftrightarrow B \models A \vee B$.

e. $A \Leftrightarrow B \models \neg A \vee B$.

f. $(A \wedge B) \Rightarrow C \models (A \Rightarrow C) \vee (B \Rightarrow C)$.

g. $(C \vee (\neg A \wedge \neg B)) \equiv ((A \Rightarrow C) \wedge (B \Rightarrow C))$.

h. $(A \vee B) \wedge (\neg C \vee \neg D \vee E) \models (A \vee B)$.

i. $(A \vee B) \wedge (\neg C \vee \neg D \vee E) \models (A \vee B) \wedge (\neg D \vee E)$.

j. $(A \vee B) \wedge \neg(A \Rightarrow B)$ is satisfiable.

k. $(A \Leftrightarrow B) \wedge (\neg A \vee B)$ is satisfiable.

l. $(A \Leftrightarrow B) \Leftrightarrow C$ has the same number of models as $(A \Leftrightarrow B)$ for any fixed set of proposition symbols that includes A, B, C.

5 Prove each of the following assertions:

a. α is valid if and only if $True \models \alpha$.
b. For any α, $False \models \alpha$.
c. $\alpha \models \beta$ if and only if the sentence $(\alpha \Rightarrow \beta)$ is valid.
d. $\alpha \equiv \beta$ if and only if the sentence $(\alpha \Leftrightarrow \beta)$ is valid.
e. $\alpha \models \beta$ if and only if the sentence $(\alpha \wedge \neg\beta)$ is unsatisfiable.

6 Prove, or find a counterexample to, each of the following assertions:

a. If $\alpha \models \gamma$ or $\beta \models \gamma$ (or both) then $(\alpha \wedge \beta) \models \gamma$
b. If $\alpha \models (\beta \wedge \gamma)$ then $\alpha \models \beta$ and $\alpha \models \gamma$.
c. If $\alpha \models (\beta \vee \gamma)$ then $\alpha \models \beta$ or $\alpha \models \gamma$ (or both).

7 Consider a vocabulary with only four propositions, A, B, C, and D. How many models are there for the following sentences?

a. $B \vee C$.
b. $\neg A \vee \neg B \vee \neg C \vee \neg D$.
c. $(A \Rightarrow B) \wedge A \wedge \neg B \wedge C \wedge D$.

8 We have defined four binary logical connectives.

a. Are there any others that might be useful?
b. How many binary connectives can there be?
c. Why are some of them not very useful?

9 Using a method of your choice, verify each of the equivalences in Figure 11.

10 Decide whether each of the following sentences is valid, unsatisfiable, or neither. Verify your decisions using truth tables or the equivalence rules of Figure 11.

a. $Smoke \Rightarrow Smoke$
b. $Smoke \Rightarrow Fire$
c. $(Smoke \Rightarrow Fire) \Rightarrow (\neg Smoke \Rightarrow \neg Fire)$
d. $Smoke \vee Fire \vee \neg Fire$
e. $((Smoke \wedge Heat) \Rightarrow Fire) \Leftrightarrow ((Smoke \Rightarrow Fire) \vee (Heat \Rightarrow Fire))$
f. $(Smoke \Rightarrow Fire) \Rightarrow ((Smoke \wedge Heat) \Rightarrow Fire)$
g. $Big \vee Dumb \vee (Big \Rightarrow Dumb)$

11 Any propositional logic sentence is logically equivalent to the assertion that each possible world in which it would be false is not the case. From this observation, prove that any sentence can be written in CNF.

12 Use resolution to prove the sentence $\neg A \wedge \neg B$ from the clauses in Exercise 20.

13 This exercise looks into the relationship between clauses and implication sentences.

a. Show that the clause $(\neg P_1 \vee \cdots \vee \neg P_m \vee Q)$ is logically equivalent to the implication sentence $(P_1 \wedge \cdots \wedge P_m) \Rightarrow Q$.

b. Show that every clause (regardless of the number of positive literals) can be written in the form $(P_1 \wedge \cdots \wedge P_m) \Rightarrow (Q_1 \vee \cdots \vee Q_n)$, where the Ps and Qs are proposition symbols. A knowledge base consisting of such sentences is in **implicative normal form** or **Kowalski form** (Kowalski, 1979).

IMPLICATIVE NORMAL FORM

c. Write down the full resolution rule for sentences in implicative normal form.

14 According to some political pundits, a person who is radical (R) is electable (E) if he/she is conservative (C), but otherwise is not electable.

a. Which of the following are correct representations of this assertion?

(i) $(R \wedge E) \iff C$
(ii) $R \Rightarrow (E \iff C)$
(iii) $R \Rightarrow ((C \Rightarrow E) \vee \neg E)$

b. Which of the sentences in (a) can be expressed in Horn form?

15 This question considers representing satisfiability (SAT) problems as CSPs.

a. Draw the constraint graph corresponding to the SAT problem

$$(\neg X_1 \vee X_2) \wedge (\neg X_2 \vee X_3) \wedge \ldots \wedge (\neg X_{n-1} \vee X_n)$$

for the particular case $n = 5$.

b. How many solutions are there for this general SAT problem as a function of n?

c. Suppose we apply BACKTRACKING-SEARCH to find *all* solutions to a SAT CSP of CSP of the type given in (a). (To find *all* solutions to a CSP, we simply modify the basic algorithm so it continues searching after each solution is found.) Assume that variables are ordered $X_1, \ldots, X_n$ and *false* is ordered before *true*. How much time will the algorithm take to terminate? (Write an $O(\cdot)$ expression as a function of n.)

d. We know that SAT problems in Horn form can be solved in linear time by forward chaining (unit propagation). We also know that every tree-structured binary CSP with discrete, finite domains can be solved in time linear in the number of variables. Are these two facts connected? Discuss.

16 Explain why every nonempty propositional clause, by itself, is satisfiable. Prove rigorously that every set of five 3-SAT clauses is satisfiable, provided that each clause mentions discrete, finite domains can be solved in time linear in the number of variables. Are these two facts connected? Discuss.

17 A propositional *2-CNF* expression is a conjunction of clauses, each containing *exactly* 2 literals, e.g.,

$$(A \vee B) \wedge (\neg A \vee C) \wedge (\neg B \vee D) \wedge (\neg C \vee G) \wedge (\neg D \vee G) .$$

a. Prove using resolution that the above sentence entails G.

b. Two clauses are *semantically distinct* if they are not logically equivalent. How many semantically distinct 2-CNF clauses can be constructed from n proposition symbols?

c. Using your answer to (b), prove that propositional resolution always terminates in time polynomial in n given a 2-CNF sentence containing no more than n distinct symbols.

d. Explain why your argument in (c) does not apply to 3-CNF.

18 Consider the following sentence:

$$[(Food \Rightarrow Party) \lor (Drinks \Rightarrow Party)] \Rightarrow [(Food \land Drinks) \Rightarrow Party] .$$

a. Determine, using enumeration, whether this sentence is valid, satisfiable (but not valid), or unsatisfiable.

b. Convert the left-hand and right-hand sides of the main implication into CNF, showing each step, and explain how the results confirm your answer to (a).

c. Prove your answer to (a) using resolution.

DISJUNCTIVE NORMAL FORM

19 A sentence is in **disjunctive normal form** (DNF) if it is the disjunction of conjunctions of literals. For example, the sentence $(A \land B \land \neg C) \lor (\neg A \land C) \lor (B \land \neg C)$ is in DNF.

a. Any propositional logic sentence is logically equivalent to the assertion that some possible world in which it would be true is in fact the case. From this observation, prove that any sentence can be written in DNF.

b. Construct an algorithm that converts any sentence in propositional logic into DNF. (*Hint*: The algorithm is similar to the algorithm for conversion to CNF given in Section 5.2.)

c. Construct a simple algorithm that takes as input a sentence in DNF and returns a satisfying assignment if one exists, or reports that no satisfying assignment exists.

d. Apply the algorithms in (b) and (c) to the following set of sentences:

$$A \Rightarrow B$$
$$B \Rightarrow C$$
$$C \Rightarrow \neg A .$$

e. Since the algorithm in (b) is very similar to the algorithm for conversion to CNF, and since the algorithm in (c) is much simpler than any algorithm for solving a set of sentences in CNF, why is this technique not used in automated reasoning?

20 Convert the following set of sentences to clausal form.

S1: $A \Leftrightarrow (B \lor E)$.
S2: $E \Rightarrow D$.
S3: $C \land F \Rightarrow \neg B$.
S4: $E \Rightarrow B$.
S5: $B \Rightarrow F$.
S6: $B \Rightarrow C$

Give a trace of the execution of DPLL on the conjunction of these clauses.

21 Is a randomly generated 4-CNF sentence with n symbols and m clauses more or less likely to be solvable than a randomly generated 3-CNF sentence with n symbols and m clauses? Explain.

22 Minesweeper, the well-known computer game, is closely related to the wumpus world. A minesweeper world is a rectangular grid of N squares with M invisible mines scattered among them. Any square may be probed by the agent; instant death follows if a mine is probed. Minesweeper indicates the presence of mines by revealing, in each probed square, the *number* of mines that are directly or diagonally adjacent. The goal is to probe every unmined square.

a. Let $X_{i,j}$ be true iff square $[i, j]$ contains a mine. Write down the assertion that exactly two mines are adjacent to [1,1] as a sentence involving some logical combination of $X_{i,j}$ propositions.

b. Generalize your assertion from (a) by explaining how to construct a CNF sentence asserting that k of n neighbors contain mines.

c. Explain precisely how an agent can use DPLL to prove that a given square does (or does not) contain a mine, ignoring the global constraint that there are exactly M mines in all.

d. Suppose that the global constraint is constructed from your method from part (b). How does the number of clauses depend on M and N? Suggest a way to modify DPLL so that the global constraint does not need to be represented explicitly.

e. Are any conclusions derived by the method in part (c) invalidated when the global constraint is taken into account?

f. Give examples of configurations of probe values that induce *long-range dependencies* such that the contents of a given unprobed square would give information about the contents of a far-distant square. (*Hint*: consider an $N \times 1$ board.)

23 How long does it take to prove $KB \models \alpha$ using DPLL when α is a literal *already contained in KB*? Explain.

24 Trace the behavior of DPLL on the knowledge base in Figure 16 when trying to prove Q, and compare this behavior with that of the forward-chaining algorithm.

25 Write a successor-state axiom for the *Locked* predicate, which applies to doors, assuming the only actions available are *Lock* and *Unlock*.

26 Section 7.1 provides some of the successor-state axioms required for the wumpus world. Write down axioms for all remaining fluent symbols.

27 Modify the HYBRID-WUMPUS-AGENT to use the 1-CNF logical state estimation method. We noted on that page that such an agent will not be able to acquire, maintain, and use more complex beliefs such as the disjunction $P_{3,1} \vee P_{2,2}$. Sugest a method for overcoming this problem by defining additional proposition symbols ,and try it out in the wumpus world. Does it improve the performance of the agent?

CONSTRAINT SATISFACTION PROBLEMS

CONSTRAINT SATISFACTION PROBLEMS

In which we see how treating states as more than just little black boxes leads to the invention of a range of powerful new search methods and a deeper understanding of problem structure and complexity.

Problems can be solved by searching in a space of **states**. These states can be evaluated by domain-specific heuristics and tested to see whether they are goal states. From the point of view of the search algorithm, however, each state is atomic, or indivisible—a black box with no internal structure.

This chapter describes a way to solve a wide variety of problems more efficiently. We use a **factored representation** for each state: a set of variables, each of which has a value. A problem is solved when each variable has a value that satisfies all the constraints on the variable. A problem described this way is called a **constraint satisfaction problem**, or CSP.

CONSTRAINT SATISFACTION PROBLEM

CSP search algorithms take advantage of the structure of states and use *general-purpose* rather than *problem-specific* heuristics to enable the solution of complex problems. The main idea is to eliminate large portions of the search space all at once by identifying variable/value combinations that violate the constraints.

1 DEFINING CONSTRAINT SATISFACTION PROBLEMS

A constraint satisfaction problem consists of three components, X, D, and C:

X is a set of variables, $\{X_1, \ldots, X_n\}$.

D is a set of domains, $\{D_1, \ldots, D_n\}$, one for each variable.

C is a set of constraints that specify allowable combinations of values.

Each domain D_i consists of a set of allowable values, $\{v_1, \ldots, v_k\}$ for variable X_i. Each constraint C_i consists of a pair $\langle scope, rel \rangle$, where *scope* is a tuple of variables that participate in the constraint and *rel* is a relation that defines the values that those variables can take on. A relation can be represented as an explicit list of all tuples of values that satisfy the constraint, or as an abstract relation that supports two operations: testing if a tuple is a member of the relation and enumerating the members of the relation. For example, if X_1 and X_2 both have the domain {A,B}, then the constraint saying the two variables must have different values can be written as $\langle (X_1, X_2), [(A, B), (B, A)] \rangle$ or as $\langle (X_1, X_2), X_1 \neq X_2 \rangle$.

To solve a CSP, we need to define a state space and the notion of a solution. Each state in a CSP is defined by an **assignment** of values to some or all of the variables, $\{X_i = v_i, X_j = v_j, \ldots\}$. An assignment that does not violate any constraints is called a **consistent** or legal assignment. A **complete assignment** is one in which every variable is assigned, and a **solution** to a CSP is a consistent, complete assignment. A **partial assignment** is one that assigns values to only some of the variables.

ASSIGNMENT

CONSISTENT

COMPLETE ASSIGNMENT

SOLUTION

PARTIAL ASSIGNMENT

1.1 Example problem: Map coloring

Suppose that we are looking at a map of Australia showing each of its states and territories (Figure 1(a)). We are given the task of coloring each region either red, green, or blue in such a way that no neighboring regions have the same color. To formulate this as a CSP, we define the variables to be the regions

$$X = \{ WA, NT, Q, NSW, V, SA, T\} .$$

The domain of each variable is the set $D_i = \{red, green, blue\}$. The constraints require neighboring regions to have distinct colors. Since there are nine places where regions border, there are nine constraints:

$$\begin{aligned} C = \{ & SA \neq WA, SA \neq NT, SA \neq Q, SA \neq NSW, SA \neq V, \\ & WA \neq NT, NT \neq Q, Q \neq NSW, NSW \neq V\} . \end{aligned}$$

Here we are using abbreviations; $SA \neq WA$ is a shortcut for $\langle (SA, WA), SA \neq WA \rangle$, where $SA \neq WA$ can be fully enumerated in turn as

$$\{(red, green), (red, blue), (green, red), (green, blue), (blue, red), (blue, green)\} .$$

There are many possible solutions to this problem, such as

$$\{ WA = red, NT = green, Q = red, NSW = green, V = red, SA = blue, T = red \}.$$

CONSTRAINT GRAPH

It can be helpful to visualize a CSP as a **constraint graph**, as shown in Figure 1(b). The nodes of the graph correspond to variables of the problem, and a link connects any two variables that participate in a constraint.

Why formulate a problem as a CSP? One reason is that the CSPs yield a natural representation for a wide variety of problems; if you already have a CSP-solving system, it is often easier to solve a problem using it than to design a custom solution using another search technique. In addition, CSP solvers can be faster than state-space searchers because the CSP solver can quickly eliminate large swatches of the search space. For example, once we have chosen $\{SA = blue\}$ in the Australia problem, we can conclude that none of the five neighboring variables can take on the value $blue$. Without taking advantage of constraint propagation, a search procedure would have to consider $3^5 = 243$ assignments for the five neighboring variables; with constraint propagation we never have to consider $blue$ as a value, so we have only $2^5 = 32$ assignments to look at, a reduction of 87%.

In regular state-space search we can only ask: is this specific state a goal? No? What about this one? With CSPs, once we find out that a partial assignment is not a solution, we can

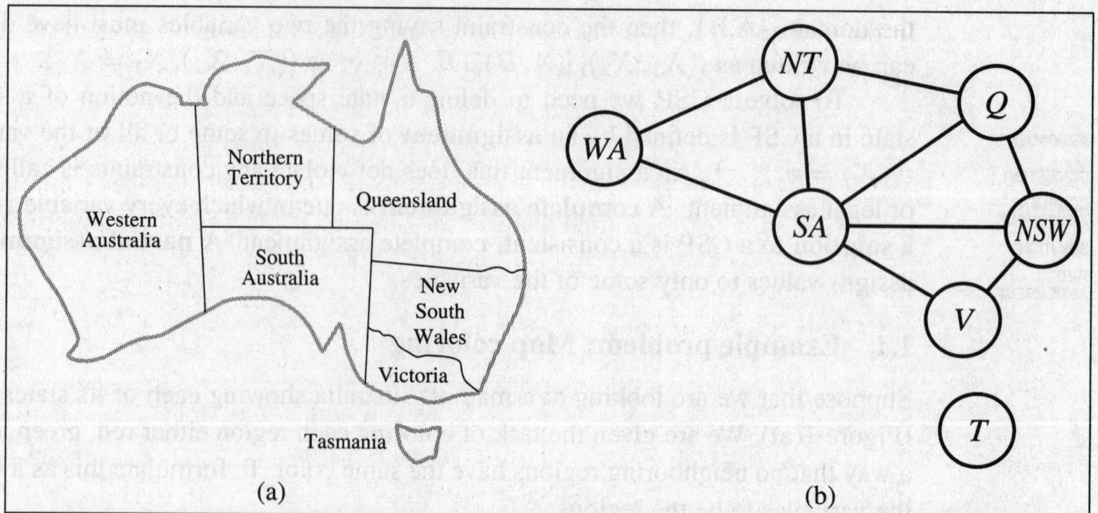

Figure 1 (a) The principal states and territories of Australia. Coloring this map can be viewed as a constraint satisfaction problem (CSP). The goal is to assign colors to each region so that no neighboring regions have the same color. (b) The map-coloring problem represented as a constraint graph.

immediately discard further refinements of the partial assignment. Furthermore, we can see *why* the assignment is not a solution—we see which variables violate a constraint—so we can focus attention on the variables that matter. As a result, many problems that are intractable for regular state-space search can be solved quickly when formulated as a CSP.

1.2 Example problem: Job-shop scheduling

Factories have the problem of scheduling a day's worth of jobs, subject to various constraints. In practice, many of these problems are solved with CSP techniques. Consider the problem of scheduling the assembly of a car. The whole job is composed of tasks, and we can model each task as a variable, where the value of each variable is the time that the task starts, expressed as an integer number of minutes. Constraints can assert that one task must occur before another—for example, a wheel must be installed before the hubcap is put on—and that only so many tasks can go on at once. Constraints can also specify that a task takes a certain amount of time to complete.

We consider a small part of the car assembly, consisting of 15 tasks: install axles (front and back), affix all four wheels (right and left, front and back), tighten nuts for each wheel, affix hubcaps, and inspect the final assembly. We can represent the tasks with 15 variables:

$$X = \{Axle_F, Axle_B, Wheel_{RF}, Wheel_{LF}, Wheel_{RB}, Wheel_{LB}, Nuts_{RF}, Nuts_{LF}, Nuts_{RB}, Nuts_{LB}, Cap_{RF}, Cap_{LF}, Cap_{RB}, Cap_{LB}, Inspect\} .$$

The value of each variable is the time that the task starts. Next we represent **precedence constraints** between individual tasks. Whenever a task T_1 must occur before task T_2, and task T_1 takes duration d_1 to complete, we add an arithmetic constraint of the form

PRECEDENCE CONSTRAINTS

$$T_1 + d_1 \leq T_2 .$$

In our example, the axles have to be in place before the wheels are put on, and it takes 10 minutes to install an axle, so we write

$$Axle_F + 10 \leq Wheel_{RF}; \quad Axle_F + 10 \leq Wheel_{LF};$$
$$Axle_B + 10 \leq Wheel_{RB}; \quad Axle_B + 10 \leq Wheel_{LB}.$$

Next we say that, for each wheel, we must affix the wheel (which takes 1 minute), then tighten the nuts (2 minutes), and finally attach the hubcap (1 minute, but not represented yet):

$$Wheel_{RF} + 1 \leq Nuts_{RF}; \quad Nuts_{RF} + 2 \leq Cap_{RF};$$
$$Wheel_{LF} + 1 \leq Nuts_{LF}; \quad Nuts_{LF} + 2 \leq Cap_{LF};$$
$$Wheel_{RB} + 1 \leq Nuts_{RB}; \quad Nuts_{RB} + 2 \leq Cap_{RB};$$
$$Wheel_{LB} + 1 \leq Nuts_{LB}; \quad Nuts_{LB} + 2 \leq Cap_{LB}.$$

Suppose we have four workers to install wheels, but they have to share one tool that helps put the axle in place. We need a **disjunctive constraint** to say that $Axle_F$ and $Axle_B$ must not overlap in time; either one comes first or the other does:

DISJUNCTIVE CONSTRAINT

$$(Axle_F + 10 \leq Axle_B) \quad \textbf{or} \quad (Axle_B + 10 \leq Axle_F).$$

This looks like a more complicated constraint, combining arithmetic and logic. But it still reduces to a set of pairs of values that $Axle_F$ and $Axle_F$ can take on.

We also need to assert that the inspection comes last and takes 3 minutes. For every variable except *Inspect* we add a constraint of the form $X + d_X \leq Inspect$. Finally, suppose there is a requirement to get the whole assembly done in 30 minutes. We can achieve that by limiting the domain of all variables:

$$D_i = \{1, 2, 3, \ldots, 27\}.$$

This particular problem is trivial to solve, but CSPs have been applied to job-shop scheduling problems like this with thousands of variables. In some cases, there are complicated constraints that are difficult to specify in the CSP formalism, and more advanced planning techniques are used.

1.3 Variations on the CSP formalism

DISCRETE DOMAIN

FINITE DOMAIN

The simplest kind of CSP involves variables that have **discrete, finite domains**. Map-coloring problems and scheduling with time limits are both of this kind. The 8-queens problem, that you may be familiar with, can also be viewed as a finite-domain CSP, where the variables $Q_1, \ldots, Q_8$ are the positions of each queen in columns 1, . . . , 8 and each variable has the domain $D_i = \{1, 2, 3, 4, 5, 6, 7, 8\}$.

INFINITE

A discrete domain can be **infinite**, such as the set of integers or strings. (If we didn't put a deadline on the job-scheduling problem, there would be an infinite number of start times for each variable.) With infinite domains, it is no longer possible to describe constraints by enumerating all allowed combinations of values. Instead, a **constraint language** must be used that understands constraints such as $T_1 + d_1 \leq T_2$ directly, without enumerating the set of pairs of allowable values for (T_1, T_2). Special solution algorithms (which we do not discuss here) exist for **linear constraints** on integer variables—that is, constraints, such as the one just given, in which each variable appears only in linear form. It can be shown that no algorithm exists for solving general **nonlinear constraints** on integer variables.

CONSTRAINT LANGUAGE

LINEAR CONSTRAINTS

NONLINEAR CONSTRAINTS

CONTINUOUS DOMAINS

Constraint satisfaction problems with **continuous domains** are common in the real world and are widely studied in the field of operations research. For example, the scheduling of experiments on the Hubble Space Telescope requires very precise timing of observations; the start and finish of each observation and maneuver are continuous-valued variables that must obey a variety of astronomical, precedence, and power constraints. The best-known category of continuous-domain CSPs is that of **linear programming** problems, where constraints must be linear equalities or inequalities. Linear programming problems can be solved in time polynomial in the number of variables. Problems with different types of constraints and objective functions have also been studied—quadratic programming, second-order conic programming, and so on.

UNARY CONSTRAINT

In addition to examining the types of variables that can appear in CSPs, it is useful to look at the types of constraints. The simplest type is the **unary constraint**, which restricts the value of a single variable. For example, in the map-coloring problem it could be the case that South Australians won't tolerate the color green; we can express that with the unary constraint $\langle (SA), SA \neq green \rangle$

BINARY CONSTRAINT

A **binary constraint** relates two variables. For example, $SA \neq NSW$ is a binary constraint. A binary CSP is one with only binary constraints; it can be represented as a constraint graph, as in Figure 1(b).

We can also describe higher-order constraints, such as asserting that the value of Y is between X and Z, with the ternary constraint $Between(X, Y, Z)$.

GLOBAL CONSTRAINT

A constraint involving an arbitrary number of variables is called a **global constraint.** (The name is traditional but confusing because it need not involve *all* the variables in a problem). One of the most common global constraints is *Alldiff*, which says that all of the variables involved in the constraint must have different values. In Sudoku problems (see Section 2.6), all variables in a row or column must satisfy an *Alldiff* constraint. Another example is provided by **cryptarithmetic** puzzles. (See Figure 2(a).) Each letter in a cryptarithmetic puzzle represents a different digit. For the case in Figure 2(a), this would be represented as the global constraint $Alldiff(F, T, U, W, R, O)$. The addition constraints on the four columns of the puzzle can be written as the following n-ary constraints:

CRYPTARITHMETIC

$$
\begin{aligned}
&O + O = R + 10 \cdot C_{10} \\
&C_{10} + W + W = U + 10 \cdot C_{100} \\
&C_{100} + T + T = O + 10 \cdot C_{1000} \\
&C_{1000} = F\,,
\end{aligned}
$$

where C_{10}, C_{100}, and C_{1000} are auxiliary variables representing the digit carried over into the tens, hundreds, or thousands column. These constraints can be represented in a **constraint hypergraph**, such as the one shown in Figure 2(b). A hypergraph consists of ordinary nodes (the circles in the figure) and hypernodes (the squares), which represent n-ary constraints.

CONSTRAINT HYPERGRAPH

Alternatively, as Exercise 6 asks you to prove, every finite-domain constraint can be reduced to a set of binary constraints if enough auxiliary variables are introduced, so we could transform any CSP into one with only binary constraints; this makes the algorithms simpler. Another way to convert an n-ary CSP to a binary one is the **dual graph** transformation: create a new graph in which there will be one variable for each constraint in the original graph, and

DUAL GRAPH

$$\begin{array}{r} T\ W\ O \\ +\ T\ W\ O \\ \hline F\ O\ U\ R \end{array}$$

(a)

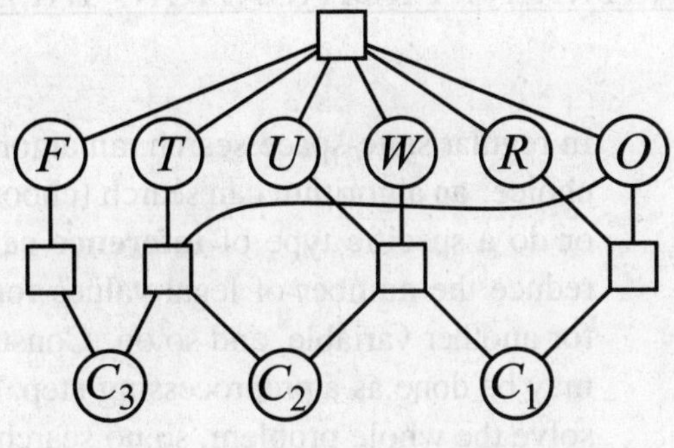

(b)

Figure 2 (a) A cryptarithmetic problem. Each letter stands for a distinct digit; the aim is to find a substitution of digits for letters such that the resulting sum is arithmetically correct, with the added restriction that no leading zeroes are allowed. (b) The constraint hypergraph for the cryptarithmetic problem, showing the *Alldiff* constraint (square box at the top) as well as the column addition constraints (four square boxes in the middle). The variables C_1, C_2, and C_3 represent the carry digits for the three columns.

one binary constraint for each pair of constraints in the original graph that share variables. For example, if the original graph has variables $\{X, Y, Z\}$ and constraints $\langle (X, Y, Z), C_1 \rangle$ and $\langle (X, Y), C_2 \rangle$ then the dual graph would have variables $\{C_1, C_2\}$ with the binary constraint $\langle (X, Y), R_1 \rangle$, where (X, Y) are the shared variables and R_1 is a new relation that defines the constraint between the shared variables, as specified by the original C_1 and C_2.

There are however two reasons why we might prefer a global constraint such as *Alldiff* rather than a set of binary constraints. First, it is easier and less error-prone to write the problem description using *Alldiff*. Second, it is possible to design special-purpose inference algorithms for global constraints that are not available for a set of more primitive constraints. We describe these inference algorithms in Section 2.5.

PREFERENCE CONSTRAINTS

The constraints we have described so far have all been absolute constraints, violation of which rules out a potential solution. Many real-world CSPs include **preference constraints** indicating which solutions are preferred. For example, in a university class-scheduling problem there are absolute constraints that no professor can teach two classes at the same time. But we also may allow preference constraints: Prof. R might prefer teaching in the morning, whereas Prof. N prefers teaching in the afternoon. A schedule that has Prof. R teaching at 2 p.m. would still be an allowable solution (unless Prof. R happens to be the department chair) but would not be an optimal one. Preference constraints can often be encoded as costs on individual variable assignments—for example, assigning an afternoon slot for Prof. R costs 2 points against the overall objective function, whereas a morning slot costs 1. With this formulation, CSPs with preferences can be solved with optimization search methods, either path-based or local. We call such a problem a **constraint optimization problem**, or COP. Linear programming problems do this kind of optimization.

CONSTRAINT OPTIMIZATION PROBLEM

2 CONSTRAINT PROPAGATION: INFERENCE IN CSPS

INFERENCE

CONSTRAINT PROPAGATION

In regular state-space search, an algorithm can do only one thing: search. In CSPs there is a choice: an algorithm can search (choose a new variable assignment from several possibilities) or do a specific type of **inference** called **constraint propagation**: using the constraints to reduce the number of legal values for a variable, which in turn can reduce the legal values for another variable, and so on. Constraint propagation may be intertwined with search, or it may be done as a preprocessing step, before search starts. Sometimes this preprocessing can solve the whole problem, so no search is required at all.

LOCAL CONSISTENCY

The key idea is **local consistency**. If we treat each variable as a node in a graph (see Figure 1(b)) and each binary constraint as an arc, then the process of enforcing local consistency in each part of the graph causes inconsistent values to be eliminated throughout the graph. There are different types of local consistency, which we now cover in turn.

2.1 Node consistency

NODE CONSISTENCY

A single variable (corresponding to a node in the CSP network) is **node-consistent** if all the values in the variable's domain satisfy the variable's unary constraints. For example, in the variant of the Australia map-coloring problem (Figure 1) where South Australians dislike green, the variable SA starts with domain $\{red, green, blue\}$, and we can make it node consistent by eliminating $green$, leaving SA with the reduced domain $\{red, blue\}$. We say that a network is node-consistent if every variable in the network is node-consistent.

It is always possible to eliminate all the unary constraints in a CSP by running node consistency. It is also possible to transform all n-ary constraints into binary ones (see Exercise 6). Because of this, it is common to define CSP solvers that work with only binary constraints; we make that assumption for the rest of this chapter, except where noted.

2.2 Arc consistency

ARC CONSISTENCY

A variable in a CSP is **arc-consistent** if every value in its domain satisfies the variable's binary constraints. More formally, X_i is arc-consistent with respect to another variable X_j if for every value in the current domain D_i there is some value in the domain D_j that satisfies the binary constraint on the arc (X_i, X_j). A network is arc-consistent if every variable is arc consistent with every other variable. For example, consider the constraint $Y = X^2$ where the domain of both X and Y is the set of digits. We can write this constraint explicitly as

$$\langle (X,Y), \{(0,0),(1,1),(2,4),(3,9)\} \rangle .$$

To make X arc-consistent with respect to Y, we reduce X's domain to $\{0,1,2,3\}$. If we also make Y arc-consistent with respect to X, then Y's domain becomes $\{0,1,4,9\}$ and the whole CSP is arc-consistent.

On the other hand, arc consistency can do nothing for the Australia map-coloring problem. Consider the following inequality constraint on (SA, WA):

$$\{(red, green), (red, blue), (green, red), (green, blue), (blue, red), (blue, green)\} .$$

```
function AC-3(csp) returns false if an inconsistency is found and true otherwise
  inputs: csp, a binary CSP with components (X, D, C)
  local variables: queue, a queue of arcs, initially all the arcs in csp

  while queue is not empty do
    (X_i, X_j) ← REMOVE-FIRST(queue)
    if REVISE(csp, X_i, X_j) then
      if size of D_i = 0 then return false
      for each X_k in X_i.NEIGHBORS - {X_j} do
        add (X_k, X_i) to queue
  return true
```

```
function REVISE(csp, X_i, X_j) returns true iff we revise the domain of X_i
  revised ← false
  for each x in D_i do
    if no value y in D_j allows (x,y) to satisfy the constraint between X_i and X_j then
      delete x from D_i
      revised ← true
  return revised
```

Figure 3 The arc-consistency algorithm AC-3. After applying AC-3, either every arc is arc-consistent, or some variable has an empty domain, indicating that the CSP cannot be solved. The name "AC-3" was used by the algorithm's inventor (Mackworth, 1977) because it's the third version developed in the paper.

No matter what value you choose for *SA* (or for *WA*), there is a valid value for the other variable. So applying arc consistency has no effect on the domains of either variable.

The most popular algorithm for arc consistency is called AC-3 (see Figure 3). To make every variable arc-consistent, the AC-3 algorithm maintains a queue of arcs to consider. (Actually, the order of consideration is not important, so the data structure is really a set, but tradition calls it a queue.) Initially, the queue contains all the arcs in the CSP. AC-3 then pops off an arbitrary arc (X_i, X_j) from the queue and makes X_i arc-consistent with respect to X_j. If this leaves D_i unchanged, the algorithm just moves on to the next arc. But if this revises D_i (makes the domain smaller), then we add to the queue all arcs (X_k, X_i) where X_k is a neighbor of X_i. We need to do that because the change in D_i might enable further reductions in the domains of D_k, even if we have previously considered X_k. If D_i is revised down to nothing, then we know the whole CSP has no consistent solution, and AC-3 can immediately return failure. Otherwise, we keep checking, trying to remove values from the domains of variables until no more arcs are in the queue. At that point, we are left with a CSP that is equivalent to the original CSP—they both have the same solutions—but the arc-consistent CSP will in most cases be faster to search because its variables have smaller domains.

The complexity of AC-3 can be analyzed as follows. Assume a CSP with n variables, each with domain size at most d, and with c binary constraints (arcs). Each arc (X_k, X_i) can be inserted in the queue only d times because X_i has at most d values to delete. Checking consistency of an arc can be done in $O(d^2)$ time, so we get $O(cd^3)$ total worst-case time.[1]

It is possible to extend the notion of arc consistency to handle n-ary rather than just binary constraints; this is called generalized arc consistency or sometimes hyperarc consistency, depending on the author. A variable X_i is **generalized arc consistent** with respect to an n-ary constraint if for every value v in the domain of X_i there exists a tuple of values that is a member of the constraint, has all its values taken from the domains of the corresponding variables, and has its X_i component equal to v. For example, if all variables have the domain $\{0, 1, 2, 3\}$, then to make the variable X consistent with the constraint $X < Y < Z$, we would have to eliminate 2 and 3 from the domain of X because the constraint cannot be satisfied when X is 2 or 3.

GENERALIZED ARC CONSISTENT

2.3 Path consistency

Arc consistency can go a long way toward reducing the domains of variables, sometimes finding a solution (by reducing every domain to size 1) and sometimes finding that the CSP cannot be solved (by reducing some domain to size 0). But for other networks, arc consistency fails to make enough inferences. Consider the map-coloring problem on Australia, but with only two colors allowed, red and blue. Arc consistency can do nothing because every variable is already arc consistent: each can be red with blue at the other end of the arc (or vice versa). But clearly there is no solution to the problem: because Western Australia, Northern Territory and South Australia all touch each other, we need at least three colors for them alone.

Arc consistency tightens down the domains (unary constraints) using the arcs (binary constraints). To make progress on problems like map coloring, we need a stronger notion of consistency. **Path consistency** tightens the binary constraints by using implicit constraints that are inferred by looking at triples of variables.

PATH CONSISTENCY

A two-variable set $\{X_i, X_j\}$ is path-consistent with respect to a third variable X_m if, for every assignment $\{X_i = a, X_j = b\}$ consistent with the constraints on $\{X_i, X_j\}$, there is an assignment to X_m that satisfies the constraints on $\{X_i, X_m\}$ and $\{X_m, X_j\}$. This is called path consistency because one can think of it as looking at a path from X_i to X_j with X_m in the middle.

Let's see how path consistency fares in coloring the Australia map with two colors. We will make the set $\{WA, SA\}$ path consistent with respect to NT. We start by enumerating the consistent assignments to the set. In this case, there are only two: $\{WA = red, SA = blue\}$ and $\{WA = blue, SA = red\}$. We can see that with both of these assignments NT can be neither *red* nor *blue* (because it would conflict with either WA or SA). Because there is no valid choice for NT, we eliminate both assignments, and we end up with no valid assignments for $\{WA, SA\}$. Therefore, we know that there can be no solution to this problem. The PC-2 algorithm (Mackworth, 1977) achieves path consistency in much the same way that AC-3 achieves arc consistency. Because it is so similar, we do not show it here.

[1] The AC-4 algorithm (Mohr and Henderson, 1986) runs in $O(cd^2)$ worst-case time but can be slower than AC-3 on average cases. See Exercise 13.

2.4 *K*-consistency

K-CONSISTENCY

Stronger forms of propagation can be defined with the notion of **k-consistency**. A CSP is k-consistent if, for any set of $k-1$ variables and for any consistent assignment to those variables, a consistent value can always be assigned to any kth variable. 1-consistency says that, given the empty set, we can make any set of one variable consistent: this is what we called node consistency. 2-consistency is the same as arc consistency. For binary constraint networks, 3-consistency is the same as path consistency.

STRONGLY K-CONSISTENT

A CSP is **strongly k-consistent** if it is k-consistent and is also $(k-1)$-consistent, $(k-2)$-consistent, ... all the way down to 1-consistent. Now suppose we have a CSP with n nodes and make it strongly n-consistent (i.e., strongly k-consistent for $k=n$). We can then solve the problem as follows: First, we choose a consistent value for X_1. We are then guaranteed to be able to choose a value for X_2 because the graph is 2-consistent, for X_3 because it is 3-consistent, and so on. For each variable X_i, we need only search through the d values in the domain to find a value consistent with $X_1, \ldots, X_{i-1}$. We are guaranteed to find a solution in time $O(n^2d)$. Of course, there is no free lunch: any algorithm for establishing n-consistency must take time exponential in n in the worst case. Worse, n-consistency also requires space that is exponential in n. The memory issue is even more severe than the time. In practice, determining the appropriate level of consistency checking is mostly an empirical science. It can be said practitioners commonly compute 2-consistency and less commonly 3-consistency.

2.5 Global constraints

Remember that a **global constraint** is one involving an arbitrary number of variables (but not necessarily all variables). Global constraints occur frequently in real problems and can be handled by special-purpose algorithms that are more efficient than the general-purpose methods described so far. For example, the *Alldiff* constraint says that all the variables involved must have distinct values (as in the cryptarithmetic problem above and Sudoku puzzles below). One simple form of inconsistency detection for *Alldiff* constraints works as follows: if m variables are involved in the constraint, and if they have n possible distinct values altogether, and $m > n$, then the constraint cannot be satisfied.

This leads to the following simple algorithm: First, remove any variable in the constraint that has a singleton domain, and delete that variable's value from the domains of the remaining variables. Repeat as long as there are singleton variables. If at any point an empty domain is produced or there are more variables than domain values left, then an inconsistency has been detected.

This method can detect the inconsistency in the assignment $\{WA = red, NSW = red\}$ for Figure 1. Notice that the variables SA, NT, and Q are effectively connected by an *Alldiff* constraint because each pair must have two different colors. After applying AC-3 with the partial assignment, the domain of each variable is reduced to $\{green, blue\}$. That is, we have three variables and only two colors, so the *Alldiff* constraint is violated. Thus, a simple consistency procedure for a higher-order constraint is sometimes more effective than applying arc consistency to an equivalent set of binary constraints. There are more complex inference algorithms for *Alldiff* (see van Hoeve and Katriel, 2006) that propagate more constraints but are more computationally expensive to run.

RESOURCE CONSTRAINT

Another important higher-order constraint is the **resource constraint**, sometimes called the *atmost* constraint. For example, in a scheduling problem, let $P_1, \ldots, P_4$ denote the numbers of personnel assigned to each of four tasks. The constraint that no more than 10 personnel are assigned in total is written as $Atmost(10, P_1, P_2, P_3, P_4)$. We can detect an inconsistency simply by checking the sum of the minimum values of the current domains; for example, if each variable has the domain $\{3, 4, 5, 6\}$, the $Atmost$ constraint cannot be satisfied. We can also enforce consistency by deleting the maximum value of any domain if it is not consistent with the minimum values of the other domains. Thus, if each variable in our example has the domain $\{2, 3, 4, 5, 6\}$, the values 5 and 6 can be deleted from each domain.

For large resource-limited problems with integer values—such as logistical problems involving moving thousands of people in hundreds of vehicles—it is usually not possible to represent the domain of each variable as a large set of integers and gradually reduce that set by consistency-checking methods. Instead, domains are represented by upper and lower bounds and are managed by **bounds propagation**. For example, in an airline-scheduling problem, let's suppose there are two flights, F_1 and F_2, for which the planes have capacities 165 and 385, respectively. The initial domains for the numbers of passengers on each flight are then

BOUNDS PROPAGATION

$$D_1 = [0, 165] \quad \text{and} \quad D_2 = [0, 385] .$$

Now suppose we have the additional constraint that the two flights together must carry 420 people: $F_1 + F_2 = 420$. Propagating bounds constraints, we reduce the domains to

$$D_1 = [35, 165] \quad \text{and} \quad D_2 = [255, 385] .$$

BOUNDS CONSISTENT

We say that a CSP is **bounds consistent** if for every variable X, and for both the lower-bound and upper-bound values of X, there exists some value of Y that satisfies the constraint between X and Y for every variable Y. This kind of bounds propagation is widely used in practical constraint problems.

2.6 Sudoku example

SUDOKU

The popular **Sudoku** puzzle has introduced millions of people to constraint satisfaction problems, although they may not recognize it. A Sudoku board consists of 81 squares, some of which are initially filled with digits from 1 to 9. The puzzle is to fill in all the remaining squares such that no digit appears twice in any row, column, or 3×3 box (see Figure 4). A row, column, or box is called a **unit**.

The Sudoku puzzles that are printed in newspapers and puzzle books have the property that there is exactly one solution. Although some can be tricky to solve by hand, taking tens of minutes, even the hardest Sudoku problems yield to a CSP solver in less than 0.1 second.

A Sudoku puzzle can be considered a CSP with 81 variables, one for each square. We use the variable names *A1* through *A9* for the top row (left to right), down to *I1* through *I9* for the bottom row. The empty squares have the domain $\{1, 2, 3, 4, 5, 6, 7, 8, 9\}$ and the pre-filled squares have a domain consisting of a single value. In addition, there are 27 different

(a)

	1	2	3	4	5	6	7	8	9
A			3		2		6		
B	9			3		5			1
C			1	8		6	4		
D			8	1		2	9		
E	7								8
F			6	7		8	2		
G			2	6		9	5		
H	8			2		3			9
I			5		1		3		

(b)

	1	2	3	4	5	6	7	8	9
A	4	8	3	9	2	1	6	5	7
B	9	6	7	3	4	5	8	2	1
C	2	5	1	8	7	6	4	9	3
D	5	4	8	1	3	2	9	7	6
E	7	2	9	5	6	4	1	3	8
F	1	3	6	7	9	8	2	4	5
G	3	7	2	6	8	9	5	1	4
H	8	1	4	2	5	3	7	6	9
I	6	9	5	4	1	7	3	8	2

Figure 4 (a) A Sudoku puzzle and (b) its solution.

Alldiff constraints: one for each row, column, and box of 9 squares.

$$Alldiff(A1, A2, A3, A4, A5, A6, A7, A8, A9)$$
$$Alldiff(B1, B2, B3, B4, B5, B6, B7, B8, B9)$$
$$\cdots$$
$$Alldiff(A1, B1, C1, D1, E1, F1, G1, H1, I1)$$
$$Alldiff(A2, B2, C2, D2, E2, F2, G2, H2, I2)$$
$$\cdots$$
$$Alldiff(A1, A2, A3, B1, B2, B3, C1, C2, C3)$$
$$Alldiff(A4, A5, A6, B4, B5, B6, C4, C5, C6)$$
$$\cdots$$

Let us see how far arc consistency can take us. Assume that the *Alldiff* constraints have been expanded into binary constraints (such as $A1 \neq A2$) so that we can apply the AC-3 algorithm directly. Consider variable $E6$ from Figure 4(a)—the empty square between the 2 and the 8 in the middle box. From the constraints in the box, we can remove not only 2 and 8 but also 1 and 7 from $E6$'s domain. From the constraints in its column, we can eliminate 5, 6, 2, 8, 9, and 3. That leaves $E6$ with a domain of $\{4\}$; in other words, we know the answer for $E6$. Now consider variable $I6$—the square in the bottom middle box surrounded by 1, 3, and 3. Applying arc consistency in its column, we eliminate 5, 6, 2, 4 (since we now know $E6$ must be 4), 8, 9, and 3. We eliminate 1 by arc consistency with $I5$, and we are left with only the value 7 in the domain of $I6$. Now there are 8 known values in column 6, so arc consistency can infer that $A6$ must be 1. Inference continues along these lines, and eventually, AC-3 can solve the entire puzzle—all the variables have their domains reduced to a single value, as shown in Figure 4(b).

Of course, Sudoku would soon lose its appeal if every puzzle could be solved by a mechanical application of AC-3, and indeed AC-3 works only for the easiest Sudoku puzzles. Slightly harder ones can be solved by PC-2, but at a greater computational cost: there are 255,960 different path constraints to consider in a Sudoku puzzle. To solve the hardest puzzles and to make efficient progress, we will have to be more clever.

Indeed, the appeal of Sudoku puzzles for the human solver is the need to be resourceful in applying more complex inference strategies. Aficionados give them colorful names, such as "naked triples." That strategy works as follows: in any unit (row, column or box), find three squares that each have a domain that contains the same three numbers or a subset of those numbers. For example, the three domains might be $\{1, 8\}$, $\{3, 8\}$, and $\{1, 3, 8\}$. From that we don't know which square contains 1, 3, or 8, but we do know that the three numbers must be distributed among the three squares. Therefore we can remove 1, 3, and 8 from the domains of every *other* square in the unit.

It is interesting to note how far we can go without saying much that is specific to Sudoku. We do of course have to say that there are 81 variables, that their domains are the digits 1 to 9, and that there are 27 *Alldiff* constraints. But beyond that, all the strategies—arc consistency, path consistency, etc.—apply generally to all CSPs, not just to Sudoku problems. Even naked triples is really a strategy for enforcing consistency of *Alldiff* constraints and has nothing to do with Sudoku *per se*. This is the power of the CSP formalism: for each new problem area, we only need to define the problem in terms of constraints; then the general constraint-solving mechanisms can take over.

3 BACKTRACKING SEARCH FOR CSPS

Sudoku problems are designed to be solved by inference over constraints. But many other CSPs cannot be solved by inference alone; there comes a time when we must search for a solution. In this section we look at backtracking search algorithms that work on partial assignments; in the next section we look at local search algorithms over complete assignments.

We could apply a standard depth-limited search. A state would be a partial assignment, and an action would be adding $var = value$ to the assignment. But for a CSP with n variables of domain size d, we quickly notice something terrible: the branching factor at the top level is nd because any of d values can be assigned to any of n variables. At the next level, the branching factor is $(n - 1)d$, and so on for n levels. We generate a tree with $n! \cdot d^n$ leaves, even though there are only d^n possible complete assignments!

Our seemingly reasonable but naive formulation ignores crucial property common to all CSPs: **commutativity**. A problem is commutative if the order of application of any given set of actions has no effect on the outcome. CSPs are commutative because when assigning values to variables, we reach the same partial assignment regardless of order. Therefore, we need only consider a *single* variable at each node in the search tree. For example, at the root node of a search tree for coloring the map of Australia, we might make a choice between $SA = red$, $SA = green$, and $SA = blue$, but we would never choose between $SA = red$ and $WA = blue$. With this restriction, the number of leaves is d^n, as we would hope.

COMMUTATIVITY

```
function BACKTRACKING-SEARCH(csp) returns a solution, or failure
  return BACKTRACK({ }, csp)

function BACKTRACK(assignment, csp) returns a solution, or failure
  if assignment is complete then return assignment
  var ← SELECT-UNASSIGNED-VARIABLE(csp)
  for each value in ORDER-DOMAIN-VALUES(var, assignment, csp) do
      if value is consistent with assignment  then
          add {var = value} to assignment
          inferences ← INFERENCE(csp, var, value)
          if inferences ≠ failure then
            add inferences to assignment
            result ← BACKTRACK(assignment, csp)
            if result ≠ failure then
                return result
      remove {var = value} and inferences from assignment
  return failure
```

Figure 5 A simple backtracking algorithm for constraint satisfaction problems. By varying the functions SELECT-UNNASSIGNED-VARIABLE and ORDER-DOMAIN-VALUES, we can implement the general-purpose heuristics discussed in the text. The function INFERENCE can optionally be used to impose arc-, path-, or *k*-consistency, as desired. If a value choice leads to failure (noticed either by INFERENCE or by BACKTRACK), then value assignments (including those made by INFERENCE) are removed from the current assignment and a new value is tried.

BACKTRACKING SEARCH

The term **backtracking search** is used for a depth-first search that chooses values for one variable at a time and backtracks when a variable has no legal values left to assign. The algorithm is shown in Figure 5. It repeatedly chooses an unassigned variable, and then tries all values in the domain of that variable in turn, trying to find a solution. If an inconsistency is detected, then BACKTRACK returns failure, causing the previous call to try another value. Part of the search tree for the Australia problem is shown in Figure 6, where we have assigned variables in the order $WA, NT, Q, \ldots$. Because the representation of CSPs is standardized, there is no need to supply BACKTRACKING-SEARCH with a domain-specific initial state, action function, transition model, or goal test.

Notice that BACKTRACKING-SEARCH keeps only a single representation of a state and alters that representation rather than creating new ones.

The poor performance of uninformed search algorithms can be improved by supplying them with domain-specific heuristic functions derived from our knowledge of the problem. It turns out that we can solve CSPs efficiently *without* such domain-specific knowledge. Instead, we can add some sophistication to the unspecified functions in Figure 5, using them to address the following questions;

1. Which variable should be assigned next (SELECT-UNASSIGNED-VARIABLE), and in what order should its values be tried (ORDER-DOMAIN-VALUES)?

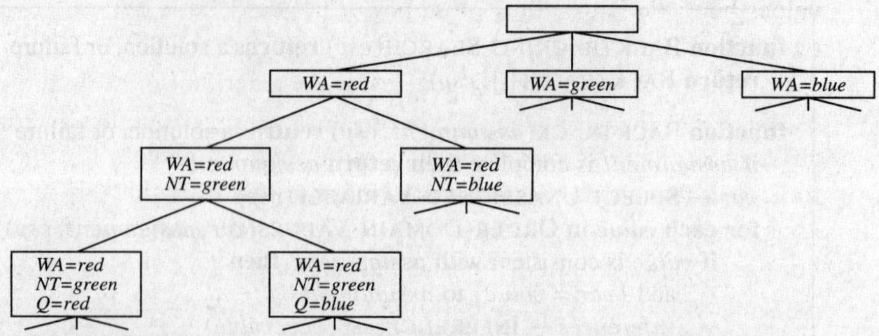

Figure 6 Part of the search tree for the map-coloring problem in Figure 1.

2. What inferences should be performed at each step in the search (INFERENCE)?
3. When the search arrives at an assignment that violates a constraint, can the search avoid repeating this failure?

The subsections that follow answer each of these questions in turn.

3.1 Variable and value ordering

The backtracking algorithm contains the line

$var \leftarrow$ SELECT-UNASSIGNED-VARIABLE(csp) .

The simplest strategy for SELECT-UNASSIGNED-VARIABLE is to choose the next unassigned variable in order, $\{X_1, X_2, \ldots\}$. This static variable ordering seldom results in the most efficient search. For example, after the assignments for $WA = red$ and $NT = green$ in Figure 6, there is only one possible value for SA, so it makes sense to assign $SA = blue$ next rather than assigning Q. In fact, after SA is assigned, the choices for Q, NSW, and V are all forced. This intuitive idea—choosing the variable with the fewest "legal" values—is called the **minimum-remaining-values** (MRV) heuristic. It also has been called the "most constrained variable" or "fail-first" heuristic, the latter because it picks a variable that is most likely to cause a failure soon, thereby pruning the search tree. If some variable X has no legal values left, the MRV heuristic will select X and failure will be detected immediately—avoiding pointless searches through other variables. The MRV heuristic usually performs better than a random or static ordering, sometimes by a factor of 1,000 or more, although the results vary widely depending on the problem.

MINIMUM-REMAINING-VALUES

The MRV heuristic doesn't help at all in choosing the first region to color in Australia, because initially every region has three legal colors. In this case, the **degree heuristic** comes in handy. It attempts to reduce the branching factor on future choices by selecting the variable that is involved in the largest number of constraints on other unassigned variables. In Figure 1, SA is the variable with highest degree, 5; the other variables have degree 2 or 3, except for T, which has degree 0. In fact, once SA is chosen, applying the degree heuristic solves the problem without any false steps—you can choose *any* consistent color at each choice point and still arrive at a solution with no backtracking. The minimum-remaining-

DEGREE HEURISTIC

values heuristic is usually a more powerful guide, but the degree heuristic can be useful as a tie-breaker.

LEAST-CONSTRAINING-VALUE

Once a variable has been selected, the algorithm must decide on the order in which to examine its values. For this, the **least-constraining-value** heuristic can be effective in some cases. It prefers the value that rules out the fewest choices for the neighboring variables in the constraint graph. For example, suppose that in Figure 1 we have generated the partial assignment with $WA = red$ and $NT = green$ and that our next choice is for Q. Blue would be a bad choice because it eliminates the last legal value left for Q's neighbor, SA. The least-constraining-value heuristic therefore prefers red to blue. In general, the heuristic is trying to leave the maximum flexibility for subsequent variable assignments. Of course, if we are trying to find all the solutions to a problem, not just the first one, then the ordering does not matter because we have to consider every value anyway. The same holds if there are no solutions to the problem.

Why should variable selection be fail-first, but value selection be fail-last? It turns out that, for a wide variety of problems, a variable ordering that chooses a variable with the minimum number of remaining values helps minimize the number of nodes in the search tree by pruning larger parts of the tree earlier. For value ordering, the trick is that we only need one solution; therefore it makes sense to look for the most likely values first. If we wanted to enumerate all solutions rather than just find one, then value ordering would be irrelevant.

3.2 Interleaving search and inference

So far we have seen how AC-3 and other algorithms can infer reductions in the domain of variables *before* we begin the search. But inference can be even more powerful in the course of a search: every time we make a choice of a value for a variable, we have a brand-new opportunity to infer new domain reductions on the neighboring variables.

FORWARD CHECKING

One of the simplest forms of inference is called **forward checking**. Whenever a variable X is assigned, the forward-checking process establishes arc consistency for it: for each unassigned variable Y that is connected to X by a constraint, delete from Y's domain any value that is inconsistent with the value chosen for X. Because forward checking only does arc consistency inferences, there is no reason to do forward checking if we have already done arc consistency as a preprocessing step.

Figure 7 shows the progress of backtracking search on the Australia CSP with forward checking. There are two important points to notice about this example. First, notice that after $WA = red$ and $Q = green$ are assigned, the domains of NT and SA are reduced to a single value; we have eliminated branching on these variables altogether by propagating information from WA and Q. A second point to notice is that after $V = blue$, the domain of SA is empty. Hence, forward checking has detected that the partial assignment $\{WA = red, Q = green, V = blue\}$ is inconsistent with the constraints of the problem, and the algorithm will therefore backtrack immediately.

For many problems the search will be more effective if we combine the MRV heuristic with forward checking. Consider Figure 7 after assigning $\{WA = red\}$. Intuitively, it seems that that assignment constrains its neighbors, NT and SA, so we should handle those

	WA	*NT*	*Q*	*NSW*	*V*	*SA*	*T*
Initial domains	R G B	R G B	R G B	R G B	R G B	R G B	R G B
After *WA*=*red*	Ⓡ	G B	R G B	R G B	R G B	G B	R G B
After *Q*=*green*	Ⓡ	B	Ⓖ	R B	R G B	B	R G B
After *V*=*blue*	Ⓡ	B	Ⓖ	R	Ⓑ		R G B

Figure 7 The progress of a map-coloring search with forward checking. $WA = red$ is assigned first; then forward checking deletes *red* from the domains of the neighboring variables NT and SA. After $Q = green$ is assigned, *green* is deleted from the domains of NT, SA, and NSW. After $V = blue$ is assigned, *blue* is deleted from the domains of NSW and SA, leaving SA with no legal values.

variables next, and then all the other variables will fall into place. That's exactly what happens with MRV: NT and SA have two values, so one of them is chosen first, then the other, then Q, NSW, and V in order. Finally T still has three values, and any one of them works. We can view forward checking as an efficient way to incrementally compute the information that the MRV heuristic needs to do its job.

Although forward checking detects many inconsistencies, it does not detect all of them. The problem is that it makes the current variable arc-consistent, but doesn't look ahead and make all the other variables arc-consistent. For example, consider the third row of Figure 7. It shows that when WA is *red* and Q is *green*, both NT and SA are forced to be blue. Forward checking does not look far enough ahead to notice that this is an inconsistency: NT and SA are adjacent and so cannot have the same value.

MAINTAINING ARC CONSISTENCY (MAC)

The algorithm called MAC (for **Maintaining Arc Consistency (MAC)**) detects this inconsistency. After a variable X_i is assigned a value, the INFERENCE procedure calls AC-3, but instead of a queue of all arcs in the CSP, we start with only the arcs (X_j, X_i) for all X_j that are unassigned variables that are neighbors of X_i. From there, AC-3 does constraint propagation in the usual way, and if any variable has its domain reduced to the empty set, the call to AC-3 fails and we know to backtrack immediately. We can see that MAC is strictly more powerful than forward checking because forward checking does the same thing as MAC on the initial arcs in MAC's queue; but unlike MAC, forward checking does not recursively propagate constraints when changes are made to the domains of variables.

3.3 Intelligent backtracking: Looking backward

The BACKTRACKING-SEARCH algorithm in Figure 5 has a very simple policy for what to do when a branch of the search fails: back up to the preceding variable and try a different value for it. This is called **chronological backtracking** because the *most recent* decision point is revisited. In this subsection, we consider better possibilities.

CHRONOLOGICAL BACKTRACKING

Consider what happens when we apply simple backtracking in Figure 1 with a fixed variable ordering Q, NSW, V, T, SA, WA, NT. Suppose we have generated the partial assignment $\{Q = red, NSW = green, V = blue, T = red\}$. When we try the next variable, SA, we see that every value violates a constraint. We back up to T and try a new color for

Tasmania! Obviously this is silly—recoloring Tasmania cannot possibly resolve the problem with South Australia.

A more intelligent approach to backtracking is to backtrack to a variable that might fix the problem—a variable that was responsible for making one of the possible values of SA impossible. To do this, we will keep track of a set of assignments that are in conflict with some value for SA. The set (in this case $\{Q = red, NSW = green, V = blue,\}$), is called the **conflict set** for SA. The **backjumping** method backtracks to the *most recent* assignment in the conflict set; in this case, backjumping would jump over Tasmania and try a new value for V. This method is easily implemented by a modification to BACKTRACK such that it accumulates the conflict set while checking for a legal value to assign. If no legal value is found, the algorithm should return the most recent element of the conflict set along with the failure indicator.

CONFLICT SET

BACKJUMPING

The sharp-eyed reader will have noticed that forward checking can supply the conflict set with no extra work: whenever forward checking based on an assignment $X = x$ deletes a value from Y's domain, it should add $X = x$ to Y's conflict set. If the last value is deleted from Y's domain, then the assignments in the conflict set of Y are added to the conflict set of X. Then, when we get to Y, we know immediately where to backtrack if needed.

The eagle-eyed reader will have noticed something odd: backjumping occurs when every value in a domain is in conflict with the current assignment; but forward checking detects this event and prevents the search from ever reaching such a node! In fact, it can be shown that *every* branch pruned by backjumping is also pruned by forward checking. Hence, simple backjumping is redundant in a forward-checking search or, indeed, in a search that uses stronger consistency checking, such as MAC.

Despite the observations of the preceding paragraph, the idea behind backjumping remains a good one: to backtrack based on the reasons for failure. Backjumping notices failure when a variable's domain becomes empty, but in many cases a branch is doomed long before this occurs. Consider again the partial assignment $\{WA = red, NSW = red\}$ (which, from our earlier discussion, is inconsistent). Suppose we try $T = red$ next and then assign NT, Q, V, SA. We know that no assignment can work for these last four variables, so eventually we run out of values to try at NT. Now, the question is, where to backtrack? Backjumping cannot work, because NT *does* have values consistent with the preceding assigned variables—NT doesn't have a complete conflict set of preceding variables that caused it to fail. We know, however, that the four variables NT, Q, V, and SA, *taken together*, failed because of a set of preceding variables, which must be those variables that directly conflict with the four. This leads to a deeper notion of the conflict set for a variable such as NT: it is that set of preceding variables that caused NT, *together with any subsequent variables*, to have no consistent solution. In this case, the set is WA and NSW, so the algorithm should backtrack to NSW and skip over Tasmania. A backjumping algorithm that uses conflict sets defined in this way is called **conflict-directed backjumping**.

CONFLICT-DIRECTED BACKJUMPING

We must now explain how these new conflict sets are computed. The method is in fact quite simple. The "terminal" failure of a branch of the search always occurs because a variable's domain becomes empty; that variable has a standard conflict set. In our example, SA fails, and its conflict set is (say) $\{WA, NT, Q\}$. We backjump to Q, and Q *absorbs* the conflict set from SA (minus Q itself, of course) into its own direct conflict set, which is $\{NT, NSW\}$; the new conflict set is $\{WA, NT, NSW\}$. That is, there is no solution from Q onward, given the preceding assignment to $\{WA, NT, NSW\}$. Therefore, we backtrack to NT, the most recent of these. NT absorbs $\{WA, NT, NSW\} - \{NT\}$ into its own direct conflict set $\{WA\}$, giving $\{WA, NSW\}$ (as stated in the previous paragraph). Now the algorithm backjumps to NSW, as we would hope. To summarize: let X_j be the current variable, and let $conf(X_j)$ be its conflict set. If every possible value for X_j fails, backjump to the most recent variable X_i in $conf(X_j)$, and set

$$conf(X_i) \leftarrow conf(X_i) \cup conf(X_j) - \{X_i\}\ .$$

When we reach a contradiction, backjumping can tell us how far to back up, so we don't waste time changing variables that won't fix the problem. But we would also like to avoid running into the same problem again. When the search arrives at a contradiction, we know that some subset of the conflict set is responsible for the problem. **Constraint learning** is the idea of finding a minimum set of variables from the conflict set that causes the problem. This set of variables, along with their corresponding values, is called a **no-good**. We then record the no-good, either by adding a new constraint to the CSP or by keeping a separate cache of no-goods.

CONSTRAINT LEARNING

NO-GOOD

For example, consider the state $\{WA = red, NT = green, Q = blue\}$ in the bottom row of Figure 6. Forward checking can tell us this state is a no-good because there is no valid assignment to SA. In this particular case, recording the no-good would not help, because once we prune this branch from the search tree, we will never encounter this combination again. But suppose that the search tree in Figure 6 were actually part of a larger search tree that started by first assigning values for V and T. Then it would be worthwhile to record $\{WA = red, NT = green, Q = blue\}$ as a no-good because we are going to run into the same problem again for each possible set of assignments to V and T.

No-goods can be effectively used by forward checking or by backjumping. Constraint learning is one of the most important techniques used by modern CSP solvers to achieve efficiency on complex problems.

4 Local Search for CSPs

Local search algorithms turn out to be effective in solving many CSPs. They use a complete-state formulation: the initial state assigns a value to every variable, and the search changes the value of one variable at a time. For example, in the 8-queens problem, the initial state might be a random configuration of 8 queens in 8 columns, and each step moves a single queen to a new position in its column. Typically, the initial guess violates several constraints. The point of local search is to eliminate the violated constraints.[2]

In choosing a new value for a variable, the most obvious heuristic is to select the value that results in the minimum number of conflicts with other variables—the **min-conflicts**

MIN-CONFLICTS

[2] Local search can easily be extended to constraint optimization problems (COPs). In that case, all the techniques for hill climbing and simulated annealing can be applied to optimize the objective function.

```
function MIN-CONFLICTS(csp, max_steps) returns a solution or failure
  inputs: csp, a constraint satisfaction problem
          max_steps, the number of steps allowed before giving up

  current ← an initial complete assignment for csp
  for i = 1 to max_steps do
     if current is a solution for csp then return current
     var ← a randomly chosen conflicted variable from csp.VARIABLES
     value ← the value v for var that minimizes CONFLICTS(var, v, current, csp)
     set var = value in current
  return failure
```

Figure 8 The MIN-CONFLICTS algorithm for solving CSPs by local search. The initial state may be chosen randomly or by a greedy assignment process that chooses a minimal-conflict value for each variable in turn. The CONFLICTS function counts the number of constraints violated by a particular value, given the rest of the current assignment.

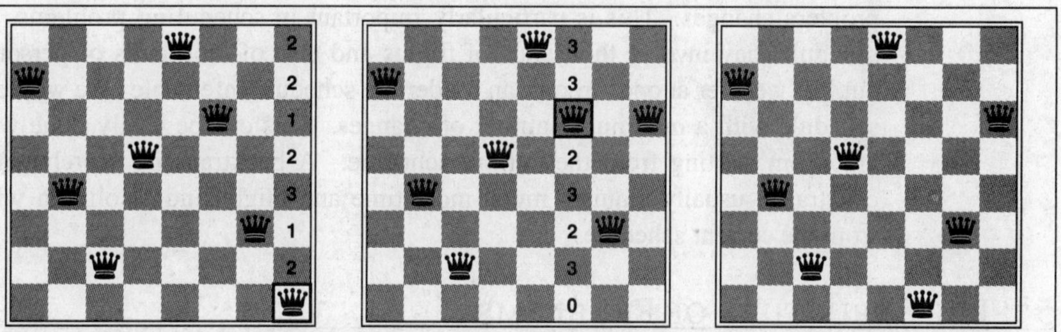

Figure 9 A two-step solution using min-conflicts for an 8-queens problem. At each stage, a queen is chosen for reassignment in its column. The number of conflicts (in this case, the number of attacking queens) is shown in each square. The algorithm moves the queen to the min-conflicts square, breaking ties randomly.

heuristic. The algorithm is shown in Figure 8 and its application to an 8-queens problem is diagrammed in Figure 9.

Min-conflicts is surprisingly effective for many CSPs. Amazingly, on the n-queens problem, if you don't count the initial placement of queens, the run time of min-conflicts is roughly *independent of problem size*. It solves even the *million*-queens problem in an average of 50 steps (after the initial assignment). This remarkable observation was the stimulus leading to a great deal of research in the 1990s on local search and the distinction between easy and hard problems. Roughly speaking, n-queens is easy for local search because solutions are densely distributed throughout the state space. Min-conflicts also works well for hard problems. For example, it has been used to schedule observations for the Hubble Space Telescope, reducing the time taken to schedule a week of observations from three weeks (!) to around 10 minutes.

Local search techniques can be candidates for application to CSPs, and some of those have proved especially effective. The landscape of a CSP under the min-conflicts heuristic usually has a series of plateaux. There may be millions of variable assignments that are only one conflict away from a solution. Plateau search—allowing sideways moves to another state with the same score—can help local search find its way off this plateau. This wandering on the plateau can be directed with **tabu search:** keeping a small list of recently visited states and forbidding the algorithm to return to those states. Simulated annealing can also be used to escape from plateaux.

CONSTRAINT WEIGHTING

Another technique, called **constraint weighting**, can help concentrate the search on the important constraints. Each constraint is given a numeric weight, W_i, initially all 1. At each step of the search, the algorithm chooses a variable/value pair to change that will result in the lowest total weight of all violated constraints. The weights are then adjusted by incrementing the weight of each constraint that is violated by the current assignment. This has two benefits: it adds topography to plateaux, making sure that it is possible to improve from the current state, and it also, over time, adds weight to the constraints that are proving difficult to solve.

Another advantage of local search is that it can be used in an online setting when the problem changes. This is particularly important in scheduling problems. A week's airline schedule may involve thousands of flights and tens of thousands of personnel assignments, but bad weather at one airport can render the schedule infeasible. We would like to repair the schedule with a minimum number of changes. This can be easily done with a local search algorithm starting from the current schedule. A backtracking search with the new set of constraints usually requires much more time and might find a solution with many changes from the current schedule.

5 THE STRUCTURE OF PROBLEMS

In this section, we examine ways in which the *structure* of the problem, as represented by the constraint graph, can be used to find solutions quickly. Most of the approaches here also apply to other problems besides CSPs, such as probabilistic reasoning. After all, the only way we can possibly hope to deal with the real world is to decompose it into many subproblems. Looking again at the constraint graph for Australia (Figure 1(b), repeated as Figure 12(a)), one fact stands out: Tasmania is not connected to the mainland.[3] Intuitively, it is obvious that coloring Tasmania and coloring the mainland are **independent subproblems**—any solution for the mainland combined with any solution for Tasmania yields a solution for the whole map. Independence can be ascertained simply by finding **connected components** of the constraint graph. Each component corresponds to a subproblem CSP_i. If assignment S_i is a solution of CSP_i, then $\bigcup_i S_i$ is a solution of $\bigcup_i CSP_i$. Why is this important? Consider the following: suppose each CSP_i has c variables from the total of n variables, where c is a constant. Then there are n/c subproblems, each of which takes at most d^c work to solve,

INDEPENDENT SUBPROBLEMS

CONNECTED COMPONENT

[3] A careful cartographer or patriotic Tasmanian might object that Tasmania should not be colored the same as its nearest mainland neighbor, to avoid the impression that it *might* be part of that state.

where d is the size of the domain. Hence, the total work is $O(d^c n/c)$, which is *linear* in n; without the decomposition, the total work is $O(d^n)$, which is exponential in n. Let's make this more concrete: dividing a Boolean CSP with 80 variables into four subproblems reduces the worst-case solution time from the lifetime of the universe down to less than a second.

Completely independent subproblems are delicious, then, but rare. Fortunately, some other graph structures are also easy to solve. For example, a constraint graph is a **tree** when any two variables are connected by only one path. We show that *any tree-structured CSP can be solved in time linear in the number of variables.*[4] The key is a new notion of consistency, called **directed arc consistency** or DAC. A CSP is defined to be directed arc-consistent under an ordering of variables $X_1, X_2, \ldots, X_n$ if and only if every X_i is arc-consistent with each X_j for $j > i$.

DIRECTED ARC CONSISTENCY

To solve a tree-structured CSP, first pick any variable to be the root of the tree, and choose an ordering of the variables such that each variable appears after its parent in the tree. Such an ordering is called a **topological sort**. Figure 10(a) shows a sample tree and (b) shows one possible ordering. Any tree with n nodes has $n-1$ arcs, so we can make this graph directed arc-consistent in $O(n)$ steps, each of which must compare up to d possible domain values for two variables, for a total time of $O(nd^2)$. Once we have a directed arc-consistent graph, we can just march down the list of variables and choose any remaining value. Since each link from a parent to its child is arc consistent, we know that for any value we choose for the parent, there will be a valid value left to choose for the child. That means we won't have to backtrack; we can move linearly through the variables. The complete algorithm is shown in Figure 11.

TOPOLOGICAL SORT

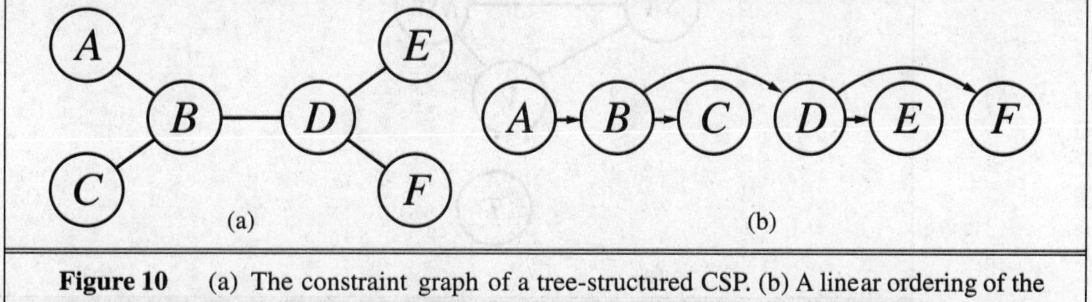

Figure 10 (a) The constraint graph of a tree-structured CSP. (b) A linear ordering of the variables consistent with the tree with A as the root. This is known as a **topological sort** of the variables.

Now that we have an efficient algorithm for trees, we can consider whether more general constraint graphs can be *reduced* to trees somehow. There are two primary ways to do this, one based on removing nodes and one based on collapsing nodes together.

The first approach involves assigning values to some variables so that the remaining variables form a tree. Consider the constraint graph for Australia, shown again in Figur 12(a). If we could delete South Australia, the graph would become a tree, as in (b). Fortunately, we can do this (in the graph, not the continent) by fixing a value for SA and

[4] Sadly, very few regions of the world have tree-structured maps, although Sulawesi comes close.

```
function TREE-CSP-SOLVER( csp) returns a solution, or failure
  inputs: csp, a CSP with components X, D, C

  n ← number of variables in X
  assignment ← an empty assignment
  root ← any variable in X
  X ← TOPOLOGICALSORT(X, root)
  for j = n down to 2 do
    MAKE-ARC-CONSISTENT(PARENT(X_j), X_j)
    if it cannot be made consistent then return failure
  for i = 1 to n do
    assignment[X_i] ← any consistent value from D_i
    if there is no consistent value then return failure
  return assignment
```

Figure 11 The TREE-CSP-SOLVER algorithm for solving tree-structured CSPs. If the CSP has a solution, we will find it in linear time; if not, we will detect a contradiction.

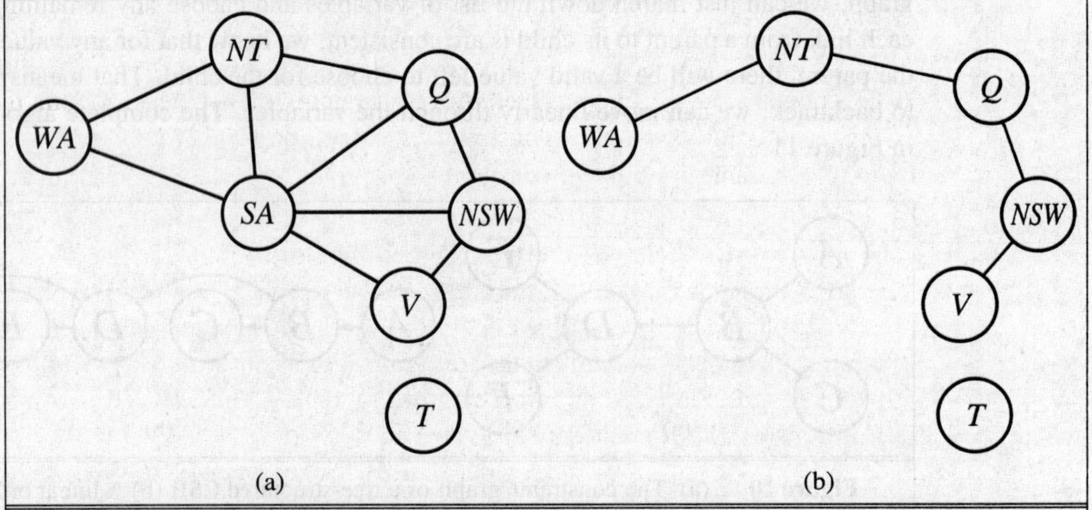

Figure 12 (a) The original constraint graph from Figure 1. (b) The constraint graph after the removal of SA.

deleting from the domains of the other variables any values that are inconsistent with the value chosen for SA.

Now, any solution for the CSP after SA and its constraints are removed will be consistent with the value chosen for SA. (This works for binary CSPs; the situation is more complicated with higher-order constraints.) Therefore, we can solve the remaining tree with the algorithm given above and thus solve the whole problem. Of course, in the general case (as opposed to map coloring), the value chosen for SA could be the wrong one, so we would need to try each possible value. The general algorithm is as follows:

1. Choose a subset S of the CSP's variables such that the constraint graph becomes a tree after removal of S. S is called a **cycle cutset**.
2. For each possible assignment to the variables in S that satisfies all constraints on S,
   (a) remove from the domains of the remaining variables any values that are inconsistent with the assignment for S, and
   (b) If the remaining CSP has a solution, return it together with the assignment for S.

CYCLE CUTSET

If the cycle cutset has size c, then the total run time is $O(d^c \cdot (n - c)d^2)$: we have to try each of the d^c combinations of values for the variables in S, and for each combination we must solve a tree problem of size $n - c$. If the graph is "nearly a tree," then c will be small and the savings over straight backtracking will be huge. In the worst case, however, c can be as large as $(n - 2)$. Finding the *smallest* cycle cutset is NP-hard, but several efficient approximation algorithms are known. The overall algorithmic approach is called **cutset conditioning**.

CUTSET CONDITIONING

TREE DECOMPOSITION

The second approach is based on constructing a **tree decomposition** of the constraint graph into a set of connected subproblems. Each subproblem is solved independently, and the resulting solutions are then combined. Like most divide-and-conquer algorithms, this works well if no subproblem is too large. Figure 13 shows a tree decomposition of the map-coloring problem into five subproblems. A tree decomposition must satisfy the following three requirements:

- Every variable in the original problem appears in at least one of the subproblems.
- If two variables are connected by a constraint in the original problem, they must appear together (along with the constraint) in at least one of the subproblems.
- If a variable appears in two subproblems in the tree, it must appear in every subproblem along the path connecting those subproblems.

The first two conditions ensure that all the variables and constraints are represented in the decomposition. The third condition seems rather technical, but simply reflects the constraint that any given variable must have the same value in every subproblem in which it appears; the links joining subproblems in the tree enforce this constraint. For example, SA appears in all four of the connected subproblems in Figure 13. You can verify from Figure 12 that this decomposition makes sense.

We solve each subproblem independently; if any one has no solution, we know the entire problem has no solution. If we can solve all the subproblems, then we attempt to construct a global solution as follows. First, we view each subproblem as a "mega-variable" whose domain is the set of all solutions for the subproblem. For example, the leftmost subproblem in Figure 13 is a map-coloring problem with three variables and hence has six solutions—one is $\{WA = red, SA = blue, NT = green\}$. Then, we solve the constraints connecting the subproblems, using the efficient algorithm for trees given earlier. The constraints between subproblems simply insist that the subproblem solutions agree on their shared variables. For example, given the solution $\{WA = red, SA = blue, NT = green\}$ for the first subproblem, the only consistent solution for the next subproblem is $\{SA = blue, NT = green, Q = red\}$.

A given constraint graph admits many tree decompositions; in choosing a decomposition, the aim is to make the subproblems as small as possible. The **tree width** of a tree

TREE WIDTH

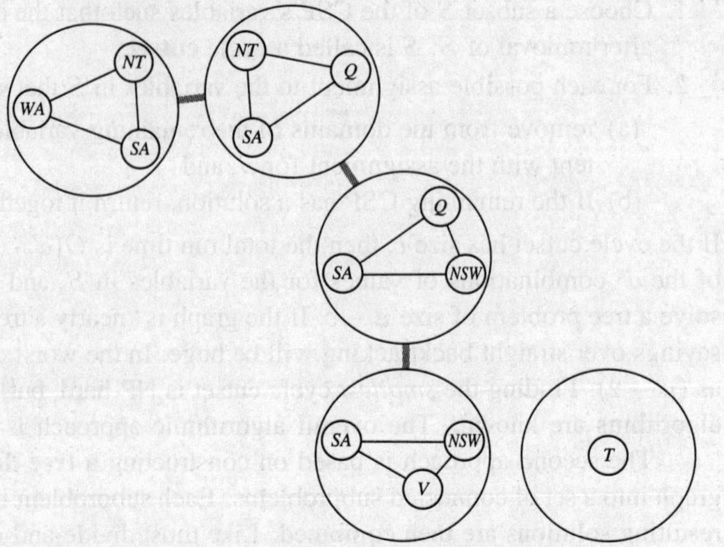

Figure 13 A tree decomposition of the constraint graph in Figure 12(a).

decomposition of a graph is one less than the size of the largest subproblem; the tree width of the graph itself is defined to be the minimum tree width among all its tree decompositions. If a graph has tree width w and we are given the corresponding tree decomposition, then the problem can be solved in $O(nd^{w+1})$ time. Hence, *CSPs with constraint graphs of bounded tree width are solvable in polynomial time.* Unfortunately, finding the decomposition with minimal tree width is NP-hard, but there are heuristic methods that work well in practice.

So far, we have looked at the structure of the constraint graph. There can be important structure in the *values* of variables as well. Consider the map-coloring problem with n colors. For every consistent solution, there is actually a set of $n!$ solutions formed by permuting the color names. For example, on the Australia map we know that WA, NT, and SA must all have different colors, but there are $3! = 6$ ways to assign the three colors to these three regions. This is called **value symmetry**. We would like to reduce the search space by a factor of $n!$ by breaking the symmetry. We do this by introducing a **symmetry-breaking constraint**. For our example, we might impose an arbitrary ordering constraint, $NT < SA < WA$, that requires the three values to be in alphabetical order. This constraint ensures that only one of the $n!$ solutions is possible: $\{NT = blue, SA = green, WA = red\}$.

VALUE SYMMETRY

SYMMETRY-BREAKING CONSTRAINT

For map coloring, it was easy to find a constraint that eliminates the symmetry, and in general it is possible to find constraints that eliminate all but one symmetric solution in polynomial time, but it is NP-hard to eliminate all symmetry among intermediate sets of values during search. In practice, breaking value symmetry has proved to be important and effective on a wide range of problems.

6 SUMMARY

- **Constraint satisfaction problems** (CSPs) represent a state with a set of variable/value pairs and represent the conditions for a solution by a set of constraints on the variables. Many important real-world problems can be described as CSPs.
- A number of inference techniques use the constraints to infer which variable/value pairs are consistent and which are not. These include node, arc, path, and k-consistency.
- **Backtracking search**, a form of depth-first search, is commonly used for solving CSPs. Inference can be interwoven with search.
- The **minimum-remaining-values** and **degree** heuristics are domain-independent methods for deciding which variable to choose next in a backtracking search. The **least-constraining-value** heuristic helps in deciding which value to try first for a given variable. Backtracking occurs when no legal assignment can be found for a variable. **Conflict-directed backjumping** backtracks directly to the source of the problem.
- Local search using the **min-conflicts** heuristic has also been applied to constraint satisfaction problems with great success.
- The complexity of solving a CSP is strongly related to the structure of its constraint graph. Tree-structured problems can be solved in linear time. **Cutset conditioning** can reduce a general CSP to a tree-structured one and is quite efficient if a small cutset can be found. **Tree decomposition** techniques transform the CSP into a tree of subproblems and are efficient if the **tree width** of the constraint graph is small.

BIBLIOGRAPHICAL AND HISTORICAL NOTES

The earliest work related to constraint satisfaction dealt largely with numerical constraints. Equational constraints with integer domains were studied by the Indian mathematician Brahmagupta in the seventh century; they are often called **Diophantine equations**, after the Greek mathematician Diophantus (c. 200–284), who actually considered the domain of positive rationals. Systematic methods for solving linear equations by variable elimination were studied by Gauss (1829); the solution of linear inequality constraints goes back to Fourier (1827).

DIOPHANTINE EQUATIONS

Finite-domain constraint satisfaction problems also have a long history. For example, **graph coloring** (of which map coloring is a special case) is an old problem in mathematics. The four-color conjecture (that every planar graph can be colored with four or fewer colors) was first made by Francis Guthrie, a student of De Morgan, in 1852. It resisted solution—despite several published claims to the contrary—until a proof was devised by Appel and Haken (1977) (see the book *Four Colors Suffice* (Wilson, 2004)). Purists were disappointed that part of the proof relied on a computer, so Georges Gonthier (2008), using the COQ theorem prover, derived a formal proof that Appel and Haken's proof was correct.

GRAPH COLORING

Specific classes of constraint satisfaction problems occur throughout the history of computer science. One of the most influential early examples was the SKETCHPAD system (Sutherland, 1963), which solved geometric constraints in diagrams and was the forerunner of modern drawing programs and CAD tools. The identification of CSPs as a *general* class is due to Ugo Montanari (1974). The reduction of higher-order CSPs to purely binary CSPs with auxiliary variables (see Exercise 6) is due originally to the 19th-century logician Charles Sanders Peirce. It was introduced into the CSP literature by Dechter (1990b) and was elaborated by Bacchus and van Beek (1998). CSPs with preferences among solutions are studied widely in the optimization literature; see Bistarelli *et al.* (1997) for a generalization of the CSP framework to allow for preferences. The bucket-elimination algorithm (Dechter, 1999) can also be applied to optimization problems.

Constraint propagation methods were popularized by Waltz's (1975) success on polyhedral line-labeling problems for computer vision. Waltz showed that, in many problems, propagation completely eliminates the need for backtracking. Montanari (1974) introduced the notion of constraint networks and propagation by path consistency. Alan Mackworth (1977) proposed the AC-3 algorithm for enforcing arc consistency as well as the general idea of combining backtracking with some degree of consistency enforcement. AC-4, a more efficient arc-consistency algorithm, was developed by Mohr and Henderson (1986). Soon after Mackworth's paper appeared, researchers began experimenting with the tradeoff between the cost of consistency enforcement and the benefits in terms of search reduction. Haralick and Elliot (1980) favored the minimal forward-checking algorithm described by McGregor (1979), whereas Gaschnig (1979) suggested full arc-consistency checking after each variable assignment—an algorithm later called MAC by Sabin and Freuder (1994). The latter paper provides somewhat convincing evidence that, on harder CSPs, full arc-consistency checking pays off. Freuder (1978, 1982) investigated the notion of k-consistency and its relationship to the complexity of solving CSPs. Apt (1999) describes a generic algorithmic framework within which consistency propagation algorithms can be analyzed, and Bessière (2006) presents a current survey.

Special methods for handling higher-order or global constraints were developed first within the context of **constraint logic programming**. Marriott and Stuckey (1998) provide excellent coverage of research in this area. The *Alldiff* constraint was studied by Regin (1994), Stergiou and Walsh (1999), and van Hoeve (2001). Bounds constraints were incorporated into constraint logic programming by Van Hentenryck *et al.* (1998). A survey of global constraints is provided by van Hoeve and Katriel (2006).

Sudoku has become the most widely known CSP and was described as such by Simonis (2005). Agerbeck and Hansen (2008) describe some of the strategies and show that Sudoku on an $n^2 \times n^2$ board is in the class of *NP*-hard problems. Reeson *et al.* (2007) show an interactive solver based on CSP techniques.

The idea of backtracking search goes back to Golomb and Baumert (1965), and its application to constraint satisfaction is due to Bitner and Reingold (1975), although they trace the basic algorithm back to the 19th century. Bitner and Reingold also introduced the MRV heuristic, which they called the *most-constrained-variable* heuristic. Brelaz (1979) used the degree heuristic as a tiebreaker after applying the MRV heuristic. The resulting algorithm, despite its simplicity, is still the best method for k-coloring arbitrary graphs. Haralick and Elliot (1980) proposed the least-constraining-value heuristic.

The basic backjumping method is due to John Gaschnig (1977, 1979). Kondrak and van Beek (1997) showed that this algorithm is essentially subsumed by forward checking. Conflict-directed backjumping was devised by Prosser (1993). The most general and powerful form of intelligent backtracking was actually developed very early on by Stallman and Sussman (1977). Their technique of **dependency-directed backtracking** led to the development of **truth maintenance systems** (Doyle, 1979). The connection between the two areas is analyzed by de Kleer (1989).

DEPENDENCY-DIRECTED BACKTRACKING

The work of Stallman and Sussman also introduced the idea of **constraint learning**, in which partial results obtained by search can be saved and reused later in the search. The idea was formalized Dechter (1990a). **Backmarking** (Gaschnig, 1979) is a particularly simple method in which consistent and inconsistent pairwise assignments are saved and used to avoid rechecking constraints. Backmarking can be combined with conflict-directed backjumping; Kondrak and van Beek (1997) present a hybrid algorithm that provably subsumes either method taken separately. The method of **dynamic backtracking** (Ginsberg, 1993) retains successful partial assignments from later subsets of variables when backtracking over an earlier choice that does not invalidate the later success.

BACKMARKING

DYNAMIC BACKTRACKING

Empirical studies of several randomized backtracking methods were done by Gomes *et al.* (2000) and Gomes and Selman (2001). Van Beek (2006) surveys backtracking.

Local search in constraint satisfaction problems was popularized by the work of Kirkpatrick *et al.* (1983) on simulated annealing, which is widely used for scheduling problems. The min-conflicts heuristic was first proposed by Gu (1989) and was developed independently by Minton *et al.* (1992). Sosic and Gu (1994) showed how it could be applied to solve the 3,000,000 queens problem in less than a minute. The astounding success of local search using min-conflicts on the *n*-queens problem led to a reappraisal of the nature and prevalence of "easy" and "hard" problems. Peter Cheeseman *et al.* (1991) explored the difficulty of randomly generated CSPs and discovered that almost all such problems either are trivially easy or have no solutions. Only if the parameters of the problem generator are set in a certain narrow range, within which roughly half of the problems are solvable, do we find "hard" problem instances. Konolige (1994) showed that local search is inferior to backtracking search on problems with a certain degree of local structure; this led to work that combined local search and inference, such as that by Pinkas and Dechter (1995). Hoos and Tsang (2006) survey local search techniques.

Work relating the structure and complexity of CSPs originates with Freuder (1985), who showed that search on arc consistent trees works without any backtracking. A similar result, with extensions to acyclic hypergraphs, was developed in the database community (Beeri *et al.*, 1983). Bayardo and Miranker (1994) present an algorithm for tree-structured CSPs that runs in linear time without any preprocessing.

Since those papers were published, there has been a great deal of progress in developing more general results relating the complexity of solving a CSP to the structure of its constraint graph. The notion of tree width was introduced by the graph theorists Robertson and Seymour (1986). Dechter and Pearl (1987, 1989), building on the work of Freuder, applied a related notion (which they called **induced width**) to constraint satisfaction problems and developed the tree decomposition approach sketched in Section 5. Drawing on this work and on results from database theory, Gottlob *et al.* (1999a, 1999b) developed a notion, **hypertree width**, that is based on the characterization of the CSP as a hypergraph. In addition to showing that any CSP with hypertree width w can be solved in time $O(n^{w+1} \log n)$, they also showed that hypertree width subsumes all previously defined measures of "width" in the sense that there are cases where the hypertree width is bounded and the other measures are unbounded.

Interest in look-back approaches to backtracking was rekindled by the work of Bayardo and Schrag (1997), whose RELSAT algorithm combined constraint learning and backjumping and was shown to outperform many other algorithms of the time. This led to AND/OR search algorithms applicable to both CSPs and probabilistic reasoning (Dechter and Mateescu, 2007). Brown *et al.* (1988) introduce the idea of symmetry breaking in CSPs, and Gent *et al.* (2006) give a recent survey.

DISTRIBUTED CONSTRAINT SATISFACTION

The field of **distributed constraint satisfaction** looks at solving CSPs when there is a collection of agents, each of which controls a subset of the constraint variables. There have been annual workshops on this problem since 2000, and good coverage elsewhere (Collin *et al.*, 1999; Pearce *et al.*, 2008; Shoham and Leyton-Brown, 2009).

Comparing CSP algorithms is mostly an empirical science: few theoretical results show that one algorithm dominates another on all problems; instead, we need to run experiments to see which algorithms perform better on typical instances of problems. As Hooker (1995) points out, we need to be careful to distinguish between competitive testing—as occurs in competitions among algorithms based on run time—and scientific testing, whose goal is to identify the properties of an algorithm that determine its efficacy on a class of problems.

The recent textbooks by Apt (2003) and Dechter (2003), and the collection by Rossi *et al.* (2006) are excellent resources on constraint processing. There are several good earlier surveys, including those by Kumar (1992), Dechter and Frost (2002), and Bartak (2001); and the encyclopedia articles by Dechter (1992) and Mackworth (1992). Pearson and Jeavons (1997) survey tractable classes of CSPs, covering both structural decomposition methods and methods that rely on properties of the domains or constraints themselves. Kondrak and van Beek (1997) give an analytical survey of backtracking search algorithms, and Bacchus and van Run (1995) give a more empirical survey. Constraint programming is covered in the books by Apt (2003) and Fruhwirth and Abdennadher (2003). Several interesting applications are described in the collection edited by Freuder and Mackworth (1994). Papers on constraint satisfaction appear regularly in *Artificial Intelligence* and in the specialist journal *Constraints*. The primary conference venue is the International Conference on Principles and Practice of Constraint Programming, often called *CP*.

EXERCISES

1 How many solutions are there for the map-coloring problem in Figure 1? How many solutions if four colors are allowed? Two colors?

2 Consider the problem of placing k knights on an $n \times n$ chessboard such that no two knights are attacking each other, where k is given and $k \leq n^2$.

a. Choose a CSP formulation. In your formulation, what are the variables?

b. What are the possible values of each variable?

c. What sets of variables are constrained, and how?

d. Now consider the problem of putting *as many knights as possible* on the board without any attacks. Explain how to solve this with local search by defining appropriate ACTIONS and RESULT functions and a sensible objective function.

3 Consider the problem of constructing (not solving) crossword puzzles:[5] fitting words into a rectangular grid. The grid, which is given as part of the problem, specifies which squares are blank and which are shaded. Assume that a list of words (i.e., a dictionary) is provided and that the task is to fill in the blank squares by using any subset of the list. Formulate this problem precisely in two ways:

a. As a general search problem. Choose an appropriate search algorithm and specify a heuristic function. Is it better to fill in blanks one letter at a time or one word at a time?

b. As a constraint satisfaction problem. Should the variables be words or letters?

Which formulation do you think will be better? Why?

4 Give precise formulations for each of the following as constraint satisfaction problems:

a. Rectilinear floor-planning: find non-overlapping places in a large rectangle for a number of smaller rectangles.

b. Class scheduling: There is a fixed number of professors and classrooms, a list of classes to be offered, and a list of possible time slots for classes. Each professor has a set of classes that he or she can teach.

c. Hamiltonian tour: given a network of cities connected by roads, choose an order to visit all cities in a country without repeating any.

5 Solve the cryptarithmetic problem in Figure 2 by hand, using the strategy of backtracking with forward checking and the MRV and least-constraining-value heuristics.

6 Show how a single ternary constraint such as "$A + B = C$" can be turned into three binary constraints by using an auxiliary variable. You may assume finite domains. (*Hint:* Consider a new variable that takes on values that are pairs of other values, and consider constraints such as "X is the first element of the pair Y.") Next, show how constraints with more than three variables can be treated similarly. Finally, show how unary constraints can be eliminated by altering the domains of variables. This completes the demonstration that any CSP can be transformed into a CSP with only binary constraints.

7 Consider the following logic puzzle: In five houses, each with a different color, live five persons of different nationalities, each of whom prefers a different brand of candy, a different drink, and a different pet. Given the following facts, the questions to answer are "Where does the zebra live, and in which house do they drink water?"

---

[5] Ginsberg *et al.* (1990) discuss several methods for constructing crossword puzzles. Littman *et al.* (1999) tackle the harder problem of solving them.

The Englishman lives in the red house.
The Spaniard owns the dog.
The Norwegian lives in the first house on the left.
The green house is immediately to the right of the ivory house.
The man who eats Hershey bars lives in the house next to the man with the fox.
Kit Kats are eaten in the yellow house.
The Norwegian lives next to the blue house.
The Smarties eater owns snails.
The Snickers eater drinks orange juice.
The Ukrainian drinks tea.
The Japanese eats Milky Ways.
Kit Kats are eaten in a house next to the house where the horse is kept.
Coffee is drunk in the green house.
Milk is drunk in the middle house.

Discuss different representations of this problem as a CSP. Why would one prefer one representation over another?

8 Consider the graph with 8 nodes A_1, A_2, A_3, A_4, H, T, F_1, F_2. A_i is connected to A_{i+1} for all i, each A_i is connected to H, H is connected to T, and T is connected to each F_i. Find a 3-coloring of this graph by hand using the following strategy: backtracking with conflict-directed backjumping, the variable order A_1, H, A_4, F_1, A_2, F_2, A_3, T, and the value order R, G, B.

9 Explain why it is a good heuristic to choose the variable that is *most* constrained but the value that is *least* constraining in a CSP search.

10 Generate random instances of map-coloring problems as follows: scatter n points on the unit square; select a point X at random, connect X by a straight line to the nearest point Y such that X is not already connected to Y and the line crosses no other line; repeat the previous step until no more connections are possible. The points represent regions on the map and the lines connect neighbors. Now try to find k-colorings of each map, for both $k=3$ and $k=4$, using min-conflicts, backtracking, backtracking with forward checking, and backtracking with MAC. Construct a table of average run times for each algorithm for values of n up to the largest you can manage. Comment on your results.

11 Use the AC-3 algorithm to show that arc consistency can detect the inconsistency of the partial assignment $\{WA = green, V = red\}$ for the problem shown in Figure 1.

12 What is the worst-case complexity of running AC-3 on a tree-structured CSP?

13 AC-3 puts back on the queue *every* arc (X_k, X_i) whenever *any* value is deleted from the domain of X_i, even if each value of X_k is consistent with several remaining values of X_i. Suppose that, for every arc (X_k, X_i), we keep track of the number of remaining values of X_i that are consistent with each value of X_k. Explain how to update these numbers efficiently and hence show that arc consistency can be enforced in total time $O(n^2d^2)$.

14 The TREE-CSP-SOLVER (Figure 10) makes arcs consistent starting at the leaves and working backwards towards the root. Why does it do that? What would happen if it went in the opposite direction?

15 We introduced Sudoku as a CSP to be solved by search over partial assignments because that is the way people generally undertake solving Sudoku problems. It is also possible, of course, to attack these problems with local search over complete assignments. How well would a local solver using the min-conflicts heuristic do on Sudoku problems?

16 Define in your own words the terms constraint, backtracking search, arc consistency, backjumping, min-conflicts, and cycle cutset.

17 Suppose that a graph is known to have a cycle cutset of no more than k nodes. Describe a simple algorithm for finding a minimal cycle cutset whose run time is not much more than $O(n^k)$ for a CSP with n variables. Search the literature for methods for finding approximately minimal cycle cutsets in time that is polynomial in the size of the cutset. Does the existence of such algorithms make the cycle cutset method practical?

FIRST-ORDER LOGIC

In which we notice that the world is blessed with many objects, some of which are related to other objects, and in which we endeavor to reason about them.

A knowledge-based agent can represent the world in which it operates and deduce what actions to take. We can use propositional logic as our representation language because it sufficiently illustrates the basic concepts of logic and knowledge-based agents. Unfortunately, propositional logic is too puny a language to represent knowledge of complex environments in a concise way. FIRST-ORDER LOGIC In this chapter, we examine **first-order logic**,[1] which is sufficiently expressive to represent a good deal of our commonsense knowledge. It also either subsumes or forms the foundation of many other representation languages and has been studied intensively for many decades. We begin in Section 1 with a discussion of representation languages in general; Section 2 covers the syntax and semantics of first-order logic; Sections 3 and 4 illustrate the use of first-order logic for simple representations.

1 REPRESENTATION REVISITED

In this section, we discuss the nature of representation languages. Our discussion motivates the development of first-order logic, a much more expressive language than propositional logic. We look at propositional logic and at other kinds of languages to understand what works and what fails. Our discussion will be cursory, compressing centuries of thought, trial, and error into a few paragraphs.

Programming languages (such as C++ or Java or Lisp) are by far the largest class of formal languages in common use. Programs themselves represent, in a direct sense, only computational processes. Data structures within programs can represent facts; for example, a program could use a 4×4 array to represent the contents of the wumpus world. Thus, the programming language statement $World[2,2] \leftarrow Pit$ is a fairly natural way to assert that there is a pit in square [2,2]. (Such representations might be considered *ad hoc*; database systems were developed precisely to provide a more general, domain-independent way to store and

[1] Also called **first-order predicate calculus**, sometimes abbreviated as **FOL** or **FOPC**.

retrieve facts.) What programming languages lack is any general mechanism for deriving facts from other facts; each update to a data structure is done by a domain-specific procedure whose details are derived by the programmer from his or her own knowledge of the domain. This procedural approach can be contrasted with the **declarative** nature of propositional logic, in which knowledge and inference are separate, and inference is entirely domain independent.

A second drawback of data structures in programs (and of databases, for that matter) is the lack of any easy way to say, for example, "There is a pit in [2,2] or [3,1]" or "If the wumpus is in [1,1] then he is not in [2,2]." Programs can store a single value for each variable, and some systems allow the value to be "unknown," but they lack the expressiveness required to handle partial information.

Propositional logic is a declarative language because its semantics is based on a truth relation between sentences and possible worlds. It also has sufficient expressive power to deal with partial information, using disjunction and negation. Propositional logic has a third

COMPOSITIONALITY

property that is desirable in representation languages, namely, **compositionality**. In a compositional language, the meaning of a sentence is a function of the meaning of its parts. For example, the meaning of "$S_{1,4} \wedge S_{1,2}$" is related to the meanings of "$S_{1,4}$" and "$S_{1,2}$." It would be very strange if "$S_{1,4}$" meant that there is a stench in square [1,4] and "$S_{1,2}$" meant that there is a stench in square [1,2], but "$S_{1,4} \wedge S_{1,2}$" meant that France and Poland drew 1–1 in last week's ice hockey qualifying match. Clearly, noncompositionality makes life much more difficult for the reasoning system.

However, propositional logic lacks the expressive power to *concisely* describe an environment with many objects. For example, we were forced to write a separate rule about breezes and pits for each square, such as

$$B_{1,1} \Leftrightarrow (P_{1,2} \vee P_{2,1}) .$$

In English, on the other hand, it seems easy enough to say, once and for all, "Squares adjacent to pits are breezy." The syntax and semantics of English somehow make it possible to describe the environment concisely.

1.1 The language of thought

Natural languages (such as English or Spanish) are very expressive indeed. We managed to write almost this whole text in natural language, with only occasional lapses into other languages (including logic, mathematics, and the language of diagrams). There is a long tradition in linguistics and the philosophy of language that views natural language as a declarative knowledge representation language. If we could uncover the rules for natural language, we could use it in representation and reasoning systems and gain the benefit of the billions of pages that have been written in natural language.

The modern view of natural language is that it serves a as a medium for **communication** rather than pure representation. When a speaker points and says, "Look!" the listener comes to know that, say, Superman has finally appeared over the rooftops. Yet we would not want to say that the sentence "Look!" represents that fact. Rather, the meaning of the sentence depends both on the sentence itself and on the **context** in which the sentence was spoken. Clearly, one could not store a sentence such as "Look!" in a knowledge base and expect to recover its meaning without also storing a representation of the context—which raises the question of how the context itself can be represented. Natural languages also suffer from AMBIGUITY **ambiguity**, a problem for a representation language. As Pinker (1995) puts it: "When people think about *spring*, surely they are not confused as to whether they are thinking about a season or something that goes *boing*—and if one word can correspond to two thoughts, thoughts can't be words."

The famous **Sapir–Whorf hypothesis** claims that our understanding of the world *is* strongly influenced by the language we speak. Whorf (1956) wrote "We cut nature up, organize it into concepts, and ascribe significances as we do, largely because we are parties to an agreement to organize it this way—an agreement that holds throughout our speech community and is codified in the patterns of our language." It is certainly true that different speech communities divide up the world differently. The French have two words "chaise" and "fauteuil," for a concept that English speakers cover with one: "chair." But English speakers can easily recognize the category fauteuil and give it a name—roughly "open-arm chair"—so does language really make a difference? Whorf relied mainly on intuition and speculation, but in the intervening years we actually have real data from anthropological, psychological and neurological studies.

For example, can you remember which of the following two phrases formed the opening of Section 1?

"In this section, we discuss the nature of representation languages . . ."

"This section covers the topic of knowledge representation languages . . ."

Wanner (1974) did a similar experiment and found that subjects made the right choice at chance level—about 50% of the time—but remembered the content of what they read with better than 90% accuracy. This suggests that people process the words to form some kind of *nonverbal* representation.

More interesting is the case in which a concept is completely absent in a language. Speakers of the Australian aboriginal language Guugu Yimithirr have no words for relative directions, such as front, back, right, or left. Instead they use absolute directions, saying, for example, the equivalent of "I have a pain in my north arm." This difference in language makes a difference in behavior: Guugu Yimithirr speakers are better at navigating in open terrain, while English speakers are better at placing the fork to the right of the plate.

Language also seems to influence thought through seemingly arbitrary grammatical features such as the gender of nouns. For example, "bridge" is masculine in Spanish and feminine in German. Boroditsky (2003) asked subjects to choose English adjectives to describe a photograph of a particular bridge. Spanish speakers chose *big*, *dangerous*, *strong*, and *towering*, whereas German speakers chose *beautiful*, *elegant*, *fragile*, and *slender*. Words can serve as anchor points that affect how we perceive the world. Loftus and Palmer (1974) showed experimental subjects a movie of an auto accident. Subjects who were asked "How fast were the cars going when they contacted each other?" reported an average of 32 mph, while subjects who were asked the question with the word "smashed" instead of "contacted" reported 41mph for the same cars in the same movie.

In a first-order logic reasoning system that uses CNF, we can see that the linguistic form "$\neg(A \vee B)$" and "$\neg A \wedge \neg B$" are the same because we can look inside the system and see that the two sentences are stored as the same canonical CNF form. Can we do that with the human brain? Until recently the answer was "no," but now it is "maybe." Mitchell *et al.* (2008) put subjects in an fMRI (functional magnetic resonance imaging) machine, showed them words such as "celery," and imaged their brains. The researchers were then able to train a computer program to predict, from a brain image, what word the subject had been presented with. Given two choices (e.g., "celery" or "airplane"), the system predicts correctly 77% of the time. The system can even predict at above-chance levels for words it has never seen an fMRI image of before (by considering the images of related words) and for people it has never seen before (proving that fMRI reveals some level of common representation across people). This type of work is still in its infancy, but fMRI (and other imaging technology such as intracranial electrophysiology (Sahin *et al.*, 2009)) promises to give us much more concrete ideas of what human knowledge representations are like.

From the viewpoint of formal logic, representing the same knowledge in two different ways makes absolutely no difference; the same facts will be derivable from either representation. In practice, however, one representation might require fewer steps to derive a conclusion, meaning that a reasoner with limited resources could get to the conclusion using one representation but not the other. For *nondeductive* tasks such as learning from experience, outcomes are *necessarily* dependent on the form of the representations used. When a learning program considers two possible theories of the world, both of which are consistent with all the data, the most common way of breaking the tie is to choose the most succinct theory—and that depends on the language used to represent theories. Thus, the influence of language on thought is unavoidable for any agent that does learning.

1.2 Combining the best of formal and natural languages

We can adopt the foundation of propositional logic—a declarative, compositional semantics that is context-independent and unambiguous—and build a more expressive logic on that foundation, borrowing representational ideas from natural language while avoiding its drawbacks. When we look at the syntax of natural language, the most obvious elements are nouns and noun phrases that refer to **objects** (squares, pits, wumpuses) and verbs and verb phrases that refer to **relations** among objects (is breezy, is adjacent to, shoots). Some of these relations are **functions**—relations in which there is only one "value" for a given "input." It is easy to start listing examples of objects, relations, and functions:

OBJECT

RELATION

FUNCTION

- Objects: people, houses, numbers, theories, Ronald McDonald, colors, baseball games, wars, centuries ...
- Relations: these can be unary relations or **properties** such as red, round, bogus, prime, multistoried ..., or more general n-ary relations such as brother of, bigger than, inside, part of, has color, occurred after, owns, comes between, ...
- Functions: father of, best friend, third inning of, one more than, beginning of ...

PROPERTY

Indeed, almost any assertion can be thought of as referring to objects and properties or relations. Some examples follow:

- "One plus two equals three."
  Objects: one, two, three, one plus two; Relation: equals; Function: plus. ("One plus two" is a name for the object that is obtained by applying the function "plus" to the objects "one" and "two." "Three" is another name for this object.)
- "Squares neighboring the wumpus are smelly."
  Objects: wumpus, squares; Property: smelly; Relation: neighboring.
- "Evil King John ruled England in 1200."
  Objects: John, England, 1200; Relation: ruled; Properties: evil, king.

The language of **first-order logic**, whose syntax and semantics we define in the next section, is built around objects and relations. It has been so important to mathematics, philosophy, and artificial intelligence precisely because those fields—and indeed, much of everyday human existence—can be usefully thought of as dealing with objects and the relations among them. First-order logic can also express facts about *some* or *all* of the objects in the universe. This enables one to represent general laws or rules, such as the statement "Squares neighboring the wumpus are smelly."

ONTOLOGICAL COMMITMENT

The primary difference between propositional and first-order logic lies in the **ontological commitment** made by each language—that is, what it assumes about the nature of *reality*. Mathematically, this commitment is expressed through the nature of the formal **models** with respect to which the truth of sentences is defined. For example, propositional logic assumes that there are facts that either hold or do not hold in the world. Each fact can be in one of two states: true or false, and each model assigns *true* or *false* to each proposition symbol.[2] First-order logic assumes more; namely, that the world consists of objects with certain relations among them that do or do not hold. The formal models are correspondingly more complicated than those for propositional logic. Special-purpose logics make still further ontological commitments; for example, **temporal logic** assumes that facts hold at particular *times* and that those times (which may be points or intervals) are ordered. Thus, special-purpose logics give certain kinds of objects (and the axioms about them) "first class" status within the logic, rather than simply defining them within the knowledge base. **Higher-order logic** views the relations and functions referred to by first-order logic as objects in themselves. This allows one to make assertions about *all* relations—for example, one could wish to define what it means for a relation to be transitive. Unlike most special-purpose logics, higher-order logic is strictly more expressive than first-order logic, in the sense that some sentences of higher-order logic cannot be expressed by any finite number of first-order logic sentences.

TEMPORAL LOGIC

HIGHER-ORDER LOGIC

EPISTEMOLOGICAL COMMITMENT

A logic can also be characterized by its **epistemological commitments**—the possible states of knowledge that it allows with respect to each fact. In both propositional and first-order logic, a sentence represents a fact and the agent either believes the sentence to be true, believes it to be false, or has no opinion. These logics therefore have three possible states of knowledge regarding any sentence. Systems using **probability theory**, on the other hand,

[2] In contrast, facts in **fuzzy logic** have a **degree of truth** between 0 and 1. For example, the sentence "Vienna is a large city" might be true in our world only to degree 0.6 in fuzzy logic.

can have any *degree of belief*, ranging from 0 (total disbelief) to 1 (total belief).[3] For example, a probabilistic wumpus-world agent might believe that the wumpus is in [1,3] with probability 0.75. The ontological and epistemological commitments of five different logics are summarized in Figure 1.

Language	Ontological Commitment (What exists in the world)	Epistemological Commitment (What an agent believes about facts)
Propositional logic	facts	true/false/unknown
First-order logic	facts, objects, relations	true/false/unknown
Temporal logic	facts, objects, relations, times	true/false/unknown
Probability theory	facts	degree of belief $\in [0, 1]$
Fuzzy logic	facts with degree of truth $\in [0, 1]$	known interval value

Figure 1 Formal languages and their ontological and epistemological commitments.

In the next section, we will launch into the details of first-order logic. Just as a student of physics requires some familiarity with mathematics, a student of AI must develop a talent for working with logical notation. On the other hand, it is also important *not* to get too concerned with the *specifics* of logical notation—after all, there are dozens of different versions. The main things to keep hold of are how the language facilitates concise representations and how its semantics leads to sound reasoning procedures.

2 Syntax and Semantics of First-Order Logic

We begin this section by specifying more precisely the way in which the possible worlds of first-order logic reflect the ontological commitment to objects and relations. Then we introduce the various elements of the language, explaining their semantics as we go along.

2.1 Models for first-order logic

The models of a logical language are the formal structures that constitute the possible worlds under consideration. Each model links the vocabulary of the logical sentences to elements of the possible world, so that the truth of any sentence can be determined. Thus, models for propositional logic link proposition symbols to predefined truth values. Models for first-order logic are much more interesting. First, they have objects in them! The

DOMAIN

DOMAIN ELEMENTS

domain of a model is the set of objects or **domain elements** it contains. The domain is required to be *nonempty*—every possible world must contain at least one object. (See Exercise 7 for a discussion of empty worlds.) Mathematically speaking, it doesn't matter *what* these objects are—all that matters is *how many* there are in each particular model—but for pedagogical purposes we'll use a concrete example. Figure 2 shows a model with five

[3] It is important not to confuse the degree of belief in probability theory with the degree of truth in fuzzy logic. Indeed, some fuzzy systems allow uncertainty (degree of belief) about degrees of truth.

objects: Richard the Lionheart, King of England from 1189 to 1199; his younger brother, the evil King John, who ruled from 1199 to 1215; the left legs of Richard and John; and a crown.

The objects in the model may be *related* in various ways. In the figure, Richard and John are brothers. Formally speaking, a relation is just the set of **tuples** of objects that are related. (A tuple is a collection of objects arranged in a fixed order and is written with angle brackets surrounding the objects.) Thus, the brotherhood relation in this model is the set

TUPLE

$$\{ \langle \text{Richard the Lionheart, King John} \rangle, \langle \text{King John, Richard the Lionheart} \rangle \} . \quad (1)$$

(Here we have named the objects in English, but you may, if you wish, mentally substitute the pictures for the names.) The crown is on King John's head, so the "on head" relation contains just one tuple, ⟨the crown, King John⟩. The "brother" and "on head" relations are binary relations—that is, they relate pairs of objects. The model also contains unary relations, or properties: the "person" property is true of both Richard and John; the "king" property is true only of John (presumably because Richard is dead at this point); and the "crown" property is true only of the crown.

Certain kinds of relationships are best considered as functions, in that a given object must be related to exactly one object in this way. For example, each person has one left leg, so the model has a unary "left leg" function that includes the following mappings:

$$\begin{aligned} &\langle \text{Richard the Lionheart} \rangle \rightarrow \text{Richard's left leg} \\ &\langle \text{King John} \rangle \rightarrow \text{John's left leg} . \end{aligned} \quad (2)$$

TOTAL FUNCTIONS

Strictly speaking, models in first-order logic require **total functions**, that is, there must be a value for every input tuple. Thus, the crown must have a left leg and so must each of the left legs. There is a technical solution to this awkward problem involving an additional "invisible"

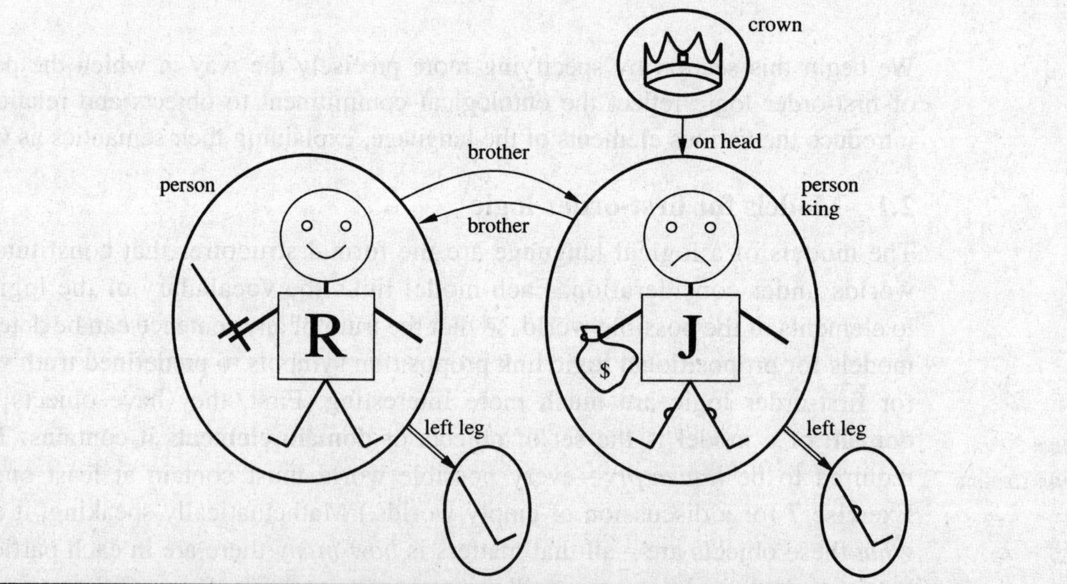

Figure 2 A model containing five objects, two binary relations, three unary relations (indicated by labels on the objects), and one unary function, left-leg.

object that is the left leg of everything that has no left leg, including itself. Fortunately, as long as one makes no assertions about the left legs of things that have no left legs, these technicalities are of no import.

So far, we have described the elements that populate models for first-order logic. The other essential part of a model is the link between those elements and the vocabulary of the logical sentences, which we explain next.

2.2 Symbols and interpretations

We turn now to the syntax of first-order logic. The impatient reader can obtain a complete description from the formal grammar in Figure 3.

The basic syntactic elements of first-order logic are the symbols that stand for objects, relations, and functions. The symbols, therefore, come in three kinds: **constant symbols**, which stand for objects; **predicate symbols**, which stand for relations; and **function symbols**, which stand for functions. We adopt the convention that these symbols will begin with uppercase letters. For example, we might use the constant symbols *Richard* and *John*; the predicate symbols *Brother*, *OnHead*, *Person*, *King*, and *Crown*; and the function symbol *LeftLeg*. As with proposition symbols, the choice of names is entirely up to the user. Each predicate and function symbol comes with an **arity** that fixes the number of arguments.

CONSTANT SYMBOL
PREDICATE SYMBOL
FUNCTION SYMBOL
ARITY

As in propositional logic, every model must provide the information required to determine if any given sentence is true or false. Thus, in addition to its objects, relations, and functions, each model includes an **interpretation** that specifies exactly which objects, relations and functions are referred to by the constant, predicate, and function symbols. One possible interpretation for our example—which a logician would call the **intended interpretation**—is as follows:

INTERPRETATION
INTENDED INTERPRETATION

- *Richard* refers to Richard the Lionheart and *John* refers to the evil King John.
- *Brother* refers to the brotherhood relation, that is, the set of tuples of objects given in Equation (1); *OnHead* refers to the "on head" relation that holds between the crown and King John; *Person*, *King*, and *Crown* refer to the sets of objects that are persons, kings, and crowns.
- *LeftLeg* refers to the "left leg" function, that is, the mapping given in Equation (2).

There are many other possible interpretations, of course. For example, one interpretation maps *Richard* to the crown and *John* to King John's left leg. There are five objects in the model, so there are 25 possible interpretations just for the constant symbols *Richard* and *John*. Notice that not all the objects need have a name—for example, the intended interpretation does not name the crown or the legs. It is also possible for an object to have several names; there is an interpretation under which both *Richard* and *John* refer to the crown.[4] If you find this possibility confusing, remember that, in propositional logic, it is perfectly possible to have a model in which *Cloudy* and *Sunny* are both true; it is the job of the knowledge base to rule out models that are inconsistent with our knowledge.

[4] Later, in Section 2.8, we examine a semantics in which every object has exactly one name.

$$
\begin{array}{rcl}
\textit{Sentence} & \rightarrow & \textit{AtomicSentence} \mid \textit{ComplexSentence} \\
\textit{AtomicSentence} & \rightarrow & \textit{Predicate} \mid \textit{Predicate}(\textit{Term}, \ldots) \mid \textit{Term} = \textit{Term} \\
\textit{ComplexSentence} & \rightarrow & (\ \textit{Sentence}\ ) \mid [\ \textit{Sentence}\ ] \\
 & \mid & \neg\ \textit{Sentence} \\
 & \mid & \textit{Sentence} \wedge \textit{Sentence} \\
 & \mid & \textit{Sentence} \vee \textit{Sentence} \\
 & \mid & \textit{Sentence} \Rightarrow \textit{Sentence} \\
 & \mid & \textit{Sentence} \Leftrightarrow \textit{Sentence} \\
 & \mid & \textit{Quantifier}\ \textit{Variable}, \ldots\ \textit{Sentence} \\
 & & \\
\textit{Term} & \rightarrow & \textit{Function}(\textit{Term}, \ldots) \\
 & \mid & \textit{Constant} \\
 & \mid & \textit{Variable} \\
 & & \\
\textit{Quantifier} & \rightarrow & \forall \mid \exists \\
\textit{Constant} & \rightarrow & A \mid X_1 \mid \textit{John} \mid \cdots \\
\textit{Variable} & \rightarrow & a \mid x \mid s \mid \cdots \\
\textit{Predicate} & \rightarrow & \textit{True} \mid \textit{False} \mid \textit{After} \mid \textit{Loves} \mid \textit{Raining} \mid \cdots \\
\textit{Function} & \rightarrow & \textit{Mother} \mid \textit{LeftLeg} \mid \cdots \\
 & & \\
\text{OPERATOR PRECEDENCE} & : & \neg, =, \wedge, \vee, \Rightarrow, \Leftrightarrow
\end{array}
$$

Figure 3 The syntax of first-order logic with equality, specified in Backus–Naur form. Operator precedences are specified, from highest to lowest. The precedence of quantifiers is such that a quantifier holds over everything to the right of it.

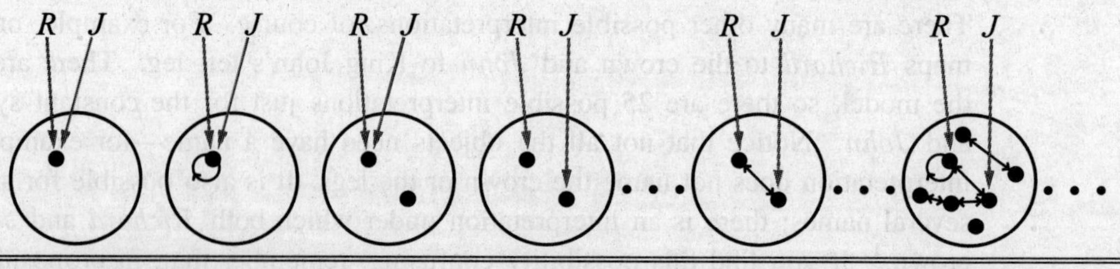

Figure 4 Some members of the set of all models for a language with two constant symbols, R and J, and one binary relation symbol. The interpretation of each constant symbol is shown by a gray arrow. Within each model, the related objects are connected by arrows.

In summary, a model in first-order logic consists of a set of objects and an interpretation that maps constant symbols to objects, predicate symbols to relations on those objects, and function symbols to functions on those objects. Just as with propositional logic, entailment, validity, and so on are defined in terms of *all possible models*. To get an idea of what the set of all possible models looks like, see Figure 4. It shows that models vary in how many objects they contain—from one up to infinity—and in the way the constant symbols map to objects. If there are two constant symbols and one object, then both symbols must refer to the same object; but this can still happen even with more objects. When there are more objects than constant symbols, some of the objects will have no names. Because the number of possible models is unbounded, checking entailment by the enumeration of all possible models is not feasible for first-order logic (unlike propositional logic). Even if the number of objects is restricted, the number of combinations can be very large. (See Exercise 5.) For the example in Figure 4, there are 137,506,194,466 models with six or fewer objects.

2.3 Terms

TERM A **term** is a logical expression that refers to an object. Constant symbols are therefore terms, but it is not always convenient to have a distinct symbol to name every object. For example, in English we might use the expression "King John's left leg" rather than giving a name to his leg. This is what function symbols are for: instead of using a constant symbol, we use $LeftLeg(John)$. In the general case, a complex term is formed by a function symbol followed by a parenthesized list of terms as arguments to the function symbol. It is important to remember that a complex term is just a complicated kind of name. It is not a "subroutine call" that "returns a value." There is no *LeftLeg* subroutine that takes a person as input and returns a leg. We can reason about left legs (e.g., stating the general rule that everyone has one and then deducing that John must have one) without ever providing a definition of *LeftLeg*. This is something that cannot be done with subroutines in programming languages.[5]

The formal semantics of terms is straightforward. Consider a term $f(t_1, \ldots, t_n)$. The function symbol f refers to some function in the model (call it F); the argument terms refer to objects in the domain (call them $d_1, \ldots, d_n$); and the term as a whole refers to the object that is the value of the function F applied to $d_1, \ldots, d_n$. For example, suppose the *LeftLeg* function symbol refers to the function shown in Equation (2) and *John* refers to King John, then $LeftLeg(John)$ refers to King John's left leg. In this way, the interpretation fixes the referent of every term.

2.4 Atomic sentences

Now that we have both terms for referring to objects and predicate symbols for referring to relations, we can put them together to make **atomic sentences** that state facts. An **atomic**

[5] **λ-expressions** provide a useful notation in which new function symbols are constructed "on the fly." For example, the function that squares its argument can be written as $(\lambda x\ x \times x)$ and can be applied to arguments just like any other function symbol. A λ-expression can also be defined and used as a predicate symbol. The `lambda` operator in Lisp plays exactly the same role. Notice that the use of λ in this way does *not* increase the formal expressive power of first-order logic, because any sentence that includes a λ-expression can be rewritten by "plugging in" its arguments to yield an equivalent sentence.

ATOMIC SENTENCE ATOM **sentence** (or **atom** for short) is formed from a predicate symbol optionally followed by a parenthesized list of terms, such as

$$Brother(Richard, John).$$

This states, under the intended interpretation given earlier, that Richard the Lionheart is the brother of King John.[6] Atomic sentences can have complex terms as arguments. Thus,

$$Married(Father(Richard), Mother(John))$$

states that Richard the Lionheart's father is married to King John's mother (again, under a suitable interpretation).

*An atomic sentence is **true** in a given model if the relation referred to by the predicate symbol holds among the objects referred to by the arguments.*

2.5 Complex sentences

We can use **logical connectives** to construct more complex sentences, with the same syntax and semantics as in propositional calculus. Here are four sentences that are true in the model of Figure 2 under our intended interpretation:

$$\neg Brother(LeftLeg(Richard), John)$$
$$Brother(Richard, John) \land Brother(John, Richard)$$
$$King(Richard) \lor King(John)$$
$$\neg King(Richard) \Rightarrow King(John).$$

2.6 Quantifiers

QUANTIFIER Once we have a logic that allows objects, it is only natural to want to express properties of entire collections of objects, instead of enumerating the objects by name. **Quantifiers** let us do this. First-order logic contains two standard quantifiers, called *universal* and *existential*.

Universal quantification (∀)

It is difficult to express general rules in propositional logic. Rules such as "Squares neighboring the wumpus are smelly" and "All kings are persons" are the bread and butter of first-order logic. We deal with the first of these in Section 3. The second rule, "All kings are persons," is written in first-order logic as

$$\forall x \ King(x) \Rightarrow Person(x).$$

∀ is usually pronounced "For all ...". (Remember that the upside-down A stands for "all.") Thus, the sentence says, "For all x, if x is a king, then x is a person." The symbol x is called

VARIABLE a **variable**. By convention, variables are lowercase letters. A variable is a term all by itself, and as such can also serve as the argument of a function—for example, $LeftLeg(x)$. A term

GROUND TERM with no variables is called a **ground term**.

Intuitively, the sentence $\forall x \ P$, where P is any logical expression, says that P is true for every object x. More precisely, $\forall x \ P$ is true in a given model if P is true in all possible

EXTENDED INTERPRETATION **extended interpretations** constructed from the interpretation given in the model, where each

[6] We usually follow the argument-ordering convention that $P(x, y)$ is read as "x is a P of y."

extended interpretation specifies a domain element to which x refers.

This sounds complicated, but it is really just a careful way of stating the intuitive meaning of universal quantification. Consider the model shown in Figure 2 and the intended interpretation that goes with it. We can extend the interpretation in five ways:

$x \rightarrow$ Richard the Lionheart,
$x \rightarrow$ King John,
$x \rightarrow$ Richard's left leg,
$x \rightarrow$ John's left leg,
$x \rightarrow$ the crown.

The universally quantified sentence $\forall x \;\; King(x) \Rightarrow Person(x)$ is true in the original model if the sentence $King(x) \Rightarrow Person(x)$ is true under each of the five extended interpretations. That is, the universally quantified sentence is equivalent to asserting the following five sentences:

Richard the Lionheart is a king $\Rightarrow$ Richard the Lionheart is a person.
King John is a king $\Rightarrow$ King John is a person.
Richard's left leg is a king $\Rightarrow$ Richard's left leg is a person.
John's left leg is a king $\Rightarrow$ John's left leg is a person.
The crown is a king $\Rightarrow$ the crown is a person.

Let us look carefully at this set of assertions. Since, in our model, King John is the only king, the second sentence asserts that he is a person, as we would hope. But what about the other four sentences, which appear to make claims about legs and crowns? Is that part of the meaning of "All kings are persons"? In fact, the other four assertions are true in the model, but make no claim whatsoever about the personhood qualifications of legs, crowns, or indeed Richard. This is because none of these objects is a king. Looking at the truth table for $\Rightarrow$ (Figure 8 in the chapter "Logical Agents"), we see that the implication is true whenever its premise is false—*regardless* of the truth of the conclusion. Thus, by asserting the universally quantified sentence, which is equivalent to asserting a whole list of individual implications, we end up asserting the conclusion of the rule just for those objects for whom the premise is true and saying nothing at all about those individuals for whom the premise is false. Thus, the truth-table definition of $\Rightarrow$ turns out to be perfect for writing general rules with universal quantifiers.

A common mistake, made frequently even by diligent readers who have read this paragraph several times, is to use conjunction instead of implication. The sentence

$$\forall x \;\; King(x) \land Person(x)$$

would be equivalent to asserting

Richard the Lionheart is a king $\land$ Richard the Lionheart is a person,
King John is a king $\land$ King John is a person,
Richard's left leg is a king $\land$ Richard's left leg is a person,

and so on. Obviously, this does not capture what we want.

Existential quantification ($\exists$)

Universal quantification makes statements about every object. Similarly, we can make a statement about *some* object in the universe without naming it, by using an existential quantifier. To say, for example, that King John has a crown on his head, we write

$$\exists x \;\; Crown(x) \wedge OnHead(x, John)\,.$$

$\exists x$ is pronounced "There exists an x such that ..." or "For some x ...".

Intuitively, the sentence $\exists x \;\; P$ says that P is true for at least one object x. More precisely, $\exists x \;\; P$ is true in a given model if P is true in *at least one* extended interpretation that assigns x to a domain element. That is, at least one of the following is true:

Richard the Lionheart is a crown $\wedge$ Richard the Lionheart is on John's head;
King John is a crown $\wedge$ King John is on John's head;
Richard's left leg is a crown $\wedge$ Richard's left leg is on John's head;
John's left leg is a crown $\wedge$ John's left leg is on John's head;
The crown is a crown $\wedge$ the crown is on John's head.

The fifth assertion is true in the model, so the original existentially quantified sentence is true in the model. Notice that, by our definition, the sentence would also be true in a model in which King John was wearing two crowns. This is entirely consistent with the original sentence "King John has a crown on his head." [7]

Just as $\Rightarrow$ appears to be the natural connective to use with $\forall$, $\wedge$ is the natural connective to use with $\exists$. Using $\wedge$ as the main connective with $\forall$ led to an overly strong statement in the example in the previous section; using $\Rightarrow$ with $\exists$ usually leads to a very weak statement, indeed. Consider the following sentence:

$$\exists x \;\; Crown(x) \Rightarrow OnHead(x, John)\,.$$

On the surface, this might look like a reasonable rendition of our sentence. Applying the semantics, we see that the sentence says that at least one of the following assertions is true:

Richard the Lionheart is a crown $\Rightarrow$ Richard the Lionheart is on John's head;
King John is a crown $\Rightarrow$ King John is on John's head;
Richard's left leg is a crown $\Rightarrow$ Richard's left leg is on John's head;

and so on. Now an implication is true if both premise and conclusion are true, *or if its premise is false*. So if Richard the Lionheart is not a crown, then the first assertion is true and the existential is satisfied. So, an existentially quantified implication sentence is true whenever *any* object fails to satisfy the premise; hence such sentences really do not say much at all.

Nested quantifiers

We will often want to express more complex sentences using multiple quantifiers. The simplest case is where the quantifiers are of the same type. For example, "Brothers are siblings" can be written as

$$\forall x \;\; \forall y \;\; Brother(x, y) \Rightarrow Sibling(x, y)\,.$$

[7] There is a variant of the existential quantifier, usually written $\exists^1$ or $\exists!$, that means "There exists exactly one." The same meaning can be expressed using equality statements.

Consecutive quantifiers of the same type can be written as one quantifier with several variables. For example, to say that siblinghood is a symmetric relationship, we can write

$$\forall\, x, y \;\; Sibling(x, y) \Leftrightarrow Sibling(y, x)\;.$$

In other cases we will have mixtures. "Everybody loves somebody" means that for every person, there is someone that person loves:

$$\forall\, x \;\exists\, y \;\; Loves(x, y)\;.$$

On the other hand, to say "There is someone who is loved by everyone," we write

$$\exists\, y \;\forall\, x \;\; Loves(x, y)\;.$$

The order of quantification is therefore very important. It becomes clearer if we insert parentheses. $\forall\, x\; (\exists\, y\; Loves(x, y))$ says that *everyone* has a particular property, namely, the property that they love someone. On the other hand, $\exists\, y\; (\forall\, x\; Loves(x, y))$ says that *someone* in the world has a particular property, namely the property of being loved by everybody.

Some confusion can arise when two quantifiers are used with the same variable name. Consider the sentence

$$\forall\, x \;\; (Crown(x) \lor (\exists\, x \;\; Brother(Richard, x)))\;.$$

Here the x in $Brother(Richard, x)$ is *existentially* quantified. The rule is that the variable belongs to the innermost quantifier that mentions it; then it will not be subject to any other quantification. Another way to think of it is this: $\exists\, x\; Brother(Richard, x)$ is a sentence about Richard (that he has a brother), not about x; so putting a $\forall\, x$ outside it has no effect. It could equally well have been written $\exists\, z\; Brother(Richard, z)$. Because this can be a source of confusion, we will always use different variable names with nested quantifiers.

Connections between $\forall$ and $\exists$

The two quantifiers are actually intimately connected with each other, through negation. Asserting that everyone dislikes parsnips is the same as asserting there does not exist someone who likes them, and vice versa:

$$\forall\, x \;\neg Likes(x, Parsnips) \quad \text{is equivalent to} \quad \neg\exists\, x \;\; Likes(x, Parsnips)\;.$$

We can go one step further: "Everyone likes ice cream" means that there is no one who does not like ice cream:

$$\forall\, x \;\; Likes(x, IceCream) \quad \text{is equivalent to} \quad \neg\exists\, x \;\neg Likes(x, IceCream)\;.$$

Because $\forall$ is really a conjunction over the universe of objects and $\exists$ is a disjunction, it should not be surprising that they obey De Morgan's rules. The De Morgan rules for quantified and unquantified sentences are as follows:

$$\begin{array}{llll}
\forall\, x \;\neg P \;\equiv\; \neg\exists\, x \;\; P & \qquad & \neg(P \lor Q) & \equiv\; \neg P \land \neg Q \\
\neg\forall\, x \;\; P \;\equiv\; \exists\, x \;\neg P & & \neg(P \land Q) & \equiv\; \neg P \lor \neg Q \\
\forall\, x \;\; P \;\;\; \equiv\; \neg\exists\, x \;\neg P & & P \land Q & \equiv\; \neg(\neg P \lor \neg Q) \\
\exists\, x \;\; P \;\;\; \equiv\; \neg\forall\, x \;\neg P & & P \lor Q & \equiv\; \neg(\neg P \land \neg Q)\;.
\end{array}$$

Thus, we do not really need both $\forall$ and $\exists$, just as we do not really need both $\land$ and $\lor$. Still, readability is more important than parsimony, so we will keep both of the quantifiers.

2.7 Equality

First-order logic includes one more way to make atomic sentences, other than using a predicate and terms as described earlier. We can use the **equality symbol** to signify that two terms refer to the same object. For example,

EQUALITY SYMBOL

$$Father(John) = Henry$$

says that the object referred to by *Father*(*John*) and the object referred to by *Henry* are the same. Because an interpretation fixes the referent of any term, determining the truth of an equality sentence is simply a matter of seeing that the referents of the two terms are the same object.

The equality symbol can be used to state facts about a given function, as we just did for the *Father* symbol. It can also be used with negation to insist that two terms are not the same object. To say that Richard has at least two brothers, we would write

$$\exists\, x, y \;\; Brother(x, Richard) \land Brother(y, Richard) \land \neg(x = y)\,.$$

The sentence

$$\exists\, x, y \;\; Brother(x, Richard) \land Brother(y, Richard)$$

does not have the intended meaning. In particular, it is true in the model of Figure 2, where Richard has only one brother. To see this, consider the extended interpretation in which both x and y are assigned to King John. The addition of $\neg(x = y)$ rules out such models. The notation $x \neq y$ is sometimes used as an abbreviation for $\neg(x = y)$.

2.8 An alternative semantics?

Continuing the example from the previous section, suppose that we believe that Richard has two brothers, John and Geoffrey.[8] Can we capture this state of affairs by asserting

$$Brother(John, Richard) \land Brother(Geoffrey, Richard)\ ? \tag{3}$$

Not quite. First, this assertion is true in a model where Richard has only one brother—we need to add $John \neq Geoffrey$. Second, the sentence doesn't rule out models in which Richard has many more brothers besides John and Geoffrey. Thus, the correct translation of "Richard's brothers are John and Geoffrey" is as follows:

$$\begin{aligned} &Brother(John, Richard) \land Brother(Geoffrey, Richard) \land John \neq Geoffrey \\ &\quad \land \forall\, x \;\; Brother(x, Richard) \Rightarrow (x = John \lor x = Geoffrey)\,. \end{aligned}$$

For many purposes, this seems much more cumbersome than the corresponding natural-language expression. As a consequence, humans may make mistakes in translating their knowledge into first-order logic, resulting in unintuitive behaviors from logical reasoning systems that use the knowledge. Can we devise a semantics that allows a more straightforward logical expression?

One proposal that is very popular in database systems works as follows. First, we insist that every constant symbol refer to a distinct object—the so-called **unique-names assumption**. Second, we assume that atomic sentences not known to be true are in fact false—the **closed-world assumption**. Finally, we invoke **domain closure**, meaning that each model

UNIQUE-NAMES ASSUMPTION
CLOSED-WORLD ASSUMPTION
DOMAIN CLOSURE

8 Actually he had four, the others being William and Henry.

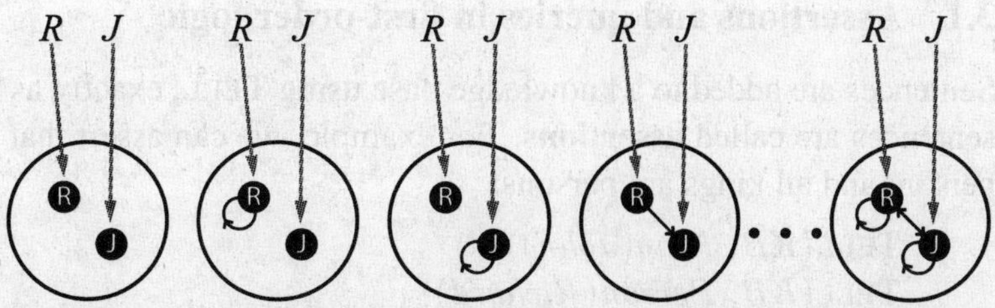

Figure 5 Some members of the set of all models for a language with two constant symbols, R and J, and one binary relation symbol, under database semantics. The interpretation of the constant symbols is fixed, and there is a distinct object for each constant symbol.

contains no more domain elements than those named by the constant symbols. Under the resulting semantics, which we call **database semantics** to distinguish it from the standard semantics of first-order logic, the sentence Equation (3) does indeed state that Richard's two brothers are John and Geoffrey. Database semantics is also used in logic programming systems.

DATABASE SEMANTICS

It is instructive to consider the set of all possible models under database semantics for the same case as shown in Figure 4. Figure 5 shows some of the models, ranging from the model with no tuples satisfying the relation to the model with all tuples satisfying the relation. With two objects, there are four possible two-element tuples, so there are $2^4 = 16$ different subsets of tuples that can satisfy the relation. Thus, there are 16 possible models in all—a lot fewer than the infinitely many models for the standard first-order semantics. On the other hand, the database semantics requires definite knowledge of what the world contains.

This example brings up an important point: there is no one "correct" semantics for logic. The usefulness of any proposed semantics depends on how concise and intuitive it makes the expression of the kinds of knowledge we want to write down, and on how easy and natural it is to develop the corresponding rules of inference. Database semantics is most useful when we are certain about the identity of all the objects described in the knowledge base and when we have all the facts at hand; in other cases, it is quite awkward. For the rest of this chapter, we assume the standard semantics while noting instances in which this choice leads to cumbersome expressions.

3 USING FIRST-ORDER LOGIC

Now that we have defined an expressive logical language, it is time to learn how to use it. The best way to do this is through examples. We have seen some simple sentences illustrating the various aspects of logical syntax; in this section, we provide more systematic representations of some simple **domains**. In knowledge representation, a domain is just some part of the world about which we wish to express some knowledge.

DOMAIN

We begin with a brief description of the TELL/ASK interface for first-order knowledge bases. Then we look at the domains of family relationships, numbers, sets, and lists, and at the wumpus world. The next section contains a more substantial example (electronic circuits).

3.1 Assertions and queries in first-order logic

Sentences are added to a knowledge base using TELL, exactly as in propositional logic. Such sentences are called **assertions**. For example, we can assert that John is a king, Richard is a person, and all kings are persons:

ASSERTION

$$\text{TELL}(KB,\ King(John))\ .$$
$$\text{TELL}(KB,\ Person(Richard))\ .$$
$$\text{TELL}(KB,\ \forall x\ \ King(x) \Rightarrow\ Person(x))\ .$$

We can ask questions of the knowledge base using ASK. For example,

$$\text{ASK}(KB,\ King(John))$$

QUERY
GOAL

returns *true*. Questions asked with ASK are called **queries** or **goals**. Generally speaking, any query that is logically entailed by the knowledge base should be answered affirmatively. For example, given the two preceding assertions, the query

$$\text{ASK}(KB,\ Person(John))$$

should also return *true*. We can ask quantified queries, such as

$$\text{ASK}(KB,\ \exists x\ \ Person(x))\ .$$

The answer is *true*, but this is perhaps not as helpful as we would like. It is rather like answering "Can you tell me the time?" with "Yes." If we want to know what value of x makes the sentence true, we will need a different function, ASKVARS, which we call with

$$\text{ASKVARS}(KB, Person(x))$$

SUBSTITUTION
BINDING LIST

and which yields a stream of answers. In this case there will be two answers: $\{x/John\}$ and $\{x/Richard\}$. Such an answer is called a **substitution** or **binding list**. ASKVARS is usually reserved for knowledge bases consisting solely of Horn clauses, because in such knowledge bases every way of making the query true will bind the variables to specific values. That is not the case with first-order logic; if KB has been told $King(John) \lor King(Richard)$, then there is no binding to x for the query $\exists x\ \ King(x)$, even though the query is true.

3.2 The kinship domain

The first example we consider is the domain of family relationships, or kinship. This domain includes facts such as "Elizabeth is the mother of Charles" and "Charles is the father of William" and rules such as "One's grandmother is the mother of one's parent."

Clearly, the objects in our domain are people. We have two unary predicates, *Male* and *Female*. Kinship relations—parenthood, brotherhood, marriage, and so on—are represented by binary predicates: *Parent*, *Sibling*, *Brother*, *Sister*, *Child*, *Daughter*, *Son*, *Spouse*, *Wife*, *Husband*, *Grandparent*, *Grandchild*, *Cousin*, *Aunt*, and *Uncle*. We use functions for *Mother* and *Father*, because every person has exactly one of each of these (at least according to nature's design).

We can go through each function and predicate, writing down what we know in terms of the other symbols. For example, one's mother is one's female parent:

$$\forall m, c \;\; Mother(c) = m \;\Leftrightarrow\; Female(m) \land Parent(m, c) \,.$$

One's husband is one's male spouse:

$$\forall w, h \;\; Husband(h, w) \;\Leftrightarrow\; Male(h) \land Spouse(h, w) \,.$$

Male and female are disjoint categories:

$$\forall x \;\; Male(x) \;\Leftrightarrow\; \neg Female(x) \,.$$

Parent and child are inverse relations:

$$\forall p, c \;\; Parent(p, c) \;\Leftrightarrow\; Child(c, p) \,.$$

A grandparent is a parent of one's parent:

$$\forall g, c \;\; Grandparent(g, c) \;\Leftrightarrow\; \exists p \;\; Parent(g, p) \land Parent(p, c) \,.$$

A sibling is another child of one's parents:

$$\forall x, y \;\; Sibling(x, y) \;\Leftrightarrow\; x \neq y \land \exists p \;\; Parent(p, x) \land Parent(p, y) \,.$$

We could go on for several more pages like this, and Exercise 14 asks you to do just that.

Each of these sentences can be viewed as an **axiom** of the kinship domain. Axioms are commonly associated with purely mathematical domains—we will see some axioms for numbers shortly—but they are needed in all domains. They provide the basic factual information from which useful conclusions can be derived. Our kinship axioms are also **definitions**; they have the form $\forall x, y \;\; P(x, y) \Leftrightarrow \ldots$. The axioms define the *Mother* function and the *Husband, Male, Parent, Grandparent,* and *Sibling* predicates in terms of other predicates. Our definitions "bottom out" at a basic set of predicates (*Child, Spouse,* and *Female*) in terms of which the others are ultimately defined. This is a natural way in which to build up the representation of a domain, and it is analogous to the way in which software packages are built up by successive definitions of subroutines from primitive library functions. Notice that there is not necessarily a unique set of primitive predicates; we could equally well have used *Parent, Spouse,* and *Male*. In some domains, as we show, there is no clearly identifiable basic set.

DEFINITION

THEOREM

Not all logical sentences about a domain are axioms. Some are **theorems**—that is, they are entailed by the axioms. For example, consider the assertion that siblinghood is symmetric:

$$\forall x, y \;\; Sibling(x, y) \;\Leftrightarrow\; Sibling(y, x) \,.$$

Is this an axiom or a theorem? In fact, it is a theorem that follows logically from the axiom that defines siblinghood. If we ASK the knowledge base this sentence, it should return *true*.

From a purely logical point of view, a knowledge base need contain only axioms and no theorems, because the theorems do not increase the set of conclusions that follow from the knowledge base. From a practical point of view, theorems are essential to reduce the computational cost of deriving new sentences. Without them, a reasoning system has to start from first principles every time, rather like a physicist having to rederive the rules of calculus for every new problem.

Not all axioms are definitions. Some provide more general information about certain predicates without constituting a definition. Indeed, some predicates have no complete definition because we do not know enough to characterize them fully. For example, there is no obvious definitive way to complete the sentence

$$\forall x \;\; Person(x) \Leftrightarrow \;\; \ldots$$

Fortunately, first-order logic allows us to make use of the *Person* predicate without completely defining it. Instead, we can write partial specifications of properties that every person has and properties that make something a person:

$$\forall x \;\; Person(x) \Rightarrow \;\; \ldots$$
$$\forall x \;\; \ldots \;\; \Rightarrow \; Person(x) \, .$$

Axioms can also be "just plain facts," such as *Male*(*Jim*) and *Spouse*(*Jim*, *Laura*). Such facts form the descriptions of specific problem instances, enabling specific questions to be answered. The answers to these questions will then be theorems that follow from the axioms. Often, one finds that the expected answers are not forthcoming—for example, from *Spouse*(*Jim*, *Laura*) one expects (under the laws of many countries) to be able to infer ¬*Spouse*(*George*, *Laura*); but this does not follow from the axioms given earlier—even after we add $Jim \neq George$ as suggested in Section 2.8. This is a sign that an axiom is missing. Exercise 8 asks the reader to supply it.

3.3 Numbers, sets, and lists

Numbers are perhaps the most vivid example of how a large theory can be built up from a tiny kernel of axioms. We describe here the theory of **natural numbers** or non-negative integers. We need a predicate *NatNum* that will be true of natural numbers; we need one constant symbol, 0; and we need one function symbol, S (successor). The **Peano axioms** define natural numbers and addition.[9] Natural numbers are defined recursively:

NATURAL NUMBERS

PEANO AXIOMS

$$NatNum(0) \, .$$
$$\forall n \;\; NatNum(n) \;\Rightarrow\; NatNum(S(n)) \, .$$

That is, 0 is a natural number, and for every object n, if n is a natural number, then $S(n)$ is a natural number. So the natural numbers are 0, $S(0)$, $S(S(0))$, and so on. (After reading Section 2.8, you will notice that these axioms allow for other natural numbers besides the usual ones; see Exercise 12.) We also need axioms to constrain the successor function:

$$\forall n \;\; 0 \neq S(n) \, .$$
$$\forall m, n \;\; m \neq n \;\Rightarrow\; S(m) \neq S(n) \, .$$

Now we can define addition in terms of the successor function:

$$\forall m \;\; NatNum(m) \Rightarrow +(0, m) = m \, .$$
$$\forall m, n \;\; NatNum(m) \wedge NatNum(n) \;\Rightarrow\; +(S(m), n) = S(+(m, n)) \, .$$

The first of these axioms says that adding 0 to any natural number m gives m itself. Notice the use of the binary function symbol "+" in the term $+(m, 0)$; in ordinary mathematics, the term would be written $m + 0$ using **infix** notation. (The notation we have used for first-order

INFIX

[9] The Peano axioms also include the principle of induction, which is a sentence of second-order logic rather than of first-order logic.

PREFIX logic is called **prefix**.) To make our sentences about numbers easier to read, we allow the use of infix notation. We can also write $S(n)$ as $n+1$, so the second axiom becomes

$$\forall\, m, n \;\; NatNum(m) \land NatNum(n) \;\Rightarrow\; (m+1)+n = (m+n)+1 \,.$$

This axiom reduces addition to repeated application of the successor function.

SYNTACTIC SUGAR The use of infix notation is an example of **syntactic sugar**, that is, an extension to or abbreviation of the standard syntax that does not change the semantics. Any sentence that uses sugar can be "desugared" to produce an equivalent sentence in ordinary first-order logic.

Once we have addition, it is straightforward to define multiplication as repeated addition, exponentiation as repeated multiplication, integer division and remainders, prime numbers, and so on. Thus, the whole of number theory (including cryptography) can be built up from one constant, one function, one predicate and four axioms.

SET The domain of **sets** is also fundamental to mathematics as well as to commonsense reasoning. (In fact, it is possible to define number theory in terms of set theory.) We want to be able to represent individual sets, including the empty set. We need a way to build up sets by adding an element to a set or taking the union or intersection of two sets. We will want to know whether an element is a member of a set and we will want to distinguish sets from objects that are not sets.

We will use the normal vocabulary of set theory as syntactic sugar. The empty set is a constant written as $\{\,\}$. There is one unary predicate, Set, which is true of sets. The binary predicates are $x \in s$ (x is a member of set s) and $s_1 \subseteq s_2$ (set s_1 is a subset, not necessarily proper, of set s_2). The binary functions are $s_1 \cap s_2$ (the intersection of two sets), $s_1 \cup s_2$ (the union of two sets), and $\{x|s\}$ (the set resulting from adjoining element x to set s). One possible set of axioms is as follows:

1. The only sets are the empty set and those made by adjoining something to a set:

   $$\forall\, s \;\; Set(s) \Leftrightarrow (s = \{\,\}) \lor (\exists\, x, s_2 \;\; Set(s_2) \land s = \{x|s_2\}) \,.$$

2. The empty set has no elements adjoined into it. In other words, there is no way to decompose $\{\,\}$ into a smaller set and an element:

   $$\neg \exists\, x, s \; \{x|s\} = \{\,\} \,.$$

3. Adjoining an element already in the set has no effect:

   $$\forall\, x, s \;\; x \in s \Leftrightarrow s = \{x|s\} \,.$$

4. The only members of a set are the elements that were adjoined into it. We express this recursively, saying that x is a member of s if and only if s is equal to some set s_2 adjoined with some element y, where either y is the same as x or x is a member of s_2:

   $$\forall\, x, s \;\; x \in s \;\Leftrightarrow\; \exists\, y, s_2 \;\; (s = \{y|s_2\} \land (x = y \lor x \in s_2)) \,.$$

5. A set is a subset of another set if and only if all of the first set's members are members of the second set:

   $$\forall\, s_1, s_2 \;\; s_1 \subseteq s_2 \;\Leftrightarrow\; (\forall\, x \;\; x \in s_1 \Rightarrow x \in s_2) \,.$$

6. Two sets are equal if and only if each is a subset of the other:

   $$\forall\, s_1, s_2 \;\; (s_1 = s_2) \;\Leftrightarrow\; (s_1 \subseteq s_2 \land s_2 \subseteq s_1) \,.$$

7. An object is in the intersection of two sets if and only if it is a member of both sets:

$$\forall x, s_1, s_2 \;\; x \in (s_1 \cap s_2) \;\Leftrightarrow\; (x \in s_1 \wedge x \in s_2) .$$

8. An object is in the union of two sets if and only if it is a member of either set:

$$\forall x, s_1, s_2 \;\; x \in (s_1 \cup s_2) \;\Leftrightarrow\; (x \in s_1 \vee x \in s_2) .$$

LIST

Lists are similar to sets. The differences are that lists are ordered and the same element can appear more than once in a list. We can use the vocabulary of Lisp for lists: *Nil* is the constant list with no elements; *Cons*, *Append*, *First*, and *Rest* are functions; and *Find* is the predicate that does for lists what *Member* does for sets. *List*? is a predicate that is true only of lists. As with sets, it is common to use syntactic sugar in logical sentences involving lists. The empty list is [ ]. The term $Cons(x, y)$, where y is a nonempty list, is written $[x|y]$. The term $Cons(x, Nil)$ (i.e., the list containing the element x) is written as $[x]$. A list of several elements, such as $[A, B, C]$, corresponds to the nested term $Cons(A, Cons(B, Cons(C, Nil)))$. Exercise 16 asks you to write out the axioms for lists.

3.4 The wumpus world

You may be familiar with some propositional logic axioms for the wumpus world. The first-order axioms in this section are much more concise, capturing in a natural way exactly what we want to say.

The wumpus agent receives a percept vector with five elements. The corresponding first-order sentence stored in the knowledge base must include both the percept and the time at which it occurred; otherwise, the agent will get confused about when it saw what. We use integers for time steps. A typical percept sentence would be

$$Percept([Stench, Breeze, Glitter, None, None], 5) .$$

Here, *Percept* is a binary predicate, and *Stench* and so on are constants placed in a list. The actions in the wumpus world can be represented by logical terms:

$$Turn(Right),\;\; Turn(Left),\;\; Forward,\;\; Shoot,\;\; Grab,\;\; Climb .$$

To determine which is best, the agent program executes the query

$$\text{ASKVARS}(\exists\, a \;\; BestAction(a, 5)) ,$$

which returns a binding list such as $\{a/Grab\}$. The agent program can then return *Grab* as the action to take. The raw percept data implies certain facts about the current state. For example:

$$\forall t, s, g, m, c \;\; Percept([s, Breeze, g, m, c], t) \;\Rightarrow\; Breeze(t) ,$$
$$\forall t, s, b, m, c \;\; Percept([s, b, Glitter, m, c], t) \;\Rightarrow\; Glitter(t) ,$$

and so on. These rules exhibit a trivial form of the reasoning process called **perception**. Notice the quantification over time *t*. In propositional logic, we would need copies of each sentence for each time step.

Simple "reflex" behavior can also be implemented by quantified implication sentences. For example, we have

$$\forall t \;\; Glitter(t) \;\Rightarrow\; BestAction(Grab, t) .$$

Given the percept and rules from the preceding paragraphs, this would yield the desired conclusion $BestAction(Grab, 5)$—that is, *Grab* is the right thing to do.

We have represented the agent's inputs and outputs; now it is time to represent the environment itself. Let us begin with objects. Obvious candidates are squares, pits, and the wumpus. We could name each square—$Square_{1,2}$ and so on—but then the fact that $Square_{1,2}$ and $Square_{1,3}$ are adjacent would have to be an "extra" fact, and we would need one such fact for each pair of squares. It is better to use a complex term in which the row and column appear as integers; for example, we can simply use the list term $[1, 2]$. Adjacency of any two squares can be defined as

$$\forall\, x, y, a, b \;\; Adjacent([x, y], [a, b]) \Leftrightarrow$$
$$(x = a \land (y = b - 1 \lor y = b + 1)) \lor (y = b \land (x = a - 1 \lor x = a + 1)) \,.$$

We could name each pit, but this would be inappropriate for a different reason: there is no reason to distinguish among pits.[10] It is simpler to use a unary predicate *Pit* that is true of squares containing pits. Finally, since there is exactly one wumpus, a constant *Wumpus* is just as good as a unary predicate (and perhaps more dignified from the wumpus's viewpoint).

The agent's location changes over time, so we write $At(Agent, s, t)$ to mean that the agent is at square s at time t. We can fix the wumpus's location with $\forall t\; At(Wumpus, [2, 2], t)$. We can then say that objects can only be at one location at a time:

$$\forall\, x, s_1, s_2, t \;\; At(x, s_1, t) \land At(x, s_2, t) \;\Rightarrow\; s_1 = s_2 \,.$$

Given its current location, the agent can infer properties of the square from properties of its current percept. For example, if the agent is at a square and perceives a breeze, then that square is breezy:

$$\forall\, s, t \;\; At(Agent, s, t) \land Breeze(t) \;\Rightarrow\; Breezy(s) \,.$$

It is useful to know that a *square* is breezy because we know that the pits cannot move about. Notice that *Breezy* has no time argument.

Having discovered which places are breezy (or smelly) and, very important, *not* breezy (or *not* smelly), the agent can deduce where the pits are (and where the wumpus is). Whereas propositional logic necessitates a separate axiom for each square (see R2 and R3 in section 4.3 of the chapter "Logical Agents") and would need a different set of axioms for each geographical layout of the world, first-order logic just needs one axiom:

$$\forall\, s \;\; Breezy(s) \Leftrightarrow \exists\, r \;\; Adjacent(r, s) \land Pit(r) \,. \qquad (4)$$

Similarly, in first-order logic we can quantify over time, so we need just one successor-state axiom for each predicate, rather than a different copy for each time step. For example, the axiom for the arrow (Equation 2 of the chapter "Logical Agents") becomes

$$\forall\, t \;\; HaveArrow(t + 1) \;\Leftrightarrow\; (HaveArrow(t) \land \neg Action(Shoot, t)) \,.$$

From these two example sentences, we can see that the first-order logic formulation is no less concise than the original English-language description given in the chapter "Logical Agents."

[10] Similarly, most of us do not name each bird that flies overhead as it migrates to warmer regions in winter. An ornithologist wishing to study migration patterns, survival rates, and so on *does* name each bird, by means of a ring on its leg, because individual birds must be tracked.

The reader is invited to construct analogous axioms for the agent's location and orientation; in these cases, the axioms quantify over both space and time. As in the case of propositional state estimation, an agent can use logical inference with axioms of this kind to keep track of aspects of the world that are not directly observed.

4 Knowledge Engineering in First-Order Logic

The preceding section illustrated the use of first-order logic to represent knowledge in three simple domains. This section describes the general process of knowledge-base construction—a process called **knowledge engineering**. A knowledge engineer is someone who investigates a particular domain, learns what concepts are important in that domain, and creates a formal representation of the objects and relations in the domain. We illustrate the knowledge engineering process in an electronic circuit domain that should already be fairly familiar, so that we can concentrate on the representational issues involved. The approach we take is suitable for developing *special-purpose* knowledge bases whose domain is carefully circumscribed and whose range of queries is known in advance. *General-purpose* knowledge bases cover a broad range of human knowledge and are intended to support tasks such as natural language understanding.

KNOWLEDGE ENGINEERING

4.1 The knowledge-engineering process

Knowledge engineering projects vary widely in content, scope, and difficulty, but all such projects include the following steps:

1. *Identify the task.* The knowledge engineer must delineate the range of questions that the knowledge base will support and the kinds of facts that will be available for each specific problem instance. For example, does the wumpus knowledge base need to be able to choose actions or is it required to answer questions only about the contents of the environment? Will the sensor facts include the current location? The task will determine what knowledge must be represented in order to connect problem instances to answers.

2. *Assemble the relevant knowledge.* The knowledge engineer might already be an expert in the domain, or might need to work with real experts to extract what they know—a process called **knowledge acquisition**. At this stage, the knowledge is not represented formally. The idea is to understand the scope of the knowledge base, as determined by the task, and to understand how the domain actually works.

   KNOWLEDGE ACQUISITION

   For the wumpus world, which is defined by an artificial set of rules, the relevant knowledge is easy to identify. (Notice, however, that the definition of adjacency was not supplied explicitly in the wumpus-world rules.) For real domains, the issue of relevance can be quite difficult—for example, a system for simulating VLSI designs might or might not need to take into account stray capacitances and skin effects.

3. *Decide on a vocabulary of predicates, functions, and constants.* That is, translate the important domain-level concepts into logic-level names. This involves many questions of knowledge-engineering *style*. Like programming style, this can have a significant impact on the eventual success of the project. For example, should pits be represented by objects or by a unary predicate on squares? Should the agent's orientation be a function or a predicate? Should the wumpus's location depend on time? Once the choices have been made, the result is a vocabulary that is known as the **ontology** of the domain. The word *ontology* means a particular theory of the nature of being or existence. The ontology determines what kinds of things exist, but does not determine their specific properties and interrelationships.

ONTOLOGY

4. *Encode general knowledge about the domain.* The knowledge engineer writes down the axioms for all the vocabulary terms. This pins down (to the extent possible) the meaning of the terms, enabling the expert to check the content. Often, this step reveals misconceptions or gaps in the vocabulary that must be fixed by returning to step 3 and iterating through the process.
5. *Encode a description of the specific problem instance.* If the ontology is well thought out, this step will be easy. It will involve writing simple atomic sentences about instances of concepts that are already part of the ontology. For a logical agent, problem instances are supplied by the sensors, whereas a "disembodied" knowledge base is supplied with additional sentences in the same way that traditional programs are supplied with input data.
6. *Pose queries to the inference procedure and get answers.* This is where the reward is: we can let the inference procedure operate on the axioms and problem-specific facts to derive the facts we are interested in knowing. Thus, we avoid the need for writing an application-specific solution algorithm.
7. *Debug the knowledge base.* Alas, the answers to queries will seldom be correct on the first try. More precisely, the answers will be correct *for the knowledge base as written*, assuming that the inference procedure is sound, but they will not be the ones that the user is expecting. For example, if an axiom is missing, some queries will not be answerable from the knowledge base. A considerable debugging process could ensue. Missing axioms or axioms that are too weak can be easily identified by noticing places where the chain of reasoning stops unexpectedly. For example, if the knowledge base includes a diagnostic rule (see Exercise 13) for finding the wumpus,

$$\forall s \ Smelly(s) \Rightarrow Adjacent(Home(Wumpus), s) ,$$

instead of the biconditional, then the agent will never be able to prove the *absence* of wumpuses. Incorrect axioms can be identified because they are false statements about the world. For example, the sentence

$$\forall x \ NumOfLegs(x, 4) \Rightarrow Mammal(x)$$

is false for reptiles, amphibians, and, more importantly, tables. *The falsehood of this sentence can be determined independently of the rest of the knowledge base.* In contrast, a typical error in a program looks like this:

```
offset = position + 1.
```

It is impossible to tell whether this statement is correct without looking at the rest of the program to see whether, for example, `offset` is used to refer to the current position, or to one beyond the current position, or whether the value of `position` is changed by another statement and so `offset` should also be changed again.

To understand this seven-step process better, we now apply it to an extended example—the domain of electronic circuits.

4.2 The electronic circuits domain

We will develop an ontology and knowledge base that allow us to reason about digital circuits of the kind shown in Figure 6. We follow the seven-step process for knowledge engineering.

Identify the task

There are many reasoning tasks associated with digital circuits. At the highest level, one analyzes the circuit's functionality. For example, does the circuit in Figure 6 actually add properly? If all the inputs are high, what is the output of gate A2? Questions about the circuit's structure are also interesting. For example, what are all the gates connected to the first input terminal? Does the circuit contain feedback loops? These will be our tasks in this section. There are more detailed levels of analysis, including those related to timing delays, circuit area, power consumption, production cost, and so on. Each of these levels would require additional knowledge.

Assemble the relevant knowledge

What do we know about digital circuits? For our purposes, they are composed of wires and gates. Signals flow along wires to the input terminals of gates, and each gate produces a

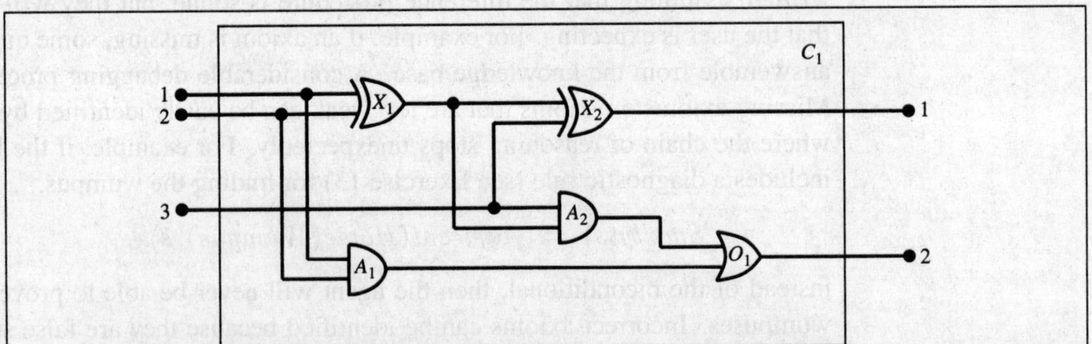

Figure 6 A digital circuit C1, purporting to be a one-bit full adder. The first two inputs are the two bits to be added, and the third input is a carry bit. The first output is the sum, and the second output is a carry bit for the next adder. The circuit contains two XOR gates, two AND gates, and one OR gate.

signal on the output terminal that flows along another wire. To determine what these signals will be, we need to know how the gates transform their input signals. There are four types of gates: AND, OR, and XOR gates have two input terminals, and NOT gates have one. All gates have one output terminal. Circuits, like gates, have input and output terminals.

To reason about functionality and connectivity, we do not need to talk about the wires themselves, the paths they take, or the junctions where they come together. All that matters is the connections between terminals—we can say that one output terminal is connected to another input terminal without having to say what actually connects them. Other factors such as the size, shape, color, or cost of the various components are irrelevant to our analysis.

If our purpose were something other than verifying designs at the gate level, the ontology would be different. For example, if we were interested in debugging faulty circuits, then it would probably be a good idea to include the wires in the ontology, because a faulty wire can corrupt the signal flowing along it. For resolving timing faults, we would need to include gate delays. If we were interested in designing a product that would be profitable, then the cost of the circuit and its speed relative to other products on the market would be important.

Decide on a vocabulary

We now know that we want to talk about circuits, terminals, signals, and gates. The next step is to choose functions, predicates, and constants to represent them. First, we need to be able to distinguish gates from each other and from other objects. Each gate is represented as an object named by a constant, about which we assert that it is a gate with, say, $Gate(X_1)$. The behavior of each gate is determined by its type: one of the constants AND, OR, XOR, or NOT. Because a gate has exactly one type, a function is appropriate: $Type(X_1) = XOR$. Circuits, like gates, are identified by a predicate: $Circuit(C_1)$.

Next we consider terminals, which are identified by the predicate $Terminal(x)$. A gate or circuit can have one or more input terminals and one or more output terminals. We use the function $In(1, X_1)$ to denote the first input terminal for gate X_1. A similar function Out is used for output terminals. The function $Arity(c, i, j)$ says that circuit c has i input and j output terminals. The connectivity between gates can be represented by a predicate, $Connected$, which takes two terminals as arguments, as in $Connected(Out(1, X_1), In(1, X_2))$.

Finally, we need to know whether a signal is on or off. One possibility is to use a unary predicate, $On(t)$, which is true when the signal at a terminal is on. This makes it a little difficult, however, to pose questions such as "What are all the possible values of the signals at the output terminals of circuit C_1 ?" We therefore introduce as objects two signal values, 1 and 0, and a function $Signal(t)$ that denotes the signal value for the terminal t.

Encode general knowledge of the domain

One sign that we have a good ontology is that we require only a few general rules, which can be stated clearly and concisely. These are all the axioms we will need:

1. If two terminals are connected, then they have the same signal:
$$\forall t_1, t_2 \;\; Terminal(t_1) \land Terminal(t_2) \land Connected(t_1, t_2) \Rightarrow$$
$$Signal(t_1) = Signal(t_2) \,.$$

2. The signal at every terminal is either 1 or 0:
$$\forall t \;\; Terminal(t) \;\Rightarrow\; Signal(t) = 1 \lor Signal(t) = 0 \;.$$
3. Connected is commutative:
$$\forall t_1, t_2 \;\; Connected(t_1, t_2) \;\Leftrightarrow\; Connected(t_2, t_1) \;.$$
4. There are four types of gates:
$$\forall g \;\; Gate(g) \land k = Type(g) \;\Rightarrow\; k = AND \lor k = OR \lor k = XOR \lor k = NOT \;.$$
5. An AND gate's output is 0 if and only if any of its inputs is 0:
$$\forall g \;\; Gate(g) \land Type(g) = AND \;\Rightarrow \\ Signal(Out(1, g)) = 0 \;\Leftrightarrow\; \exists n \;\; Signal(In(n, g)) = 0 \;.$$
6. An OR gate's output is 1 if and only if any of its inputs is 1:
$$\forall g \;\; Gate(g) \land Type(g) = OR \;\Rightarrow \\ Signal(Out(1, g)) = 1 \;\Leftrightarrow\; \exists n \;\; Signal(In(n, g)) = 1 \;.$$
7. An XOR gate's output is 1 if and only if its inputs are different:
$$\forall g \;\; Gate(g) \land Type(g) = XOR \;\Rightarrow \\ Signal(Out(1, g)) = 1 \;\Leftrightarrow\; Signal(In(1, g)) \neq Signal(In(2, g)) \;.$$
8. A NOT gate's output is different from its input:
$$\forall g \;\; Gate(g) \land (Type(g) = NOT) \;\Rightarrow \\ Signal(Out(1, g)) \neq Signal(In(1, g)) \;.$$
9. The gates (except for NOT) have two inputs and one output.
$$\forall g \;\; Gate(g) \land Type(g) = NOT \;\Rightarrow\; Arity(g, 1, 1)$$
$$\forall g \;\; Gate(g) \land k = Type(g) \land (k = AND \lor k = OR \lor k = XOR) \;\Rightarrow \\ Arity(g, 2, 1)$$
10. A circuit has terminals, up to its input and output arity, and nothing beyond its arity:
$$\forall c, i, j \;\; Circuit(c) \land Arity(c, i, j) \;\Rightarrow \\ \forall n \;\; (n \leq i \Rightarrow Terminal(In(c, n))) \land (n > i \Rightarrow In(c, n) = Nothing) \land \\ \forall n \;\; (n \leq j \Rightarrow Terminal(Out(c, n))) \land (n > j \Rightarrow Out(c, n) = Nothing)$$
11. Gates, terminals, signals, gate types, and *Nothing* are all distinct.
$$\forall g, t \;\; Gate(g) \land Terminal(t) \;\Rightarrow \\ g \neq t \neq 1 \neq 0 \neq OR \neq AND \neq XOR \neq NOT \neq Nothing \;.$$
12. Gates are circuits.
$$\forall g \;\; Gate(g) \;\Rightarrow\; Circuit(g)$$

Encode the specific problem instance

The circuit shown in Figure 6 is encoded as circuit C_1 with the following description. First, we categorize the circuit and its component gates:

$$Circuit(C_1) \land Arity(C_1, 3, 2) \\ Gate(X_1) \land Type(X_1) = XOR \\ Gate(X_2) \land Type(X_2) = XOR \\ Gate(A_1) \land Type(A_1) = AND \\ Gate(A_2) \land Type(A_2) = AND \\ Gate(O_1) \land Type(O_1) = OR \;.$$

Then, we show the connections between them:

$$\begin{array}{ll} Connected(Out(1,X_1), In(1,X_2)) & Connected(In(1,C_1), In(1,X_1)) \\ Connected(Out(1,X_1), In(2,A_2)) & Connected(In(1,C_1), In(1,A_1)) \\ Connected(Out(1,A_2), In(1,O_1)) & Connected(In(2,C_1), In(2,X_1)) \\ Connected(Out(1,A_1), In(2,O_1)) & Connected(In(2,C_1), In(2,A_1)) \\ Connected(Out(1,X_2), Out(1,C_1)) & Connected(In(3,C_1), In(2,X_2)) \\ Connected(Out(1,O_1), Out(2,C_1)) & Connected(In(3,C_1), In(1,A_2)) . \end{array}$$

Pose queries to the inference procedure

What combinations of inputs would cause the first output of C_1 (the sum bit) to be 0 and the second output of C_1 (the carry bit) to be 1?

$$\exists\, i_1, i_2, i_3 \;\; Signal(In(1,C_1)) = i_1 \wedge Signal(In(2,C_1)) = i_2 \wedge Signal(In(3,C_1)) = i_3 \\ \wedge\, Signal(Out(1,C_1)) = 0 \wedge Signal(Out(2,C_1)) = 1 .$$

The answers are substitutions for the variables i_1, i_2, and i_3 such that the resulting sentence is entailed by the knowledge base. ASKVARS will give us three such substitutions:

$$\{i_1/1,\ i_2/1,\ i_3/0\} \quad \{i_1/1,\ i_2/0,\ i_3/1\} \quad \{i_1/0,\ i_2/1,\ i_3/1\} .$$

What are the possible sets of values of all the terminals for the adder circuit?

$$\exists\, i_1, i_2, i_3, o_1, o_2 \;\; Signal(In(1,C_1)) = i_1 \wedge Signal(In(2,C_1)) = i_2 \\ \wedge\, Signal(In(3,C_1)) = i_3 \wedge Signal(Out(1,C_1)) = o_1 \wedge Signal(Out(2,C_1)) = o_2 .$$

This final query will return a complete input–output table for the device, which can be used to check that it does in fact add its inputs correctly. This is a simple example of **circuit verification**. We can also use the definition of the circuit to build larger digital systems, for which the same kind of verification procedure can be carried out. (See Exercise 26.) Many domains are amenable to the same kind of structured knowledge-base development, in which more complex concepts are defined on top of simpler concepts.

CIRCUIT VERIFICATION

Debug the knowledge base

We can perturb the knowledge base in various ways to see what kinds of erroneous behaviors emerge. For example, suppose we fail to read Section 2.8 and hence forget to assert that $1 \neq 0$. Suddenly, the system will be unable to prove any outputs for the circuit, except for the input cases 000 and 110. We can pinpoint the problem by asking for the outputs of each gate. For example, we can ask

$$\exists\, i_1, i_2, o \;\; Signal(In(1,C_1)) = i_1 \wedge Signal(In(2,C_1)) = i_2 \wedge Signal(Out(1,X_1)) ,$$

which reveals that no outputs are known at X_1 for the input cases 10 and 01. Then, we look at the axiom for XOR gates, as applied to X_1:

$$Signal(Out(1,X_1)) = 1 \Leftrightarrow Signal(In(1,X_1)) \neq Signal(In(2,X_1)) .$$

If the inputs are known to be, say, 1 and 0, then this reduces to

$$Signal(Out(1,X_1)) = 1 \Leftrightarrow 1 \neq 0 .$$

Now the problem is apparent: the system is unable to infer that $Signal(Out(1,X_1)) = 1$, so we need to tell it that $1 \neq 0$.

5 SUMMARY

This chapter has introduced **first-order logic**, a representation language that is far more powerful than propositional logic. The important points are as follows:

- Knowledge representation languages should be declarative, compositional, expressive, context independent, and unambiguous.
- Logics differ in their **ontological commitments** and **epistemological commitments**. While propositional logic commits only to the existence of facts, first-order logic commits to the existence of objects and relations and thereby gains expressive power.
- The syntax of first-order logic builds on that of propositional logic. It adds terms to represent objects, and has universal and existential quantifiers to construct assertions about all or some of the possible values of the quantified variables.
- A **possible world**, or **model**, for first-order logic includes a set of objects and an **interpretation** that maps constant symbols to objects, predicate symbols to relations among objects, and function symbols to functions on objects.
- An atomic sentence is true just when the relation named by the predicate holds between the objects named by the terms. **Extended interpretations**, which map quantifier variables to objects in the model, define the truth of quantified sentences.
- Developing a knowledge base in first-order logic requires a careful process of analyzing the domain, choosing a vocabulary, and encoding the axioms required to support the desired inferences.

BIBLIOGRAPHICAL AND HISTORICAL NOTES

Although Aristotle's logic deals with generalizations over objects, it fell far short of the expressive power of first-order logic. A major barrier to its further development was its concentration on one-place predicates to the exclusion of many-place relational predicates. The first systematic treatment of relations was given by Augustus De Morgan (1864), who cited the following example to show the sorts of inferences that Aristotle's logic could not handle: "All horses are animals; therefore, the head of a horse is the head of an animal." This inference is inaccessible to Aristotle because any valid rule that can support this inference must first analyze the sentence using the two-place predicate "x is the head of y." The logic of relations was studied in depth by Charles Sanders Peirce (1870, 2004).

True first-order logic dates from the introduction of quantifiers in Gottlob Frege's (1879) *Begriffschrift* ("Concept Writing" or "Conceptual Notation"). Peirce (1883) also developed first-order logic independently of Frege, although slightly later. Frege's ability to nest quantifiers was a big step forward, but he used an awkward notation. The present notation for first-order logic is due substantially to Giuseppe Peano (1889), but the semantics is virtually identical to Frege's. Oddly enough, Peano's axioms were due in large measure to Grassmann (1861) and Dedekind (1888).

Leopold Löwenheim (1915) gave a systematic treatment of model theory for first-order logic, including the first proper treatment of the equality symbol. Löwenheim's results were further extended by Thoralf Skolem (1920). Alfred Tarski (1935, 1956) gave an explicit definition of truth and model-theoretic satisfaction in first-order logic, using set theory.

McCarthy (1958) was primarily responsible for the introduction of first-order logic as a tool for building AI systems. The prospects for logic-based AI were advanced significantly by Robinson's (1965) development of resolution, a complete procedure for first-order inference. The logicist approach took root at Stanford University. Cordell Green (1969a, 1969b) developed a first-order reasoning system, QA3, leading to the first attempts to build a logical robot at SRI (Fikes and Nilsson, 1971). First-order logic was applied by Zohar Manna and Richard Waldinger (1971) for reasoning about programs and later by Michael Genesereth (1984) for reasoning about circuits. In Europe, logic programming (a restricted form of first-order reasoning) was developed for linguistic analysis (Colmerauer *et al.*, 1973) and for general declarative systems (Kowalski, 1974). Computational logic was also well entrenched at Edinburgh through the LCF (Logic for Computable Functions) project (Gordon *et al.*, 1979).

Practical applications built with first-order logic include a system for evaluating the manufacturing requirements for electronic products (Mannion, 2002), a system for reasoning about policies for file access and digital rights management (Halpern and Weissman, 2008), and a system for the automated composition of Web services (McIlraith and Zeng, 2001).

Reactions to the Whorf hypothesis (Whorf, 1956) and the problem of language and thought in general, appear in several recent books (Gumperz and Levinson, 1996; Bowerman and Levinson, 2001; Pinker, 2003; Gentner and Goldin-Meadow, 2003). The "theory" theory (Gopnik and Glymour, 2002; Tenenbaum *et al.*, 2007) views children's learning about the world as analogous to the construction of scientific theories. Just as the predictions of a machine learning algorithm depend strongly on the vocabulary supplied to it, so will the child's formulation of theories depend on the linguistic environment in which learning occurs.

There are a number of good introductory texts on first-order logic, including some by leading figures in the history of logic: Alfred Tarski (1941), Alonzo Church (1956), and W.V. Quine (1982) (which is one of the most readable). Enderton (1972) gives a more mathematically oriented perspective. A highly formal treatment of first-order logic, along with many more advanced topics in logic, is provided by Bell and Machover (1977). Manna and Waldinger (1985) give a readable introduction to logic from a computer science perspective, as do Huth and Ryan (2004), who concentrate on program verification. Barwise and Etchemendy (2002) take an approach similar to the one used here. Smullyan (1995) presents results concisely, using the tableau format. Gallier (1986) provides an extremely rigorous mathematical exposition of first-order logic, along with a great deal of material on its use in automated reasoning. *Logical Foundations of Artificial Intelligence* (Genesereth and Nilsson, 1987) is both a solid introduction to logic and the first systematic treatment of logical agents with percepts and actions, and there are two good handbooks: van Bentham and ter Meulen (1997) and Robinson and Voronkov (2001). The journal of record for the field of pure mathematical logic is the *Journal of Symbolic Logic*, whereas the *Journal of Applied Logic* deals with concerns closer to those of artificial intelligence.

Exercises

1 A logical knowledge base represents the world using a set of sentences with no explicit structure. An **analogical** representation, on the other hand, has physical structure that corresponds directly to the structure of the thing represented. Consider a road map of your country as an analogical representation of facts about the country—it represents facts with a map language. The two-dimensional structure of the map corresponds to the two-dimensional surface of the area.

a. Give five examples of *symbols* in the map language.

b. An *explicit* sentence is a sentence that the creator of the representation actually writes down. An *implicit* sentence is a sentence that results from explicit sentences because of properties of the analogical representation. Give three examples each of *implicit* and *explicit* sentences in the map language.

c. Give three examples of facts about the physical structure of your country that cannot be represented in the map language.

d. Give two examples of facts that are much easier to express in the map language than in first-order logic.

e. Give two other examples of useful analogical representations. What are the advantages and disadvantages of each of these languages?

2 Consider a knowledge base containing just two sentences: $P(a)$ and $P(b)$. Does this knowledge base entail $\forall\, x\ P(x)$? Explain your answer in terms of models.

3 Is the sentence $\exists\, x, y\ \ x = y$ valid? Explain.

4 Write down a logical sentence such that every world in which it is true contains exactly one object.

5 Consider a symbol vocabulary that contains c constant symbols, p_k predicate symbols of each arity k, and f_k function symbols of each arity k, where $1 \leq k \leq A$. Let the domain size be fixed at D. For any given model, each predicate or function symbol is mapped onto a relation or function, respectively, of the same arity. You may assume that the functions in the model allow some input tuples to have no value for the function (i.e., the value is the invisible object). Derive a formula for the number of possible models for a domain with D elements. Don't worry about eliminating redundant combinations.

6 Which of the following are valid (necessarily true) sentences?

a. $(\exists x\ x = x) \Rightarrow (\forall\, y\ \exists z\ y = z)$.

b. $\forall\, x\ \ P(x) \lor \neg P(x)$.

c. $\forall\, x\ \ Smart(x) \lor (x = x)$.

7 Consider a version of the semantics for first-order logic in which models with empty domains are allowed. Give at least two examples of sentences that are valid according to the standard semantics but not according to the new semantics. Discuss which outcome makes more intuitive sense for your examples.

8 Does the fact $\neg Spouse(George, Laura)$ follow from the facts $Jim \neq George$ and $Spouse(Jim, Laura)$? If so, give a proof; if not, supply additional axioms as needed. What happens if we use *Spouse* as a unary function symbol instead of a binary predicate?

9 This exercise uses the function *MapColor* and predicates $In(x, y)$, $Borders(x, y)$, and $Country(x)$, whose arguments are geographical regions, along with constant symbols for various regions. In each of the following we give an English sentence and a number of candidate logical expressions. For each of the logical expressions, state whether it (1) correctly expresses the English sentence; (2) is syntactically invalid and therefore meaningless; or (3) is syntactically valid but does not express the meaning of the English sentence.

a. Paris and Marseilles are both in France.

(i) $In(Paris \wedge Marseilles, France)$.

(ii) $In(Paris, France) \wedge In(Marseilles, France)$.

(iii) $In(Paris, France) \vee In(Marseilles, France)$.

b. There is a country that borders both Iraq and Pakistan.

(i) $\exists c \;\; Country(c) \wedge Border(c, Iraq) \wedge Border(c, Pakistan)$.

(ii) $\exists c \;\; Country(c) \;\Rightarrow\; [Border(c, Iraq) \wedge Border(c, Pakistan)]$.

(iii) $[\exists c \;\; Country(c)] \;\Rightarrow\; [Border(c, Iraq) \wedge Border(c, Pakistan)]$.

(iv) $\exists c \;\; Border(Country(c), Iraq \wedge Pakistan)$.

c. All countries that border Ecuador are in South America.

(i) $\forall c \;\; Country(c) \wedge Border(c, Ecuador) \;\Rightarrow\; In(c, SouthAmerica)$.

(ii) $\forall c \;\; Country(c) \;\Rightarrow\; [Border(c, Ecuador) \;\Rightarrow\; In(c, SouthAmerica)]$.

(iii) $\forall c \;\; [Country(c) \;\Rightarrow\; Border(c, Ecuador)] \;\Rightarrow\; In(c, SouthAmerica)$.

(iv) $\forall c \;\; Country(c) \wedge Border(c, Ecuador) \wedge In(c, SouthAmerica)$.

d. No region in South America borders any region in Europe.

(i) $\neg[\exists c, d \;\; In(c, SouthAmerica) \wedge In(d, Europe) \wedge Borders(c, d)]$.

(ii) $\forall c, d \;\; [In(c, SouthAmerica) \wedge In(d, Europe)] \;\Rightarrow\; \neg Borders(c, d)]$.

(iii) $\neg\forall c \;\; In(c, SouthAmerica) \;\Rightarrow\; \exists d \;\; In(d, Europe) \wedge \neg Borders(c, d)$.

(iv) $\forall c \;\; In(c, SouthAmerica) \;\Rightarrow\; \forall d \;\; In(d, Europe) \;\Rightarrow\; \neg Borders(c, d)$.

e. No two adjacent countries have the same map color.

(i) $\forall x, y \;\; \neg Country(x) \vee \neg Country(y) \vee \neg Borders(x, y) \vee$
$\neg(MapColor(x) = MapColor(y))$.

(ii) $\forall x, y \;\; (Country(x) \wedge Country(y) \wedge Borders(x, y) \wedge \neg(x = y)) \;\Rightarrow$
$\neg(MapColor(x) = MapColor(y))$.

(iii) $\forall x, y \;\; Country(x) \wedge Country(y) \wedge Borders(x, y) \wedge$
$\neg(MapColor(x) = MapColor(y))$.

(iv) $\forall x, y \;\; (Country(x) \wedge Country(y) \wedge Borders(x, y)) \;\Rightarrow\; MapColor(x \neq y)$.

10 Consider a vocabulary with the following symbols:

$Occupation(p, o)$: Predicate. Person p has occupation o.
$Customer(p1, p2)$: Predicate. Person $p1$ is a customer of person $p2$.
$Boss(p1, p2)$: Predicate. Person $p1$ is a boss of person $p2$.
$Doctor$, $Surgeon$, $Lawyer$, $Actor$: Constants denoting occupations.
$Emily$, Joe: Constants denoting people.

Use these symbols to write the following assertions in first-order logic:

a. Emily is either a surgeon or a lawyer.
b. Joe is an actor, but he also holds another job.
c. All surgeons are doctors.
d. Joe does not have a lawyer (i.e., is not a customer of any lawyer).
e. Emily has a boss who is a lawyer.
f. There exists a lawyer all of whose customers are doctors.
g. Every surgeon has a lawyer.

11 Complete the following exercises about logical senntences:

a. Translate into *good, natural* English (no xs or ys!):

$$\forall x, y, l \; SpeaksLanguage(x, l) \land SpeaksLanguage(y, l) \Rightarrow Understands(x, y) \land Understands(y, x).$$

b. Explain why this sentence is entailed by the sentence

$$\forall x, y, l \; SpeaksLanguage(x, l) \land SpeaksLanguage(y, l) \Rightarrow Understands(x, y).$$

c. Translate into first-order logic the following sentences:

(i) Understanding leads to friendship.
(ii) Friendship is transitive.

Remember to define all predicates, functions, and constants you use.

12 Rewrite the first two Peano axioms in Section 3.3 as a single axiom that defines $NatNum(x)$ so as to exclude the possibility of natural numbers except for those generated by the successor function.

13 Equation (4) defines the conditions under which a square is breezy. Here we consider two other ways to describe this aspect of the wumpus world.

DIAGNOSTIC RULE

a. We can write **diagnostic rules** leading from observed effects to hidden causes. For finding pits, the obvious diagnostic rules say that if a square is breezy, some adjacent square must contain a pit; and if a square is not breezy, then no adjacent square contains a pit. Write these two rules in first-order logic and show that their conjunction is logically equivalent to Equation (4).

CAUSAL RULE

b. We can write **causal rules** leading from cause to effect. One obvious causal rule is that a pit causes all adjacent squares to be breezy. Write this rule in first-order logic, explain why it is incomplete compared to Equation (4), and supply the missing axiom.

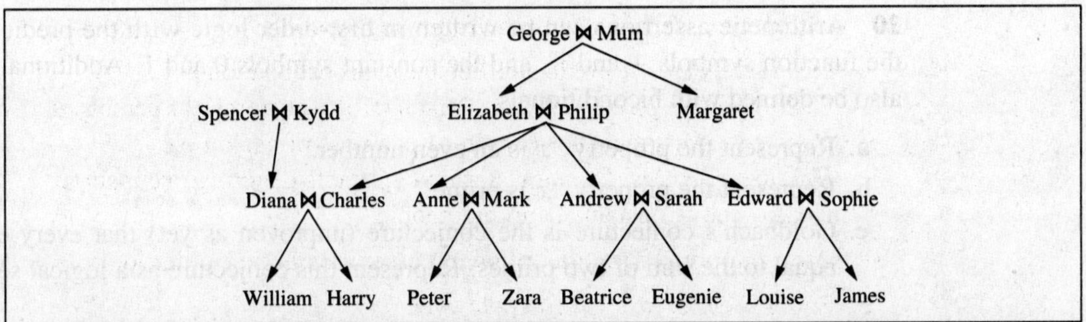

Figure 7 A typical family tree. The symbol "⋈" connects spouses and arrows point to children.

14 Write axioms describing the predicates *Grandchild*, *Greatgrandparent*, *Ancestor*, *Brother*, *Sister*, *Daughter*, *Son*, *FirstCousin*, *BrotherInLaw*, *SisterInLaw*, *Aunt*, and *Uncle*. Find out the proper definition of mth cousin n times removed, and write the definition in first-order logic. Now write down the basic facts depicted in the family tree in Figure 7. Using a suitable logical reasoning system, TELL it all the sentences you have written down, and ASK it who are Elizabeth's grandchildren, Diana's brothers-in-law, Zara's great-grandparents, and Eugenie's ancestors.

15 Explain what is wrong with the following proposed definition of the set membership predicate $\in$:

$$\begin{aligned}&\forall\, x, s \;\; x \in \{x|s\}\\ &\forall\, x, s \;\; x \in s \;\Rightarrow\; \forall\, y \;\; x \in \{y|s\}\,.\end{aligned}$$

16 Using the set axioms as examples, write axioms for the list domain, including all the constants, functions, and predicates mentioned in the chapter.

17 Explain what is wrong with the following proposed definition of adjacent squares in the wumpus world:

$$\forall\, x, y \;\; Adjacent([x, y], [x + 1, y]) \wedge Adjacent([x, y], [x, y + 1])\,.$$

18 Write out the axioms required for reasoning about the wumpus's location, using a constant symbol *Wumpus* and a binary predicate *At*(*Wumpus*, *Location*). Remember that there is only one wumpus.

19 Assuming predicates $Parent(p, q)$ and $Female(p)$ and constants *Joan* and *Kevin*, with the obvious meanings, express each of the following sentences in first-order logic. (You may use the abbreviation $\exists^1$ to mean "there exists exactly one.")

a. Joan has a daughter (possibly more than one, and possibly sons as well).

b. Joan has exactly one daughter (but may have sons as well).

c. Joan has exactly one child, a daughter.

d. Joan and Kevin have exactly one child together.

e. Joan has at least one child with Kevin, and no children with anyone else.

20 Arithmetic assertions can be written in first-order logic with the predicate symbol $<$, the function symbols $+$ and $\times$, and the constant symbols 0 and 1. Additional predicates can also be defined with biconditionals.

a. Represent the property "x is an even number."

b. Represent the property "x is prime."

c. Goldbach's conjecture is the conjecture (unproven as yet) that every even number is equal to the sum of two primes. Represent this conjecture as a logical sentence.

21 Equality can be used to indicate the relation between a variable and its value. For instance, *WA* = *red* means that Western Australia is colored red. Representing this in first-order logic, we must write more verbosely *ColorOf*(*WA*) = *red*. What incorrect inference could be drawn if we wrote sentences such as *WA* = *red* directly as logical assertions?

22 Write in first-order logic the assertion that every key and at least one of every pair of socks will eventually be lost forever, using only the following vocabulary: $Key(x)$, x is a key; $Sock(x)$, x is a sock; $Pair(x, y)$, x and y are a pair; Now, the current time; $Before(t_1, t_2)$, time t_1 comes before time t_2; $Lost(x, t)$, object x is lost at time t.

23 For each of the following sentences in English, decide if the accompanying first-order logic sentence is a good translation. If not, explain why not and correct it. (Some sentences may have more than one error!)

a. No two people have the same social security number.

$$\neg\exists\, x, y, n \;\; Person(x) \land Person(y) \;\Rightarrow\; [HasSS\#(x, n) \land HasSS\#(y, n)].$$

b. John's social security number is the same as Mary's.

$$\exists\, n \;\; HasSS\#(John, n) \land HasSS\#(Mary, n).$$

c. Everyone's social security number has nine digits.

$$\forall\, x, n \;\; Person(x) \;\Rightarrow\; [HasSS\#(x, n) \land Digits(n, 9)].$$

d. Rewrite each of the above (uncorrected) sentences using a function symbol $SS\#$ instead of the predicate $HasSS\#$.

24 Represent the following sentences in first-order logic, using a consistent vocabulary (which you must define):

a. Some students took French in spring 2001.

b. Every student who takes French passes it.

c. Only one student took Greek in spring 2001.

d. The best score in Greek is always higher than the best score in French.

e. Every person who buys a policy is smart.

f. No person buys an expensive policy.

g. There is an agent who sells policies only to people who are not insured.

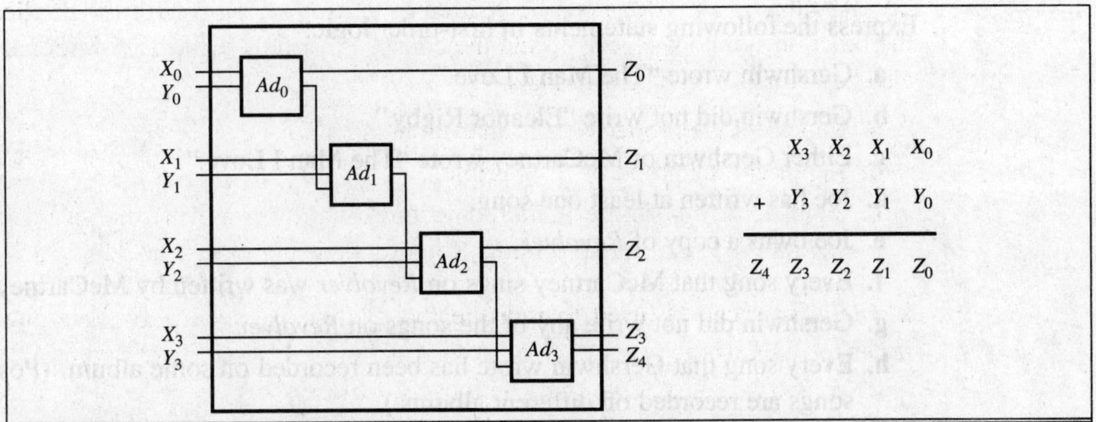

Figure 8 A four-bit adder. Each Ad_i is a one-bit adder, as in Figure 6.

h. There is a barber who shaves all men in town who do not shave themselves.

i. A person born in the UK, each of whose parents is a UK citizen or a UK resident, is a UK citizen by birth.

j. A person born outside the UK, one of whose parents is a UK citizen by birth, is a UK citizen by descent.

k. Politicians can fool some of the people all of the time, and they can fool all of the people some of the time, but they can't fool all of the people all of the time.

l. All Greeks speak the same language. (Use $\mathit{Speaks}(x, l)$ to mean that person x speaks language l.)

25 Write a general set of facts and axioms to represent the assertion "Wellington heard about Napoleon's death" and to correctly answer the question "Did Napoleon hear about Wellington's death?"

26 Extend the vocabulary from Section 4 to define addition for n-bit binary numbers. Then encode the description of the four-bit adder in Figure 8, and pose the queries needed to verify that it is in fact correct.

27 Obtain a passport application for your country, identify the rules determining eligibility for a passport, and translate them into first-order logic, following the steps outlined in Section 4.

28 Consider a first-order logical knowledge base that describes worlds containing people, songs, albums (e.g., "Meet the Beatles") and disks (i.e., particular physical instances of CDs). The vocabulary contains the following symbols:

$\mathit{CopyOf}(d, a)$: Predicate. Disk d is a copy of album a.
$\mathit{Owns}(p, d)$: Predicate. Person p owns disk d.
$\mathit{Sings}(p, s, a)$: Album a includes a recording of song s sung by person p.
$\mathit{Wrote}(p, s)$: Person p wrote song s.
$\mathit{McCartney}$, $\mathit{Gershwin}$, $\mathit{BHoliday}$, Joe, $\mathit{EleanorRigby}$, $\mathit{TheManILove}$, $\mathit{Revolver}$: Constants with the obvious meanings.

Express the following statements in first-order logic:

a. Gershwin wrote "The Man I Love."

b. Gershwin did not write "Eleanor Rigby."

c. Either Gershwin or McCartney wrote "The Man I Love."

d. Joe has written at least one song.

e. Joe owns a copy of *Revolver*.

f. Every song that McCartney sings on *Revolver* was written by McCartney.

g. Gershwin did not write any of the songs on *Revolver*.

h. Every song that Gershwin wrote has been recorded on some album. (Possibly different songs are recorded on different albums.)

i. There is a single album that contains every song that Joe has written.

j. Joe owns a copy of an album that has Billie Holiday singing "The Man I Love."

k. Joe owns a copy of every album that has a song sung by McCartney. (Of course, each different album is instantiated in a different physical CD.)

l. Joe owns a copy of every album on which all the songs are sung by Billie Holiday.

INFERENCE IN FIRST-ORDER LOGIC

INFERENCE IN FIRST-ORDER LOGIC

In which we define effective procedures for answering questions posed in first-order logic.

Sound and complete inference can be achieved for propositional logic. In this chapter, we build on that to obtain algorithms that can answer any answerable question stated in first-order logic. Section 1 introduces inference rules for quantifiers and shows how to reduce first-order inference to propositional inference, albeit at potentially great expense. Section 2 describes the idea of **unification**, showing how it can be used to construct inference rules that work directly with first-order sentences. We then discuss three major families of first-order inference algorithms. **Forward chaining** and its applications to **deductive databases** and **production systems** are covered in Section 3; **backward chaining** and **logic programming** systems are developed in Section 4. Forward and backward chaining can be very efficient, fibut are applicable only to knowledge bases that can be expressed as sets of Horn clauses. General first-order sentences require resolution-based **theorem proving**, which is described in Section 5.

1 Propositional vs. First-Order Inference

This section and the next introduce the ideas underlying modern logical inference systems. We begin with some simple inference rules that can be applied to sentences with quantifiers to obtain sentences without quantifiers. These rules lead naturally to the idea that *first-order* inference can be done by converting the knowledge base to *propositional* logic and using *propositional* inference, which we already know how to do. The next section points out an obvious shortcut, leading to inference methods that manipulate first-order sentences directly.

1.1 Inference rules for quantifiers

Let us begin with universal quantifiers. Suppose our knowledge base contains the standard folkloric axiom stating that all greedy kings are evil:

$$\forall x \;\; King(x) \land Greedy(x) \;\Rightarrow\; Evil(x) \,.$$

Then it seems quite permissible to infer any of the following sentences:

$$King(John) \land Greedy(John) \Rightarrow Evil(John)$$
$$King(Richard) \land Greedy(Richard) \Rightarrow Evil(Richard)$$
$$King(Father(John)) \land Greedy(Father(John)) \Rightarrow Evil(Father(John)) .$$
$$\vdots$$

UNIVERSAL INSTANTIATION

GROUND TERM

The rule of **Universal Instantiation** (**UI** for short) says that we can infer any sentence obtained by substituting a **ground term** (a term without variables) for the variable.[1] To write out the inference rule formally, we use the notion of **substitutions**. Let $\text{SUBST}(\theta, \alpha)$ denote the result of applying the substitution θ to the sentence α. Then the rule is written

$$\frac{\forall v \;\; \alpha}{\text{SUBST}(\{v/g\}, \alpha)}$$

for any variable v and ground term g. For example, the three sentences given earlier are obtained with the substitutions $\{x/John\}$, $\{x/Richard\}$, and $\{x/Father(John)\}$.

EXISTENTIAL INSTANTIATION

In the rule for **Existential Instantiation**, the variable is replaced by a single *new constant symbol*. The formal statement is as follows: for any sentence α, variable v, and constant symbol k that does not appear elsewhere in the knowledge base,

$$\frac{\exists v \;\; \alpha}{\text{SUBST}(\{v/k\}, \alpha)} .$$

For example, from the sentence

$$\exists x \;\; Crown(x) \land OnHead(x, John)$$

we can infer the sentence

$$Crown(C_1) \land OnHead(C_1, John)$$

as long as C_1 does not appear elsewhere in the knowledge base. Basically, the existential sentence says there is some object satisfying a condition, and applying the existential instantiation rule just gives a name to that object. Of course, that name must not already belong to another object. Mathematics provides a nice example: suppose we discover that there is a number that is a little bigger than 2.71828 and that satisfies the equation $d(x^y)/dy = x^y$ for x. We can give this number a name, such as e, but it would be a mistake to give it the name of an existing object, such as π. In logic, the new name is called a **Skolem constant**. Existential Instantiation is a special case of a more general process called **skolemization**, which we cover in Section 5.

SKOLEM CONSTANT

Whereas Universal Instantiation can be applied many times to produce many different consequences, Existential Instantiation can be applied once, and then the existentially quantified sentence can be discarded. For example, we no longer need $\exists x \; Kill(x, Victim)$ once we have added the sentence $Kill(Murderer, Victim)$. Strictly speaking, the new knowledge base is not logically equivalent to the old, but it can be shown to be **inferentially equivalent** in the sense that it is satisfiable exactly when the original knowledge base is satisfiable.

INFERENTIAL EQUIVALENCE

1 Do not confuse these substitutions with the extended interpretations used to define the semantics of quantifiers. The substitution replaces a variable with a term (a piece of syntax) to produce a new sentence, whereas an interpretation maps a variable to an object in the domain.

1.2 Reduction to propositional inference

Once we have rules for inferring nonquantified sentences from quantified sentences, it becomes possible to reduce first-order inference to propositional inference. In this section we give the main ideas; the details are given in Section 5.

The first idea is that, just as an existentially quantified sentence can be replaced by one instantiation, a universally quantified sentence can be replaced by the set of *all possible* instantiations. For example, suppose our knowledge base contains just the sentences

$$\begin{aligned}&\forall x\ King(x) \wedge Greedy(x) \Rightarrow Evil(x)\\&King(John)\\&Greedy(John)\\&Brother(Richard, John)\,.\end{aligned} \tag{1}$$

Then we apply UI to the first sentence using all possible ground-term substitutions from the vocabulary of the knowledge base—in this case, $\{x/John\}$ and $\{x/Richard\}$. We obtain

$$\begin{aligned}&King(John) \wedge Greedy(John) \Rightarrow Evil(John)\\&King(Richard) \wedge Greedy(Richard) \Rightarrow Evil(Richard)\,,\end{aligned}$$

and we discard the universally quantified sentence. Now, the knowledge base is essentially propositional if we view the ground atomic sentences—$King(John)$, $Greedy(John)$, and so on—as proposition symbols. Therefore, we can apply complete propositional algorithms to obtain conclusions such as $Evil(John)$.

This technique of **propositionalization** can be made completely general, as we show in Section 5; that is, every first-order knowledge base and query can be propositionalized in such a way that entailment is preserved. Thus, we have a complete decision procedure for entailment ... or perhaps not. There is a problem: when the knowledge base includes a function symbol, the set of possible ground-term substitutions is infinite! For example, if the knowledge base mentions the *Father* symbol, then infinitely many nested terms such as $Father(Father(Father(John)))$ can be constructed. Our propositional algorithms will have difficulty with an infinitely large set of sentences.

Fortunately, there is a famous theorem due to Jacques Herbrand (1930) to the effect that if a sentence is entailed by the original, first-order knowledge base, then there is a proof involving just a *finite* subset of the propositionalized knowledge base. Since any such subset has a maximum depth of nesting among its ground terms, we can find the subset by first generating all the instantiations with constant symbols ($Richard$ and $John$), then all terms of depth 1 ($Father(Richard)$ and $Father(John)$), then all terms of depth 2, and so on, until we are able to construct a propositional proof of the entailed sentence.

We have sketched an approach to first-order inference via propositionalization that is **complete**—that is, any entailed sentence can be proved. This is a major achievement, given that the space of possible models is infinite. On the other hand, we do not know until the proof is done that the sentence *is* entailed! What happens when the sentence is *not* entailed? Can we tell? Well, for first-order logic, it turns out that we cannot. Our proof procedure can go on and on, generating more and more deeply nested terms, but we will not know whether it is stuck in a hopeless loop or whether the proof is just about to pop out. This is very much like the halting problem for Turing machines. Alan Turing (1936) and Alonzo Church (1936) both proved, in rather different ways, the inevitability of this state of affairs. *The question of entailment for first-order logic is* ***semidecidable****—that is, algorithms exist that say yes to every entailed sentence, but no algorithm exists that also says no to every nonentailed sentence.*

2 Unification and Lifting

The preceding section described the understanding of first-order inference that existed up to the early 1960s. The sharp-eyed reader (and certainly the computational logicians of the early 1960s) will have noticed that the propositionalization approach is rather inefficient. For example, given the query $Evil(x)$ and the knowledge base in Equation (1), it seems perverse to generate sentences such as $King(Richard) \land Greedy(Richard) \Rightarrow Evil(Richard)$. Indeed, the inference of $Evil(John)$ from the sentences

$$\forall x \;\; King(x) \land Greedy(x) \;\Rightarrow\;\; Evil(x)$$
$$King(John)$$
$$Greedy(John)$$

seems completely obvious to a human being. We now show how to make it completely obvious to a computer.

2.1 A first-order inference rule

The inference that John is evil—that is, that $\{x/John\}$ solves the query $Evil(x)$—works like this: to use the rule that greedy kings are evil, find some x such that x is a king and x is greedy, and then infer that this x is evil. More generally, if there is some substitution θ that makes each of the conjuncts of the premise of the implication identical to sentences already in the knowledge base, then we can assert the conclusion of the implication, after applying θ. In this case, the substitution $\theta = \{x/John\}$ achieves that aim.

We can actually make the inference step do even more work. Suppose that instead of knowing $Greedy(John)$, we know that *everyone* is greedy:

$$\forall y \;\; Greedy(y)\,. \qquad (2)$$

Then we would still like to be able to conclude that $Evil(John)$, because we know that John is a king (given) and John is greedy (because everyone is greedy). What we need for this to work is to find a substitution both for the variables in the implication sentence and for the variables in the sentences that are in the knowledge base. In this case, applying the substitution $\{x/John, y/John\}$ to the implication premises $King(x)$ and $Greedy(x)$ and the knowledge-base sentences $King(John)$ and $Greedy(y)$ will make them identical. Thus, we can infer the conclusion of the implication.

GENERALIZED MODUS PONENS

This inference process can be captured as a single inference rule that we call **Generalized Modus Ponens:**[2] For atomic sentences p_i, $p_i{}'$, and q, where there is a substitution θ

such that $\text{SUBST}(\theta, p\ ) = \text{SUBST}(\theta, p\ )$, for all i,

$$\frac{p_1{}',\ p_2{}',\ \ldots,\ p_n{}',\ (p_1 \wedge p_2 \wedge \ldots \wedge p_n \Rightarrow q)}{\text{SUBST}(\theta, q)}\,.$$

There are $n+1$ premises to this rule: the n atomic sentences $p_i{}'$ and the one implication. The conclusion is the result of applying the substitution θ to the consequent q. For our example:

$p_1{}'$ is $King(John)$ $\qquad$ p_1 is $King(x)$
$p_2{}'$ is $Greedy(y)$ $\qquad$ p_2 is $Greedy(x)$
θ is $\{x/John, y/John\}$ $\qquad$ q is $Evil(x)$
$\text{SUBST}(\theta, q)$ is $Evil(John)$.

It is easy to show that Generalized Modus Ponens is a sound inference rule. First, we observe that, for any sentence p (whose variables are assumed to be universally quantified) and for any substitution θ,

$$p \models \text{SUBST}(\theta, p)$$

holds by Universal Instantiation. It holds in particular for a θ that satisfies the conditions of the Generalized Modus Ponens rule. Thus, from $p_1{}', \ldots, p_n{}'$ we can infer

$$\text{SUBST}(\theta, p_1{}') \wedge \ldots \wedge \text{SUBST}(\theta, p_n{}')$$

and from the implication $p_1 \wedge \ldots \wedge p_n \Rightarrow q$ we can infer

$$\text{SUBST}(\theta, p_1) \wedge \ldots \wedge \text{SUBST}(\theta, p_n) \ \Rightarrow\ \text{SUBST}(\theta, q)\,.$$

Now, θ in Generalized Modus Ponens is defined so that $\text{SUBST}(\theta, p_i{}') = \text{SUBST}(\theta, p_i)$, for all i; therefore the first of these two sentences matches the premise of the second exactly. Hence, $\text{SUBST}(\theta, q)$ follows by Modus Ponens.

LIFTING

Generalized Modus Ponens is a **lifted** version of Modus Ponens—it raises Modus Ponens from ground (variable-free) propositional logic to first-order logic. We will see in the rest of this chapter that we can develop that you may already be familiar with lifted versions of forward chaining, backward chaining, and resolution algorithms. The key advantage of lifted inference rules over propositionalization is that they make only those substitutions that are required to allow particular inferences to proceed.

2.2 Unification

UNIFICATION

UNIFIER

Lifted inference rules require finding substitutions that make different logical expressions look identical. This process is called **unification** and is a key component of all first-order inference algorithms. The UNIFY algorithm takes two sentences and returns a **unifier** for them if one exists:

$$\text{UNIFY}(p, q) = \theta \text{ where } \text{SUBST}(\theta, p) = \text{SUBST}(\theta, q)\,.$$

Let us look at some examples of how UNIFY should behave. Suppose we have a query $AskVars(Knows(John, x))$: whom does John know? Answers to this query can be found

[2] Generalized Modus Ponens is more general than Modus Ponens in the sense that the known facts and the premise of the implication need match only up to a substitution, rather than exactly. On the other hand, Modus Ponens allows any sentence α as the premise, rather than just a conjunction of atomic sentences.

by finding all sentences in the knowledge base that unify with $Knows(John, x)$. Here are the results of unification with four different sentences that might be in the knowledge base:

$$\text{UNIFY}(Knows(John, x),\ Knows(John, Jane)) = \{x/Jane\}$$
$$\text{UNIFY}(Knows(John, x),\ Knows(y, Bill)) = \{x/Bill, y/John\}$$
$$\text{UNIFY}(Knows(John, x),\ Knows(y, Mother(y))) = \{y/John, x/Mother(John)\}$$
$$\text{UNIFY}(Knows(John, x),\ Knows(x, Elizabeth)) = fail\ .$$

The last unification fails because x cannot take on the values *John* and *Elizabeth* at the same time. Now, remember that $Knows(x, Elizabeth)$ means "Everyone knows Elizabeth," so we *should* be able to infer that John knows Elizabeth. The problem arises only because the two sentences happen to use the same variable name, x. The problem can be avoided by **standardizing apart** one of the two sentences being unified, which means renaming its variables to avoid name clashes. For example, we can rename x in $Knows(x, Elizabeth)$ to x_{17} (a new variable name) without changing its meaning. Now the unification will work:

STANDARDIZING APART

$$\text{UNIFY}(Knows(John, x),\ Knows(x_{17}, Elizabeth)) = \{x/Elizabeth, x_{17}/John\}\ .$$

Exercise 12 delves further into the need for standardizing apart.

There is one more complication: we said that UNIFY should return a substitution that makes the two arguments look the same. But there could be more than one such unifier. For example, $\text{UNIFY}(Knows(John, x), Knows(y, z))$ could return $\{y/John, x/z\}$ or $\{y/John, x/John, z/John\}$. The first unifier gives $Knows(John, z)$ as the result of unification, whereas the second gives $Knows(John, John)$. The second result could be obtained from the first by an additional substitution $\{z/John\}$; we say that the first unifier is *more general* than the second, because it places fewer restrictions on the values of the variables. It turns out that, for every unifiable pair of expressions, there is a single **most general unifier** (or MGU) that is unique up to renaming and substitution of variables. (For example, $\{x/John\}$ and $\{y/John\}$ are considered equivalent, as are $\{x/John, y/John\}$ and $\{x/John, y/x\}$.) In this case it is $\{y/John, x/z\}$.

MOST GENERAL UNIFIER

An algorithm for computing most general unifiers is shown in Figure 1. The process is simple: recursively explore the two expressions simultaneously "side by side," building up a unifier along the way, but failing if two corresponding points in the structures do not match. There is one expensive step: when matching a variable against a complex term, one must check whether the variable itself occurs inside the term; if it does, the match fails because no consistent unifier can be constructed. For example, $S(x)$ can't unify with $S(S(x))$. This so-called **occur check** makes the complexity of the entire algorithm quadratic in the size of the expressions being unified. Some systems, including all logic programming systems, simply omit the occur check and sometimes make unsound inferences as a result; other systems use more complex algorithms with linear-time complexity.

OCCUR CHECK

2.3 Storage and retrieval

Underlying the TELL and ASK functions used to inform and interrogate a knowledge base are the more primitive STORE and FETCH functions. STORE(s) stores a sentence s into the knowledge base and FETCH(q) returns all unifiers such that the query q unifies with some

```
function UNIFY(x, y, θ) returns a substitution to make x and y identical
  inputs: x, a variable, constant, list, or compound expression
          y, a variable, constant, list, or compound expression
          θ, the substitution built up so far (optional, defaults to empty)

  if θ = failure then return failure
  else if x = y then return θ
  else if VARIABLE?(x) then return UNIFY-VAR(x, y, θ)
  else if VARIABLE?(y) then return UNIFY-VAR(y, x, θ)
  else if COMPOUND?(x) and COMPOUND?(y) then
      return UNIFY(x.ARGS, y.ARGS, UNIFY(x.OP, y.OP, θ))
  else if LIST?(x) and LIST?(y) then
      return UNIFY(x.REST, y.REST, UNIFY(x.FIRST, y.FIRST, θ))
  else return failure

function UNIFY-VAR(var, x, θ) returns a substitution

  if {var/val} ∈ θ then return UNIFY(val, x, θ)
  else if {x/val} ∈ θ then return UNIFY(var, val, θ)
  else if OCCUR-CHECK?(var, x) then return failure
  else return add {var/x} to θ
```

Figure 1 The unification algorithm. The algorithm works by comparing the structures of the inputs, element by element. The substitution θ that is the argument to UNIFY is built up along the way and is used to make sure that later comparisons are consistent with bindings that were established earlier. In a compound expression such as $F(A, B)$, the OP field picks out the function symbol F and the ARGS field picks out the argument list (A, B).

sentence in the knowledge base. The problem we used to illustrate unification—finding all facts that unify with $Knows(John, x)$—is an instance of FETCHing.

The simplest way to implement STORE and FETCH is to keep all the facts in one long list and unify each query against every element of the list. Such a process is inefficient, but it works, and it's all you need to understand the rest of the chapter. The remainder of this section outlines ways to make retrieval more efficient; it can be skipped on first reading.

We can make FETCH more efficient by ensuring that unifications are attempted only with sentences that have *some* chance of unifying. For example, there is no point in trying to unify $Knows(John, x)$ with $Brother(Richard, John)$. We can avoid such unifications by **indexing** the facts in the knowledge base. A simple scheme called **predicate indexing** puts all the $Knows$ facts in one bucket and all the $Brother$ facts in another. The buckets can be stored in a hash table for efficient access.

INDEXING

PREDICATE INDEXING

Predicate indexing is useful when there are many predicate symbols but only a few clauses for each symbol. Sometimes, however, a predicate has many clauses. For example, suppose that the tax authorities want to keep track of who employs whom, using a predicate $Employs(x, y)$. This would be a very large bucket with perhaps millions of employers

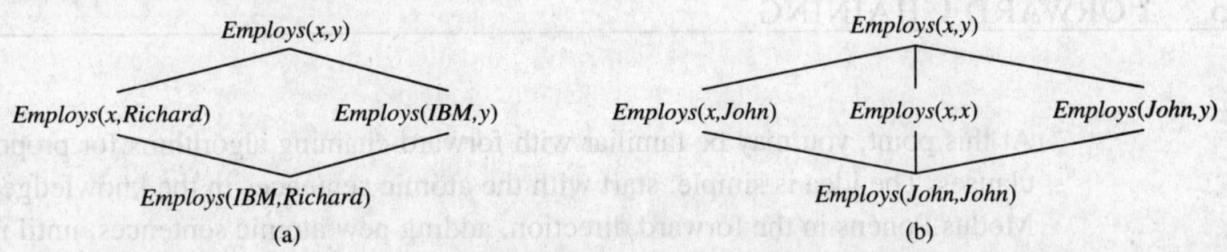

Figure 2 (a) The subsumption lattice whose lowest node is $Employs(IBM, Richard)$. (b) The subsumption lattice for the sentence $Employs(John, John)$.

and tens of millions of employees. Answering a query such as $Employs(x, Richard)$ with predicate indexing would require scanning the entire bucket.

For this particular query, it would help if facts were indexed both by predicate and by second argument, perhaps using a combined hash table key. Then we could simply construct the key from the query and retrieve exactly those facts that unify with the query. For other queries, such as $Employs(IBM, y)$, we would need to have indexed the facts by combining the predicate with the first argument. Therefore, facts can be stored under multiple index keys, rendering them instantly accessible to various queries that they might unify with.

Given a sentence to be stored, it is possible to construct indices for *all possible* queries that unify with it. For the fact $Employs(IBM, Richard)$, the queries are

$Employs(IBM, Richard)$	Does IBM employ Richard?
$Employs(x, Richard)$	Who employs Richard?
$Employs(IBM, y)$	Whom does IBM employ?
$Employs(x, y)$	Who employs whom?

SUBSUMPTION LATTICE

These queries form a **subsumption lattice**, as shown in Figure 2(a). The lattice has some interesting properties. For example, the child of any node in the lattice is obtained from its parent by a single substitution; and the "highest" common descendant of any two nodes is the result of applying their most general unifier. The portion of the lattice above any ground fact can be constructed systematically (Exercise 5). A sentence with repeated constants has a slightly different lattice, as shown in Figure 2(b). Function symbols and variables in the sentences to be stored introduce still more interesting lattice structures.

The scheme we have described works very well whenever the lattice contains a small number of nodes. For a predicate with n arguments, however, the lattice contains $O(2^n)$ nodes. If function symbols are allowed, the number of nodes is also exponential in the size of the terms in the sentence to be stored. This can lead to a huge number of indices. At some point, the benefits of indexing are outweighed by the costs of storing and maintaining all the indices. We can respond by adopting a fixed policy, such as maintaining indices only on keys composed of a predicate plus each argument, or by using an adaptive policy that creates indices to meet the demands of the kinds of queries being asked. For most AI systems, the number of facts to be stored is small enough that efficient indexing is considered a solved problem. For commercial databases, where facts number in the billions, the problem has been the subject of intensive study and technology development..

3 Forward Chaining

At this point, you may be familiar with forward-chaining algorithms for propositional definite clauses. The idea is simple: start with the atomic sentences in the knowledge base and apply Modus Ponens in the forward direction, adding new atomic sentences, until no further inferences can be made. Here, we explain how the algorithm is applied to first-order definite clauses. Definite clauses such as $Situation \Rightarrow Response$ are especially useful for systems that make inferences in response to newly arrived information. Many systems can be defined this way, and forward chaining can be implemented very efficiently.

3.1 First-order definite clauses

First-order definite clauses closely resemble propositional definite clauses: they are disjunctions of literals of which *exactly one is positive*. A definite clause either is atomic or is an implication whose antecedent is a conjunction of positive literals and whose consequent is a single positive literal. The following are first-order definite clauses:

$$King(x) \wedge Greedy(x) \Rightarrow Evil(x) .$$
$$King(John) .$$
$$Greedy(y) .$$

Unlike propositional literals, first-order literals can include variables, in which case those variables are assumed to be universally quantified. (Typically, we omit universal quantifiers when writing definite clauses.) Not every knowledge base can be converted into a set of definite clauses because of the single-positive-literal restriction, but many can. Consider the following problem:

> The law says that it is a crime for an American to sell weapons to hostile nations. The country Nono, an enemy of America, has some missiles, and all of its missiles were sold to it by Colonel West, who is American.

We will prove that West is a criminal. First, we will represent these facts as first-order definite clauses. The next section shows how the forward-chaining algorithm solves the problem.

"... it is a crime for an American to sell weapons to hostile nations":

$$American(x) \wedge Weapon(y) \wedge Sells(x, y, z) \wedge Hostile(z) \Rightarrow Criminal(x) . \quad (3)$$

"Nono ... has some missiles." The sentence $\exists\, x\ Owns(Nono, x) \wedge Missile(x)$ is transformed into two definite clauses by Existential Instantiation, introducing a new constant M_1:

$$Owns(Nono, M_1) \quad (4)$$
$$Missile(M_1) \quad (5)$$

"All of its missiles were sold to it by Colonel West":

$$Missile(x) \wedge Owns(Nono, x) \Rightarrow Sells(West, x, Nono) . \quad (6)$$

We will also need to know that missiles are weapons:

$$Missile(x) \Rightarrow Weapon(x) \quad (7)$$

and we must know that an enemy of America counts as "hostile":

$$Enemy(x, America) \Rightarrow Hostile(x) . \tag{8}$$

"West, who is American ...":

$$American(West) . \tag{9}$$

"The country Nono, an enemy of America ...":

$$Enemy(Nono, America) . \tag{10}$$

This knowledge base contains no function symbols and is therefore an instance of the class of **Datalog** knowledge bases. Datalog is a language that is restricted to first-order definite clauses with no function symbols. Datalog gets its name because it can represent the type of statements typically made in relational databases. We will see that the absence of function symbols makes inference much easier.

DATALOG

3.2 A simple forward-chaining algorithm

The first forward-chaining algorithm we consider is a simple one, shown in Figure 3. Starting from the known facts, it triggers all the rules whose premises are satisfied, adding their conclusions to the known facts. The process repeats until the query is answered (assuming that just one answer is required) or no new facts are added. Notice that a fact is not "new" if it is just a **renaming** of a known fact. One sentence is a renaming of another if they are identical except for the names of the variables. For example, $Likes(x, IceCream)$ and $Likes(y, IceCream)$ are renamings of each other because they differ only in the choice of x or y; their meanings are identical: everyone likes ice cream.

RENAMING

We use our crime problem to illustrate how FOL-FC-ASK works. The implication sentences are (3), (6), (7), and (8). Two iterations are required:

- On the first iteration, rule (3) has unsatisfied premises.
  Rule (6) is satisfied with $\{x/M_1\}$, and $Sells(West, M_1, Nono)$ is added.
  Rule (7) is satisfied with $\{x/M_1\}$, and $Weapon(M_1)$ is added.
  Rule (8) is satisfied with $\{x/Nono\}$, and $Hostile(Nono)$ is added.
- On the second iteration, rule (3) is satisfied with $\{x/West, y/M_1, z/Nono\}$, and $Criminal(West)$ is added.

Figure 4 shows the proof tree that is generated. Notice that no new inferences are possible at this point because every sentence that could be concluded by forward chaining is already contained explicitly in the KB. Such a knowledge base is called a **fixed point** of the inference process. Fixed points reached by forward chaining with first-order definite clauses are similar to those for propositional forward chaining; the principal difference is that a first-order fixed point can include universally quantified atomic sentences.

FOL-FC-ASK is easy to analyze. First, it is **sound**, because every inference is just an application of Generalized Modus Ponens, which is sound. Second, it is **complete** for definite clause knowledge bases; that is, it answers every query whose answers are entailed by any knowledge base of definite clauses. For Datalog knowledge bases, which contain no function symbols, the proof of completeness is fairly easy. We begin by counting the number of

```
function FOL-FC-ASK(KB, α) returns a substitution or false
  inputs: KB, the knowledge base, a set of first-order definite clauses
          α, the query, an atomic sentence
  local variables: new, the new sentences inferred on each iteration

  repeat until new is empty
     new ← { }
     for each rule in KB do
        (p1 ∧ . . . ∧ pn ⇒ q) ← STANDARDIZE-VARIABLES(rule)
        for each θ such that SUBST(θ, p1 ∧ . . . ∧ pn) = SUBST(θ, p'1 ∧ . . . ∧ p'n)
                     for some p'1, . . . , p'n in KB
           q' ← SUBST(θ, q)
           if q' does not unify with some sentence already in KB or new then
              add q' to new
              φ ← UNIFY(q', α)
              if φ is not fail then return φ
     add new to KB
  return false
```

Figure 3 A conceptually straightforward, but very inefficient, forward-chaining algorithm. On each iteration, it adds to KB all the atomic sentences that can be inferred in one step from the implication sentences and the atomic sentences already in KB. The function STANDARDIZE-VARIABLES replaces all variables in its arguments with new ones that have not been used before.

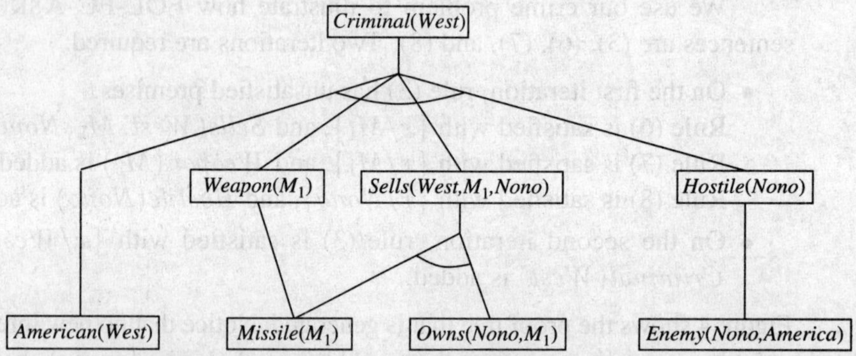

Figure 4 The proof tree generated by forward chaining on the crime example. The initial facts appear at the bottom level, facts inferred on the first iteration in the middle level, and facts inferred on the second iteration at the top level.

possible facts that can be added, which determines the maximum number of iterations. Let k be the maximum **arity** (number of arguments) of any predicate, p be the number of predicates, and n be the number of constant symbols. Clearly, there can be no more than pn^k distinct ground facts, so after this many iterations the algorithm must have reached a fixed point. Then we can make an argument very similar to the proof of completeness for propositional forward chaining. The details of how to make the transition from propositional to first-order completeness are given for the resolution algorithm in Section 5.

For general definite clauses with function symbols, FOL-FC-ASK can generate infinitely many new facts, so we need to be more careful. For the case in which an answer to the query sentence q is entailed, we must appeal to Herbrand's theorem to establish that the algorithm will find a proof. (See Section 5 for the resolution case.) If the query has no answer, the algorithm could fail to terminate in some cases. For example, if the knowledge base includes the Peano axioms

$$NatNum(0)$$
$$\forall n \;\; NatNum(n) \Rightarrow NatNum(S(n)) \; ,$$

then forward chaining adds $NatNum(S(0))$, $NatNum(S(S(0)))$, $NatNum(S(S(S(0))))$, and so on. This problem is unavoidable in general. As with general first-order logic, entailment with definite clauses is semidecidable.

3.3 Efficient forward chaining

The forward-chaining algorithm in Figure 3 is designed for ease of understanding rather than for efficiency of operation. There are three possible sources of inefficiency. First, the "inner loop" of the algorithm involves finding all possible unifiers such that the premise of a rule unifies with a suitable set of facts in the knowledge base. This is often called **pattern matching** and can be very expensive. Second, the algorithm rechecks every rule on every iteration to see whether its premises are satisfied, even if very few additions are made to the knowledge base on each iteration. Finally, the algorithm might generate many facts that are irrelevant to the goal. We address each of these issues in turn.

PATTERN MATCHING

Matching rules against known facts

The problem of matching the premise of a rule against the facts in the knowledge base might seem simple enough. For example, suppose we want to apply the rule

$$Missile(x) \Rightarrow Weapon(x) \; .$$

Then we need to find all the facts that unify with $Missile(x)$; in a suitably indexed knowledge base, this can be done in constant time per fact. Now consider a rule such as

$$Missile(x) \land Owns(Nono, x) \Rightarrow Sells(West, x, Nono) \; .$$

Again, we can find all the objects owned by Nono in constant time per object; then, for each object, we could check whether it is a missile. If the knowledge base contains many objects owned by Nono and very few missiles, however, it would be better to find all the missiles first and then check whether they are owned by Nono. This is the **conjunct ordering** problem: find an ordering to solve the conjuncts of the rule premise so that the total cost is minimized. It turns out that finding the optimal ordering is NP-hard, but good heuristics are available. For example, the **minimum-remaining-values** (MRV) heuristic would suggest ordering the conjuncts to look for missiles first if fewer missiles than objects are owned by Nono.

CONJUNCT ORDERING

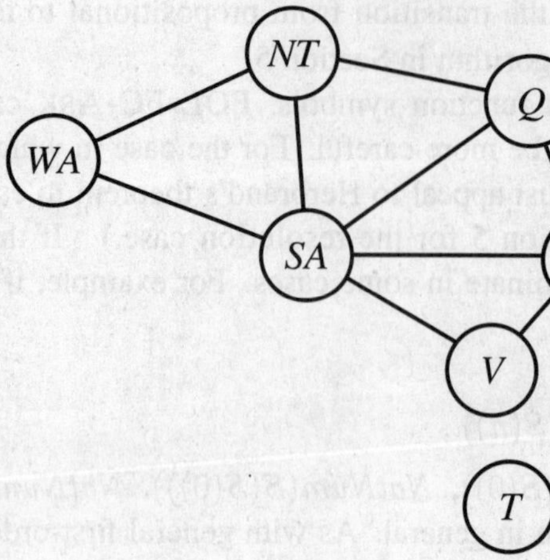

(a)

$$\begin{aligned}&Diff(wa, nt) \wedge Diff(wa, sa) \wedge\\ &\quad Diff(nt, q) \wedge Diff(nt, sa) \wedge\\ &\quad Diff(q, nsw) \wedge Diff(q, sa) \wedge\\ &\quad Diff(nsw, v) \wedge Diff(nsw, sa) \wedge\\ &\quad Diff(v, sa) \Rightarrow Colorable()\end{aligned}$$

$$Diff(Red, Blue) \quad Diff(Red, Green)$$

$$Diff(Green, Red) \quad Diff(Green, Blue)$$

$$Diff(Blue, Red) \quad Diff(Blue, Green)$$

(b)

Figure 5 (a) Constraint graph for coloring the map of Australia. (b) The map-coloring CSP expressed as a single definite clause. Each map region is represented as a variable whose value can be one of the constants *Red*, *Green* or *Blue*.

The connection between pattern matching and constraint satisfaction is actually very close. We can view each conjunct as a constraint on the variables that it contains—for example, $Missile(x)$ is a unary constraint on x. Extending this idea, *we can express every finite-domain CSP as a single definite clause together with some associated ground facts*. Consider the map-coloring problem shown in Figure 5(a). An equivalent formulation as a single definite clause is given in Figure 5(b). Clearly, the conclusion $Colorable()$ can be inferred only if the CSP has a solution. Because CSPs in general include 3-SAT problems as special cases, we can conclude that *matching a definite clause against a set of facts is NP-hard*.

It might seem rather depressing that forward chaining has an NP-hard matching problem in its inner loop. There are three ways to cheer ourselves up:

- We can remind ourselves that most rules in real-world knowledge bases are small and simple (like the rules in our crime example) rather than large and complex (like the CSP formulation in Figure 5). It is common in the database world to assume that both the sizes of rules and the arities of predicates are bounded by a constant and to worry only about **data complexity**—that is, the complexity of inference as a function of the number of ground facts in the knowledge base. It is easy to show that the data complexity of forward chaining is polynomial.

DATA COMPLEXITY

- We can consider subclasses of rules for which matching is efficient. Essentially every Datalog clause can be viewed as defining a CSP, so matching will be tractable just when the corresponding CSP is tractable. For example, if the constraint graph (the graph whose nodes are variables and whose links are constraints) forms a tree, then the CSP can be solved in linear time. Exactly the same result holds for rule matching. For instance, if we remove South

Australia from the map in Figure 5, the resulting clause is

$$Diff(wa, nt) \wedge Diff(nt, q) \wedge Diff(q, nsw) \wedge Diff(nsw, v) \Rightarrow Colorable().$$

Algorithms for solving tree-structured CSPs can be applied directly to the problem of rule matching.

- We can try to to eliminate redundant rule-matching attempts in the forward-chaining algorithm, as described next.

Incremental forward chaining

When we showed how forward chaining works on the crime example, we cheated; in particular, we omitted some of the rule matching done by the algorithm shown in Figure 3. For example, on the second iteration, the rule

$$Missile(x) \Rightarrow Weapon(x)$$

matches against $Missile(M_1)$ (again), and of course the conclusion $Weapon(M_1)$ is already known so nothing happens. Such redundant rule matching can be avoided if we make the following observation: *Every new fact inferred on iteration t must be derived from at least one new fact inferred on iteration $t-1$.* This is true because any inference that does not require a new fact from iteration $t-1$ could have been done at iteration $t-1$ already.

This observation leads naturally to an incremental forward-chaining algorithm where, at iteration t, we check a rule only if its premise includes a conjunct p_i that unifies with a fact p'_i newly inferred at iteration $t-1$. The rule-matching step then fixes p_i to match with p'_i, but allows the other conjuncts of the rule to match with facts from any previous iteration. This algorithm generates exactly the same facts at each iteration as the algorithm in Figure 3, but is much more efficient.

With suitable indexing, it is easy to identify all the rules that can be triggered by any given fact, and indeed many real systems operate in an "update" mode wherein forward chaining occurs in response to each new fact that is TELLed to the system. Inferences cascade through the set of rules until the fixed point is reached, and then the process begins again for the next new fact.

Typically, only a small fraction of the rules in the knowledge base are actually triggered by the addition of a given fact. This means that a great deal of redundant work is done in repeatedly constructing partial matches that have some unsatisfied premises. Our crime example is rather too small to show this effectively, but notice that a partial match is constructed on the first iteration between the rule

$$American(x) \wedge Weapon(y) \wedge Sells(x, y, z) \wedge Hostile(z) \Rightarrow Criminal(x)$$

and the fact $American(West)$. This partial match is then discarded and rebuilt on the second iteration (when the rule succeeds). It would be better to retain and gradually complete the partial matches as new facts arrive, rather than discarding them.

RETE

The **rete** algorithm[3] was the first to address this problem. The algorithm preprocesses the set of rules in the knowledge base to construct a sort of dataflow network in which each

[3] Rete is Latin for net. The English pronunciation rhymes with treaty.

node is a literal from a rule premise. Variable bindings flow through the network and are filtered out when they fail to match a literal. If two literals in a rule share a variable—for example, $Sells(x, y, z) \land Hostile(z)$ in the crime example—then the bindings from each literal are filtered through an equality node. A variable binding reaching a node for an n-ary literal such as $Sells(x, y, z)$ might have to wait for bindings for the other variables to be established before the process can continue. At any given point, the state of a rete network captures all the partial matches of the rules, avoiding a great deal of recomputation.

PRODUCTION SYSTEM

Rete networks, and various improvements thereon, have been a key component of so-called **production systems**, which were among the earliest forward-chaining systems in widespread use.[4] The XCON system (originally called R1; McDermott, 1982) was built with a production-system architecture. XCON contained several thousand rules for designing configurations of computer components for customers of the Digital Equipment Corporation. It was one of the first clear commercial successes in the emerging field of expert systems. Many other similar systems have been built with the same underlying technology, which has been implemented in the general-purpose language OPS-5.

COGNITIVE ARCHITECTURES

Production systems are also popular in **cognitive architectures**—that is, models of human reasoning—such as ACT (Anderson, 1983) and SOAR (Laird *et al.*, 1987). In such systems, the "working memory" of the system models human short-term memory, and the productions are part of long-term memory. On each cycle of operation, productions are matched against the working memory of facts. A production whose conditions are satisfied can add or delete facts in working memory. In contrast to the typical situation in databases, production systems often have many rules and relatively few facts. With suitably optimized matching technology, some modern systems can operate in real time with tens of millions of rules.

Irrelevant facts

The final source of inefficiency in forward chaining appears to be intrinsic to the approach and also arises in the propositional context. Forward chaining makes all allowable inferences based on the known facts, *even if they are irrelevant to the goal at hand.* In our crime example, there were no rules capable of drawing irrelevant conclusions, so the lack of directedness was not a problem. In other cases (e.g., if many rules describe the eating habits of Americans and the prices of missiles), FOL-FC-ASK will generate many irrelevant conclusions.

One way to avoid drawing irrelevant conclusions is to use backward chaining, as described in Section 4. Another solution is to restrict forward chaining to a selected subset of rules, as in PL-FC-ENTAILS?. A third approach has emerged in the field of **deductive databases**, which are large-scale databases, like relational databases, but which use forward chaining as the standard inference tool rather than SQL queries. The idea is to rewrite the rule set, using information from the goal, so that only relevant variable bindings—those belonging to a so-called **magic set**—are considered during forward inference. For example, if the goal is $Criminal(West)$, the rule that concludes $Criminal(x)$ will be rewritten to include an extra conjunct that constrains the value of x:

DEDUCTIVE DATABASES

MAGIC SET

$$Magic(x) \land American(x) \land Weapon(y) \land Sells(x, y, z) \land Hostile(z) \Rightarrow Criminal(x) .$$

[4] The word **production** in **production systems** denotes a condition–action rule.

The fact $Magic(West)$ is also added to the KB. In this way, even if the knowledge base contains facts about millions of Americans, only Colonel West will be considered during the forward inference process. The complete process for defining magic sets and rewriting the knowledge base is too complex to go into here, but the basic idea is to perform a sort of "generic" backward inference from the goal in order to work out which variable bindings need to be constrained. The magic sets approach can therefore be thought of as a kind of hybrid between forward inference and backward preprocessing.

4 BACKWARD CHAINING

The second major family of logical inference algorithms uses the **backward chaining** approach for definite clauses. These algorithms work backward from the goal, chaining through rules to find known facts that support the proof. We describe the basic algorithm, and then we describe how it is used in **logic programming**, which is the most widely used form of automated reasoning. We also see that backward chaining has some disadvantages compared with forward chaining, and we look at ways to overcome them. Finally, we look at the close connection between logic programming and constraint satisfaction problems.

4.1 A backward-chaining algorithm

Figure 6 shows a backward-chaining algorithm for definite clauses. FOL-BC-ASK(*KB*, *goal*) will be proved if the knowledge base contains a clause of the form $lhs \Rightarrow goal$, where lhs (left-hand side) is a list of conjuncts. An atomic fact like $American(West)$ is considered as a clause whose lhs is the empty list. Now a query that contains variables might be proved in multiple ways. For example, the query $Person(x)$ could be proved with the substitution
GENERATOR
$\{x/John\}$ as well as with $\{x/Richard\}$. So we implement FOL-BC-ASK as a **generator**—a function that returns multiple times, each time giving one possible result.

Backward chaining is a kind of AND/OR search—the OR part because the goal query can be proved by any rule in the knowledge base, and the AND part because all the conjuncts in the lhs of a clause must be proved. FOL-BC-OR works by fetching all clauses that might unify with the goal, standardizing the variables in the clause to be brand-new variables, and then, if the rhs of the clause does indeed unify with the goal, proving every conjunct in the lhs, using FOL-BC-AND. That function in turn works by proving each of the conjuncts in turn, keeping track of the accumulated substitution as we go. Figure 7 is the proof tree for deriving $Criminal(West)$ from sentences (3) through (10).

Backward chaining, as we have written it, is clearly a depth-first search algorithm. This means that its space requirements are linear in the size of the proof (neglecting, for now, the space required to accumulate the solutions). It also means that backward chaining (unlike forward chaining) suffers from problems with repeated states and incompleteness. We will discuss these problems and some potential solutions, but first we show how backward chaining is used in logic programming systems.

```
function FOL-BC-ASK(KB, query) returns a generator of substitutions
  return FOL-BC-OR(KB, query, { })

generator FOL-BC-OR(KB, goal, θ) yields a substitution
  for each rule (lhs ⇒ rhs) in FETCH-RULES-FOR-GOAL(KB, goal) do
    (lhs, rhs) ← STANDARDIZE-VARIABLES((lhs, rhs))
    for each θ′ in FOL-BC-AND(KB, lhs, UNIFY(rhs, goal, θ)) do
      yield θ′

generator FOL-BC-AND(KB, goals, θ) yields a substitution
  if θ = failure then return
  else if LENGTH(goals) = 0 then yield θ
  else do
    first,rest ← FIRST(goals), REST(goals)
    for each θ′ in FOL-BC-OR(KB, SUBST(θ, first), θ) do
      for each θ″ in FOL-BC-AND(KB, rest, θ′) do
        yield θ″
```

Figure 6 A simple backward-chaining algorithm for first-order knowledge bases.

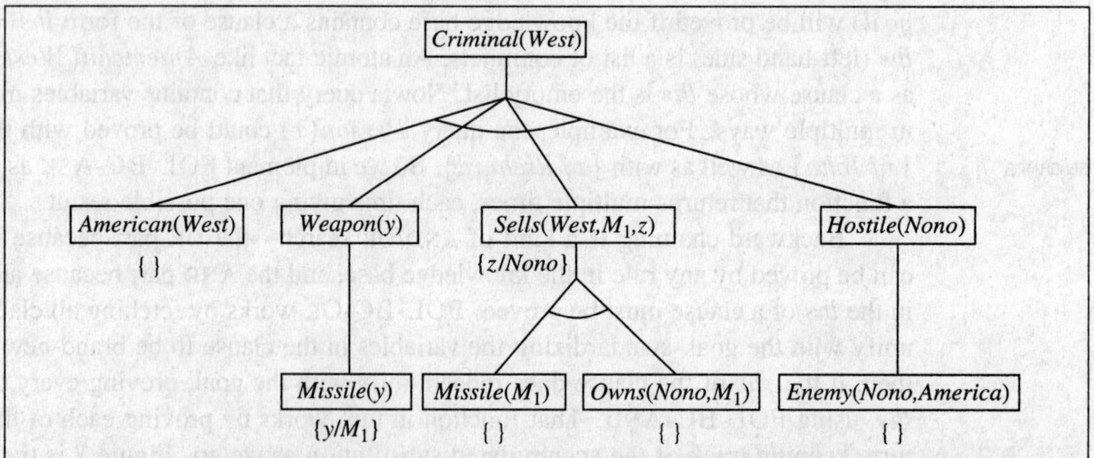

Figure 7 Proof tree constructed by backward chaining to prove that West is a criminal. The tree should be read depth first, left to right. To prove $Criminal(West)$, we have to prove the four conjuncts below it. Some of these are in the knowledge base, and others require further backward chaining. Bindings for each successful unification are shown next to the corresponding subgoal. Note that once one subgoal in a conjunction succeeds, its substitution is applied to subsequent subgoals. Thus, by the time FOL-BC-ASK gets to the last conjunct, originally $Hostile(z)$, z is already bound to $Nono$.

4.2 Logic programming

Logic programming is a technology that comes fairly close to embodying the declarative ideal: that systems should be constructed by expressing knowledge in a formal language and that problems should be solved by running inference processes on that knowledge. The ideal is summed up in Robert Kowalski's equation,

$$Algorithm = Logic + Control \, .$$

PROLOG **Prolog** is the most widely used logic programming language. It is used primarily as a rapid-prototyping language and for symbol-manipulation tasks such as writing compilers (Van Roy, 1990) and parsing natural language (Pereira and Warren, 1980). Many expert systems have been written in Prolog for legal, medical, financial, and other domains.

Prolog programs are sets of definite clauses written in a notation somewhat different from standard first-order logic. Prolog uses uppercase letters for variables and lowercase for constants—the opposite of our convention for logic. Commas separate conjuncts in a clause, and the clause is written "backwards" from what we are used to; instead of $A \wedge B \;\Rightarrow\; C$ in Prolog we have `C :- A, B`. Here is a typical example:

```
criminal(X) :- american(X), weapon(Y), sells(X,Y,Z), hostile(Z).
```

The notation `[E|L]` denotes a list whose first element is `E` and whose rest is `L`. Here is a Prolog program for `append(X,Y,Z)`, which succeeds if list `Z` is the result of appending lists `X` and `Y`:

```
append([],Y,Y).
append([A|X],Y,[A|Z]) :- append(X,Y,Z).
```

In English, we can read these clauses as (1) appending an empty list with a list `Y` produces the same list `Y` and (2) `[A|Z]` is the result of appending `[A|X]` onto `Y`, provided that `Z` is the result of appending `X` onto `Y`. In most high-level languages we can write a similar recursive function that describes how to append two lists. The Prolog definition is actually much more powerful, however, because it describes a *relation* that holds among three arguments, rather than a *function* computed from two arguments. For example, we can ask the query `append(X,Y,[1,2])`: what two lists can be appended to give `[1,2]`? We get back the solutions

```
X=[]      Y=[1,2];
X=[1]     Y=[2];
X=[1,2]   Y=[]
```

The execution of Prolog programs is done through depth-first backward chaining, where clauses are tried in the order in which they are written in the knowledge base. Some aspects of Prolog fall outside standard logical inference:

- Prolog uses database semantics rather than first-order semantics, and this is apparent in its treatment of equality and negation (see Section 4.5).
- There is a set of built-in functions for arithmetic. Literals using these function symbols are "proved" by executing code rather than doing further inference. For example, the

goal "X is 4+3" succeeds with X bound to 7. On the other hand, the goal "5 is X+Y" fails, because the built-in functions do not do arbitrary equation solving.[5]

- There are built-in predicates that have side effects when executed. These include input–output predicates and the assert/retract predicates for modifying the knowledge base. Such predicates have no counterpart in logic and can produce confusing results—for example, if facts are asserted in a branch of the proof tree that eventually fails.
- The **occur check** is omitted from Prolog's unification algorithm. This means that some unsound inferences can be made; these are almost never a problem in practice.
- Prolog uses depth-first backward-chaining search with no checks for infinite recursion. This makes it very fast when given the right set of axioms, but incomplete when given the wrong ones.

Prolog's design represents a compromise between declarativeness and execution efficiency—inasmuch as efficiency was understood at the time Prolog was designed.

4.3 Efficient implementation of logic programs

The execution of a Prolog program can happen in two modes: interpreted and compiled. Interpretation essentially amounts to running the FOL-BC-ASK algorithm from Figure 6, with the program as the knowledge base. We say "essentially" because Prolog interpreters contain a variety of improvements designed to maximize speed. Here we consider only two.

First, our implementation had to explicitly manage the iteration over possible results generated by each of the subfunctions. Prolog interpreters have a global data structure, a stack of **choice points**, to keep track of the multiple possibilities that we considered in FOL-BC-OR. This global stack is more efficient, and it makes debugging easier, because the debugger can move up and down the stack.

CHOICE POINT

Second, our simple implementation of FOL-BC-ASK spends a good deal of time generating substitutions. Instead of explicitly constructing substitutions, Prolog has logic variables that remember their current binding. At any point in time, every variable in the program either is unbound or is bound to some value. Together, these variables and values implicitly define the substitution for the current branch of the proof. Extending the path can only add new variable bindings, because an attempt to add a different binding for an already bound variable results in a failure of unification. When a path in the search fails, Prolog will back up to a previous choice point, and then it might have to unbind some variables. This is done by keeping track of all the variables that have been bound in a stack called the **trail**. As each new variable is bound by UNIFY-VAR, the variable is pushed onto the trail. When a goal fails and it is time to back up to a previous choice point, each of the variables is unbound as it is removed from the trail.

TRAIL

Even the most efficient Prolog interpreters require several thousand machine instructions per inference step because of the cost of index lookup, unification, and building the recursive call stack. In effect, the interpreter always behaves as if it has never seen the program before; for example, it has to *find* clauses that match the goal. A compiled Prolog

[5] Note that if the Peano axioms are provided, such goals can be solved by inference within a Prolog program.

```
procedure APPEND(ax, y, az, continuation)

  trail ← GLOBAL-TRAIL-POINTER()
  if ax = [] and UNIFY(y, az) then CALL(continuation)
  RESET-TRAIL(trail)
  a, x, z ← NEW-VARIABLE(), NEW-VARIABLE(), NEW-VARIABLE()
  if UNIFY(ax, [a | x]) and UNIFY(az, [a | z]) then APPEND(x, y, z, continuation)
```

Figure 8 Pseudocode representing the result of compiling the Append predicate. The function NEW-VARIABLE returns a new variable, distinct from all other variables used so far. The procedure CALL(*continuation*) continues execution with the specified continuation.

program, on the other hand, is an inference procedure for a specific set of clauses, so it *knows* what clauses match the goal. Prolog basically generates a miniature theorem prover for each different predicate, thereby eliminating much of the overhead of interpretation. It is also possible to **open-code** the unification routine for each different call, thereby avoiding explicit analysis of term structure. (For details of open-coded unification, see Warren *et al.* (1977).)

OPEN-CODE

The instruction sets of today's computers give a poor match with Prolog's semantics, so most Prolog compilers compile into an intermediate language rather than directly into machine language. The most popular intermediate language is the Warren Abstract Machine, or WAM, named after David H. D. Warren, one of the implementers of the first Prolog compiler. The WAM is an abstract instruction set that is suitable for Prolog and can be either interpreted or translated into machine language. Other compilers translate Prolog into a high-level language such as Lisp or C and then use that language's compiler to translate to machine language. For example, the definition of the Append predicate can be compiled into the code shown in Figure 8. Several points are worth mentioning:

- Rather than having to search the knowledge base for Append clauses, the clauses become a procedure and the inferences are carried out simply by calling the procedure.
- As described earlier, the current variable bindings are kept on a trail. The first step of the procedure saves the current state of the trail, so that it can be restored by RESET-TRAIL if the first clause fails. This will undo any bindings generated by the first call to UNIFY.
- CONTINUATION The trickiest part is the use of **continuations** to implement choice points. You can think of a continuation as packaging up a procedure and a list of arguments that together define what should be done next whenever the current goal succeeds. It would not do just to return from a procedure like APPEND when the goal succeeds, because it could succeed in several ways, and each of them has to be explored. The continuation argument solves this problem because it can be called each time the goal succeeds. In the APPEND code, if the first argument is empty and the second argument unifies with the third, then the APPEND predicate has succeeded. We then CALL the continuation, with the appropriate bindings on the trail, to do whatever should be done next. For example, if the call to APPEND were at the top level, the continuation would print the bindings of the variables.

Before Warren's work on the compilation of inference in Prolog, logic programming was too slow for general use. Compilers by Warren and others allowed Prolog code to achieve speeds that are competitive with C on a variety of standard benchmarks (Van Roy, 1990). Of course, the fact that one can write a planner or natural language parser in a few dozen lines of Prolog makes it somewhat more desirable than C for prototyping most small-scale AI research projects.

Parallelization can also provide substantial speedup. There are two principal sources of parallelism. The first, called **OR-parallelism**, comes from the possibility of a goal unifying with many different clauses in the knowledge base. Each gives rise to an independent branch in the search space that can lead to a potential solution, and all such branches can be solved in parallel. The second, called **AND-parallelism**, comes from the possibility of solving each conjunct in the body of an implication in parallel. AND-parallelism is more difficult to achieve, because solutions for the whole conjunction require consistent bindings for all the variables. Each conjunctive branch must communicate with the other branches to ensure a global solution.

OR-PARALLELISM

AND-PARALLELISM

4.4 Redundant inference and infinite loops

We now turn to the Achilles heel of Prolog: the mismatch between depth-first search and search trees that include repeated states and infinite paths. Consider the following logic program that decides if a path exists between two points on a directed graph:

```
path(X,Z) :- link(X,Z).
path(X,Z) :- path(X,Y), link(Y,Z).
```

A simple three-node graph, described by the facts `link(a,b)` and `link(b,c)`, is shown in Figure 9(a). With this program, the query `path(a,c)` generates the proof tree shown in Figure 10(a). On the other hand, if we put the two clauses in the order

```
path(X,Z) :- path(X,Y), link(Y,Z).
path(X,Z) :- link(X,Z).
```

then Prolog follows the infinite path shown in Figure 10(b). Prolog is therefore **incomplete** as a theorem prover for definite clauses—even for Datalog programs, as this example shows—because, for some knowledge bases, it fails to prove sentences that are entailed. Notice that forward chaining does not suffer from this problem: once `path(a,b)`, `path(b,c)`, and `path(a,c)` are inferred, forward chaining halts.

Depth-first backward chaining also has problems with redundant computations. For example, when finding a path from A_1 to J_4 in Figure 9(b), Prolog performs 877 inferences, most of which involve finding all possible paths to nodes from which the goal is unreachable. The total amount of inference can be exponential in the number of ground facts that are generated. If we apply forward chaining instead, at most n^2 `path(X,Y)` facts can be generated linking n nodes. For the problem in Figure 9(b), only 62 inferences are needed.

DYNAMIC PROGRAMMING

Forward chaining on graph search problems is an example of **dynamic programming**, in which the solutions to subproblems are constructed incrementally from those of smaller

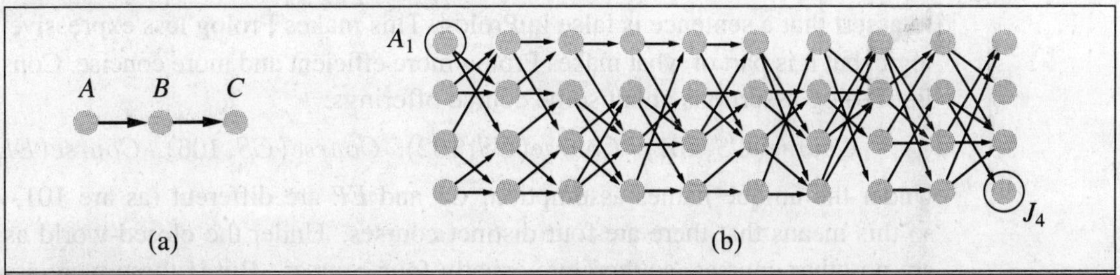

Figure 9 (a) Finding a path from A to C can lead Prolog into an infinite loop. (b) A graph in which each node is connected to two random successors in the next layer. Finding a path from A_1 to J_4 requires 877 inferences.

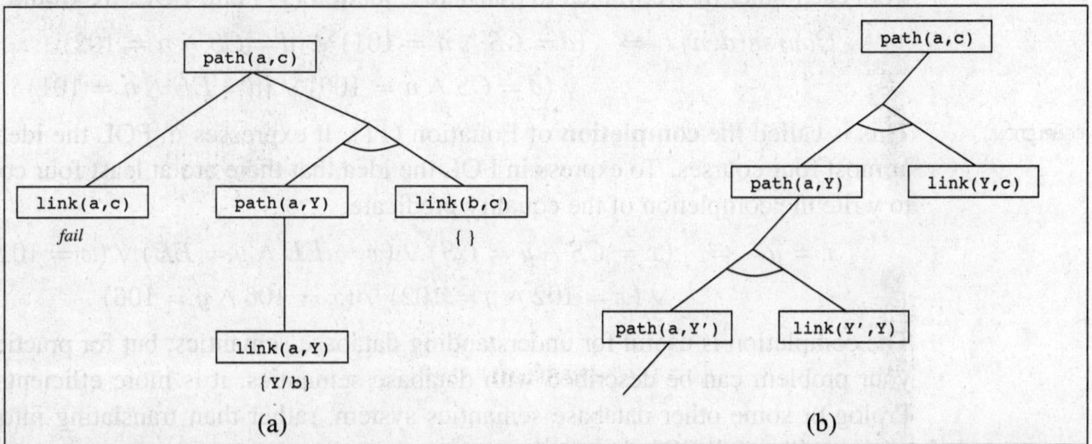

Figure 10 (a) Proof that a path exists from A to C. (b) Infinite proof tree generated when the clauses are in the "wrong" order.

subproblems and are cached to avoid recomputation. We can obtain a similar effect in a backward chaining system using **memoization**—that is, caching solutions to subgoals as they are found and then reusing those solutions when the subgoal recurs, rather than repeating the previous computation. This is the approach taken by **tabled logic programming** systems, which use efficient storage and retrieval mechanisms to perform memoization. Tabled logic programming combines the goal-directedness of backward chaining with the dynamic-programming efficiency of forward chaining. It is also complete for Datalog knowledge bases, which means that the programmer need worry less about infinite loops. (It is still possible to get an infinite loop with predicates like `father(X,Y)` that refer to a potentially unbounded number of objects.)

TABLED LOGIC PROGRAMMING

4.5 Database semantics of Prolog

Prolog uses database semantics. The unique names assumption says that every Prolog constant and every ground term refers to a distinct object, and the closed world assumption says that the only sentences that are true are those that are entailed by the knowledge base. There is no way to assert that a sentence is false in Prolog. This makes Prolog less expressive than first-order logic, but it is part of what makes Prolog more efficient and more concise. Consider the following Prolog assertions about some course offerings:

$$Course(CS, 101),\ Course(CS, 102),\ Course(CS, 106),\ Course(EE, 101). \quad (11)$$

Under the unique names assumption, *CS* and *EE* are different (as are 101, 102, and 106), so this means that there are four distinct courses. Under the closed-world assumption there are no other courses, so there are exactly four courses. But if these were assertions in FOL rather than in Prolog, then all we could say is that there are somewhere between one and infinity courses. That's because the assertions (in FOL) do not deny the possibility that other unmentioned courses are also offered, nor do they say that the courses mentioned are different from each other. If we wanted to translate Equation (11) into FOL, we would get this:

$$\begin{aligned} Course(d, n) \quad \Leftrightarrow \quad & (d = CS \wedge n = 101) \vee (d = CS \wedge n = 102) \\ & \vee (d = CS \wedge n = 106) \vee (d = EE \wedge n = 101)\,. \end{aligned} \quad (12)$$

COMPLETION

This is called the **completion** of Equation (11). It expresses in FOL the idea that there are at most four courses. To express in FOL the idea that there are at least four courses, we need to write the completion of the equality predicate:

$$\begin{aligned} x = y \quad \Leftrightarrow \quad & (x = CS \wedge y = CS) \vee (x = EE \wedge y = EE) \vee (x = 101 \wedge y = 101) \\ & \vee (x = 102 \wedge y = 102) \vee (x = 106 \wedge y = 106)\,. \end{aligned}$$

The completion is useful for understanding database semantics, but for practical purposes, if your problem can be described with database semantics, it is more efficient to reason with Prolog or some other database semantics system, rather than translating into FOL and reasoning with a full FOL theorem prover.

4.6 Constraint logic programming

In our discussion of forward chaining (Section 3), we showed how constraint satisfaction problems (CSPs) can be encoded as definite clauses. Standard Prolog solves such problems in exactly the same way as a simple backtracking algorithm.

Because backtracking enumerates the domains of the variables, it works only for **finite-domain** CSPs. In Prolog terms, there must be a finite number of solutions for any goal with unbound variables. (For example, the goal `diff(Q,SA)`, which says that Queensland and South Australia must be different colors, has six solutions if three colors are allowed.) Infinite-domain CSPs—for example, with integer or real-valued variables—require quite different algorithms, such as bounds propagation or linear programming.

Consider the following example. We define `triangle(X,Y,Z)` as a predicate that holds if the three arguments are numbers that satisfy the triangle inequality:

```
triangle(X,Y,Z) :-
    X>0, Y>0, Z>0, X+Y>=Z, Y+Z>=X, X+Z>=Y.
```

If we ask Prolog the query `triangle(3,4,5)`, it succeeds. On the other hand, if we ask `triangle(3,4,Z)`, no solution will be found, because the subgoal `Z>=0` cannot be handled by Prolog; we can't compare an unbound value to 0.

CONSTRAINT LOGIC PROGRAMMING

Constraint logic programming (CLP) allows variables to be *constrained* rather than *bound*. A CLP solution is the most specific set of constraints on the query variables that can be derived from the knowledge base. For example, the solution to the `triangle(3,4,Z)` query is the constraint `7 >= Z >= 1`. Standard logic programs are just a special case of CLP in which the solution constraints must be equality constraints—that is, bindings.

CLP systems incorporate various constraint-solving algorithms for the constraints allowed in the language. For example, a system that allows linear inequalities on real-valued variables might include a linear programming algorithm for solving those constraints. CLP systems also adopt a much more flexible approach to solving standard logic programming queries. For example, instead of depth-first, left-to-right backtracking, they might use more efficient algorithms, including heuristic conjunct ordering, backjumping, cutset conditioning, and so on. CLP systems therefore combine elements of constraint satisfaction algorithms, logic programming, and deductive databases.

METARULE

Several systems that allow the programmer more control over the search order for inference have been defined. The MRS language (Genesereth and Smith, 1981; Russell, 1985) allows the programmer to write **metarules** to determine which conjuncts are tried first. The user could write a rule saying that the goal with the fewest variables should be tried first or could write domain-specific rules for particular predicates.

5 RESOLUTION

The last of our three families of logical systems is based on **resolution**. Propositional resolution using refutation is a complete inference procedure for propositional logic. In this section, we describe how to extend resolution to first-order logic.

5.1 Conjunctive normal form for first-order logic

As in the propositional case, first-order resolution requires that sentences be in **conjunctive normal form** (CNF)—that is, a conjunction of clauses, where each clause is a disjunction of literals.[6] Literals can contain variables, which are assumed to be universally quantified. For example, the sentence

$$\forall x \;\; American(x) \land Weapon(y) \land Sells(x,y,z) \land Hostile(z) \;\Rightarrow\; Criminal(x)$$

becomes, in CNF,

$$\neg American(x) \lor \neg Weapon(y) \lor \neg Sells(x,y,z) \lor \neg Hostile(z) \lor Criminal(x)\,.$$

Every sentence of first-order logic can be converted into an inferentially equivalent CNF sentence. In particular, the CNF sentence will be unsatisfiable just when the original sentence is unsatisfiable, so we have a basis for doing proofs by contradiction on the CNF sentences.

[6] A clause can also be represented as an implication with a conjunction of atoms in the premise and a disjunction of atoms in the conclusion. This is called **implicative normal form** or **Kowalski form** (especially when written with a right-to-left implication symbol (Kowalski, 1979)) and is often much easier to read.

The procedure for conversion to CNF is similar to the propositional case. The principal difference arises from the need to eliminate existential quantifiers. We illustrate the procedure by translating the sentence "Everyone who loves all animals is loved by someone," or

$$\forall x \ [\forall y \ Animal(y) \Rightarrow Loves(x,y)] \Rightarrow [\exists y \ Loves(y,x)] .$$

The steps are as follows:

- **Eliminate implications**:
$$\forall x \ [\neg\forall y \ \neg Animal(y) \lor Loves(x,y)] \lor [\exists y \ Loves(y,x)] .$$
- **Move $\neg$ inwards**: In addition to the usual rules for negated connectives, we need rules for negated quantifiers. Thus, we have

  $\neg\forall x \ p$ becomes $\exists x \ \neg p$

  $\neg\exists x \ p$ becomes $\forall x \ \neg p$.

  Our sentence goes through the following transformations:
$$\forall x \ [\exists y \ \neg(\neg Animal(y) \lor Loves(x,y))] \lor [\exists y \ Loves(y,x)] .$$
$$\forall x \ [\exists y \ \neg\neg Animal(y) \land \neg Loves(x,y)] \lor [\exists y \ Loves(y,x)] .$$
$$\forall x \ [\exists y \ Animal(y) \land \neg Loves(x,y)] \lor [\exists y \ Loves(y,x)] .$$
  Notice how a universal quantifier ($\forall y$) in the premise of the implication has become an existential quantifier. The sentence now reads "Either there is some animal that x doesn't love, or (if this is not the case) someone loves x." Clearly, the meaning of the original sentence has been preserved.
- **Standardize variables**: For sentences like $(\exists x \, P(x)) \lor (\exists x \, Q(x))$ which use the same variable name twice, change the name of one of the variables. This avoids confusion later when we drop the quantifiers. Thus, we have
$$\forall x \ [\exists y \ Animal(y) \land \neg Loves(x,y)] \lor [\exists z \ Loves(z,x)] .$$
- SKOLEMIZATION **Skolemize**: **Skolemization** is the process of removing existential quantifiers by elimination. In the simple case, it is just like the Existential Instantiation rule of Section 1: translate $\exists x \ P(x)$ into $P(A)$, where A is a new constant. However, we can't apply Existential Instantiation to our sentence above because it doesn't match the pattern $\exists v \ \alpha$; only parts of the sentence match the pattern. If we blindly apply the rule to the two matching parts we get
$$\forall x \ [Animal(A) \land \neg Loves(x,A)] \lor Loves(B,x) ,$$
  which has the wrong meaning entirely: it says that everyone either fails to love a particular animal A or is loved by some particular entity B. In fact, our original sentence allows each person to fail to love a different animal or to be loved by a different person. Thus, we want the Skolem entities to depend on x and z:
$$\forall x \ [Animal(F(x)) \land \neg Loves(x,F(x))] \lor Loves(G(z),x) .$$
  SKOLEM FUNCTION Here F and G are **Skolem functions**. The general rule is that the arguments of the Skolem function are all the universally quantified variables in whose scope the existential quantifier appears. As with Existential Instantiation, the Skolemized sentence is satisfiable exactly when the original sentence is satisfiable.

- **Drop universal quantifiers**: At this point, all remaining variables must be universally quantified. Moreover, the sentence is equivalent to one in which all the universal quantifiers have been moved to the left. We can therefore drop the universal quantifiers:

$$[Animal(F(x)) \land \neg Loves(x, F(x))] \lor Loves(G(z), x) .$$

- **Distribute $\lor$ over $\land$**:

$$[Animal(F(x)) \lor Loves(G(z), x)] \land [\neg Loves(x, F(x)) \lor Loves(G(z), x)] .$$

  This step may also require flattening out nested conjunctions and disjunctions.

The sentence is now in CNF and consists of two clauses. It is quite unreadable. (It may help to explain that the Skolem function $F(x)$ refers to the animal potentially unloved by x, whereas $G(z)$ refers to someone who might love x.) Fortunately, humans seldom need look at CNF sentences—the translation process is easily automated.

5.2 The resolution inference rule

The resolution rule for first-order clauses is simply a lifted version of the propositional resolution rule. Two clauses, which are assumed to be standardized apart so that they share no variables, can be resolved if they contain complementary literals. Propositional literals are complementary if one is the negation of the other; first-order literals are complementary if one *unifies with* the negation of the other. Thus, we have

$$\frac{\ell_1 \lor \cdots \lor \ell_k, \qquad m_1 \lor \cdots \lor m_n}{\textsc{Subst}(\theta, \ell_1 \lor \cdots \lor \ell_{i-1} \lor \ell_{i+1} \lor \cdots \lor \ell_k \lor m_1 \lor \cdots \lor m_{j-1} \lor m_{j+1} \lor \cdots \lor m_n)}$$

where $\textsc{Unify}(\ell_i, \neg m_j) = \theta$. For example, we can resolve the two clauses

$$[Animal(F(x)) \lor Loves(G(x), x)] \quad \text{and} \quad [\neg Loves(u, v) \lor \neg Kills(u, v)]$$

by eliminating the complementary literals $Loves(G(x), x)$ and $\neg Loves(u, v)$, with unifier $\theta = \{u/G(x), v/x\}$, to produce the **resolvent** clause

$$[Animal(F(x)) \lor \neg Kills(G(x), x)] .$$

BINARY RESOLUTION

This rule is called the **binary resolution** rule because it resolves exactly two literals. The binary resolution rule by itself does not yield a complete inference procedure. The full resolution rule resolves subsets of literals in each clause that are unifiable. An alternative approach is to extend **factoring**—the removal of redundant literals—to the first-order case. Propositional factoring reduces two literals to one if they are *identical*; first-order factoring reduces two literals to one if they are *unifiable*. The unifier must be applied to the entire clause. The combination of binary resolution and factoring is complete.

5.3 Example proofs

Resolution proves that $KB \models \alpha$ by proving $KB \land \neg\alpha$ unsatisfiable, that is, by deriving the empty clause. The algorithmic approach is identical to the propositional case, so we need not

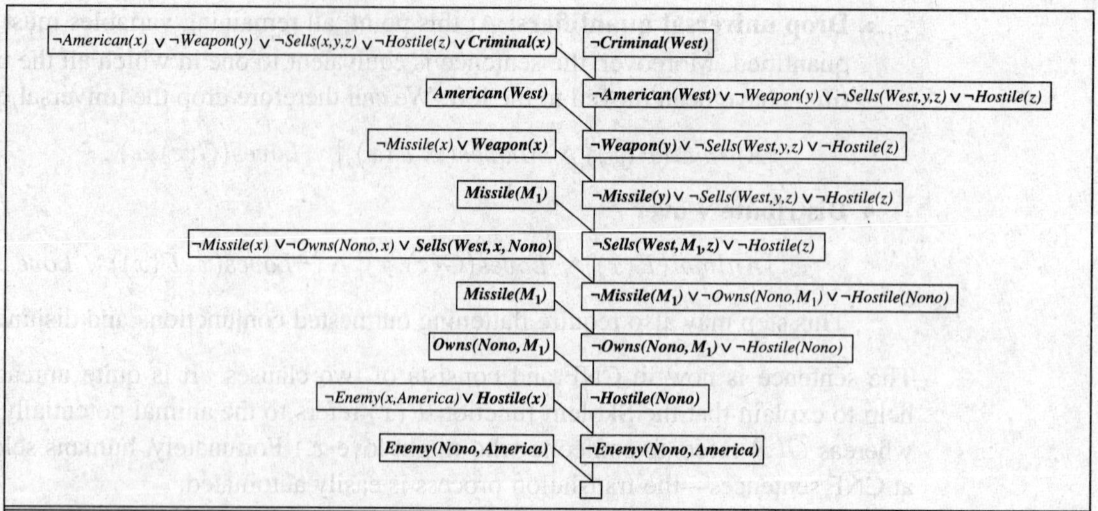

Figure 11 A resolution proof that West is a criminal. At each step, the literals that unify are in bold.

repeat it here. Instead, we give two example proofs. The first is the crime example from Section 3. The sentences in CNF are

$$\neg American(x) \vee \neg Weapon(y) \vee \neg Sells(x, y, z) \vee \neg Hostile(z) \vee Criminal(x)$$
$$\neg Missile(x) \vee \neg Owns(Nono, x) \vee Sells(West, x, Nono)$$
$$\neg Enemy(x, America) \vee Hostile(x)$$
$$\neg Missile(x) \vee Weapon(x)$$
$$Owns(Nono, M_1) \qquad\qquad Missile(M_1)$$
$$American(West) \qquad\qquad Enemy(Nono, America)\,.$$

We also include the negated goal $\neg Criminal(West)$. The resolution proof is shown in Figure 11. Notice the structure: single "spine" beginning with the goal clause, resolving against clauses from the knowledge base until the empty clause is generated. This is characteristic of resolution on Horn clause knowledge bases. In fact, the clauses along the main spine correspond *exactly* to the consecutive values of the *goals* variable in the backward-chaining algorithm of Figure 6. This is because we always choose to resolve with a clause whose positive literal unified with the leftmost literal of the "current" clause on the spine; this is exactly what happens in backward chaining. Thus, backward chaining is just a special case of resolution with a particular control strategy to decide which resolution to perform next.

Our second example makes use of Skolemization and involves clauses that are not definite clauses. This results in a somewhat more complex proof structure. In English, the problem is as follows:

Everyone who loves all animals is loved by someone.
Anyone who kills an animal is loved by no one.
Jack loves all animals.
Either Jack or Curiosity killed the cat, who is named Tuna.
Did Curiosity kill the cat?

First, we express the original sentences, some background knowledge, and the negated goal G in first-order logic:

A. $\forall x\ [\forall y\ Animal(y) \Rightarrow Loves(x,y)] \Rightarrow [\exists y\ Loves(y,x)]$

B. $\forall x\ [\exists z\ Animal(z) \wedge Kills(x,z)] \Rightarrow [\forall y\ \neg Loves(y,x)]$

C. $\forall x\ Animal(x) \Rightarrow Loves(Jack, x)$

D. $Kills(Jack, Tuna) \vee Kills(Curiosity, Tuna)$

E. $Cat(Tuna)$

F. $\forall x\ Cat(x) \Rightarrow Animal(x)$

¬G. $\neg Kills(Curiosity, Tuna)$

Now we apply the conversion procedure to convert each sentence to CNF:

A1. $Animal(F(x)) \vee Loves(G(x), x)$

A2. $\neg Loves(x, F(x)) \vee Loves(G(x), x)$

B. $\neg Loves(y,x) \vee \neg Animal(z) \vee \neg Kills(x,z)$

C. $\neg Animal(x) \vee Loves(Jack, x)$

D. $Kills(Jack, Tuna) \vee Kills(Curiosity, Tuna)$

E. $Cat(Tuna)$

F. $\neg Cat(x) \vee Animal(x)$

¬G. $\neg Kills(Curiosity, Tuna)$

The resolution proof that Curiosity killed the cat is given in Figure 12. In English, the proof could be paraphrased as follows:

> Suppose Curiosity did not kill Tuna. We know that either Jack or Curiosity did; thus Jack must have. Now, Tuna is a cat and cats are animals, so Tuna is an animal. Because anyone who kills an animal is loved by no one, we know that no one loves Jack. On the other hand, Jack loves all animals, so someone loves him; so we have a contradiction. Therefore, Curiosity killed the cat.

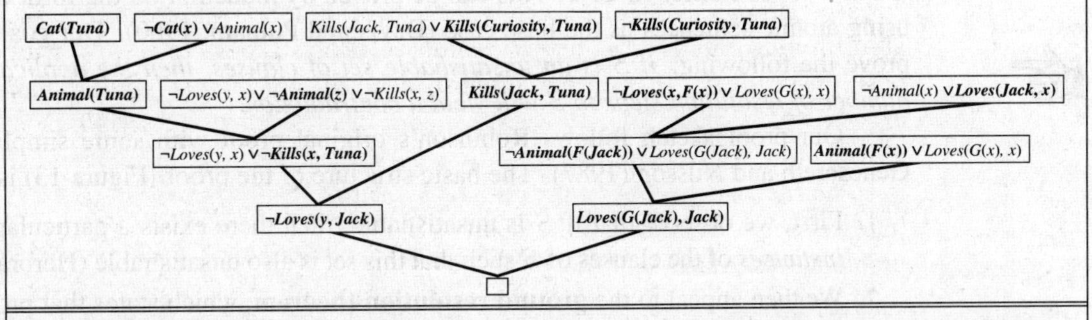

Figure 12 A resolution proof that Curiosity killed the cat. Notice the use of factoring in the derivation of the clause $Loves(G(Jack), Jack)$. Notice also in the upper right, the unification of $Loves(x, F(x))$ and $Loves(Jack, x)$ can only succeed after the variables have been standardized apart.

The proof answers the question "Did Curiosity kill the cat?" but often we want to pose more general questions, such as "Who killed the cat?" Resolution can do this, but it takes a little more work to obtain the answer. The goal is $\exists\, w\ Kills(w, Tuna)$, which, when negated, becomes $\neg Kills(w, Tuna)$ in CNF. Repeating the proof in Figure 12 with the new negated goal, we obtain a similar proof tree, but with the substitution $\{w/Curiosity\}$ in one of the steps. So, in this case, finding out who killed the cat is just a matter of keeping track of the bindings for the query variables in the proof.

NONCONSTRUCTIVE PROOF

Unfortunately, resolution can produce **nonconstructive proofs** for existential goals. For example, $\neg Kills(w, Tuna)$ resolves with $Kills(Jack, Tuna) \lor Kills(Curiosity, Tuna)$ to give $Kills(Jack, Tuna)$, which resolves again with $\neg Kills(w, Tuna)$ to yield the empty clause. Notice that w has two different bindings in this proof; resolution is telling us that, yes, someone killed Tuna—either Jack or Curiosity. This is no great surprise! One solution is to restrict the allowed resolution steps so that the query variables can be bound only once in a given proof; then we need to be able to backtrack over the possible bindings. Another solution is to add a special **answer literal** to the negated goal, which becomes $\neg Kills(w, Tuna) \lor Answer(w)$. Now, the resolution process generates an answer whenever a clause is generated containing just a *single* answer literal. For the proof in Figure 12, this is $Answer(Curiosity)$. The nonconstructive proof would generate the clause $Answer(Curiosity) \lor Answer(Jack)$, which does not constitute an answer.

ANSWER LITERAL

5.4 Completeness of resolution

This section gives a completeness proof of resolution. It can be safely skipped by those who are willing to take it on faith.

REFUTATION COMPLETENESS

We show that resolution is **refutation-complete**, which means that *if* a set of sentences is unsatisfiable, then resolution will always be able to derive a contradiction. Resolution cannot be used to generate all logical consequences of a set of sentences, but it can be used to establish that a given sentence is entailed by the set of sentences. Hence, it can be used to find all answers to a given question, $Q(x)$, by proving that $KB \land \neg Q(x)$ is unsatisfiable.

We take it as given that any sentence in first-order logic (without equality) can be rewritten as a set of clauses in CNF. This can be proved by induction on the form of the sentence, using atomic sentences as the base case (Davis and Putnam, 1960). Our goal therefore is to prove the following: *if S is an unsatisfiable set of clauses, then the application of a finite number of resolution steps to S will yield a contradiction.*

Our proof sketch follows Robinson's original proof with some simplifications from Genesereth and Nilsson (1987). The basic structure of the proof (Figure 13) is as follows:

1. First, we observe that if S is unsatisfiable, then there exists a particular set of *ground instances* of the clauses of S such that this set is also unsatisfiable (Herbrand's theorem).
2. We then appeal to the **ground resolution theorem,** which states that propositional resolution is complete for ground sentences.
3. We then use a **lifting lemma** to show that, for any propositional resolution proof using the set of ground sentences, there is a corresponding first-order resolution proof using the first-order sentences from which the ground sentences were obtained.

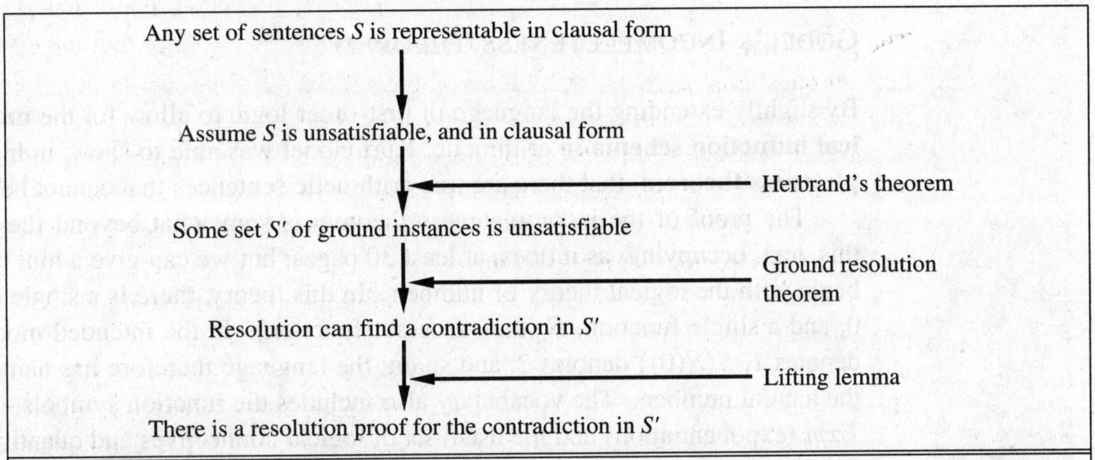

Figure 13 Structure of a completeness proof for resolution.

To carry out the first step, we need three new concepts:

HERBRAND UNIVERSE

- **Herbrand universe**: If S is a set of clauses, then H_S, the Herbrand universe of S, is the set of all ground terms constructable from the following:
  a. The function symbols in S, if any.
  b. The constant symbols in S, if any; if none, then the constant symbol A.

  For example, if S contains just the clause $\neg P(x, F(x, A)) \vee \neg Q(x, A) \vee R(x, B)$, then H_S is the following infinite set of ground terms:
  $$\{A, B, F(A, A), F(A, B), F(B, A), F(B, B), F(A, F(A, A)), \ldots\}.$$

SATURATION

- **Saturation**: If S is a set of clauses and P is a set of ground terms, then $P(S)$, the saturation of S with respect to P, is the set of all ground clauses obtained by applying all possible consistent substitutions of ground terms in P with variables in S.

HERBRAND BASE

- **Herbrand base**: The saturation of a set S of clauses with respect to its Herbrand universe is called the Herbrand base of S, written as $H_S(S)$. For example, if S contains solely the clause just given, then $H_S(S)$ is the infinite set of clauses
  $$\begin{aligned}\{&\neg P(A, F(A, A)) \vee \neg Q(A, A) \vee R(A, B),\\ &\neg P(B, F(B, A)) \vee \neg Q(B, A) \vee R(B, B),\\ &\neg P(F(A, A), F(F(A, A), A)) \vee \neg Q(F(A, A), A) \vee R(F(A, A), B),\\ &\neg P(F(A, B), F(F(A, B), A)) \vee \neg Q(F(A, B), A) \vee R(F(A, B), B), \ldots\}\end{aligned}$$

HERBRAND'S THEOREM

These definitions allow us to state a form of **Herbrand's theorem** (Herbrand, 1930):

> If a set S of clauses is unsatisfiable, then there exists a finite subset of $H_S(S)$ that is also unsatisfiable.

Let S' be this finite subset of ground sentences. Now, we can appeal to the ground resolution theorem to show that the **resolution closure** $RC(S')$ contains the empty clause. That is, running propositional resolution to completion on S' will derive a contradiction.

Now that we have established that there is always a resolution proof involving some finite subset of the Herbrand base of S, the next step is to show that there is a resolution

GÖDEL'S INCOMPLETENESS THEOREM

By slightly extending the language of first-order logic to allow for the **mathematical induction schema** in arithmetic, Kurt Gödel was able to show, in his **incompleteness theorem**, that there are true arithmetic sentences that cannot be proved.

The proof of the incompleteness theorem is somewhat beyond the scope of this text, occupying, as it does, at least 30 pages, but we can give a hint here. We begin with the logical theory of numbers. In this theory, there is a single constant, 0, and a single function, S (the successor function). In the intended model, $S(0)$ denotes 1, $S(S(0))$ denotes 2, and so on; the language therefore has names for all the natural numbers. The vocabulary also includes the function symbols $+$, $\times$, and *Expt* (exponentiation) and the usual set of logical connectives and quantifiers. The first step is to notice that the set of sentences that we can write in this language can be enumerated. (Imagine defining an alphabetical order on the symbols and then arranging, in alphabetical order, each of the sets of sentences of length 1, 2, and so on.) We can then number each sentence α with a unique natural number $\#\alpha$ (the **Gödel number**). This is crucial: number theory contains a name for each of its own sentences. Similarly, we can number each possible proof P with a Gödel number $G(P)$, because a proof is simply a finite sequence of sentences.

Now suppose we have a recursively enumerable set A of sentences that are true statements about the natural numbers. Recalling that A can be named by a given set of integers, we can imagine writing in our language a sentence $\alpha(j, A)$ of the following sort:

> $\forall i$ i is not the Gödel number of a proof of the sentence whose Gödel number is j, where the proof uses only premises in A.

Then let σ be the sentence $\alpha(\#\sigma, A)$, that is, a sentence that states its own unprovability from A. (That this sentence always exists is true but not entirely obvious.)

Now we make the following ingenious argument: Suppose that σ *is* provable from A; then σ is false (because σ says it cannot be proved). But then we have a false sentence that is provable from A, so A cannot consist of only true sentences—a violation of our premise. Therefore, σ is *not* provable from A. But this is exactly what σ itself claims; hence σ is a true sentence.

So, we have shown (barring $29\frac{1}{2}$ pages) that for any set of true sentences of number theory, and in particular any set of basic axioms, there are other true sentences that *cannot* be proved from those axioms. This establishes, among other things, that we can never prove all the theorems of mathematics *within any given system of axioms*. Clearly, this was an important discovery for mathematics. Its significance for AI has been widely debated, beginning with speculations by Gödel himself.

proof using the clauses of S itself, which are not necessarily ground clauses. We start by considering a single application of the resolution rule. Robinson stated this lemma:

> Let C_1 and C_2 be two clauses with no shared variables, and let C_1' and C_2' be ground instances of C_1 and C_2. If C' is a resolvent of C_1' and C_2', then there exists a clause C such that (1) C is a resolvent of C_1 and C_2 and (2) C' is a ground instance of C.

LIFTING LEMMA

This is called a **lifting lemma**, because it lifts a proof step from ground clauses up to general first-order clauses. In order to prove his basic lifting lemma, Robinson had to invent unification and derive all of the properties of most general unifiers. Rather than repeat the proof here, we simply illustrate the lemma:

$$\begin{aligned}
C_1 &= \neg P(x, F(x, A)) \lor \neg Q(x, A) \lor R(x, B) \\
C_2 &= \neg N(G(y), z) \lor P(H(y), z) \\
C_1' &= \neg P(H(B), F(H(B), A)) \lor \neg Q(H(B), A) \lor R(H(B), B) \\
C_2' &= \neg N(G(B), F(H(B), A)) \lor P(H(B), F(H(B), A)) \\
C' &= \neg N(G(B), F(H(B), A)) \lor \neg Q(H(B), A) \lor R(H(B), B) \\
C &= \neg N(G(y), F(H(y), A)) \lor \neg Q(H(y), A) \lor R(H(y), B)\,.
\end{aligned}$$

We see that indeed C' is a ground instance of C. In general, for C_1' and C_2' to have any resolvents, they must be constructed by first applying to C_1 and C_2 the most general unifier of a pair of complementary literals in C_1 and C_2. From the lifting lemma, it is easy to derive a similar statement about any sequence of applications of the resolution rule:

> For any clause C' in the resolution closure of S' there is a clause C in the resolution closure of S such that C' is a ground instance of C and the derivation of C is the same length as the derivation of C'.

From this fact, it follows that if the empty clause appears in the resolution closure of S', it must also appear in the resolution closure of S. This is because the empty clause cannot be a ground instance of any other clause. To recap: we have shown that if S is unsatisfiable, then there is a finite derivation of the empty clause using the resolution rule.

The lifting of theorem proving from ground clauses to first-order clauses provides a vast increase in power. This increase comes from the fact that the first-order proof need instantiate variables only as far as necessary for the proof, whereas the ground-clause methods were required to examine a huge number of arbitrary instantiations.

5.5 Equality

None of the inference methods described so far in this chapter handle an assertion of the form $x = y$. Three distinct approaches can be taken. The first approach is to axiomatize equality—to write down sentences about the equality relation in the knowledge base. We need to say that equality is reflexive, symmetric, and transitive, and we also have to say that we can substitute equals for equals in any predicate or function. So we need three basic axioms, and then one for each predicate and function:

$$\forall x \; x = x$$
$$\forall x, y \; x = y \Rightarrow y = x$$
$$\forall x, y, z \; x = y \wedge y = z \Rightarrow x = z$$

$$\forall x, y \; x = y \Rightarrow (P_1(x) \Leftrightarrow P_1(y))$$
$$\forall x, y \; x = y \Rightarrow (P_2(x) \Leftrightarrow P_2(y))$$
$$\vdots$$
$$\forall w, x, y, z \; w = y \wedge x = z \Rightarrow (F_1(w, x) = F_1(y, z))$$
$$\forall w, x, y, z \; w = y \wedge x = z \Rightarrow (F_2(w, x) = F_2(y, z))$$
$$\vdots$$

Given these sentences, a standard inference procedure such as resolution can perform tasks requiring equality reasoning, such as solving mathematical equations. However, these axioms will generate a lot of conclusions, most of them not helpful to a proof. So there has been a search for more efficient ways of handling equality. One alternative is to add inference rules rather than axioms. The simplest rule, **demodulation**, takes a unit clause $x = y$ and some clause α that contains the term x, and yields a new clause formed by substituting y for x within α. It works if the term within α unifies with x; it need not be exactly equal to x. Note that demodulation is directional; given $x = y$, the x always gets replaced with y, never vice versa. That means that demodulation can be used for simplifying expressions using demodulators such as $x + 0 = x$ or $x^1 = x$. As another example, given

$$Father(Father(x)) = PaternalGrandfather(x)$$
$$Birthdate(Father(Father(Bella)), 1926)$$

we can conclude by demodulation

$$Birthdate(PaternalGrandfather(Bella), 1926) .$$

More formally, we have

DEMODULATION

- **Demodulation**: For any terms x, y, and z, where z appears somewhere in literal m_i and where $\text{UNIFY}(x, z) = \theta$,

$$\frac{x = y, \qquad m_1 \vee \cdots \vee m_n}{\text{SUB}(\text{SUBST}(\theta, x), \text{SUBST}(\theta, y), m_1 \vee \cdots \vee m_n)} .$$

where SUBST is the usual substitution of a binding list, and $\text{SUB}(x, y, m)$ means to replace x with y everywhere that x occurs within m.

The rule can also be extended to handle non-unit clauses in which an equality literal appears:

PARAMODULATION

- **Paramodulation**: For any terms x, y, and z, where z appears somewhere in literal m_i, and where $\text{UNIFY}(x, z) = \theta$,

$$\frac{\ell_1 \vee \cdots \vee \ell_k \vee x = y, \qquad m_1 \vee \cdots \vee m_n}{\text{SUB}(\text{SUBST}(\theta, x), \text{SUBST}(\theta, y), \text{SUBST}(\theta, \ell_1 \vee \cdots \vee \ell_k \vee m_1 \vee \cdots \vee m_n)} .$$

For example, from

$$P(F(x, B), x) \vee Q(x) \quad \text{and} \quad F(A, y) = y \vee R(y)$$

we have $\theta = \text{UNIFY}(F(A, y), F(x, B)) = \{x/A, y/B\}$, and we can conclude by paramodulation the sentence

$$P(B, A) \vee Q(A) \vee R(B) .$$

Paramodulation yields a complete inference procedure for first-order logic with equality.

A third approach handles equality reasoning entirely within an extended unification algorithm. That is, terms are unifiable if they are *provably* equal under some substitution, where "provably" allows for equality reasoning. For example, the terms $1 + 2$ and $2 + 1$ normally are not unifiable, but a unification algorithm that knows that $x + y = y + x$ could unify them with the empty substitution. **Equational unification** of this kind can be done with efficient algorithms designed for the particular axioms used (commutativity, associativity, and so on) rather than through explicit inference with those axioms. Theorem provers using this technique are closely related to the CLP systems described in Section 4.

EQUATIONAL UNIFICATION

5.6 Resolution strategies

We know that repeated applications of the resolution inference rule will eventually find a proof if one exists. In this subsection, we examine strategies that help find proofs *efficiently*.

UNIT PREFERENCE

Unit preference: This strategy prefers to do resolutions where one of the sentences is a single literal (also known as a **unit clause**). The idea behind the strategy is that we are trying to produce an empty clause, so it might be a good idea to prefer inferences that produce shorter clauses. Resolving a unit sentence (such as P) with any other sentence (such as $\neg P \vee \neg Q \vee R$) always yields a clause (in this case, $\neg Q \vee R$) that is shorter than the other clause. When the unit preference strategy was first tried for propositional inference in 1964, it led to a dramatic speedup, making it feasible to prove theorems that could not be handled without the preference. **Unit resolution** is a restricted form of resolution in which every resolution step must involve a unit clause. Unit resolution is incomplete in general, but complete for Horn clauses. Unit resolution proofs on Horn clauses resemble forward chaining.

The OTTER theorem prover (Organized Techniques for Theorem-proving and Effective Research, McCune, 1992), uses a form of best-first search. Its heuristic function measures the "weight" of each clause, where lighter clauses are preferred. The exact choice of heuristic is up to the user, but generally, the weight of a clause should be correlated with its size or difficulty. Unit clauses are treated as light; the search can thus be seen as a generalization of the unit preference strategy.

SET OF SUPPORT

Set of support: Preferences that try certain resolutions first are helpful, but in general it is more effective to try to eliminate some potential resolutions altogether. For example, we can insist that every resolution step involve at least one element of a special set of clauses—the *set of support*. The resolvent is then added into the set of support. If the set of support is small relative to the whole knowledge base, the search space will be reduced dramatically.

We have to be careful with this approach because a bad choice for the set of support will make the algorithm incomplete. However, if we choose the set of support S so that the remainder of the sentences are jointly satisfiable, then set-of-support resolution is complete. For example, one can use the negated query as the set of support, on the assumption that the original knowledge base is consistent. (After all, if it is not consistent, then the fact that the query follows from it is vacuous.) The set-of-support strategy has the additional advantage of generating goal-directed proof trees that are often easy for humans to understand.

INPUT RESOLUTION **Input resolution**: In this strategy, every resolution combines one of the input sentences (from the KB or the query) with some other sentence. The proof in Figure 11 uses only input resolutions and has the characteristic shape of a single "spine" with single sentences combining onto the spine. Clearly, the space of proof trees of this shape is smaller than the space of all proof graphs. In Horn knowledge bases, Modus Ponens is a kind of input resolution strategy, because it combines an implication from the original KB with some other sentences. Thus, it is no surprise that input resolution is complete for knowledge bases that are in Horn form, but LINEAR RESOLUTION incomplete in the general case. The **linear resolution** strategy is a slight generalization that allows P and Q to be resolved together either if P is in the original KB or if P is an ancestor of Q in the proof tree. Linear resolution is complete.

SUBSUMPTION **Subsumption**: The subsumption method eliminates all sentences that are subsumed by (that is, more specific than) an existing sentence in the KB. For example, if $P(x)$ is in the KB, then there is no sense in adding $P(A)$ and even less sense in adding $P(A) \vee Q(B)$. Subsumption helps keep the KB small and thus helps keep the search space small.

Practical uses of resolution theorem provers

SYNTHESIS VERIFICATION Theorem provers can be applied to the problems involved in the **synthesis** and **verification** of both hardware and software. Thus, theorem-proving research is carried out in the fields of hardware design, programming languages, and software engineering—not just in AI.

In the case of hardware, the axioms describe the interactions between signals and circuit elements. Logical reasoners designed specially for verification have been able to verify entire CPUs, including their timing properties (Srivas and Bickford, 1990). The AURA theorem prover has been applied to design circuits that are more compact than any previous design (Wojciechowski and Wojcik, 1983).

In the case of software, reasoning about programs is quite similar to reasoning about actions: axioms describe the preconditions and effects of each statement. The formal synthesis of algorithms was one of the first uses of theorem provers, as outlined by Cordell Green (1969a), who built on earlier ideas by Herbert Simon (1963). The idea is to constructively DEDUCTIVE SYNTHESIS prove a theorem to the effect that "there exists a program p satisfying a certain specification." Although fully automated deductive synthesis, as it is called, has not yet become feasible for general-purpose programming, hand-guided **deductive synthesis** has been successful in designing several novel and sophisticated algorithms. Synthesis of special-purpose programs, such as scientific computing code, is also an active area of research.

Similar techniques are now being applied to software verification by systems such as the SPIN model checker (Holzmann, 1997). For example, the Remote Agent spacecraft control program was verified before and after flight (Havelund *et al.*, 2000). The RSA public key encryption algorithm and the Boyer–Moore string-matching algorithm have been verified this way (Boyer and Moore, 1984).

6 SUMMARY

We have presented an analysis of logical inference in first-order logic and a number of algorithms for doing it.

- A first approach uses inference rules (**universal instantiation** and **existential instantiation**) to **propositionalize** the inference problem. Typically, this approach is slow, unless the domain is small.
- The use of **unification** to identify appropriate substitutions for variables eliminates the instantiation step in first-order proofs, making the process more efficient in many cases.
- A lifted version of **Modus Ponens** uses unification to provide a natural and powerful inference rule, **generalized Modus Ponens**. The **forward-chaining** and **backward-chaining** algorithms apply this rule to sets of definite clauses.
- Generalized Modus Ponens is complete for definite clauses, although the entailment problem is **semidecidable**. For **Datalog** knowledge bases consisting of function-free definite clauses, entailment is decidable.
- Forward chaining is used in **deductive databases**, where it can be combined with relational database operations. It is also used in **production systems**, which perform efficient updates with very large rule sets. Forward chaining is complete for Datalog and runs in polynomial time.
- Backward chaining is used in **logic programming systems**, which employ sophisticated compiler technology to provide very fast inference. Backward chaining suffers from redundant inferences and infinite loops; these can be alleviated by **memoization**.
- Prolog, unlike first-order logic, uses a closed world with the unique names assumption and negation as failure. These make Prolog a more practical programming language, but bring it further from pure logic.
- The generalized **resolution** inference rule provides a complete proof system for first-order logic, using knowledge bases in conjunctive normal form.
- Several strategies exist for reducing the search space of a resolution system without compromising completeness. One of the most important issues is dealing with equality; we showed how **demodulation** and **paramodulation** can be used.
- Efficient resolution-based theorem provers have been used to prove interesting mathematical theorems and to verify and synthesize software and hardware.

BIBLIOGRAPHICAL AND HISTORICAL NOTES

Gottlob Frege, who developed full first-order logic in 1879, based his system of inference on a collection of valid schemas plus a single inference rule, Modus Ponens. Whitehead and Russell (1910) expounded the so-called *rules of passage* (the actual term is from Herbrand (1930)) that are used to move quantifiers to the front of formulas. Skolem constants and Skolem functions were introduced, appropriately enough, by Thoralf Skolem (1920). Oddly enough, it was Skolem who introduced the Herbrand universe (Skolem, 1928).

Herbrand's theorem (Herbrand, 1930) has played a vital role in the development of automated reasoning. Herbrand is also the inventor of unification. Gödel (1930) built on the ideas of Skolem and Herbrand to show that first-order logic has a complete proof procedure. Alan Turing (1936) and Alonzo Church (1936) simultaneously showed, using very different proofs, that validity in first-order logic was not decidable. The excellent text by Enderton (1972) explains all of these results in a rigorous yet understandable fashion.

Abraham Robinson proposed that an automated reasoner could be built using propositionalization and Herbrand's theorem, and Paul Gilmore (1960) wrote the first program. Davis and Putnam (1960) introduced the propositionalization method of Section 1. Prawitz (1960) developed the key idea of letting the quest for propositional inconsistency drive the search, and generating terms from the Herbrand universe only when they were necessary to establish propositional inconsistency. After further development by other researchers, this idea led J. A. Robinson (no relation) to develop resolution (Robinson, 1965).

In AI, resolution was adopted for question-answering systems by Cordell Green and Bertram Raphael (1968). Early AI implementations put a good deal of effort into data structures that would allow efficient retrieval of facts; this work is covered in AI programming texts (Charniak *et al.*, 1987; Norvig, 1992; Forbus and de Kleer, 1993). By the early 1970s, **forward chaining** was well established in AI as an easily understandable alternative to resolution. AI applications typically involved large numbers of rules, so it was important to develop efficient rule-matching technology, particularly for incremental updates. The technology for **production systems** was developed to support such applications. The production system language OPS-5 (Forgy, 1981; Brownston *et al.*, 1985), incorporating the efficient
RETE **rete** match process (Forgy, 1982), was used for applications such as the R1 expert system for minicomputer configuration (McDermott, 1982).

The SOAR cognitive architecture (Laird *et al.*, 1987; Laird, 2008) was designed to handle very large rule sets—up to a million rules (Doorenbos, 1994). Example applications of SOAR include controlling simulated fighter aircraft (Jones *et al.*, 1998), airspace management (Taylor *et al.*, 2007), AI characters for computer games (Wintermute *et al.*, 2007), and training tools for soldiers (Wray and Jones, 2005).

The field of **deductive databases** began with a workshop in Toulouse in 1977 that brought together experts in logical inference and database systems (Gallaire and Minker, 1978). Influential work by Chandra and Harel (1980) and Ullman (1985) led to the adoption of Datalog as a standard language for deductive databases. The development of the **magic sets** technique for rule rewriting by Bancilhon *et al.* (1986) allowed forward chaining to borrow the advantage of goal-directedness from backward chaining. Current work includes the idea of integrating multiple databases into a consistent dataspace (Halevy, 2007).

Backward chaining for logical inference appeared first in Hewitt's PLANNER language (1969). Meanwhile, in 1972, Alain Colmerauer had developed and implemented **Prolog** for the purpose of parsing natural language—Prolog's clauses were intended initially as context-free grammar rules (Roussel, 1975; Colmerauer *et al.*, 1973). Much of the theoretical background for logic programming was developed by Robert Kowalski, working with Colmerauer; see Kowalski (1988) and Colmerauer and Roussel (1993) for a historical overview. Efficient Prolog compilers are generally based on the Warren Abstract Machine (WAM) model of computation developed by David H. D. Warren (1983). Van Roy (1990) showed that Prolog programs can be competitive with C programs in terms of speed.

Methods for avoiding unnecessary looping in recursive logic programs were developed independently by Smith *et al.* (1986) and Tamaki and Sato (1986). The latter paper also included memoization for logic programs, a method developed extensively as **tabled logic programming** by David S. Warren. Swift and Warren (1994) show how to extend the WAM to handle tabling, enabling Datalog programs to execute an order of magnitude faster than forward-chaining deductive database systems.

Early work on constraint logic programming was done by Jaffar and Lassez (1987). Jaffar *et al.* (1992) developed the CLP(R) system for handling real-valued constraints. There are now commercial products for solving large-scale configuration and optimization problems with constraint programming; one of the best known is ILOG (Junker, 2003). Answer set programming (Gelfond, 2008) extends Prolog, allowing disjunction and negation.

Texts on logic programming and Prolog, including Shoham (1994), Bratko (2001), Clocksin (2003), and Clocksin and Mellish (2003). Prior to 2000, the *Journal of Logic Programming* was the journal of record; it has now been replaced by *Theory and Practice of Logic Programming*. Logic programming conferences include the International Conference on Logic Programming (ICLP) and the International Logic Programming Symposium (ILPS).

Research into **mathematical theorem proving** began even before the first complete first-order systems were developed. Herbert Gelernter's Geometry Theorem Prover (Gelernter, 1959) used heuristic search methods combined with diagrams for pruning false subgoals and was able to prove some quite intricate results in Euclidean geometry. The demodulation and paramodulation rules for equality reasoning were introduced by Wos *et al.* (1967) and Wos and Robinson (1968), respectively. These rules were also developed independently in the context of term-rewriting systems (Knuth and Bendix, 1970). The incorporation of equality reasoning into the unification algorithm is due to Gordon Plotkin (1972). Jouannaud and Kirchner (1991) survey equational unification from a term-rewriting perspective. An overview of unification is given by Baader and Snyder (2001).

A number of control strategies have been proposed for resolution, beginning with the unit preference strategy (Wos *et al.*, 1964). The set-of-support strategy was proposed by Wos *et al.* (1965) to provide a degree of goal-directedness in resolution. Linear resolution first appeared in Loveland (1970). Genesereth and Nilsson (1987, Chapter 5) provide a short but thorough analysis of a wide variety of control strategies.

A Computational Logic (Boyer and Moore, 1979) is the basic reference on the Boyer-Moore theorem prover. Stickel (1992) covers the Prolog Technology Theorem Prover (PTTP), which combines the advantages of Prolog compilation with the completeness of model elimination. SETHEO (Letz *et al.*, 1992) is another widely used theorem prover based on this approach. LEANTAP (Beckert and Posegga, 1995) is an efficient theorem prover implemented in only 25 lines of Prolog. Weidenbach (2001) describes SPASS, one of the strongest current theorem provers. The most successful theorem prover in recent annual competitions has been VAMPIRE (Riazanov and Voronkov, 2002). The COQ system (Bertot *et al.*, 2004) and the E equational solver (Schulz, 2004) have also proven to be valuable tools for proving correctness. Theorem provers have been used to automatically synthesize and verify software for controlling spacecraft (Denney *et al.*, 2006), including NASA's new Orion capsule (Lowry, 2008). The design of the FM9001 32-bit microprocessor was proved correct by the NQTHM system (Hunt and Brock, 1992). The Conference on Automated Deduction (CADE) runs an annual contest for automated theorem provers. From 2002 through 2008, the most successful system has been VAMPIRE (Riazanov and Voronkov, 2002). Wiedijk (2003) compares the strength of 15 mathematical provers. TPTP (Thousands of Problems for Theorem Provers) is a library of theorem-proving problems, useful for comparing the performance of systems (Sutcliffe and Suttner, 1998; Sutcliffe *et al.*, 2006).

Theorem provers have come up with novel mathematical results that eluded human mathematicians for decades, as detailed in the book *Automated Reasoning and the Discovery of Missing Elegant Proofs* (Wos and Pieper, 2003). The SAM (Semi-Automated Mathematics) program was the first, proving a lemma in lattice theory (Guard *et al.*, 1969). The AURA program has also answered open questions in several areas of mathematics (Wos and Winker, 1983). The Boyer–Moore theorem prover (Boyer and Moore, 1979) was used by Natarajan Shankar to give the first fully rigorous formal proof of Gödel's Incompleteness Theorem (Shankar, 1986). The NUPRL system proved Girard's paradox (Howe, 1987) and Higman's Lemma (Murthy and Russell, 1990). In 1933, Herbert Robbins proposed a simple set of axioms—the **Robbins algebra**—that appeared to define Boolean algebra, but no proof could be found (despite serious work by Alfred Tarski and others). On October 10, 1996, after eight days of computation, EQP (a version of OTTER) found a proof (McCune, 1997).

ROBBINS ALGEBRA

Many early papers in mathematical logic are to be found in *From Frege to Gödel: A Source Book in Mathematical Logic* (van Heijenoort, 1967). Textbooks geared toward automated deduction include the classic *Symbolic Logic and Mechanical Theorem Proving* (Chang and Lee, 1973), as well as more recent works by Duffy (1991), Wos *et al.* (1992), Bibel (1993), and Kaufmann *et al.* (2000). The principal journal for theorem proving is the *Journal of Automated Reasoning*; the main conferences are the annual Conference on Automated Deduction (CADE) and the International Joint Conference on Automated Reasoning (IJCAR). The *Handbook of Automated Reasoning* (Robinson and Voronkov, 2001) collects papers in the field. MacKenzie's *Mechanizing Proof* (2004) covers the history and technology of theorem proving for the popular audience.

EXERCISES

1 Prove that Universal Instantiation is sound and that Existential Instantiation produces an inferentially equivalent knowledge base.

2 From $Likes(Jerry, IceCream)$ it seems reasonable to infer $\exists\, x\ Likes(x, IceCream)$. Write down a general inference rule, **Existential Introduction**, that sanctions this inference. State carefully the conditions that must be satisfied by the variables and terms involved.

EXISTENTIAL INTRODUCTION

3 Suppose a knowledge base contains just one sentence, $\exists x\ AsHighAs(x, Everest)$. Which of the following are legitimate results of applying Existential Instantiation?

a. $AsHighAs(Everest, Everest)$.

b. $AsHighAs(Kilimanjaro, Everest)$.

c. $AsHighAs(Kilimanjaro, Everest) \land AsHighAs(BenNevis, Everest)$ (after two applications).

4 For each pair of atomic sentences, give the most general unifier if it exists:

a. $P(A, B, B), P(x, y, z)$.

b. $Q(y, G(A, B)), Q(G(x, x), y)$.

c. $Older(Father(y), y), Older(Father(x), John)$.

d. $Knows(Father(y), y), Knows(x, x)$.

5 Consider the subsumption lattices shown in Figure 2.

a. Construct the lattice for the sentence $Employs(Mother(John), Father(Richard))$.

b. Construct the lattice for the sentence $Employs(IBM, y)$ ("Everyone works for IBM"). Remember to include every kind of query that unifies with the sentence.

c. Assume that STORE indexes each sentence under every node in its subsumption lattice. Explain how FETCH should work when some of these sentences contain variables; use as examples the sentences in (a) and (b) and the query $Employs(x, Father(x))$.

6 Write down logical representations for the following sentences, suitable for use with Generalized Modus Ponens:

a. Horses, cows, and pigs are mammals.

b. An offspring of a horse is a horse.

c. Bluebeard is a horse.

d. Bluebeard is Charlie's parent.

e. Offspring and parent are inverse relations.

f. Every mammal has a parent.

7 These questions concern concern issues with substitution and Skolemization.

a. Given the premise $\forall x\ \exists y\ P(x, y)$, it is not valid to conclude that $\exists q\ P(q, q)$. Give an example of a predicate P where the first is true but the second is false.

b. Suppose that an inference engine is incorrectly written with the occurs check omitted, so that it allows a literal like $P(x, F(x))$ to be unified with $P(q, q)$. (As mentioned, most standard implementations of Prolog actually do allow this.) Show that such an inference engine will allow the conclusion $\exists y\ P(q, q)$ to be inferred from the premise $\forall x\ \exists y\ P(x, y)$.

c. Suppose that a procedure that converts first-order logic to clausal form incorrectly Skolemizes $\forall x\ \exists y\ \ P(x, y)$ to $P(x, Sk0)$—that is, it replaces y by a Skolem constant rather than by a Skolem function of x. Show that an inference engine that uses such a procedure will likewise allow $\exists q\ \ P(q, q)$ to be inferred from the premise $\forall x\ \exists y\ P(x, y)$.

d. A common error among students is to suppose that, in unification, one is allowed to substitute a term for a Skolem constant instead of for a variable. For instance, they will say that the formulas $P(Sk1)$ and $P(A)$ can be unified under the substitution $\{Sk1/A\}$. Give an example where this leads to an invalid inference.

8 Explain how to write any given 3-SAT problem of arbitrary size using a single first-order definite clause and no more than 30 ground facts.

9 Suppose you are given the following axioms:

1. $0 \le 3$.
2. $7 \le 9$.
3. $\forall x \quad x \le x$.
4. $\forall x \quad x \le x + 0$.
5. $\forall x \quad x + 0 \le x$.
6. $\forall x, y \quad x + y \le y + x$.
7. $\forall w, x, y, z \quad w \le y \land x \le z \;\Rightarrow\; w + x \le y + z$.
8. $\forall x, y, z \quad x \le y \land y \le z \;\Rightarrow\; x \le z$

a. Give a backward-chaining proof of the sentence $7 \le 3 + 9$. (Be sure, of course, to use only the axioms given here, not anything else you may know about arithmetic.) Show only the steps that leads to success, not the irrelevant steps.

b. Give a forward-chaining proof of the sentence $7 \le 3 + 9$. Again, show only the steps that lead to success.

10 A popular children's riddle is "Brothers and sisters have I none, but that man's father is my father's son." Use the rules of the family domain (Section 3.2 of the chapter "First Order Logic") to show who that man is. You may apply any of the inference methods described in this chapter. Why do you think that this riddle is difficult?

11 Suppose we put into a logical knowledge base a segment of the U.S. census data listing the age, city of residence, date of birth, and mother of every person, using social security numbers as identifying constants for each person. Thus, George's age is given by Age(443-65-1282, 56). Which of the following indexing schemes S1–S5 enable an efficient solution for which of the queries Q1–Q4 (assuming normal backward chaining)?

- **S1**: an index for each atom in each position.
- **S2**: an index for each first argument.
- **S3**: an index for each predicate atom.
- **S4**: an index for each *combination* of predicate and first argument.

- **S5**: an index for each *combination* of predicate and second argument and an index for each first argument.
- **Q1**: $Age(443\text{-}44\text{-}4321, x)$
- **Q2**: $ResidesIn(x, Houston)$
- **Q3**: $Mother(x, y)$
- **Q4**: $Age(x, 34) \land ResidesIn(x, TinyTownUSA)$

12 One might suppose that we can avoid the problem of variable conflict in unification during backward chaining by standardizing apart all of the sentences in the knowledge base once and for all. Show that, for some sentences, this approach cannot work. (*Hint*: Consider a sentence in which one part unifies with another.)

13 In this exercise, use the sentences you wrote in Exercise 6 to answer a question by using a backward-chaining algorithm.

a. Draw the proof tree generated by an exhaustive backward-chaining algorithm for the query $\exists h \;\; Horse(h)$, where clauses are matched in the order given.

b. What do you notice about this domain?

c. How many solutions for h actually follow from your sentences?

d. Can you think of a way to find all of them? (*Hint*: See Smith *et al.* (1986).)

14 Trace the execution of the backward-chaining algorithm in Figure 6 when it is applied to solve the crime problem. Show the sequence of values taken on by the *goals* variable, and arrange them into a tree.

15 The following Prolog code defines a predicate `P`. (Remember that uppercase terms are variables, not constants, in Prolog.)

```
P(X,[X|Y]).
P(X,[Y|Z]) :- P(X,Z).
```

a. Show proof trees and solutions for the queries `P(A,[2,1,3])` and `P(2,[1,A,3])`.

b. What standard list operation does `P` represent?

16 This exercise looks at sorting in Prolog.

a. Write Prolog clauses that define the predicate `sorted(L)`, which is true if and only if list `L` is sorted in ascending order.

b. Write a Prolog definition for the predicate `perm(L,M)`, which is true if and only if `L` is a permutation of `M`.

c. Define `sort(L,M)` (`M` is a sorted version of `L`) using `perm` and `sorted`.

d. Run `sort` on longer and longer lists until you lose patience. What is the time complexity of your program?

e. Write a faster sorting algorithm, such as insertion sort or quicksort, in Prolog.

17 This exercise looks at the recursive application of rewrite rules, using logic programming. A rewrite rule (or **demodulator** in OTTER terminology) is an equation with a specified direction. For example, the rewrite rule $x + 0 \rightarrow x$ suggests replacing any expression that matches $x+0$ with the expression x. Rewrite rules are a key component of equational reasoning systems. Use the predicate `rewrite(X,Y)` to represent rewrite rules. For example, the earlier rewrite rule is written as `rewrite(X+0,X)`. Some terms are *primitive* and cannot be further simplified; thus, we write `primitive(0)` to say that 0 is a primitive term.

a. Write a definition of a predicate `simplify(X,Y)`, that is true when `Y` is a simplified version of `X`—that is, when no further rewrite rules apply to any subexpression of `Y`.

b. Write a collection of rules for the simplification of expressions involving arithmetic operators, and apply your simplification algorithm to some sample expressions.

c. Write a collection of rewrite rules for symbolic differentiation, and use them along with your simplification rules to differentiate and simplify expressions involving arithmetic expressions, including exponentiation.

18 This exercise considers the implementation of search algorithms in Prolog. Suppose that `successor(X,Y)` is true when state `Y` is a successor of state `X`; and that `goal(X)` is true when `X` is a goal state. Write a definition for `solve(X,P)`, which means that `P` is a path (list of states) beginning with `X`, ending in a goal state, and consisting of a sequence of legal steps as defined by `successor`. You will find that depth-first search is the easiest way to do this. How easy would it be to add heuristic search control?

19 Suppose a knowledge base contains just the following first-order Horn clauses:

$$Ancestor(Mother(x), x)$$
$$Ancestor(x, y) \wedge Ancestor(y, z) \Rightarrow Ancestor(x, z)$$

Consider a forward chaining algorithm that, on the jth iteration, terminates if the KB contains a sentence that unifies with the query, else adds to the KB every atomic sentence that can be inferred from the sentences already in the KB after iteration $j - 1$.

a. For each of the following queries, say whether the algorithm will (1) give an answer (if so, write down that answer); or (2) terminate with no answer; or (3) never terminate.

(i) $Ancestor(Mother(y), John)$
(ii) $Ancestor(Mother(Mother(y)), John)$
(iii) $Ancestor(Mother(Mother(Mother(y))), Mother(y))$
(iv) $Ancestor(Mother(John), Mother(Mother(John)))$

b. Can a resolution algorithm prove the sentence $\neg Ancestor(John, John)$ from the original knowledge base? Explain how, or why not.

c. Suppose we add the assertion that $\neg(Mother(x) = x)$ and augment the resolution algorithm with inference rules for equality. Now what is the answer to (b)?

20 Let $\mathcal{L}$ be the first-order language with a single predicate $S(p, q)$, meaning "p shaves q." Assume a domain of people.

a. Consider the sentence "There exists a person P who shaves every one who does not shave themselves, and only people that do not shave themselves." Express this in $\mathcal{L}$.

b. Convert the sentence in (a) to clausal form.

c. Construct a resolution proof to show that the clauses in (b) are inherently inconsistent. (Note: you do not need any additional axioms.)

21 How can resolution be used to show that a sentence is valid? Unsatisfiable?

22 Construct an example of two clauses that can be resolved together in two different ways giving two different outcomes.

23 From "Horses are animals," it follows that "The head of a horse is the head of an animal." Demonstrate that this inference is valid by carrying out the following steps:

a. Translate the premise and the conclusion into the language of first-order logic. Use three predicates: $HeadOf(h, x)$ (meaning "h is the head of x"), $Horse(x)$, and $Animal(x)$.

b. Negate the conclusion, and convert the premise and the negated conclusion into conjunctive normal form.

c. Use resolution to show that the conclusion follows from the premise.

24 Here are two sentences in the language of first-order logic:

(A) $\forall x\ \exists y\ (x \geq y)$

(B) $\exists y\ \forall x\ (x \geq y)$

a. Assume that the variables range over all the natural numbers $0, 1, 2, \ldots, \infty$ and that the "$\geq$" predicate means "is greater than or equal to." Under this interpretation, translate (A) and (B) into English.

b. Is (A) true under this interpretation?

c. Is (B) true under this interpretation?

d. Does (A) logically entail (B)?

e. Does (B) logically entail (A)?

f. Using resolution, try to prove that (A) follows from (B). Do this even if you think that (B) does not logically entail (A); continue until the proof breaks down and you cannot proceed (if it does break down). Show the unifying substitution for each resolution step. If the proof fails, explain exactly where, how, and why it breaks down.

g. Now try to prove that (B) follows from (A).

25 Resolution can produce nonconstructive proofs for queries with variables, so we had to introduce special mechanisms to extract definite answers. Explain why this issue does not arise with knowledge bases containing only definite clauses.

26 We said in this chapter that resolution cannot be used to generate all logical consequences of a set of sentences. Can any algorithm do this?

CLASSICAL PLANNING

CLASSICAL PLANNING

In which we see how an agent can take advantage of the structure of a problem to construct complex plans of action.

We define AI as the study of rational action, which means that **planning**—devising a plan of action to achieve one's goals—is a critical part of AI. Two examples of planning agents include: the search-based problem-solving agent and the hybrid logical agent. In this chapter we introduce a representation for planning problems that scales up to problems that could not be handled by those earlier approaches.

Section 1 develops an expressive yet carefully constrained language for representing planning problems. Section 2 shows how forward and backward search algorithms can take advantage of this representation, primarily through accurate heuristics that can be derived automatically from the structure of the representation. (This is analogous to the way in which effective domain-independent heuristics can be constructed for constraint satisfaction problems.) Section 3 shows how a data structure called the planning graph can make the search for a plan more efficient. We then describe a few of the other approaches to planning, and conclude by comparing the various approaches.

This chapter covers fully observable, deterministic, static environments with single agents.

1 DEFINITION OF CLASSICAL PLANNING

A problem-solving agent can find sequences of actions that result in a goal state. But it deals with atomic representations of states and thus needs good domain-specific heuristics to perform well. A hybrid propositional logical agent can find plans without domain-specific heuristics because it uses domain-independent heuristics based on the logical structure of the problem. But it relies on ground (variable-free) propositional inference, which means that it may be swamped when there are many actions and states. For example, in the wumpus world, the simple action of moving a step forward had to be repeated for all four agent orientations, T time steps, and n^2 current locations.

In response to this, planning researchers have settled on a **factored representation**—one in which a state of the world is represented by a collection of variables. We use a language called **PDDL**, the Planning Domain Definition Language, that allows us to express all $4Tn^2$ actions with one action schema. There have been several versions of PDDL; we select a simple version and alter its syntax to be consistent with the rest of the book.[1] We now show how PDDL describes the four things we need to define a search problem: the initial state, the actions that are available in a state, the result of applying an action, and the goal test.

PDDL

Each **state** is represented as a conjunction of fluents that are ground, functionless atoms. For example, $Poor \land Unknown$ might represent the state of a hapless agent, and a state in a package delivery problem might be $At(Truck_1, Melbourne) \land At(Truck_2, Sydney)$. **Database semantics** is used: the closed-world assumption means that any fluents that are not mentioned are false, and the unique names assumption means that $Truck_1$ and $Truck_2$ are distinct. The following fluents are *not* allowed in a state: $At(x, y)$ (because it is non-ground), $\neg Poor$ (because it is a negation), and $At(Father(Fred), Sydney)$ (because it uses a function symbol). The representation of states is carefully designed so that a state can be treated either as a conjunction of fluents, which can be manipulated by logical inference, or as a *set* of fluents, which can be manipulated with set operations. The **set semantics** is sometimes easier to deal with.

SET SEMANTICS

Actions are described by a set of action schemas that implicitly define the ACTIONS(s) and RESULT(s, a) functions needed to do a problem-solving search. Any system for action description needs to solve the frame problem—to say what changes and what stays the same as the result of the action. Classical planning concentrates on problems where most actions leave most things unchanged. Think of a world consisting of a bunch of object on a flat surface. The action of nudging an object causes that object to change its location by a vector Δ.A concise description of the action should mention onlyΔ; it shouldn't have to mention all the object that stay in place. PDDL does that by specifying the result of an action in terms of what changes; everything that stays the same is left unmentioned.

ACTION SCHEMA

A set of ground (variable-free) actions can be represented by a single **action schema**. The schema is a **lifted** representation—it lifts the level of reasoning from propositional logic to a restricted subset of first-order logic. For example, here is an action schema for flying a plane from one location to another:

$$
\begin{aligned}
&Action(Fly(p, from, to),\\
&\quad \text{PRECOND:} At(p, from) \land Plane(p) \land Airport(from) \land Airport(to)\\
&\quad \text{EFFECT:} \neg At(p, from) \land At(p, to))
\end{aligned}
$$

The schema consists of the action name, a list of all the variables used in the schema, a **precondition** and an **effect**. Although we haven't said yet how the action schema converts into logical sentences, think of the variables as being universally quantified. We are free to choose whatever values we want to instantiate the variables. For example, here is one ground

PRECONDITION

EFFECT

[1] PDDL was derived from the original STRIPS planning language(Fikes and Nilsson, 1971). which is slightly more restricted than PDDL: STRIPS preconditions and goals cannot contain negative literals.

action that results from substituting values for all the variables:

$$\begin{aligned}&Action(Fly(P_1, SFO, JFK),\\&\quad \text{PRECOND}: At(P_1, SFO) \wedge Plane(P_1) \wedge Airport(SFO) \wedge Airport(JFK)\\&\quad \text{EFFECT}: \neg At(P_1, SFO) \wedge At(P_1, JFK))\end{aligned}$$

The precondition and effect of an action are each conjunctions of literals (positive or negated atomic sentences). The precondition defines the states in which the action can be executed, and the effect defines the result of executing the action. An action a can be executed in state s if s entails the precondition of a. Entailment can also be expressed with the set semantics: $s \models q$ iff every positive literal in q is in s and every negated literal in q is not. In formal notation we say

$$(a \in \text{ACTIONS}(s)) \Leftrightarrow s \models \text{PRECOND}(a),$$

where any variables in a are universally quantified. For example,

$$\begin{aligned}&\forall\, p, from, to\ \ (Fly(p, from, to) \in \text{ACTIONS}(s)) \Leftrightarrow\\&\quad s \models (At(p, from) \wedge Plane(p) \wedge Airport(from) \wedge Airport(to))\end{aligned}$$

APPLICABLE

We say that action a is **applicable** in state s if the preconditions are satisfied by s. When an action schema a contains variables, it may have multiple applicable instantiations. For example, with the initial state defined in Figure 1, the *Fly* action can be instantiated as $Fly(P_1, SFO, JFK)$ or as $Fly(P_2, JFK, SFO)$, both of which are applicable in the initial state. If an action a has v variables, then, in a domain with k unique names of objects, it takes $O(v^k)$ time in the worst case to find the applicable ground actions.

PROPOSITIONALIZE

Sometimes we want to **propositionalize** a PDDL problem—replace each action schema with a set of ground actions and then use a propositional solver such as SATPLAN to find a solution. However, this is impractical when v and k are large.

DELETE LIST

ADD LIST

The **result** of executing action a in state s is defined as a state s' which is represented by the set of fluents formed by starting with s, removing the fluents that appear as negative literals in the action's effects (what we call the **delete list** or $\text{DEL}(a)$), and adding the fluents that are positive literals in the action's effects (what we call the **add list** or $\text{ADD}(a)$):

$$\text{RESULT}(s, a) = (s - \text{DEL}(a)) \cup \text{ADD}(a)\,. \qquad (1)$$

For example, with the action $Fly(P_1, SFO, JFK)$, we would remove $At(P_1, SFO)$ and add $At(P_1, JFK)$. It is a requirement of action schemas that any variable in the effect must also appear in the precondition. That way, when the precondition is matched against the state s, all the variables will be bound, and $\text{RESULT}(s, a)$ will therefore have only ground atoms. In other words, ground states are closed under the RESULT operation.

Also note that the fluents do not explicitly refer to time. They don't need superscripts for time, and successor-state axioms of the form

$$F^{t+1} \Leftrightarrow ActionCausesF^t \vee (F^t \wedge \neg ActionCausesNotF^t)\,.$$

In PDDL the times and states are implicit in the action schemas: the precondition always refers to time t and the effect to time $t + 1$.

A set of action schemas serves as a definition of a planning *domain*. A specific *problem* within the domain is defined with the addition of an initial state and a goal. The **initial**

$$\begin{array}{l} Init(At(C_1,\ SFO) \wedge At(C_2,\ JFK) \wedge At(P_1,\ SFO) \wedge At(P_2,\ JFK) \\ \quad \wedge\ Cargo(C_1) \wedge Cargo(C_2) \wedge Plane(P_1) \wedge Plane(P_2) \\ \quad \wedge\ Airport(JFK) \wedge Airport(SFO)) \\ Goal(At(C_1,\ JFK) \wedge At(C_2,\ SFO)) \\ Action(Load(c,\ p,\ a), \\ \quad \text{PRECOND: } At(c,\ a) \wedge At(p,\ a) \wedge Cargo(c) \wedge Plane(p) \wedge Airport(a) \\ \quad \text{EFFECT: } \neg\ At(c,\ a) \wedge In(c,\ p)) \\ Action(Unload(c,\ p,\ a), \\ \quad \text{PRECOND: } In(c,\ p) \wedge At(p,\ a) \wedge Cargo(c) \wedge Plane(p) \wedge Airport(a) \\ \quad \text{EFFECT: } At(c,\ a) \wedge \neg\ In(c,\ p)) \\ Action(Fly(p,\ from,\ to), \\ \quad \text{PRECOND: } At(p,\ from) \wedge Plane(p) \wedge Airport(from) \wedge Airport(to) \\ \quad \text{EFFECT: } \neg\ At(p,\ from) \wedge At(p,\ to)) \end{array}$$

Figure 1 A PDDL description of an air cargo transportation planning problem.

INITIAL STATE

GOAL

state is a conjunction of ground atoms. (As with all states, the closed-world assumption is used, which means that any atoms that are not mentioned are false.) The **goal** is just like a precondition: a conjunction of literals (positive or negative) that may contain variables, such as $At(p, SFO) \wedge Plane(p)$. Any variables are treated as existentially quantified, so this goal is to have *any* plane at SFO. The problem is solved when we can find a sequence of actions that end in a state s that entails the goal. For example, the state $Rich \wedge Famous \wedge Miserable$ entails the goal $Rich \wedge Famous$, and the state $Plane(Plane_1) \wedge At(Plane_1, SFO)$ entails the goal $At(p, SFO) \wedge Plane(p)$.

Now we have defined planning as a search problem: we have an initial state, an ACTIONS function, a RESULT function, and a goal test. We'll look at some example problems before investigating efficient search algorithms.

1.1 Example: Air cargo transport

Figure 1 shows an air cargo transport problem involving loading and unloading cargo and flying it from place to place. The problem can be defined with three actions: *Load*, *Unload*, and *Fly*. The actions affect two predicates: $In(c, p)$ means that cargo c is inside plane p, and $At(x, a)$ means that object x (either plane or cargo) is at airport a. Note that some care must be taken to make sure the At predicates are maintained properly. When a plane flies from one airport to another, all the cargo inside the plane goes with it. In first-order logic it would be easy to quantify over all objects that are inside the plane. But basic PDDL does not have a universal quantifier, so we need a different solution. The approach we use is to say that a piece of cargo ceases to be At anywhere when it is In a plane; the cargo only becomes At the new airport when it is unloaded. So At really means "available for use at a given location." The following plan is a solution to the problem:

$$[Load(C_1, P_1, SFO), Fly(P_1, SFO, JFK), Unload(C_1, P_1, JFK), \\ Load(C_2, P_2, JFK), Fly(P_2, JFK, SFO), Unload(C_2, P_2, SFO)]\ .$$

Finally, there is the problem of spurious actions such as $Fly(P_1, JFK, JFK)$, which should be a no-op, but which has contradictory effects (according to the definition, the effect would include $At(P_1, JFK) \wedge \neg At(P_1, JFK)$). It is common to ignore such problems, because they seldom cause incorrect plans to be produced. The correct approach is to add inequality preconditions saying that the *from* and *to* airports must be different; see another example of this in Figure 3.

1.2 Example: The spare tire problem

Consider the problem of changing a flat tire (Figure 2). The goal is to have a good spare tire properly mounted onto the car's axle, where the initial state has a flat tire on the axle and a good spare tire in the trunk. To keep it simple, our version of the problem is an abstract one, with no sticky lug nuts or other complications. There are just four actions: removing the spare from the trunk, removing the flat tire from the axle, putting the spare on the axle, and leaving the car unattended overnight. We assume that the car is parked in a particularly bad neighborhood, so that the effect of leaving it overnight is that the tires disappear. A solution to the problem is $[Remove(Flat, Axle), Remove(Spare, Trunk), PutOn(Spare, Axle)]$.

$Init(Tire(Flat) \wedge Tire(Spare) \wedge At(Flat, Axle) \wedge At(Spare, Trunk))$
$Goal(At(Spare, Axle))$
$Action(Remove(obj, loc),$
  PRECOND: $At(obj, loc)$
  EFFECT: $\neg At(obj, loc) \wedge At(obj, Ground))$
$Action(PutOn(t, Axle),$
  PRECOND: $Tire(t) \wedge At(t, Ground) \wedge \neg At(Flat, Axle)$
  EFFECT: $\neg At(t, Ground) \wedge At(t, Axle))$
$Action(LeaveOvernight,$
  PRECOND:
  EFFECT: $\neg At(Spare, Ground) \wedge \neg At(Spare, Axle) \wedge \neg At(Spare, Trunk)$
  $\wedge \neg At(Flat, Ground) \wedge \neg At(Flat, Axle) \wedge \neg At(Flat, Trunk))$

Figure 2 The simple spare tire problem.

1.3 Example: The blocks world

BLOCKS WORLD

One of the most famous planning domains is known as the **blocks world**. This domain consists of a set of cube-shaped blocks sitting on a table.[2] The blocks can be stacked, but only one block can fit directly on top of another. A robot arm can pick up a block and move it to another position, either on the table or on top of another block. The arm can pick up only one block at a time, so it cannot pick up a block that has another one on it. The goal will always be to build one or more stacks of blocks, specified in terms of what blocks are on top

[2] The blocks world used in planning research is much simpler than SHRDLU's version, which you may be familiar with.

$Init(On(A, Table) \land On(B, Table) \land On(C, A)$
$\quad \land Block(A) \land Block(B) \land Block(C) \land Clear(B) \land Clear(C))$
$Goal(On(A, B) \land On(B, C))$
$Action(Move(b, x, y),$
$\quad$ PRECOND: $On(b, x) \land Clear(b) \land Clear(y) \land Block(b) \land Block(y) \land$
$\qquad (b{\neq}x) \land (b{\neq}y) \land (x{\neq}y),$
$\quad$ EFFECT: $On(b, y) \land Clear(x) \land \neg On(b, x) \land \neg Clear(y))$
$Action(MoveToTable(b, x),$
$\quad$ PRECOND: $On(b, x) \land Clear(b) \land Block(b) \land (b{\neq}x),$
$\quad$ EFFECT: $On(b, Table) \land Clear(x) \land \neg On(b, x))$

Figure 3 A planning problem in the blocks world: building a three-block tower. One solution is the sequence $[MoveToTable(C, A), Move(B, Table, C), Move(A, Table, B)]$.

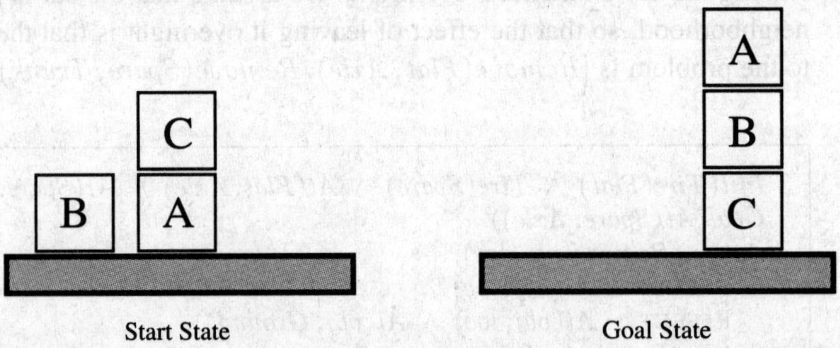

Figure 4 Diagram of the blocks-world problem in Figure 3.

of what other blocks. For example, a goal might be to get block A on B and block B on C (see Figure 4).

We use $On(b, x)$ to indicate that block b is on x, where x is either another block or the table. The action for moving block b from the top of x to the top of y will be $Move(b, x, y)$. Now, one of the preconditions on moving b is that no other block be on it. In first-order logic, this would be $\neg\exists\, x\ On(x, b)$ or, alternatively, $\forall\, x\ \neg On(x, b)$. Basic PDDL does not allow quantifiers, so instead we introduce a predicate $Clear(x)$ that is true when nothing is on x. (The complete problem description is in Figure 3.)

The action *Move* moves a block b from x to y if both b and y are clear. After the move is made, b is still clear but y is not. A first attempt at the *Move* schema is

$$\begin{aligned}&Action(Move(b, x, y),\\ &\quad \text{PRECOND:}\, On(b, x) \land Clear(b) \land Clear(y),\\ &\quad \text{EFFECT:}\, On(b, y) \land Clear(x) \land \neg On(b, x) \land \neg Clear(y))\,.\end{aligned}$$

Unfortunately, this does not maintain *Clear* properly when x or y is the table. When x is the *Table*, this action has the effect $Clear(Table)$, but the table should not become clear; and when $y = Table$, it has the precondition $Clear(Table)$, but the table does not have to be clear for us to move a block onto it. To fix this, we do two things. First, we introduce another action to move a block b from x to the table:

$$\begin{array}{l} Action(MoveToTable(b, x), \\ \quad \text{PRECOND:} On(b, x) \land Clear(b), \\ \quad \text{EFFECT:} On(b, Table) \land Clear(x) \land \neg On(b, x)) \,. \end{array}$$

Second, we take the interpretation of $Clear(x)$ to be "there is a clear space on x to hold a block." Under this interpretation, $Clear(Table)$ will always be true. The only problem is that nothing prevents the planner from using $Move(b, x, Table)$ instead of $MoveToTable(b, x)$. We could live with this problem—it will lead to a larger-than-necessary search space, but will not lead to incorrect answers—or we could introduce the predicate *Block* and add $Block(b) \land Block(y)$ to the precondition of *Move*.

1.4 The complexity of classical planning

In this subsection we consider the theoretical complexity of planning and distinguish two decision problems. **PlanSAT** is the question of whether there exists any plan that solves a planning problem. **Bounded PlanSAT** asks whether there is a solution of length k or less; this can be used to find an optimal plan.

PLANSAT

BOUNDED PLANSAT

The first result is that both decision problems are decidable for classical planning. The proof follows from the fact that the number of states is finite. But if we add function symbols to the language, then the number of states becomes infinite, and PlanSAT becomes only semidecidable: an algorithm exists that will terminate with the correct answer for any solvable problem, but may not terminate on unsolvable problems. The Bounded PlanSAT problem remains decidable even in the presence of function symbols. For proofs of the assertions in this section, see Ghallab *et al.* (2004).

Both PlanSAT and Bounded PlanSAT are in the complexity class PSPACE, a class that is larger (and hence more difficult) than NP and refers to problems that can be solved by a deterministic Turing machine with a polynomial amount of space. Even if we make some rather severe restrictions, the problems remain quite difficult. For example, if we disallow negative effects, both problems are still NP-hard. However, if we also disallow negative preconditions, PlanSAT reduces to the class P.

These worst-case results may seem discouraging. We can take solace in the fact that agents are usually not asked to find plans for arbitrary worst-case problem instances, but rather are asked for plans in specific domains (such as blocks-world problems with n blocks), which can be much easier than the theoretical worst case. For many domains (including the blocks world and the air cargo world), Bounded PlanSAT is NP-complete while PlanSAT is in P; in other words, optimal planning is usually hard, but sub-optimal planning is sometimes easy. To do well on easier-than-worst-case problems, we will need good search heuristics. That's the true advantage of the classical planning formalism: it has facilitated the development of very accurate domain-independent heuristics, whereas systems based on successor-state axioms in first-order logic have had less success in coming up with good heuristics.

2 ALGORITHMS FOR PLANNING AS STATE-SPACE SEARCH

Now we turn our attention to planning algorithms. We saw how the description of a planning problem defines a search problem: we can search from the initial state through the space of states, looking for a goal. One of the nice advantages of the declarative representation of action schemas is that we can also search backward from the goal, looking for the initial state. Figure 5 compares forward and backward searches.

2.1 Forward (progression) state-space search

Now that we have shown how a planning problem maps into a search problem, we can solve planning problems with heuristic search algorithms or a local search algorithm (provided we keep track of the actions used to reach the goal). From the earliest days of planning research (around 1961) until around 1998 it was assumed that forward state-space search was too inefficient to be practical. It is not hard to come up with reasons why.

First, forward search is prone to exploring irrelevant actions. Consider the noble task of buying a copy of *AI: A Modern Approach* from an online bookseller. Suppose there is an

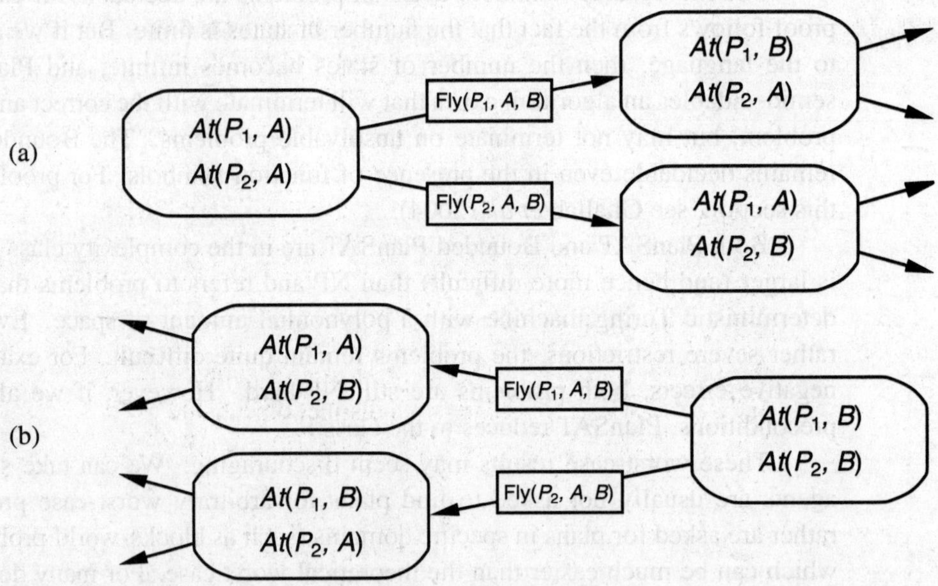

Figure 5 Two approaches to searching for a plan. (a) Forward (progression) search through the space of states, starting in the initial state and using the problem's actions to search forward for a member of the set of goal states. (b) Backward (regression) search through sets of relevant states, starting at the set of states representing the goal and using the inverse of the actions to search backward for the initial state.

action schema $Buy(isbn)$ with effect $Own(isbn)$. ISBNs are 10 digits, so this action schema represents 10 billion ground actions. An uninformed forward-search algorithm would have to start enumerating these 10 billion actions to find one that leads to the goal.

Second, planning problems often have large state spaces. Consider an air cargo problem with 10 airports, where each airport has 5 planes and 20 pieces of cargo. The goal is to move all the cargo at airport A to airport B. There is a simple solution to the problem: load the 20 pieces of cargo into one of the planes at A, fly the plane to B, and unload the cargo. Finding the solution can be difficult because the average branching factor is huge: each of the 50 planes can fly to 9 other airports, and each of the 200 packages can be either unloaded (if it is loaded) or loaded into any plane at its airport (if it is unloaded). So in any state there is a minimum of 450 actions (when all the packages are at airports with no planes) and a maximum of 10,450 (when all packages and planes are at the same airport). On average, let's say there are about 2000 possible actions per state, so the search graph up to the depth of the obvious solution has about 2000^{41} nodes.

Clearly, even this relatively small problem instance is hopeless without an accurate heuristic. Although many real-world applications of planning have relied on domain-specific heuristics, it turns out (as we see in Section 2.3) that strong domain-independent heuristics can be derived automatically; that is what makes forward search feasible.

2.2 Backward (regression) relevant-states search

RELEVANT-STATES

In regression search we start at the goal and apply the actions backward until we find a sequence of steps that reaches the initial state. It is called **relevant-states** search because we only consider actions that are relevant to the goal (or current state). As in belief-state search, there is a *set* of relevant states to consider at each step, not just a single state.

We start with the goal, which is a conjunction of literals forming a description of a set of states—for example, the goal $\neg Poor \wedge Famous$ describes those states in which $Poor$ is false, $Famous$ is true, and any other fluent can have any value. If there are n ground fluents in a domain, then there are 2^n ground states (each fluent can be true or false), but 3^n descriptions of sets of goal states (each fluent can be positive, negative, or not mentioned).

In general, backward search works only when we know how to regress from a state description to the predecessor state description. For example, it is hard to search backwards for a solution to the n-queens problem because there is no easy way to describe the states that are one move away from the goal. Happily, the PDDL representation was designed to make it easy to regress actions—if a domain can be expressed in PDDL, then we can do regression search on it. Given a ground goal description g and a ground action a, the regression from g over a gives us a state description g' defined by

$$g' = (g - \text{ADD}(a)) \cup Precond(a) .$$

That is, the effects that were added by the action need not have been true before, and also the preconditions must have held before, or else the action could not have been executed. Note that $\text{DEL}(a)$ does not appear in the formula; that's because while we know the fluents in $\text{DEL}(a)$ are no longer true after the action, we don't know whether or not they were true before, so there's nothing to be said about them.

To get the full advantage of backward search, we need to deal with partially uninstantiated actions and states, not just ground ones. For example, suppose the goal is to deliver a specific piece of cargo to SFO: $At(C_2, SFO)$. That suggests the action $Unload(C_2, p', SFO)$:

$$\begin{array}{l} Action(Unload(C_2, p', SFO), \\ \quad \text{PRECOND:} In(C_2, p') \wedge At(p', SFO) \wedge Cargo(C_2) \wedge Plane(p') \wedge Airport(SFO) \\ \quad \text{EFFECT:} At(C_2, SFO) \wedge \neg In(C_2, p') \, . \end{array}$$

(Note that we have **standardized** variable names (changing p to p' in this case) so that there will be no confusion between variable names if we happen to use the same action schema twice in a plan. The same approach can be used for first-order logical inference.) This represents unloading the package from an *unspecified* plane at SFO; any plane will do, but we need not say which one now. We can take advantage of the power of first-order representations: a single description summarizes the possibility of using *any* of the planes by implicitly quantifying over p'. The regressed state description is

$$g' = In(C_2, p') \wedge At(p', SFO) \wedge Cargo(C_2) \wedge Plane(p') \wedge Airport(SFO) \, .$$

The final issue is deciding which actions are candidates to regress over. In the forward direction we chose actions that were **applicable**—those actions that could be the next step in the plan. In backward search we want actions that are **relevant**—those actions that could be the *last* step in a plan leading up to the current goal state.

RELEVANCE

For an action to be relevant to a goal it obviously must contribute to the goal: at least one of the action's effects (either positive or negative) must unify with an element of the goal. What is less obvious is that the action must not have any effect (positive or negative) that negates an element of the goal. Now, if the goal is $A \wedge B \wedge C$ and an action has the effect $A \wedge B \wedge \neg C$ then there is a colloquial sense in which that action is very relevant to the goal—it gets us two-thirds of the way there. But it is not relevant in the technical sense defined here, because this action could not be the *final* step of a solution—we would always need at least one more step to achieve C.

Given the goal $At(C_2, SFO)$, several instantiations of $Unload$ are relevant: we could chose any specific plane to unload from, or we could leave the plane unspecified by using the action $Unload(C_2, p', SFO)$. We can reduce the branching factor without ruling out any solutions by always using the action formed by substituting the most general unifier into the (standardized) action schema.

As another example, consider the goal $Own(0136042597)$, given an initial state with 10 billion ISBNs, and the single action schema

$$A = Action(Buy(i), \text{PRECOND:} ISBN(i), \text{EFFECT:} Own(i)) \, .$$

As we mentioned before, forward search without a heuristic would have to start enumerating the 10 billion ground Buy actions. But with backward search, we would unify the goal $Own(0136042597)$ with the (standardized) effect $Own(i')$, yielding the substitution $\theta = \{i'/0136042597\}$. Then we would regress over the action $Subst(\theta, A')$ to yield the predecessor state description $ISBN(0136042597)$. This is part of, and thus entailed by, the initial state, so we are done.

We can make this more formal. Assume a goal description g which contains a goal literal g_i and an action schema A that is standardized to produce A'. If A' has an effect literal e'_j where $Unify(g_i, e'_j) = \theta$ and where we define $a' = \text{SUBST}(\theta, A')$ and if there is no effect in a' that is the negation of a literal in g, then a' is a relevant action towards g.

Backward search keeps the branching factor lower than forward search, for most problem domains. However, the fact that backward search uses state sets rather than individual states makes it harder to come up with good heuristics. That is the main reason why the majority of current systems favor forward search.

2.3 Heuristics for planning

Neither forward nor backward search is efficient without a good heuristic function. A heuristic function $h(s)$ estimates the distance from a state s to the goal and that if we can derive an **admissible** heuristic for this distance—one that does not overestimate—then we can use A* search to find optimal solutions. An admissible heuristic can be derived by defining a **relaxed problem** that is easier to solve. The exact cost of a solution to this easier problem then becomes the heuristic for the original problem.

By definition, there is no way to analyze an atomic state, and thus it it requires some ingenuity by a human analyst to define good domain-specific heuristics for search problems with atomic states. Planning uses a factored representation for states and action schemas. That makes it possible to define good domain-independent heuristics and for programs to automatically apply a good domain-independent heuristic for a given problem.

Think of a search problem as a graph where the nodes are states and the edges are actions. The problem is to find a path connecting the initial state to a goal state. There are two ways we can relax this problem to make it easier: by adding more edges to the graph, making it strictly easier to find a path, or by grouping multiple nodes together, forming an abstraction of the state space that has fewer states, and thus is easier to search.

IGNORE PRECONDITIONS HEURISTIC

We look first at heuristics that add edges to the graph. For example, the **ignore preconditions heuristic** drops all preconditions from actions. Every action becomes applicable in every state, and any single goal fluent can be achieved in one step (if there is an applicable action—if not, the problem is impossible). This almost implies that the number of steps required to solve the relaxed problem is the number of unsatisfied goals—almost but not quite, because (1) some action may achieve multiple goals and (2) some actions may undo the effects of others. For many problems an accurate heuristic is obtained by considering (1) and ignoring (2). First, we relax the actions by removing all preconditions and all effects except those that are literals in the goal. Then, we count the minimum number of actions required such that the union of those actions' effects satisfies the goal. This is an instance of the **set-cover problem**. There is one minor irritation: the set-cover problem is NP-hard. Fortunately a simple greedy algorithm is guaranteed to return a set covering whose size is within a factor of $\log n$ of the true minimum covering, where n is the number of literals in the goal. Unfortunately, the greedy algorithm loses the guarantee of admissibility.

SET-COVER PROBLEM

It is also possible to ignore only *selected* preconditions of actions. Consider the sliding-block puzzle (8-puzzle or 15-puzzle) from Section 2 of the chapter "Solving Problems by

Searching." We could encode this as a planning problem involving tiles with a single schema *Slide*:

$$\begin{aligned}&Action(Slide(t, s_1, s_2),\\&\quad \text{PRECOND}: On(t, s_1) \wedge Tile(t) \wedge Blank(s_2) \wedge Adjacent(s_1, s_2)\\&\quad \text{EFFECT}: On(t, s_2) \wedge Blank(s_1) \wedge \neg On(t, s_1) \wedge \neg Blank(s_2))\end{aligned}$$

If we remove the preconditions $Blank(s_2) \wedge Adjacent(s_1, s_2)$ then any tile can move in one action to any space and we get the number-of-misplaced-tiles heuristic. If we remove $Blank(s_2)$ then we get the Manhattan-distance heuristic. It is easy to see how these heuristics could be derived automatically from the action schema description. The ease of manipulating the schemas is the great advantage of the factored representation of planning problems, as compared with the atomic representation of search problems.

IGNORE DELETE LISTS

Another possibility is the **ignore delete lists** heuristic. Assume for a moment that all goals and preconditions contain only positive literals[3] We want to create a relaxed version of the original problem that will be easier to solve, and where the length of the solution will serve as a good heuristic. We can do that by removing the delete lists from all actions (i.e., removing all negative literals from effects). That makes it possible to make monotonic progress towards the goal—no action will ever undo progress made by another action. It turns out it is still NP-hard to find the optimal solution to this relaxed problem, but an approximate solution can be found in polynomial time by hill-climbing. Figure 6 diagrams part of the state space for two planning problems using the ignore-delete-lists heuristic. The dots represent states and the edges actions, and the height of each dot above the bottom plane represents the heuristic value. States on the bottom plane are solutions. In both these problems, there is a wide path to the goal. There are no dead ends, so no need for backtracking; a simple hillclimbing search will easily find a solution to these problems (although it may not be an optimal solution).

The relaxed problems leave us with a simplified—but still expensive—planning problem just to calculate the value of the heuristic function. Many planning problems have 10^{100} states or more, and relaxing the *actions* does nothing to reduce the number of states. Therefore, we now look at relaxations that decrease the number of states by forming a **state abstraction**—a many-to-one mapping from states in the ground representation of the problem to the abstract representation.

STATE ABSTRACTION

The easiest form of state abstraction is to ignore some fluents. For example, consider an air cargo problem with 10 airports, 50 planes, and 200 pieces of cargo. Each plane can be at one of 10 airports and each package can be either in one of the planes or unloaded at one of the airports. So there are $50^{10} \times 200^{50+10} \approx 10^{155}$ states. Now consider a particular problem in that domain in which it happens that all the packages are at just 5 of the airports, and all packages at a given airport have the same destination. Then a useful abstraction of the problem is to drop all the *At* fluents except for the ones involving one plane and one package at each of the 5 airports. Now there are only $5^{10} \times 5^{5+10} \approx 10^{17}$ states. A solution in this abstract state space will be shorter than a solution in the original space (and thus will be an admissible heuristic), and the abstract solution is easy to extend to a solution to the original problem (by adding additional *Load* and *Unload* actions).

[3] Many problems are written with this convention. For problems that aren't, replace every negative literal $\neg P$ in a goal or precondition with a new positive literal, P'.

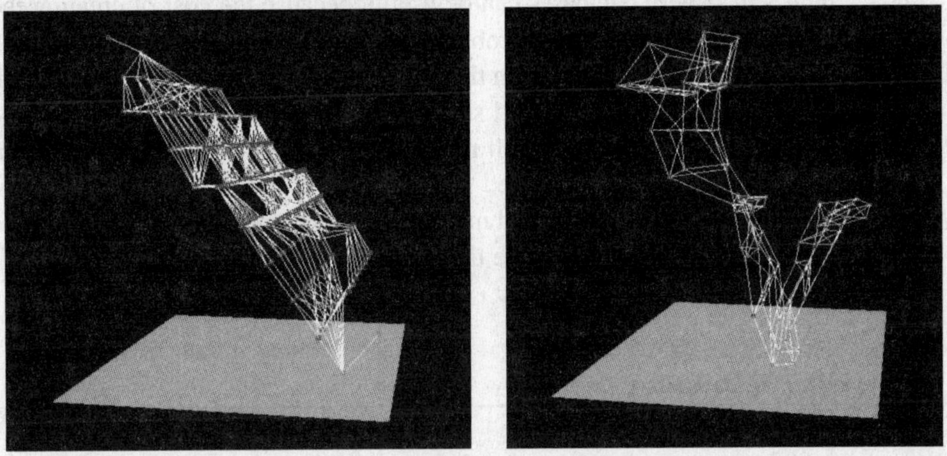

Figure 6 Two state spaces from planning problems with the ignore-delete-lists heuristic. The height above the bottom plane is the heuristic score of a state; states on the bottom plane are goals. There are no local minima, so search for the goal is straightforward. From Hoffmann (2005).

DECOMPOSITION

SUBGOAL INDEPENDENCE

A key idea in defining heuristics is **decomposition**: dividing a problem into parts, solving each part independently, and then combining the parts. The **subgoal independence** assumption is that the cost of solving a conjunction of subgoals is approximated by the sum of the costs of solving each subgoal *independently*. The subgoal independence assumption can be optimistic or pessimistic. It is optimistic when there are negative interactions between the subplans for each subgoal—for example, when an action in one subplan deletes a goal achieved by another subplan. It is pessimistic, and therefore inadmissible, when subplans contain redundant actions—for instance, two actions that could be replaced by a single action in the merged plan.

Suppose the goal is a set of fluents G, which we divide into disjoint subsets $G_1, \ldots, G_n$. We then find plans $P_1, \ldots, P_n$ that solve the respective subgoals. What is an estimate of the cost of the plan for achieving all of G? We can think of each $Cost(P_i)$ as a heuristic estimate, and we know that if we combine estimates by taking their maximum value, we always get an admissible heuristic. So $\max_i \textsc{Cost}(P_i)$ is admissible, and sometimes it is exactly correct: it could be that P_1 serendipitously achieves all the G_i. But in most cases, in practice the estimate is too low. Could we sum the costs instead? For many problems that is a reasonable estimate, but it is not admissible. The best case is when we can determine that G_i and G_j are **independent**. If the effects of P_i leave all the preconditions and goals of P_j unchanged, then the estimate $\textsc{Cost}(P_i) + \textsc{Cost}(P_j)$ is admissible, and more accurate than the max estimate. We show in Section 3.1 that planning graphs can help provide better heuristic estimates.

It is clear that there is great potential for cutting down the search space by forming abstractions. The trick is choosing the right abstractions and using them in a way that makes the total cost—defining an abstraction, doing an abstract search, and mapping the abstraction back to the original problem—less than the cost of solving the original problem. The techniques of **pattern databases** can be useful, because the cost of creating the pattern database can be amortized over multiple problem instances.

An example of a system that makes use of effective heuristics is FF, or FASTFORWARD (Hoffmann, 2005), a forward state-space searcher that uses the ignore-delete-lists heuristic, estimating the heuristic with the help of a planning graph (see Section 3). FF then uses hill-climbing search (modified to keep track of the plan) with the heuristic to find a solution. When it hits a plateau or local maximum—when no action leads to a state with better heuristic score—then FF uses iterative deepening search until it finds a state that is better, or it gives up and restarts hill-climbing.

3 PLANNING GRAPHS

All of the heuristics we have suggested can suffer from inaccuracies. This section shows how a special data structure called a **planning graph** can be used to give better heuristic estimates. These heuristics can be applied to any of the search techniques we have seen so far. Alternatively, we can search for a solution over the space formed by the planning graph, using an algorithm called GRAPHPLAN.

PLANNING GRAPH

A planning problem asks if we can reach a goal state from the initial state. Suppose we are given a tree of all possible actions from the initial state to successor states, and their successors, and so on. If we indexed this tree appropriately, we could answer the planning question "can we reach state G from state S_0" immediately, just by looking it up. Of course, the tree is of exponential size, so this approach is impractical. A planning graph is polynomial-size approximation to this tree that can be constructed quickly. The planning graph can't answer definitively whether G is reachable from S_0, but it can *estimate* how many steps it takes to reach G. The estimate is always correct when it reports the goal is not reachable, and it never overestimates the number of steps, so it is an admissible heuristic.

LEVEL

A planning graph is a directed graph organized into **levels**: first a level S_0 for the initial state, consisting of nodes representing each fluent that holds in S_0; then a level A_0 consisting of nodes for each ground action that might be applicable in S_0; then alternating levels S_i followed by A_i; until we reach a termination condition (to be discussed later).

Roughly speaking, S_i contains all the literals that *could* hold at time i, depending on the actions executed at preceding time steps. If it is possible that either P or $\neg P$ could hold, then both will be represented in S_i. Also roughly speaking, A_i contains all the actions that *could* have their preconditions satisfied at time i. We say "roughly speaking" because the planning graph records only a restricted subset of the possible negative interactions among actions; therefore, a literal might show up at level S_j when actually it could not be true until a later level, if at all. (A literal will never show up too late.) Despite the possible error, the level j at which a literal first appears is a good estimate of how difficult it is to achieve the literal from the initial state.

Planning graphs work only for propositional planning problems—ones with no variables. As we mentioned earlier in this chapter, it is straightforward to propositionalize a set of ac-

Init(*Have*(*Cake*))
Goal(*Have*(*Cake*) ∧ *Eaten*(*Cake*))
Action(*Eat*(*Cake*)
  PRECOND: *Have*(*Cake*)
  EFFECT: ¬ *Have*(*Cake*) ∧ *Eaten*(*Cake*))
Action(*Bake*(*Cake*)
  PRECOND: ¬ *Have*(*Cake*)
  EFFECT: *Have*(*Cake*))

Figure 7 The "have cake and eat cake too" problem.

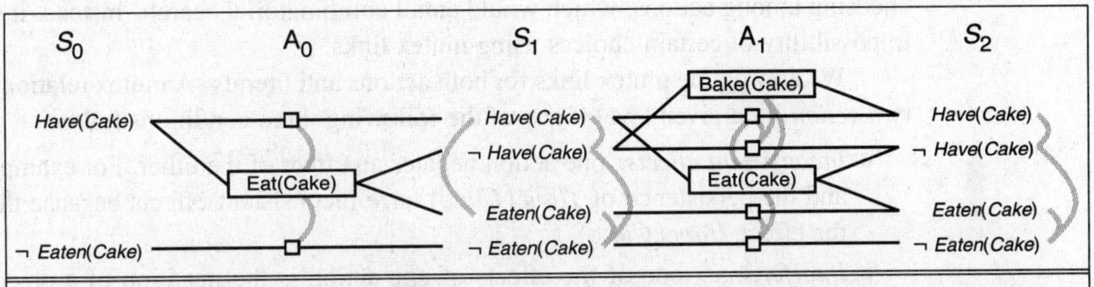

Figure 8 The planning graph for the "have cake and eat cake too" problem up to level S_2. Rectangles indicate actions (small squares indicate persistence actions), and straight lines indicate preconditions and effects. Mutex links are shown as curved gray lines. Not all mutex links are shown, because the graph would be too cluttered. In general, if two literals are mutex at S_i, then the persistence actions for those literals will be mutex at A_i and we need not draw that mutex link.

tion schemas. Despite the resulting increase in the size of the problem description, planning graphs have proved to be effective tools for solving hard planning problems.

Figure 7 shows a simple planning problem, and Figure 8 shows its planning graph. Each action at level A_i is connected to its preconditions at S_i and its effects at S_{i+1}. So a literal appears because an action caused it, but we also want to say that a literal can persist if no action negates it. This is represented by a **persistence action** (sometimes called a *no-op*). For every literal C, we add to the problem a persistence action with precondition C and effect C. Level A_0 in Figure 8 shows one "real" action, *Eat*(*Cake*), along with two persistence actions drawn as small square boxes.

PERSISTENCE ACTION

Level A_0 contains all the actions that *could* occur in state S_0, but just as important it records conflicts between actions that would prevent them from occurring together. The gray lines in Figure 8 indicate **mutual exclusion** (or **mutex**) links. For example, *Eat*(*Cake*) is mutually exclusive with the persistence of either *Have*(*Cake*) or ¬*Eaten*(*Cake*). We shall see shortly how mutex links are computed.

MUTUAL EXCLUSION

MUTEX

Level S_1 contains all the literals that could result from picking any subset of the actions in A_0, as well as mutex links (gray lines) indicating literals that could not appear together, regardless of the choice of actions. For example, *Have*(*Cake*) and *Eaten*(*Cake*) are mutex:

depending on the choice of actions in A_0, either, but not both, could be the result. In other words, S_1 represents a belief state: a set of possible states. The members of this set are all subsets of the literals such that there is no mutex link between any members of the subset.

We continue in this way, alternating between state level S_i and action level A_i until we reach a point where two consecutive levels are identical. At this point, we say that the graph has **leveled off**. The graph in Figure 8 levels off at S_2.

LEVELED OFF

What we end up with is a structure where every A_i level contains all the actions that are applicable in S_i, along with constraints saying that two actions cannot both be executed at the same level. Every S_i level contains all the literals that could result from any possible choice of actions in A_{i-1}, along with constraints saying which pairs of literals are not possible. It is important to note that the process of constructing the planning graph does *not* require choosing among actions, which would entail combinatorial search. Instead, it just records the impossibility of certain choices using mutex links.

We now define mutex links for both actions and literals. A mutex relation holds between two *actions* at a given level if any of the following three conditions holds:

- *Inconsistent effects:* one action negates an effect of the other. For example, $Eat(Cake)$ and the persistence of $Have(Cake)$ have inconsistent effects because they disagree on the effect $Have(Cake)$.
- *Interference:* one of the effects of one action is the negation of a precondition of the other. For example $Eat(Cake)$ interferes with the persistence of $Have(Cake)$ by negating its precondition.
- *Competing needs:* one of the preconditions of one action is mutually exclusive with a precondition of the other. For example, $Bake(Cake)$ and $Eat(Cake)$ are mutex because they compete on the value of the $Have(Cake)$ precondition.

A mutex relation holds between two *literals* at the same level if one is the negation of the other or if each possible pair of actions that could achieve the two literals is mutually exclusive. This condition is called *inconsistent support*. For example, $Have(Cake)$ and $Eaten(Cake)$ are mutex in S_1 because the only way of achieving $Have(Cake)$, the persistence action, is mutex with the only way of achieving $Eaten(Cake)$, namely $Eat(Cake)$. In S_2 the two literals are not mutex, because there are new ways of achieving them, such as $Bake(Cake)$ and the persistence of $Eaten(Cake)$, that are not mutex.

A planning graph is polynomial in the size of the planning problem. For a planning problem with l literals and a actions, each S_i has no more than l nodes and l^2 mutex links, and each A_i has no more than $a + l$ nodes (including the no-ops), $(a + l)^2$ mutex links, and $2(al + l)$ precondition and effect links. Thus, an entire graph with n levels has a size of $O(n(a + l)^2)$. The time to build the graph has the same complexity.

3.1 Planning graphs for heuristic estimation

A planning graph, once constructed, is a rich source of information about the problem. First, if any goal literal fails to appear in the final level of the graph, then the problem is unsolvable. Second, we can estimate the cost of achieving any goal literal g_i from state s as the level at which g_i first appears in the planning graph constructed from initial state s. We call this the

LEVEL COST **level cost** of g_i. In Figure 8, $Have(Cake)$ has level cost 0 and $Eaten(Cake)$ has level cost 1. It is easy to show (Exercise 10) that these estimates are admissible for the individual goals. The estimate might not always be accurate, however, because planning graphs allow several actions at each level, whereas the heuristic counts just the level and not the number of actions. For this reason, it is common to use a **serial planning graph** for computing heuristics. A serial graph insists that only one action can actually occur at any given time step; this is done by adding mutex links between every pair of nonpersistence actions. Level costs extracted from serial graphs are often quite reasonable estimates of actual costs.

SERIAL PLANNING GRAPH

To estimate the cost of a *conjunction* of goals, there are three simple approaches. The **max-level** heuristic simply takes the maximum level cost of any of the goals; this is admissible, but not necessarily accurate.

MAX-LEVEL

LEVEL SUM

The **level sum** heuristic, following the subgoal independence assumption, returns the sum of the level costs of the goals; this can be inadmissible but works well in practice for problems that are largely decomposable. It is much more accurate than the number-of-unsatisfied-goals heuristic from Section 2. For our problem, the level-sum heuristic estimate for the conjunctive goal $Have(Cake) \wedge Eaten(Cake)$ will be $0 + 1 = 1$, whereas the correct answer is 2, achieved by the plan $[Eat(Cake), Bake(Cake)]$. That doesn't seem so bad. A more serious error is that if $Bake(Cake)$ were not in the set of actions, then the estimate would still be 1, when in fact the conjunctive goal would be impossible.

SET-LEVEL

Finally, the **set-level** heuristic finds the level at which all the literals in the conjunctive goal appear in the planning graph without any pair of them being mutually exclusive. This heuristic gives the correct values of 2 for our original problem and infinity for the problem without $Bake(Cake)$. It is admissible, it dominates the max-level heuristic, and it works extremely well on tasks in which there is a good deal of interaction among subplans. It is not perfect, of course; for example, it ignores interactions among three or more literals.

As a tool for generating accurate heuristics, we can view the planning graph as a relaxed problem that is efficiently solvable. To understand the nature of the relaxed problem, we need to understand exactly what it means for a literal g to appear at level S_i in the planning graph. Ideally, we would like it to be a guarantee that there exists a plan with i action levels that achieves g, and also that if g does not appear, there is no such plan. Unfortunately, making that guarantee is as difficult as solving the original planning problem. So the planning graph makes the second half of the guarantee (if g does not appear, there is no plan), but if g does appear, then all the planning graph promises is that there is a plan that *possibly* achieves g and has no "obvious" flaws. An obvious flaw is defined as a flaw that can be detected by considering two actions or two literals at a time—in other words, by looking at the mutex relations. There could be more subtle flaws involving three, four, or more actions, but experience has shown that it is not worth the computational effort to keep track of these possible flaws. This is similar to a lesson learned from constraint satisfaction problems—that it is often worthwhile to compute 2-consistency before searching for a solution, but less often worthwhile to compute 3-consistency or higher.

One example of an unsolvable problem that cannot be recognized as such by a planning graph is the blocks-world problem where the goal is to get block A on B, B on C, and C on A. This is an impossible goal; a tower with the bottom on top of the top. But a planning graph cannot detect the impossibility, because any two of the three subgoals are achievable. There are no mutexes between any pair of literals, only between the three as a whole. To detect that this problem is impossible, we would have to search over the planning graph.

3.2 The GRAPHPLAN algorithm

This subsection shows how to extract a plan directly from the planning graph, rather than just using the graph to provide a heuristic. The GRAPHPLAN algorithm (Figure 9) repeatedly adds a level to a planning graph with EXPAND-GRAPH. Once all the goals show up as non-mutex in the graph, GRAPHPLAN calls EXTRACT-SOLUTION to search for a plan that solves the problem. If that fails, it expands another level and tries again, terminating with failure when there is no reason to go on.

```
function GRAPHPLAN(problem) returns solution or failure
  graph ← INITIAL-PLANNING-GRAPH(problem)
  goals ← CONJUNCTS(problem.GOAL)
  nogoods ← an empty hash table
  for tl = 0 to ∞ do
    if goals all non-mutex in S_t of graph then
       solution ← EXTRACT-SOLUTION(graph, goals, NUMLEVELS(graph), nogoods)
       if solution ≠ failure then return solution
    if graph and nogoods have both leveled off then return failure
    graph ← EXPAND-GRAPH(graph, problem)
```

Figure 9 The GRAPHPLAN algorithm. GRAPHPLAN calls EXPAND-GRAPH to add a level until either a solution is found by EXTRACT-SOLUTION, or no solution is possible.

Let us now trace the operation of GRAPHPLAN on the spare tire problem from section 1.2. The graph is shown in Figure 10. The first line of GRAPHPLAN initializes the planning graph to a one-level (S_0) graph representing the initial state. The positive fluents from the problem description's initial state are shown, as are the relevant negative fluents. Not shown are the unchanging positive literals (such as *Tire*(*Spare*)) and the irrelevant negative literals. The goal *At*(*Spare*,*Axle*) is not present in S_0, so we need not call EXTRACT-SOLUTION—we are certain that there is no solution yet. Instead, EXPAND-GRAPH adds into A_0 the three actions whose preconditions exist at level S_0(i.e., all the actions except *PutOn*(*Spare*,*Axle*)), along with persistence actions for all the literals in S_0. The effects of the actions are added at level S_1. EXPAND-GRAPH then looks for mutex relations and adds them to the graph.

At(*Spare*, *Axle*) is still not present in S_1, so again we do not call EXTRACT-SOLUTION. We call EXPAND-GRAPH again, adding A_1 and S_1 and giving us the planning graph shown in Figure 10. Now that we have the full complement of actions, it is worthwhile to look at some of the examples of mutex relations and their causes:

- *Inconsistent effects:* *Remove*(*Spare*, *Trunk*) is mutex with *LeaveOvernight* because one has the effect *At*(*Spare*, *Ground*) and the other has its negation.

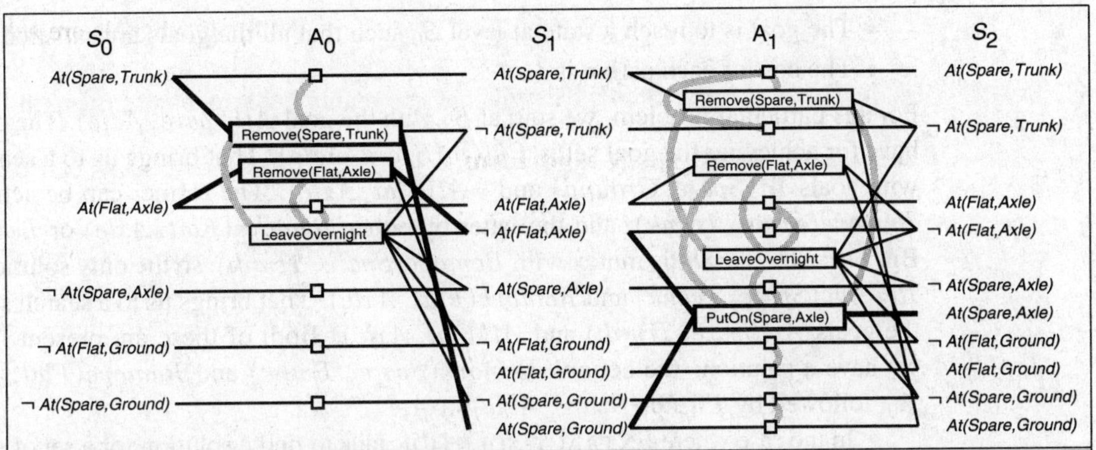

Figure 10 The planning graph for the spare tire problem after expansion to level S_2. Mutex links are shown as gray lines. Not all links are shown, because the graph would be too cluttered if we showed them all. The solution is indicated by bold lines and outlines.

- *Interference:* $Remove(Flat, Axle)$ is mutex with $LeaveOvernight$ because one has the precondition $At(Flat, Axle)$ and the other has its negation as an effect.
- *Competing needs:* $PutOn(Spare, Axle)$ is mutex with $Remove(Flat, Axle)$ because one has $At(Flat, Axle)$ as a precondition and the other has its negation.
- *Inconsistent support:* $At(Spare, Axle)$ is mutex with $At(Flat, Axle)$ in S_2 because the only way of achieving $At(Spare, Axle)$ is by $PutOn(Spare, Axle)$, and that is mutex with the persistence action that is the only way of achieving $At(Flat, Axle)$. Thus, the mutex relations detect the immediate conflict that arises from trying to put two objects in the same place at the same time.

This time, when we go back to the start of the loop, all the literals from the goal are present in S_2, and none of them is mutex with any other. That means that a solution might exist, and EXTRACT-SOLUTION will try to find it. We can formulate EXTRACT-SOLUTION as a Boolean constraint satisfaction problem (CSP) where the variables are the actions at each level, the values for each variable are *in* or *out* of the plan, and the constraints are the mutexes and the need to satisfy each goal and precondition.

Alternatively, we can define EXTRACT-SOLUTION as a backward search problem, where each state in the search contains a pointer to a level in the planning graph and a set of unsatisfied goals. We define this search problem as follows:

- The initial state is the last level of the planning graph, S_n, along with the set of goals from the planning problem.
- The actions available in a state at level S_i are to select any conflict-free subset of the actions in A_{i-1} whose effects cover the goals in the state. The resulting state has level S_{i-1} and has as its set of goals the preconditions for the selected set of actions. By "conflict free," we mean a set of actions such that no two of them are mutex and no two of their preconditions are mutex.

- The goal is to reach a state at level S_0 such that all the goals are satisfied.
- The cost of each action is 1.

For this particular problem, we start at S_2 with the goal $At(Spare, Axle)$. The only choice we have for achieving the goal set is $PutOn(Spare, Axle)$. That brings us to a search state at S_1 with goals $At(Spare, Ground)$ and $\neg At(Flat, Axle)$. The former can be achieved only by $Remove(Spare, Trunk)$, and the latter by either $Remove(Flat, Axle)$ or $LeaveOvernight$. But $LeaveOvernight$ is mutex with $Remove(Spare, Trunk)$, so the only solution is to choose $Remove(Spare, Trunk)$ and $Remove(Flat, Axle)$. That brings us to a search state at S_0 with the goals $At(Spare, Trunk)$ and $At(Flat, Axle)$. Both of these are present in the state, so we have a solution: the actions $Remove(Spare, Trunk)$ and $Remove(Flat, Axle)$ in level A_0, followed by $PutOn(Spare, Axle)$ in A_1.

In the case where EXTRACT-SOLUTION fails to find a solution for a set of goals at a given level, we record the $(level, goals)$ pair as a **no-good**, just as we did in constraint learning for CSPs. Whenever EXTRACT-SOLUTION is called again with the same level and goals, we can find the recorded no-good and immediately return failure rather than searching again. We see shortly that no-goods are also used in the termination test.

We know that planning is PSPACE-complete and that constructing the planning graph takes polynomial time, so it must be the case that solution extraction is intractable in the worst case. Therefore, we will need some heuristic guidance for choosing among actions during the backward search. One approach that works well in practice is a greedy algorithm based on the level cost of the literals. For any set of goals, we proceed in the following order:

1. Pick first the literal with the highest level cost.
2. To achieve that literal, prefer actions with easier preconditions. That is, choose an action such that the sum (or maximum) of the level costs of its preconditions is smallest.

3.3 Termination of GRAPHPLAN

So far, we have skated over the question of termination. Here we show that GRAPHPLAN will in fact terminate and return failure when there is no solution.

The first thing to understand is why we can't stop expanding the graph as soon as it has leveled off. Consider an air cargo domain with one plane and n pieces of cargo at airport A, all of which have airport B as their destination. In this version of the problem, only one piece of cargo can fit in the plane at a time. The graph will level off at level 4, reflecting the fact that for any single piece of cargo, we can load it, fly it, and unload it at the destination in three steps. But that does not mean that a solution can be extracted from the graph at level 4; in fact a solution will require $4n - 1$ steps: for each piece of cargo we load, fly, and unload, and for all but the last piece we need to fly back to airport A to get the next piece.

How long do we have to keep expanding after the graph has leveled off? If the function EXTRACT-SOLUTION fails to find a solution, then there must have been at least one set of goals that were not achievable and were marked as a no-good. So if it is possible that there might be fewer no-goods in the next level, then we should continue. As soon as the graph itself and the no-goods have both leveled off, with no solution found, we can terminate with failure because there is no possibility of a subsequent change that could add a solution.

Now all we have to do is prove that the graph and the no-goods will always level off. The key to this proof is that certain properties of planning graphs are monotonically increasing or decreasing. "X increases monotonically" means that the set of Xs at level $i + 1$ is a superset (not necessarily proper) of the set at level i. The properties are as follows:

- *Literals increase monotonically:* Once a literal appears at a given level, it will appear at all subsequent levels. This is because of the persistence actions; once a literal shows up, persistence actions cause it to stay forever.
- *Actions increase monotonically:* Once an action appears at a given level, it will appear at all subsequent levels. This is a consequence of the monotonic increase of literals; if the preconditions of an action appear at one level, they will appear at subsequent levels, and thus so will the action.
- *Mutexes decrease monotonically:* If two actions are mutex at a given level A_i, then they will also be mutex for all *previous* levels at which they both appear. The same holds for mutexes between literals. It might not always appear that way in the figures, because the figures have a simplification: they display neither literals that cannot hold at level S_i nor actions that cannot be executed at level A_i. We can see that "mutexes decrease monotonically" is true if you consider that these invisible literals and actions are mutex with everything.

  The proof can be handled by cases: if actions A and B are mutex at level A_i, it must be because of one of the three types of mutex. The first two, inconsistent effects and interference, are properties of the actions themselves, so if the actions are mutex at A_i, they will be mutex at every level. The third case, competing needs, depends on conditions at level S_i: that level must contain a precondition of A that is mutex with a precondition of B. Now, these two preconditions can be mutex if they are negations of each other (in which case they would be mutex in every level) or if all actions for achieving one are mutex with all actions for achieving the other. But we already know that the available actions are increasing monotonically, so, by induction, the mutexes must be decreasing.
- *No-goods decrease monotonically:* If a set of goals is not achievable at a given level, then they are not achievable in any *previous* level. The proof is by contradiction: if they were achievable at some previous level, then we could just add persistence actions to make them achievable at a subsequent level.

Because the actions and literals increase monotonically and because there are only a finite number of actions and literals, there must come a level that has the same number of actions and literals as the previous level. Because mutexes and no-goods decrease, and because there can never be fewer than zero mutexes or no-goods, there must come a level that has the same number of mutexes and no-goods as the previous level. Once a graph has reached this state, then if one of the goals is missing or is mutex with another goal, then we can stop the GRAPHPLAN algorithm and return failure. That concludes a sketch of the proof; for more details see Ghallab *et al.* (2004).

Year	Track	Winning Systems (approaches)
2008	Optimal	GAMER (model checking, bidirectional search)
2008	Satisficing	LAMA (fast downward search with FF heuristic)
2006	Optimal	SATPLAN, MAXPLAN (Boolean satisfiability)
2006	Satisficing	SGPLAN (forward search; partitions into independent subproblems)
2004	Optimal	SATPLAN (Boolean satisfiability)
2004	Satisficing	FAST DIAGONALLY DOWNWARD (forward search with causal graph)
2002	Automated	LPG (local search, planning graphs converted to CSPs)
2002	Hand-coded	TLPLAN (temporal action logic with control rules for forward search)
2000	Automated	FF (forward search)
2000	Hand-coded	TALPLANNER (temporal action logic with control rules for forward search)
1998	Automated	IPP (planning graphs); HSP (forward search)

Figure 11 Some of the top-performing systems in the International Planning Competition. Each year there are various tracks: "Optimal" means the planners must produce the shortest possible plan, while "Satisficing" means nonoptimal solutions are accepted. "Hand-coded" means domain-specific heuristics are allowed; "Automated" means they are not.

4 OTHER CLASSICAL PLANNING APPROACHES

Currently the most popular and effective approaches to fully automated planning are:

- Translating to a Boolean satisfiability (SAT) problem
- Forward state-space search with carefully crafted heuristics (Section 2)
- Search using a planning graph (Section 3)

These three approaches are not the only ones tried in the 40-year history of automated planning. Figure 11 shows some of the top systems in the International Planning Competitions, which have been held every even year since 1998. In this section we first describe the translation to a satisfiability problem and then describe three other influential approaches: planning as first-order logical deduction; as constraint satisfaction; and as plan refinement.

4.1 Classical planning as Boolean satisfiability

Recall how SATPLAN solves planning problems that are expressed in propositional logic. Here we show how to translate a PDDL description into a form that can be processed by SATPLAN. The translation is a series of straightforward steps:

- Propositionalize the actions: replace each action schema with a set of ground actions formed by substituting constants for each of the variables. These ground actions are not part of the translation, but will be used in subsequent steps.
- Define the initial state: assert F^0 for every fluent F in the problem's initial state, and $\neg F$ for every fluent not mentioned in the initial state.
- Propositionalize the goal: for every variable in the goal, replace the literals that contain the variable with a disjunction over constants. For example, the goal of having block A

on another block, $On(A, x) \wedge Block(x)$ in a world with objects A, B and C, would be replaced by the goal

$$(On(A, A) \wedge Block(A)) \vee (On(A, B) \wedge Block(B)) \vee (On(A, C) \wedge Block(C)).$$

- Add successor-state axioms: For each fluent F, add an axiom of the form

$$F^{t+1} \Leftrightarrow ActionCausesF^t \vee (F^t \wedge \neg ActionCausesNotF^t),$$

where $ActionCausesF$ is a disjunction of all the ground actions that have F in their add list, and $ActionCausesNotF$ is a disjunction of all the ground actions that have F in their delete list.

- Add precondition axioms: For each ground action A, add the axiom $A^t \Rightarrow \text{PRE}(A)^t$, that is, if an action is taken at time t, then the preconditions must have been true.
- Add action exclusion axioms: say that every action is distinct from every other action.

The resulting translation is in the form that we can hand to SATPLAN to find a solution.

4.2 Planning as first-order logical deduction: Situation calculus

PDDL is a language that carefully balances the expressiveness of the language with the complexity of the algorithms that operate on it. But some problems remain difficult to express in PDDL. For example, we can't express the goal "move all the cargo from A to B regardless of how many pieces of cargo there are" in PDDL, but we can do it in first-order logic, using a universal quantifier. Likewise, first-order logic can concisely express global constraints such as "no more than four robots can be in the same place at the same time." PDDL can only say this with repetitious preconditions on every possible action that involves a move.

The propositional logic representation of planning problems also has limitations, such as the fact that the notion of time is tied directly to fluents. For example, $South^2$ means "the agent is facing south at time 2." With that representation, there is no way to say "the agent would be facing south at time 2 if it executed a right turn at time 1; otherwise it would be facing east." First-order logic lets us get around this limitation by replacing the notion of linear time with a notion of branching *situations*, using a representation called **situation calculus** that works like this:

SITUATION CALCULUS

SITUATION

- The initial state is called a **situation**. If s is a situation and a is an action, then $\text{RESULT}(s, a)$ is also a situation. There are no other situations. Thus, a situation corresponds to a sequence, or history, of actions. You can also think of a situation as the result of applying the actions, but note that two situations are the same only if their start and actions are the same: $(\text{RESULT}(s, a) = \text{RESULT}(s', a')) \Leftrightarrow (s = s' \wedge a = a')$. Some examples of actions and situations are shown in Figure 12.
- A function or relation that can vary from one situation to the next is a **fluent**. By convention, the situation s is always the last argument to the fluent, for example $At(x, l, s)$ is a relational fluent that is true when object x is at location l in situation s, and $Location$ is a functional fluent such that $Location(x, s) = l$ holds in the same situations as $At(x, l, s)$.

POSSIBILITY AXIOM

- Each action's preconditions are described with a **possibility axiom** that says when the action can be taken. It has the form $\Phi(s) \Rightarrow Poss(a, s)$ where $\Phi(s)$ is some formula

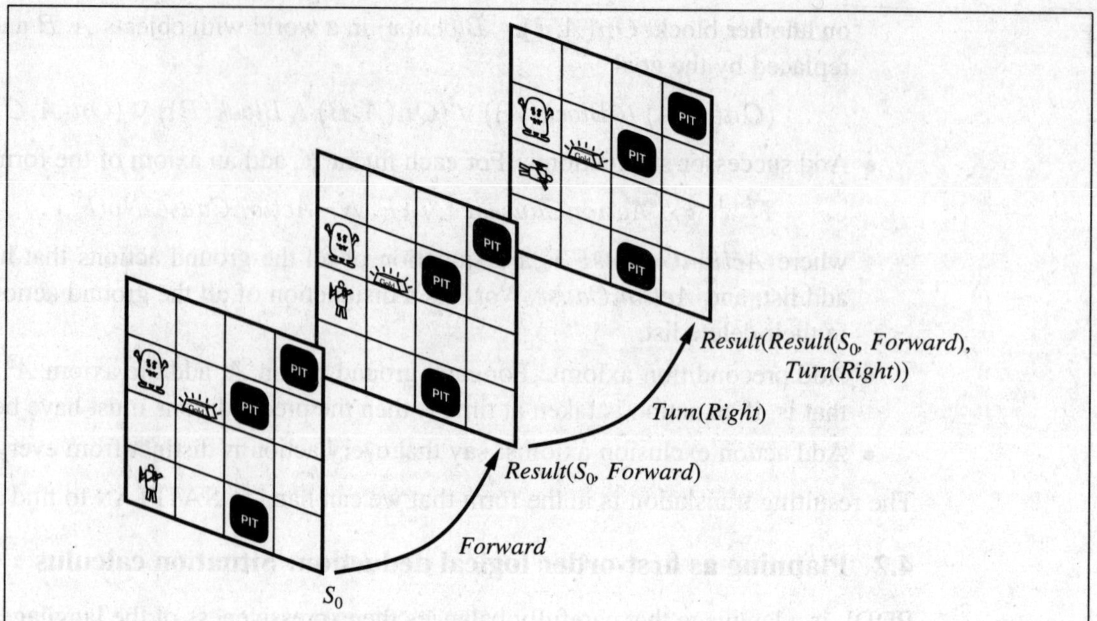

Figure 12 Situations as the results of actions in the wumpus world.

involving s that describes the preconditions. An example from the wumpus world says that it is possible to shoot if the agent is alive and has an arrow:

$$Alive(Agent, s) \land Have(Agent, Arrow, s) \Rightarrow Poss(Shoot, s)$$

- Each fluent is described with a **successor-state axiom** that says what happens to the fluent, depending on what action is taken. This is similar to the approach we took for propositional logic. The axiom has the form

$$\begin{aligned}&Action\ is\ possible \Rightarrow\\&\quad (Fluent\ is\ true\ in\ result\ state \Leftrightarrow Action\text{'s}\ effect\ made\ it\ true\\&\qquad\qquad\qquad\qquad\qquad\qquad\quad \lor It\ was\ true\ before\ and\ action\ left\ it\ alone)\,.\end{aligned}$$

For example, the axiom for the relational fluent *Holding* says that the agent is holding some gold g after executing a possible action if and only if the action was a *Grab* of g or if the agent was already holding g and the action was not releasing it:

$$\begin{aligned}&Poss(a, s) \Rightarrow\\&\quad (Holding(Agent, g, Result(a, s)) \Leftrightarrow\\&\qquad a = Grab(g) \lor (Holding(Agent, g, s) \land a \neq Release(g)))\,.\end{aligned}$$

UNIQUE ACTION AXIOMS

- We need **unique action axioms** so that the agent can deduce that, for example, $a \neq Release(g)$. For each distinct pair of action names A_i and A_j we have an axiom that says the actions are different:

$$A_i(x, \ldots) \neq A_j(y, \ldots)$$

and for each action name A_i we have an axiom that says two uses of that action name are equal if and only if all their arguments are equal:

$$A_i(x_1,\ldots,x_n) = A_i(y_1,\ldots,y_n) \Leftrightarrow x_1 = y_1 \wedge \ldots \wedge x_n = y_n\,.$$

- A solution is a situation (and hence a sequence of actions) that satisfies the goal.

Work in situation calculus has done a lot to define the formal semantics of planning and to open up new areas of investigation. But so far there have not been any practical large-scale planning programs based on logical deduction over the situation calculus. This is in part because of the difficulty of doing efficient inference in FOL, but is mainly because the field has not yet developed effective heuristics for planning with situation calculus.

4.3 Planning as constraint satisfaction

We have seen that constraint satisfaction has a lot in common with Boolean satisfiability, and we have seen that CSP techniques are effective for scheduling problems, so it is not surprising that it is possible to encode a bounded planning problem (i.e., the problem of finding a plan of length k) as a constraint satisfaction problem (CSP). The encoding is similar to the encoding to a SAT problem (Section 4.1), with one important simplification: at each time step we need only a single variable, $Action^t$, whose domain is the set of possible actions. We no longer need one variable for every action, and we don't need the action exclusion axioms. It is also possible to encode a planning graph into a CSP. This is the approach taken by GP-CSP (Do and Kambhampati, 2003).

4.4 Planning as refinement of partially ordered plans

All the approaches we have seen so far construct *totally ordered* plans consisting of a strictly linear sequences of actions. This representation ignores the fact that many subproblems are independent. A solution to an air cargo problem consists of a totally ordered sequence of actions, yet if 30 packages are being loaded onto one plane in one airport and 50 packages are being loaded onto another at another airport, it seems pointless to come up with a strict linear ordering of 80 load actions; the two subsets of actions should be thought of independently.

An alternative is to represent plans as *partially ordered* structures: a plan is a set of actions and a set of constraints of the form $Before(a_i, a_j)$ saying that one action occurs before another. In the bottom of Figure 13, we see a partially ordered plan that is a solution to the spare tire problem. Actions are boxes and ordering constraints are arrows. Note that $Remove(Spare, Trunk)$ and $Remove(Flat, Axle)$ can be done in either order as long as they are both completed before the $PutOn(Spare, Axle)$ action.

Partially ordered plans are created by a *search through the space of plans* rather than through the state space. We start with the empty plan consisting of just the initial state and the goal, with no actions in between, as in the top of Figure 13. The search procedure then looks for a **flaw** in the plan, and makes an addition to the plan to correct the flaw (or if no correction can be made, the search backtracks and tries something else). A flaw is anything that keeps the partial plan from being a solution. For example, one flaw in the empty plan is that no action achieves $At(Spare, Axle)$. One way to correct the flaw is to insert into the plan

FLAW

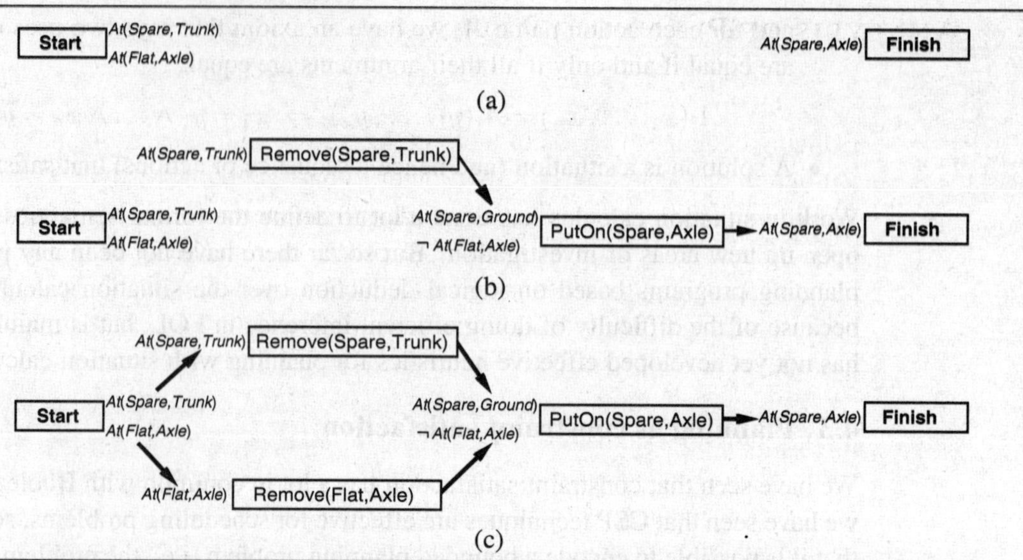

Figure 13 (a) the tire problem expressed as an empty plan. (b) an incomplete partially ordered plan for the tire problem. Boxes represent actions and arrows indicate that one action must occur before another. (c) a complete partially-ordered solution.

the action *PutOn*(*Spare*, *Axle*). Of course that introduces some new flaws: the preconditions of the new action are not achieved. The search keeps adding to the plan (backtracking if necessary) until all flaws are resolved, as in the bottom of Figure 13. At every step, we make the **least commitment** possible to fix the flaw. For example, in adding the action *Remove*(*Spare*, *Trunk*) we need to commit to having it occur before *PutOn*(*Spare*, *Axle*), but we make no other commitment that places it before or after other actions. If there were a variable in the action schema that could be left unbound, we would do so.

LEAST COMMITMENT

In the 1980s and 90s, partial-order planning was seen as the best way to handle planning problems with independent subproblems—after all, it was the only approach that explicitly represents independent branches of a plan. On the other hand, it has the disadvantage of not having an explicit representation of states in the state-transition model. That makes some computations cumbersome. By 2000, forward-search planners had developed excellent heuristics that allowed them to efficiently discover the independent subproblems that partial-order planning was designed for. As a result, partial-order planners are not competitive on fully automated classical planning problems.

However, partial-order planning remains an important part of the field. For some specific tasks, such as operations scheduling, partial-order planning with domain specific heuristics is the technology of choice. Many of these systems use libraries of high-level plans. Partial-order planning is also often used in domains where it is important for humans to understand the plans. Operational plans for spacecraft and Mars rovers are generated by partial-order planners and are then checked by human operators before being uploaded to the vehicles for execution. The plan refinement approach makes it easier for the humans to understand what the planning algorithms are doing and verify that they are correct.

5 ANALYSIS OF PLANNING APPROACHES

Planning combines two major areas of AI: *search and logic*. A planner can be seen either as a program that searches for a solution or as one that (constructively) proves the existence of a solution. The cross-fertilization of ideas from the two areas has led both to improvements in performance amounting to several orders of magnitude in the last decade and to an increased use of planners in industrial applications. Unfortunately, we do not yet have a clear understanding of which techniques work best on which kinds of problems. Quite possibly, new techniques will emerge that dominate existing methods.

Planning is foremost an exercise in controlling combinatorial explosion. If there are n propositions in a domain, then there are 2^n states. As we have seen, planning is PSPACE-hard. Against such pessimism, the identification of independent subproblems can be a powerful weapon. In the best case—full decomposability of the problem—we get an exponential speedup. Decomposability is destroyed, however, by negative interactions between actions. GRAPHPLAN records mutexes to point out where the difficult interactions are. SATPLAN represents a similar range of mutex relations, but does so by using the general CNF form rather than a specific data structure. Forward search addresses the problem heuristically by trying to find patterns (subsets of propositions) that cover the independent subproblems. Since this approach is heuristic, it can work even when the subproblems are not completely independent.

Sometimes it is possible to solve a problem efficiently by recognizing that negative interactions can be ruled out. We say that a problem has **serializable subgoals** if there exists an order of subgoals such that the planner can achieve them in that order without having to undo any of the previously achieved subgoals. For example, in the blocks world, if the goal is to build a tower (e.g., *A* on *B*, which in turn is on *C*, which in turn is on the *Table*, as in Figure 4), then the subgoals are serializable bottom to top: if we first achieve *C* on *Table*, we will never have to undo it while we are achieving the other subgoals. A planner that uses the bottom-to-top trick can solve any problem in the blocks world without backtracking (although it might not always find the shortest plan).

SERIALIZABLE SUBGOAL

As a more complex example, for the Remote Agent planner that commanded NASA's Deep Space One spacecraft, it was determined that the propositions involved in commanding a spacecraft are serializable. This is perhaps not too surprising, because a spacecraft is *designed* by its engineers to be as easy as possible to control (subject to other constraints). Taking advantage of the serialized ordering of goals, the Remote Agent planner was able to eliminate most of the search. This meant that it was fast enough to control the spacecraft in real time, something previously considered impossible.

Planners such as GRAPHPLAN, SATPLAN, and FF have moved the field of planning forward, by raising the level of performance of planning systems, by clarifying the representational and combinatorial issues involved, and by the development of useful heuristics. However, there is a question of how far these techniques will scale. It seems likely that further progress on larger problems cannot rely only on factored and propositional representations, and will require some kind of synthesis of first-order and hierarchical representations with the efficient heuristics currently in use.

6 SUMMARY

In this chapter, we defined the problem of planning in deterministic, fully observable, static environments. We described the PDDL representation for planning problems and several algorithmic approaches for solving them. The points to remember:

- Planning systems are problem-solving algorithms that operate on explicit propositional or relational representations of states and actions. These representations make possible the derivation of effective heuristics and the development of powerful and flexible algorithms for solving problems.
- PDDL, the Planning Domain Definition Language, describes the initial and goal states as conjunctions of literals, and actions in terms of their preconditions and effects.
- State-space search can operate in the forward direction (**progression**) or the backward direction (**regression**). Effective heuristics can be derived by subgoal independence assumptions and by various relaxations of the planning problem.
- A **planning graph** can be constructed incrementally, starting from the initial state. Each layer contains a superset of all the literals or actions that could occur at that time step and encodes mutual exclusion (mutex) relations among literals or actions that cannot co-occur. Planning graphs yield useful heuristics for state-space and partial-order planners and can be used directly in the GRAPHPLAN algorithm.
- Other approaches include first-order deduction over situation calculus axioms; encoding a planning problem as a Boolean satisfiability problem or as a constraint satisfaction problem; and explicitly searching through the space of partially ordered plans.
- Each of the major approaches to planning has its adherents, and there is as yet no consensus on which is best. Competition and cross-fertilization among the approaches have resulted in significant gains in efficiency for planning systems.

BIBLIOGRAPHICAL AND HISTORICAL NOTES

AI planning arose from investigations into state-space search, theorem proving, and control theory and from the practical needs of robotics, scheduling, and other domains. STRIPS (Fikes and Nilsson, 1971), the first major planning system, illustrates the interaction of these influences. STRIPS was designed as the planning component of the software for the Shakey robot project at SRI. Its overall control structure was modeled on that of GPS, the General Problem Solver (Newell and Simon, 1961), a state-space search system that used means–ends analysis. Bylander (1992) shows simple STRIPS planning to be PSPACE-complete. Fikes and Nilsson (1993) give a historical retrospective on the STRIPS project and its relationship to more recent planning efforts.

The representation language used by STRIPS has been far more influential than its algorithmic approach; what we call the "classical" language is close to what STRIPS used.

The Action Description Language, or ADL (Pednault, 1986), relaxed some of the STRIPS restrictions and made it possible to encode more realistic problems. Nebel (2000) explores schemes for compiling ADL into STRIPS. The Problem Domain Description Language, or PDDL (Ghallab *et al.*, 1998), was introduced as a computer-parsable, standardized syntax for representing planning problems and has been used as the standard language for the International Planning Competition since 1998. There have been several extensions; the most recent version, PDDL 3.0, includes plan constraints and preferences (Gerevini and Long, 2005).

Planners in the early 1970s generally considered totally ordered action sequences. Problem decomposition was achieved by computing a subplan for each subgoal and then stringing

LINEAR PLANNING

the subplans together in some order. This approach, called **linear planning** by Sacerdoti (1975), was soon discovered to be incomplete. It cannot solve some very simple problems, such as the Sussman anomaly (see Exercise 7), found by Allen Brown during experimentation with the HACKER system (Sussman, 1975). A complete planner must allow for **interleaving** of actions from different subplans within a single sequence. The notion of serializable subgoals (Korf, 1987) corresponds exactly to the set of problems for which noninterleaved planners are complete.

INTERLEAVING

One solution to the interleaving problem was goal-regression planning, a technique in which steps in a totally ordered plan are reordered so as to avoid conflict between subgoals. This was introduced by Waldinger (1975) and also used by Warren's (1974) WARPLAN. WARPLAN is also notable in that it was the first planner to be written in a logic programming language (Prolog) and is one of the best examples of the remarkable economy that can sometimes be gained with logic programming: WARPLAN is only 100 lines of code, a small fraction of the size of comparable planners of the time.

The ideas underlying partial-order planning include the detection of conflicts (Tate, 1975a) and the protection of achieved conditions from interference (Sussman, 1975). The construction of partially ordered plans (then called **task networks**) was pioneered by the NOAH planner (Sacerdoti, 1975, 1977) and by Tate's (1975b, 1977) NONLIN system.

Partial-order planning dominated the next 20 years of research, yet the first clear formal exposition was TWEAK (Chapman, 1987), a planner that was simple enough to allow proofs of completeness and intractability (NP-hardness and undecidability) of various planning problems. Chapman's work led to a straightforward description of a complete partial-order planner (McAllester and Rosenblitt, 1991), then to the widely distributed implementations SNLP (Soderland and Weld, 1991) and UCPOP (Penberthy and Weld, 1992). Partial-order planning fell out of favor in the late 1990s as faster methods emerged. Nguyen and Kambhampati (2001) suggest that a reconsideration is merited: with accurate heuristics derived from a planning graph, their REPOP planner scales up much better than GRAPHPLAN in parallelizable domains and is competitive with the fastest state-space planners.

The resurgence of interest in state-space planning was pioneered by Drew McDermott's UNPOP program (1996), which was the first to suggest the ignore-delete-list heuristic, The name UNPOP was a reaction to the overwhelming concentration on partial-order planning at the time; McDermott suspected that other approaches were not getting the attention they deserved. Bonet and Geffner's Heuristic Search Planner (HSP) and its later derivatives (Bonet and Geffner, 1999; Haslum *et al.*, 2005; Haslum, 2006) were the first to make state-space search practical for large planning problems. HSP searches in the forward direction while HSPR (Bonet and Geffner, 1999) searches backward. The most successful state-space searcher to date is FF (Hoffmann, 2001; Hoffmann and Nebel, 2001; Hoffmann, 2005), winner of the AIPS 2000 planning competition. FASTDOWNWARD (Helmert, 2006) is a forward state-space search planner that preprocesses the action schemas into an alternative representation which makes some of the constraints more explicit. FASTDOWNWARD (Helmert and Richter, 2004; Helmert, 2006) won the 2004 planning competition, and LAMA (Richter and Westphal, 2008), a planner based on FASTDOWNWARD with improved heuristics, won the 2008 competition.

Bylander (1994) and Ghallab *et al.* (2004) discuss the computational complexity of several variants of the planning problem. Helmert (2003) proves complexity bounds for many of the standard benchmark problems, and Hoffmann (2005) analyzes the search space of the ignore-delete-list heuristic. Heuristics for the set-covering problem are discussed by Caprara *et al.* (1995) for scheduling operations of the Italian railway. Edelkamp (2009) and Haslum *et al.* (2007) describe how to construct pattern databases for planning heuristics. Felner *et al.* (2004) show encouraging results using pattern databases for sliding blocks puzzles, which can be thought of as a planning domain, but Hoffmann *et al.* (2006) show some limitations of abstraction for classical planning problems.

Avrim Blum and Merrick Furst (1995, 1997) revitalized the field of planning with their GRAPHPLAN system, which was orders of magnitude faster than the partial-order planners of the time. Other graph-planning systems, such as IPP (Koehler *et al.*, 1997), STAN (Fox and Long, 1998), and SGP (Weld *et al.*, 1998), soon followed. A data structure closely resembling the planning graph had been developed slightly earlier by Ghallab and Laruelle (1994), whose IXTET partial-order planner used it to derive accurate heuristics to guide searches. Nguyen *et al.* (2001) thoroughly analyze heuristics derived from planning graphs. Our discussion of planning graphs is based partly on this work and on lecture notes and articles by Subbarao Kambhampati (Bryce and Kambhampati, 2007). As mentioned in the chapter, a planning graph can be used in many different ways to guide the search for a solution. The winner of the 2002 AIPS planning competition, LPG (Gerevini and Serina, 2002, 2003), searched planning graphs using a local search technique inspired by WALKSAT.

The situation calculus approach to planning was introduced by John McCarthy (1963). The version we show here was proposed by Ray Reiter (1991, 2001).

Kautz *et al.* (1996) investigated various ways to propositionalize action schemas, finding that the most compact forms did not necessarily lead to the fastest solution times. A systematic analysis was carried out by Ernst *et al.* (1997), who also developed an automatic "compiler" for generating propositional representations from PDDL problems. The BLACKBOX planner, which combines ideas from GRAPHPLAN and SATPLAN, was developed by Kautz and Selman (1998). CPLAN, a planner based on constraint satisfaction, was described by van Beek and Chen (1999).

BINARY DECISION DIAGRAM

Most recently, there has been interest in the representation of plans as **binary decision diagrams**, compact data structures for Boolean expressions widely studied in the hardware verification community (Clarke and Grumberg, 1987; McMillan, 1993). There are techniques for proving properties of binary decision diagrams, including the property of being a solution to a planning problem. Cimatti *et al.* (1998) present a planner based on this approach. Other representations have also been used; for example, Vossen *et al.* (2001) survey the use of integer programming for planning.

The jury is still out, but there are now some interesting comparisons of the various approaches to planning. Helmert (2001) analyzes several classes of planning problems, and shows that constraint-based approaches such as GRAPHPLAN and SATPLAN are best for NP-hard domains, while search-based approaches do better in domains where feasible solutions can be found without backtracking. GRAPHPLAN and SATPLAN have trouble in domains with many objects because that means they must create many actions. In some cases the problem can be delayed or avoided by generating the propositionalized actions dynamically, only as needed, rather than instantiating them all before the search begins.

Readings in Planning (Allen *et al.*, 1990) is a comprehensive anthology of early work in the field. Weld (1994, 1999) provides two excellent surveys of planning algorithms of the 1990s. It is interesting to see the change in the five years between the two surveys: the first concentrates on partial-order planning, and the second introduces GRAPHPLAN and SATPLAN. *Automated Planning* (Ghallab *et al.*, 2004) is an excellent textbook on all aspects of planning. LaValle's text *Planning Algorithms* (2006) covers both classical and stochastic planning, with extensive coverage of robot motion planning.

Planning research has been central to AI since its inception, and papers on planning are a staple of mainstream AI journals and conferences. There are also specialized conferences such as the International Conference on AI Planning Systems, the International Workshop on Planning and Scheduling for Space, and the European Conference on Planning.

EXERCISES

1 Describe the differences and similarities between problem solving and planning.

2 Given the action schemas and initial state from Figure 1, what are all the applicable concrete instances of $Fly(p, from, to)$ in the state described by

$$At(P_1, JFK) \land At(P_2, SFO) \land Plane(P_1) \land Plane(P_2)$$
$$\land\ Airport(JFK) \land Airport(SFO)\ ?$$

3 The monkey-and-bananas problem is faced by a monkey in a laboratory with some bananas hanging out of reach from the ceiling. A box is available that will enable the monkey to reach the bananas if he climbs on it. Initially, the monkey is at A, the bananas at B, and the box at C. The monkey and box have height Low, but if the monkey climbs onto the box he will have height $High$, the same as the bananas. The actions available to the monkey include Go from one place to another, $Push$ an object from one place to another, $ClimbUp$ onto or $ClimbDown$ from an object, and $Grasp$ or $Ungrasp$ an object. The result of a $Grasp$ is that the monkey holds the object if the monkey and object are in the same place at the same height.

a. Write down the initial state description.

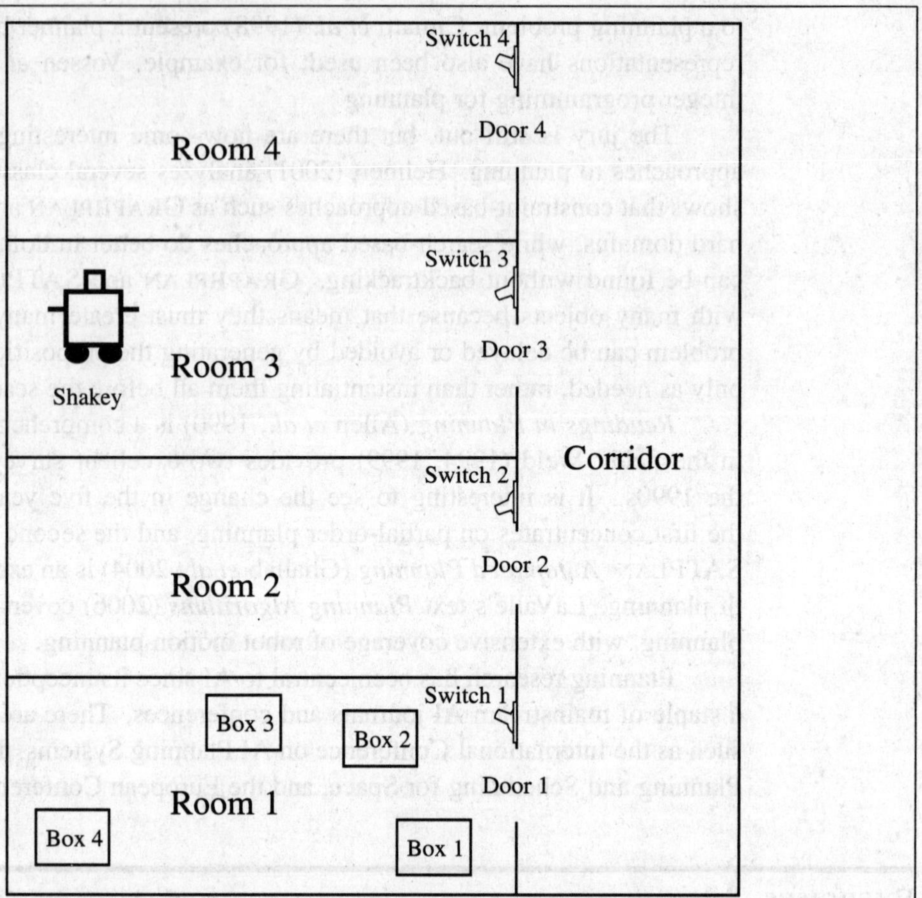

Figure 14 Shakey's world. Shakey can move between landmarks within a room, can pass through the door between rooms, can climb climbable objects and push pushable objects, and can flip light switches.

b. Write the six action schemas.

c. Suppose the monkey wants to fool the scientists, who are off to tea, by grabbing the bananas, but leaving the box in its original place. Write this as a general goal (i.e., not assuming that the box is necessarily at C) in the language of situation calculus. Can this goal be solved by a classical planning system?

d. Your schema for pushing is probably incorrect, because if the object is too heavy, its position will remain the same when the *Push* schema is applied. Fix your action schema to account for heavy objects.

4 The original STRIPS planner was designed to control Shakey the robot. Figure 14 shows a version of Shakey's world consisting of four rooms lined up along a corridor, where each room has a door and a light switch. The actions in Shakey's world include moving from place to place, pushing movable objects (such as boxes), climbing onto and down from rigid objects (such as boxes), and turning light switches on and off. The robot itself could not climb on a box or toggle a switch, but the planner was capable of finding and printing out plans that were beyond the robot's abilities. Shakey's six actions are the following:

- $Go(x, y, r)$, which requires that Shakey be $At\ x$ and that x and y are locations In the same room r. By convention a door between two rooms is in both of them.
- Push a box b from location x to location y within the same room: $Push(b, x, y, r)$. You will need the predicate Box and constants for the boxes.
- Climb onto a box from position x: $ClimbUp(x, b)$; climb down from a box to position x: $ClimbDown(b, x)$. We will need the predicate On and the constant $Floor$.
- Turn a light switch on or off: $TurnOn(s, b)$; $TurnOff(s, b)$. To turn a light on or off, Shakey must be on top of a box at the light switch's location.

Write PDDL sentences for Shakey's six actions and the initial state from Figure 14. Construct a plan for Shakey to get Box_2 into $Room_2$.

5 A finite Turing machine has a finite one-dimensional tape of cells, each cell containing one of a finite number of symbols. One cell has a read and write head above it. There is a finite set of states the machine can be in, one of which is the accept state. At each time step, depending on the symbol on the cell under the head and the machine's current state, there are a set of actions we can choose from. Each action involves writing a symbol to the cell under the head, transitioning the machine to a state, and optionally moving the head left or right. The mapping that determines which actions are allowed is the Turing machine's program. Your goal is to control the machine into the accept state.

Represent the Turing machine acceptance problem as a planning problem. If you can do this, it demonstrates that determining whether a planning problem has a solution is at least as hard as the Turing acceptance problem, which is PSPACE-hard.

6 Explain why dropping negative effects from every action schema in a planning problem results in a relaxed problem.

SUSSMAN ANOMALY

7 Figure 4 shows a blocks-world problem that is known as the **Sussman anomaly.** The problem was considered anomalous because the noninterleaved planners of the early 1970s could not solve it. Write a definition of the problem and solve it, either by hand or with a planning program. A noninterleaved planner is a planner that, when given two subgoals $G1$ and $G2$, produces either a plan for $G1$ concatenated with a plan for $G2$, or vice versa. Explain why a noninterleaved planner cannot solve this problem.

8 Prove that backward search with PDDL problems is complete.

9 Construct levels 0, 1, and 2 of the planning graph for the problem in Figure 1.

10 Prove the following assertions about planning graphs:

a. A literal that does not appear in the final level of the graph cannot be achieved.

b. The level cost of a literal in a serial graph is no greater than the actual cost of an optimal plan for achieving it.

11 The set-level heuristic uses a planning graph to estimate the cost of achieving a conjunctive goal from the current state. What relaxed problem is the set-level heuristic the solution to?

12 Examine the definition of **bidirectional search** in the chapter "Solving Problems by Searching."

a. Would bidirectional state-space search be a good idea for planning?

b. What about bidirectional search in the space of partial-order plans?

c. Devise a version of partial-order planning in which an action can be added to a plan if its preconditions can be achieved by the effects of actions already in the plan. Explain how to deal with conflicts and ordering constraints. Is the algorithm essentially identical to forward state-space search?

13 We contrasted forward and backward state-space searchers with partial-order planners, saying that the latter is a plan-space searcher. Explain how forward and backward state-space search can also be considered plan-space searchers, and say what the plan refinement operators are.

14 Up to now we have assumed that the plans we create always make sure that an action's preconditions are satisfied. Let us now investigate what propositional successor-state axioms such as $HaveArrow^{t+1} \Leftrightarrow (HaveArrow^t \wedge \neg Shoot^t)$ have to say about actions whose preconditions are not satisfied.

a. Show that the axioms predict that nothing will happen when an action is executed in a state where its preconditions are not satisfied.

b. Consider a plan p that contains the actions required to achieve a goal but also includes illegal actions. Is it the case that

$$initial\ state \wedge successor\text{-}state\ axioms \wedge p \models goal\ ?$$

c. With first-order successor-state axioms in situation calculus, is it possible to prove that a plan containing illegal actions will achieve the goal?

15 Consider how to translate a set of action schemas into the successor-state axioms of situation calculus.

a. Consider the schema for $Fly(p, from, to)$. Write a logical definition for the predicate $Poss(Fly(p, from, to), s)$, which is true if the preconditions for $Fly(p, from, to)$ are satisfied in situation s.

b. Next, assuming that $Fly(p, from, to)$ is the only action schema available to the agent, write down a successor-state axiom for $At(p, x, s)$ that captures the same information as the action schema.

c. Now suppose there is an additional method of travel: $Teleport(p, from, to)$. It has the additional precondition $\neg Warped(p)$ and the additional effect $Warped(p)$. Explain how the situation calculus knowledge base must be modified.

d. Finally, develop a general and precisely specified procedure for carrying out the translation from a set of action schemas to a set of successor-state axioms.

16 In the SATPLAN algorithm in Figure 22 of the chapter "Logical Agents," each call to the satisfiability algorithm asserts a goal g^T, where T ranges from 0 to $T_{\max}$. Suppose instead that the satisfiability algorithm is called only once, with the goal $g^0 \vee g^1 \vee \cdots \vee g^{T_{\max}}$.

a. Will this always return a plan if one exists with length less than or equal to $T_{\max}$?

b. Does this approach introduce any new spurious "solutions"?

c. Discuss how one might modify a satisfiability algorithm such as WALKSAT so that it finds short solutions (if they exist) when given a disjunctive goal of this form.

PLANNING AND ACTING IN THE REAL WORLD

In which we see how more expressive representations and more interactive agent architectures lead to planners that are useful in the real world.

Planners that are are used in the real world for planning and scheduling the operations of spacecraft, factories, and military campaigns go beyond the most basic concepts, representations, and algorithms for planning; they extend both the representation language and the way the planner interacts with the environment. This chapter shows how. Section 1 extends the classical language for planning to talk about actions with durations and resource constraints. Section 2 describes methods for constructing plans that are organized hierarchically. This allows human experts to communicate to the planner what they know about how to solve the problem. Hierarchy also lends itself to efficient plan construction because the planner can solve a problem at an abstract level before delving into details. Section 3 presents agent architectures that can handle uncertain environments and interleave deliberation with execution, and gives some examples of real-world systems. Section 4 shows how to plan when the environment contains other agents.

1 Time, Schedules, and Resources

The classical planning representation talks about *what to do*, and in *what order*, but the representation cannot talk about time: *how long* an action takes and *when* it occurs. For example, planners can produce a schedule for an airline that says which planes are assigned to which flights, but we really need to know departure and arrival times as well. This is the subject matter of **scheduling.** The real world also imposes many **resource constraints**; for example, an airline has a limited number of staff—and staff who are on one flight cannot be on another at the same time. This section covers methods for representing and solving planning problems that include temporal and resource constraints.

The approach we take in this section is "plan first, schedule later": that is, we divide the overall problem into a *planning* phase in which actions are selected, with some ordering constraints, to meet the goals of the problem, and a later *scheduling* phase, in which temporal information is added to the plan to ensure that it meets resource and deadline constraints.

$Jobs(\{AddEngine1 \prec AddWheels1 \prec Inspect1\},$
$\quad \{AddEngine2 \prec AddWheels2 \prec Inspect2\})$

$Resources(EngineHoists(1), WheelStations(1), Inspectors(2), LugNuts(500))$

$Action(AddEngine1, \text{DURATION}{:}30,$
$\quad \text{USE}{:}EngineHoists(1))$
$Action(AddEngine2, \text{DURATION}{:}60,$
$\quad \text{USE}{:}EngineHoists(1))$
$Action(AddWheels1, \text{DURATION}{:}30,$
$\quad \text{CONSUME}{:}LugNuts(20), \text{USE}{:}\ WheelStations(1))$
$Action(AddWheels2, \text{DURATION}{:}15,$
$\quad \text{CONSUME}{:}LugNuts(20), \text{USE}{:}\ WheelStations(1))$
$Action(Inspect_i, \text{DURATION}{:}10,$
$\quad \text{USE}{:}Inspectors(1))$

Figure 1 A job-shop scheduling problem for assembling two cars, with resource constraints. The notation $A \prec B$ means that action A must precede action B.

This approach is common in real-world manufacturing and logistical settings, where the planning phase is often performed by human experts. Automated methods can also be used for the planning phase, provided that they produce plans with just the minimal ordering constraints required for correctness. GRAPHPLAN, SATPLAN, and partial-order planners can do this; search-based methods produce totally ordered plans, but these can easily be converted to plans with minimal ordering constraints.

1.1 Representing temporal and resource constraints

JOB
DURATION

A typical **job-shop scheduling problem** consists of a set of **jobs**, each of which consists a collection of **actions** with ordering constraints among them. Each action has a **duration** and a set of resource constraints required by the action. Each constraint specifies a *type* of resource (e.g., bolts, wrenches, or pilots), the number of that resource required, and whether that resource is **consumable** (e.g., the bolts are no longer available for use) or **reusable** (e.g., a pilot is occupied during a flight but is available again when the flight is over). Resources can also be *produced* by actions with negative consumption, including manufacturing, growing, and resupply actions. A solution to a job-shop scheduling problem must specify the start times for each action and must satisfy all the temporal ordering constraints and resource constraints. As with search and planning problems, solutions can be evaluated according to a cost function; this can be quite complicated, with nonlinear resource costs, time-dependent delay costs, and so on. For simplicity, we assume that the cost function is just the total duration of the plan, which is called the **makespan**.

CONSUMABLE
REUSABLE
MAKESPAN

Figure 1 shows a simple example: a problem involving the assembly of two cars. The problem consists of two jobs, each of the form $[AddEngine, AddWheels, Inspect]$. Then the

Resources statement declares that there are four types of resources, and gives the number of each type available at the start: 1 engine hoist, 1 wheel station, 2 inspectors, and 500 lug nuts. The action schemas give the duration and resource needs of each action. The lug nuts are *consumed* as wheels are added to the car, whereas the other resources are "borrowed" at the start of an action and released at the action's end.

The representation of resources as numerical quantities, such as $Inspectors(2)$ rather than as named entities, such as $Inspector(I_1)$ and $Inspector(I_2)$, is an example of a very general technique called **aggregation**. The central idea of aggregation is to group individual objects into quantities when the objects are all indistinguishable with respect to the purpose at hand. In our assembly problem, it does not matter *which* inspector inspects the car, so there is no need to make the distinction. Aggregation is essential for reducing complexity. Consider what happens when a proposed schedule has 10 concurrent *Inspect* actions but only 9 inspectors are available. With inspectors represented as quantities, a failure is detected immediately and the algorithm backtracks to try another schedule. With inspectors represented as individuals, the algorithm backtracks to try all 10! ways of assigning inspectors to actions.

AGGREGATION

1.2 Solving scheduling problems

We begin by considering just the temporal scheduling problem, ignoring resource constraints. To minimize makespan (plan duration), we must find the earliest start times for all the actions consistent with the ordering constraints supplied with the problem. It is helpful to view these ordering constraints as a directed graph relating the actions, as shown in Figure 2. We can apply the **critical path method** (CPM) to this graph to determine the possible start and end times of each action. A **path** through a graph representing a partial-order plan is a linearly ordered sequence of actions beginning with *Start* and ending with *Finish*. (For example, there are two paths in the partial-order plan in Figure 2.)

CRITICAL PATH METHOD

The **critical path** is that path whose total duration is longest; the path is "critical" because it determines the duration of the entire plan—shortening other paths doesn't shorten the plan as a whole, but delaying the start of any action on the critical path slows down the whole plan. Actions that are off the critical path have a window of time in which they can be executed. The window is specified in terms of an earliest possible start time, ES, and a latest possible start time, LS. The quantity $LS - ES$ is known as the **slack** of an action. We can see in Figure 2 that the whole plan will take 85 minutes, that each action in the top job has 15 minutes of slack, and that each action on the critical path has no slack (by definition). Together the ES and LS times for all the actions constitute a **schedule** for the problem.

CRITICAL PATH

SLACK

SCHEDULE

The following formulas serve as a definition for ES and LS and also as the outline of a dynamic-programming algorithm to compute them. A and B are actions, and $A \prec B$ means that A comes before B:

$$ES(Start) = 0$$
$$ES(B) = \max_{A \prec B} ES(A) + Duration(A)$$
$$LS(Finish) = ES(Finish)$$
$$LS(A) = \min_{B \succ A} LS(B) - Duration(A)\ .$$

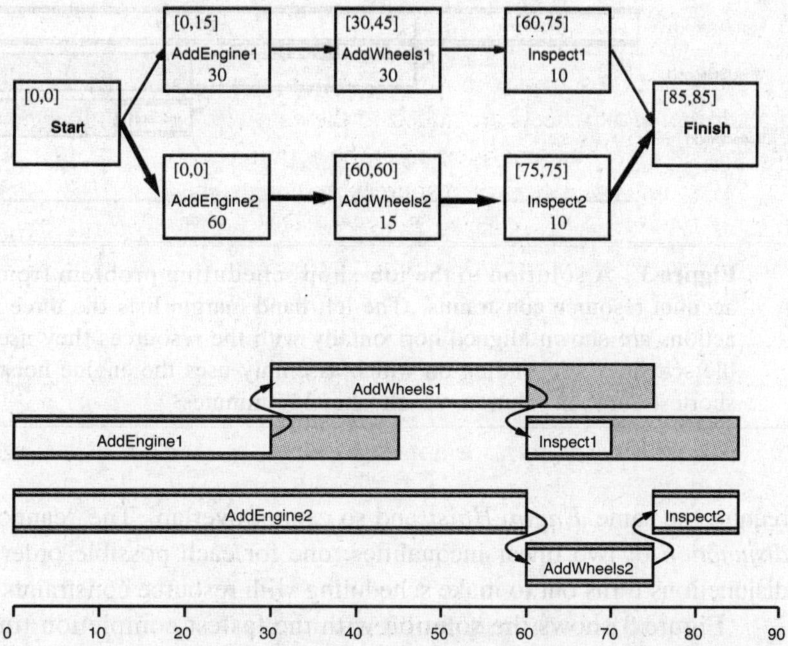

Figure 2 Top: a representation of the temporal constraints for the job-shop scheduling problem of Figure 1. The duration of each action is given at the bottom of each rectangle. In solving the problem, we compute the earliest and latest start times as the pair $[ES, LS]$, displayed in the upper left. The difference between these two numbers is the *slack* of an action; actions with zero slack are on the critical path, shown with bold arrows. Bottom: the same solution shown as a timeline. Grey rectangles represent time intervals during which an action may be executed, provided that the ordering constraints are respected. The unoccupied portion of a gray rectangle indicates the slack.

The idea is that we start by assigning $ES(Start)$ to be 0. Then, as soon as we get an action B such that all the actions that come immediately before B have ES values assigned, we set $ES(B)$ to be the maximum of the earliest finish times of those immediately preceding actions, where the earliest finish time of an action is defined as the earliest start time plus the duration. This process repeats until every action has been assigned an ES value. The LS values are computed in a similar manner, working backward from the *Finish* action.

The complexity of the critical path algorithm is just $O(Nb)$, where N is the number of actions and b is the maximum branching factor into or out of an action. (To see this, note that the LS and ES computations are done once for each action, and each computation iterates over at most b other actions.) Therefore, finding a minimum-duration schedule, given a partial ordering on the actions and no resource constraints, is quite easy.

Mathematically speaking, critical-path problems are easy to solve because they are defined as a *conjunction* of *linear* inequalities on the start and end times. When we introduce resource constraints, the resulting constraints on start and end times become more complicated. For example, the $AddEngine$ actions, which begin at the same time in Figure 2,

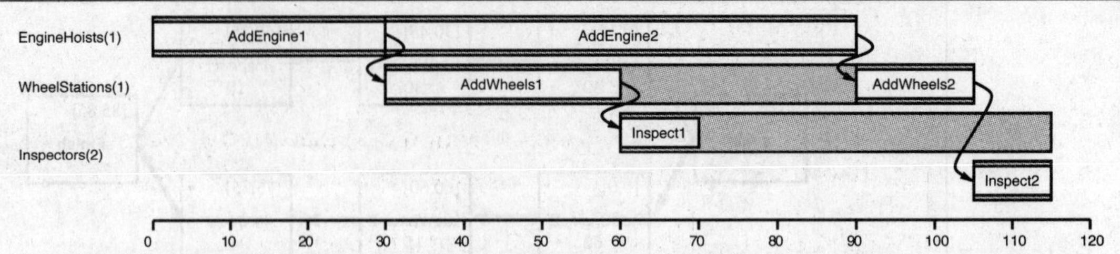

Figure 3 A solution to the job-shop scheduling problem from Figure 1, taking into account resource constraints. The left-hand margin lists the three reusable resources, and actions are shown aligned horizontally with the resources they use. There are two possible schedules, depending on which assembly uses the engine hoist first; we've shown the shortest-duration solution, which takes 115 minutes.

require the same *EngineHoist* and so cannot overlap. The "cannot overlap" constraint is a *disjunction* of two linear inequalities, one for each possible ordering. The introduction of disjunctions turns out to make scheduling with resource constraints NP-hard.

Figure 3 shows the solution with the fastest completion time, 115 minutes. This is 30 minutes longer than the 85 minutes required for a schedule without resource constraints. Notice that there is no time at which both inspectors are required, so we can immediately move one of our two inspectors to a more productive position.

The complexity of scheduling with resource constraints is often seen in practice as well as in theory. A challenge problem posed in 1963—to find the optimal schedule for a problem involving just 10 machines and 10 jobs of 100 actions each—went unsolved for 23 years (Lawler *et al.*, 1993). Many approaches have been tried, including branch-and bound, simulated annealing, tabu search, and constraint satisfaction. One simple but popular heuristic is the **minimum slack** algorithm: on each iteration, schedule for the earliest possible start whichever unscheduled action has all its predecessors scheduled and has the least slack; then update the *ES* and *LS* times for each affected action and repeat. The heuristic resembles the minimum-remaining-values (MRV) heuristic in constraint satisfaction. It often works well in practice, but for our assembly problem it yields a 130–minute solution, not the 115–minute solution of Figure 3.

MINIMUM SLACK

Up to this point, we have assumed that the set of actions and ordering constraints is fixed. Under these assumptions, every scheduling problem can be solved by a nonoverlapping sequence that avoids all resource conflicts, provided that each action is feasible by itself. If a scheduling problem is proving very difficult, however, it may not be a good idea to solve it this way—it may be better to reconsider the actions and constraints, in case that leads to a much easier scheduling problem. Thus, it makes sense to *integrate* planning and scheduling by taking into account durations and overlaps during the construction of a partial-order plan. Several planning algorithms can be augmented to handle this information. For example, partial-order planners can detect resource constraint violations in much the same way they detect conflicts with causal links. Heuristics can be devised to estimate the total completion time of a plan. This is currently an active area of research.

2 HIERARCHICAL PLANNING

Most likely, the problem-solving and planning methods that you are familiar with all operate with a fixed set of atomic actions. Actions can be strung together into sequences or branching networks; state-of-the-art algorithms can generate solutions containing thousands of actions.

For plans executed by the human brain, atomic actions are muscle activations. In very round numbers, we have about 10^3 muscles to activate (639, by some counts, but many of them have multiple subunits); we can modulate their activation perhaps 10 times per second; and we are alive and awake for about 10^9 seconds in all. Thus, a human life contains about 10^{13} actions, give or take one or two orders of magnitude. Even if we restrict ourselves to planning over much shorter time horizons—for example, a two-week vacation in Hawaii—a detailed motor plan would contain around 10^{10} actions. This is a lot more than 1000.

To bridge this gap, AI systems will probably have to do what humans appear to do: plan at higher levels of abstraction. A reasonable plan for the Hawaii vacation might be "Go to San Francisco airport; take Hawaiian Airlines flight 11 to Honolulu; do vacation stuff for two weeks; take Hawaiian Airlines flight 12 back to San Francisco; go home." Given such a plan, the action "Go to San Francisco airport" can be viewed as a planning task in itself, with a solution such as "Drive to the long-term parking lot; park; take the shuttle to the terminal." Each of these actions, in turn, can be decomposed further, until we reach the level of actions that can be executed without deliberation to generate the required motor control sequences.

In this example, we see that planning can occur both before and during the execution of the plan; for example, one would probably defer the problem of planning a route from a parking spot in long-term parking to the shuttle bus stop until a particular parking spot has been found during execution. Thus, that particular action will remain at an abstract level prior to the execution phase. We defer discussion of this topic until Section 3. Here, we concentrate on the aspect of **hierarchical decomposition**, an idea that pervades almost all attempts to manage complexity. For example, complex software is created from a hierarchy of subroutines or object classes; armies operate as a hierarchy of units; governments and corporations have hierarchies of departments, subsidiaries, and branch offices. The key benefit of hierarchical structure is that, at each level of the hierarchy, a computational task, military mission, or administrative function is reduced to a *small* number of activities at the next lower level, so the computational cost of finding the correct way to arrange those activities for the current problem is small. Nonhierarchical methods, on the other hand, reduce a task to a *large* number of individual actions; for large-scale problems, this is completely impractical.

HIERARCHICAL DECOMPOSITION

2.1 High-level actions

The basic formalism we adopt to understand hierarchical decomposition comes from the area of **hierarchical task networks** or HTN planning. As in classical planning, we assume full observability and determinism and the availability of a set of actions, now called **primitive actions**, with standard precondition–effect schemas. The key additional concept is the **high-level action** or HLA—for example, the action "Go to San Francisco airport" in the example

HIERARCHICAL TASK NETWORK

PRIMITIVE ACTION

HIGH-LEVEL ACTION

$$\begin{array}{l} Refinement(Go(Home, SFO), \\ \quad \text{STEPS: } [Drive(Home, SFOLongTermParking), \\ \qquad\qquad Shuttle(SFOLongTermParking, SFO)]\,) \\ Refinement(Go(Home, SFO), \\ \quad \text{STEPS: } [Taxi(Home, SFO)]\,) \end{array}$$

$$\begin{array}{l} Refinement(Navigate([a, b], [x, y]), \\ \quad \text{PRECOND: } a = x \land b = y \\ \quad \text{STEPS: } [\,]\,) \\ Refinement(Navigate([a, b], [x, y]), \\ \quad \text{PRECOND: } Connected([a, b], [a-1, b]) \\ \quad \text{STEPS: } [Left, Navigate([a-1, b], [x, y])]\,) \\ Refinement(Navigate([a, b], [x, y]), \\ \quad \text{PRECOND: } Connected([a, b], [a+1, b]) \\ \quad \text{STEPS: } [Right, Navigate([a+1, b], [x, y])]\,) \\ \ldots \end{array}$$

Figure 4 Definitions of possible refinements for two high-level actions: going to San Francisco airport and navigating in the vacuum world. In the latter case, note the recursive nature of the refinements and the use of preconditions.

REFINEMENT

given earlier. Each HLA has one or more possible **refinements**, into a sequence[1] of actions, each of which may be an HLA or a primitive action (which has no refinements by definition). For example, the action "Go to San Francisco airport," represented formally as *Go*(*Home SFO*), might have two possible refinements, as shown in Figure 4. The same figure shows a **recursive** refinement for navigation in the vacuum world: to get to a destination, take a step, and then go to the destination.

These examples show that high-level actions and their refinements embody knowledge about *how to do things*. For instance, the refinements for $Go(Home, SFO)$ say that to get to the airport you can drive or take a taxi; buying milk, sitting down, and moving the knight to e4 are not to be considered.

IMPLEMENTATION

An HLA refinement that contains only primitive actions is called an **implementation** of the HLA. For example, in the vacuum world, the sequences $[Right, Right, Down]$ and $[Down, Right, Right]$ both implement the HLA $Navigate([1, 3], [3, 2])$. An implementation of a high-level plan (a sequence of HLAs) is the concatenation of implementations of each HLA in the sequence. Given the precondition–effect definitions of each primitive action, it is straightforward to determine whether any given implementation of a high-level plan achieves the goal. We can say, then, that *a high-level plan achieves the goal from a given state if at least one of its implementations achieves the goal from that state.* The "at least one" in this definition is crucial—not *all* implementations need to achieve the goal, because the agent gets

[1] HTN planners often allow refinement into partially ordered plans, and they allow the refinements of two different HLAs in a plan to *share* actions. We omit these important complications in the interest of understanding the basic concepts of hierarchical planning.

to decide which implementation it will execute. Thus, the set of possible implementations in HTN planning—each of which may have a different outcome—is not the same as the set of possible outcomes in nondeterministic planning. There, we required that a plan work for *all* outcomes because the agent doesn't get to choose the outcome; nature does.

The simplest case is an HLA that has exactly one implementation. In that case, we can compute the preconditions and effects of the HLA from those of the implementation (see Exercise 3) and then treat the HLA exactly as if it were a primitive action itself. It can be shown that the right collection of HLAs can result in the time complexity of blind search dropping from exponential in the solution depth to linear in the solution depth, although devising such a collection of HLAs may be a nontrivial task in itself. When HLAs have multiple possible implementations, there are two options: one is to search among the implementations for one that works, as in Section 2.2; the other is to reason directly about the HLAs—despite the multiplicity of implementations—as explained in Section 2.3. The latter method enables the derivation of provably correct abstract plans, without the need to consider their implementations.

2.2 Searching for primitive solutions

HTN planning is often formulated with a single "top level" action called *Act*, where the aim is to find an implementation of *Act* that achieves the goal. This approach is entirely general. For example, classical planning problems can be defined as follows: for each primitive action a_i, provide one refinement of *Act* with steps $[a_i, Act]$. That creates a recursive definition of *Act* that lets us add actions. But we need some way to stop the recursion; we do that by providing one more refinement for *Act*, one with an empty list of steps and with a precondition equal to the goal of the problem. This says that if the goal is already achieved, then the right implementation is to do nothing.

The approach leads to a simple algorithm: repeatedly choose an HLA in the current plan and replace it with one of its refinements, until the plan achieves the goal. One possible implementation based on breadth-first tree search is shown in Figure 5. Plans are considered in order of depth of nesting of the refinements, rather than number of primitive steps. It is straightforward to design a graph-search version of the algorithm as well as depth-first and iterative deepening versions.

In essence, this form of hierarchical search explores the space of sequences that conform to the knowledge contained in the HLA library about how things are to be done. A great deal of knowledge can be encoded, not just in the action sequences specified in each refinement but also in the preconditions for the refinements. For some domains, HTN planners have been able to generate huge plans with very little search. For example, O-PLAN (Bell and Tate, 1985), which combines HTN planning with scheduling, has been used to develop production plans for Hitachi. A typical problem involves a product line of 350 different products, 35 assembly machines, and over 2000 different operations. The planner generates a 30-day schedule with three 8-hour shifts a day, involving tens of millions of steps. Another important aspect of HTN plans is that they are, by definition, hierarchically structured; usually this makes them easy for humans to understand.

```
function HIERARCHICAL-SEARCH(problem, hierarchy) returns a solution, or failure
  frontier ← a FIFO queue with [Act] as the only element
  loop do
     if EMPTY?(frontier) then return failure
     plan ← POP(frontier)  /* chooses the shallowest plan in frontier */
     hla ← the first HLA in plan, or null if none
     prefix,suffix ← the action subsequences before and after hla in plan
     outcome ← RESULT(problem.INITIAL-STATE, prefix)
     if hla is null then  /* so plan is primitive and outcome is its result */
        if outcome satisfies problem.GOAL  then return plan
     else for each sequence in REFINEMENTS(hla, outcome, hierarchy) do
        frontier ← INSERT(APPEND(prefix, sequence, suffix), frontier)
```

Figure 5 A breadth-first implementation of hierarchical forward planning search. The initial plan supplied to the algorithm is [*Act*]. The REFINEMENTS function returns a set of action sequences, one for each refinement of the HLA whose preconditions are satisfied by the specified state, *outcome*.

The computational benefits of hierarchical search can be seen by examining an idealized case. Suppose that a planning problem has a solution with d primitive actions. For a nonhierarchical, forward state-space planner with b allowable actions at each state, the cost is $O(b^d)$. For an HTN planner, let us suppose a very regular refinement structure: each nonprimitive action has r possible refinements, each into k actions at the next lower level. We want to know how many different refinement trees there are with this structure. Now, if there are d actions at the primitive level, then the number of levels below the root is $\log_k d$, so the number of internal refinement nodes is $1 + k + k^2 + \cdots + k^{\log_k d - 1} = (d-1)/(k-1)$. Each internal node has r possible refinements, so $r^{(d-1)/(k-1)}$ possible regular decomposition trees could be constructed. Examining this formula, we see that keeping r small and k large can result in huge savings: essentially we are taking the kth root of the nonhierarchical cost, if b and r are comparable. Small r and large k means a library of HLAs with a small number of refinements each yielding a long action sequence (that nonetheless allows us to solve any problem). This is not always possible: long action sequences that are usable across a wide range of problems are extremely precious.

The key to HTN planning, then, is the construction of a plan library containing known methods for implementing complex, high-level actions. One method of constructing the library is to *learn* the methods from problem-solving experience. After the excruciating experience of constructing a plan from scratch, the agent can save the plan in the library as a method for implementing the high-level action defined by the task. In this way, the agent can become more and more competent over time as new methods are built on top of old methods. One important aspect of this learning process is the ability to *generalize* the methods that are constructed, eliminating detail that is specific to the problem instance (e.g., the name of the builder or the address of the plot of land) and keeping just the key elements of the plan. It seems to us inconceivable that humans could be as competent as they are without some such mechanism.

2.3 Searching for abstract solutions

The hierarchical search algorithm in the preceding section refines HLAs all the way to primitive action sequences to determine if a plan is workable. This contradicts common sense: one should be able to determine that the two-HLA high-level plan

$$[Drive(Home, SFOLongTermParking), Shuttle(SFOLongTermParking, SFO)]$$

gets one to the airport without having to determine a precise route, choice of parking spot, and so on. The solution seems obvious: write precondition–effect descriptions of the HLAs, just as we write down what the primitive actions do. From the descriptions, it ought to be easy to prove that the high-level plan achieves the goal. This is the holy grail, so to speak, of hierarchical planning because if we derive a high-level plan that provably achieves the goal, working in a small search space of high-level actions, then we can commit to that plan and work on the problem of refining each step of the plan. This gives us the exponential reduction we seek. For this to work, it has to be the case that every high-level plan that "claims" to achieve the goal (by virtue of the descriptions of its steps) does in fact achieve the goal in the sense defined earlier: it must have at least one implementation that does achieve the goal.

DOWNWARD REFINEMENT PROPERTY

This property has been called the **downward refinement property** for HLA descriptions.

Writing HLA descriptions that satisfy the downward refinement property is, in principle, easy: as long as the descriptions are *true*, then any high-level plan that claims to achieve the goal must in fact do so—otherwise, the descriptions are making some false claim about what the HLAs do. We have already seen how to write true descriptions for HLAs that have exactly one implementation (Exercise 3); a problem arises when the HLA has *multiple* implementations. How can we describe the effects of an action that can be implemented in many different ways?

One safe answer (at least for problems where all preconditions and goals are positive) is to include only the positive effects that are achieved by *every* implementation of the HLA and the negative effects of *any* implementation. Then the downward refinement property would be satisfied. Unfortunately, this semantics for HLAs is much too conservative. Consider again the HLA $Go(Home, SFO)$, which has two refinements, and suppose, for the sake of argument, a simple world in which one can always drive to the airport and park, but taking a taxi requires $Cash$ as a precondition. In that case, $Go(Home, SFO)$ doesn't always get you to the airport. In particular, it fails if $Cash$ is false, and so we cannot assert $At(Agent, SFO)$ as an effect of the HLA. This makes no sense, however; if the agent didn't have $Cash$, it would drive itself. Requiring that an effect hold for *every* implementation is equivalent to assuming that *someone else*—an adversary—will choose the implementation. It treats the HLA's multiple outcomes exactly as if the HLA were a **nondeterministic** action. For our case, the agent itself will choose the implementation.

DEMONIC NONDETERMINISM

The programming languages community has coined the term **demonic nondeterminism** for the case where an adversary makes the choices, contrasting this with **angelic nonde-**

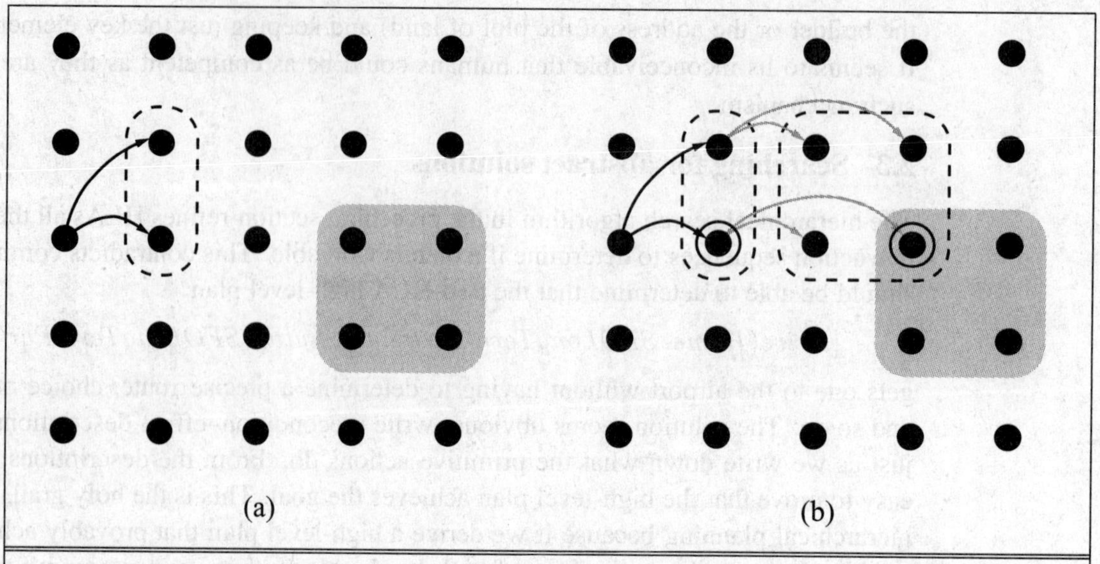

Figure 6 Schematic examples of reachable sets. The set of goal states is shaded. Black and gray arrows indicate possible implementations of h_1 and h_2, respectively. (a) The reachable set of an HLA h_1 in a state s. (b) The reachable set for the sequence $[h_1, h_2]$. Because this intersects the goal set, the sequence achieves the goal.

ANGELIC NONDETERMINISM

ANGELIC SEMANTICS

REACHABLE SET

terminism, where the agent itself makes the choices. We borrow this term to define **angelic semantics** for HLA descriptions. The basic concept required for understanding angelic semantics is the **reachable set** of an HLA: given a state s, the reachable set for an HLA h, written as $\text{REACH}(s, h)$, is the set of states reachable by any of the HLA's implementations. The key idea is that the agent can choose *which* element of the reachable set it ends up in when it executes the HLA; thus, an HLA with multiple refinements is more "powerful" than the same HLA with fewer refinements. We can also define the reachable set of a sequences of HLAs. For example, the reachable set of a sequence $[h_1, h_2]$ is the union of all the reachable sets obtained by applying h_2 in each state in the reachable set of h_1:

$$\text{REACH}(s, [h_1, h_2]) = \bigcup_{s' \in \text{REACH}(s, h_1)} \text{REACH}(s', h_2).$$

Given these definitions, a high-level plan—a sequence of HLAs—achieves the goal if its reachable set *intersects* the set of goal states. (Compare this to the much stronger condition for demonic semantics, where every member of the reachable set has to be a goal state.) Conversely, if the reachable set doesn't intersect the goal, then the plan definitely doesn't work. Figure 6 illustrates these ideas.

The notion of reachable sets yields a straightforward algorithm: search among high-level plans, looking for one whose reachable set intersects the goal; once that happens, the algorithm can *commit* to that abstract plan, knowing that it works, and focus on refining the plan further. We will come back to the algorithmic issues later; first, we consider the question of how the effects of an HLA—the reachable set for each possible initial state—are represented. As with classical action schemas, we represent the *changes* made to each fluent. Think of a fluent as a state variable. A primitive action can *add* or *delete* a variable or leave it *unchanged.* (With conditional effects (see Section 3.1) there is a fourth possibility: flipping a variable to its opposite.)

An HLA under angelic semantics can do more: it can *control* the value of a variable, setting it to true or false depending on which implementation is chosen. In fact, an HLA can have nine different effects on a variable: if the variable starts out true, it can always keep it true, always make it false, or have a choice; if the variable starts out false, it can always keep it false, always make it true, or have a choice; and the three choices for each case can be combined arbitrarily, making nine. Notationally, this is a bit challenging. We'll use the $\tilde{}$ symbol to mean "possibly, if the agent so chooses." Thus, an effect $\tilde{+}A$ means "possibly add A," that is, either leave A unchanged or make it true. Similarly, $\tilde{-}A$ means "possibly delete A" and $\tilde{\pm}A$ means "possibly add or delete A." For example, the HLA $Go(Home, SFO)$, with the two refinements shown in Figure 4, possibly deletes *Cash* (if the agent decides to take a taxi), so it should have the effect $\tilde{-}Cash$. Thus, we see that the descriptions of HLAs are *derivable*, in principle, from the descriptions of their refinements—in fact, this is required if we want true HLA descriptions, such that the downward refinement property holds. Now, suppose we have the following schemas for the HLAs h_1 and h_2:

$$Action(h_1, \text{PRECOND:}\neg A, \text{EFFECT:} A \wedge \tilde{-}B)\,,$$
$$Action(h_2, \text{PRECOND:}\neg B, \text{EFFECT:}\tilde{+}A \wedge \tilde{\pm}C)\,.$$

That is, h_1 adds A and possible deletes B, while h_2 possibly adds A and has full control over C. Now, if only B is true in the initial state and the goal is $A \wedge C$ then the sequence $[h_1, h_2]$ achieves the goal: we choose an implementation of h_1 that makes B false, then choose an implementation of h_2 that leaves A true and makes C true.

The preceding discussion assumes that the effects of an HLA—the reachable set for any given initial state—can be described exactly by describing the effect on each variable. It would be nice if this were always true, but in many cases we can only approximate the effects because an HLA may have infinitely many implementations and may produce arbitrarily wiggly reachable sets. For example, we said that $Go(Home, SFO)$ possibly deletes *Cash*; it also possibly adds *At*(*Car*, *SFOLongTermParking*); but it cannot do both—in fact, it must do exactly one. As with belief states, we may need to write *approximate* descriptions. We will use two kinds of approximation: an **optimistic description** $\text{REACH}^+(s, h)$ of an HLA h may overstate the reachable set, while a **pessimistic description** $\text{REACH}^-(s, h)$ may understate the reachable set. Thus, we have

OPTIMISTIC DESCRIPTION
PESSIMISTIC DESCRIPTION

$$\text{REACH}^-(s,h) \subseteq \text{REACH}(s,h) \subseteq \text{REACH}^+(s,h)\,.$$

For example, an optimistic description of $Go(Home, SFO)$ says that it possible deletes $Cash$ *and* possibly adds $At(Car, SFOLongTermParking)$.

With approximate descriptions, the test for whether a plan achieves the goal needs to be modified slightly. If the optimistic reachable set for the plan doesn't intersect the goal,

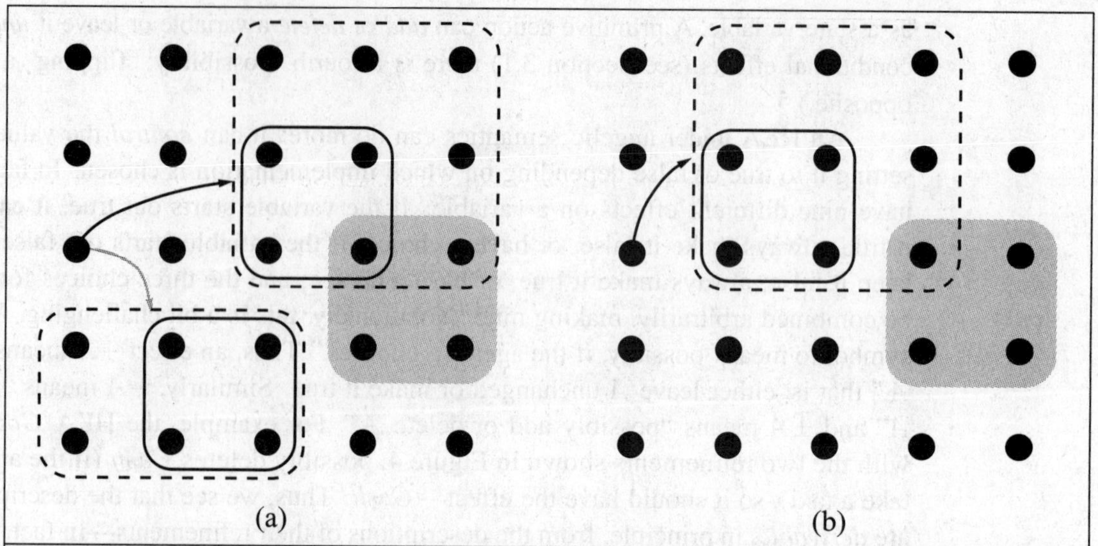

Figure 7 Goal achievement for high-level plans with approximate descriptions. The set of goal states is shaded. For each plan, the pessimistic (solid lines) and optimistic (dashed lines) reachable sets are shown. (a) The plan indicated by the black arrow definitely achieves the goal, while the plan indicated by the gray arrow definitely doesn't. (b) A plan that would need to be refined further to determine if it really does achieve the goal.

then the plan doesn't work; if the pessimistic reachable set intersects the goal, then the plan does work (Figure 7(a)). With exact descriptions, a plan either works or it doesn't, but with approximate descriptions, there is a middle ground: if the optimistic set intersects the goal but the pessimistic set doesn't, then we cannot tell if the plan works (Figure 7(b)). When this circumstance arises, the uncertainty can be resolved by refining the plan. This is a very common situation in human reasoning. For example, in planning the aforementioned two-week Hawaii vacation, one might propose to spend two days on each of seven islands. Prudence would indicate that this ambitious plan needs to be refined by adding details of inter-island transportation.

An algorithm for hierarchical planning with approximate angelic descriptions is shown in Figure 8. For simplicity, we have kept to the same overall scheme used previously in Figure 5, that is, a breadth-first search in the space of refinements. As just explained, the algorithm can detect plans that will and won't work by checking the intersections of the optimistic and pessimistic reachable sets with the goal. (The details of how to compute the reachable sets of a plan, given approximate descriptions of each step, are covered in Exercise 5.) When a workable abstract plan is found, the algorithm *decomposes* the original problem into subproblems, one for each step of the plan. The initial state and goal for each subproblem are obtained by regressing a guaranteed-reachable goal state through the action schemas for each step of the plan. Figure 6(b) illustrates the basic idea: the right-hand circled state is the guaranteed-reachable goal state, and the left-hand circled state is the intermediate

```
function ANGELIC-SEARCH(problem, hierarchy, initialPlan) returns solution or fail
  frontier ← a FIFO queue with initialPlan as the only element
  loop do
     if EMPTY?(frontier) then return fail
     plan ← POP(frontier)  /* chooses the shallowest node in frontier */
     if REACH+(problem.INITIAL-STATE, plan) intersects problem.GOAL then
        if plan is primitive then return plan  /* REACH+ is exact for primitive plans */
        guaranteed ← REACH−(problem.INITIAL-STATE, plan) ∩ problem.GOAL
        if guaranteed≠{ } and MAKING-PROGRESS(plan, initialPlan) then
           finalState ← any element of guaranteed
           return DECOMPOSE(hierarchy, problem.INITIAL-STATE, plan, finalState)
        hla ← some HLA in plan
        prefix,suffix ← the action subsequences before and after hla in plan
        for each sequence in REFINEMENTS(hla, outcome, hierarchy) do
           frontier ← INSERT(APPEND(prefix, sequence, suffix), frontier)
```

```
function DECOMPOSE(hierarchy, s0, plan, sf) returns a solution
  solution ← an empty plan
  while plan is not empty do
     action ← REMOVE-LAST(plan)
     si ← a state in REACH−(s0, plan) such that sf ∈REACH−(si, action)
     problem ← a problem with INITIAL-STATE = si and GOAL = sf
     solution ← APPEND(ANGELIC-SEARCH(problem, hierarchy, action), solution)
     sf ← si
  return solution
```

Figure 8 A hierarchical planning algorithm that uses angelic semantics to identify and commit to high-level plans that work while avoiding high-level plans that don't. The predicate MAKING-PROGRESS checks to make sure that we aren't stuck in an infinite regression of refinements. At top level, call ANGELIC-SEARCH with $[Act]$ as the *initialPlan*.

goal obtained by regressing the goal through the final action.

The ability to commit to or reject high-level plans can give ANGELIC-SEARCH a significant computational advantage over HIERARCHICAL-SEARCH, which in turn may have a large advantage over plain old BREADTH-FIRST-SEARCH. Consider, for example, cleaning up a large vacuum world consisting of rectangular rooms connected by narrow corridors. It makes sense to have an HLA for *Navigate* (as shown in Figure 4) and one for *CleanWholeRoom*. (Cleaning the room could be implemented with the repeated application of another HLA to clean each row.) Since there are five actions in this domain, the cost for BREADTH-FIRST-SEARCH grows as 5^d, where d is the length of the shortest solution (roughly twice the total number of squares); the algorithm cannot manage even two 2×2 rooms. HIERARCHICAL-SEARCH is more efficient, but still suffers from exponential growth because it tries all ways of cleaning that are consistent with the hierarchy. ANGELIC-SEARCH scales approximately linearly in the number of squares—it commits to a good high-level sequence and prunes away the other options. Notice that cleaning a set of rooms by cleaning each room in turn is hardly rocket science: it is easy for humans precisely because of the hierarchical structure of the task. When we consider how difficult humans find it to solve small puzzles such as the 8-puzzle, it seems likely that the human capacity for solving complex problems derives to a great extent from their skill in abstracting and decomposing the problem to eliminate combinatorics.

The angelic approach can be extended to find least-cost solutions by generalizing the notion of reachable set. Instead of a state being reachable or not, it has a cost for the most efficient way to get there. (The cost is ∞ for unreachable states.) The optimistic and pessimistic descriptions bound these costs. In this way, angelic search can find provably optimal abstract plans without considering their implementations. The same approach can be used to obtain effective **hierarchical lookahead** algorithms for online search, in the style of LRTA*. In some ways, such algorithms mirror aspects of human deliberation in tasks such as planning a vacation to Hawaii—consideration of alternatives is done initially at an abstract level over long time scales; some parts of the plan are left quite abstract until execution time, such as how to spend two lazy days on Molokai, while others parts are planned in detail, such as the flights to be taken and lodging to be reserved—without these refinements, there is no guarantee that the plan would be feasible.

HIERARCHICAL LOOKAHEAD

3 PLANNING AND ACTING IN NONDETERMINISTIC DOMAINS

In this section we extend planning to handle partially observable, nondeterministic, and unknown environments. Methods include: **sensorless planning** (also known as **conformant planning**) for environments with no observations; **contingency planning** for partially observable and nondeterministic environments; and **online planning** and **replanning** for unknown environments.

Here, planners deal with factored representations rather than atomic representations. This affects the way we represent the agent's capability for action and observation and the way we represent **belief states**—the sets of possible physical states the agent might be in—for unobservable and partially observable environments. We can also take advantage of many domain-independent methods for calculating search heuristics.

Consider this problem: given a chair and a table, the goal is to have them match—have the same color. In the initial state we have two cans of paint, but the colors of the paint and the furniture are unknown. Only the table is initially in the agent's field of view:

$$Init(Object(Table) \land Object(Chair) \land Can(C_1) \land Can(C_2) \land InView(Table))$$
$$Goal(Color(Chair, c) \land Color(Table, c))$$

There are two actions: removing the lid from a paint can and painting an object using the paint from an open can. The action schemas are straightforward, with one exception: we now allow preconditions and effects to contain variables that are not part of the action's variable list. That is, $Paint(x, can)$ does not mention the variable c, representing the color of the paint in the can. In the fully observable case, this is not allowed—we would have to name the action $Paint(x, can, c)$. But in the partially observable case, we might or might not know what color is in the can. (The variable c is universally quantified, just like all the other variables in an action schema.)

$$\begin{array}{l} Action(RemoveLid(can), \\ \quad \text{PRECOND}: Can(can) \\ \quad \text{EFFECT}: Open(can)) \\ Action(Paint(x, can), \\ \quad \text{PRECOND}: Object(x) \wedge Can(can) \wedge Color(can, c) \wedge Open(can) \\ \quad \text{EFFECT}: Color(x, c)) \end{array}$$

To solve a partially observable problem, the agent will have to reason about the percepts it will obtain when it is executing the plan. The percept will be supplied by the agent's sensors when it is actually acting, but when it is planning it will need a model of its sensors. For planning,

PERCEPT SCHEMA we augment PDDL with a new type of schema, the **percept schema**:

$$\begin{array}{l} Percept(Color(x, c), \\ \quad \text{PRECOND}: Object(x) \wedge InView(x) \\ Percept(Color(can, c), \\ \quad \text{PRECOND}: Can(can) \wedge InView(can) \wedge Open(can) \end{array}$$

The first schema says that whenever an object is in view, the agent will perceive the color of the object (that is, for the object x, the agent will learn the truth value of $Color(x, c)$ for all c). The second schema says that if an open can is in view, then the agent perceives the color of the paint in the can. Because there are no exogenous events in this world, the color of an object will remain the same, even if it is not being perceived, until the agent performs an action to change the object's color. Of course, the agent will need an action that causes objects (one at a time) to come into view:

$$\begin{array}{l} Action(LookAt(x), \\ \quad \text{PRECOND}: InView(y) \wedge (x \neq y) \\ \quad \text{EFFECT}: InView(x) \wedge \neg InView(y)) \end{array}$$

For a fully observable environment, we would have a $Percept$ axiom with no preconditions for each fluent. A sensorless agent, on the other hand, has no $Percept$ axioms at all. Note that even a sensorless agent can solve the painting problem. One solution is to open any can of paint and apply it to both chair and table, thus **coercing** them to be the same color (even though the agent doesn't know what the color is).

A contingent planning agent with sensors can generate a better plan. First, look at the table and chair to obtain their colors; if they are already the same then the plan is done. If not, look at the paint cans; if the paint in a can is the same color as one piece of furniture, then apply that paint to the other piece. Otherwise, paint both pieces with any color.

Finally, an online planning agent might generate a contingent plan with fewer branches at first—perhaps ignoring the possibility that no cans match any of the furniture—and deal with problems when they arise by replanning. It could also deal with incorrectness of its action schemas. Whereas a contingent planner simply assumes that the effects of an action always succeed—that painting the chair does the job—a replanning agent would check the result and make an additional plan to fix any unexpected failure, such as an unpainted area or the original color showing through.

In the real world, agents use a combination of approaches. Car manufacturers sell spare tires and air bags, which are physical embodiments of contingent plan branches designed to handle punctures or crashes. On the other hand, most car drivers never consider these possibilities; when a problem arises they respond as replanning agents. In general, agents plan only for contingencies that have important consequences and a nonnegligible chance of happening. Thus, a car driver contemplating a trip across the Sahara desert should make explicit contingency plans for breakdowns, whereas a trip to the supermarket requires less advance planning. We next look at each of the three approaches in more detail.

3.1 Sensorless planning

You should be familiar with the basic idea of searching in belief-state space to find a solution for sensorless problems. Conversion of a sensorless planning problem to a belief-state planning problem works much the same way; the main differences are that the underlying physical transition model is represented by a collection of action schemas and the belief state can be represented by a logical formula instead of an explicitly enumerated set of states. For simplicity, we assume that the underlying planning problem is deterministic.

The initial belief state for the sensorless painting problem can ignore $InView$ fluents because the agent has no sensors. Furthermore, we take as given the unchanging facts $Object(Table) \land Object(Chair) \land Can(C_1) \land Can(C_2)$ because these hold in every belief state. The agent doesn't know the colors of the cans or the objects, or whether the cans are open or closed, but it does know that objects and cans have colors: $\forall x \;\exists c \;\; Color(x, c)$. After Skolemizing, we obtain the initial belief state:

$$b_0 = Color(x, C(x)) \,.$$

In classical planning, where the **closed-world assumption** is made, we would assume that any fluent not mentioned in a state is false, but in sensorless (and partially observable) planning we have to switch to an **open-world assumption** in which states contain both positive and negative fluents, and if a fluent does not appear, its value is unknown. Thus, the belief state corresponds exactly to the set of possible worlds that satisfy the formula. Given this initial belief state, the following action sequence is a solution:

$$[RemoveLid(Can_1), Paint(Chair, Can_1), Paint(Table, Can_1)] \,.$$

We now show how to progress the belief state through the action sequence to show that the final belief state satisfies the goal.

First, note that in a given belief state b, the agent can consider any action whose preconditions are satisfied by b. (The other actions cannot be used because the transition model doesn't define the effects of actions whose preconditions might be unsatisfied.) The general formula for updating the belief state b given an applicable action a in a deterministic world is as follows

$$b' = \text{RESULT}(b, a) = \{s' : s' = \text{RESULT}_P(s, a) \text{ and } s \in b\}$$

where RESULT_P defines the physical transition model. For the time being, we assume that the initial belief state is always a conjunction of literals, that is, a 1-CNF formula. To construct the new belief state b', we must consider what happens to each literal ℓ in each physical state s in b when action a is applied. For literals whose truth value is already known in b, the truth value in b' is computed from the current value and the add list and delete list of the action. (For example, if ℓ is in the delete list of the action, then $\neg\ell$ is added to b'.) What about a literal whose truth value is unknown in b? There are three cases:

1. If the action adds ℓ, then ℓ will be true in b' regardless of its initial value.
2. If the action deletes ℓ, then ℓ will be false in b' regardless of its initial value.
3. If the action does not affect ℓ, then ℓ will retain its initial value (which is unknown) and will not appear in b'.

Hence, we see that the calculation of b' is almost identical to the observable case, specified by the following equation:

$$b' = \text{RESULT}(b, a) = (b - \text{DEL}(a)) \cup \text{ADD}(a) .$$

We cannot quite use the set semantics because (1) we must make sure that b' does not contain both ℓ and $\neg\ell$, and (2) atoms may contain unbound variables. But it is still the case that $\text{RESULT}(b, a)$ is computed by starting with b, setting any atom that appears in $\text{DEL}(a)$ to false, and setting any atom that appears in $\text{ADD}(a)$ to true. For example, if we apply $RemoveLid(Can_1)$ to the initial belief state b_0, we get

$$b_1 = Color(x, C(x)) \land Open(Can_1) .$$

When we apply the action $Paint(Chair, Can_1)$, the precondition $Color(Can_1, c)$ is satisfied by the known literal $Color(x, C(x))$ with binding $\{x/Can_1, c/C(Can_1)\}$ and the new belief state is

$$b_2 = Color(x, C(x)) \land Open(Can_1) \land Color(Chair, C(Can_1)) .$$

Finally, we apply the action $Paint(Table, Can_1)$ to obtain

$$b_3 = Color(x, C(x)) \land Open(Can_1) \land Color(Chair, C(Can_1)) \\ \land Color(Table, C(Can_1)) .$$

The final belief state satisfies the goal, $Color(Table, c) \land Color(Chair, c)$, with the variable c bound to $C(Can_1)$.

The preceding analysis of the update rule has shown a very important fact: *the family of belief states defined as conjunctions of literals is closed under updates defined by PDDL action schemas.* That is, if the belief state starts as a conjunction of literals, then any update will yield a conjunction of literals. That means that in a world with n fluents, any belief state can be represented by a conjunction of size $O(n)$. This is a very comforting result, considering that there are 2^n states in the world. It says we can compactly represent all the subsets of those 2^n states that we will ever need. Moreover, the process of checking for belief states that are subsets or supersets of previously visited belief states is also easy, at least in the propositional case.

The fly in the ointment of this pleasant picture is that it only works for action schemas that have the *same effects* for all states in which their preconditions are satisfied. It is this property that enables the preservation of the 1-CNF belief-state representation. As soon as the effect can depend on the state, dependencies are introduced between fluents and the 1-CNF property is lost. Consider, for example, the simple vacuum world defined in Section 2.1 of the chapter "Solving Problems by Searching." Let the fluents be *AtL* and *AtR* for the location of the robot and *CleanL* and *CleanR* for the state of the squares. According to the definition of the problem, the *Suck* action has no precondition—it can always be done. The difficulty is that its effect depends on the robot's location: when the robot is *AtL*, the result is *CleanL*, but when it is *AtR*, the result is *CleanR*. For such actions, our action schemas will need something new: a **conditional effect**. These have the syntax "**when** *condition*:*effect*," where *condition* is a logical formula to be compared against the current state, and *effect* is a formula describing the resulting state. For the vacuum world, we have

CONDITIONAL EFFECT

$$Action(Suck,$$
$$\text{EFFECT:}\,\textbf{when}\ AtL\text{:}\ CleanL \wedge \textbf{when}\ AtR\text{:}\ CleanR)\,.$$

When applied to the initial belief state *True*, the resulting belief state is $(AtL \wedge CleanL) \vee CleanR)$,which is no longer in 1-CNF. In general, conditional effects can induce arbitrary dependencies among the fluents in a belief state, leading to belief states of exponential size in the worst case.

It is important to understand the difference between preconditions and conditional effects. *All* conditional effects whose conditions are satisfied have their effects applied to generate the resulting state; if none are satisfied, then the resulting state is unchanged. On the other hand, if a *precondition* is unsatisfied, then the action is inapplicable and the resulting state is undefined. From the point of view of sensorless planning, it is better to have conditional effects than an inapplicable action. For example, we could split *Suck* into two actions with unconditional effects as follows:

$$Action(SuckL,$$
$$\text{PRECOND:}\,AtL;\ \text{EFFECT:}\,CleanL)$$
$$Action(SuckR,$$
$$\text{PRECOND:}\,AtR;\ \text{EFFECT:}\,CleanR)\,.$$

Now we have only unconditional schemas, so the belief states all remain in 1-CNF; unfortunately, we cannot determine the applicability of *SuckL* and *SuckR* in the initial belief state.

It seems inevitable, then, that nontrivial problems will involve wiggly belief states, just like those encountered when we consider the problem of state estimation for the wumpus world. The solution suggested then was to use a **conservative approximation** to the exact belief state; for example, the belief state can remain in 1-CNF if it contains all literals whose truth values can be determined and treats all other literals as unknown. While this approach is *sound*, in that it never generates an incorrect plan, it is *incomplete* because it may be unable to find solutions to problems that necessarily involve interactions among literals. To give a trivial example, if the goal is for the robot to be on a clean square, then $[Suck]$ is a solution but a sensorless agent that insists on 1-CNF belief states will not find it.

Perhaps a better solution is to look for action sequences that keep the belief state as simple as possible. For example, in the sensorless vacuum world, the action sequence $[Right, Suck, Left, Suck]$ generates the following sequence of belief states:

$$\begin{aligned} b_0 &= \mathit{True} \\ b_1 &= \mathit{AtR} \\ b_2 &= \mathit{AtR} \wedge \mathit{CleanR} \\ b_3 &= \mathit{AtL} \wedge \mathit{CleanR} \\ b_4 &= \mathit{AtL} \wedge \mathit{CleanR} \wedge \mathit{CleanL} \end{aligned}$$

That is, the agent *can* solve the problem while retaining a 1-CNF belief state, even though some sequences (e.g., those beginning with *Suck*) go outside 1-CNF. The general lesson is not lost on humans: we are always performing little actions (checking the time, patting our pockets to make sure we have the car keys, reading street signs as we navigate through a city) to eliminate uncertainty and keep our belief state manageable.

There is another, quite different approach to the problem of unmanageably wiggly belief states: don't bother computing them at all. Suppose the initial belief state is b_0 and we would like to know the belief state resulting from the action sequence $[a_1, \ldots, a_m]$. Instead of computing it explicitly, just represent it as "b_0 then $[a_1, \ldots, a_m]$." This is a lazy but unambiguous representation of the belief state, and it's quite concise—$O(n + m)$ where n is the size of the initial belief state (assumed to be in 1-CNF) and m is the maximum length of an action sequence. As a belief-state representation, it suffers from one drawback, however: determining whether the goal is satisfied, or an action is applicable, may require a lot of computation.

The computation can be implemented as an entailment test: if A_m represents the collection of successor-state axioms required to define occurrences of the actions $a_1,...,a_m$, and G_m asserts that the goal is true after m steps, then the plan achieves the goal if $b_0 \wedge A_m \models G_m$, that is, if $b_0 \wedge A_m \wedge \neg G_m$ is unsatisfiable. Given a modern SAT solver, it may be possible to do this much more quickly than computing the full belief state. For example, if none of the actions in the sequence has a particular goal fluent in its add list, the solver will detect this immediately. It also helps if partial results about the belief state—for example, fluents known to be true or false—are cached to simplify subsequent computations.

The final piece of the sensorless planning puzzle is a heuristic function to guide the search. The meaning of the heuristic function is the same as for classical planning: an estimate (perhaps admissible) of the cost of achieving the goal from the given belief state. With belief states, we have one additional fact: solving any subset of a belief state is necessarily easier than solving the belief state:

$$\text{if } b_1 \subseteq b_2 \text{ then } h^*(b_1) \leq h^*(b_2) .$$

Hence, any admissible heuristic computed for a subset is admissible for the belief state itself. The most obvious candidates are the singleton subsets, that is, individual physical states. We can take any random collection of states $s_1, \ldots, s_N$ that are in the belief state b, apply an admissible heuristic h, and return

$$H(b) = \max\{h(s_1), \ldots, h(s_N)\}$$

as the heuristic estimate for solving b. We could also use a planning graph directly on b itself: if it is a conjunction of literals (1-CNF), simply set those literals to be the initial state layer of the graph. If b is not in 1-CNF, it may be possible to find sets of literals that together entail b. For example, if b is in disjunctive normal form (DNF), each term of the DNF formula is a conjunction of literals that entails b and can form the initial layer of a planning graph. As before, we can take the maximum of the heuristics obtained from each set of literals. We can also use inadmissible heuristics such as the ignore-delete-lists heuristic, which seems to work quite well in practice.

3.2 Contingent planning

Contingent planning—the generation of plans with conditional branching based on percepts—is appropriate for environments with partial observability, non-determinism, or both. For the partially observable painting problem with the percept axioms given earlier, one possible contingent solution is as follows:

$[LookAt(Table), LookAt(Chair),$
  if $Color(Table, c) \wedge Color(Chair, c)$ **then** $NoOp$
    else $[RemoveLid(Can_1), LookAt(Can_1), RemoveLid(Can_2), LookAt(Can_2),$
      if $Color(Table, c) \wedge Color(can, c)$ **then** $Paint(Chair, can)$
      else if $Color(Chair, c) \wedge Color(can, c)$ **then** $Paint(Table, can)$
      else $[Paint(Chair, Can_1), Paint(Table, Can_1)]]]$

Variables in this plan should be considered existentially quantified; the second line says that if there exists some color c that is the color of the table and the chair, then the agent need not do anything to achieve the goal. When executing this plan, a contingent-planning agent can maintain its belief state as a logical formula and evaluate each branch condition by determining if the belief state entails the condition formula or its negation. (It is up to the contingent-planning algorithm to make sure that the agent will never end up in a belief state where the condition formula's truth value is unknown.) Note that with first-order conditions, the formula may be satisfied in more than one way; for example, the condition $Color(Table, c) \wedge Color(can, c)$ might be satisfied by $\{can/Can_1\}$ and by $\{can/Can_2\}$ if both cans are the same color as the table. In that case, the agent can choose any satisfying substitution to apply to the rest of the plan.

Calculating the new belief state after an action and subsequent percept is done in two stages. The first stage calculates the belief state after the action, just as for the sensorless agent:

$$\hat{b} = (b - \text{DEL}(a)) \cup \text{ADD}(a)$$

where, as before, we have assumed a belief state represented as a conjunction of literals. The second stage is a little trickier. Suppose that percept literals $p_1, \ldots, p_k$ are received. One might think that we simply need to add these into the belief state; in fact, we can also infer that the preconditions for sensing are satisfied. Now, if a percept p has exactly one percept axiom, $Percept(p, \text{PRECOND}{:}c)$, where c is a conjunction of literals, then those literals can be thrown into the belief state along with p. On the other hand, if p has more than one percept axiom whose preconditions might hold according to the predicted belief state $\hat{b}$, then we have to add in the *disjunction* of the preconditions. Obviously, this takes the belief state outside 1-CNF and brings up the same complications as conditional effects, with much the same classes of solutions.

Given a mechanism for computing exact or approximate belief states, we can generate contingent plans with an extension of the AND–OR forward search over belief states, which you may be familiar with. Actions with nondeterministic effects—which are defined simply by using a disjunction in the EFFECT of the action schema—can be accommodated with minor changes to the belief-state update calculation and no change to the search algorithm.[2] For the heuristic function, many of the methods suggested for sensorless planning are also applicable in the partially observable, nondeterministic case.

3.3 Online replanning

Imagine watching a spot-welding robot in a car plant. The robot's fast, accurate motions are repeated over and over again as each car passes down the line. Although technically impressive, the robot probably does not seem at all *intelligent* because the motion is a fixed, preprogrammed sequence; the robot obviously doesn't "know what it's doing" in any meaningful sense. Now suppose that a poorly attached door falls off the car just as the robot is about to apply a spot-weld. The robot quickly replaces its welding actuator with a gripper, picks up the door, checks it for scratches, reattaches it to the car, sends an email to the floor supervisor, switches back to the welding actuator, and resumes its work. All of a sudden, the robot's behavior seems *purposive* rather than rote; we assume it results not from a vast, precomputed contingent plan but from an online replanning process—which means that the robot *does* need to know what it's trying to do.

EXECUTION MONITORING

Replanning presupposes some form of **execution monitoring** to determine the need for a new plan. One such need arises when a contingent planning agent gets tired of planning for every little contingency, such as whether the sky might fall on its head.[3] Some branches of a partially constructed contingent plan can simply say *Replan*; if such a branch is reached during execution, the agent reverts to planning mode. As we mentioned earlier, the decision as to how much of the problem to solve in advance and how much to leave to replanning is one that involves tradeoffs among possible events with different costs and probabilities of occurring. Nobody wants to have their car break down in the middle of the Sahara desert and only then think about having enough water.

2 If cyclic solutions are required for a nondeterministic problem, AND–OR search must be generalized to a loopy version such as LAO* (Hansen and Zilberstein, 2001).

3 In 1954, a Mrs. Hodges of Alabama was hit by meteorite that crashed through her roof. In 1992, a piece of the Mbale meteorite hit a small boy on the head; fortunately, its descent was slowed by banana leaves (Jenniskens *et al.*, 1994). And in 2009, a German boy claimed to have been hit in the hand by a pea-sized meteorite. No serious injuries resulted from any of these incidents, suggesting that the need for preplanning against such contingencies is sometimes overstated.

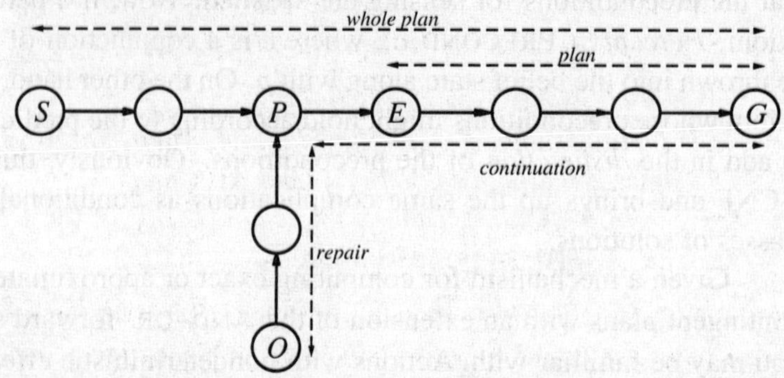

Figure 9 Before execution, the planner comes up with a plan, here called *whole plan*, to get from S to G. The agent executes steps of the plan until it expects to be in state E, but observes it is actually in O. The agent then replans for the minimal repair plus continuation to reach G.

MISSING PRECONDITION

MISSING EFFECT

MISSING STATE VARIABLE

EXOGENOUS EVENT

Replanning may also be needed if the agent's model of the world is incorrect. The model for an action may have a **missing precondition**—for example, the agent may not know that removing the lid of a paint can often requires a screwdriver; the model may have a **missing effect**—for example, painting an object may get paint on the floor as well; or the model may have a **missing state variable**—for example, the model given earlier has no notion of the amount of paint in a can, of how its actions affect this amount, or of the need for the amount to be nonzero. The model may also lack provision for **exogenous events** such as someone knocking over the paint can. Exogenous events can also include changes in the goal, such as the addition of the requirement that the table and chair not be painted black. Without the ability to monitor and replan, an agent's behavior is likely to be extremely fragile if it relies on absolute correctness of its model.

The online agent has a choice of how carefully to monitor the environment. We distinguish three levels:

ACTION MONITORING

- **Action monitoring**: before executing an action, the agent verifies that all the preconditions still hold.

PLAN MONITORING

- **Plan monitoring**: before executing an action, the agent verifies that the remaining plan will still succeed.

GOAL MONITORING

- **Goal monitoring**: before executing an action, the agent checks to see if there is a better set of goals it could be trying to achieve.

In Figure 9 we see a schematic of action monitoring. The agent keeps track of both its original plan, *wholeplan*, and the part of the plan that has not been executed yet, which is denoted by *plan*. After executing the first few steps of the plan, the agent expects to be in state E. But the agent observes it is actually in state O. It then needs to repair the plan by finding some point P on the original plan that it can get back to. (It may be that P is the goal state, G.) The agent tries to minimize the total cost of the plan: the repair part (from O to P) plus the continuation (from P to G).

Now let's return to the example problem of achieving a chair and table of matching color. Suppose the agent comes up with this plan:

$$[LookAt(Table), LookAt(Chair),\\ \textbf{if } Color(Table, c) \land Color(Chair, c) \textbf{ then } NoOp\\ \textbf{else } [RemoveLid(Can_1), LookAt(Can_1),\\ \textbf{if } Color(Table, c) \land Color(Can_1, c) \textbf{ then } Paint(Chair, Can_1)\\ \textbf{else } \text{REPLAN}]].$$

Now the agent is ready to execute the plan. Suppose the agent observes that the table and can of paint are white and the chair is black. It then executes $Paint(Chair, Can_1)$. At this point a classical planner would declare victory; the plan has been executed. But an online execution monitoring agent needs to check the preconditions of the remaining empty plan—that the table and chair are the same color. Suppose the agent perceives that they do not have the same color—in fact, the chair is now a mottled gray because the black paint is showing through. The agent then needs to figure out a position in *whole plan* to aim for and a repair action sequence to get there. The agent notices that the current state is identical to the precondition before the $Paint(Chair, Can_1)$ action, so the agent chooses the empty sequence for *repair* and makes its *plan* be the same $[Paint]$ sequence that it just attempted. With this new plan in place, execution monitoring resumes, and the *Paint* action is retried. This behavior will loop until the chair is perceived to be completely painted. But notice that the loop is created by a process of plan–execute–replan, rather than by an explicit loop in a plan. Note also that the original plan need not cover every contingency. If the agent reaches the step marked REPLAN, it can then generate a new plan (perhaps involving Can_2).

Action monitoring is a simple method of execution monitoring, but it can sometimes lead to less than intelligent behavior. For example, suppose there is no black or white paint, and the agent constructs a plan to solve the painting problem by painting both the chair and table red. Suppose that there is only enough red paint for the chair. With action monitoring, the agent would go ahead and paint the chair red, then notice that it is out of paint and cannot paint the table, at which point it would replan a repair—perhaps painting both chair and table green. A plan-monitoring agent can detect failure whenever the current state is such that the remaining plan no longer works. Thus, it would not waste time painting the chair red. Plan monitoring achieves this by checking the preconditions for success of the entire remaining plan—that is, the preconditions of each step in the plan, except those preconditions that are achieved by another step in the remaining plan. Plan monitoring cuts off execution of a doomed plan as soon as possible, rather than continuing until the failure actually occurs.[4] Plan monitoring also allows for **serendipity**—accidental success. If someone comes along and paints the table red at the same time that the agent is painting the chair red, then the final plan preconditions are satisfied (the goal has been achieved), and the agent can go home early.

It is straightforward to modify a planning algorithm so that each action in the plan is annotated with the action's preconditions, thus enabling action monitoring. It is slightly

[4] Plan monitoring means that we have an agent that is smarter than a dung beetle. A plan-monitoring agent would notice that the dung ball was missing from its grasp and would replan to get another ball and plug its hole.

more complex to enable plan monitoring. Partial-order and planning-graph planners have the advantage that they have already built up structures that contain the relations necessary for plan monitoring. Augmenting state-space planners with the necessary annotations can be done by careful bookkeeping as the goal fluents are regressed through the plan.

Now that we have described a method for monitoring and replanning, we need to ask, "Does it work?" This is a surprisingly tricky question. If we mean, "Can we guarantee that the agent will always achieve the goal?" then the answer is no, because the agent could inadvertently arrive at a dead end from which there is no repair. For example, the vacuum agent might have a faulty model of itself and not know that its batteries can run out. Once they do, it cannot repair any plans. If we rule out dead ends—assume that there exists a plan to reach the goal from *any* state in the environment—and assume that the environment is really nondeterministic, in the sense that such a plan always has *some* chance of success on any given execution attempt, then the agent will eventually reach the goal.

Trouble occurs when an action is actually not nondeterministic, but rather depends on some precondition that the agent does not know about. For example, sometimes a paint can may be empty, so painting from that can has no effect. No amount of retrying is going to change this. One solution is to choose randomly from among the set of possible repair plans, rather than to try the same one each time. In this case, the repair plan of opening another can might work. A better approach is to **learn** a better model. Every prediction failure is an opportunity for learning; an agent should be able to modify its model of the world to accord with its percepts. From then on, the replanner will be able to come up with a repair that gets at the root problem, rather than relying on luck to choose a good repair.

4 Multiagent Planning

So far, we have assumed that only one agent is doing the sensing, planning, and acting. When there are multiple agents in the environment, each agent faces a **multiagent planning problem** in which it tries to achieve its own goals with the help or hindrance of others.

MULTIAGENT PLANNING PROBLEM

Between the purely single-agent and truly multiagent cases is a wide spectrum of problems that exhibit various degrees of decomposition of the monolithic agent. An agent with multiple effectors that can operate concurrently—for example, a human who can type and speak at the same time—needs to do **multieffector planning** to manage each effector while handling positive and negative interactions among the effectors. When the effectors are physically decoupled into detached units—as in a fleet of delivery robots in a factory—multieffector planning becomes **multibody planning**. A multibody problem is still a "standard" single-agent problem as long as the relevant sensor information collected by each body can be pooled—either centrally or within each body—to form a common estimate of the world state that then informs the execution of the overall plan; in this case, the multiple bodies act as a single body. When communication constraints make this impossible, we have

MULTIEFFECTOR PLANNING

MULTIBODY PLANNING

DECENTRALIZED PLANNING what is sometimes called a **decentralized planning** problem; this is perhaps a misnomer, because the planning phase is centralized but the execution phase is at least partially decoupled. In this case, the subplan constructed for each body may need to include explicit communicative actions with other bodies. For example, multiple reconnaissance robots covering a wide area may often be out of radio contact with each other and should share their findings during times when communication is feasible.

When a single entity is doing the planning, there is really only one goal, which all the bodies necessarily share. When the bodies are distinct agents that do their own planning, they may still share identical goals; for example, two human tennis players who form a doubles team share the goal of winning the match. Even with shared goals, however, the multibody and multiagent cases are quite different. In a multibody robotic doubles team, a single plan dictates which body will go where on the court and which body will hit the ball. In a multiagent doubles team, on the other hand, each agent decides what to do; without some method for **coordination**, both agents may decide to cover the same part of the court and each may leave the ball for the other to hit.

COORDINATION

The clearest case of a multiagent problem, of course, is when the agents have different goals. In tennis, the goals of two opposing teams are in direct conflict, leading to a zerosum situation. Spectators could be viewed as agents if their support or disdain is a significant factor and can be influenced by the players' conduct; otherwise, they can be treated as an aspect of nature—just like the weather—that is assumed to be indifferent to the players' intentions.[5]

Finally, some systems are a mixture of centralized and multiagent planning. For example, a delivery company may do centralized, offline planning for the routes of its trucks and planes each day, but leave some aspects open for autonomous decisions by drivers and pilots who can respond individually to traffic and weather situations. Also, the goals of the company and its employees are brought into alignment, to some extent, by the payment of **incentives** (salaries and bonuses)—a sure sign that this is a true multiagent system.

INCENTIVE

The issues involved in multiagent planning can be divided roughly into two sets. The first, covered in Section 4.1, involves issues of representing and planning for multiple simultaneous actions; these issues occur in all settings from multieffector to multiagent planning. The second, covered in Section 4.2, involves issues of cooperation, coordination, and competition arising in true multiagent settings.

4.1 Planning with multiple simultaneous actions

MULTIACTOR

ACTOR

For the time being, we will treat the multieffector, multibody, and multiagent settings in the same way, labeling them generically as **multiactor** settings, using the generic term **actor** to cover effectors, bodies, and agents. The goal of this section is to work out how to define transition models, correct plans, and efficient planning algorithms for the multiactor setting. A correct plan is one that, if executed by the actors, achieves the goal. (In the true multiagent setting, of course, the agents may not agree to execute any particular plan, but at least they

[5] We apologize to residents of the United Kingdom, where the mere act of contemplating a game of tennis guarantees rain.

$Actors(A, B)$
$Init(At(A, LeftBaseline) \wedge At(B, RightNet) \wedge$
$\quad Approaching(Ball, RightBaseline)) \wedge Partner(A, B) \wedge Partner(B, A)$
$Goal(Returned(Ball) \wedge (At(a, RightNet) \vee At(a, LeftNet))$
$Action(Hit(actor, Ball),$
$\quad$ PRECOND: $Approaching(Ball, loc) \wedge At(actor, loc)$
$\quad$ EFFECT: $Returned(Ball))$
$Action(Go(actor, to),$
$\quad$ PRECOND: $At(actor, loc) \wedge to \neq loc,$
$\quad$ EFFECT: $At(actor, to) \wedge \neg At(actor, loc))$

Figure 10 The doubles tennis problem. Two actors A and B are playing together and can be in one of four locations: *LeftBaseline*, *RightBaseline*, *LeftNet*, and *RightNet*. The ball can be returned only if a player is in the right place. Note that each action must include the actor as an argument.

will know what plans *would* work if they *did* agree to execute them.) For simplicity, we assume perfect **synchronization**: each action takes the same amount of time and actions at each point in the joint plan are simultaneous.

SYNCHRONIZATION

We begin with the transition model; for the deterministic case, this is the function RESULT(s, a). In the single-agent setting, there might be b different choices for the action; b can be quite large, especially for first-order representations with many objects to act on, but action schemas provide a concise representation nonetheless. In the multiactor setting with n actors, the single action a is replaced by a **joint action** $\langle a_1, \ldots, a_n \rangle$, where a_i is the action taken by the ith actor. Immediately, we see two problems: first, we have to describe the transition model for b^n different joint actions; second, we have a joint planning problem with a branching factor of b^n.

JOINT ACTION

Having put the actors together into a multiactor system with a huge branching factor, the principal focus of research on multiactor planning has been to *decouple* the actors to the extent possible, so that the complexity of the problem grows linearly with n rather than exponentially. If the actors have no interaction with one another—for example, n actors each playing a game of solitaire—then we can simply solve n separate problems. If the actors are **loosely coupled**, can we attain something close to this exponential improvement? This is, of course, a central question in many areas of AI. We can see it explicitly in the context of CSPs, where "tree like" constraint graphs yield efficient solution methods, as well as in the context of disjoint pattern databases and additive heuristics for planning.

LOOSELY COUPLED

The standard approach to loosely coupled problems is to pretend the problems are completely decoupled and then fix up the interactions. For the transition model, this means writing action schemas as if the actors acted independently. Let's see how this works for the doubles tennis problem. Let's suppose that at one point in the game, the team has the goal of returning the ball that has been hit to them and ensuring that at least one of them is covering the net.

A first pass at a multiactor definition might look like Figure 10. With this definition, it is easy to see that the following **joint plan** plan works:

JOINT PLAN

PLAN 1:

$$A: \; [Go(A, RightBaseline), Hit(A, Ball)]$$
$$B: \; [NoOp(B), NoOp(B)]\,.$$

Problems arise, however, when a plan has both agents hitting the ball at the same time. In the real world, this won't work, but the action schema for *Hit* says that the ball will be returned successfully. Technically, the difficulty is that preconditions constrain the *state* in which an action can be executed successfully, but do not constrain other actions that might mess it up. We solve this by augmenting action schemas with one new feature: a **concurrent action list** stating which actions must or must not be executed concurrently. For example, the *Hit* action could be described as follows:

CONCURRENT ACTION LIST

$$\begin{aligned}&Action(Hit(a, Ball),\\&\quad \text{CONCURRENT:} b \neq a \;\Rightarrow\; \neg Hit(b, Ball)\\&\quad \text{PRECOND:} Approaching(Ball, loc) \wedge At(a, loc)\\&\quad \text{EFFECT:} Returned(Ball))\,.\end{aligned}$$

In other words, the *Hit* action has its stated effect only if no other *Hit* action by another agent occurs at the same time. (In the SATPLAN approach, this would be handled by a partial **action exclusion axiom.**) For some actions, the desired effect is achieved *only* when another action occurs concurrently. For example, two agents are needed to carry a cooler full of beverages to the tennis court:

$$\begin{aligned}&Action(Carry(a, cooler, here, there),\\&\quad \text{CONCURRENT:} b \neq a \wedge Carry(b, cooler, here, there)\\&\quad \text{PRECOND:} At(a, here) \wedge At(cooler, here) \wedge Cooler(cooler)\\&\quad \text{EFFECT:} At(a, there) \wedge At(cooler, there) \wedge \neg At(a, here) \wedge \neg At(cooler, here))\,.\end{aligned}$$

With these kinds of action schemas, planning algorithms can be adapted with only minor modifications to generate multiactor plans. To the extent that the coupling among subplans is loose—meaning that concurrency constraints come into play only rarely during plan search—one would expect the various heuristics derived for single-agent planning to also be effective in the multiactor context.

4.2 Planning with multiple agents: Cooperation and coordination

Now let us consider the true multiagent setting in which each agent makes its own plan. To start with, let us assume that the goals and knowledge base are shared. One might think that this reduces to the multibody case—each agent simply computes the joint solution and executes its own part of that solution. Alas, the "*the*" in "*the joint solution*" is misleading. For our doubles team, more than one joint solution exists:

PLAN 2:

$$A: \; [Go(A, LeftNet), NoOp(A)]$$
$$B: \; [Go(B, RightBaseline), Hit(B, Ball)]\,.$$

If both agents can agree on either plan 1 or plan 2, the goal will be achieved. But if A chooses plan 2 and B chooses plan 1, then nobody will return the ball. Conversely, if A chooses 1 and B chooses 2, then they will both try to hit the ball. The agents may realize this, but how can they coordinate to make sure they agree on the plan?

CONVENTION One option is to adopt a **convention** before engaging in joint activity. A convention is any constraint on the selection of joint plans. For example, the convention "stick to your side of the court" would rule out plan 1, causing the doubles partners to select plan 2. Drivers on a road face the problem of not colliding with each other; this is (partially) solved by adopting the convention "stay on the right side of the road" in most countries; the alternative, "stay on the left side," works equally well as long as all agents in an environment agree. Similar considerations apply to the development of human language, where the important thing is not which language each individual should speak, but the fact that a community all speaks the same language. When conventions are widespread, they are called **social laws**. SOCIAL LAWS

In the absence of a convention, agents can use **communication** to achieve common knowledge of a feasible joint plan. For example, a tennis player could shout "Mine!" or "Yours!" to indicate a preferred joint plan. Communication does not necessarily involve a verbal exchange. For example, one player can communicate a preferred joint plan to the other simply by executing the first part of it. If agent A heads for the net, then agent B is obliged to go back to the baseline to hit the ball, because plan 2 is the only joint plan that begins with A's heading for the net. This approach to coordination, sometimes called **plan recognition**, works when a single action (or short sequence of actions) is enough to determine a joint plan unambiguously. Note that communication can work as well with competitive agents as with cooperative ones. PLAN RECOGNITION

Conventions can also arise through evolutionary processes. For example, seed-eating harvester ants are social creatures that evolved from the less social wasps. Colonies of ants execute very elaborate joint plans without any centralized control—the queen's job is to reproduce, not to do centralized planning—and with very limited computation, communication, and memory capabilities in each ant (Gordon, 2000, 2007). The colony has many roles, including interior workers, patrollers, and foragers. Each ant chooses to perform a role according to the local conditions it observes. For example, foragers travel away from the nest, search for a seed, and when they find one, bring it back immediately. Thus, the rate at which foragers return to the nest is an approximation of the availability of food today. When the rate is high, other ants abandon their current role and take on the role of scavenger. The ants appear to have a convention on the importance of roles—foraging is the most important—and ants will easily switch into the more important roles, but not into the less important. There is some learning mechanism: a colony learns to make more successful and prudent actions over the course of its decades-long life, even though individual ants live only about a year.

One final example of cooperative multiagent behavior appears in the flocking behavior of birds. We can obtain a reasonable simulation of a flock if each bird agent (sometimes called a **boid**) observes the positions of its nearest neighbors and then chooses the heading and acceleration that maximizes the weighted sum of these three components: BOID

(a) (b) (c)

Figure 11 (a) A simulated flock of birds, using Reynold's boids model. Image courtesy Giuseppe Randazzo, novastructura.net. (b) An actual flock of starlings. Image by Eduardo (pastaboy sleeps on flickr). (c) Two competitive teams of agents attempting to capture the towers in the NERO game. Image courtesy Risto Miikkulainen.

1. Cohesion: a positive score for getting closer to the average position of the neighbors
2. Separation: a negative score for getting too close to any one neighbor
3. Alignment: a positive score for getting closer to the average heading of the neighbors

EMERGENT BEHAVIOR

If all the boids execute this policy, the flock exhibits the **emergent behavior** of flying as a pseudorigid body with roughly constant density that does not disperse over time, and that occasionally makes sudden swooping motions. You can see a still images in Figure 11(a) and compare it to an actual flock in (b). As with ants, there is no need for each agent to possess a joint plan that models the actions of other agents.

The most difficult multiagent problems involve both cooperation with members of one's own team and competition against members of opposing teams, all without centralized control. We see this in games such as robotic soccer or the NERO game shown in Figure 11(c), in which two teams of software agents compete to capture the control towers. As yet, methods for efficient planning in these kinds of environments—for example, taking advantage of loose coupling—are in their infancy.

5 SUMMARY

This chapter has addressed some of the complications of planning and acting in the real world. The main points:

- Many actions consume **resources**, such as money, gas, or raw materials. It is convenient to treat these resources as numeric measures in a pool rather than try to reason about, say, each individual coin and bill in the world. Actions can generate and consume resources, and it is usually cheap and effective to check partial plans for satisfaction of resource constraints before attempting further refinements.
- Time is one of the most important resources. It can be handled by specialized scheduling algorithms, or scheduling can be integrated with planning.

- **Hierarchical task network** (HTN) planning allows the agent to take advice from the domain designer in the form of **high-level actions** (HLAs) that can be implemented in various ways by lower-level action sequences. The effects of HLAs can be defined with **angelic semantics**, allowing provably correct high-level plans to be derived without consideration of lower-level implementations. HTN methods can create the very large plans required by many real-world applications.
- Standard planning algorithms assume complete and correct information and deterministic, fully observable environments. Many domains violate this assumption.
- **Contingent plans** allow the agent to sense the world during execution to decide what branch of the plan to follow. In some cases, **sensorless** or **conformant planning** can be used to construct a plan that works without the need for perception. Both conformant and contingent plans can be constructed by search in the space of **belief states**. Efficient representation or computation of belief states is a key problem.
- An **online planning agent** uses execution monitoring and splices in repairs as needed to recover from unexpected situations, which can be due to nondeterministic actions, exogenous events, or incorrect models of the environment.
- **Multiagent** planning is necessary when there are other agents in the environment with which to cooperate or compete. Joint plans can be constructed, but must be augmented with some form of coordination if two agents are to agree on which joint plan to execute.
- This chapter extends classic planning to cover nondeterministic environments (where outcomes of actions are uncertain), but it is not the last word on planning.

BIBLIOGRAPHICAL AND HISTORICAL NOTES

Planning with time constraints was first dealt with by DEVISER (Vere, 1983). The representation of time in plans was addressed by Allen (1984) and by Dean *et al.* (1990) in the FORBIN system. NONLIN+ (Tate and Whiter, 1984) and SIPE (Wilkins, 1988, 1990) could reason about the allocation of limited resources to various plan steps. O-PLAN (Bell and Tate, 1985), an HTN planner, had a uniform, general representation for constraints on time and resources. In addition to the Hitachi application mentioned in the text, O-PLAN has been applied to software procurement planning at Price Waterhouse and back-axle assembly planning at Jaguar Cars.

The two planners SAPA (Do and Kambhampati, 2001) and T4 (Haslum and Geffner, 2001) both used forward state-space search with sophisticated heuristics to handle actions with durations and resources. An alternative is to use very expressive action languages, but guide them by human-written domain-specific heuristics, as is done by ASPEN (Fukunaga *et al.*, 1997), HSTS (Jonsson *et al.*, 2000), and IxTeT (Ghallab and Laruelle, 1994).

A number of hybrid planning-and-scheduling systems have been deployed: ISIS (Fox *et al.*, 1982; Fox, 1990) has been used for job shop scheduling at Westinghouse, GARI (Descotte and Latombe, 1985) planned the machining and construction of mechanical parts, FORBIN was used for factory control, and NONLIN+ was used for naval logistics planning. We chose to present planning and scheduling as two separate problems; (Cushing *et al.*, 2007) show that this can lead to incompleteness on certain problems. There is a long history of scheduling in aerospace. T-SCHED (Drabble, 1990) was used to schedule mission-command sequences for the UOSAT-II satellite. OPTIMUM-AIV (Aarup *et al.*, 1994) and PLAN-ERS1 (Fuchs *et al.*, 1990), both based on O-PLAN, were used for spacecraft assembly and observation planning, respectively, at the European Space Agency. SPIKE (Johnston and Adorf, 1992) was used for observation planning at NASA for the Hubble Space Telescope, while the Space Shuttle Ground Processing Scheduling System (Deale *et al.*, 1994) does job-shop scheduling of up to 16,000 worker-shifts. Remote Agent (Muscettola *et al.*, 1998) became the first autonomous planner–scheduler to control a spacecraft when it flew onboard the Deep Space One probe in 1999. Space applications have driven the development of algorithms for resource allocations; see Laborie (2003) and Muscettola (2002). The literature on scheduling is presented in a classic survey article (Lawler *et al.*, 1993), a recent book (Pinedo, 2008), and an edited handbook (Blazewicz *et al.*, 2007).

MACROPS

The facility in the STRIPS program for learning **macrops**—"macro-operators" consisting of a sequence of primitive steps—could be considered the first mechanism for hierarchical planning (Fikes *et al.*, 1972). Hierarchy was also used in the LAWALY system (Siklossy and Dreussi, 1973). The ABSTRIPS system (Sacerdoti, 1974) introduced the idea of an **abstraction hierarchy**, whereby planning at higher levels was permitted to ignore lower-level preconditions of actions in order to derive the general structure of a working plan. Austin Tate's Ph.D. thesis (1975b) and work by Earl Sacerdoti (1977) developed the basic ideas of HTN planning in its modern form. Many practical planners, including O-PLAN and SIPE, are HTN planners. Yang (1990) discusses properties of actions that make HTN planning efficient. Erol, Hendler, and Nau (1994, 1996) present a complete hierarchical decomposition planner as well as a range of complexity results for pure HTN planners. Our presentation of HLAs and angelic semantics is due to Marthi *et al.* (2007, 2008). Kambhampati *et al.* (1998) have proposed an approach in which decompositions are just another form of plan refinement, similar to the refinements for non-hierarchical partial-order planning.

ABSTRACTION HIERARCHY

Beginning with the work on macro-operators in STRIPS, one of the goals of hierarchical planning has been the reuse of previous planning experience in the form of generalized plans. The technique of **explanation-based learning** has been applied in several systems as a means of generalizing previously computed plans, including SOAR (Laird *et al.*, 1986) and PRODIGY (Carbonell *et al.*, 1989). An alternative approach is to store previously computed plans in their original form and then reuse them to solve new, similar problems by analogy to the original problem. This is the approach taken by the field called **case-based planning** (Carbonell, 1983; Alterman, 1988; Hammond, 1989). Kambhampati (1994) argues that case-based planning should be analyzed as a form of refinement planning and provides a formal foundation for case-based partial-order planning.

CASE-BASED PLANNING

Early planners lacked conditionals and loops, but some could use coercion to form conformant plans. Sacerdoti's NOAH solved the "keys and boxes" problem, a planning challenge problem in which the planner knows little about the initial state, using coercion. Mason (1993) argued that sensing often can and should be dispensed with in robotic planning, and described a sensorless plan that can move a tool into a specific position on a table by a sequence of tilting actions, *regardless* of the initial position.

Goldman and Boddy (1996) introduced the term **conformant planning**, noting that sensorless plans are often effective even if the agent has sensors. The first moderately efficient conformant planner was Smith and Weld's (1998) Conformant Graphplan or CGP. Ferraris and Giunchiglia (2000) and Rintanen (1999) independently developed SATPLAN-based conformant planners. Bonet and Geffner (2000) describe a conformant planner based on heuristic search in the space of belief states, drawing on ideas first developed in the 1960s for partially observable Markov decision processes, or POMDPs.

Currently, there are three main approaches to conformant planning. The first two use heuristic search in belief-state space: HSCP (Bertoli *et al.*, 2001a) uses binary decision diagrams (BDDs) to represent belief states, whereas Hoffmann and Brafman (2006) adopt the lazy approach of computing precondition and goal tests on demand using a SAT solver. The third approach, championed primarily by Jussi Rintanen (2007), formulates the entire sensorless planning problem as a quantified Boolean formula (QBF) and solves it using a general-purpose QBF solver. Current conformant planners are five orders of magnitude faster than CGP. The winner of the 2006 conformant-planning track at the International Planning Competition was T_0 (Palacios and Geffner, 2007), which uses heuristic search in belief-state space while keeping the belief-state representation simple by defining derived literals that cover conditional effects. Bryce and Kambhampati (2007) discuss how a planning graph can be generalized to generate good heuristics for conformant and contingent planning.

There has been some confusion in the literature between the terms "conditional" and "contingent" planning. Following Majercik and Littman (2003), we use "conditional" to mean a plan (or action) that has different effects depending on the actual state of the world, and "contingent" to mean a plan in which the agent can choose different actions depending on the results of sensing. The problem of contingent planning received more attention after the publication of Drew McDermott's (1978a) influential article, *Planning and Acting*.

The contingent-planning approach described in the chapter is based on Hoffmann and Brafman (2005), and was influenced by the efficient search algorithms for cyclic AND–OR graphs developed by Jimenez and Torras (2000) and Hansen and Zilberstein (2001). Bertoli *et al.* (2001b) describe MBP (Model-Based Planner), which uses binary decision diagrams to do conformant and contingent planning.

In retrospect, it is now possible to see how the major classical planning algorithms led to extended versions for uncertain domains. Fast-forward heuristic search through state space led to forward search in belief space (Bonet and Geffner, 2000; Hoffmann and Brafman, 2005); SATPLAN led to stochastic SATPLAN (Majercik and Littman, 2003) and to planning with quantified Boolean logic (Rintanen, 2007); partial order planning led to UWL (Etzioni *et al.*, 1992) and CNLP (Peot and Smith, 1992); GRAPHPLAN led to Sensory Graphplan or SGP (Weld *et al.*, 1998).

The first online planner with execution monitoring was PLANEX (Fikes *et al.*, 1972), which worked with the STRIPS planner to control the robot Shakey. The NASL planner (McDermott, 1978a) treated a planning problem simply as a specification for carrying out a complex action, so that execution and planning were completely unified. SIPE (System for Interactive Planning and Execution monitoring) (Wilkins, 1988, 1990) was the first planner to deal systematically with the problem of replanning. It has been used in demonstration projects in several domains, including planning operations on the flight deck of an aircraft carrier, job-shop scheduling for an Australian beer factory, and planning the construction of multistory buildings (Kartam and Levitt, 1990).

In the mid-1980s, pessimism about the slow run times of planning systems led to the proposal of reflex agents called **reactive planning** systems (Brooks, 1986; Agre and Chapman, 1987). PENGI (Agre and Chapman, 1987) could play a (fully observable) video game by using Boolean circuits combined with a "visual" representation of current goals and the agent's internal state. "Universal plans" (Schoppers, 1987, 1989) were developed as a lookup-table method for reactive planning, but turned out to be a rediscovery of the idea of **policies** that had long been used in Markov decision processes. A universal plan (or a policy) contains a mapping from any state to the action that should be taken in that state. Koenig (2001) surveys online planning techniques, under the name *Agent-Centered Search*.

REACTIVE PLANNING

POLICY

Multiagent planning has leaped in popularity in recent years, although it does have a long history. Konolige (1982) formalizes multiagent planning in first-order logic, while Pednault (1986) gives a STRIPS-style description. The notion of joint intention, which is essential if agents are to execute a joint plan, comes from work on communicative acts (Cohen and Levesque, 1990; Cohen *et al.*, 1990). Boutilier and Brafman (2001) show how to adapt partial-order planning to a multiactor setting. Brafman and Domshlak (2008) devise a multiactor planning algorithm whose complexity grows only linearly with the number of actors, provided that the degree of coupling (measured partly by the **tree width** of the graph of interactions among agents) is bounded. Petrik and Zilberstein (2009) show that an approach based on bilinear programming outperforms the cover-set approach we outlined in the chapter.

We have barely skimmed the surface of work on negotiation in multiagent planning. Durfee and Lesser (1989) discuss how tasks can be shared out among agents by negotiation. Kraus *et al.* (1991) describe a system for playing Diplomacy, a board game requiring negotiation, coalition formation, and dishonesty. Stone (2000) shows how agents can cooperate as teammates in the competitive, dynamic, partially observable environment of robotic soccer. In a later article, Stone (2003) analyzes two competitive multiagent environments—RoboCup, a robotic soccer competition, and TAC, the auction-based Trading Agents Competition—and finds that the computational intractability of our current theoretically well-founded approaches has led to many multiagent systems being designed by *ad hoc* methods.

In his highly influential *Society of Mind* theory, Marvin Minsky (1986, 2007) proposes that human minds are constructed from an ensemble of agents. Livnat and Pippenger (2006) prove that, for the problem of optimal path-finding, and given a limitation on the total amount of computing resources, the best architecture for an agent is an ensemble of subagents, each of which tries to optimize its own objective, and all of which are in conflict with one another.

The boid model is due to Reynolds (1987), who won an Academy Award for its application to swarms of penguins in *Batman Returns*. The NERO game and the methods for learning strategies are described by Bryant and Miikkulainen (2007).

Recent book on multiagent systems include those by Weiss (2000a), Young (2004), Vlassis (2008), and Shoham and Leyton-Brown (2009). There is an annual conference on autonomous agents and multiagent systems (AAMAS).

EXERCISES

1 The goals we have considered so far all ask the planner to make the world satisfy the goal at just one time step. Not all goals can be expressed this way: you do not achieve the goal of suspending a chandelier above the ground by throwing it in the air. More seriously, you wouldn't want your spacecraft life-support system to supply oxygen one day but not the next. A *maintenance goal* is achieved when the agent's plan causes a condition to hold continuously from a given state onward. Describe how to extend the formalism of this chapter to support maintenance goals.

2 You have a number of trucks with which to deliver a set of packages. Each package starts at some location on a grid map, and has a destination somewhere else. Each truck is directly controlled by moving forward and turning. Construct a hierarchy of high-level actions for this problem. What knowledge about the solution does your hierarchy encode?

3 Suppose that a high-level action has exactly one implementation as a sequence of primitive actions. Give an algorithm for computing its preconditions and effects, given the complete refinement hierarchy and schemas for the primitive actions.

4 Suppose that the optimistic reachable set of a high-level plan is a superset of the goal set; can anything be concluded about whether the plan achieves the goal? What if the pessimistic reachable set doesn't intersect the goal set? Explain.

5 Write an algorithm that takes an initial state (specified by a set of propositional literals) and a sequence of HLAs (each defined by preconditions and angelic specifications of optimistic and pessimistic reachable sets) and computes optimistic and pessimistic descriptions of the reachable set of the sequence.

6 In Figure 2 we showed how to describe actions in a scheduling problem by using separate fields for DURATION, USE, and CONSUME. Now suppose we wanted to combine scheduling with nondeterministic planning, which requires nondeterministic and conditional effects. Consider each of the three fields and explain if they should remain separate fields, or if they should become effects of the action. Give an example for each of the three.

7 Some of the operations in standard programming languages can be modeled as actions that change the state of the world. For example, the assignment operation changes the contents of a memory location, and the print operation changes the state of the output stream. A program consisting of these operations can also be considered as a plan, whose goal is given by the specification of the program. Therefore, planning algorithms can be used to construct programs that achieve a given specification.

a. Write an action schema for the assignment operator (assigning the value of one variable to another). Remember that the original value will be overwritten!

b. Show how object creation can be used by a planner to produce a plan for exchanging the values of two variables by using a temporary variable.

8 Suppose the *Flip* action always changes the truth value of variable L. Show how to define its effects by using an action schema with conditional effects. Show that, despite the use of conditional effects, a 1-CNF belief state representation remains in 1-CNF after a *Flip*.

9 In the blocks world we were forced to introduce two action schemas, *Move* and *MoveToTable*, in order to maintain the *Clear* predicate properly. Show how conditional effects can be used to represent both of these cases with a single action.

10 Conditional effects were illustrated for the *Suck* action in the vacuum world—which square becomes clean depends on which square the robot is in. Can you think of a new set of propositional variables to define states of the vacuum world, such that *Suck* has an *unconditional* description? Write out the descriptions of *Suck*, *Left*, and *Right*, using your propositions, and demonstrate that they suffice to describe all possible states of the world.

11 Find a suitably dirty carpet, free of obstacles, and vacuum it. Draw the path taken by the vacuum cleaner as accurately as you can. Explain it, with reference to the forms of planning discussed in this chapter.

12 To the medication problem in the previous exercise, add a *Test* action that has the conditional effect *CultureGrowth* when *Disease* is true and in any case has the perceptual effect *Known*(*CultureGrowth*). Diagram a conditional plan that solves the problem and minimizes the use of the *Medicate* action.

KNOWLEDGE REPRESENTATION

In which we show how to use first-order logic to represent the most important aspects of the real world, such as action, space, time, thoughts, and shopping.

The technology for knowledge-based agents includes the syntax, semantics, proof theory of propositional and first-order logic, and the implementation of agents that use these logics. In this chapter we address the question of what *content* to put into such an agent's knowledge base—how to represent facts about the world.

Section 1 introduces the idea of a general ontology, which organizes everything in the world into a hierarchy of categories. Section 2 covers the basic categories of objects, substances, and measures; Section 3 covers events, and Section 4 discusses knowledge about beliefs. We then return to consider the technology for reasoning with this content: Section 5 discusses reasoning systems designed for efficient inference with categories, and Section 6 discusses reasoning with default information. Section 7 brings all the knowledge together in the context of an Internet shopping environment.

1 ONTOLOGICAL ENGINEERING

In "toy" domains, the choice of representation is not that important; many choices will work. Complex domains such as shopping on the Internet or driving a car in traffic require more general and flexible representations. This chapter shows how to create these representations, concentrating on general concepts—such as *Events, Time, Physical Objects*, and *Beliefs*—that occur in many different domains. Representing these abstract concepts is sometimes called **ontological engineering**.

ONTOLOGICAL ENGINEERING

The prospect of representing *everything* in the world is daunting. Of course, we won't actually write a complete description of everything—that would be far too much for even a 1000-page textbook—but we will leave placeholders where new knowledge for any domain can fit in. For example, we will define what it means to be a physical object, and the details of different types of objects—robots, televisions, books, or whatever—can be filled in later. This is analogous to the way that designers of an object-oriented programming framework (such as the Java Swing graphical framework) define general concepts like *Window*, expecting users to

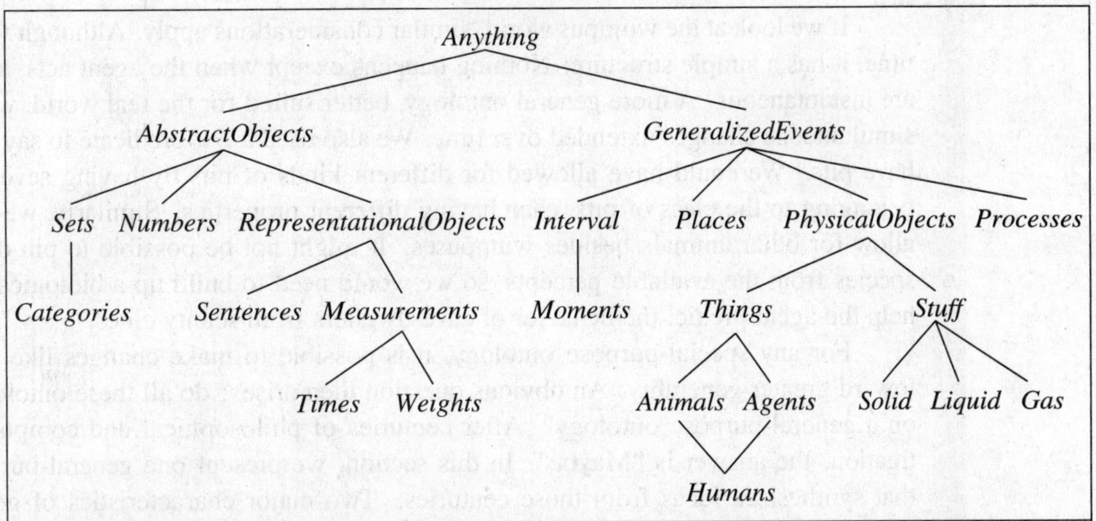

Figure 1 The upper ontology of the world, showing the topics to be covered later in the chapter. Each link indicates that the lower concept is a specialization of the upper one. Specializations are not necessarily disjoint; a human is both an animal and an agent, for example. We will see in Section 3.3 why physical objects come under generalized events.

use these to define more specific concepts like *SpreadsheetWindow*. The general framework of concepts is called an **upper ontology** because of the convention of drawing graphs with the general concepts at the top and the more specific concepts below them, as in Figure 1.

UPPER ONTOLOGY

Before considering the ontology further, we should state one important caveat. We have elected to use first-order logic to discuss the content and organization of knowledge, although certain aspects of the real world are hard to capture in FOL. The principal difficulty is that most generalizations have exceptions or hold only to a degree. For example, although "tomatoes are red" is a useful rule, some tomatoes are green, yellow, or orange. Similar exceptions can be found to almost all the rules in this chapter. The ability to handle exceptions and uncertainty is extremely important, but is orthogonal to the task of understanding the general ontology. For this reason, we delay the discussion of exceptions until Section 5 of this chapter.

Of what use is an upper ontology? Certain ontologies make many simplifying assumptions: time is omitted completely; signals are fixed and do not propagate; the structure of the circuit remains constant. A more general ontology would consider signals at particular times, and would include the wire lengths and propagation delays. This would allow us to simulate the timing properties of the circuit, and indeed such simulations are often carried out by circuit designers. We could also introduce more interesting classes of gates, for example, by describing the technology (TTL, CMOS, and so on) as well as the input–output specification. If we wanted to discuss reliability or diagnosis, we would include the possibility that the structure of the circuit or the properties of the gates might change spontaneously. To account for stray capacitances, we would need to represent where the wires are on the board.

If we look at the wumpus world, similar considerations apply. Although we do represent time, it has a simple structure: Nothing happens except when the agent acts, and all changes are instantaneous. A more general ontology, better suited for the real world, would allow for simultaneous changes extended over time. We also used a *Pit* predicate to say which squares have pits. We could have allowed for different kinds of pits by having several individuals belonging to the class of pits, each having different properties. Similarly, we might want to allow for other animals besides wumpuses. It might not be possible to pin down the exact species from the available percepts, so we would need to build up a biological taxonomy to help the agent predict the behavior of cave-dwellers from scanty clues.

For any special-purpose ontology, it is possible to make changes like these to move toward greater generality. An obvious question then arises: do all these ontologies converge on a general-purpose ontology? After centuries of philosophical and computational investigation, the answer is "Maybe." In this section, we present one general-purpose ontology that synthesizes ideas from those centuries. Two major characteristics of general-purpose ontologies distinguish them from collections of special-purpose ontologies:

- A general-purpose ontology should be applicable in more or less any special-purpose domain (with the addition of domain-specific axioms). This means that no representational issue can be finessed or brushed under the carpet.
- In any sufficiently demanding domain, different areas of knowledge must be *unified*, because reasoning and problem solving could involve several areas simultaneously. A robot circuit-repair system, for instance, needs to reason about circuits in terms of electrical connectivity and physical layout, and about time, both for circuit timing analysis and estimating labor costs. The sentences describing time therefore must be capable of being combined with those describing spatial layout and must work equally well for nanoseconds and minutes and for angstroms and meters.

We should say up front that the enterprise of general ontological engineering has so far had only limited success. None of the top AI applications make use of a shared ontology—they all use special-purpose knowledge engineering. Social/political considerations can make it difficult for competing parties to agree on an ontology. As Tom Gruber (2004) says, "Every ontology is a treaty—a social agreement—among people with some common motive in sharing." When competing concerns outweigh the motivation for sharing, there can be no common ontology. Those ontologies that do exist have been created along four routes:

1. By a team of trained ontologist/logicians, who architect the ontology and write axioms. The CYC system was mostly built this way (Lenat and Guha, 1990).
2. By importing categories, attributes, and values from an existing database or databases. DBPEDIA was built by importing structured facts from Wikipedia (Bizer *et al.*, 2007).
3. By parsing text documents and extracting information from them. TEXTRUNNER was built by reading a large corpus of Web pages (Banko and Etzioni, 2008).
4. By enticing unskilled amateurs to enter commonsense knowledge. The OPENMIND system was built by volunteers who proposed facts in English (Singh *et al.*, 2002; Chklovski and Gil, 2005).

2 CATEGORIES AND OBJECTS

CATEGORY

The organization of objects into **categories** is a vital part of knowledge representation. Although interaction with the world takes place at the level of individual objects, *much reasoning takes place at the level of categories.* For example, a shopper would normally have the goal of buying a basketball, rather than a *particular* basketball such as BB_9. Categories also serve to make predictions about objects once they are classified. One infers the presence of certain objects from perceptual input, infers category membership from the perceived properties of the objects, and then uses category information to make predictions about the objects. For example, from its green and yellow mottled skin, one-foot diameter, ovoid shape, red flesh, black seeds, and presence in the fruit aisle, one can infer that an object is a watermelon; from this, one infers that it would be useful for fruit salad.

REIFICATION

There are two choices for representing categories in first-order logic: predicates and objects. That is, we can use the predicate $Basketball(b)$, or we can **reify**[1] the category as an object, $Basketballs$. We could then say $Member(b, Basketballs)$, which we will abbreviate as $b \in Basketballs$, to say that b is a member of the category of basketballs. We say $Subset(Basketballs, Balls)$, abbreviated as $Basketballs \subset Balls$, to say that $Basketballs$ is a **subcategory** of $Balls$. We will use subcategory, subclass, and subset interchangeably.

SUBCATEGORY

INHERITANCE

Categories serve to organize and simplify the knowledge base through **inheritance**. If we say that all instances of the category $Food$ are edible, and if we assert that $Fruit$ is a subclass of $Food$ and $Apples$ is a subclass of $Fruit$, then we can infer that every apple is edible. We say that the individual apples **inherit** the property of edibility, in this case from their membership in the $Food$ category.

TAXONOMY

Subclass relations organize categories into a **taxonomy**, or **taxonomic hierarchy**. Taxonomies have been used explicitly for centuries in technical fields. The largest such taxonomy organizes about 10 million living and extinct species, many of them beetles,[2] into a single hierarchy; library science has developed a taxonomy of all fields of knowledge, encoded as the Dewey Decimal system; and tax authorities and other government departments have developed extensive taxonomies of occupations and commercial products. Taxonomies are also an important aspect of general commonsense knowledge.

First-order logic makes it easy to state facts about categories, either by relating objects to categories or by quantifying over their members. Here are some types of facts, with examples of each:

- An object is a member of a category.
  $BB_9 \in Basketballs$
- A category is a subclass of another category.
  $Basketballs \subset Balls$
- All members of a category have some properties.
  $(x \in Basketballs) \Rightarrow Spherical(x)$

1 Turning a proposition into an object is called **reification**, from the Latin word *res*, or thing. John McCarthy proposed the term "thingification," but it never caught on.

2 The famous biologist J. B. S. Haldane deduced "An inordinate fondness for beetles" on the part of the Creator.

- Members of a category can be recognized by some properties.
  $Orange(x) \land Round(x) \land Diameter(x) = 9.5'' \land x \in Balls \Rightarrow x \in Basketballs$
- A category as a whole has some properties.
  $Dogs \in DomesticatedSpecies$

Notice that because *Dogs* is a category and is a member of *DomesticatedSpecies*, the latter must be a category of categories. Of course there are exceptions to many of the above rules (punctured basketballs are not spherical); we deal with these exceptions later.

Although subclass and member relations are the most important ones for categories, we also want to be able to state relations between categories that are not subclasses of each other. For example, if we just say that *Males* and *Females* are subclasses of *Animals*, then we have not said that a male cannot be a female. We say that two or more categories are

DISJOINT

disjoint if they have no members in common. And even if we know that males and females are disjoint, we will not know that an animal that is not a male must be a female, unless

EXHAUSTIVE DECOMPOSITION

we say that males and females constitute an **exhaustive decomposition** of the animals. A

PARTITION

disjoint exhaustive decomposition is known as a **partition**. The following examples illustrate these three concepts:

$$Disjoint(\{Animals, Vegetables\})$$
$$ExhaustiveDecomposition(\{Americans, Canadians, Mexicans\}, NorthAmericans)$$
$$Partition(\{Males, Females\}, Animals) .$$

(Note that the *ExhaustiveDecomposition* of *NorthAmericans* is not a *Partition*, because some people have dual citizenship.) The three predicates are defined as follows:

$$Disjoint(s) \Leftrightarrow (\forall c_1, c_2 \;\; c_1 \in s \land c_2 \in s \land c_1 \neq c_2 \Rightarrow Intersection(c_1, c_2) = \{\,\})$$
$$ExhaustiveDecomposition(s, c) \Leftrightarrow (\forall i \;\; i \in c \Leftrightarrow \exists c_2 \;\; c_2 \in s \land i \in c_2)$$
$$Partition(s, c) \Leftrightarrow Disjoint(s) \land ExhaustiveDecomposition(s, c) .$$

Categories can also be *defined* by providing necessary and sufficient conditions for membership. For example, a bachelor is an unmarried adult male:

$$x \in Bachelors \Leftrightarrow Unmarried(x) \land x \in Adults \land x \in Males .$$

As we discuss in the sidebar on natural kinds strict logical definitions for categories are neither always possible nor always necessary.

2.1 Physical composition

The idea that one object can be part of another is a familiar one. One's nose is part of one's head, and Romania is part of Europe. We use the general *PartOf* relation to say that one thing is part of another. Objects can be grouped into *PartOf* hierarchies, reminiscent of the *Subset* hierarchy:

$$PartOf(Bucharest, Romania)$$
$$PartOf(Romania, EasternEurope)$$
$$PartOf(EasternEurope, Europe)$$
$$PartOf(Europe, Earth) .$$

The $PartOf$ relation is transitive and reflexive; that is,

$$PartOf(x,y) \land PartOf(y,z) \Rightarrow PartOf(x,z) .$$
$$PartOf(x,x) .$$

Therefore, we can conclude $PartOf(Bucharest, Earth)$.

COMPOSITE OBJECT

Categories of **composite objects** are often characterized by structural relations among parts. For example, a biped has two legs attached to a body:

$$\begin{aligned} Biped(a) \quad \Rightarrow \quad & \exists\, l_1, l_2, b \;\; Leg(l_1) \land Leg(l_2) \land Body(b) \land \\ & PartOf(l_1,a) \land PartOf(l_2,a) \land PartOf(b,a) \land \\ & Attached(l_1,b) \land Attached(l_2,b) \land \\ & l_1 \neq l_2 \land [\forall\, l_3 \;\; Leg(l_3) \land PartOf(l_3,a) \Rightarrow (l_3 = l_1 \lor l_3 = l_2)] . \end{aligned}$$

The notation for "exactly two" is a little awkward; we are forced to say that there are two legs, that they are not the same, and that if anyone proposes a third leg, it must be the same as one of the other two. In Section 5.2, we describe a formalism called description logic makes it easier to represent constraints like "exactly two."

We can define a $PartPartition$ relation analogous to the $Partition$ relation for categories. (See Exercise 8.) An object is composed of the parts in its $PartPartition$ and can be viewed as deriving some properties from those parts. For example, the mass of a composite object is the sum of the masses of the parts. Notice that this is not the case with categories, which have no mass, even though their elements might.

It is also useful to define composite objects with definite parts but no particular structure. For example, we might want to say "The apples in this bag weigh two pounds." The temptation would be to ascribe this weight to the *set* of apples in the bag, but this would be a mistake because the set is an abstract mathematical concept that has elements but does not

BUNCH

have weight. Instead, we need a new concept, which we will call a **bunch**. For example, if the apples are $Apple_1$, $Apple_2$, and $Apple_3$, then

$$BunchOf(\{Apple_1, Apple_2, Apple_3\})$$

denotes the composite object with the three apples as parts (not elements). We can then use the bunch as a normal, albeit unstructured, object. Notice that $BunchOf(\{x\}) = x$. Furthermore, $BunchOf(Apples)$ is the composite object consisting of all apples—not to be confused with $Apples$, the category or set of all apples.

We can define $BunchOf$ in terms of the $PartOf$ relation. Obviously, each element of s is part of $BunchOf(s)$:

$$\forall\, x \;\; x \in s \Rightarrow PartOf(x, BunchOf(s)) .$$

Furthermore, $BunchOf(s)$ *is the smallest object satisfying this condition.* In other words, $BunchOf(s)$ must be part of any object that has all the elements of s as parts:

$$\forall\, y \;\; [\forall\, x \;\; x \in s \Rightarrow PartOf(x,y)] \Rightarrow PartOf(BunchOf(s), y) .$$

LOGICAL MINIMIZATION

These axioms are an example of a general technique called **logical minimization**, which means defining an object as the smallest one satisfying certain conditions.

NATURAL KINDS

Some categories have strict definitions: an object is a triangle if and only if it is a polygon with three sides. On the other hand, most categories in the real world have no clear-cut definition; these are called **natural kind** categories. For example, tomatoes tend to be a dull scarlet; roughly spherical; with an indentation at the top where the stem was; about two to four inches in diameter; with a thin but tough skin; and with flesh, seeds, and juice inside. There is, however, variation: some tomatoes are yellow or orange, unripe tomatoes are green, some are smaller or larger than average, and cherry tomatoes are uniformly small. Rather than having a complete definition of tomatoes, we have a set of features that serves to identify objects that are clearly typical tomatoes, but might not be able to decide for other objects. (Could there be a tomato that is fuzzy like a peach?)

This poses a problem for a logical agent. The agent cannot be sure that an object it has perceived is a tomato, and even if it were sure, it could not be certain which of the properties of typical tomatoes this one has. This problem is an inevitable consequence of operating in partially observable environments.

One useful approach is to separate what is true of all instances of a category from what is true only of typical instances. So in addition to the category *Tomatoes*, we will also have the category *Typical*(*Tomatoes*). Here, the *Typical* function maps a category to the subclass that contains only typical instances:

$$Typical(c) \subseteq c\,.$$

Most knowledge about natural kinds will actually be about their typical instances:

$$x \in Typical(Tomatoes) \;\Rightarrow\; Red(x) \wedge Round(x)\,.$$

Thus, we can write down useful facts about categories without exact definitions. The difficulty of providing exact definitions for most natural categories was explained in depth by Wittgenstein (1953). He used the example of *games* to show that members of a category shared "family resemblances" rather than necessary and sufficient characteristics: what strict definition encompasses chess, tag, solitaire, and dodgeball?

The utility of the notion of strict definition was also challenged by Quine (1953). He pointed out that even the definition of "bachelor" as an unmarried adult male is suspect; one might, for example, question a statement such as "the Pope is a bachelor." While not strictly *false*, this usage is certainly *infelicitous* because it induces unintended inferences on the part of the listener. The tension could perhaps be resolved by distinguishing between logical definitions suitable for internal knowledge representation and the more nuanced criteria for felicitous linguistic usage. The latter may be achieved by "filtering" the assertions derived from the former. It is also possible that failures of linguistic usage serve as feedback for modifying internal definitions, so that filtering becomes unnecessary.

2.2 Measurements

In both scientific and commonsense theories of the world, objects have height, mass, cost, and so on. The values that we assign for these properties are called **measures**. Ordinary quantitative measures are quite easy to represent. We imagine that the universe includes abstract "measure objects," such as the *length* that is the length of this line segment: ⊢——⊣. We can call this length 1.5 inches or 3.81 centimeters. Thus, the same length has different names in our language.We represent the length with a **units function** that takes a number as argument. (An alternative scheme is explored in Exercise 9.) If the line segment is called L , we can write

MEASURE

UNITS FUNCTION

$$Length(L_1) = Inches(1.5) = Centimeters(3.81) .$$

Conversion between units is done by equating multiples of one unit to another:

$$Centimeters(2.54 \times d) = Inches(d) .$$

Similar axioms can be written for pounds and kilograms, seconds and days, and dollars and cents. Measures can be used to describe objects as follows:

$$Diameter(Basketball_{12}) = Inches(9.5) .$$
$$ListPrice(Basketball_{12}) = \$(19) .$$
$$d \in Days \Rightarrow Duration(d) = Hours(24) .$$

Note that $\$(1)$ is *not* a dollar bill! One can have two dollar bills, but there is only one object named $\$(1)$. Note also that, while $Inches(0)$ and $Centimeters(0)$ refer to the same zero length, they are not identical to other zero measures, such as $Seconds(0)$.

Simple, quantitative measures are easy to represent. Other measures present more of a problem, because they have no agreed scale of values. Exercises have difficulty, desserts have deliciousness, and poems have beauty, yet numbers cannot be assigned to these qualities. One might, in a moment of pure accountancy, dismiss such properties as useless for the purpose of logical reasoning; or, still worse, attempt to impose a numerical scale on beauty. This would be a grave mistake, because it is unnecessary. The most important aspect of measures is not the particular numerical values, but the fact that measures can be *ordered*.

Although measures are not numbers, we can still compare them, using an ordering symbol such as $>$. For example, we might well believe that Norvig's exercises are tougher than Russell's, and that one scores less on tougher exercises:

$$e_1 \in Exercises \land e_2 \in Exercises \land Wrote(Norvig, e_1) \land Wrote(Russell, e_2) \Rightarrow$$
$$Difficulty(e_1) > Difficulty(e_2) .$$
$$e_1 \in Exercises \land e_2 \in Exercises \land Difficulty(e_1) > Difficulty(e_2) \Rightarrow$$
$$ExpectedScore(e_1) < ExpectedScore(e_2) .$$

This is enough to allow one to decide which exercises to do, even though no numerical values for difficulty were ever used. (One does, however, have to discover who wrote which exercises.) These sorts of monotonic relationships among measures form the basis for the field of **qualitative physics**, a subfield of AI that investigates how to reason about physical systems without plunging into detailed equations and numerical simulations. Qualitative physics is discussed in the historical notes section.

2.3 Objects: Things and stuff

The real world can be seen as consisting of primitive objects (e.g., atomic particles) and composite objects built from them. By reasoning at the level of large objects such as apples and cars, we can overcome the complexity involved in dealing with vast numbers of primitive objects individually. There is, however, a significant portion of reality that seems to defy any

INDIVIDUATION

obvious **individuation**—division into distinct objects. We give this portion the generic name

STUFF

stuff. For example, suppose I have some butter and an aardvark in front of me. I can say there is one aardvark, but there is no obvious number of "butter-objects," because any part of a butter-object is also a butter-object, at least until we get to very small parts indeed. This is the major distinction between *stuff* and *things*. If we cut an aardvark in half, we do not get two aardvarks (unfortunately).

The English language distinguishes clearly between *stuff* and *things*. We say "an aardvark," but, except in pretentious California restaurants, one cannot say "a butter." Linguists

COUNT NOUNS

MASS NOUN

distinguish between **count nouns**, such as aardvarks, holes, and theorems, and **mass nouns**, such as butter, water, and energy. Several competing ontologies claim to handle this distinction. Here we describe just one; the others are covered in the historical notes section.

To represent *stuff* properly, we begin with the obvious. We need to have as objects in our ontology at least the gross "lumps" of *stuff* we interact with. For example, we might recognize a lump of butter as the one left on the table the night before; we might pick it up, weigh it, sell it, or whatever. In these senses, it is an object just like the aardvark. Let us call it $Butter_3$. We also define the category $Butter$. Informally, its elements will be all those things of which one might say "It's butter," including $Butter_3$. With some caveats about very small parts that we w omit for now, any part of a butter-object is also a butter-object:

$$b \in Butter \land PartOf(p, b) \Rightarrow p \in Butter .$$

We can now say that butter melts at around 30 degrees centigrade:

$$b \in Butter \Rightarrow MeltingPoint(b, Centigrade(30)) .$$

We could go on to say that butter is yellow, is less dense than water, is soft at room temperature, has a high fat content, and so on. On the other hand, butter has no particular size, shape, or weight. We can define more specialized categories of butter such as $UnsaltedButter$, which is also a kind of *stuff*. Note that the category $PoundOfButter$, which includes as members all butter-objects weighing one pound, is not a kind of *stuff*. If we cut a pound of butter in half, we do not, alas, get two pounds of butter.

INTRINSIC

What is actually going on is this: some properties are **intrinsic**: they belong to the very substance of the object, rather than to the object as a whole. When you cut an instance of *stuff* in half, the two pieces retain the intrinsic properties—things like density, boiling point,

EXTRINSIC

flavor, color, ownership, and so on. On the other hand, their **extrinsic** properties—weight, length, shape, and so on—are not retained under subdivision. A category of objects that includes in its definition only *intrinsic* properties is then a substance, or mass noun; a class that includes *any* extrinsic properties in its definition is a count noun. The category $Stuff$ is the most general substance category, specifying no intrinsic properties. The category $Thing$ is the most general discrete object category, specifying no extrinsic properties.

3 EVENTS

Situation calculus represents actions and their effects, but is limited in its applicability: it was designed to describe a world in which actions are discrete, instantaneous, and happen one at a time. Consider a continuous action, such as filling a bathtub. Situation calculus can say that the tub is empty before the action and full when the action is done, but it can't talk about what happens *during* the action. It also can't describe two actions happening at the same time—such as brushing one's teeth while waiting for the tub to fill. To handle such cases we introduce an alternative formalism known as **event calculus**, which is based on points of time rather than on situations.[3]

EVENT CALCULUS

Event calculus reifies fluents and events. The fluent $At(Shankar, Berkeley)$ is an object that refers to the fact of Shankar being in Berkeley, but does not by itself say anything about whether it is true. To assert that a fluent is actually true at some point in time we use the predicate T, as in $T(At(Shankar, Berkeley), t)$.

Events are described as instances of event categories.[4] The event E_1 of Shankar flying from San Francisco to Washington, D.C. is described as

$$E_1 \in Flyings \land Flyer(E_1, Shankar) \land Origin(E_1, SF) \land Destination(E_1, DC)\,.$$

If this is too verbose, we can define an alternative three-argument version of the category of flying events and say

$$E_1 \in Flyings(Shankar, SF, DC)\,.$$

We then use $Happens(E_1, i)$ to say that the event E_1 took place over the time interval i, and we say the same thing in functional form with $Extent(E_1) = i$. We represent time intervals by a (start, end) pair of times; that is, $i = (t_1, t_2)$ is the time interval that starts at t_1 and ends at t_2. The complete set of predicates for one version of the event calculus is

$T(f, t)$	Fluent f is true at time t
$Happens(e, i)$	Event e happens over the time interval i
$Initiates(e, f, t)$	Event e causes fluent f to start to hold at time t
$Terminates(e, f, t)$	Event e causes fluent f to cease to hold at time t
$Clipped(f, i)$	Fluent f ceases to be true at some point during time interval i
$Restored(f, i)$	Fluent f becomes true sometime during time interval i

We assume a distinguished event, *Start*, that describes the initial state by saying which fluents are initiated or terminated at the start time. We define T by saying that a fluent holds at a point in time if the fluent was initiated by an event at some time in the past and was not made false (clipped) by an intervening event. A fluent does not hold if it was terminated by an event and

3 The terms "event" and "action" may be used interchangeably. Informally, "action" connotes an agent while "event" connotes the possibility of agentless actions.

4 Some versions of event calculus do not distinguish event categories from instances of the categories.

not made true (restored) by another event. Formally, the axioms are:

$$Happens(e,(t_1,t_2)) \land Initiates(e,f,t_1) \land \neg Clipped(f,(t_1,t)) \land t_1 < t \Rightarrow T(f,t)$$

$$Happens(e,(t_1,t_2)) \land Terminates(e,f,t_1) \land \neg Restored(f,(t_1,t)) \land t_1 < t \Rightarrow \neg T(f,t)$$

where *Clipped* and *Restored* are defined by

$$Clipped(f,(t_1,t_2)) \Leftrightarrow \exists\, e,t,t_3 \;\; Happens(e,(t,t_3)) \land t_1 \le t < t_2 \land Terminates(e,f,t)$$

$$Restored(f,(t_1,t_2)) \Leftrightarrow \exists\, e,t,t_3 \;\; Happens(e,(t,t_3)) \land t_1 \le t < t_2 \land Initiates(e,f,t)$$

It is convenient to extend T to work over intervals as well as time points; a fluent holds over an interval if it holds on every point within the interval:

$$T(f,(t_1,t_2)) \Leftrightarrow [\forall t \;\; (t_1 \le t < t_2) \Rightarrow T(f,t)]$$

Fluents and actions are defined with domain-specific axioms that are similar to successor-state axioms. For example, we can say that the only way a wumpus-world agent gets an arrow is at the start, and the only way to use up an arrow is to shoot it:

$$Initiates(e, HaveArrow(a), t) \Leftrightarrow e = Start$$

$$Terminates(e, HaveArrow(a), t) \Leftrightarrow e \in Shootings(a)$$

By reifying events we make it possible to add any amount of arbitrary information about them. For example, we can say that Shankar's flight was bumpy with $Bumpy(E_1)$. In an ontology where events are n-ary predicates, there would be no way to add extra information like this; moving to an $n+1$-ary predicate isn't a scalable solution.

We can extend event calculus to make it possible to represent simultaneous events (such as two people being necessary to ride a seesaw), exogenous events (such as the wind blowing and changing the location of an object), continuous events (such as the level of water in the bathtub continuously rising) and other complications.

3.1 Processes

DISCRETE EVENTS

The events we have seen so far are what we call **discrete events**—they have a definite structure. Shankar's trip has a beginning, middle, and end. If interrupted halfway, the event would be something different—it would not be a trip from San Francisco to Washington, but instead a trip from San Francisco to somewhere over Kansas. On the other hand, the category of events denoted by *Flyings* has a different quality. If we take a small interval of Shankar's flight, say, the third 20-minute segment (while he waits anxiously for a bag of peanuts), that event is still a member of *Flyings*. In fact, this is true for any subinterval.

PROCESS

LIQUID EVENT

Categories of events with this property are called **process** categories or **liquid event** categories. Any process e that happens over an interval also happens over any subinterval:

$$(e \in Processes) \land Happens(e,(t_1,t_4)) \land (t_1 < t_2 < t_3 < t_4) \Rightarrow Happens(e,(t_2,t_3)).$$

TEMPORAL SUBSTANCE

SPATIAL SUBSTANCE

The distinction between liquid and nonliquid events is exactly analogous to the difference between substances, or *stuff*, and individual objects, or *things*. In fact, some have called liquid events **temporal substances**, whereas substances like butter are **spatial substances**.

3.2 Time intervals

Event calculus opens us up to the possibility of talking about time, and time intervals. We will consider two kinds of time intervals: moments and extended intervals. The distinction is that only moments have zero duration:

$$Partition(\{Moments, ExtendedIntervals\}, Intervals)$$
$$i \in Moments \Leftrightarrow Duration(i) = Seconds(0)\ .$$

Next we invent a time scale and associate points on that scale with moments, giving us absolute times. The time scale is arbitrary; we measure it in seconds and say that the moment at midnight (GMT) on January 1, 1900, has time 0. The functions *Begin* and *End* pick out the earliest and latest moments in an interval, and the function *Time* delivers the point on the time scale for a moment. The function *Duration* gives the difference between the end time and the start time.

$$Interval(i) \Rightarrow Duration(i) = (Time(End(i)) - Time(Begin(i)))\ .$$
$$Time(Begin(AD1900)) = Seconds(0)\ .$$
$$Time(Begin(AD2001)) = Seconds(3187324800)\ .$$
$$Time(End(AD2001)) = Seconds(3218860800)\ .$$
$$Duration(AD2001) = Seconds(31536000)\ .$$

To make these numbers easier to read, we also introduce a function *Date*, which takes six arguments (hours, minutes, seconds, day, month, and year) and returns a time point:

$$Time(Begin(AD2001)) = Date(0, 0, 0, 1, Jan, 2001)$$
$$Date(0, 20, 21, 24, 1, 1995) = Seconds(3000000000)\ .$$

Two intervals *Meet* if the end time of the first equals the start time of the second. The complete set of interval relations, as proposed by Allen (1983), is shown graphically in Figure 2 and logically below:

$$\begin{array}{lcl}
Meet(i,j) & \Leftrightarrow & End(i) = Begin(j) \\
Before(i,j) & \Leftrightarrow & End(i) < Begin(j) \\
After(j,i) & \Leftrightarrow & Before(i,j) \\
During(i,j) & \Leftrightarrow & Begin(j) < Begin(i) < End(i) < End(j) \\
Overlap(i,j) & \Leftrightarrow & Begin(i) < Begin(j) < End(i) < End(j) \\
Begins(i,j) & \Leftrightarrow & Begin(i) = Begin(j) \\
Finishes(i,j) & \Leftrightarrow & End(i) = End(j) \\
Equals(i,j) & \Leftrightarrow & Begin(i) = Begin(j) \wedge End(i) = End(j)
\end{array}$$

These all have their intuitive meaning, with the exception of *Overlap*: we tend to think of overlap as symmetric (if *i* overlaps *j* then *j* overlaps *i*), but in this definition, $Overlap(i, j)$ only holds if *i* begins before *j*. To say that the reign of Elizabeth II immediately followed that of George VI, and the reign of Elvis overlapped with the 1950s, we can write the following:

$$Meets(ReignOf(GeorgeVI), ReignOf(ElizabethII))\ .$$
$$Overlap(Fifties, ReignOf(Elvis))\ .$$
$$Begin(Fifties) = Begin(AD1950)\ .$$
$$End(Fifties) = End(AD1959)\ .$$

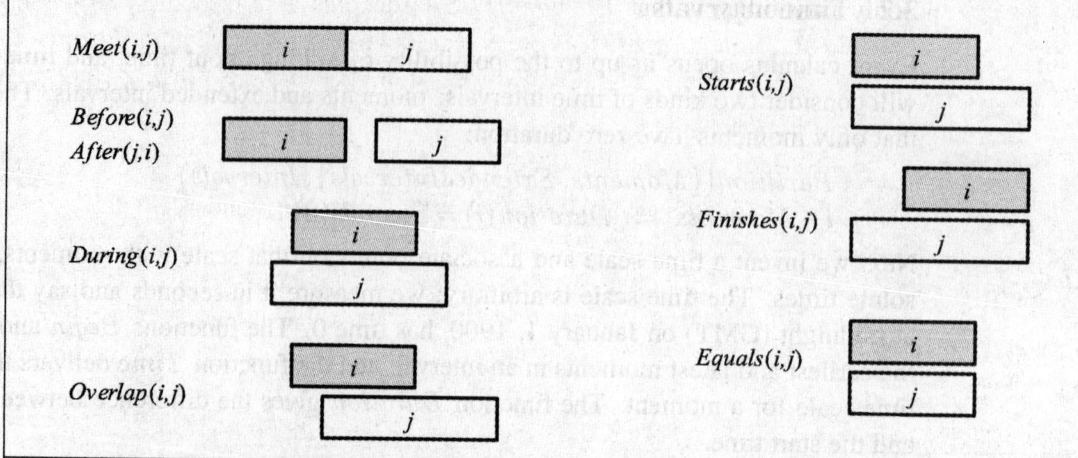

Figure 2 Predicates on time intervals.

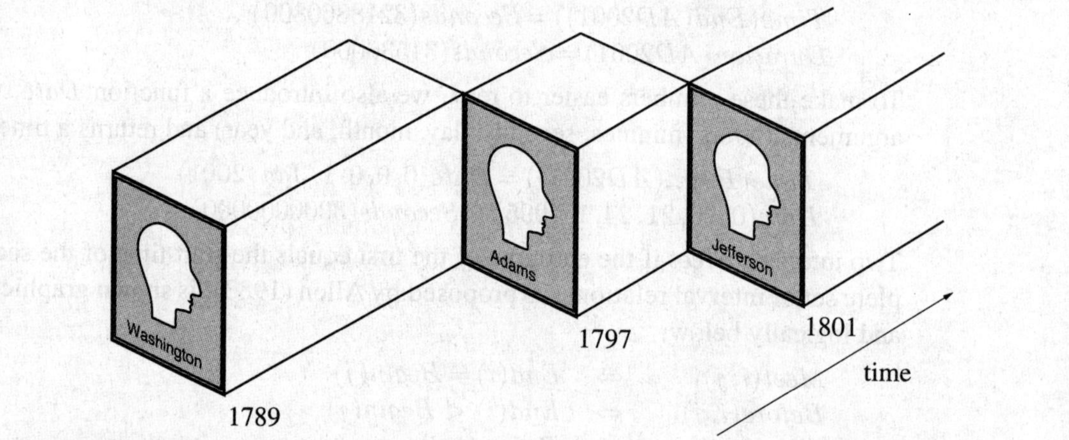

Figure 3 A schematic view of the object $President(USA)$ for the first 15 years of its existence.

3.3 Fluents and objects

Physical objects can be viewed as generalized events, in the sense that a physical object is a chunk of space–time. For example, USA can be thought of as an event that began in, say, 1776 as a union of 13 states and is still in progress today as a union of 50. We can describe the changing properties of USA using state fluents, such as $Population(USA)$. A property of the USA that changes every four or eight years, barring mishaps, is its president. One might propose that $President(USA)$ is a logical term that denotes a different object at different times. Unfortunately, this is not possible, because a term denotes exactly one object in a given model structure. (The term $President(USA, t)$ can denote different objects, depending on the value of t, but our ontology keeps time indices separate from fluents.) The only possibility is that $President(USA)$ denotes a single object that consists of different people at different times. It is the object that is George Washington from 1789 to 1797, John Adams from 1797 to 1801, and so on, as in Figure 3. To say that George Washington was president throughout 1790, we can write

$$T(Equals(President(USA), GeorgeWashington), AD1790) .$$

We use the function symbol $Equals$ rather than the standard logical predicate =, because we cannot have a predicate as an argument to T, and because the interpretation is *not* that $GeorgeWashington$ and $President(USA)$ are logically identical in 1790; logical identity is not something that can change over time. The identity is between the subevents of each object that are defined by the period 1790.

4 MENTAL EVENTS AND MENTAL OBJECTS

The agents we have constructed so far have beliefs and can deduce new beliefs. Yet none of them has any knowledge *about* beliefs or *about* deduction. Knowledge about one's own knowledge and reasoning processes is useful for controlling inference. For example, suppose Alice asks "what is the square root of 1764" and Bob replies "I don't know." If Alice insists "think harder," Bob should realize that with some more thought, this question can in fact be answered. On the other hand, if the question were "Is your mother sitting down right now?" then Bob should realize that thinking harder is unlikely to help. Knowledge about the knowledge of other agents is also important; Bob should realize that his mother knows whether she is sitting or not, and that asking her would be a way to find out.

What we need is a model of the mental objects that are in someone's head (or something's knowledge base) and of the mental processes that manipulate those mental objects. The model does not have to be detailed. We do not have to be able to predict how many milliseconds it will take for a particular agent to make a deduction. We will be happy just to be able to conclude that mother knows whether or not she is sitting.

PROPOSITIONAL ATTITUDE

We begin with the **propositional attitudes** that an agent can have toward mental objects: attitudes such as $Believes$, $Knows$, $Wants$, $Intends$, and $Informs$. The difficulty is that these attitudes do not behave like "normal" predicates. For example, suppose we try to assert that Lois knows that Superman can fly:

$$Knows(Lois, CanFly(Superman)) .$$

One minor issue with this is that we normally think of $CanFly(Superman)$ as a sentence, but here it appears as a term. That issue can be patched up just be reifying $CanFly(Superman)$; making it a fluent. A more serious problem is that, if it is true that Superman is Clark Kent, then we must conclude that Lois knows that Clark can fly:

$$(Superman = Clark) \wedge Knows(Lois, CanFly(Superman))$$
$$\models Knows(Lois, CanFly(Clark)) .$$

This is a consequence of the fact that equality reasoning is built into logic. Normally that is a good thing; if our agent knows that $2 + 2 = 4$ and $4 < 5$, then we want our agent to know

REFERENTIAL TRANSPARENCY

that $2 + 2 < 5$. This property is called **referential transparency**—it doesn't matter what term a logic uses to refer to an object, what matters is the object that the term names. But for propositional attitudes like *believes* and *knows*, we would like to have referential opacity—the terms used *do* matter, because not all agents know which terms are co-referential.

MODAL LOGIC

Modal logic is designed to address this problem. Regular logic is concerned with a single modality, the modality of truth, allowing us to express "P is true." Modal logic includes special modal operators that take sentences (rather than terms) as arguments. For example, "A knows P" is represented with the notation $\mathbf{K}_A P$, where $\mathbf{K}$ is the modal operator for knowledge. It takes two arguments, an agent (written as the subscript) and a sentence. The syntax of modal logic is the same as first-order logic, except that sentences can also be formed with modal operators.

The semantics of modal logic is more complicated. In first-order logic a **model** contains a set of objects and an interpretation that maps each name to the appropriate object, relation, or function. In modal logic we want to be able to consider both the possibility that Superman's secret identity is Clark and that it isn't. Therefore, we will need a more complicated model, one that consists of a collection of **possible worlds** rather than just one true world. The worlds are connected in a graph by **accessibility relations**, one relation for each modal operator. We say that world w_1 is accessible from world w_0 with respect to the modal operator $\mathbf{K}_A$ if everything in w_1 is consistent with what A knows in w_0, and we write this as $Acc(\mathbf{K}_A, w_0, w_1)$. In diagrams such as Figure 4 we show accessibility as an arrow between possible worlds. As an example, in the real world, Bucharest is the capital of Romania, but for an agent that did not know that, other possible worlds are accessible, including ones where the capital of Romania is Sibiu or Sofia. Presumably a world where $2 + 2 = 5$ would not be accessible to any agent.

POSSIBLE WORLD

ACCESSIBILITY RELATIONS

In general, a knowledge atom $\mathbf{K}_A P$ is true in world w if and only if P is true in every world accessible from w. The truth of more complex sentences is derived by recursive application of this rule and the normal rules of first-order logic. That means that modal logic can be used to reason about nested knowledge sentences: what one agent knows about another agent's knowledge. For example, we can say that, even though Lois doesn't know whether Superman's secret identity is Clark Kent, she does know that Clark knows:

$$\mathbf{K}_{Lois}[\mathbf{K}_{Clark}\, Identity(Superman, Clark) \lor \mathbf{K}_{Clark} \neg Identity(Superman, Clark)]$$

Figure 4 shows some possible worlds for this domain, with accessibility relations for Lois and Superman.

In the TOP-LEFT diagram, it is common knowledge that Superman knows his own identity, and neither he nor Lois has seen the weather report. So in w_0 the worlds w_0 and w_2 are accessible to Superman; maybe rain is predicted, maybe not. For Lois all four worlds are accessible from each other; she doesn't know anything about the report or if Clark is Superman. But she does know that Superman knows whether he is Clark, because in every world that is accessible to Lois, either Superman knows I, or he knows $\neg I$. Lois does not know which is the case, but either way she knows Superman knows.

In the TOP-RIGHT diagram it is common knowledge that Lois has seen the weather report. So in w_4 she knows rain is predicted and in w_6 she knows rain is not predicted.

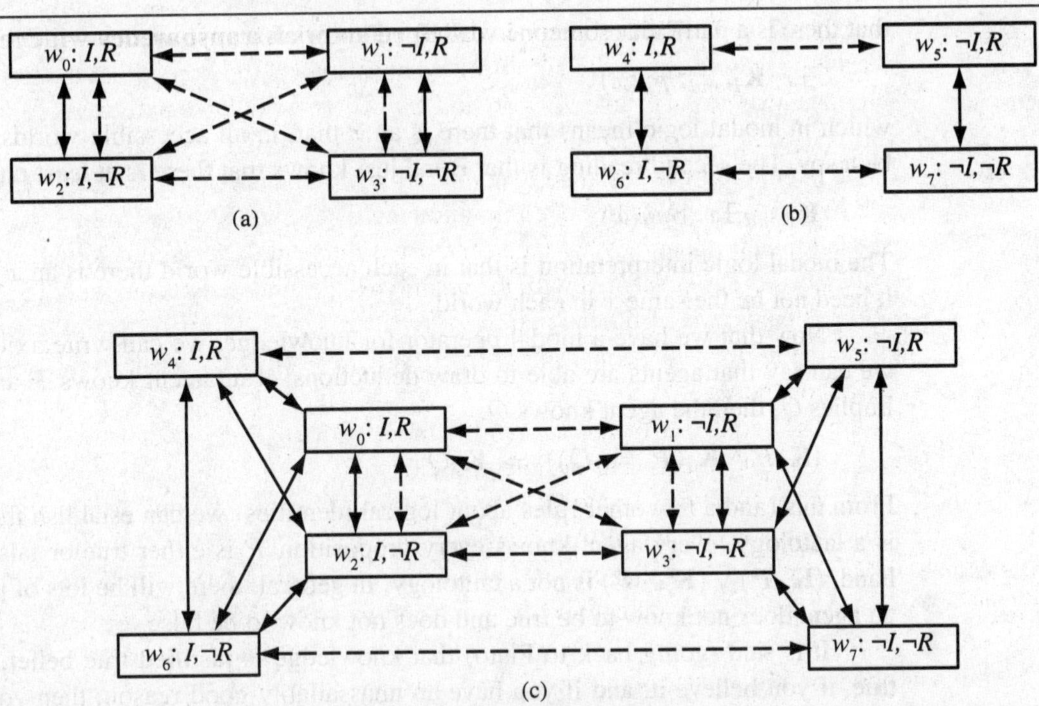

Figure 4 Possible worlds with accessibility relations $\mathbf{K}_{Superman}$ (solid arrows) and $\mathbf{K}_{Lois}$ (dotted arrows). The proposition R means "the weather report for tomorrow is rain" and I means "Superman's secret identity is Clark Kent." All worlds are accessible to themselves; the arrows from a world to itself are not shown.

Superman does not know the report, but he knows that Lois knows, because in every world that is accessible to him, either she knows R or she knows $\neg R$.

In the BOTTOM diagram we represent the scenario where it is common knowledge that Superman knows his identity, and Lois might or might not have seen the weather report. We represent this by combining the two top scenarios, and adding arrows to show that Superman does not know which scenario actually holds. Lois does know, so we don't need to add any arrows for her. In w_0 Superman still knows I but not R, and now he does not know whether Lois knows R. From what Superman knows, he might be in w_0 or w_2, in which case Lois does not know whether R is true, or he could be in w_4, in which case she knows R, or w_6, in which case she knows $\neg R$.

There are an infinite number of possible worlds, so the trick is to introduce just the ones you need to represent what you are trying to model. A new possible world is needed to talk about different possible facts (e.g., rain is predicted or not), or to talk about different states of knowledge (e.g., does Lois know that rain is predicted). That means two possible worlds, such as w_4 and w_0 in Figure 4, might have the same base facts about the world, but differ in their accessibility relations, and therefore in facts about knowledge.

Modal logic solves some tricky issues with the interplay of quantifiers and knowledge. The English sentence "Bond knows that someone is a spy" is ambiguous. The first reading is that there is a particular someone who Bond knows is a spy; we can write this as

$$\exists x \;\; \mathbf{K}_{Bond} Spy(x) \, ,$$

which in modal logic means that there is an x that, in all accessible worlds, Bond knows to be a spy. The second reading is that Bond just knows that there is at least one spy:

$$\mathbf{K}_{Bond} \exists x \;\; Spy(x) \, .$$

The modal logic interpretation is that in each accessible world there is an x that is a spy, but it need not be the same x in each world.

Now that we have a modal operator for knowledge, we can write axioms for it. First, we can say that agents are able to draw deductions; if an agent knows P and knows that P implies Q, then the agent knows Q:

$$(\mathbf{K}_a P \wedge \mathbf{K}_a(P \;\Rightarrow\; Q)) \;\Rightarrow\; \mathbf{K}_a Q \, .$$

From this (and a few other rules about logical identities) we can establish that $\mathbf{K}_A(P \vee \neg P)$ is a tautology; every agent knows every proposition P is either true or false. On the other hand, $(\mathbf{K}_A P) \vee (\mathbf{K}_A \neg P)$ is not a tautology; in general, there will be lots of propositions that an agent does not know to be true and does not know to be false.

It is said (going back to Plato) that knowledge is justified true belief. That is, if it is true, if you believe it, and if you have an unassailably good reason, then you know it. That means that if you know something, it must be true, and we have the axiom:

$$\mathbf{K}_a P \;\Rightarrow\; P \, .$$

Furthermore, logical agents should be able to introspect on their own knowledge. If they know something, then they know that they know it:

$$\mathbf{K}_a P \;\Rightarrow\; \mathbf{K}_a(\mathbf{K}_a P) \, .$$

We can define similar axioms for belief (often denoted by **B**) and other modalities. However, one problem with the modal logic approach is that it assumes **logical omniscience** on the part of agents. That is, if an agent knows a set of axioms, then it knows all consequences of those axioms. This is on shaky ground even for the somewhat abstract notion of knowledge, but it seems even worse for belief, because belief has more connotation of referring to things that are physically represented in the agent, not just potentially derivable. There have been attempts to define a form of limited rationality for agents; to say that agents believe those assertions that can be derived with the application of no more than k reasoning steps, or no more than s seconds of computation. These attempts have been generally unsatisfactory.

LOGICAL OMNISCIENCE

5 Reasoning Systems for Categories

Categories are the primary building blocks of large-scale knowledge representation schemes. This section describes systems specially designed for organizing and reasoning with categories. There are two closely related families of systems: **semantic networks** provide graphical aids for visualizing a knowledge base and efficient algorithms for inferring properties of an object on the basis of its category membership; and **description logics** provide a formal language for constructing and combining category definitions and efficient algorithms for deciding subset and superset relationships between categories.

5.1 Semantic networks

EXISTENTIAL GRAPHS

In 1909, Charles S. Peirce proposed a graphical notation of nodes and edges called **existential graphs** that he called "the logic of the future." Thus began a long-running debate between advocates of "logic" and advocates of "semantic networks." Unfortunately, the debate obscured the fact that semantics networks—at least those with well-defined semantics—*are* a form of logic. The notation that semantic networks provide for certain kinds of sentences is often more convenient, but if we strip away the "human interface" issues, the underlying concepts—objects, relations, quantification, and so on—are the same.

There are many variants of semantic networks, but all are capable of representing individual objects, categories of objects, and relations among objects. A typical graphical notation displays object or category names in ovals or boxes, and connects them with labeled links. For example, Figure 5 has a $MemberOf$ link between $Mary$ and $FemalePersons$, corresponding to the logical assertion $Mary \in FemalePersons$; similarly, the $SisterOf$ link between $Mary$ and $John$ corresponds to the assertion $SisterOf(Mary, John)$. We can connect categories using $SubsetOf$ links, and so on. It is such fun drawing bubbles and arrows that one can get carried away. For example, we know that persons have female persons as mothers, so can we draw a $HasMother$ link from $Persons$ to $FemalePersons$? The answer is no, because $HasMother$ is a relation between a person and his or her mother, and categories do not have mothers.[5]

For this reason, we have used a special notation—the double-boxed link—in Figure 5. This link asserts that

$$\forall x \;\; x \in Persons \;\Rightarrow\; [\forall y \;\; HasMother(x,y) \;\Rightarrow\; y \in FemalePersons] .$$

We might also want to assert that persons have two legs—that is,

$$\forall x \;\; x \in Persons \;\Rightarrow\; Legs(x,2) .$$

As before, we need to be careful not to assert that a category has legs; the single-boxed link in Figure 5 is used to assert properties of every member of a category.

The semantic network notation makes it convenient to perform **inheritance** reasoning of the kind introduced in Section 2. For example, by virtue of being a person, Mary inherits the property of having two legs. Thus, to find out how many legs Mary has, the inheritance algorithm follows the $MemberOf$ link from $Mary$ to the category she belongs to, and then follows $SubsetOf$ links up the hierarchy until it finds a category for which there is a boxed $Legs$ link—in this case, the $Persons$ category. The simplicity and efficiency of this inference

[5] Several early systems failed to distinguish between properties of members of a category and properties of the category as a whole. This can lead directly to inconsistencies, as pointed out by Drew McDermott (1976) in his article "Artificial Intelligence Meets Natural Stupidity." Another common problem was the use of IsA links for both subset and membership relations, in correspondence with English usage: "a cat is a mammal" and "Fifi is a cat." See Exercise 22 for more on these issues.

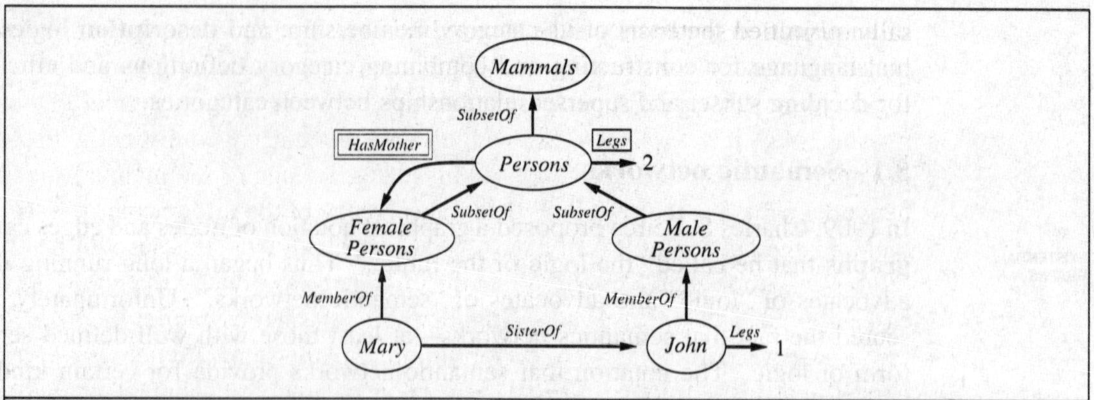

Figure 5 A semantic network with four objects (John, Mary, 1, and 2) and four categories. Relations are denoted by labeled links.

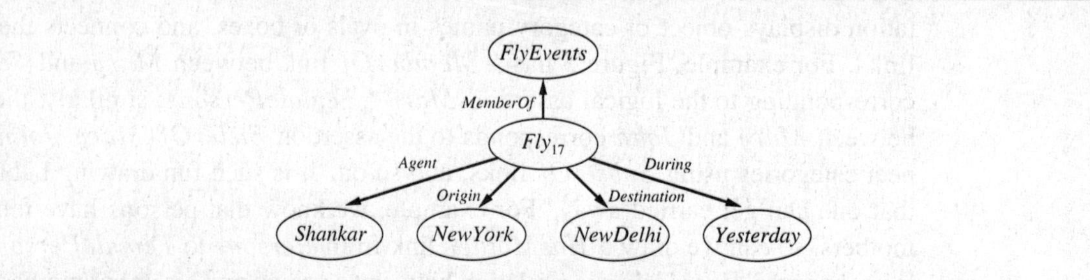

Figure 6 A fragment of a semantic network showing the representation of the logical assertion *Fly*(*Shankar*, *NewYork*, *NewDelhi*, *Yesterday*).

mechanism, compared with logical theorem proving, has been one of the main attractions of semantic networks.

Inheritance becomes complicated when an object can belong to more than one category or when a category can be a subset of more than one other category; this is called **multiple inheritance**. In such cases, the inheritance algorithm might find two or more conflicting values answering the query. For this reason, multiple inheritance is banned in some **object-oriented programming** (OOP) languages, such as Java, that use inheritance in a class hierarchy. It is usually allowed in semantic networks, but we defer discussion of that until Section 6.

MULTIPLE INHERITANCE

The reader might have noticed an obvious drawback of semantic network notation, compared to first-order logic: the fact that links between bubbles represent only *binary* relations. For example, the sentence *Fly*(*Shankar*, *NewYork*, *NewDelhi*, *Yesterday*) cannot be asserted directly in a semantic network. Nonetheless, we *can* obtain the effect of n-ary assertions by reifying the proposition itself as an event belonging to an appropriate event category. Figure 6 shows the semantic network structure for this particular event. Notice that the restriction to binary relations forces the creation of a rich ontology of reified concepts.

Reification of propositions makes it possible to represent every ground, function-free atomic sentence of first-order logic in the semantic network notation. Certain kinds of universally quantified sentences can be asserted using inverse links and the singly boxed and doubly boxed arrows applied to categories, but that still leaves us a long way short of full first-order logic. Negation, disjunction, nested function symbols, and existential quantification are all missing. Now it is *possible* to extend the notation to make it equivalent to first-order logic—as in Peirce's existential graphs—but doing so negates one of the main advantages of semantic networks, which is the simplicity and transparency of the inference processes. Designers can build a large network and still have a good idea about what queries will be efficient, because (a) it is easy to visualize the steps that the inference procedure will go through and (b) in some cases the query language is so simple that difficult queries cannot be posed. In cases where the expressive power proves to be too limiting, many semantic network systems provide for **procedural attachment** to fill in the gaps. Procedural attachment is a technique whereby a query about (or sometimes an assertion of) a certain relation results in a call to a special procedure designed for that relation rather than a general inference algorithm.

DEFAULT VALUE

One of the most important aspects of semantic networks is their ability to represent **default values** for categories. Examining Figure 5 carefully, one notices that John has one leg, despite the fact that he is a person and all persons have two legs. In a strictly logical KB, this would be a contradiction, but in a semantic network, the assertion that all persons have two legs has only default status; that is, a person is assumed to have two legs unless this is contradicted by more specific information. The default semantics is enforced naturally by the inheritance algorithm, because it follows links upwards from the object itself (John in this case) and stops as soon as it finds a value. We say that the default is **overridden** by the more specific value. Notice that we could also override the default number of legs by creating a category of $OneLeggedPersons$, a subset of $Persons$ of which $John$ is a member.

OVERRIDING

We can retain a strictly logical semantics for the network if we say that the $Legs$ assertion for $Persons$ includes an exception for John:

$$\forall x \;\; x \in Persons \land x \neq John \;\Rightarrow\; Legs(x, 2)\,.$$

For a *fixed* network, this is semantically adequate but will be much less concise than the network notation itself if there are lots of exceptions. For a network that will be updated with more assertions, however, such an approach fails—we really want to say that any persons as yet unknown with one leg are exceptions too. Section 6 goes into more depth on this issue and on default reasoning in general.

5.2 Description logics

DESCRIPTION LOGIC

The syntax of first-order logic is designed to make it easy to say things about objects. **Description logics** are notations that are designed to make it easier to describe definitions and properties of categories. Description logic systems evolved from semantic networks in response to pressure to formalize what the networks mean while retaining the emphasis on taxonomic structure as an organizing principle.

SUBSUMPTION

CLASSIFICATION

The principal inference tasks for description logics are **subsumption** (checking if one category is a subset of another by comparing their definitions) and **classification** (checking whether an object belongs to a category).. Some systems also include **consistency** of a category definition—whether the membership criteria are logically satisfiable.

$$
\begin{aligned}
\textit{Concept} \;\rightarrow\; & \textbf{Thing} \mid \textit{ConceptName} \\
\mid\; & \textbf{And}(\textit{Concept}, \ldots) \\
\mid\; & \textbf{All}(\textit{RoleName}, \textit{Concept}) \\
\mid\; & \textbf{AtLeast}(\textit{Integer}, \textit{RoleName}) \\
\mid\; & \textbf{AtMost}(\textit{Integer}, \textit{RoleName}) \\
\mid\; & \textbf{Fills}(\textit{RoleName}, \textit{IndividualName}, \ldots) \\
\mid\; & \textbf{SameAs}(\textit{Path}, \textit{Path}) \\
\mid\; & \textbf{OneOf}(\textit{IndividualName}, \ldots) \\
\textit{Path} \;\rightarrow\; & [\textit{RoleName}, \ldots]
\end{aligned}
$$

Figure 7 The syntax of descriptions in a subset of the CLASSIC language.

The CLASSIC language (Borgida *et al.*, 1989) is a typical description logic. The syntax of CLASSIC descriptions is shown in Figure 7.[6] For example, to say that bachelors are unmarried adult males we would write

$$Bachelor = And(Unmarried, Adult, Male)\,.$$

The equivalent in first-order logic would be

$$Bachelor(x) \;\Leftrightarrow\; Unmarried(x) \wedge Adult(x) \wedge Male(x)\,.$$

Notice that the description logic has an an algebra of operations on predicates, which of course we can't do in first-order logic. Any description in CLASSIC can be translated into an equivalent first-order sentence, but some descriptions are more straightforward in CLASSIC. For example, to describe the set of men with at least three sons who are all unemployed and married to doctors, and at most two daughters who are all professors in physics or math departments, we would use

$$
\begin{aligned}
& And(Man, AtLeast(3, Son), AtMost(2, Daughter), \\
& \quad All(Son, And(Unemployed, Married, All(Spouse, Doctor))), \\
& \quad All(Daughter, And(Professor, Fills(Department, Physics, Math))))\,.
\end{aligned}
$$

We leave it as an exercise to translate this into first-order logic.

Perhaps the most important aspect of description logics is their emphasis on tractability of inference. A problem instance is solved by describing it and then asking if it is subsumed by one of several possible solution categories. In standard first-order logic systems, predicting the solution time is often impossible. It is frequently left to the user to engineer the representation to detour around sets of sentences that seem to be causing the system to take several weeks to solve a problem. The thrust in description logics, on the other hand, is to ensure that subsumption-testing can be solved in time polynomial in the size of the descriptions.[7]

[6] Notice that the language does *not* allow one to simply state that one concept, or category, is a subset of another. This is a deliberate policy: subsumption between categories must be derivable from some aspects of the descriptions of the categories. If not, then something is missing from the descriptions.

[7] CLASSIC provides efficient subsumption testing in practice, but the worst-case run time is exponential.

This sounds wonderful in principle, until one realizes that it can only have one of two consequences: either hard problems cannot be stated at all, or they require exponentially large descriptions! However, the tractability results do shed light on what sorts of constructs cause problems and thus help the user to understand how different representations behave. For example, description logics usually lack *negation* and *disjunction*. Each forces first-order logical systems to go through a potentially exponential case analysis in order to ensure completeness. CLASSIC allows only a limited form of disjunction in the *Fills* and *OneOf* constructs, which permit disjunction over explicitly enumerated individuals but not over descriptions. With disjunctive descriptions, nested definitions can lead easily to an exponential number of alternative routes by which one category can subsume another.

6 REASONING WITH DEFAULT INFORMATION

In the preceding section, we saw a simple example of an assertion with default status: people have two legs. This default can be overridden by more specific information, such as that Long John Silver has one leg. We saw that the inheritance mechanism in semantic networks implements the overriding of defaults in a simple and natural way. In this section, we study defaults more generally, with a view toward understanding the *semantics* of defaults rather than just providing a procedural mechanism.

6.1 Circumscription and default logic

The following are two examples of reasoning processes that violate the **monotonicity** property of logic.[8] In this chapter we saw that a property inherited by all members of a category in a semantic network could be overridden by more specific information for a subcategory. Also under the closed-world assumption, if a proposition α is not mentioned in *KB* then $KB \models \neg\alpha$, but $KB \land \alpha \models \alpha$.

Simple introspection suggests that these failures of monotonicity are widespread in commonsense reasoning. It seems that humans often "jump to conclusions." For example, when one sees a car parked on the street, one is normally willing to believe that it has four wheels even though only three are visible. Now, probability theory can certainly provide a conclusion that the fourth wheel exists with high probability, yet, for most people, the possibility of the car's not having four wheels *does not arise unless some new evidence presents itself*. Thus, it seems that the four-wheel conclusion is reached *by default*, in the absence of any reason to doubt it. If new evidence arrives—for example, if one sees the owner carrying a wheel and notices that the car is jacked up—then the conclusion can be retracted. This kind of reasoning is said to exhibit **nonmonotonicity**, because the set of beliefs does not grow monotonically over time as new evidence arrives. **Nonmonotonic logics** have been devised with modified notions of truth and entailment in order to capture such behavior. We will look at two such logics that have been studied extensively: circumscription and default logic.

NONMONOTONICITY

NONMONOTONIC LOGIC

[8] Monotonicity requires all entailed sentences to remain entailed after new sentences are added to the KB. That is, if $KB \models \alpha$ then $KB \land \beta \models \alpha$.

CIRCUMSCRIPTION **Circumscription** can be seen as a more powerful and precise version of the closed-world assumption. The idea is to specify particular predicates that are assumed to be "as false as possible"—that is, false for every object except those for which they are known to be true. For example, suppose we want to assert the default rule that birds fly. We would introduce a predicate, say $Abnormal_1(x)$, and write

$$Bird(x) \land \neg Abnormal_1(x) \Rightarrow Flies(x) .$$

If we say that $Abnormal_1$ is to be **circumscribed**, a circumscriptive reasoner is entitled to assume $\neg Abnormal_1(x)$ unless $Abnormal_1(x)$ is known to be true. This allows the conclusion $Flies(Tweety)$ to be drawn from the premise $Bird(Tweety)$, but the conclusion no longer holds if $Abnormal_1(Tweety)$ is asserted.

MODEL PREFERENCE Circumscription can be viewed as an example of a **model preference** logic. In such logics, a sentence is entailed (with default status) if it is true in all *preferred* models of the KB, as opposed to the requirement of truth in *all* models in classical logic. For circumscription, one model is preferred to another if it has fewer abnormal objects.[9] Let us see how this idea works in the context of multiple inheritance in semantic networks. The standard example for which multiple inheritance is problematic is called the "Nixon diamond." It arises from the observation that Richard Nixon was both a Quaker (and hence by default a pacifist) and a Republican (and hence by default not a pacifist). We can write this as follows:

$$\begin{aligned}
&Republican(Nixon) \land Quaker(Nixon) .\\
&Republican(x) \land \neg Abnormal_2(x) \Rightarrow \neg Pacifist(x) .\\
&Quaker(x) \land \neg Abnormal_3(x) \Rightarrow Pacifist(x) .
\end{aligned}$$

If we circumscribe $Abnormal_2$ and $Abnormal_3$, there are two preferred models: one in which $Abnormal_2(Nixon)$ and $Pacifist(Nixon)$ hold and one in which $Abnormal_3(Nixon)$ and $\neg Pacifist(Nixon)$ hold. Thus, the circumscriptive reasoner remains properly agnostic as to whether Nixon was a pacifist. If we wish, in addition, to assert that religious beliefs take precedence over political beliefs, we can use a formalism called **prioritized circumscription** to give preference to models where $Abnormal_3$ is minimized.

PRIORITIZED CIRCUMSCRIPTION

DEFAULT LOGIC

DEFAULT RULES

Default logic is a formalism in which **default rules** can be written to generate contingent, nonmonotonic conclusions. A default rule looks like this:

$$Bird(x) : Flies(x)/Flies(x) .$$

This rule means that if $Bird(x)$ is true, and if $Flies(x)$ is consistent with the knowledge base, then $Flies(x)$ may be concluded by default. In general, a default rule has the form

$$P : J_1, \ldots, J_n/C$$

where P is called the prerequisite, C is the conclusion, and J_i are the justifications—if any one of them can be proven false, then the conclusion cannot be drawn. Any variable that

9 For the closed-world assumption, one model is preferred to another if it has fewer true atoms—that is, preferred models are **minimal** models. There is a natural connection between the closed-world assumption and definite-clause KBs, because the fixed point reached by forward chaining on definite-clause KBs is the unique minimal model.

appears in J_i or C must also appear in P. The Nixon-diamond example can be represented in default logic with one fact and two default rules:

$$Republican(Nixon) \land Quaker(Nixon) .$$
$$Republican(x) : \neg Pacifist(x) / \neg Pacifist(x) .$$
$$Quaker(x) : Pacifist(x) / Pacifist(x) .$$

EXTENSION

To interpret what the default rules mean, we define the notion of an **extension** of a default theory to be a maximal set of consequences of the theory. That is, an extension S consists of the original known facts and a set of conclusions from the default rules, such that no additional conclusions can be drawn from S and the justifications of every default conclusion in S are consistent with S. As in the case of the preferred models in circumscription, we have two possible extensions for the Nixon diamond: one wherein he is a pacifist and one wherein he is not. Prioritized schemes exist in which some default rules can be given precedence over others, allowing some ambiguities to be resolved.

Since 1980, when nonmonotonic logics were first proposed, a great deal of progress has been made in understanding their mathematical properties. There are still unresolved questions, however. For example, if "Cars have four wheels" is false, what does it mean to have it in one's knowledge base? What is a good set of default rules to have? If we cannot decide, for each rule separately, whether it belongs in our knowledge base, then we have a serious problem of nonmodularity. Finally, how can beliefs that have default status be used to make decisions? This is probably the hardest issue for default reasoning. Decisions often involve tradeoffs, and one therefore needs to compare the *strengths* of belief in the outcomes of different actions, and the *costs* of making a wrong decision. In cases where the same kinds of decisions are being made repeatedly, it is possible to interpret default rules as "threshold probability" statements. For example, the default rule "My brakes are always OK" really means "The probability that my brakes are OK, given no other information, is sufficiently high that the optimal decision is for me to drive without checking them." When the decision context changes—for example, when one is driving a heavily laden truck down a steep mountain road—the default rule suddenly becomes inappropriate, even though there is no new evidence of faulty brakes. These considerations have led some researchers to consider how to embed default reasoning within probability theory or utility theory.

6.2 Truth maintenance systems

Many of the inferences drawn by a knowledge representation system will have only default status, rather than being absolutely certain. Inevitably, some of these inferred facts will turn out to be wrong and will have to be retracted in the face of new information. This process

BELIEF REVISION

is called **belief revision.**[10] Suppose that a knowledge base KB contains a sentence P—perhaps a default conclusion recorded by a forward-chaining algorithm, or perhaps just an incorrect assertion—and we want to execute TELL(KB, $\neg P$). To avoid creating a contradiction, we must first execute RETRACT(KB, P). This sounds easy enough. Problems arise,

[10] Belief revision is often contrasted with **belief update**, which occurs when a knowledge base is revised to reflect a change in the world rather than new information about a fixed world. Belief update combines belief revision with reasoning about time and change; it is also related to the process of **filtering.**

however, if any *additional sentences* were inferred from P and asserted in the KB. For example, the implication $P \Rightarrow Q$ might have been used to add Q. The obvious "solution"—retracting all sentences inferred from P—fails because such sentences may have other justifications besides P. For example, if R and $R \Rightarrow Q$ are also in the KB, then Q does not have to be removed after all. **Truth maintenance systems,** or TMSs, are designed to handle exactly these kinds of complications.

TRUTH MAINTENANCE SYSTEM

One simple approach to truth maintenance is to keep track of the order in which sentences are told to the knowledge base by numbering them from P_1 to P_n. When the call RETRACT(KB, P_i) is made, the system reverts to the state just before P_i was added, thereby removing both P_i and any inferences that were derived from P_i. The sentences P_{i+1} through P_n can then be added again. This is simple, and it guarantees that the knowledge base will be consistent, but retracting P_i requires retracting and reasserting $n - i$ sentences as well as undoing and redoing all the inferences drawn from those sentences. For systems to which many facts are being added—such as large commercial databases—this is impractical.

JTMS

JUSTIFICATION

A more efficient approach is the justification-based truth maintenance system, or **JTMS**. In a JTMS, each sentence in the knowledge base is annotated with a **justification** consisting of the set of sentences from which it was inferred. For example, if the knowledge base already contains $P \Rightarrow Q$, then TELL(P) will cause Q to be added with the justification $\{P,\ P \Rightarrow Q\}$. In general, a sentence can have any number of justifications. Justifications make retraction efficient. Given the call RETRACT(P), the JTMS will delete exactly those sentences for which P is a member of every justification. So, if a sentence Q had the single justification $\{P,\ P \Rightarrow Q\}$, it would be removed; if it had the additional justification $\{P,\ P \vee R \Rightarrow Q\}$, it would still be removed; but if it also had the justification $\{R,\ P \vee R \Rightarrow Q\}$, then it would be spared. In this way, the time required for retraction of P depends only on the number of sentences derived from P rather than on the number of other sentences added since P entered the knowledge base.

The JTMS assumes that sentences that are considered once will probably be considered again, so rather than deleting a sentence from the knowledge base entirely when it loses all justifications, we merely mark the sentence as being *out* of the knowledge base. If a subsequent assertion restores one of the justifications, then we mark the sentence as being back *in*. In this way, the JTMS retains all the inference chains that it uses and need not rederive sentences when a justification becomes valid again.

In addition to handling the retraction of incorrect information, TMSs can be used to speed up the analysis of multiple hypothetical situations. Suppose, for example, that the Romanian Olympic Committee is choosing sites for the swimming, athletics, and equestrian events at the 2048 Games to be held in Romania. For example, let the first hypothesis be $Site(Swimming, Pitesti)$, $Site(Athletics, Bucharest)$, and $Site(Equestrian, Arad)$. A great deal of reasoning must then be done to work out the logistical consequences and hence the desirability of this selection. If we want to consider $Site(Athletics, Sibiu)$ instead, the TMS avoids the need to start again from scratch. Instead, we simply retract $Site(Athletics, Bucharest)$ and assert $Site(Athletics, Sibiu)$ and the TMS takes care of the necessary revisions. Inference chains generated from the choice of Bucharest can be reused with Sibiu, provided that the conclusions are the same.

ATMS An assumption-based truth maintenance system, or **ATMS**, makes this type of context-switching between hypothetical worlds particularly efficient. In a JTMS, the maintenance of justifications allows you to move quickly from one state to another by making a few retractions and assertions, but at any time only one state is represented. An ATMS represents *all* the states that have ever been considered at the same time. Whereas a JTMS simply labels each sentence as being *in* or *out*, an ATMS keeps track, for each sentence, of which assumptions would cause the sentence to be true. In other words, each sentence has a label that consists of a set of assumption sets. The sentence holds just in those cases in which all the assumptions in one of the assumption sets hold.

EXPLANATION Truth maintenance systems also provide a mechanism for generating **explanations**. Technically, an explanation of a sentence P is a set of sentences E such that E entails P. If the sentences in E are already known to be true, then E simply provides a sufficient basis for proving that P must be the case. But explanations can also include **assumptions**— ASSUMPTION sentences that are not known to be true, but would suffice to prove P if they were true. For example, one might not have enough information to prove that one's car won't start, but a reasonable explanation might include the assumption that the battery is dead. This, combined with knowledge of how cars operate, explains the observed nonbehavior. In most cases, we will prefer an explanation E that is minimal, meaning that there is no proper subset of E that is also an explanation. An ATMS can generate explanations for the "car won't start" problem by making assumptions (such as "gas in car" or "battery dead") in any order we like, even if some assumptions are contradictory. Then we look at the label for the sentence "car won't start" to read off the sets of assumptions that would justify the sentence.

The exact algorithms used to implement truth maintenance systems are a little complicated, and we do not cover them here. The computational complexity of the truth maintenance problem is at least as great as that of propositional inference—that is, NP-hard. Therefore, you should not expect truth maintenance to be a panacea. When used carefully, however, a TMS can provide a substantial increase in the ability of a logical system to handle complex environments and hypotheses.

7 The Internet Shopping World

In this final section we put together all we have learned to encode knowledge for a shopping research agent that helps a buyer find product offers on the Internet. The shopping agent is given a product description by the buyer and has the task of producing a list of Web pages that offer such a product for sale, and ranking which offers are best. In some cases the buyer's product description will be precise, as in *Canon Rebel XTi digital camera*, and the task is then to find the store(s) with the best offer. In other cases the description will be only partially specified, as in *digital camera for under $300*, and the agent will have to compare different products.

The shopping agent's environment is the entire World Wide Web in its full complexity— not a toy simulated environment. The agent's percepts are Web pages, but whereas a human

Example Online Store

Select from our fine line of products:

- Computers
- Cameras
- Books
- Videos
- Music

```
<h1>Example Online Store</h1>
<i>Select</i> from our fine line of products:
<ul>
<li> <a href="http://example.com/compu">Computers</a>
<li> <a href="http://example.com/camer">Cameras</a>
<li> <a href="http://example.com/books">Books</a>
<li> <a href="http://example.com/video">Videos</a>
<li> <a href="http://example.com/music">Music</a>
</ul>
```

Figure 8 A Web page from a generic online store in the form perceived by the human user of a browser (top), and the corresponding HTML string as perceived by the browser or the shopping agent (bottom). In HTML, characters between < and > are markup directives that specify how the page is displayed. For example, the string `<i>Select</i>` means to switch to italic font, display the word *Select*, and then end the use of italic font. A page identifier such as `http://example.com/books` is called a **uniform resource locator (URL)**. The markup `<a href="`*url*`">`*Books*`</a>` means to create a hypertext link to *url* with the **anchor text** *Books*..

Web user would see pages displayed as an array of pixels on a screen, the shopping agent will perceive a page as a character string consisting of ordinary words interspersed with formatting commands in the HTML markup language. Figure 8 shows a Web page and a corresponding HTML character string. The perception problem for the shopping agent involves extracting useful information from percepts of this kind.

Clearly, perception on Web pages is easier than, say, perception while driving a taxi in Cairo. Nonetheless, there are complications to the Internet perception task. The Web page in Figure 8 is simple compared to real shopping sites, which may include CSS, cookies, Java, Javascript, Flash, robot exclusion protocols, malformed HTML, sound files, movies, and text that appears only as part of a JPEG image. An agent that can deal with *all* of the Internet is almost as complex as a robot that can move in the real world. We concentrate on a simple agent that ignores most of these complications.

The agent's first task is to collect product offers that are relevant to a query. If the query is "laptops," then a Web page with a review of the latest high-end laptop would be relevant, but if it doesn't provide a way to buy, it isn't an offer. For now, we can say a page is an offer if it contains the words "buy" or "price" or "add to cart" within an HTML link or form on the page. For example, if the page contains a string of the form "<a...add to cart...</a>" then it is an offer. This could be represented in first-order logic, but it is more straightforward to encode it into program code.

7.1 Following links

The strategy is to start at the home page of an online store and consider all pages that can be reached by following relevant links.[11] The agent will have knowledge of a number of stores, for example:

$$\begin{aligned}&Amazon \in OnlineStores \land Homepage(Amazon, \text{“}amazon.com\text{”})\,.\\&Ebay \in OnlineStores \land Homepage(Ebay, \text{“}ebay.com\text{”})\,.\\&ExampleStore \in OnlineStores \land Homepage(ExampleStore, \text{“}example.com\text{”})\,.\end{aligned}$$

These stores classify their goods into product categories, and provide links to the major categories from their home page. Minor categories can be reached through a chain of relevant links, and eventually we will reach offers. In other words, a page is relevant to the query if it can be reached by a chain of zero or more relevant category links from a store's home page, and then from one more link to the product offer. We can define relevance:

$$\begin{aligned}&Relevant(page, query) \Leftrightarrow\\&\qquad \exists\, store, home \;\; store \in OnlineStores \land Homepage(store, home)\\&\qquad \land \exists\, url, url_2 \;\; RelevantChain(home, url_2, query) \land Link(url_2, url)\\&\qquad\quad \land\, page = Contents(url)\,.\end{aligned}$$

Here the predicate $Link(from, to)$ means that there is a hyperlink from the *from* URL to the *to* URL. To define what counts as a *RelevantChain*, we need to follow not just any old hyperlinks, but only those links whose associated anchor text indicates that the link is relevant to the product query. For this, we use $LinkText(from, to, text)$ to mean that there is a link between *from* and *to* with *text* as the anchor text. A chain of links between two URLs, *start* and *end*, is relevant to a description d if the anchor text of each link is a relevant category name for d. The existence of the chain itself is determined by a recursive definition, with the empty chain ($start = end$) as the base case:

$$\begin{aligned}&RelevantChain(start, end, query) \Leftrightarrow (start = end)\\&\qquad \lor (\exists\, u, text \;\; LinkText(start, u, text) \land RelevantCategoryName(query, text)\\&\qquad\quad \land\, RelevantChain(u, end, query))\,.\end{aligned}$$

Now we must define what it means for *text* to be a *RelevantCategoryName* for *query*. First, we need to relate strings to the categories they name. This is done using the predicate $Name(s, c)$, which says that string s is a name for category c—for example, we might assert that $Name(\text{“}laptops\text{”}, LaptopComputers)$. Some more examples of the *Name* predicate appear in Figure 9(b). Next, we define relevance. Suppose that *query* is "laptops." Then $RelevantCategoryName(query, text)$ is true when one of the following holds:

- The *text* and *query* name the same category—e.g., "notebooks" and "laptops."

[11] An alternative to the link-following strategy is to use an Internet search engine.

$Books \subset Products$
$MusicRecordings \subset Products$
$\quad MusicCDs \subset MusicRecordings$
$Electronics \subset Products$
$\quad DigitalCameras \subset Electronics$
$\quad StereoEquipment \subset Electronics$
$\quad Computers \subset Electronics$
$\quad\quad DesktopComputers \subset Computers$
$\quad\quad LaptopComputers \subset Computers$
$\quad\quad \ldots$

(a)

$Name(\text{“books”}, Books)$
$Name(\text{“music”}, MusicRecordings)$
$\quad Name(\text{“CDs”}, MusicCDs)$
$Name(\text{“electronics”}, Electronics)$
$\quad Name(\text{“digital cameras”}, DigitalCameras)$
$\quad Name(\text{“stereos”}, StereoEquipment)$
$\quad Name(\text{“computers”}, Computers)$
$\quad\quad Name(\text{“desktops”}, DesktopComputers)$
$\quad\quad Name(\text{“laptops”}, LaptopComputers)$
$\quad\quad Name(\text{“notebooks”}, LaptopComputers)$
$\quad\quad \ldots$

(b)

Figure 9 (a) Taxonomy of product categories. (b) Names for those categories.

- The *text* names a supercategory such as “computers.”
- The *text* names a subcategory such as “ultralight notebooks.”

The logical definition of *RelevantCategoryName* is as follows:

$$RelevantCategoryName(query, text) \Leftrightarrow$$
$$\exists\, c_1, c_2\ \ Name(query, c_1) \wedge Name(text, c_2) \wedge (c_1 \subseteq c_2 \vee c_2 \subseteq c_1)\,. \qquad (1)$$

Otherwise, the anchor text is irrelevant because it names a category outside this line, such as “clothes” or “lawn & garden.”

To follow relevant links, then, it is essential to have a rich hierarchy of product categories. The top part of this hierarchy might look like Figure 9(a). It will not be feasible to list *all* possible shopping categories, because a buyer could always come up with some new desire and manufacturers will always come out with new products to satisfy them (electric kneecap warmers?). Nonetheless, an ontology of about a thousand categories will serve as a very useful tool for most buyers.

In addition to the product hierarchy itself, we also need to have a rich vocabulary of names for categories. Life would be much easier if there were a one-to-one correspondence between categories and the character strings that name them. We have already seen the problem of **synonymy**—two names for the same category, such as “laptop computers” and “laptops.” There is also the problem of **ambiguity**—one name for two or more different categories. For example, if we add the sentence

$$Name(\text{“CDs”}, CertificatesOfDeposit)$$

to the knowledge base in Figure 9(b), then “CDs” will name two different categories.

Synonymy and ambiguity can cause a significant increase in the number of paths that the agent has to follow, and can sometimes make it difficult to determine whether a given page is indeed relevant. A much more serious problem is the very broad range of descriptions that a user can type and category names that a store can use. For example, the link might say “laptop” when the knowledge base has only “laptops” or the user might ask for “a computer

I can fit on the tray table of an economy-class airline seat." It is impossible to enumerate in advance all the ways a category can be named, so the agent will have to be able to do additional reasoning in some cases to determine if the *Name* relation holds. In the worst case, this requires full natural language understanding. In practice, a few simple rules—such as allowing "laptop" to match a category named "laptops"—go a long way. Exercise 10 asks you to develop a set of such rules after doing some research into online stores.

Given the logical definitions from the preceding paragraphs and suitable knowledge bases of product categories and naming conventions, are we ready to apply an inference algorithm to obtain a set of relevant offers for our query? Not quite! The missing element is the $Contents(url)$ function, which refers to the HTML page at a given URL. The agent doesn't have the page contents of every URL in its knowledge base; nor does it have explicit rules for deducing what those contents might be. Instead, we can arrange for the right HTTP procedure to be executed whenever a subgoal involves the *Contents* function. In this way, it appears to the inference engine as if the entire Web is inside the knowledge base. This is an example of a general technique called **procedural attachment**, whereby particular predicates and functions can be handled by special-purpose methods.

PROCEDURAL ATTACHMENT

7.2 Comparing offers

Let us assume that the reasoning processes of the preceding section have produced a set of offer pages for our "laptops" query. To compare those offers, the agent must extract the relevant information—price, speed, disk size, weight, and so on—from the offer pages. This can be a difficult task with real Web pages, for all the reasons mentioned previously. A common way of dealing with this problem is to use programs called **wrappers** to extract information from a page. For now we assume that wrappers exist, and when given a page and a knowledge base, they add assertions to the knowledge base. Typically, a hierarchy of wrappers would be applied to a page: a very general one to extract dates and prices, a more specific one to extract attributes for computer-related products, and if necessary a site-specific one that knows the format of a particular store. Given a page on the example.com site with the text

WRAPPER

```
IBM ThinkBook 970.  Our price:  $399.00
```

followed by various technical specifications, we would like a wrapper to extract information such as the following:

$$\begin{aligned}
&\exists\, c, \mathit{offer}\;\; c \in \mathit{LaptopComputers} \wedge \mathit{offer} \in \mathit{ProductOffers} \wedge \\
&\quad \mathit{Manufacturer}(c, \mathit{IBM}) \wedge \mathit{Model}(c, \mathit{ThinkBook970}) \wedge \\
&\quad \mathit{ScreenSize}(c, \mathit{Inches}(14)) \wedge \mathit{ScreenType}(c, \mathit{ColorLCD}) \wedge \\
&\quad \mathit{MemorySize}(c, \mathit{Gigabytes}(2)) \wedge \mathit{CPUSpeed}(c, \mathit{GHz}(1.2)) \wedge \\
&\quad \mathit{OfferedProduct}(\mathit{offer}, c) \wedge \mathit{Store}(\mathit{offer}, \mathit{GenStore}) \wedge \\
&\quad \mathit{URL}(\mathit{offer}, \text{“}\texttt{example.com/computers/34356.html}\text{”}) \wedge \\
&\quad \mathit{Price}(\mathit{offer}, \$(399)) \wedge \mathit{Date}(\mathit{offer}, \mathit{Today})\,.
\end{aligned}$$

This example illustrates several issues that arise when we take seriously the task of knowledge engineering for commercial transactions. For example, notice that the price is an attribute of the *offer*, not the product itself. This is important because the offer at a given store may change from day to day even for the same individual laptop; for some categories—such as houses and paintings—the same individual object may even be offered simultaneously by different intermediaries at different prices. There are still more complications that we have not handled, such as the possibility that the price depends on the method of payment and on the buyer's qualifications for certain discounts. The final task is to compare the offers that have been extracted. For example, consider these three offers:

A : 1.4 GHz CPU, 2GB RAM, 250 GB disk, \$299 .
B : 1.2 GHz CPU, 4GB RAM, 350 GB disk, \$500 .
C : 1.2 GHz CPU, 2GB RAM, 250 GB disk, \$399 .

C is **dominated** by A; that is, A is cheaper and faster, and they are otherwise the same. In general, X dominates Y if X has a better value on at least one attribute, and is not worse on any attribute. But neither A nor B dominates the other. To decide which is better we need to know how the buyer weighs CPU speed and price against memory and disk space. For now, our shopping agent will simply return a list of all undominated offers that meet the buyer's description. In this example, both A and B are undominated. Notice that this outcome relies on the assumption that everyone prefers cheaper prices, faster processors, and more storage. Some attributes, such as screen size on a notebook, depend on the user's particular preference (portability versus visibility); for these, the shopping agent will just have to ask the user.

The shopping agent we have described here is a simple one; many refinements are possible. Still, it has enough capability that with the right domain-specific knowledge it can actually be of use to a shopper. Because of its declarative construction, it extends easily to more complex applications. The main point of this section is to show that some knowledge representation—in particular, the product hierarchy—is necessary for such an agent, and that once we have some knowledge in this form, the rest follows naturally.

8 SUMMARY

By delving into the details of how one represents a variety of knowledge, we hope we have given the reader a sense of how real knowledge bases are constructed and a feeling for the interesting philosophical issues that arise. The major points are as follows:

- Large-scale knowledge representation requires a general-purpose ontology to organize and tie together the various specific domains of knowledge.
- A general-purpose ontology needs to cover a wide variety of knowledge and should be capable, in principle, of handling any domain.
- Building a large, general-purpose ontology is a significant challenge that has yet to be fully realized, although current frameworks seem to be quite robust.
- We presented an **upper ontology** based on categories and the event calculus. We covered categories, subcategories, parts, structured objects, measurements, substances, events, time and space, change, and beliefs.

- Natural kinds cannot be defined completely in logic, but properties of natural kinds can be represented.
- Actions, events, and time can be represented either in situation calculus or in more expressive representations such as event calculus. Such representations enable an agent to construct plans by logical inference.
- We presented a detailed analysis of the Internet shopping domain, exercising the general ontology and showing how the domain knowledge can be used by a shopping agent.
- Special-purpose representation systems, such as **semantic networks** and **description logics**, have been devised to help in organizing a hierarchy of categories. **Inheritance** is an important form of inference, allowing the properties of objects to be deduced from their membership in categories.
- The **closed-world assumption**, as implemented in logic programs, provides a simple way to avoid having to specify lots of negative information. It is best interpreted as a **default** that can be overridden by additional information.
- **Nonmonotonic logics**, such as **circumscription** and **default logic**, are intended to capture default reasoning in general.
- **Truth maintenance systems** handle knowledge updates and revisions efficiently.

BIBLIOGRAPHICAL AND HISTORICAL NOTES

Briggs (1985) claims that formal knowledge representation research began with classical Indian theorizing about the grammar of Shastric Sanskrit, which dates back to the first millennium B.C. In the West, the use of definitions of terms in ancient Greek mathematics can be regarded as the earliest instance: Aristotle's *Metaphysics* (literally, what comes after the book on physics) is a near-synonym for *Ontology*. Indeed, the development of technical terminology in any field can be regarded as a form of knowledge representation.

Early discussions of representation in AI tended to focus on "*problem* representation" rather than "*knowledge* representation." (See, for example, Amarel's (1968) discussion of the Missionaries and Cannibals problem.) In the 1970s, AI emphasized the development of "expert systems" (also called "knowledge-based systems") that could, if given the appropriate domain knowledge, match or exceed the performance of human experts on narrowly defined tasks. For example, the first expert system, DENDRAL (Feigenbaum *et al.*, 1971; Lindsay *et al.*, 1980), interpreted the output of a mass spectrometer (a type of instrument used to analyze the structure of organic chemical compounds) as accurately as expert chemists. Although the success of DENDRAL was instrumental in convincing the AI research community of the importance of knowledge representation, the representational formalisms used in DENDRAL are highly specific to the domain of chemistry. Over time, researchers became interested in standardized knowledge representation formalisms and ontologies that could streamline the process of creating new expert systems. In so doing, they ventured into territory previously explored by philosophers of science and of language. The discipline imposed in AI by the need for one's theories to "work" has led to more rapid and deeper progress than was the case when these problems were the exclusive domain of philosophy (although it has at times also led to the repeated reinvention of the wheel).

The creation of comprehensive taxonomies or classifications dates back to ancient times. Aristotle (384–322 B.C.) strongly emphasized classification and categorization schemes. His *Organon*, a collection of works on logic assembled by his students after his death, included a treatise called *Categories* in which he attempted to construct what we would now call an upper ontology. He also introduced the notions of **genus** and **species** for lower-level classification. Our present system of biological classification, including the use of "binomial nomenclature" (classification via genus and species in the technical sense), was invented by the Swedish biologist Carolus Linnaeus, or Carl von Linne (1707–1778). The problems associated with natural kinds and inexact category boundaries have been addressed by Wittgenstein (1953), Quine (1953), Lakoff (1987), and Schwartz (1977), among others.

Interest in larger-scale ontologies is increasing, as documented by the *Handbook on Ontologies* (Staab, 2004). The OPENCYC project (Lenat and Guha, 1990; Matuszek *et al.*, 2006) has released a 150,000-concept ontology, with an upper ontology similar to the one in Figure 1 as well as specific concepts like "OLED Display" and "iPhone," which is a type of "cellular phone," which in turn is a type of "consumer electronics," "phone," "wireless communication device," and other concepts. The DBPEDIA project extracts structured data from Wikipedia; specifically from Infoboxes: the boxes of attribute/value pairs that accompany many Wikipedia articles (Wu and Weld, 2008; Bizer *et al.*, 2007). As of mid-2009, DBPEDIA contains 2.6 million concepts, with about 100 facts per concept. The IEEE working group P1600.1 created the Suggested Upper Merged Ontology (SUMO) (Niles and Pease, 2001; Pease and Niles, 2002), which contains about 1000 terms in the upper ontology and links to over 20,000 domain-specific terms. Stoffel *et al.* (1997) describe algorithms for efficiently managing a very large ontology. A survey of techniques for extracting knowledge from Web pages is given by Etzioni *et al.* (2008).

On the Web, representation languages are emerging. RDF (Brickley and Guha, 2004) allows for assertions to be made in the form of relational triples, and provides some means for evolving the meaning of names over time. OWL (Smith *et al.*, 2004) is a description logic that supports inferences over these triples. So far, usage seems to be inversely proportional to representational complexity: the traditional HTML and CSS formats account for over 99% of Web content, followed by the simplest representation schemes, such as microformats (Khare, 2006) and RDFa (Adida and Birbeck, 2008), which use HTML and XHTML markup to add attributes to literal text. Usage of sophisticated RDF and OWL ontologies is not yet widespread, and the full vision of the Semantic Web (Berners-Lee *et al.*, 2001) has not yet been realized. The conferences on *Formal Ontology in Information Systems* (FOIS) contain many interesting papers on both general and domain-specific ontologies.

The taxonomy used in this chapter was developed by the authors and is based in part on their experience in the CYC project and in part on work by Hwang and Schubert (1993) and Davis (1990, 2005). An inspirational discussion of the general project of commonsense knowledge representation appears in Hayes's (1978, 1985b) "Naive Physics Manifesto."

Successful deep ontologies within a specific field include the Gene Ontology project (Consortium, 2008) and CML, the Chemical Markup Language (Murray-Rust *et al.*, 2003).

Doubts about the feasibility of a single ontology for *all* knowledge are expressed by Doctorow (2001), Gruber (2004), Halevy *et al.* (2009), and Smith (2004), who states, "the initial project of building one single ontology . . . has . . . largely been abandoned."

The event calculus was introduced by Kowalski and Sergot (1986) to handle continuous time, and there have been several variations (Sadri and Kowalski, 1995; Shanahan, 1997) and overviews (Shanahan, 1999; Mueller, 2006). van Lambalgen and Hamm (2005) show how the logic of events maps onto the language we use to talk about events. An alternative to the event and situation calculi is the fluent calculus (Thielscher, 1999). James Allen introduced time intervals for the same reason (Allen, 1984), arguing that intervals were much more natural than situations for reasoning about extended and concurrent events. Peter Ladkin (1986a, 1986b) introduced "concave" time intervals (intervals with gaps; essentially, unions of ordinary "convex" time intervals) and applied the techniques of mathematical abstract algebra to time representation. Allen (1991) systematically investigates the wide variety of techniques available for time representation; van Beek and Manchak (1996) analyze algorithms for temporal reasoning. There are significant commonalities between the event-based ontology given in this chapter and an analysis of events due to the philosopher Donald Davidson (1980). The **histories** in Pat Hayes's (1985a) ontology of liquids and the **chronicles** in McDermott's (1985) theory of plans were also important influences on the field and this chapter.

The question of the ontological status of substances has a long history. Plato proposed that substances were abstract entities entirely distinct from physical objects; he would say $MadeOf(Butter_3, Butter)$ rather than $Butter_3 \in Butter$. This leads to a substance hierarchy in which, for example, $UnsaltedButter$ is a more specific substance than $Butter$. The position adopted in this chapter, in which substances are categories of objects, was championed by Richard Montague (1973). It has also been adopted in the CYC project. Copeland (1993) mounts a serious, but not invincible, attack. The alternative approach mentioned in the chapter, in which butter is one object consisting of all buttery objects in the universe, was proposed

MEREOLOGY originally by the Polish logician Leśniewski (1916). His **mereology** (the name is derived from the Greek word for "part") used the part–whole relation as a substitute for mathematical set theory, with the aim of eliminating abstract entities such as sets. A more readable exposition of these ideas is given by Leonard and Goodman (1940), and Goodman's *The Structure of Appearance* (1977) applies the ideas to various problems in knowledge representation. While some aspects of the mereological approach are awkward—for example, the need for a separate inheritance mechanism based on part–whole relations—the approach gained the support of Quine (1960). Harry Bunt (1985) has provided an extensive analysis of its use in knowledge representation. Casati and Varzi (1999) cover parts, wholes, and the spatial locations.

Mental objects have been the subject of intensive study in philosophy and AI. There are three main approaches. The one taken in this chapter, based on modal logic and possible worlds, is the classical approach from philosophy (Hintikka, 1962; Kripke, 1963; Hughes and Cresswell, 1996). The book *Reasoning about Knowledge* (Fagin *et al.*, 1995) provides a thorough introduction. The second approach is a first-order theory in which mental objects are fluents. Davis (2005) and Davis and Morgenstern (2005) describe this approach. It relies on the possible-worlds formalism, and builds on work by Robert Moore (1980, 1985). The

SYNTACTIC THEORY third approach is a **syntactic theory**, in which mental objects are represented by character strings. A string is just a complex term denoting a list of symbols, so $CanFly(Clark)$ can be represented by the list of symbols $[C, a, n, F, l, y, (, C, l, a, r, k,)]$. The syntactic theory of mental objects was first studied in depth by Kaplan and Montague (1960), who showed that it led to paradoxes if not handled carefully. Ernie Davis (1990) provides an excellent comparison of the syntactic and modal theories of knowledge.

The Greek philosopher Porphyry (c. 234–305 A.D.), commenting on Aristotle's *Categories*, drew what might qualify as the first semantic network. Charles S. Peirce (1909) developed existential graphs as the first semantic network formalism using modern logic. Ross Quillian (1961), driven by an interest in human memory and language processing, initiated work on semantic networks within AI. An influential paper by Marvin Minsky (1975) presented a version of semantic networks called **frames**; a frame was a representation of an object or category, with attributes and relations to other objects or categories. The question of semantics arose quite acutely with respect to Quillian's semantic networks (and those of others who followed his approach), with their ubiquitous and very vague "IS-A links" Woods's (1975) famous article "What's In a Link?" drew the attention of AI researchers to the need for precise semantics in knowledge representation formalisms. Brachman (1979) elaborated on this point and proposed solutions. Patrick Hayes's (1979) "The Logic of Frames" cut even deeper, claiming that "Most of 'frames' is just a new syntax for parts of first-order logic." Drew McDermott's (1978b) "Tarskian Semantics, or, No Notation without Denotation!" argued that the model-theoretic approach to semantics used in first-order logic should be applied to all knowledge representation formalisms. This remains a controversial idea; notably, McDermott himself has reversed his position in "A Critique of Pure Reason" (McDermott, 1987). Selman and Levesque (1993) discuss the complexity of inheritance with exceptions, showing that in most formulations it is NP-complete.

The development of description logics is the most recent stage in a long line of research aimed at finding useful subsets of first-order logic for which inference is computationally tractable. Hector Levesque and Ron Brachman (1987) showed that certain logical constructs—notably, certain uses of disjunction and negation—were primarily responsible for the intractability of logical inference. Building on the KL-ONE system (Schmolze and Lipkis, 1983), several researchers developed systems that incorporate theoretical complexity analysis, most notably KRYPTON (Brachman *et al.*, 1983) and Classic (Borgida *et al.*, 1989). The result has been a marked increase in the speed of inference and a much better understanding of the interaction between complexity and expressiveness in reasoning systems. Calvanese *et al.* (1999) summarize the state of the art, and Baader *et al.* (2007) present a comprehensive handbook of description logic. Against this trend, Doyle and Patil (1991) have argued that restricting the expressiveness of a language either makes it impossible to solve certain problems or encourages the user to circumvent the language restrictions through nonlogical means.

The three main formalisms for dealing with nonmonotonic inference—circumscription (McCarthy, 1980), default logic (Reiter, 1980), and modal nonmonotonic logic (McDermott and Doyle, 1980)—were all introduced in one special issue of the AI Journal. Delgrande and Schaub (2003) discuss the merits of the variants, given 25 years of hindsight. Answer set programming can be seen as an extension of negation as failure or as a refinement of circumscription; the underlying theory of stable model semantics was introduced by Gelfond and Lifschitz (1988), and the leading answer set programming systems are DLV (Eiter *et al.*, 1998) and SMODELS (Niemelä *et al.*, 2000). The disk drive example comes from the SMODELS user manual (Syrjänen, 2000). Lifschitz (2001) discusses the use of answer set programming for planning. Brewka *et al.* (1997) give a good overview of the various approaches to nonmonotonic logic. Clark (1978) covers the negation-as-failure approach to logic programming and Clark completion. Van Emden and Kowalski (1976) show that every Prolog program without negation has a unique minimal model. Recent years have seen renewed interest in applications of nonmonotonic logics to large-scale knowledge representation systems. The BENINQ systems for handling insurance-benefit inquiries was perhaps the first commercially successful application of a nonmonotonic inheritance system (Morgenstern, 1998). Lifschitz (2001) discusses the application of answer set programming to planning. A variety of nonmonotonic reasoning systems based on logic programming are documented in the proceedings of the conferences on *Logic Programming and Nonmonotonic Reasoning* (LPNMR).

The study of truth maintenance systems began with the TMS (Doyle, 1979) and RUP (McAllester, 1980) systems, both of which were essentially JTMSs. Forbus and de Kleer (1993) explain in depth how TMSs can be used in AI applications. Nayak and Williams (1997) show how an efficient incremental TMS called an ITMS makes it feasible to plan the operations of a NASA spacecraft in real time.

This chapter could not cover *every* area of knowledge representation in depth. The three principal topics omitted are the following:

QUALITATIVE PHYSICS

Qualitative physics: Qualitative physics is a subfield of knowledge representation concerned specifically with constructing a logical, nonnumeric theory of physical objects and processes. The term was coined by Johan de Kleer (1975), although the enterprise could be said to have started in Fahlman's (1974) BUILD, a sophisticated planner for constructing complex towers of blocks. Fahlman discovered in the process of designing it that most of the effort (80%, by his estimate) went into modeling the physics of the blocks world to calculate the stability of various subassemblies of blocks, rather than into planning per se. He sketches a hypothetical naive-physics-like process to explain why young children can solve BUILD-like problems without access to the high-speed floating-point arithmetic used in BUILD's physical modeling. Hayes (1985a) uses "histories"—four-dimensional slices of space-time similar to Davidson's events—to construct a fairly complex naive physics of liquids. Hayes was the first to prove that a bath with the plug in will eventually overflow if the tap keeps running and that a person who falls into a lake will get wet all over. Davis (2008) gives an update to the ontology of liquids that describes the pouring of liquids into containers.

De Kleer and Brown (1985), Ken Forbus (1985), and Benjamin Kuipers (1985) independently and almost simultaneously developed systems that can reason about a physical system based on qualitative abstractions of the underlying equations. Qualitative physics soon developed to the point where it became possible to analyze an impressive variety of complex physical systems (Yip, 1991). Qualitative techniques have been used to construct novel designs for clocks, windshield wipers, and six-legged walkers (Subramanian and Wang, 1994). The collection *Readings in Qualitative Reasoning about Physical Systems* (Weld and de Kleer, 1990) an encyclopedia article by Kuipers (2001), and a handbook article by Davis (2007) introduce to the field.

SPATIAL REASONING

Spatial reasoning: The reasoning necessary to navigate in the wumpus world and shopping world is trivial in comparison to the rich spatial structure of the real world. The earliest serious attempt to capture commonsense reasoning about space appears in the work of Ernest Davis (1986, 1990). The region connection calculus of Cohn *et al.* (1997) supports a form of qualitative spatial reasoning and has led to new kinds of geographical information systems; see also (Davis, 2006). As with qualitative physics, an agent can go a long way, so to speak, without resorting to a full metric representation. When such a representation is necessary, techniques developed in robotics can be used.

PSYCHOLOGICAL REASONING

Psychological reasoning: Psychological reasoning involves the development of a working *psychology* for artificial agents to use in reasoning about themselves and other agents. This is often based on so-called folk psychology, the theory that humans in general are believed to use in reasoning about themselves and other humans. When AI researchers provide their artificial agents with psychological theories for reasoning about other agents, the theories are frequently based on the researchers' description of the logical agents' own design. Psychological reasoning is currently most useful within the context of natural language understanding, where divining the speaker's intentions is of paramount importance.

Minker (2001) collects papers by leading researchers in knowledge representation, summarizing 40 years of work in the field. The proceedings of the international conferences on *Principles of Knowledge Representation and Reasoning* provide the most up-to-date sources for work in this area. *Readings in Knowledge Representation* (Brachman and Levesque, 1985) and *Formal Theories of the Commonsense World* (Hobbs and Moore, 1985) are excellent anthologies on knowledge representation; the former focuses more on historically important papers in representation languages and formalisms, the latter on the accumulation of the knowledge itself. Davis (1990), Stefik (1995), and Sowa (1999) provide textbook introductions to knowledge representation, van Harmelen *et al.* (2007) contributes a handbook, and a special issue of AI Journal covers recent progress (Davis and Morgenstern, 2004). The biennial conference on *Theoretical Aspects of Reasoning About Knowledge* (TARK) covers applications of the theory of knowledge in AI, economics, and distributed systems.

EXERCISES

1 Define an ontology in first-order logic for tic-tac-toe. The ontology should contain situations, actions, squares, players, marks (X, O, or blank), and the notion of winning, losing, or drawing a game. Also define the notion of a forced win (or draw): a position from which a player can force a win (or draw) with the right sequence of actions. Write axioms for the domain. (Note: The axioms that enumerate the different squares and that characterize the winning positions are rather long. You need not write these out in full, but indicate clearly what they look like.)

2 Figure 1 shows the top levels of a hierarchy for everything. Extend it to include as many real categories as possible. A good way to do this is to cover all the things in your everyday life. This includes objects and events. Start with waking up, and proceed in an orderly fashion noting everything that you see, touch, do, and think about. For example, a random sampling produces music, news, milk, walking, driving, gas, Soda Hall, carpet, talking, Professor Fateman, chicken curry, tongue, $7, sun, the daily newspaper, and so on.

You should produce both a single hierarchy chart (on a large sheet of paper) and a listing of objects and categories with the relations satisfied by members of each category. Every object should be in a category, and every category should be in the hierarchy.

3 Develop a representational system for reasoning about windows in a window-based computer interface. In particular, your representation should be able to describe:

- The state of a window: minimized, displayed, or nonexistent.
- Which window (if any) is the active window.
- The position of every window at a given time.
- The order (front to back) of overlapping windows.
- The actions of creating, destroying, resizing, and moving windows; changing the state of a window; and bringing a window to the front. Treat these actions as atomic; that is, do not deal with the issue of relating them to mouse actions. Give axioms describing the effects of actions on fluents. You may use either event or situation calculus.

Assume an ontology containing *situations, actions, integers* (for x and y coordinates) and *windows*. Define a language over this ontology; that is, a list of constants, function symbols, and predicates with an English description of each. If you need to add more categories to the ontology (e.g., pixels), you may do so, but be sure to specify these in your write-up. You may (and should) use symbols defined in the text, but be sure to list these explicitly.

4 State the following in the language you developed for the previous exercise:

a. In situation S_0, window W_1 is behind W_2 but sticks out on the left and right. Do *not* state exact coordinates for these; describe the *general* situation.

b. If a window is displayed, then its top edge is higher than its bottom edge.

c. After you create a window w, it is displayed.

d. A window can be minimized if it is displayed.

5 (Adapted from an example by Doug Lenat.) Your mission is to capture, in logical form, enough knowledge to answer a series of questions about the following simple scenario:

> Yesterday John went to the North Berkeley Safeway supermarket and bought two pounds of tomatoes and a pound of ground beef.

Start by trying to represent the content of the sentence as a series of assertions. You should write sentences that have straightforward logical structure (e.g., statements that objects have certain properties, that objects are related in certain ways, that all objects satisfying one property satisfy another). The following might help you get started:

- Which classes, objects, and relations would you need? What are their parents, siblings and so on? (You will need events and temporal ordering, among other things.)
- Where would they fit in a more general hierarchy?
- What are the constraints and interrelationships among them?
- How detailed must you be about each of the various concepts?

To answer the questions below, your knowledge base must include background knowledge. You'll have to deal with what kind of things are at a supermarket, what is involved with purchasing the things one selects, what the purchases will be used for, and so on. Try to make your representation as general as possible. To give a trivial example: don't say "People buy food from Safeway," because that won't help you with those who shop at another supermarket. Also, don't turn the questions into answers; for example, question (c) asks "Did John buy any meat?"—not "Did John buy a pound of ground beef?"

Sketch the chains of reasoning that would answer the questions. If possible, use a logical reasoning system to demonstrate the sufficiency of your knowledge base. Many of the things you write might be only approximately correct in reality, but don't worry too much; the idea is to extract the common sense that lets you answer these questions at all. A truly complete answer to this question is *extremely* difficult, probably beyond the state of the art of current knowledge representation. But you should be able to put together a consistent set of axioms for the limited questions posed here.

a. Is John a child or an adult? [Adult]

b. Does John now have at least two tomatoes? [Yes]

c. Did John buy any meat? [Yes]

d. If Mary was buying tomatoes at the same time as John, did he see her? [Yes]

e. Are the tomatoes made in the supermarket? [No]

f. What is John going to do with the tomatoes? [Eat them]

g. Does Safeway sell deodorant? [Yes]

h. Did John bring some money or a credit card to the supermarket? [Yes]

i. Does John have less money after going to the supermarket? [Yes]

6 Make the necessary additions or changes to your knowledge base from the previous exercise so that the questions that follow can be answered. Include in your report a discussion of your changes, explaining why they were needed, whether they were minor or major, and what kinds of questions would necessitate further changes.

a. Are there other people in Safeway while John is there? [Yes—staff!]

b. Is John a vegetarian? [No]

c. Who owns the deodorant in Safeway? [Safeway Corporation]

d. Did John have an ounce of ground beef? [Yes]

e. Does the Shell station next door have any gas? [Yes]

f. Do the tomatoes fit in John's car trunk? [Yes]

7 Represent the following seven sentences using and extending the representations developed in the chapter:

a. Water is a liquid between 0 and 100 degrees.

b. Water boils at 100 degrees.

c. The water in John's water bottle is frozen.

d. Perrier is a kind of water.

e. John has Perrier in his water bottle.

f. All liquids have a freezing point.

g. A liter of water weighs more than a liter of alcohol.

8 Write definitions for the following:

a. $ExhaustivePartDecomposition$

b. $PartPartition$

c. $PartwiseDisjoint$

These should be analogous to the definitions for $ExhaustiveDecomposition$, $Partition$, and $Disjoint$. Is it the case that $PartPartition(s, BunchOf(s))$? If so, prove it; if not, give a counterexample and define sufficient conditions under which it does hold.

9 An alternative scheme for representing measures involves applying the units function to an abstract length object. In such a scheme, one would write $Inches(Length(L_1)) = 1.5$. How does this scheme compare with the one in the chapter? Issues include conversion axioms, names for abstract quantities (such as "50 dollars"), and comparisons of abstract measures in different units (50 inches is more than 50 centimeters).

10 Add sentences to extend the definition of the predicate $Name(s, c)$ so that a string such as "laptop computer" matches the appropriate category names from a variety of stores. Try to make your definition general. Test it by looking at ten online stores, and at the category names they give for three different categories. For example, for the category of laptops, we found the names "Notebooks," "Laptops," "Notebook Computers," "Notebook," "Laptops and Notebooks," and "Notebook PCs." Some of these can be covered by explicit $Name$ facts, while others could be covered by sentences for handling plurals, conjunctions, etc.

11 Write event calculus axioms to describe the actions in the wumpus world.

12 State the interval-algebra relation that holds between every pair of the following real-world events:

LK: The life of President Kennedy.
IK: The infancy of President Kennedy.
PK: The presidency of President Kennedy.
LJ: The life of President Johnson.
PJ: The presidency of President Johnson.
LO: The life of President Obama.

13 Investigate ways to extend the event calculus to handle *simultaneous* events. Is it possible to avoid a combinatorial explosion of axioms?

14 Construct a representation for exchange rates between currencies that allows for daily fluctuations.

15 Define the predicate *Fixed*, where $Fixed(Location(x))$ means that the location of object x is fixed over time.

16 Describe the event of trading something for something else. Describe buying as a kind of trading in which one of the objects traded is a sum of money.

17 The two preceding exercises assume a fairly primitive notion of ownership. For example, the buyer starts by *owning* the dollar bills. This picture begins to break down when, for example, one's money is in the bank, because there is no longer any specific collection of dollar bills that one owns. The picture is complicated still further by borrowing, leasing, renting, and bailment. Investigate the various commonsense and legal concepts of ownership, and propose a scheme by which they can be represented formally.

18 (Adapted from Fagin *et al.* (1995).) Consider a game played with a deck of just 8 cards, 4 aces and 4 kings. The three players, Alice, Bob, and Carlos, are dealt two cards each. Without looking at them, they place the cards on their foreheads so that the other players can see them. Then the players take turns either announcing that they know what cards are on their own forehead, thereby winning the game, or saying "I don't know." Everyone knows the players are truthful and are perfect at reasoning about beliefs.

a. Game 1. Alice and Bob have both said "I don't know." Carlos sees that Alice has two aces (A-A) and Bob has two kings (K-K). What should Carlos say? (*Hint*: consider all three possible cases for Carlos: A-A, K-K, A-K.)

b. Describe each step of Game 1 using the notation of modal logic.

c. Game 2. Carlos, Alice, and Bob all said "I don't know" on their first turn. Alice holds K-K and Bob holds A-K. What should Carlos say on his second turn?

d. Game 3. Alice, Carlos, and Bob all say "I don't know" on their first turn, as does Alice on her second turn. Alice and Bob both hold A-K. What should Carlos say?

e. Prove that there will always be a winner to this game.

19 The assumption of *logical omniscience,* discussed in section 4, is of course not true of any actual reasoners. Rather, it is an *idealization* of the reasoning process that may be more or less acceptable depending on the applications. Discuss the reasonableness of the assumption for each of the following applications of reasoning about knowledge:

a. Partial knowledge adversary games, such as card games. Here one player wants to reason about what his opponent knows about the state of the game.

b. Chess with a clock. Here the player may wish to reason about the limits of his opponent's or his own ability to find the best move in the time available. For instance, if player A has much more time left than player B, then A will sometimes make a move that greatly complicates the situation, in the hopes of gaining an advantage because he has more time to work out the proper strategy.

c. A shopping agent in an environment in which there are costs of gathering information.

d. Reasoning about public key cryptography, which rests on the intractability of certain computational problems.

20 Translate the following description logic expression into first-order logic, and comment on the result:

$$\begin{aligned}&And(Man, AtLeast(3, Son), AtMost(2, Daughter),\\&\quad All(Son, And(Unemployed, Married, All(Spouse, Doctor))),\\&\quad All(Daughter, And(Professor, Fills(Department, Physics, Math)))) .\end{aligned}$$

21 Recall that inheritance information in semantic networks can be captured logically by suitable implication sentences. This exercise investigates the efficiency of using such sentences for inheritance.

a. Consider the information in a used-car catalog such as Kelly's Blue Book—for example, that 1973 Dodge vans are (or perhaps were once) worth $575. Suppose all this information (for 11,000 models) is encoded as logical sentences, as suggested in the chapter. Write down three such sentences, including that for 1973 Dodge vans. How would you use the sentences to find the value of a *particular* car, given a backward-chaining theorem prover such as Prolog?

b. Compare the time efficiency of the backward-chaining method for solving this problem with the inheritance method used in semantic nets.

c. Explain how forward chaining allows a logic-based system to solve the same problem efficiently, assuming that the KB contains only the 11,000 sentences about prices.

d. Describe a situation in which neither forward nor backward chaining on the sentences will allow the price query for an individual car to be handled efficiently.

e. Can you suggest a solution enabling this type of query to be solved efficiently in all cases in logic systems? (*Hint:* Remember that two cars of the same year and model have the same price.)

22 One might suppose that the syntactic distinction between unboxed links and singly boxed links in semantic networks is unnecessary, because singly boxed links are always attached to categories; an inheritance algorithm could simply assume that an unboxed link attached to a category is intended to apply to all members of that category. Show that this argument is fallacious, giving examples of errors that would arise.

23 One part of the shopping process that was not covered in this chapter is checking for compatibility between items. For example, if a digital camera is ordered, what accessory batteries, memory cards, and cases are compatible with the camera? Write a knowledge base that can determine the compatibility of a set of items and suggest replacements or additional items if the shopper makes a choice that is not compatible. The knowledge base should works with at least one line of products and extend easily to other lines.

24 A complete solution to the problem of inexact matches to the buyer's description in shopping is very difficult and requires a full array of natural language processing and information retrieval techniques. One small step is to allow the user to specify minimum and maximum values for various attributes. The buyer must use the following grammar for product descriptions:

Description	→	*Category* [*Connector Modifier*]∗
Connector	→	"*with*" | "*and*" | ","
Modifier	→	*Attribute* | *Attribute Op Value*
Op	→	"=" | ">" | "<"

Here, *Category* names a product category, *Attribute* is some feature such as "CPU" or "price," and *Value* is the target value for the attribute. So the query "computer with at least a 2.5 GHz CPU for under $500" must be re-expressed as "computer with CPU > 2.5 GHz and price < $500." Implement a shopping agent that accepts descriptions in this language.

25 Our description of Internet shopping omitted the all-important step of actually *buying* the product. Provide a formal logical description of buying, using event calculus. That is, define the sequence of events that occurs when a buyer submits a credit-card purchase and then eventually gets billed and receives the product.

QUANTIFYING UNCERTAINTY

QUANTIFYING UNCERTAINTY

In which we see how an agent can tame uncertainty with degrees of belief.

1 Acting under Uncertainty

UNCERTAINTY

Agents may need to handle **uncertainty**, whether due to partial observability, nondeterminism, or a combination of the two. An agent may never know for certain what state it's in or where it will end up after a sequence of actions.

Problem-solving agents and logical agents are designed to handle uncertainty by keeping track of a **belief state**—a representation of the set of all possible world states that it might be in—and generating a contingency plan that handles every possible eventuality that its sensors may report during execution. Despite its many virtues, however, this approach has significant drawbacks when taken literally as a recipe for creating agent programs:

- When interpreting partial sensor information, a logical agent must consider *every logically possible* explanation for the observations, no matter how unlikely. This leads to impossible large and complex belief-state representations.
- A correct contingent plan that handles every eventuality can grow arbitrarily large and must consider arbitrarily unlikely contingencies.
- Sometimes there is no plan that is guaranteed to achieve the goal—yet the agent must act. It must have some way to compare the merits of plans that are not guaranteed.

Suppose, for example, that an automated taxi!automated has the goal of delivering a passenger to the airport on time. The agent forms a plan, A_{90}, that involves leaving home 90 minutes before the flight departs and driving at a reasonable speed. Even though the airport is only about 5 miles away, a logical taxi agent will not be able to conclude with certainty that "Plan A_{90} will get us to the airport in time." Instead, it reaches the weaker conclusion "Plan A_{90} will get us to the airport in time, as long as the car doesn't break down or run out of gas, and I don't get into an accident, and there are no accidents on the bridge, and the plane doesn't leave early, and no meteorite hits the car, and . . . ." None of these conditions can be deduced for sure, so the plan's success cannot be inferred. This is the **qualification problem,** for which we so far have seen no real solution.

Nonetheless, in some sense A_{90} *is* in fact the right thing to do. What do we mean by this? We mean that out of all the plans that could be executed, A_{90} is expected to maximize the agent's performance measure (where the expectation is relative to the agent's knowledge about the environment). The performance measure includes getting to the airport in time for the flight, avoiding a long, unproductive wait at the airport, and avoiding speeding tickets along the way. The agent's knowledge cannot guarantee any of these outcomes for A_{90}, but it can provide some degree of belief that they will be achieved. Other plans, such as A_{180}, might increase the agent's belief that it will get to the airport on time, but also increase the likelihood of a long wait. *The right thing to do—the* ***rational decision****—therefore depends on both the relative importance of various goals and the likelihood that, and degree to which, they will be achieved.* The remainder of this section hones these ideas, in preparation for the development of the general theories of uncertain reasoning and rational decisions.

1.1 Summarizing uncertainty

Let's consider an example of uncertain reasoning: diagnosing a dental patient's toothache. Diagnosis—whether for medicine, automobile repair, or whatever—almost always involves uncertainty. Let us try to write rules for dental diagnosis using propositional logic, so that we can see how the logical approach breaks down. Consider the following simple rule:

$$Toothache \Rightarrow Cavity\ .$$

The problem is that this rule is wrong. Not all patients with toothaches have cavities; some of them have gum disease, an abscess, or one of several other problems:

$$Toothache \Rightarrow Cavity \lor GumProblem \lor Abscess \ldots$$

Unfortunately, in order to make the rule true, we have to add an almost unlimited list of possible problems. We could try turning the rule into a causal rule:

$$Cavity \Rightarrow Toothache\ .$$

But this rule is not right either; not all cavities cause pain. The only way to fix the rule is to make it logically exhaustive: to augment the left-hand side with all the qualifications required for a cavity to cause a toothache. Trying to use logic to cope with a domain like medical diagnosis thus fails for three main reasons:

LAZINESS

- **Laziness**: It is too much work to list the complete set of antecedents or consequents needed to ensure an exceptionless rule and too hard to use such rules.

THEORETICAL IGNORANCE

- **Theoretical ignorance**: Medical science has no complete theory for the domain.

PRACTICAL IGNORANCE

- **Practical ignorance**: Even if we know all the rules, we might be uncertain about a particular patient because not all the necessary tests have been or can be run.

The connection between toothaches and cavities is just not a logical consequence in either direction. This is typical of the medical domain, as well as most other judgmental domains: law, business, design, automobile repair, gardening, dating, and so on. The agent's knowledge

DEGREE OF BELIEF
PROBABILITY THEORY

can at best provide only a **degree of belief** in the relevant sentences. Our main tool for dealing with degrees of belief is **probability theory**. The **ontological commitments** of logic and probability theory are the same—that the world is composed of facts that do or do not hold in any particular case—but the **epistemological commitments** are different: a logical agent believes each sentence to be true or false or has no opinion, whereas a probabilistic agent may have a numerical degree of belief between 0 (for sentences that are certainly false) and 1 (certainly true).

Probability provides a way of **summarizing** *the uncertainty that comes from our laziness and ignorance,* thereby solving the qualification problem. We might not know for sure what afflicts a particular patient, but we believe that there is, say, an 80% chance—that is, a probability of 0.8—that the patient who has a toothache has a cavity. That is, we expect that out of all the situations that are indistinguishable from the current situation as far as our knowledge goes, the patient will have a cavity in 80% of them. This belief could be derived from statistical data—80% of the toothache patients seen so far have had cavities—or from some general dental knowledge, or from a combination of evidence sources.

One confusing point is that at the time of our diagnosis, there is no uncertainty in the actual world: the patient either has a cavity or doesn't. So what does it mean to say the probability of a cavity is 0.8? Shouldn't it be either 0 or 1? The answer is that probability statements are made with respect to a knowledge state, not with respect to the real world. We say "The probability that the patient has a cavity, *given that she has a toothache*, is 0.8." If we later learn that the patient has a history of gum disease, we can make a different statement: "The probability that the patient has a cavity, given that she has a toothache and a history of gum disease, is 0.4." If we gather further conclusive evidence against a cavity, we can say "The probability that the patient has a cavity, given all we now know, is almost 0." Note that these statements do not contradict each other; each is a separate assertion about a different knowledge state.

1.2 Uncertainty and rational decisions

Consider again the A_{90} plan for getting to the airport. Suppose it gives us a 97% chance of catching our flight. Does this mean it is a rational choice? Not necessarily: there might be other plans, such as A_{180}, with higher probabilities. If it is vital not to miss the flight, then it is worth risking the longer wait at the airport. What about A_{1440}, a plan that involves leaving home 24 hours in advance? In most circumstances, this is not a good choice, because although it almost guarantees getting there on time, it involves an intolerable wait—not to mention a possibly unpleasant diet of airport food.

PREFERENCE
OUTCOME
UTILITY THEORY

To make such choices, an agent must first have **preferences** between the different possible **outcomes** of the various plans. An outcome is a completely specified state, including such factors as whether the agent arrives on time and the length of the wait at the airport. We use **utility theory** to represent and reason with preferences. (The term **utility** is used here in the sense of "the quality of being useful," not in the sense of the electric company or water works.) Utility theory says that every state has a degree of usefulness, or utility, to an agent and that the agent will prefer states with higher utility.

The utility of a state is relative to an agent. For example, the utility of a state in which White has checkmated Black in a game of chess is obviously high for the agent playing White, but low for the agent playing Black. But we can't go strictly by the scores of 1, 1/2, and 0 that are dictated by the rules of tournament chess—some players (including the authors) might be thrilled with a draw against the world champion, whereas other players (including the former world champion) might not. There is no accounting for taste or preferences: you might think that an agent who prefers jalapeño bubble-gum ice cream to chocolate chocolate chip is odd or even misguided, but you could not say the agent is irrational. A utility function can account for any set of preferences—quirky or typical, noble or perverse. Note that utilities can account for altruism, simply by including the welfare of others as one of the factors.

DECISION THEORY

Preferences, as expressed by utilities, are combined with probabilities in the general theory of rational decisions called **decision theory**:

$$\textit{Decision theory} = \textit{probability theory} + \textit{utility theory} .$$

MAXIMUM EXPECTED UTILITY

The fundamental idea of decision theory is that *an agent is rational if and only if it chooses the action that yields the highest expected utility, averaged over all the possible outcomes of the action.* This is called the principle of **maximum expected utility** (MEU). Note that "expected" might seem like a vague, hypothetical term, but as it is used here it has a precise meaning: it means the "average," or "statistical mean" of the outcomes, weighted by the probability of the outcome.

Figure 1 sketches the structure of an agent that uses decision theory to select actions. The agent is identical, at an abstract level, to agents that maintain a belief state reflecting the history of percepts to date. The primary difference is that the decision-theoretic agent's belief state represents not just the *possibilities* for world states but also their *probabilities*. Given the belief state, the agent can make probabilistic predictions of action outcomes and hence select the action with highest expected utility. This chapter concentrates on the task of representing and computing with probabilistic information in general.

2 Basic Probability Notation

For our agent to represent and use probabilistic information, we need a formal language. The language of probability theory has traditionally been informal, written by human mathematicians to other human mathematicians. Here, we take an approach more suited to the needs of AI and more consistent with the concepts of formal logic.

```
function DT-AGENT(percept) returns an action
  persistent: belief_state, probabilistic beliefs about the current state of the world
              action, the agent's action

  update belief_state based on action and percept
  calculate outcome probabilities for actions,
      given action descriptions and current belief_state
  select action with highest expected utility
      given probabilities of outcomes and utility information
  return action
```

Figure 1 A decision-theoretic agent that selects rational actions.

2.1 What probabilities are about

Like logical assertions, probabilistic assertions are about possible worlds. Whereas logical assertions say which possible worlds are strictly ruled out (all those in which the assertion is false), probabilistic assertions talk about how probable the various worlds are. In probability theory, the set of all possible worlds is called the **sample space**. The possible worlds are *mutually exclusive* and *exhaustive*—two possible worlds cannot both be the case, and one possible world must be the case. For example, if we are about to roll two (distinguishable) dice, there are 36 possible worlds to consider: (1,1), (1,2), ..., (6,6). The Greek letter Ω (uppercase omega) is used to refer to the sample space, and ω (lowercase omega) refers to elements of the space, that is, particular possible worlds.

SAMPLE SPACE

PROBABILITY MODEL

A fully specified **probability model** associates a numerical probability $P(\omega)$ with each possible world.[1] The basic axioms of probability theory say that every possible world has a probability between 0 and 1 and that the total probability of the set of possible worlds is 1:

$$0 \leq P(\omega) \leq 1 \text{ for every } \omega \text{ and } \sum_{\omega \in \Omega} P(\omega) = 1 . \tag{1}$$

For example, if we assume that each die is fair and the rolls don't interfere with each other, then each of the possible worlds (1,1), (1,2), ..., (6,6) has probability 1/36. On the other hand, if the dice conspire to produce the same number, then the worlds (1,1), (2,2), (3,3), etc., might have higher probabilities, leaving the others with lower probabilities.

Probabilistic assertions and queries are not usually about particular possible worlds, but about sets of them. For example, we might be interested in the cases where the two dice add up to 11, the cases where doubles are rolled, and so on. In probability theory, these sets are called **events**. In AI, the sets are always described by **propositions** in a formal language. (One such language is described in Section 2.2.) For each proposition, the corresponding set contains just those possible worlds in which the proposition holds. The probability associated with a proposition

EVENT

[1] For now, we assume a discrete, countable set of worlds. The proper treatment of the continuous case brings in certain complications that are less relevant for most purposes in AI.

is defined to be the sum of the probabilities of the worlds in which it holds:

$$\text{For any proposition } \phi,\ P(\phi) = \sum_{\omega \in \phi} P(\omega) . \tag{2}$$

For example, when rolling fair dice, we have $P(Total = 11) = P((5,6)) + P((6,5)) = 1/36 + 1/36 = 1/18$. Note that probability theory does not require complete knowledge of the probabilities of each possible world. For example, if we believe the dice conspire to produce the same number, we might *assert* that $P(doubles) = 1/4$ without knowing whether the dice prefer double 6 to double 2. Just as with logical assertions, this assertion *constrains* the underlying probability model without fully determining it.

UNCONDITIONAL PROBABILITY

PRIOR PROBABILITY

Probabilities such as $P(Total = 11)$ and $P(doubles)$ are called **unconditional** or **prior probabilities** (and sometimes just "priors" for short); they refer to degrees of belief in propositions *in the absence of any other information*. Most of the time, however, we have *some* information, usually called **evidence**, that has already been revealed. For example, the first die may already be showing a 5 and we are waiting with bated breath for the other one to stop spinning. In that case, we are interested not in the unconditional probability of rolling doubles, but the **conditional** or **posterior** probability (or just "posterior" for short) of rolling doubles *given that the first die is a 5*. This probability is written $P(doubles \mid Die_1 = 5)$, where the "$\mid$" is pronounced "given." Similarly, if I am going to the dentist for a regular checkup, the probability $P(cavity) = 0.2$ might be of interest; but if I go to the dentist because I have a toothache, it's $P(cavity \mid toothache) = 0.6$ that matters. Note that the precedence of "$\mid$" is such that any expression of the form $P(\ldots \mid \ldots)$ always means $P((\ldots)|(\ldots))$.

EVIDENCE

CONDITIONAL PROBABILITY

POSTERIOR PROBABILITY

It is important to understand that $P(cavity) = 0.2$ is still *valid* after *toothache* is observed; it just isn't especially useful. When making decisions, an agent needs to condition on *all* the evidence it has observed. It is also important to understand the difference between conditioning and logical implication. The assertion that $P(cavity \mid toothache) = 0.6$ does not mean "Whenever *toothache* is true, conclude that *cavity* is true with probability 0.6" rather it means "Whenever *toothache* is true *and we have no further information*, conclude that *cavity* is true with probability 0.6." The extra condition is important; for example, if we had the further information that the dentist found no cavities, we definitely would not want to conclude that *cavity* is true with probability 0.6; instead we need to use $P(cavity|toothache \wedge \neg cavity) = 0$.

Mathematically speaking, conditional probabilities are defined in terms of unconditional probabilities as follows: for any propositions a and b, we have

$$P(a \mid b) = \frac{P(a \wedge b)}{P(b)} , \tag{3}$$

which holds whenever $P(b) > 0$. For example,

$$P(doubles \mid Die_1 = 5) = \frac{P(doubles \wedge Die_1 = 5)}{P(Die_1 = 5)} .$$

The definition makes sense if you remember that observing b rules out all those possible worlds where b is false, leaving a set whose total probability is just $P(b)$. Within that set, the a-worlds satisfy $a \wedge b$ and constitute a fraction $P(a \wedge b)/P(b)$.

The definition of conditional probability, Equation (3), can be written in a different form called the **product rule**:

PRODUCT RULE

$$P(a \wedge b) = P(a \mid b)P(b) ,$$

The product rule is perhaps easier to remember: it comes from the fact that, for a and b to be true, we need b to be true, and we also need a to be true given b.

2.2 The language of propositions in probability assertions

In this chapter, propositions describing sets of possible worlds are written in a notation that combines elements of propositional logic and constraint satisfaction notation. It is a **factored representation**, in which a possible world is represented by a set of variable/value pairs.

RANDOM VARIABLE

Variables in probability theory are called **random variables** and their names begin with an uppercase letter. Thus, in the dice example, $Total$ and Die_1 are random variables. Every random variable has a **domain**—the set of possible values it can take on. The domain of $Total$ for two dice is the set $\{2, \ldots, 12\}$ and the domain of Die_1 is $\{1, \ldots, 6\}$. A Boolean random variable has the domain $\{true, false\}$ (notice that values are always lowercase); for example, the proposition that doubles are rolled can be written as $Doubles = true$. By convention, propositions of the form $A = true$ are abbreviated simply as a, while $A = false$ is abbreviated as $\neg a$. (The uses of *doubles*, *cavity*, and *toothache* in the preceding section are abbreviations of this kind.) As in CSPs, domains can be sets of arbitrary tokens; we might choose the domain of Age to be $\{juvenile, teen, adult\}$ and the domain of $Weather$ might be $\{sunny, rain, cloudy, snow\}$. When no ambiguity is possible, it is common to use a value by itself to stand for the proposition that a particular variable has that value; thus, *sunny* can stand for $Weather = sunny$.

DOMAIN

The preceding examples all have finite domains. Variables can have infinite domains, too—either discrete (like the integers) or continuous (like the reals). For any variable with an ordered domain, inequalities are also allowed, such as $NumberOfAtomsInUniverse \geq 10^{70}$.

Finally, we can combine these sorts of elementary propositions (including the abbreviated forms for Boolean variables) by using the connectives of propositional logic. For example, we can express "The probability that the patient has a cavity, given that she is a teenager with no toothache, is 0.1" as follows:

$$P(cavity \mid \neg toothache \wedge teen) = 0.1 .$$

Sometimes we will want to talk about the probabilities of *all* the possible values of a random variable. We could write:

$$\begin{aligned} &P(Weather = sunny) = 0.6 \\ &P(Weather = rain) = 0.1 \\ &P(Weather = cloudy) = 0.29 \\ &P(Weather = snow) = 0.01 , \end{aligned}$$

but as an abbreviation we will allow

$$\mathbf{P}(Weather) = \langle 0.6, 0.1, 0.29, 0.01 \rangle ,$$

where the bold **P** indicates that the result is a vector of numbers, and where we assume a predefined ordering $\langle sunny, rain, cloudy, snow\rangle$ on the domain of $Weather$. We say that the **P** statement defines a **probability distribution** for the random variable $Weather$. The **P** notation is also used for conditional distributions: $\mathbf{P}(X \mid Y)$ gives the values of $P(X = x_i \mid Y = y_j)$ for each possible i, j pair.

PROBABILITY DISTRIBUTION

For continuous variables, it is not possible to write out the entire distribution as a vector, because there are infinitely many values. Instead, we can define the probability that a random variable takes on some value x as a parameterized function of x. For example, the sentence

$$P(NoonTemp = x) = Uniform_{[18C,26C]}(x)$$

expresses the belief that the temperature at noon is distributed uniformly between 18 and 26 degrees Celsius. We call this a **probability density function**.

PROBABILITY DENSITY FUNCTION

Probability density functions (sometimes called **pdfs**) differ in meaning from discrete distributions. Saying that the probability density is uniform from $18C$ to $26C$ means that there is a 100% chance that the temperature will fall somewhere in that $8C$-wide region and a 50% chance that it will fall in any $4C$-wide region, and so on. We write the probability density for a continuous random variable X at value x as $P(X = x)$ or just $P(x)$; the intuitive definition of $P(x)$ is the probability that X falls within an arbitrarily small region beginning at x, divided by the width of the region:

$$P(x) = \lim_{dx \to 0} P(x \le X \le x + dx)/dx \,.$$

For $NoonTemp$ we have

$$P(NoonTemp = x) = Uniform_{[18C,26C]}(x) = \begin{cases} \frac{1}{8C} \text{ if } 18C \le x \le 26C \\ 0 \text{ otherwise} \end{cases} ,$$

where C stands for centigrade (not for a constant). In $P(NoonTemp = 20.18C) = \frac{1}{8C}$, note that $\frac{1}{8C}$ is not a probability, it is a probability density. The probability that $NoonTemp$ is *exactly* $20.18C$ is zero, because $20.18C$ is a region of width 0. Some authors use different symbols for discrete distributions and density functions; we use P in both cases, since confusion seldom arises and the equations are usually identical. Note that probabilities are unitless numbers, whereas density functions are measured with a unit, in this case reciprocal degrees.

In addition to distributions on single variables, we need notation for distributions on multiple variables. Commas are used for this. For example, $\mathbf{P}(Weather, Cavity)$ denotes the probabilities of all combinations of the values of $Weather$ and $Cavity$. This is a 4×2 table of probabilities called the **joint probability distribution** of $Weather$ and $Cavity$. We can also mix variables with and without values; $\mathbf{P}(sunny, Cavity)$ would be a two-element vector giving the probabilities of a sunny day with a cavity and a sunny day with no cavity. The **P** notation makes certain expressions much more concise than they might otherwise be. For example, the product rules for all possible values of $Weather$ and $Cavity$ can be written as a single equation:

JOINT PROBABILITY DISTRIBUTION

$$\mathbf{P}(Weather, Cavity) = \mathbf{P}(Weather \mid Cavity)\mathbf{P}(Cavity) \,,$$

instead of as these $4 \times 2 = 8$ equations (using abbreviations W and C):

$$
\begin{aligned}
&P(W = sunny \land C = true) = P(W = sunny|C = true)\, P(C = true)\\
&P(W = rain \land C = true) = P(W = rain|C = true)\, P(C = true)\\
&P(W = cloudy \land C = true) = P(W = cloudy|C = true)\, P(C = true)\\
&P(W = snow \land C = true) = P(W = snow|C = true)\, P(C = true)\\
&P(W = sunny \land C = false) = P(W = sunny|C = false)\, P(C = false)\\
&P(W = rain \land C = false) = P(W = rain|C = false)\, P(C = false)\\
&P(W = cloudy \land C = false) = P(W = cloudy|C = false)\, P(C = false)\\
&P(W = snow \land C = false) = P(W = snow|C = false)\, P(C = false)\,.
\end{aligned}
$$

As a degenerate case, $\mathbf{P}(sunny, cavity)$ has no variables and thus is a one-element vector that is the probability of a sunny day with a cavity, which could also be written as $P(sunny, cavity)$ or $P(sunny \land cavity)$. We will sometimes use **P** notation to derive results about individual P values, and when we say "$\mathbf{P}(sunny) = 0.6$" it is really an abbreviation for "$\mathbf{P}(sunny)$ is the one-element vector $\langle 0.6 \rangle$, which means that $P(sunny) = 0.6$."

Now we have defined a syntax for propositions and probability assertions and we have given part of the semantics: Equation (2) defines the probability of a proposition as the sum of the probabilities of worlds in which it holds. To complete the semantics, we need to say what the worlds are and how to determine whether a proposition holds in a world. We borrow this part directly from the semantics of propositional logic, as follows. *A possible world is defined to be an assignment of values to all of the random variables under consideration.* It is easy to see that this definition satisfies the basic requirement that possible worlds be mutually exclusive and exhaustive (Exercise 5). For example, if the random variables are $Cavity$, $Toothache$, and $Weather$, then there are $2 \times 2 \times 4 = 16$ possible worlds. Furthermore, the truth of any given proposition, no matter how complex, can be determined easily in such worlds using the same recursive definition of truth as for formulas in propositional logic.

FULL JOINT PROBABILITY DISTRIBUTION

From the preceding definition of possible worlds, it follows that a probability model is completely determined by the joint distribution for all of the random variables—the so-called **full joint probability distribution**. For example, if the variables are $Cavity$, $Toothache$, and $Weather$, then the full joint distribution is given by $\mathbf{P}(Cavity, Toothache, Weather)$. This joint distribution can be represented as a $2 \times 2 \times 4$ table with 16 entries. Because every proposition's probability is a sum over possible worlds, a full joint distribution suffices, in principle, for calculating the probability of any proposition.

2.3 Probability axioms and their reasonableness

The basic axioms of probability (Equations (1) and (2)) imply certain relationships among the degrees of belief that can be accorded to logically related propositions. For example, we can derive the familiar relationship between the probability of a proposition and the probability of its negation:

$$
\begin{aligned}
P(\neg a) &= \textstyle\sum_{\omega \in \neg a} P(\omega) && \text{by Equation (2)}\\
&= \textstyle\sum_{\omega \in \neg a} P(\omega) + \sum_{\omega \in a} P(\omega) - \sum_{\omega \in a} P(\omega) &&\\
&= \textstyle\sum_{\omega \in \Omega} P(\omega) - \sum_{\omega \in a} P(\omega) && \text{grouping the first two terms}\\
&= 1 - P(a) && \text{by (1) and (2).}
\end{aligned}
$$

INCLUSION–EXCLUSION PRINCIPLE

We can also derive the well-known formula for the probability of a disjunction, sometimes called the **inclusion–exclusion principle**:

$$P(a \lor b) = P(a) + P(b) - P(a \land b) . \tag{4}$$

This rule is easily remembered by noting that the cases where a holds, together with the cases where b holds, certainly cover all the cases where $a \lor b$ holds; but summing the two sets of cases counts their intersection twice, so we need to subtract $P(a \land b)$. The proof is left as an exercise (Exercise 6).

KOLMOGOROV'S AXIOMS

Equations (1) and (4) are often called **Kolmogorov's axioms** in honor of the Russian mathematician Andrei Kolmogorov, who showed how to build up the rest of probability theory from this simple foundation and how to handle the difficulties caused by continuous variables.[2] While Equation (2) has a definitional flavor, Equation (4) reveals that the axioms really do constrain the degrees of belief an agent can have concerning logically related propositions. This is analogous to the fact that a logical agent cannot simultaneously believe A, B, and $\neg(A \land B)$, because there is no possible world in which all three are true. With probabilities, however, statements refer not to the world directly, but to the agent's own state of knowledge. Why, then, can an agent not hold the following set of beliefs (even though they violate Kolmogorov's axioms)?

$$\begin{aligned} P(a) &= 0.4 \qquad & P(a \land b) &= 0.0 \\ P(b) &= 0.3 \qquad & P(a \lor b) &= 0.8 . \end{aligned} \tag{5}$$

This kind of question has been the subject of decades of intense debate between those who advocate the use of probabilities as the only legitimate form for degrees of belief and those who advocate alternative approaches.

One argument for the axioms of probability, first stated in 1931 by Bruno de Finetti (and translated into English in de Finetti (1993)), is as follows: If an agent has some degree of belief in a proposition a, then the agent should be able to state odds at which it is indifferent to a bet for or against a.[3] Think of it as a game between two agents: Agent 1 states, "my degree of belief in event a is 0.4." Agent 2 is then free to choose whether to wager for or against a at stakes that are consistent with the stated degree of belief. That is, Agent 2 could choose to accept Agent 1's bet that a will occur, offering \$6 against Agent 1's \$4. Or Agent 2 could accept Agent 1's bet that $\neg a$ will occur, offering \$4 against Agent 1's \$6. Then we observe the outcome of a, and whoever is right collects the money. If an agent's degrees of belief do not accurately reflect the world, then you would expect that it would tend to lose money over the long run to an opposing agent whose beliefs more accurately reflect the state of the world.

But de Finetti proved something much stronger: *If Agent 1 expresses a set of degrees of belief that violate the axioms of probability theory then there is a combination of bets by Agent 2 that guarantees that Agent 1 will lose money every time.* For example, suppose that Agent 1 has the set of degrees of belief from Equation (5). Figure 2 shows that if Agent

[2] The difficulties include the **Vitali set**, a well-defined subset of the interval [0, 1] with no well-defined size.

[3] One might argue that the agent's preferences for different bank balances are such that the possibility of losing \$1 is not counterbalanced by an equal possibility of winning \$1. One possible response is to make the bet amounts small enough to avoid this problem. Savage's analysis (1954) circumvents the issue altogether.

2 chooses to bet \$4 on a, \$3 on b, and \$2 on $\neg(a \vee b)$, then Agent 1 always loses money, regardless of the outcomes for a and b. De Finetti's theorem implies that no rational agent can have beliefs that violate the axioms of probability.

Agent 1		Agent 2		Outcomes and payoffs to Agent 1			
Proposition	Belief	Bet	Stakes	a, b	$a, \neg b$	$\neg a, b$	$\neg a, \neg b$
a	0.4	a	4 to 6	−6	−6	4	4
b	0.3	b	3 to 7	−7	3	−7	3
$a \vee b$	0.8	$\neg(a \vee b)$	2 to 8	2	2	2	−8
				−11	−1	−1	−1

Figure 2 Because Agent 1 has inconsistent beliefs, Agent 2 is able to devise a set of bets that guarantees a loss for Agent 1, no matter what the outcome of a and b.

One common objection to de Finetti's theorem is that this betting game is rather contrived. For example, what if one refuses to bet? Does that end the argument? The answer is that the betting game is an abstract model for the decision-making situation in which every agent is *unavoidably* involved at every moment. Every action (including inaction) is a kind of bet, and every outcome can be seen as a payoff of the bet. Refusing to bet is like refusing to allow time to pass.

Other strong philosophical arguments have been put forward for the use of probabilities, most notably those of Cox (1946), Carnap (1950), and Jaynes (2003). They each construct a set of axioms for reasoning with degrees of beliefs: no contradictions, correspondence with ordinary logic (for example, if belief in A goes up, then belief in $\neg A$ must go down), and so on. The only controversial axiom is that degrees of belief must be numbers, or at least act like numbers in that they must be transitive (if belief in A is greater than belief in B, which is greater than belief in C, then belief in A must be greater than C) and comparable (the belief in A must be one of equal to, greater than, or less than belief in B). It can then be proved that probability is the only approach that satisfies these axioms.

The world being the way it is, however, practical demonstrations sometimes speak louder than proofs. The success of reasoning systems based on probability theory has been much more effective in making converts. We now look at how the axioms can be deployed to make inferences.

3 Inference Using Full Joint Distributions

PROBABILISTIC INFERENCE

In this section we describe a simple method for **probabilistic inference**—that is, the computation of posterior probabilities for query propositions given observed evidence. We use the full joint distribution as the "knowledge base" from which answers to all questions may be derived. Along the way we also introduce several useful techniques for manipulating equations involving probabilities.

Where Do Probabilities Come From?

There has been endless debate over the source and status of probability numbers. The **frequentist** position is that the numbers can come only from *experiments*: if we test 100 people and find that 10 of them have a cavity, then we can say that the probability of a cavity is approximately 0.1. In this view, the assertion "the probability of a cavity is 0.1" means that 0.1 is the fraction that would be observed in the limit of infinitely many samples. From any finite sample, we can estimate the true fraction and also calculate how accurate our estimate is likely to be.

The **objectivist** view is that probabilities are real aspects of the universe—propensities of objects to behave in certain ways—rather than being just descriptions of an observer's degree of belief. For example, the fact that a fair coin comes up heads with probability 0.5 is a propensity of the coin itself. In this view, frequentist measurements are attempts to observe these propensities. Most physicists agree that quantum phenomena are objectively probabilistic, but uncertainty at the macroscopic scale—e.g., in coin tossing—usually arises from ignorance of initial conditions and does not seem consistent with the propensity view.

The **subjectivist** view describes probabilities as a way of characterizing an agent's beliefs, rather than as having any external physical significance. The subjective **Bayesian** view allows any self-consistent ascription of prior probabilities to propositions, but then insists on proper Bayesian updating as evidence arrives.

In the end, even a strict frequentist position involves subjective analysis because of the **reference class** problem: in trying to determine the outcome probability of a *particular* experiment, the frequentist has to place it in a reference class of "similar" experiments with known outcome frequencies. I. J. Good (1983, p. 27) wrote, "every event in life is unique, and every real-life probability that we estimate in practice is that of an event that has never occurred before." For example, given a particular patient, a frequentist who wants to estimate the probability of a cavity will consider a reference class of other patients who are similar in important ways—age, symptoms, diet—and see what proportion of them had a cavity. If the dentist considers everything that is known about the patient—weight to the nearest gram, hair color, mother's maiden name—then the reference class becomes empty. This has been a vexing problem in the philosophy of science.

The **principle of indifference** attributed to Laplace (1816) states that propositions that are syntactically "symmetric" with respect to the evidence should be accorded equal probability. Various refinements have been proposed, culminating in the attempt by Carnap and others to develop a rigorous **inductive logic**, capable of computing the correct probability for any proposition from any collection of observations. Currently, it is believed that no unique inductive logic exists; rather, any such logic rests on a subjective prior probability distribution whose effect is diminished as more observations are collected.

	toothache		*¬toothache*	
	catch	*¬catch*	*catch*	*¬catch*
cavity	0.108	0.012	0.072	0.008
¬cavity	0.016	0.064	0.144	0.576

Figure 3 A full joint distribution for the *Toothache*, *Cavity*, *Catch* world.

We begin with a simple example: a domain consisting of just the three Boolean variables *Toothache*, *Cavity*, and *Catch* (the dentist's nasty steel probe catches in my tooth). The full joint distribution is a $2 \times 2 \times 2$ table as shown in Figure 3.

Notice that the probabilities in the joint distribution sum to 1, as required by the axioms of probability. Notice also that Equation (2) gives us a direct way to calculate the probability of any proposition, simple or complex: simply identify those possible worlds in which the proposition is true and add up their probabilities. For example, there are six possible worlds in which $cavity \lor toothache$ holds:

$$P(cavity \lor toothache) = 0.108 + 0.012 + 0.072 + 0.008 + 0.016 + 0.064 = 0.28\,.$$

One particularly common task is to extract the distribution over some subset of variables or a single variable. For example, adding the entries in the first row gives the unconditional or

MARGINAL PROBABILITY

marginal probability[4] of *cavity*:

$$P(cavity) = 0.108 + 0.012 + 0.072 + 0.008 = 0.2\,.$$

MARGINALIZATION

This process is called **marginalization**, or **summing out**—because we sum up the probabilities for each possible value of the other variables, thereby taking them out of the equation. We can write the following general marginalization rule for any sets of variables **Y** and **Z**:

$$\mathbf{P}(\mathbf{Y}) = \sum_{\mathbf{z} \in \mathbf{Z}} \mathbf{P}(\mathbf{Y}, \mathbf{z})\,, \tag{6}$$

where $\sum_{\mathbf{z} \in \mathbf{Z}}$ means to sum over all the possible combinations of values of the set of variables **Z**. We sometimes abbreviate this as $\sum_{\mathbf{z}}$, leaving **Z** implicit. We just used the rule as

$$\mathbf{P}(Cavity) = \sum_{\mathbf{z} \in \{Catch, Toothache\}} \mathbf{P}(Cavity, \mathbf{z})\,. \tag{7}$$

A variant of this rule involves conditional probabilities instead of joint probabilities, using the product rule:

$$\mathbf{P}(\mathbf{Y}) = \sum_{\mathbf{z}} \mathbf{P}(\mathbf{Y} \mid \mathbf{z}) P(\mathbf{z})\,. \tag{8}$$

CONDITIONING

This rule is called **conditioning**. Marginalization and conditioning turn out to be useful rules for all kinds of derivations involving probability expressions.

In most cases, we are interested in computing *conditional* probabilities of some variables, given evidence about others. Conditional probabilities can be found by first using

[4] So called because of a common practice among actuaries of writing the sums of observed frequencies in the margins of insurance tables.

Equation (3) to obtain an expression in terms of unconditional probabilities and then evaluating the expression from the full joint distribution. For example, we can compute the probability of a cavity, given evidence of a toothache, as follows:

$$\begin{aligned} P(cavity \mid toothache) &= \frac{P(cavity \wedge toothache)}{P(toothache)} \\ &= \frac{0.108 + 0.012}{0.108 + 0.012 + 0.016 + 0.064} = 0.6\,. \end{aligned}$$

Just to check, we can also compute the probability that there is no cavity, given a toothache:

$$\begin{aligned} P(\neg cavity \mid toothache) &= \frac{P(\neg cavity \wedge toothache)}{P(toothache)} \\ &= \frac{0.016 + 0.064}{0.108 + 0.012 + 0.016 + 0.064} = 0.4\,. \end{aligned}$$

The two values sum to 1.0, as they should. Notice that in these two calculations the term $1/P(toothache)$ remains constant, no matter which value of *Cavity* we calculate. In fact,

NORMALIZATION it can be viewed as a **normalization** constant for the distribution $\mathbf{P}(Cavity \mid toothache)$, ensuring that it adds up to 1. Throughout the chapters dealing with probability, we use α to denote such constants. With this notation, we can write the two preceding equations in one:

$$\begin{aligned} \mathbf{P}(Cavity \mid toothache) &= \alpha\, \mathbf{P}(Cavity, toothache) \\ &= \alpha\, [\mathbf{P}(Cavity, toothache, catch) + \mathbf{P}(Cavity, toothache, \neg catch)] \\ &= \alpha\, [\langle 0.108, 0.016\rangle + \langle 0.012, 0.064\rangle] = \alpha\, \langle 0.12, 0.08\rangle = \langle 0.6, 0.4\rangle\,. \end{aligned}$$

In other words, we can calculate $\mathbf{P}(Cavity \mid toothache)$ even if we don't know the value of $P(toothache)$! We temporarily forget about the factor $1/P(toothache)$ and add up the values for *cavity* and $\neg cavity$, getting 0.12 and 0.08. Those are the correct relative proportions, but they don't sum to 1, so we normalize them by dividing each one by $0.12 + 0.08$, getting the true probabilities of 0.6 and 0.4. Normalization turns out to be a useful shortcut in many probability calculations, both to make the computation easier and to allow us to proceed when some probability assessment (such as $P(toothache)$) is not available.

From the example, we can extract a general inference procedure. We begin with the case in which the query involves a single variable, X (*Cavity* in the example). Let $\mathbf{E}$ be the list of evidence variables (just *Toothache* in the example), let $\mathbf{e}$ be the list of observed values for them, and let $\mathbf{Y}$ be the remaining unobserved variables (just *Catch* in the example). The query is $\mathbf{P}(X \mid \mathbf{e})$ and can be evaluated as

$$\mathbf{P}(X \mid \mathbf{e}) = \alpha\, \mathbf{P}(X, \mathbf{e}) = \alpha \sum_{\mathbf{y}} \mathbf{P}(X, \mathbf{e}, \mathbf{y})\,, \tag{9}$$

where the summation is over all possible $\mathbf{y}$s (i.e., all possible combinations of values of the unobserved variables $\mathbf{Y}$). Notice that together the variables X, $\mathbf{E}$, and $\mathbf{Y}$ constitute the complete set of variables for the domain, so $\mathbf{P}(X, \mathbf{e}, \mathbf{y})$ is simply a subset of probabilities from the full joint distribution.

Given the full joint distribution to work with, Equation (9) can answer probabilistic queries for discrete variables. It does not scale well, however: for a domain described by n Boolean variables, it requires an input table of size $O(2^n)$ and takes $O(2^n)$ time to process the table. In a realistic problem we could easily have $n > 100$, making $O(2^n)$ impractical. The full joint distribution in tabular form is just not a practical tool for building reasoning systems. Instead, it should be viewed as the theoretical foundation on which more effective approaches may be built, just as truth tables formed a theoretical foundation for more practical algorithms like DPLL. The remainder of this chapter introduces some of the basic ideas required in preparation for the development of realistic systems.

4 INDEPENDENCE

Let us expand the full joint distribution in Figure 3 by adding a fourth variable, *Weather*. The full joint distribution then becomes $\mathbf{P}(Toothache, Catch, Cavity, Weather)$, which has $2 \times 2 \times 2 \times 4 = 32$ entries. It contains four "editions" of the table shown in Figure 3, one for each kind of weather. What relationship do these editions have to each other and to the original three-variable table? For example, how are $P(toothache, catch, cavity, cloudy)$ and $P(toothache, catch, cavity)$ related? We can use the product rule:

$$\begin{aligned} & P(toothache, catch, cavity, cloudy) \\ & \quad = P(cloudy \mid toothache, catch, cavity) P(toothache, catch, cavity) . \end{aligned}$$

Now, unless one is in the deity business, one should not imagine that one's dental problems influence the weather. And for indoor dentistry, at least, it seems safe to say that the weather does not influence the dental variables. Therefore, the following assertion seems reasonable:

$$P(cloudy \mid toothache, catch, cavity) = P(cloudy) . \tag{10}$$

From this, we can deduce

$$P(toothache, catch, cavity, cloudy) = P(cloudy) P(toothache, catch, cavity) .$$

A similar equation exists for *every entry* in $\mathbf{P}(Toothache, Catch, Cavity, Weather)$. In fact, we can write the general equation

$$\mathbf{P}(Toothache, Catch, Cavity, Weather) = \mathbf{P}(Toothache, Catch, Cavity) \mathbf{P}(Weather) .$$

Thus, the 32-element table for four variables can be constructed from one 8-element table and one 4-element table. This decomposition is illustrated schematically in Figure 4(a).

INDEPENDENCE

The property we used in Equation (10) is called **independence** (also **marginal independence** and **absolute independence**). In particular, the weather is independent of one's dental problems. Independence between propositions a and b can be written as

$$P(a \mid b) = P(a) \quad \text{or} \quad P(b \mid a) = P(b) \quad \text{or} \quad P(a \wedge b) = P(a) P(b) . \tag{11}$$

All these forms are equivalent (Exercise 12). Independence between variables X and Y can be written as follows (again, these are all equivalent):

$$\mathbf{P}(X \mid Y) = \mathbf{P}(X) \quad \text{or} \quad \mathbf{P}(Y \mid X) = \mathbf{P}(Y) \quad \text{or} \quad \mathbf{P}(X, Y) = \mathbf{P}(X) \mathbf{P}(Y) .$$

Independence assertions are usually based on knowledge of the domain. As the toothache–weather example illustrates, they can dramatically reduce the amount of information necessary to specify the full joint distribution. If the complete set of variables can be divided

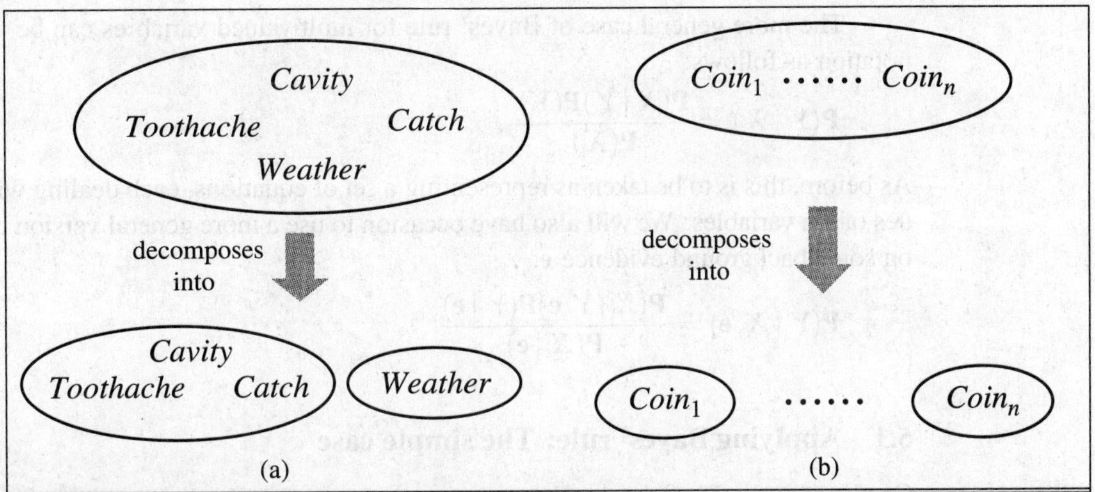

Figure 4 Two examples of factoring a large joint distribution into smaller distributions, using absolute independence. (a) Weather and dental problems are independent. (b) Coin flips are independent.

into independent subsets, then the full joint distribution can be *factored* into separate joint distributions on those subsets. For example, the full joint distribution on the outcome of n independent coin flips, $\mathbf{P}(C_1, \ldots, C_n)$, has 2^n entries, but it can be represented as the product of n single-variable distributions $\mathbf{P}(C_i)$. In a more practical vein, the independence of dentistry and meteorology is a good thing, because otherwise the practice of dentistry might require intimate knowledge of meteorology, and vice versa.

When they are available, then, independence assertions can help in reducing the size of the domain representation and the complexity of the inference problem. Unfortunately, clean separation of entire sets of variables by independence is quite rare. Whenever a connection, however indirect, exists between two variables, independence will fail to hold. Moreover, even independent subsets can be quite large—for example, dentistry might involve dozens of diseases and hundreds of symptoms, all of which are interrelated. To handle such problems, we need more subtle methods than the straightforward concept of independence.

5 Bayes' Rule and Its Use

In section 2.1, we defined the **product rule**. It can actually be written in two forms:

$$P(a \wedge b) = P(a \mid b)P(b) \qquad \text{and} \qquad P(a \wedge b) = P(b \mid a)P(a) .$$

Equating the two right-hand sides and dividing by $P(a)$, we get

$$P(b \mid a) = \frac{P(a \mid b)P(b)}{P(a)} . \tag{12}$$

BAYES' RULE This equation is known as **Bayes' rule** (also Bayes' law or Bayes' theorem). This simple equation underlies most modern AI systems for probabilistic inference.

The more general case of Bayes' rule for multivalued variables can be written in the **P** notation as follows:

$$\mathbf{P}(Y \mid X) = \frac{\mathbf{P}(X \mid Y)\mathbf{P}(Y)}{\mathbf{P}(X)},$$

As before, this is to be taken as representing a set of equations, each dealing with specific values of the variables. We will also have occasion to use a more general version conditionalized on some background evidence **e**:

$$\mathbf{P}(Y \mid X, \mathbf{e}) = \frac{\mathbf{P}(X \mid Y, \mathbf{e})\mathbf{P}(Y \mid \mathbf{e})}{\mathbf{P}(X \mid \mathbf{e})}. \tag{13}$$

5.1 Applying Bayes' rule: The simple case

On the surface, Bayes' rule does not seem very useful. It allows us to compute the single term $P(b \mid a)$ in terms of three terms: $P(a \mid b)$, $P(b)$, and $P(a)$. That seems like two steps backwards, but Bayes' rule is useful in practice because there are many cases where we do have good probability estimates for these three numbers and need to compute the fourth. Often, we perceive as evidence the *effect* of some unknown *cause* and we would like to determine that cause. In that case, Bayes' rule becomes

$$P(\mathit{cause} \mid \mathit{effect}) = \frac{P(\mathit{effect} \mid \mathit{cause})P(\mathit{cause})}{P(\mathit{effect})}.$$

CAUSAL DIAGNOSTIC

The conditional probability $P(\mathit{effect} \mid \mathit{cause})$ quantifies the relationship in the **causal** direction, whereas $P(\mathit{cause} \mid \mathit{effect})$ describes the **diagnostic** direction. In a task such as medical diagnosis, we often have conditional probabilities on causal relationships (that is, the doctor knows $P(\mathit{symptoms} \mid \mathit{disease})$) and want to derive a diagnosis, $P(\mathit{disease} \mid \mathit{symptoms})$. For example, a doctor knows that the disease meningitis causes the patient to have a stiff neck, say, 70% of the time. The doctor also knows some unconditional facts: the prior probability that a patient has meningitis is 1/50,000, and the prior probability that any patient has a stiff neck is 1%. Letting s be the proposition that the patient has a stiff neck and m be the proposition that the patient has meningitis, we have

$$\begin{aligned} P(s \mid m) &= 0.7 \\ P(m) &= 1/50000 \\ P(s) &= 0.01 \\ P(m \mid s) &= \frac{P(s \mid m)P(m)}{P(s)} = \frac{0.7 \times 1/50000}{0.01} = 0.0014\,. \end{aligned} \tag{14}$$

That is, we expect less than 1 in 700 patients with a stiff neck to have meningitis. Notice that even though a stiff neck is quite strongly indicated by meningitis (with probability 0.7), the probability of meningitis in the patient remains small. This is because the prior probability of stiff necks is much higher than that of meningitis.

Section 3 illustrated a process by which one can avoid assessing the prior probability of the evidence (here, $P(s)$) by instead computing a posterior probability for each value of the query variable (here, m and $\neg m$) and then normalizing the results. The same process can be applied when using Bayes' rule. We have

$$\mathbf{P}(M \mid s) = \alpha \, \langle P(s \mid m)P(m), P(s \mid \neg m)P(\neg m) \rangle \; .$$

Thus, to use this approach we need to estimate $P(s \mid \neg m)$ instead of $P(s)$. There is no free lunch—sometimes this is easier, sometimes it is harder. The general form of Bayes' rule with normalization is

$$\mathbf{P}(Y \mid X) = \alpha \, \mathbf{P}(X \mid Y)\mathbf{P}(Y) \; , \tag{15}$$

where α is the normalization constant needed to make the entries in $\mathbf{P}(Y \mid X)$ sum to 1.

One obvious question to ask about Bayes' rule is why one might have available the conditional probability in one direction, but not the other. In the meningitis domain, perhaps the doctor knows that a stiff neck implies meningitis in 1 out of 5000 cases; that is, the doctor has quantitative information in the **diagnostic** direction from symptoms to causes. Such a doctor has no need to use Bayes' rule. Unfortunately, *diagnostic knowledge is often more fragile than causal knowledge.* If there is a sudden epidemic of meningitis, the unconditional probability of meningitis, $P(m)$, will go up. The doctor who derived the diagnostic probability $P(m \mid s)$ directly from statistical observation of patients before the epidemic will have no idea how to update the value, but the doctor who computes $P(m \mid s)$ from the other three values will see that $P(m \mid s)$ should go up proportionately with $P(m)$. Most important, the causal information $P(s \mid m)$ is *unaffected* by the epidemic, because it simply reflects the way meningitis works. The use of this kind of direct causal or model-based knowledge provides the crucial robustness needed to make probabilistic systems feasible in the real world.

5.2 Using Bayes' rule: Combining evidence

We have seen that Bayes' rule can be useful for answering probabilistic queries conditioned on one piece of evidence—for example, the stiff neck. In particular, we have argued that probabilistic information is often available in the form $P(\mathit{effect} \mid \mathit{cause})$. What happens when we have two or more pieces of evidence? For example, what can a dentist conclude if her nasty steel probe catches in the aching tooth of a patient? If we know the full joint distribution (Figure 3), we can read off the answer:

$$\mathbf{P}(\mathit{Cavity} \mid \mathit{toothache} \wedge \mathit{catch}) = \alpha \, \langle 0.108, 0.016 \rangle \approx \langle 0.871, 0.129 \rangle \; .$$

We know, however, that such an approach does not scale up to larger numbers of variables. We can try using Bayes' rule to reformulate the problem:

$$\begin{aligned} &\mathbf{P}(\mathit{Cavity} \mid \mathit{toothache} \wedge \mathit{catch}) \\ &\quad = \alpha \, \mathbf{P}(\mathit{toothache} \wedge \mathit{catch} \mid \mathit{Cavity}) \, \mathbf{P}(\mathit{Cavity}) \; . \end{aligned} \tag{16}$$

For this reformulation to work, we need to know the conditional probabilities of the conjunction *toothache* $\wedge$ *catch* for each value of *Cavity*. That might be feasible for just two evidence variables, but again it does not scale up. If there are n possible evidence variables (X rays, diet, oral hygiene, etc.), then there are 2^n possible combinations of observed values for which we would need to know conditional probabilities. We might as well go back to using the full joint distribution. This is what first led researchers away from probability theory toward approximate methods for evidence combination that, while giving incorrect answers, require fewer numbers to give any answer at all.

Rather than taking this route, we need to find some additional assertions about the domain that will enable us to simplify the expressions. The notion of **independence** in Section 4 provides a clue, but needs refining. It would be nice if *Toothache* and *Catch* were independent, but they are not: if the probe catches in the tooth, then it is likely that the tooth has a cavity and that the cavity causes a toothache. These variables *are* independent, however, *given the presence or the absence of a cavity*. Each is directly caused by the cavity, but neither has a direct effect on the other: toothache depends on the state of the nerves in the tooth, whereas the probe's accuracy depends on the dentist's skill, to which the toothache is irrelevant.[5] Mathematically, this property is written as

$$\mathbf{P}(toothache \wedge catch \mid Cavity) = \mathbf{P}(toothache \mid Cavity)\mathbf{P}(catch \mid Cavity)\,. \qquad (17)$$

CONDITIONAL INDEPENDENCE

This equation expresses the **conditional independence** of *toothache* and *catch* given *Cavity*. We can plug it into Equation (16) to obtain the probability of a cavity:

$$\mathbf{P}(Cavity \mid toothache \wedge catch)$$
$$= \alpha\,\mathbf{P}(toothache \mid Cavity)\,\mathbf{P}(catch \mid Cavity)\,\mathbf{P}(Cavity)\,. \qquad (18)$$

Now the information requirements are the same as for inference, using each piece of evidence separately: the prior probability $\mathbf{P}(Cavity)$ for the query variable and the conditional probability of each effect, given its cause.

The general definition of **conditional independence** of two variables X and Y, given a third variable Z, is

$$\mathbf{P}(X, Y \mid Z) = \mathbf{P}(X \mid Z)\mathbf{P}(Y \mid Z)\,.$$

In the dentist domain, for example, it seems reasonable to assert conditional independence of the variables *Toothache* and *Catch*, given *Cavity*:

$$\mathbf{P}(Toothache, Catch \mid Cavity) = \mathbf{P}(Toothache \mid Cavity)\mathbf{P}(Catch \mid Cavity)\,. \qquad (19)$$

Notice that this assertion is somewhat stronger than Equation (17), which asserts independence only for specific values of *Toothache* and *Catch*. As with absolute independence in Equation (11), the equivalent forms

$$\mathbf{P}(X \mid Y, Z) = \mathbf{P}(X \mid Z) \quad \text{and} \quad \mathbf{P}(Y \mid X, Z) = \mathbf{P}(Y \mid Z)$$

can also be used (see Exercise 17). Section 4 showed that absolute independence assertions allow a decomposition of the full joint distribution into much smaller pieces. It turns out that the same is true for conditional independence assertions. For example, given the assertion in Equation (19), we can derive a decomposition as follows:

$$\mathbf{P}(Toothache, Catch, Cavity)$$
$$= \mathbf{P}(Toothache, Catch \mid Cavity)\mathbf{P}(Cavity) \quad \text{(product rule)}$$
$$= \mathbf{P}(Toothache \mid Cavity)\mathbf{P}(Catch \mid Cavity)\mathbf{P}(Cavity) \quad \text{(using 19).}$$

(The reader can easily check that this equation does in fact hold in Figure 3.) In this way, the original large table is decomposed into three smaller tables. The original table has seven

[5] We assume that the patient and dentist are distinct individuals.

independent numbers ($2^3 = 8$ entries in the table, but they must sum to 1, so 7 are independent). The smaller tables contain five independent numbers (for a conditional probability distributions such as $\mathbf{P}(T|C$ there are two rows of two numbers, and each row sums to 1, so that's two independent numbers; for a prior distribution like $\mathbf{P}(C)$ there is only one independent number). Going from seven to five might not seem like a major triumph, but the point is that, for n symptoms that are all conditionally independent given $Cavity$, the size of the representation grows as $O(n)$ instead of $O(2^n)$. That means that *conditional independence assertions can allow probabilistic systems to scale up; moreover, they are much more commonly available than absolute independence assertions.* Conceptually, $Cavity$ **separates** $Toothache$ and $Catch$ because it is a direct cause of both of them. The decomposition of large probabilistic domains into weakly connected subsets through conditional independence is one of the most important developments in the recent history of AI.

SEPARATION

The dentistry example illustrates a commonly occurring pattern in which a single cause directly influences a number of effects, all of which are conditionally independent, given the cause. The full joint distribution can be written as

$$\mathbf{P}(Cause, Effect_1, \ldots, Effect_n) = \mathbf{P}(Cause) \prod_i \mathbf{P}(Effect_i \mid Cause) .$$

NAIVE BAYES

Such a probability distribution is called a **naive Bayes** model—"naive" because it is often used (as a simplifying assumption) in cases where the "effect" variables are *not* actually conditionally independent given the cause variable. (The naive Bayes model is sometimes called a **Bayesian classifier**, a somewhat careless usage that has prompted true Bayesians to call it the **idiot Bayes** model.) In practice, naive Bayes systems can work surprisingly well, even when the conditional independence assumption is not true.

6 THE WUMPUS WORLD REVISITED

We can combine of the ideas in this chapter to solve probabilistic reasoning problems in the wumpus world. Uncertainty arises in the wumpus world because the agent's sensors give only partial information about the world. For example, Figure 5 shows a situation in which each of the three reachable squares—[1,3], [2,2], and [3,1]—might contain a pit. Pure logical inference can conclude nothing about which square is most likely to be safe, so a logical agent might have to choose randomly. We will see that a probabilistic agent can do much better than the logical agent.

Our aim is to calculate the probability that each of the three squares contains a pit. (For this example we ignore the wumpus and the gold.) The relevant properties of the wumpus world are that (1) a pit causes breezes in all neighboring squares, and (2) each square other than [1,1] contains a pit with probability 0.2. The first step is to identify the set of random variables we need:

- As in the propositional logic case, we want one Boolean variable P_{ij} for each square, which is true iff square $[i, j]$ actually contains a pit.

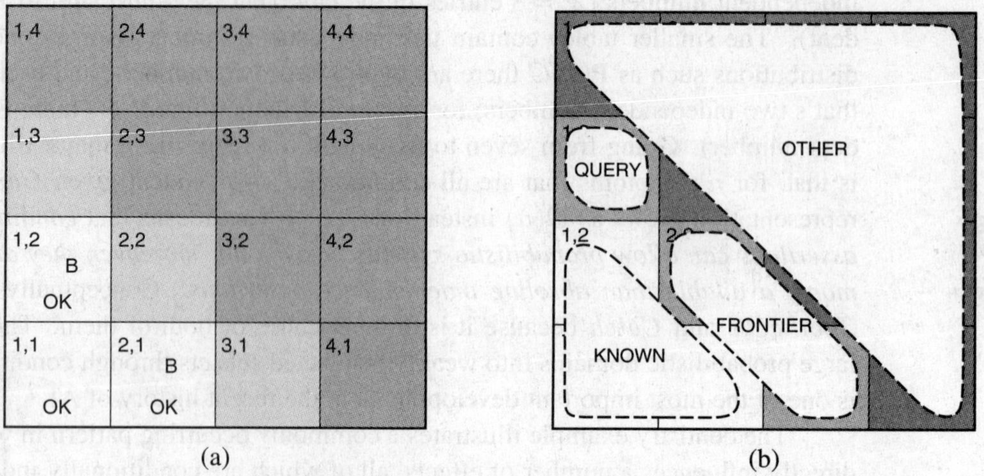

Figure 5 (a) After finding a breeze in both [1,2] and [2,1], the agent is stuck—there is no safe place to explore. (b) Division of the squares into *Known*, *Frontier*, and *Other*, for a query about [1,3].

- We also have Boolean variables B_{ij} that are true iff square $[i, j]$ is breezy; we include these variables only for the observed squares—in this case, [1,1], [1,2], and [2,1].

The next step is to specify the full joint distribution, $\mathbf{P}(P_{1,1}, \ldots, P_{4,4}, B_{1,1}, B_{1,2}, B_{2,1})$. Applying the product rule, we have

$$\mathbf{P}(P_{1,1}, \ldots, P_{4,4}, B_{1,1}, B_{1,2}, B_{2,1}) = \mathbf{P}(B_{1,1}, B_{1,2}, B_{2,1} \mid P_{1,1}, \ldots, P_{4,4})\mathbf{P}(P_{1,1}, \ldots, P_{4,4}) .$$

This decomposition makes it easy to see what the joint probability values should be. The first term is the conditional probability distribution of a breeze configuration, given a pit configuration; its values are 1 if the breezes are adjacent to the pits and 0 otherwise. The second term is the prior probability of a pit configuration. Each square contains a pit with probability 0.2, independently of the other squares; hence,

$$\mathbf{P}(P_{1,1}, \ldots, P_{4,4}) = \prod_{i,j=1,1}^{4,4} \mathbf{P}(P_{i,j}) . \tag{20}$$

For a particular configuration with exactly n pits, $P(P_{1,1}, \ldots, P_{4,4}) = 0.2^n \times 0.8^{16-n}$.

In the situation in Figure 5(a), the evidence consists of the observed breeze (or its absence) in each square that is visited, combined with the fact that each such square contains no pit. We abbreviate these facts as $b = \neg b_{1,1} \wedge b_{1,2} \wedge b_{2,1}$ and $known = \neg p_{1,1} \wedge \neg p_{1,2} \wedge \neg p_{2,1}$. We are interested in answering queries such as $\mathbf{P}(P_{1,3} \mid known, b)$: how likely is it that [1,3] contains a pit, given the observations so far?

To answer this query, we can follow the standard approach of Equation (9), namely, summing over entries from the full joint distribution. Let *Unknown* be the set of $P_{i,j}$ variables for squares other than the *Known* squares and the query square [1,3]. Then, by Equation (9), we have

$$\mathbf{P}(P_{1,3} \mid known, b) = \alpha \sum_{unknown} \mathbf{P}(P_{1,3}, unknown, known, b) .$$

The full joint probabilities have already been specified, so we are done—that is, unless we care about computation. There are 12 unknown squares; hence the summation contains $2^{12} = 4096$ terms. In general, the summation grows exponentially with the number of squares.

Surely, one might ask, aren't the other squares irrelevant? How could [4,4] affect whether [1,3] has a pit? Indeed, this intuition is correct. Let *Frontier* be the pit variables (other than the query variable) that are adjacent to visited squares, in this case just [2,2] and [3,1]. Also, let *Other* be the pit variables for the other unknown squares; in this case, there are 10 other squares, as shown in Figure 5(b). The key insight is that the observed breezes are *conditionally independent* of the other variables, given the known, frontier, and query variables. To use the insight, we manipulate the query formula into a form in which the breezes are conditioned on all the other variables, and then we apply conditional independence:

$$\begin{aligned}
&\mathbf{P}(P_{1,3} \mid known, b) \\
&= \alpha \sum_{unknown} \mathbf{P}(P_{1,3}, known, b, unknown) \quad \text{(by Equation (9))} \\
&= \alpha \sum_{unknown} \mathbf{P}(b \mid P_{1,3}, known, unknown)\mathbf{P}(P_{1,3}, known, unknown) \\
&\qquad \text{(by the product rule)} \\
&= \alpha \sum_{frontier} \sum_{other} \mathbf{P}(b \mid known, P_{1,3}, frontier, other)\mathbf{P}(P_{1,3}, known, frontier, other) \\
&= \alpha \sum_{frontier} \sum_{other} \mathbf{P}(b \mid known, P_{1,3}, frontier)\mathbf{P}(P_{1,3}, known, frontier, other) ,
\end{aligned}$$

where the final step uses conditional independence: b is independent of *other* given *known*, $P_{1,3}$, and *frontier*. Now, the first term in this expression does not depend on the *Other* variables, so we can move the summation inward:

$$\begin{aligned}
&\mathbf{P}(P_{1,3} \mid known, b) \\
&= \alpha \sum_{frontier} \mathbf{P}(b \mid known, P_{1,3}, frontier) \sum_{other} \mathbf{P}(P_{1,3}, known, frontier, other) .
\end{aligned}$$

By independence, as in Equation (20), the prior term can be factored, and then the terms can be reordered:

$$\begin{aligned}
&\mathbf{P}(P_{1,3} \mid known, b) \\
&= \alpha \sum_{frontier} \mathbf{P}(b \mid known, P_{1,3}, frontier) \sum_{other} \mathbf{P}(P_{1,3})P(known)P(frontier)P(other) \\
&= \alpha\, P(known)\mathbf{P}(P_{1,3}) \sum_{frontier} \mathbf{P}(b \mid known, P_{1,3}, frontier)P(frontier) \sum_{other} P(other) \\
&= \alpha' \,\mathbf{P}(P_{1,3}) \sum_{frontier} \mathbf{P}(b \mid known, P_{1,3}, frontier)P(frontier) ,
\end{aligned}$$

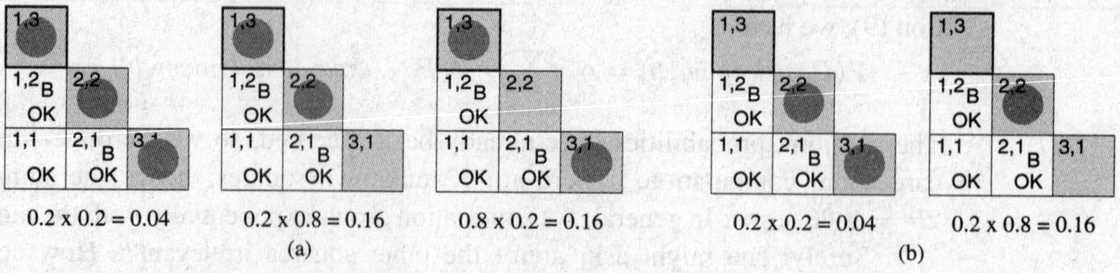

Figure 6 Consistent models for the frontier variables $P_{2,2}$ and $P_{3,1}$, showing $P(frontier)$ for each model: (a) three models with $P_{1,3} = true$ showing two or three pits, and (b) two models with $P_{1,3} = false$ showing one or two pits.

where the last step folds $P(known)$ into the normalizing constant and uses the fact that $\sum_{other} P(other)$ equals 1.

Now, there are just four terms in the summation over the frontier variables $P_{2,2}$ and $P_{3,1}$. The use of independence and conditional independence has completely eliminated the other squares from consideration.

Notice that the expression $\mathbf{P}(b \mid known, P_{1,3}, frontier)$ is 1 when the frontier is consistent with the breeze observations, and 0 otherwise. Thus, for each value of $P_{1,3}$, we sum over the *logical models* for the frontier variables that are consistent with the known facts. The models and their associated prior probabilities—$P(frontier)$—are shown in Figure 6. We have

$$\mathbf{P}(P_{1,3} \mid known, b) = \alpha' \langle 0.2(0.04 + 0.16 + 0.16),\ 0.8(0.04 + 0.16) \rangle \approx \langle 0.31, 0.69 \rangle .$$

That is, [1,3] (and [3,1] by symmetry) contains a pit with roughly 31% probability. A similar calculation, which the reader might wish to perform, shows that [2,2] contains a pit with roughly 86% probability. The wumpus agent should definitely avoid [2,2]! Logic can tell us that it is unknown whether there is a pit in [2, 2], but we need probability to tell us how likely it is.

What this section has shown is that even seemingly complicated problems can be formulated precisely in probability theory and solved with simple algorithms. To get *efficient* solutions, independence and conditional independence relationships can be used to simplify the summations required. These relationships often correspond to our natural understanding of how the problem should be decomposed. In the next chapter, we develop formal representations for such relationships as well as algorithms that operate on those representations to perform probabilistic inference efficiently.

7 SUMMARY

This chapter has suggested probability theory as a suitable foundation for uncertain reasoning and provided a gentle introduction to its use.

- Uncertainty arises because of both laziness and ignorance. It is inescapable in complex, nondeterministic, or partially observable environments.
- Probabilities express the agent's inability to reach a definite decision regarding the truth of a sentence. Probabilities summarize the agent's beliefs relative to the evidence.
- Decision theory combines the agent's beliefs and desires, defining the best action as the one that maximizes expected utility.
- Basic probability statements include **prior probabilities** and **conditional probabilities** over simple and complex propositions.
- The axioms of probability constrain the possible assignments of probabilities to propositions. An agent that violates the axioms must behave irrationally in some cases.
- The **full joint probability distribution** specifies the probability of each complete assignment of values to random variables. It is usually too large to create or use in its explicit form, but when it is available it can be used to answer queries simply by adding up entries for the possible worlds corresponding to the query propositions.
- **Absolute independence** between subsets of random variables allows the full joint distribution to be factored into smaller joint distributions, greatly reducing its complexity. Absolute independence seldom occurs in practice.
- **Bayes' rule** allows unknown probabilities to be computed from known conditional probabilities, usually in the causal direction. Applying Bayes' rule with many pieces of evidence runs into the same scaling problems as does the full joint distribution.
- **Conditional independence** brought about by direct causal relationships in the domain might allow the full joint distribution to be factored into smaller, conditional distributions. The **naive Bayes** model assumes the conditional independence of all effect variables, given a single cause variable, and grows linearly with the number of effects.
- A wumpus-world agent can calculate probabilities for unobserved aspects of the world, thereby improving on the decisions of a purely logical agent. Conditional independence makes these calculations tractable.

BIBLIOGRAPHICAL AND HISTORICAL NOTES

Probability theory was invented as a way of analyzing games of chance. In about 850 A.D. the Indian mathematician Mahaviracarya described how to arrange a set of bets that can't lose (what we now call a Dutch book). In Europe, the first significant systematic analyses were produced by Girolamo Cardano around 1565, although publication was posthumous (1663). By that time, probability had been established as a mathematical discipline due to a series of results established in a famous correspondence between Blaise Pascal and Pierre de Fermat in 1654. As with probability itself, the results were initially motivated by gambling problems (see Exercise 9). The first published textbook on probability was *De Ratiociniis in Ludo Aleae* (Huygens, 1657). The "laziness and ignorance" view of uncertainty was described by John Arbuthnot in the preface of his translation of Huygens (Arbuthnot, 1692): "It is impossible for a Die, with such determin'd force and direction, not to fall on such determin'd side, only I don't know the force and direction which makes it fall on such determin'd side, and therefore I call it Chance, which is nothing but the want of art..."

Laplace (1816) gave an exceptionally accurate and modern overview of probability; he was the first to use the example "take two urns, A and B, the first containing four white and two black balls, ..." The Rev. Thomas Bayes (1702–1761) introduced the rule for reasoning about conditional probabilities that was named after him (Bayes, 1763). Bayes only considered the case of uniform priors; it was Laplace who independently developed the general case. Kolmogorov (1950, first published in German in 1933) presented probability theory in a rigorously axiomatic framework for the first time. Rényi (1970) later gave an axiomatic presentation that took conditional probability, rather than absolute probability, as primitive.

Pascal used probability in ways that required both the objective interpretation, as a property of the world based on symmetry or relative frequency, and the subjective interpretation, based on degree of belief—the former in his analyses of probabilities in games of chance, the latter in the famous "Pascal's wager" argument about the possible existence of God. However, Pascal did not clearly realize the distinction between these two interpretations. The distinction was first drawn clearly by James Bernoulli (1654–1705).

Leibniz introduced the "classical" notion of probability as a proportion of enumerated, equally probable cases, which was also used by Bernoulli, although it was brought to prominence by Laplace (1749–1827). This notion is ambiguous between the frequency interpretation and the subjective interpretation. The cases can be thought to be equally probable either because of a natural, physical symmetry between them, or simply because we do not have any knowledge that would lead us to consider one more probable than another. The use of this latter, subjective consideration to justify assigning equal probabilities is known as the

PRINCIPLE OF INDIFFERENCE

principle of indifference. The principle is often attributed to Laplace, but he never isolated the principle explicitly. George Boole and John Venn both referred to it as the **principle of**

PRINCIPLE OF INSUFFICIENT REASON

insufficient reason; the modern name is due to Keynes (1921).

The debate between objectivists and subjectivists became sharper in the 20th century. Kolmogorov (1963), R. A. Fisher (1922), and Richard von Mises (1928) were advocates of the relative frequency interpretation. Karl Popper's (1959, first published in German in 1934) "propensity" interpretation traces relative frequencies to an underlying physical symmetry. Frank Ramsey (1931), Bruno de Finetti (1937), R. T. Cox (1946), Leonard Savage (1954), Richard Jeffrey (1983), and E. T. Jaynes (2003) interpreted probabilities as the degrees of belief of specific individuals. Their analyses of degree of belief were closely tied to utilities and to behavior—specifically, to the willingness to place bets. Rudolf Carnap, following Leibniz and Laplace, offered a different kind of subjective interpretation of probability—not as any actual individual's degree of belief, but as the degree of belief that an idealized individual *should* have in a particular proposition a, given a particular body of evidence $\mathbf{e}$.

CONFIRMATION INDUCTIVE LOGIC Carnap attempted to go further than Leibniz or Laplace by making this notion of degree of **confirmation** mathematically precise, as a logical relation between a and $\mathbf{e}$. The study of this relation was intended to constitute a mathematical discipline called **inductive logic**, analogous to ordinary deductive logic (Carnap, 1948, 1950). Carnap was not able to extend his inductive logic much beyond the propositional case, and Putnam (1963) showed by adversarial arguments that some fundamental difficulties would prevent a strict extension to languages capable of expressing arithmetic.

Cox's theorem (1946) shows that any system for uncertain reasoning that meets his set of assumptions is equivalent to probability theory. This gave renewed confidence to those who already favored probability, but others were not convinced, pointing to the assumptions (primarily that belief must be represented by a single number, and thus the belief in $\neg p$ must be a function of the belief in p). Halpern (1999) describes the assumptions and shows some gaps in Cox's original formulation. Horn (2003) shows how to patch up the difficulties. Jaynes (2003) has a similar argument that is easier to read.

The question of reference classes is closely tied to the attempt to find an inductive logic. The approach of choosing the "most specific" reference class of sufficient size was formally proposed by Reichenbach (1949). Various attempts have been made, notably by Henry Kyburg (1977, 1983), to formulate more sophisticated policies in order to avoid some obvious fallacies that arise with Reichenbach's rule, but such approaches remain somewhat *ad hoc*. More recent work by Bacchus, Grove, Halpern, and Koller (1992) extends Carnap's methods to first-order theories, thereby avoiding many of the difficulties associated with the straightforward reference-class method. Kyburg and Teng (2006) contrast probabilistic inference with nonmonotonic logic.

Bayesian probabilistic reasoning has been used in AI since the 1960s, especially in medical diagnosis. It was used not only to make a diagnosis from available evidence, but also to select further questions and tests by using the theory of information value when available evidence was inconclusive (Gorry, 1968; Gorry *et al.*, 1973). One system outperformed human experts in the diagnosis of acute abdominal illnesses (de Dombal *et al.*, 1974). Lucas *et al.* (2004) gives an overview. These early Bayesian systems suffered from a number of problems, however. Because they lacked any theoretical model of the conditions they were diagnosing, they were vulnerable to unrepresentative data occurring in situations for which only a small sample was available (de Dombal *et al.*, 1981). Even more fundamentally, because they lacked a concise formalism for representing and using conditional independence information, they depended on the acquisition, storage, and processing of enormous tables of probabilistic data. Because of these difficulties, probabilistic methods for coping with uncertainty fell out of favor in AI from the 1970s to the mid-1980s.

The naive Bayes model for joint distributions has been studied extensively in the pattern recognition literature since the 1950s (Duda and Hart, 1973). It has also been used, often unwittingly, in information retrieval, beginning with the work of Maron (1961). The probabilistic foundations of this technique, described further in Exercise 22, were elucidated by Robertson and Sparck Jones (1976). Domingos and Pazzani (1997) provide an explanation for the surprising success of naive Bayesian reasoning even in domains where the independence assumptions are clearly violated.

There are many good introductory textbooks on probability theory, including those by Bertsekas and Tsitsiklis (2008) and Grinstead and Snell (1997). DeGroot and Schervish (2001) offer a combined introduction to probability and statistics from a Bayesian standpoint. Richard Hamming's (1991) textbook gives a mathematically sophisticated introduction to probability theory from the standpoint of a propensity interpretation based on physical symmetry. Hacking (1975) and Hald (1990) cover the early history of the concept of probability. Bernstein (1996) gives an entertaining popular account of the story of risk.

EXERCISES

1 Show from first principles that $P(a \mid b \wedge a) = 1$.

2 Using the axioms of probability, prove that any probability distribution on a discrete random variable must sum to 1.

3 For each of the following statements, either prove it is true or give a counterexample.

a. If $P(a \mid b, c) = P(b \mid a, c)$, then $P(a \mid c) = P(b \mid c)$

b. If $P(a \mid b, c) = P(a)$, then $P(b \mid c) = P(b)$

c. If $P(a \mid b) = P(a)$, then $P(a \mid b, c) = P(a \mid c)$

4 Would it be rational for an agent to hold the three beliefs $P(A) = 0.4$, $P(B) = 0.3$, and $P(A \vee B) = 0.5$? If so, what range of probabilities would be rational for the agent to hold for $A \wedge B$? Make up a table like the one in Figure 2, and show how it supports your argument about rationality. Then draw another version of the table where $P(A \vee B) = 0.7$. Explain why it is rational to have this probability, even though the table shows one case that is a loss and three that just break even. (*Hint:* what is Agent 1 committed to about the probability of each of the four cases, especially the case that is a loss?)

5 This question deals with the properties of possible worlds, defined as assignments to all random variables. We will work with propositions that correspond to exactly one possible world because they pin down the assignments of all the variables. In probability

ATOMIC EVENT

theory, such propositions are called **atomic events**. For example, with Boolean variables X_1, X_2, X_3, the proposition $x_1 \wedge \neg x_2 \wedge \neg x_3$ fixes the assignment of the variables; in the language of propositional logic, we would say it has exactly one model.

a. Prove, for the case of n Boolean variables, that any two distinct atomic events are mutually exclusive; that is, their conjunction is equivalent to *false*.

b. Prove that the disjunction of all possible atomic events is logically equivalent to *true*.

c. Prove that any proposition is logically equivalent to the disjunction of the atomic events that entail its truth.

6 Prove Equation (4) from Equations (1) and (2).

7 Consider the set of all possible five-card poker hands dealt fairly from a standard deck of fifty-two cards.

a. How many atomic events are there in the joint probability distribution (i.e., how many five-card hands are there)?

b. What is the probability of each atomic event?

c. What is the probability of being dealt a royal straight flush? Four of a kind?

8 Given the full joint distribution shown in Figure 3, calculate the following:

a. $\mathbf{P}(toothache)$.

b. $\mathbf{P}(Cavity)$.

c. $\mathbf{P}(Toothache \mid cavity)$.

d. $\mathbf{P}(Cavity \mid toothache \vee catch)$.

9 In his letter of August 24, 1654, Pascal was trying to show how a pot of money should be allocated when a gambling game must end prematurely. Imagine a game where each turn consists of the roll of a die, player E gets a point when the die is even, and player O gets a point when the die is odd. The first player to get 7 points wins the pot. Suppose the game is interrupted with E leading 4–2. How should the money be fairly split in this case? What is the general formula? (Fermat and Pascal made several errors before solving the problem, but you should be able to get it right the first time.)

10 Deciding to put probability theory to good use, we encounter a slot machine with three independent wheels, each producing one of the four symbols BAR, BELL, LEMON, or CHERRY with equal probability. The slot machine has the following payout scheme for a bet of 1 coin (where "?" denotes that we don't care what comes up for that wheel):

BAR/BAR/BAR pays 20 coins
BELL/BELL/BELL pays 15 coins
LEMON/LEMON/LEMON pays 5 coins
CHERRY/CHERRY/CHERRY pays 3 coins
CHERRY/CHERRY/? pays 2 coins
CHERRY/?/? pays 1 coin

a. Compute the expected "payback" percentage of the machine. In other words, for each coin played, what is the expected coin return?

b. Compute the probability that playing the slot machine once will result in a win.

c. Estimate the mean and median number of plays you can expect to make until you go broke, if you start with 10 coins. You can run a simulation to estimate this, rather than trying to compute an exact answer.

11 We wish to transmit an n-bit message to a receiving agent. The bits in the message are independently corrupted (flipped) during transmission with ϵ probability each. With an extra parity bit sent along with the original information, a message can be corrected by the receiver if at most one bit in the entire message (including the parity bit) has been corrupted. Suppose we want to ensure that the correct message is received with probability at least $1 - \delta$. What is the maximum feasible value of n? Calculate this value for the case $\epsilon = 0.001$, $\delta = 0.01$.

12 Show that the three forms of independence in Equation (11) are equivalent.

13 Consider two medical tests, A and B, for a virus. Test A is 95% effective at recognizing the virus when it is present, but has a 10% false positive rate (indicating that the virus is present, when it is not). Test B is 90% effective at recognizing the virus, but has a 5% false positive rate. The two tests use independent methods of identifying the virus. The virus is carried by 1% of all people. Say that a person is tested for the virus using only one of the tests, and that test comes back positive for carrying the virus. Which test returning positive is more indicative of someone really carrying the virus? Justify your answer mathematically.

14 Suppose you are given a coin that lands *heads* with probability x and *tails* with probability $1 - x$. Are the outcomes of successive flips of the coin independent of each other given that you know the value of x? Are the outcomes of successive flips of the coin independent of each other if you do *not* know the value of x? Justify your answer.

15 After your yearly checkup, the doctor has bad news and good news. The bad news is that you tested positive for a serious disease and that the test is 99% accurate (i.e., the probability of testing positive when you do have the disease is 0.99, as is the probability of testing negative when you don't have the disease). The good news is that this is a rare disease, striking only 1 in 10,000 people of your age. Why is it good news that the disease is rare? What are the chances that you actually have the disease?

16 It is quite often useful to consider the effect of some specific propositions in the context of some general background evidence that remains fixed, rather than in the complete absence of information. The following questions ask you to prove more general versions of the product rule and Bayes' rule, with respect to some background evidence **e**:

a. Prove the conditionalized version of the general product rule:

$$\mathbf{P}(X, Y \mid \mathbf{e}) = \mathbf{P}(X \mid Y, \mathbf{e})\mathbf{P}(Y \mid \mathbf{e}) .$$

b. Prove the conditionalized version of Bayes' rule in Equation (13).

17 Show that the statement of conditional independence

$$\mathbf{P}(X, Y \mid Z) = \mathbf{P}(X \mid Z)\mathbf{P}(Y \mid Z)$$

is equivalent to each of the statements

$$\mathbf{P}(X \mid Y, Z) = \mathbf{P}(X \mid Z) \quad \text{and} \quad \mathbf{P}(B \mid X, Z) = \mathbf{P}(Y \mid Z) .$$

18 Suppose you are given a bag containing n unbiased coins. You are told that $n - 1$ of these coins are normal, with heads on one side and tails on the other, whereas one coin is a fake, with heads on both sides.

a. Suppose you reach into the bag, pick out a coin at random, flip it, and get a head. What is the (conditional) probability that the coin you chose is the fake coin?

b. Suppose you continue flipping the coin for a total of k times after picking it and see k heads. Now what is the conditional probability that you picked the fake coin?

c. Suppose you wanted to decide whether the chosen coin was fake by flipping it k times. The decision procedure returns *fake* if all k flips come up heads; otherwise it returns *normal*. What is the (unconditional) probability that this procedure makes an error?

19 In this exercise, you will complete the normalization calculation for the meningitis example. First, make up a suitable value for $P(s \mid \neg m)$, and use it to calculate unnormalized values for $P(m \mid s)$ and $P(\neg m \mid s)$ (i.e., ignoring the $P(s)$ term in the Bayes' rule expression, Equation (14)). Now normalize these values so that they add to 1.

20 Let X, Y, Z be Boolean random variables. Label the eight entries in the joint distribution $\mathbf{P}(X, Y, Z)$ as a through h. Express the statement that X and Y are conditionally independent given Z, as a set of equations relating a through h. How many *nonredundant* equations are there?

21 (Adapted from Pearl (1988).) Suppose you are a witness to a nighttime hit-and-run accident involving a taxi in Athens. All taxis in Athens are blue or green. You swear, under oath, that the taxi was blue. Extensive testing shows that, under the dim lighting conditions, discrimination between blue and green is 75% reliable.

a. Is it possible to calculate the most likely color for the taxi? (*Hint:* distinguish carefully between the proposition that the taxi *is* blue and the proposition that it *appears* blue.)

b. What if you know that 9 out of 10 Athenian taxis are green?

22 Text categorization is the task of assigning a given document to one of a fixed set of categories on the basis of the text it contains. Naive Bayes models are often used for this task. In these models, the query variable is the document category, and the "effect" variables are the presence or absence of each word in the language; the assumption is that words occur independently in documents, with frequencies determined by the document category.

a. Explain precisely how such a model can be constructed, given as "training data" a set of documents that have been assigned to categories.

b. Explain precisely how to categorize a new document.

c. Is the conditional independence assumption reasonable? Discuss.

23 In our analysis of the wumpus world, we used the fact that each square contains a pit with probability 0.2, independently of the contents of the other squares. Suppose instead that exactly $N/5$ pits are scattered at random among the N squares other than [1,1]. Are the variables $P_{i,j}$ and $P_{k,l}$ still independent? What is the joint distribution $\mathbf{P}(P_{1,1}, \ldots, P_{4,4})$ now? Redo the calculation for the probabilities of pits in [1,3] and [2,2].

24 Redo the probability calculation for pits in [1,3] and [2,2], assuming that each square contains a pit with probability 0.01, independent of the other squares. What can you say about the relative performance of a logical versus a probabilistic agent in this case?

25 Implement a hybrid probabilistic agent for the wumpus world, based on a hybrid agent, which you should be familiar with, and the probabilistic inference procedure outlined in this chapter.

PROBABILISTIC REASONING

PROBABILISTIC REASONING

In which we explain how to build network models to reason under uncertainty according to the laws of probability theory.

Introduced the basic elements of probability theory and noted the importance of Independence and conditional independence relationships are important when simplifying probabilistic representations of the world. This chapter introduces a systematic way to represent such relationships explicitly in the form of **Bayesian networks**. We define the syntax and semantics of these networks and show how they can be used to capture uncertain knowledge in a natural and efficient way. We then show how probabilistic inference, although computationally intractable in the worst case, can be done efficiently in many practical situations. We also describe a variety of approximate inference algorithms that are often applicable when exact inference is infeasible. We explore ways in which probability theory can be applied to worlds with objects and relations—that is, to *first-order*, as opposed to *propositional*, representations. Finally, we survey alternative approaches to uncertain reasoning.

1 Representing Knowledge in an Uncertain Domain

The full joint probability distribution can answer any question about the domain, but can become intractably large as the number of variables grows. Furthermore, specifying probabilities for possible worlds one by one is unnatural and tedious.

Independence and conditional independence relationships among variables can greatly reduce the number of probabilities that need to be specified in order to define the full joint distribution. This section introduces a data structure called a **Bayesian network**[1] to represent the dependencies among variables. Bayesian networks can represent essentially *any* full joint probability distribution and in many cases can do so very concisely.

BAYESIAN NETWORK

[1] This is the most common name, but there are many synonyms, including **belief network**, **probabilistic network**, **causal network**, and **knowledge map**. In statistics, the term **graphical model** refers to a somewhat broader class that includes Bayesian networks.

A Bayesian network is a directed graph in which each node is annotated with quantitative probability information. The full specification is as follows:

1. Each node corresponds to a random variable, which may be discrete or continuous.
2. A set of directed links or arrows connects pairs of nodes. If there is an arrow from node X to node Y, X is said to be a *parent* of Y. The graph has no directed cycles (and hence is a directed acyclic graph, or DAG.
3. Each node X_i has a conditional probability distribution $\mathbf{P}(X_i \mid Parents(X_i))$ that quantifies the effect of the parents on the node.

The topology of the network—the set of nodes and links—specifies the conditional independence relationships that hold in the domain, in a way that will be made precise shortly. The *intuitive* meaning of an arrow is typically that X has a *direct influence* on Y, which suggests that causes should be parents of effects. It is usually easy for a domain expert to decide what direct influences exist in the domain—much easier, in fact, than actually specifying the probabilities themselves. Once the topology of the Bayesian network is laid out, we need only specify a conditional probability distribution for each variable, given its parents. We will see that the combination of the topology and the conditional distributions suffices to specify (implicitly) the full joint distribution for all the variables.

Consider a simple world, consisting of the variables *Toothache*, *Cavity*, *Catch*, and *Weather*. *Weather* is independent of the other variables; furthermore, *Toothache* and *Catch* are conditionally independent, given *Cavity*. These relationships are represented by the Bayesian network structure shown in Figure 1. Formally, the conditional independence of *Toothache* and *Catch*, given *Cavity*, is indicated by the *absence* of a link between *Toothache* and *Catch*. Intuitively, the network represents the fact that *Cavity* is a direct cause of *Toothache* and *Catch*, whereas no direct causal relationship exists between *Toothache* and *Catch*.

Now consider the following example, which is just a little more complex. You have a new burglar alarm installed at home. It is fairly reliable at detecting a burglary, but also responds on occasion to minor earthquakes. (This example is due to Judea Pearl, a resident of Los Angeles—hence the acute interest in earthquakes.) You also have two neighbors, John and Mary, who have promised to call you at work when they hear the alarm. John nearly always calls when he hears the alarm, but sometimes confuses the telephone ringing with

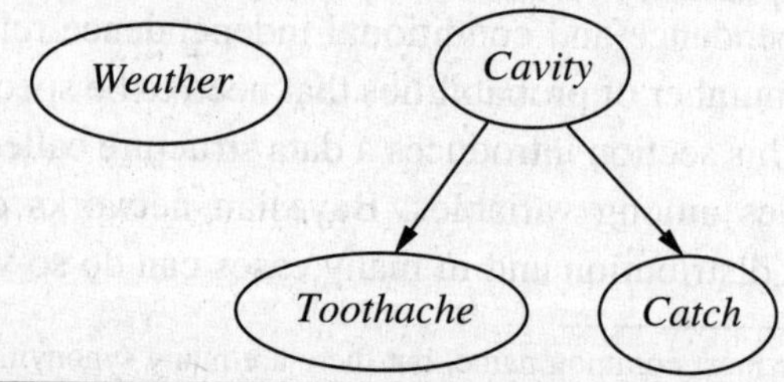

Figure 1 A simple Bayesian network in which *Weather* is independent of the other three variables and *Toothache* and *Catch* are conditionally independent, given *Cavity*.

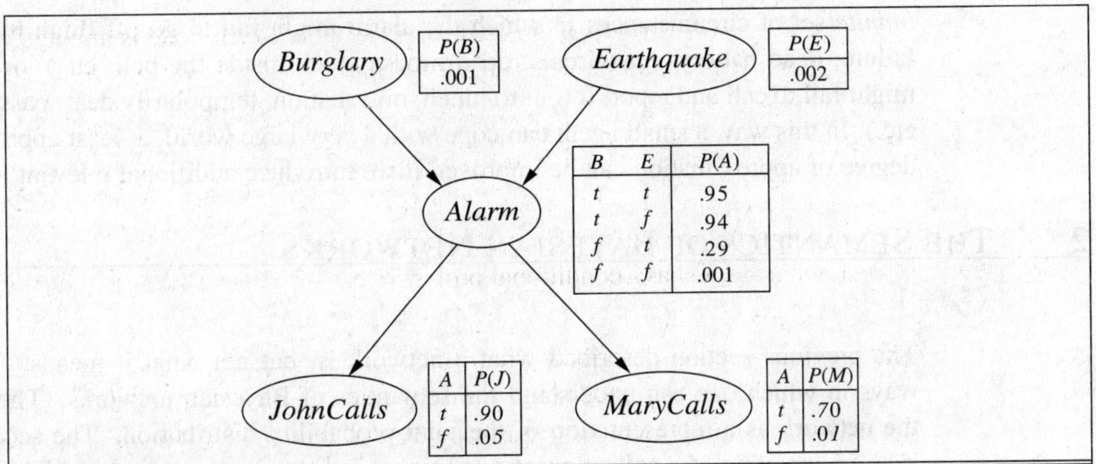

Figure 2 A typical Bayesian network, showing both the topology and the conditional probability tables (CPTs). In the CPTs, the letters B, E, A, J, and M stand for *Burglary*, *Earthquake*, *Alarm*, *JohnCalls*, and *MaryCalls*, respectively.

the alarm and calls then, too. Mary, on the other hand, likes rather loud music and often misses the alarm altogether. Given the evidence of who has or has not called, we would like to estimate the probability of a burglary.

A Bayesian network for this domain appears in Figure 2. The network structure shows that burglary and earthquakes directly affect the probability of the alarm's going off, but whether John and Mary call depends only on the alarm. The network thus represents our assumptions that they do not perceive burglaries directly, they do not notice minor earthquakes, and they do not confer before calling.

CONDITIONAL PROBABILITY TABLE

The conditional distributions in Figure 2 are shown as a **conditional probability table**, or CPT. (This form of table can be used for discrete variables; other representations, including those suitable for continuous variables, are described in Section 2.) Each row

CONDITIONING CASE

in a CPT contains the conditional probability of each node value for a **conditioning case**. A conditioning case is just a possible combination of values for the parent nodes—a miniature possible world, if you like. Each row must sum to 1, because the entries represent an exhaustive set of cases for the variable. For Boolean variables, once you know that the probability of a true value is p, the probability of false must be $1 - p$, so we often omit the second number, as in Figure 2. In general, a table for a Boolean variable with k Boolean parents contains 2^k independently specifiable probabilities. A node with no parents has only one row, representing the prior probabilities of each possible value of the variable.

Notice that the network does not have nodes corresponding to Mary's currently listening to loud music or to the telephone ringing and confusing John. These factors are summarized in the uncertainty associated with the links from *Alarm* to *JohnCalls* and *MaryCalls*. This shows both laziness and ignorance in operation: it would be a lot of work to find out why those factors would be more or less likely in any particular case, and we have no reasonable way to obtain the relevant information anyway. The probabilities actually summarize a *potentially infinite* set of circumstances in which the alarm might fail to go off (high humidity, power failure, dead battery, cut wires, a dead mouse stuck inside the bell, etc.) or John or Mary might fail to call and report it (out to lunch, on vacation, temporarily deaf, passing helicopter, etc.). In this way, a small agent can cope with a very large world, at least approximately. The degree of approximation can be improved if we introduce additional relevant information.

2 THE SEMANTICS OF BAYESIAN NETWORKS

The previous section described what a network is, but not what it means. There are two ways in which one can understand the semantics of Bayesian networks. The first is to see the network as a representation of the joint probability distribution. The second is to view it as an encoding of a collection of conditional independence statements. The two views are equivalent, but the first turns out to be helpful in understanding how to *construct* networks, whereas the second is helpful in designing inference procedures.

2.1 Representing the full joint distribution

Viewed as a piece of "syntax," a Bayesian network is a directed acyclic graph with some numeric parameters attached to each node. One way to define what the network means—its semantics—is to define the way in which it represents a specific joint distribution over all the variables. To do this, we first need to retract (temporarily) what we said earlier about the parameters associated with each node. We said that those parameters correspond to conditional probabilities $\mathbf{P}(X_i \mid Parents(X_i))$; this is a true statement, but until we assign semantics to the network as a whole, we should think of them just as numbers $\theta(X_i \mid Parents(X_i))$.

A generic entry in the joint distribution is the probability of a conjunction of particular assignments to each variable, such as $P(X_1 = x_1 \wedge \ldots \wedge X_n = x_n)$. We use the notation $P(x_1, \ldots, x_n)$ as an abbreviation for this. The value of this entry is given by the formula

$$P(x_1, \ldots, x_n) = \prod_{i=1}^{n} \theta(x_i \mid parents(X_i)) , \tag{1}$$

where $parents(X_i)$ denotes the values of $Parents(X_i)$ that appear in $x_1, \ldots, x_n$. Thus, each entry in the joint distribution is represented by the product of the appropriate elements of the conditional probability tables (CPTs) in the Bayesian network.

From this definition, it is easy to prove that the parameters $\theta(X_i \mid Parents(X_i))$ are exactly the conditional probabilities $\mathbf{P}(X_i \mid Parents(X_i))$ implied by the joint distribution (see Exercise 2). Hence, we can rewrite Equation (1) as

$$P(x_1, \ldots, x_n) = \prod_{i=1}^{n} P(x_i \mid parents(X_i)) . \tag{2}$$

In other words, the tables we have been calling conditional probability tables really *are* conditional probability tables according to the semantics defined in Equation (1).

To illustrate this, we can calculate the probability that the alarm has sounded, but neither a burglary nor an earthquake has occurred, and both John and Mary call. We multiply entries from the joint distribution (using single-letter names for the variables):

$$\begin{aligned} P(j, m, a, \neg b, \neg e) &= P(j \mid a)P(m \mid a)P(a \mid \neg b \wedge \neg e)P(\neg b)P(\neg e) \\ &= 0.90 \times 0.70 \times 0.001 \times 0.999 \times 0.998 = 0.000628 . \end{aligned}$$

The full joint distribution can be used to answer any query about the domain. If a Bayesian network is a representation of the joint distribution, then it too can be used to answer any query, by summing all the relevant joint entries. Section 4 explains how to do this, but also describes methods that are much more efficient.

A method for constructing Bayesian networks

Equation (2) defines what a given Bayesian network means. The next step is to explain how to *construct* a Bayesian network in such a way that the resulting joint distribution is a good representation of a given domain. We will now show that Equation (2) implies certain conditional independence relationships that can be used to guide the knowledge engineer in constructing the topology of the network. First, we rewrite the entries in the joint distribution in terms of conditional probability, using the product rule.

$$P(x_1, \ldots, x_n) = P(x_n \mid x_{n-1}, \ldots, x_1)P(x_{n-1}, \ldots, x_1) .$$

Then we repeat the process, reducing each conjunctive probability to a conditional probability and a smaller conjunction. We end up with one big product:

$$\begin{aligned} P(x_1, \ldots, x_n) &= P(x_n \mid x_{n-1}, \ldots, x_1)P(x_{n-1} \mid x_{n-2}, \ldots, x_1) \cdots P(x_2 \mid x_1)P(x_1) \\ &= \prod_{i=1}^{n} P(x_i \mid x_{i-1}, \ldots, x_1) . \end{aligned}$$

CHAIN RULE

This identity is called the **chain rule**. It holds for any set of random variables. Comparing it with Equation (2), we see that the specification of the joint distribution is equivalent to the general assertion that, for every variable X_i in the network,

$$\mathbf{P}(X_i \mid X_{i-1}, \ldots, X_1) = \mathbf{P}(X_i \mid Parents(X_i)) , \tag{3}$$

provided that $Parents(X_i) \subseteq \{X_{i-1}, \ldots, X_1\}$. This last condition is satisfied by numbering the nodes in a way that is consistent with the partial order implicit in the graph structure.

What Equation (3) says is that the Bayesian network is a correct representation of the domain only if each node is conditionally independent of its other predecessors in the node ordering, given its parents. We can satisfy this condition with this methodology:

1. *Nodes:* First determine the set of variables that are required to model the domain. Now order them, $\{X_1, \ldots, X_n\}$. Any order will work, but the resulting network will be more compact if the variables are ordered such that causes precede effects.
2. *Links:* For $i = 1$ to n do:
   - Choose, from $X_1, \ldots, X_{i-1}$, a minimal set of parents for X_i, such that Equation (3) is satisfied.
   - For each parent insert a link from the parent to X_i.
   - CPTs: Write down the conditional probability table, $\mathbf{P}(X_i|Parents(X_i))$.

Intuitively, the parents of node X_i should contain all those nodes in $X_1, \ldots, X_{i-1}$ that *directly influence* X_i. For example, suppose we have completed the network in Figure 2 except for the choice of parents for *MaryCalls*. *MaryCalls* is certainly influenced by whether there is a *Burglary* or an *Earthquake*, but not *directly* influenced. Intuitively, our knowledge of the domain tells us that these events influence Mary's calling behavior only through their effect on the alarm. Also, given the state of the alarm, whether John calls has no influence on Mary's calling. Formally speaking, we believe that the following conditional independence statement holds:

$$\mathbf{P}(MaryCalls \mid JohnCalls, Alarm, Earthquake, Burglary) = \mathbf{P}(MaryCalls \mid Alarm)\,.$$

Thus, *Alarm* will be the only parent node for *MaryCalls*.

Because each node is connected only to earlier nodes, this construction method guarantees that the network is acyclic. Another important property of Bayesian networks is that they contain no redundant probability values. If there is no redundancy, then there is no chance for inconsistency: *it is impossible for the knowledge engineer or domain expert to create a Bayesian network that violates the axioms of probability.*

Compactness and node ordering

As well as being a complete and nonredundant representation of the domain, a Bayesian network can often be far more *compact* than the full joint distribution. This property is what makes it feasible to handle domains with many variables. The compactness of Bayesian networks is an example of a general property of **locally structured** (also called **sparse**) systems. In a locally structured system, each subcomponent interacts directly with only a bounded number of other components, regardless of the total number of components. Local structure is usually associated with linear rather than exponential growth in complexity. In the case of Bayesian networks, it is reasonable to suppose that in most domains each random variable is directly influenced by at most k others, for some constant k. If we assume n Boolean variables for simplicity, then the amount of information needed to specify each conditional probability table will be at most 2^k numbers, and the complete network can be specified by $n2^k$ numbers. In contrast, the joint distribution contains 2^n numbers. To make this concrete, suppose we have $n = 30$ nodes, each with five parents ($k = 5$). Then the Bayesian network requires 960 numbers, but the full joint distribution requires over a billion.

LOCALLY STRUCTURED

SPARSE

There are domains in which each variable can be influenced directly by all the others, so that the network is fully connected. Then specifying the conditional probability tables requires the same amount of information as specifying the joint distribution. In some domains, there will be slight dependencies that should strictly be included by adding a new link. But if these dependencies are tenuous, then it may not be worth the additional complexity in the network for the small gain in accuracy. For example, one might object to our burglary network on the grounds that if there is an earthquake, then John and Mary would not call even if they heard the alarm, because they assume that the earthquake is the cause. Whether to add the link from *Earthquake* to *JohnCalls* and *MaryCalls* (and thus enlarge the tables) depends on comparing the importance of getting more accurate probabilities with the cost of specifying the extra information.

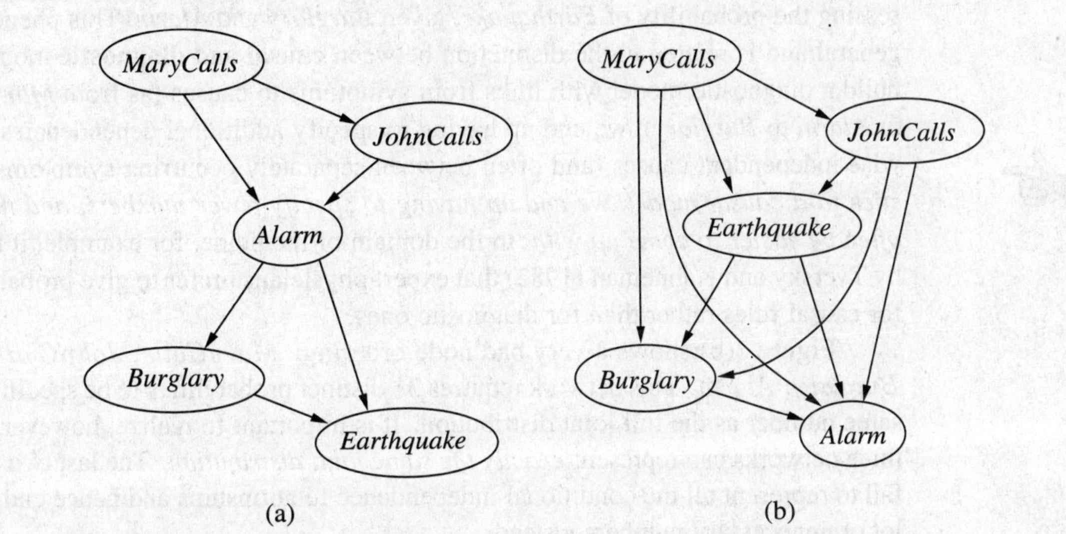

Figure 3 Network structure depends on order of introduction. In each network, we have introduced nodes in top-to-bottom order.

Even in a locally structured domain, we will get a compact Bayesian network only if we choose the node ordering well. What happens if we happen to choose the wrong order? Consider the burglary example again. Suppose we decide to add the nodes in the order $MaryCalls$, $JohnCalls$, $Alarm$, $Burglary$, $Earthquake$. We then get the somewhat more complicated network shown in Figure 3(a). The process goes as follows:

- Adding $MaryCalls$: No parents.
- Adding $JohnCalls$: If Mary calls, that probably means the alarm has gone off, which of course would make it more likely that John calls. Therefore, $JohnCalls$ needs $MaryCalls$ as a parent.
- Adding $Alarm$: Clearly, if both call, it is more likely that the alarm has gone off than if just one or neither calls, so we need both $MaryCalls$ and $JohnCalls$ as parents.
- Adding $Burglary$: If we know the alarm state, then the call from John or Mary might give us information about our phone ringing or Mary's music, but not about burglary:

$$\mathbf{P}(Burglary \mid Alarm, JohnCalls, MaryCalls) = \mathbf{P}(Burglary \mid Alarm) .$$

  Hence we need just $Alarm$ as parent.
- Adding $Earthquake$: If the alarm is on, it is more likely that there has been an earthquake. (The alarm is an earthquake detector of sorts.) But if we know that there has been a burglary, then that explains the alarm, and the probability of an earthquake would be only slightly above normal. Hence, we need both $Alarm$ and $Burglary$ as parents.

The resulting network has two more links than the original network in Figure 2 and requires three more probabilities to be specified. What's worse, some of the links represent tenuous relationships that require difficult and unnatural probability judgments, such as assessing the probability of *Earthquake*, given *Burglary* and *Alarm*. This phenomenon is quite general and is related to the distinction between **causal** and **diagnostic** models. If we try to build a diagnostic model with links from symptoms to causes (as from *MaryCalls* to *Alarm* or *Alarm* to *Burglary*), we end up having to specify additional dependencies between otherwise independent causes (and often between separately occurring symptoms as well). *If we stick to a causal model, we end up having to specify fewer numbers, and the numbers will often be easier to come up with.* In the domain of medicine, for example, it has been shown by Tversky and Kahneman (1982) that expert physicians prefer to give probability judgments for causal rules rather than for diagnostic ones.

Figure 3(b) shows a very bad node ordering: $MaryCalls$, $JohnCalls$, $Earthquake$, $Burglary$, $Alarm$. This network requires 31 distinct probabilities to be specified—exactly the same number as the full joint distribution. It is important to realize, however, that any of the three networks can represent *exactly the same joint distribution*. The last two versions simply fail to represent all the conditional independence relationships and hence end up specifying a lot of unnecessary numbers instead.

2.2 Conditional independence relations in Bayesian networks

We have provided a "numerical" semantics for Bayesian networks in terms of the representation of the full joint distribution, as in Equation (2). Using this semantics to derive a method for constructing Bayesian networks, we were led to the consequence that a node is conditionally independent of its other predecessors, given its parents. It turns out that we can also go in the other direction. We can start from a "topological" semantics that specifies the conditional independence relationships encoded by the graph structure, and from this we can derive the "numerical" semantics. The topological semantics[2] specifies that each variable is conditionally independent of its non-**descendants**, given its parents. For example, in Figure 2, $JohnCalls$ is independent of $Burglary$, $Earthquake$, and $MaryCalls$ given the value of $Alarm$. The definition is illustrated in Figure 4(a). From these conditional independence assertions and the interpretation of the network parameters $\theta(X_i \,|\, Parents(X_i))$ as specifications of conditional probabilities $\mathbf{P}(X_i \,|\, Parents(X_i))$, the full joint distribution given in Equation (2) can be reconstructed. In this sense, the "numerical" semantics and the "topological" semantics are equivalent.

DESCENDANT

Another important independence property is implied by the topological semantics: a node is conditionally independent of all other nodes in the network, given its parents, children, and children's parents—that is, given its **Markov blanket**. (Exercise 7 asks you to prove this.) For example, $Burglary$ is independent of $JohnCalls$ and $MaryCalls$, given $Alarm$ and $Earthquake$. This property is illustrated in Figure 4(b).

MARKOV BLANKET

[2] There is also a general topological criterion called **d-separation** for deciding whether a set of nodes $\mathbf{X}$ is conditionally independent of another set $\mathbf{Y}$, given a third set $\mathbf{Z}$. The criterion is rather complicated and is not needed for deriving the algorithms in this chapter, so we omit it. Details may be found in Pearl (1988) or Darwiche (2009). Shachter (1998) gives a more intuitive method of ascertaining d-separation.

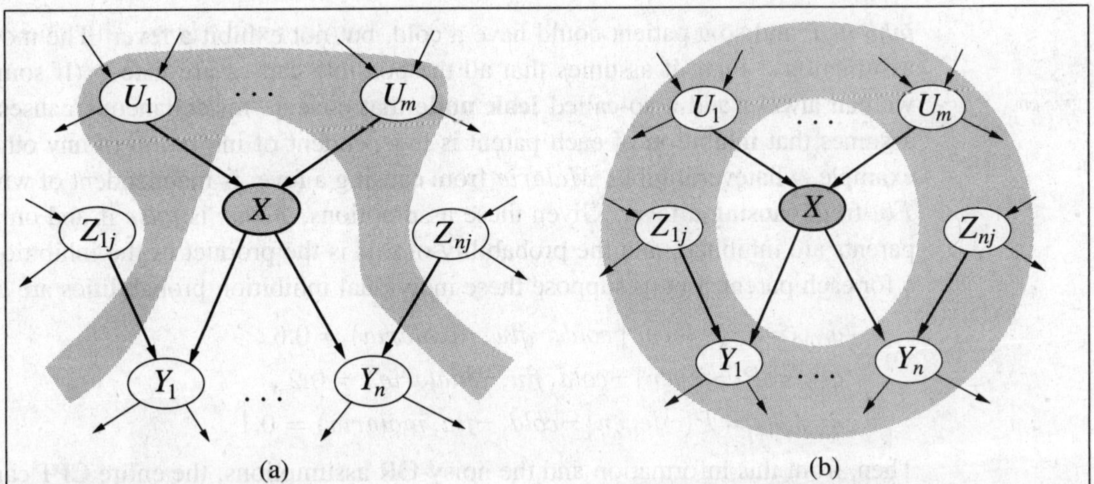

Figure 4 (a) A node X is conditionally independent of its non-descendants (e.g., the Z_{ij}s) given its parents (the U_is shown in the gray area). (b) A node X is conditionally independent of all other nodes in the network given its Markov blanket (the gray area).

3 Efficient Representation of Conditional Distributions

Even if the maximum number of parents k is smallish, filling in the CPT for a node requires up to $O(2^k)$ numbers and perhaps a great deal of experience with all the possible conditioning cases. In fact, this is a worst-case scenario in which the relationship between the parents and the child is completely arbitrary. Usually, such relationships are describable by a **canonical distribution** that fits some standard pattern. In such cases, the complete table can be specified by naming the pattern and perhaps supplying a few parameters—much easier than supplying an exponential number of parameters.

CANONICAL DISTRIBUTION

DETERMINISTIC NODES

The simplest example is provided by **deterministic nodes**. A deterministic node has its value specified exactly by the values of its parents, with no uncertainty. The relationship can be a logical one: for example, the relationship between the parent nodes *Canadian*, *US*, *Mexican* and the child node *NorthAmerican* is simply that the child is the disjunction of the parents. The relationship can also be numerical: for example, if the parent nodes are the prices of a particular model of car at several dealers and the child node is the price that a bargain hunter ends up paying, then the child node is the minimum of the parent values; or if the parent nodes are a lake's inflows (rivers, runoff, precipitation) and outflows (rivers, evaporation, seepage) and the child is the change in the water level of the lake, then the value of the child is the sum of the inflow parents minus the sum of the outflow parents.

NOISY-OR

Uncertain relationships can often be characterized by so-called **noisy** logical relationships. The standard example is the **noisy-OR** relation, which is a generalization of the logical OR. In propositional logic, we might say that *Fever* is true if and only if *Cold*, *Flu*, or *Malaria* is true. The noisy-OR model allows for uncertainty about the ability of each parent to cause the child to be true—the causal relationship between parent and child may be *inhibited*, and so a patient could have a cold, but not exhibit a fever. The model makes two assumptions. First, it assumes that all the possible causes are listed. (If some are missing, we can always add a so-called **leak node** that covers "miscellaneous causes.") Second, it assumes that inhibition of each parent is independent of inhibition of any other parents: for example, whatever inhibits $Malaria$ from causing a fever is independent of whatever inhibits Flu from causing a fever. Given these assumptions, $Fever$ is *false* if and only if all its *true* parents are inhibited, and the probability of this is the product of the inhibition probabilities q for each parent. Let us suppose these individual inhibition probabilities are as follows:

LEAK NODE

$$q_{\text{cold}} = P(\neg fever \mid cold, \neg flu, \neg malaria) = 0.6 ,$$
$$q_{\text{flu}} = P(\neg fever \mid \neg cold, flu, \neg malaria) = 0.2 ,$$
$$q_{\text{malaria}} = P(\neg fever \mid \neg cold, \neg flu, malaria) = 0.1 .$$

Then, from this information and the noisy-OR assumptions, the entire CPT can be built. The general rule is that

$$P(x_i \mid parents(X_i)) = 1 - \prod_{\{j : X_j = true\}} q_j ,$$

where the product is taken over the parents that are set to true for that row of the CPT. The following table illustrates this calculation:

$Cold$	Flu	$Malaria$	$P(Fever)$	$P(\neg Fever)$
F	F	F	0.0	1.0
F	F	T	0.9	**0.1**
F	T	F	0.8	**0.2**
F	T	T	0.98	$0.02 = 0.2 \times 0.1$
T	F	F	0.4	**0.6**
T	F	T	0.94	$0.06 = 0.6 \times 0.1$
T	T	F	0.88	$0.12 = 0.6 \times 0.2$
T	T	T	0.988	$0.012 = 0.6 \times 0.2 \times 0.1$

In general, noisy logical relationships in which a variable depends on k parents can be described using $O(k)$ parameters instead of $O(2^k)$ for the full conditional probability table. This makes assessment and learning much easier. For example, the CPCS network (Pradhan *et al.*, 1994) uses noisy-OR and noisy-MAX distributions to model relationships among diseases and symptoms in internal medicine. With 448 nodes and 906 links, it requires only 8,254 values instead of 133,931,430 for a network with full CPTs.

Bayesian nets with continuous variables

Many real-world problems involve continuous quantities, such as height, mass, temperature, and money; in fact, much of statistics deals with random variables whose domains are continuous. By definition, continuous variables have an infinite number of possible values, so it is impossible to specify conditional probabilities explicitly for each value. One possible way to handle continuous variables is to avoid them by using **discretization**—that is, dividing up the

DISCRETIZATION

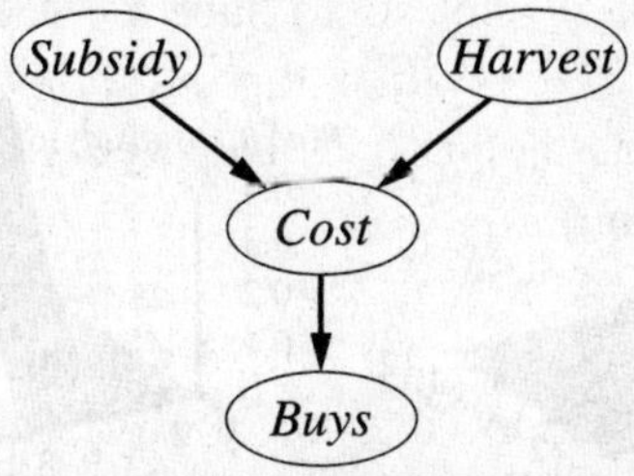

Figure 5 A simple network with discrete variables ($Subsidy$ and $Buys$) and continuous variables ($Harvest$ and $Cost$).

possible values into a fixed set of intervals. For example, temperatures could be divided into (<0°C), (0°C−100°C), and (>100°C). Discretization is sometimes an adequate solution, but often results in a considerable loss of accuracy and very large CPTs. The most common solution is to define standard families of probability density functions (see Appendix A) that are specified by a finite number of **parameters**. For example, a Gaussian (or normal) distribution $N(\mu, \sigma^2)(x)$ has the mean μ and the variance σ^2 as parameters. Yet another solution—sometimes called a **nonparametric** representation—is to define the conditional distribution implicitly with a collection of instances, each containing specific values of the parent and child variables.

PARAMETER

NONPARAMETRIC

A network with both discrete and continuous variables is called a **hybrid Bayesian network**. To specify a hybrid network, we have to specify two new kinds of distributions: the conditional distribution for a continuous variable given discrete or continuous parents; and the conditional distribution for a discrete variable given continuous parents. Consider the simple example in Figure 5, in which a customer buys some fruit depending on its cost, which depends in turn on the size of the harvest and whether the government's subsidy scheme is operating. The variable $Cost$ is continuous and has continuous and discrete parents; the variable $Buys$ is discrete and has a continuous parent.

HYBRID BAYESIAN NETWORK

For the $Cost$ variable, we need to specify $\mathbf{P}(Cost \mid Harvest, Subsidy)$. The discrete parent is handled by enumeration—that is, by specifying both $P(Cost \mid Harvest, subsidy)$ and $P(Cost \mid Harvest, \neg subsidy)$. To handle $Harvest$, we specify how the distribution over the cost c depends on the continuous value h of $Harvest$. In other words, we specify the *parameters* of the cost distribution as a function of h. The most common choice is the **linear Gaussian** distribution, in which the child has a Gaussian distribution whose mean μ varies linearly with the value of the parent and whose standard deviation σ is fixed. We need two distributions, one for $subsidy$ and one for $\neg subsidy$, with different parameters:

LINEAR GAUSSIAN

$$P(c \mid h, subsidy) = N(a_t h + b_t, \sigma_t^2)(c) = \frac{1}{\sigma_t \sqrt{2\pi}} e^{-\frac{1}{2}\left(\frac{c-(a_t h + b_t)}{\sigma_t}\right)^2}$$

$$P(c \mid h, \neg subsidy) = N(a_f h + b_f, \sigma_f^2)(c) = \frac{1}{\sigma_f \sqrt{2\pi}} e^{-\frac{1}{2}\left(\frac{c-(a_f h + b_f)}{\sigma_f}\right)^2} .$$

For this example, then, the conditional distribution for $Cost$ is specified by naming the linear Gaussian distribution and providing the parameters a_t, b_t, σ_t, a_f, b_f, and σ_f. Figures 6(a)

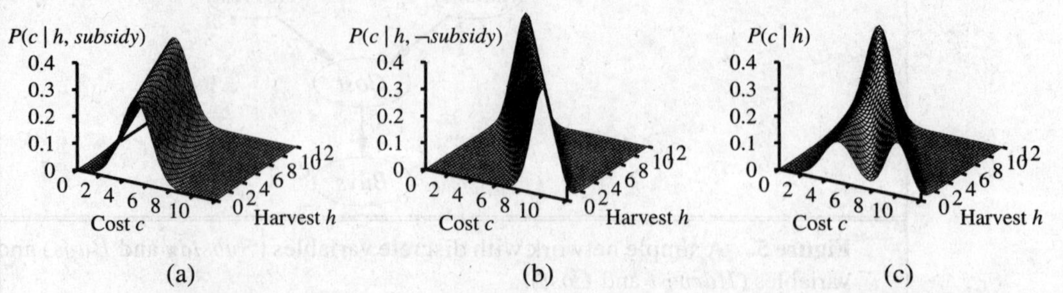

Figure 6 The graphs in (a) and (b) show the probability distribution over *Cost* as a function of *Harvest* size, with *Subsidy* true and false, respectively. Graph (c) shows the distribution $P(Cost \mid Harvest)$, obtained by summing over the two subsidy cases.

and (b) show these two relationships. Notice that in each case the slope is negative, because cost decreases as supply increases. (Of course, the assumption of linearity implies that the cost becomes negative at some point; the linear model is reasonable only if the harvest size is limited to a narrow range.) Figure 6(c) shows the distribution $P(c \mid h)$, averaging over the two possible values of *Subsidy* and assuming that each has prior probability 0.5. This shows that even with very simple models, quite interesting distributions can be represented.

The linear Gaussian conditional distribution has some special properties. A network containing only continuous variables with linear Gaussian distributions has a joint distribution that is a multivariate Gaussian distribution over all the variables (Exercise 9). Furthermore, the posterior distribution given any evidence also has this property.[3] When discrete variables are added as parents (not as children) of continuous variables, the network defines a **conditional Gaussian**, or CG, distribution: given any assignment to the discrete variables, the distribution over the continuous variables is a multivariate Gaussian.

CONDITIONAL GAUSSIAN

Now we turn to the distributions for discrete variables with continuous parents. Consider, for example, the *Buys* node in Figure 5. It seems reasonable to assume that the customer will buy if the cost is low and will not buy if it is high and that the probability of buying varies smoothly in some intermediate region. In other words, the conditional distribution is like a "soft" threshold function. One way to make soft thresholds is to use the *integral* of the standard normal distribution:

$$\Phi(x) = \int_{-\infty}^{x} N(0,1)(x)dx \; .$$

Then the probability of *Buys* given *Cost* might be

$$P(buys \mid Cost = c) = \Phi((-c + \mu)/\sigma) \; ,$$

which means that the cost threshold occurs around μ, the width of the threshold region is proportional to σ, and the probability of buying decreases as cost increases. This **probit distri-**

[3] It follows that inference in linear Gaussian networks takes only $O(n^3)$ time in the worst case, regardless of the network topology. In Section 4, we see that inference for networks of discrete variables is NP-hard.

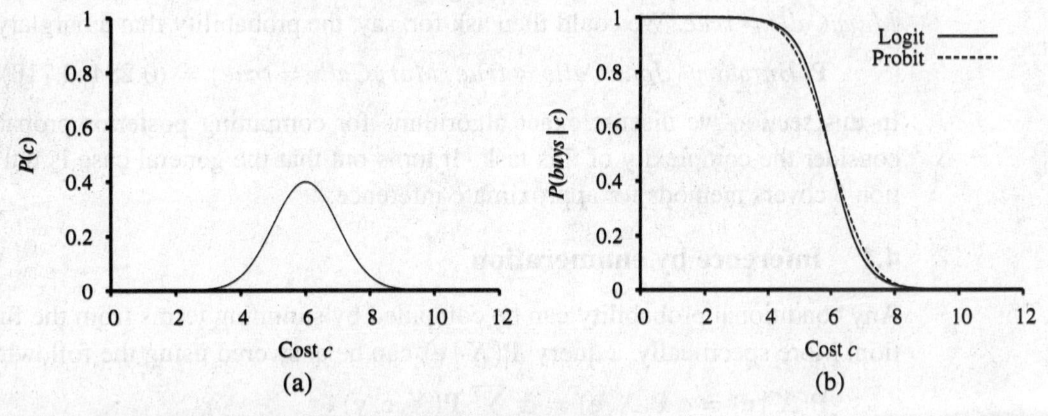

Figure 7 (a) A normal (Gaussian) distribution for the cost threshold, centered on $\mu = 6.0$ with standard deviation $\sigma = 1.0$. (b) Logit and probit distributions for the probability of *buys* given *cost*, for the parameters $\mu = 6.0$ and $\sigma = 1.0$.

PROBIT DISTRIBUTION

bution (pronounced "pro-bit" and short for "probability unit") is illustrated in Figure 7(a). The form can be justified by proposing that the underlying decision process has a hard threshold, but that the precise location of the threshold is subject to random Gaussian noise.

LOGIT DISTRIBUTION

LOGISTIC FUNCTION

An alternative to the probit model is the **logit distribution** (pronounced "low-jit"). It uses the **logistic function** $1/(1 + e^{-x})$ to produce a soft threshold:

$$P(buys \mid Cost = c) = \frac{1}{1 + exp(-2\frac{-c+\mu}{\sigma})} .$$

This is illustrated in Figure 7(b). The two distributions look similar, but the logit actually has much longer "tails." The probit is often a better fit to real situations, but the logit is sometimes easier to deal with mathematically. It is used widely in neural networks. Both probit and logit can be generalized to handle multiple continuous parents by taking a linear combination of the parent values.

4 EXACT INFERENCE IN BAYESIAN NETWORKS

EVENT

The basic task for any probabilistic inference system is to compute the posterior probability distribution for a set of **query variables**, given some observed **event**—that is, some assignment of values to a set of **evidence variables**. To simplify the presentation, we will consider only one query variable at a time; the algorithms can easily be extended to queries with multiple variables. X denotes the query variable; **E** denotes the set of evidence variables $E1,...,Em$, and **e** is a particular observed event; **Y** will denotes the nonevidence, nonquery variables $Y1,...,Yl$ (called the **hidden variables**). Thus, the complete set of variables is $\mathbf{X} = \{X\}$? **E** ? **Y**. A typical query asks for the posterior probability distribution $\mathbf{P}(X| \mathbf{e})$.

HIDDEN VARIABLE

In the burglary network, we might observe the event in which $JohnCalls = true$ and $MaryCalls = true$. We could then ask for, say, the probability that a burglary has occurred:

$$\mathbf{P}(Burglary \mid JohnCalls = true, MaryCalls = true) = \langle 0.284, 0.716 \rangle .$$

In this section we discuss exact algorithms for computing posterior probabilities and will consider the complexity of this task. It turns out that the general case is intractable, so Section 5 covers methods for approximate inference.

4.1 Inference by enumeration

Any conditional probability can be computed by summing terms from the full joint distribution. More specifically, a query $\mathbf{P}(X \mid \mathbf{e})$ can be answered using the following equation:

$$\mathbf{P}(X \mid \mathbf{e}) = \alpha\, \mathbf{P}(X, \mathbf{e}) = \alpha \sum_{\mathbf{y}} \mathbf{P}(X, \mathbf{e}, \mathbf{y}) .$$

Now, a Bayesian network gives a complete representation of the full joint distribution. More specifically, Equation (2) shows that the terms $P(x, \mathbf{e}, \mathbf{y})$ in the joint distribution can be written as products of conditional probabilities from the network. Therefore, *a query can be answered using a Bayesian network by computing sums of products of conditional probabilities from the network.*

Consider the query $\mathbf{P}(Burglary \mid JohnCalls = true, MaryCalls = true)$. The hidden variables for this query are *Earthquake* and *Alarm*. From Equation 9, in the chapter "Knowledge Representation," using initial letters for the variables to shorten the expressions, we have[4]

$$\mathbf{P}(B \mid j, m) = \alpha\, \mathbf{P}(B, j, m) = \alpha \sum_{e} \sum_{a} \mathbf{P}(B, j, m, e, a,) .$$

The semantics of Bayesian networks (Equation (2)) then gives us an expression in terms of CPT entries. For simplicity, we do this just for $Burglary = true$:

$$P(b \mid j, m) = \alpha \sum_{e} \sum_{a} P(b) P(e) P(a \mid b, e) P(j \mid a) P(m \mid a) .$$

To compute this expression, we have to add four terms, each computed by multiplying five numbers. In the worst case, where we have to sum out almost all the variables, the complexity of the algorithm for a network with n Boolean variables is $O(n2^n)$.

An improvement can be obtained from the following simple observations: the $P(b)$ term is a constant and can be moved outside the summations over a and e, and the $P(e)$ term can be moved outside the summation over a. Hence, we have

$$P(b \mid j, m) = \alpha\, P(b) \sum_{e} P(e) \sum_{a} P(a \mid b, e) P(j \mid a) P(m \mid a) . \quad (4)$$

This expression can be evaluated by looping through the variables in order, multiplying CPT entries as we go. For each summation, we also need to loop over the variable's possible

[4] An expression such as $\sum_e P(a, e)$ means to sum $P(A = a, E = e)$ for all possible values of e. When E is Boolean, there is an ambiguity in that $P(e)$ is used to mean both $P(E = true)$ and $P(E = e)$, but it should be clear from context which is intended; in particular, in the context of a sum the latter is intended.

values. The structure of this computation is shown in Figure 8. Using the numbers from Figure 2, we obtain $P(b \mid j, m) = \alpha \times 0.00059224$. The corresponding computation for $\neg b$ yields $\alpha \times 0.0014919$; hence,

$$\mathbf{P}(B \mid j, m) = \alpha \langle 0.00059224, 0.0014919 \rangle \approx \langle 0.284, 0.716 \rangle .$$

That is, the chance of a burglary, given calls from both neighbors, is about 28%.

The evaluation process for the expression in Equation (4) is shown as an expression tree in Figure 8. The ENUMERATION-ASK algorithm in Figure 9 evaluates such trees using depth-first recursion. The algorithm is very similar in structure to the backtracking algorithm for solving CSPs and the DPLL algorithm for satisfiability.

The space complexity of ENUMERATION-ASK is only linear in the number of variables: the algorithm sums over the full joint distribution without ever constructing it explicitly. Unfortunately, its time complexity for a network with n Boolean variables is always $O(2^n)$—better than the $O(n\,2^n)$ for the simple approach described earlier, but still rather grim.

Note that the tree in Figure 8 makes explicit the *repeated subexpressions* evaluated by the algorithm. The products $P(j \mid a)P(m \mid a)$ and $P(j \mid \neg a)P(m \mid \neg a)$ are computed twice, once for each value of e. The next section describes a general method that avoids such wasted computations.

4.2 The variable elimination algorithm

The enumeration algorithm can be improved substantially by eliminating repeated calculations of the kind illustrated in Figure 8. The idea is simple: do the calculation once and save the results for later use. This is a form of dynamic programming. There are several versions of this approach; we present the **variable elimination** algorithm, which is the simplest. Variable elimination works by evaluating expressions such as Equation (4) in *right-to-left* order (that is, *bottom up* in Figure 8). Intermediate results are stored, and summations over each variable are done only for those portions of the expression that depend on the variable.

VARIABLE ELIMINATION

Let us illustrate this process for the burglary network. We evaluate the expression

$$\mathbf{P}(B \mid j, m) = \alpha \underbrace{\mathbf{P}(B)}_{\mathbf{f}_1(B)} \sum_e \underbrace{P(e)}_{\mathbf{f}_2(E)} \sum_a \underbrace{\mathbf{P}(a \mid B, e)}_{\mathbf{f}_3(A,B,E)} \underbrace{P(j \mid a)}_{\mathbf{f}_4(A)} \underbrace{P(m \mid a)}_{\mathbf{f}_5(A)} .$$

Notice that we have annotated each part of the expression with the name of the corresponding **factor**; each factor is a matrix indexed by the values of its argument variables. For example, the factors $\mathbf{f}_4(A)$ and $\mathbf{f}_5(A)$ corresponding to $P(j \mid a)$ and $P(m \mid a)$ depend just on A because J and M are fixed by the query. They are therefore two-element vectors:

FACTOR

$$\mathbf{f}_4(A) = \begin{pmatrix} P(j \mid a) \\ P(j \mid \neg a) \end{pmatrix} = \begin{pmatrix} 0.90 \\ 0.05 \end{pmatrix} \qquad \mathbf{f}_5(A) = \begin{pmatrix} P(m \mid a) \\ P(m \mid \neg a) \end{pmatrix} = \begin{pmatrix} 0.70 \\ 0.01 \end{pmatrix} .$$

$\mathbf{f}_3(A, B, E)$ will be a $2 \times 2 \times 2$ matrix, which is hard to show on the printed page. (The "first" element is given by $P(a \mid b, e) = 0.95$ and the "last" by $P(\neg a \mid \neg b, \neg e) = 0.999$.) In terms of factors, the query expression is written as

$$\mathbf{P}(B \mid j, m) = \alpha\, \mathbf{f}_1(B) \times \sum_e \mathbf{f}_2(E) \times \sum_a \mathbf{f}_3(A, B, E) \times \mathbf{f}_4(A) \times \mathbf{f}_5(A)$$

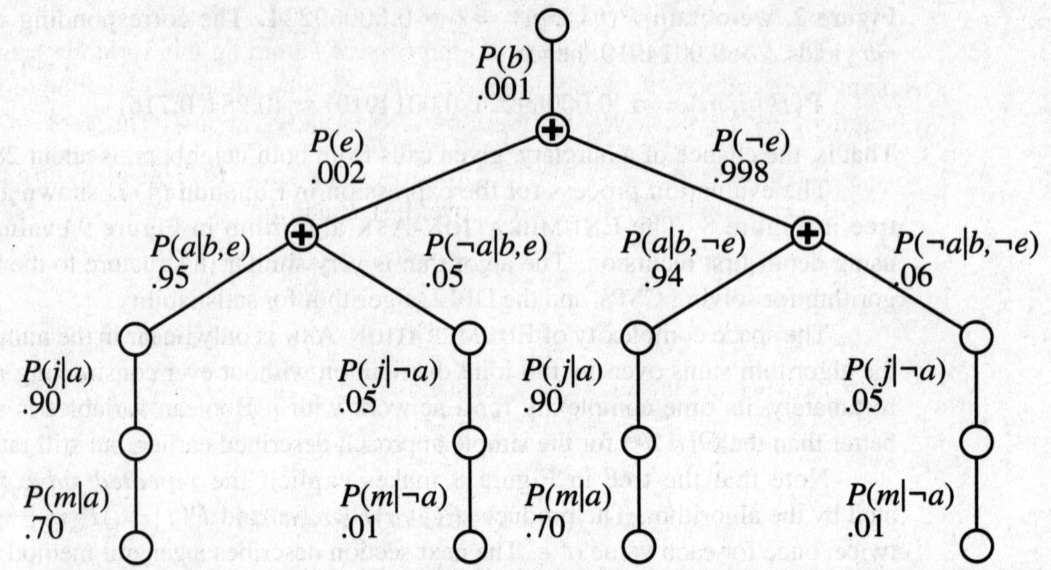

Figure 8 The structure of the expression shown in Equation (4). The evaluation proceeds top down, multiplying values along each path and summing at the "+" nodes. Notice the repetition of the paths for j and m.

```
function ENUMERATION-ASK(X, e, bn) returns a distribution over X
  inputs: X, the query variable
          e, observed values for variables E
          bn, a Bayes net with variables {X} ∪ E ∪ Y   /* Y = hidden variables */

  Q(X) ← a distribution over X, initially empty
  for each value x_i of X do
      Q(x_i) ← ENUMERATE-ALL(bn.VARS, e_{x_i})
         where e_{x_i} is e extended with X = x_i
  return NORMALIZE(Q(X))

function ENUMERATE-ALL(vars, e) returns a real number
  if EMPTY?(vars) then return 1.0
  Y ← FIRST(vars)
  if Y has value y in e
      then return P(y | parents(Y)) × ENUMERATE-ALL(REST(vars), e)
      else return Σ_y P(y | parents(Y)) × ENUMERATE-ALL(REST(vars), e_y)
         where e_y is e extended with Y = y
```

Figure 9 The enumeration algorithm for answering queries on Bayesian networks.

where the "×" operator is not ordinary matrix multiplication but instead the **pointwise product** operation, to be described shortly.

POINTWISE PRODUCT

The process of evaluation is a process of summing out variables (right to left) from pointwise products of factors to produce new factors, eventually yielding a factor that is the solution, i.e., the posterior distribution over the query variable. The steps are as follows:

- First, we sum out A from the product of $\mathbf{f}_3$, $\mathbf{f}_4$, and $\mathbf{f}_5$. This gives us a new 2×2 factor $\mathbf{f}_6(B, E)$ whose indices range over just B and E:

$$\begin{aligned}\mathbf{f}_6(B,E) &= \sum_a \mathbf{f}_3(A,B,E) \times \mathbf{f}_4(A) \times \mathbf{f}_5(A) \\ &= (\mathbf{f}_3(a,B,E) \times \mathbf{f}_4(a) \times \mathbf{f}_5(a)) + (\mathbf{f}_3(\neg a,B,E) \times \mathbf{f}_4(\neg a) \times \mathbf{f}_5(\neg a)).\end{aligned}$$

Now we are left with the expression

$$\mathbf{P}(B \mid j,m) = \alpha\, \mathbf{f}_1(B) \times \sum_e \mathbf{f}_2(E) \times \mathbf{f}_6(B,E).$$

- Next, we sum out E from the product of $\mathbf{f}_2$ and $\mathbf{f}_6$:

$$\begin{aligned}\mathbf{f}_7(B) &= \sum_e \mathbf{f}_2(E) \times \mathbf{f}_6(B,E) \\ &= \mathbf{f}_2(e) \times \mathbf{f}_6(B,e) + \mathbf{f}_2(\neg e) \times \mathbf{f}_6(B,\neg e).\end{aligned}$$

This leaves the expression

$$\mathbf{P}(B \mid j,m) = \alpha\, \mathbf{f}_1(B) \times \mathbf{f}_7(B)$$

which can be evaluated by taking the pointwise product and normalizing the result.

Examining this sequence, we see that two basic computational operations are required: pointwise product of a pair of factors, and summing out a variable from a product of factors. The next section describes each of these operations.

Operations on factors

The pointwise product of two factors $\mathbf{f}_1$ and $\mathbf{f}_2$ yields a new factor $\mathbf{f}$ whose variables are the *union* of the variables in $\mathbf{f}_1$ and $\mathbf{f}_2$ and whose elements are given by the product of the corresponding elements in the two factors. Suppose the two factors have variables $Y_1, \ldots, Y_k$ in common. Then we have

$$\mathbf{f}(X_1 \ldots X_j, Y_1 \ldots Y_k, Z_1 \ldots Z_l) = \mathbf{f}_1(X_1 \ldots X_j, Y_1 \ldots Y_k)\, \mathbf{f}_2(Y_1 \ldots Y_k, Z, \ldots Z_l).$$

If all the variables are binary, then $\mathbf{f}_1$ and $\mathbf{f}_2$ have 2^{j+k} and 2^{k+l} entries, respectively, and the pointwise product has 2^{j+k+l} entries. For example, given two factors $\mathbf{f}_1(A,B)$ and $\mathbf{f}_2(B,C)$, the pointwise product $\mathbf{f}_1 \times \mathbf{f}_2 = \mathbf{f}_3(A,B,C)$ has $2^{1+1+1} = 8$ entries, as illustrated in Figure 10. Notice that the factor resulting from a pointwise product can contain more variables than any of the factors being multiplied and that the size of a factor is exponential in the number of variables. This is where both space and time complexity arise in the variable elimination algorithm.

A	B	$\mathbf{f}_1(A,B)$	B	C	$\mathbf{f}_2(B,C)$	A	B	C	$\mathbf{f}_3(A,B,C)$
T	T	.3	T	T	.2	T	T	T	$.3\times.2=.06$
T	F	.7	T	F	.8	T	T	F	$.3\times.8=.24$
F	T	.9	F	T	.6	T	F	T	$.7\times.6=.42$
F	F	.1	F	F	.4	T	F	F	$.7\times.4=.28$
						F	T	T	$.9\times.2=.18$
						F	T	F	$.9\times.8=.72$
						F	F	T	$.1\times.6=.06$
						F	F	F	$.1\times.4=.04$

Figure 10 Illustrating pointwise multiplication: $\mathbf{f}_1(A,B)\times\mathbf{f}_2(B,C)=\mathbf{f}_3(A,B,C)$.

Summing out a variable from a product of factors is done by adding up the submatrices formed by fixing the variable to each of its values in turn. For example, to sum out A from $\mathbf{f}_3(A,B,C)$, we write

$$\begin{aligned}\mathbf{f}(B,C) &= \sum_a \mathbf{f}_3(A,B,C) = \mathbf{f}_3(a,B,C)+\mathbf{f}_3(\neg a,B,C)\\ &= \begin{pmatrix} .06 & .24\\ .42 & .28\end{pmatrix} + \begin{pmatrix} .18 & .72\\ .06 & .04\end{pmatrix} = \begin{pmatrix} .24 & .96\\ .48 & .32\end{pmatrix}.\end{aligned}$$

The only trick is to notice that any factor that does *not* depend on the variable to be summed out can be moved outside the summation. For example, if we were to sum out E first in the burglary network, the relevant part of the expression would be

$$\sum_e \mathbf{f}_2(E)\times\mathbf{f}_3(A,B,E)\times\mathbf{f}_4(A)\times\mathbf{f}_5(A) = \mathbf{f}_4(A)\times\mathbf{f}_5(A)\times\sum_e \mathbf{f}_2(E)\times\mathbf{f}_3(A,B,E).$$

Now the pointwise product inside the summation is computed, and the variable is summed out of the resulting matrix.

Notice that matrices are *not* multiplied until we need to sum out a variable from the accumulated product. At that point, we multiply just those matrices that include the variable to be summed out. Given functions for pointwise product and summing out, the variable elimination algorithm itself can be written quite simply, as shown in Figure 11.

Variable ordering and variable relevance

The algorithm in Figure 11 includes an unspecified ORDER function to choose an ordering for the variables. Every choice of ordering yields a valid algorithm, but different orderings cause different intermediate factors to be generated during the calculation. For example, in the calculation shown previously, we eliminated A before E; if we do it the other way, the calculation becomes

$$\mathbf{P}(B\,|\,j,m) = \alpha\,\mathbf{f}_1(B)\times\sum_a \mathbf{f}_4(A)\times\mathbf{f}_5(A)\times\sum_e \mathbf{f}_2(E)\times\mathbf{f}_3(A,B,E),$$

during which a new factor $\mathbf{f}_6(A,B)$ will be generated.

In general, the time and space requirements of variable elimination are dominated by the size of the largest factor constructed during the operation of the algorithm. This in turn

```
function ELIMINATION-ASK(X, e, bn) returns a distribution over X
  inputs: X, the query variable
          e, observed values for variables E
          bn, a Bayesian network specifying joint distribution P(X_1, ..., X_n)

  factors ← []
  for each var in ORDER(bn.VARS) do
      factors ← [MAKE-FACTOR(var, e)|factors]
      if var is a hidden variable then factors ← SUM-OUT(var, factors)
  return NORMALIZE(POINTWISE-PRODUCT(factors))
```

Figure 11 The variable elimination algorithm for inference in Bayesian networks.

is determined by the order of elimination of variables and by the structure of the network. It turns out to be intractable to determine the optimal ordering, but several good heuristics are available. One fairly effective method is a greedy one: eliminate whichever variable minimizes the size of the next factor to be constructed.

Let us consider one more query: $\mathbf{P}(JohnCalls \mid Burglary = true)$. As usual, the first step is to write out the nested summation:

$$\mathbf{P}(J \mid b) = \alpha\, P(b) \sum_{e} P(e) \sum_{a} P(a \mid b, e)\mathbf{P}(J \mid a) \sum_{m} P(m \mid a)\,.$$

Evaluating this expression from right to left, we notice something interesting: $\sum_m P(m \mid a)$ is equal to 1 by definition! Hence, there was no need to include it in the first place; the variable M is *irrelevant* to this query. Another way of saying this is that the result of the query $P(JohnCalls \mid Burglary = true)$ is unchanged if we remove $MaryCalls$ from the network altogether. In general, we can remove any leaf node that is not a query variable or an evidence variable. After its removal, there may be some more leaf nodes, and these too may be irrelevant. Continuing this process, we eventually find that *every variable that is not an ancestor of a query variable or evidence variable is irrelevant to the query.* A variable elimination algorithm can therefore remove all these variables before evaluating the query.

4.3 The complexity of exact inference

The complexity of exact inference in Bayesian networks depends strongly on the structure of the network. The burglary network of Figure 2 belongs to the family of networks in which there is at most one undirected path between any two nodes in the network. These are called

SINGLY CONNECTED

POLYTREE

singly connected networks or **polytrees**, and they have a particularly nice property: *The time and space complexity of exact inference in polytrees is linear in the size of the network.* Here, the size is defined as the number of CPT entries; if the number of parents of each node is bounded by a constant, then the complexity will also be linear in the number of nodes.

MULTIPLY CONNECTED

For **multiply connected** networks, such as that of Figure 12(a), variable elimination can have exponential time and space complexity in the worst case, even when the number of parents per node is bounded. This is not surprising when one considers that *because it*

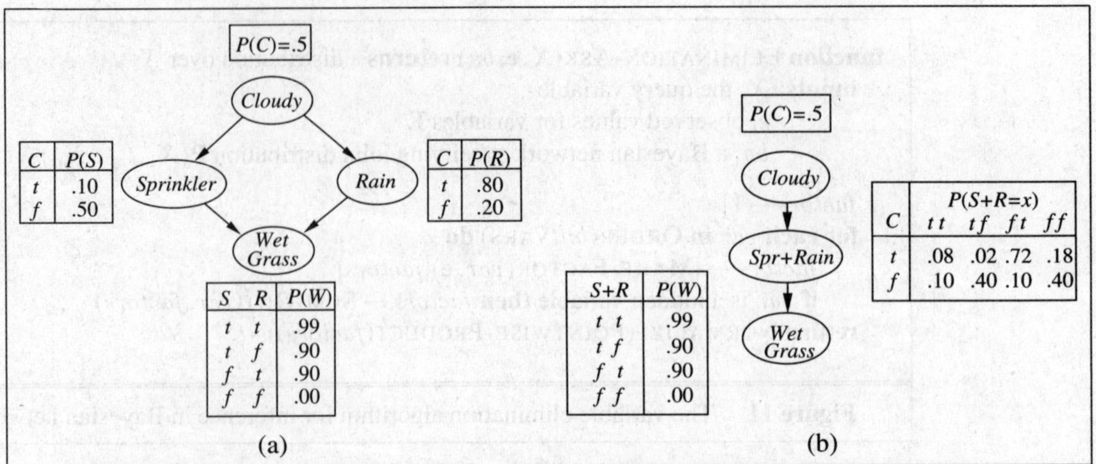

Figure 12 (a) A multiply connected network with conditional probability tables. (b) A clustered equivalent of the multiply connected network.

includes inference in propositional logic as a special case, inference in Bayesian networks is NP-hard. In fact, it can be shown (Exercise 16) that the problem is as hard as that of computing the *number* of satisfying assignments for a propositional logic formula. This means that it is #P-hard ("number-P hard")—that is, strictly harder than NP-complete problems.

There is a close connection between the complexity of Bayesian network inference and the complexity of constraint satisfaction problems (CSPs). The difficulty of solving a discrete CSP is related to how "treelike" its constraint graph is. Measures such as **tree width**, which bound the complexity of solving a CSP, can also be applied directly to Bayesian networks. Moreover, the variable elimination algorithm can be generalized to solve CSPs as well as Bayesian networks.

4.4 Clustering algorithms

The variable elimination algorithm is simple and efficient for answering individual queries. If we want to compute posterior probabilities for all the variables in a network, however, it can be less efficient. For example, in a polytree network, one would need to issue $O(n)$ queries costing $O(n)$ each, for a total of $O(n^2)$ time. Using **clustering** algorithms (also known as **join tree** algorithms), the time can be reduced to $O(n)$. For this reason, these algorithms are widely used in commercial Bayesian network tools.

CLUSTERING

JOIN TREE

The basic idea of clustering is to join individual nodes of the network to form cluster nodes in such a way that the resulting network is a polytree. For example, the multiply connected network shown in Figure 12(a) can be converted into a polytree by combining the *Sprinkler* and *Rain* node into a cluster node called *Sprinkler+Rain*, as shown in Figure 12(b). The two Boolean nodes are replaced by a "meganode" that takes on four possible values: tt, tf, ft, and ff. The meganode has only one parent, the Boolean variable *Cloudy*, so there are two conditioning cases. Although this example doesn't show it, the process of clustering often produces meganodes that share some variables.

Once the network is in polytree form, a special-purpose inference algorithm is required, because ordinary inference methods cannot handle meganodes that share variables with each other. Essentially, the algorithm is a form of constraint propagation where the constraints ensure that neighboring meganodes agree on the posterior probability of any variables that they have in common. With careful bookkeeping, this algorithm is able to compute posterior probabilities for all the nonevidence nodes in the network in time *linear* in the size of the clustered network. However, the NP-hardness of the problem has not disappeared: if a network requires exponential time and space with variable elimination, then the CPTs in the clustered network will necessarily be exponentially large.

5 Approximate Inference in Bayesian Networks

Given the intractability of exact inference in large, multiply connected networks, it is essential to consider approximate inference methods. This section describes randomized sampling algorithms, also called **Monte Carlo** algorithms, that provide approximate answers whose accuracy depends on the number of samples generated. Monte Carlo algorithms, of which simulated annealing is an example, are used in many branches of science to estimate quantities that are difficult to calculate exactly. In this section, we are interested in sampling applied to the computation of posterior probabilities. We describe two families of algorithms: direct sampling and Markov chain sampling. Two other approaches—variational methods and loopy propagation—are mentioned in the notes at the end of the chapter.

MONTE CARLO

5.1 Direct sampling methods

The primitive element in any sampling algorithm is the generation of samples from a known probability distribution. For example, an unbiased coin can be thought of as a random variable $Coin$ with values $\langle heads, tails \rangle$ and a prior distribution $\mathbf{P}(Coin) = \langle 0.5, 0.5 \rangle$. Sampling from this distribution is exactly like flipping the coin: with probability 0.5 it will return *heads*, and with probability 0.5 it will return $tails$. Given a source of random numbers uniformly distributed in the range $[0, 1]$, it is a simple matter to sample any distribution on a single variable, whether discrete or continuous. (See Exercise 17.)

The simplest kind of random sampling process for Bayesian networks generates events from a network that has no evidence associated with it. The idea is to sample each variable in turn, in topological order. The probability distribution from which the value is sampled is conditioned on the values already assigned to the variable's parents. This algorithm is shown in Figure 13. We can illustrate its operation on the network in Figure 12(a), assuming an ordering $[Cloudy, Sprinkler, Rain, WetGrass]$:

1. Sample from $\mathbf{P}(Cloudy) = \langle 0.5, 0.5 \rangle$, value is *true*.
2. Sample from $\mathbf{P}(Sprinkler \mid Cloudy = true) = \langle 0.1, 0.9 \rangle$, value is *false*.
3. Sample from $\mathbf{P}(Rain \mid Cloudy = true) = \langle 0.8, 0.2 \rangle$, value is *true*.
4. Sample from $\mathbf{P}(WetGrass \mid Sprinkler = false, Rain = true) = \langle 0.9, 0.1 \rangle$, value is *true*.

In this case, PRIOR-SAMPLE returns the event $[true, false, true, true]$.

```
function PRIOR-SAMPLE(bn) returns an event sampled from the prior specified by bn
  inputs: bn, a Bayesian network specifying joint distribution P(X_1, ..., X_n)

  x ← an event with n elements
  foreach variable X_i in X_1, ..., X_n do
     x[i] ← a random sample from P(X_i | parents(X_i))
  return x
```

Figure 13 A sampling algorithm that generates events from a Bayesian network. Each variable is sampled according to the conditional distribution given the values already sampled for the variable's parents.

It is easy to see that PRIOR-SAMPLE generates samples from the prior joint distribution specified by the network. First, let $S_{PS}(x_1, \ldots, x_n)$ be the probability that a specific event is generated by the PRIOR-SAMPLE algorithm. *Just looking at the sampling process*, we have

$$S_{PS}(x_1 \ldots x_n) = \prod_{i=1}^{n} P(x_i \mid parents(X_i))$$

because each sampling step depends only on the parent values. This expression should look familiar, because it is also the probability of the event according to the Bayesian net's representation of the joint distribution, as stated in Equation (2). That is, we have

$$S_{PS}(x_1 \ldots x_n) = P(x_1 \ldots x_n) .$$

This simple fact makes it easy to answer questions by using samples.

In any sampling algorithm, the answers are computed by counting the actual samples generated. Suppose there are N total samples, and let $N_{PS}(x_1, \ldots, x_n)$ be the number of times the specific event $x_1, \ldots, x_n$ occurs in the set of samples. We expect this number, as a fraction of the total, to converge in the limit to its expected value according to the sampling probability:

$$\lim_{N\to\infty} \frac{N_{PS}(x_1, \ldots, x_n)}{N} = S_{PS}(x_1, \ldots, x_n) = P(x_1, \ldots, x_n) . \tag{5}$$

For example, consider the event produced earlier: $[true, false, true, true]$. The sampling probability for this event is

$$S_{PS}(true, false, true, true) = 0.5 \times 0.9 \times 0.8 \times 0.9 = 0.324 .$$

Hence, in the limit of large N, we expect 32.4% of the samples to be of this event.

Whenever we use an approximate equality ("$\approx$") in what follows, we mean it in exactly this sense—that the estimated probability becomes exact in the large-sample limit. Such an

CONSISTENT

estimate is called **consistent**. For example, one can produce a consistent estimate of the probability of any partially specified event $x_1, \ldots, x_m$, where $m \leq n$, as follows:

$$P(x_1, \ldots, x_m) \approx N_{PS}(x_1, \ldots, x_m)/N . \tag{6}$$

That is, the probability of the event can be estimated as the fraction of all complete events generated by the sampling process that match the partially specified event. For example, if we generate 1000 samples from the sprinkler network, and 511 of them have $Rain = true$, then the estimated probability of rain, written as $\hat{P}(Rain = true)$, is 0.511.

Rejection sampling in Bayesian networks

REJECTION SAMPLING

Rejection sampling is a general method for producing samples from a hard-to-sample distribution given an easy-to-sample distribution. In its simplest form, it can be used to compute conditional probabilities—that is, to determine $P(X \mid \mathbf{e})$. The REJECTION-SAMPLING algorithm is shown in Figure 14. First, it generates samples from the prior distribution specified by the network. Then, it rejects all those that do not match the evidence. Finally, the estimate $\hat{P}(X = x \mid \mathbf{e})$ is obtained by counting how often $X = x$ occurs in the remaining samples.

Let $\hat{\mathbf{P}}(X \mid \mathbf{e})$ be the estimated distribution that the algorithm returns. From the definition of the algorithm, we have

$$\hat{\mathbf{P}}(X \mid \mathbf{e}) = \alpha\, \mathbf{N}_{PS}(X, \mathbf{e}) = \frac{\mathbf{N}_{PS}(X, \mathbf{e})}{N_{PS}(\mathbf{e})} .$$

From Equation (6), this becomes

$$\hat{\mathbf{P}}(X \mid \mathbf{e}) \approx \frac{\mathbf{P}(X, \mathbf{e})}{P(\mathbf{e})} = \mathbf{P}(X \mid \mathbf{e}) .$$

That is, rejection sampling produces a consistent estimate of the true probability.

Continuing with our example from Figure 12(a), let us assume that we wish to estimate $\mathbf{P}(Rain \mid Sprinkler = true)$, using 100 samples. Of the 100 that we generate, suppose that 73 have $Sprinkler = false$ and are rejected, while 27 have $Sprinkler = true$; of the 27, 8 have $Rain = true$ and 19 have $Rain = false$. Hence,

$$\mathbf{P}(Rain \mid Sprinkler = true) \approx \text{NORMALIZE}(\langle 8, 19 \rangle) = \langle 0.296, 0.704 \rangle .$$

The true answer is $\langle 0.3, 0.7 \rangle$. As more samples are collected, the estimate will converge to the true answer. The standard deviation of the error in each probability will be proportional to $1/\sqrt{n}$, where n is the number of samples used in the estimate.

The biggest problem with rejection sampling is that it rejects so many samples! The fraction of samples consistent with the evidence $\mathbf{e}$ drops exponentially as the number of evidence variables grows, so the procedure is simply unusable for complex problems.

Notice that rejection sampling is very similar to the estimation of conditional probabilities directly from the real world. For example, to estimate $\mathbf{P}(Rain \mid RedSkyAtNight = true)$, one can simply count how often it rains after a red sky is observed the previous evening—ignoring those evenings when the sky is not red. (Here, the world itself plays the role of the sample-generation algorithm.) Obviously, this could take a long time if the sky is very seldom red, and that is the weakness of rejection sampling.

Likelihood weighting

LIKELIHOOD WEIGHTING

Likelihood weighting avoids the inefficiency of rejection sampling by generating only events that are consistent with the evidence $\mathbf{e}$. It is a particular instance of the general statistical technique of **importance sampling**, tailored for inference in Bayesian networks. We begin by

IMPORTANCE SAMPLING

```
function REJECTION-SAMPLING(X, e, bn, N) returns an estimate of P(X|e)
  inputs: X, the query variable
          e, observed values for variables E
          bn, a Bayesian network
          N, the total number of samples to be generated
  local variables: N, a vector of counts for each value of X, initially zero

  for j = 1 to N do
     x ← PRIOR-SAMPLE(bn)
     if x is consistent with e then
        N[x] ← N[x]+1 where x is the value of X in x
  return NORMALIZE(N)
```

Figure 14 The rejection-sampling algorithm for answering queries given evidence in a Bayesian network.

describing how the algorithm works; then we show that it works correctly—that is, generates consistent probability estimates.

LIKELIHOOD-WEIGHTING (see Figure 15) fixes the values for the evidence variables **E** and samples only the nonevidence variables. This guarantees that each event generated is consistent with the evidence. Not all events are equal, however. Before tallying the counts in the distribution for the query variable, each event is weighted by the *likelihood* that the event accords to the evidence, as measured by the product of the conditional probabilities for each evidence variable, given its parents. Intuitively, events in which the actual evidence appears unlikely should be given less weight.

Let us apply the algorithm to the network shown in Figure 12(a), with the query $\mathbf{P}(Rain \mid Cloudy = true, WetGrass = true)$ and the ordering *Cloudy*, *Sprinkler*, *Rain*, *WetGrass*. (Any topological ordering will do.) The process goes as follows: First, the weight w is set to 1.0. Then an event is generated:

1. *Cloudy* is an evidence variable with value *true*. Therefore, we set
$$w \leftarrow w \times P(Cloudy = true) = 0.5 .$$
2. *Sprinkler* is not an evidence variable, so sample from $\mathbf{P}(Sprinkler \mid Cloudy = true) = \langle 0.1, 0.9 \rangle$; suppose this returns *false*.
3. Similarly, sample from $\mathbf{P}(Rain \mid Cloudy = true) = \langle 0.8, 0.2 \rangle$; suppose this returns *true*.
4. *WetGrass* is an evidence variable with value *true*. Therefore, we set
$$w \leftarrow w \times P(WetGrass = true \mid Sprinkler = false, Rain = true) = 0.45 .$$

Here WEIGHTED-SAMPLE returns the event [*true*, *false*, *true*, *true*] with weight 0.45, and this is tallied under *Rain* = *true*.

To understand why likelihood weighting works, we start by examining the sampling probability S_{WS} for WEIGHTED-SAMPLE. Remember that the evidence variables **E** are fixed

```
function LIKELIHOOD-WEIGHTING(X, e, bn, N) returns an estimate of P(X|e)
  inputs: X, the query variable
          e, observed values for variables E
          bn, a Bayesian network specifying joint distribution P(X1, ..., Xn)
          N, the total number of samples to be generated
  local variables: W, a vector of weighted counts for each value of X, initially zero

  for j = 1 to N do
     x, w ← WEIGHTED-SAMPLE(bn, e)
     W[x] ← W[x] + w where x is the value of X in x
  return NORMALIZE(W)
```

```
function WEIGHTED-SAMPLE(bn, e) returns an event and a weight

  w ← 1; x ← an event with n elements initialized from e
  foreach variable Xi in X1, ..., Xn do
     if Xi is an evidence variable with value xi in e
        then w ← w × P(Xi = xi | parents(Xi))
        else x[i] ← a random sample from P(Xi | parents(Xi))
  return x, w
```

Figure 15 The likelihood-weighting algorithm for inference in Bayesian networks. In WEIGHTED-SAMPLE, each nonevidence variable is sampled according to the conditional distribution given the values already sampled for the variable's parents, while a weight is accumulated based on the likelihood for each evidence variable.

with values **e**. We call the nonevidence variables **Z** (including the query variable X). The algorithm samples each variable in **Z** given its parent values:

$$S_{WS}(\mathbf{z}, \mathbf{e}) = \prod_{i=1}^{l} P(z_i \mid parents(Z_i)) \,. \tag{7}$$

Notice that $Parents(Z_i)$ can include both nonevidence variables and evidence variables. Unlike the prior distribution $P(\mathbf{z})$, the distribution S_{WS} pays some attention to the evidence: the sampled values for each Z_i will be influenced by evidence among Z_i's ancestors. For example, when sampling *Sprinkler* the algorithm pays attention to the evidence $Cloudy = true$ in its parent variable. On the other hand, S_{WS} pays less attention to the evidence than does the true posterior distribution $P(\mathbf{z} \mid \mathbf{e})$, because the sampled values for each Z_i *ignore* evidence among Z_i's non-ancestors.[5] For example, when sampling *Sprinkler* and *Rain* the algorithm ignores the evidence in the child variable $WetGrass = true$; this means it will generate many samples with $Sprinkler = false$ and $Rain = false$ despite the fact that the evidence actually rules out this case.

[5] Ideally, we would like to use a sampling distribution equal to the true posterior $P(\mathbf{z} \mid \mathbf{e})$, to take all the evidence into account. This cannot be done efficiently, however. If it could, then we could approximate the desired probability to arbitrary accuracy with a polynomial number of samples. It can be shown that no such polynomial-time approximation scheme can exist.

The likelihood weight w makes up for the difference between the actual and desired sampling distributions. The weight for a given sample $\mathbf{x}$, composed from $\mathbf{z}$ and $\mathbf{e}$, is the product of the likelihoods for each evidence variable given its parents (some or all of which may be among the Z_is):

$$w(\mathbf{z},\mathbf{e}) = \prod_{i=1}^{m} P(e_i \,|\, parents(E_i)) \,. \tag{8}$$

Multiplying Equations (7) and (8), we see that the *weighted* probability of a sample has the particularly convenient form

$$\begin{aligned} S_{WS}(\mathbf{z},\mathbf{e})w(\mathbf{z},\mathbf{e}) &= \prod_{i=1}^{l} P(z_i \,|\, parents(Z_i)) \prod_{i=1}^{m} P(e_i \,|\, parents(E_i)) \\ &= P(\mathbf{z},\mathbf{e}) \end{aligned} \tag{9}$$

because the two products cover all the variables in the network, allowing us to use Equation (2) for the joint probability.

Now it is easy to show that likelihood weighting estimates are consistent. For any particular value x of X, the estimated posterior probability can be calculated as follows:

$$\begin{aligned} \hat{P}(x \,|\, \mathbf{e}) &= \alpha \sum_{\mathbf{y}} N_{WS}(x,\mathbf{y},\mathbf{e})w(x,\mathbf{y},\mathbf{e}) && \text{from LIKELIHOOD-WEIGHTING} \\ &\approx \alpha' \sum_{\mathbf{y}} S_{WS}(x,\mathbf{y},\mathbf{e})w(x,\mathbf{y},\mathbf{e}) && \text{for large } N \\ &= \alpha' \sum_{\mathbf{y}} P(x,\mathbf{y},\mathbf{e}) && \text{by Equation (9)} \\ &= \alpha' P(x,\mathbf{e}) = P(x \,|\, \mathbf{e}) \,. \end{aligned}$$

Hence, likelihood weighting returns consistent estimates.

Because likelihood weighting uses all the samples generated, it can be much more efficient than rejection sampling. It will, however, suffer a degradation in performance as the number of evidence variables increases. This is because most samples will have very low weights and hence the weighted estimate will be dominated by the tiny fraction of samples that accord more than an infinitesimal likelihood to the evidence. The problem is exacerbated if the evidence variables occur late in the variable ordering, because then the nonevidence variables will have no evidence in their parents and ancestors to guide the generation of samples. This means the samples will be simulations that bear little resemblance to the reality suggested by the evidence.

5.2 Inference by Markov chain simulation

MARKOV CHAIN MONTE CARLO

Markov chain Monte Carlo (MCMC) algorithms work quite differently from rejection sampling and likelihood weighting. Instead of generating each sample from scratch, MCMC algorithms generate each sample by making a random change to the preceding sample. It is therefore helpful to think of an MCMC algorithm as being in a particular *current state* specifying a value for every variable and generating a *next state* by making random changes to the current state. (If this reminds you of simulated annealing or WALKSAT, that is because both are members of the MCMC family.) Here we describe a particular form of MCMC called **Gibbs sampling**, which is especially well suited for Bayesian networks. (Other forms, some of them significantly more powerful, are discussed in the notes at the end of the chapter.) We will first describe what the algorithm does, then we will explain why it works.

GIBBS SAMPLING

Gibbs sampling in Bayesian networks

The Gibbs sampling algorithm for Bayesian networks starts with an arbitrary state (with the evidence variables fixed at their observed values) and generates a next state by randomly sampling a value for one of the nonevidence variables Xi. The sampling for Xi is done *conditioned on the current values of the variables in the Markov blanket of* Xi. (Recall that the Markov blanket of a variable consists of its parents, children, and children's parents.) The algorithm therefore wanders randomly around the state space—the space of possible complete assignments—flipping one variable at a time, but keeping the evidence variables fixed.

Consider the query $\mathbf{P}(Rain \mid Sprinkler = true, WetGrass = true)$ applied to the network in Figure 12(a). The evidence variables *Sprinkler* and *WetGrass* are fixed to their observed values and the nonevidence variables *Cloudy* and *Rain* are initialized randomly—let us say to *true* and *false* respectively. Thus, the initial state is $[true, true, false, true]$. Now the nonevidence variables are sampled repeatedly in an arbitrary order. For example:

1. *Cloudy* is sampled, given the current values of its Markov blanket variables: in this case, we sample from $\mathbf{P}(Cloudy \mid Sprinkler = true, Rain = false)$. (Shortly, we will show how to calculate this distribution.) Suppose the result is $Cloudy = false$. Then the new current state is $[false, true, false, true]$.
2. *Rain* is sampled, given the current values of its Markov blanket variables: in this case, we sample from $\mathbf{P}(Rain \mid Cloudy = false, Sprinkler = true, WetGrass = true)$. Suppose this yields $Rain = true$. The new current state is $[false, true, true, true]$.

Each state visited during this process is a sample that contributes to the estimate for the query variable *Rain*. If the process visits 20 states where *Rain* is true and 60 states where *Rain* is false, then the answer to the query is $\text{NORMALIZE}(\langle 20, 60\rangle) = \langle 0.25, 0.75\rangle$. The complete algorithm is shown in Figure 16.

Why Gibbs sampling works

We will now show that Gibbs sampling returns consistent estimates for posterior probabilities. The material in this section is quite technical, but the basic claim is straightforward: *the sampling process settles into a "dynamic equilibrium" in which the long-run fraction of time spent in each state is exactly proportional to its posterior probability.* This remarkable property follows from the specific **transition probability** with which the process moves from one state to another, as defined by the conditional distribution given the Markov blanket of the variable being sampled.

TRANSITION PROBABILITY

```
function GIBBS-ASK(X, e, bn, N) returns an estimate of P(X|e)
  local variables: N, a vector of counts for each value of X, initially zero
                   Z, the nonevidence variables in bn
                   x, the current state of the network, initially copied from e

  initialize x with random values for the variables in Z
  for j = 1 to N do
      for each Z_i in Z do
          set the value of Z_i in x by sampling from P(Z_i|mb(Z_i))
          N[x] ← N[x] + 1 where x is the value of X in x
  return NORMALIZE(N)
```

Figure 16 The Gibbs sampling algorithm for approximate inference in Bayesian networks; this version cycles through the variables, but choosing variables at random also works.

Let $q(\mathbf{x} \to \mathbf{x}')$ be the probability that the process makes a transition from state $\mathbf{x}$ to state $\mathbf{x}'$. This transition probability defines what is called a **Markov chain** on the state space. Now suppose that we run the Markov chain for t steps, and let $\pi_t(\mathbf{x})$be the probability that the system is in state $\mathbf{x}$ at time t. Similarly, let $\pi_{t+1}(\mathbf{x}')$ be the probability of being in state $\mathbf{x}'$ at time $t+1$. Given $\pi_t(\mathbf{x})$, we can calculate $\pi_{t+1}(\mathbf{x}')$ by summing, for all states the system could be in at time t, the probability of being in that state times the probability of making the transition to $\mathbf{x}'$:

MARKOV CHAIN

$$\pi_{t+1}(\mathbf{x}') = \sum_{\mathbf{x}} \pi_t(\mathbf{x}) q(\mathbf{x} \to \mathbf{x}') .$$

STATIONARY DISTRIBUTION

We say that the chain has reached its **stationary distribution** if $\pi_t = \pi_{t+1}$. Let us call this stationary distribution π; its defining equation is therefore

$$\pi(\mathbf{x}') = \sum_{\mathbf{x}} \pi(\mathbf{x}) q(\mathbf{x} \to \mathbf{x}') \qquad \text{for all } \mathbf{x}' . \tag{10}$$

ERGODIC

Provided the transition probability distribution q is **ergodic**—that is, every state is reachable from every other and there are no strictly periodic cycles—there is exactly one distribution π satisfying this equation for any given q.

Equation (10) can be read as saying that the expected "outflow" from each state (i.e., its current "population") is equal to the expected "inflow" from all the states. One obvious way to satisfy this relationship is if the expected flow between any pair of states is the same in both directions; that is,

$$\pi(\mathbf{x}) q(\mathbf{x} \to \mathbf{x}') = \pi(\mathbf{x}') q(\mathbf{x}' \to \mathbf{x}) \qquad \text{for all } \mathbf{x},\ \mathbf{x}' . \tag{11}$$

DETAILED BALANCE

When these equations hold, we say that $q(\mathbf{x} \to \mathbf{x}')$ is in **detailed balance** with $\pi(\mathbf{x})$.

We can show that detailed balance implies stationarity simply by summing over $\mathbf{x}$ in Equation (11). We have

$$\sum_{\mathbf{x}} \pi(\mathbf{x}) q(\mathbf{x} \to \mathbf{x}') = \sum_{\mathbf{x}} \pi(\mathbf{x}') q(\mathbf{x}' \to \mathbf{x}) = \pi(\mathbf{x}') \sum_{\mathbf{x}} q(\mathbf{x}' \to \mathbf{x}) = \pi(\mathbf{x}')$$

where the last step follows because a transition from $\mathbf{x}'$ is guaranteed to occur.

The transition probability $q(\mathbf{x} \rightarrow \mathbf{x}')$ defined by the sampling step in GIBBS-ASK is actually a special case of the more general definition of Gibbs sampling, according to which each variable is sampled conditionally on the current values of *all* the other variables. We start by showing that this general definition of Gibbs sampling satisfies the detailed balance equation with a stationary distribution equal to $P(\mathbf{x} \mid \mathbf{e})$, (the true posterior distribution on the nonevidence variables). Then, we simply observe that, for Bayesian networks, sampling conditionally on all variables is equivalent to sampling conditionally on the variable's Markov blanket (see section 2.2).

To analyze the general Gibbs sampler, which samples each X_i in turn with a transition probability q_i that conditions on all the other variables, we define $\overline{\mathbf{X}_i}$ to be these other variables (except the evidence variables); their values in the current state are $\overline{\mathbf{x}_i}$. If we sample a new value x'_i for X_i conditionally on all the other variables, including the evidence, we have

$$q_i(\mathbf{x} \rightarrow \mathbf{x}') = q_i((x_i, \overline{\mathbf{x}_i}) \rightarrow (x'_i, \overline{\mathbf{x}_i})) = P(x'_i \mid \overline{\mathbf{x}_i}, \mathbf{e}) .$$

Now we show that the transition probability for each step of the Gibbs sampler is in detailed balance with the true posterior:

$$\begin{aligned}
\pi(\mathbf{x}) q_i(\mathbf{x} \rightarrow \mathbf{x}') &= P(\mathbf{x} \mid \mathbf{e}) P(x'_i \mid \overline{\mathbf{x}_i}, \mathbf{e}) = P(x_i, \overline{\mathbf{x}_i} \mid \mathbf{e}) P(x'_i \mid \overline{\mathbf{x}_i}, \mathbf{e}) \\
&= P(x_i \mid \overline{\mathbf{x}_i}, \mathbf{e}) P(\overline{\mathbf{x}_i} \mid \mathbf{e}) P(x'_i \mid \overline{\mathbf{x}_i}, \mathbf{e}) \qquad \text{(using the chain rule on the first term)} \\
&= P(x_i \mid \overline{\mathbf{x}_i}, \mathbf{e}) P(x'_i, \overline{\mathbf{x}_i} \mid \mathbf{e}) \qquad \text{(using the chain rule backward)} \\
&= \pi(\mathbf{x}') q_i(\mathbf{x}' \rightarrow \mathbf{x}) .
\end{aligned}$$

We can think of the loop "**for each** Z_i **in Z do**" in Figure 16 as defining one large transition probability q that is the sequential composition $q_1 \circ q_2 \circ \cdots \circ q_n$ of the transition probabilities for the individual variables. It is easy to show (Exercise 19) that if each of q_i and q_j has π as its stationary distribution, then the sequential composition $q_i \circ q_j$ does too; hence the transition probability q for the whole loop has $P(\mathbf{x} \mid \mathbf{e})$ as its stationary distribution. Finally, unless the CPTs contain probabilities of 0 or 1—which can cause the state space to become disconnected—it is easy to see that q is ergodic. Hence, the samples generated by Gibbs sampling will eventually be drawn from the true posterior distribution.

The final step is to show how to perform the general Gibbs sampling step—sampling X_i from $\mathbf{P}(X_i \mid \overline{\mathbf{x}_i}, \mathbf{e})$—in a Bayesian network. Recall from section 2.2 that a variable is independent of all other variables given its Markov blanket; hence,

$$P(x'_i \mid \overline{\mathbf{x}_i}, \mathbf{e}) = P(x'_i \mid mb(X_i)) ,$$

where $mb(X_i)$ denotes the values of the variables in X_i's Markov blanket, $MB(X_i)$. As shown in Exercise 7, the probability of a variable given its Markov blanket is proportional to the probability of the variable given its parents times the probability of each child given its respective parents:

$$P(x'_i \mid mb(X_i)) = \alpha\, P(x'_i \mid parents(X_i)) \times \prod_{Y_j \in Children(X_i)} P(y_j \mid parents(Y_j)) . \qquad (12)$$

Hence, to flip each variable X_i conditioned on its Markov blanket, the number of multiplications required is equal to the number of X_i's children.

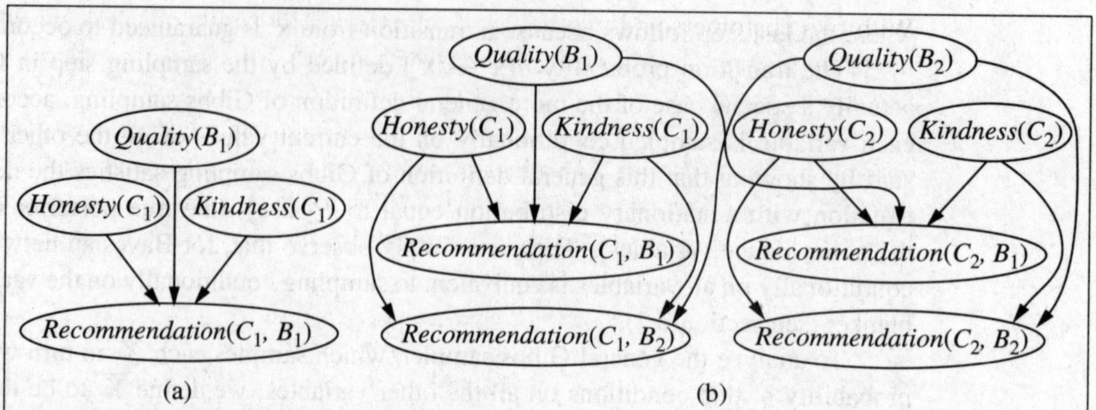

Figure 17 (a) Bayes net for a single customer C_1 recommending a single book B_1. $Honest(C_1)$ is Boolean, while the other variables have integer values from 1 to 5. (b) Bayes net with two customers and two books.

6 RELATIONAL AND FIRST-ORDER PROBABILITY MODELS

There exist representational advantages possessed by first-order logic in comparison to propositional logic. First-order logic commits to the existence of objects and relations among them and can express facts about *some* or *all* of the objects in a domain. This often results in representations that are vastly more concise than the equivalent propositional descriptions. Now, Bayesian networks are essentially propositional: the set of random variables is fixed and finite, and each has a fixed domain of possible values. This fact limits the applicability of Bayesian networks. *If we can find a way to combine probability theory with the expressive power of first-order representations, we expect to be able to increase dramatically the range of problems that can be handled.*

For example, suppose that an online book retailer would like to provide overall evaluations of products based on recommendations received from its customers. The evaluation will take the form of a posterior distribution over the quality of the book, given the available evidence. The simplest solution to base the evaluation on the average recommendation, perhaps with a variance determined by the number of recommendations, but this fails to take into account the fact that some customers are kinder than others and some are less honest than others. Kind customers tend to give high recommendations even to fairly mediocre books, while dishonest customers give very high or very low recommendations for reasons other than quality—for example, they might work for a publisher.[6]

For a single customer $C1$, recommending a single book $B1$, the Bayes net might look like the one shown in Figure 17(a). (Expressions with parentheses such as *Honest*($C1$) are just fancy symbols—in this case, fancy names for random variables.)

[6] A game theorist would advise a dishonest customer to avoid detection by occasionally recommending a good book from a competitor.

With two customers and two books, the Bayes net looks like the one in Figure 17(b). For larger numbers of books and customers, it becomes completely impractical to specify the network by hand.

Fortunately, the network has a lot of repeated structure. Each $Recommendation(c, b)$ variable has as its parents the variables $Honest(c)$, $Kindness(c)$, and $Quality(b)$. Moreover, the CPTs for all the $Recommendation(c, b)$ variables are identical, as are those for all the $Honest(c)$ variables, and so on. The situation seems tailor-made for a first-order language. We would like to say something like

$$Recommendation(c, b) \sim RecCPT(Honest(c), Kindness(c), Quality(b))$$

with the intended meaning that a customer's recommendation for a book depends on the customer's honesty and kindness and the book's quality according to some fixed CPT. This section develops a language that lets us say exactly this, and a lot more besides.

6.1 Possible worlds

A probability model defines a set Ω of possible worlds with a probability $P(\omega)$ for each world ω. For Bayesian networks, the possible worlds are assignments of values to variables; for the Boolean case in particular, the possible worlds are identical to those of propositional logic. For a first-order probability model, then, it seems we need the possible worlds to be those of first-order logic—that is, a set of objects with relations among them and an interpretation that maps constant symbols to objects, predicate symbols to relations, and function symbols to functions on those objects. The model also needs to define a probability for each such possible world, just as a Bayesian network defines a probability for each assignment of values to variables.

Let us suppose, for a moment, that we have figured out how to do this. Then, as usual, we can obtain the probability of any first-order logical sentence ϕ as a sum over the possible worlds where it is true:

$$P(\phi) = \sum_{\omega:\phi \text{ is true in } \omega} P(\omega) . \tag{13}$$

Conditional probabilities $P(\phi \mid \mathbf{e})$ can be obtained similarly, so we can, in principle, ask any question we want of our model—e.g., "Which books are most likely to be recommended highly by dishonest customers?"—and get an answer. So far, so good.

There is, however, a problem: the set of first-order models is infinite. We see this in Figure 18 (top). This means that (1) the summation in Equation (13) could be infeasible, and (2) specifying a complete, consistent distribution over an infinite set of worlds could be very difficult.

Section 6.2 explores one approach to dealing with this problem. The idea is to borrow not from the standard semantics of first-order logic but from the **database semantics.** The database semantics makes the **unique names assumption**—here, we adopt it for the constant symbols. It also assumes **domain closure**—there are no more objects than those that are named. We can then guarantee a finite set of possible worlds by making the set of objects in each world be exactly the set of constant symbols that are used; as shown in Figure 18 (bot-

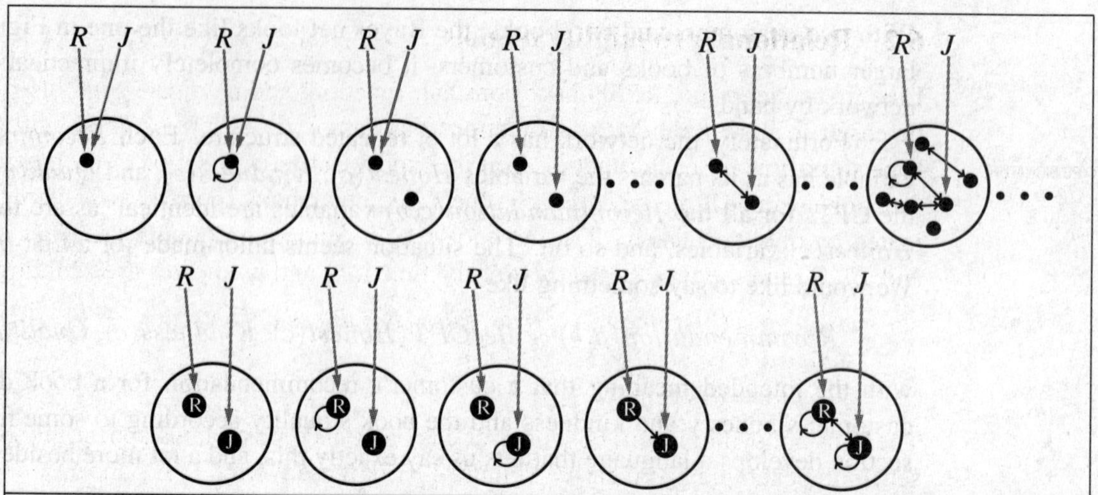

Figure 18 Top: Some members of the set of all possible worlds for a language with two constant symbols, R and J, and one binary relation symbol, under the standard semantics for first-order logic. Bottom: the possible worlds under database semantics. The interpretation of the constant symbols is fixed, and there is a distinct object for each constant symbol.

tom), there is no uncertainty about the mapping from symbols to objects or about the objects that exist. We will call models defined in this way **relational probability models**, or RPMs.[7] The most significant difference between the semantics of RPMs and database semantics is that RPMs do not make the closed-world assumption—obviously, assuming that every unknown fact is false doesn't make sense in a probabilistic reasoning system!

RELATIONAL PROBABILITY MODEL

When the underlying assumptions of database semantics fail to hold, RPMs won't work well. For example, a book retailer might use an ISBN (International Standard Book Number) as a constant symbol to name each book, even though a given "logical" book (e.g., "Gone With the Wind") may have several ISBNs. It would make sense to aggregate recommendations across multiple ISBNs, but the retailer may not know for sure which ISBNs are really the same book. (Note that we are not reifying the *individual copies* of the book, which might be necessary for used-book sales, car sales, and so on.) Worse still, each customer is identified by a login ID, but a dishonest customer may have thousands of IDs! In the computer security field, these multiple IDs are called **sibyls** and their use to confound a reputation system is called a **sibyl attack**. Thus, even a simple application in a relatively well-defined, online domain involves both **existence uncertainty** (what are the real books and customers underlying the observed data) and **identity uncertainty** (which symbol really refer to the same object). We need to bite the bullet and define probability models based on the standard semantics of first-order logic, for which the possible worlds vary in the objects they contain and in the mappings from symbols to objects. Section 6.3 shows how to do this.

SIBYL

SIBYL ATTACK

EXISTENCE UNCERTAINTY

IDENTITY UNCERTAINTY

---

[7] The name *relational probability model* was given by Pfeffer (2000) to a slightly different representation, but the underlying ideas are the same.

6.2 Relational probability models

Like first-order logic, RPMs have constant, function, and predicate symbols. (It turns out to be easier to view predicates as functions that return *true* or *false*.) We will also assume a **type signature** for each function, that is, a specification of the type of each argument and the function's value. If the type of each object is known, many spurious possible worlds are eliminated by this mechanism. For the book-recommendation domain, the types are *Customer* and *Book*, and the type signatures for the functions and predicates are as follows:

TYPE SIGNATURE

$$Honest : Customer \rightarrow \{true, false\} Kindness : Customer \rightarrow \{1,2,3,4,5\}$$
$$Quality : Book \rightarrow \{1,2,3,4,5\}$$
$$Recommendation : Customer \times Book \rightarrow \{1,2,3,4,5\}$$

The constant symbols will be whatever customer and book names appear in the retailer's data set. In the example given earlier (Figure 17(b)), these were C_1, C_2 and B_1, B_2.

Given the constants and their types, together with the functions and their type signatures, the random variables of the RPM are obtained by instantiating each function with each possible combination of objects: $Honest(C_1)$, $Quality(B_2)$, $Recommendation(C_1, B_2)$, and so on. These are exactly the variables appearing in Figure 17(b). Because each type has only finitely many instances, the number of basic random variables is also finite.

To complete the RPM, we have to write the dependencies that govern these random variables. There is one dependency statement for each function, where each argument of the function is a logical variable (i.e., a variable that ranges over objects, as in first-order logic):

$$Honest(c) \sim \langle 0.99, 0.01 \rangle$$
$$Kindness(c) \sim \langle 0.1, 0.1, 0.2, 0.3, 0.3 \rangle$$
$$Quality(b) \sim \langle 0.05, 0.2, 0.4, 0.2, 0.15 \rangle$$
$$Recommendation(c,b) \sim RecCPT(Honest(c), Kindness(c), Quality(b))$$

where *RecCPT* is a separately defined conditional distribution with $2 \times 5 \times 5 = 50$ rows, each with 5 entries. The semantics of the RPM can be obtained by instantiating these dependencies for all known constants, giving a Bayesian network (as in Figure 17(b)) that defines a joint distribution over the RPM's random variables.[8]

CONTEXT-SPECIFIC INDEPENDENCE

We can refine the model by introducing a **context-specific independence** to reflect the fact that dishonest customers ignore quality when giving a recommendation; moreover, kindness plays no role in their decisions. A context-specific independence allows a variable to be independent of some of its parents given certain values of others; thus, $Recommendation(c, b)$ is independent of $Kindness(c)$ and $Quality(b)$ when $Honest(c) = false$:

$$\begin{aligned} Recommendation(c,b) \sim\ & \textbf{if } Honest(c) \textbf{ then} \\ & \quad HonestRecCPT(Kindness(c), Quality(b)) \\ & \textbf{else } \langle 0.4, 0.1, 0.0, 0.1, 0.4 \rangle . \end{aligned}$$

[8] Some technical conditions must be observed to guarantee that the RPM defines a proper distribution. First, the dependencies must be *acyclic*, otherwise the resulting Bayesian network will have cycles and will not define a proper distribution. Second, the dependencies must be *well-founded*, that is, there can be no infinite ancestor chains, such as might arise from recursive dependencies. Under some circumstances (see Exercise 6), a fixed-point calculation yields a well-defined probability model for a recursive RPM.

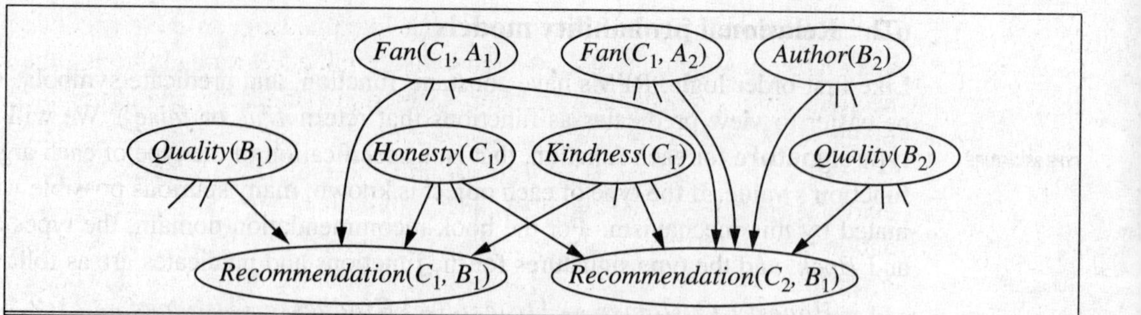

Figure 19 Fragment of the equivalent Bayes net when $Author(B_2)$ is unknown.

This kind of dependency may look like an ordinary if–then–else statement on a programming language, but there is a key difference: the inference engine *doesn't necessarily know the value of the conditional test*!

We can elaborate this model in endless ways to make it more realistic. For example, suppose that an honest customer who is a fan of a book's author always gives the book a 5, regardless of quality:

$$
\begin{aligned}
Recommendation(c, b) \sim\ & \textbf{if } Honest(c) \textbf{ then} \\
& \quad \textbf{if } Fan(c, Author(b)) \textbf{ then } Exactly(5) \\
& \quad \textbf{else } HonestRecCPT(Kindness(c), Quality(b)) \\
& \textbf{else } \langle 0.4, 0.1, 0.0, 0.1, 0.4 \rangle
\end{aligned}
$$

Again, the conditional test $Fan(c, Author(b))$ is unknown, but if a customer gives only 5s to a particular author's books and is not otherwise especially kind, then the posterior probability that the customer is a fan of that author will be high. Furthermore, the posterior distribution will tend to discount the customer's 5s in evaluating the quality of that author's books.

In the preceding example, we implicitly assumed that the value of $Author(b)$ is known for every b, but this may not be the case. How can the system reason about whether, say, C_1 is a fan of $Author(B_2)$ when $Author(B_2)$ is unknown? The answer is that the system may have to reason about *all possible authors*. Suppose (to keep things simple) that there are just two authors, A_1 and A_2. Then $Author(B_2)$ is a random variable with two possible values, A_1 and A_2, and it is a parent of $Recommendation(C_1, B_2)$. The variables $Fan(C_1, A_1)$ and $Fan(C_1, A_2)$ are parents too. The conditional distribution for $Recommendation(C_1, B_2)$ is MULTIPLEXER then essentially a **multiplexer** in which the $Author(B_2)$ parent acts as a selector to choose which of $Fan(C_1, A_1)$ and $Fan(C_1, A_2)$ actually gets to influence the recommendation. A fragment of the equivalent Bayes net is shown in Figure 19. Uncertainty in the value of $Author(B_2)$, which affects the dependency structure of the network, is an instance of RELATIONAL UNCERTAINTY **relational uncertainty**.

In case you are wondering how the system can possibly work out who the author of B_2 is: consider the possibility that three other customers are fans of A_1 (and have no other favorite authors in common) and all three have given B_2 a 5, even though most other customers find it quite dismal. In that case, it is extremely likely that A_1 is the author of B_2.

The emergence of sophisticated reasoning like this from an RPM model of just a few lines is an intriguing example of how probabilistic influences spread through the web of interconnections among objects in the model. As more dependencies and more objects are added, the picture conveyed by the posterior distribution often becomes clearer and clearer.

The next question is how to do inference in RPMs. One approach is to collect the evidence and query and the constant symbols therein, construct the equivalent Bayes net, and apply any of the inference methods discussed in this chapter. This technique is called

UNROLLING

unrolling. The obvious drawback is that the resulting Bayes net may be very large. Furthermore, if there are many candidate objects for an unknown relation or function—for example, the unknown author of B_2—then some variables in the network may have many parents.

Fortunately, much can be done to improve on generic inference algorithms. First, the presence of repeated substructure in the unrolled Bayes net means that many of the factors constructed during variable elimination (and similar kinds of tables constructed by clustering algorithms) will be identical; effective caching schemes have yielded speedups of three orders of magnitude for large networks. Second, inference methods developed to take advantage of context-specific independence in Bayes nets find many applications in RPMs. Third, MCMC inference algorithms have some interesting properties when applied to RPMs with relational uncertainty. MCMC works by sampling complete possible worlds, so in each state the relational structure is completely known. In the example given earlier, each MCMC state would specify the value of $Author(B_2)$, and so the other potential authors are no longer parents of the recommendation nodes for B_2. For MCMC, then, relational uncertainty causes no increase in network complexity; instead, the MCMC process includes transitions that change the relational structure, and hence the dependency structure, of the unrolled network.

All of the methods just described assume that the RPM has to be partially or completely unrolled into a Bayesian network. This is exactly analogous to the method of **propositionalization** for first-order logical inference. Resolution theorem-provers and logic programming systems avoid propositionalizing by instantiating the logical variables only as needed to make the inference go through; that is, they *lift* the inference process above the level of ground propositional sentences and make each lifted step do the work of many ground steps. The same idea applied in probabilistic inference. For example, in the variable elimination algorithm, a lifted factor can represent an entire set of ground factors that assign probabilities to random variables in the RPM, where those random variables differ only in the constant symbols used to construct them. References, containing details of this method, are given at the end of this chapter.

6.3 Open-universe probability models

We argued earlier that database semantics was appropriate for situations in which we know exactly the set of relevant objects that exist and can identify them unambiguously. (In particular, all observations about an object are correctly associated with the constant symbol that names it.) In many real-world settings, however, these assumptions are simply untenable. We gave the examples of multiple ISBNs and sibyl attacks in the book-recommendation domain (to which we will return in a moment), but the phenomenon is far more pervasive:

- A vision system doesn't know what exists, if anything, around the next corner, and may not know if the object it sees now is the same one it saw a few minutes ago.
- A text-understanding system does not know in advance the entities that will be featured in a text, and must reason about whether phrases such as "Mary," "Dr. Smith," "she," "his cardiologist," "his mother," and so on refer to the same object.
- An intelligence analyst hunting for spies never knows how many spies there really are and can only guess whether various pseudonyms, phone numbers, and sightings belong to the same individual.

In fact, a major part of human cognition seems to require learning what objects exist and being able to connect observations—which almost never come with unique IDs attached—to hypothesized objects in the world.

OPEN UNIVERSE

For these reasons, we need to be able to write so-called **open-universe** probability models or OUPMs based on the standard semantics of first-order logic, as illustrated at the top of Figure 18. A language for OUPMs provides a way of writing such models easily while guaranteeing a unique, consistent probability distribution over the infinite space of possible worlds.

The basic idea is to understand how ordinary Bayesian networks and RPMs manage to define a unique probability model and to transfer that insight to the first-order setting. In essence, a Bayes net *generates* each possible world, event by event, in the topological order defined by the network structure, where each event is an assignment of a value to a variable. An RPM extends this to entire sets of events, defined by the possible instantiations of the logical variables in a given predicate or function. OUPMs go further by allowing generative steps that *add objects* to the possible world under construction, where the number and type of objects may depend on the objects that are already in that world. That is, the event being generated is not the assignment of a value to a variable, but the very *existence* of objects.

One way to do this in OUPMs is to add statements that define conditional distributions over the numbers of objects of various kinds. For example, in the book-recommendation domain, we might want to distinguish between *customers* (real people) and their *login IDs*. Suppose we expect somewhere between 100 and 10,000 distinct customers (whom we cannot observe directly). We can express this as a prior log-normal distribution[9] as follows:

$$\#\, Customer \sim LogNormal[6.9, 2.3^2]() .$$

We expect honest customers to have just one ID, whereas dishonest customers might have anywhere between 10 and 1000 IDs:

$$\begin{aligned}\#\, LoginID(Owner = c) \sim \quad & \textbf{if } Honest(c) \textbf{ then } Exactly(1) \\ & \textbf{else } LogNormal[6.9, 2.3^2]() .\end{aligned}$$

ORIGIN FUNCTION

This statement defines the number of login IDs for a given owner, who is a customer. The *Owner* function is called an **origin function** because it says where each generated object came from. In the formal semantics of BLOG (as distinct from first-order logic), the domain elements in each possible world are actually generation histories (e.g., "the fourth login ID of the seventh customer") rather than simple tokens.

[9] A distribution $LogNormal[\mu, \sigma^2](x)$ is equivalent to a distribution $N[\mu, \sigma^2](x)$ over $\log_e(x)$.

Subject to technical conditions of acyclicity and well-foundedness similar to those for RPMs, open-universe models of this kind define a unique distribution over possible worlds. Furthermore, there exist inference algorithms such that, for every such well-defined model and every first-order query, the answer returned approaches the true posterior arbitrarily closely in the limit. There are some tricky issues involved in designing these algorithms. For example, an MCMC algorithm cannot sample directly in the space of possible worlds when the size of those worlds is unbounded; instead, it samples finite, partial worlds, relying on the fact that only finitely many objects can be relevant to the query in distinct ways. Moreover, transitions must allow for merging two objects into one or splitting one into two. (Details are given in the references at the end of the chapter.) Despite these complications, the basic principle established in Equation (13) still holds: the probability of any sentence is well defined and can be calculated.

Research in this area is still at an early stage, but already it is becoming clear that first-order probabilistic reasoning yields a tremendous increase in the effectiveness of AI systems at handling uncertain information. Potential applications include those mentioned above—computer vision, text understanding, and intelligence analysis—as well as many other kinds of sensor interpretation.

7 Other Approaches to Uncertain Reasoning

Other sciences (e.g., physics, genetics, and economics) have long favored probability as a model for uncertainty. In 1819, Pierre Laplace said, "Probability theory is nothing but common sense reduced to calculation." In 1850, James Maxwell said, "The true logic for this world is the calculus of Probabilities, which takes account of the magnitude of the probability which is, or ought to be, in a reasonable man's mind."

Given this long tradition, it is perhaps surprising that AI has considered many alternatives to probability. The earliest expert systems of the 1970s ignored uncertainty and used strict logical reasoning, but it soon became clear that this was impractical for most real-world domains. The next generation of expert systems (especially in medical domains) used probabilistic techniques. Initial results were promising, but they did not scale up because of the exponential number of probabilities required in the full joint distribution. (Efficient Bayesian network algorithms were unknown then.) As a result, probabilistic approaches fell out of favor from roughly 1975 to 1988, and a variety of alternatives to probability were tried for a variety of reasons:

- One common view is that probability theory is essentially numerical, whereas human judgmental reasoning is more "qualitative." Certainly, we are not consciously aware of doing numerical calculations of degrees of belief. (Neither are we aware of doing unification, yet we seem to be capable of some kind of logical reasoning.) It might be that we have some kind of numerical degrees of belief encoded directly in strengths of connections and activations in our neurons. In that case, the difficulty of conscious access to those strengths is not surprising. One should also note that qualitative reasoning mechanisms can be built directly on top of probability theory, so the "no numbers" argument against probability has little force. Nonetheless, some qualitative schemes have a good deal of appeal in their own right. One of the best studied is **default reasoning**, which treats conclusions not as "believed to a certain degree," but as "believed until a better reason is found to believe something else."

- **Rule-based** approaches to uncertainty have also been tried. Such approaches hope to build on the success of logical rule-based systems, but add a sort of "fudge factor" to each rule to accommodate uncertainty. These methods were developed in the mid-1970s and formed the basis for a large number of expert systems in medicine and other areas.
- One area that we have not addressed so far is the question of **ignorance**, as opposed to uncertainty. Consider the flipping of a coin. If we know that the coin is fair, then a probability of 0.5 for heads is reasonable. If we know that the coin is biased, but we do not know which way, then 0.5 for heads is again reasonable. Obviously, the two cases are different, yet the outcome probability seems not to distinguish them. The **Dempster–Shafer theory** uses **interval-valued** degrees of belief to represent an agent's knowledge of the probability of a proposition.
- Probability makes the same ontological commitment as logic: that propositions are true or false in the world, even if the agent is uncertain as to which is the case. Researchers in **fuzzy logic** have proposed an ontology that allows **vagueness**: that a proposition can be "sort of" true. Vagueness and uncertainty are in fact orthogonal issues.

The next three subsections treat some of these approaches in slightly more depth. We will not provide detailed technical material, but we cite references for further study.

7.1 Rule-based methods for uncertain reasoning

Rule-based systems emerged from early work on practical and intuitive systems for logical inference. Logical systems in general, and logical rule-based systems in particular, have three desirable properties:

LOCALITY

- **Locality**: In logical systems, whenever we have a rule of the form $A \Rightarrow B$, we can conclude B, given evidence A, *without worrying about any other rules.* In probabilistic systems, we need to consider *all* the evidence.

DETACHMENT

- **Detachment**: Once a logical proof is found for a proposition B, the proposition can be used regardless of how it was derived. That is, it can be **detached** from its justification. In dealing with probabilities, on the other hand, the source of the evidence for a belief is important for subsequent reasoning.

TRUTH-FUNCTIONALITY

- **Truth-functionality**: In logic, the truth of complex sentences can be computed from the truth of the components. Probability combination does not work this way, except under strong global independence assumptions.

There have been several attempts to devise uncertain reasoning schemes that retain these advantages. The idea is to attach degrees of belief to propositions and rules and to devise purely local schemes for combining and propagating those degrees of belief. The schemes are also truth-functional; for example, the degree of belief in $A \vee B$ is a function of the belief in A and the belief in B.

The bad news for rule-based systems is that the properties of *locality, detachment, and truth-functionality are simply not appropriate for uncertain reasoning.* Let us look at truth-functionality first. Let H_1 be the event that a fair coin flip comes up heads, let T_1 be the event that the coin comes up tails on that same flip, and let H_2 be the event that the coin comes up heads on a second flip. Clearly, all three events have the same probability, 0.5, and so a truth-functional system must assign the same belief to the disjunction of any two of them. But we can see that the probability of the disjunction depends on the events themselves and not just on their probabilities:

$P(A)$	$P(B)$	$P(A \vee B)$
	$P(H_1) = 0.5$	$P(H_1 \vee H_1) = 0.50$
$P(H_1) = 0.5$	$P(T_1) = 0.5$	$P(H_1 \vee T_1) = 1.00$
	$P(H_2) = 0.5$	$P(H_1 \vee H_2) = 0.75$

It gets worse when we chain evidence together. Truth-functional systems have **rules** of the form $A \mapsto B$ that allow us to compute the belief in B as a function of the belief in the rule and the belief in A. Both forward- and backward-chaining systems can be devised. The belief in the rule is assumed to be constant and is usually specified by the knowledge engineer—for example, as $A \mapsto_{0.9} B$.

Consider the wet-grass situation from Figure 12(a). If we wanted to be able to do both causal and diagnostic reasoning, we would need the two rules

$$Rain \mapsto WetGrass \qquad \text{and} \qquad WetGrass \mapsto Rain\ .$$

These two rules form a feedback loop: evidence for *Rain* increases the belief in *WetGrass*, which in turn increases the belief in *Rain* even more. Clearly, uncertain reasoning systems need to keep track of the paths along which evidence is propagated.

Intercausal reasoning (or explaining away) is also tricky. Consider what happens when we have the two rules

$$Sprinkler \mapsto WetGrass \qquad \text{and} \qquad WetGrass \mapsto Rain\ .$$

Suppose we see that the sprinkler is on. Chaining forward through our rules, this increases the belief that the grass will be wet, which in turn increases the belief that it is raining. But this is ridiculous: the fact that the sprinkler is on explains away the wet grass and should *reduce* the belief in rain. A truth-functional system acts as if it also believes $Sprinkler \mapsto Rain$.

Given these difficulties, how can truth-functional systems be made useful in practice? The answer lies in restricting the task and in carefully engineering the rule base so that undesirable interactions do not occur. The most famous example of a truth-functional system for uncertain reasoning is the **certainty factors** model, which was developed for the MYCIN medical diagnosis program and was widely used in expert systems of the late 1970s and 1980s. Almost all uses of certainty factors involved rule sets that were either purely diagnostic (as in MYCIN) or purely causal. Furthermore, evidence was entered only at the "roots" of the rule set, and most rule sets were singly connected. Heckerman (1986) has shown that,

CERTAINTY FACTOR

under these circumstances, a minor variation on certainty-factor inference was exactly equivalent to Bayesian inference on polytrees. In other circumstances, certainty factors could yield disastrously incorrect degrees of belief through overcounting of evidence. As rule sets became larger, undesirable interactions between rules became more common, and practitioners found that the certainty factors of many other rules had to be "tweaked" when new rules were added. For these reasons, Bayesian networks have largely supplanted rule-based methods for uncertain reasoning.

7.2 Representing ignorance: Dempster–Shafer theory

DEMPSTER–SHAFER THEORY

The **Dempster–Shafer theory** is designed to deal with the distinction between **uncertainty** and **ignorance**. Rather than computing the probability of a proposition, it computes the probability that the evidence supports the proposition. This measure of belief is called a **belief function**, written $Bel(X)$.

BELIEF FUNCTION

We return to coin flipping for an example of belief functions. Suppose you pick a coin from a magician's pocket. Given that the coin might or might not be fair, what belief should you ascribe to the event that it comes up heads? Dempster–Shafer theory says that because you have no evidence either way, you have to say that the belief $Bel(Heads) = 0$ and also that $Bel(\neg Heads) = 0$. This makes Dempster–Shafer reasoning systems skeptical in a way that has some intuitive appeal. Now suppose you have an expert at your disposal who testifies with 90% certainty that the coin is fair (i.e., he is 90% sure that $P(Heads) = 0.5$). Then Dempster–Shafer theory gives $Bel(Heads) = 0.9 \times 0.5 = 0.45$ and likewise $Bel(\neg Heads) = 0.45$. There is still a 10 percentage point "gap" that is not accounted for by the evidence.

The mathematical underpinnings of Dempster–Shafer theory have a similar flavor to those of probability theory; the main difference is that, instead of assigning probabilities to possible worlds, the theory assigns **masses** to *sets* of possible world, that is, to events. The masses still must add to 1 over all possible events. $Bel(A)$ is defined to be the sum of masses for all events that are subsets of (i.e., that entail) A, including A itself. With this definition, $Bel(A)$ and $Bel(\neg A)$ sum to *at most* 1, and the gap—the interval between $Bel(A)$ and $1 - Bel(\neg A)$—is often interpreted as bounding the probability of A.

MASS

As with default reasoning, there is a problem in connecting beliefs to actions. Whenever there is a gap in the beliefs, then a decision problem can be defined such that a Dempster–Shafer system is unable to make a decision. In fact, the notion of utility in the Dempster–Shafer model is not yet well understood because the meanings of masses and beliefs themselves have yet to be understood. Pearl (1988) has argued that $Bel(A)$ should be interpreted not as a degree of belief in A but as the probability assigned to all the possible worlds (now interpreted as logical theories) in which A is *provable*. While there are cases in which this quantity might be of interest, it is not the same as the probability that A is true.

A Bayesian analysis of the coin-flipping example would suggest that no new formalism is necessary to handle such cases. The model would have two variables: the *Bias* of the coin (a number between 0 and 1, where 0 is a coin that always shows tails and 1 a coin that always shows heads) and the outcome of the next *Flip*. The prior probability distribution for *Bias* would reflect our beliefs based on the source of the coin (the magician's pocket): some small probability that it is fair and some probability that it is heavily biased toward heads or tails. The conditional distribution $\mathbf{P}(Flip \mid Bias)$ simply defines how the bias operates. If $\mathbf{P}(Bias)$ is symmetric about 0.5, then our prior probability for the flip is

$$P(Flip = heads) = \int_0^1 P(Bias = x)P(Flip = heads \mid Bias = x)\, dx = 0.5 \,.$$

This is the same prediction as if we believe strongly that the coin is fair, but that does *not* mean that probability theory treats the two situations identically. The difference arises *after* the flips in computing the posterior distribution for $Bias$. If the coin came from a bank, then seeing it come up heads three times running would have almost no effect on our strong prior belief in its fairness; but if the coin comes from the magician's pocket, the same evidence will lead to a stronger posterior belief that the coin is biased toward heads. Thus, a Bayesian approach expresses our "ignorance" in terms of how our beliefs would change in the face of future information gathering.

7.3 Representing vagueness: Fuzzy sets and fuzzy logic

FUZZY SET THEORY

Fuzzy set theory is a means of specifying how well an object satisfies a vague description. For example, consider the proposition "Nate is tall." Is this true if Nate is 5′ 10″? Most people would hesitate to answer "true" or "false," preferring to say, "sort of." Note that this is not a question of uncertainty about the external world—we are sure of Nate's height. The issue is that the linguistic term "tall" does not refer to a sharp demarcation of objects into two classes—there are *degrees* of tallness. For this reason, *fuzzy set theory is not a method for uncertain reasoning at all.* Rather, fuzzy set theory treats $Tall$ as a fuzzy predicate and says that the truth value of $Tall(Nate)$ is a number between 0 and 1, rather than being just *true* or *false*. The name "fuzzy set" derives from the interpretation of the predicate as implicitly defining a set of its members—a set that does not have sharp boundaries.

FUZZY LOGIC

Fuzzy logic is a method for reasoning with logical expressions describing membership in fuzzy sets. For example, the complex sentence $Tall(Nate) \land Heavy(Nate)$ has a fuzzy truth value that is a function of the truth values of its components. The standard rules for evaluating the fuzzy truth, T, of a complex sentence are

$$\begin{aligned} T(A \land B) &= \min(T(A), T(B)) \\ T(A \lor B) &= \max(T(A), T(B)) \\ T(\lnot A) &= 1 - T(A)\,. \end{aligned}$$

Fuzzy logic is therefore a truth-functional system—a fact that causes serious difficulties. For example, suppose that $T(Tall(Nate)) = 0.6$ and $T(Heavy(Nate)) = 0.4$. Then we have $T(Tall(Nate) \land Heavy(Nate)) = 0.4$, which seems reasonable, but we also get the result $T(Tall(Nate) \land \lnot Tall(Nate)) = 0.4$, which does not. Clearly, the problem arises from the inability of a truth-functional approach to take into account the correlations or anticorrelations among the component propositions.

FUZZY CONTROL

Fuzzy control is a methodology for constructing control systems in which the mapping between real-valued input and output parameters is represented by fuzzy rules. Fuzzy control has been very successful in commercial products such as automatic transmissions, video cameras, and electric shavers. Critics (see, e.g., Elkan, 1993) argue that these applications are successful because they have small rule bases, no chaining of inferences, and tunable parameters that can be adjusted to improve the system's performance. The fact that they are implemented with fuzzy operators might be incidental to their success; the key is simply to provide a concise and intuitive way to specify a smoothly interpolated, real-valued function.

There have been attempts to provide an explanation of fuzzy logic in terms of probability theory. One idea is to view assertions such as "Nate is Tall" as discrete observations made concerning a continuous hidden variable, Nate's actual Height. The probability model specifies P(Observer says Nate is tall | *Height*), perhaps using a **probit distribution** as described in section 3. A posterior distribution over Nate's height can then be calculated in the usual way, for example, if the model is part of a hybrid Bayesian network. Such an approach is not truth-functional, of course. For example, the conditional distribution

$$P(\text{Observer says Nate is tall and heavy} \mid Height, Weight)$$

allows for interactions between height and weight in the causing of the observation. Thus, someone who is eight feet tall and weighs 190 pounds is very unlikely to be called "tall and heavy," even though "eight feet" counts as "tall" and "190 pounds" counts as "heavy."

Fuzzy predicates can also be given a probabilistic interpretation in terms of **random sets**—that is, random variables whose possible values are sets of objects. For example, *Tall* is a random set whose possible values are sets of people. The probability $P(Tall = S_1)$, where S_1 is some particular set of people, is the probability that exactly that set would be identified as "tall" by an observer. Then the probability that "Nate is tall" is the sum of the probabilities of all the sets of which Nate is a member.

RANDOM SET

Both the hybrid Bayesian network approach and the random sets approach appear to capture aspects of fuzziness without introducing degrees of truth. Nonetheless, there remain many open issues concerning the proper representation of linguistic observations and continuous quantities—issues that have been neglected by most outside the fuzzy community.

8 SUMMARY

This chapter has described **Bayesian networks**, a well-developed representation for uncertain knowledge. Bayesian networks play a role roughly analogous to that of propositional logic for definite knowledge.

- A Bayesian network is a directed acyclic graph whose nodes correspond to random variables; each node has a conditional distribution for the node, given its parents.
- Bayesian networks provide a concise way to represent **conditional independence** relationships in the domain.
- A Bayesian network specifies a full joint distribution; each joint entry is defined as the product of the corresponding entries in the local conditional distributions. A Bayesian network is often exponentially smaller than an explicitly enumerated joint distribution.
- Many conditional distributions can be represented compactly by canonical families of

distributions. **Hybrid Bayesian networks**, which include both discrete and continuous variables, use a variety of canonical distributions.

- Inference in Bayesian networks means computing the probability distribution of a set of query variables, given a set of evidence variables. Exact inference algorithms, such as **variable elimination**, evaluate sums of products of conditional probabilities as efficiently as possible.
- In **polytrees** (singly connected networks), exact inference takes time linear in the size of the network. In the general case, the problem is intractable.
- Stochastic approximation techniques such as **likelihood weighting** and **Markov chain Monte Carlo** can give reasonable estimates of the true posterior probabilities in a network and can cope with much larger networks than can exact algorithms.
- Probability theory can be combined with representational ideas from first-order logic to produce very powerful systems for reasoning under uncertainty. **Relational probability models** (RPMs) include representational restrictions that guarantee a well-defined probability distribution that can be expressed as an equivalent Bayesian network. **Open-universe probability models** handle **existence** and **identity uncertainty**, defining probabilty distributions over the infinite space of first-order possible worlds.
- Various alternative systems for reasoning under uncertainty have been suggested. Generally speaking, **truth-functional** systems are not well suited for such reasoning.

BIBLIOGRAPHICAL AND HISTORICAL NOTES

The use of networks to represent probabilistic information began early in the 20th century, with the work of Sewall Wright on the probabilistic analysis of genetic inheritance and animal growth factors (Wright, 1921, 1934). I. J. Good (1961), in collaboration with Alan Turing, developed probabilistic representations and Bayesian inference methods that could be regarded as a forerunner of modern Bayesian networks—although the paper is not often cited in this context.[10] The same paper is the original source for the noisy-OR model.

The **influence diagram** representation for decision problems, which incorporated a DAG representation for random variables, was used in decision analysis in the late 1970s, but only enumeration was used for evaluation. Judea Pearl developed the message-passing method for carrying out inference in tree networks (Pearl, 1982a) and poly-tree networks (Kim and Pearl, 1983) and explained the importance of causal rather than diagnostic probability models, in contrast to the certainty-factor systems then in vogue.

The first expert system using Bayesian networks was CONVINCE (Kim, 1983). Early applications in medicine included the MUNIN system for diagnosing neuromuscular disorders (Andersen *et al.*, 1989) and the PATHFINDER system for pathology (Heckerman, 1991). The CPCS system (Pradhan *et al.*, 1994) is a Bayesian network for internal medicine consisting

[10] I. J. Good was chief statistician for Turing's code-breaking team in World War II. In *2001: A Space Odyssey* (Clarke, 1968a), Good and Minsky are credited with making the breakthrough that led to the development of the HAL 9000 computer.

of 448 nodes, 906 links and 8,254 conditional probability values.

Applications in engineering include the Electric Power Research Institute's work on monitoring power generators (Morjaria *et al.*, 1995), NASA's work on displaying time-critical information at Mission Control in Houston (Horvitz and Barry, 1995), and the general field of **network tomography**, which aims to infer unobserved local properties of nodes and links in the Internet from observations of end-to-end message performance (Castro *et al.*, 2004). Perhaps the most widely used Bayesian network systems have been the diagnosis-and-repair modules (e.g., the Printer Wizard) in Microsoft Windows (Breese and Heckerman, 1996) and the Office Assistant in Microsoft Office (Horvitz *et al.*, 1998). Another important application area is biology: Bayesian networks have been used for identifying human genes by reference to mouse genes (Zhang *et al.*, 2003), inferring cellular networks Friedman (2004), and many other tasks in bioinformatics. We could go on, but instead we'll refer you to Pourret *et al.* (2008), a 400-page guide to applications of Bayesian networks.

Ross Shachter (1986), working in the influence diagram community, developed the first complete algorithm for general Bayesian networks. His method was based on goal-directed reduction of the network using posterior-preserving transformations. Pearl (1986) developed a clustering algorithm for exact inference in general Bayesian networks, utilizing a conversion to a directed polytree of clusters in which message passing was used to achieve consistency over variables shared between clusters. A similar approach, developed by the statisticians David Spiegelhalter and Steffen Lauritzen (Lauritzen and Spiegelhalter, 1988), is based on conversion to an undirected form of graphical model called a **Markov network**. This approach is implemented in the HUGIN system, an efficient and widely used tool for uncertain reasoning (Andersen *et al.*, 1989). Boutilier *et al.* (1996) show how to exploit context-specific independence in clustering algorithms.

MARKOV NETWORK

The basic idea of variable elimination—that repeated computations within the overall sum-of-products expression can be avoided by caching—appeared in the symbolic probabilistic inference (SPI) algorithm (Shachter *et al.*, 1990). The elimination algorithm we describe is closest to that developed by Zhang and Poole (1994). Criteria for pruning irrelevant variables were developed by Geiger *et al.* (1990) and by Lauritzen *et al.* (1990); the criterion we give is a simple special case of these. Dechter (1999) shows how the variable elimination idea is essentially identical to **nonserial dynamic programming** (Bertele and Brioschi, 1972), an algorithmic approach that can be applied to solve a range of inference problems in Bayesian networks—for example, finding the **most likely explanation** for a set of observations. This connects Bayesian network algorithms to related methods for solving CSPs and gives a direct measure of the complexity of exact inference in terms of the tree width of the network. Wexler and Meek (2009) describe a method of preventing exponential growth in the size of factors computed in variable elimination; their algorithm breaks down large factors into products of smaller factors and simultaneously computes an error bound for the resulting approximation.

NONSERIAL DYNAMIC PROGRAMMING

The inclusion of continuous random variables in Bayesian networks was considered by Pearl (1988) and Shachter and Kenley (1989); these papers discussed networks containing only continuous variables with linear Gaussian distributions. The inclusion of discrete variables has been investigated by Lauritzen and Wermuth (1989) and implemented in the cHUGIN system (Olesen, 1993). Further analysis of linear Gaussian models, with connections to many other models used in statistics, appears in Roweis and Ghahramani (1999) The probit distribution is usually attributed to Gaddum (1933) and Bliss (1934), although it had been discovered several times in the 19th century. Bliss's work was expanded considerably by Finney (1947). The probit has been used widely for modeling discrete choice phenomena and can be extended to handle more than two choices (Daganzo, 1979). The logit model was introduced by Berkson (1944); initially much derided, it eventually became more popular than the probit model. Bishop (1995) gives a simple justification for its use.

Cooper (1990) showed that the general problem of inference in unconstrained Bayesian networks is NP-hard, and Paul Dagum and Mike Luby (1993) showed the corresponding approximation problem to be NP-hard. Space complexity is also a serious problem in both clustering and variable elimination methods. The method of **cutset conditioning**, avoids the construction of exponentially large tables. In a Bayesian network, a cutset is a set of nodes that, when instantiated, reduces the remaining nodes to a polytree that can be solved in linear time and space. The query is answered by summing over all the instantiations of the cutset, so the overall space requirement is still linear (Pearl, 1988). Darwiche (2001) describes a recursive conditioning algorithm that allows a complete range of space/time tradeoffs.

The development of fast approximation algorithms for Bayesian network inference is a very active area, with contributions from statistics, computer science, and physics. The rejection sampling method is a general technique that is long known to statisticians; it was first applied to Bayesian networks by Max Henrion (1988), who called it **logic sampling**. Likelihood weighting, which was developed by Fung and Chang (1989) and Shachter and Peot (1989), is an example of the well-known statistical method of **importance sampling**. Cheng and Druzdzel (2000) describe an adaptive version of likelihood weighting that works well even when the evidence has very low prior likelihood.

Markov chain Monte Carlo (MCMC) algorithms began with the Metropolis algorithm, due to Metropolis *et al.* (1953), which is also the source of the simulated annealing algorithm. The Gibbs sampler was devised by Geman and Geman (1984) for inference in undirected Markov networks. The application of MCMC to Bayesian networks is due to Pearl (1987). The papers collected by Gilks *et al.* (1996) cover a wide variety of applications of MCMC, several of which were developed in the well-known BUGS package (Gilks *et al.*, 1994).

There are two very important families of approximation methods that we did not cover in the chapter. The first is the family of **variational approximation** methods, which can be used to simplify complex calculations of all kinds. The basic idea is to propose a reduced version of the original problem that is simple to work with, but that resembles the original problem as closely as possible. The reduced problem is described by some **variational parameters** $\boldsymbol{\lambda}$ that are adjusted to minimize a distance function D between the original and the reduced problem, often by solving the system of equations $\partial D/\partial\boldsymbol{\lambda}=0$. In many cases, strict upper and lower bounds can be obtained. Variational methods have long been used in statistics (Rustagi, 1976). In statistical physics, the **mean-field** method is a particular variational approximation in which the individual variables making up the model are assumed

VARIATIONAL APPROXIMATION

VARIATIONAL PARAMETER

MEAN FIELD

to be completely independent. This idea was applied to solve large undirected Markov networks (Peterson and Anderson, 1987; Parisi, 1988). Saul *et al.* (1996) developed the mathematical foundations for applying variational methods to Bayesian networks and obtained accurate lower-bound approximations for sigmoid networks with the use of mean-field methods. Jaakkola and Jordan (1996) extended the methodology to obtain both lower and upper bounds. Since these early papers, variational methods have been applied to many specific families of models. The remarkable paper by Wainwright and Jordan (2008) provides a unifying theoretical analysis of the literature on variational methods.

A second important family of approximation algorithms is based on Pearl's polytree message-passing algorithm (1982a). This algorithm can be applied to general networks, as suggested by Pearl (1988). The results might be incorrect, or the algorithm might fail to terminate, but in many cases, the values obtained are close to the true values. Little attention was paid to this so-called **belief propagation** (or BP) approach until McEliece *et al.* (1998) observed that message passing in a multiply connected Bayesian network was exactly the computation performed by the **turbo decoding** algorithm (Berrou *et al.*, 1993), which provided a major breakthrough in the design of efficient error-correcting codes. The implication is that BP is both fast and accurate on the very large and very highly connected networks used for decoding and might therefore be useful more generally. Murphy *et al.* (1999) presented a promising empirical study of BP's performance, and Weiss and Freeman (2001) established strong convergence results for BP on linear Gaussian networks. Weiss (2000b) shows how an approximation called loopy belief propagation works, and when the approximation is correct. Yedidia *et al.* (2005) made further connections between loopy propagation and ideas from statistical physics.

BELIEF PROPAGATION

TURBO DECODING

The connection between probability and first-order languages was first studied by Carnap (1950). Gaifman (1964) and Scott and Krauss (1966) defined a language in which probabilities could be associated with first-order sentences and for which models were probability measures on possible worlds. Within AI, this idea was developed for propositional logic by Nilsson (1986) and for first-order logic by Halpern (1990). The first extensive investigation of knowledge representation issues in such languages was carried out by Bacchus (1990). The basic idea is that each sentence in the knowledge base expressed a *constraint* on the distribution over possible worlds; one sentence entails another if it expresses a stronger constraint. For example, the sentence $\forall x \quad P(Hungry(x)) > 0.2$ rules out distributions in which any object is hungry with probability less than 0.2; thus, it entails the sentence $\forall x \quad P(Hungry(x)) > 0.1$. It turns out that writing a *consistent* set of sentences in these languages is quite difficult and constructing a unique probability model nearly impossible unless one adopts the representation approach of Bayesian networks by writing suitable sentences about conditional probabilities.

Beginning in the early 1990s, researchers working on complex applications noticed the expressive limitations of Bayesian networks and developed various languages for writing "templates" with logical variables, from which large networks could be constructed automatically for each problem instance (Breese, 1992; Wellman *et al.*, 1992). The most important such language was BUGS (Bayesian inference Using Gibbs Sampling) (Gilks *et al.*, 1994), which combined Bayesian networks with the **indexed random variable** notation common in

INDEXED RANDOM VARIABLE

statistics. (In BUGS, an indexed random variable looks like $X[i]$, where i has a defined integer range.) These languages inherited the key property of Bayesian networks: every well-formed knowledge base defines a unique, consistent probability model. Languages with well-defined semantics based on unique names and domain closure drew on the representational capabilities of logic programming (Poole, 1993; Sato and Kameya, 1997; Kersting *et al.*, 2000) and semantic networks (Koller and Pfeffer, 1998; Pfeffer, 2000). Pfeffer (2007) went on to develop IBAL, which represents first-order probability models as probabilistic programs in a programming language extended with a randomization primitive. Another important thread was the combination of relational and first-order notations with (undirected) Markov networks (Taskar *et al.*, 2002; Domingos and Richardson, 2004), where the emphasis has been less on knowledge representation and more on learning from large data sets.

Initially, inference in these models was performed by generating an equivalent Bayesian network. Pfeffer *et al.* (1999) introduced a variable elimination algorithm that cached each computed factor for reuse by later computations involving the same relations but different objects, thereby realizing some of the computational gains of lifting. The first truly lifted inference algorithm was a lifted form of variable elimination described by Poole (2003) and subsequently improved by de Salvo Braz *et al.* (2007). Further advances, including cases where certain aggregate probabilities can be computed in closed form, are described by Milch *et al.* (2008) and Kisynski and Poole (2009). Pasula and Russell (2001) studied the application of MCMC to avoid building the complete equivalent Bayes net in cases of relational and identity uncertainty. Getoor and Taskar (2007) collect many important papers on first-order probability models and their use in machine learning.

Probabilistic reasoning about identity uncertainty has two distinct origins. In statistics, the problem of **record linkage** arises when data records do not contain standard unique identifiers—for example, various citations of this book might name its first author "Stuart Russell" or "S. J. Russell" or even "Stewart Russle," and other authors may use the some of the same names. Literally hundreds of companies exist solely to solve record linkage problems in financial, medical, census, and other data. Probabilistic analysis goes back to work by Dunn (1946); the Fellegi–Sunter model (1969), which is essentially naive Bayes applied to matching, still dominates current practice. The second origin for work on identity uncertainty is multitarget tracking (Sittler, 1964). For most of its history, work in symbolic AI assumed erroneously that sensors could supply sentences with unique identifiers for objects. The issue was studied in the context of language understanding by Charniak and Goldman (1992) and in the context of surveillance by (Huang and Russell, 1998) and Pasula *et al.* (1999). Pasula *et al.* (2003) developed a complex generative model for authors, papers, and citation strings, involving both relational and identity uncertainty, and demonstrated high accuracy for citation information extraction. The first formally defined language for open-universe probability models was BLOG (Milch *et al.*, 2005), which came with a complete (albeit slow) MCMC inference algorithm for all well-defined models. Laskey (2008) describes another open-universe modeling language called **multi-entity Bayesian networks**.

Early probabilistic systems fell out of favor in the early 1970s, leaving a partial vacuum to be filled by alternative methods. Certainty factors were invented for use in the medical expert system MYCIN (Shortliffe, 1976), which was intended both as an engineering solution and as a model of human judgment under uncertainty. The collection *Rule-Based Expert Systems* (Buchanan and Shortliffe, 1984) provides a complete overview of MYCIN and its descendants (see also Stefik, 1995). David Heckerman (1986) showed that a slightly modified version of certainty factor calculations gives correct probabilistic results in some cases, but results in serious overcounting of evidence in other cases. The PROSPECTOR expert system (Duda *et al.*, 1979) used a rule-based approach in which the rules were justified by a (seldom tenable) global independence assumption.

Dempster–Shafer theory originates with a paper by Arthur Dempster (1968) proposing a generalization of probability to interval values and a combination rule for using them. Later work by Glenn Shafer (1976) led to the Dempster-Shafer theory's being viewed as a competing approach to probability. Pearl (1988) and Ruspini *et al.* (1992) analyze the relationship between the Dempster–Shafer theory and standard probability theory.

Fuzzy sets were developed by Lotfi Zadeh (1965) in response to the perceived difficulty of providing exact inputs to intelligent systems. The text by Zimmermann (2001) provides a thorough introduction to fuzzy set theory; papers on fuzzy applications are collected in Zimmermann (1999). As we mentioned in the text, fuzzy logic has often been perceived incorrectly as a direct competitor to probability theory, whereas in fact it addresses a different set of issues. **Possibility theory** (Zadeh, 1978) was introduced to handle uncertainty in fuzzy systems and has much in common with probability. Dubois and Prade (1994) survey the connections between possibility theory and probability theory.

POSSIBILITY THEORY

The resurgence of probability depended mainly on Pearl's development of Bayesian networks as a method for representing and using conditional independence information. This resurgence did not come without a fight; Peter Cheeseman's (1985) pugnacious "In Defense of Probability" and his later article "An Inquiry into Computer Understanding" (Cheeseman, 1988, with commentaries) give something of the flavor of the debate. Eugene Charniak helped present the ideas to AI researchers with a popular article, "Bayesian networks without tears"[11] (1991), and book (1993). The book by Dean and Wellman (1991) also helped introduce Bayesian networks to AI researchers. One of the principal philosophical objections of the logicists was that the numerical calculations that probability theory was thought to require were not apparent to introspection and presumed an unrealistic level of precision in our uncertain knowledge. The development of **qualitative probabilistic networks** (Wellman, 1990a) provided a purely qualitative abstraction of Bayesian networks, using the notion of positive and negative influences between variables. Wellman shows that in many cases such information is sufficient for optimal decision making without the need for the precise specification of probability values. Goldszmidt and Pearl (1996) take a similar approach. Work by Adnan Darwiche and Matt Ginsberg (1992) extracts the basic properties of conditioning and evidence combination from probability theory and shows that they can also be applied in logical and default reasoning. Often, programs speak louder than words, and the ready avail-

[11] The title of the original version of the article was "Pearl for swine."

ability of high-quality software such as the Bayes Net toolkit (Murphy, 2001) accelerated the adoption of the technology.

The most important single publication in the growth of Bayesian networks was undoubtedly the text *Probabilistic Reasoning in Intelligent Systems* (Pearl, 1988). Several excellent texts (Lauritzen, 1996; Jensen, 2001; Korb and Nicholson, 2003; Jensen, 2007; Darwiche, 2009; Koller and Friedman, 2009) provide thorough treatments of the topics we have covered in this chapter. New research on probabilistic reasoning appears both in mainstream AI journals, such as *Artificial Intelligence* and the *Journal of AI Research*, and in more specialized journals, such as the *International Journal of Approximate Reasoning*. Many papers on graphical models, which include Bayesian networks, appear in statistical journals. The proceedings of the conferences on Uncertainty in Artificial Intelligence (UAI), Neural Information Processing Systems (NIPS), and Artificial Intelligence and Statistics (AISTATS) are excellent sources for current research.

EXERCISES

1 We have a bag of three biased coins a, b, and c with probabilities of coming up heads of 20%, 60%, and 80%, respectively. One coin is drawn randomly from the bag (with equal likelihood of drawing each of the three coins), and then the coin is flipped three times to generate the outcomes X_1, X_2, and X_3.

a. Draw the Bayesian network corresponding to this setup and define the necessary CPTs.

b. Calculate which coin was most likely to have been drawn from the bag if the observed flips come out heads twice and tails once.

2 Equation (1) defines the joint distribution represented by a Bayesian network in terms of the parameters $\theta(X_i \mid Parents(X_i))$. This exercise asks you to derive the equivalence between the parameters and the conditional probabilities $\mathbf{P}(X_i \mid Parents(X_i))$ from this definition.

a. Consider a simple network $X \to Y \to Z$ with three Boolean variables. Use Equations (3) and (6) from the chapter "Quantifying Uncertainity" to express the conditional probability $P(z \mid y)$ as the ratio of two sums, each over entries in the joint distribution $\mathbf{P}(X, Y, Z)$.

b. Now use Equation (1) to write this expression in terms of the network parameters $\theta(X)$, $\theta(Y \mid X)$, and $\theta(Z \mid Y)$.

c. Next, expand out the summations in your expression from part (b), writing out explicitly the terms for the true and false values of each summed variable. Assuming that all network parameters satisfy the constraint $\sum_{x_i} \theta(x_i \mid parents(X_i)) = 1$, show that the resulting expression reduces to $\theta(x \mid y)$.

d. Generalize this derivation to show that $\theta(X_i \mid Parents(X_i)) = \mathbf{P}(X_i \mid Parents(X_i))$ for any Bayesian network.

ARC REVERSAL **3** The operation of **arc reversal** in a Bayesian network allows us to change the direction of an arc $X \rightarrow Y$ while preserving the joint probability distribution that the network represents (Shachter, 1986). Arc reversal may require introducing new arcs: all the parents of X also become parents of Y, and all parents of Y also become parents of X.

a. Assume that X and Y start with m and n parents, respectively, and that all variables have k values. By calculating the change in size for the CPTs of X and Y, show that the total number of parameters in the network cannot decrease during arc reversal. (*Hint*: the parents of X and Y need not be disjoint.)

b. Under what circumstances can the total number remain constant?

c. Let the parents of X be $\mathbf{U} \cup \mathbf{V}$ and the parents of Y be $\mathbf{V} \cup \mathbf{W}$, where $\mathbf{U}$ and $\mathbf{W}$ are disjoint. The formulas for the new CPTs after arc reversal are as follows:

$$\mathbf{P}(Y \mid \mathbf{U}, \mathbf{V}, \mathbf{W}) = \sum_x \mathbf{P}(Y \mid \mathbf{V}, \mathbf{W}, x)\mathbf{P}(x \mid \mathbf{U}, \mathbf{V})$$

$$\mathbf{P}(X \mid \mathbf{U}, \mathbf{V}, \mathbf{W}, Y) = \mathbf{P}(Y \mid X, \mathbf{V}, \mathbf{W})\mathbf{P}(X \mid \mathbf{U}, \mathbf{V})/\mathbf{P}(Y \mid \mathbf{U}, \mathbf{V}, \mathbf{W}) .$$

Prove that the new network expresses the same joint distribution over all variables as the original network.

4 Consider the Bayesian network in Figure 2.

a. If no evidence is observed, are *Burglary* and *Earthquake* independent? Prove this from the numerical semantics and from the topological semantics.

b. If we observe $Alarm = true$, are *Burglary* and *Earthquake* independent? Justify your answer by calculating whether the probabilities involved satisfy the definition of conditional independence.

5 Suppose that in a Bayesian network containing an unobserved variable Y, all the variables in the Markov blanket $MB(Y)$ have been observed.

a. Prove that removing the node Y from the network will not affect the posterior distribution for any other unobserved variable in the network.

b. Discuss whether we can remove Y if we are planning to use (i) rejection sampling and (ii) likelihood weighting.

6 Let H_x be a random variable denoting the handedness of an individual x, with possible values l or r. A common hypothesis is that left- or right-handedness is inherited by a simple mechanism; that is, perhaps there is a gene G_x, also with values l or r, and perhaps actual handedness turns out mostly the same (with some probability s) as the gene an individual possesses. Furthermore, perhaps the gene itself is equally likely to be inherited from either of an individual's parents, with a small nonzero probability m of a random mutation flipping the handedness.

a. Which of the three networks in Figure 20 claim that $\mathbf{P}(G_{father}, G_{mother}, G_{child}) = \mathbf{P}(G_{father})\mathbf{P}(G_{mother})\mathbf{P}(G_{child})$?

b. Which of the three networks make independence claims that are consistent with the hypothesis about the inheritance of handedness?

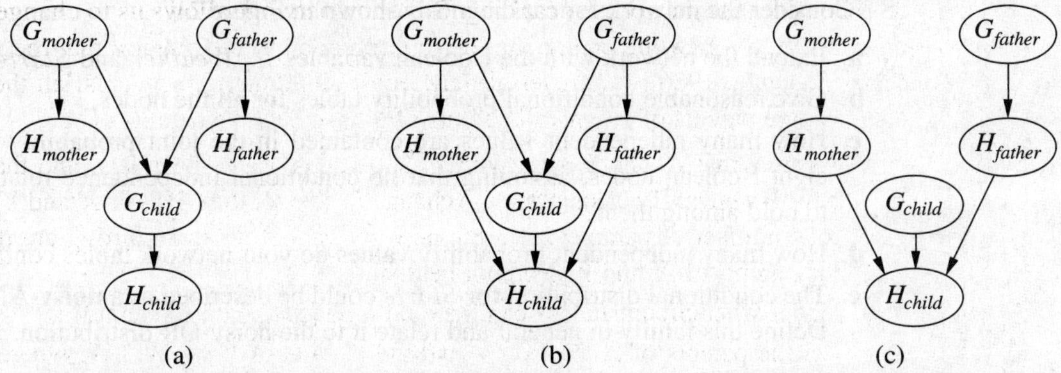

Figure 20 Three possible structures for a Bayesian network describing genetic inheritance of handedness.

c. Which of the three networks is the best description of the hypothesis?

d. Write down the CPT for the G_{child} node in network (a), in terms of s and m.

e. Suppose that $P(G_{father} = l) = P(G_{mother} = l) = q$. In network (a), derive an expression for $P(G_{child} = l)$ in terms of m and q only, by conditioning on its parent nodes.

f. Under conditions of genetic equilibrium, we expect the distribution of genes to be the same across generations. Use this to calculate the value of q, and, given what you know about handedness in humans, explain why the hypothesis described at the beginning of this question must be wrong.

7 The **Markov blanket** of a variable is defined in section 2.2. Prove that a variable is independent of all other variables in the network, given its Markov blanket and derive Equation (12).

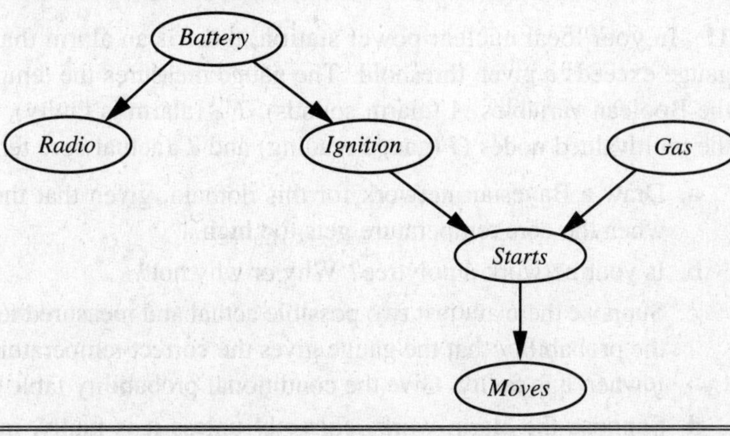

Figure 21 A Bayesian network describing some features of a car's electrical system and engine. Each variable is Boolean, and the *true* value indicates that the corresponding aspect of the vehicle is in working order.

8 Consider the network for car diagnosis shown in Figure 21.

a. Extend the network with the Boolean variables *IcyWeather* and *StarterMotor*.

b. Give reasonable conditional probability tables for all the nodes.

c. How many independent values are contained in the joint probability distribution for eight Boolean nodes, assuming that no conditional independence relations are known to hold among them?

d. How many independent probability values do your network tables contain?

e. The conditional distribution for *Starts* could be described as a **noisy-AND** distribution. Define this family in general and relate it to the noisy-OR distribution.

9 Consider the family of linear Gaussian networks, as defined in section 3.

a. In a two-variable network, let X_1 be the parent of X_2, let X_1 have a Gaussian prior, and let $\mathbf{P}(X_2 \mid X_1)$ be a linear Gaussian distribution. Show that the joint distribution $P(X_1, X_2)$ is a multivariate Gaussian, and calculate its covariance matrix.

b. Prove by induction that the joint distribution for a general linear Gaussian network on $X_1, \ldots, X_n$ is also a multivariate Gaussian.

10 The probit distribution defined in section 3 describes the probability distribution for a Boolean child, given a single continuous parent.

a. How might the definition be extended to cover multiple continuous parents?

b. How might it be extended to handle a *multivalued* child variable? Consider both cases where the child's values are ordered (as in selecting a gear while driving, depending on speed, slope, desired acceleration, etc.) and cases where they are unordered (as in selecting bus, train, or car to get to work). (*Hint*: Consider ways to divide the possible values into two sets, to mimic a Boolean variable.)

11 In your local nuclear power station, there is an alarm that senses when a temperature gauge exceeds a given threshold. The gauge measures the temperature of the core. Consider the Boolean variables A (alarm sounds), F_A (alarm is faulty), and F_G (gauge is faulty) and the multivalued nodes G (gauge reading) and T (actual core temperature).

a. Draw a Bayesian network for this domain, given that the gauge is more likely to fail when the core temperature gets too high.

b. Is your network a polytree? Why or why not?

c. Suppose there are just two possible actual and measured temperatures, normal and high; the probability that the gauge gives the correct temperature is x when it is working, but y when it is faulty. Give the conditional probability table associated with G.

d. Suppose the alarm works correctly unless it is faulty, in which case it never sounds. Give the conditional probability table associated with A.

e. Suppose the alarm and gauge are working and the alarm sounds. Calculate an expression for the probability that the temperature of the core is too high, in terms of the various conditional probabilities in the network.

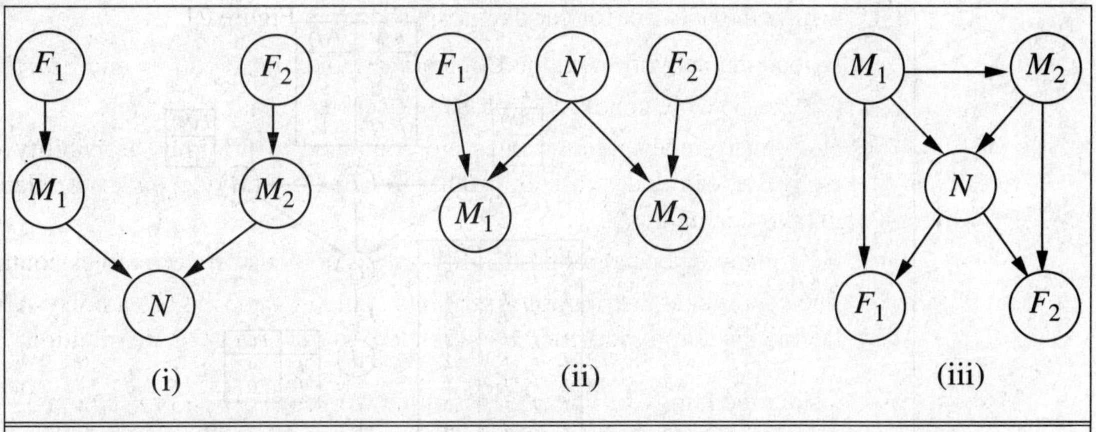

Figure 22 Three possible networks for the telescope problem.

12 Two astronomers in different parts of the world make measurements M_1 and M_2 of the number of stars N in some small region of the sky, using their telescopes. Normally, there is a small possibility e of error by up to one star in each direction. Each telescope can also (with a much smaller probability f) be badly out of focus (events F_1 and F_2), in which case the scientist will undercount by three or more stars (or if N is less than 3, fail to detect any stars at all). Consider the three networks shown in Figure 22.

a. Which of these Bayesian networks are correct (but not necessarily efficient) representations of the preceding information?

b. Which is the best network? Explain.

c. Write out a conditional distribution for $\mathbf{P}(M_1 \mid N)$, for the case where $N \in \{1, 2, 3\}$ and $M_1 \in \{0, 1, 2, 3, 4\}$. Each entry in the conditional distribution should be expressed as a function of the parameters e and/or f.

d. Suppose $M_1 = 1$ and $M_2 = 3$. What are the *possible* numbers of stars if you assume no prior constraint on the values of N?

e. What is the *most likely* number of stars, given these observations? Explain how to compute this, or if it is not possible to compute, explain what additional information is needed and how it would affect the result.

13 Consider the network shown in Figure 22(ii), and assume that the two telescopes work identically. $N \in \{1, 2, 3\}$ and $M_1, M_2 \in \{0, 1, 2, 3, 4\}$, with the symbolic CPTs as described in Exercise 12. Using the enumeration algorithm (Figure 9), calculate the probability distribution $\mathbf{P}(N \mid M_1 = 2, M_2 = 2)$.

14 Consider the Bayes net shown in Figure 23.

a. Which of the following are asserted by the network *structure*?

(i) $\mathbf{P}(B, I, M) = \mathbf{P}(B)\mathbf{P}(I)\mathbf{P}(M)$.

(ii) $\mathbf{P}(J \mid G) = \mathbf{P}(J \mid G, I)$.

(iii) $\mathbf{P}(M \mid G, B, I) = \mathbf{P}(M \mid G, B, I, J)$.

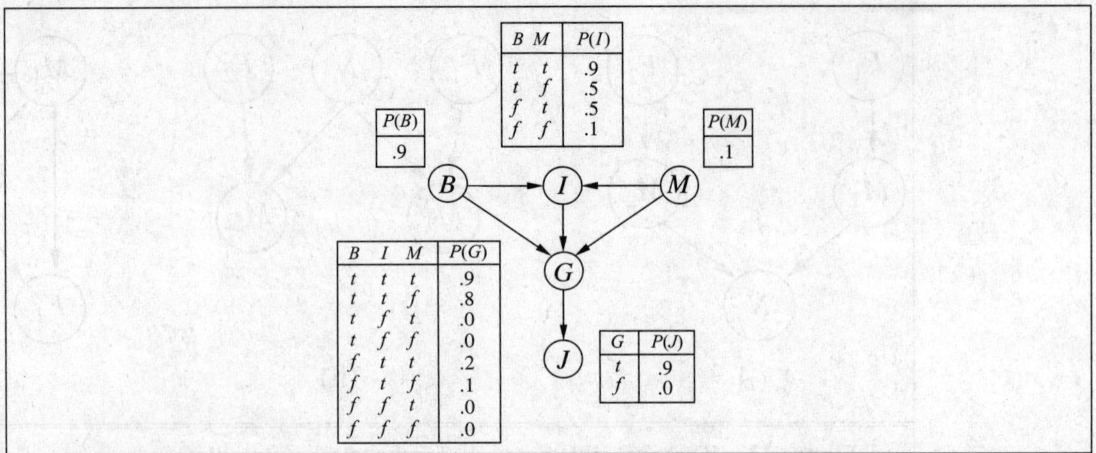

Figure 23 A simple Bayes net with Boolean variables $B = BrokeElectionLaw$, $I = Indicted$, $M = PoliticallyMotivatedProsecutor$, $G = FoundGuilty$, $J = Jailed$.

b. Calculate the value of $P(b, i, \neg m, g, j)$.

c. Calculate the probability that someone goes to jail given that they broke the law, have been indicted, and face a politically motivated prosecutor.

d. **context-specific independence** allows a variable to be independent of some of its parents given certain values of others. In addition to the usual conditional independences given by the graph structure, what context-specific independences exist in the Bayes net in Figure 23?

e. Suppose we want to add the variable $P = PresidentialPardon$ to the network; draw the new network and briefly explain any links you add.

15 Consider the variable elimination algorithm in Figure 11.

a. Section 4 applies variable elimination to the query

$$\mathbf{P}(Burglary \mid JohnCalls = true, MaryCalls = true)\,.$$

Perform the calculations indicated and check that the answer is correct.

b. Count the number of arithmetic operations performed, and compare it with the number performed by the enumeration algorithm.

c. Suppose a network has the form of a *chain*: a sequence of Boolean variables $X_1, \ldots, X_n$ where $Parents(X_i) = \{X_{i-1}\}$ for $i = 2, \ldots, n$. What is the complexity of computing $\mathbf{P}(X_1 \mid X_n = true)$ using enumeration? Using variable elimination?

d. Prove that the complexity of running variable elimination on a polytree network is linear in the size of the tree for any variable ordering consistent with the network structure.

16 Investigate the complexity of exact inference in general Bayesian networks:

a. Prove that any 3-SAT problem can be reduced to exact inference in a Bayesian network constructed to represent the particular problem and hence that exact inference is NP-hard. (*Hint*: Consider a network with one variable for each proposition symbol, one for each clause, and one for the conjunction of clauses.)

b. The problem of counting the number of satisfying assignments for a 3-SAT problem is #P-complete. Show that exact inference is at least as hard as this.

17 Consider the problem of generating a random sample from a specified distribution on a single variable. Assume you have a random number generator that returns a random number uniformly distributed between 0 and 1.

a. Let X be a discrete variable with $P(X=x_i)=p_i$ for $i \in \{1,\ldots,k\}$. The **cumulative distribution** of X gives the probability that $X \in \{x_1,\ldots,x_j\}$ for each possible j. (See also Appendix A.) Explain how to calculate the cumulative distribution in $O(k)$ time and how to generate a single sample of X from it. Can the latter be done in less than $O(k)$ time?

CUMULATIVE DISTRIBUTION

b. Now suppose we want to generate N samples of X, where $N \gg k$. Explain how to do this with an expected run time per sample that is *constant* (i.e., independent of k).

c. Now consider a continuous-valued variable with a parameterized distribution (e.g., Gaussian). How can samples be generated from such a distribution?

d. Suppose you want to query a continuous-valued variable and you are using a sampling algorithm such as LIKELIHOODWEIGHTING to do the inference. How would you have to modify the query-answering process?

18 Consider the query $\mathbf{P}(Rain \mid Sprinkler = true, WetGrass = true)$ in Figure 12(a) and how Gibbs sampling can answer it.

a. How many states does the Markov chain have?

b. Calculate the **transition matrix Q** containing $q(\mathbf{y} \to \mathbf{y}')$ for all $\mathbf{y}, \mathbf{y}'$.

c. What does $\mathbf{Q}^2$, the square of the transition matrix, represent?

d. What about $\mathbf{Q}^n$ as $n \to \infty$?

e. Explain how to do probabilistic inference in Bayesian networks, assuming that $\mathbf{Q}^n$ is available. Is this a practical way to do inference?

19 This exercise explores the stationary distribution for Gibbs sampling methods.

a. The convex composition $[\alpha, q_1; 1-\alpha, q_2]$ of q_1 and q_2 is a transition probability distribution that first chooses one of q_1 and q_2 with probabilities α and $1-\alpha$, respectively, and then applies whichever is chosen. Prove that if q_1 and q_2 are in detailed balance with π, then their convex composition is also in detailed balance with π. (*Note*: this result justifies a variant of GIBBS-ASK in which variables are chosen at random rather than sampled in a fixed sequence.)

b. Prove that if each of q_1 and q_2 has π as its stationary distribution, then the sequential composition $q = q_1 \circ q_2$ also has π as its stationary distribution.

METROPOLIS–HASTINGS

20 The **Metropolis–Hastings** algorithm is a member of the MCMC family; as such, it is designed to generate samples $\mathbf{x}$ (eventually) according to target probabilities $\pi(\mathbf{x})$. (Typically

PROPOSAL DISTRIBUTION

ACCEPTANCE PROBABILITY

we are interested in sampling from $\pi(\mathbf{x}) = P(\mathbf{x} \mid \mathbf{e})$.) Like simulated annealing, Metropolis–Hastings operates in two stages. First, it samples a new state $\mathbf{x}'$ from a **proposal distribution** $q(\mathbf{x}' \mid \mathbf{x})$, given the current state $\mathbf{x}$. Then, it probabilistically accepts or rejects $\mathbf{x}'$ according to the **acceptance probability**

$$\alpha(\mathbf{x}' \mid \mathbf{x}) = \min\left(1, \frac{\pi(\mathbf{x}')q(\mathbf{x} \mid \mathbf{x}')}{\pi(\mathbf{x})q(\mathbf{x}' \mid \mathbf{x})}\right).$$

If the proposal is rejected, the state remains at $\mathbf{x}$.

a. Consider an ordinary Gibbs sampling step for a specific variable X_i. Show that this step, considered as a proposal, is guaranteed to be accepted by Metropolis–Hastings. (Hence, Gibbs sampling is a special case of Metropolis–Hastings.)

b. Show that the two-step process above, viewed as a transition probability distribution, is in detailed balance with π.

21 Three soccer teams A, B, and C, play each other once. Each match is between two teams, and can be won, drawn, or lost. Each team has a fixed, unknown degree of quality—an integer ranging from 0 to 3—and the outcome of a match depends probabilistically on the difference in quality between the two teams.

a. Construct a relational probability model to describe this domain, and suggest numerical values for all the necessary probability distributions.

b. Construct the equivalent Bayesian network for the three matches.

c. Suppose that in the first two matches A beats B and draws with C. Using an exact inference algorithm of your choice, compute the posterior distribution for the outcome of the third match.

d. Suppose there are n teams in the league and we have the results for all but the last match. How does the complexity of predicting the last game vary with n?

e. Investigate the application of MCMC to this problem. How quickly does it converge in practice and how well does it scale?

PROBABILISTIC REASONING OVER TIME

PROBABILISTIC REASONING OVER TIME

In which we try to interpret the present, understand the past, and perhaps predict the future, even when very little is crystal clear.

Agents in partially observable environments must be able to keep track of the current state, to the extent that their sensors allow. An agent can achieve this by maintaining a **belief state** that represents which states of the world are currently possible. From the belief state and a **transition model**, the agent can predict how the world might evolve in the next time step. From the percepts observed and a **sensor model**, the agent can update the belief state. This is a pervasive idea. Belief states can be represented by explicitly enumerated sets of states, as well as logical formulas. Those approaches defined belief states in terms of which world states were *possible*, but could say nothing about which states were *likely* or *unlikely*. In this chapter, we use probability theory to quantify the degree of belief in elements of the belief state.

As we show in Section 1, time itself is handled in the following way: a changing world is modeled using a variable for each aspect of the world state *at each point in time*. The transition and sensor models may be uncertain: the transition model describes the probability distribution of the variables at time t, given the state of the world at past times, while the sensor model describes the probability of each percept at time t, given the current state of the world. Section 2 defines the basic inference tasks and describes the general structure of inference algorithms for temporal models. Then we describe three specific kinds of models: **hidden Markov models**, **Kalman filters**, and **dynamic Bayesian networks** (which include hidden Markov models and Kalman filters as special cases). Finally, Section 6 examines the problems faced when keeping track of more than one thing.

1 TIME AND UNCERTAINTY

Techniques have been developed for probabilistic reasoning in the context of *static* worlds, in which each random variable has a single fixed value. For example, when repairing a car, we assume that whatever is broken remains broken during the process of diagnosis; our job is to infer the state of the car from observed evidence, which also remains fixed.

Now consider a slightly different problem: treating a diabetic patient. As in the case of car repair, we have evidence such as recent insulin doses, food intake, blood sugar measurements, and other physical signs. The task is to assess the current state of the patient, including the actual blood sugar level and insulin level. Given this information, we can make a decision about the patient's food intake and insulin dose. Unlike the case of car repair, here the *dynamic* aspects of the problem are essential. Blood sugar levels and measurements thereof can change rapidly over time, depending on recent food intake and insulin doses, metabolic activity, the time of day, and so on. To assess the current state from the history of evidence and to predict the outcomes of treatment actions, we must model these changes.

The same considerations arise in many other contexts, such as tracking the location of a robot, tracking the economic activity of a nation, and making sense of a spoken or written sequence of words. How can dynamic situations like these be modeled?

1.1 States and observations

TIME SLICE

We view the world as a series of snapshots, or **time slices**, each of which contains a set of random variables, some observable and some not.[1] For simplicity, we will assume that the same subset of variables is observable in each time slice (although this is not strictly necessary in anything that follows). We will use $\mathbf{X}_t$ to denote the set of state variables at time t, which are assumed to be unobservable, and $\mathbf{E}_t$ to denote the set of observable evidence variables. The observation at time t is $\mathbf{E}_t = \mathbf{e}_t$ for some set of values $\mathbf{e}_t$.

Consider the following example: You are the security guard stationed at a secret underground installation. You want to know whether it's raining today, but your only access to the outside world occurs each morning when you see the director coming in with, or without, an umbrella. For each day t, the set $\mathbf{E}_t$ thus contains a single evidence variable $Umbrella_t$ or U_t for short (whether the umbrella appears), and the set $\mathbf{X}_t$ contains a single state variable $Rain_t$ or R_t for short (whether it is raining). Other problems can involve larger sets of variables. In the diabetes example, we might have evidence variables, such as $MeasuredBloodSugar_t$ and $PulseRate_t$, and state variables, such as $BloodSugar_t$ and $StomachContents_t$. (Notice that $BloodSugar_t$ and $MeasuredBloodSugar_t$ are not the same variable; this is how we deal with noisy measurements of actual quantities.)

The interval between time slices also depends on the problem. For diabetes monitoring, a suitable interval might be an hour rather than a day. In this chapter we assume the interval between slices is fixed, so we can label times by integers. We will assume that the state sequence starts at $t=0$; for various uninteresting reasons, we will assume that evidence starts arriving at $t=1$ rather than $t=0$. Hence, our umbrella world is represented by state variables $R_0, R_1, R_2, \ldots$ and evidence variables $U_1, U_2, \ldots$. We will use the notation $a{:}b$ to denote the sequence of integers from a to b (inclusive), and the notation $\mathbf{X}_{a:b}$ to denote the set of variables from $\mathbf{X}_a$ to $\mathbf{X}_b$. For example, $U_{1:3}$ corresponds to the variables U_1, U_2, U_3.

---

[1] Uncertainty over *continuous* time can be modeled by **stochastic differential equations** (SDEs). The models studied in this chapter can be viewed as discrete-time approximations to SDEs.

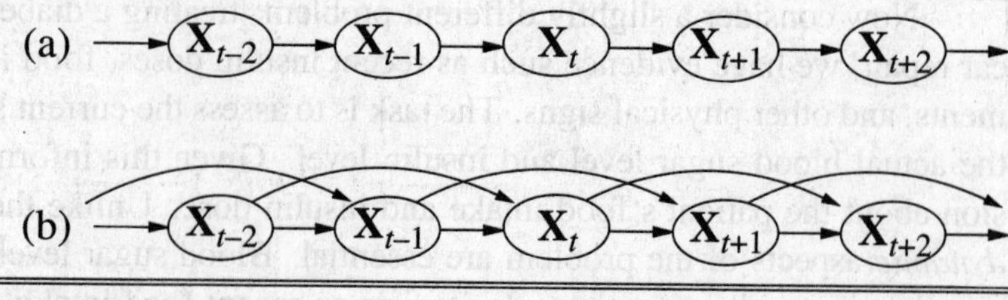

Figure 1 (a) Bayesian network structure corresponding to a first-order Markov process with state defined by the variables $\mathbf{X}_t$. (b) A second-order Markov process.

1.2 Transition and sensor models

With the set of state and evidence variables for a given problem decided on, the next step is to specify how the world evolves (the transition model) and how the evidence variables get their values (the sensor model).

MARKOV ASSUMPTION

MARKOV PROCESS

FIRST-ORDER MARKOV PROCESS

The transition model specifies the probability distribution over the latest state variables, given the previous values, that is, $\mathbf{P}(\mathbf{X}_t \mid \mathbf{X}_{0:t-1})$. Now we face a problem: the set $\mathbf{X}_{0:t-1}$ is unbounded in size as t increases. We solve the problem by making a **Markov assumption**—that the current state depends on only a *finite fixed number* of previous states. Processes satisfying this assumption were first studied in depth by the Russian statistician Andrei Markov (1856–1922) and are called **Markov processes** or **Markov chains**. They come in various flavors; the simplest is the **first-order Markov process**, in which the current state depends only on the previous state and not on any earlier states. In other words, a state provides enough information to make the future conditionally independent of the past, and we have

$$\mathbf{P}(\mathbf{X}_t \mid \mathbf{X}_{0:t-1}) = \mathbf{P}(\mathbf{X}_t \mid \mathbf{X}_{t-1}) \,. \tag{1}$$

Hence, in a first-order Markov process, the transition model is the conditional distribution $\mathbf{P}(\mathbf{X}_t \mid \mathbf{X}_{t-1})$. The transition model for a second-order Markov process is the conditional distribution $\mathbf{P}(\mathbf{X}_t \mid \mathbf{X}_{t-2}, \mathbf{X}_{t-1})$. Figure 1 shows the Bayesian network structures corresponding to first-order and second-order Markov processes.

STATIONARY PROCESS

Even with the Markov assumption there is still a problem: there are infinitely many possible values of t. Do we need to specify a different distribution for each time step? We avoid this problem by assuming that changes in the world state are caused by a **stationary process**—that is, a process of change that is governed by laws that do not themselves change over time. (Don't confuse *stationary* with *static*: in a *static* process, the state itself does not change.) In the umbrella world, then, the conditional probability of rain, $\mathbf{P}(R_t \mid R_{t-1})$, is the same for all t, and we only have to specify one conditional probability table.

SENSOR MARKOV ASSUMPTION

Now for the sensor model. The evidence variables $\mathbf{E}_t$ *could* depend on previous variables as well as the current state variables, but any state that's worth its salt should suffice to generate the current sensor values. Thus, we make a **sensor Markov assumption** as follows:

$$\mathbf{P}(\mathbf{E}_t \mid \mathbf{X}_{0:t}, \mathbf{E}_{0:t-1}) = \mathbf{P}(\mathbf{E}_t \mid \mathbf{X}_t) \,. \tag{2}$$

Thus, $\mathbf{P}(\mathbf{E}_t \mid \mathbf{X}_t)$ is our sensor model (sometimes called the **observation model**). Figure 2 shows both the transition model and the sensor model for the umbrella example. Notice the

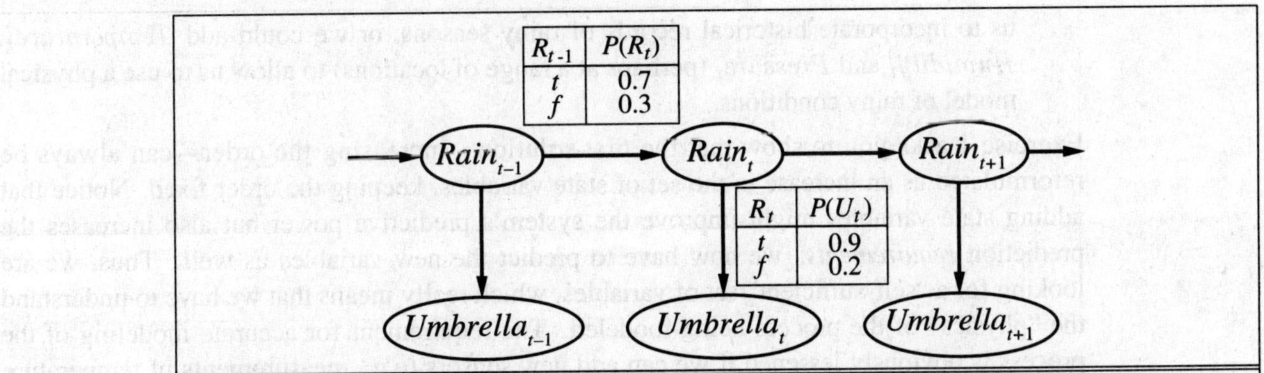

Figure 2 Bayesian network structure and conditional distributions describing the umbrella world. The transition model is $P(Rain_t \mid Rain_{t-1})$ and the sensor model is $P(Umbrella_t \mid Rain_t)$.

direction of the dependence between state and sensors: the arrows go from the actual state of the world to sensor values because the state of the world *causes* the sensors to take on particular values: the rain *causes* the umbrella to appear. (The inference process, of course, goes in the other direction; the distinction between the direction of modeled dependencies and the direction of inference is one of the principal advantages of Bayesian networks.)

In addition to specifying the transition and sensor models, we need to say how everything gets started—the prior probability distribution at time 0, $\mathbf{P}(\mathbf{X}_0)$. With that, we have a specification of the complete joint distribution over all the variables. For any t,

$$\mathbf{P}(\mathbf{X}_{0:t}, \mathbf{E}_{1:t}) = \mathbf{P}(\mathbf{X}_0) \prod_{i=1}^{t} \mathbf{P}(\mathbf{X}_i \mid \mathbf{X}_{i-1})\, \mathbf{P}(\mathbf{E}_i \mid \mathbf{X}_i)\,. \tag{3}$$

The three terms on the right-hand side are the initial state model $\mathbf{P}(\mathbf{X}_0)$, the transition model $\mathbf{P}(\mathbf{X}_i \mid \mathbf{X}_{i-1})$, and the sensor model $\mathbf{P}(\mathbf{E}_i \mid \mathbf{X}_i)$.

The structure in Figure 2 is a first-order Markov process—the probability of rain is assumed to depend only on whether it rained the previous day. Whether such an assumption is reasonable depends on the domain itself. The first-order Markov assumption says that the state variables contain *all* the information needed to characterize the probability distribution for the next time slice. Sometimes the assumption is exactly true—for example, if a particle is executing a random walk along the x-axis, changing its position by ± 1 at each time step, then using the x-coordinate as the state gives a first-order Markov process. Sometimes the assumption is only approximate, as in the case of predicting rain only on the basis of whether it rained the previous day. There are two ways to improve the accuracy of the approximation:

1. Increasing the order of the Markov process model. For example, we could make a second-order model by adding $Rain_{t-2}$ as a parent of $Rain_t$, which might give slightly more accurate predictions. For example, in Palo Alto, California, it very rarely rains more than two days in a row.
2. Increasing the set of state variables. For example, we could add $Season_t$ to allow

us to incorporate historical records of rainy seasons, or we could add $Temperature_t$, $Humidity_t$ and $Pressure_t$ (perhaps at a range of locations) to allow us to use a physical model of rainy conditions.

Exercise 1 asks you to show that the first solution—increasing the order—can always be reformulated as an increase in the set of state variables, keeping the order fixed. Notice that adding state variables might improve the system's predictive power but also increases the prediction *requirements*: we now have to predict the new variables as well. Thus, we are looking for a "self-sufficient" set of variables, which really means that we have to understand the "physics" of the process being modeled. The requirement for accurate modeling of the process is obviously lessened if we can add new sensors (e.g., measurements of temperature and pressure) that provide information directly about the new state variables.

Consider, for example, the problem of tracking a robot wandering randomly on the X–Y plane. One might propose that the position and velocity are a sufficient set of state variables: one can simply use Newton's laws to calculate the new position, and the velocity may change unpredictably. If the robot is battery-powered, however, then battery exhaustion would tend to have a systematic effect on the change in velocity. Because this in turn depends on how much power was used by all previous maneuvers, the Markov property is violated. We can restore the Markov property by including the charge level $Battery_t$ as one of the state variables that make up $\mathbf{X}_t$. This helps in predicting the motion of the robot, but in turn requires a model for predicting $Battery_t$ from $Battery_{t-1}$ and the velocity. In some cases, that can be done reliably, but more often we find that error accumulates over time. In that case, accuracy can be improved by *adding a new sensor* for the battery level.

2 Inference in Temporal Models

Having set up the structure of a generic temporal model, we can formulate the basic inference tasks that must be solved:

FILTERING
BELIEF STATE
STATE ESTIMATION

- **Filtering**: This is the task of computing the **belief state**—the posterior distribution over the most recent state—given all evidence to date. Filtering[2] is also called **state estimation**. In our example, we wish to compute $\mathbf{P}(\mathbf{X}_t \mid \mathbf{e}_{1:t})$. In the umbrella example, this would mean computing the probability of rain today, given all the observations of the umbrella carrier made so far. Filtering is what a rational agent does to keep track of the current state so that rational decisions can be made. It turns out that an almost identical calculation provides the likelihood of the evidence sequence, $P(\mathbf{e}_{1:t})$.

PREDICTION

- **Prediction**: This is the task of computing the posterior distribution over the *future* state, given all evidence to date. That is, we wish to compute $\mathbf{P}(\mathbf{X}_{t+k} \mid \mathbf{e}_{1:t})$ for some $k > 0$. In the umbrella example, this might mean computing the probability of rain three days from now, given all the observations to date. Prediction is useful for evaluating possible courses of action based on their expected outcomes.

[2] The term "filtering" refers to the roots of this problem in early work on signal processing, where the problem is to filter out the noise in a signal by estimating its underlying properties.

SMOOTHING

- **Smoothing**: This is the task of computing the posterior distribution over a *past* state, given all evidence up to the present. That is, we wish to compute $\mathbf{P}(\mathbf{X}_k \mid \mathbf{e}_{1:t})$ for some k such that $0 \leq k < t$. In the umbrella example, it might mean computing the probability that it rained last Wednesday, given all the observations of the umbrella carrier made up to today. Smoothing provides a better estimate of the state than was available at the time, because it incorporates more evidence.[3]
- **Most likely explanation**: Given a sequence of observations, we might wish to find the sequence of states that is most likely to have generated those observations. That is, we wish to compute $\text{argmax}_{\mathbf{x}_{1:t}} P(\mathbf{x}_{1:t} \mid \mathbf{e}_{1:t})$. For example, if the umbrella appears on each of the first three days and is absent on the fourth, then the most likely explanation is that it rained on the first three days and did not rain on the fourth. Algorithms for this task are useful in many applications, including speech recognition—where the aim is to find the most likely sequence of words, given a series of sounds—and the reconstruction of bit strings transmitted over a noisy channel.

In addition to these inference tasks, we also have

- **Learning**: The transition and sensor models, if not yet known, can be learned from observations. Just as with static Bayesian networks, dynamic Bayes net learning can be done as a by-product of inference. Inference provides an estimate of what transitions actually occurred and of what states generated the sensor readings, and these estimates can be used to update the models. The updated models provide new estimates, and the process iterates to convergence. The overall process is an instance of the expectation-maximization or **EM algorithm.**

Note that learning requires smoothing, rather than filtering, because smoothing provides better estimates of the states of the process. Learning with filtering can fail to converge correctly; consider, for example, the problem of learning to solve murders: unless you are an eyewitness, smoothing is *always* required to infer what happened at the murder scene from the observable variables.

The remainder of this section describes generic algorithms for the four inference tasks, independent of the particular kind of model employed. Improvements specific to each model are described in subsequent sections.

2.1 Filtering and prediction

A useful filtering algorithm needs to maintain a current state estimate and update it, rather than going back over the entire history of percepts for each update. (Otherwise, the cost of each update increases as time goes by.) In other words, given the result of filtering up to time t, the agent needs to compute the result for $t+1$ from the new evidence $\mathbf{e}_t$+1,

$$\mathbf{P}(\mathbf{X}_{t+1} \mid \mathbf{e}_{1:t+1}) = f(\mathbf{e}_{t+1}, \mathbf{P}(\mathbf{X}_t \mid \mathbf{e}_{1:t}))\ ,$$

RECURSIVE ESTIMATION

for some function f. This process is called **recursive estimation**. We can view the calculation

[3] In particular, when tracking a moving object with inaccurate position observations, smoothing gives a smoother estimated trajectory than filtering—hence the name.

as being composed of two parts: first, the current state distribution is projected forward from t to $t+1$; then it is updated using the new evidence $\mathbf{e}_{t+1}$. This two-part process emerges quite simply when the formula is rearranged:

$$\begin{aligned}\mathbf{P}(\mathbf{X}_{t+1} \mid \mathbf{e}_{1:t+1}) &= \mathbf{P}(\mathbf{X}_{t+1} \mid \mathbf{e}_{1:t}, \mathbf{e}_{t+1}) \quad \text{(dividing up the evidence)} \\ &= \alpha\, \mathbf{P}(\mathbf{e}_{t+1} \mid \mathbf{X}_{t+1}, \mathbf{e}_{1:t})\, \mathbf{P}(\mathbf{X}_{t+1} \mid \mathbf{e}_{1:t}) \quad \text{(using Bayes' rule)} \\ &= \alpha\, \mathbf{P}(\mathbf{e}_{t+1} \mid \mathbf{X}_{t+1})\, \mathbf{P}(\mathbf{X}_{t+1} \mid \mathbf{e}_{1:t}) \quad \text{(by the sensor Markov assumption).} \qquad (4)\end{aligned}$$

Here and throughout this chapter, α is a normalizing constant used to make probabilities sum up to 1. The second term, $\mathbf{P}(\mathbf{X}_{t+1} \mid \mathbf{e}_{1:t})$ represents a one-step prediction of the next state, and the first term updates this with the new evidence; notice that $\mathbf{P}(\mathbf{e}_{t+1} \mid \mathbf{X}_{t+1})$ is obtainable directly from the sensor model. Now we obtain the one-step prediction for the next state by conditioning on the current state $\mathbf{X}_t$:

$$\begin{aligned}\mathbf{P}(\mathbf{X}_{t+1} \mid \mathbf{e}_{1:t+1}) &= \alpha\, \mathbf{P}(\mathbf{e}_{t+1} \mid \mathbf{X}_{t+1}) \sum_{\mathbf{x}_t} \mathbf{P}(\mathbf{X}_{t+1} \mid \mathbf{x}_t, \mathbf{e}_{1:t}) P(\mathbf{x}_t \mid \mathbf{e}_{1:t}) \\ &= \alpha\, \mathbf{P}(\mathbf{e}_{t+1} \mid \mathbf{X}_{t+1}) \sum_{\mathbf{x}_t} \mathbf{P}(\mathbf{X}_{t+1} \mid \mathbf{x}_t) P(\mathbf{x}_t \mid \mathbf{e}_{1:t}) \quad \text{(Markov assumption).} \qquad (5)\end{aligned}$$

Within the summation, the first factor comes from the transition model and the second comes from the current state distribution. Hence, we have the desired recursive formulation. We can think of the filtered estimate $\mathbf{P}(\mathbf{X}_t \mid \mathbf{e}_{1:t})$ as a "message" $\mathbf{f}_{1:t}$ that is propagated forward along the sequence, modified by each transition and updated by each new observation. The process is given by

$$\mathbf{f}_{1:t+1} = \alpha\, \text{FORWARD}(\mathbf{f}_{1:t}, \mathbf{e}_{t+1}),$$

where FORWARD implements the update described in Equation (5) and the process begins with $\mathbf{f}_{1:0} = \mathbf{P}(\mathbf{X}_0)$. When all the state variables are discrete, the time for each update is constant (i.e., independent of t), and the space required is also constant. (The constants depend, of course, on the size of the state space and the specific type of the temporal model in question.) *The time and space requirements for updating must be constant if an agent with limited memory is to keep track of the current state distribution over an unbounded sequence of observations.*

Let us illustrate the filtering process for two steps in the basic umbrella example (Figure 2.) That is, we will compute $\mathbf{P}(R_2 \mid u_{1:2})$ as follows:

- On day 0, we have no observations, only the security guard's prior beliefs; let's assume that consists of $\mathbf{P}(R_0) = \langle 0.5, 0.5 \rangle$.
- On day 1, the umbrella appears, so $U_1 = true$. The prediction from $t=0$ to $t=1$ is

$$\begin{aligned}\mathbf{P}(R_1) &= \sum_{r_0} \mathbf{P}(R_1 \mid r_0) P(r_0) \\ &= \langle 0.7, 0.3 \rangle \times 0.5 + \langle 0.3, 0.7 \rangle \times 0.5 = \langle 0.5, 0.5 \rangle\,.\end{aligned}$$

Then the update step simply multiplies by the probability of the evidence for $t=1$ and normalizes, as shown in Equation (4):

$$\begin{aligned}\mathbf{P}(R_1 \mid u_1) &= \alpha\, \mathbf{P}(u_1 \mid R_1) \mathbf{P}(R_1) = \alpha\, \langle 0.9, 0.2 \rangle \langle 0.5, 0.5 \rangle \\ &= \alpha\, \langle 0.45, 0.1 \rangle \approx \langle 0.818, 0.182 \rangle\,.\end{aligned}$$

- On day 2, the umbrella appears, so $U_2 = true$. The prediction from $t=1$ to $t=2$ is

$$\begin{aligned}\mathbf{P}(R_2 \mid u_1) &= \sum_{r_1} \mathbf{P}(R_2 \mid r_1) P(r_1 \mid u_1) \\ &= \langle 0.7, 0.3 \rangle \times 0.818 + \langle 0.3, 0.7 \rangle \times 0.182 \approx \langle 0.627, 0.373 \rangle ,\end{aligned}$$

and updating it with the evidence for $t=2$ gives

$$\begin{aligned}\mathbf{P}(R_2 \mid u_1, u_2) &= \alpha\, \mathbf{P}(u_2 \mid R_2) \mathbf{P}(R_2 \mid u_1) = \alpha \langle 0.9, 0.2 \rangle \langle 0.627, 0.373 \rangle \\ &= \alpha \langle 0.565, 0.075 \rangle \approx \langle 0.883, 0.117 \rangle .\end{aligned}$$

Intuitively, the probability of rain increases from day 1 to day 2 because rain persists. Exercise 2(a) asks you to investigate this tendency further.

The task of **prediction** can be seen simply as filtering without the addition of new evidence. In fact, the filtering process already incorporates a one-step prediction, and it is easy to derive the following recursive computation for predicting the state at $t+k+1$ from a prediction for $t+k$:

$$\mathbf{P}(\mathbf{X}_{t+k+1} \mid \mathbf{e}_{1:t}) = \sum_{\mathbf{x}_{t+k}} \mathbf{P}(\mathbf{X}_{t+k+1} \mid \mathbf{x}_{t+k}) P(\mathbf{x}_{t+k} \mid \mathbf{e}_{1:t}) . \tag{6}$$

Naturally, this computation involves only the transition model and not the sensor model.

It is interesting to consider what happens as we try to predict further and further into the future. As Exercise 2(b) shows, the predicted distribution for rain converges to a fixed point $\langle 0.5, 0.5 \rangle$, after which it remains constant for all time. This is the **stationary distribution** of the Markov process defined by the transition model. A great deal is known about the properties of such distributions and about the **mixing time**— roughly, the time taken to reach the fixed point. In practical terms, this dooms to failure any attempt to predict the *actual* state for a number of steps that is more than a small fraction of the mixing time, unless the stationary distribution itself is strongly peaked in a small area of the state space. The more uncertainty there is in the transition model, the shorter will be the mixing time and the more the future is obscured.

MIXING TIME

In addition to filtering and prediction, we can use a forward recursion to compute the **likelihood** of the evidence sequence, $P(\mathbf{e}_{1:t})$. This is a useful quantity if we want to compare different temporal models that might have produced the same evidence sequence (e.g., two different models for the persistence of rain). For this recursion, we use a likelihood message $\boldsymbol{\ell}_{1:t}(\mathbf{X}_t) = \mathbf{P}(\mathbf{X}_t, \mathbf{e}_{1:t})$. It is a simple exercise to show that the message calculation is identical to that for filtering:

$$\boldsymbol{\ell}_{1:t+1} = \text{FORWARD}(\boldsymbol{\ell}_{1:t}, \mathbf{e}_{t+1}) .$$

Having computed $\boldsymbol{\ell}_{1:t}$, we obtain the actual likelihood by summing out $\mathbf{X}_t$:

$$L_{1:t} = P(\mathbf{e}_{1:t}) = \sum_{\mathbf{x}_t} \boldsymbol{\ell}_{1:t}(\mathbf{x}_t) . \tag{7}$$

Notice that the likelihood message represents the probabilities of longer and longer evidence sequences as time goes by and so becomes numerically smaller and smaller, leading to underflow problems with floating-point arithmetic. This is an important problem in practice, but we shall not go into solutions here.

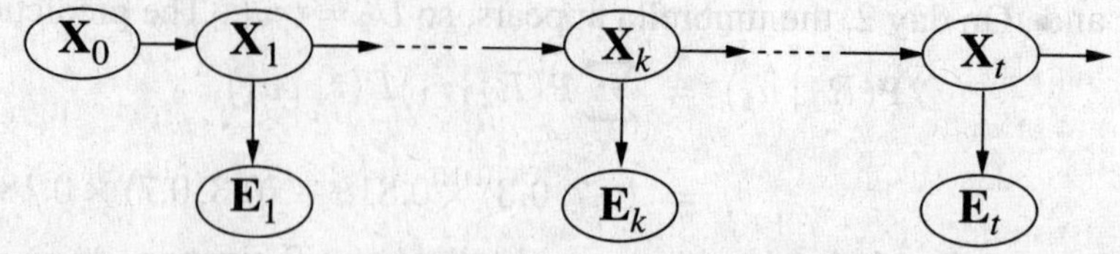

Figure 3 Smoothing computes $\mathbf{P}(\mathbf{X}_k \mid \mathbf{e}_{1:t})$, the posterior distribution of the state at some past time k given a complete sequence of observations from 1 to t.

2.2 Smoothing

As we said earlier, smoothing is the process of computing the distribution over past states given evidence up to the present; that is, $\mathbf{P}(\mathbf{X}_k \mid \mathbf{e}_{1:t})$ for $0 \le k < t$. (See Figure 3.) In anticipation of another recursive message-passing approach, we can split the computation into two parts—the evidence up to k and the evidence from $k+1$ to t,

$$\begin{aligned}
\mathbf{P}(\mathbf{X}_k \mid \mathbf{e}_{1:t}) &= \mathbf{P}(\mathbf{X}_k \mid \mathbf{e}_{1:k}, \mathbf{e}_{k+1:t}) \\
&= \alpha\, \mathbf{P}(\mathbf{X}_k \mid \mathbf{e}_{1:k}) \mathbf{P}(\mathbf{e}_{k+1:t} \mid \mathbf{X}_k, \mathbf{e}_{1:k}) \quad \text{(using Bayes' rule)} \\
&= \alpha\, \mathbf{P}(\mathbf{X}_k \mid \mathbf{e}_{1:k}) \mathbf{P}(\mathbf{e}_{k+1:t} \mid \mathbf{X}_k) \quad \text{(using conditional independence)} \\
&= \alpha\, \mathbf{f}_{1:k} \times \mathbf{b}_{k+1:t}\,. \qquad (8)
\end{aligned}$$

where "$\times$" represents pointwise multiplication of vectors. Here we have defined a "backward" message $\mathbf{b}_{k+1:t} = \mathbf{P}(\mathbf{e}_{k+1:t} \mid \mathbf{X}_k)$, analogous to the forward message $\mathbf{f}_{1:k}$. The forward message $\mathbf{f}_{1:k}$ can be computed by filtering forward from 1 to k, as given by Equation (5). It turns out that the backward message $\mathbf{b}_{k+1:t}$ can be computed by a recursive process that runs *backward* from t:

$$\begin{aligned}
\mathbf{P}(\mathbf{e}_{k+1:t} \mid \mathbf{X}_k) &= \sum_{\mathbf{x}_{k+1}} \mathbf{P}(\mathbf{e}_{k+1:t} \mid \mathbf{X}_k, \mathbf{x}_{k+1}) \mathbf{P}(\mathbf{x}_{k+1} \mid \mathbf{X}_k) \quad \text{(conditioning on } \mathbf{X}_{k+1}\text{)} \\
&= \sum_{\mathbf{x}_{k+1}} P(\mathbf{e}_{k+1:t} \mid \mathbf{x}_{k+1}) \mathbf{P}(\mathbf{x}_{k+1} \mid \mathbf{X}_k) \quad \text{(by conditional independence)} \\
&= \sum_{\mathbf{x}_{k+1}} P(\mathbf{e}_{k+1}, \mathbf{e}_{k+2:t} \mid \mathbf{x}_{k+1}) \mathbf{P}(\mathbf{x}_{k+1} \mid \mathbf{X}_k) \\
&= \sum_{\mathbf{x}_{k+1}} P(\mathbf{e}_{k+1} \mid \mathbf{x}_{k+1}) P(\mathbf{e}_{k+2:t} \mid \mathbf{x}_{k+1}) \mathbf{P}(\mathbf{x}_{k+1} \mid \mathbf{X}_k)\,, \qquad (9)
\end{aligned}$$

where the last step follows by the conditional independence of $\mathbf{e}_{k+1}$ and $\mathbf{e}_{k+2:t}$, given $\mathbf{X}_{k+1}$. Of the three factors in this summation, the first and third are obtained directly from the model, and the second is the "recursive call." Using the message notation, we have

$$\mathbf{b}_{k+1:t} = \text{BACKWARD}(\mathbf{b}_{k+2:t}, \mathbf{e}_{k+1})\,,$$

where BACKWARD implements the update described in Equation (9). As with the forward recursion, the time and space needed for each update are constant and thus independent of t.

We can now see that the two terms in Equation (8) can both be computed by recursions through time, one running forward from 1 to k and using the filtering equation (5) and the other running backward from t to $k+1$ and using Equation (9). Note that the backward phase is initialized with $\mathbf{b}_{t+1:t} = \mathbf{P}(\mathbf{e}_{t+1:t} \mid \mathbf{X}_t) = \mathbf{P}(\ \mid \mathbf{X}_t)\mathbf{1}$, where $\mathbf{1}$ is a vector of 1s. (Because $\mathbf{e}_{t+1:t}$ is an empty sequence, the probability of observing it is 1.)

Let us now apply this algorithm to the umbrella example, computing the smoothed estimate for the probability of rain at time $k=1$, given the umbrella observations on days 1 and 2. From Equation (8), this is given by

$$\mathbf{P}(R_1 \mid u_1, u_2) = \alpha\, \mathbf{P}(R_1 \mid u_1)\, \mathbf{P}(u_2 \mid R_1)\,. \tag{10}$$

The first term we already know to be $\langle .818, .182\rangle$, from the forward filtering process described earlier. The second term can be computed by applying the backward recursion in Equation (9):

$$\begin{aligned}\mathbf{P}(u_2 \mid R_1) &= \sum_{r_2} P(u_2 \mid r_2) P(\ \mid r_2) \mathbf{P}(r_2 \mid R_1) \\ &= (0.9 \times 1 \times \langle 0.7, 0.3\rangle) + (0.2 \times 1 \times \langle 0.3, 0.7\rangle) = \langle 0.69, 0.41\rangle\,.\end{aligned}$$

Plugging this into Equation (10), we find that the smoothed estimate for rain on day 1 is

$$\mathbf{P}(R_1 \mid u_1, u_2) = \alpha\, \langle 0.818, 0.182\rangle \times \langle 0.69, 0.41\rangle \approx \langle 0.883, 0.117\rangle\,.$$

Thus, the smoothed estimate for rain on day 1 is *higher* than the filtered estimate (0.818) in this case. This is because the umbrella on day 2 makes it more likely to have rained on day 2; in turn, because rain tends to persist, that makes it more likely to have rained on day 1.

Both the forward and backward recursions take a constant amount of time per step; hence, the time complexity of smoothing with respect to evidence $\mathbf{e}_{1:t}$ is $O(t)$. This is the complexity for smoothing at a particular time step k. If we want to smooth the whole sequence, one obvious method is simply to run the whole smoothing process once for each time step to be smoothed. This results in a time complexity of $O(t^2)$. A better approach uses a simple application of dynamic programming to reduce the complexity to $O(t)$. A clue appears in the preceding analysis of the umbrella example, where we were able to reuse the results of the forward-filtering phase. The key to the linear-time algorithm is to *record the results* of forward filtering over the whole sequence. Then we run the backward recursion from t down to 1, computing the smoothed estimate at each step k from the computed backward message $\mathbf{b}_{k+1:t}$ and the stored forward message $\mathbf{f}_{1:k}$. The algorithm, aptly called the **forward–backward algorithm**, is shown in Figure 4.

FORWARD–BACKWARD ALGORITHM

The alert reader will have spotted that the Bayesian network structure shown in Figure 3 is a *polytree*. This means that a straightforward application of the clustering algorithm also yields a linear-time algorithm that computes smoothed estimates for the entire sequence. It is now understood that the forward–backward algorithm is in fact a special case of the polytree propagation algorithm used with clustering methods (although the two were developed independently).

The forward–backward algorithm forms the computational backbone for many applications that deal with sequences of noisy observations. As described so far, it has two practical drawbacks. The first is that its space complexity can be too high when the state space is large and the sequences are long. It uses $O(|\mathbf{f}|t)$ space where $|\mathbf{f}|$ is the size of the representation of the forward message. The space requirement can be reduced to $O(|\mathbf{f}|\log t)$ with a concomitant increase in the time complexity by a factor of $\log t$, as shown in Exercise 3. In some cases (see Section 3), a constant-space algorithm can be used.

The second drawback of the basic algorithm is that it needs to be modified to work in an *online* setting where smoothed estimates must be computed for earlier time slices as new observations are continuously added to the end of the sequence. The most common requirement is for **fixed-lag smoothing**, which requires computing the smoothed estimate $\mathbf{P}(\mathbf{X}_{t-d} \mid \mathbf{e}_{1:t})$ for fixed d. That is, smoothing is done for the time slice d steps behind the current time t; as t increases, the smoothing has to keep up. Obviously, we can run the forward–backward algorithm over the d-step "window" as each new observation is added, but this seems inefficient. In Section 3, we will see that fixed-lag smoothing can, in some cases, be done in constant time per update, independent of the lag d.

FIXED-LAG SMOOTHING

2.3 Finding the most likely sequence

Suppose that $[true, true, false, true, true]$ is the umbrella sequence for the security guard's first five days on the job. What is the weather sequence most likely to explain this? Does the absence of the umbrella on day 3 mean that it wasn't raining, or did the director forget to bring it? If it didn't rain on day 3, perhaps (because weather tends to persist) it didn't rain on day 4 either, but the director brought the umbrella just in case. In all, there are 2^5 possible weather sequences we could pick. Is there a way to find the most likely one, short of enumerating all of them?

We could try this linear-time procedure: use smoothing to find the posterior distribution for the weather at each time step; then construct the sequence, using at each step the weather that is most likely according to the posterior. Such an approach should set off alarm bells in the reader's head, because the posterior distributions computed by smoothing are distri-

```
function FORWARD-BACKWARD(ev, prior) returns a vector of probability distributions
  inputs: ev, a vector of evidence values for steps 1,...,t
          prior, the prior distribution on the initial state, P(X_0)
  local variables: fv, a vector of forward messages for steps 0,...,t
                   b, a representation of the backward message, initially all 1s
                   sv, a vector of smoothed estimates for steps 1,...,t

  fv[0] ← prior
  for i = 1 to t do
     fv[i] ← FORWARD(fv[i − 1], ev[i])
  for i = t downto 1 do
     sv[i] ← NORMALIZE(fv[i] × b)
     b ← BACKWARD(b, ev[i])
  return sv
```

Figure 4 The forward–backward algorithm for smoothing: computing posterior probabilities of a sequence of states given a sequence of observations. The FORWARD and BACKWARD operators are defined by Equations (5) and (9), respectively.

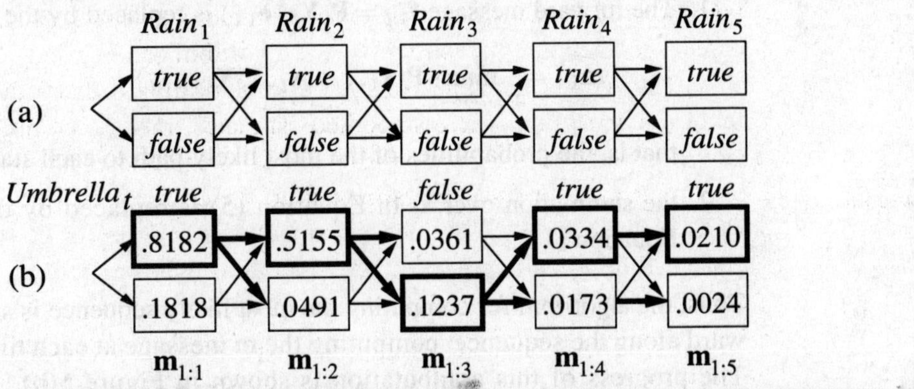

Figure 5 (a) Possible state sequences for $Rain_t$ can be viewed as paths through a graph of the possible states at each time step. (States are shown as rectangles to avoid confusion with nodes in a Bayes net.) (b) Operation of the Viterbi algorithm for the umbrella observation sequence [*true*, *true*, *false*, *true*, *true*]. For each t, we have shown the values of the message $\mathbf{m}_{1:t}$, which gives the probability of the best sequence reaching each state at time t. Also, for each state, the bold arrow leading into it indicates its best predecessor as measured by the product of the preceding sequence probability and the transition probability. Following the bold arrows back from the most likely state in $\mathbf{m}_{1:5}$ gives the most likely sequence.

butions over *single* time steps, whereas to find the most likely *sequence* we must consider *joint* probabilities over all the time steps. The results can in fact be quite different. (See Exercise 4.)

There *is* a linear-time algorithm for finding the most likely sequence, but it requires a little more thought. It relies on the same Markov property that yielded efficient algorithms for filtering and smoothing. The easiest way to think about the problem is to view each sequence as a *path* through a graph whose nodes are the possible *states* at each time step. Such a graph is shown for the umbrella world in Figure 5(a). Now consider the task of finding the most likely path through this graph, where the likelihood of any path is the product of the transition probabilities along the path and the probabilities of the given observations at each state. Let's focus in particular on paths that reach the state $Rain_5 = true$. Because of the Markov property, it follows that the most likely path to the state $Rain_5 = true$ consists of the most likely path to *some* state at time 4 followed by a transition to $Rain_5 = true$; and the state at time 4 that will become part of the path to $Rain_5 = true$ is whichever maximizes the likelihood of that path. In other words, *there is a recursive relationship between most likely paths to each state* $\mathbf{x}_{t+1}$ *and most likely paths to each state* $\mathbf{x}_t$. We can write this relationship as an equation connecting the probabilities of the paths:

$$\max_{\mathbf{x}_1\ldots\mathbf{x}_t} \mathbf{P}(\mathbf{x}_1,\ldots,\mathbf{x}_t,\mathbf{X}_{t+1} \mid \mathbf{e}_{1:t+1})$$
$$= \alpha\,\mathbf{P}(\mathbf{e}_{t+1} \mid \mathbf{X}_{t+1}) \max_{\mathbf{x}_t}\left(\mathbf{P}(\mathbf{X}_{t+1} \mid \mathbf{x}_t) \max_{\mathbf{x}_1\ldots\mathbf{x}_{t-1}} P(\mathbf{x}_1,\ldots,\mathbf{x}_{t-1},\mathbf{x}_t \mid \mathbf{e}_{1:t})\right). \quad (11)$$

Equation (11) is *identical* to the filtering equation (5) except that

1. The forward message $\mathbf{f}_{1:t} = \mathbf{P}(\mathbf{X}_t \mid \mathbf{e}_{1:t})$ is replaced by the message

$$\mathbf{m}_{1:t} = \max_{\mathbf{x}_1 \ldots \mathbf{x}_{t-1}} \mathbf{P}(\mathbf{x}_1, \ldots, \mathbf{x}_{t-1}, \mathbf{X}_t \mid \mathbf{e}_{1:t}) ,$$

that is, the probabilities of the most likely path to each state $\mathbf{x}_t$; and

2. the summation over $\mathbf{x}_t$ in Equation (5) is replaced by the maximization over $\mathbf{x}_t$ in Equation (11).

Thus, the algorithm for computing the most likely sequence is similar to filtering: it runs forward along the sequence, computing the **m** message at each time step, using Equation (11). The progress of this computation is shown in Figure 5(b). At the end, it will have the probability for the most likely sequence reaching *each* of the final states. One can thus easily select the most likely sequence overall (the states outlined in bold). In order to identify the actual sequence, as opposed to just computing its probability, the algorithm will also need to record, for each state, the best state that leads to it; these are indicated by the bold arrows in Figure 5(b). The optimal sequence is identified by following these bold arrows backwards from the best final state.

VITERBI ALGORITHM

The algorithm we have just described is called the **Viterbi algorithm**, after its inventor. Like the filtering algorithm, its time complexity is linear in t, the length of the sequence. Unlike filtering, which uses constant space, its space requirement is also linear in t. This is because the Viterbi algorithm needs to keep the pointers that identify the best sequence leading to each state.

3 Hidden Markov Models

The preceding section developed algorithms for temporal probabilistic reasoning using a general framework that was independent of the specific form of the transition and sensor models. In this and the next two sections, we discuss more concrete models and applications that illustrate the power of the basic algorithms and in some cases allow further improvements.

HIDDEN MARKOV MODEL

We begin with the **hidden Markov model**, or **HMM**. An HMM is a temporal probabilistic model in which the state of the process is described by a *single discrete* random variable. The possible values of the variable are the possible states of the world. The umbrella example described in the preceding section is therefore an HMM, since it has just one state variable: $Rain_t$. What happens if you have a model with two or more state variables? You can still fit it into the HMM framework by combining the variables into a single "megavariable" whose values are all possible tuples of values of the individual state variables. We will see that the restricted structure of HMMs allows for a simple and elegant matrix implementation of all the basic algorithms.

3.1 Simplified matrix algorithms

With a single, discrete state variable X_t, we can give concrete form to the representations of the transition model, the sensor model, and the forward and backward messages. Let the state variable X_t have values denoted by integers $1, \ldots, S$, where S is the number of possible states. The transition model $\mathbf{P}(X_t \mid X_{t-1})$ becomes an $S \times S$ matrix $\mathbf{T}$, where

$$\mathbf{T}_{ij} = P(X_t = j \mid X_{t-1} = i) .$$

That is, $\mathbf{T}_{ij}$ is the probability of a transition from state i to state j. For example, the transition matrix for the umbrella world is

$$\mathbf{T} = \mathbf{P}(X_t \mid X_{t-1}) = \begin{pmatrix} 0.7 & 0.3 \\ 0.3 & 0.7 \end{pmatrix} .$$

We also put the sensor model in matrix form. In this case, because the value of the evidence variable E_t is known at time t (call it e_t), we need only specify, for each state, how likely it is that the state causes e_t to appear: we need $P(e_t \mid X_t = i)$ for each state i. For mathematical convenience we place these values into an $S \times S$ diagonal matrix, $\mathbf{O}_t$ whose ith diagonal entry is $P(e_t \mid X_t = i)$ and whose other entries are 0. For example, on day 1 in the umbrella world of Figure 5, $U_1 = true$, and on day 3, $U_3 = false$, so, from Figure 2, we have

$$\mathbf{O}_1 = \begin{pmatrix} 0.9 & 0 \\ 0 & 0.2 \end{pmatrix}; \qquad \mathbf{O}_3 = \begin{pmatrix} 0.1 & 0 \\ 0 & 0.8 \end{pmatrix} .$$

Now, if we use column vectors to represent the forward and backward messages, all the computations become simple matrix–vector operations. The forward equation (5) becomes

$$\mathbf{f}_{1:t+1} = \alpha\, \mathbf{O}_{t+1} \mathbf{T}^{\top} \mathbf{f}_{1:t} \tag{12}$$

and the backward equation (9) becomes

$$\mathbf{b}_{k+1:t} = \mathbf{T}\mathbf{O}_{k+1} \mathbf{b}_{k+2:t} . \tag{13}$$

From these equations, we can see that the time complexity of the forward–backward algorithm (Figure 4) applied to a sequence of length t is $O(S^2 t)$, because each step requires multiplying an S-element vector by an $S \times S$ matrix. The space requirement is $O(St)$, because the forward pass stores t vectors of size S.

Besides providing an elegant description of the filtering and smoothing algorithms for HMMs, the matrix formulation reveals opportunities for improved algorithms. The first is a simple variation on the forward–backward algorithm that allows smoothing to be carried out in *constant* space, independently of the length of the sequence. The idea is that smoothing for any particular time slice k requires the simultaneous presence of both the forward and backward messages, $\mathbf{f}_{1:k}$ and $\mathbf{b}_{k+1:t}$, according to Equation (8). The forward–backward algorithm achieves this by storing the **f**s computed on the forward pass so that they are available during the backward pass. Another way to achieve this is with a single pass that propagates both **f** and **b** in the same direction. For example, the "forward" message **f** can be propagated backward if we manipulate Equation (12) to work in the other direction:

$$\mathbf{f}_{1:t} = \alpha' (\mathbf{T}^{\top})^{-1} \mathbf{O}_{t+1}^{-1} \mathbf{f}_{1:t+1} .$$

The modified smoothing algorithm works by first running the standard forward pass to compute $\mathbf{f}_{t:t}$ (forgetting all the intermediate results) and then running the backward pass for both

```
function FIXED-LAG-SMOOTHING(e_t, hmm, d) returns a distribution over X_{t-d}
  inputs: e_t, the current evidence for time step t
          hmm, a hidden Markov model with S × S transition matrix T
          d, the length of the lag for smoothing
  persistent: t, the current time, initially 1
              f, the forward message P(X_t|e_{1:t}), initially hmm.PRIOR
              B, the d-step backward transformation matrix, initially the identity matrix
              e_{t-d:t}, double-ended list of evidence from t − d to t, initially empty
  local variables: O_{t-d}, O_t, diagonal matrices containing the sensor model information

  add e_t to the end of e_{t-d:t}
  O_t ← diagonal matrix containing P(e_t|X_t)
  if t > d then
      f ← FORWARD(f, e_t)
      remove e_{t-d-1} from the beginning of e_{t-d:t}
      O_{t-d} ← diagonal matrix containing P(e_{t-d}|X_{t-d})
      B ← O_{t-d}^{-1} T^{-1} B T O_t
  else B ← B T O_t
  t ← t + 1
  if t > d then return NORMALIZE(f × B1) else return null
```

Figure 6 An algorithm for smoothing with a fixed time lag of d steps, implemented as an online algorithm that outputs the new smoothed estimate given the observation for a new time step. Notice that the final output NORMALIZE($\mathbf{f} \times \mathbf{B1}$) is just $\alpha\,\mathbf{f} \times \mathbf{b}$, by Equation (14).

b and **f** together, using them to compute the smoothed estimate at each step. Since only one copy of each message is needed, the storage requirements are constant (i.e., independent of t, the length of the sequence). There are two significant restrictions on this algorithm: it requires that the transition matrix be invertible and that the sensor model have no zeroes—that is, that every observation be possible in every state.

A second area in which the matrix formulation reveals an improvement is in *online* smoothing with a fixed lag. The fact that smoothing can be done in constant space suggests that there should exist an efficient recursive algorithm for online smoothing—that is, an algorithm whose time complexity is independent of the length of the lag. Let us suppose that the lag is d; that is, we are smoothing at time slice $t-d$, where the current time is t. By Equation (8), we need to compute

$$\alpha\, \mathbf{f}_{1:t-d} \times \mathbf{b}_{t-d+1:t}$$

for slice $t-d$. Then, when a new observation arrives, we need to compute

$$\alpha\, \mathbf{f}_{1:t-d+1} \times \mathbf{b}_{t-d+2:t+1}$$

for slice $t-d+1$. How can this be done incrementally? First, we can compute $\mathbf{f}_{1:t-d+1}$ from $\mathbf{f}_{1:t-d}$, using the standard filtering process, Equation (5).

Computing the backward message incrementally is trickier, because there is no simple relationship between the old backward message $\mathbf{b}_{t-d+1:t}$ and the new backward message $\mathbf{b}_{t-d+2:t+1}$. Instead, we will examine the relationship between the old backward message $\mathbf{b}_{t-d+1:t}$ and the backward message at the front of the sequence, $\mathbf{b}_{t+1:t}$. To do this, we apply Equation (13) d times to get

$$\mathbf{b}_{t-d+1:t} = \left(\prod_{i=t-d+1}^{t} \mathbf{TO}_i \right) \mathbf{b}_{t+1:t} = \mathbf{B}_{t-d+1:t}\mathbf{1}\,, \tag{14}$$

where the matrix $\mathbf{B}_{t-d+1:t}$ is the product of the sequence of $\mathbf{T}$ and $\mathbf{O}$ matrices. $\mathbf{B}$ can be thought of as a "transformation operator" that transforms a later backward message into an earlier one. A similar equation holds for the new backward messages *after* the next observation arrives:

$$\mathbf{b}_{t-d+2:t+1} = \left(\prod_{i=t-d+2}^{t+1} \mathbf{TO}_i \right) \mathbf{b}_{t+2:t+1} = \mathbf{B}_{t-d+2:t+1}\mathbf{1}\,. \tag{15}$$

Examining the product expressions in Equations (14) and (15), we see that they have a simple relationship: to get the second product, "divide" the first product by the first element $\mathbf{TO}_{t-d+1}$, and multiply by the new last element $\mathbf{TO}_{t+1}$. In matrix language, then, there is a simple relationship between the old and new $\mathbf{B}$ matrices:

$$\mathbf{B}_{t-d+2:t+1} = \mathbf{O}_{t-d+1}^{-1}\mathbf{T}^{-1}\mathbf{B}_{t-d+1:t}\mathbf{TO}_{t+1}\,. \tag{16}$$

This equation provides an incremental update for the $\mathbf{B}$ matrix, which in turn (through Equation (15)) allows us to compute the new backward message $\mathbf{b}_{t-d+2:t+1}$. The complete algorithm, which requires storing and updating $\mathbf{f}$ and $\mathbf{B}$, is shown in Figure 6.

3.2 Hidden Markov model example: Localization

In a simple form of the **localization** problem for the vacuum world, a robot has a single nondeterministic *Move* action and its sensors report perfectly whether or not obstacles lay immediately to the north, south, east, and west; the robot's belief state is the set of possible locations it could be in.

Here we make the problem slightly more realistic by including a simple probability model for the robot's motion and by allowing for noise in the sensors. The state variable X_t represents the location of the robot on the discrete grid; the domain of this variable is the set of empty squares $\{s_1, \ldots, s_n\}$. Let $\text{NEIGHBORS}(s)$ be the set of empty squares that are adjacent to s and let $N(s)$ be the size of that set. Then the transition model for *Move* action says that the robot is equally likely to end up at any neighboring square:

$$P(X_{t+1} = j \mid X_t = i) = \mathbf{T}_{ij} = (1/N(i) \text{ if } j \in \text{NEIGHBORS}(i) \text{ else } 0)\,.$$

We don't know where the robot starts, so we will assume a uniform distribution over all the squares; that is, $P(X_0 = i) = 1/n$. For the particular environment we consider (Figure 7), $n = 42$ and the transition matrix $\mathbf{T}$ has $42 \times 42 = 1764$ entries.

The sensor variable E_t has 16 possible values, each a four-bit sequence giving the presence or absence of an obstacle in a particular compass direction. We will use the notation

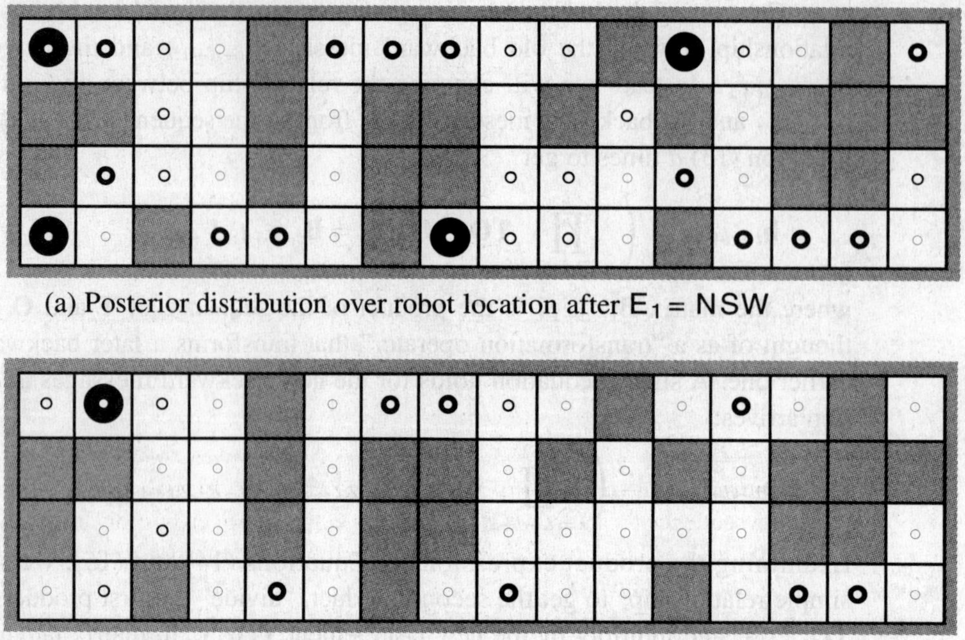

(a) Posterior distribution over robot location after $E_1 = NSW$

(b) Posterior distribution over robot location after $E_1 = NSW, E_2 = NS$

Figure 7 Posterior distribution over robot location: (a) one observation $E_1 = NSW$; (b) after a second observation $E_2 = NS$. The size of each disk corresponds to the probability that the robot is at that location. The sensor error rate is $\epsilon = 0.2$.

NS, for example, to mean that the north and south sensors report an obstacle and the east and west do not. Suppose that each sensor's error rate is ϵ and that errors occur independently for the four sensor directions. In that case, the probability of getting all four bits right is $(1-\epsilon)^4$ and the probability of getting them all wrong is ϵ^4. Furthermore, if d_{it} is the discrepancy—the number of bits that are different—between the true values for square i and the actual reading e_t, then the probability that a robot in square i would receive a sensor reading e_t is

$$P(E_t = e_t \mid X_t = i) = \mathbf{O}_{t_{ii}} = (1-\epsilon)^{4-d_{it}}\epsilon^{d_{it}} .$$

For example, the probability that a square with obstacles to the north and south would produce a sensor reading NSE is $(1-\epsilon)^3\epsilon^1$.

Given the matrices $\mathbf{T}$ and $\mathbf{O}_t$, the robot can use Equation (12) to compute the posterior distribution over locations—that is, to work out where it is. Figure 7 shows the distributions $\mathbf{P}(X_1 \mid E_1 = NSW)$ and $\mathbf{P}(X_2 \mid E_1 = NSW, E_2 = NS)$. Using logical filtering we can find the locations that are *possible*, assuming perfect sensing. Those same locations are still the most *likely* with noisy sensing, but now *every* location has some nonzero probability.

In addition to filtering to estimate its current location, the robot can use smoothing (Equation (13)) to work out where it was at any given past time—for example, where it began at time 0—and it can use the Viterbi algorithm to work out the most likely path it has

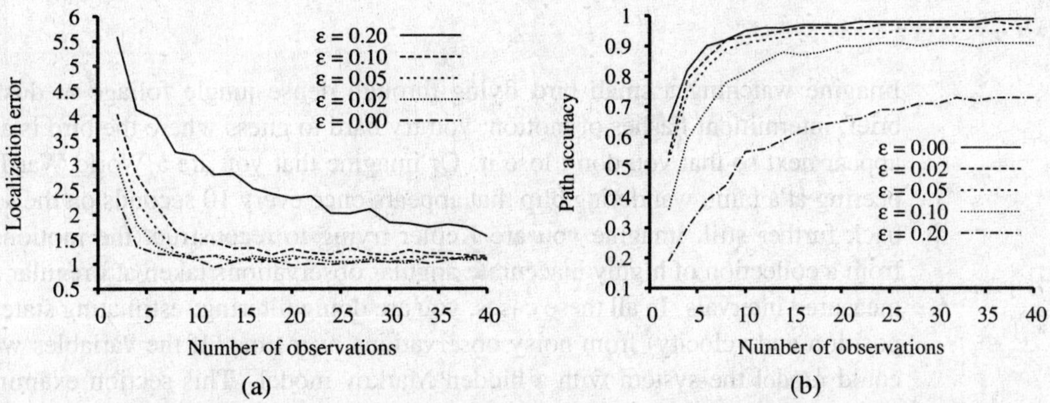

Figure 8 Performance of HMM localization as a function of the length of the observation sequence for various different values of the sensor error probability ϵ; data averaged over 400 runs. (a) The localization error, defined as the Manhattan distance from the true location. (b) The Viterbi path accuracy, defined as the fraction of correct states on the Viterbi path.

taken to get where it is now. Figure 8 shows the localization error and Viterbi path accuracy for various values of the per-bit sensor error rate ϵ. Even when ϵ is 20%—which means that the overall sensor reading is wrong 59% of the time—the robot is usually able to work out its location within two squares after 25 observations. This is because of the algorithm's ability to integrate evidence over time and to take into account the probabilistic constraints imposed on the location sequence by the transition model. When ϵ is 10%, the performance after a half-dozen observations is hard to distinguish from the performance with perfect sensing. Exercise 7 asks you to explore how robust the HMM localization algorithm is to errors in the prior distribution $\mathbf{P}(X_0)$ and in the transition model itself. Broadly speaking, high levels of localization and path accuracy are maintained even in the face of substantial errors in the models used.

The state variable for the example we have considered in this section is a physical location in the world. Other problems can, of course, include other aspects of the world. Exercise 8 asks you to consider a version of the vacuum robot that has the policy of going straight for as long as it can; only when it encounters an obstacle does it change to a new (randomly selected) heading. To model this robot, each state in the model consists of a *(location, heading)* pair. For the environment in Figure 7, which has 42 empty squares, this leads to 168 states and a transition matrix with $168^2 = 28,224$ entries—still a manageable number. If we add the possibility of dirt in the squares, the number of states is multiplied by 2^{42} and the transition matrix ends up with more than 10^{29} entries—no longer a manageable number; Section 5 shows how to use dynamic Bayesian networks to model domains with many state variables. If we allow the robot to move continuously rather than in a discrete grid, the number of states becomes infinite; the next section shows how to handle this case.

4 KALMAN FILTERS

Imagine watching a small bird flying through dense jungle foliage at dusk: you glimpse brief, intermittent flashes of motion; you try hard to guess where the bird is and where it will appear next so that you don't lose it. Or imagine that you are a World War II radar operator peering at a faint, wandering blip that appears once every 10 seconds on the screen. Or, going back further still, imagine you are Kepler trying to reconstruct the motions of the planets from a collection of highly inaccurate angular observations taken at irregular and imprecisely measured intervals. In all these cases, you are doing filtering: estimating state variables (here, position and velocity) from noisy observations over time. If the variables were discrete, we could model the system with a hidden Markov model. This section examines methods for handling continuous variables, using an algorithm called **Kalman filtering**, after one of its inventors, Rudolf E. Kalman.

KALMAN FILTERING

The bird's flight might be specified by six continuous variables at each time point; three for position (X_t, Y_t, Z_t) and three for velocity $(\dot{X}_t, \dot{Y}_t, \dot{Z}_t)$. We will need suitable conditional densities to represent the transition and sensor models; we will use **linear Gaussian** distributions. This means that the next state $\mathbf{X}_{t+1}$ must be a linear function of the current state $\mathbf{X}_t$, plus some Gaussian noise, a condition that turns out to be quite reasonable in practice. Consider, for example, the X-coordinate of the bird, ignoring the other coordinates for now. Let the time interval between observations be Δ, and assume constant velocity during the interval; then the position update is given by $X_{t+\Delta} = X_t + \dot{X}\,\Delta$. Adding Gaussian noise (to account for wind variation, etc.), we obtain a linear Gaussian transition model:

$$P(X_{t+\Delta} = x_{t+\Delta} \mid X_t = x_t, \dot{X}_t = \dot{x}_t) = N(x_t + \dot{x}_t\,\Delta, \sigma^2)(x_{t+\Delta})\,.$$

The Bayesian network structure for a system with position vector $\mathbf{X}_t$ and velocity $\dot{\mathbf{X}}_t$ is shown in Figure 9. Note that this is a very specific form of linear Gaussian model; the general form will be described later in this section and covers a vast array of applications beyond the simple motion examples of the first paragraph. The reader might wish to consult the mathematical properties of Gaussian distributions; for our immediate purposes, the most important is that a **multivariate Gaussian** distribution for d variables is specified by a d-element mean $\boldsymbol{\mu}$ and a $d \times d$ covariance matrix $\boldsymbol{\Sigma}$.

MULTIVARIATE GAUSSIAN

4.1 Updating Gaussian distributions

A key property of the linear Gaussian family of distributions is that it remains closed under the standard Bayesian network operations. Here, we make this claim precise in the context of filtering in a temporal probability model. The required properties correspond to the two-step filtering calculation in Equation (5):

1. If the current distribution $\mathbf{P}(\mathbf{X}_t \mid \mathbf{e}_{1:t})$ is Gaussian and the transition model $\mathbf{P}(\mathbf{X}_{t+1} \mid \mathbf{x}_t)$ is linear Gaussian, then the one-step predicted distribution given by

$$\mathbf{P}(\mathbf{X}_{t+1} \mid \mathbf{e}_{1:t}) = \int_{\mathbf{x}_t} \mathbf{P}(\mathbf{X}_{t+1} \mid \mathbf{x}_t) P(\mathbf{x}_t \mid \mathbf{e}_{1:t})\, d\mathbf{x}_t \qquad (17)$$

   is also a Gaussian distribution.

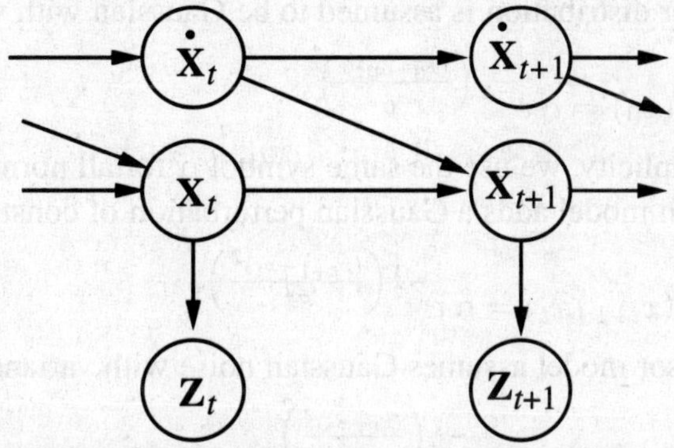

Figure 9 Bayesian network structure for a linear dynamical system with position $\mathbf{X}_t$, velocity $\dot{\mathbf{X}}_t$, and position measurement $\mathbf{Z}_t$.

2. If the prediction $\mathbf{P}(\mathbf{X}_{t+1} \mid \mathbf{e}_{1:t})$ is Gaussian and the sensor model $\mathbf{P}(\mathbf{e}_{t+1} \mid \mathbf{X}_{t+1})$ is linear Gaussian, then, after conditioning on the new evidence, the updated distribution

$$\mathbf{P}(\mathbf{X}_{t+1} \mid \mathbf{e}_{1:t+1}) = \alpha\, \mathbf{P}(\mathbf{e}_{t+1} \mid \mathbf{X}_{t+1})\mathbf{P}(\mathbf{X}_{t+1} \mid \mathbf{e}_{1:t}) \tag{18}$$

is also a Gaussian distribution.

Thus, the FORWARD operator for Kalman filtering takes a Gaussian forward message $\mathbf{f}_{1:t}$, specified by a mean $\boldsymbol{\mu}_t$ and covariance matrix $\boldsymbol{\Sigma}_t$, and produces a new multivariate Gaussian forward message $\mathbf{f}_{1:t+1}$, specified by a mean $\boldsymbol{\mu}_{t+1}$ and covariance matrix $\boldsymbol{\Sigma}_{t+1}$. So, if we start with a Gaussian prior $\mathbf{f}_{1:0} = \mathbf{P}(\mathbf{X}_0) = N(\boldsymbol{\mu}_0, \boldsymbol{\Sigma}_0)$, filtering with a linear Gaussian model produces a Gaussian state distribution for all time.

This seems to be a nice, elegant result, but why is it so important? The reason is that, except for a few special cases such as this, *filtering with continuous or hybrid (discrete and continuous) networks generates state distributions whose representation grows without bound over time.* This statement is not easy to prove in general, but Exercise 10 shows what happens for a simple example.

4.2 A simple one-dimensional example

We have said that the FORWARD operator for the Kalman filter maps a Gaussian into a new Gaussian. This translates into computing a new mean and covariance matrix from the previous mean and covariance matrix. Deriving the update rule in the general (multivariate) case requires rather a lot of linear algebra, so we will stick to a very simple univariate case for now; and later give the results for the general case. Even for the univariate case, the calculations are somewhat tedious, but we feel that they are worth seeing because the usefulness of the Kalman filter is tied so intimately to the mathematical properties of Gaussian distributions.

The temporal model we consider describes a **random walk** of a single continuous state variable X_t with a noisy observation Z_t. An example might be the "consumer confidence" index, which can be modeled as undergoing a random Gaussian-distributed change each month and is measured by a random consumer survey that also introduces Gaussian sampling noise.

The prior distribution is assumed to be Gaussian with variance σ_0^2:

$$P(x_0) = \alpha\, e^{-\frac{1}{2}\left(\frac{(x_0-\mu_0)^2}{\sigma_0^2}\right)}.$$

(For simplicity, we use the same symbol α for all normalizing constants in this section.) The transition model adds a Gaussian perturbation of constant variance σ_x^2 to the current state:

$$P(x_{t+1}\,|\,x_t) = \alpha\, e^{-\frac{1}{2}\left(\frac{(x_{t+1}-x_t)^2}{\sigma_x^2}\right)}.$$

The sensor model assumes Gaussian noise with variance σ_z^2:

$$P(z_t\,|\,x_t) = \alpha\, e^{-\frac{1}{2}\left(\frac{(z_t-x_t)^2}{\sigma_z^2}\right)}.$$

Now, given the prior $\mathbf{P}(X_0)$, the one-step predicted distribution comes from Equation (17):

$$\begin{aligned} P(x_1) &= \int_{-\infty}^{\infty} P(x_1\,|\,x_0)P(x_0)\,dx_0 = \alpha \int_{-\infty}^{\infty} e^{-\frac{1}{2}\left(\frac{(x_1-x_0)^2}{\sigma_x^2}\right)} e^{-\frac{1}{2}\left(\frac{(x_0-\mu_0)^2}{\sigma_0^2}\right)}\,dx_0 \\ &= \alpha \int_{-\infty}^{\infty} e^{-\frac{1}{2}\left(\frac{\sigma_0^2(x_1-x_0)^2+\sigma_x^2(x_0-\mu_0)^2}{\sigma_0^2\sigma_x^2}\right)}\,dx_0\,. \end{aligned}$$

This integral looks rather complicated. The key to progress is to notice that the exponent is the sum of two expressions that are *quadratic* in x_0 and hence is itself a quadratic in x_0. A simple trick known as **completing the square** allows the rewriting of any quadratic $ax_0^2 + bx_0 + c$ as the sum of a squared term $a(x_0 - \frac{-b}{2a})^2$ and a residual term $c - \frac{b^2}{4a}$ that is independent of x_0. The residual term can be taken outside the integral, giving us

COMPLETING THE SQUARE

$$P(x_1) = \alpha\, e^{-\frac{1}{2}\left(c-\frac{b^2}{4a}\right)} \int_{-\infty}^{\infty} e^{-\frac{1}{2}\left(a(x_0-\frac{-b}{2a})^2\right)}\,dx_0\,.$$

Now the integral is just the integral of a Gaussian over its full range, which is simply 1. Thus, we are left with only the residual term from the quadratic. Then, we notice that the residual term is a quadratic in x_1; in fact, after simplification, we obtain

$$P(x_1) = \alpha\, e^{-\frac{1}{2}\left(\frac{(x_1-\mu_0)^2}{\sigma_0^2+\sigma_x^2}\right)}.$$

That is, the one-step predicted distribution is a Gaussian with the same mean μ_0 and a variance equal to the sum of the original variance σ_0^2 and the transition variance σ_x^2.

To complete the update step, we need to condition on the observation at the first time step, namely, z_1. From Equation (18), this is given by

$$\begin{aligned} P(x_1\,|\,z_1) &= \alpha\, P(z_1\,|\,x_1)P(x_1) \\ &= \alpha\, e^{-\frac{1}{2}\left(\frac{(z_1-x_1)^2}{\sigma_z^2}\right)} e^{-\frac{1}{2}\left(\frac{(x_1-\mu_0)^2}{\sigma_0^2+\sigma_x^2}\right)}. \end{aligned}$$

Once again, we combine the exponents and complete the square (Exercise 11), obtaining

$$P(x_1\,|\,z_1) = \alpha\, e^{-\frac{1}{2}\left(\frac{\left(x_1-\frac{(\sigma_0^2+\sigma_x^2)z_1+\sigma_z^2\mu_0}{\sigma_0^2+\sigma_x^2+\sigma_z^2}\right)^2}{(\sigma_0^2+\sigma_x^2)\sigma_z^2/(\sigma_0^2+\sigma_x^2+\sigma_z^2)}\right)}. \qquad (19)$$

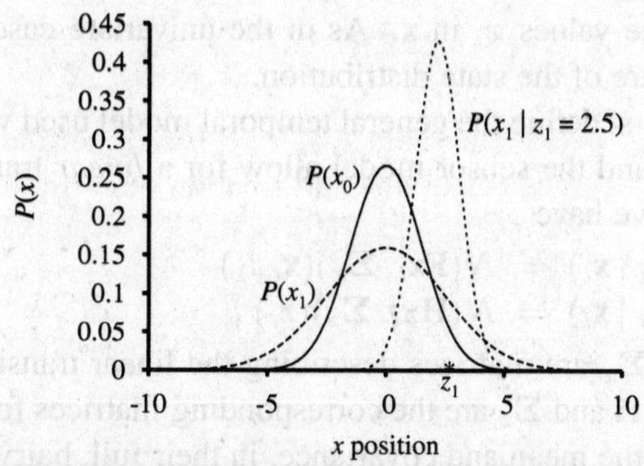

Figure 10 Stages in the Kalman filter update cycle for a random walk with a prior given by $\mu_0 = 0.0$ and $\sigma_0 = 1.0$, transition noise given by $\sigma_x = 2.0$, sensor noise given by $\sigma_z = 1.0$, and a first observation $z_1 = 2.5$ (marked on the x-axis). Notice how the prediction $P(x_1)$ is flattened out, relative to $P(x_0)$, by the transition noise. Notice also that the mean of the posterior distribution $P(x_1 \mid z_1)$ is slightly to the left of the observation z_1 because the mean is a weighted average of the prediction and the observation.

Thus, after one update cycle, we have a new Gaussian distribution for the state variable.

From the Gaussian formula in Equation (19), we see that the new mean and standard deviation can be calculated from the old mean and standard deviation as follows:

$$\mu_{t+1} = \frac{(\sigma_t^2 + \sigma_x^2) z_{t+1} + \sigma_z^2 \mu_t}{\sigma_t^2 + \sigma_x^2 + \sigma_z^2} \quad \text{and} \quad \sigma_{t+1}^2 = \frac{(\sigma_t^2 + \sigma_x^2)\sigma_z^2}{\sigma_t^2 + \sigma_x^2 + \sigma_z^2}. \tag{20}$$

Figure 10 shows one update cycle for particular values of the transition and sensor models.

Equation (20) plays exactly the same role as the general filtering equation (5) or the HMM filtering equation (12). Because of the special nature of Gaussian distributions, however, the equations have some interesting additional properties. First, we can interpret the calculation for the new mean μ_{t+1} as simply a *weighted mean* of the new observation z_{t+1} and the old mean μ_t. If the observation is unreliable, then σ_z^2 is large and we pay more attention to the old mean; if the old mean is unreliable (σ_t^2 is large) or the process is highly unpredictable (σ_x^2 is large), then we pay more attention to the observation. Second, notice that the update for the variance σ_{t+1}^2 is *independent of the observation*. We can therefore compute in advance what the sequence of variance values will be. Third, the sequence of variance values converges quickly to a fixed value that depends only on σ_x^2 and σ_z^2, thereby substantially simplifying the subsequent calculations. (See Exercise 12.)

4.3 The general case

The preceding derivation illustrates the key property of Gaussian distributions that allows Kalman filtering to work: the fact that the exponent is a quadratic form. This is true not just for the univariate case; the full multivariate Gaussian distribution has the form

$$N(\boldsymbol{\mu}, \boldsymbol{\Sigma})(\mathbf{x}) = \alpha\, e^{-\frac{1}{2}\left((\mathbf{x}-\boldsymbol{\mu})^\top \boldsymbol{\Sigma}^{-1}(\mathbf{x}-\boldsymbol{\mu})\right)}.$$

Multiplying out the terms in the exponent makes it clear that the exponent is also a quadratic function of the values x_i in $\mathbf{x}$. As in the univariate case, the filtering update preserves the Gaussian nature of the state distribution.

Let us first define the general temporal model used with Kalman filtering. Both the transition model and the sensor model allow for a *linear* transformation with additive Gaussian noise. Thus, we have

$$\begin{aligned} P(\mathbf{x}_{t+1} \mid \mathbf{x}_t) &= N(\mathbf{F}\mathbf{x}_t, \boldsymbol{\Sigma}_x)(\mathbf{x}_{t+1}) \\ P(\mathbf{z}_t \mid \mathbf{x}_t) &= N(\mathbf{H}\mathbf{x}_t, \boldsymbol{\Sigma}_z)(\mathbf{z}_t)\,, \end{aligned} \tag{21}$$

where $\mathbf{F}$ and $\boldsymbol{\Sigma}_x$ are matrices describing the linear transition model and transition noise covariance, and $\mathbf{H}$ and $\boldsymbol{\Sigma}_z$ are the corresponding matrices for the sensor model. Now the update equations for the mean and covariance, in their full, hairy horribleness, are

$$\begin{aligned} \boldsymbol{\mu}_{t+1} &= \mathbf{F}\boldsymbol{\mu}_t + \mathbf{K}_{t+1}(\mathbf{z}_{t+1} - \mathbf{H}\mathbf{F}\boldsymbol{\mu}_t) \\ \boldsymbol{\Sigma}_{t+1} &= (\mathbf{I} - \mathbf{K}_{t+1}\mathbf{H})(\mathbf{F}\boldsymbol{\Sigma}_t\mathbf{F}^\top + \boldsymbol{\Sigma}_x)\,, \end{aligned} \tag{22}$$

where $\mathbf{K}_{t+1} = (\mathbf{F}\boldsymbol{\Sigma}_t\mathbf{F}^\top + \boldsymbol{\Sigma}_x)\mathbf{H}^\top(\mathbf{H}(\mathbf{F}\boldsymbol{\Sigma}_t\mathbf{F}^\top + \boldsymbol{\Sigma}_x)\mathbf{H}^\top + \boldsymbol{\Sigma}_z)^{-1}$ is called the **Kalman gain matrix**. Believe it or not, these equations make some intuitive sense. For example, consider the update for the mean state estimate $\boldsymbol{\mu}$. The term $\mathbf{F}\boldsymbol{\mu}_t$ is the *predicted* state at $t+1$, so $\mathbf{H}\mathbf{F}\boldsymbol{\mu}_t$ is the *predicted* observation. Therefore, the term $\mathbf{z}_{t+1} - \mathbf{H}\mathbf{F}\boldsymbol{\mu}_t$ represents the error in the predicted observation. This is multiplied by $\mathbf{K}_{t+1}$ to correct the predicted state; hence, $\mathbf{K}_{t+1}$ is a measure of *how seriously to take the new observation* relative to the prediction. As in Equation (20), we also have the property that the variance update is independent of the observations. The sequence of values for $\boldsymbol{\Sigma}_t$ and $\mathbf{K}_t$ can therefore be computed offline, and the actual calculations required during online tracking are quite modest.

KALMAN GAIN MATRIX

To illustrate these equations at work, we have applied them to the problem of tracking an object moving on the X–Y plane. The state variables are $\mathbf{X} = (X, Y, \dot{X}, \dot{Y})^\top$, so $\mathbf{F}$, $\boldsymbol{\Sigma}_x$, $\mathbf{H}$, and $\boldsymbol{\Sigma}_z$ are 4×4 matrices. Figure 11(a) shows the true trajectory, a series of noisy observations, and the trajectory estimated by Kalman filtering, along with the covariances indicated by the one-standard-deviation contours. The filtering process does a good job of tracking the actual motion, and, as expected, the variance quickly reaches a fixed point.

We can also derive equations for *smoothing* as well as filtering with linear Gaussian models. The smoothing results are shown in Figure 11(b). Notice how the variance in the position estimate is sharply reduced, except at the ends of the trajectory (why?), and that the estimated trajectory is much smoother.

4.4 Applicability of Kalman filtering

The Kalman filter and its elaborations are used in a vast array of applications. The "classical" application is in radar tracking of aircraft and missiles. Related applications include acoustic tracking of submarines and ground vehicles and visual tracking of vehicles and people. In a slightly more esoteric vein, Kalman filters are used to reconstruct particle trajectories from bubble-chamber photographs and ocean currents from satellite surface measurements. The range of application is much larger than just the tracking of motion: any system characterized by continuous state variables and noisy measurements will do. Such systems include pulp mills, chemical plants, nuclear reactors, plant ecosystems, and national economies.

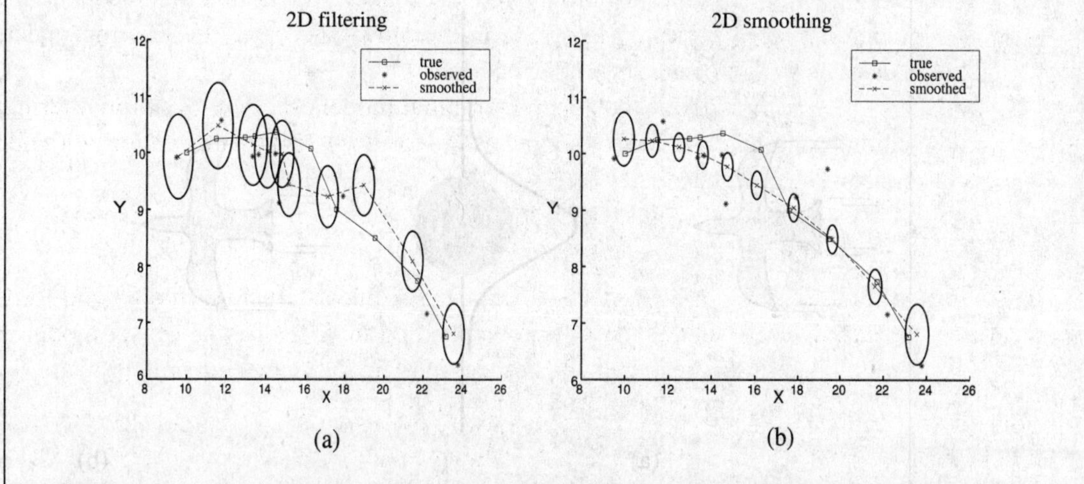

Figure 11 (a) Results of Kalman filtering for an object moving on the X–Y plane, showing the true trajectory (left to right), a series of noisy observations, and the trajectory estimated by Kalman filtering. Variance in the position estimate is indicated by the ovals. (b) The results of Kalman smoothing for the same observation sequence.

The fact that Kalman filtering can be applied to a system does not mean that the results will be valid or useful. The assumptions made—a linear Gaussian transition and sensor models—are very strong. The **extended Kalman filter (EKF)** attempts to overcome nonlinearities in the system being modeled. A system is **nonlinear** if the transition model cannot be described as a matrix multiplication of the state vector, as in Equation (21). The EKF works by modeling the system as *locally* linear in $\mathbf{x}_t$ in the region of $\mathbf{x}_t = \boldsymbol{\mu}_t$, the mean of the current state distribution. This works well for smooth, well-behaved systems and allows the tracker to maintain and update a Gaussian state distribution that is a reasonable approximation to the true posterior.

EXTENDED KALMAN FILTER (EKF)

NONLINEAR

What does it mean for a system to be "unsmooth" or "poorly behaved"? Technically, it means that there is significant nonlinearity in system response within the region that is "close" (according to the covariance Σ_t) to the current mean $\boldsymbol{\mu}_t$. To understand this idea in nontechnical terms, consider the example of trying to track a bird as it flies through the jungle. The bird appears to be heading at high speed straight for a tree trunk. The Kalman filter, whether regular or extended, can make only a Gaussian prediction of the location of the bird, and the mean of this Gaussian will be centered on the trunk, as shown in Figure 12(a). A reasonable model of the bird, on the other hand, would predict evasive action to one side or the other, as shown in Figure 12(b). Such a model is highly nonlinear, because the bird's decision varies sharply depending on its precise location relative to the trunk.

To handle examples like these, we clearly need a more expressive language for representing the behavior of the system being modeled. Within the control theory community, for which problems such as evasive maneuvering by aircraft raise the same kinds of difficulties, the standard solution is the **switching Kalman filter**. In this approach, multiple Kalman fil-

SWITCHING KALMAN FILTER

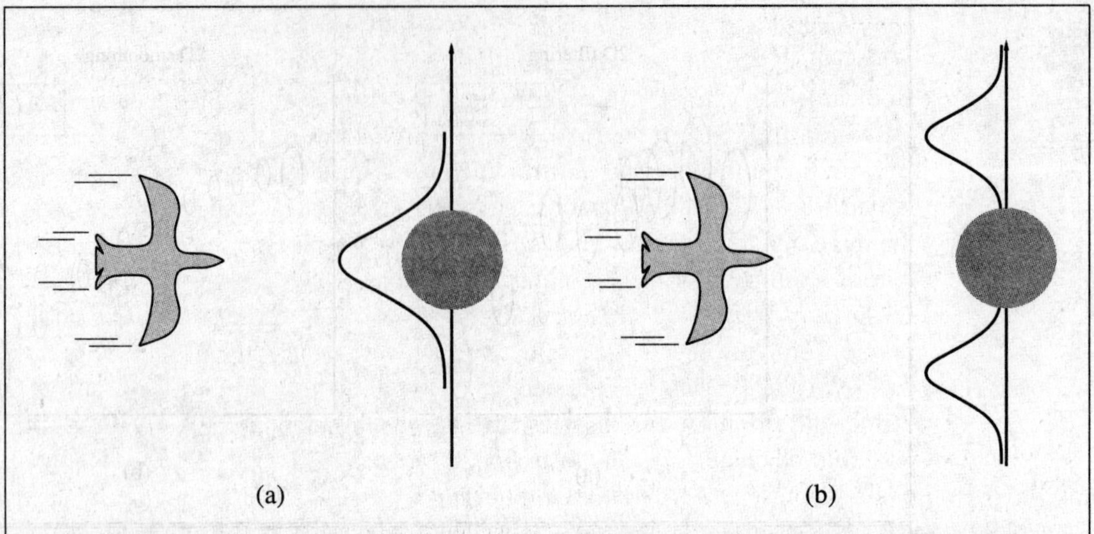

Figure 12 A bird flying toward a tree (top views). (a) A Kalman filter will predict the location of the bird using a single Gaussian centered on the obstacle. (b) A more realistic model allows for the bird's evasive action, predicting that it will fly to one side or the other.

ters run in parallel, each using a different model of the system—for example, one for straight flight, one for sharp left turns, and one for sharp right turns. A weighted sum of predictions is used, where the weight depends on how well each filter fits the current data. We will see in the next section that this is simply a special case of the general dynamic Bayesian network model, obtained by adding a discrete "maneuver" state variable to the network shown in Figure 9. Switching Kalman filters are discussed further in Exercise 10.

5 Dynamic Bayesian Networks

DYNAMIC BAYESIAN NETWORK

A **dynamic Bayesian network**, or **DBN**, is a Bayesian network that represents a temporal probability model of the kind described in Section 1. We have already seen examples of DBNs: the umbrella network in Figure 2 and the Kalman filter network in Figure 9. In general, each slice of a DBN can have any number of state variables $\mathbf{X}_t$ and evidence variables $\mathbf{E}_t$. For simplicity, we assume that the variables and their links are exactly replicated from slice to slice and that the DBN represents a first-order Markov process, so that each variable can have parents only in its own slice or the immediately preceding slice.

It should be clear that every hidden Markov model can be represented as a DBN with a single state variable and a single evidence variable. It is also the case that every discrete-variable DBN can be represented as an HMM; as explained in Section 3, we can combine all the state variables in the DBN into a single state variable whose values are all possible tuples of values of the individual state variables. Now, if every HMM is a DBN and every DBN can be translated into an HMM, what's the difference? The difference is that, *by de-*

composing the state of a complex system into its constituent variables, the can take advantage of sparseness *in the temporal probability model.* Suppose, for example, that a DBN has 20 Boolean state variables, each of which has three parents in the preceding slice. Then the DBN transition model has $20 \times 2^3 = 160$ probabilities, whereas the corresponding HMM has 2^{20} states and therefore 2^{40}, or roughly a trillion, probabilities in the transition matrix. This is bad for at least three reasons: first, the HMM itself requires much more space; second, the huge transition matrix makes HMM inference much more expensive; and third, the problem of learning such a huge number of parameters makes the pure HMM model unsuitable for large problems. The relationship between DBNs and HMMs is roughly analogous to the relationship between ordinary Bayesian networks and full tabulated joint distributions.

We have already explained that every Kalman filter model can be represented in a DBN with continuous variables and linear Gaussian conditional distributions (Figure 9). It should be clear from the discussion at the end of the preceding section that *not* every DBN can be represented by a Kalman filter model. In a Kalman filter, the current state distribution is always a single multivariate Gaussian distribution—that is, a single "bump" in a particular location. DBNs, on the other hand, can model arbitrary distributions. For many real-world applications, this flexibility is essential. Consider, for example, the current location of my keys. They might be in my pocket, on the bedside table, on the kitchen counter, dangling from the front door, or locked in the car. A single Gaussian bump that included all these places would have to allocate significant probability to the keys being in mid-air in the front hall. Aspects of the real world such as purposive agents, obstacles, and pockets introduce "nonlinearities" that require combinations of discrete and continuous variables in order to get reasonable models.

5.1 Constructing DBNs

To construct a DBN, one must specify three kinds of information: the prior distribution over the state variables, $\mathbf{P}(\mathbf{X}_0)$; the transition model $\mathbf{P}(\mathbf{X}_{t+1} \mid \mathbf{X}_t)$; and the sensor model $\mathbf{P}(\mathbf{E}_t \mid \mathbf{X}_t)$. To specify the transition and sensor models, one must also specify the topology of the connections between successive slices and between the state and evidence variables. Because the transition and sensor models are assumed to be stationary—the same for all t—it is most convenient simply to specify them for the first slice. For example, the complete DBN specification for the umbrella world is given by the three-node network shown in Figure 13(a). From this specification, the complete DBN with an unbounded number of time slices can be constructed as needed by copying the first slice.

Let us now consider a more interesting example: monitoring a battery-powered robot moving in the X–Y plane, as introduced at the end of Section 1. First, we need state variables, which will include both $\mathbf{X}_t = (X_t, Y_t)$ for position and $\dot{\mathbf{X}}_t = (\dot{X}_t, \dot{Y}_t)$ for velocity. We assume some method of measuring position—perhaps a fixed camera or onboard GPS (Global Positioning System)—yielding measurements $\mathbf{Z}_t$. The position at the next time step depends on the current position and velocity, as in the standard Kalman filter model. The velocity at the next step depends on the current velocity and the state of the battery. We add $Battery_t$ to represent the actual battery charge level, which has as parents the previous

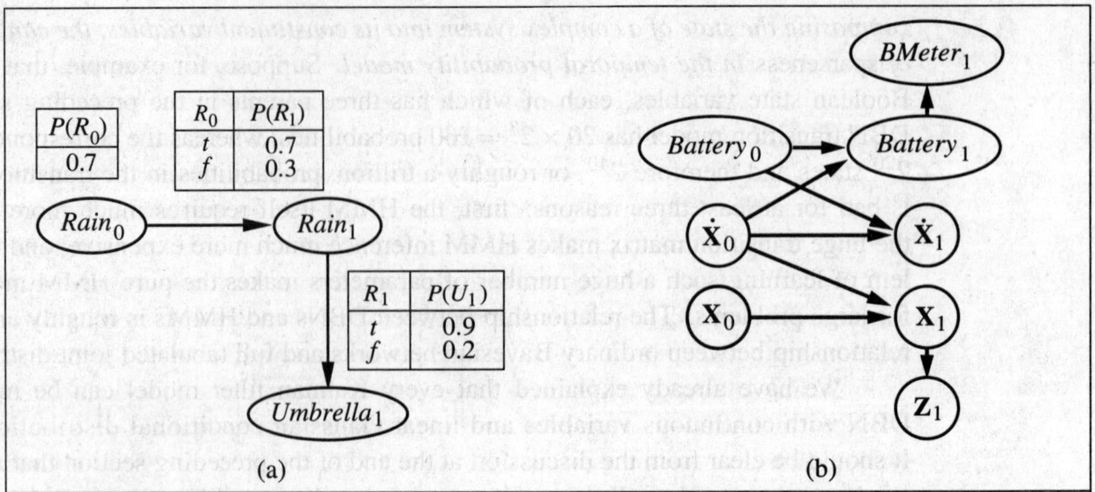

Figure 13 (a) Specification of the prior, transition model, and sensor model for the umbrella DBN. All subsequent slices are assumed to be copies of slice 1. (b) A simple DBN for robot motion in the X–Y plane.

battery level and the velocity, and we add $BMeter_t$, which measures the battery charge level. This gives us the basic model shown in Figure 13(b).

It is worth looking in more depth at the nature of the sensor model for $BMeter_t$. Let us suppose, for simplicity, that both $Battery_t$ and $BMeter_t$ can take on discrete values 0 through 5. If the meter is always accurate, then the CPT $\mathbf{P}(BMeter_t \mid Battery_t)$ should have probabilities of 1.0 "along the diagonal" and probabilities of 0.0 elsewhere. In reality, noise always creeps into measurements. For continuous measurements, a Gaussian distribution with a small variance might be used.[4] For our discrete variables, we can approximate a Gaussian using a distribution in which the probability of error drops off in the appropriate way, so that the probability of a large error is very small. We use the term **Gaussian error model** to cover both the continuous and discrete versions.

GAUSSIAN ERROR MODEL

Anyone with hands-on experience of robotics, computerized process control, or other forms of automatic sensing will readily testify to the fact that small amounts of measurement noise are often the least of one's problems. Real sensors *fail*. When a sensor fails, it does not necessarily send a signal saying, "Oh, by the way, the data I'm about to send you is a load of nonsense." Instead, it simply sends the nonsense. The simplest kind of failure is called a **transient failure**, where the sensor occasionally decides to send some nonsense. For example, the battery level sensor might have a habit of sending a zero when someone bumps the robot, even if the battery is fully charged.

TRANSIENT FAILURE

Let's see what happens when a transient failure occurs with a Gaussian error model that doesn't accommodate such failures. Suppose, for example, that the robot is sitting quietly and observes 20 consecutive battery readings of 5. Then the battery meter has a temporary seizure

[4] Strictly speaking, a Gaussian distribution is problematic because it assigns nonzero probability to large negative charge levels. The **beta distribution** is sometimes a better choice for a variable whose range is restricted.

and the next reading is $BMeter_{21} = 0$. What will the simple Gaussian error model lead us to believe about $Battery_{21}$? According to Bayes' rule, the answer depends on both the sensor model $\mathbf{P}(BMeter_{21} = 0 \mid Battery_{21})$ and the prediction $\mathbf{P}(Battery_{21} \mid BMetcr_{1:20})$. If the probability of a large sensor error is significantly less likely than the probability of a transition to $Battery_{21} = 0$, even if the latter is very unlikely, then the posterior distribution will assign a high probability to the battery's being empty. A second reading of 0 at $t = 22$ will make this conclusion almost certain. If the transient failure then disappears and the reading returns to 5 from $t = 23$ onwards, the estimate for the battery level will quickly return to 5, as if by magic. This course of events is illustrated in the upper curve of Figure 14(a), which shows the expected value of $Battery_t$ over time, using a discrete Gaussian error model.

Despite the recovery, there is a time ($t = 22$) when the robot is convinced that its battery is empty; presumably, then, it should send out a mayday signal and shut down. Alas, its oversimplified sensor model has led it astray. How can this be fixed? Consider a familiar example from everyday human driving: on sharp curves or steep hills, one's "fuel tank empty" warning light sometimes turns on. Rather than looking for the emergency phone, one simply recalls that the fuel gauge sometimes gives a very large error when the fuel is sloshing around in the tank. The moral of the story is the following: *for the system to handle sensor failure properly, the sensor model must include the possibility of failure.*

The simplest kind of failure model for a sensor allows a certain probability that the sensor will return some completely incorrect value, regardless of the true state of the world. For example, if the battery meter fails by returning 0, we might say that

$$P(BMeter_t = 0 \mid Battery_t = 5) = 0.03 ,$$

TRANSIENT FAILURE MODEL

which is presumably much larger than the probability assigned by the simple Gaussian error model. Let's call this the **transient failure model**. How does it help when we are faced with a reading of 0? Provided that the *predicted* probability of an empty battery, according to the readings so far, is much less than 0.03, then the best explanation of the observation $BMeter_{21} = 0$ is that the sensor has temporarily failed. Intuitively, we can think of the belief about the battery level as having a certain amount of "inertia" that helps to overcome temporary blips in the meter reading. The upper curve in Figure 14(b) shows that the transient failure model can handle transient failures without a catastrophic change in beliefs.

So much for temporary blips. What about a persistent sensor failure? Sadly, failures of this kind are all too common. If the sensor returns 20 readings of 5 followed by 20 readings of 0, then the transient sensor failure model described in the preceding paragraph will result in the robot gradually coming to believe that its battery is empty when in fact it may be that the meter has failed. The lower curve in Figure 14(b) shows the belief "trajectory" for this case. By $t = 25$—five readings of 0—the robot is convinced that its battery is empty. Obviously, we would prefer the robot to believe that its battery meter is broken—if indeed this is the more likely event.

PERSISTENT FAILURE MODEL

Unsurprisingly, to handle persistent failure, we need a **persistent failure model** that describes how the sensor behaves under normal conditions and after failure. To do this, we need to augment the state of the system with an additional variable, say, *BMBroken*, that describes the status of the battery meter. The persistence of failure must be modeled by an

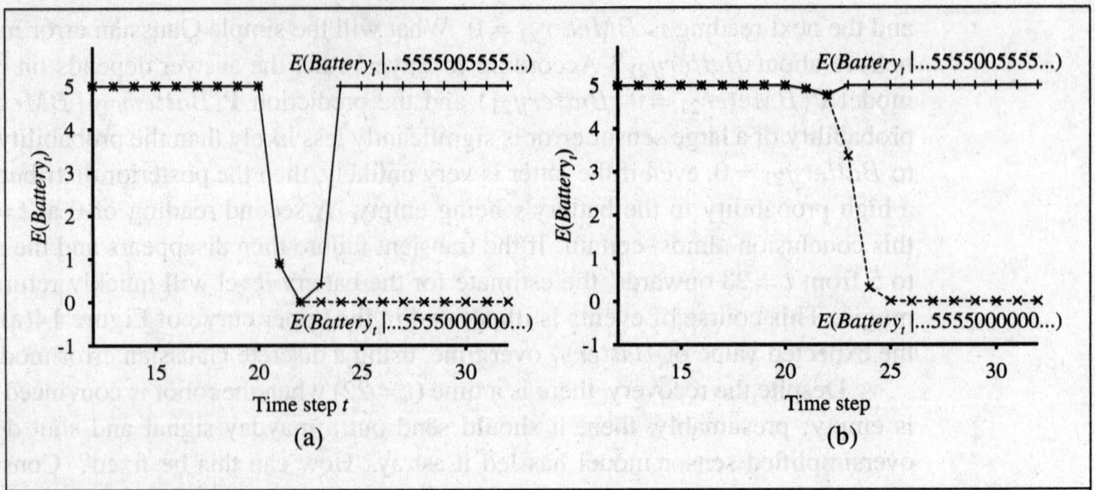

Figure 14 (a) Upper curve: trajectory of the expected value of $Battery_t$ for an observation sequence consisting of all 5s except for 0s at $t = 21$ and $t = 22$, using a simple Gaussian error model. Lower curve: trajectory when the observation remains at 0 from $t = 21$ onwards. (b) The same experiment run with the transient failure model. Notice that the transient failure is handled well, but the persistent failure results in excessive pessimism about the battery charge.

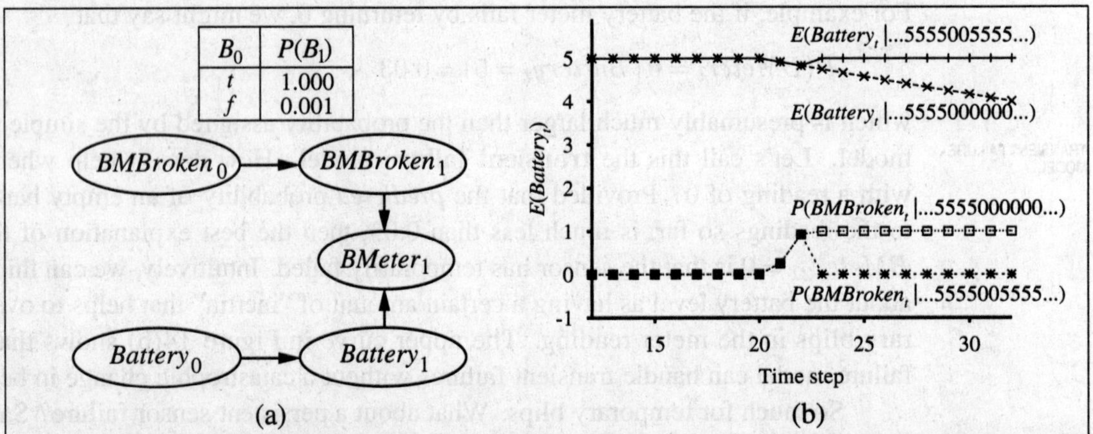

Figure 15 (a) A DBN fragment showing the sensor status variable required for modeling persistent failure of the battery sensor. (b) Upper curves: trajectories of the expected value of $Battery_t$ for the "transient failure" and "permanent failure" observations sequences. Lower curves: probability trajectories for $BMBroken$ given the two observation sequences.

PERSISTENCE ARC arc linking $BMBroken_0$ to $BMBroken_1$. This **persistence arc** has a CPT that gives a small probability of failure in any given time step, say, 0.001, but specifies that the sensor stays broken once it breaks. When the sensor is OK, the sensor model for $BMeter$ is identical to the transient failure model; when the sensor is broken, it says $BMeter$ is always 0, regardless of the actual battery charge.

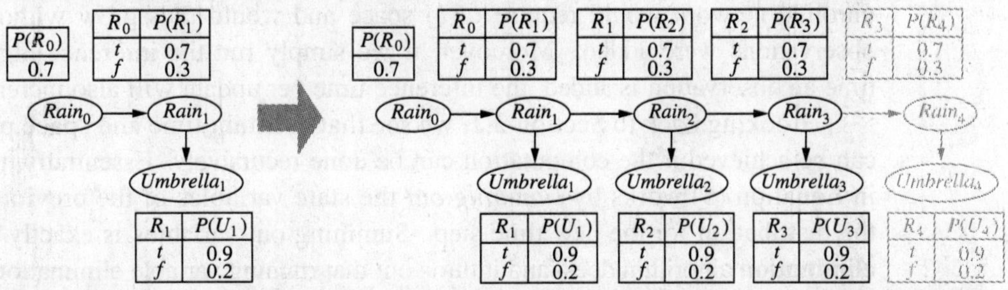

Figure 16 Unrolling a dynamic Bayesian network: slices are replicated to accommodate the observation sequence $Umbrella_{1:3}$. Further slices have no effect on inferences within the observation period.

The persistent failure model for the battery sensor is shown in Figure 15(a). Its performance on the two data sequences (temporary blip and persistent failure) is shown in Figure 15(b). There are several things to notice about these curves. First, in the case of the temporary blip, the probability that the sensor is broken rises significantly after the second 0 reading, but immediately drops back to zero once a 5 is observed. Second, in the case of persistent failure, the probability that the sensor is broken rises quickly to almost 1 and stays there. Finally, once the sensor is known to be broken, the robot can only assume that its battery discharges at the "normal" rate, as shown by the gradually descending level of $E(Battery_t \mid \ldots)$.

So far, we have merely scratched the surface of the problem of representing complex processes. The variety of transition models is huge, encompassing topics as disparate as modeling the human endocrine system and modeling multiple vehicles driving on a freeway. Sensor modeling is also a vast subfield in itself, but even subtle phenomena, such as sensor drift, sudden decalibration, and the effects of exogenous conditions (such as weather) on sensor readings, can be handled by explicit representation within dynamic Bayesian networks.

5.2 Exact inference in DBNs

Having sketched some ideas for representing complex processes as DBNs, we now turn to the question of inference. In a sense, this question has already been answered: dynamic Bayesian networks *are* Bayesian networks, and we already have algorithms for inference in Bayesian networks. Given a sequence of observations, one can construct the full Bayesian network representation of a DBN by replicating slices until the network is large enough to accommodate the observations, as in Figure 16. This technique is called **unrolling**. (Technically, the DBN is equivalent to the semi-infinite network obtained by unrolling forever. Slices added beyond the last observation have no effect on inferences within the observation period and can be omitted.) Once the DBN is unrolled, one can use any of the inference algorithms—variable elimination, clustering methods, and so on.

Unfortunately, a naive application of unrolling would not be particularly efficient. If we want to perform filtering or smoothing with a long sequence of observations $\mathbf{e}_{1:t}$, the unrolled network would require $O(t)$ space and would thus grow without bound as more observations were added. Moreover, if we simply run the inference algorithm anew each time an observation is added, the inference time per update will also increase as $O(t)$.

Looking back to Section 2.1, we see that constant time and space per filtering update can be achieved if the computation can be done recursively. Essentially, the filtering update in Equation (5) works by *summing out* the state variables of the previous time step to get the distribution for the new time step. Summing out variables is exactly what the **variable elimination** algorithm does, and it turns out that running variable elimination with the variables in temporal order exactly mimics the operation of the recursive filtering update in Equation (5). The modified algorithm keeps at most two slices in memory at any one time: starting with slice 0, we add slice 1, then sum out slice 0, then add slice 2, then sum out slice 1, and so on. In this way, we can achieve constant space and time per filtering update. (The same performance can be achieved by suitable modifications to the clustering algorithm.) Exercise 17 asks you to verify this fact for the umbrella network.

So much for the good news; now for the bad news: It turns out that the "constant" for the per-update time and space complexity is, in almost all cases, exponential in the number of state variables. What happens is that, as the variable elimination proceeds, the factors grow to include all the state variables (or, more precisely, all those state variables that have parents in the previous time slice). The maximum factor size is $O(d^{n+k})$ and the total update cost per step is $O(nd^{n+k})$, where d is the domain size of the variables and k is the maximum number of parents of any state variable.

Of course, this is much less than the cost of HMM updating, which is $O(d^{2n})$, but it is still infeasible for large numbers of variables. This grim fact is somewhat hard to accept. What it means is that *even though we can use DBNs to* represent *very complex temporal processes with many sparsely connected variables, we cannot* reason *efficiently and exactly about those processes.* The DBN model itself, which represents the prior joint distribution over all the variables, is factorable into its constituent CPTs, but the posterior joint distribution conditioned on an observation sequence—that is, the forward message—is generally *not* factorable. So far, no one has found a way around this problem, despite the fact that many important areas of science and engineering would benefit enormously from its solution. Thus, we must fall back on approximate methods.

5.3 Approximate inference in DBNs

Two approximation algorithms that you may be familiar with are likelihood weighting and Markov chain Monte Carlo. Of the two, the former is most easily adapted to the DBN context. (An MCMC filtering algorithm is described briefly in the notes at the end of the chapter.) We will see, however, that several improvements are required over the standard likelihood weighting algorithm before a practical method emerges.

Likelihood weighting works by sampling the nonevidence nodes of the network in topological order, weighting each sample by the likelihood it accords to the observed evidence variables. As with the exact algorithms, we could apply likelihood weighting directly to an unrolled DBN, but this would suffer from the same problems of increasing time and space requirements per update as the observation sequence grows. The problem is that the standard algorithm runs each sample in turn, all the way through the network. Instead, we can simply run all N samples together through the DBN, one slice at a time. The modified algorithm fits the general pattern of filtering algorithms, with the set of N samples as the forward message. The first key innovation, then, is to *use the samples themselves as an approximate representation of the current state distribution.* This meets the requirement of a "constant" time per update, although the constant depends on the number of samples required to maintain an accurate approximation. There is also no need to unroll the DBN, because we need to have in memory only the current slice and the next slice.

When using likelihood weighting, the algorithm's accuracy suffers if the evidence variables are "downstream" from the variables being sampled, because in that case the samples are generated without any influence from the evidence. Looking at the typical structure of a DBN—say, the umbrella DBN in Figure 16—we see that indeed the early state variables will be sampled without the benefit of the later evidence. In fact, looking more carefully, we see that *none* of the state variables has *any* evidence variables among its ancestors! Hence, although the weight of each sample will depend on the evidence, the actual set of samples generated will be *completely independent* of the evidence. For example, even if the boss brings in the umbrella every day, the sampling process could still hallucinate endless days of sunshine. What this means in practice is that the fraction of samples that remain reasonably close to the actual series of events (and therefore have nonnegligible weights) drops exponentially with t, the length of the observation sequence. In other words, to maintain a given level of accuracy, we need to increase the number of samples exponentially with t. Given that a filtering algorithm that works in real time can use only a fixed number of samples, what happens in practice is that the error blows up after a very small number of update steps.

Clearly, we need a better solution. The second key innovation is to *focus the set of samples on the high-probability regions of the state space.* This can be done by throwing away samples that have very low weight, according to the observations, while replicating those that have high weight. In that way, the population of samples will stay reasonably close to reality. If we think of samples as a resource for modeling the posterior distribution, then it makes sense to use more samples in regions of the state space where the posterior is higher.

PARTICLE FILTERING

A family of algorithms called **particle filtering** is designed to do just that. Particle filtering works as follows: First, a population of N initial-state samples is created by sampling from the prior distribution $\mathbf{P}(\mathbf{X}_0)$. Then the update cycle is repeated for each time step:

1. Each sample is propagated forward by sampling the next state value $\mathbf{x}_{t+1}$ given the current value $\mathbf{x}_t$ for the sample, based on the transition model $\mathbf{P}(\mathbf{X}_{t+1} \mid \mathbf{x}_t)$.
2. Each sample is weighted by the likelihood it assigns to the new evidence, $P(\mathbf{e}_{t+1} \mid \mathbf{x}_{t+1})$.
3. The population is *resampled* to generate a new population of N samples. Each new sample is selected from the current population; the probability that a particular sample is selected is proportional to its weight. The new samples are unweighted.

The algorithm is shown in detail in Figure 17, and its operation for the umbrella DBN is illustrated in Figure 18.

```
function PARTICLE-FILTERING(e, N, dbn) returns a set of samples for the next time step
  inputs: e, the new incoming evidence
          N, the number of samples to be maintained
          dbn, a DBN with prior P(X0), transition model P(X1|X0), sensor model P(E1|X1)
  persistent: S, a vector of samples of size N, initially generated from P(X0)
  local variables: W, a vector of weights of size N

  for i = 1 to N do
     S[i] ← sample from P(X1 | X0 = S[i])   /* step 1 */
     W[i] ← P(e | X1 = S[i])                 /* step 2 */
  S ← WEIGHTED-SAMPLE-WITH-REPLACEMENT(N, S, W)        /* step 3 */
  return S
```

Figure 17 The particle filtering algorithm implemented as a recursive update operation with state (the set of samples). Each of the sampling operations involves sampling the relevant slice variables in topological order, much as in PRIOR-SAMPLE. The WEIGHTED-SAMPLE-WITH-REPLACEMENT operation can be implemented to run in $O(N)$ expected time. The step numbers refer to the description in the text.

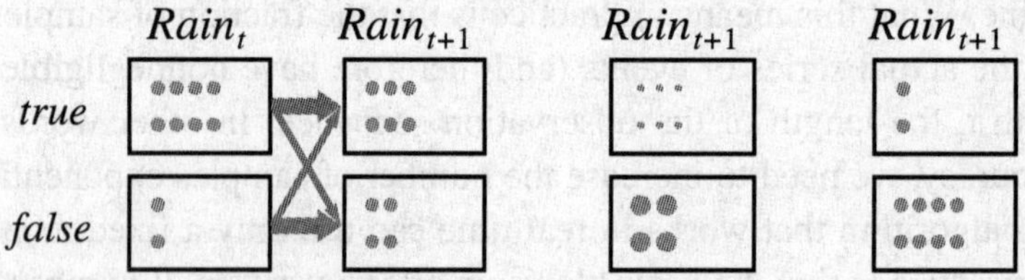

(a) Propagate (b) Weight (c) Resample

Figure 18 The particle filtering update cycle for the umbrella DBN with $N = 10$, showing the sample populations of each state. (a) At time t, 8 samples indicate *rain* and 2 indicate $\neg rain$. Each is propagated forward by sampling the next state through the transition model. At time $t+1$, 6 samples indicate *rain* and 4 indicate $\neg rain$. (b) $\neg umbrella$ is observed at $t+1$. Each sample is weighted by its likelihood for the observation, as indicated by the size of the circles. (c) A new set of 10 samples is generated by weighted random selection from the current set, resulting in 2 samples that indicate *rain* and 8 that indicate $\neg rain$.

We can show that this algorithm is consistent—gives the correct probabilities as N tends to infinity—by considering what happens during one update cycle. We assume that the sample population starts with a correct representation of the forward message $\mathbf{f}_{1:t} = \mathbf{P}(\mathbf{X}_t \mid \mathbf{e}_{1:t})$ at time t. Writing $N(\mathbf{x}_t \mid \mathbf{e}_{1:t})$ for the number of samples occupying state $\mathbf{x}_t$ after observations $\mathbf{e}_{1:t}$ have been processed, we therefore have

$$N(\mathbf{x}_t \mid \mathbf{e}_{1:t})/N = P(\mathbf{x}_t \mid \mathbf{e}_{1:t}) \tag{23}$$

for large N. Now we propagate each sample forward by sampling the state variables at $t+1$, given the values for the sample at t. The number of samples reaching state $\mathbf{x}_{t+1}$ from each

$\mathbf{x}_t$ is the transition probability times the population of $\mathbf{x}_t$; hence, the total number of samples reaching $\mathbf{x}_{t+1}$ is

$$N(\mathbf{x}_{t+1} \mid \mathbf{e}_{1:t}) = \sum_{\mathbf{x}_t} P(\mathbf{x}_{t+1} \mid \mathbf{x}_t) N(\mathbf{x}_t \mid \mathbf{e}_{1:t}) .$$

Now we weight each sample by its likelihood for the evidence at $t+1$. A sample in state $\mathbf{x}_{t+1}$ receives weight $P(\mathbf{e}_{t+1} \mid \mathbf{x}_{t+1})$. The total weight of the samples in $\mathbf{x}_{t+1}$ after seeing $\mathbf{e}_{t+1}$ is therefore

$$W(\mathbf{x}_{t+1} \mid \mathbf{e}_{1:t+1}) = P(\mathbf{e}_{t+1} \mid \mathbf{x}_{t+1}) N(\mathbf{x}_{t+1} \mid \mathbf{e}_{1:t}) .$$

Now for the resampling step. Since each sample is replicated with probability proportional to its weight, the number of samples in state $\mathbf{x}_{t+1}$ after resampling is proportional to the total weight in $\mathbf{x}_{t+1}$ before resampling:

$$\begin{aligned}
N(\mathbf{x}_{t+1} \mid \mathbf{e}_{1:t+1})/N &= \alpha W(\mathbf{x}_{t+1} \mid \mathbf{e}_{1:t+1}) \\
&= \alpha P(\mathbf{e}_{t+1} \mid \mathbf{x}_{t+1}) N(\mathbf{x}_{t+1} \mid \mathbf{e}_{1:t}) \\
&= \alpha P(\mathbf{e}_{t+1} \mid \mathbf{x}_{t+1}) \sum_{\mathbf{x}_t} P(\mathbf{x}_{t+1} \mid \mathbf{x}_t) N(\mathbf{x}_t \mid \mathbf{e}_{1:t}) \\
&= \alpha N P(\mathbf{e}_{t+1} \mid \mathbf{x}_{t+1}) \sum_{\mathbf{x}_t} P(\mathbf{x}_{t+1} \mid \mathbf{x}_t) P(\mathbf{x}_t \mid \mathbf{e}_{1:t}) \quad \text{(by 23)} \\
&= \alpha' P(\mathbf{e}_{t+1} \mid \mathbf{x}_{t+1}) \sum_{\mathbf{x}_t} P(\mathbf{x}_{t+1} \mid \mathbf{x}_t) P(\mathbf{x}_t \mid \mathbf{e}_{1:t}) \\
&= P(\mathbf{x}_{t+1} \mid \mathbf{e}_{1:t+1}) \quad \text{(by 5)}.
\end{aligned}$$

Therefore the sample population after one update cycle correctly represents the forward message at time $t+1$.

Particle filtering is *consistent*, therefore, but is it *efficient*? In practice, it seems that the answer is yes: particle filtering seems to maintain a good approximation to the true posterior using a constant number of samples. Under certain assumptions—in particular, that the probabilities in the transition and sensor models are strictly greater than 0 and less than 1—it is possible to prove that the approximation maintains bounded error with high probability. On the practical side, the range of applications has grown to include many fields of science and engineering; some references are given at the end of the chapter.

6 Keeping Track of Many Objects

The preceding sections have considered—without mentioning it—state estimation problems involving a single object. In this section, we see what happens when two or more objects generate the observations. What makes this case different from plain old state estimation is that there is now the possibility of *uncertainty* about which object generated which observation. This is the **identity uncertainty** problem now viewed in a temporal context. In the control theory literature, this is the **data association** problem—that is, the problem of associating observation data with the objects that generated them.

DATA ASSOCIATION

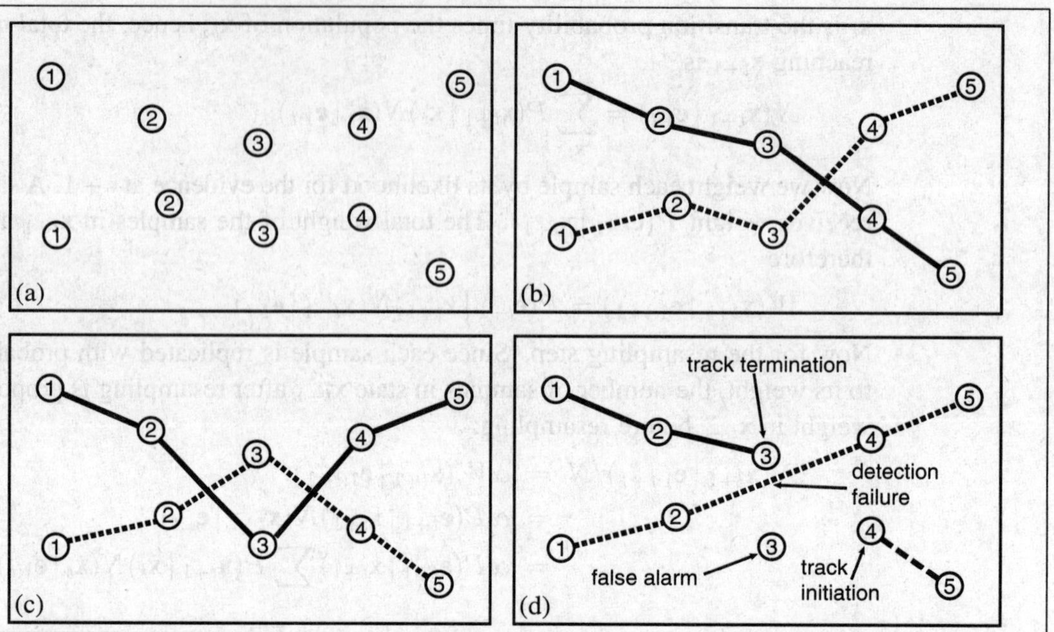

Figure 19 (a) Observations made of object locations in 2D space over five time steps. Each observation is labeled with the time step but does not identify the object that produced it. (b–c) Possible hypotheses about the underlying object tracks. (d) A hypothesis for the case in which false alarms, detection failures, and track initiation/termination are possible.

The data association problem was studied originally in the context of radar tracking, where reflected pulses are detected at fixed time intervals by a rotating radar antenna. At each time step, multiple blips may appear on the screen, but there is no direct observation of which blips at time t belong to which blips at time $t-1$. Figure 19(a) shows a simple example with two blips per time step for five steps. Let the two blip locations at time t be e_t^1 and e_t^2. (The labeling of blips within a time step as "1" and "2" is completely arbitrary and carries no information.) Let us assume, for the time being, that exactly two aircraft, A and B, generated the blips; their true positions are X_t^A and X_t^B. Just to keep things simple, we'll also assume that the each aircraft moves independently according to a known transition model—e.g., a linear Gaussian model as used in the Kalman filter (Section 4).

Suppose we try to write down the overall probability model for this scenario, just as we did for general temporal processes in Equation (3). As usual, the joint distribution factors into contributions for each time step as follows:

$$P(x_{0:t}^A, x_{0:t}^B, e_{1:t}^1, e_{1:t}^2) =$$
$$P(x_0^A)P(x_0^B)\prod_{i=1}^{t} P(x_i^A \mid x_{i-1}^A)P(x_i^B \mid x_{i-1}^B)\, P(e_i^1, e_i^2 \mid x_i^A, x_i^B)\,. \qquad (24)$$

We would like to factor the observation term $P(e_i^1, e_i^2 \mid x_i^A, x_i^B)$ into a product of two terms, one for each object, but this would require knowing which observation was generated by which object. Instead, we have to sum over all possible ways of associating the observations with the objects. Some of those ways are shown in Figure 19(b–c); in general, for n objects and T time steps, there are $(n!)^T$ ways of doing it—an awfully large number.

Mathematically speaking, the "way of associating the observations with the objects" is a collection of unobserved random variable that identify the source of each observation. We'll write ω_t to denote the one-to-one mapping from objects to observations at time t, with $\omega_t(A)$ and $\omega_t(B)$ denoting the specific observations (1 or 2) that ω_t assigns to A and B. (For n objects, ω_t will have $n!$ possible values; here, $n! = 2$.) Because the labels "1" ad "2" on the observations are assigned arbitrarily, the prior on ω_t is uniform and ω_t is independent of the states of the objects, x_t^A and x_t^B). So we can condition the observation term $P(e_i^1, e_i^2 \mid x_i^A, x_i^B)$ on ω_t and then simplify:

$$
\begin{aligned}
P(e_i^1, e_i^2 \mid x_i^A, x_i^B) &= \sum_{\omega_i} P(e_i^1, e_i^2 \mid x_i^A, x_i^B, \omega_i) P(\omega_i \mid x_i^A, x_i^B) \\
&= \sum_{\omega_i} P(e_i^{\omega_i(A)} \mid x_i^A) P(e_i^{\omega_i(B)} \mid x_i^B) P(\omega_i \mid x_i^A, x_i^B) \\
&= \frac{1}{2} \sum_{\omega_i} P(e_i^{\omega_i(A)} \mid x_i^A) P(e_i^{\omega_i(B)} \mid x_i^B) .
\end{aligned}
$$

Plugging this into Equation (24), we get an expression that is only in terms of transition and sensor models for individual objects and observations.

As for all probability models, inference means summing out the variables other than the query and the evidence. For filtering in HMMs and DBNs, we were able to sum out the state variables from 1 to $t-1$ by a simple dynamic programming trick; for Kalman filters, we took advantage of special properties of Gaussians. For data association, we are less fortunate. There is no (known) efficient exact algorithm, for the same reason that there is none for the switching Kalman filter: the filtering distribution $P(x_t^A \mid e_{1:t}^1, e_{1:t}^2)$ for object A ends up as a mixture of exponentially many distributions, one for each way of picking a sequence of observations to assign to A.

As a result of the complexity of exact inference, many different approximate methods have been used. The simplest approach is to choose a single "best" assignment at each time step, given the predicted positions of the objects at the current time step. This assignment associates observations with objects and enables the track of each object to be updated and a prediction made for the next time step. For choosing the "best" assignment, it is common to use the so-called **nearest-neighbor filter**, which repeatedly chooses the closest pairing of predicted position and observation and adds that pairing to the assignment. The nearest-neighbor filter works well when the objects are well separated in state space and the prediction uncertainty and observation error are small—in other words, when there is no possibility of confusion. When there is more uncertainty as to the correct assignment, a better approach is to choose the assignment that maximizes the joint probability of the current observations given the predicted positions. This can be done very efficiently using the **Hungarian algorithm** (Kuhn, 1955), even though there are $n!$ assignments to choose from.

NEAREST-NEIGHBOR FILTER

HUNGARIAN ALGORITHM

Any method that commits to a single best assignment at each time step fails miserably under more difficult conditions. In particular, if the algorithm commits to an incorrect assignment, the prediction at the next time step may be significantly wrong, leading to more

(a) (b)

Figure 20 Images from (a) upstream and (b) downstream surveillance cameras roughly two miles apart on Highway 99 in Sacramento, California. The boxed vehicle has been identified at both cameras.

incorrect assignments, and so on. Two modern approaches turn out to be much more effective. A **particle filtering** algorithm for data association works by maintaining a large collection of possible current assignments. An **MCMC** algorithm explores the space of assignment histories—for example, Figure 19(b–c) might be states in the MCMC state space—and can change its mind about previous assignment decisions. Current MCMC data association methods can handle many hundreds of objects in real time while giving a good approximation to the true posterior distributions.

The scenario described so far involved n known objects generating n observations at each time step. Real application of data association are typically much more complicated. Often, the reported observations include **false alarms** (also known as **clutter**), which are not caused by real objects. **Detection failures** can occur, meaning that no observation is reported for a real object. Finally, new objects arrive and old ones disappear. These phenomena, which create even more possible worlds to worry about, are illustrated in Figure 19(d).

FALSE ALARM

CLUTTER

DETECTION FAILURE

Figure 20 shows two images from widely separated cameras on a California freeway. In this application, we are interested in two goals: estimating the time it takes, under current traffic conditions, to go from one place to another in the freeway system; and measuring *demand*, i.e., how many vehicles travel between any two points in the system at particular times of the day and on particular days of the week. Both goals require solving the data association problem over a wide area with many cameras and tens of thousands of vehicles per hour. With visual surveillance, false alarms are caused by moving shadows, articulated vehicles, reflections in puddles, etc.; detection failures are caused by occlusion, fog, darkness, and lack of visual contrast; and vehicles are constantly entering and leaving the freeway system. Furthermore, the appearance of any given vehicle can change dramatically between cameras depending on lighting conditions and vehicle pose in the image, and the transition model changes as traffic jams come and go. Despite these problems, modern data association algorithms have been successful in estimating traffic parameters in real-world settings.

Data association is an essential foundation for keeping track of a complex world, because without it there is no way to combine multiple observations of any given object. When objects in the world interact with each other in complex activities, understanding the world requires combining data association with relational and open-universe probability models. This is currently an active area of research.

7 SUMMARY

This chapter has addressed the general problem of representing and reasoning about probabilistic temporal processes. The main points are as follows:

- The changing state of the world is handled by using a set of random variables to represent the state at each point in time.
- Representations can be designed to satisfy the **Markov property**, so that the future is independent of the past given the present. Combined with the assumption that the process is **stationary**—that is, the dynamics do not change over time—this greatly simplifies the representation.
- A temporal probability model can be thought of as containing a **transition model** describing the state evolution and a **sensor model** describing the observation process.
- The principal inference tasks in temporal models are **filtering**, **prediction**, **smoothing**, and computing the **most likely explanation**. Each of these can be achieved using simple, recursive algorithms whose run time is linear in the length of the sequence.
- Three families of temporal models were studied in more depth: **hidden Markov models**, **Kalman filters**, and **dynamic Bayesian networks** (which include the other two as special cases).
- Unless special assumptions are made, as in Kalman filters, exact inference with many state variables is intractable. In practice, the **particle filtering** algorithm seems to be an effective approximation algorithm.
- When trying to keep track of many objects, uncertainty arises as to which observations belong to which objects—the **data association** problem. The number of association hypotheses is typically intractably large, but MCMC and particle filtering algorithms for data association work well in practice.

BIBLIOGRAPHICAL AND HISTORICAL NOTES

Many of the basic ideas for estimating the state of dynamical systems came from the mathematician C. F. Gauss (1809), who formulated a deterministic least-squares algorithm for the problem of estimating orbits from astronomical observations. A. A. Markov (1913) developed what was later called the **Markov assumption** in his analysis of stochastic processes;

he estimated a first-order Markov chain on letters from the text of *Eugene Onegin*. The general theory of Markov chains and their mixing times is covered by Levin *et al.* (2008).

Significant classified work on filtering was done during World War II by Wiener (1942) for continuous-time processes and by Kolmogorov (1941) for discrete-time processes. Although this work led to important technological developments over the next 20 years, its use of a frequency-domain representation made many calculations quite cumbersome. Direct state-space modeling of the stochastic process turned out to be simpler, as shown by Peter Swerling (1959) and Rudolf Kalman (1960). The latter paper described what is now known as the Kalman filter for forward inference in linear systems with Gaussian noise; Kalman's results had, however, been obtained previously by the Danish statistician Thorvold Thiele (1880) and by the Russian mathematician Ruslan Stratonovich (1959), whom Kalman met in Moscow in 1960. After a visit to NASA Ames Research Center in 1960, Kalman saw the applicability of the method to the tracking of rocket trajectories, and the filter was later implemented for the Apollo missions. Important results on smoothing were derived by Rauch *et al.* (1965), and the impressively named Rauch–Tung–Striebel smoother is still a standard technique today. Many early results are gathered in Gelb (1974). Bar-Shalom and Fortmann (1988) give a more modern treatment with a Bayesian flavor, as well as many references to the vast literature on the subject. Chatfield (1989) and Box *et al.* (1994) cover the control theory approach to time series analysis.

The hidden Markov model and associated algorithms for inference and learning, including the forward–backward algorithm, were developed by Baum and Petrie (1966). The Viterbi algorithm first appeared in (Viterbi, 1967). Similar ideas also appeared independently in the Kalman filtering community (Rauch *et al.*, 1965). The forward–backward algorithm was one of the main precursors of the general formulation of the EM algorithm (Dempster *et al.*, 1977). Constant-space smoothing appears in Binder *et al.* (1997b), as does the divide-and-conquer algorithm developed in Exercise 3. Constant-time fixed-lag smoothing for HMMs first appeared in Russell and Norvig (2003). HMMs have found many applications in language processing (Charniak, 1993), speech recognition (Rabiner and Juang, 1993), machine translation (Och and Ney, 2003), computational biology (Krogh *et al.*, 1994; Baldi *et al.*, 1994), financial economics Bhar and Hamori (2004) and other fields. There have been several extensions to the basic HMM model, for example the Hierarchical HMM (Fine *et al.*, 1998) and Layered HMM (Oliver *et al.*, 2004) introduce structure back into the model, replacing the single state variable of HMMs.

Dynamic Bayesian networks (DBNs) can be viewed as a sparse encoding of a Markov process and were first used in AI by Dean and Kanazawa (1989b), Nicholson and Brady (1992), and Kjaerulff (1992). The last work extends the HUGIN Bayes net system to accommodate dynamic Bayesian networks. The book by Dean and Wellman (1991) helped popularize DBNs and the probabilistic approach to planning and control within AI. Murphy (2002) provides a thorough analysis of DBNs.

Dynamic Bayesian networks have become popular for modeling a variety of complex motion processes in computer vision (Huang *et al.*, 1994; Intille and Bobick, 1999). Like HMMs, they have found applications in speech recognition (Zweig and Russell, 1998; Richardson *et al.*, 2000; Stephenson *et al.*, 2000; Nefian *et al.*, 2002; Livescu *et al.*, 2003), genomics (Murphy and Mian, 1999; Perrin *et al.*, 2003; Husmeier, 2003) and robot localization (Theocharous *et al.*, 2004). The link between HMMs and DBNs, and between the forward–backward algorithm and Bayesian network propagation, was made explicitly by Smyth *et al.* (1997). A further unification with Kalman filters (and other statistical models) appears in Roweis and Ghahramani (1999). Procedures exist for learning the parameters (Binder *et al.*, 1997a; Ghahramani, 1998) and structures (Friedman *et al.*, 1998) of DBNs.

The particle filtering algorithm described in Section 5 has a particularly interesting history. The first sampling algorithms for particle filtering (also called sequential Monte Carlo methods) were developed in the control theory community by Handschin and Mayne (1969), and the resampling idea that is the core of particle filtering appeared in a Russian control journal (Zaritskii *et al.*, 1975). It was later reinvented in statistics as **sequential importance-sampling resampling**, or **SIR** (Rubin, 1988; Liu and Chen, 1998), in control theory as particle filtering (Gordon *et al.*, 1993; Gordon, 1994), in AI as **survival of the fittest** (Kanazawa *et al.*, 1995), and in computer vision as **condensation** (Isard and Blake, 1996). The paper by Kanazawa *et al.* (1995) includes an improvement called **evidence reversal** whereby the state at time $t + 1$ is sampled conditional on both the state at time *t and the evidence at time* $t + 1$. This allows the evidence to influence sample generation directly and was proved by Doucet (1997) and Liu and Chen (1998) to reduce the approximation error. Particle filtering has been applied in many areas, including tracking complex motion patterns in video (Isard and Blake, 1996), predicting the stock market (de Freitas *et al.*, 2000), and diagnosing faults on planetary rovers (Verma *et al.*, 2004). A variant called the **Rao-Blackwellized particle filter** or RBPF (Doucet *et al.*, 2000; Murphy and Russell, 2001) applies particle filtering to a subset of state variables and, for each particle, performs exact inference on the remaining variables conditioned on the value sequence in the particle. In some cases RBPF works well with thousands of state variables. The book by Doucet *et al.* (2001) collects many important papers on **sequential Monte Carlo** (SMC) algorithms, of which particle filtering is the most important instance. Pierre Del Moral and colleagues have performed extensive theoretical analyses of SMC algorithms (Del Moral, 2004; Del Moral *et al.*, 2006).

EVIDENCE REVERSAL

RAO-BLACKWELLIZED PARTICLE FILTER

SEQUENTIAL MONTE CARLO

MCMC methods can be applied to the filtering problem; for example, Gibbs sampling can be applied directly to an unrolled DBN. To avoid the problem of increasing update times as the unrolled network grows, the **decayed MCMC** filter (Marthi *et al.*, 2002) prefers to sample more recent state variables, with a probability that decays as $1/k^2$ for a variable k steps into the past. Decayed MCMC is a provably nondivergent filter. Nondivergence theorems can also be obtained for certain types of **assumed-density filter**. An assumed-density filter assumes that the posterior distribution over states at time t belongs to a particular finitely parameterized family; if the projection and update steps take it outside this family, the distribution is projected back to give the best approximation within the family. For DBNs, the Boyen–Koller algorithm (Boyen *et al.*, 1999) and the **factored frontier** algorithm (Murphy and Weiss, 2001) assume that the posterior distribution can be approximated well by a product of small factors. Variational techniques have also been developed for temporal models. Ghahramani and Jordan (1997) discuss an approximation algorithm for the **factorial HMM**, a DBN in which two or more independently evolving Markov chains are linked by a shared

DECAYED MCMC

ASSUMED-DENSITY FILTER

FACTORED FRONTIER

FACTORIAL HMM

observation stream. Jordan *et al.* (1998) cover a number of other applications.

Data association for multitarget tracking was first described in a probabilistic setting by Sittler (1964). The first practical algorithm for large-scale problems was the "multiple hypothesis tracker" or MHT algorithm (Reid, 1979). Many important papers are collected by Bar-Shalom and Fortmann (1988) and Bar-Shalom (1992). The development of an MCMC algorithm for data association is due to Pasula *et al.* (1999), who applied it to traffic surveillance problems. Oh *et al.* (2009) provide a formal analysis and extensive experimental comparisons to other methods. Schulz *et al.* (2003) describe a data association method based on particle filtering. Ingemar Cox analyzed the complexity of data association (Cox, 1993; Cox and Hingorani, 1994) and brought the topic to the attention of the vision community. He also noted the applicability of the polynomial-time Hungarian algorithm to the problem of finding most-likely assignments, which had long been considered an intractable problem in the tracking community. The algorithm itself was published by Kuhn (1955), based on translations of papers published in 1931 by two Hungarian mathematicians, Dénes König and Jenö Egerváry. The basic theorem had been derived previously, however, in an unpublished Latin manuscript by the famous Prussian mathematician Carl Gustav Jacobi (1804–1851).

EXERCISES

1 Show that any second-order Markov process can be rewritten as a first-order Markov process with an augmented set of state variables. Can this always be done *parsimoniously*, i.e., without increasing the number of parameters needed to specify the transition model?

2 In this exercise, we examine what happens to the probabilities in the umbrella world in the limit of long time sequences.

a. Suppose we observe an unending sequence of days on which the umbrella appears. Show that, as the days go by, the probability of rain on the current day increases monotonically toward a fixed point. Calculate this fixed point.

b. Now consider *forecasting* further and further into the future, given just the first two umbrella observations. First, compute the probability $P(r_{2+k}|u_1, u_2)$ for $k=1\ldots20$ and plot the results. You should see that the probability converges towards a fixed point. Prove that the exact value of this fixed point is 0.5.

3 This exercise develops a space-efficient variant of the forward–backward algorithm described in Figure 4. We wish to compute $\mathbf{P}(\mathbf{X}_k|\mathbf{e}_{1:t})$ for $k=1,\ldots,t$. This will be done with a divide-and-conquer approach.

a. Suppose, for simplicity, that t is odd, and let the halfway point be $h=(t+1)/2$. Show that $\mathbf{P}(\mathbf{X}_k|\mathbf{e}_{1:t})$ can be computed for $k=1,\ldots,h$ given just the initial forward message $\mathbf{f}_{1:0}$, the backward message $\mathbf{b}_{h+1:t}$, and the evidence $\mathbf{e}_{1:h}$.

b. Show a similar result for the second half of the sequence.

c. Given the results of (a) and (b), a recursive divide-and-conquer algorithm can be constructed by first running forward along the sequence and then backward from the end, storing just the required messages at the middle and the ends. Then the algorithm is called on each half. Write out the algorithm in detail.

d. Compute the time and space complexity of the algorithm as a function of t, the length of the sequence. How does this change if we divide the input into more than two pieces?

4 In section 2.3, we outlined a flawed procedure for finding the most likely state sequence, given an observation sequence. The procedure involves finding the most likely state at each time step, using smoothing, and returning the sequence composed of these states. Show that, for some temporal probability models and observation sequences, this procedure returns an impossible state sequence (i.e., the posterior probability of the sequence is zero).

5 Equation (12) describes the filtering process for the matrix formulation of HMMs. Give a similar equation for the calculation of likelihoods, which was described generically in Equation (7).

6 Consider the vacuum world of Figure 7 (noisy sensing). Suppose that the robot receives an observation sequence such that, with perfect sensing, there is exactly one possible location it could be in. Is this location necessarily the most probable location under noisy sensing for sufficiently small noise probability ϵ? Prove your claim or find a counterexample.

7 In Section 3.2, the prior distribution over locations is uniform and the transition model assumes an equal probability of moving to any neighboring square. What if those assumptions are wrong? Suppose that the initial location is actually chosen uniformly from the northwest quadrant of the room and the *Move* action actually tends to move southeast. Keeping the HMM model fixed, explore the effect on localization and path accuracy as the southeasterly tendency increases, for different values of ϵ.

8 Consider a version of the vacuum robot that has the policy of going straight for as long as it can; only when it encounters an obstacle does it change to a new (randomly selected) heading. To model this robot, each state in the model consists of a *(location, heading)* pair. Implement this model and see how well the Viterbi algorithm can track a robot with this model. The robot's policy is more constrained than the random-walk robot; does that mean that predictions of the most likely path are more accurate?

9 This exercise is concerned with filtering in an environment with no landmarks. Consider a vacuum robot in an empty room, represented by an $n \times m$ rectangular grid. The robot's location is hidden; the only evidence available to the observer is a noisy location sensor that gives an approximation to the robot's location. If the robot is at location (x, y) then with probability .1 the sensor gives the correct location, with probability .05 each it reports one of the 8 locations immediately surrounding (x, y), with probability .025 each it reports one of the 16 locations that surround those 8, and with the remaining probability of .1 it reports "no reading." The robot's policy is to pick a direction and follow it with probability .8 on each step; the robot switches to a randomly selected new heading with probability .2 (or with

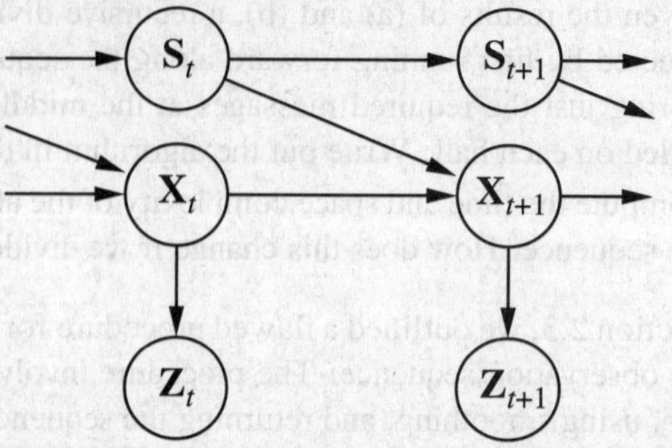

Figure 21 A Bayesian network representation of a switching Kalman filter. The switching variable S_t is a discrete state variable whose value determines the transition model for the continuous state variables $\mathbf{X}_t$. For any discrete state i, the transition model $\mathbf{P}(\mathbf{X}_{t+1}|\mathbf{X}_t, S_t = i)$ is a linear Gaussian model, just as in a regular Kalman filter. The transition model for the discrete state, $\mathbf{P}(S_{t+1}|S_t)$, can be thought of as a matrix, as in a hidden Markov model.

probability 1 if it encounters a wall). Implement this as an HMM and do filtering to track the robot. How accurately can we track the robot's path?

10 Often, we wish to monitor a continuous-state system whose behavior switches unpredictably among a set of k distinct "modes." For example, an aircraft trying to evade a missile can execute a series of distinct maneuvers that the missile may attempt to track. A Bayesian network representation of such a **switching Kalman filter** model is shown in Figure 21.

a. Suppose that the discrete state S_t has k possible values and that the prior continuous state estimate $\mathbf{P}(\mathbf{X}_0)$ is a multivariate Gaussian distribution. Show that the prediction $\mathbf{P}(\mathbf{X}_1)$ is a **mixture of Gaussians**—that is, a weighted sum of Gaussians such that the weights sum to 1.

b. Show that if the current continuous state estimate $\mathbf{P}(\mathbf{X}_t|\mathbf{e}_{1:t})$ is a mixture of m Gaussians, then in the general case the updated state estimate $\mathbf{P}(\mathbf{X}_{t+1}|\mathbf{e}_{1:t+1})$ will be a mixture of km Gaussians.

c. What aspect of the temporal process do the weights in the Gaussian mixture represent?

The results in (a) and (b) show that the representation of the posterior grows without limit even for switching Kalman filters, which are among the simplest hybrid dynamic models.

11 Complete the missing step in the derivation of Equation (19), the first update step for the one-dimensional Kalman filter.

12 Let us examine the behavior of the variance update in Equation (20).

a. Plot the value of σ_t^2 as a function of t, given various values for σ_x^2 and σ_z^2.

b. Show that the update has a fixed point σ^2 such that $\sigma_t^2 \to \sigma^2$ as $t \to \infty$, and calculate the value of σ^2.

c. Give a qualitative explanation for what happens as $\sigma_x^2 \to 0$ and as $\sigma_z^2 \to 0$.

13 A professor wants to know if students are getting enough sleep. Each day, the professor observes whether the students sleep in class, and whether they have red eyes. The professor has the following domain theory:

- The prior probability of getting enough sleep, with no observations, is 0.7.
- The probability of getting enough sleep on night t is 0.8 given that the student got enough sleep the previous night, and 0.3 if not.
- The probability of having red eyes is 0.2 if the student got enough sleep, and 0.7 if not.
- The probability of sleeping in class is 0.1 if the student got enough sleep, and 0.3 if not.

Formulate this information as a dynamic Bayesian network that the professor could use to filter or predict from a sequence of observations. Then reformulate it as a hidden Markov model that has only a single observation variable. Give the complete probability tables for the model.

14 For the DBN specified in Exercise 13 and for the evidence values

$\mathbf{e}_1 =$ not red eyes, not sleeping in class
$\mathbf{e}_2 =$ red eyes, not sleeping in class
$\mathbf{e}_3 =$ red eyes, sleeping in class

perform the following computations:

a. State estimation: Compute $P(EnoughSleep_t|\mathbf{e}_{1:t})$ for each of $t = 1, 2, 3$.
b. Smoothing: Compute $P(EnoughSleep_t|\mathbf{e}_{1:3})$ for each of $t = 1, 2, 3$.
c. Compare the filtered and smoothed probabilities for $t = 1$ and $t = 2$.

15 Suppose that a particular student shows up with red eyes and sleeps in class every day. Given the model described in Exercise 13, explain why the probability that the student had enough sleep the previous night converges to a fixed point rather than continuing to go down as we gather more days of evidence. What is the fixed point? Answer this both numerically (by computation) and analytically.

16 This exercise analyzes in more detail the persistent-failure model for the battery sensor in Figure 15(a).

a. Figure 15(b) stops at $t = 32$. Describe qualitatively what should happen as $t \to \infty$ if the sensor continues to read 0.
b. Suppose that the external temperature affects the battery sensor in such a way that transient failures become more likely as temperature increases. Show how to augment the DBN structure in Figure 15(a), and explain any required changes to the CPTs.
c. Given the new network structure, can battery readings be used by the robot to infer the current temperature?

17 Consider applying the variable elimination algorithm to the umbrella DBN unrolled for three slices, where the query is $\mathbf{P}(R_3|u_1, u_2, u_3)$. Show that the space complexity of the algorithm—the size of the largest factor—is the same, regardless of whether the rain variables are eliminated in forward or backward order.

MAKING SIMPLE DECISIONS

MAKING SIMPLE DECISIONS

In which we see how an agent should make decisions so that it gets what it wants—on average, at least.

In this chapter, we fill in the details of how utility theory combines with probability theory to yield a decision-theoretic agent—an agent that can make rational decisions based on what it believes and what it wants. Such an agent can make decisions in contexts in which uncertainty and conflicting goals leave a logical agent with no way to decide: a goal-based agent has a binary distinction between good (goal) and bad (non-goal) states, while a decision-theoretic agent has a continuous measure of outcome quality.

Section 1 introduces the basic principle of decision theory: the maximization of expected utility. Section 2 shows that the behavior of any rational agent can be captured by supposing a utility function that is being maximized. Section 3 discusses the nature of utility functions in more detail, and in particular their relation to individual quantities such as money. Section 4 shows how to handle utility functions that depend on several quantities. In Section 5, we describe the implementation of decision-making systems. In particular, we introduce a formalism called a **decision network** (also known as an **influence diagram**) that extends Bayesian networks by incorporating actions and utilities. The remainder of the chapter discusses issues that arise in applications of decision theory to expert systems.

1 COMBINING BELIEFS AND DESIRES UNDER UNCERTAINTY

Decision theory, in its simplest form, deals with choosing among actions based on the desirability of their *immediate* outcomes; that is, the environment is assumed to be episodic. The notation RESULT (s_0, a) can be used for the state that is the deterministic outcome of taking action a in state s_0. In this chapter we deal with nondeterministic partially observable environments. Since the agent may not know the current state, we omit it and define RESULT (a) as a *random variable* whose values are the possible outcome states. The probability of outcome s', given evidence observations $\mathbf{e}$, is written

$$P(\text{RESULT}(a) = s' \mid a, \mathbf{e}) ,$$

where the a on the right-hand side of the conditioning bar stands for the event that action a is executed.[1]

UTILITY FUNCTION

EXPECTED UTILITY

The agent's preferences are captured by a **utility function**, $U(s)$, which assigns a single number to express the desirability of a state. The **expected utility** of an action given the evidence, $EU(a|\mathbf{e})$, is just the average utility value of the outcomes, weighted by the probability that the outcome occurs:

$$EU(a|\mathbf{e}) = \sum_{s'} P(\textrm{RESULT}(a) = s' \mid a, \mathbf{e})\, U(s')\,. \tag{1}$$

MAXIMUM EXPECTED UTILITY

The principle of **maximum expected utility** (MEU) says that a rational agent should choose the action that maximizes the agent's expected utility:

$$action = \operatorname*{argmax}_{a} EU(a|\mathbf{e})$$

In a sense, the MEU principle could be seen as defining all of AI. All an intelligent agent has to do is calculate the various quantities, maximize utility over its actions, and away it goes. But this does not mean that the AI problem is *solved* by the definition!

The MEU principle *formalizes* the general notion that the agent should "do the right thing," but goes only a small distance toward a full *operationalization* of that advice. Estimating the state of the world requires perception, learning, knowledge representation, and inference. Computing $P(\textrm{RESULT}(a) \mid a, \mathbf{e})$ requires a complete causal model of the world and NP-hard inference in (very large) Bayesian networks. Computing the outcome utilities $U(s')$ often requires searching or planning, because an agent may not know how good a state is until it knows where it can get to from that state. So, decision theory is not a panacea that solves the AI problem—but it does provide a useful framework.

The MEU principle has a clear relation to the idea of performance measures. The basic idea is simple. Consider the environments that could lead to an agent having a given percept history, and consider the different agents that we could design. *If an agent acts so as to maximize a utility function that correctly reflects the performance measure, then the agent will achieve the highest possible performance score (averaged over all the possible environments).* This is the central justification for the MEU principle itself. While the claim may seem tautological, it does in fact embody a very important transition from a global, external criterion of rationality—the performance measure over environment histories—to a local, internal criterion involving the maximization of a utility function applied to the next state.

2 THE BASIS OF UTILITY THEORY

Intuitively, the principle of Maximum Expected Utility (MEU) seems like a reasonable way to make decisions, but it is by no means obvious that it is the *only* rational way. After all, why should maximizing the *average* utility be so special? What's wrong with an agent that

[1] Classical decision theory leaves the current state S_0 implicit, but we could make it explicit by writing $P(\textrm{RESULT}(a) = s' \mid a, \mathbf{e}) = \sum_s P(\textrm{RESULT}(s, a) = s' \mid a) P(S_0 = s \mid \mathbf{e})$.

maximizes the weighted sum of the cubes of the possible utilities, or tries to minimize the worst possible loss? Could an agent act rationally just by expressing preferences between states, without giving them numeric values? Finally, why should a utility function with the required properties exist at all? We shall see.

2.1 Constraints on rational preferences

These questions can be answered by writing down some constraints on the preferences that a rational agent should have and then showing that the MEU principle can be derived from the constraints. We use the following notation to describe an agent's preferences:

$A \succ B$ the agent prefers A over B.
$A \sim B$ the agent is indifferent between A and B.
$A \succsim B$ the agent prefers A over B or is indifferent between them.

Now the obvious question is, what sorts of things are A and B? They could be states of the world, but more often than not there is uncertainty about what is really being offered. For example, an airline passenger who is offered "the pasta dish or the chicken" does not know what lurks beneath the tinfoil cover.[2] The pasta could be delicious or congealed, the chicken juicy or overcooked beyond recognition. We can think of the set of outcomes for each action as a **lottery**—think of each action as a ticket. A lottery L with possible outcomes $S_1, \ldots, S_n$ that occur with probabilities $p_1, \ldots, p_n$ is written

LOTTERY

$$L = [p_1, S_1;\ p_2, S_2;\ \ldots\ p_n, S_n]$$

In general, each outcome S_i of a lottery can be either an atomic state or another lottery. The primary issue for utility theory is to understand how preferences between complex lotteries are related to preferences between the underlying states in those lotteries. To address this issue we list six constraints that we require any reasonable preference relation to obey:

ORDERABILITY

- **Orderability**: Given any two lotteries, a rational agent must either prefer one to the other or else rate the two as equally preferable. That is, the agent cannot avoid deciding. Refusing to bet is like refusing to allow time to pass.

$$\text{Exactly one of } (A \succ B),\ (B \succ A),\ \text{ or } (A \sim B) \text{ holds.}$$

TRANSITIVITY

- **Transitivity**: Given any three lotteries, if an agent prefers A to B and prefers B to C, then the agent must prefer A to C.

$$(A \succ B) \land (B \succ C) \Rightarrow (A \succ C)\,.$$

CONTINUITY

- **Continuity**: If some lottery B is between A and C in preference, then there is some probability p for which the rational agent will be indifferent between getting B for sure and the lottery that yields A with probability p and C with probability $1 - p$.

$$A \succ B \succ C \Rightarrow \exists p\ [p, A;\ 1-p, C] \sim B\,.$$

SUBSTITUTABILITY

- **Substitutability**: If an agent is indifferent between two lotteries A and B, then the agent is indifferent between two more complex lotteries that are the same except that B

2 We apologize to readers whose local airlines no longer offer food on long flights.

is substituted for A in one of them. This holds regardless of the probabilities and the other outcome(s) in the lotteries.

$$A \sim B \Rightarrow [p, A;\ 1-p, C] \sim [p, B; 1-p, C]\ .$$

This also holds if we substitute $\succ$ for $\sim$ in this axiom.

MONOTONICITY

- **Monotonicity**: Suppose two lotteries have the same two possible outcomes, A and B. If an agent prefers A to B, then the agent must prefer the lottery that has a higher probability for A (and vice versa).

$$A \succ B \Rightarrow (p > q \Leftrightarrow [p, A;\ 1-p, B] \succ [q, A;\ 1-q, B])\ .$$

DECOMPOSABILITY

- **Decomposability**: Compound lotteries can be reduced to simpler ones using the laws of probability. This has been called the "no fun in gambling" rule because it says that two consecutive lotteries can be compressed into a single equivalent lottery, as shown in Figure 1(b).[3]

$$[p, A;\ 1-p, [q, B;\ 1-q, C]] \sim [p, A;\ (1-p)q, B;\ (1-p)(1-q), C]\ .$$

These constraints are known as the axioms of utility theory. Each axiom can be motivated by showing that an agent that violates it will exhibit patently irrational behavior in some situations. For example, we can motivate transitivity by making an agent with nontransitive preferences give us all its money. Suppose that the agent has the nontransitive preferences $A \succ B \succ C \succ A$, where A, B, and C are goods that can be freely exchanged. If the agent currently has A, then we could offer to trade C for A plus one cent. The agent prefers C, and so would be willing to make this trade. We could then offer to trade B for C, extracting another cent, and finally trade A for B. This brings us back where we started from, except that the agent has given us three cents (Figure 1(a)). We can keep going around the cycle until the agent has no money at all. Clearly, the agent has acted irrationally in this case.

2.2 Preferences lead to utility

Notice that the axioms of utility theory are really axioms about preferences—they say nothing about a utility function. But in fact from the axioms of utility we can derive the following consequences (for the proof, see von Neumann and Morgenstern, 1944):

- **Existence of Utility Function**: If an agent's preferences obey the axioms of utility, then there exists a function U such that $U(A) > U(B)$ if and only if A is preferred to B, and $U(A) = U(B)$ if and only if the agent is indifferent between A and B.

$$U(A) > U(B) \Leftrightarrow A \succ B$$
$$U(A) = U(B) \Leftrightarrow A \sim B$$

- **Expected Utility of a Lottery**: The utility of a lottery is the sum of the probability of each outcome times the utility of that outcome.

$$U([p_1, S_1; \ldots ; p_n, S_n]) = \sum_i p_i U(S_i)\ .$$

[3] We can account for the enjoyment of gambling by encoding gambling events into the state description; for example, "Have \$10 and gambled" could be preferred to "Have \$10 and didn't gamble."

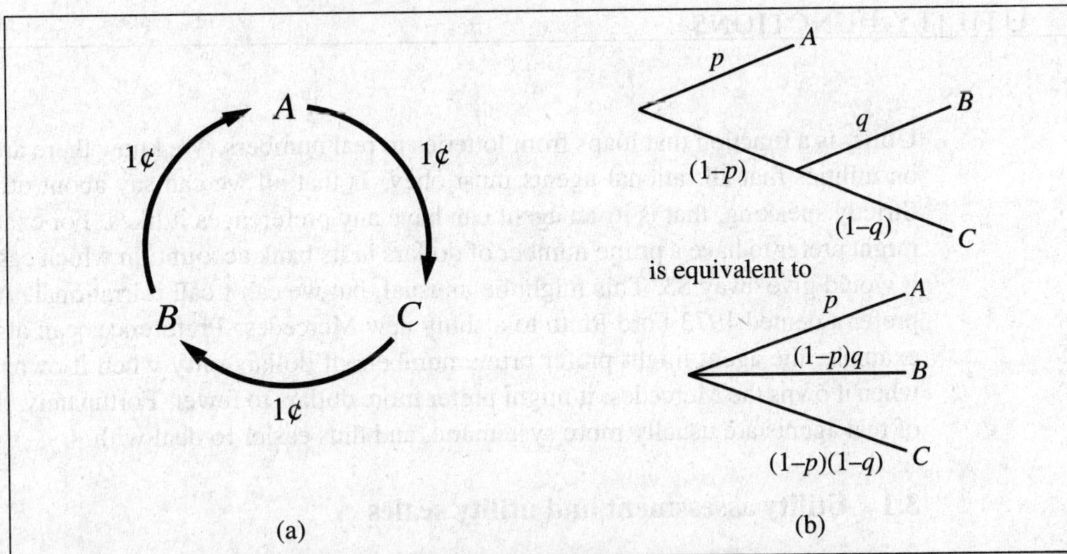

Figure 1 (a) A cycle of exchanges showing that the nontransitive preferences $A \succ B \succ C \succ A$ result in irrational behavior. (b) The decomposability axiom.

In other words, once the probabilities and utilities of the possible outcome states are specified, the utility of a compound lottery involving those states is completely determined. Because the outcome of a nondeterministic action is a lottery, it follows that an agent can act rationally—that is, consistently with its preferences—only by choosing an action that maximizes expected utility according to Equation (1).

The preceding theorems establish that a utility function *exists* for any rational agent, but they do not establish that it is *unique*. It is easy to see, in fact, that an agent's behavior would not change if its utility function $U(S)$ were transformed according to

$$U'(S) = aU(S) + b\,, \tag{2}$$

where a and b are constants and $a > 0$; an affine transformation.[4]

As in game-playing, in a deterministic environment an agent just needs a preference ranking on states—the numbers don't matter. This is called a **value function** or **ordinal utility function**.

VALUE FUNCTION

ORDINAL UTILITY FUNCTION

It is important to remember that the existence of a utility function that describes an agent's preference behavior does not necessarily mean that the agent is *explicitly* maximizing that utility function in its own deliberations. Rational behavior can be generated in any number of ways. By observing a rational agent's preferences, however, an observer can construct the utility function that represents what the agent is actually trying to achieve (even if the agent doesn't know it).

[4] In this sense, utilities resemble temperatures: a temperature in Fahrenheit is 1.8 times the Celsius temperature plus 32. You get the same results in either measurement system.

3 UTILITY FUNCTIONS

Utility is a function that maps from lotteries to real numbers. We know there are some axioms on utilities that all rational agents must obey. Is that all we can say about utility functions? Strictly speaking, that is it: an agent can have any preferences it likes. For example, an agent might prefer to have a prime number of dollars in its bank account; in which case, if it had \$16 it would give away \$3. This might be unusual, but we can't call it irrational. An agent might prefer a dented 1973 Ford Pinto to a shiny new Mercedes. Preferences can also interact: for example, the agent might prefer prime numbers of dollars only when it owns the Pinto, but when it owns the Mercedes, it might prefer more dollars to fewer. Fortunately, the preferences of real agents are usually more systematic, and thus easier to deal with.

3.1 Utility assessment and utility scales

If we want to build a decision-theoretic system that helps the agent make decisions or acts on his or her behalf, we must first work out what the agent's utility function is. This process, often called **preference elicitation**, involves presenting choices to the agent and using the observed preferences to pin down the underlying utility function.

PREFERENCE ELICITATION

Equation (2) says that there is no absolute scale for utilities, but it is helpful, nonetheless, to establish *some* scale on which utilities can be recorded and compared for any particular problem. A scale can be established by fixing the utilities of any two particular outcomes, just as we fix a temperature scale by fixing the freezing point and boiling point of water. Typically, we fix the utility of a "best possible prize" at $U(S) = u_\top$ and a "worst possible catastrophe" at $U(S) = u_\bot$. **Normalized utilities** use a scale with $u_\bot = 0$ and $u_\top = 1$.

NORMALIZED UTILITIES

Given a utility scale between $u_\top$ and $u_\bot$, we can assess the utility of any particular prize S by asking the agent to choose between S and a **standard lottery** $[p, u_\top;\ (1-p), u_\bot]$. The probability p is adjusted until the agent is indifferent between S and the standard lottery. Assuming normalized utilities, the utility of S is given by p. Once this is done for each prize, the utilities for all lotteries involving those prizes are determined.

STANDARD LOTTERY

In medical, transportation, and environmental decision problems, among others, people's lives are at stake. In such cases, $u_\bot$ is the value assigned to immediate death (or perhaps many deaths). *Although nobody feels comfortable with putting a value on human life, it is a fact that tradeoffs are made all the time.* Aircraft are given a complete overhaul at intervals determined by trips and miles flown, rather than after every trip. Cars are manufactured in a way that trades off costs against accident survival rates. Paradoxically, a refusal to "put a monetary value on life" means that life is often *undervalued.* Ross Shachter relates an experience with a government agency that commissioned a study on removing asbestos from schools. The decision analysts performing the study assumed a particular dollar value for the life of a school-age child, and argued that the rational choice under that assumption was to remove the asbestos. The agency, morally outraged at the idea of setting the value of a life, rejected the report out of hand. It then decided against asbestos removal—implicitly asserting a lower value for the life of a child than that assigned by the analysts.

Some attempts have been made to find out the value that people place on their own lives. One common "currency" used in medical and safety analysis is the **micromort**, a one in a million chance of death. If you ask people how much they would pay to avoid a risk—for example, to avoid playing Russian roulette with a million-barreled revolver—they will respond with very large numbers, perhaps tens of thousands of dollars, but their actual behavior reflects a much lower monetary value for a micromort. For example, driving in a car for 230 miles incurs a risk of one micromort; over the life of your car—say, 92,000 miles—that's 400 micromorts. People appear to be willing to pay about $10,000 (at 2009 prices) more for a safer car that halves the risk of death, or about $50 per micromort. A number of studies have confirmed a figure in this range across many individuals and risk types. Of course, this argument holds only for small risks. Most people won't agree to kill themselves for $50 million.

MICROMORT

Another measure is the **QALY**, or quality-adjusted life year. Patients with a disability are willing to accept a shorter life expectancy to be restored to full health. For example, kidney patients on average are indifferent between living two years on a dialysis machine and one year at full health.

QALY

3.2 The utility of money

Utility theory has its roots in economics, and economics provides one obvious candidate for a utility measure: money (or more specifically, an agent's total net assets). The almost universal exchangeability of money for all kinds of goods and services suggests that money plays a significant role in human utility functions.

It will usually be the case that an agent prefers more money to less, all other things being equal. We say that the agent exhibits a **monotonic preference** for more money. This does not mean that money behaves as a utility function, because it says nothing about preferences between *lotteries* involving money.

MONOTONIC PREFERENCE

Suppose you have triumphed over the other competitors in a television game show. The host now offers you a choice: either you can take the $1,000,000 prize or you can gamble it on the flip of a coin. If the coin comes up heads, you end up with nothing, but if it comes up tails, you get $2,500,000. If you're like most people, you would decline the gamble and pocket the million. Are you being irrational?

Assuming the coin is fair, the **expected monetary value** (EMV) of the gamble is $\frac{1}{2}$($0) + $\frac{1}{2}$($2,500,000) = $1,250,000, which is more than the original $1,000,000. But that does not necessarily mean that accepting the gamble is a better decision. Suppose we use S_n to denote the state of possessing total wealth $\$n$, and that your current wealth is $\$k$. Then the expected utilities of the two actions of accepting and declining the gamble are

EXPECTED MONETARY VALUE

$$\begin{aligned} EU(Accept) &= \tfrac{1}{2}U(S_k) + \tfrac{1}{2}U(S_{k+2{,}500{,}000}) \,, \\ EU(Decline) &= U(S_{k+1{,}000{,}000}) \,. \end{aligned}$$

To determine what to do, we need to assign utilities to the outcome states. Utility is not directly proportional to monetary value, because the utility for your first million is very high (or so they say), whereas the utility for an additional million is smaller. Suppose you assign a utility of 5 to your current financial status (S_k), a 9 to the state $S_{k+2{,}500{,}000}$, and an 8 to the

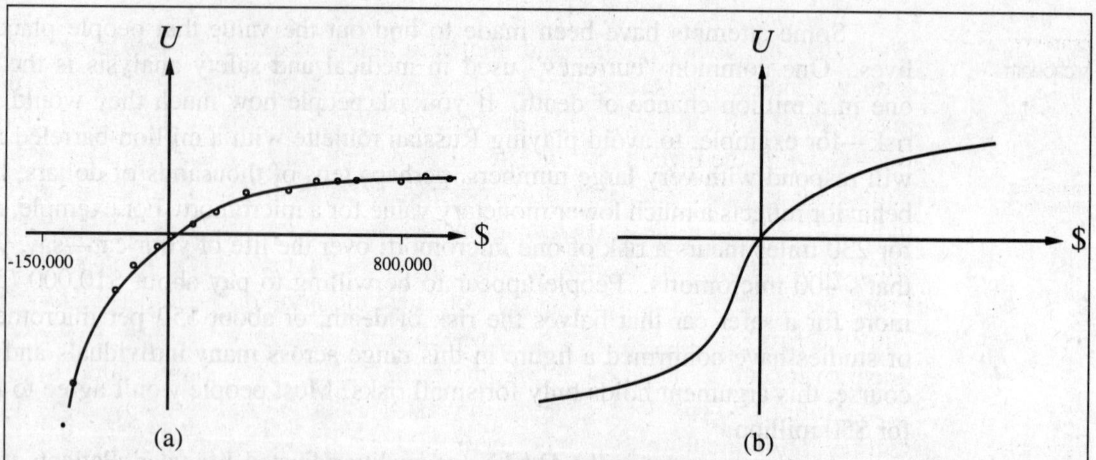

Figure 2 The utility of money. (a) Empirical data for Mr. Beard over a limited range. (b) A typical curve for the full range.

state $S_{k+1,000,000}$. Then the rational action would be to decline, because the expected utility of accepting is only 7 (less than the 8 for declining). On the other hand, a billionaire would most likely have a utility function that is locally linear over the range of a few million more, and thus would accept the gamble.

In a pioneering study of actual utility functions, Grayson (1960) found that the utility of money was almost exactly proportional to the *logarithm* of the amount. (This idea was first suggested by Bernoulli (1738); see Exercise 3.) One particular utility curve, for a certain Mr. Beard, is shown in Figure 2(a). The data obtained for Mr. Beard's preferences are consistent with a utility function

$$U(S_{k+n}) = -263.31 + 22.09 \log(n + 150,000)$$

for the range between $n = -\$150,000$ and $n = \$800,000$.

We should not assume that this is the definitive utility function for monetary value, but it is likely that most people have a utility function that is concave for positive wealth. Going into debt is bad, but preferences between different levels of debt can display a reversal of the concavity associated with positive wealth. For example, someone already $10,000,000 in debt might well accept a gamble on a fair coin with a gain of $10,000,000 for heads and a loss of $20,000,000 for tails.[5] This yields the S-shaped curve shown in Figure 2(b).

If we restrict our attention to the positive part of the curves, where the slope is decreasing, then for any lottery L, the utility of being faced with that lottery is less than the utility of being handed the expected monetary value of the lottery as a sure thing:

$$U(L) < U(S_{EMV(L)}) .$$

RISK-AVERSE

That is, agents with curves of this shape are **risk-averse**: they prefer a sure thing with a payoff that is less than the expected monetary value of a gamble. On the other hand, in the "desperate" region at large negative wealth in Figure 2(b), the behavior is **risk-seeking**.

RISK-SEEKING

[5] Such behavior might be called desperate, but it is rational if one is already in a desperate situation.

CERTAINTY EQUIVALENT

The value an agent will accept in lieu of a lottery is called the **certainty equivalent** of the lottery. Studies have shown that most people will accept about \$400 in lieu of a gamble that gives \$1000 half the time and \$0 the other half—that is, the certainty equivalent of the lottery is \$400, while the EMV is \$500. The difference between the EMV of a lottery and its certainty equivalent is called the **insurance premium**. Risk aversion is the basis for the insurance industry, because it means that insurance premiums are positive. People would rather pay a small insurance premium than gamble the price of their house against the chance of a fire. From the insurance company's point of view, the price of the house is very small compared with the firm's total reserves. This means that the insurer's utility curve is approximately linear over such a small region, and the gamble costs the company almost nothing.

INSURANCE PREMIUM

Notice that for *small* changes in wealth relative to the current wealth, almost any curve will be approximately linear. An agent that has a linear curve is said to be **risk-neutral**. For gambles with small sums, therefore, we expect risk neutrality.

RISK-NEUTRAL

3.3 Expected utility and post-decision disappointment

The rational way to choose the best action, a^*, is to maximize expected utility:

$$a^* = \underset{a}{\operatorname{argmax}}\, EU(a|\mathbf{e}) .$$

If we have calculated the expected utility correctly according to our probability model, and if the probability model correctly reflects the underlying stochastic processes that generate the outcomes, then, on average, we will get the utility we expect if the whole process is repeated many times.

In reality, however, our model usually oversimplifies the real situation, either because we don't know enough (e.g., when making a complex investment decision) or because the computation of the true expected utility is too difficult (e.g., when estimating the utility of successor states of the root node in backgammon). In that case, we are really working with *estimates* $\widehat{EU}(a|\mathbf{e})$ of the true expected utility. We will assume, kindly perhaps, that the estimates are **unbiased**, that is, the expected value of the error, $E(\widehat{EU}(a|\mathbf{e}) - EU(a|\mathbf{e}))$, is zero. In that case, it still seems reasonable to choose the action with the highest estimated utility and to expect to receive that utility, on average, when the action is executed.

UNBIASED

Unfortunately, the real outcome will usually be significantly *worse* than we estimated, even though the estimate was unbiased! To see why, consider a decision problem in which there are k choices, each of which has true estimated utility of 0. Suppose that the error in each utility estimate has zero mean and standard deviation of 1, shown as the bold curve in Figure 3. Now, as we actually start to generate the estimates, some of the errors will be negative (pessimistic) and some will be positive (optimistic). Because we select the action with the *highest* utility estimate, we are obviously favoring the overly optimistic estimates, and that is the source of the bias. It is a straightforward matter to calculate the distribution of the maximum of the k estimates (see Exercise 11) and hence quantify the extent of our disappointment. The curve in Figure 3 for $k=3$ has a mean around 0.85, so the average disappointment will be about 85% of the standard deviation in the utility estimates.

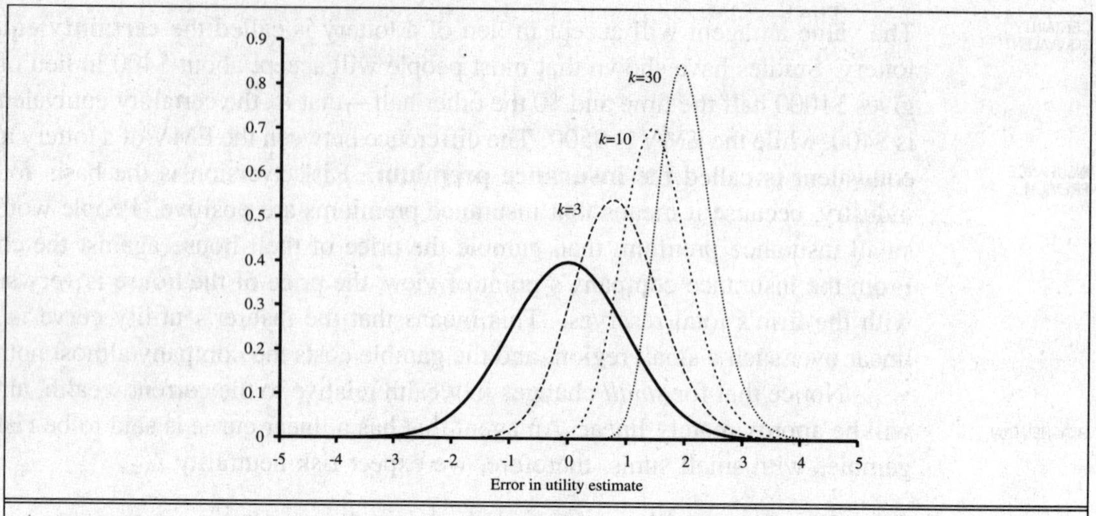

Figure 3 Plot of the error in each of k utility estimates and of the distribution of the maximum of k estimates for $k = 3$, 10, and 30.

With more choices, extremely optimistic estimates are more likely to arise: for $k = 30$, the disappointment will be around twice the standard deviation in the estimates.

OPTIMIZER'S CURSE

This tendency for the estimated expected utility of the best choice to be too high is called the **optimizer's curse** (Smith and Winkler, 2006). It afflicts even the most seasoned decision analysts and statisticians. Serious manifestations include believing that an exciting new drug that has cured 80% patients in a trial will cure 80% of patients (it's been chosen from $k =$ thousands of candidate drugs) or that a mutual fund advertised as having above-average returns will continue to have them (it's been chosen to appear in the advertisement out of $k =$ dozens of funds in the company's overall portfolio). It can even be the case that what appears to be the best choice may not be, if the variance in the utility estimate is high: a drug, selected from thousands tried, that has cured 9 of 10 patients is probably *worse* than one that has cured 800 of 1000.

The optimizer's curse crops up everywhere because of the ubiquity of utility-maximizing selection processes, so taking the utility estimates at face value is a bad idea. We can avoid the curse by using an explicit probability model $\mathbf{P}(\widehat{EU} \mid EU)$ of the error in the utility estimates. Given this model and a prior $\mathbf{P}(EU)$ on what we might reasonably expect the utilities to be, we treat the utility estimate, once obtained, as evidence and compute the posterior distribution for the true utility using Bayes' rule.

3.4 Human judgment and irrationality

NORMATIVE THEORY

DESCRIPTIVE THEORY

Decision theory is a **normative theory**: it describes how a rational agent *should* act. A **descriptive theory**, on the other hand, describes how actual agents—for example, humans—really do act. The application of economic theory would be greatly enhanced if the two coincided, but there appears to be some experimental evidence to the contrary. The evidence suggests that humans are "predictably irrational" (Ariely, 2009).

The best-known problem is the Allais paradox (Allais, 1953). People are given a choice between lotteries A and B and then between C and D, which have the following prizes:

$$A: \ 80\% \text{ chance of } \$4000 \qquad C: \ 20\% \text{ chance of } \$4000$$
$$B: \ 100\% \text{ chance of } \$3000 \qquad D: \ 25\% \text{ chance of } \$3000$$

Most people consistently prefer B over A (taking the sure thing), and C over D (taking the higher EMV). The normative analysis disagrees! We can see this most easily if we use the freedom implied by Equation (2) to set $U(\$0) = 0$. In that case, then $B \succ A$ implies that $U(\$3000) > 0.8\,U(\$4000)$, whereas $C \succ D$ implies exactly the reverse. In other words, there is no utility function that is consistent with these choices. One explanation for the apparently irrational preferences is the **certainty effect** (Kahneman and Tversky, 1979): people are strongly attracted to gains that are certain. There are several reasons why this may be so. First, people may prefer to reduce their computational burden; by choosing certain outcomes, they don't have to compute with probabilities. But the effect persists even when the computations involved are very easy ones. Second, people may distrust the legitimacy of the stated probabilities. I trust that a coin flip is roughly 50/50 if I have control over the coin and the flip, but I may distrust the result if the flip is done by someone with a vested interest in the outcome.[6] In the presence of distrust, it might be better to go for the sure thing.[7] Third, people may be accounting for their emotional state as well as their financial state. People know they would experience **regret** if they gave up a certain reward (B) for an 80% chance at a higher reward and then lost. In other words, if A is chosen, there is a 20% chance of getting no money *and feeling like a complete idiot*, which is worse than just getting no money. So perhaps people who choose B over A and C over D are not being irrational; they are just saying that they are willing to give up \$200 of EMV to avoid a 20% chance of feeling like an idiot.

CERTAINTY EFFECT

REGRET

A related problem is the Ellsberg paradox. Here the prizes are fixed, but the probabilities are underconstrained. Your payoff will depend on the color of a ball chosen from an urn. You are told that the urn contains 1/3 red balls, and 2/3 either black or yellow balls, but you don't know how many black and how many yellow. Again, you are asked whether you prefer lottery A or B; and then C or D:

$$A: \ \$100 \text{ for a red ball} \qquad C: \ \$100 \text{ for a red or yellow ball}$$
$$B: \ \$100 \text{ for a black ball} \qquad D: \ \$100 \text{ for a black or yellow ball}.$$

It should be clear that if you think there are more red than black balls then you should prefer A over B and C over D; if you think there are fewer red than black you should prefer the opposite. But it turns out that most people prefer A over B and also prefer D over C, even though there is no state of the world for which this is rational. It seems that people have **ambiguity aversion**: A gives you a 1/3 chance of winning, while B could be anywhere between 0 and 2/3. Similarly, D gives you a 2/3 chance, while C could be anywhere between 1/3 and 3/3. Most people elect the known probability rather than the unknown unknowns.

AMBIGUITY AVERSION

6 For example, the mathematician/magician Persi Diaconis can make a coin flip come out the way he wants every time (Landhuis, 2004).

7 Even the sure thing may not be certain. Despite cast-iron promises, we have not yet received that \$27,000,000 from the Nigerian bank account of a previously unknown deceased relative.

Yet another problem is that the exact wording of a decision problem can have a big impact on the agent's choices; this is called the **framing effect**. Experiments show that people like a medical procedure that it is described as having a "90% survival rate" about twice as much as one described as having a "10% death rate," even though these two statements mean exactly the same thing. This discrepancy in judgment has been found in multiple experiments and is about the same whether the subjects were patients in a clinic, statistically sophisticated business school students, or experienced doctors.

FRAMING EFFECT

People feel more comfortable making *relative* utility judgments rather than absolute ones. I may have little idea how much I might enjoy the various wines offered by a restaurant. The restaurant takes advantage of this by offering a $200 bottle that it knows nobody will buy, but which serves to skew upward the customer's estimate of the value of all wines and make the $55 bottle seem like a bargain. This is called the **anchoring effect**.

ANCHORING EFFECT

If human informants insist on contradictory preference judgments, there is nothing that automated agents can do to be consistent with them. Fortunately, preference judgments made by humans are often open to revision in the light of further consideration. Paradoxes like the Allais paradox are greatly reduced (but not eliminated) if the choices are explained better. In work at the Harvard Business School on assessing the utility of money, Keeney and Raiffa (1976, p. 210) found the following:

> Subjects tend to be too risk-averse in the small and therefore . . . the fitted utility functions exhibit unacceptably large risk premiums for lotteries with a large spread. . . . Most of the subjects, however, can reconcile their inconsistencies and feel that they have learned an important lesson about how they want to behave. As a consequence, some subjects cancel their automobile collision insurance and take out more term insurance on their lives.

The evidence for human irrationality is also questioned by researchers in the field of **evolutionary psychology**, who point to the fact that our brain's decision-making mechanisms did not evolve to solve word problems with probabilities and prizes stated as decimal numbers. Let us grant, for the sake of argument, that the brain has built-in neural mechanism for computing with probabilities and utilities, or something functionally equivalent; if so, the required inputs would be obtained through accumulated experience of outcomes and rewards rather than through linguistic presentations of numerical values. It is far from obvious that we can directly access the brain's built-in neural mechanisms by presenting decision problems in linguistic/numerical form. The very fact that different wordings of the *same decision problem* elicit different choices suggests that the decision problem itself is not getting through. Spurred by this observation, psychologists have tried presenting problems in uncertain reasoning and decision making in "evolutionarily appropriate" forms; for example, instead of saying "90% survival rate," the experimenter might show 100 stick-figure animations of the operation, where the patient dies in 10 of them and survives in 90. (Boredom is a complicating factor in these experiments!) With decision problems posed in this way, people seem to be much closer to rational behavior than previously suspected.

EVOLUTIONARY PSYCHOLOGY

4 MULTIATTRIBUTE UTILITY FUNCTIONS

Decision making in the field of public policy involves high stakes, in both money and lives. For example, in deciding what levels of harmful emissions to allow from a power plant, policy makers must weigh the prevention of death and disability against the benefit of the power and the economic burden of mitigating the emissions. Siting a new airport requires consideration of the disruption caused by construction; the cost of land; the distance from centers of population; the noise of flight operations; safety issues arising from local topography and weather conditions; and so on. Problems like these, in which outcomes are characterized by two or more attributes, are handled by **multiattribute utility theory**.

MULTIATTRIBUTE UTILITY THEORY

We will call the attributes $\mathbf{X} = X_1, \ldots, X_n$; a complete vector of assignments will be $\mathbf{x} = \langle x_1, \ldots, x_n \rangle$, where each x_i is either a numeric value or a discrete value with an assumed ordering on values. We will assume that higher values of an attribute correspond to higher utilities, all other things being equal. For example, if we choose *AbsenceOfNoise* as an attribute in the airport problem, then the greater its value, the better the solution.[8] We begin by examining cases in which decisions can be made *without* combining the attribute values into a single utility value. Then we look at cases in which the utilities of attribute combinations can be specified very concisely.

4.1 Dominance

STRICT DOMINANCE

Suppose that airport site S_1 costs less, generates less noise pollution, and is safer than site S_2. One would not hesitate to reject S_2. We then say that there is **strict dominance** of S_1 over S_2. In general, if an option is of lower value on all attributes than some other option, it need not be considered further. Strict dominance is often very useful in narrowing down the field of choices to the real contenders, although it seldom yields a unique choice. Figure 4(a) shows a schematic diagram for the two-attribute case.

That is fine for the deterministic case, in which the attribute values are known for sure. What about the general case, where the outcomes are uncertain? A direct analog of strict dominance can be constructed, where, despite the uncertainty, all possible concrete outcomes for S_1 strictly dominate all possible outcomes for S_2. (See Figure 4(b).) Of course, this will probably occur even less often than in the deterministic case.

STOCHASTIC DOMINANCE

Fortunately, there is a more useful generalization called **stochastic dominance**, which occurs very frequently in real problems. Stochastic dominance is easiest to understand in the context of a single attribute. Suppose we believe that the cost of siting the airport at S_1 is uniformly distributed between \$2.8 billion and \$4.8 billion and that the cost at S_2 is uniformly distributed between \$3 billion and \$5.2 billion. Figure 5(a) shows these distributions, with cost plotted as a negative value. Then, given only the information that utility decreases with

[8] In some cases, it may be necessary to subdivide the range of values so that utility varies monotonically within each range. For example, if the *RoomTemperature* attribute has a utility peak at 70°F, we would split it into two attributes measuring the difference from the ideal, one colder and one hotter. Utility would then be monotonically increasing in each attribute.

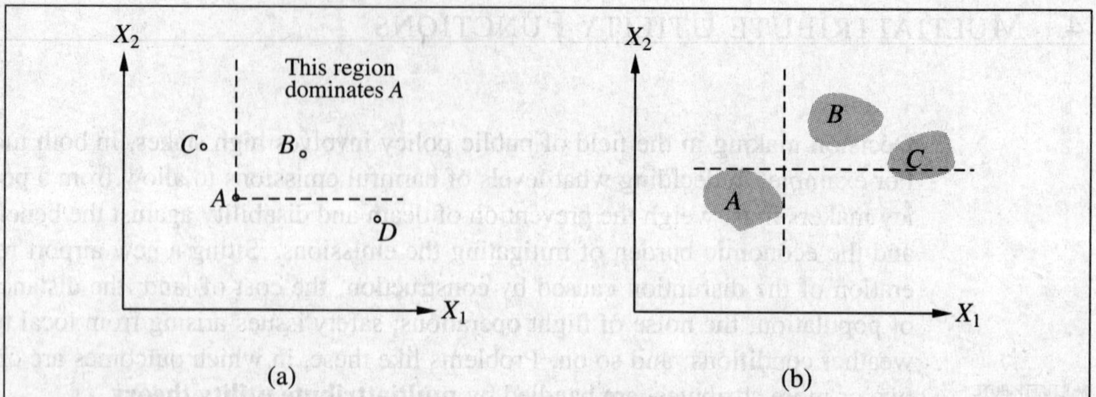

Figure 4 Strict dominance. (a) Deterministic: Option A is strictly dominated by B but not by C or D. (b) Uncertain: A is strictly dominated by B but not by C.

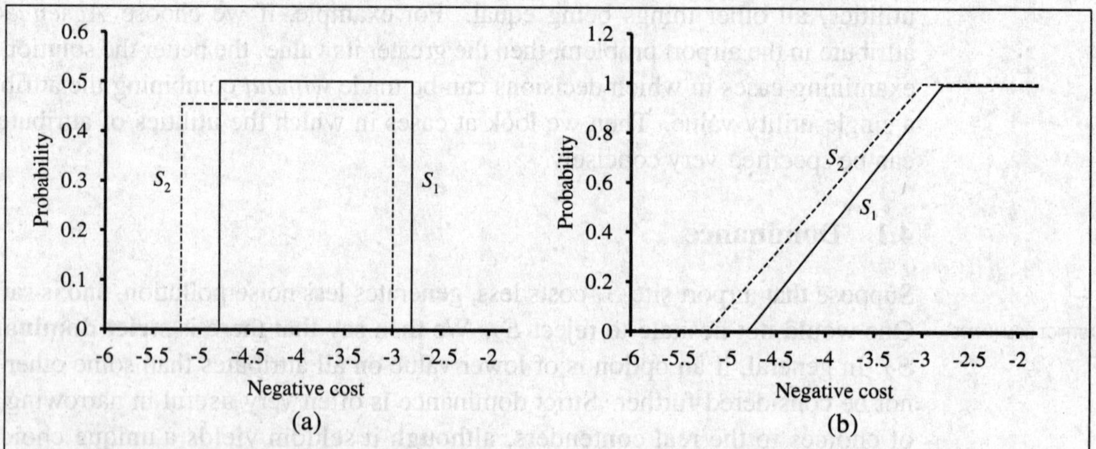

Figure 5 Stochastic dominance. (a) S_1 stochastically dominates S_2 on cost. (b) Cumulative distributions for the negative cost of S_1 and S_2.

cost, we can say that S_1 stochastically dominates S_2 (i.e., S_2 can be discarded). It is important to note that this does *not* follow from comparing the expected costs. For example, if we knew the cost of S_1 to be *exactly* \$3.8 billion, then we would be *unable* to make a decision without additional information on the utility of money. (It might seem odd that *more* information on the cost of S_1 could make the agent *less* able to decide. The paradox is resolved by noting that in the absence of exact cost information, the decision is easier to make but is more likely to be wrong.)

The exact relationship between the attribute distributions needed to establish stochastic dominance is best seen by examining the **cumulative distributions**, shown in Figure 5(b). The cumulative distribution measures the probability that the cost is less than or equal to any given amount—that is, it integrates the original distribution. If the cumulative distribution for S_1 is always to the right of the cumulative distribution for S_2, then, stochastically speaking, S_1 is cheaper than S_2. Formally, if two actions A_1 and A_2 lead to probability distributions $p_1(x)$ and $p_2(x)$ on attribute X, then A_1 stochastically dominates A_2 on X if

$$\forall\, x \int_{-\infty}^{x} p_1(x')\, dx' \leq \int_{-\infty}^{x} p_2(x')\, dx' .$$

The relevance of this definition to the selection of optimal decisions comes from the following property: *if A_1 stochastically dominates A_2, then for any monotonically nondecreasing utility function $U(x)$, the expected utility of A_1 is at least as high as the expected utility of A_2.* Hence, if an action is stochastically dominated by another action on all attributes, then it can be discarded.

The stochastic dominance condition might seem rather technical and perhaps not so easy to evaluate without extensive probability calculations. In fact, it can be decided very easily in many cases. Suppose, for example, that the construction transportation cost depends on the distance to the supplier. The cost itself is uncertain, but the greater the distance, the greater the cost. If S_1 is closer than S_2, then S_1 will dominate S_2 on cost. Although we will not present them here, there exist algorithms for propagating this kind of qualitative information among uncertain variables in **qualitative probabilistic networks**, enabling a system to make rational decisions based on stochastic dominance, without using any numeric values.

QUALITATIVE PROBABILISTIC NETWORKS

4.2 Preference structure and multiattribute utility

Suppose we have n attributes, each of which has d distinct possible values. To specify the complete utility function $U(x_1, \ldots, x_n)$, we need d^n values in the worst case. Now, the worst case corresponds to a situation in which the agent's preferences have no regularity at all. Multiattribute utility theory is based on the supposition that the preferences of typical agents have much more structure than that. The basic approach is to identify regularities in the preference behavior we would expect to see and to use what are called **representation theorems** to show that an agent with a certain kind of preference structure has a utility function

REPRESENTATION THEOREM

$$U(x_1, \ldots, x_n) = F[f_1(x_1), \ldots, f_n(x_n)] ,$$

where F is, we hope, a simple function such as addition. Notice the similarity to the use of Bayesian networks to decompose the joint probability of several random variables.

Preferences without uncertainty

Let us begin with the deterministic case. Remember that for deterministic environments the agent has a value function $V(x_1, \ldots, x_n)$; the aim is to represent this function concisely. The basic regularity that arises in deterministic preference structures is called **preference independence**. Two attributes X_1 and X_2 are preferentially independent of a third attribute X_3 if the preference between outcomes $\langle x_1, x_2, x_3 \rangle$ and $\langle x'_1, x'_2, x_3 \rangle$ does not depend on the particular value x_3 for attribute X_3.

PREFERENCE INDEPENDENCE

Going back to the airport example, where we have (among other attributes) *Noise*, *Cost*, and *Deaths* to consider, one may propose that *Noise* and *Cost* are preferentially independent of *Deaths*. For example, if we prefer a state with 20,000 people residing in the flight path and a construction cost of \$4 billion over a state with 70,000 people residing in the flight path and a cost of \$3.7 billion when the safety level is 0.06 deaths per million passenger miles in both cases, then we would have the same preference when the safety level is 0.12 or 0.03; and the same independence would hold for preferences between any other pair of values for *Noise* and *Cost*. It is also apparent that *Cost* and *Deaths* are preferentially independent of *Noise* and that *Noise* and *Deaths* are preferentially independent of *Cost*. We say that the set of attributes $\{Noise, Cost, Deaths\}$ exhibits **mutual preferential independence** (MPI). MPI says that, whereas each attribute may be important, it does not affect the way in which one trades off the other attributes against each other.

MUTUAL PREFERENTIAL INDEPENDENCE

Mutual preferential independence is something of a mouthful, but thanks to a remarkable theorem due to the economist Gérard Debreu (1960), we can derive from it a very simple form for the agent's value function: *If attributes $X_1, \ldots, X_n$ are mutually preferentially independent, then the agent's preference behavior can be described as maximizing the function*

$$V(x_1, \ldots, x_n) = \sum_i V_i(x_i) \,,$$

where each V_i is a value function referring only to the attribute X_i. For example, it might well be the case that the airport decision can be made using a value function

$$V(noise, cost, deaths) = -noise \times 10^4 - cost - deaths \times 10^{12} \,.$$

ADDITIVE VALUE FUNCTION

A value function of this type is called an **additive value function**. Additive functions are an extremely natural way to describe an agent's preferences and are valid in many real-world situations. For n attributes, assessing an additive value function requires assessing n separate one-dimensional value functions rather than one n-dimensional function; typically, this represents an exponential reduction in the number of preference experiments that are needed. Even when MPI does not strictly hold, as might be the case at extreme values of the attributes, an additive value function might still provide a good approximation to the agent's preferences. This is especially true when the violations of MPI occur in portions of the attribute ranges that are unlikely to occur in practice.

To understand MPI better, it helps to look at cases where it *doesn't* hold. Suppose you are at a medieval market, considering the purchase of some hunting dogs, some chickens, and some wicker cages for the chickens. The hunting dogs are very valuable, but if you don't have enough cages for the chickens, the dogs will eat the chickens; hence, the tradeoff between dogs and chickens depends strongly on the number of cages, and MPI is violated. The existence of these kinds of interactions among various attributes makes it much harder to assess the overall value function.

Preferences with uncertainty

When uncertainty is present in the domain, we also need to consider the structure of preferences between lotteries and to understand the resulting properties of utility functions, rather than just value functions. The mathematics of this problem can become quite complicated, so we present just one of the main results to give a flavor of what can be done. The reader is referred to Keeney and Raiffa (1976) for a thorough survey of the field.

UTILITY INDEPENDENCE

The basic notion of **utility independence** extends preference independence to cover lotteries: a set of attributes **X** is utility independent of a set of attributes **Y** if preferences between lotteries on the attributes in **X** are independent of the particular values of the attributes in **Y**. A set of attributes is **mutually utility independent** (MUI) if each of its subsets is utility-independent of the remaining attributes. Again, it seems reasonable to propose that the airport attributes are MUI.

MUTUALLY UTILITY INDEPENDENT

MULTIPLICATIVE UTILITY FUNCTION

MUI implies that the agent's behavior can be described using a **multiplicative utility function** (Keeney, 1974). The general form of a multiplicative utility function is best seen by looking at the case for three attributes. For conciseness, we use U_i to mean $U_i(x_i)$:

$$U = k_1U_1 + k_2U_2 + k_3U_3 + k_1k_2U_1U_2 + k_2k_3U_2U_3 + k_3k_1U_3U_1 + k_1k_2k_3U_1U_2U_3 .$$

Although this does not look very simple, it contains just three single-attribute utility functions and three constants. In general, an n-attribute problem exhibiting MUI can be modeled using n single-attribute utilities and n constants. Each of the single-attribute utility functions can be developed independently of the other attributes, and this combination will be guaranteed to generate the correct overall preferences. Additional assumptions are required to obtain a purely additive utility function.

5 DECISION NETWORKS

In this section, we look at a general mechanism for making rational decisions. The notation is often called an **influence diagram** (Howard and Matheson, 1984), but we will use the more descriptive term **decision network**. Decision networks combine Bayesian networks with additional node types for actions and utilities. We use airport siting as an example.

INFLUENCE DIAGRAM

DECISION NETWORK

5.1 Representing a decision problem with a decision network

In its most general form, a decision network represents information about the agent's current state, its possible actions, the state that will result from the agent's action, and the utility of that state. It therefore provides a substrate for implementing certain utility-based agents. Figure 6 shows a decision network for the airport siting problem. It illustrates the three types of nodes used:

CHANCE NODES

- **Chance nodes** (ovals) represent random variables, just as they do in Bayesian networks. The agent could be uncertain about the construction cost, the level of air traffic and the potential for litigation, and the *Deaths*, *Noise*, and total *Cost* variables, each of which also depends on the site chosen. Each chance node has associated with it a conditional distribution that is indexed by the state of the parent nodes. In decision networks, the parent nodes can include decision nodes as well as chance nodes. Note that each of the current-state chance nodes could be part of a large Bayesian network for assessing construction costs, air traffic levels, or litigation potentials.

DECISION NODES

- **Decision nodes** (rectangles) represent points where the decision maker has a choice of

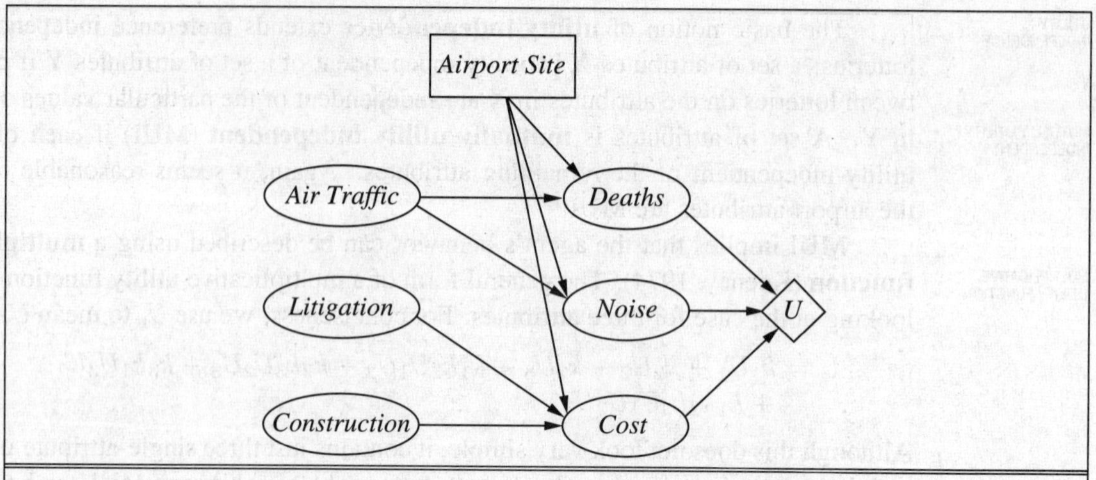

Figure 6 A simple decision network for the airport-siting problem.

actions. In this case, the *AirportSite* action can take on a different value for each site under consideration. The choice influences the cost, safety, and noise that will result. In this chapter, we assume that we are dealing with a single decision node.

UTILITY NODES

- **Utility nodes** (diamonds) represent the agent's utility function.[9] The utility node has as parents all variables describing the outcome that directly affect utility. Associated with the utility node is a description of the agent's utility as a function of the parent attributes. The description could be just a tabulation of the function, or it might be a parameterized additive or linear function of the attribute values.

A simplified form is also used in many cases. The notation remains identical, but the chance nodes describing the outcome state are omitted. Instead, the utility node is connected directly to the current-state nodes and the decision node. In this case, rather than representing a utility function on outcome states, the utility node represents the *expected* utility associated with each action, as defined in Equation (1); that is, the node is associated with an **action-utility function** (also known as a **Q-function** in reinforcement learning). Figure 7 shows the action-utility representation of the airport siting problem.

ACTION-UTILITY FUNCTION

Notice that, because the *Noise*, *Deaths*, and *Cost* chance nodes in Figure 6 refer to future states, they can never have their values set as evidence variables. Thus, the simplified version that omits these nodes can be used whenever the more general form can be used. Although the simplified form contains fewer nodes, the omission of an explicit description of the outcome of the siting decision means that it is less flexible with respect to changes in circumstances. For example, in Figure 6, a change in aircraft noise levels can be reflected by a change in the conditional probability table associated with the *Noise* node, whereas a change in the weight accorded to noise pollution in the utility function can be reflected by

[9] These nodes are also called **value nodes** in the literature.

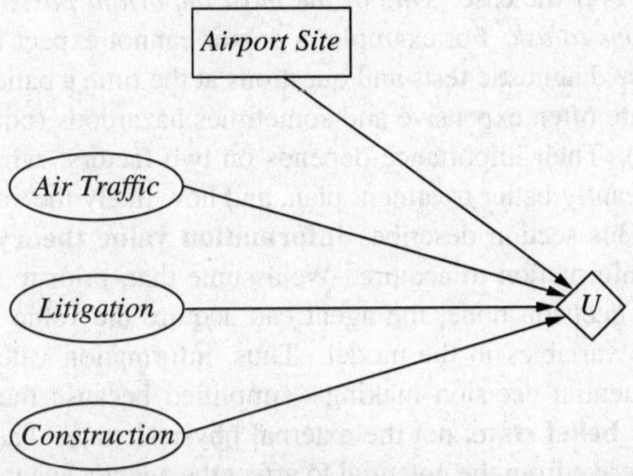

Figure 7 A simplified representation of the airport-siting problem. Chance nodes corresponding to outcome states have been factored out.

a change in the utility table. In the action-utility diagram, Figure 7, on the other hand, all such changes have to be reflected by changes to the action-utility table. Essentially, the action-utility formulation is a *compiled* version of the original formulation.

5.2 Evaluating decision networks

Actions are selected by evaluating the decision network for each possible setting of the decision node. Once the decision node is set, it behaves exactly like a chance node that has been set as an evidence variable. The algorithm for evaluating decision networks is the following:

1. Set the evidence variables for the current state.
2. For each possible value of the decision node:
   (a) Set the decision node to that value.
   (b) Calculate the posterior probabilities for the parent nodes of the utility node, using a standard probabilistic inference algorithm.
   (c) Calculate the resulting utility for the action.
3. Return the action with the highest utility.

This is a straightforward extension of the Bayesian network algorithm. The possibility of executing several actions in sequence makes the problem much more interesting.

6 THE VALUE OF INFORMATION

In the preceding analysis, we have assumed that all relevant information, or at least all available information, is provided to the agent before it makes its decision. In practice, this is hardly ever the case. *One of the most important parts of decision making is knowing what questions to ask.* For example, a doctor cannot expect to be provided with the results of *all possible* diagnostic tests and questions at the time a patient first enters the consulting room.[10] Tests are often expensive and sometimes hazardous (both directly and because of associated delays). Their importance depends on two factors: whether the test results would lead to a significantly better treatment plan, and how likely the various test results are.

INFORMATION VALUE THEORY

This section describes **information value theory**, which enables an agent to choose what information to acquire. We assume that, prior to selecting a "real" action represented by the decision node, the agent can acquire the value of any of the potentially observable chance variables in the model. Thus, information value theory involves a simplified form of sequential decision making—simplified because the observation actions affect only the agent's **belief state**, not the external physical state. The value of any particular observation must derive from the potential to affect the agent's eventual physical action; and this potential can be estimated directly from the decision model itself.

6.1 A simple example

Suppose an oil company is hoping to buy one of n indistinguishable blocks of ocean-drilling rights. Let us assume further that exactly one of the blocks contains oil worth C dollars, while the others are worthless. The asking price of each block is C/n dollars. If the company is risk-neutral, then it will be indifferent between buying a block and not buying one.

Now suppose that a seismologist offers the company the results of a survey of block number 3, which indicates definitively whether the block contains oil. How much should the company be willing to pay for the information? The way to answer this question is to examine what the company would do if it had the information:

- With probability $1/n$, the survey will indicate oil in block 3. In this case, the company will buy block 3 for C/n dollars and make a profit of $C - C/n = (n-1)C/n$ dollars.
- With probability $(n-1)/n$, the survey will show that the block contains no oil, in which case the company will buy a different block. Now the probability of finding oil in one of the other blocks changes from $1/n$ to $1/(n-1)$, so the company makes an expected profit of $C/(n-1) - C/n = C/n(n-1)$ dollars.

Now we can calculate the expected profit, given the survey information:

$$\frac{1}{n} \times \frac{(n-1)C}{n} + \frac{n-1}{n} \times \frac{C}{n(n-1)} = C/n\,.$$

Therefore, the company should be willing to pay the seismologist up to C/n dollars for the information: the information is worth as much as the block itself.

The value of information derives from the fact that *with* the information, one's course of action can be changed to suit the *actual* situation. One can discriminate according to the situation, whereas without the information, one has to do what's best on average over the possible situations. In general, the value of a given piece of information is defined to be the difference in expected value between best actions before and after information is obtained.

[10] In the United States, the only question that is always asked beforehand is whether the patient has insurance.

6.2 A general formula for perfect information

It is simple to derive a general mathematical formula for the value of information. We assume that exact evidence can be obtained about the value of some random variable E_j (that is, we learn $E_j = e_j$), so the phrase **value of perfect information** (VPI) is used.[11]

VALUE OF PERFECT INFORMATION

Let the agent's initial evidence be $\mathbf{e}$. Then the value of the current best action α is defined by

$$EU(\alpha|\mathbf{e}) = \max_a \sum_{s'} P(\text{RESULT}(a) = s' \mid a, \mathbf{e})\, U(s')\,,$$

and the value of the new best action (after the new evidence $E_j = e_j$ is obtained) will be

$$EU(\alpha_{e_j}|\mathbf{e}, e_j) = \max_a \sum_{s'} P(\text{RESULT}(a) = s' \mid a, \mathbf{e}, e_j)\, U(s')\,.$$

But E_j is a random variable whose value is *currently* unknown, so to determine the value of discovering E_j, given current information $\mathbf{e}$ we must average over all possible values e_{jk} that we might discover for E_j, using our *current* beliefs about its value:

$$VPI_{\mathbf{e}}(E_j) = \left(\sum_k P(E_j = e_{jk}|\mathbf{e})\, EU(\alpha_{e_{jk}}|\mathbf{e}, E_j = e_{jk})\right) - EU(\alpha|\mathbf{e})\,.$$

To get some intuition for this formula, consider the simple case where there are only two actions, a_1 and a_2, from which to choose. Their current expected utilities are U_1 and U_2. The information $E_j = e_{jk}$ will yield some new expected utilities U_1' and U_2' for the actions, but before we obtain E_j, we will have some probability distributions over the possible values of U_1' and U_2' (which we assume are independent).

Suppose that a_1 and a_2 represent two different routes through a mountain range in winter. a_1 is a nice, straight highway through a low pass, and a_2 is a winding dirt road over the top. Just given this information, a_1 is clearly preferable, because it is quite possible that a_2 is blocked by avalanches, whereas it is unlikely that anything blocks a_1. U_1 is therefore clearly higher than U_2. It is possible to obtain satellite reports E_j on the actual state of each road that would give new expectations, U_1' and U_2', for the two crossings. The distributions for these expectations are shown in Figure 8(a). Obviously, in this case, it is not worth the expense of obtaining satellite reports, because it is unlikely that the information derived from them will change the plan. With no change, information has no value.

Now suppose that we are choosing between two different winding dirt roads of slightly different lengths and we are carrying a seriously injured passenger. Then, even when U_1 and U_2 are quite close, the distributions of U_1' and U_2' are very broad. There is a significant possibility that the second route will turn out to be clear while the first is blocked, and in this

[11] There is no loss of expressiveness in requiring perfect information. Suppose we wanted to model the case in which we become somewhat more certain about a variable. We can do that by introducing *another* variable about which we learn perfect information. For example, suppose we initially have broad uncertainty about the variable *Temperature*. Then we gain the perfect knowledge *Thermometer* = 37; this gives us imperfect information about the true *Temperature*, and the uncertainty due to measurement error is encoded in the sensor model $\mathbf{P}(Thermometer \mid Temperature)$. See Exercise 17 for another example.

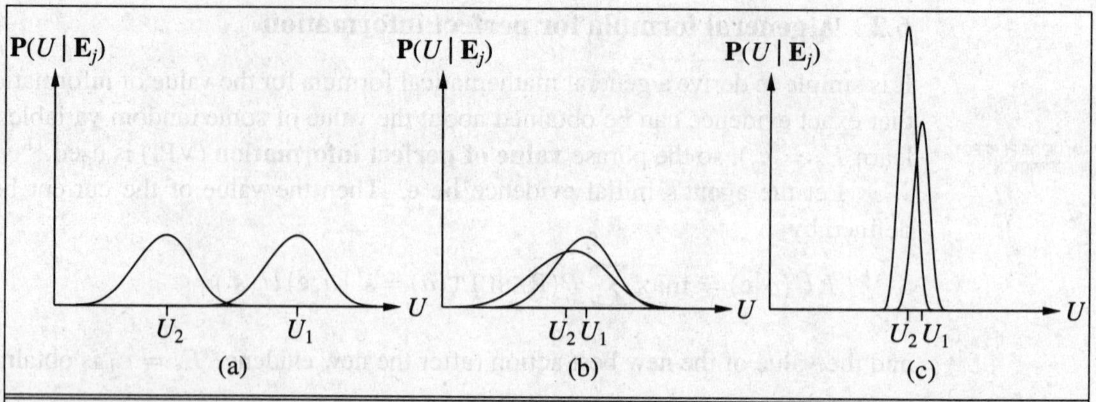

Figure 8 Three generic cases for the value of information. In (a), a_1 will almost certainly remain superior to a_2, so the information is not needed. In (b), the choice is unclear and the information is crucial. In (c), the choice is unclear, but because it makes little difference, the information is less valuable. (Note: The fact that U_2 has a high peak in (c) means that its expected value is known with higher certainty than U_1.)

case the difference in utilities will be very high. The VPI formula indicates that it might be worthwhile getting the satellite reports. Such a situation is shown in Figure 8(b).

Finally, suppose that we are choosing between the two dirt roads in summertime, when blockage by avalanches is unlikely. In this case, satellite reports might show one route to be more scenic than the other because of flowering alpine meadows, or perhaps wetter because of errant streams. It is therefore quite likely that we would change our plan if we had the information. In this case, however, the difference in value between the two routes is still likely to be very small, so we will not bother to obtain the reports. This situation is shown in Figure 8(c).

In sum, *information has value to the extent that it is likely to cause a change of plan and to the extent that the new plan will be significantly better than the old plan.*

6.3 Properties of the value of information

One might ask whether it is possible for information to be deleterious: can it actually have negative expected value? Intuitively, one should expect this to be impossible. After all, one could in the worst case just ignore the information and pretend that one has never received it. This is confirmed by the following theorem, which applies to any decision-theoretic agent: *The expected value of information is nonnegative:*

$$\forall \mathbf{e}, E_j \quad VPI_{\mathbf{e}}(E_j) \geq 0 .$$

The theorem follows directly from the definition of VPI, and we leave the proof as an exercise (Exercise 18). It is, of course, a theorem about *expected* value, not *actual* value. Additional information can easily lead to a plan that *turns out to* be worse than the original plan if the information happens to be misleading. For example, a medical test that gives a false positive result may lead to unnecessary surgery; but that does not mean that the test shouldn't be done.

It is important to remember that VPI depends on the current state of information, which is why it is subscripted. It can change as more information is acquired. For any given piece of evidence E_j, the value of acquiring it can go down (e.g., if another variable strongly constrains the posterior for E_j) or up (e.g., if another variable provides a clue on which E_j builds, enabling a new and better plan to be devised). Thus, VPI is not additive. That is,

$$VPI_{\mathbf{e}}(E_j, E_k) \neq VPI_{\mathbf{e}}(E_j) + VPI_{\mathbf{e}}(E_k) \quad \text{(in general)}\ .$$

VPI is, however, order independent. That is,

$$VPI_{\mathbf{e}}(E_j, E_k) = VPI_{\mathbf{e}}(E_j) + VPI_{\mathbf{e},e_j}(E_k) = VPI_{\mathbf{e}}(E_k) + VPI_{\mathbf{e},e_k}(E_j)\ .$$

Order independence distinguishes sensing actions from ordinary actions and simplifies the problem of calculating the value of a sequence of sensing actions.

6.4 Implementation of an information-gathering agent

A sensible agent should ask questions in a reasonable order, should avoid asking questions that are irrelevant, should take into account the importance of each piece of information in relation to its cost, and should stop asking questions when that is appropriate. All of these capabilities can be achieved by using the value of information as a guide.

Figure 9 shows the overall design of an agent that can gather information intelligently before acting. For now, we assume that with each observable evidence variable E_j, there is an associated cost, $Cost(E_j)$, which reflects the cost of obtaining the evidence through tests, consultants, questions, or whatever. The agent requests what appears to be the most efficient observation in terms of utility gain per unit cost. We assume that the result of the action $Request(E_j)$ is that the next percept provides the value of E_j. If no observation is worth its cost, the agent selects a "real" action.

The agent algorithm we have described implements a form of information gathering that is called **myopic**. This is because it uses the VPI formula shortsightedly, calculating the value of information as if only a single evidence variable will be acquired. Myopic control is based on the same heuristic idea as greedy search and often works well in practice. (For example, it has been shown to outperform expert physicians in selecting diagnostic tests.)

MYOPIC

```
function INFORMATION-GATHERING-AGENT(percept) returns an action
  persistent: D, a decision network

  integrate percept into D
  j ← the value that maximizes VPI(E_j) / Cost(E_j)
  if VPI(E_j) > Cost(E_j)
     return REQUEST(E_j)
  else return the best action from D
```

Figure 9 Design of a simple information-gathering agent. The agent works by repeatedly selecting the observation with the highest information value, until the cost of the next observation is greater than its expected benefit.

However, if there is no single evidence variable that will help a lot, a myopic agent might hastily take an action when it would have been better to request two or more variables first and then take action. A better approach in this situation would be to construct a *conditional plan* that asks for variable values and takes different next steps depending on the answer.

One final consideration is the effect a series of questions will have on a human respondent. People may respond better to a series of questions if they "make sense," so some expert systems are built to take this into account, asking questions in an order that maximizes the total utility of the system and human rather than an order that maximizes value of information.

7 DECISION-THEORETIC EXPERT SYSTEMS

DECISION ANALYSIS

The field of **decision analysis**, which evolved in the 1950s and 1960s, studies the application of decision theory to actual decision problems. It is used to help make rational decisions in important domains where the stakes are high, such as business, government, law, military strategy, medical diagnosis and public health, engineering design, and resource management. The process involves a careful study of the possible actions and outcomes, as well as the preferences placed on each outcome. It is traditional in decision analysis to talk about two roles: the **decision maker** states preferences between outcomes, and the **decision analyst** enumerates the possible actions and outcomes and elicits preferences from the decision maker to determine the best course of action. Until the early 1980s, the main purpose of decision analysis was to help humans make decisions that actually reflect their own preferences. As more and more decision processes become automated, decision analysis is increasingly used to ensure that the automated processes are behaving as desired.

DECISION MAKER

DECISION ANALYST

Early expert system research concentrated on answering questions, rather than on making decisions. Those systems that did recommend actions rather than providing opinions on matters of fact generally did so using condition-action rules, rather than with explicit representations of outcomes and preferences. The emergence of Bayesian networks in the late 1980s made it possible to build large-scale systems that generated sound probabilistic inferences from evidence. The addition of decision networks means that expert systems can be developed that recommend optimal decisions, reflecting the preferences of the agent as well as the available evidence.

A system that incorporates utilities can avoid one of the most common pitfalls associated with the consultation process: confusing likelihood and importance. A common strategy in early medical expert systems, for example, was to rank possible diagnoses in order of likelihood and report the most likely. Unfortunately, this can be disastrous! For the majority of patients in general practice, the two most *likely* diagnoses are usually "There's nothing wrong with you" and "You have a bad cold," but if the third most likely diagnosis for a given patient is lung cancer, that's a serious matter. Obviously, a testing or treatment plan should depend both on probabilities and utilities. Current medical expert systems can take into account the value of information to recommend tests, and then describe a differential diagnosis.

We now describe the knowledge engineering process for decision-theoretic expert systems. As an example we consider the problem of selecting a medical treatment for a kind of congenital heart disease in children (see Lucas, 1996).

About 0.8% of children are born with a heart anomaly, the most common being **aortic coarctation** (a constriction of the aorta). It can be treated with surgery, angioplasty (expanding the aorta with a balloon placed inside the artery), or medication. The problem is to decide what treatment to use and when to do it: the younger the infant, the greater the risks of certain treatments, but one mustn't wait too long. A decision-theoretic expert system for this problem can be created by a team consisting of at least one domain expert (a pediatric cardiologist) and one knowledge engineer. The process can be broken down into the following steps:

AORTIC COARCTATION

Create a causal model. Determine the possible symptoms, disorders, treatments, and outcomes. Then draw arcs between them, indicating what disorders cause what symptoms, and what treatments alleviate what disorders. Some of this will be well known to the domain expert, and some will come from the literature. Often the model will match well with the informal graphical descriptions given in medical textbooks.

Simplify to a qualitative decision model. Since we are using the model to make treatment decisions and not for other purposes (such as determining the joint probability of certain symptom/disorder combinations), we can often simplify by removing variables that are not involved in treatment decisions. Sometimes variables will have to be split or joined to match the expert's intuitions. For example, the original aortic coarctation model had a *Treatment* variable with values *surgery*, *angioplasty*, and *medication*, and a separate variable for *Timing* of the treatment. But the expert had a hard time thinking of these separately, so they were combined, with *Treatment* taking on values such as *surgery in 1 month*. This gives us the model of Figure 10.

Assign probabilities. Probabilities can come from patient databases, literature studies, or the expert's subjective assessments. Note that a diagnostic system will reason from symptoms and other observations to the disease or other cause of the problems. Thus, in the early years of building these systems, experts were asked for the probability of a cause given an effect. In general they found this difficult to do, and were better able to assess the probability of an effect given a cause. So modern systems usually assess causal knowledge and encode it directly in the Bayesian network structure of the model, leaving the diagnostic reasoning to the Bayesian network inference algorithms (Shachter and Heckerman, 1987).

Assign utilities. When there are a small number of possible outcomes, they can be enumerated and evaluated individually using the methods of Section 3.1. We would create a scale from best to worst outcome and give each a numeric value, for example 0 for death and 1 for complete recovery. We would then place the other outcomes on this scale. This can be done by the expert, but it is better if the patient (or in the case of infants, the patient's parents) can be involved, because different people have different preferences. If there are exponentially many outcomes, we need some way to combine them using multiattribute utility functions. For example, we may say that the costs of various complications are additive.

Verify and refine the model. To evaluate the system we need a set of correct (input, output) pairs; a so-called **gold standard** to compare against. For medical expert systems this usually means assembling the best available doctors, presenting them with a few cases,

GOLD STANDARD

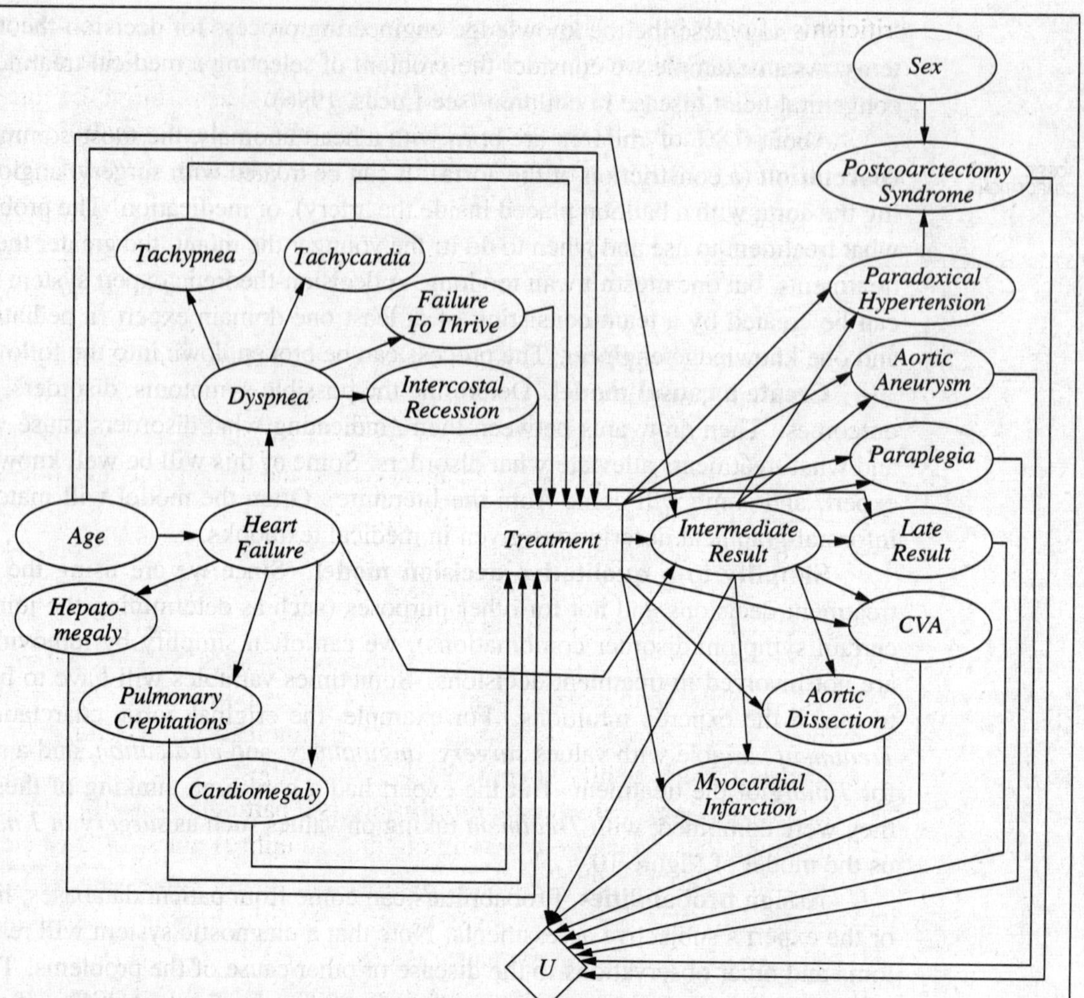

Figure 10 Influence diagram for aortic coarctation (courtesy of Peter Lucas).

and asking them for their diagnosis and recommended treatment plan. We then see how well the system matches their recommendations. If it does poorly, we try to isolate the parts that are going wrong and fix them. It can be useful to run the system "backward." Instead of presenting the system with symptoms and asking for a diagnosis, we can present it with a diagnosis such as "heart failure," examine the predicted probability of symptoms such as tachycardia, and compare with the medical literature.

SENSITIVITY ANALYSIS

Perform sensitivity analysis. This important step checks whether the best decision is sensitive to small changes in the assigned probabilities and utilities by systematically varying those parameters and running the evaluation again. If small changes lead to significantly different decisions, then it could be worthwhile to spend more resources to collect better data. If all variations lead to the same decision, then the agent will have more confidence that it is the right decision. Sensitivity analysis is particularly important, because one of the main criticisms of probabilistic approaches to expert systems is that it is too difficult to assess the numerical probabilities required. Sensitivity analysis often reveals that many of the numbers need be specified only very approximately. For example, we might be uncertain about the conditional probability $P(tachycardia \mid dyspnea)$, but if the optimal decision is reasonably robust to small variations in the probability, then our ignorance is less of a concern.

8 SUMMARY

This chapter shows how to combine utility theory with probability to enable an agent to select actions that will maximize its expected performance.

- **Probability theory** describes what an agent should believe on the basis of evidence, **utility theory** describes what an agent wants, and **decision theory** puts the two together to describe what an agent should do.
- We can use decision theory to build a system that makes decisions by considering all possible actions and choosing the one that leads to the best expected outcome. Such a system is known as a **rational agent**.
- Utility theory shows that an agent whose preferences between lotteries are consistent with a set of simple axioms can be described as possessing a utility function; furthermore, the agent selects actions as if maximizing its expected utility.
- **Multiattribute utility theory** deals with utilities that depend on several distinct attributes of states. **Stochastic dominance** is a particularly useful technique for making unambiguous decisions, even without precise utility values for attributes.
- **Decision networks** provide a simple formalism for expressing and solving decision problems. They are a natural extension of Bayesian networks, containing decision and utility nodes in addition to chance nodes.
- Sometimes, solving a problem involves finding more information before making a decision. The **value of information** is defined as the expected improvement in utility compared with making a decision without the information.
- **Expert systems** that incorporate utility information have additional capabilities compared with pure inference systems. In addition to being able to make decisions, they can use the value of information to decide which questions to ask, if any; they can recommend contingency plans; and they can calculate the sensitivity of their decisions to small changes in probability and utility assessments.

BIBLIOGRAPHICAL AND HISTORICAL NOTES

The book *L'art de Penser*, also known as the *Port-Royal Logic* (Arnauld, 1662) states:

> To judge what one must do to obtain a good or avoid an evil, it is necessary to consider not only the good and the evil in itself, but also the probability that it happens or does not happen; and to view geometrically the proportion that all these things have together.

Modern texts talk of *utility* rather than good and evil, but this statement correctly notes that one should multiply utility by probability ("view geometrically") to give expected utility, and maximize that over all outcomes ("all these things") to "judge what one must do." It is remarkable how much this got right, 350 years ago, and only 8 years after Pascal and Fermat showed how to use probability correctly. The Port-Royal Logic also marked the first publication of Pascal's wager.

Daniel Bernoulli (1738), investigating the St. Petersburg paradox (see Exercise 3), was the first to realize the importance of preference measurement for lotteries, writing "the *value* of an item must not be based on its *price*, but rather on the *utility* that it yields" (italics his). Utilitarian philosopher Jeremy Bentham (1823) proposed the **hedonic calculus** for weighing "pleasures" and "pains," arguing that all decisions (not just monetary ones) could be reduced to utility comparisons.

The derivation of numerical utilities from preferences was first carried out by Ramsey (1931); the axioms for preference in the present text are closer in form to those rediscovered in *Theory of Games and Economic Behavior* (von Neumann and Morgenstern, 1944). A good presentation of these axioms, in the course of a discussion on risk preference, is given by Howard (1977). Ramsey had derived subjective probabilities (not just utilities) from an agent's preferences; Savage (1954) and Jeffrey (1983) carry out more recent constructions of this kind. Von Winterfeldt and Edwards (1986) provide a modern perspective on decision analysis and its relationship to human preference structures. The micromort utility measure is discussed by Howard (1989). A 1994 survey by the *Economist* set the value of a life at between $750,000 and $2.6 million. However, Richard Thaler (1992) found irrational framing effects on the price one is willing to pay to avoid a risk of death versus the price one is willing to be paid to accept a risk. For a 1/1000 chance, a respondent wouldn't pay more than $200 to remove the risk, but wouldn't accept $50,000 to take on the risk. How much are people willing to pay for a QALY? When it comes down to a specific case of saving oneself or a family member, the number is approximately "whatever I've got." But we can ask at a societal level: suppose there is a vaccine that would yield X QALYs but costs Y dollars; is it worth it? In this case people report a wide range of values from around $10,000 to $150,000 per QALY (Prades *et al.*, 2008). QALYs are much more widely used in medical and social policy decision making than are micromorts; see (Russell, 1990) for a typical example of an argument for a major change in public health policy on grounds of increased expected utility measured in QALYs.

The **optimizer's curse** was brought to the attention of decision analysts in a forceful way by Smith and Winkler (2006), who pointed out that the financial benefits to the client projected by analysts for their proposed course of action almost never materialized. They trace this directly to the bias introduced by selecting an optimal action and show that a more complete Bayesian analysis eliminates the problem. The same underlying concept has been called **post-decision disappointment** by Harrison and March (1984) and was noted in the context of analyzing capital investment projects by Brown (1974). The optimizer's curse is also closely related to the **winner's curse** (Capen *et al.*, 1971; Thaler, 1992), which applies to competitive bidding in auctions: whoever wins the auction is very likely to have overestimated the value of the object in question. Capen *et al.* quote a petroleum engineer on the

POST-DECISION DISAPPOINTMENT

WINNER'S CURSE

topic of bidding for oil-drilling rights: "If one wins a tract against two or three others he may feel fine about his good fortune. But how should he feel if he won against 50 others? Ill."

REGRESSION TO THE MEAN

Finally, behind both curses is the general phenomenon of **regression to the mean**, whereby individuals selected on the basis of exceptional characteristics previously exhibited will, with high probability, become less exceptional in future.

The Allais paradox, due to Nobel Prize-winning economist Maurice Allais (1953) was tested experimentally (Tversky and Kahneman, 1982; Conlisk, 1989) to show that people are consistently inconsistent in their judgments. The Ellsberg paradox on ambiguity aversion was introduced in the Ph.D. thesis of Daniel Ellsberg (Ellsberg, 1962), who went on to become a military analyst at the RAND Corporation and to leak documents known as The Pentagon Papers, which contributed to the end of the Vietnam war and the resignation of President Nixon. Fox and Tversky (1995) describe a further study of ambiguity aversion. Mark Machina (2005) gives an overview of choice under uncertainty and how it can vary from expected utility theory.

There has been a recent outpouring of more-or-less popular books on human irrationality. The best known is *Predictably Irrational* (Ariely, 2009); others include *Sway* (Brafman and Brafman, 2009), *Nudge* (Thaler and Sunstein, 2009), *Kluge* (Marcus, 2009), *How We Decide* (Lehrer, 2009) and *On Being Certain* (Burton, 2009). They complement the classic (Kahneman *et al.*, 1982) and the article that started it all (Kahneman and Tversky, 1979). The field of evolutionary psychology (Buss, 2005), on the other hand, has run counter to this literature, arguing that humans are quite rational in evolutionarily appropriate contexts. Its adherents point out that irrationality is penalized by definition in an evolutionary context and show that in some cases it is an artifact of the experimental setup (Cummins and Allen, 1998). There has been a recent resurgence of interest in Bayesian models of cognition, overturning decades of pessimism (Oaksford and Chater, 1998; Elio, 2002; Chater and Oaksford, 2008).

Keeney and Raiffa (1976) give a thorough introduction to multiattribute utility theory. They describe early computer implementations of methods for eliciting the necessary parameters for a multiattribute utility function and include extensive accounts of real applications of the theory. In AI, the principal reference for MAUT is Wellman's (1985) paper, which includes a system called URP (Utility Reasoning Package) that can use a collection of statements about preference independence and conditional independence to analyze the structure of decision problems. The use of stochastic dominance together with qualitative probability models was investigated extensively by Wellman (1988, 1990a). Wellman and Doyle (1992) provide a preliminary sketch of how a complex set of utility-independence relationships might be used to provide a structured model of a utility function, in much the same way that Bayesian networks provide a structured model of joint probability distributions. Bacchus and Grove (1995, 1996) and La Mura and Shoham (1999) give further results along these lines.

Decision theory has been a standard tool in economics, finance, and management science since the 1950s. Until the 1980s, decision trees were the main tool used for representing simple decision problems. Smith (1988) gives an overview of the methodology of decision analysis. Influence diagrams were introduced by Howard and Matheson (1984), based on earlier work at SRI (Miller *et al.*, 1976). Howard and Matheson's method involved the derivation of a decision tree from a decision network, but in general the tree is of exponential size. Shachter (1986) developed a method for making decisions based directly on a decision network, without the creation of an intermediate decision tree. This algorithm was also one of the first to provide complete inference for multiply connected Bayesian networks. Zhang *et al.* (1994) showed how to take advantage of conditional independence of information to reduce the size of trees in practice; they use the term *decision network* for networks that use this approach (although others use it as a synonym for influence diagram). Nilsson and Lauritzen (2000) link algorithms for decision networks to ongoing developments in clustering algorithms for Bayesian networks. Koller and Milch (2003) show how influence diagrams can be used to solve games that involve gathering information by opposing players, and Detwarasiti and Shachter (2005) show how influence diagrams can be used as an aid to decision making for a team that shares goals but is unable to share all information perfectly. The collection by Oliver and Smith (1990) has a number of useful articles on decision networks, as does the 1990 special issue of the journal *Networks*. Papers on decision networks and utility modeling also appear regularly in the journals *Management Science* and *Decision Analysis*.

The theory of information value was explored first in the context of statistical experiments, where a quasi-utility (entropy reduction) was used (Lindley, 1956). The Russian control theorist Ruslan Stratonovich (1965) developed the more general theory presented here, in which information has value by virtue of its ability to affect decisions. Stratonovich's work was not known in the West, where Ron Howard (1966) pioneered the same idea. His paper ends with the remark "If information value theory and associated decision theoretic structures do not in the future occupy a large part of the education of engineers, then the engineering profession will find that its traditional role of managing scientific and economic resources for the benefit of man has been forfeited to another profession." To date, the implied revolution in managerial methods has not occurred.

Recent work by Krause and Guestrin (2009) shows that computing the exact nonmyopic value of information is intractable even in polytree networks. There are other cases—more restricted than general value of information—in which the myopic algorithm does provide a provably good approximation to the optimal sequence of observations (Krause *et al.*, 2008). In some cases—for example, looking for treasure buried in one of n places—ranking experiments in order of success probability divided by cost gives an optimal solution (Kadane and Simon, 1977).

Surprisingly few early AI researchers adopted decision-theoretic tools after the early applications in medical decision making. One of the few exceptions was Jerry Feldman, who applied decision theory to problems in vision (Feldman and Yakimovsky, 1974) and planning (Feldman and Sproull, 1977). After the resurgence of interest in probabilistic methods in AI in the 1980s, decision-theoretic expert systems gained widespread acceptance (Horvitz *et al.*, 1988; Cowell *et al.*, 2002). In fact, from 1991 onward, the cover design of the journal *Artificial Intelligence* has depicted a decision network, although some artistic license appears to have been taken with the direction of the arrows.

EXERCISES

1 (Adapted from David Heckerman.) This exercise concerns the **Almanac Game**, which is used by decision analysts to calibrate numeric estimation. For each of the questions that follow, give your best guess of the answer, that is, a number that you think is as likely to be too high as it is to be too low. Also give your guess at a 25th percentile estimate, that is, a number that you think has a 25% chance of being too high, and a 75% chance of being too low. Do the same for the 75th percentile. (Thus, you should give three estimates in all—low, median, and high—for each question.)

a. Number of passengers who flew between New York and Los Angeles in 1989.

b. Population of Warsaw in 1992.

c. Year in which Coronado discovered the Mississippi River.

d. Number of votes received by Jimmy Carter in the 1976 presidential election.

e. Age of the oldest living tree, as of 2002.

f. Height of the Hoover Dam in feet.

g. Number of eggs produced in Oregon in 1985.

h. Number of Buddhists in the world in 1992.

i. Number of deaths due to AIDS in the United States in 1981.

j. Number of U.S. patents granted in 1901.

The correct answers appear after the last exercise of this chapter. From the point of view of decision analysis, the interesting thing is not how close your median guesses came to the real answers, but rather how often the real answer came within your 25% and 75% bounds. If it was about half the time, then your bounds are accurate. But if you're like most people, you will be more sure of yourself than you should be, and fewer than half the answers will fall within the bounds. With practice, you can calibrate yourself to give realistic bounds, and thus be more useful in supplying information for decision making. Try this second set of questions and see if there is any improvement:

a. Year of birth of Zsa Zsa Gabor.

b. Maximum distance from Mars to the sun in miles.

c. Value in dollars of exports of wheat from the United States in 1992.

d. Tons handled by the port of Honolulu in 1991.

e. Annual salary in dollars of the governor of California in 1993.

f. Population of San Diego in 1990.

g. Year in which Roger Williams founded Providence, Rhode Island.

h. Height of Mt. Kilimanjaro in feet.

i. Length of the Brooklyn Bridge in feet.

j. Number of deaths due to automobile accidents in the United States in 1992.

2 Chris considers four used cars before buying the one with maximum expected utility. Pat considers ten cars and does the same. All other things being equal, which one is more likely to have the better car? Which is more likely to be disappointed with their car's quality? By how much (in terms of standard deviations of expected quality)?

3 In 1713, Nicolas Bernoulli stated a puzzle, now called the St. Petersburg paradox, which works as follows. You have the opportunity to play a game in which a fair coin is tossed repeatedly until it comes up heads. If the first heads appears on the nth toss, you win 2^n dollars.

- **a.** Show that the expected monetary value of this game is infinite.
- **b.** How much would you, personally, pay to play the game?
- **c.** Nicolas's cousin Daniel Bernoulli resolved the apparent paradox in 1738 by suggesting that the utility of money is measured on a logarithmic scale (i.e., $U(S_n) = a \log_2 n + b$, where S_n is the state of having \$$n$). What is the expected utility of the game under this assumption?
- **d.** What is the maximum amount that it would be rational to pay to play the game, assuming that one's initial wealth is \$$k$?

4 Write a computer program to automate the process in Exercise 9. Try your program out on several people of different net worth and political outlook. Comment on the consistency of your results, both for an individual and across individuals.

5 The Surprise Candy Company makes candy in two flavors: 70% are strawberry flavor and 30% are anchovy flavor. Each new piece of candy starts out with a round shape; as it moves along the production line, a machine randomly selects a certain percentage to be trimmed into a square; then, each piece is wrapped in a wrapper whose color is chosen randomly to be red or brown. 80% of the strawberry candies are round and 80% have a red wrapper, while 90% of the anchovy candies are square and 90% have a brown wrapper. All candies are sold individually in sealed, identical, black boxes.

Now you, the customer, have just bought a Surprise candy at the store but have not yet opened the box. Consider the three Bayes nets in Figure 11.

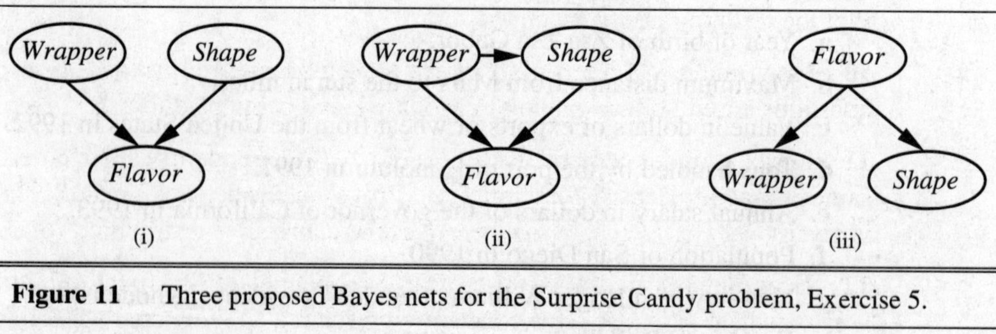

Figure 11 Three proposed Bayes nets for the Surprise Candy problem, Exercise 5.

- **a.** Which network(s) can correctly represent $\mathbf{P}(Flavor, Wrapper, Shape)$?
- **b.** Which network is the best representation for this problem?

c. Does network (i) assert that $\mathbf{P}(Wrapper|Shape) = \mathbf{P}(Wrapper)$?

d. What is the probability that your candy has a red wrapper?

e. In the box is a round candy with a red wrapper. What is the probability that its flavor is strawberry?

f. A unwrapped strawberry candy is worth s on the open market and an unwrapped anchovy candy is worth a. Write an expression for the value of an unopened candy box.

g. A new law prohibits trading of unwrapped candies, but it is still legal to trade wrapped candies (out of the box). Is an unopened candy box now worth more than less than, or the same as before?

6 Prove that the judgments $B \succ A$ and $C \succ D$ in the Allais paradox violate the axiom of substitutability.

7 Consider the Allais paradox: an agent who prefers B over A (taking the sure thing), and C over D (taking the higher EMV) is not acting rationally, according to utility theory. Do you think this indicates a problem for the agent, a problem for the theory, or no problem at all? Explain.

8 Tickets to a lottery cost \$1. There are two possible prizes: a \$10 payoff with probability 1/50, and a \$1,000,000 payoff with probability 1/2,000,000. What is the expected monetary value of a lottery ticket? When (if ever) is it rational to buy a ticket? Be precise—show an equation involving utilities. You may assume current wealth of \$$k$ and that $U(S_k) = 0$. You may also assume that $U(S_{k+10}) = 10 \times U(S_{k+1})$, but you may not make any assumptions about $U(S_{k+1,000,000})$. Sociological studies show that people with lower income buy a disproportionate number of lottery tickets. Do you think this is because they are worse decision makers or because they have a different utility function? Consider the value of contemplating the possibility of winning the lottery versus the value of contemplating becoming an action hero while watching an adventure movie.

9 Assess your own utility for different incremental amounts of money by running a series of preference tests between some definite amount M_1 and a lottery $[p, M_2; (1-p), 0]$. Choose different values of M_1 and M_2, and vary p until you are indifferent between the two choices. Plot the resulting utility function.

10 How much is a micromort worth to you? Devise a protocol to determine this. Ask questions based both on paying to avoid risk and being paid to accept risk.

11 Let continuous variables $X_1, \ldots, X_k$ be independently distributed according to the same probability density function $f(x)$. Prove that the density function for $\max\{X_1, \ldots, X_k\}$ is given by $kf(x)(F(x))^{k-1}$, where F is the cumulative distribution for f.

12 Economists often make use of an exponential utility function for money: $U(x) = -e^{x/R}$, where R is a positive constant representing an individual's risk tolerance. Risk tolerance reflects how likely an individual is to accept a lottery with a particular expected monetary value (EMV) versus some certain payoff. As R (which is measured in the same units as x) becomes larger, the individual becomes less risk-averse.

a. Assume Mary has an exponential utility function with $R = \$500$. Mary is given the choice between receiving \$500 with certainty (probability 1) or participating in a lottery which has a 60% probability of winning \$5000 and a 40% probability of winning nothing. Assuming Marry acts rationally, which option would she choose? Show how you derived your answer.

b. Consider the choice between receiving \$100 with certainty (probability 1) or participating in a lottery which has a 50% probability of winning \$500 and a 50% probability of winning nothing. Approximate the value of R (to 3 significant digits) in an exponential utility function that would cause an individual to be indifferent to these two alternatives. (You might find it helpful to write a short program to help you solve this problem.)

13 Repeat Exercise 16, using the action-utility representation shown in Figure 7.

14 For either of the airport-siting diagrams from Exercises 16 and 13, to which conditional probability table entry is the utility most sensitive, given the available evidence?

15 Consider a student who has the choice to buy or not buy a textbook for a course. We'll model this as a decision problem with one Boolean decision node, B, indicating whether the agent chooses to buy the book, and two Boolean chance nodes, M, indicating whether the student has mastered the material in the book, and P, indicating whether the student passes the course. Of course, there is also a utility node, U. A certain student, Sam, has an additive utility function: 0 for not buying the book and -\$100 for buying it; and \$2000 for passing the course and 0 for not passing. Sam's conditional probability estimates are as follows:

$$P(p|b,m) = 0.9 \qquad P(m|b) = 0.9$$
$$P(p|b,\neg m) = 0.5 \qquad P(m|\neg b) = 0.7$$
$$P(p|\neg b,m) = 0.8$$
$$P(p|\neg b,\neg m) = 0.3$$

You might think that P would be independent of B given M, But this course has an open-book final—so having the book helps.

a. Draw the decision network for this problem.

b. Compute the expected utility of buying the book and of not buying it.

c. What should Sam do?

16 This exercise completes the analysis of the airport-siting problem in Figure 6.

a. Provide reasonable variable domains, probabilities, and utilities for the network, assuming that there are three possible sites.

b. Solve the decision problem.

c. What happens if changes in technology mean that each aircraft generates half the noise?

d. What if noise avoidance becomes three times more important?

e. Calculate the VPI for *AirTraffic*, *Litigation*, and *Construction* in your model.

17 (Adapted from Pearl (1988).) A used-car buyer can decide to carry out various tests with various costs (e.g., kick the tires, take the car to a qualified mechanic) and then, depending on the outcome of the tests, decide which car to buy. We will assume that the buyer is deciding whether to buy car c_1, that there is time to carry out at most one test, and that t_1 is the test of c_1 and costs \$50.

A car can be in good shape (quality q^+) or bad shape (quality q^-), and the tests might help indicate what shape the car is in. Car c_1 costs \$1,500, and its market value is \$2,000 if it is in good shape; if not, \$700 in repairs will be needed to make it in good shape. The buyer's estimate is that c_1 has a 70% chance of being in good shape.

a. Draw the decision network that represents this problem.

b. Calculate the expected net gain from buying c_1, given no test.

c. Tests can be described by the probability that the car will pass or fail the test given that the car is in good or bad shape. We have the following information:
$P(pass(c_1, t_1)|q^+(c_1)) = 0.8$
$P(pass(c_1, t_1)|q^-(c_1)) = 0.35$
Use Bayes' theorem to calculate the probability that the car will pass (or fail) its test and hence the probability that it is in good (or bad) shape given each possible test outcome.

d. Calculate the optimal decisions given either a pass or a fail, and their expected utilities.

e. Calculate the value of information of the test, and derive an optimal conditional plan for the buyer.

18 Recall the definition of *value of information* in Section 6.

a. Prove that the value of information is nonnegative and order independent.

b. Explain why it is that some people would prefer not to get some information—for example, not wanting to know the sex of their baby when an ultrasound is done.

SUBMODULARITY

c. A function f on sets is **submodular** if, for any element x and any sets A and B such that $A \subseteq B$, adding x to A gives a greater increase in f than adding x to B:

$$A \subseteq B \Rightarrow (f(A \cup \{x\}) - f(A)) \geq (f(B \cup \{x\}) - f(B)).$$

Submodularity captures the intuitive notion of *diminishing returns*. Is the value of information, viewed as a function f on sets of possible observations, submodular? Prove this or find a counterexample.

The answers to Exercise 1 (where M stands for million): First set: 3M, 1.6M, 1541, 41M, 4768, 221, 649M, 295M, 132, 25,546. Second set: 1917, 155M, 4,500M, 11M, 120,000, 1.1M, 1636, 19,340, 1,595, 41,710.

MAKING COMPLEX DECISIONS

In which we examine methods for deciding what to do today, given that we may decide again tomorrow.

In this chapter, we address the computational issues involved in making decisions in a stochastic environment. Instead of concerning ourselves with one-shot or episodic decision problems, in which the utility of each action's outcome was well known, we are concerned here with **sequential decision problems**, in which the agent's utility depends on a sequence of decisions. Sequential decision problems incorporate utilities, uncertainty, and sensing, and include search and planning problems as special cases. Section 1 explains how sequential decision problems are defined, and Sections 2 and 3 explain how they can be solved to produce optimal behavior that balances the risks and rewards of acting in an uncertain environment. Section 4 extends these ideas to the case of partially observable environments, and Section 4.3 develops a complete design for decision-theoretic agents in partially observable environments, combining dynamic Bayesian networks with decision networks.

SEQUENTIAL DECISION PROBLEM

The second part of the chapter covers environments with multiple agents. In such environments, the notion of optimal behavior is complicated by the interactions among the agents. Section 5 introduces the main ideas of **game theory**, including the idea that rational agents might need to behave randomly. Section 6 looks at how multiagent systems can be designed so that multiple agents can achieve a common goal.

1 SEQUENTIAL DECISION PROBLEMS

Suppose that an agent is situated in the 4×3 environment shown in Figure 1(a). Beginning in the start state, it must choose an action at each time step. The interaction with the environment terminates when the agent reaches one of the goal states, marked +1 or –1. Just as for search problems, the actions available to the agent in each state are given by $\text{ACTIONS}(s)$, sometimes abbreviated to $A(s)$; in the 4×3 environment, the actions in every state are *Up*, *Down*, *Left*, and *Right*. We assume for now that the environment is **fully observable**, so that the agent always knows where it is.

From Chapter 17 of *Artificial Intelligence: A Modern Approach*, Third Edition. Stuart Russell and Peter Norvig.

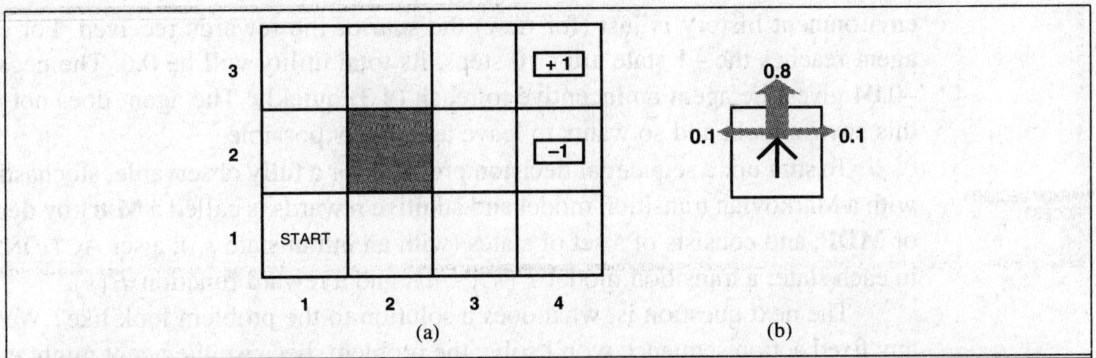

Figure 1 (a) A simple 4×3 environment that presents the agent with a sequential decision problem. (b) Illustration of the transition model of the environment: the "intended" outcome occurs with probability 0.8, but with probability 0.2 the agent moves at right angles to the intended direction. A collision with a wall results in no movement. The two terminal states have reward +1 and –1, respectively, and all other states have a reward of –0.04.

If the environment were deterministic, a solution would be easy: [*Up, Up, Right, Right, Right*]. Unfortunately, the environment won't always go along with this solution, because the actions are unreliable. The particular model of stochastic motion that we adopt is illustrated in Figure 1(b). Each action achieves the intended effect with probability 0.8, but the rest of the time, the action moves the agent at right angles to the intended direction. Furthermore, if the agent bumps into a wall, it stays in the same square. For example, from the start square (1,1), the action *Up* moves the agent to (1,2) with probability 0.8, but with probability 0.1, it moves right to (2,1), and with probability 0.1, it moves left, bumps into the wall, and stays in (1,1). In such an environment, the sequence $[Up, Up, Right, Right, Right]$ goes up around the barrier and reaches the goal state at (4,3) with probability $0.8^5 = 0.32768$. There is also a small chance of accidentally reaching the goal by going the other way around with probability $0.1^4 \times 0.8$, for a grand total of 0.32776. (See also Exercise 1.)

The **transition model** (or just "model," whenever no confusion can arise) describes the outcome of each action in each state. Here, the outcome is stochastic, so we write $P(s' \mid s, a)$ to denote the probability of reaching state s' if action a is done in state s. We will assume that transitions are **Markovian,** that is, the probability of reaching s' from s depends only on s and not on the history of earlier states. For now, you can think of $P(s' \mid s, a)$ as a big three-dimensional table containing probabilities. Later, in Section 4.3, we will see that the transition model can be represented as a **dynamic Bayesian network**.

To complete the definition of the task environment, we must specify the utility function for the agent. Because the decision problem is sequential, the utility function will depend on a sequence of states—an **environment history**—rather than on a single state. Later in this section, we investigate how such utility functions can be specified in general; for now, REWARD we simply stipulate that in each state s, the agent receives a **reward** $R(s)$, which may be positive or negative, but must be bounded. For our particular example, the reward is -0.04 in all states except the terminal states (which have rewards +1 and –1). The utility of an environment history is just (for now) the *sum* of the rewards received. For example, if the agent reaches the +1 state after 10 steps, its total utility will be 0.6. The negative reward of –0.04 gives the agent an incentive to reach (4,3) quickly. The agent does not enjoy living in this environment and so wants to leave as soon as possible.

MARKOV DECISION PROCESS

To sum up: a sequential decision problem for a fully observable, stochastic environment with a Markovian transition model and additive rewards is called a **Markov decision process**, or **MDP**, and consists of a set of states (with an initial state s_0); a set $\text{ACTIONS}(s)$ of actions in each state; a transition model $P(s' \mid s, a)$; and a reward function $R(s)$.[1]

POLICY

The next question is, what does a solution to the problem look like? We have seen that any fixed action sequence won't solve the problem, because the agent might end up in a state other than the goal. Therefore, a solution must specify what the agent should do for *any* state that the agent might reach. A solution of this kind is called a **policy**. It is traditional to denote a policy by π, and $\pi(s)$ is the action recommended by the policy π for state s. If the agent has a complete policy, then no matter what the outcome of any action, the agent will always know what to do next.

OPTIMAL POLICY

Each time a given policy is executed starting from the initial state, the stochastic nature of the environment may lead to a different environment history. The quality of a policy is therefore measured by the *expected* utility of the possible environment histories generated by that policy. An **optimal policy** is a policy that yields the highest expected utility. We use π^* to denote an optimal policy. Given π^*, the agent decides what to do by consulting its current percept, which tells it the current state s, and then executing the action $\pi^*(s)$. A policy represents the agent function explicitly and is therefore a description of a simple reflex agent, computed from the information used for a utility-based agent.

An optimal policy for the world of Figure 1 is shown in Figure 2(a). Notice that, because the cost of taking a step is fairly small compared with the penalty for ending up in (4,2) by accident, the optimal policy for the state (3,1) is conservative. The policy recommends taking the long way round, rather than taking the shortcut and thereby risking entering (4,2).

The balance of risk and reward changes depending on the value of $R(s)$ for the nonterminal states. Figure 2(b) shows optimal policies for four different ranges of $R(s)$. When $R(s) \leq -1.6284$, life is so painful that the agent heads straight for the nearest exit, even if the exit is worth –1. When $-0.4278 \leq R(s) \leq -0.0850$, life is quite unpleasant; the agent takes the shortest route to the +1 state and is willing to risk falling into the –1 state by accident. In particular, the agent takes the shortcut from (3,1). When life is only slightly dreary $(-0.0221 < R(s) < 0)$, the optimal policy takes *no risks at all*. In (4,1) and (3,2), the agent heads directly away from the –1 state so that it cannot fall in by accident, even though this means banging its head against the wall quite a few times. Finally, if $R(s) > 0$, then life is positively enjoyable and the agent avoids *both* exits. As long as the actions in (4,1), (3,2),

[1] Some definitions of MDPs allow the reward to depend on the action and outcome too, so the reward function is $R(s, a, s')$. This simplifies the description of some environments but does not change the problem in any fundamental way, as shown in Exercise 4.

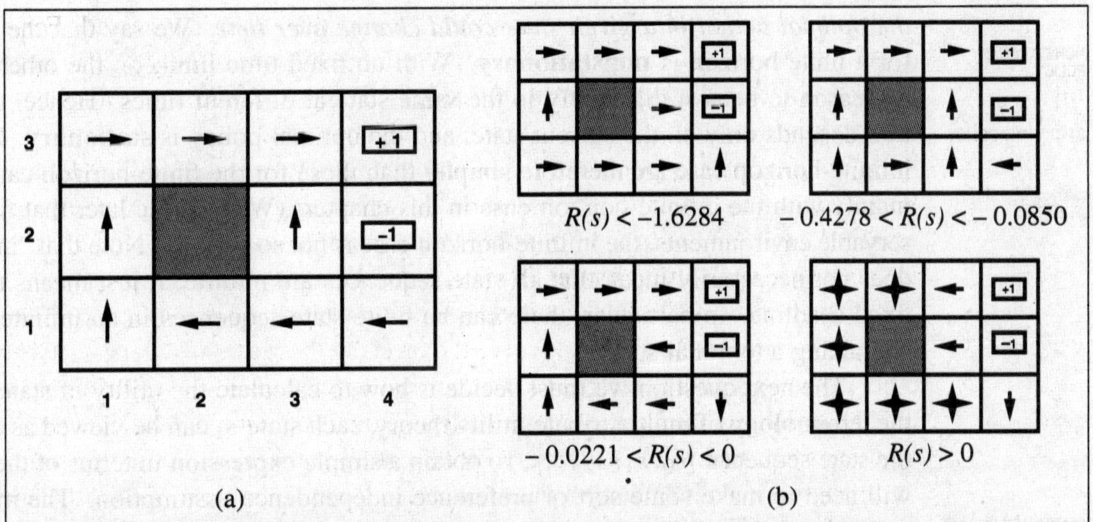

Figure 2 (a) An optimal policy for the stochastic environment with $R(s) = -0.04$ in the nonterminal states. (b) Optimal policies for four different ranges of $R(s)$.

and (3,3) are as shown, every policy is optimal, and the agent obtains infinite total reward because it never enters a terminal state. Surprisingly, it turns out that there are six other optimal policies for various ranges of $R(s)$; Exercise 5 asks you to find them.

The careful balancing of risk and reward is a characteristic of MDPs that does not arise in deterministic search problems; moreover, it is a characteristic of many real-world decision problems. For this reason, MDPs have been studied in several fields, including AI, operations research, economics, and control theory. Dozens of algorithms have been proposed for calculating optimal policies. In sections 2 and 3 we describe two of the most important algorithm families. First, however, we must complete our investigation of utilities and policies for sequential decision problems.

1.1 Utilities over time

In the MDP example in Figure 1, the performance of the agent was measured by a sum of rewards for the states visited. This choice of performance measure is not arbitrary, but it is not the only possibility for the utility function on environment histories, which we write as $U_h([s_0, s_1, \ldots, s_n])$. Our analysis draws on **multiattribute utility theory** and is somewhat technical; the impatient reader may wish to skip to the next section.

FINITE HORIZON
INFINITE HORIZON

The first question to answer is whether there is a **finite horizon** or an **infinite horizon** for decision making. A finite horizon means that there is a *fixed* time N after which nothing matters—the game is over, so to speak. Thus, $U_h([s_0, s_1, \ldots, s_{N+k}]) = U_h([s_0, s_1, \ldots, s_N])$ for all $k > 0$. For example, suppose an agent starts at (3,1) in the 4×3 world of Figure 1, and suppose that $N = 3$. Then, to have any chance of reaching the +1 state, the agent must head directly for it, and the optimal action is to go *Up*. On the other hand, if $N = 100$, then there is plenty of time to take the safe route by going *Left*. *So, with a finite horizon,*

NONSTATIONARY POLICY

the optimal action in a given state could change over time. We say that the optimal policy for a finite horizon is **nonstationary**. With no fixed time limit, on the other hand, there is no reason to behave differently in the same state at different times. Hence, the optimal action depends only on the current state, and the optimal policy is **stationary**. Policies for the infinite-horizon case are therefore simpler than those for the finite-horizon case, and we deal mainly with the infinite-horizon case in this chapter. (We will see later that for partially observable environments, the infinite-horizon case is not so simple.) Note that "infinite horizon" does not necessarily mean that all state sequences are infinite; it just means that there is no fixed deadline. In particular, there can be finite state sequences in an infinite-horizon MDP containing a terminal state.

STATIONARY POLICY

The next question we must decide is how to calculate the utility of state sequences. In the terminology of multiattribute utility theory, each state s_i can be viewed as an **attribute** of the state sequence $[s_0, s_1, s_2 \ldots]$. To obtain a simple expression in terms of the attributes, we will need to make some sort of preference-independence assumption. The most natural assumption is that the agent's preferences between state sequences are **stationary**. Stationarity for preferences means the following: if two state sequences $[s_0, s_1, s_2, \ldots]$ and $[s'_0, s'_1, s'_2, \ldots]$ begin with the same state (i.e., $s_0 = s'_0$), then the two sequences should be preference-ordered the same way as the sequences $[s_1, s_2, \ldots]$ and $[s'_1, s'_2, \ldots]$. In English, this means that if you prefer one future to another starting tomorrow, then you should still prefer that future if it were to start today instead. Stationarity is a fairly innocuous-looking assumption with very strong consequences: it turns out that under stationarity there are just two coherent ways to assign utilities to sequences:

STATIONARY PREFERENCE

ADDITIVE REWARD

1. **Additive rewards**: The utility of a state sequence is

$$U_h([s_0, s_1, s_2, \ldots]) = R(s_0) + R(s_1) + R(s_2) + \cdots .$$

The 4×3 world in Figure 1 uses additive rewards. Notice that additivity was used implicitly in our use of path cost functions in heuristic search algorithms.

DISCOUNTED REWARD

2. **Discounted rewards**: The utility of a state sequence is

$$U_h([s_0, s_1, s_2, \ldots]) = R(s_0) + \gamma R(s_1) + \gamma^2 R(s_2) + \cdots ,$$

DISCOUNT FACTOR

where the **discount factor** γ is a number between 0 and 1. The discount factor describes the preference of an agent for current rewards over future rewards. When γ is close to 0, rewards in the distant future are viewed as insignificant. When γ is 1, discounted rewards are exactly equivalent to additive rewards, so additive rewards are a special case of discounted rewards. Discounting appears to be a good model of both animal and human preferences over time. A discount factor of γ is equivalent to an interest rate of $(1/\gamma) - 1$.

For reasons that will shortly become clear, we assume discounted rewards in the remainder of the chapter, although sometimes we allow $\gamma = 1$.

Lurking beneath our choice of infinite horizons is a problem: if the environment does not contain a terminal state, or if the agent never reaches one, then all environment histories will be infinitely long, and utilities with additive, undiscounted rewards will generally be infinite. While we can agree that $+\infty$ is better than $-\infty$, comparing two state sequences with $+\infty$ utility is more difficult. There are three solutions, two of which we have seen already:

1. With discounted rewards, the utility of an infinite sequence is *finite*. In fact, if $\gamma < 1$ and rewards are bounded by $\pm R_{\max}$, we have
$$U_h([s_0, s_1, s_2, \ldots]) = \sum_{t=0}^{\infty} \gamma^t R(s_t) \leq \sum_{t=0}^{\infty} \gamma^t R_{\max} = R_{\max}/(1-\gamma)\,, \qquad (1)$$
using the standard formula for the sum of an infinite geometric series.

2. If the environment contains terminal states *and if the agent is guaranteed to get to one eventually*, then we will never need to compare infinite sequences. A policy that is guaranteed to reach a terminal state is called a **proper policy**. With proper policies, we can use $\gamma = 1$ (i.e., additive rewards). The first three policies shown in Figure 2(b) are proper, but the fourth is improper. It gains infinite total reward by staying away from the terminal states when the reward for the nonterminal states is positive. The existence of improper policies can cause the standard algorithms for solving MDPs to fail with additive rewards, and so provides a good reason for using discounted rewards.

PROPER POLICY

AVERAGE REWARD

3. Infinite sequences can be compared in terms of the **average reward** obtained per time step. Suppose that square (1,1) in the 4×3 world has a reward of 0.1 while the other nonterminal states have a reward of 0.01. Then a policy that does its best to stay in (1,1) will have higher average reward than one that stays elsewhere. Average reward is a useful criterion for some problems, but the analysis of average-reward algorithms is beyond the scope of this text.

In sum, discounted rewards present the fewest difficulties in evaluating state sequences.

1.2 Optimal policies and the utilities of states

Having decided that the utility of a given state sequence is the sum of discounted rewards obtained during the sequence, we can compare policies by comparing the *expected* utilities obtained when executing them. We assume the agent is in some initial state s and define S_t (a random variable) to be the state the agent reaches at time t when executing a particular policy π. (Obviously, $S_0 = s$, the state the agent is in now.) The probability distribution over state sequences $S_1, S_2, \ldots$, is determined by the initial state s, the policy π, and the transition model for the environment.

The expected utility obtained by executing π starting in s is given by
$$U^{\pi}(s) = E\left[\sum_{t=0}^{\infty} \gamma^t R(S_t)\right]\,, \qquad (2)$$
where the expectation is with respect to the probability distribution over state sequences determined by s and π. Now, out of all the policies the agent could choose to execute starting in s, one (or more) will have higher expected utilities than all the others. We'll use π_s^* to denote one of these policies:
$$\pi_s^* = \operatorname*{argmax}_{\pi} U^{\pi}(s)\,. \qquad (3)$$

Remember that π^*_s is a policy, so it recommends an action for every state; its connection with s in particular is that it's an optimal policy when s is the starting state. A remarkable consequence of using discounted utilities with infinite horizons is that the optimal policy is *independent* of the starting state. (Of course, the *action sequence* won't be independent; remember that a policy is a function specifying an action for each state.) This fact seems intuitively obvious: if policy π^*_a is optimal starting in a and policy π^*_b is optimal starting in b, then, when they reach a third state c, there's no good reason for them to disagree with each other, or with π^*_c, about what to do next.[2] So we can simply write π^* for an optimal policy.

Given this definition, the true utility of a state is just $U^{\pi^*}(s)$—that is, the expected sum of discounted rewards if the agent executes an optimal policy. We write this as $U(s)$, matching the notation for the utility of an outcome. Notice that $U(s)$ and $R(s)$ are quite different quantities; $R(s)$ is the "short term" reward for being in s, whereas $U(s)$ is the "long term" total reward from s onward. Figure 3 shows the utilities for the 4×3 world. Notice that the utilities are higher for states closer to the +1 exit, because fewer steps are required to reach the exit.

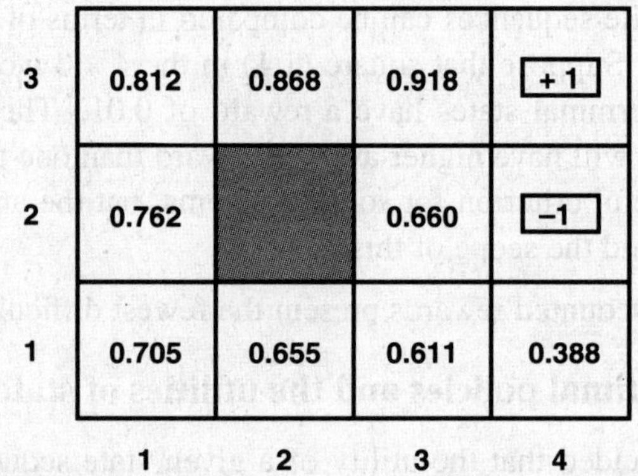

Figure 3 The utilities of the states in the 4×3 world, calculated with $\gamma = 1$ and $R(s) = -0.04$ for nonterminal states.

The utility function $U(s)$ allows the agent to select actions by using the principle of maximum expected utility—that is, choose the action that maximizes the expected utility of the subsequent state:

$$\pi^*(s) = \underset{a \in A(s)}{\operatorname{argmax}} \sum_{s'} P(s' \mid s, a) U(s') . \tag{4}$$

The next two sections describe algorithms for finding optimal policies.

[2] Although this seems obvious, it does not hold for finite-horizon policies or for other ways of combining rewards over time. The proof follows directly from the uniqueness of the utility function on states, as shown in Section 2.

2 VALUE ITERATION

VALUE ITERATION

In this section, we present an algorithm, called **value iteration**, for calculating an optimal policy. The basic idea is to calculate the utility of each state and then use the state utilities to select an optimal action in each state.

2.1 The Bellman equation for utilities

Section 1.2 defined the utility of being in a state as the expected sum of discounted rewards from that point onwards. From this, it follows that there is a direct relationship between the utility of a state and the utility of its neighbors: *the utility of a state is the immediate reward for that state plus the expected discounted utility of the next state, assuming that the agent chooses the optimal action.* That is, the utility of a state is given by

$$U(s) = R(s) + \gamma \max_{a \in A(s)} \sum_{s'} P(s' \mid s, a) U(s') . \tag{5}$$

BELLMAN EQUATION

This is called the **Bellman equation**, after Richard Bellman (1957). The utilities of the states—defined by Equation (2) as the expected utility of subsequent state sequences—are solutions of the set of Bellman equations. In fact, they are the *unique* solutions, as we show in Section 2.3.

Let us look at one of the Bellman equations for the 4×3 world. The equation for the state (1,1) is

$$\begin{aligned} U(1,1) = -0.04 + \gamma \max[\ & 0.8U(1,2) + 0.1U(2,1) + 0.1U(1,1), && (Up)\\ & 0.9U(1,1) + 0.1U(1,2), && (Left)\\ & 0.9U(1,1) + 0.1U(2,1), && (Down)\\ & 0.8U(2,1) + 0.1U(1,2) + 0.1U(1,1)\ ]. && (Right) \end{aligned}$$

When we plug in the numbers from Figure 3, we find that *Up* is the best action.

2.2 The value iteration algorithm

The Bellman equation is the basis of the value iteration algorithm for solving MDPs. If there are n possible states, then there are n Bellman equations, one for each state. The n equations contain n unknowns—the utilities of the states. So we would like to solve these simultaneous equations to find the utilities. There is one problem: the equations are *nonlinear*, because the "max" operator is not a linear operator. Whereas systems of linear equations can be solved quickly using linear algebra techniques, systems of nonlinear equations are more problematic. One thing to try is an *iterative* approach. We start with arbitrary initial values for the utilities, calculate the right-hand side of the equation, and plug it into the left-hand side—thereby updating the utility of each state from the utilities of its neighbors. We repeat this until we reach an equilibrium. Let $U_i(s)$ be the utility value for state s at the ith iteration. The iteration step, called a **Bellman update**, looks like this:

BELLMAN UPDATE

$$U_{i+1}(s) \leftarrow R(s) + \gamma \max_{a \in A(s)} \sum_{s'} P(s' \mid s, a) U_i(s') , \tag{6}$$

function VALUE-ITERATION(mdp, ϵ) **returns** a utility function
  inputs: mdp, an MDP with states S, actions $A(s)$, transition model $P(s' \mid s, a)$,
    rewards $R(s)$, discount γ
    ϵ, the maximum error allowed in the utility of any state
  local variables: U, U', vectors of utilities for states in S, initially zero
    δ, the maximum change in the utility of any state in an iteration

  repeat
    $U \leftarrow U'$; $\delta \leftarrow 0$
    for each state s **in** S **do**
      $U'[s] \leftarrow R(s) + \gamma \max_{a \in A(s)} \sum_{s'} P(s' \mid s, a)\, U[s']$
      if $|U'[s] - U[s]| > \delta$ **then** $\delta \leftarrow |U'[s] - U[s]|$
  until $\delta < \epsilon(1-\gamma)/\gamma$
  return U

Figure 4 The value iteration algorithm for calculating utilities of states. The termination condition is from Equation (8).

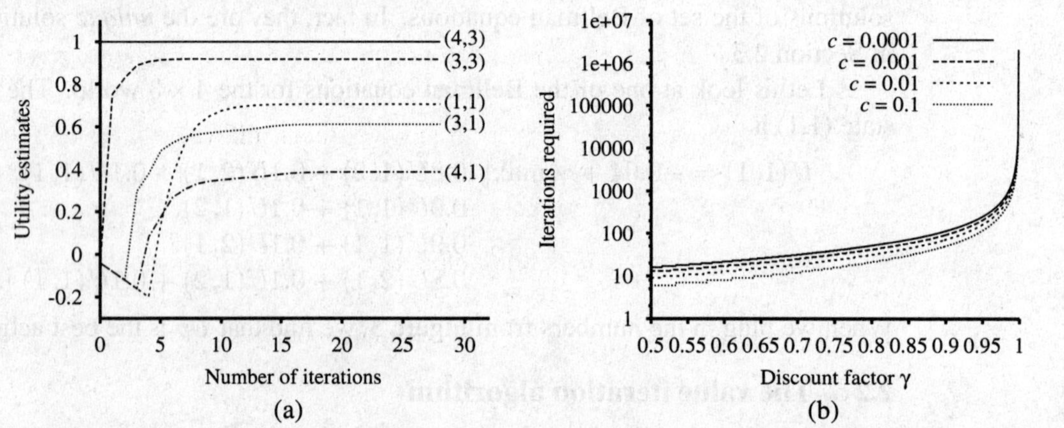

Figure 5 (a) Graph showing the evolution of the utilities of selected states using value iteration. (b) The number of value iterations k required to guarantee an error of at most $\epsilon = c \cdot R_{\max}$, for different values of c, as a function of the discount factor γ.

where the update is assumed to be applied simultaneously to all the states at each iteration. If we apply the Bellman update infinitely often, we are guaranteed to reach an equilibrium (see Section 2.3), in which case the final utility values must be solutions to the Bellman equations. In fact, they are also the *unique* solutions, and the corresponding policy (obtained using Equation (4)) is optimal. The algorithm, called VALUE-ITERATION, is shown in Figure 4.

We can apply value iteration to the 4×3 world in Figure 1(a). Starting with initial values of zero, the utilities evolve as shown in Figure 5(a). Notice how the states at different distances from (4,3) accumulate negative reward until a path is found to (4,3), whereupon the utilities start to increase. We can think of the value iteration algorithm as *propagating information* through the state space by means of local updates.

2.3 Convergence of value iteration

We said that value iteration eventually converges to a unique set of solutions of the Bellman equations. In this section, we explain why this happens. We introduce some useful mathematical ideas along the way, and we obtain some methods for assessing the error in the utility function returned when the algorithm is terminated early; this is useful because it means that we don't have to run forever. This section is quite technical.

CONTRACTION

The basic concept used in showing that value iteration converges is the notion of a **contraction**. Roughly speaking, a contraction is a function of one argument that, when applied to two different inputs in turn, produces two output values that are "closer together," by at least some constant factor, than the original inputs. For example, the function "divide by two" is a contraction, because, after we divide any two numbers by two, their difference is halved. Notice that the "divide by two" function has a fixed point, namely zero, that is unchanged by the application of the function. From this example, we can discern two important properties of contractions:

- A contraction has only one fixed point; if there were two fixed points they would not get closer together when the function was applied, so it would not be a contraction.
- When the function is applied to any argument, the value must get closer to the fixed point (because the fixed point does not move), so repeated application of a contraction always reaches the fixed point in the limit.

Now, suppose we view the Bellman update (Equation (6)) as an operator B that is applied simultaneously to update the utility of every state. Let U_i denote the vector of utilities for all the states at the ith iteration. Then the Bellman update equation can be written as

$$U_{i+1} \leftarrow B\,U_i\,.$$

MAX NORM

Next, we need a way to measure distances between utility vectors. We will use the **max norm**, which measures the "length" of a vector by the absolute value of its biggest component:

$$||U|| = \max_s |U(s)|\,.$$

With this definition, the "distance" between two vectors, $||U - U'||$, is the maximum difference between any two corresponding elements. The main result of this section is the following: *Let U_i and U_i' be any two utility vectors. Then we have*

$$||B\,U_i - B\,U_i'|| \leq \gamma\,||U_i - U_i'||\,. \tag{7}$$

That is, the Bellman update is a contraction by a factor of γ on the space of utility vectors. (Exercise 6 provides some guidance on proving this claim.) Hence, from the properties of contractions in general, it follows that value iteration always converges to a unique solution of the Bellman equations whenever $\gamma < 1$.

We can also use the contraction property to analyze the *rate* of convergence to a solution. In particular, we can replace U_i' in Equation (7) with the *true* utilities U, for which $B\,U = U$. Then we obtain the inequality

$$||B\,U_i - U|| \leq \gamma\,||U_i - U||\,.$$

So, if we view $||U_i - U||$ as the *error* in the estimate U_i, we see that the error is reduced by a factor of at least γ on each iteration. This means that value iteration converges exponentially fast. We can calculate the number of iterations required to reach a specified error bound ϵ as follows: First, recall from Equation (1) that the utilities of all states are bounded by $\pm R_{\max}/(1-\gamma)$. This means that the maximum initial error $||U_0 - U|| \leq 2R_{\max}/(1-\gamma)$. Suppose we run for N iterations to reach an error of at most ϵ. Then, because the error is reduced by at least γ each time, we require $\gamma^N \cdot 2R_{\max}/(1-\gamma) \leq \epsilon$. Taking logs, we find

$$N = \lceil \log(2R_{\max}/\epsilon(1-\gamma))/\log(1/\gamma)\rceil$$

iterations suffice. Figure 5(b) shows how N varies with γ, for different values of the ratio $\epsilon/R_{\max}$. The good news is that, because of the exponentially fast convergence, N does not depend much on the ratio $\epsilon/R_{\max}$. The bad news is that N grows rapidly as γ becomes close to 1. We can get fast convergence if we make γ small, but this effectively gives the agent a short horizon and could miss the long-term effects of the agent's actions.

The error bound in the preceding paragraph gives some idea of the factors influencing the run time of the algorithm, but is sometimes overly conservative as a method of deciding when to stop the iteration. For the latter purpose, we can use a bound relating the error to the size of the Bellman update on any given iteration. From the contraction property (Equation (7)), it can be shown that if the update is small (i.e., no state's utility changes by much), then the error, compared with the true utility function, also is small. More precisely,

$$\text{if} \quad ||U_{i+1} - U_i|| < \epsilon(1-\gamma)/\gamma \quad \text{then} \quad ||U_{i+1} - U|| < \epsilon\,. \qquad (8)$$

This is the termination condition used in the VALUE-ITERATION algorithm of Figure 4.

So far, we have analyzed the error in the utility function returned by the value iteration algorithm. *What the agent really cares about, however, is how well it will do if it makes its decisions on the basis of this utility function.* Suppose that after i iterations of value iteration, the agent has an estimate U_i of the true utility U and obtains the MEU policy π_i based on one-step look-ahead using U_i (as in Equation (4)). Will the resulting behavior be nearly as good as the optimal behavior? This is a crucial question for any real agent, and it turns out that the answer is yes. $U^{\pi_i}(s)$ is the utility obtained if π_i is executed starting in s, and the

POLICY LOSS

policy loss $||U^{\pi_i} - U||$ is the most the agent can lose by executing π_i instead of the optimal policy π^*. The policy loss of π_i is connected to the error in U_i by the following inequality:

$$\text{if} \quad ||U_i - U|| < \epsilon \quad \text{then} \quad ||U^{\pi_i} - U|| < 2\epsilon\gamma/(1-\gamma)\,. \qquad (9)$$

In practice, it often occurs that π_i becomes optimal long before U_i has converged. Figure 6 shows how the maximum error in U_i and the policy loss approach zero as the value iteration process proceeds for the 4×3 environment with $\gamma = 0.9$. The policy π_i is optimal when $i = 4$, even though the maximum error in U_i is still 0.46.

Now we have everything we need to use value iteration in practice. We know that it converges to the correct utilities, we can bound the error in the utility estimates if we stop after a finite number of iterations, and we can bound the policy loss that results from executing the corresponding MEU policy. As a final note, all of the results in this section depend on discounting with $\gamma < 1$. If $\gamma = 1$ and the environment contains terminal states, then a similar set of convergence results and error bounds can be derived whenever certain technical conditions are satisfied.

3 POLICY ITERATION

In the previous section, we observed that it is possible to get an optimal policy even when the utility function estimate is inaccurate. If one action is clearly better than all others, then the exact magnitude of the utilities on the states involved need not be precise. This insight suggests an alternative way to find optimal policies. The **policy iteration** algorithm alternates the following two steps, beginning from some initial policy π_0:

POLICY ITERATION

- **Policy evaluation**: given a policy π_i, calculate $U_i = U^{\pi_i}$, the utility of each state if π_i were to be executed.

POLICY EVALUATION

- **Policy improvement**: Calculate a new MEU policy π_{i+1}, using one-step look-ahead based on U_i (as in Equation (4)).

POLICY IMPROVEMENT

The algorithm terminates when the policy improvement step yields no change in the utilities. At this point, we know that the utility function U_i is a fixed point of the Bellman update, so it is a solution to the Bellman equations, and π_i must be an optimal policy. Because there are only finitely many policies for a finite state space, and each iteration can be shown to yield a better policy, policy iteration must terminate. The algorithm is shown in Figure 7.

The policy improvement step is obviously straightforward, but how do we implement the POLICY-EVALUATION routine? It turns out that doing so is much simpler than solving the standard Bellman equations (which is what value iteration does), because the action in each state is fixed by the policy. At the ith iteration, the policy π_i specifies the action $\pi_i(s)$ in

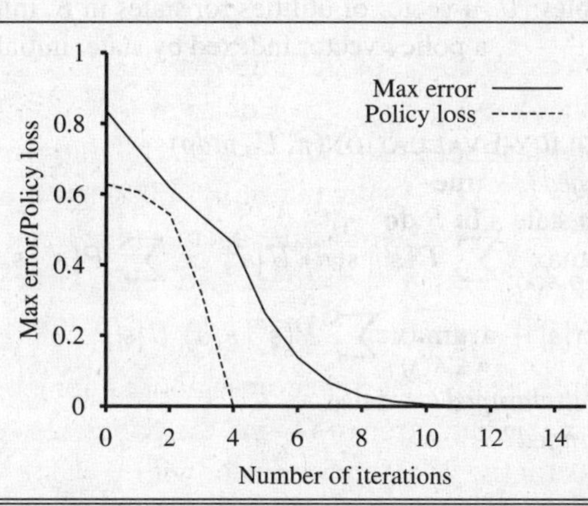

Figure 6 The maximum error $||U_i - U||$ of the utility estimates and the policy loss $||U^{\pi_i} - U||$, as a function of the number of iterations of value iteration.

state s. This means that we have a simplified version of the Bellman equation (5) relating the utility of s (under π_i) to the utilities of its neighbors:

$$U_i(s) = R(s) + \gamma \sum_{s'} P(s' \mid s, \pi_i(s)) U_i(s') . \qquad (10)$$

For example, suppose π_i is the policy shown in Figure 2(a). Then we have $\pi_i(1,1) = Up$, $\pi_i(1,2) = Up$, and so on, and the simplified Bellman equations are

$$\begin{aligned} U_i(1,1) &= -0.04 + 0.8U_i(1,2) + 0.1U_i(1,1) + 0.1U_i(2,1) , \\ U_i(1,2) &= -0.04 + 0.8U_i(1,3) + 0.2U_i(1,2) , \\ &\vdots \end{aligned}$$

The important point is that these equations are *linear*, because the "max" operator has been removed. For n states, we have n linear equations with n unknowns, which can be solved exactly in time $O(n^3)$ by standard linear algebra methods.

For small state spaces, policy evaluation using exact solution methods is often the most efficient approach. For large state spaces, $O(n^3)$ time might be prohibitive. Fortunately, it is not necessary to do *exact* policy evaluation. Instead, we can perform some number of simplified value iteration steps (simplified because the policy is fixed) to give a reasonably good approximation of the utilities. The simplified Bellman update for this process is

$$U_{i+1}(s) \leftarrow R(s) + \gamma \sum_{s'} P(s' \mid s, \pi_i(s)) U_i(s') ,$$

and this is repeated k times to produce the next utility estimate. The resulting algorithm is called **modified policy iteration**. It is often much more efficient than standard policy iteration or value iteration.

MODIFIED POLICY ITERATION

```
function POLICY-ITERATION(mdp) returns a policy
  inputs: mdp, an MDP with states S, actions A(s), transition model P(s' | s, a)
  local variables: U, a vector of utilities for states in S, initially zero
                   π, a policy vector indexed by state, initially random

  repeat
     U ← POLICY-EVALUATION(π, U, mdp)
     unchanged? ← true
     for each state s in S do
        if max_{a ∈ A(s)} Σ_{s'} P(s' | s, a) U[s'] > Σ_{s'} P(s' | s, π[s]) U[s'] then do
           π[s] ← argmax_{a ∈ A(s)} Σ_{s'} P(s' | s, a) U[s']
           unchanged? ← false
  until unchanged?
  return π
```

Figure 7 The policy iteration algorithm for calculating an optimal policy.

The algorithms we have described so far require updating the utility or policy for all states at once. It turns out that this is not strictly necessary. In fact, on each iteration, we can pick *any subset* of states and apply *either* kind of updating (policy improvement or simplified value iteration) to that subset. This very general algorithm is called **asynchronous policy iteration**. Given certain conditions on the initial policy and initial utility function, asynchronous policy iteration is guaranteed to converge to an optimal policy. The freedom to choose any states to work on means that we can design much more efficient heuristic algorithms—for example, algorithms that concentrate on updating the values of states that are likely to be reached by a good policy. This makes a lot of sense in real life: if one has no intention of throwing oneself off a cliff, one should not spend time worrying about the exact value of the resulting states.

ASYNCHRONOUS POLICY ITERATION

4 Partially Observable MDPs

The description of Markov decision processes in Section 1 assumed that the environment was **fully observable**. With this assumption, the agent always knows which state it is in. This, combined with the Markov assumption for the transition model, means that the optimal policy depends only on the current state. When the environment is only **partially observable**, the situation is, one might say, much less clear. The agent does not necessarily know which state it is in, so it cannot execute the action $\pi(s)$ recommended for that state. Furthermore, the utility of a state s and the optimal action in s depend not just on s, but also on *how much the agent knows* when it is in s. For these reasons, **partially observable MDPs** (or POMDPs—pronounced "pom-dee-pees") are usually viewed as much more difficult than ordinary MDPs. We cannot avoid POMDPs, however, because the real world is one.

PARTIALLY OBSERVABLE MDP

4.1 Definition of POMDPs

To get a handle on POMDPs, we must first define them properly. A POMDP has the same elements as an MDP—the transition model $P(s' \mid s, a)$, actions $A(s)$, and reward function $R(s)$—but it also has a **sensor model** $P(e \mid s)$. Here the sensor model specifies the probability of perceiving evidence e in state s.[3] For example, we can convert the 4×3 world of Figure 1 into a POMDP by adding a noisy or partial sensor instead of assuming that the agent knows its location exactly. Such a sensor might measure the *number of adjacent walls*, which happens to be 2 in all the nonterminal squares except for those in the third column, where the value is 1; a noisy version might give the wrong value with probability 0.1.

Recall that the **belief state**—the set of actual states the agent might be in—is a key concept for describing and calculating solutions. In POMDPs, the belief state b becomes a *probability distribution* over all possible states. For example, the initial

[3] As with the reward function for MDPs, the sensor model can also depend on the action and outcome state, but again this change is not fundamental.

belief state for the 4×3 POMDP could be the uniform distribution over the nine nonterminal states, i.e., $\langle \frac{1}{9}, \frac{1}{9}, \frac{1}{9}, \frac{1}{9}, \frac{1}{9}, \frac{1}{9}, \frac{1}{9}, \frac{1}{9}, \frac{1}{9}, 0, 0 \rangle$. We write $b(s)$ for the probability assigned to the actual state s by belief state b. The agent can calculate its current belief state as the conditional probability distribution over the actual states given the sequence of percepts and actions so far. For POMDPs, we also have an action to consider, but the result is essentially the same. If $b(s)$ was the previous belief state, and the agent does action a and then perceives evidence e, then the new belief state is given by

$$b'(s') = \alpha\, P(e \mid s') \sum_{s} P(s' \mid s, a) b(s) ,$$

where α is a normalizing constant that makes the belief state sum to 1. By analogy with the update operator for filtering, we can write this as

$$b' = \text{FORWARD}(b, a, e) . \tag{11}$$

In the 4×3 POMDP, suppose the agent moves *Left* and its sensor reports 1 adjacent wall; then it's quite likely (although not guaranteed, because both the motion and the sensor are noisy) that the agent is now in (3,1). Exercise 13 asks you to calculate the exact probability values for the new belief state.

The fundamental insight required to understand POMDPs is this: *the optimal action depends only on the agent's current belief state.* That is, the optimal policy can be described by a mapping $\pi^*(b)$ from belief states to actions. It does *not* depend on the *actual* state the agent is in. This is a good thing, because the agent does not know its actual state; all it knows is the belief state. Hence, the decision cycle of a POMDP agent can be broken down into the following three steps:

1. Given the current belief state b, execute the action $a = \pi^*(b)$.
2. Receive percept e.
3. Set the current belief state to $\text{FORWARD}(b, a, e)$ and repeat.

Now we can think of POMDPs as requiring a search in belief-state space, just like the methods for sensorless and contingency problems. The main difference is that the POMDP belief-state space is *continuous*, because a POMDP belief state is a probability distribution. For example, a belief state for the 4×3 world is a point in an 11-dimensional continuous space. An action changes the belief state, not just the physical state. Hence, the action is evaluated at least in part according to the information the agent acquires as a result. POMDPs therefore include the value of information as one component of the decision problem.

Let's look more carefully at the outcome of actions. In particular, let's calculate the probability that an agent in belief state b reaches belief state b' after executing action a. Now, if we knew the action *and the subsequent percept*, then Equation (11) would provide a *deterministic* update to the belief state: $b' = \text{FORWARD}(b, a, e)$. Of course, the subsequent percept is not yet known, so the agent might arrive in one of several possible belief states b', depending on the percept that is received. The probability of perceiving e, given that a was performed starting in belief state b, is given by summing over all the actual states s' that the agent might reach:

$$\begin{aligned} P(e|a,b) &= \sum_{s'} P(e|a,s',b)P(s'|a,b) \\ &= \sum_{s'} P(e \mid s')P(s'|a,b) \\ &= \sum_{s'} P(e \mid s') \sum_{s} P(s' \mid s,a)b(s) \,. \end{aligned}$$

Let us write the probability of reaching b' from b, given action a, as $P(b' \mid b, a))$. Then that gives us

$$\begin{aligned} P(b' \mid b,a) \;=\; P(b'|a,b) &= \sum_{e} P(b'|e,a,b)P(e|a,b) \\ &= \sum_{e} P(b'|e,a,b) \sum_{s'} P(e \mid s') \sum_{s} P(s' \mid s,a)b(s) \,, \end{aligned} \qquad (12)$$

where $P(b'|e, a, b)$ is 1 if $b' = \text{FORWARD}(b, a, e)$ and 0 otherwise.

Equation (12) can be viewed as defining a transition model for the belief-state space. We can also define a reward function for belief states (i.e., the expected reward for the actual states the agent might be in):

$$\rho(b) = \sum_{s} b(s)R(s) \,.$$

Together, $P(b' \mid b, a)$ and $\rho(b)$ define an *observable* MDP on the space of belief states. Furthermore, it can be shown that an optimal policy for this MDP, $\pi^*(b)$, is also an optimal policy for the original POMDP. In other words, *solving a POMDP on a physical state space can be reduced to solving an MDP on the corresponding belief-state space.* This fact is perhaps less surprising if we remember that the belief state is always observable to the agent, by definition.

Notice that, although we have reduced POMDPs to MDPs, the MDP we obtain has a continuous (and usually high-dimensional) state space. None of the MDP algorithms described in Sections 2 and 3 applies directly to such MDPs. The next two subsections describe a value iteration algorithm designed specifically for POMDPs and an online decision-making algorithm.

4.2 Value iteration for POMDPs

Section 2 described a value iteration algorithm that computed one utility value for each state. With infinitely many belief states, we need to be more creative. Consider an optimal policy π^* and its application in a specific belief state b: the policy generates an action, then, for each subsequent percept, the belief state is updated and a new action is generated, and so on. For this specific b, therefore, the policy is exactly equivalent to a **conditional plan**, as defined for nondeterministic and partially observable problems. Instead of thinking about policies, let us think about conditional plans and how the expected utility of executing a fixed conditional plan varies with the initial belief state. We make two observations:

1. Let the utility of executing a *fixed* conditional plan p starting in physical state s be $\alpha_p(s)$. Then the expected utility of executing p in belief state b is just $\sum_s b(s)\alpha_p(s)$, or $b \cdot \alpha_p$ if we think of them both as vectors. Hence, the expected utility of a fixed conditional plan varies *linearly* with b; that is, it corresponds to a hyperplane in belief space.
2. At any given belief state b, the optimal policy will choose to execute the conditional plan with highest expected utility; and the expected utility of b under the optimal policy is just the utility of that conditional plan:

$$U(b) = U^{\pi^*}(b) = \max_p b \cdot \alpha_p .$$

If the optimal policy π^* chooses to execute p starting at b, then it is reasonable to expect that it might choose to execute p in belief states that are very close to b; in fact, if we bound the depth of the conditional plans, then there are only finitely many such plans and the continuous space of belief states will generally be divided into *regions*, each corresponding to a particular conditional plan that is optimal in that region.

From these two observations, we see that the utility function $U(b)$ on belief states, being the maximum of a collection of hyperplanes, will be *piecewise linear* and *convex*.

To illustrate this, we use a simple two-state world. The states are labeled 0 and 1, with $R(0) = 0$ and $R(1) = 1$. There are two actions: *Stay* stays put with probability 0.9 and *Go* switches to the other state with probability 0.9. For now we will assume the discount factor $\gamma = 1$. The sensor reports the correct state with probability 0.6. Obviously, the agent should *Stay* when it thinks it's in state 1 and *Go* when it thinks it's in state 0.

The advantage of a two-state world is that the belief space can be viewed as one-dimensional, because the two probabilities must sum to 1. In Figure 8(a), the x-axis represents the belief state, defined by $b(1)$, the probability of being in state 1. Now let us consider the one-step plans $[Stay]$ and $[Go]$, each of which receives the reward for the current state followed by the (discounted) reward for the state reached after the action:

$$\begin{aligned}
\alpha_{[Stay]}(0) &= R(0) + \gamma(0.9R(0) + 0.1R(1)) = 0.1 \\
\alpha_{[Stay]}(1) &= R(1) + \gamma(0.9R(1) + 0.1R(0)) = 1.9 \\
\alpha_{[Go]}(0) &= R(0) + \gamma(0.9R(1) + 0.1R(0)) = 0.9 \\
\alpha_{[Go]}(1) &= R(1) + \gamma(0.9R(0) + 0.1R(1)) = 1.1
\end{aligned}$$

The hyperplanes (lines, in this case) for $b \cdot \alpha_{[Stay]}$ and $b \cdot \alpha_{[Go]}$ are shown in Figure 8(a) and their maximum is shown in bold. The bold line therefore represents the utility function for the finite-horizon problem that allows just one action, and in each "piece" of the piecewise linear utility function the optimal action is the first action of the corresponding conditional plan. In this case, the optimal one-step policy is to *Stay* when $b(1) > 0.5$ and *Go* otherwise.

Once we have utilities $\alpha_p(s)$ for all the conditional plans p of depth 1 in each physical state s, we can compute the utilities for conditional plans of depth 2 by considering each possible first action, each possible subsequent percept, and then each way of choosing a depth-1 plan to execute for each percept:

[*Stay*; **if** *Percept* = 0 **then** *Stay* **else** *Stay*]

[*Stay*; **if** *Percept* = 0 **then** *Stay* **else** *Go*] . . .

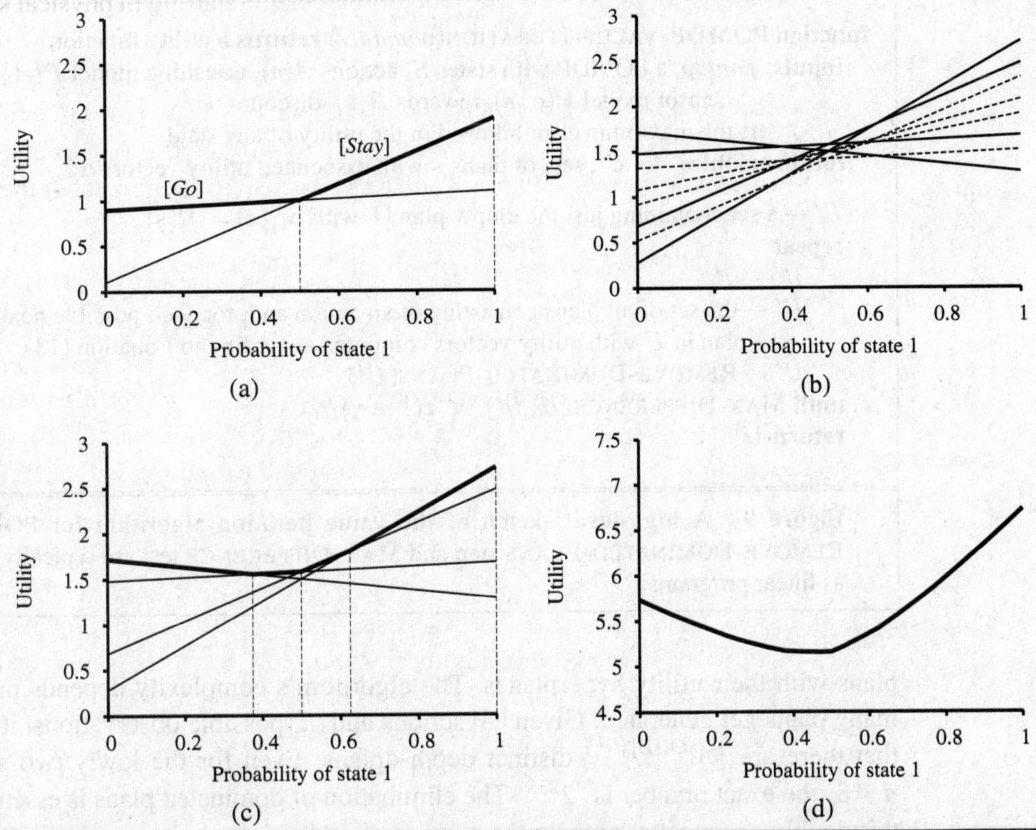

Figure 8 (a) Utility of two one-step plans as a function of the initial belief state $b(1)$ for the two-state world, with the corresponding utility function shown in bold. (b) Utilities for 8 distinct two-step plans. (c) Utilities for four undominated two-step plans. (d) Utility function for optimal eight-step plans.

There are eight distinct depth-2 plans in all, and their utilities are shown in Figure 8(b). Notice that four of the plans, shown as dashed lines, are suboptimal across the entire belief space—we say these plans are **dominated**, and they need not be considered further. There are four undominated plans, each of which is optimal in a specific region, as shown in Figure 8(c). The regions partition the belief-state space.

DOMINATED PLAN

We repeat the process for depth 3, and so on. In general, let p be a depth-d conditional plan whose initial action is a and whose depth-$d-1$ subplan for percept e is $p.e$; then

$$\alpha_p(s) = R(s) + \gamma \left(\sum_{s'} P(s' \mid s, a) \sum_{e} P(e \mid s') \alpha_{p.e}(s') \right) . \tag{13}$$

This recursion naturally gives us a value iteration algorithm, which is sketched in Figure 9. The structure of the algorithm and its error analysis are similar to those of the basic value iteration algorithm in Figure 4; the main difference is that instead of computing one utility number for each state, POMDP-VALUE-ITERATION maintains a collection of undominated

```
function POMDP-VALUE-ITERATION(pomdp, ε) returns a utility function
  inputs: pomdp, a POMDP with states S, actions A(s), transition model P(s' | s, a),
            sensor model P(e | s), rewards R(s), discount γ
          ε, the maximum error allowed in the utility of any state
  local variables: U, U', sets of plans p with associated utility vectors α_p

  U' ← a set containing just the empty plan [], with α_[](s) = R(s)
  repeat
      U ← U'
      U' ← the set of all plans consisting of an action and, for each possible next percept,
          a plan in U with utility vectors computed according to Equation (13)
      U' ← REMOVE-DOMINATED-PLANS(U')
  until MAX-DIFFERENCE(U, U') < ε(1 − γ)/γ
  return U
```

Figure 9 A high-level sketch of the value iteration algorithm for POMDPs. The REMOVE-DOMINATED-PLANS step and MAX-DIFFERENCE test are typically implemented as linear programs.

plans with their utility hyperplanes. The algorithm's complexity depends primarily on how many plans get generated. Given $|A|$ actions and $|E|$ possible observations, it is easy to show that there are $|A|^{O(|E|^{d\ 1})}$ distinct depth-dplans. Even for the lowly two-state world with $d=8$, the exact number is 2^{255}. The elimination of dominated plans is essential for reducing this doubly exponential growth: the number of undominated plans with $d=8$ is just 144. The utility function for these 144 plans is shown in Figure 8(d).

Notice that even though state 0 has lower utility than state 1, the intermediate belief states have even lower utility because the agent lacks the information needed to choose a good action. This is why information has value and optimal policies in POMDPs often include information-gathering actions.

Given such a utility function, an executable policy can be extracted by looking at which hyperplane is optimal at any given belief state b and executing the first action of the corresponding plan. In Figure 8(d), the corresponding optimal policy is still the same as for depth-1 plans: *Stay* when $b(1) > 0.5$ and *Go* otherwise.

In practice, the value iteration algorithm in Figure 9 is hopelessly inefficient for larger problems—even the 4×3 POMDP is too hard. The main reason is that, given n conditional plans at level d, the algorithm constructs $|A| \cdot n^{|E|}$ conditional plans at level $d+1$ before eliminating the dominated ones. Since the 1970s, when this algorithm was developed, there have been several advances including more efficient forms of value iteration and various kinds of policy iteration algorithms. Some of these are discussed in the notes at the end of the chapter. For general POMDPs, however, finding optimal policies is very difficult (PSPACE-hard, in fact—i.e., very hard indeed). Problems with a few dozen states are often infeasible. The next section describes a different, approximate method for solving POMDPs, one based on look-ahead search.

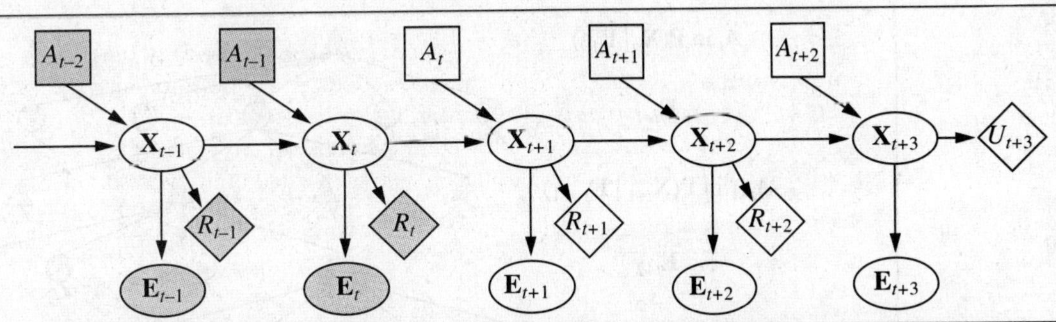

Figure 10 The generic structure of a dynamic decision network. Variables with known values are shaded. The current time is t and the agent must decide what to do—that is, choose a value for A_t. The network has been unrolled into the future for three steps and represents future rewards, as well as the utility of the state at the look-ahead horizon.

4.3 Online agents for POMDPs

In this section, we outline a simple approach to agent design for partially observable, stochastic environments. The basic elements of the design are already familiar:

- The transition and sensor models are represented by a **dynamic Bayesian network** (DBN).
- The dynamic Bayesian network is extended with decision and utility nodes, as used in **decision networks**. The resulting model is called a **dynamic decision network**, or DDN.

DYNAMIC DECISION NETWORK

- A filtering algorithm is used to incorporate each new percept and action and to update the belief state representation.
- Decisions are made by projecting forward possible action sequences and choosing the best one.

DBNs are **factored representations:** they typically have an exponential complexity advantage over atomic representations and can model quite substantial real-world problems. The agent design is therefore a practical implementation of the **utility-based agent**.

In the DBN, the single state S_t becomes a set of state variables $\mathbf{X}_t$, and there may be multiple evidence variables $\mathbf{E}_t$. We will use A_t to refer to the action at time t, so the transition model becomes $\mathbf{P}(\mathbf{X}_{t+1}|\mathbf{X}_t, A_t)$ and the sensor model becomes $\mathbf{P}(\mathbf{E}_t|\mathbf{X}_t)$. We will use R_t to refer to the reward received at time t and U_t to refer to the utility of the state at time t. (Both of these are random variables.) With this notation, a dynamic decision network looks like the one shown in Figure 10.

Dynamic decision networks can be used as inputs for any POMDP algorithm, including those for value and policy iteration methods. In this section, we focus on look-ahead methods that project action sequences forward from the current belief state. The network in Figure 10 has been projected three steps into the future; the current and future decisions A and the future observations

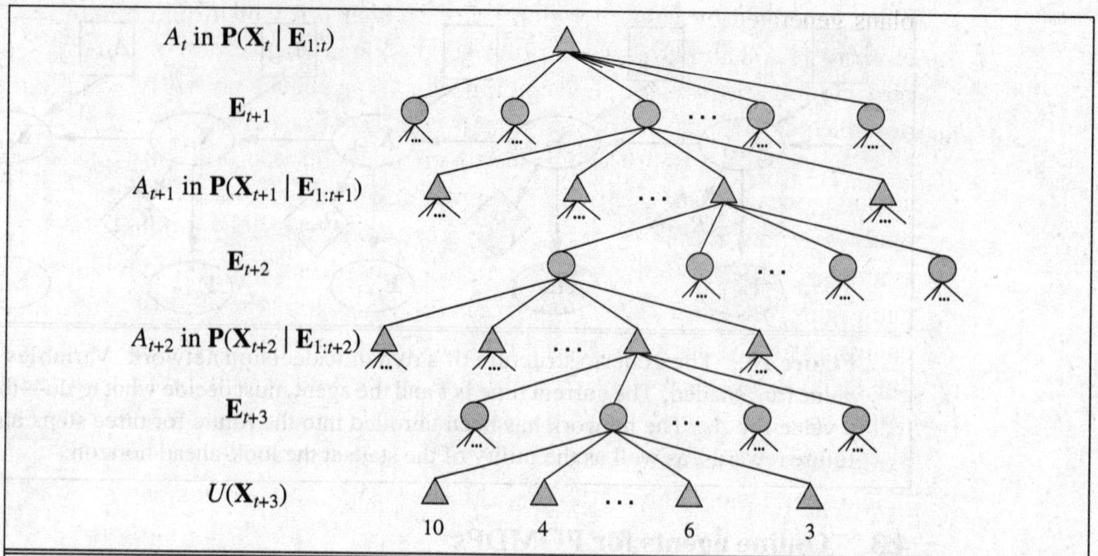

Figure 11 Part of the look-ahead solution of the DDN in Figure 10. Each decision will be taken in the belief state indicated.

$\mathbf{E}$ and rewards R are all unknown. Notice that the network includes nodes for the *rewards* for $\mathbf{X}_{t+1}$ and $\mathbf{X}_{t+2}$, but the *utility* for $\mathbf{X}_{t+3}$. This is because the agent must maximize the (discounted) sum of all future rewards, and $U(\mathbf{X}_{t+3})$ represents the reward for $\mathbf{X}_{t+3}$ and all subsequent rewards. We assume that U is available only in some approximate form: if exact utility values were available, look-ahead beyond depth 1 would be unnecessary.

Figure 11 shows part of the search tree corresponding to the three-step look-ahead DDN in Figure 10. Each of the triangular nodes is a belief state in which the agent makes a decision A_{t+i} for $i=0,1,2,\ldots$. The round (chance) nodes correspond to choices by the environment, namely, what evidence $\mathbf{E}_{t+i}$ arrives. Notice that there are no chance nodes corresponding to the action outcomes; this is because the belief-state update for an action is deterministic regardless of the actual outcome.

The belief state at each triangular node can be computed by applying a filtering algorithm to the sequence of percepts and actions leading to it. In this way, the algorithm takes into account the fact that, for decision A_{t+i}, the agent *will* have available percepts $\mathbf{E}_{t+1},\ldots,\mathbf{E}_{t+i}$, even though at time t it does not know what those percepts will be. In this way, a decision-theoretic agent automatically takes into account the value of information and will execute information-gathering actions where appropriate.

A decision can be extracted from the search tree by backing up the utility values from the leaves, taking an average at the chance nodes and taking the maximum at the decision nodes. This is similar to the EXPECTIMINIMAX algorithm for game trees with chance nodes, except that (1) there can also be rewards at non-leaf states and (2) the decision nodes correspond to belief states rather than actual states. The time complexity of an exhaustive search to depth d is $O(|A|^d \cdot |\mathbf{E}|^d)$, where $|A|$ is the number of available actions and $|\mathbf{E}|$ is the number of possible percepts. (Notice that this is far less than the number of depth-d conditional plans generated by value iteration.) For problems in which the discount factor γ is not too close to 1, a shallow search is often good enough to give near-optimal decisions. It is also possible to approximate the averaging step at the chance nodes, by sampling from the set of possible percepts instead of summing over all possible percepts.

Decision-theoretic agents based on dynamic decision networks have a number of advantages compared with other, simpler agent designs. In particular, they handle partially observable, uncertain environments and can easily revise their "plans" to handle unexpected evidence. With appropriate sensor models, they can handle sensor failure and can plan to gather information. They exhibit "graceful degradation" under time pressure and in complex environments, using various approximation techniques. So what is missing? One defect of our DDN-based algorithm is its reliance on forward search through state space, rather than using hierarchical and other advanced planning techniques. There have been attempts to extend these techniques into the probabilistic domain, but so far they have proved to be inefficient. A second, related problem is the basically propositional nature of the DDN language. We would like to be able to extend some of the ideas for first-order probabilistic languages to the problem of decision making. Current research has shown that this extension is possible and has significant benefits, as discussed in the notes at the end of the chapter.

5 Decisions with Multiple Agents: Game Theory

This chapter has concentrated on making decisions in uncertain environments. But what if the uncertainty is due to other agents and the decisions they make? And what if the decisions of those agents are in turn influenced by our decisions? In this section we study the aspects of **game theory** that analyze games with simultaneous moves and other sources of partial observability. (Game theorists use the terms **perfect information** and **imperfect information** rather than fully and partially observable.) Game theory can be used in at least two ways:

GAME THEORY

1. **Agent design**: Game theory can analyze the agent's decisions and compute the expected utility for each decision (under the assumption that other agents are acting optimally according to game theory). For example, in the game **two-finger Morra**, two players, O and E, simultaneously display one or two fingers. Let the total number of fingers be f. If f is odd, O collects f dollars from E; and if f is even, E collects f dollars from O. Game theory can determine the best strategy against a rational player and the expected return for each player.[4]

[4] Morra is a recreational version of an **inspection game**. In such games, an inspector chooses a day to inspect a facility (such as a restaurant or a biological weapons plant), and the facility operator chooses a day to hide all the nasty stuff. The inspector wins if the days are different, and the facility operator wins if they are the same.

2. **Mechanism design**: When an environment is inhabited by many agents, it might be possible to define the rules of the environment (i.e., the game that the agents must play) so that the collective good of all agents is maximized when each agent adopts the game-theoretic solution that maximizes its own utility. For example, game theory can help design the protocols for a collection of Internet traffic routers so that each router has an incentive to act in such a way that global throughput is maximized. Mechanism design can also be used to construct intelligent **multiagent systems** that solve complex problems in a distributed fashion.

5.1 Single-move games

We start by considering a restricted set of games: ones where all players take action simultaneously and the result of the game is based on this single set of actions. (Actually, it is not crucial that the actions take place at exactly the same time; what matters is that no player has knowledge of the other players' choices.) The restriction to a single move (and the very use of the word "game") might make this seem trivial, but in fact, game theory is serious business. It is used in decision-making situations including the auctioning of oil drilling rights and wireless frequency spectrum rights, bankruptcy proceedings, product development and pricing decisions, and national defense—situations involving billions of dollars and hundreds of thousands of lives. A single-move game is defined by three components:

PLAYER

- **Players** or agents who will be making decisions. Two-player games have received the most attention, although n-player games for $n > 2$ are also common. We give players capitalized names, like *Alice* and *Bob* or O and E.

ACTION

- **Actions** that the players can choose. We will give actions lowercase names, like *one* or *testify*. The players may or may not have the same set of actions available.

PAYOFF FUNCTION

STRATEGIC FORM

- A **payoff function** that gives the utility to each player for each combination of actions by all the players. For single-move games the payoff function can be represented by a matrix, a representation known as the **strategic form** (also called **normal form**). The payoff matrix for two-finger Morra is as follows:

	O: one	*O: two*
E: one	$E = +2, O = -2$	$E = -3, O = +3$
E: two	$E = -3, O = +3$	$E = +4, O = -4$

  For example, the lower-right corner shows that when player O chooses action *two* and E also chooses *two*, the payoff is +4 for E and -4 for O.

STRATEGY

PURE STRATEGY

MIXED STRATEGY

STRATEGY PROFILE

OUTCOME

Each player in a game must adopt and then execute a **strategy** (which is the name used in game theory for a *policy*). A **pure strategy** is a deterministic policy; for a single-move game, a pure strategy is just a single action. For many games an agent can do better with a **mixed strategy**, which is a randomized policy that selects actions according to a probability distribution. The mixed strategy that chooses action a with probability p and action b otherwise is written $[p\colon a; (1-p)\colon b]$. For example, a mixed strategy for two-finger Morra might be $[0.5\colon one; 0.5\colon two]$. A **strategy profile** is an assignment of a strategy to each player; given the strategy profile, the game's **outcome** is a numeric value for each player.

SOLUTION

A **solution** to a game is a strategy profile in which each player adopts a rational strategy. We will see that the most important issue in game theory is to define what "rational" means when each agent chooses only part of the strategy profile that determines the outcome. It is important to realize that outcomes are actual results of playing a game, while solutions are theoretical constructs used to analyze a game. We will see that some games have a solution only in mixed strategies. But that does not mean that a player must literally be adopting a mixed strategy to be rational.

Consider the following story: Two alleged burglars, Alice and Bob, are caught red-handed near the scene of a burglary and are interrogated separately. A prosecutor offers each a deal: if you testify against your partner as the leader of a burglary ring, you'll go free for being the cooperative one, while your partner will serve 10 years in prison. However, if you both testify against each other, you'll both get 5 years. Alice and Bob also know that if both refuse to testify they will serve only 1 year each for the lesser charge of possessing stolen property. Now Alice and Bob face the so-called **prisoner's dilemma**: should they testify or refuse? Being rational agents, Alice and Bob each want to maximize their own expected utility. Let's assume that Alice is callously unconcerned about her partner's fate, so her utility decreases in proportion to the number of years she will spend in prison, regardless of what happens to Bob. Bob feels exactly the same way. To help reach a rational decision, they both construct the following payoff matrix:

PRISONER'S DILEMMA

	Alice:testify	*Alice:refuse*
Bob:testify	$A = -5, B = -5$	$A = -10, B = 0$
Bob:refuse	$A = 0, B = -10$	$A = -1, B = -1$

Alice analyzes the payoff matrix as follows: "Suppose Bob testifies. Then I get 5 years if I testify and 10 years if I don't, so in that case testifying is better. On the other hand, if Bob refuses, then I get 0 years if I testify and 1 year if I refuse, so in that case as well testifying is better. So in either case, it's better for me to testify, so that's what I must do."

DOMINANT STRATEGY
STRONG DOMINATION

Alice has discovered that *testify* is a **dominant strategy** for the game. We say that a strategy s for player p **strongly dominates** strategy s' if the outcome for s is better for p than the outcome for s', for every choice of strategies by the other player(s). Strategy s **weakly dominates** s' if s is better than s' on at least one strategy profile and no worse on any other. A dominant strategy is a strategy that dominates all others. It is irrational to play a dominated strategy, and irrational not to play a dominant strategy if one exists. Being rational, Alice chooses the dominant strategy. We need just a bit more terminology: we say that an outcome is **Pareto optimal**[5] if there is no other outcome that all players would prefer. An outcome is **Pareto dominated** by another outcome if all players would prefer the other outcome.

WEAK DOMINATION

PARETO OPTIMAL

PARETO DOMINATED

If Alice is clever as well as rational, she will continue to reason as follows: Bob's dominant strategy is also to testify. Therefore, he will testify and we will both get five years. When each player has a dominant strategy, the combination of those strategies is called a **dominant strategy equilibrium**. In general, a strategy profile forms an **equilibrium** if no player can benefit by switching strategies, given that every other player sticks with the same

DOMINANT STRATEGY EQUILIBRIUM
EQUILIBRIUM

[5] Pareto optimality is named after the economist Vilfredo Pareto (1848–1923).

strategy. An equilibrium is essentially a **local optimum** in the space of policies; it is the top of a peak that slopes downward along every dimension, where a dimension corresponds to a player's strategy choices.

NASH EQUILIBRIUM

The mathematician John Nash (1928–) proved that *every game has at least one equilibrium.* The general concept of equilibrium is now called **Nash equilibrium** in his honor. Clearly, a dominant strategy equilibrium is a Nash equilibrium (Exercise 16), but some games have Nash equilibria but no dominant strategies.

The *dilemma* in the prisoner's dilemma is that the equilibrium outcome is worse for both players than the outcome they would get if they both refused to testify. In other words, $(testify, testify)$ is Pareto dominated by the (-1, -1) outcome of $(refuse, refuse)$. Is there any way for Alice and Bob to arrive at the (-1, -1) outcome? It is certainly an *allowable* option for both of them to refuse to testify, but is is hard to see how rational agents can get there, given the definition of the game. Either player contemplating playing *refuse* will realize that he or she would do better by playing *testify*. That is the attractive power of an equilibrium point. Game theorists agree that being a Nash equilibrium is a necessary condition for being a solution—although they disagree whether it is a sufficient condition.

It is easy enough to get to the $(refuse, refuse)$ solution if we modify the game. For example, we could change to a **repeated game** in which the players know that they will meet again. Or the agents might have moral beliefs that encourage cooperation and fairness. That means they have a different utility function, necessitating a different payoff matrix, making it a different game. We will see later that agents with limited computational powers, rather than the ability to reason absolutely rationally, can reach non-equilibrium outcomes, as can an agent that knows that the other agent has limited rationality. In each case, we are considering a different game than the one described by the payoff matrix above.

Now let's look at a game that has no dominant strategy. Acme, a video game console manufacturer, has to decide whether its next game machine will use Blu-ray discs or DVDs. Meanwhile, the video game software producer Best needs to decide whether to produce its next game on Blu-ray or DVD. The profits for both will be positive if they agree and negative if they disagree, as shown in the following payoff matrix:

	$Acme{:}bluray$	$Acme{:}dvd$
$Best{:}bluray$	$A = +9, B = +9$	$A = -4, B = -1$
$Best{:}dvd$	$A = -3, B = -1$	$A = +5, B = +5$

There is no dominant strategy equilibrium for this game, but there are *two* Nash equilibria: (*bluray, bluray*) and (*dvd, dvd*). We know these are Nash equilibria because if either player unilaterally moves to a different strategy, that player will be worse off. Now the agents have a problem: *there are multiple acceptable solutions, but if each agent aims for a different solution, then both agents will suffer.* How can they agree on a solution? One answer is that both should choose the Pareto-optimal solution (*bluray, bluray*); that is, we can restrict the definition of "solution" to the unique Pareto-optimal Nash equilibrium *provided that one exists.* Every game has at least one Pareto-optimal solution, but a game might have several, or they might not be equilibrium points. For example, if (*bluray, bluray*) had payoff (5, 5), then there would be two equal Pareto-optimal equilibrium points. To choose between them the agents can either guess or *communicate*, which can be done either by establishing a convention that orders the solutions before the game begins or by negotiating to reach a mutually beneficial solution during the game (which would mean including communicative actions as part of a sequential game). Communication thus arises in game theory for exactly the same reasons that it arises in multiagent planning. Games in which players need to communicate like this are called **coordination games**.

COORDINATION GAME

A game can have more than one Nash equilibrium; how do we know that every game must have at least one? Some games have no *pure-strategy* Nash equilibria. Consider, for example, any pure-strategy profile for two-finger Morra. If the total number of fingers is even, then O will want to switch; on the other hand (so to speak), if the total is odd, then E will want to switch. Therefore, no pure strategy profile can be an equilibrium and we must look to mixed strategies instead.

ZERO-SUM GAME

But *which* mixed strategy? In 1928, von Neumann developed a method for finding the *optimal* mixed strategy for two-player, **zero-sum games**—games in which the sum of the payoffs is always zero. Clearly, Morra is such a game. For two-player, zero-sum games, we know that the payoffs are equal and opposite, so we need consider the payoffs of only one player, who will be the maximizer. For Morra, we pick the even player E to be the maximizer, so we can define the payoff matrix by the values $U_E(e, o)$—the payoff to E if E does e and O does o. (For convenience we call player E "her" and O "him.") Von Neumann's method is called the the **maximin** technique, and it works as follows:

MAXIMIN

- Suppose we change the rules as follows: first E picks her strategy and reveals it to O. Then O picks his strategy, with knowledge of E's strategy. Finally, we evaluate the expected payoff of the game based on the chosen strategies. This gives us a turn-taking game to which we can apply the standard **minimax** algorithm. Let's suppose this gives an outcome $U_{E,O}$. Clearly, this game favors O, so the true utility U of the original game (from E's point of view) is *at least* $U_{E,O}$. For example, if we just look at pure strategies, the minimax game tree has a root value of -3 (see Figure 12(a)), so we know that $U \geq -3$.
- Now suppose we change the rules to force O to reveal his strategy first, followed by E. Then the minimax value of this game is $U_{O,E}$, and because this game favors E we know that U is *at most* $U_{O,E}$. With pure strategies, the value is $+2$ (see Figure 12(b)), so we know $U \leq +2$.

Combining these two arguments, we see that the true utility U of the solution to the original game must satisfy

$$U_{E,O} \leq U \leq U_{O,E} \qquad \text{or in this case,} \qquad -3 \leq U \leq 2\,.$$

To pinpoint the value of U, we need to turn our analysis to mixed strategies. First, observe the following: *once the first player has revealed his or her strategy, the second player might as well choose a pure strategy.* The reason is simple: if the second player plays a mixed strategy, $[p\text{: } one; (1-p)\text{: } two]$, its expected utility is a linear combination $(p \cdot u_{one} + (1-p) \cdot u_{two})$ of

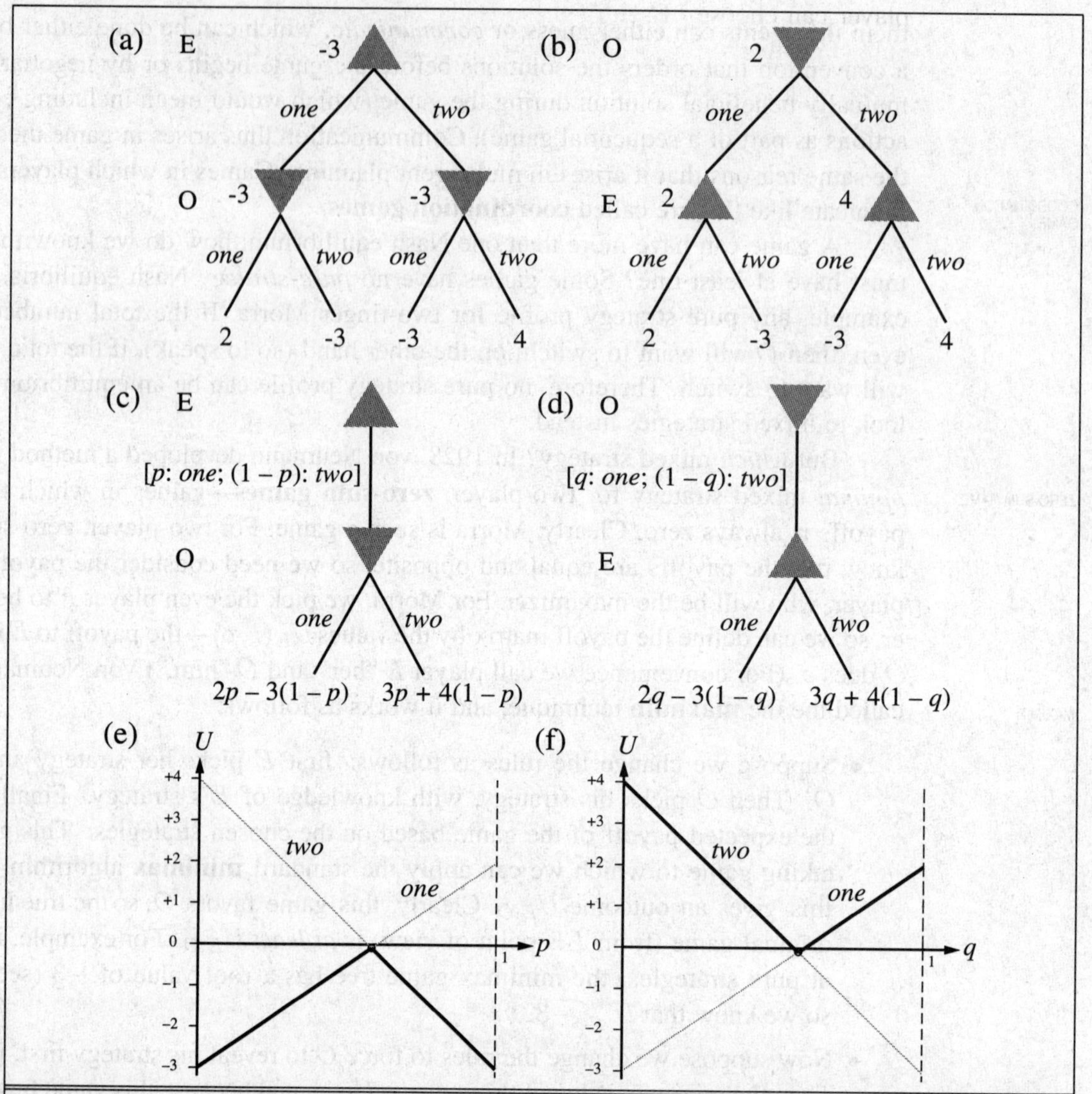

Figure 12 (a) and (b): Minimax game trees for two-finger Morra if the players take turns playing pure strategies. (c) and (d): Parameterized game trees where the first player plays a mixed strategy. The payoffs depend on the probability parameter (p or q) in the mixed strategy. (e) and (f): For any particular value of the probability parameter, the second player will choose the "better" of the two actions, so the value of the first player's mixed strategy is given by the heavy lines. The first player will choose the probability parameter for the mixed strategy at the intersection point.

the utilities of the pure strategies, u_{one} and u_{two}. This linear combination can never be better than the better of u_{one} and u_{two}, so the second player can just choose the better one.

With this observation in mind, the minimax trees can be thought of as having infinitely many branches at the root, corresponding to the infinitely many mixed strategies the first player can choose. Each of these leads to a node with two branches corresponding to the pure strategies for the second player. We can depict these infinite trees finitely by having one "parameterized" choice at the root:

- If E chooses first, the situation is as shown in Figure 12(c). E chooses the strategy $[p\text{: } one; (1-p)\text{: } two]$ at the root, and then O chooses a pure strategy (and hence a move) given the value of p. If O chooses *one*, the expected payoff (to E) is $2p-3(1-p)=5p-3$; if O chooses *two*, the expected payoff is $-3p+4(1-p)=4-7p$. We can draw these two payoffs as straight lines on a graph, where p ranges from 0 to 1 on the x-axis, as shown in Figure 12(e). O, the minimizer, will always choose the lower of the two lines, as shown by the heavy lines in the figure. Therefore, the best that E can do at the root is to choose p to be at the intersection point, which is where
$$5p-3=4-7p \qquad \Rightarrow \qquad p=7/12\,.$$
The utility for E at this point is $U_{E,O}=-1/12$.
- If O moves first, the situation is as shown in Figure 12(d). O chooses the strategy $[q\text{: } one; (1-q)\text{: } two]$ at the root, and then E chooses a move given the value of q. The payoffs are $2q-3(1-q)=5q-3$ and $-3q+4(1-q)=4-7q$.[6] Again, Figure 12(f) shows that the best O can do at the root is to choose the intersection point:
$$5q-3=4-7q \qquad \Rightarrow \qquad q=7/12\,.$$
The utility for E at this point is $U_{O,E}=-1/12$.

Now we know that the true utility of the original game lies between $-1/12$ and $-1/12$, that is, it is exactly $-1/12$! (The moral is that it is better to be O than E if you are playing this game.) Furthermore, the true utility is attained by the mixed strategy $[7/12\text{: } one; 5/12\text{: } two]$, which should be played by both players. This strategy is called the **maximin equilibrium** of the game, and is a Nash equilibrium. Note that each component strategy in an equilibrium mixed strategy has the same expected utility. In this case, both *one* and *two* have the same expected utility, $-1/12$, as the mixed strategy itself.

MAXIMIN EQUILIBRIUM

Our result for two-finger Morra is an example of the general result by von Neumann: *every two-player zero-sum game has a maximin equilibrium when you allow mixed strategies.* Furthermore, every Nash equilibrium in a zero-sum game is a maximin for both players. A player who adopts the maximin strategy has two guarantees: First, no other strategy can do better against an opponent who plays well (although some other strategies might be better at exploiting an opponent who makes irrational mistakes). Second, the player continues to do just as well even if the strategy is revealed to the opponent.

The general algorithm for finding maximin equilibria in zero-sum games is somewhat more involved than Figures 12(e) and (f) might suggest. When there are n possible actions, a mixed strategy is a point in n-dimensional space and the lines become hyperplanes. It's also possible for some pure strategies for the second player to be dominated by others, so that they are not optimal against *any* strategy for the first player. After removing all such strategies (which might have to be done repeatedly), the optimal choice at the root is the

[6] It is a coincidence that these equations are the same as those for p; the coincidence arises because $U_E(one, two)=U_E(two, one)=-3$. This also explains why the optimal strategy is the same for both players.

highest (or lowest) intersection point of the remaining hyperplanes. Finding this choice is an example of a **linear programming** problem: maximizing an objective function subject to linear constraints. Such problems can be solved by standard techniques in time polynomial in the number of actions (and in the number of bits used to specify the reward function, if you want to get technical).

The question remains, what should a rational agent actually *do* in playing a single game of Morra? The rational agent will have derived the fact that $[7/12\colon one; 5/12\colon two]$ is the maximin equilibrium strategy, and will assume that this is mutual knowledge with a rational opponent. The agent could use a 12-sided die or a random number generator to pick randomly according to this mixed strategy, in which case the expected payoff would be -1/12 for E. Or the agent could just decide to play *one*, or *two*. In either case, the expected payoff remains -1/12 for E. Curiously, unilaterally choosing a particular action does not harm one's expected payoff, but allowing the other agent to know that one has made such a unilateral decision *does* affect the expected payoff, because then the opponent can adjust his strategy accordingly.

Finding equilibria in non-zero-sum games is somewhat more complicated. The general approach has two steps: (1) Enumerate all possible subsets of actions that might form mixed strategies. For example, first try all strategy profiles where each player uses a single action, then those where each player uses either one or two actions, and so on. This is exponential in the number of actions, and so only applies to relatively small games. (2) For each strategy profile enumerated in (1), check to see if it is an equilibrium. This is done by solving a set of equations and inequalities that are similar to the ones used in the zero-sum case. For two players these equations are linear and can be solved with basic linear programming techniques, but for three or more players they are nonlinear and may be very difficult to solve.

5.2 Repeated games

So far we have looked only at games that last a single move. The simplest kind of multiple-move game is the **repeated game**, in which players face the same choice repeatedly, but each time with knowledge of the history of all players' previous choices. A strategy profile for a repeated game specifies an action choice for each player at each time step for every possible history of previous choices. As with MDPs, payoffs are additive over time.

REPEATED GAME

Let's consider the repeated version of the prisoner's dilemma. Will Alice and Bob work together and refuse to testify, knowing they will meet again? The answer depends on the details of the engagement. For example, suppose Alice and Bob know that they must play exactly 100 rounds of prisoner's dilemma. Then they both know that the 100th round will not be a repeated game—that is, its outcome can have no effect on future rounds—and therefore they will both choose the dominant strategy, *testify*, in that round. But once the 100th round is determined, the 99th round can have no effect on subsequent rounds, so it too will have a dominant strategy equilibrium at (*testify*, *testify*). By induction, both players will choose *testify* on every round, earning a total jail sentence of 500 years each.

We can get different solutions by changing the rules of the interaction. For example, suppose that after each round there is a 99% chance that the players will meet again. Then the expected number of rounds is still 100, but neither player knows for sure which round will be the last. Under these conditions, more cooperative behavior is possible. For example, one equilibrium strategy is for each player to *refuse* unless the other player has ever played *testify*. This strategy could be called **perpetual punishment**. Suppose both players have adopted this strategy, and this is mutual knowledge. Then as long as neither player has played *testify*, then at any point in time the expected future total payoff for each player is

PERPETUAL PUNISHMENT

$$\sum_{t=0}^{\infty} 0.99^t \cdot (-1) = -100 .$$

A player who deviates from the strategy and chooses *testify* will gain a score of 0 rather than -1 on the very next move, but from then on both players will play *testify* and the player's total expected future payoff becomes

$$0 + \sum_{t=1}^{\infty} 0.99^t \cdot (-5) = -495 .$$

Therefore, at every step, there is no incentive to deviate from (*refuse*, *refuse*). Perpetual punishment is the "mutually assured destruction" strategy of the prisoner's dilemma: once either player decides to *testify*, it ensures that both players suffer a great deal. But it works as a deterrent only if the other player believes you have adopted this strategy—or at least that you might have adopted it.

TIT-FOR-TAT

Other strategies are more forgiving. The most famous, called **tit-for-tat**, calls for starting with *refuse* and then echoing the other player's previous move on all subsequent moves. So Alice would refuse as long as Bob refuses and would testify the move after Bob testified, but would go back to refusing if Bob did. Although very simple, this strategy has proven to be highly robust and effective against a wide variety of strategies.

We can also get different solutions by changing the agents, rather than changing the rules of engagement. Suppose the agents are finite-state machines with n states and they are playing a game with $m > n$ total steps. The agents are thus incapable of representing the number of remaining steps, and must treat it as an unknown. Therefore, they cannot do the induction, and are free to arrive at the more favorable (*refuse, refuse*) equilibrium. In this case, ignorance *is* bliss—or rather, having your opponent believe that you are ignorant is bliss. Your success in these repeated games depends on the other player's *perception* of you as a bully or a simpleton, and not on your actual characteristics.

5.3 Sequential games

EXTENSIVE FORM

In the general case, a game consists of a sequence of turns that need not be all the same. Such games are best represented by a game tree, which game theorists call the **extensive form**. The tree includes the following information: an initial state S_0, a function PLAYER (s) that tells which player has the move, a function ACTIONS (s) enumerating the possible actions, a function RESULT(s, a) that defines the transition to a new state, and a partial function UTILITY(s, p), which is defined only on terminal states, to give the payoff for each player.

To represent stochastic games, such as backgammon, we add a distinguished player, *chance*, that can take random actions. *Chance*'s "strategy" is part of the definition of the game, specified as a probability distribution over actions (the other players get to choose their own strategy). To represent games with nondeterministic actions, such as billiards, we break the action into two pieces: the player's action itself has a deterministic result, and then *chance* has a turn to react to the action in its own capricious way. To represent simultaneous moves, as in the prisoner's dilemma or two-finger Morra, we impose an arbitrary order on the players, but we have the option of asserting that the earlier player's actions are not observable to the subsequent players: e.g., Alice must choose *refuse* or *testify* first, then Bob chooses, but Bob does not know what choice Alice made at that time (we can also represent the fact that the move is revealed later). However, we assume the players always remember all their *own* previous actions; this assumption is called **perfect recall**.

The key idea of extensive form that sets it apart from other game trees is the representation of partial observability. A player in a partially observable game such as Kriegspiel can create a game tree over the space of **belief states**. With that tree, in some cases a player can find a sequence of moves (a strategy) that leads to a forced checkmate regardless of what actual state we started in, and regardless of what strategy the opponent uses. However, that game tree could not tell a player what to do when there is no guaranteed checkmate. If the player's best strategy depends on the opponent's strategy and vice versa, then minimax (or alpha–beta) by itself cannot find a solution. The extensive form *does* allow us to find solutions because it represents the belief states (game theorists call them **information sets**) of *all* players at once. From that representation we can find equilibrium solutions, just as we did with normal-form games.

INFORMATION SETS

As a simple example of a sequential game, place two agents in the 4×3 world of Figure 1 and have them move simultaneously until one agent reaches an exit square, and gets the payoff for that square. If we specify that no movement occurs when the two agents try to move into the same square simultaneously (a common problem at many traffic intersections), then certain pure strategies can get stuck forever. Thus, agents need a mixed strategy to perform well in this game: randomly choose between moving ahead and staying put. This is exactly what is done to resolve packet collisions in Ethernet networks.

Next we'll consider a very simple variant of poker. The deck has only four cards, two aces and two kings. One card is dealt to each player. The first player then has the option to *raise* the stakes of the game from 1 point to 2, or to *check*. If player 1 checks, the game is over. If he raises, then player 2 has the option to *call*, accepting that the game is worth 2 points, or *fold*, conceding the 1 point. If the game does not end with a fold, then the payoff depends on the cards: it is zero for both players if they have the same card; otherwise the player with the king pays the stakes to the player with the ace.

The extensive-form tree for this game is shown in Figure 13. Nonterminal states are shown as circles, with the player to move inside the circle; player 0 is *chance*. Each action is depicted as an arrow with a label, corresponding to a *raise, check, call,* or *fold*, or, for *chance*, the four possible deals ("AK" means that player 1 gets an ace and player 2 a king). Terminal states are rectangles labeled by their payoff to player 1 and player 2. Information sets are shown as labeled dashed boxes; for example, $I_{1,1}$ is the information set where it is player 1's turn, and he knows he has an ace (but does not know what player 2 has). In information set $I_{2,1}$, it is player 2's turn and she knows that she has an ace and that player 1 has raised,

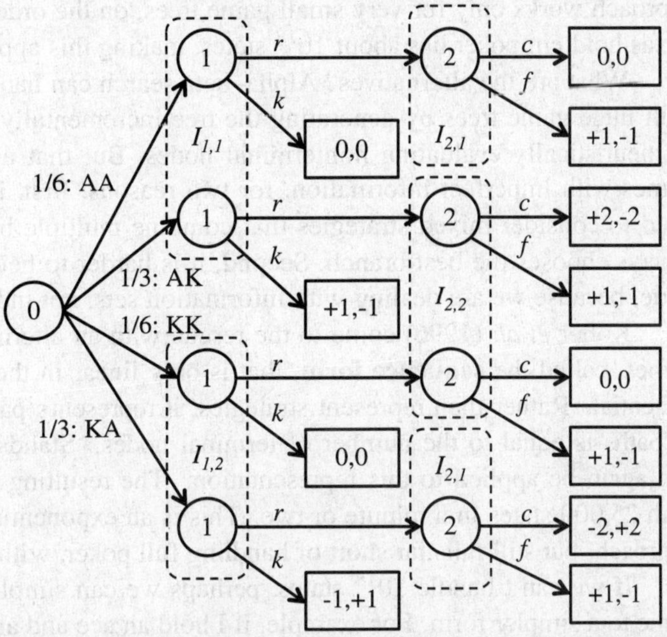

Figure 13 Extensive form of a simplified version of poker.

but does not know what card player 1 has. (Due to the limits of two-dimensional paper, this information set is shown as two boxes rather than one.)

One way to solve an extensive game is to convert it to a normal-form game. Recall that the normal form is a matrix, each row of which is labeled with a pure strategy for player 1, and each column by a pure strategy for player 2. In an extensive game a pure strategy for player i corresponds to an action for each information set involving that player. So in Figure 13, one pure strategy for player 1 is "raise when in $I_{1,1}$ (that is, when I have an ace), and check when in $I_{1,2}$ (when I have a king)." In the payoff matrix below, this strategy is called *rk*. Similarly, strategy *cf* for player 2 means "call when I have an ace and fold when I have a king." Since this is a zero-sum game, the matrix below gives only the payoff for player 1; player 2 always has the opposite payoff:

	2:*cc*	2:*cf*	2:*ff*	2:*fc*
1:*rr*	0	-1/6	1	7/6
1:*kr*	-1/3	-1/6	5/6	2/3
1:*rk*	1/3	**0**	1/6	1/2
1:*kk*	0	**0**	0	0

This game is so simple that it has two pure-strategy equilibria, shown in bold: *cf* for player 2 and *rk* or *kk* for player 1. But in general we can solve extensive games by converting to normal form and then finding a solution (usually a mixed strategy) using standard linear programming methods. That works in theory. But if a player has I information sets and a actions per set, then that player will have a^I pure strategies. In other words, the size of the normal-form matrix is exponential in the number of information sets, so in practice the approach works only for very small game trees, on the order of a dozen states. A game like Texas hold'em poker has about 10^{18} states, making this approach completely infeasible.

What are the alternatives? Alpha–beta search can handle games of perfect information with huge game trees by generating the tree incrementally, by pruning some branches, and by heuristically evaluating nonterminal nodes. But that approach does not work well for games with imperfect information, for two reasons: first, it is harder to prune, because we need to consider mixed strategies that combine multiple branches, not a pure strategy that always chooses the best branch. Second, it is harder to heuristically evaluate a nonterminal node, because we are dealing with information sets, not individual states.

Koller *et al.* (1996) come to the rescue with an alternative representation of extensive games, called the **sequence form**, that is only linear in the size of the tree, rather than exponential. Rather than represent strategies, it represents paths through the tree; the number of paths is equal to the number of terminal nodes. Standard linear programming methods can again be applied to this representation. The resulting system can solve poker variants with 25,000 states in a minute or two. This is an exponential speedup over the normal-form approach, but still falls far short of handling full poker, with 10^{18} states.

SEQUENCE FORM

If we can't handle 10^{18} states, perhaps we can simplify the problem by changing the game to a simpler form. For example, if I hold an ace and am considering the possibility that the next card will give me a pair of aces, then I don't care about the suit of the next card; any suit will do equally well. This suggests forming an **abstraction** of the game, one in which suits are ignored. The resulting game tree will be smaller by a factor of $4! = 24$. Suppose I can solve this smaller game; how will the solution to that game relate to the original game? If no player is going for a flush (or bluffing so), then the suits don't matter to any player, and the solution for the abstraction will also be a solution for the original game. However, if any player is contemplating a flush, then the abstraction will be only an approximate solution (but it is possible to compute bounds on the error).

ABSTRACTION

There are many opportunities for abstraction. For example, at the point in a game where each player has two cards, if I hold a pair of queens, then the other players' hands could be abstracted into three classes: *better* (only a pair of kings or a pair of aces), *same* (pair of queens) or *worse* (everything else). However, this abstraction might be too coarse. A better abstraction would divide *worse* into, say, *medium pair* (nines through jacks), *low pair*, and *no pair*. These examples are abstractions of states; it is also possible to abstract actions. For example, instead of having a bet action for each integer from 1 to 1000, we could restrict the bets to 10^0, 10^1, 10^2 and 10^3. Or we could cut out one of the rounds of betting altogether. We can also abstract over chance nodes, by considering only a subset of the possible deals. This is equivalent to the rollout technique used in Go programs. Putting all these abstractions together, we can reduce the 10^{18} states of poker to 10^7 states, a size that can be solved with current techniques.

Poker programs based on this approach can easily defeat novice and some experienced human players, but are not yet at the level of master players. Part of the problem is that the solution these programs approximate—the equilibrium solution—is optimal only against an opponent who also plays the equilibrium strategy. Against fallible human players it is important to be able to exploit an opponent's deviation from the equilibrium strategy. As

Gautam Rao (aka "The Count"), the world's leading online poker player, said (Billings *et al.*, 2003), "You have a very strong program. Once you add opponent modeling to it, it will kill everyone." However, good models of human fallability remain elusive.

In a sense, extensive game form is the one of the most complete representations we have seen so far: it can handle partially observable, multiagent, stochastic, sequential, dynamic environments—most of the hard cases from the list of environment properties. However, there are two limitations of game theory. First, it does not deal well with continuous states and actions (although there have been some extensions to the continuous case; for example, the theory of **Cournot competition** uses game theory to solve problems where two companies choose prices for their products from a continuous space). Second, game theory assumes the game is *known*. Parts of the game may be specified as unobservable to some of the players, but it must be known what parts are unobservable. In cases in which the players learn the unknown structure of the game over time, the model begins to break down. Let's examine each source of uncertainty, and whether each can be represented in game theory.

COURNOT COMPETITION

Actions: There is no easy way to represent a game where the players have to discover what actions are available. Consider the game between computer virus writers and security experts. Part of the problem is anticipating what action the virus writers will try next.

Strategies: Game theory is very good at representing the idea that the other players' strategies are initially unknown—as long as we assume all agents are rational. The theory itself does not say what to do when the other players are less than fully rational. The notion of a **Bayes–Nash equilibrium** partially addresses this point: it is an equilibrium with respect to a player's prior probability distribution over the other players' strategies—in other words, it expresses a player's beliefs about the other players' likely strategies.

BAYES–NASH EQUILIBRIUM

Chance: If a game depends on the roll of a die, it is easy enough to model a chance node with uniform distribution over the outcomes. But what if it is possible that the die is unfair? We can represent that with another chance node, higher up in the tree, with two branches for "die is fair" and "die is unfair," such that the corresponding nodes in each branch are in the same information set (that is, the players don't know if the die is fair or not). And what if we suspect the other opponent does know? Then we add *another* chance node, with one branch representing the case where the opponent does know, and one where he doesn't.

Utilities: What if we don't know our opponent's utilities? Again, that can be modeled with a chance node, such that the other agent knows its own utilities in each branch, but we don't. But what if we don't know our *own* utilities? For example, how do I know if it is rational to order the Chef's salad if I don't know how much I will like it? We can model that with yet another chance node specifying an unobservable "intrinsic quality" of the salad.

Thus, we see that game theory is good at representing most sources of uncertainty—but at the cost of doubling the size of the tree every time we add another node; a habit which quickly leads to intractably large trees. Because of these and other problems, game theory has been used primarily to *analyze* environments that are at equilibrium, rather than to *control* agents within an environment. Next we shall see how it can help *design* environments.

6 Mechanism Design

In the previous section, we asked, "Given a game, what is a rational strategy?" In this section, we ask, "Given that agents pick rational strategies, what game should we design?" More specifically, we would like to design a game whose solutions, consisting of each agent pursuing its own rational strategy, result in the maximization of some global utility function. This problem is called **mechanism design**, or sometimes **inverse game theory**. Mechanism design is a staple of economics and political science. Capitalism 101 says that if everyone tries to get rich, the total wealth of society will increase. But the examples we will discuss show that proper mechanism design is necessary to keep the invisible hand on track. For collections of agents, mechanism design allows us to construct smart systems out of a collection of more limited systems—even uncooperative systems—in much the same way that teams of humans can achieve goals beyond the reach of any individual.

MECHANISM DESIGN

Examples of mechanism design include auctioning off cheap airline tickets, routing TCP packets between computers, deciding how medical interns will be assigned to hospitals, and deciding how robotic soccer players will cooperate with their teammates. Mechanism design became more than an academic subject in the 1990s when several nations, faced with the problem of auctioning off licenses to broadcast in various frequency bands, lost hundreds of millions of dollars in potential revenue as a result of poor mechanism design. Formally, a **mechanism** consists of (1) a language for describing the set of allowable strategies that agents may adopt, (2) a distinguished agent, called the **center**, that collects reports of strategy choices from the agents in the game, and (3) an outcome rule, known to all agents, that the center uses to determine the payoffs to each agent, given their strategy choices.

MECHANISM

CENTER

6.1 Auctions

AUCTION

Let's consider **auctions** first. An auction is a mechanism for selling some goods to members of a pool of bidders. For simplicity, we concentrate on auctions with a single item for sale. Each bidder i has a utility value v_i for having the item. In some cases, each bidder has a **private value** for the item. For example, the first item sold on eBay was a broken laser pointer, which sold for \$14.83 to a collector of broken laser pointers. Thus, we know that the collector has $v_i \geq \$14.83$, but most other people would have $v_j \ll \$14.83$. In other cases, such as auctioning drilling rights for an oil tract, the item has a **common value**—the tract will produce some amount of money, X, and all bidders value a dollar equally—but there is uncertainty as to what the actual value of X is. Different bidders have different information, and hence different estimates of the item's true value. In either case, bidders end up with their own v_i. Given v_i, each bidder gets a chance, at the appropriate time or times in the auction, to make a bid b_i. The highest bid, b_{max} wins the item, but the price paid need not be b_{max}; that's part of the mechanism design.

ASCENDING-BID

ENGLISH AUCTION

The best-known auction mechanism is the **ascending-bid**,[7] or **English auction**, in which the center starts by asking for a minimum (or **reserve**) bid b_{min}. If some bidder is

7 The word "auction" comes from the Latin *augere*, to increase.

willing to pay that amount, the center then asks for $b_{min} + d$, for some increment d, and continues up from there. The auction ends when nobody is willing to bid anymore; then the last bidder wins the item, paying the price he bid.

How do we know if this is a good mechanism? One goal is to maximize expected revenue for the seller. Another goal is to maximize a notion of global utility. These goals overlap to some extent, because one aspect of maximizing global utility is to ensure that the winner of the auction is the agent who values the item the most (and thus is willing to pay the most). We say an auction is **efficient** if the goods go to the agent who values them most. The ascending-bid auction is usually both efficient and revenue maximizing, but if the reserve price is set too high, the bidder who values it most may not bid, and if the reserve is set too low, the seller loses net revenue.

EFFICIENT

Probably the most important things that an auction mechanism can do is encourage a sufficient number of bidders to enter the game and discourage them from engaging in **collusion**. Collusion is an unfair or illegal agreement by two or more bidders to manipulate prices. It can happen in secret backroom deals or tacitly, within the rules of the mechanism.

COLLUSION

For example, in 1999, Germany auctioned ten blocks of cell-phone spectrum with a simultaneous auction (bids were taken on all ten blocks at the same time), using the rule that any bid must be a minimum of a 10% raise over the previous bid on a block. There were only two credible bidders, and the first, Mannesman, entered the bid of 20 million deutschmark on blocks 1-5 and 18.18 million on blocks 6-10. Why 18.18M? One of T-Mobile's managers said they "interpreted Mannesman's first bid as an offer." Both parties could compute that a 10% raise on 18.18M is 19.99M; thus Mannesman's bid was interpreted as saying "we can each get half the blocks for 20M; let's not spoil it by bidding the prices up higher." And in fact T-Mobile bid 20M on blocks 6-10 and that was the end of the bidding. The German government got less than they expected, because the two competitors were able to use the bidding mechanism to come to a tacit agreement on how not to compete. From the government's point of view, a better result could have been obtained by any of these changes to the mechanism: a higher reserve price; a sealed-bid first-price auction, so that the competitors could not communicate through their bids; or incentives to bring in a third bidder. Perhaps the 10% rule was an error in mechanism design, because it facilitated the precise signaling from Mannesman to T-Mobile.

In general, both the seller and the global utility function benefit if there are more bidders, although global utility can suffer if you count the cost of wasted time of bidders that have no chance of winning. One way to encourage more bidders is to make the mechanism easier for them. After all, if it requires too much research or computation on the part of the bidders, they may decide to take their money elsewhere. So it is desirable that the bidders have a **dominant strategy**. Recall that "dominant" means that the strategy works against all other strategies, which in turn means that an agent can adopt it without regard for the other strategies. An agent with a dominant strategy can just bid, without wasting time contemplating other agents' possible strategies. A mechanism where agents have a dominant strategy is called a **strategy-proof** mechanism. If, as is usually the case, that strategy involves the bidders revealing their true value, v_i, then it is called a **truth-revealing**, or **truthful**, auction; the term **incentive compatible** is also used. The **revelation principle** states that any mecha-

STRATEGY-PROOF

TRUTH-REVEALING

REVELATION PRINCIPLE

nism can be transformed into an equivalent truth-revealing mechanism, so part of mechanism design is finding these equivalent mechanisms.

It turns out that the ascending-bid auction has most of the desirable properties. The bidder with the highest value v_i gets the goods at a price of $b_o + d$, where b_o is the highest bid among all the other agents and d is the auctioneer's increment.[8] Bidders have a simple dominant strategy: keep bidding as long as the current cost is below your v_i. The mechanism is not quite truth-revealing, because the winning bidder reveals only that his $v_i \geq b_o + d$; we have a lower bound on v_i but not an exact amount.

A disadvantage (from the point of view of the seller) of the ascending-bid auction is that it can discourage competition. Suppose that in a bid for cell-phone spectrum there is one advantaged company that everyone agrees would be able to leverage existing customers and infrastructure, and thus can make a larger profit than anyone else. Potential competitors can see that they have no chance in an ascending-bid auction, because the advantaged company can always bid higher. Thus, the competitors may not enter at all, and the advantaged company ends up winning at the reserve price.

Another negative property of the English auction is its high communication costs. Either the auction takes place in one room or all bidders have to have high-speed, secure communication lines; in either case they have to have the time available to go through several rounds of bidding. An alternative mechanism, which requires much less communication, is the **sealed-bid auction**. Each bidder makes a single bid and communicates it to the auctioneer, without the other bidders seeing it. With this mechanism, there is no longer a simple dominant strategy. If your value is v_i and you believe that the maximum of all the other agents' bids will be b_o, then you should bid $b_o + \epsilon$, for some small ϵ, if that is less than v_i. Thus, your bid depends on your estimation of the other agents' bids, requiring you to do more work. Also, note that the agent with the highest v_i might not win the auction. This is offset by the fact that the auction is more competitive, reducing the bias toward an advantaged bidder.

SEALED-BID AUCTION

A small change in the mechanism for sealed-bid auctions produces the **sealed-bid second-price auction**, also known as a **Vickrey auction**.[9] In such auctions, the winner pays the price of the *second*-highest bid, b_o, rather than paying his own bid. This simple modification completely eliminates the complex deliberations required for standard (or **first-price**) sealed-bid auctions, because the dominant strategy is now simply to bid v_i; the mechanism is truth-revealing. Note that the utility of agent i in terms of his bid b_i, his value v_i, and the best bid among the other agents, b_o, is

SEALED-BID SECOND-PRICE AUCTION

VICKREY AUCTION

$$u_i = \begin{cases} (v_i - b_o) & \text{if } b_i > b_o \\ 0 & \text{otherwise.} \end{cases}$$

To see that $b_i = v_i$ is a dominant strategy, note that when $(v_i - b_o)$ is positive, any bid that wins the auction is optimal, and bidding v_i in particular wins the auction. On the other hand, when $(v_i - b_o)$ is negative, any bid that loses the auction is optimal, and bidding v_i in

[8] There is actually a small chance that the agent with highest v_i fails to get the goods, in the case in which $b_o < v_i < b_o + d$. The chance of this can be made arbitrarily small by decreasing the increment d.

[9] Named after William Vickrey (1914–1996), who won the 1996 Nobel Prize in economics for this work and died of a heart attack three days later.

particular loses the auction. So bidding v_i is optimal for all possible values of b_o, and in fact, v_i is the only bid that has this property. Because of its simplicity and the minimal computation requirements for both seller and bidders, the Vickrey auction is widely used in constructing distributed AI systems. Also, Internet search engines conduct over a billion auctions a day to sell advertisements along with their search results, and online auction sites handle $100 billion a year in goods, all using variants of the Vickrey auction. Note that the expected value to the seller is b_o, which is the same expected return as the limit of the English auction as the increment d goes to zero. This is actually a very general result: the **revenue equivalence theorem** states that, with a few minor caveats, any auction mechanism where risk-neutral bidders have values v_i known only to themselves (but know a probability distribution from which those values are sampled), will yield the same expected revenue. This principle means that the various mechanisms are not competing on the basis of revenue generation, but rather on other qualities.

REVENUE EQUIVALENCE THEOREM

Although the second-price auction is truth-revealing, it turns out that extending the idea to multiple goods and using a next-price auction is not truth-revealing. Many Internet search engines use a mechanism where they auction k slots for ads on a page. The highest bidder wins the top spot, the second highest gets the second spot, and so on. Each winner pays the price bid by the next-lower bidder, with the understanding that payment is made only if the searcher actually clicks on the ad. The top slots are considered more valuable because they are more likely to be noticed and clicked on. Imagine that three bidders, b_1, b_2 and b_3, have valuations for a click of $v_1 = 200$, $v_2 = 180$, and $v_3 = 100$, and that$k = 2$ slots are available, where it is known that the top spot is clicked on 5% of the time and the bottom spot 2%. If all bidders bid truthfully, then b_1 wins the top slot and pays 180, and has an expected return of $(200 - 180) \times 0.05 = 1$. The second slot goes to b_2. But b_1 can see that if she were to bid anything in the range 101–179, she would concede the top slot to b_2, win the second slot, and yield an expected return of $(200 - 100) \times .02 = 2$. Thus, b_1 can double her expected return by bidding less than her true value in this case. In general, bidders in this multislot auction must spend a lot of energy analyzing the bids of others to determine their best strategy; there is no simple dominant strategy. Aggarwal *et al.* (2006) show that there is a unique truthful auction mechanism for this multislot problem, in which the winner of slot j pays the full price for slot j just for those additional clicks that are available at slot j and not at slot $j + 1$. The winner pays the price for the lower slot for the remaining clicks. In our example, b_1 would bid 200 truthfully, and would pay 180 for the additional $.05 - .02 = .03$ clicks in the top slot, but would pay only the cost of the bottom slot, 100, for the remaining .02 clicks. Thus, the total return to b_1 would be $(200 - 180) \times .03 + (200 - 100) \times .02 = 2.6$.

Another example of where auctions can come into play within AI is when a collection of agents are deciding whether to cooperate on a joint plan. Hunsberger and Grosz (2000) show that this can be accomplished efficiently with an auction in which the agents bid for roles in the joint plan.

6.2 Common goods

Now let's consider another type of game, in which countries set their policy for controlling air pollution. Each country has a choice: they can reduce pollution at a cost of -10 points for implementing the necessary changes, or they can continue to pollute, which gives them a net utility of -5 (in added health costs, etc.) and also contributes -1 points to every other country (because the air is shared across countries). Clearly, the dominant strategy for each country is "continue to pollute," but if there are 100 countries and each follows this policy, then each country gets a total utility of -104, whereas if every country reduced pollution, they would each have a utility of -10. This situation is called the **tragedy of the commons**: if nobody has to pay for using a common resource, then it tends to be exploited in a way that leads to a lower total utility for all agents. It is similar to the prisoner's dilemma: there is another solution to the game that is better for all parties, but there appears to be no way for rational agents to arrive at that solution.

TRAGEDY OF THE COMMONS

The standard approach for dealing with the tragedy of the commons is to change the mechanism to one that charges each agent for using the commons. More generally, we need to ensure that all **externalities**—effects on global utility that are not recognized in the individual agents' transactions—are made explicit. Setting the prices correctly is the difficult part. In the limit, this approach amounts to creating a mechanism in which each agent is effectively required to maximize global utility, but can do so by making a local decision. For this example, a carbon tax would be an example of a mechanism that charges for use of the commons in a way that, if implemented well, maximizes global utility.

EXTERNALITIES

As a final example, consider the problem of allocating some common goods. Suppose a city decides it wants to install some free wireless Internet transceivers. However, the number of transceivers they can afford is less than the number of neighborhoods that want them. The city wants to allocate the goods efficiently, to the neighborhoods that would value them the most. That is, they want to maximize the global utility $V = \sum_i v_i$. The problem is that if they just ask each neighborhood council "how much do you value this free gift?" they would all have an incentive to lie, and report a high value. It turns out there is a mechanism, known as the **Vickrey-Clarke-Groves**, or **VCG**, mechanism, that makes it a dominant strategy for each agent to report its true utility and that achieves an efficient allocation of the goods. The trick is that each agent pays a tax equivalent to the loss in global utility that occurs because of the agent's presence in the game. The mechanism works like this:

VICKREY-CLARKE-GROVES

VCG

1. The center asks each agent to report its value for receiving an item. Call this b_i.
2. The center allocates the goods to a subset of the bidders. We call this subset A, and use the notation $b_i(A)$ to mean the result to i under this allocation: b_i if i is in A (that is, i is a winner), and 0 otherwise. The center chooses A to maximize total reported utility $B = \sum_i b_i(A)$.
3. The center calculates (for each i) the sum of the reported utilities for all the winners except i. We use the notation $B_{-i} = \sum_{j \neq i} b_j(A)$. The center also computes (for each i) the allocation that would maximize total global utility if i were not in the game; call that sum W_{-i}.
4. Each agent i pays a tax equal to $W_{-i} - B_{-i}$.

In this example, the VCG rule means that each winner would pay a tax equal to the highest reported value among the losers. That is, if I report my value as 5, and that causes someone with value 2 to miss out on an allocation, then I pay a tax of 2. All winners should be happy because they pay a tax that is less than their value, and all losers are as happy as they can be, because they value the goods less than the required tax.

Why is it that this mechanism is truth-revealing? First, consider the payoff to agent i, which is the value of getting an item, minus the tax:

$$v_i(A) - (W_{-i} - B_{-i}) . \tag{14}$$

Here we distinguish the agent's true utility, v_i, from his reported utility b_i (but we are trying to show that a dominant strategy is $b_i = v_i$). Agent i knows that the center will maximize global utility using the reported values,

$$\sum_j b_j(A) = b_i(A) + \sum_{j \neq i} b_j(A)$$

whereas agent i wants the center to maximize (14), which can be rewritten as

$$v_i(A) + \sum_{j \neq i} b_j(A) - W_{-i} .$$

Since agent i cannot affect the value of W_{-i} (it depends only on the other agents), the only way i can make the center optimize what i wants is to report the true utility, $b_i = v_i$.

7 SUMMARY

This chapter shows how to use knowledge about the world to make decisions even when the outcomes of an action are uncertain and the rewards for acting might not be reaped until many actions have passed. The main points are as follows:

- Sequential decision problems in uncertain environments, also called **Markov decision processes**, or MDPs, are defined by a **transition model** specifying the probabilistic outcomes of actions and a **reward function** specifying the reward in each state.
- The utility of a state sequence is the sum of all the rewards over the sequence, possibly discounted over time. The solution of an MDP is a **policy** that associates a decision with every state that the agent might reach. An optimal policy maximizes the utility of the state sequences encountered when it is executed.
- The utility of a state is the expected utility of the state sequences encountered when an optimal policy is executed, starting in that state. The **value iteration** algorithm for solving MDPs works by iteratively solving the equations relating the utility of each state to those of its neighbors.
- **Policy iteration** alternates between calculating the utilities of states under the current policy and improving the current policy with respect to the current utilities.
- Partially observable MDPs, or POMDPs, are much more difficult to solve than are MDPs. They can be solved by conversion to an MDP in the continuous space of belief

states; both value iteration and policy iteration algorithms have been devised. Optimal behavior in POMDPs includes information gathering to reduce uncertainty and therefore make better decisions in the future.

- A decision-theoretic agent can be constructed for POMDP environments. The agent uses a **dynamic decision network** to represent the transition and sensor models, to update its belief state, and to project forward possible action sequences.
- **Game theory** describes rational behavior for agents in situations in which multiple agents interact simultaneously. Solutions of games are **Nash equilibria**—strategy profiles in which no agent has an incentive to deviate from the specified strategy.
- **Mechanism design** can be used to set the rules by which agents will interact, in order to maximize some global utility through the operation of individually rational agents. Sometimes, mechanisms exist that achieve this goal without requiring each agent to consider the choices made by other agents.

BIBLIOGRAPHICAL AND HISTORICAL NOTES

Richard Bellman developed the ideas underlying the modern approach to sequential decision problems while working at the RAND Corporation beginning in 1949. According to his autobiography (Bellman, 1984), he coined the exciting term "dynamic programming" to hide from a research-phobic Secretary of Defense, Charles Wilson, the fact that his group was doing mathematics. (This cannot be strictly true, because his first paper using the term (Bellman, 1952) appeared before Wilson became Secretary of Defense in 1953.) Bellman's book, *Dynamic Programming* (1957), gave the new field a solid foundation and introduced the basic algorithmic approaches. Ron Howard's Ph.D. thesis (1960) introduced policy iteration and the idea of average reward for solving infinite-horizon problems. Several additional results were introduced by Bellman and Dreyfus (1962). Modified policy iteration is due to van Nunen (1976) and Puterman and Shin (1978). Asynchronous policy iteration was analyzed by Williams and Baird (1993), who also proved the policy loss bound in Equation (9). The analysis of discounting in terms of stationary preferences is due to Koopmans (1972). The texts by Bertsekas (1987), Puterman (1994), and Bertsekas and Tsitsiklis (1996) provide a rigorous introduction to sequential decision problems. Papadimitriou and Tsitsiklis (1987) describe results on the computational complexity of MDPs.

Seminal work by Sutton (1988) and Watkins (1989) on reinforcement learning methods for solving MDPs played a significant role in introducing MDPs into the AI community, as did the later survey by Barto *et al.* (1995). (Earlier work by Werbos (1977) contained many similar ideas, but was not taken up to the same extent.) The connection between MDPs and AI planning problems was made first by Sven Koenig (1991), who showed how probabilistic STRIPS operators provide a compact representation for transition models (see also Wellman,

1990b). Work by Dean *et al.* (1993) and Tash and Russell (1994) attempted to overcome the combinatorics of large state spaces by using a limited search horizon and abstract states. Heuristics based on the value of information can be used to select areas of the state space where a local expansion of the horizon will yield a significant improvement in decision quality. Agents using this approach can tailor their effort to handle time pressure and generate some interesting behaviors such as using familiar "beaten paths" to find their way around the state space quickly without having to recompute optimal decisions at each point.

As one might expect, AI researchers have pushed MDPs in the direction of more expressive representations that can accommodate much larger problems than the traditional atomic representations based on transition matrices. The use of a dynamic Bayesian network to represent transition models was an obvious idea, but work on **factored MDPs** (Boutilier *et al.*, 2000; Koller and Parr, 2000; Guestrin *et al.*, 2003b) extends the idea to structured representations of the value function with provable improvements in complexity. **Relational MDPs** (Boutilier *et al.*, 2001; Guestrin *et al.*, 2003a) go one step further, using structured representations to handle domains with many related objects.

FACTORED MDP

RELATIONAL MDP

The observation that a partially observable MDP can be transformed into a regular MDP over belief states is due to Astrom (1965) and Aoki (1965). The first complete algorithm for the exact solution of POMDPs—essentially the value iteration algorithm presented in this chapter—was proposed by Edward Sondik (1971) in his Ph.D. thesis. (A later journal paper by Smallwood and Sondik (1973) contains some errors, but is more accessible.) Lovejoy (1991) surveyed the first twenty-five years of POMDP research, reaching somewhat pessimistic conclusions about the feasibility of solving large problems. The first significant contribution within AI was the Witness algorithm (Cassandra *et al.*, 1994; Kaelbling *et al.*, 1998), an improved version of POMDP value iteration. Other algorithms soon followed, including an approach due to Hansen (1998) that constructs a policy incrementally in the form of a finite-state automaton. In this policy representation, the belief state corresponds directly to a particular state in the automaton. More recent work in AI has focused on **point-based** value iteration methods that, at each iteration, generate conditional plans and α-vectors for a finite set of belief states rather than for the entire belief space. Lovejoy (1991) proposed such an algorithm for a fixed grid of points, an approach taken also by Bonet (2002). An influential paper by Pineau *et al.* (2003) suggested generating reachable points by simulating trajectories in a somewhat greedy fashion; Spaan and Vlassis (2005) observe that one need generate plans for only a small, randomly selected subset of points to improve on the plans from the previous iteration for all points in the set. Current point-based methods—such as point-based policy iteration (Ji *et al.*, 2007)—can generate near-optimal solutions for POMDPs with thousands of states. Because POMDPs are PSPACE-hard (Papadimitriou and Tsitsiklis, 1987), further progress may require taking advantage of various kinds of structure within a factored representation.

The online approach—using look-ahead search to select an action for the current belief state—was first examined by Satia and Lave (1973). The use of sampling at chance nodes was explored analytically by Kearns *et al.* (2000) and Ng and Jordan (2000). The basic ideas for an agent architecture using dynamic decision networks were proposed by Dean and Kanazawa (1989a). The book *Planning and Control* by Dean and Wellman (1991) goes into much greater depth, making connections between DBN/DDN models and the classical control literature on filtering. Tatman and Shachter (1990) showed how to apply dynamic programming algorithms to DDN models. Russell (1998) explains various ways in which such agents can be scaled up and identifies a number of open research issues.

The roots of game theory can be traced back to proposals made in the 17th century by Christiaan Huygens and Gottfried Leibniz to study competitive and cooperative human interactions scientifically and mathematically. Throughout the 19th century, several leading economists created simple mathematical examples to analyze particular examples of competitive situations. The first formal results in game theory are due to Zermelo (1913) (who had, the year before, suggested a form of minimax search for games, albeit an incorrect one). Emile Borel (1921) introduced the notion of a mixed strategy. John von Neumann (1928) proved that every two-person, zero-sum game has a maximin equilibrium in mixed strategies and a well-defined value. Von Neumann's collaboration with the economist Oskar Morgenstern led to the publication in 1944 of the *Theory of Games and Economic Behavior*, the defining book for game theory. Publication of the book was delayed by the wartime paper shortage until a member of the Rockefeller family personally subsidized its publication.

In 1950, at the age of 21, John Nash published his ideas concerning equilibria in general (non-zero-sum) games. His definition of an equilibrium solution, although originating in the work of Cournot (1838), became known as Nash equilibrium. After a long delay because of the schizophrenia he suffered from 1959 onward, Nash was awarded the Nobel Memorial Prize in Economics (along with Reinhart Selten and John Harsanyi) in 1994. The Bayes–Nash equilibrium is described by Harsanyi (1967) and discussed by Kadane and Larkey (1982). Some issues in the use of game theory for agent control are covered by Binmore (1982).

The prisoner's dilemma was invented as a classroom exercise by Albert W. Tucker in 1950 (based on an example by Merrill Flood and Melvin Dresher) and is covered extensively by Axelrod (1985) and Poundstone (1993). Repeated games were introduced by Luce and Raiffa (1957), and games of partial information in extensive form by Kuhn (1953). The first practical algorithm for sequential, partial-information games was developed within AI by Koller *et al.* (1996); the paper by Koller and Pfeffer (1997) provides a readable introduction to the field and describe a working system for representing and solving sequential games.

The use of abstraction to reduce a game tree to a size that can be solved with Koller's technique is discussed by Billings *et al.* (2003). Bowling *et al.* (2008) show how to use importance sampling to get a better estimate of the value of a strategy. Waugh *et al.* (2009) show that the abstraction approach is vulnerable to making systematic errors in approximating the equilibrium solution, meaning that the whole approach is on shaky ground: it works for some games but not others. Korb *et al.* (1999) experiment with an opponent model in the form of a Bayesian network. It plays five-card stud about as well as experienced humans. (Zinkevich *et al.*, 2008) show how an approach that minimizes regret can find approximate equilibria for abstractions with 10^{12} states, 100 times more than previous methods.

Game theory and MDPs are combined in the theory of Markov games, also called stochastic games (Littman, 1994; Hu and Wellman, 1998). Shapley (1953) actually described the value iteration algorithm independently of Bellman, but his results were not widely appreciated, perhaps because they were presented in the context of Markov games. Evolutionary game theory (Smith, 1982; Weibull, 1995) looks at strategy drift over time: if your opponent's strategy is changing, how should you react? Textbooks on game theory from an economics point of view include those by Myerson (1991), Fudenberg and Tirole (1991), Osborne (2004), and Osborne and Rubinstein (1994); Mailath and Samuelson (2006) concentrate on repeated games. From an AI perspective we have Nisan *et al.* (2007), Leyton-Brown and Shoham (2008), and Shoham and Leyton-Brown (2009).

The 2007 Nobel Memorial Prize in Economics went to Hurwicz, Maskin, and Myerson "for having laid the foundations of mechanism design theory" (Hurwicz, 1973). The tragedy of the commons, a motivating problem for the field, was presented by Hardin (1968). The revelation principle is due to Myerson (1986), and the revenue equivalence theorem was developed independently by Myerson (1981) and Riley and Samuelson (1981). Two economists, Milgrom (1997) and Klemperer (2002), write about the multibillion-dollar spectrum auctions they were involved in.

Mechanism design is used in multiagent planning (Hunsberger and Grosz, 2000; Stone *et al.*, 2009) and scheduling (Rassenti *et al.*, 1982). Varian (1995) gives a brief overview with connections to the computer science literature, and Rosenschein and Zlotkin (1994) present a book-length treatment with applications to distributed AI. Related work on distributed AI also goes under other names, including collective intelligence (Tumer and Wolpert, 2000; Segaran, 2007) and market-based control (Clearwater, 1996). Since 2001 there has been an annual Trading Agents Competition (TAC), in which agents try to make the best profit on a series of auctions (Wellman *et al.*, 2001; Arunachalam and Sadeh, 2005). Papers on computational issues in auctions often appear in the ACM Conferences on Electronic Commerce.

EXERCISES

1 For the 4×3 world shown in Figure 1, calculate which squares can be reached from (1,1) by the action sequence $[Up, Up, Right, Right, Right]$ and with what probabilities.

2 Select a specific member of the set of policies that are optimal for $R(s) > 0$ as shown in Figure 2(b), and calculate the fraction of time the agent spends in each state, in the limit, if the policy is executed forever. (*Hint*: Construct the state-to-state transition probability matrix corresponding to the policy)

3 Suppose that we define the utility of a state sequence to be the *maximum* reward obtained in any state in the sequence. Show that this utility function does not result in stationary preferences between state sequences. Is it still possible to define a utility function on states such that MEU decision making gives optimal behavior?

4 Sometimes MDPs are formulated with a reward function $R(s, a)$ that depends on the action taken or with a reward function $R(s, a, s')$ that also depends on the outcome state.

a. Write the Bellman equations for these formulations.

b. Show how an MDP with reward function $R(s, a, s')$ can be transformed into a different MDP with reward function $R(s, a)$, such that optimal policies in the new MDP correspond exactly to optimal policies in the original MDP.

c. Now do the same to convert MDPs with $R(s, a)$ into MDPs with $R(s)$.

5 For the environment shown in Figure 1, find all the threshold values for $R(s)$ such that the optimal policy changes when the threshold is crossed. You will need a way to calculate the optimal policy and its value for fixed $R(s)$. (*Hint*: Prove that the value of any fixed policy varies linearly with $R(s)$.)

6 Equation (7) states that the Bellman operator is a contraction.

a. Show that, for any functions f and g,

$$|\max_a f(a) - \max_a g(a)| \leq \max_a |f(a) - g(a)| .$$

b. Write out an expression for $|(B\,U_i - B\,U_i')(s)|$ and then apply the result from (a) to complete the proof that the Bellman operator is a contraction.

7 This exercise considers two-player MDPs that correspond to zero-sum, turn-taking games. Let the players be A and B, and let $R(s)$ be the reward for player A in state s. (The reward for B is always equal and opposite.)

a. Let $U_A(s)$ be the utility of state s when it is A's turn to move in s, and let $U_B(s)$ be the utility of state s when it is B's turn to move in s. All rewards and utilities are calculated from A's point of view (just as in a minimax game tree). Write down Bellman equations defining $U_A(s)$ and $U_B(s)$.

b. Explain how to do two-player value iteration with these equations, and define a suitable termination criterion.

c. Consider the game described in Figure 17 of the chapter "Adversarial Search." Draw the state space (rather than the game tree), showing the moves by A as solid lines and moves by B as dashed lines. Mark each state with $R(s)$. You will find it helpful to arrange the states (s_A, s_B) on a two-dimensional grid, using s_A and s_B as "coordinates."

d. Now apply two-player value iteration to solve this game, and derive the optimal policy.

8 Consider the 3×3 world shown in Figure 14(a). The transition model is the same as in the 4×3 Figure 1: 80% of the time the agent goes in the direction it selects; the rest of the time it moves at right angles to the intended direction.

Implement value iteration for this world for each value of r below. Use discounted rewards with a discount factor of 0.99. Show the policy obtained in each case. Explain intuitively why the value of r leads to each policy.

a. $r = 100$

b. $r = -3$

c. $r = 0$

d. $r = +3$

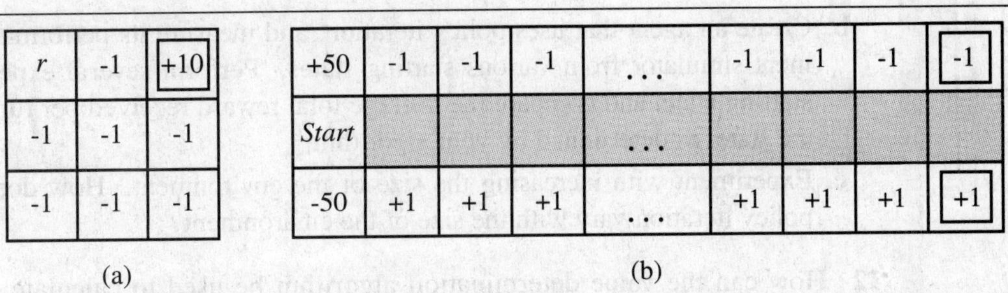

Figure 14 (a) 3 × 3 world for Exercise 8. The reward for each state is indicated. The upper right square is a terminal state. (b) 101 × 3 world for Exercise 9 (omitting 93 identical columns in the middle). The start state has reward 0.

9 Consider the 101 × 3 world shown in Figure 14(b). In the start state the agent has a choice of two deterministic actions, *Up* or *Down*, but in the other states the agent has one deterministic action, *Right*. Assuming a discounted reward function, for what values of the discount γ should the agent choose *Up* and for which *Down*? Compute the utility of each action as a function of γ. (Note that this simple example actually reflects many real-world situations in which one must weigh the value of an immediate action versus the potential continual long-term consequences, such as choosing to dump pollutants into a lake.)

10 Consider an undiscounted MDP having three states, (1, 2, 3), with rewards -1, -2, 0, respectively. State 3 is a terminal state. In states 1 and 2 there are two possible actions: a and b. The transition model is as follows:

- In state 1, action a moves the agent to state 2 with probability 0.8 and makes the agent stay put with probability 0.2.
- In state 2, action a moves the agent to state 1 with probability 0.8 and makes the agent stay put with probability 0.2.
- In either state 1 or state 2, action b moves the agent to state 3 with probability 0.1 and makes the agent stay put with probability 0.9.

Answer the following questions:

a. What can be determined *qualitatively* about the optimal policy in states 1 and 2?

b. Apply policy iteration, showing each step in full, to determine the optimal policy and the values of states 1 and 2. Assume that the initial policy has action b in both states.

c. What happens to policy iteration if the initial policy has action a in both states? Does discounting help? Does the optimal policy depend on the discount factor?

11 Consider the 4 × 3 world shown in Figure 1.

a. Implement an environment simulator for this environment, such that the specific geography of the environment is easily altered. Some code for doing this is already in the online code repository.

b. Create an agent that uses policy iteration, and measure its performance in the environment simulator from various starting states. Perform several experiments from each starting state, and compare the average total reward received per run with the utility of the state, as determined by your algorithm.

c. Experiment with increasing the size of the environment. How does the run time for policy iteration vary with the size of the environment?

12 How can the value determination algorithm be used to calculate the expected loss experienced by an agent using a given set of utility estimates U and an estimated model P, compared with an agent using correct values?

13 Let the initial belief state b_0 for the 4×3 POMDP in section 4 be the uniform distribution over the nonterminal states, i.e., $\langle \frac{1}{9}, \frac{1}{9}, \frac{1}{9}, \frac{1}{9}, \frac{1}{9}, \frac{1}{9}, \frac{1}{9}, \frac{1}{9}, \frac{1}{9}, 0, 0 \rangle$. Calculate the exact belief state b_1 after the agent moves *Left* and its sensor reports 1 adjacent wall. Also calculate b_2 assuming that the same thing happens again.

14 What is the time complexity of d steps of POMDP value iteration for a sensorless environment?

15 Consider a version of the two-state POMDP in section 4.2 in which the sensor is 90% reliable in state 0 but provides no information in state 1 (that is, it reports 0 or 1 with equal probability). Analyze, either qualitatively or quantitatively, the utility function and the optimal policy for this problem.

16 Show that a dominant strategy equilibrium is a Nash equilibrium, but not vice versa.

17 In the children's game of rock–paper–scissors each player reveals at the same time a choice of rock, paper, or scissors. Paper wraps rock, rock blunts scissors, and scissors cut paper. In the extended version rock–paper–scissors–fire–water, fire beats rock, paper, and scissors; rock, paper, and scissors beat water; and water beats fire. Write out the payoff matrix and find a mixed-strategy solution to this game.

18 The following payoff matrix, from Blinder (1983) by way of Bernstein (1996), shows a game between politicians and the Federal Reserve.

	Fed: contract	Fed: do nothing	Fed: expand
Pol: contract	$F = 7, P = 1$	$F = 9, P = 4$	$F = 6, P = 6$
Pol: do nothing	$F = 8, P = 2$	$F = 5, P = 5$	$F = 4, P = 9$
Pol: expand	$F = 3, P = 3$	$F = 2, P = 7$	$F = 1, P = 8$

Politicians can expand or contract fiscal policy, while the Fed can expand or contract monetary policy. (And of course either side can choose to do nothing.) Each side also has preferences for who should do what—neither side wants to look like the bad guys. The payoffs shown are simply the rank orderings: 9 for first choice through 1 for last choice. Find the Nash equilibrium of the game in pure strategies. Is this a Pareto-optimal solution? You might wish to analyze the policies of recent administrations in this light.

19 A Dutch auction is similar in an English auction, but rather than starting the bidding at a low price and increasing, in a Dutch auction the seller starts at a high price and gradually lowers the price until some buyer is willing to accept that price. (If multiple bidders accept the price, one is arbitrarily chosen as the winner.) More formally, the seller begins with a price p and gradually lowers p by increments of d until at least one buyer accepts the price. Assuming all bidders act rationally, is it true that for arbitrarily small d, a Dutch auction will always result in the bidder with the highest value for the item obtaining the item? If so, show mathematically why. If not, explain how it may be possible for the bidder with highest value for the item not to obtain it.

20 Imagine an auction mechanism that is just like an ascending-bid auction, except that at the end, the winning bidder, the one who bid b_{max}, pays only $b_{max}/2$ rather than b_{max}. Assuming all agents are rational, what is the expected revenue to the auctioneer for this mechanism, compared with a standard ascending-bid auction?

21 Teams in the National Hockey League historically received 2 points for winning a game and 0 for losing. If the game is tied, an overtime period is played; if nobody wins in overtime, the game is a tie and each team gets 1 point. But league officials felt that teams were playing too conservatively in overtime (to avoid a loss), and it would be more exciting if overtime produced a winner. So in 1999 the officials experimented in mechanism design: the rules were changed, giving a team that loses in overtime 1 point, not 0. It is still 2 points for a win and 1 for a tie.

a. Was hockey a zero-sum game before the rule change? After?

b. Suppose that at a certain time t in a game, the home team has probability p of winning in regulation time, probability $0.78 - p$ of losing, and probability 0.22 of going into overtime, where they have probability q of winning, $.9 - q$ of losing, and .1 of tying. Give equations for the expected value for the home and visiting teams.

c. Imagine that it were legal and ethical for the two teams to enter into a pact where they agree that they will skate to a tie in regulation time, and then both try in earnest to win in overtime. Under what conditions, in terms of p and q, would it be rational for both teams to agree to this pact?

d. Longley and Sankaran (2005) report that since the rule change, the percentage of games with a winner in overtime went up 18.2%, as desired, but the percentage of overtime games also went up 3.6%. What does that suggest about possible collusion or conservative play after the rule change?

LEARNING FROM EXAMPLES

In which we describe agents that can improve their behavior through diligent study of their own experiences.

LEARNING

An agent is **learning** if it improves its performance on future tasks after making observations about the world. Learning can range from the trivial, as exhibited by jotting down a phone number, to the profound, as exhibited by Albert Einstein, who inferred a new theory of the universe. In this chapter we will concentrate on one class of learning problem, which seems restricted but actually has vast applicability: from a collection of input–output pairs, learn a function that predicts the output for new inputs.

Why would we want an agent to learn? If the design of the agent can be improved, why wouldn't the designers just program in that improvement to begin with? There are three main reasons. First, the designers cannot anticipate all possible situations that the agent might find itself in. For example, a robot designed to navigate mazes must learn the layout of each new maze it encounters. Second, the designers cannot anticipate all changes over time; a program designed to predict tomorrow's stock market prices must learn to adapt when conditions change from boom to bust. Third, sometimes human programmers have no idea how to program a solution themselves. For example, most people are good at recognizing the faces of family members, but even the best programmers are unable to program a computer to accomplish that task, except by using learning algorithms. This chapter first gives an overview of the various forms of learning, then describes one popular approach, decision-tree learning, in Section 3, followed by a theoretical analysis of learning in Sections 4 and 5. We look at various learning systems used in practice: linear models, nonlinear models (in particular, neural networks), nonparametric models, and support vector machines. Finally we show how ensembles of models can outperform a single model.

1 FORMS OF LEARNING

Any component of an agent can be improved by learning from data. The improvements, and the techniques used to make them, depend on four major factors:

- Which *component* is to be improved.

- What *prior knowledge* the agent already has.
- What *representation* is used for the data and the component.
- What *feedback* is available to learn from.

Components to be learned

The following are common components of many agents:

1. A direct mapping from conditions on the current state to actions.
2. A means to infer relevant properties of the world from the percept sequence.
3. Information about the way the world evolves and about the results of possible actions the agent can take.
4. Utility information indicating the desirability of world states.
5. Action-value information indicating the desirability of actions.
6. Goals that describe classes of states whose achievement maximizes the agent's utility.

Each of these components can be learned. Consider, for example, an agent training to become a taxi driver. Every time the instructor shouts "Brake!" the agent might learn a condition–action rule for when to brake (component 1); the agent also learns every time the instructor does not shout. By seeing many camera images that it is told contain buses, it can learn to recognize them (2). By trying actions and observing the results—for example, braking hard on a wet road—it can learn the effects of its actions (3). Then, when it receives no tip from passengers who have been thoroughly shaken up during the trip, it can learn a useful component of its overall utility function (4).

Representation and prior knowledge

There exist several examples of representations for agent components: propositional and first-order logical sentences for the components in a logical agent; Bayesian networks for the inferential components of a decision-theoretic agent, and so on. Effective learning algorithms have been devised for all of these representations. This chapter (and most of current machine learning research) covers inputs that form a **factored representation**—a vector of attribute values—and outputs that can be either a continuous numerical value or a discrete value.

INDUCTIVE LEARNING
DEDUCTIVE LEARNING

There is another way to look at the various types of learning. We say that learning a (possibly incorrect) general function or rule from specific input–output pairs is called **inductive learning**. We can also do **analytical** or **deductive** learning: going from a known general rule to a new rule that is logically entailed, but is useful because it allows more efficient processing.

Feedback to learn from

There are three *types of feedback* that determine the three main types of learning:

UNSUPERVISED LEARNING
CLUSTERING

In **unsupervised learning** the agent learns patterns in the input even though no explicit feedback is supplied. The most common unsupervised learning task is **clustering**: detecting potentially useful clusters of input examples. For example, a taxi agent might gradually develop a concept of "good traffic days" and "bad traffic days" without ever being given labeled examples of each by a teacher.

REINFORCEMENT LEARNING

In **reinforcement learning** the agent learns from a series of reinforcements—rewards or punishments. For example, the lack of a tip at the end of the journey gives the taxi agent an indication that it did something wrong. The two points for a win at the end of a chess game tells the agent it did something right. It is up to the agent to decide which of the actions prior to the reinforcement were most responsible for it.

SUPERVISED LEARNING

In **supervised learning** the agent observes some example input–output pairs and learns a function that maps from input to output. In component 1 above, the inputs are percepts and the output are provided by a teacher who says "Brake!" or "Turn left." In component 2, the inputs are camera images and the outputs again come from a teacher who says "that's a bus." In 3, the theory of braking is a function from states and braking actions to stopping distance in feet. In this case the output value is available directly from the agent's percepts (after the fact); the environment is the teacher.

SEMI-SUPERVISED LEARNING

In practice, these distinction are not always so crisp. In **semi-supervised learning** we are given a few labeled examples and must make what we can of a large collection of unlabeled examples. Even the labels themselves may not be the oracular truths that we hope for. Imagine that you are trying to build a system to guess a person's age from a photo. You gather some labeled examples by snapping pictures of people and asking their age. That's supervised learning. But in reality some of the people lied about their age. It's not just that there is random noise in the data; rather the inaccuracies are systematic, and to uncover them is an unsupervised learning problem involving images, self-reported ages, and true (unknown) ages. Thus, both noise and lack of labels create a continuum between supervised and unsupervised learning.

2 SUPERVISED LEARNING

The task of supervised learning is this:

TRAINING SET

Given a **training set** of N example input–output pairs

$$(x_1, y_1), (x_2, y_2), \ldots (x_N, y_N)\,,$$

where each y_j was generated by an unknown function $y = f(x)$, discover a function h that approximates the true function f.

HYPOTHESIS

Here x and y can be any value; they need not be numbers. The function h is a **hypothesis.**[1] Learning is a search through the space of possible hypotheses for one that will perform well, even on new examples beyond the training set. To measure the accuracy of a hypothesis we

TEST SET

give it a **test set** of examples that are distinct from the training set. We say a hypothesis

[1] A note on notation: except where noted, we will use j to index the N examples; x_j will always be the input and y_j the output. In cases where the input is specifically a vector of attribute values (beginning with Section 3), we will use $\mathbf{x}_j$ for the jth example and we will use i to index the n attributes of each example. The elements of $\mathbf{x}_j$ are written $x_{j,1}, x_{j,2}, \ldots, x_{j,n}$.

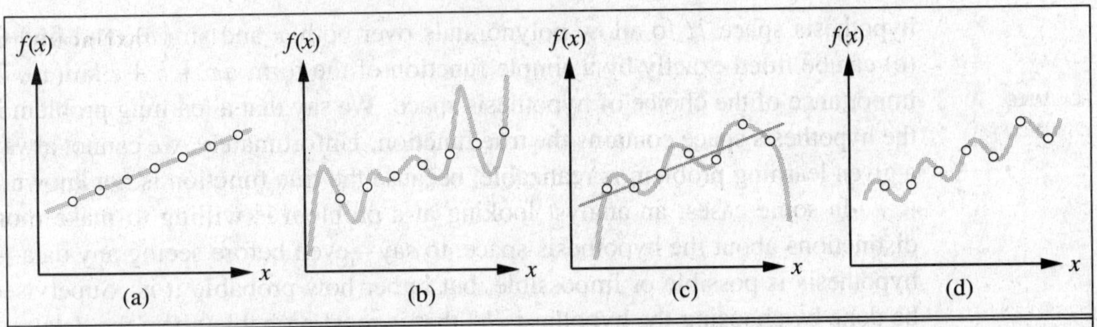

Figure 1 (a) Example $(x, f(x))$ pairs and a consistent, linear hypothesis. (b) A consistent, degree-7 polynomial hypothesis for the same data set. (c) A different data set, which admits an exact degree-6 polynomial fit or an approximate linear fit. (d) A simple, exact sinusoidal fit to the same data set.

GENERALIZATION

generalizes well if it correctly predicts the value of y for novel examples. Sometimes the function f is stochastic—it is not strictly a function of x, and what we have to learn is a conditional probability distribution, $\mathbf{P}(Y \mid x)$.

CLASSIFICATION

REGRESSION

When the output y is one of a finite set of values (such as *sunny, cloudy* or *rainy*), the learning problem is called **classification**, and is called Boolean or binary classification if there are only two values. When y is a number (such as tomorrow's temperature), the learning problem is called **regression**. (Technically, solving a regression problem is finding a conditional expectation or average value of y, because the probability that we have found *exactly* the right real-valued number for y is 0.)

HYPOTHESIS SPACE

CONSISTENT

OCKHAM'S RAZOR

Figure 1 shows a familiar example: fitting a function of a single variable to some data points. The examples are points in the (x, y) plane, where $y = f(x)$. We don't know what f is, but we will approximate it with a function h selected from a **hypothesis space**, $\mathcal{H}$, which for this example we will take to be the set of polynomials, such as x^5+3x^2+2. Figure 1(a) shows some data with an exact fit by a straight line (the polynomial $0.4x + 3$). The line is called a **consistent** hypothesis because it agrees with all the data. Figure 1(b) shows a high-degree polynomial that is also consistent with the same data. This illustrates a fundamental problem in inductive learning: *how do we choose from among multiple consistent hypotheses?* One answer is to prefer the *simplest* hypothesis consistent with the data. This principle is called **Ockham's razor**, after the 14th-century English philosopher William of Ockham, who used it to argue sharply against all sorts of complications. Defining simplicity is not easy, but it seems clear that a degree-1 polynomial is simpler than a degree-7 polynomial, and thus (a) should be preferred to (b). We will make this intuition more precise in Section 4.3.

Figure 1(c) shows a second data set. There is no consistent straight line for this data set; in fact, it requires a degree-6 polynomial for an exact fit. There are just 7 data points, so a polynomial with 7 parameters does not seem to be finding any pattern in the data and we do not expect it to generalize well. A straight line that is not consistent with any of the data points, but might generalize fairly well for unseen values of x, is also shown in (c). *In general, there is a tradeoff between complex hypotheses that fit the training data well and simpler hypotheses that may generalize better.* In Figure 1(d) we expand the hypothesis space $\mathcal{H}$ to allow polynomials over both x and $\sin(x)$, and find that the data in (c) can be fitted exactly by a simple function of the form $ax + b + c\sin(x)$. This shows the importance of the choice of hypothesis space. We say that a learning problem is **realizable** if the hypothesis space contains the true function. Unfortunately, we cannot always tell whether a given learning problem is realizable, because the true function is not known.

REALIZABLE

In some cases, an analyst looking at a problem is willing to make more fine-grained distinctions about the hypothesis space, to say—even before seeing any data—not just that a hypothesis is possible or impossible, but rather how probable it is. Supervised learning can be done by choosing the hypothesis h^* that is most probable given the data:

$$h^* = \operatorname*{argmax}_{h\in\mathcal{H}} P(h|data) .$$

By Bayes' rule this is equivalent to

$$h^* = \operatorname*{argmax}_{h\in\mathcal{H}} P(data|h)\, P(h) .$$

Then we can say that the prior probability $P(h)$ is high for a degree-1 or -2 polynomial, lower for a degree-7 polynomial, and especially low for degree-7 polynomials with large, sharp spikes as in Figure 1(b). We allow unusual-looking functions when the data say we really need them, but we discourage them by giving them a low prior probability.

Why not let $\mathcal{H}$ be the class of all Java programs, or Turing machines? After all, every computable function can be represented by some Turing machine, and that is the best we can do. One problem with this idea is that it does not take into account the computational complexity of learning. *There is a tradeoff between the expressiveness of a hypothesis space and the complexity of finding a good hypothesis within that space.* For example, fitting a straight line to data is an easy computation; fitting high-degree polynomials is somewhat harder; and fitting Turing machines is in general undecidable. A second reason to prefer simple hypothesis spaces is that presumably we will want to use h after we have learned it, and computing $h(x)$ when h is a linear function is guaranteed to be fast, while computing an arbitrary Turing machine program is not even guaranteed to terminate. For these reasons, most work on learning has focused on simple representations.

We will see that the expressiveness–complexity tradeoff is not as simple as it first seems: it is often the case that an expressive language makes it possible for a simple hypothesis to fit the data, whereas restricting the expressiveness of the language means that any consistent hypothesis must be very complex. For example, the rules of chess can be written in a page or two of first-order logic, but require thousands of pages when written in propositional logic.

3 Learning Decision Trees

Decision tree induction is one of the simplest and yet most successful forms of machine learning. We first describe the representation—the hypothesis space—and then show how to learn a good hypothesis.

3.1 The decision tree representation

DECISION TREE A **decision tree** represents a function that takes as input a vector of attribute values and returns a "decision"—a single output value. The input and output values can be discrete or continuous. For now we will concentrate on problems where the inputs have discrete values and the output has exactly two possible values; this is Boolean classification, where each example input will be classified as true (a **positive** example) or false (a **negative** example).

POSITIVE

NEGATIVE

A decision tree reaches its decision by performing a sequence of tests. Each internal node in the tree corresponds to a test of the value of one of the input attributes, A_i, and the branches from the node are labeled with the possible values of the attribute, $A_i = v_{ik}$. Each leaf node in the tree specifies a value to be returned by the function. The decision tree representation is natural for humans; indeed, many "How To" manuals (e.g., for car repair) are written entirely as a single decision tree stretching over hundreds of pages.

As an example, we will build a decision tree to decide whether to wait for a table at a restaurant. The aim here is to learn a definition for the **goal predicate** *WillWait*. First we list the attributes that we will consider as part of the input:

GOAL PREDICATE

1. *Alternate*: whether there is a suitable alternative restaurant nearby.
2. *Bar*: whether the restaurant has a comfortable bar area to wait in.
3. *Fri/Sat*: true on Fridays and Saturdays.
4. *Hungry*: whether we are hungry.
5. *Patrons*: how many people are in the restaurant (values are *None*, *Some*, and *Full*).
6. *Price*: the restaurant's price range ($, $$, $$$).
7. *Raining*: whether it is raining outside.
8. *Reservation*: whether we made a reservation.
9. *Type*: the kind of restaurant (French, Italian, Thai, or burger).
10. *WaitEstimate*: the wait estimated by the host (0–10 minutes, 10–30, 30–60, or >60).

Note that every variable has a small set of possible values; the value of *WaitEstimate*, for example, is not an integer, rather it is one of the four discrete values 0–10, 10–30, 30–60, or >60. The decision tree usually used by one of us (SR) for this domain is shown in Figure 2. Notice that the tree ignores the *Price* and *Type* attributes. Examples are processed by the tree starting at the root and following the appropriate branch until a leaf is reached. For instance, an example with *Patrons* = *Full* and *WaitEstimate* = 0–10 will be classified as positive (i.e., yes, we will wait for a table).

3.2 Expressiveness of decision trees

A Boolean decision tree is logically equivalent to the assertion that the goal attribute is true if and only if the input attributes satisfy one of the paths leading to a leaf with value *true*. Writing this out in propositional logic, we have

$$Goal \Leftrightarrow (Path_1 \vee Path_2 \vee \cdots)\,,$$

where each *Path* is a conjunction of attribute-value tests required to follow that path. Thus, the whole expression is equivalent to disjunctive normal form, which means that any function in propositional logic can be expressed as a decision tree. As an example, the rightmost path in Figure 2 is

$$Path = (Patrons = Full \wedge WaitEstimate = 0\text{–}10) .$$

For a wide variety of problems, the decision tree format yields a nice, concise result. But some functions cannot be represented concisely. For example, the majority function, which returns true if and only if more than half of the inputs are true, requires an exponentially large decision tree. In other words, decision trees are good for some kinds of functions and bad for others. Is there *any* kind of representation that is efficient for *all* kinds of functions? Unfortunately, the answer is no. We can show this in a general way. Consider the set of all Boolean functions on n attributes. How many different functions are in this set? This is just the number of different truth tables that we can write down, because the function is defined by its truth table. A truth table over n attributes has 2^n rows, one for each combination of values of the attributes. We can consider the "answer" column of the table as a 2^n-bit number that defines the function. That means there are 2^{2^n} different functions (and there will be more than that number of trees, since more than one tree can compute the same function). This is a scary number. For example, with just the ten Boolean attributes of our restaurant problem there are 2^{1024} or about 10^{308} different functions to choose from, and for 20 attributes there are over $10^{300,000}$. We will need some ingenious algorithms to find good hypotheses in such a large space.

3.3 Inducing decision trees from examples

An example for a Boolean decision tree consists of an $(\mathbf{x}, y)$ pair, where $\mathbf{x}$ is a vector of values for the input attributes, and y is a single Boolean output value. A training set of 12 examples

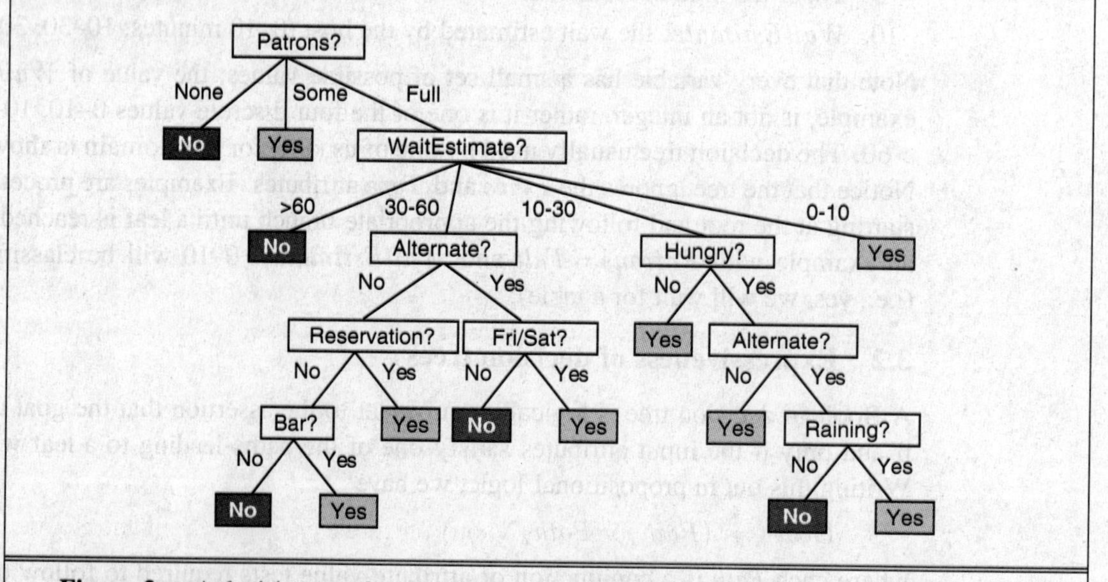

Figure 2 A decision tree for deciding whether to wait for a table.

Example	Alt	Bar	Fri	Hun	Pat	Price	Rain	Res	Type	Est	Goal: WillWait
$\mathbf{x}_1$	Yes	No	No	Yes	Some	$$$	No	Yes	French	0–10	$y_1 = Yes$
$\mathbf{x}_2$	Yes	No	No	Yes	Full	$	No	No	Thai	30–60	$y_2 = No$
$\mathbf{x}_3$	No	Yes	No	No	Some	$	No	No	Burger	0–10	$y_3 = Yes$
$\mathbf{x}_4$	Yes	No	Yes	Yes	Full	$	Yes	No	Thai	10–30	$y_4 = Yes$
$\mathbf{x}_5$	Yes	No	Yes	No	Full	$$$	No	Yes	French	>60	$y_5 = No$
$\mathbf{x}_6$	No	Yes	No	Yes	Some	$$	Yes	Yes	Italian	0–10	$y_6 = Yes$
$\mathbf{x}_7$	No	Yes	No	No	None	$	Yes	No	Burger	0–10	$y_7 = No$
$\mathbf{x}_8$	No	No	No	Yes	Some	$$	Yes	Yes	Thai	0–10	$y_8 = Yes$
$\mathbf{x}_9$	No	Yes	Yes	No	Full	$	Yes	No	Burger	>60	$y_9 = No$
$\mathbf{x}_{10}$	Yes	Yes	Yes	Yes	Full	$$$	No	Yes	Italian	10–30	$y_{10} = No$
$\mathbf{x}_{11}$	No	No	No	No	None	$	No	No	Thai	0–10	$y_{11} = No$
$\mathbf{x}_{12}$	Yes	Yes	Yes	Yes	Full	$	No	No	Burger	30–60	$y_{12} = Yes$

Figure 3 Examples for the restaurant domain.

is shown in Figure 3. The positive examples are the ones in which the goal *WillWait* is true ($\mathbf{x}_1, \mathbf{x}_3, \ldots$); the negative examples are the ones in which it is false ($\mathbf{x}_2, \mathbf{x}_5, \ldots$).

We want a tree that is consistent with the examples and is as small as possible. Unfortunately, no matter how we measure size, it is an intractable problem to find the smallest consistent tree; there is no way to efficiently search through the 2^{2^n} trees. With some simple heuristics, however, we can find a good approximate solution: a small (but not smallest) consistent tree. The DECISION-TREE-LEARNING algorithm adopts a greedy divide-and-conquer strategy: always test the most important attribute first. This test divides the problem up into smaller subproblems that can then be solved recursively. By "most important attribute," we mean the one that makes the most difference to the classification of an example. That way, we hope to get to the correct classification with a small number of tests, meaning that all paths in the tree will be short and the tree as a whole will be shallow.

Figure 4(a) shows that *Type* is a poor attribute, because it leaves us with four possible outcomes, each of which has the same number of positive as negative examples. On the other hand, in (b) we see that *Patrons* is a fairly important attribute, because if the value is *None* or *Some*, then we are left with example sets for which we can answer definitively (*No* and *Yes*, respectively). If the value is *Full*, we are left with a mixed set of examples. In general, after the first attribute test splits up the examples, each outcome is a new decision tree learning problem in itself, with fewer examples and one less attribute. There are four cases to consider for these recursive problems:

1. If the remaining examples are all positive (or all negative), then we are done: we can answer *Yes* or *No*. Figure 4(b) shows examples of this happening in the *None* and *Some* branches.
2. If there are some positive and some negative examples, then choose the best attribute to split them. Figure 4(b) shows *Hungry* being used to split the remaining examples.
3. If there are no examples left, it means that no example has been observed for this com-

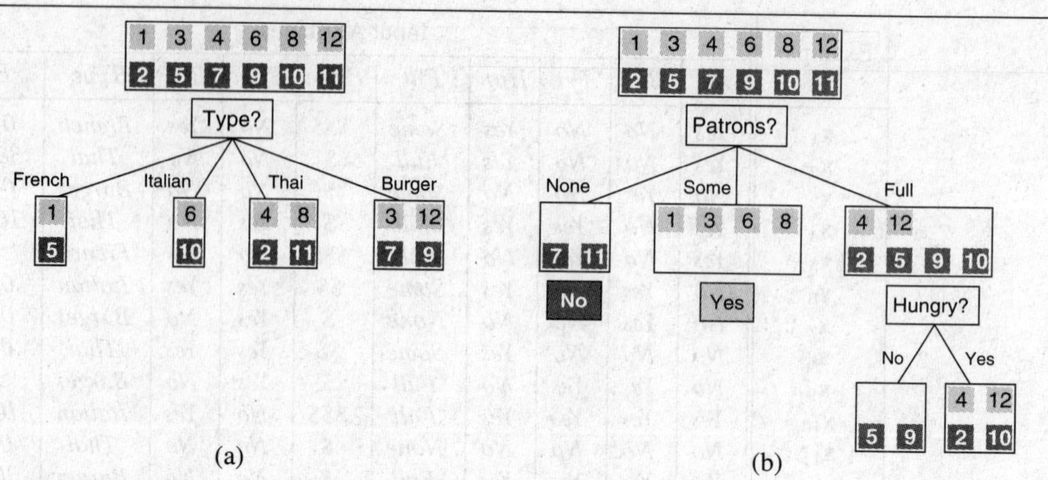

Figure 4 Splitting the examples by testing on attributes. At each node we show the positive (light boxes) and negative (dark boxes) examples remaining. (a) Splitting on *Type* brings us no nearer to distinguishing between positive and negative examples. (b) Splitting on *Patrons* does a good job of separating positive and negative examples. After splitting on *Patrons*, *Hungry* is a fairly good second test.

bination of attribute values, and we return a default value calculated from the plurality classification of all the examples that were used in constructing the node's parent. These are passed along in the variable *parent_examples*.

4. If there are no attributes left, but both positive and negative examples, it means that these examples have exactly the same description, but different classifications. This can happen because there is an error or **noise** in the data; because the domain is nondeterministic; or because we can't observe an attribute that would distinguish the examples. The best we can do is return the plurality classification of the remaining examples.

NOISE

The DECISION-TREE-LEARNING algorithm is shown in Figure 5. Note that the set of examples is crucial for *constructing* the tree, but nowhere do the examples appear in the tree itself. A tree consists of just tests on attributes in the interior nodes, values of attributes on the branches, and output values on the leaf nodes. The details of the IMPORTANCE function are given in Section 3.4. The output of the learning algorithm on our sample training set is shown in Figure 6. The tree is clearly different from the original tree shown in Figure 2. One might conclude that the learning algorithm is not doing a very good job of learning the correct function. This would be the wrong conclusion to draw, however. The learning algorithm looks at the *examples*, not at the correct function, and in fact, its hypothesis (see Figure 6) not only is consistent with all the examples, but is considerably simpler than the original tree! The learning algorithm has no reason to include tests for *Raining* and *Reservation*, because it can classify all the examples without them. It has also detected an interesting and previously unsuspected pattern: the first author will wait for Thai food on weekends. It is also bound to make some mistakes for cases where it has seen no examples. For example, it has never seen a case where the wait is 0–10 minutes but the restaurant is full.

```
function DECISION-TREE-LEARNING(examples, attributes, parent_examples) returns
a tree

  if examples is empty then return PLURALITY-VALUE(parent_examples)
  else if all examples have the same classification then return the classification
  else if attributes is empty then return PLURALITY-VALUE(examples)
  else
     A ← argmax_{a ∈ attributes} IMPORTANCE(a, examples)
     tree ← a new decision tree with root test A
     for each value v_k of A do
        exs ← {e : e ∈ examples and e.A = v_k}
        subtree ← DECISION-TREE-LEARNING(exs, attributes − A, examples)
        add a branch to tree with label (A = v_k) and subtree subtree
     return tree
```

Figure 5 The decision-tree learning algorithm. The function IMPORTANCE is described in Section 3.4. The function PLURALITY-VALUE selects the most common output value among a set of examples, breaking ties randomly.

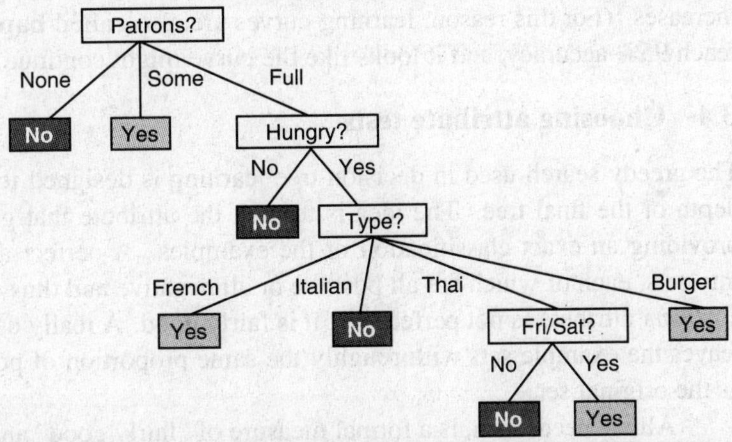

Figure 6 The decision tree induced from the 12-example training set.

In that case it says not to wait when *Hungry* is false, but I (SR) would certainly wait. With more training examples the learning program could correct this mistake.

We note there is a danger of over-interpreting the tree that the algorithm selects. When there are several variables of similar importance, the choice between them is somewhat arbitrary: with slightly different input examples, a different variable would be chosen to split on first, and the whole tree would look completely different. The function computed by the tree would still be similar, but the structure of the tree can vary widely.

LEARNING CURVE

We can evaluate the accuracy of a learning algorithm with a **learning curve**, as shown in Figure 7. We have 100 examples at our disposal, which we split into a training set and

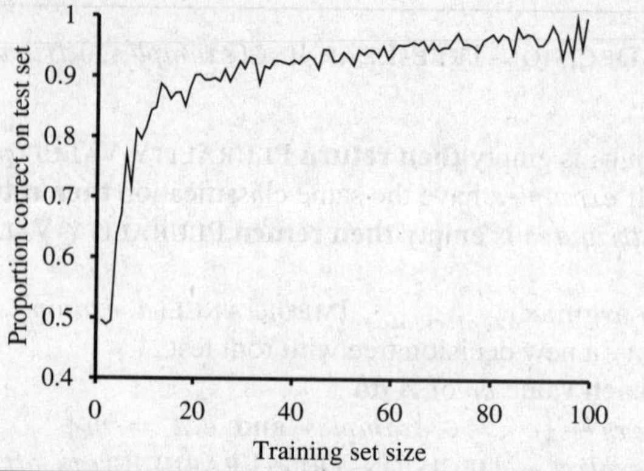

Figure 7 A learning curve for the decision tree learning algorithm on 100 randomly generated examples in the restaurant domain. Each data point is the average of 20 trials.

a test set. We learn a hypothesis h with the training set and measure its accuracy with the test set. We do this starting with a training set of size 1 and increasing one at a time up to size 99. For each size we actually repeat the process of randomly splitting 20 times, and average the results of the 20 trials. The curve shows that as the training set size grows, the accuracy increases. (For this reason, learning curves are also called **happy graphs**.) In this graph we reach 95% accuracy, and it looks like the curve might continue to increase with more data.

3.4 Choosing attribute tests

The greedy search used in decision tree learning is designed to approximately minimize the depth of the final tree. The idea is to pick the attribute that goes as far as possible toward providing an exact classification of the examples. A perfect attribute divides the examples into sets, each of which are all positive or all negative and thus will be leaves of the tree. The *Patrons* attribute is not perfect, but it is fairly good. A really useless attribute, such as *Type*, leaves the example sets with roughly the same proportion of positive and negative examples as the original set.

All we need, then, is a formal measure of "fairly good" and "really useless" and we can implement the IMPORTANCE function of Figure 5. We will use the notion of information gain, which is defined in terms of **entropy**, the fundamental quantity in information theory (Shannon and Weaver, 1949).

ENTROPY

Entropy is a measure of the uncertainty of a random variable; acquisition of information corresponds to a reduction in entropy. A random variable with only one value—a coin that always comes up heads—has no uncertainty and thus its entropy is defined as zero; thus, we gain no information by observing its value. A flip of a fair coin is equally likely to come up heads or tails, 0 or 1, and we will soon show that this counts as "1 bit" of entropy. The roll of a fair *four*-sided die has 2 bits of entropy, because it takes two bits to describe one of four equally probable choices. Now consider an unfair coin that comes up heads 99% of the time. Intuitively, this coin has less uncertainty than the fair coin—if we guess heads we'll be wrong only 1% of the time—so we would like it to have an entropy measure that is close to zero, but positive. In general, the entropy of a random variable V with values v_k, each with probability $P(v_k)$, is defined as

$$\text{Entropy:}\quad H(V) = \sum_k P(v_k)\log_2 \frac{1}{P(v_k)} = -\sum_k P(v_k)\log_2 P(v_k)\,.$$

We can check that the entropy of a fair coin flip is indeed 1 bit:

$$H(Fair) = -(0.5\log_2 0.5 + 0.5\log_2 0.5) = 1\,.$$

If the coin is loaded to give 99% heads, we get

$$H(Loaded) = -(0.99\log_2 0.99 + 0.01\log_2 0.01) \approx 0.08 \text{ bits.}$$

It will help to define $B(q)$ as the entropy of a Boolean random variable that is true with probability q:

$$B(q) = -(q\log_2 q + (1-q)\log_2(1-q))\,.$$

Thus, $H(Loaded) = B(0.99) \approx 0.08$. Now let's get back to decision tree learning. If a training set contains p positive examples and n negative examples, then the entropy of the goal attribute on the whole set is

$$H(Goal) = B\left(\frac{p}{p+n}\right)\,.$$

The restaurant training set in Figure 3 has $p = n = 6$, so the corresponding entropy is $B(0.5)$ or exactly 1 bit. A test on a single attribute A might give us only part of this 1 bit. We can measure exactly how much by looking at the entropy remaining *after* the attribute test.

An attribute A with d distinct values divides the training set E into subsets $E_1, \ldots, E_d$. Each subset E_k has p_k positive examples and n_k negative examples, so if we go along that branch, we will need an additional $B(p_k/(p_k + n_k))$ bits of information to answer the question. A randomly chosen example from the training set has the kth value for the attribute with probability $(p_k + n_k)/(p + n)$, so the expected entropy remaining after testing attribute A is

$$Remainder(A) = \sum_{k=1}^{d} \tfrac{p_k+n_k}{p+n} B\left(\tfrac{p_k}{p_k+n_k}\right)\,.$$

INFORMATION GAIN

The **information gain** from the attribute test on A is the expected reduction in entropy:

$$Gain(A) = B\left(\tfrac{p}{p+n}\right) - Remainder(A)\,.$$

In fact $Gain(A)$ is just what we need to implement the IMPORTANCE function. Returning to the attributes considered in Figure 4, we have

$$Gain(Patrons) = 1 - \left[\tfrac{2}{12}B(\tfrac{0}{2}) + \tfrac{4}{12}B(\tfrac{4}{4}) + \tfrac{6}{12}B(\tfrac{2}{6})\right] \approx 0.541 \text{ bits,}$$
$$Gain(Type) = 1 - \left[\tfrac{2}{12}B(\tfrac{1}{2}) + \tfrac{2}{12}B(\tfrac{1}{2}) + \tfrac{4}{12}B(\tfrac{2}{4}) + \tfrac{4}{12}B(\tfrac{2}{4})\right] = 0 \text{ bits,}$$

confirming our intuition that *Patrons* is a better attribute to split on. In fact, *Patrons* has the maximum gain of any of the attributes and would be chosen by the decision-tree learning algorithm as the root.

3.5 Generalization and overfitting

On some problems, the DECISION-TREE-LEARNING algorithm will generate a large tree when there is actually no pattern to be found. Consider the problem of trying to predict whether the roll of a die will come up as 6 or not. Suppose that experiments are carried out with various dice and that the attributes describing each training example include the color of the die, its weight, the time when the roll was done, and whether the experimenters had their fingers crossed. If the dice are fair, the right thing to learn is a tree with a single node that says "no," But the DECISION-TREE-LEARNING algorithm will seize on any pattern it can find in the input. If it turns out that there are 2 rolls of a 7-gram blue die with fingers crossed and they both come out 6, then the algorithm may construct a path that predicts 6 in that case. This problem is called **overfitting**. A general phenomenon, overfitting occurs with all types of learners, even when the target function is not at all random. In Figure 1(b) and (c), we saw polynomial functions overfitting the data. Overfitting becomes more likely as the hypothesis space and the number of input attributes grows, and less likely as we increase the number of training examples.

OVERFITTING

DECISION TREE PRUNING

For decision trees, a technique called **decision tree pruning** combats overfitting. Pruning works by eliminating nodes that are not clearly relevant. We start with a full tree, as generated by DECISION-TREE-LEARNING. We then look at a test node that has only leaf nodes as descendants. If the test appears to be irrelevant—detecting only noise in the data—then we eliminate the test, replacing it with a leaf node. We repeat this process, considering each test with only leaf descendants, until each one has either been pruned or accepted as is.

The question is, how do we detect that a node is testing an irrelevant attribute? Suppose we are at a node consisting of p positive and n negative examples. If the attribute is irrelevant, we would expect that it would split the examples into subsets that each have roughly the same proportion of positive examples as the whole set, $p/(p+n)$, and so the information gain will be close to zero.[2] Thus, the information gain is a good clue to irrelevance. Now the question is, how large a gain should we require in order to split on a particular attribute?

SIGNIFICANCE TEST

NULL HYPOTHESIS

We can answer this question by using a statistical **significance test**. Such a test begins by assuming that there is no underlying pattern (the so-called **null hypothesis**). Then the actual data are analyzed to calculate the extent to which they deviate from a perfect absence of pattern. If the degree of deviation is statistically unlikely (usually taken to mean a 5% probability or less), then that is considered to be good evidence for the presence of a significant pattern in the data. The probabilities are calculated from standard distributions of the amount of deviation one would expect to see in random sampling.

In this case, the null hypothesis is that the attribute is irrelevant and, hence, that the information gain for an infinitely large sample would be zero. We need to calculate the probability that, under the null hypothesis, a sample of size $v = n + p$ would exhibit the observed deviation from the expected distribution of positive and negative examples. We can measure the deviation by comparing the actual numbers of positive and negative examples in

[2] The gain will be strictly positive except for the unlikely case where all the proportions are *exactly* the same. (See Exercise 5.)

each subset, p_k and n_k, with the expected numbers, $\hat{p}_k$ and $\hat{n}_k$, assuming true irrelevance:

$$\hat{p}_k = p \times \frac{p_k + n_k}{p+n} \qquad \hat{n}_k = n \times \frac{p_k + n_k}{p+n}.$$

A convenient measure of the total deviation is given by

$$\Delta = \sum_{k=1}^{d} \frac{(p_k - \hat{p}_k)^2}{\hat{p}_k} + \frac{(n_k - \hat{n}_k)^2}{\hat{n}_k}.$$

Under the null hypothesis, the value of Δ is distributed according to the χ^2 (chi-squared) distribution with $v-1$ degrees of freedom. We can use a χ^2 table or a standard statistical library routine to see if a particular Δ value confirms or rejects the null hypothesis. For example, consider the restaurant type attribute, with four values and thus three degrees of freedom. A value of $\Delta = 7.82$ or more would reject the null hypothesis at the 5% level (and a value of $\Delta = 11.35$ or more would reject at the 1% level). Exercise 8 asks you to extend the DECISION-TREE-LEARNING algorithm to implement this form of pruning, which is known as χ^2 **pruning**.

χ^2 PRUNING

With pruning, noise in the examples can be tolerated. Errors in the example's label (e.g., an example (**x**, *Yes*) that should be (**x**, *No*)) give a linear increase in prediction error, whereas errors in the descriptions of examples (e.g., *Price* = \$ when it was actually *Price* = \$\$) have an asymptotic effect that gets worse as the tree shrinks down to smaller sets. Pruned trees perform significantly better than unpruned trees when the data contain a large amount of noise. Also, the pruned trees are often much smaller and hence easier to understand.

One final warning: You might think that χ^2 pruning and information gain look similar, so why not combine them using an approach called **early stopping**—have the decision tree algorithm stop generating nodes when there is no good attribute to split on, rather than going to all the trouble of generating nodes and then pruning them away. The problem with early stopping is that it stops us from recognizing situations where there is no one good attribute, but there are combinations of attributes that are informative. For example, consider the XOR function of two binary attributes. If there are roughly equal number of examples for all four combinations of input values, then neither attribute will be informative, yet the correct thing to do is to split on one of the attributes (it doesn't matter which one), and then at the second level we will get splits that are informative. Early stopping would miss this, but generate-and-then-prune handles it correctly.

EARLY STOPPING

3.6 Broadening the applicability of decision trees

In order to extend decision tree induction to a wider variety of problems, a number of issues must be addressed. We will briefly mention several, suggesting that a full understanding is best obtained by doing the associated exercises:

- **Missing data**: In many domains, not all the attribute values will be known for every example. The values might have gone unrecorded, or they might be too expensive to obtain. This gives rise to two problems: First, given a complete decision tree, how should one classify an example that is missing one of the test attributes? Second, how should one modify the information-gain formula when some examples have unknown values for the attribute? These questions are addressed in Exercise 9.

- **Multivalued attributes**: When an attribute has many possible values, the information gain measure gives an inappropriate indication of the attribute's usefulness. In the extreme case, an attribute such as *ExactTime* has a different value for every example, which means each subset of examples is a singleton with a unique classification, and the information gain measure would have its highest value for this attribute. But choosing this split first is unlikely to yield the best tree. One solution is to use the **gain ratio** (Exercise 10). Another possibility is to allow a Boolean test of the form $A = v_k$, that is, picking out just one of the possible values for an attribute, leaving the remaining values to possibly be tested later in the tree.

GAIN RATIO

- **Continuous and integer-valued input attributes**: Continuous or integer-valued attributes such as *Height* and *Weight*, have an infinite set of possible values. Rather than generate infinitely many branches, decision-tree learning algorithms typically find the **split point** that gives the highest information gain. For example, at a given node in the tree, it might be the case that testing on $Weight > 160$ gives the most information. Efficient methods exist for finding good split points: start by sorting the values of the attribute, and then consider only split points that are between two examples in sorted order that have different classifications, while keeping track of the running totals of positive and negative examples on each side of the split point. Splitting is the most expensive part of real-world decision tree learning applications.

SPLIT POINT

- **Continuous-valued output attributes**: If we are trying to predict a numerical output value, such as the price of an apartment, then we need a **regression tree** rather than a classification tree. A regression tree has at each leaf a linear function of some subset of numerical attributes, rather than a single value. For example, the branch for two-bedroom apartments might end with a linear function of square footage, number of bathrooms, and average income for the neighborhood. The learning algorithm must decide when to stop splitting and begin applying linear regression (see Section 6) over the attributes.

REGRESSION TREE

A decision-tree learning system for real-world applications must be able to handle all of these problems. Handling continuous-valued variables is especially important, because both physical and financial processes provide numerical data. Several commercial packages have been built that meet these criteria, and they have been used to develop thousands of fielded systems. In many areas of industry and commerce, decision trees are usually the first method tried when a classification method is to be extracted from a data set. One important property of decision trees is that it is possible for a human to understand the reason for the output of the learning algorithm. (Indeed, this is a *legal requirement* for financial decisions that are subject to anti-discrimination laws.) This is a property not shared by some other representations, such as neural networks.

4 Evaluating and Choosing the Best Hypothesis

STATIONARITY ASSUMPTION

We want to learn a hypothesis that fits the future data best. To make that precise we need to define "future data" and "best." We make the **stationarity assumption**: that there is a probability distribution over examples that remains stationary over time. Each example data point (before we see it) is a random variable E_j whose observed value $e_j = (x_j, y_j)$ is sampled from that distribution, and is independent of the previous examples:

$$\mathbf{P}(E_j|E_{j-1}, E_{j-2}, \ldots) = \mathbf{P}(E_j),$$

and each example has an identical prior probability distribution:

$$\mathbf{P}(E_j) = \mathbf{P}(E_{j-1}) = \mathbf{P}(E_{j-2}) = \cdots .$$

I.I.D.

Examples that satisfy these assumptions are called *independent and identically distributed* or **i.i.d.**. An i.i.d. assumption connects the past to the future; without some such connection, all bets are off—the future could be anything. (We will see later that learning can still occur if there are *slow* changes in the distribution.)

ERROR RATE

The next step is to define "best fit." We define the **error rate** of a hypothesis as the proportion of mistakes it makes—the proportion of times that $h(x) \neq y$ for an (x, y) example. Now, just because a hypothesis h has a low error rate on the training set does not mean that it will generalize well. A professor knows that an exam will not accurately evaluate students if they have already seen the exam questions. Similarly, to get an accurate evaluation of a hypothesis, we need to test it on a set of examples it has not seen yet. The simplest approach is the one we have seen already: randomly split the available data into a training set from which the learning algorithm produces h and a test set on which the accuracy of h is evaluated. This method, sometimes called **holdout cross-validation**, has the disadvantage that it fails to use all the available data; if we use half the data for the test set, then we are only training on half the data, and we may get a poor hypothesis. On the other hand, if we reserve only 10% of the data for the test set, then we may, by statistical chance, get a poor estimate of the actual accuracy.

HOLDOUT CROSS-VALIDATION

K-FOLD CROSS-VALIDATION

We can squeeze more out of the data and still get an accurate estimate using a technique called **k-fold cross-validation**. The idea is that each example serves double duty—as training data and test data. First we split the data into k equal subsets. We then perform k rounds of learning; on each round $1/k$ of the data is held out as a test set and the remaining examples are used as training data. The average test set score of the k rounds should then be a better estimate than a single score. Popular values for k are 5 and 10—enough to give an estimate that is statistically likely to be accurate, at a cost of 5 to 10 times longer computation time. The extreme is $k = n$, also known as **leave-one-out cross-validation** or **LOOCV**.

LEAVE-ONE-OUT CROSS-VALIDATION

LOOCV

PEEKING

Despite the best efforts of statistical methodologists, users frequently invalidate their results by inadvertently **peeking** at the test data. Peeking can happen like this: A learning algorithm has various "knobs" that can be twiddled to tune its behavior—for example, various different criteria for choosing the next attribute in decision tree learning. The researcher generates hypotheses for various different settings of the knobs, measures their error rates on the test set, and reports the error rate of the best hypothesis. Alas, peeking has occurred! The reason is that the hypothesis was selected *on the basis of its test set error rate*, so information about the test set has leaked into the learning algorithm.

Peeking is a consequence of using test-set performance to both *choose* a hypothesis and *evaluate* it. The way to avoid this is to *really* hold the test set out—lock it away until you are completely done with learning and simply wish to obtain an independent evaluation of the final hypothesis. (And then, if you don't like the results ... you have to obtain, and lock away, a completely new test set if you want to go back and find a better hypothesis.) If the test set is locked away, but you still want to measure performance on unseen data as a way of selecting a good hypothesis, then divide the available data (without the test set) into a training set and a **validation set**. The next section shows how to use validation sets to find a good tradeoff between hypothesis complexity and goodness of fit.

VALIDATION SET

4.1 Model selection: Complexity versus goodness of fit

In Figure 1 we showed that higher-degree polynomials can fit the training data better, but when the degree is to high they will overfit, and perform poorly on validation data. Choosing the degree of the polynomial is an instance of the problem of **model selection**. You can think of the task of finding the best hypothesis as two tasks: model selection defines the hypothesis space and then **optimization** finds the best hypothesis within that space.

MODEL SELECTION

OPTIMIZATION

In this section we explain how to select among models that are parameterized by *size*. For example, with polynomials we have $size = 1$ for linear functions, $size = 2$ for quadratics, and so on. For decision trees, the size could be the number of nodes in the tree. In all cases we want to find the value of the *size* parameter that best balances underfitting and overfitting to give the best test set accuracy.

An algorithm to perform model selection and optimization is shown in Figure 8. It is a **wrapper** that takes a learning algorithm as an argument (DECISION-TREE-LEARNING, for example). The wrapper enumerates models according to a parameter, *size*. For each size, it uses cross validation on *Learner* to compute the average error rate on the training and test sets. We start with the smallest, simplest models (which probably underfit the data), and iterate, considering more complex models at each step, until the models start to overfit. In Figure 9 we see typical curves: the training set error decreases monotonically (although there may in general be slight random variation), while the validation set error decreases at first, and then increases when the model begins to overfit. The cross-validation procedure picks the value of *size* with the lowest validation set error; the bottom of the U-shaped curve. We then generate a hypothesis of that *size*, using all the data (without holding out any of it). Finally, of course, we should evaluate the returned hypothesis on a separate test set.

WRAPPER

This approach requires that the learning algorithm accept a parameter, *size*, and deliver a hypothesis of that size. As we said, for decision tree learning, the size can be the number of nodes. We can modify DECISION-TREE-LEARNER so that it takes the number of nodes as an input, builds the tree breadth-first rather than depth-first (but at each level it still chooses the highest gain attribute first), and stops when it reaches the desired number of nodes.

```
function CROSS-VALIDATION-WRAPPER(Learner, k, examples) returns a hypothesis
  local variables: errT, an array, indexed by size, storing training-set error rates
                   errV, an array, indexed by size, storing validation-set error rates
  for size = 1 to ∞ do
     errT[size], errV[size] ← CROSS-VALIDATION(Learner, size, k, examples)
     if errT has converged then do
        best_size ← the value of size with minimum errV[size]
        return Learner(best_size, examples)

function CROSS-VALIDATION(Learner, size, k, examples) returns two values:
        average training set error rate, average validation set error rate

  fold_errT ← 0; fold_errV ← 0
  for fold = 1 to k do
     training_set, validation_set ← PARTITION(examples, fold, k)
     h ← Learner(size, training_set)
     fold_errT ← fold_errT + ERROR-RATE(h, training_set)
     fold_errV ← fold_errV +ERROR-RATE(h, validation_set)
  return fold_errT/k, fold_errV/k
```

Figure 8 An algorithm to select the model that has the lowest error rate on validation data by building models of increasing complexity, and choosing the one with best empirical error rate on validation data. Here *errT* means error rate on the training data, and *errV* means error rate on the validation data. *Learner*(*size*, *examples*) returns a hypothesis whose complexity is set by the parameter *size*, and which is trained on the *examples*. PARTITION(*examples*, *fold*, *k*) splits *examples* into two subsets: a validation set of size N/k and a training set with all the other examples. The split is different for each value of *fold*.

4.2 From error rates to loss

So far, we have been trying to minimize error rate. This is clearly better than maximizing error rate, but it is not the full story. Consider the problem of classifying email messages as spam or non-spam. It is worse to classify non-spam as spam (and thus potentially miss an important message) then to classify spam as non-spam (and thus suffer a few seconds of annoyance). So a classifier with a 1% error rate, where almost all the errors were classifying spam as non-spam, would be better than a classifier with only a 0.5% error rate, if most of those errors were classifying non-spam as spam. Recall that decision-makers should maximize expected utility, and utility is what learners should maximize as well. In machine learning it is traditional to express utilities by means of a **loss function**. The loss function $L(x, y, \hat{y})$ is defined as the amount of utility lost by predicting $h(x) = \hat{y}$ when the correct answer is $f(x) = y$:

LOSS FUNCTION

$$\begin{aligned} L(x, y, \hat{y}) &= Utility(\text{result of using } y \text{ given an input } x) \\ &- Utility(\text{result of using } \hat{y} \text{ given an input } x) \end{aligned}$$

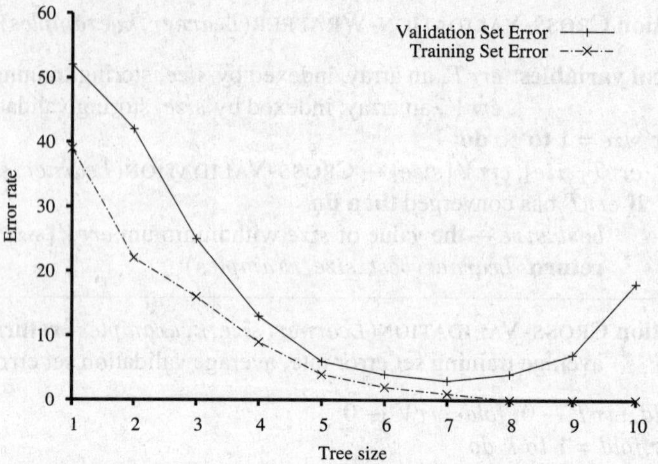

Figure 9 Error rates on training data (lower, dashed line) and validation data (upper, solid line) for different size decision trees. We stop when the training set error rate asymptotes, and then choose the tree with minimal error on the validation set; in this case the tree of size 7 nodes.

This is the most general formulation of the loss function. Often a simplified version is used, $L(y, \hat{y})$, that is independent of x. We will use the simplified version for the rest of this chapter, which means we can't say that it is worse to misclassify a letter from Mom than it is to misclassify a letter from our annoying cousin, but we can say it is 10 times worse to classify non-spam as spam than vice-versa:

$$L(spam, nospam) = 1, \quad L(nospam, spam) = 10\,.$$

Note that $L(y, y)$ is always zero; by definition there is no loss when you guess exactly right. For functions with discrete outputs, we can enumerate a loss value for each possible misclassification, but we can't enumerate all the possibilities for real-valued data. If $f(x)$ is 137.035999, we would be fairly happy with $h(x) = 137.036$, but just how happy should we be? In general small errors are better than large ones; two functions that implement that idea are the absolute value of the difference (called the L_1 loss), and the square of the difference (called the L_2 loss). If we are content with the idea of minimizing error rate, we can use the $L_{0/1}$ loss function, which has a loss of 1 for an incorrect answer and is appropriate for discrete-valued outputs:

Absolute value loss: $L_1(y, \hat{y}) = |y - \hat{y}|$
Squared error loss: $L_2(y, \hat{y}) = (y - \hat{y})^2$
0/1 loss: $L_{0/1}(y, \hat{y}) = 0$ if $y = \hat{y}$, else 1

The learning agent can theoretically maximize its expected utility by choosing the hypothesis that minimizes expected loss over all input–output pairs it will see. It is meaningless to talk about this expectation without defining a prior probability distribution, $\mathbf{P}(X, Y)$ over examples. Let $\mathcal{E}$ be the set of all possible input–output examples. Then the expected **generalization loss** for a hypothesis h (with respect to loss function L) is

GENERALIZATION LOSS

$$GenLoss_L(h) = \sum_{(x,y)\in\mathcal{E}} L(y, h(x))\, P(x, y)\,,$$

and the best hypothesis, h^*, is the one with the minimum expected generalization loss:

$$h^* = \operatorname*{argmin}_{h\in\mathcal{H}} GenLoss_L(h)\,.$$

EMPIRICAL LOSS

Because $P(x, y)$ is not known, the learning agent can only *estimate* generalization loss with **empirical loss** on a set of examples, E:

$$EmpLoss_{L,E}(h) = \frac{1}{N} \sum_{(x,y)\in E} L(y, h(x))\,.$$

The estimated best hypothesis $\hat{h}^*$ is then the one with minimum empirical loss:

$$\hat{h}^* = \operatorname*{argmin}_{h\in\mathcal{H}} EmpLoss_{L,E}(h)\,.$$

There are four reasons why $\hat{h}^*$ may differ from the true function, f: unrealizability, variance, noise, and computational complexity. First, f may not be realizable—may not be in $\mathcal{H}$—or may be present in such a way that other hypotheses are preferred. Second, a learning algorithm will return different hypotheses for different sets of examples, even if those sets are drawn from the same true function f, and those hypotheses will make different predictions on new examples. The higher the variance among the predictions, the higher the probability of significant error. Note that even when the problem is realizable, there will still be random variance, but that variance decreases towards zero as the number of training examples increases. Third, f may be nondeterministic or **noisy**—it may return different values for $f(x)$ each time x occurs. By definition, noise cannot be predicted; in many cases, it arises because the observed labels y are the result of attributes of the environment not listed in x. And finally, when $\mathcal{H}$ is complex, it can be computationally intractable to systematically search the whole hypothesis space. The best we can do is a local search (hill climbing or greedy search) that explores only part of the space. That gives us an approximation error. Combining the sources of error, we're left with an estimation of an approximation of the true function f.

NOISE

SMALL-SCALE LEARNING

Traditional methods in statistics and the early years of machine learning concentrated on **small-scale learning**, where the number of training examples ranged from dozens to the low thousands. Here the generalization error mostly comes from the approximation error of not having the true f in the hypothesis space, and from estimation error of not having enough training examples to limit variance. In recent years there has been more emphasis on **large-scale learning**, often with millions of examples. Here the generalization error is dominated by limits of computation: there is enough data and a rich enough model that we could find an h that is very close to the true f, but the computation to find it is too complex, so we settle for a sub-optimal approximation.

LARGE-SCALE LEARNING

4.3 Regularization

In Section 4.1, we saw how to do model selection with cross-validation on model size. An alternative approach is to search for a hypothesis that directly minimizes the weighted sum of empirical loss and the complexity of the hypothesis, which we will call the total cost:

$$\begin{aligned} Cost(h) &= EmpLoss(h) + \lambda\, Complexity(h) \\ h^* &= \operatorname*{argmin}_{h \in \mathcal{H}} Cost(h) . \end{aligned}$$

Here λ is a parameter, a positive number that serves as a conversion rate between loss and hypothesis complexity (which after all are not measured on the same scale). This approach combines loss and complexity into one metric, allowing us to find the best hypothesis all at once. Unfortunately we still need to do a cross-validation search to find the hypothesis that generalizes best, but this time it is with different values of λ rather than *size*. We select the value of λ that gives us the best validation set score.

REGULARIZATION

This process of explicitly penalizing complex hypotheses is called **regularization** (because it looks for a function that is more regular, or less complex). Note that the cost function requires us to make two choices: the loss function and the complexity measure, which is called a regularization function. The choice of regularization function depends on the hypothesis space. For example, a good regularization function for polynomials is the sum of the squares of the coefficients—keeping the sum small would guide us away from the wiggly polynomials in Figure 1(b) and (c). We will show an example of this type of regularization in Section 6.

FEATURE SELECTION

Another way to simplify models is to reduce the dimensions that the models work with. A process of **feature selection** can be performed to discard attributes that appear to be irrelevant. χ^2 pruning is a kind of feature selection.

MINIMUM DESCRIPTION LENGTH

It is in fact possible to have the empirical loss and the complexity measured on the same scale, without the conversion factor λ: they can both be measured in bits. First encode the hypothesis as a Turing machine program, and count the number of bits. Then count the number of bits required to encode the data, where a correctly predicted example costs zero bits and the cost of an incorrectly predicted example depends on how large the error is. The **minimum description length** or MDL hypothesis minimizes the total number of bits required. This works well in the limit, but for smaller problems there is a difficulty in that the choice of encoding for the program—for example, how best to encode a decision tree as a bit string—affects the outcome.

5 THE THEORY OF LEARNING

The main unanswered question in learning is this: How can we be sure that our learning algorithm has produced a hypothesis that will predict the correct value for previously unseen inputs? In formal terms, how do we know that the hypothesis h is close to the target function f if we don't know what f is? These questions have been pondered for several centuries. In more recent decades, other questions have emerged: how many examples do we need to get a good h? What hypothesis space should we use? If the hypothesis space is very complex, can we even find the best h, or do we have to settle for a local maximum in the space of hypotheses? How complex should h be? How do we avoid overfitting? This section examines these questions.

We'll start with the question of how many examples are needed for learning. We saw from the learning curve for decision tree learning on the restaurant problem (Figure 7) that improves with more training date. Learning curves are useful, but they are specific to a particular learning algorithm on a particular problem. Are there some more general principles governing the number of examples needed in general? Questions like this are addressed by **computational learning theory**, which lies at the intersection of AI, statistics, and theoretical computer science. The underlying principle is that *any hypothesis that is seriously wrong will almost certainly be "found out" with high probability after a small number of examples, because it will make an incorrect prediction. Thus, any hypothesis that is consistent with a sufficiently large set of training examples is unlikely to be seriously wrong: that is, it must be* ***probably approximately correct****.* Any learning algorithm that returns hypotheses that are probably approximately correct is called a **PAC learning** algorithm; we can use this approach to provide bounds on the performance of various learning algorithms.

COMPUTATIONAL LEARNING THEORY

PROBABLY APPROXIMATELY CORRECT

PAC LEARNING

PAC-learning theorems, like all theorems, are logical consequences of axioms. When a *theorem* (as opposed to, say, a political pundit) states something about the future based on the past, the axioms have to provide the "juice" to make that connection. For PAC learning, the juice is provided by the stationarity assumption, which says that future examples are going to be drawn from the same fixed distribution $\mathbf{P}(E) = \mathbf{P}(X, Y)$ as past examples. (Note that we do not have to know what distribution that is, just that it, doesn't change.) In addition, to keep things simple, we will assume that the true function f is deterministic and is a member of the hypothesis class $\mathcal{H}$ that is being considered.

The simplest PAC theorems deal with Boolean functions, for which the 0/1 loss is appropriate. The **error rate** of a hypothesis h, defined informally earlier, is defined formally here as the expected generalization error for examples drawn from the stationary distribution:

$$\text{error}(h) = GenLoss_{L_{0/1}}(h) = \sum_{x,y} L_{0/1}(y, h(x))\, P(x, y)\ .$$

In other words, $\text{error}(h)$ is the probability that h misclassifies a new example. This is the same quantity being measured experimentally by the learning curves shown earlier.

A hypothesis h is called **approximately correct** if $\text{error}(h) \leq \epsilon$, where ϵ is a small constant. We will show that we can find an N such that, after seeing N examples, with high probability, all consistent hypotheses will be approximately correct. One can think of an approximately correct hypothesis as being "close" to the true function in hypothesis space: it lies inside what is called the **ϵ-ball** around the true function f. The hypothesis space outside this ball is called $\mathcal{H}_{\text{bad}}$.

ϵ-BALL

We can calculate the probability that a "seriously wrong" hypothesis $h_b \in \mathcal{H}_{\text{bad}}$ is consistent with the first N examples as follows. We know that $\text{error}(h_b) > \epsilon$. Thus, the probability that it agrees with a given example is at most $1 - \epsilon$. Since the examples are independent, the bound for N examples is

$$P(h_b \text{ agrees with } N \text{ examples}) \leq (1 - \epsilon)^N\ .$$

The probability that $\mathcal{H}_{\text{bad}}$ contains at least one consistent hypothesis is bounded by the sum of the individual probabilities:

$$P(\mathcal{H}_{\text{bad}} \text{ contains a consistent hypothesis}) \leq |\mathcal{H}_{\text{bad}}|(1-\epsilon)^N \leq |\mathcal{H}|(1-\epsilon)^N ,$$

where we have used the fact that $|\mathcal{H}_{\text{bad}}| \leq |\mathcal{H}|$. We would like to reduce the probability of this event below some small number δ:

$$|\mathcal{H}|(1-\epsilon)^N \leq \delta .$$

Given that $1-\epsilon \leq e^{-\epsilon}$, we can achieve this if we allow the algorithm to see

$$N \geq \frac{1}{\epsilon}\left(\ln\frac{1}{\delta} + \ln|\mathcal{H}|\right) \tag{1}$$

examples. Thus, if a learning algorithm returns a hypothesis that is consistent with this many examples, then with probability at least $1-\delta$, it has error at most ϵ. In other words, it is probably approximately correct. The number of required examples, as a function of ϵ and δ, is called the **sample complexity** of the hypothesis space.

SAMPLE COMPLEXITY

If $\mathcal{H}$ is the set of all Boolean functions on n attributes, then $|\mathcal{H}| = 2^{2^n}$. Thus, the sample complexity of the space grows as 2^n. Because the number of possible examples is also 2^n, this suggests that PAC-learning in the class of all Boolean functions requires seeing all, or nearly all, of the possible examples. A moment's thought reveals the reason for this: $\mathcal{H}$ contains enough hypotheses to classify any given set of examples in all possible ways. In particular, for any set of N examples, the set of hypotheses consistent with those examples contains equal numbers of hypotheses that predict x_{N+1} to be positive and hypotheses that predict x_{N+1} to be negative.

To obtain real generalization to unseen examples, then, it seems we need to restrict the hypothesis space $\mathcal{H}$ in some way; but of course, if we do restrict the space, we might eliminate the true function altogether. There are three ways to escape this dilemma. The first, which you may not have studied yet, is to bring prior knowledgeto bear on the problem. The second, which we introduced in Section 4.3, is to insist that the algorithm return not just any consistent hypothesis, but preferably a simple one (as is done in decision tree learning). In cases where finding simple consistent hypotheses is tractable, the sample complexity results are generally better than for analyses based only on consistency. The third escape, which we pursue next, is to focus on learnable subsets of the entire hypothesis space of Boolean functions. This approach relies on the assumption that the restricted language contains a hypothesis h that is close enough to the true function f; the benefits are that the restricted hypothesis space allows for effective generalization and is typically easier to search. We now examine one such restricted language in more detail.

5.1 PAC learning example: Learning decision lists

DECISION LISTS

We now show how to apply PAC learning to a new hypothesis space: **decision lists**. A decision list consists of a series of tests, each of which is a conjunction of literals. If a test succeeds when applied to an example description, the decision list specifies the value to be returned. If the test fails, processing continues with the next test in the list. Decision lists resemble decision trees, but their overall structure is simpler: they branch only in one

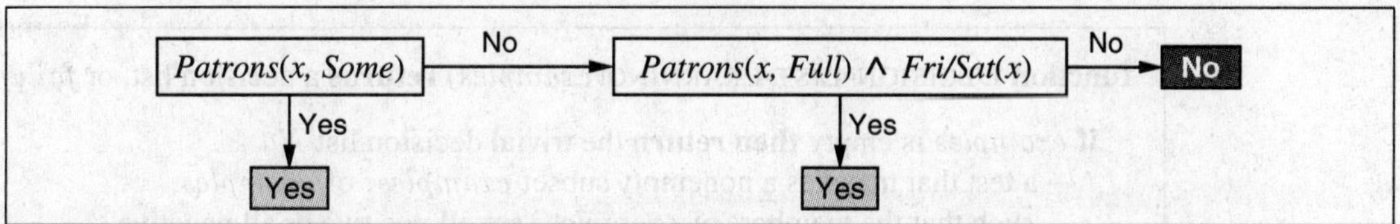

Figure 10 A decision list for the restaurant problem.

direction. In contrast, the individual tests are more complex. Figure 10 shows a decision list that represents the following hypothesis:

$$WillWait \Leftrightarrow (Patrons = Some) \lor (Patrons = Full \land Fri/Sat).$$

If we allow tests of arbitrary size, then decision lists can represent any Boolean function (Exercise 14). On the other hand, if we restrict the size of each test to at most k literals, then it is possible for the learning algorithm to generalize successfully from a small number of examples. We call this language **k-DL**. The example in Figure 10 is in 2-DL. It is easy to show (Exercise 14) that k-DL includes as a subset the language **k-DT**, the set of all decision trees of depth at most k. It is important to remember that the particular language referred to by k-DL depends on the attributes used to describe the examples. We will use the notation k-DL(n) to denote a k-DL language using n Boolean attributes.

k-DL

k-DT

The first task is to show that k-DL is learnable—that is, that any function in k-DL can be approximated accurately after training on a reasonable number of examples. To do this, we need to calculate the number of hypotheses in the language. Let the language of tests—conjunctions of at most k literals using n attributes—be $Conj(n, k)$. Because a decision list is constructed of tests, and because each test can be attached to either a *Yes* or a *No* outcome or can be absent from the decision list, there are at most $3^{|Conj(n,k)|}$ distinct sets of component tests. Each of these sets of tests can be in any order, so

$$|k\text{-DL}(n)| \leq 3^{|Conj(n,k)|} |Conj(n, k)|!.$$

The number of conjunctions of k literals from n attributes is given by

$$|Conj(n, k)| = \sum_{i=0}^{k} \binom{2n}{i} = O(n^k).$$

Hence, after some work, we obtain

$$|k\text{-DL}(n)| = 2^{O(n^k \log_2(n^k))}.$$

We can plug this into Equation (1) to show that the number of examples needed for PAC-learning a k-DL function is polynomial in n:

$$N \geq \frac{1}{\epsilon}\left(\ln\frac{1}{\delta} + O(n^k \log_2(n^k))\right)$$

Therefore, any algorithm that returns a consistent decision list will PAC-learn a k-DL function in a reasonable number of examples, for small k.

The next task is to find an efficient algorithm that returns a consistent decision list. We will use a greedy algorithm called DECISION-LIST-LEARNING that repeatedly finds a

function DECISION-LIST-LEARNING(*examples*) **returns** a decision list, or *failure*

  if *examples* is empty **then return** the trivial decision list *No*
  $t \leftarrow$ a test that matches a nonempty subset $examples_t$ of *examples*
    such that the members of $examples_t$ are all positive or all negative
  if there is no such t **then return** *failure*
  if the examples in $examples_t$ are positive **then** $o \leftarrow$ *Yes* **else** $o \leftarrow$ *No*
  return a decision list with initial test t and outcome o and remaining tests given by
    DECISION-LIST-LEARNING($examples - examples_t$)

Figure 11 An algorithm for learning decision lists.

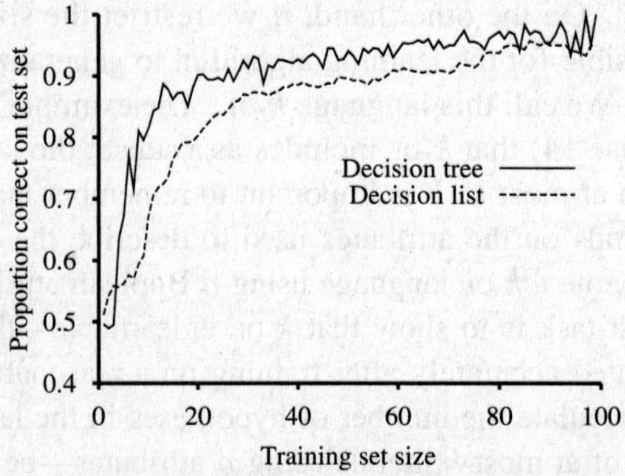

Figure 12 Learning curve for DECISION-LIST-LEARNING algorithm on the restaurant data. The curve for DECISION-TREE-LEARNING is shown for comparison.

test that agrees exactly with some subset of the training set. Once it finds such a test, it adds it to the decision list under construction and removes the corresponding examples. It then constructs the remainder of the decision list, using just the remaining examples. This is repeated until there are no examples left. The algorithm is shown in Figure 11.

This algorithm does not specify the method for selecting the next test to add to the decision list. Although the formal results given earlier do not depend on the selection method, it would seem reasonable to prefer small tests that match large sets of uniformly classified examples, so that the overall decision list will be as compact as possible. The simplest strategy is to find the smallest test t that matches any uniformly classified subset, regardless of the size of the subset. Even this approach works quite well, as Figure 12 suggests.

6 REGRESSION AND CLASSIFICATION WITH LINEAR MODELS

Now it is time to move on from decision trees and lists to a different hypothesis space, one that has been used for hundred of years: the class of **linear functions** of continuous-valued

LINEAR FUNCTION

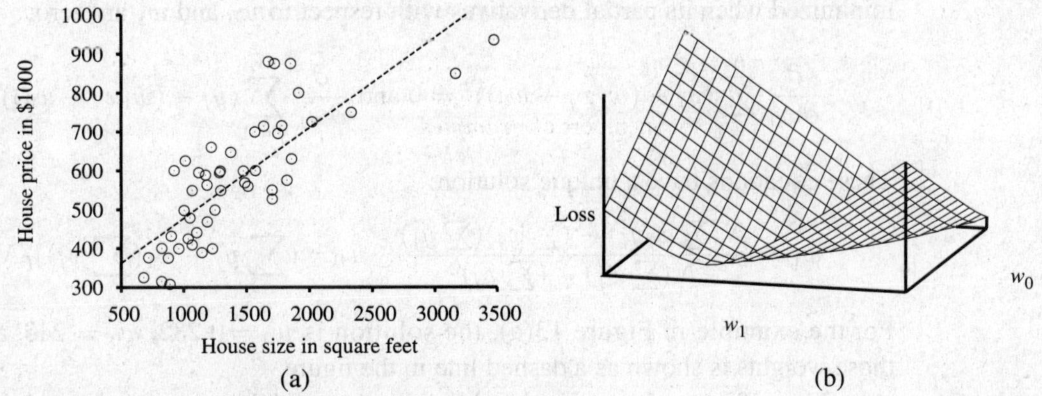

Figure 13 (a) Data points of price versus floor space of houses for sale in Berkeley, CA, in July 2009, along with the linear function hypothesis that minimizes squared error loss: $y = 0.232x + 246$. (b) Plot of the loss function $\sum_j (w_1 x_j + w_0 - y_j)^2$ for various values of w_0, w_1. Note that the loss function is convex, with a single global minimum.

inputs. We'll start with the simplest case: regression with a univariate linear function, otherwise known as "fitting a straight line." Section 6.2 covers the multivariate case. Sections 6.3 and 6.4 show how to turn linear functions into classifiers by applying hard and soft thresholds.

6.1 Univariate linear regression

A univariate linear function (a straight line) with input x and output y has the form $y = w_1 x + w_0$, where w_0 and w_1 are real-valued coefficients to be learned. We use the letter w because WEIGHT we think of the coefficients as **weights**; the value of y is changed by changing the relative weight of one term or another. We'll define **w** to be the vector $[w_0, w_1]$, and define

$$h_{\mathbf{w}}(x) = w_1 x + w_0 \,.$$

Figure 13(a) shows an example of a training set of n points in the x, y plane, each point representing the size in square feet and the price of a house offered for sale. The task of LINEAR REGRESSION finding the $h_{\mathbf{w}}$ that best fits these data is called **linear regression**. To fit a line to the data, all we have to do is find the values of the weights $[w_0, w_1]$ that minimize the empirical loss. It is traditional (going back to Gauss[3]) to use the squared loss function, L_2, summed over all the training examples:

$$Loss(h_{\mathbf{w}}) = \sum_{j=1}^{N} L_2(y_j, h_{\mathbf{w}}(x_j)) = \sum_{j=1}^{N} (y_j - h_{\mathbf{w}}(x_j))^2 = \sum_{j=1}^{N} (y_j - (w_1 x_j + w_0))^2 \,.$$

[3] Gauss showed that if the y_j values have normally distributed noise, then the most likely values of w_1 and w_0 are obtained by minimizing the sum of the squares of the errors.

We would like to find $\mathbf{w}^* = \operatorname{argmin}_{\mathbf{w}} Loss(h_{\mathbf{w}})$. The sum $\sum_{j=1}^{N}(y_j - (w_1 x_j + w_0))^2$ is minimized when its partial derivatives with respect to w_0 and w_1 are zero:

$$\frac{\partial}{\partial w_0}\sum_{j=1}^{N}(y_j - (w_1 x_j + w_0))^2 = 0 \text{ and } \frac{\partial}{\partial w_1}\sum_{j=1}^{N}(y_j - (w_1 x_j + w_0))^2 = 0 . \qquad (2)$$

These equations have a unique solution:

$$w_1 = \frac{N(\sum x_j y_j) - (\sum x_j)(\sum y_j)}{N(\sum x_j^2) - (\sum x_j)^2}; \; w_0 = (\sum y_j - w_1(\sum x_j))/N . \qquad (3)$$

For the example in Figure 13(a), the solution is $w_1 = 0.232$, $w_0 = 246$, and the line with those weights is shown as a dashed line in the figure.

Many forms of learning involve adjusting weights to minimize a loss, so it helps to have a mental picture of what's going on in **weight space**—the space defined by all possible settings of the weights. For univariate linear regression, the weight space defined by w_0 and w_1 is two-dimensional, so we can graph the loss as a function of w_0 and w_1 in a 3D plot (see Figure 13(b)). We see that the loss function is **convex**; this is true for *every* linear regression problem with an L_2 loss function, and implies that there are no local minima. In some sense that's the end of the story for linear models; if we need to fit lines to data, we apply Equation (3).[4]

WEIGHT SPACE

To go beyond linear models, we will need to face the fact that the equations defining minimum loss (as in Equation (2)) will often have no closed-form solution. Instead, we will face a general optimization search problem in a continuous weight space. Such problems can be addressed by a hill-climbing algorithm that follows the **gradient** of the function to be optimized. In this case, because we are trying to minimize the loss, we will use **gradient descent**. We choose any starting point in weight space—here, a point in the (w_0, w_1) plane—and then move to a neighboring point that is downhill, repeating until we converge on the minimum possible loss:

GRADIENT DESCENT

$\mathbf{w} \leftarrow$ any point in the parameter space
loop until convergence **do**
  for each w_i **in w do**

$$w_i \leftarrow w_i - \alpha \frac{\partial}{\partial w_i} Loss(\mathbf{w}) \qquad (4)$$

The parameter α is usually called the **learning rate** when we are trying to minimize loss in a learning problem. It can be a fixed constant, or it can decay over time as the learning process proceeds.

LEARNING RATE

For univariate regression, the loss function is a quadratic function, so the partial derivative will be a linear function. (The only calculus you need to know is that $\frac{\partial}{\partial x}x^2 = 2x$ and $\frac{\partial}{\partial x}x = 1$.) Let's first work out the partial derivatives—the slopes—in the simplified case of

[4] With some caveats: the L_2 loss function is appropriate when there is normally-distributed noise that is independent of x; all results rely on the stationarity assumption; etc.

only one training example, (x, y):

$$\frac{\partial}{\partial w_i} Loss(\mathbf{w}) = \frac{\partial}{\partial w_i}(y - h_{\mathbf{w}}(x))^2$$
$$= 2(y - h_{\mathbf{w}}(x)) \times \frac{\partial}{\partial w_i}(y - h_{\mathbf{w}}(x))$$
$$= 2(y - h_{\mathbf{w}}(x)) \times \frac{\partial}{\partial w_i}(y - (w_1 x + w_0)), \tag{5}$$

applying this to both w_0 and w_1 we get:

$$\frac{\partial}{\partial w_0} Loss(\mathbf{w}) = -2(y - h_{\mathbf{w}}(x)); \qquad \frac{\partial}{\partial w_1} Loss(\mathbf{w}) = -2(y - h_{\mathbf{w}}(x)) \times x$$

Then, plugging this back into Equation (4), and folding the 2 into the unspecified learning rate α, we get the following learning rule for the weights:

$$w_0 \leftarrow w_0 + \alpha\,(y - h_{\mathbf{w}}(x)); \quad w_1 \leftarrow w_1 + \alpha\,(y - h_{\mathbf{w}}(x)) \times x$$

These updates make intuitive sense: if $h_{\mathbf{w}}(x) > y$, i.e., the output of the hypothesis is too large, reduce w_0 a bit, and reduce w_1 if x was a positive input but increase w_1 if x was a negative input.

The preceding equations cover one training example. For N training examples, we want to minimize the sum of the individual losses for each example. The derivative of a sum is the sum of the derivatives, so we have:

$$w_0 \leftarrow w_0 + \alpha \sum_j (y_j - h_{\mathbf{w}}(x_j)); \quad w_1 \leftarrow w_1 + \alpha \sum_j (y_j - h_{\mathbf{w}}(x_j)) \times x_j\,.$$

BATCH GRADIENT DESCENT

These updates constitute the **batch gradient descent** learning rule for univariate linear regression. Convergence to the unique global minimum is guaranteed (as long as we pick α small enough) but may be very slow: we have to cycle through all the training data for every step, and there may be many steps.

STOCHASTIC GRADIENT DESCENT

There is another possibility, called **stochastic gradient descent**, where we consider only a single training point at a time, taking a step after each one using Equation (5). Stochastic gradient descent can be used in an online setting, where new data are coming in one at a time, or offline, where we cycle through the same data as many times as is necessary, taking a step after considering each single example. It is often faster than batch gradient descent. With a fixed learning rate α, however, it does not guarantee convergence; it can oscillate around the minimum without settling down. In some cases, as we see later, a schedule of decreasing learning rates (as in simulated annealing) does guarantee convergence.

6.2 Multivariate linear regression

MULTIVARIATE LINEAR REGRESSION

We can easily extend to **multivariate linear regression** problems, in which each example $\mathbf{x}_j$ is an n-element vector. Our hypothesis space is the set of functions of the form

$$h_{sw}(\mathbf{x_j}) = w_0 + w_1 x_{j,1} + \cdots + w_n x_{j,n} = w_0 + \sum_i w_i x_{j,i}\,.$$

The w_0 term, the intercept, stands out as different from the others. We can fix that by inventing a dummy input attribute, $x_{j,0}$, which is defined as always equal to 1. Then h is simply the dot product of the weights and the input vector (or equivalently, the matrix product of the transpose of the weights and the input vector):

$$h_{sw}(\mathbf{x}_j) = \mathbf{w} \cdot \mathbf{x}_j = \mathbf{w}^\top \mathbf{x}_j = \sum_i w_i x_{j,i} \,.$$

The best vector of weights, $\mathbf{w}^*$, minimizes squared-error loss over the examples:

$$\mathbf{w}^* = \underset{\mathbf{w}}{\operatorname{argmin}} \sum_j L_2(y_j, \mathbf{w} \cdot \mathbf{x}_j)\,.$$

Multivariate linear regression is actually not much more complicated than the univariate case we just covered. Gradient descent will reach the (unique) minimum of the loss function; the update equation for each weight w_i is

$$w_i \leftarrow w_i + \alpha \sum_j x_{j,i}(y_j - h_{\mathbf{w}}(\mathbf{x}_j))\,. \tag{6}$$

DATA MATRIX

It is also possible to solve analytically for the $\mathbf{w}$ that minimizes loss. Let $\mathbf{y}$ be the vector of outputs for the training examples, and $\mathbf{X}$ be the **data matrix**, i.e., the matrix of inputs with one n-dimensional example per row. Then the solution

$$\mathbf{w}^* = (\mathbf{X}^\top \mathbf{X})^{-1} \mathbf{X}^\top \mathbf{y}$$

minimizes the squared error.

With univariate linear regression we didn't have to worry about overfitting. But with multivariate linear regression in high-dimensional spaces it is possible that some dimension that is actually irrelevant appears by chance to be useful, resulting in **overfitting**.

Thus, it is common to use **regularization** on multivariate linear functions to avoid overfitting. Recall that with regularization we minimize the total cost of a hypothesis, counting both the empirical loss and the complexity of the hypothesis:

$$Cost(h) = EmpLoss(h) + \lambda\, Complexity(h)\,.$$

For linear functions the complexity can be specified as a function of the weights. We can consider a family of regularization functions:

$$Complexity(h_{\mathbf{w}}) = L_q(\mathbf{w}) = \sum_i |w_i|^q\,.$$

SPARSE MODEL

As with loss functions,[5] with $q=1$ we have L_1 regularization, which minimizes the sum of the absolute values; with $q=2$, L_2 regularization minimizes the sum of squares. Which regularization function should you pick? That depends on the specific problem, but L_5 regularization has an important advantage: it tends to produce a **sparse model**. That is, it often sets many weights to zero, effectively declaring the corresponding attributes to be irrelevant—just as DECISION-TREE-LEARNING does (although by a different mechanism). Hypotheses that discard attributes can be easier for a human to understand, and may be less likely to overfit.

[5] It is perhaps confusing that L_1 and L_2 are used for both loss functions and regularization functions. They need not be used in pairs: you could use L_2 loss with L_1 regularization, or vice versa.

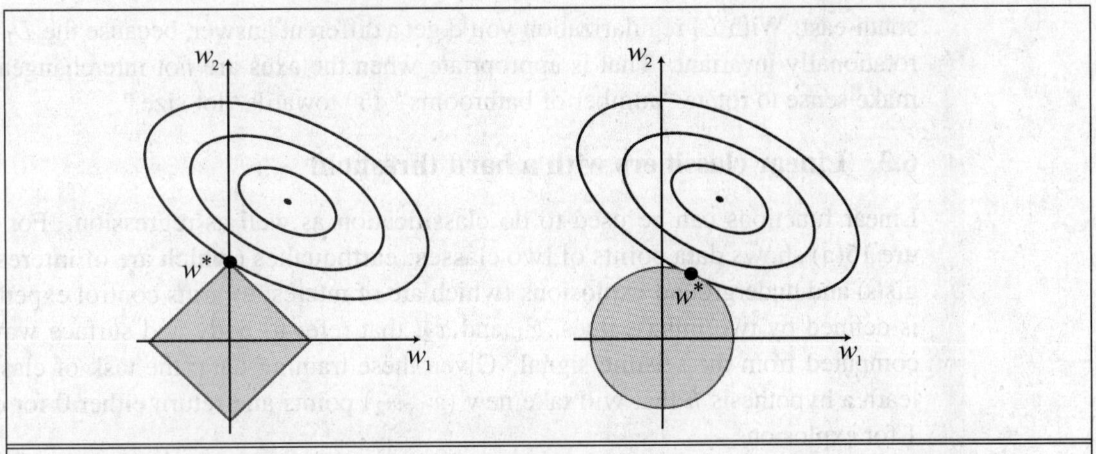

Figure 14 Why L_1 regularization tends to produce a sparse model. (a) With L_1 regularization (box), the minimal achievable loss (concentric contours) often occurs on an axis, meaning a weight of zero. (b) With L_2 regularization (circle), the minimal loss is likely to occur anywhere on the circle, giving no preference to zero weights.

Figure 14 gives an intuitive explanation of why L_1 regularization leads to weights of zero, while L_2 regularization does not. Note that minimizing $Loss(\mathbf{w}) + \lambda Complexity(\mathbf{w})$ is equivalent to minimizing $Loss(\mathbf{w})$ subject to the constraint that $Complexity(\mathbf{w}) \leq c$, for some constant c that is related to λ. Now, in Figure 14(a) the diamond-shaped box represents the set of points $\mathbf{w}$ in two-dimensional weight space that have L_1 complexity less than c; our solution will have to be somewhere inside this box. The concentric ovals represent contours of the loss function, with the minimum loss at the center. We want to find the point in the box that is closest to the minimum; you can see from the diagram that, for an arbitrary position of the minimum and its contours, it will be common for the corner of the box to find its way closest to the minimum, just because the corners are pointy. And of course the corners are the points that have a value of zero in some dimension. In Figure 14(b), we've done the same for the L_2 complexity measure, which represents a circle rather than a diamond. Here you can see that, in general, there is no reason for the intersection to appear on one of the axes; thus L_2 regularization does not tend to produce zero weights. The result is that the number of examples required to find a good h is linear in the number of irrelevant features for L_2 regularization, but only logarithmic with L_1 regularization. Empirical evidence on many problems supports this analysis.

Another way to look at it is that L_1 regularization takes the dimensional axes seriously, while L_2 treats them as arbitrary. The L_2 function is spherical, which makes it rotationally invariant: Imagine a set of points in a plane, measured by their x and y coordinates. Now imagine rotating the axes by 45°. You'd get a different set of (x', y') values representing the same points. If you apply L_2 regularization before and after rotating, you get exactly the same point as the answer (although the point would be described with the new (x', y') coordinates). That is appropriate when the choice of axes really is arbitrary—when it doesn't matter whether your two dimensions are distances north and east; or distances north-east and south-east. With L_1 regularization you'd get a different answer, because the L_1 function is not rotationally invariant. That is appropriate when the axes are not interchangeable; it doesn't make sense to rotate "number of bathrooms" 45° towards "lot size."

6.3 Linear classifiers with a hard threshold

Linear functions can be used to do classification as well as regression. For example, Figure 15(a) shows data points of two classes: earthquakes (which are of interest to seismologists) and underground explosions (which are of interest to arms control experts). Each point is defined by two input values, x_1 and x_2, that refer to body and surface wave magnitudes computed from the seismic signal. Given these training data, the task of classification is to learn a hypothesis h that will take new (x_1, x_2) points and return either 0 for earthquakes or 1 for explosions.

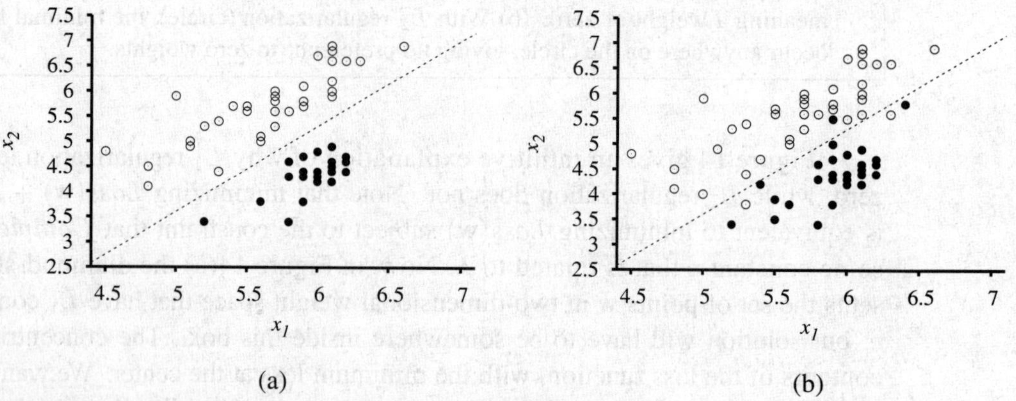

Figure 15 (a) Plot of two seismic data parameters, body wave magnitude x_1 and surface wave magnitude x_2, for earthquakes (white circles) and nuclear explosions (black circles) occurring between 1982 and 1990 in Asia and the Middle East (Kebeasy *et al.*, 1998). Also shown is a decision boundary between the classes. (b) The same domain with more data points. The earthquakes and explosions are no longer linearly separable.

DECISION BOUNDARY

LINEAR SEPARATOR

LINEAR SEPARABILITY

A **decision boundary** is a line (or a surface, in higher dimensions) that separates the two classes. In Figure 15(a), the decision boundary is a straight line. A linear decision boundary is called a **linear separator** and data that admit such a separator are called **linearly separable**. The linear separator in this case is defined by

$$x_2 = 1.7x_1 - 4.9 \quad \text{or} \quad -4.9 + 1.7x_1 - x_2 = 0\,.$$

The explosions, which we want to classify with value 1, are to the right of this line with higher values of x_1 and lower values of x_2, so they are points for which $-4.9 + 1.7x_1 - x_2 > 0$, while earthquakes have $-4.9 + 1.7x_1 - x_2 < 0$. Using the convention of a dummy input $x_0 = 1$, we can write the classification hypothesis as

$$h_{\mathbf{w}}(\mathbf{x}) = 1 \text{ if } \mathbf{w} \cdot \mathbf{x} \geq 0 \text{ and } 0 \text{ otherwise.}$$

Alternatively, we can think of h as the result of passing the linear function $\mathbf{w} \cdot \mathbf{x}$ through a

THRESHOLD FUNCTION

threshold function:

$$h_{\mathbf{w}}(\mathbf{x}) = Threshold(\mathbf{w} \cdot \mathbf{x}) \text{ where } Threshold(z) = 1 \text{ if } z \geq 0 \text{ and } 0 \text{ otherwise.}$$

The threshold function is shown in Figure 17(a).

Now that the hypothesis $h_{\mathbf{w}}(\mathbf{x})$ has a well-defined mathematical form, we can think about choosing the weights $\mathbf{w}$ to minimize the loss. In Sections 6.1 and 6.2, we did this both in closed form (by setting the gradient to zero and solving for the weights) and by gradient descent in weight space. Here, we cannot do either of those things because the gradient is zero almost everywhere in weight space except at those points where $\mathbf{w} \cdot \mathbf{x} = 0$, and at those points the gradient is undefined.

There is, however, a simple weight update rule that converges to a solution—that is, a linear separator that classifies the data perfectly–provided the data are linearly separable. For a single example $(\mathbf{x}, y)$, we have

$$w_i \leftarrow w_i + \alpha\,(y - h_{\mathbf{w}}(\mathbf{x})) \times x_i \tag{7}$$

which is essentially identical to the Equation (6), the update rule for linear regression! This

PERCEPTRON LEARNING RULE

rule is called the **perceptron learning rule**, for reasons that will become clear in Section 7. Because we are considering a 0/1 classification problem, however, the behavior is somewhat different. Both the true value y and the hypothesis output $h_{\mathbf{w}}(\mathbf{x})$ are either 0 or 1, so there are three possibilities:

- If the output is correct, i.e., $y = h_{\mathbf{w}}(\mathbf{x})$, then the weights are not changed.
- If y is 1 but $h_{\mathbf{w}}(\mathbf{x})$ is 0, then w_i is *increased* when the corresponding input x_i is positive and *decreased* when x_i is negative. This makes sense, because we want to make $\mathbf{w} \cdot \mathbf{x}$ bigger so that $h_{\mathbf{w}}(\mathbf{x})$ outputs a 1.
- If y is 0 but $h_{\mathbf{w}}(\mathbf{x})$ is 1, then w_i is *decreased* when the corresponding input x_i is positive and *increased* when x_i is negative. This makes sense, because we want to make $\mathbf{w} \cdot \mathbf{x}$ smaller so that $h_{\mathbf{w}}(\mathbf{x})$ outputs a 0.

Typically the learning rule is applied one example at a time, choosing examples at random

TRAINING CURVE

(as in stochastic gradient descent). Figure 16(a) shows a **training curve** for this learning rule applied to the earthquake/explosion data shown in Figure 15(a). A training curve measures the classifier performance on a fixed training set as the learning process proceeds on that same training set. The curve shows the update rule converging to a zero-error linear separator. The "convergence" process isn't exactly pretty, but it always works. This particular run takes 657 steps to converge, for a data set with 63 examples, so each example is presented roughly 10 times on average. Typically, the variation across runs is very large.

We have said that the perceptron learning rule converges to a perfect linear separator when the data points are linearly separable, but what if they are not? This situation is all too common in the real world. For example, Figure 15(b) adds back in the data points left out by Kebeasy *et al.* (1998) when they plotted the data shown in Figure 15(a). In Figure 16(b), we show the perceptron learning rule failing to converge even after 10,000 steps: even though it hits the minimum-error solution (three errors) many times, the algorithm keeps changing the weights. In general, the perceptron rule may not converge to a

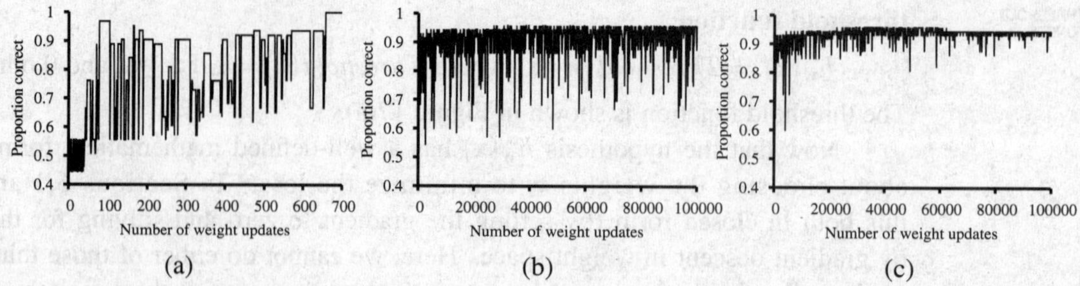

Figure 16 (a) Plot of total training-set accuracy vs. number of iterations through the training set for the perceptron learning rule, given the earthquake/explosion data in Figure 15(a). (b) The same plot for the noisy, non-separable data in Figure 15(b); note the change in scale of the x-axis. (c) The same plot as in (b), with a learning rate schedule $\alpha(t) = 1000/(1000 + t)$.

stable solution for fixed learning rate α, but if α decays as $O(1/t)$ where t is the iteration number, then the rule can be shown to converge to a minimum-error solution when examples are presented in a random sequence.[6] It can also be shown that finding the minimum-error solution is NP-hard, so one expects that many presentations of the examples will be required for convergence to be achieved. Figure 16(b) shows the training process with a learning rate schedule $\alpha(t) = 1000/(1000 + t)$: convergence is not perfect after 100,000 iterations, but it is much better than the fixed-α case.

6.4 Linear classification with logistic regression

We have seen that passing the output of a linear function through the threshold function creates a linear classifier; yet the hard nature of the threshold causes some problems: the hypothesis $h_{\mathbf{w}}(\mathbf{x})$ is not differentiable and is in fact a discontinuous function of its inputs and its weights; this makes learning with the perceptron rule a very unpredictable adventure. Furthermore, the linear classifier always announces a completely confident prediction of 1 or 0, even for examples that are very close to the boundary; in many situations, we really need more gradated predictions.

All of these issues can be resolved to a large extent by softening the threshold function—approximating the hard threshold with a continuous, differentiable function. Consider two functions that look like soft thresholds: the integral of the standard normal distribution (used for the probit model) and the logistic function (used for the logit model). Although the two functions are very similar in shape, the logistic function

$$Logistic(z) = \frac{1}{1 + e^{-z}}$$

[6] Technically, we require that $\sum_{t=1}^{\infty} \alpha(t) = \infty$ and $\sum_{t=1}^{\infty} \alpha^2(t) < \infty$. The decay $\alpha(t) = O(1/t)$ satisfies these conditions.

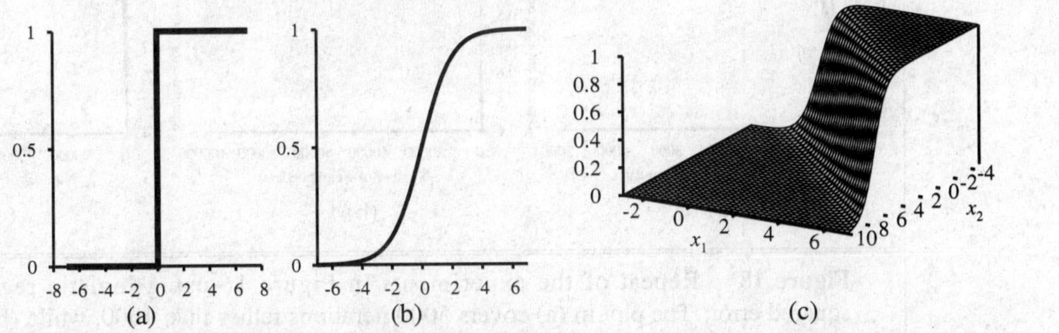

Figure 17 (a) The hard threshold function $Threshold(z)$ with 0/1 output. Note that the function is nondifferentiable at $z=0$. (b) The logistic function, $Logistic(z) = \frac{1}{1+e^{-z}}$, also known as the sigmoid function. (c) Plot of a logistic regression hypothesis $h_{\mathbf{w}}(\mathbf{x}) = Logistic(\mathbf{w} \cdot \mathbf{x})$ for the data shown in Figure 15(b).

has more convenient mathematical properties. The function is shown in Figure 17(b). With the logistic function replacing the threshold function, we now have

$$h_{\mathbf{w}}(\mathbf{x}) = Logistic(\mathbf{w} \cdot \mathbf{x}) = \frac{1}{1+e^{-\mathbf{w}\cdot\mathbf{x}}}.$$

An example of such a hypothesis for the two-input earthquake/explosion problem is shown in Figure 17(c). Notice that the output, being a number between 0 and 1, can be interpreted as a *probability* of belonging to the class labeled 1. The hypothesis forms a soft boundary in the input space and gives a probability of 0.5 for any input at the center of the boundary region, and approaches 0 or 1 as we move away from the boundary.

LOGISTIC REGRESSION

The process of fitting the weights of this model to minimize loss on a data set is called **logistic regression**. There is no easy closed-form solution to find the optimal value of **w** with this model, but the gradient descent computation is straightforward. Because our hypotheses no longer output just 0 or 1, we will use the L_2 loss function; also, to keep the formulas readable, we'll use g to stand for the logistic function, with g' its derivative.

CHAIN RULE

For a single example $(\mathbf{x}, y)$, the derivation of the gradient is the same as for linear regression (Equation (5)) up to the point where the actual form of h is inserted. (For this derivation, we will need the **chain rule**: $\partial g(f(x))/\partial x = g'(f(x))\,\partial f(x)/\partial x$.) We have

$$\begin{aligned}
\frac{\partial}{\partial w_i} Loss(\mathbf{w}) &= \frac{\partial}{\partial w_i}(y - h_{\mathbf{w}}(\mathbf{x}))^2 \\
&= 2(y - h_{\mathbf{w}}(\mathbf{x})) \times \frac{\partial}{\partial w_i}(y - h_{\mathbf{w}}(\mathbf{x})) \\
&= -2(y - h_{\mathbf{w}}(\mathbf{x})) \times g'(\mathbf{w}\cdot\mathbf{x}) \times \frac{\partial}{\partial w_i}\mathbf{w}\cdot\mathbf{x} \\
&= -2(y - h_{\mathbf{w}}(\mathbf{x})) \times g'(\mathbf{w}\cdot\mathbf{x}) \times x_i\,.
\end{aligned}$$

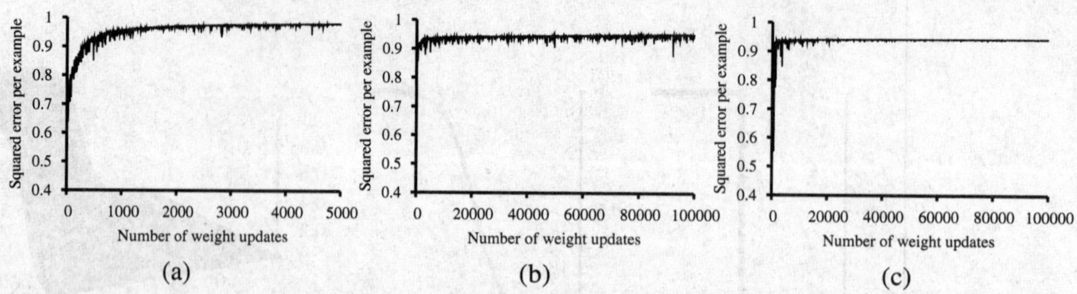

Figure 18 Repeat of the experiments in Figure 16 using logistic regression and squared error. The plot in (a) covers 5000 iterations rather than 1000, while (b) and (c) use the same scale.

The derivative g' of the logistic function satisfies $g'(z) = g(z)(1 - g(z))$, so we have

$$g'(\mathbf{w} \cdot \mathbf{x}) = g(\mathbf{w} \cdot \mathbf{x})(1 - g(\mathbf{w} \cdot \mathbf{x})) = h_{\mathbf{w}}(\mathbf{x})(1 - h_{\mathbf{w}}(\mathbf{x}))$$

so the weight update for minimizing the loss is

$$w_i \leftarrow w_i + \alpha\,(y - h_{\mathbf{w}}(\mathbf{x})) \times h_{\mathbf{w}}(\mathbf{x})(1 - h_{\mathbf{w}}(\mathbf{x})) \times x_i\,. \tag{8}$$

Repeating the experiments of Figure 16 with logistic regression instead of the linear threshold classifier, we obtain the results shown in Figure 18. In (a), the linearly separable case, logistic regression is somewhat slower to converge, but behaves much more predictably. In (b) and (c), where the data are noisy and nonseparable, logistic regression converges far more quickly and reliably. These advantages tend to carry over into real-world applications and logistic regression has become one of the most popular classification techniques for problems in medicine, marketing and survey analysis, credit scoring, public health, and other applications.

7 Artificial Neural Networks

We turn now to what seems to be a somewhat unrelated topic: the brain. In fact, as we will see, the technical ideas we have discussed so far in this chapter turn out to be useful in building mathematical models of the brain's activity; conversely, thinking about the brain has helped in extending the scope of the technical ideas.

One of the basic findings of neuroscience is the hypothesis that mental activity consists primarily of electrochemical activity in networks of brain cells called **neurons**. Inspired by this hypothesis, some of the earliest AI work aimed to create artificial **neural networks**. (Other names for the field include **connectionism, parallel distributed processing,** and **neural computation**.) Figure 19 shows a simple mathematical model of the neuron devised by McCulloch and Pitts (1943). Roughly speaking, it "fires" when a linear combination of its inputs exceeds some (hard or soft) threshold—that is, it implements a linear classifier of the

NEURAL NETWORK

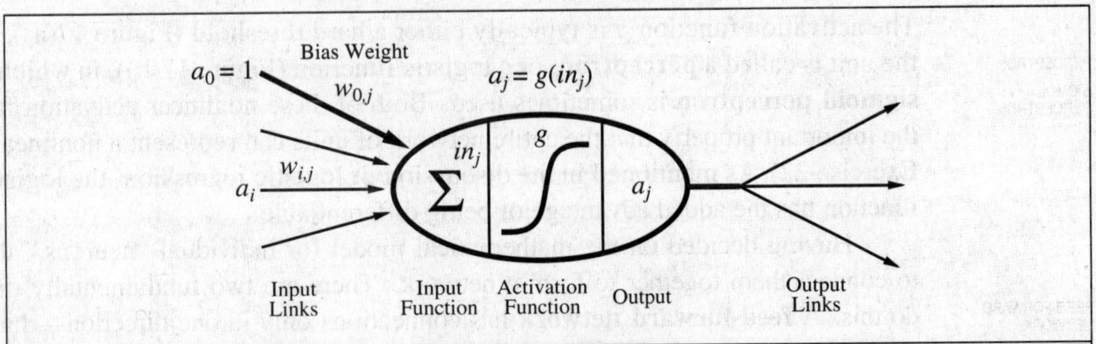

Figure 19 A simple mathematical model for a neuron. The unit's output activation is $a_j = g(\sum_{i=0}^{n} w_{i,j} a_i)$, where a_i is the output activation of unit i and $w_{i,j}$ is the weight on the link from unit i to this unit.

kind described in the preceding section. A neural network is just a collection of units connected together; the properties of the network are determined by its topology and the properties of the "neurons."

COMPUTATIONAL NEUROSCIENCE

Since 1943, much more detailed and realistic models have been developed, both for neurons and for larger systems in the brain, leading to the modern field of **computational neuroscience**. On the other hand, researchers in AI and statistics became interested in the more abstract properties of neural networks, such as their ability to perform distributed computation, to tolerate noisy inputs, and to learn. Although we understand now that other kinds of systems—including Bayesian networks—have these properties, neural networks remain one of the most popular and effective forms of learning system and are worthy of study in their own right.

7.1 Neural network structures

UNIT
LINK
ACTIVATION
WEIGHT

Neural networks are composed of nodes or **units** (see Figure 19) connected by directed **links**. A link from unit i to unit j serves to propagate the **activation** a_i from i to j.[7] Each link also has a numeric **weight** $w_{i,j}$ associated with it, which determines the strength and sign of the connection. Just as in linear regression models, each unit has a dummy input $a_0 = 1$ with an associated weight $w_{0,j}$. Each unit j first computes a weighted sum of its inputs:

$$in_j = \sum_{i=0}^{n} w_{i,j} a_i \, .$$

ACTIVATION FUNCTION

Then it applies an **activation function** g to this sum to derive the output:

$$a_j = g(in_j) = g\left(\sum_{i=0}^{n} w_{i,j} a_i\right) . \tag{9}$$

[7] A note on notation: for this section, we are forced to suspend our usual conventions. Input attributes are still indexed by i , so that an "external" activation a_i is given by input x_i; but index j will refer to internal units rather than examples. Throughout this section, the mathematical derivations concern a single generic example **x**, omitting the usual summations over examples to obtain results for the whole data set.

PERCEPTRON
SIGMOID PERCEPTRON

The activation function g is typically either a hard threshold (Figure 17(a)), in which case the unit is called a **perceptron**, or a logistic function (Figure 17(b)), in which case the term **sigmoid perceptron** is sometimes used. Both of these nonlinear activation function ensure the important property that the entire network of units can represent a nonlinear function (see Exercise 22). As mentioned in the discussion of logistic regression, the logistic activation function has the added advantage of being differentiable.

FEED-FORWARD NETWORK

RECURRENT NETWORK

Having decided on the mathematical model for individual "neurons," the next task is to connect them together to form a network. There are two fundamentally distinct ways to do this. A **feed-forward network** has connections only in one direction—that is, it forms a directed acyclic graph. Every node receives input from "upstream" nodes and delivers output to "downstream" nodes; there are no loops. A feed-forward network represents a function of its current input; thus, it has no internal state other than the weights themselves. A **recurrent network**, on the other hand, feeds its outputs back into its own inputs. This means that the activation levels of the network form a dynamical system that may reach a stable state or exhibit oscillations or even chaotic behavior. Moreover, the response of the network to a given input depends on its initial state, which may depend on previous inputs. Hence, recurrent networks (unlike feed-forward networks) can support short-term memory. This makes them more interesting as models of the brain, but also more difficult to understand. This section will concentrate on feed-forward networks; some pointers for further reading on recurrent networks are given at the end of the chapter.

LAYERS

HIDDEN UNIT

Feed-forward networks are usually arranged in **layers**, such that each unit receives input only from units in the immediately preceding layer. In the next two subsections, we will look at single-layer networks, in which every unit connects directly from the network's inputs to its outputs, and multilayer networks, which have one or more layers of **hidden units** that are not connected to the outputs of the network. So far in this chapter, we have considered only learning problems with a single output variable y, but neural networks are often used in cases where multiple outputs are appropriate. For example, if we want to train a network to add two input bits, each a 0 or a 1, we will need one output for the sum bit and one for the carry bit. Also, when the learning problem involves classification into more than two classes—for example, when learning to categorize images of handwritten digits—it is common to use one output unit for each class.

7.2 Single-layer feed-forward neural networks (perceptrons)

PERCEPTRON NETWORK

A network with all the inputs connected directly to the outputs is called a **single-layer neural network**, or a **perceptron network**. Figure 20 shows a simple two-input, two-output perceptron network. With such a network, we might hope to learn the two-bit adder function, for example. Here are all the training data we will need:

x_1	x_2	y_3 (carry)	y_4 (sum)
0	0	0	0
0	1	0	1
1	0	0	1
1	1	1	0

The first thing to notice is that a perceptron network with m outputs is really m separate networks, because each weight affects only one of the outputs. Thus, there will be m separate training processes. Furthermore, depending on the type of activation function used, the training processes will be either the **perceptron learning rule** (Equation (7) or gradient or gradient descent rule for the **logistic regression** (Equation (8)).

If you try either method on the two-bit-adder data, something interesting happens. Unit 3 learns the carry function easily, but unit 4 completely fails to learn the sum function. No, unit 4 is not defective! The problem is with the sum function itself. We saw in Section 6 that linear classifiers (whether hard or soft) can represent linear decision boundaries in the input space. This works fine for the carry function, which is a logical AND (see Figure 21(a)). The sum function, however, is an XOR (exclusive OR) of the two inputs. As Figure 21(c) illustrates, this function is not linearly separable so the perceptron cannot learn it.

The linearly separable functions constitute just a small fraction of all Boolean functions; Exercise 20 asks you to quantify this fraction. The inability of perceptrons to learn even such simple functions as XOR was a significant setback to the nascent neural network

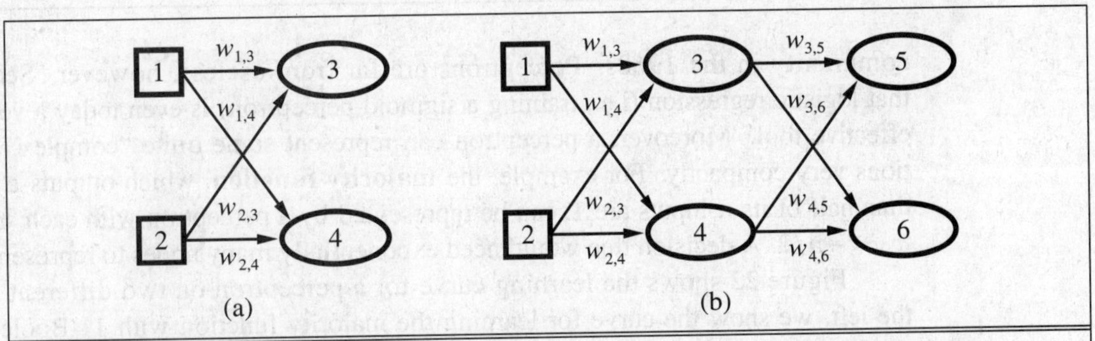

Figure 20 (a) A perceptron network with two inputs and two output units. (b) A neural network with two inputs, one hidden layer of two units, and one output unit. Not shown are the dummy inputs and their associated weights.

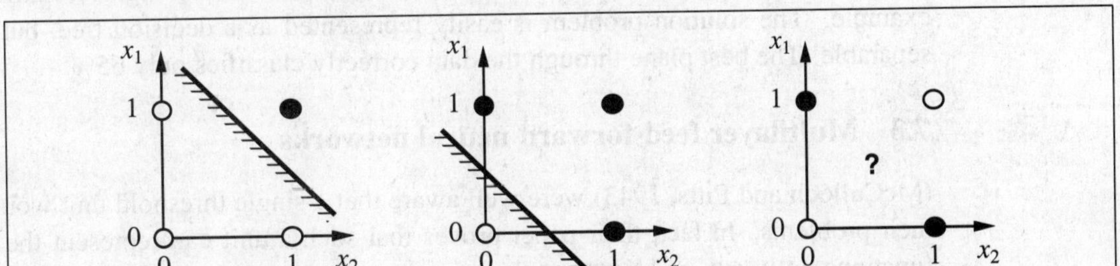

Figure 21 Linear separability in threshold perceptrons. Black dots indicate a point in the input space where the value of the function is 1, and white dots indicate a point where the value is 0. The perceptron returns 1 on the region on the non-shaded side of the line. In (c), no such line exists that correctly classifies the inputs.

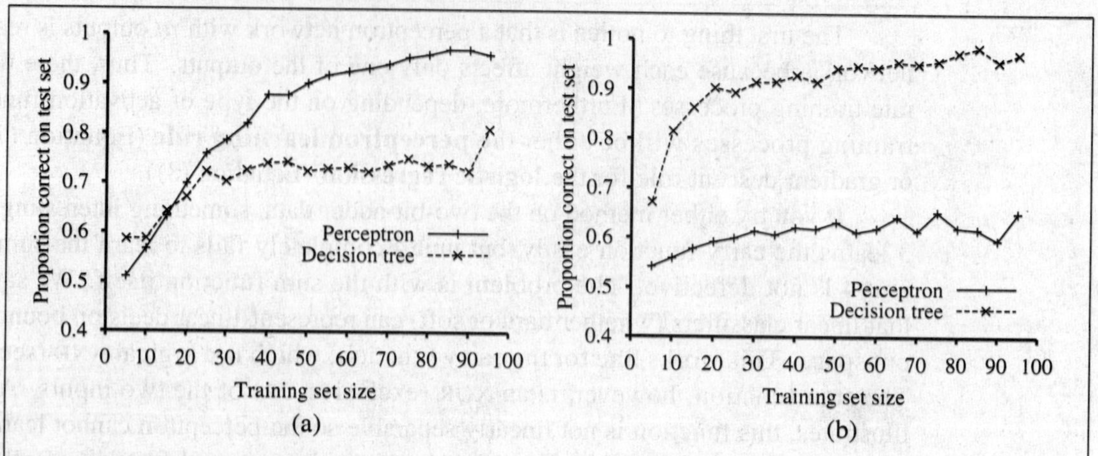

Figure 22 Comparing the performance of perceptrons and decision trees. (a) Perceptrons are better at learning the majority function of 11 inputs. (b) Decision trees are better at learning the *WillWait* predicate in the restaurant example.

community in the 1960s. Perceptrons are far from useless, however. Section 6.4 noted that logistic regression (i.e., training a sigmoid perceptron) is even today a very popular and effective tool. Moreover, a perceptron can represent some quite "complex" Boolean functions very compactly. For example, the **majority function**, which outputs a 1 only if more than half of its n inputs are 1, can be represented by a perceptron with each $w_i = 1$ and with $w_0 = -n/2$. A decision tree would need exponentially many nodes to represent this function.

Figure 22 shows the learning curve for a perceptron on two different problems. On the left, we show the curve for learning the majority function with 11 Boolean inputs (i.e., the function outputs a 1 if 6 or more inputs are 1). As we would expect, the perceptron learns the function quite quickly, because the majority function is linearly separable. On the other hand, the decision-tree learner makes no progress, because the majority function is very hard (although not impossible) to represent as a decision tree. On the right, we have the restaurant example. The solution problem is easily represented as a decision tree, but is not linearly separable. The best plane through the data correctly classifies only 65%.

7.3 Multilayer feed-forward neural networks

(McCulloch and Pitts, 1943) were well aware that a single threshold unit would not solve all their problems. In fact, their paper proves that such a unit can represent the basic Boolean functions AND, OR, and NOT and then goes on to argue that any desired functionality can be obtained by connecting large numbers of units into (possibly recurrent) networks of arbitrary depth. The problem was that nobody knew how to train such networks.

This turns out to be an easy problem if we think of a network the right way: as a function $h_{\mathbf{w}}(\mathbf{x})$ parameterized by the weights $\mathbf{w}$. Consider the simple network shown in Figure 20(b), which has two input units, two hidden units, and two output unit. (In addition, each unit has a dummy input fixed at 1.) Given an input vector $\mathbf{x} = (x_1, x_2)$, the activations

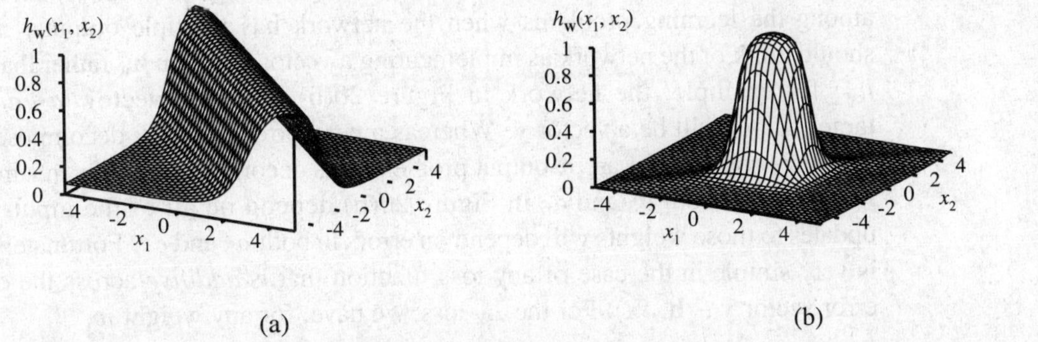

Figure 23 (a) The result of combining two opposite-facing soft threshold functions to produce a ridge. (b) The result of combining two ridges to produce a bump.

of the input units are set to $(a_1, a_2) = (x_1, x_2)$. The output at unit 5 is given by

$$\begin{aligned} a_5 &= g(w_{0,5,+} w_{3,5}\, a_3 + w_{4,5}\, a_4) \\ &= g(w_{0,5,+} w_{3,5}\, g(w_{0,3} + w_{1,3}\, a_1 + w_{2,3}\, a_2) + w_{4,5}\, g(w_0 4 + w_{1,4}\, a_1 + w_{2,4}\, a_2)) \\ &= g(w_{0,5,+} w_{3,5}\, g(w_{0,3} + w_{1,3}\, x_1 + w_{2,3}\, x_2) + w_{4,5}\, g(w_0 4 + w_{1,4}\, x_1 + w_{2,4}\, x_2)). \end{aligned}$$

Thus, we have the output expressed as a function of the inputs and the weights. A similar expression holds for unit 6. As long as we can calculate the derivatives of such expressions with respect to the weights, we can use the gradient-descent loss-minimization method to train the network. Section 7.4 shows exactly how to do this. And because the function represented by a network can be highly nonlinear—composed, as it is, of nested nonlinear soft threshold functions—we can see neural networks as a tool for doing **nonlinear regression**.

NONLINEAR REGRESSION

Before delving into learning rules, let us look at the ways in which networks generate complicated functions. First, remember that each unit in a sigmoid network represents a soft threshold in its input space, as shown in Figure 17(c). With one hidden layer and one output layer, as in Figure 20(b), each output unit computes a soft-thresholded linear combination of several such functions. For example, by adding two opposite-facing soft threshold functions and thresholding the result, we can obtain a "ridge" function as shown in Figure 23(a). Combining two such ridges at right angles to each other (i.e., combining the outputs from four hidden units), we obtain a "bump" as shown in Figure 23(b).

With more hidden units, we can produce more bumps of different sizes in more places. In fact, with a single, sufficiently large hidden layer, it is possible to represent any continuous function of the inputs with arbitrary accuracy; with two layers, even discontinuous functions can be represented.[8] Unfortunately, for any *particular* network structure, it is harder to characterize exactly which functions can be represented and which ones cannot.

[8] The proof is complex, but the main point is that the required number of hidden units grows exponentially with the number of inputs. For example, $2^n/n$ hidden units are needed to encode all Boolean functions of n inputs.

7.4 Learning in multilayer networks

First, let us dispense with one minor complication arising in multilayer networks: interactions among the learning problems when the network has multiple outputs. In such cases, we should think of the network as implementing a vector function $\mathbf{h_w}$ rather than a scalar function $h_\mathbf{w}$; for example, the network in Figure 20(b) returns a vector $[a_5, a_6]$. Similarly, the target output will be a vector $\mathbf{y}$. Whereas a perceptron network decomposes into m separate learning problems for an m-output problem, this decomposition fails in a multilayer network. For example, both a_5 and a_6 in Figure 20(b) depend on all of the input-layer weights, so updates to those weights will depend on errors in both a_5 and a_6. Fortunately, this dependency is very simple in the case of any loss function that is *additive* across the components of the error vector $\mathbf{y} - \mathbf{h_w}(\mathbf{x})$. For the L_2 loss, we have, for any weight w,

$$\frac{\partial}{\partial w} Loss(\mathbf{w}) = \frac{\partial}{\partial w} |\mathbf{y} - \mathbf{h_w}(\mathbf{x})|^2 = \frac{\partial}{\partial w} \sum_k (y_k - a_k)^2 = \sum_k \frac{\partial}{\partial w}(y_k - a_k)^2 \tag{10}$$

where the index k ranges over nodes in the output layer. Each term in the final summation is just the gradient of the loss for the kth output, computed as if the other outputs did not exist. Hence, we can decompose an m-output learning problem into m learning problems, provided we remember to add up the gradient contributions from each of them when updating the weights.

The major complication comes from the addition of hidden layers to the network. Whereas the error $\mathbf{y} - \mathbf{h_w}$ at the output layer is clear, the error at the hidden layers seems mysterious because the training data do not say what value the hidden nodes should have. Fortunately, it turns out that we can **back-propagate** the error from the output layer to the hidden layers. The back-propagation process emerges directly from a derivation of the overall error gradient. First, we will describe the process with an intuitive justification; then, we will show the derivation.

BACK-PROPAGATION

At the output layer, the weight-update rule is identical to Equation (8). We have multiple output units, so let Err_k be the kth component of the error vector $\mathbf{y} - \mathbf{h_w}$. We will also find it convenient to define a modified error $\Delta_k = Err_k \times g'(in_k)$, so that the weight-update rule becomes

$$w_{j,k} \leftarrow w_{j,k} + \alpha \times a_j \times \Delta_k \,. \tag{11}$$

To update the connections between the input units and the hidden units, we need to define a quantity analogous to the error term for output nodes. Here is where we do the error back-propagation. The idea is that hidden node j is "responsible" for some fraction of the error Δ_k in each of the output nodes to which it connects. Thus, the Δ_k values are divided according to the strength of the connection between the hidden node and the output node and are propagated back to provide the Δ_j values for the hidden layer. The propagation rule for the Δ values is the following:

$$\Delta_j = g'(in_j) \sum_k w_{j,k} \Delta_k \,. \tag{12}$$

```
function BACK-PROP-LEARNING(examples, network) returns a neural network
  inputs: examples, a set of examples, each with input vector x and output vector y
          network, a multilayer network with L layers, weights w_{i,j}, activation function g
  local variables: Δ, a vector of errors, indexed by network node

  repeat
      for each weight w_{i,j} in network do
          w_{i,j} ← a small random number
      for each example (x, y) in examples do
          /* Propagate the inputs forward to compute the outputs */
          for each node i in the input layer do
              a_i ← x_i
          for ℓ = 2 to L do
              for each node j in layer ℓ do
                  in_j ← Σ_i w_{i,j} a_i
                  a_j ← g(in_j)
          /* Propagate deltas backward from output layer to input layer */
          for each node j in the output layer do
              Δ[j] ← g′(in_j) × (y_j − a_j)
          for ℓ = L − 1 to 1 do
              for each node i in layer ℓ do
                  Δ[i] ← g′(in_i) Σ_j w_{i,j} Δ[j]
          /* Update every weight in network using deltas */
          for each weight w_{i,j} in network do
              w_{i,j} ← w_{i,j} + α × a_i × Δ[j]
  until some stopping criterion is satisfied
  return network
```

Figure 24 The back-propagation algorithm for learning in multilayer networks.

Now the weight-update rule for the weights between the inputs and the hidden layer is essentially identical to the update rule for the output layer:

$$w_{i,j} \leftarrow w_{i,j} + \alpha \times a_i \times \Delta_j .$$

The back-propagation process can be summarized as follows:

- Compute the Δ values for the output units, using the observed error.
- Starting with output layer, repeat the following for each layer in the network, until the earliest hidden layer is reached:
  - Propagate the Δ values back to the previous layer.
  - Update the weights between the two layers.

The detailed algorithm is shown in Figure 24.

For the mathematically inclined, we will now derive the back-propagation equations from first principles. The derivation is quite similar to the gradient calculation for logistic regression (leading up to Equation (8)) except that we have to use the chain rule more than once.

Following Equation (10), we compute just the gradient for $Loss_k = (y_k - a_k)^2$ at the kth output. The gradient of this loss with respect to weights connecting the hidden layer to the output layer will be zero except for weights $w_{j,k}$ that connect to the kth output unit. For those weights, we have

$$\begin{aligned}\frac{\partial Loss_k}{\partial w_{j,k}} &= -2(y_k - a_k)\frac{\partial a_k}{\partial w_{j,k}} = -2(y_k - a_k)\frac{\partial g(in_k)}{\partial w_{j,k}} \\ &= -2(y_k - a_k)g'(in_k)\frac{\partial in_k}{\partial w_{j,k}} = -2(y_k - a_k)g'(in_k)\frac{\partial}{\partial w_{j,k}}\left(\sum_j w_{j,k}a_j\right) \\ &= -2(y_k - a_k)g'(in_k)a_j = -a_j\Delta_k\ ,\end{aligned}$$

with Δ_k defined as before. To obtain the gradient with respect to the $w_{i,j}$ weights connecting the input layer to the hidden ¡layer, we have to expand out the activations a_j and reapply the chain rule. We will show the derivation in gory detail because it is interesting to see how the derivative operator propagates back through the network:

$$\begin{aligned}\frac{\partial Loss_k}{\partial w_{i,j}} &= -2(y_k - a_k)\frac{\partial a_k}{\partial w_{i,j}} = -2(y_k - a_k)\frac{\partial g(in_k)}{\partial w_{i,j}} \\ &= -2(y_k - a_k)g'(in_k)\frac{\partial in_k}{\partial w_{i,j}} = -2\Delta_k\frac{\partial}{\partial w_{i,j}}\left(\sum_j w_{j,k}a_j\right) \\ &= -2\Delta_k w_{j,k}\frac{\partial a_j}{\partial w_{i,j}} = -2\Delta_k w_{j,k}\frac{\partial g(in_j)}{\partial w_{i,j}} \\ &= -2\Delta_k w_{j,k}g'(in_j)\frac{\partial in_j}{\partial w_{i,j}} \\ &= -2\Delta_k w_{j,k}g'(in_j)\frac{\partial}{\partial w_{i,j}}\left(\sum_i w_{i,j}a_i\right) \\ &= -2\Delta_k w_{j,k}g'(in_j)a_i = -a_i\Delta_j\ ,\end{aligned}$$

where Δ_j is defined as before. Thus, we obtain the update rules obtained earlier from intuitive considerations. It is also clear that the process can be continued for networks with more than one hidden layer, which justifies the general algorithm given in Figure 24.

Having made it through (or skipped over) all the mathematics, let's see how a single-hidden-layer network performs on the restaurant problem. First, we need to determine the structure of the network. We have 10 attributes describing each example, so we will need 10 input units. Should we have one hidden layer or two? How many nodes in each layer? Should they be fully connected? There is no good theory that will tell us the answer. (See the next section.) As always, we can use cross-validation: try several different structures and see which one works best. It turns out that a network with one hidden layer containing four nodes is about right for this problem. In Figure 25, we show two curves. The first is a training curve showing the mean squared error on a given training set of 100 restaurant examples

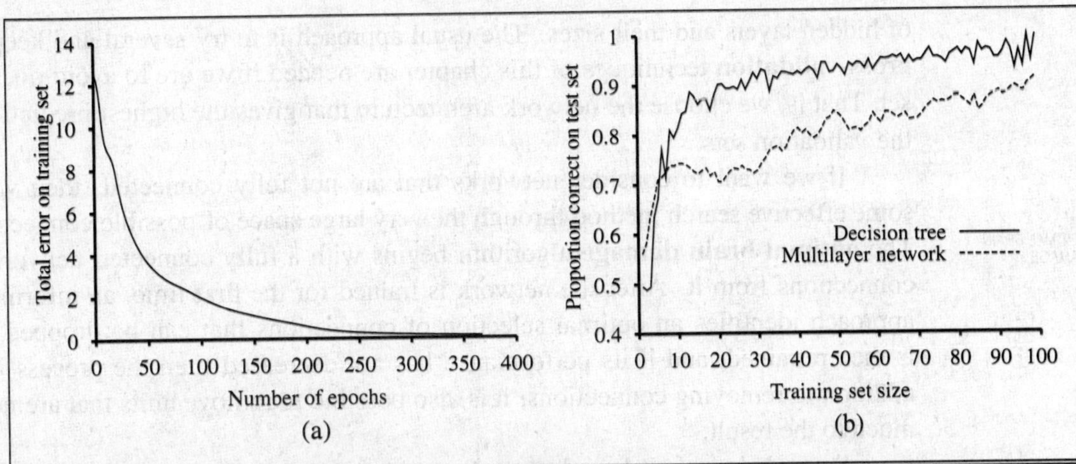

Figure 25 (a) Training curve showing the gradual reduction in error as weights are modified over several epochs, for a given set of examples in the restaurant domain. (b) Comparative learning curves showing that decision-tree learning does slightly better on the restaurant problem than back-propagation in a multilayer network.

during the weight-updating process. This demonstrates that the network does indeed converge to a perfect fit to the training data. The second curve is the standard learning curve for the restaurant data. The neural network does learn well, although not quite as fast as decision-tree learning; this is perhaps not surprising, because the data were generated from a simple decision tree in the first place.

Neural networks are capable of far more complex learning tasks of course, although it must be said that a certain amount of twiddling is needed to get the network structure right and to achieve convergence to something close to the global optimum in weight space. There are literally tens of thousands of published applications of neural networks. Section 11.1 looks at one such application in more depth.

7.5 Learning neural network structures

So far, we have considered the problem of learning weights, given a fixed network structure; just as with Bayesian networks, we also need to understand how to find the best network structure. If we choose a network that is too big, it will be able to memorize all the examples by forming a large lookup table, but will not necessarily generalize well to inputs that have not been seen before.[9] In other words, like all statistical models, neural networks are subject to **overfitting** when there are too many parameters in the model. We saw this in Figure 1, where the high-parameter models in (b) and (c) fit all the data, but might not generalize as well as the low-parameter models in (a) and (d).

If we stick to fully connected networks, the only choices to be made concern the number

[9] It has been observed that very large networks *do* generalize well *as long as the weights are kept small*. This restriction keeps the activation values in the *linear* region of the sigmoid function $g(x)$ where x is close to zero. This, in turn, means that the network behaves like a linear function (Exercise 22) with far fewer parameters.

of hidden layers and their sizes. The usual approach is to try several and keep the best. The **cross-validation** techniques of this chapter are needed if we are to avoid **peeking** at the test set. That is, we choose the network architecture that gives the highest prediction accuracy on the validation sets.

OPTIMAL BRAIN DAMAGE

If we want to consider networks that are not fully connected, then we need to find some effective search method through the very large space of possible connection topologies. The **optimal brain damage** algorithm begins with a fully connected network and removes connections from it. After the network is trained for the first time, an information-theoretic approach identifies an optimal selection of connections that can be dropped. The network is then retrained, and if its performance has not decreased then the process is repeated. In addition to removing connections, it is also possible to remove units that are not contributing much to the result.

TILING

Several algorithms have been proposed for growing a larger network from a smaller one. One, the **tiling** algorithm, resembles decision-list learning. The idea is to start with a single unit that does its best to produce the correct output on as many of the training examples as possible. Subsequent units are added to take care of the examples that the first unit got wrong. The algorithm adds only as many units as are needed to cover all the examples.

8 NONPARAMETRIC MODELS

PARAMETRIC MODEL

Linear regression and neural networks use the training data to estimate a fixed set of parameters $\mathbf{w}$. That defines our hypothesis $h_{\mathbf{w}}(\mathbf{x})$, and at that point we can throw away the training data, because they are all summarized by $\mathbf{w}$. A learning model that summarizes data with a set of parameters of fixed size (independent of the number of training examples) is called a **parametric model**.

No matter how much data you throw at a parametric model, it won't change its mind about how many parameters it needs. When data sets are small, it makes sense to have a strong restriction on the allowable hypotheses, to avoid overfitting. But when there are thousands or millions or billions of examples to learn from, it seems like a better idea to let the data speak for themselves rather than forcing them to speak through a tiny vector of parameters. If the data say that the correct answer is a very wiggly function, we shouldn't restrict ourselves to linear or slightly wiggly functions.

NONPARAMETRIC MODEL

INSTANCE-BASED LEARNING

TABLE LOOKUP

A **nonparametric model** is one that cannot be characterized by a bounded set of parameters. For example, suppose that each hypothesis we generate simply retains within itself all of the training examples and uses all of them to predict the next example. Such a hypothesis family would be nonparametric because the effective number of parameters is unbounded—it grows with the number of examples. This approach is called **instance-based learning** or **memory-based learning**. The simplest instance-based learning method is **table lookup**: take all the training examples, put them in a lookup table, and then when asked for $h(\mathbf{x})$, see if $\mathbf{x}$ is in the table; if it is, return the corresponding y. The problem with this method is that it does not generalize well: when $\mathbf{x}$ is not in the table all it can do is return some default value.

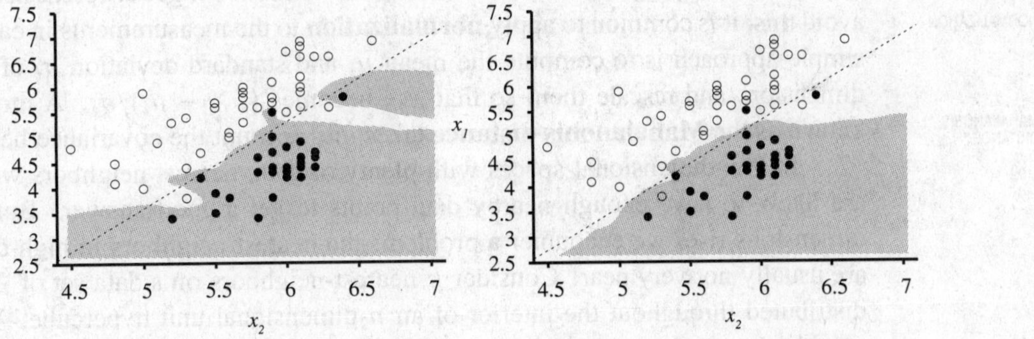

Figure 26 (a) A k-nearest-neighbor model showing the extent of the explosion class for the data in Figure 15, with $k = 1$. Overfitting is apparent. (b) With $k = 5$, the overfitting problem goes away for this data set.

8.1 Nearest neighbor models

We can improve on table lookup with a slight variation: given a query $\mathbf{x}_q$, find the k examples that are *nearest* to $\mathbf{x}_q$. This is called **k-nearest neighbors** lookup. We'll use the notation $NN(k, \mathbf{x}_q)$ to denote the set of k nearest neighbors.

NEAREST NEIGHBORS

To do classification, first find $NN(k, \mathbf{x}_q)$, then take the plurality vote of the neighbors (which is the majority vote in the case of binary classification). To avoid ties, k is always chosen to be an odd number. To do regression, we can take the mean or median of the k neighbors, or we can solve a linear regression problem on the neighbors.

In Figure 26, we show the decision boundary of k-nearest-neighbors classification for $k = 1$ and 5 on the earthquake data set from Figure 15. Nonparametric methods are still subject to underfitting and overfitting, just like parametric methods. In this case 1-nearest neighbors is overfitting; it reacts too much to the black outlier in the upper right and the white outlier at (5.4, 3.7). The 5-nearest-neighbors decision boundary is good; higher k would underfit. As usual, cross-validation can be used to select the best value of k.

The very word "nearest" implies a distance metric. How do we measure the distance from a query point $\mathbf{x}_q$ to an example point $\mathbf{x}_j$? Typically, distances are measured with a **Minkowski distance** or L^p norm, defined as

MINKOWSKI DISTANCE

$$L^p(\mathbf{x}_j, \mathbf{x}_q) = \Big(\sum_i |x_{j,i} - x_{q,i}|^p\Big)^{1/p} .$$

With $p = 2$ this is Euclidean distance and with $p = 1$ it is Manhattan distance. With Boolean attribute values, the number of attributes on which the two points differ is called the **Hamming distance**. Often $p = 2$ is used if the dimensions are measuring similar properties, such as the width, height and depth of parts on a conveyor belt, and Manhattan distance is used if they are dissimilar, such as age, weight, and gender of a patient. Note that if we use the raw numbers from each dimension then the total distance will be affected by a change in scale in any dimension. That is, if we change dimension i from measurements in centimeters to

HAMMING DISTANCE

miles while keeping the other dimensions the same, we'll get different nearest neighbors. To avoid this, it is common to apply **normalization** to the measurements in each dimension. One simple approach is to compute the mean μ_i and standard deviation σ_i of the values in each dimension, and rescale them so that $x_{j,i}$ becomes $(x_{j,i} - \mu_i)/\sigma_i$. A more complex metric known as the **Mahalanobis distance** takes into account the covariance between dimensions.

NORMALIZATION

MAHALANOBIS DISTANCE

In low-dimensional spaces with plenty of data, nearest neighbors works very well: we are likely to have enough nearby data points to get a good answer. But as the number of dimensions rises we encounter a problem: the nearest neighbors in high-dimensional spaces are usually not very near! Consider k-nearest-neighbors on a data set of N points uniformly distributed throughout the interior of an n-dimensional unit hypercube. We'll define the k-neighborhood of a point as the smallest hypercube that contains the k-nearest neighbors. Let ℓ be the average side length of a neighborhood. Then the volume of the neighborhood (which contains k points) is ℓ^n and the volume of the full cube (which contains N points) is 1. So, on average, $\ell^n = k/N$. Taking nth roots of both sides we get $\ell = (k/N)^{1/n}$.

To be concrete, let $k=10$ and $N=1,000,000$. In two dimensions ($n=2$; a unit square), the average neighborhood has $\ell=0.003$, a small fraction of the unit square, and in 3 dimensions ℓ is just 2% of the edge length of the unit cube. But by the time we get to 17 dimensions, ℓ is half the edge length of the unit hypercube, and in 200 dimensions it is 94%. This problem has been called the **curse of dimensionality**.

CURSE OF DIMENSIONALITY

Another way to look at it: consider the points that fall within a thin shell making up the outer 1% of the unit hypercube. These are outliers; in general it will be hard to find a good value for them because we will be extrapolating rather than interpolating. In one dimension, these outliers are only 2% of the points on the unit line (those points where $x < .01$ or $x > .99$), but in 200 dimensions, over 98% of the points fall within this thin shell—almost all the points are outliers. You can see an example of a poor nearest-neighbors fit on outliers if you look ahead to Figure 28(b).

The $NN(k, \mathbf{x}_q)$ function is conceptually trivial: given a set of N examples and a query $\mathbf{x}_q$, iterate through the examples, measure the distance to $\mathbf{x}_q$ from each one, and keep the best k. If we are satisfied with an implementation that takes $O(N)$ execution time, then that is the end of the story. But instance-based methods are designed for large data sets, so we would like an algorithm with sublinear run time. Elementary analysis of algorithms tells us that exact table lookup is $O(N)$ with a sequential table, $O(\log N)$ with a binary tree, and $O(1)$ with a hash table. We will now see that binary trees and hash tables are also applicable for finding nearest neighbors.

8.2 Finding nearest neighbors with k-d trees

K-D TREE

A balanced binary tree over data with an arbitrary number of dimensions is called a **k-d tree**, for k-dimensional tree. (In our notation, the number of dimensions is n, so they would be n-d trees. The construction of a k-d tree is similar to the construction of a one-dimensional balanced binary tree. We start with a set of examples and at the root node we split them along the ith dimension by testing whether $x_i \leq m$. We chose the value m to be the median of the examples along the ith dimension; thus half the examples will be in the left branch of the tree

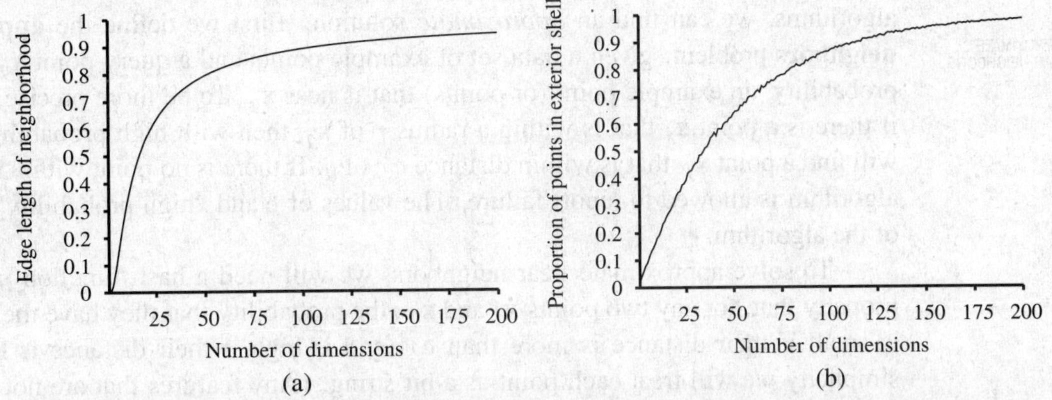

Figure 27 The curse of dimensionality: (a) The length of the average neighborhood for 10-nearest-neighbors in a unit hypercube with 1,000,000 points, as a function of the number of dimensions. (b) The proportion of points that fall within a thin shell consisting of the outer 1% of the hypercube, as a function of the number of dimensions. Sampled from 10,000 randomly distributed points.

and half in the right. We then recursively make a tree for the left and right sets of examples, stopping when there are fewer than two examples left. To choose a dimension to split on at each node of the tree, one can simply select dimension $i \bmod n$ at level i of the tree. (Note that we may need to split on any given dimension several times as we proceed down the tree.) Another strategy is to split on the dimension that has the widest spread of values.

Exact lookup from a k-d tree is just like lookup from a binary tree (with the slight complication that you need to pay attention to which dimension you are testing at each node). But nearest neighbor lookup is more complicated. As we go down the branches, splitting the examples in half, in some cases we can discard the other half of the examples. But not always. Sometimes the point we are querying for falls very close to the dividing boundary. The query point itself might be on the left hand side of the boundary, but one or more of the k nearest neighbors might actually be on the right-hand side. We have to test for this possibility by computing the distance of the query point to the dividing boundary, and then searching both sides if we can't find k examples on the left that are closer than this distance. Because of this problem, k-d trees are appropriate only when there are many more examples than dimensions, preferably at least 2^n examples. Thus, k-d trees work well with up to 10 dimensions with thousands of examples or up to 20 dimensions with millions of examples. If we don't have enough examples, lookup is no faster than a linear scan of the entire data set.

8.3 Locality-sensitive hashing

Hash tables have the potential to provide even faster lookup than binary trees. But how can we find nearest neighbors using a hash table, when hash codes rely on an *exact* match? Hash codes randomly distribute values among the bins, but we want to have near points grouped together in the same bin; we want a **locality-sensitive hash** (LSH).

LOCALITY-SENSITIVE HASH

We can't use hashes to solve $NN(k, \mathbf{x}_q)$ exactly, but with a clever use of randomized algorithms, we can find an *approximate* solution. First we define the **approximate near-neighbors** problem: given a data set of example points and a query point $\mathbf{x}_q$, find, with high probability, an example point (or points) that is near $\mathbf{x}_q$. To be more precise, we require that if there is a point $\mathbf{x}_j$ that is within a radius r of $\mathbf{x}_q$, then with high probability the algorithm will find a point $\mathbf{x}_{j'}$ that is within distance $c\,r$ of q. If there is no point within radius r then the algorithm is allowed to report failure. The values of c and "high probability" are parameters of the algorithm.

APPROXIMATE NEAR-NEIGHBORS

To solve approximate near neighbors, we will need a hash function $g(\mathbf{x})$ that has the property that, for any two points $\mathbf{x}_j$ and $\mathbf{x}_{j'}$, the probability that they have the same hash code is small if their distance is more than $c\,r$, and is high if their distance is less than r. For simplicity we will treat each point as a bit string. (Any features that are not Boolean can be encoded into a set of Boolean features.)

The intuition we rely on is that if two points are close together in an n-dimensional space, then they will necessarily be close when projected down onto a one-dimensional space (a line). In fact, we can discretize the line into bins—hash buckets—so that, with high probability, near points project down to exactly the same bin. Points that are far away from each other will tend to project down into different bins for most projections, but there will always be a few projections that coincidentally project far-apart points into the same bin. Thus, the bin for point $\mathbf{x}_q$ contains many (but not all) points that are near to $\mathbf{x}_q$, as well as some points that are far away.

The trick of LSH is to create *multiple* random projections and combine them. A random projection is just a random subset of the bit-string representation. We choose ℓ different random projections and create ℓ hash tables, $g_1(\mathbf{x}), \ldots, g_\ell(\mathbf{x})$. We then enter all the examples into each hash table. Then when given a query point $\mathbf{x}_q$, we fetch the set of points in bin $g_k(q)$ for each k, and union these sets together into a set of candidate points, C. Then we compute the actual distance to $\mathbf{x}_q$ for each of the points in C and return the k closest points. With high probability, each of the points that are near to $\mathbf{x}_q$ will show up in at least one of the bins, and although some far-away points will show up as well, we can ignore those. With large real-world problems, such as finding the near neighbors in a data set of 13 million Web images using 512 dimensions (Torralba *et al.*, 2008), locality-sensitive hashing needs to examine only a few thousand images out of 13 million to find nearest neighbors; a thousand-fold speedup over exhaustive or k-d tree approaches.

8.4 Nonparametric regression

Now we'll look at nonparametric approaches to *regression* rather than classification. Figure 28 shows an example of some different models. In (a), we have perhaps the simplest method of all, known informally as "connect-the-dots," and superciliously as "piecewise-linear nonparametric regression." This model creates a function $h(x)$ that, when given a query x_q, solves the ordinary linear regression problem with just two points: the training examples immediately to the left and right of x_q. When noise is low, this trivial method is actually not too bad, which is why it is a standard feature of charting software in spreadsheets.

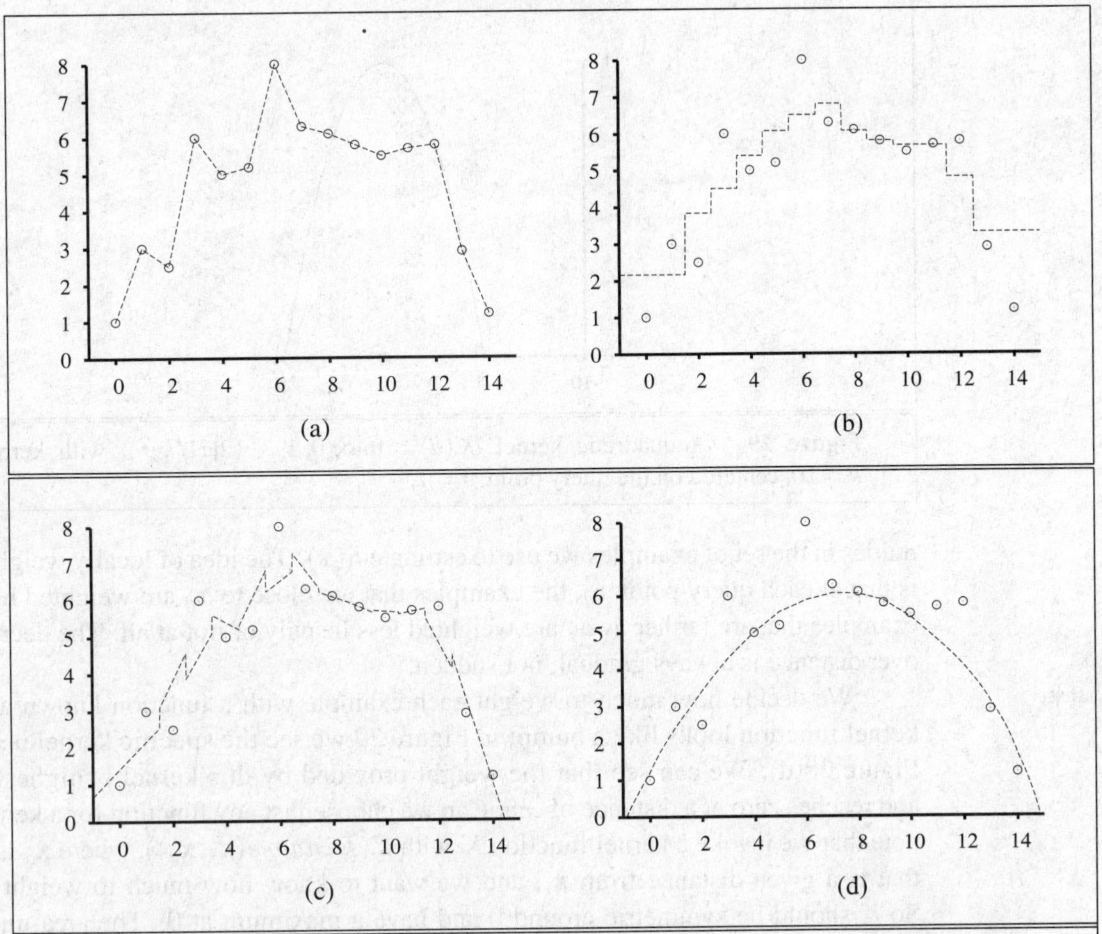

Figure 28 Nonparametric regression models: (a) connect the dots, (b) 3-nearest neighbors average, (c) 3-nearest-neighbors linear regression, (d) locally weighted regression with a quadratic kernel of width $k = 10$.

But when the data are noisy, the resulting function is spiky, and does not generalize well.

NEAREST-NEIGHBORS REGRESSION

k-nearest-neighbors regression (Figure 28(b)) improves on connect-the-dots. Instead of using just the two examples to the left and right of a query point x_q, we use the k nearest neighbors (here 3). A larger value of k tends to smooth out the magnitude of the spikes, although the resulting function has discontinuities. In (b), we have the k-nearest-neighbors average: $h(x)$ is the mean value of the k points, $\sum y_j/k$. Notice that at the outlying points, near $x = 0$ and $x = 14$, the estimates are poor because all the evidence comes from one side (the interior), and ignores the trend. In (c), we have k-nearest-neighbor linear regression, which finds the best line through the k examples. This does a better job of capturing trends at the outliers, but is still discontinuous. In both (b) and (c), we're left with the question of how to choose a good value for k. The answer, as usual, is cross-validation.

LOCALLY WEIGHTED REGRESSION

Locally weighted regression (Figure 28(d)) gives us the advantages of nearest neighbors, without the discontinuities. To avoid discontinuities in $h(x)$, we need to avoid disconti-

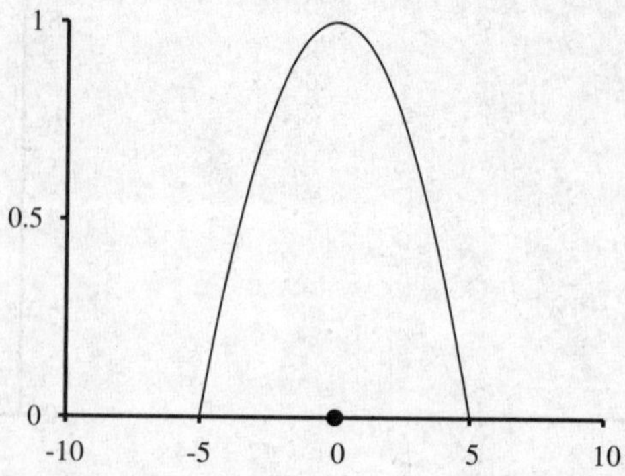

Figure 29 A quadratic kernel, $\mathcal{K}(d) = \max(0, 1 - (2|x|/k)^2)$, with kernel width $k = 10$, centered on the query point $x = 0$.

nuities in the set of examples we use to estimate $h(x)$. The idea of locally weighted regression is that at each query point x_q, the examples that are close to x_q are weighted heavily, and the examples that are farther away are weighted less heavily or not at all. The decrease in weight over distance is always gradual, not sudden.

KERNEL

We decide how much to weight each example with a function known as a **kernel**. A kernel function looks like a bump; in Figure 29 we see the specific kernel used to generate Figure 28(d). We can see that the weight provided by this kernel is highest in the center and reaches zero at a distance of ± 5. Can we choose just any function for a kernel? No. First, note that we invoke a kernel function $\mathcal{K}$ with $\mathcal{K}(Distance(\mathbf{x}_j, \mathbf{x}_q))$, where $\mathbf{x}_q$ is a query point that is a given distance from $\mathbf{x}_j$, and we want to know how much to weight that distance. So $\mathcal{K}$ should be symmetric around 0 and have a maximum at 0. The area under the kernel must remain bounded as we go to $\pm\infty$. Other shapes, such as Gaussians, have been used for kernels, but the latest research suggests that the choice of shape doesn't matter much. We do have to be careful about the width of the kernel. Again, this is a parameter of the model that is best chosen by cross-validation. Just as in choosing the k for nearest neighbors, if the kernels are too wide we'll get underfitting and if they are too narrow we'll get overfitting. In Figure 29(d), the value of $k = 10$ gives a smooth curve that looks about right—but maybe it does not pay enough attention to the outlier at $x = 6$; a narrower kernel width would be more responsive to individual points.

Doing locally weighted regression with kernels is now straightforward. For a given query point $\mathbf{x}_q$ we solve the following weighted regression problem using gradient descent:

$$\mathbf{w}^* = \underset{\mathbf{w}}{\operatorname{argmin}} \sum_j \mathcal{K}(Distance(\mathbf{x}_q, \mathbf{x}_j))\,(y_j - \mathbf{w} \cdot \mathbf{x}_j)^2\,,$$

where *Distance* is any of the distance metrics discussed for nearest neighbors. Then the answer is $h(\mathbf{x}_q) = \mathbf{w}^* \cdot \mathbf{x}_q$.

Note that we need to solve a new regression problem for *every* query point—that's what it means to be *local*. (In ordinary linear regression, we solved the regression problem once, globally, and then used the same $h_\mathbf{w}$ for any query point.) Mitigating against this extra work is the fact that each regression problem will be easier to solve, because it involves only the examples with nonzero weight—the examples whose kernels overlap the query point. When kernel widths are small, this may be just a few points.

Most nonparametric models have the advantage that it is easy to do leave-one-out cross-validation without having to recompute everything. With a k-nearest-neighbors model, for instance, when given a test example $(\mathbf{x}, y)$ we retrieve the k nearest neighbors once, compute the per-example loss $L(y, h(\mathbf{x}))$ from them, and record that as the leave-one-out result for every example that is not one of the neighbors. Then we retrieve the $k + 1$ nearest neighbors and record distinct results for leaving out each of the k neighbors. With N examples the whole process is $O(k)$, not $O(kN)$.

9 SUPPORT VECTOR MACHINES

SUPPORT VECTOR MACHINE

The **support vector machine** or SVM framework is currently the most popular approach for "off-the-shelf" supervised learning: if you don't have any specialized prior knowledge about a domain, then the SVM is an excellent method to try first. There are three properties that make SVMs attractive:

1. SVMs construct a **maximum margin separator**—a decision boundary with the largest possible distance to example points. This helps them generalize well.
2. SVMs create a linear separating hyperplane, but they have the ability to embed the data into a higher-dimensional space, using the so-called **kernel trick**. Often, data that are not linearly separable in the original input space are easily separable in the higher-dimensional space. The high-dimensional linear separator is actually nonlinear in the original space. This means the hypothesis space is greatly expanded over methods that use strictly linear representations.
3. SVMs are a nonparametric method—they retain training examples and potentially need to store them all. On the other hand, in practice they often end up retaining only a small fraction of the number of examples—sometimes as few as a small constant times the number of dimensions. Thus SVMs combine the advantages of nonparametric and parametric models: they have the flexibility to represent complex functions, but they are resistant to overfitting.

You could say that SVMs are successful because of one key insight and one neat trick. We will cover each in turn. In Figure 30(a), we have a binary classification problem with three candidate decision boundaries, each a linear separator. Each of them is consistent with all the examples, so from the point of view of 0/1 loss, each would be equally good. Logistic regression would find some separating line; the exact location of the line depends on *all* the example points. The key insight of SVMs is that some examples are more important than others, and that paying attention to them can lead to better generalization.

Consider the lowest of the three separating lines in (a). It comes very close to 5 of the black examples. Although it classifies all the examples correctly, and thus minimizes loss, it

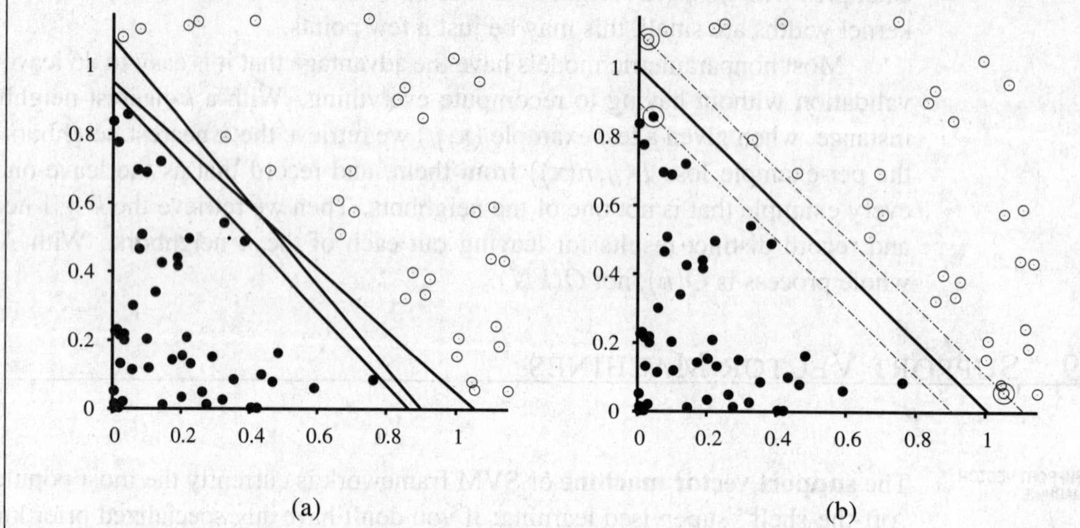

Figure 30 Support vector machine classification: (a) Two classes of points (black and white circles) and three candidate linear separators. (b) The maximum margin separator (heavy line), is at the midpoint of the **margin** (area between dashed lines). The **support vectors** (points with large circles) are the examples closest to the separator.

should make you nervous that so many examples are close to the line; it may be that other black examples will turn out to fall on the other side of the line.

SVMs address this issue: Instead of minimizing expected *empirical loss* on the training data, SVMs attempt to minimize expected *generalization* loss. We don't know where the as-yet-unseen points may fall, but under the probabilistic assumption that they are drawn from the same distribution as the previously seen examples, there are some arguments from computational learning theory (Section 5) suggesting that we minimize generalization loss by choosing the separator that is farthest away from the examples we have seen so far. We call this separator, shown in Figure 30(b) the **maximum margin separator**. The **margin** is the width of the area bounded by dashed lines in the figure—twice the distance from the separator to the nearest example point.

MAXIMUM MARGIN SEPARATOR

MARGIN

Now, how do we find this separator? Before showing the equations, some notation: Traditionally SVMs use the convention that class labels are +1 and -1, instead of the +1 and 0 we have been using so far. Also, where we put the intercept into the weight vector **w** (and a corresponding dummy 1 value into $x_{j,0}$), SVMs do not do that; they keep the intercept as a separate parameter, b. With that in mind, the separator is defined as the set of points $\{\mathbf{x} : \mathbf{w} \cdot \mathbf{x} + b = 0\}$. We could search the space of **w** and b with gradient descent to find the parameters that maximize the margin while correctly classifying all the examples.

However, it turns out there is another approach to solving this problem. We won't show the details, but will just say that there is an alternative representation called the dual representation, in which the optimal solution is found by solving

$$\underset{\alpha}{\operatorname{argmax}} \sum_j \alpha_j - \frac{1}{2} \sum_{j,k} \alpha_j \alpha_k y_j y_k (\mathbf{x}_j \cdot \mathbf{x}_k) \tag{13}$$

QUADRATIC PROGRAMMING

subject to the constraints $\alpha_j \geq 0$ and $\sum_j \alpha_j y_j = 0$. This is a **quadratic programming** optimization problem, for which there are good software packages. Once we have found the vector α we can get back to $\mathbf{w}$ with the equation $\mathbf{w} = \sum_j \alpha_j \mathbf{x}_j$, or we can stay in the dual representation. There are three important properties of Equation (13). First, the expression is convex; it has a single global maximum that can be found efficiently. Second, *the data enter the expression only in the form of dot products of pairs of points.* This second property is also true of the equation for the separator itself; once the optimal α_j have been calculated, it is

$$h(\mathbf{x}) = \operatorname{sign}\left(\sum_j \alpha_j y_j (\mathbf{x} \cdot \mathbf{x}_j) - b\right) . \tag{14}$$

SUPPORT VECTOR

A final important property is that the weights α_j associated with each data point are *zero* except for the **support vectors**—the points closest to the separator. (They are called "support" vectors because they "hold up" the separating plane.) Because there are usually many fewer support vectors than examples, SVMs gain some of the advantages of parametric models.

What if the examples are not linearly separable? Figure 31(a) shows an input space defined by attributes $\mathbf{x} = (x_1, x_2)$, with positive examples ($y = +1$) inside a circular region and negative examples ($y = -1$) outside. Clearly, there is no linear separator for this problem. Now, suppose we re-express the input data—i.e., we map each input vector $\mathbf{x}$ to a new vector of feature values, $F(\mathbf{x})$. In particular, let us use the three features

$$f_1 = x_1^2 , \qquad f_2 = x_2^2 , \qquad f_3 = \sqrt{2} x_1 x_2 . \tag{15}$$

We will see shortly where these came from, but for now, just look at what happens. Figure 31(b) shows the data in the new, three-dimensional space defined by the three features; the data are *linearly separable* in this space! This phenomenon is actually fairly general: if data are mapped into a space of sufficiently high dimension, then they will almost always be linearly separable—if you look at a set of points from enough directions, you'll find a way to make them line up. Here, we used only three dimensions;[10] Exercise 16 asks you to show that four dimensions suffice for linearly separating a circle anywhere in the plane (not just at the origin), and five dimensions suffice to linearly separate any ellipse. In general (with some special cases excepted) if we have N data points then they will always be separable in spaces of $N - 1$ dimensions or more (Exercise 25).

Now, we would not usually expect to find a linear separator in the input space $\mathbf{x}$, but we can find linear separators in the high-dimensional feature space $F(\mathbf{x})$ simply by replacing $\mathbf{x}_j \cdot \mathbf{x}_k$ in Equation (13) with $F(\mathbf{x}_j) \cdot F(\mathbf{x}_k)$. This by itself is not remarkable—replacing $\mathbf{x}$ by $F(\mathbf{x})$ in *any* learning algorithm has the required effect—but the dot product has some special properties. It turns out that $F(\mathbf{x}_j) \cdot F(\mathbf{x}_k)$ can often be computed without first computing F

[10] The reader may notice that we could have used just f_1 and f_2, but the 3D mapping illustrates the idea better.

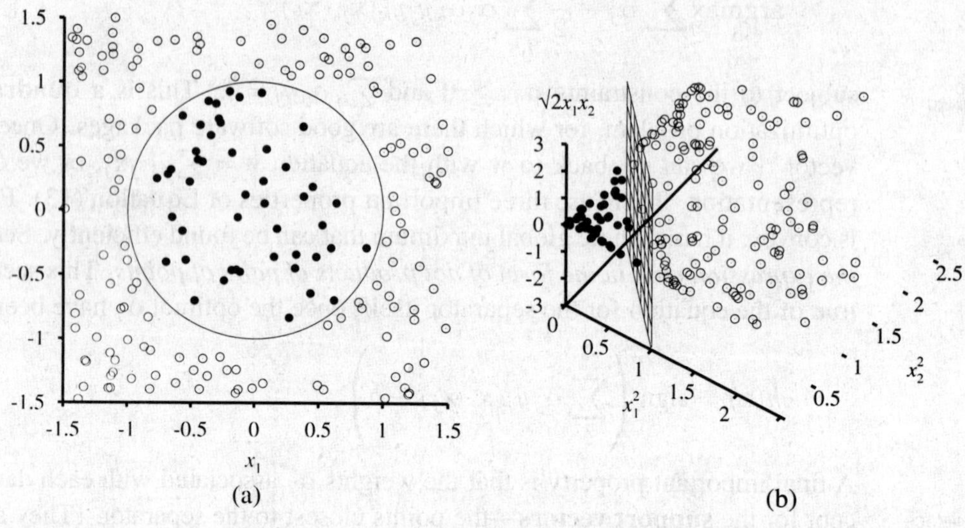

Figure 31 (a) A two-dimensional training set with positive examples as black circles and negative examples as white circles. The true decision boundary, $x_1^2 + x_2^2 \leq 1$, is also shown. (b) The same data after mapping into a three-dimensional input space $(x_1^2, x_2^2, \sqrt{2}x_1x_2)$. The circular decision boundary in (a) becomes a linear decision boundary in three dimensions. Figure 30(b) gives a closeup of the separator in (b).

for each point. In our three-dimensional feature space defined by Equation (15), a little bit of algebra shows that

$$F(\mathbf{x}_j) \cdot F(\mathbf{x}_k) = (\mathbf{x}_j \cdot \mathbf{x}_k)^2 .$$

KERNEL FUNCTION

(That's why the $\sqrt{2}$ is in f_3.) The expression $(\mathbf{x}_j \cdot \mathbf{x}_k)^2$ is called a **kernel function**,[11] and is usually written as $K(\mathbf{x}_j, \mathbf{x}_k)$. The kernel function can be applied to pairs of input data to evaluate dot products in some corresponding feature space. So, we can find linear separators in the higher-dimensional feature space $F(\mathbf{x})$ simply by replacing $\mathbf{x}_j \cdot \mathbf{x}_k$ in Equation (13) with a kernel function $K(\mathbf{x}_j, \mathbf{x}_k)$. Thus, we can learn in the higher-dimensional space, but we compute only kernel functions rather than the full list of features for each data point.

MERCER'S THEOREM

POLYNOMIAL KERNEL

The next step is to see that there's nothing special about the kernel $K(\mathbf{x}_j, \mathbf{x}_k) = (\mathbf{x}_j \cdot \mathbf{x}_k)^2$. It corresponds to a particular higher-dimensional feature space, but other kernel functions correspond to other feature spaces. A venerable result in mathematics, **Mercer's theorem** (1909), tells us that any "reasonable"[12] kernel function corresponds to *some* feature space. These feature spaces can be very large, even for innocuous-looking kernels. For example, the **polynomial kernel**, $K(\mathbf{x}_j, \mathbf{x}_k) = (1 + \mathbf{x}_j \cdot \mathbf{x}_k)^d$, corresponds to a feature space whose dimension is exponential in d.

[11] This usage of "kernel function" is slightly different from the kernels in locally weighted regression. Some SVM kernels are distance metrics, but not all are.

[12] Here, "reasonable" means that the matrix $\mathbf{K}_{jk} = K(\mathbf{x}_j, \mathbf{x}_k)$ is positive definite.

KERNEL TRICK

This then is the clever **kernel trick**: Plugging these kernels into Equation (13), *optimal linear separators can be found efficiently in feature spaces with billions of (or, in some cases, infinitely many) dimensions.* The resulting linear separators, when mapped back to the original input space, can correspond to arbitrarily wiggly, nonlinear decision boundaries between the positive and negative examples.

SOFT MARGIN

In the case of inherently noisy data, we may not want a linear separator in some high-dimensional space. Rather, we'd like a decision surface in a lower-dimensional space that does not cleanly separate the classes, but reflects the reality of the noisy data. That is possible with the **soft margin** classifier, which allows examples to fall on the wrong side of the decision boundary, but assigns them a penalty proportional to the distance required to move them back on the correct side.

KERNELIZATION

The kernel method can be applied not only with learning algorithms that find optimal linear separators, but also with any other algorithm that can be reformulated to work only with dot products of pairs of data points, as in Equations 13 and 14. Once this is done, the dot product is replaced by a kernel function and we have a **kernelized** version of the algorithm. This can be done easily for k-nearest-neighbors and perceptron learning (Section 7.2), among others.

10 ENSEMBLE LEARNING

ENSEMBLE LEARNING

So far we have looked at learning methods in which a single hypothesis, chosen from a hypothesis space, is used to make predictions. The idea of **ensemble learning** methods is to select a collection, or **ensemble**, of hypotheses from the hypothesis space and combine their predictions. For example, during cross-validation we might generate twenty different decision trees, and have them vote on the best classification for a new example.

The motivation for ensemble learning is simple. Consider an ensemble of $K = 5$ hypotheses and suppose that we combine their predictions using simple majority voting. For the ensemble to misclassify a new example, *at least three of the five hypotheses have to misclassify it.* The hope is that this is much less likely than a misclassification by a single hypothesis. Suppose we assume that each hypothesis h_k in the ensemble has an error of p—that is, the probability that a randomly chosen example is misclassified by h_k is p. Furthermore, suppose we assume that the errors made by each hypothesis are *independent*. In that case, if p is small, then the probability of a large number of misclassifications occurring is minuscule. For example, a simple calculation (Exercise 18) shows that using an ensemble of five hypotheses reduces an error rate of 1 in 10 down to an error rate of less than 1 in 100. Now, obviously the assumption of independence is unreasonable, because hypotheses are likely to be misled in the same way by any misleading aspects of the training data. But if the hypotheses are at least a little bit different, thereby reducing the correlation between their errors, then ensemble learning can be very useful.

Another way to think about the ensemble idea is as a generic way of enlarging the hypothesis space. That is, think of the ensemble itself as a hypothesis and the new hypothesis

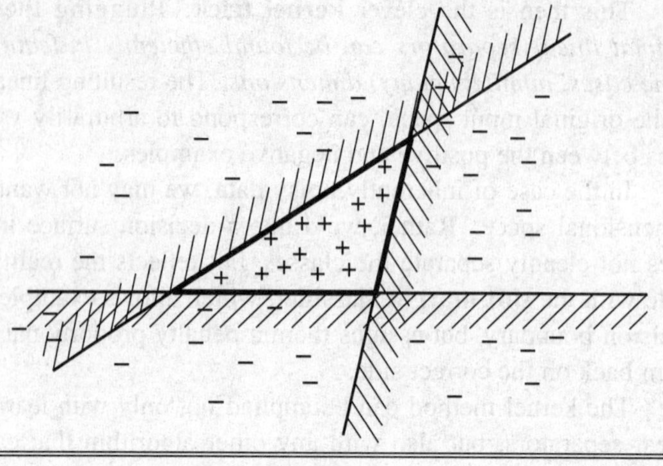

Figure 32 Illustration of the increased expressive power obtained by ensemble learning. We take three linear threshold hypotheses, each of which classifies positively on the unshaded side, and classify as positive any example classified positively by all three. The resulting triangular region is a hypothesis not expressible in the original hypothesis space.

space as the set of all possible ensembles constructable from hypotheses in the original space. Figure 32 shows how this can result in a more expressive hypothesis space. If the original hypothesis space allows for a simple and efficient learning algorithm, then the ensemble method provides a way to learn a much more expressive class of hypotheses without incurring much additional computational or algorithmic complexity.

BOOSTING

WEIGHTED TRAINING SET

The most widely used ensemble method is called **boosting**. To understand how it works, we need first to explain the idea of a **weighted training set**. In such a training set, each example has an associated weight $w_j \geq 0$. The higher the weight of an example, the higher is the importance attached to it during the learning of a hypothesis. It is straightforward to modify the learning algorithms we have seen so far to operate with weighted training sets.[13]

Boosting starts with $w_j = 1$ for all the examples (i.e., a normal training set). From this set, it generates the first hypothesis, h_1. This hypothesis will classify some of the training examples correctly and some incorrectly. We would like the next hypothesis to do better on the misclassified examples, so we increase their weights while decreasing the weights of the correctly classified examples. From this new weighted training set, we generate hypothesis h_2. The process continues in this way until we have generated K hypotheses, where K is an input to the boosting algorithm. The final ensemble hypothesis is a weighted-majority combination of all the K hypotheses, each weighted according to how well it performed on the training set. Figure 33 shows how the algorithm works conceptually. There are many variants of the basic boosting idea, with different ways of adjusting the weights and combining the hypotheses. One specific algorithm, called ADABOOST, is shown in Figure 34. ADABOOST has a very important property: if the input learning algorithm L is a **weak learning** algorithm—which

WEAK LEARNING

[13] For learning algorithms in which this is not possible, one can instead create a **replicated training set** where the jth example appears w_j times, using randomization to handle fractional weights.

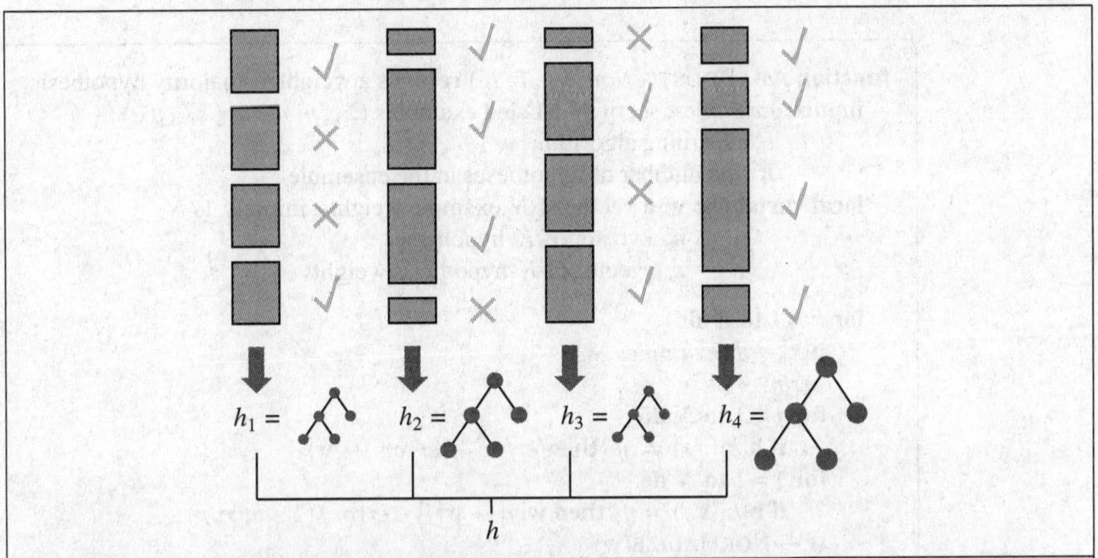

Figure 33 How the boosting algorithm works. Each shaded rectangle corresponds to an example; the height of the rectangle corresponds to the weight. The checks and crosses indicate whether the example was classified correctly by the current hypothesis. The size of the decision tree indicates the weight of that hypothesis in the final ensemble.

means that L always returns a hypothesis with accuracy on the training set that is slightly better than random guessing (i.e., $50\%+\epsilon$ for Boolean classification)—then ADABOOST will return a hypothesis that *classifies the training data perfectly* for large enough K. Thus, the algorithm *boosts* the accuracy of the original learning algorithm on the training data. This result holds no matter how inexpressive the original hypothesis space and no matter how complex the function being learned.

DECISION STUMP

Let us see how well boosting does on the restaurant data. We will choose as our original hypothesis space the class of **decision stumps**, which are decision trees with just one test, at the root. The lower curve in Figure 35(a) shows that unboosted decision stumps are not very effective for this data set, reaching a prediction performance of only 81% on 100 training examples. When boosting is applied (with $K=5$), the performance is better, reaching 93% after 100 examples.

An interesting thing happens as the ensemble size K increases. Figure 35(b) shows the training set performance (on 100 examples) as a function of K. Notice that the error reaches zero when K is 20; that is, a weighted-majority combination of 20 decision stumps suffices to fit the 100 examples exactly. As more stumps are added to the ensemble, the error remains at zero. The graph also shows that *the test set performance continues to increase long after the training set error has reached zero.* At $K = 20$, the test performance is 0.95 (or 0.05 error), and the performance increases to 0.98 as late as $K = 137$, before gradually dropping to 0.95.

This finding, which is quite robust across data sets and hypothesis spaces, came as quite a surprise when it was first noticed. Ockham's razor tells us not to make hypotheses more

```
function ADABOOST(examples, L, K) returns a weighted-majority hypothesis
  inputs: examples, set of N labeled examples (x1, y1), ..., (xN, yN)
          L, a learning algorithm
          K, the number of hypotheses in the ensemble
  local variables: w, a vector of N example weights, initially 1/N
                   h, a vector of K hypotheses
                   z, a vector of K hypothesis weights

  for k = 1 to K do
      h[k] ← L(examples, w)
      error ← 0
      for j = 1 to N do
          if h[k](xj) ≠ yj then error ← error + w[j]
      for j = 1 to N do
          if h[k](xj) = yj then w[j] ← w[j] · error/(1 − error)
      w ← NORMALIZE(w)
      z[k] ← log (1 − error)/error
  return WEIGHTED-MAJORITY(h, z)
```

Figure 34 The ADABOOST variant of the boosting method for ensemble learning. The algorithm generates hypotheses by successively reweighting the training examples. The function WEIGHTED-MAJORITY generates a hypothesis that returns the output value with the highest vote from the hypotheses in **h**, with votes weighted by **z**.

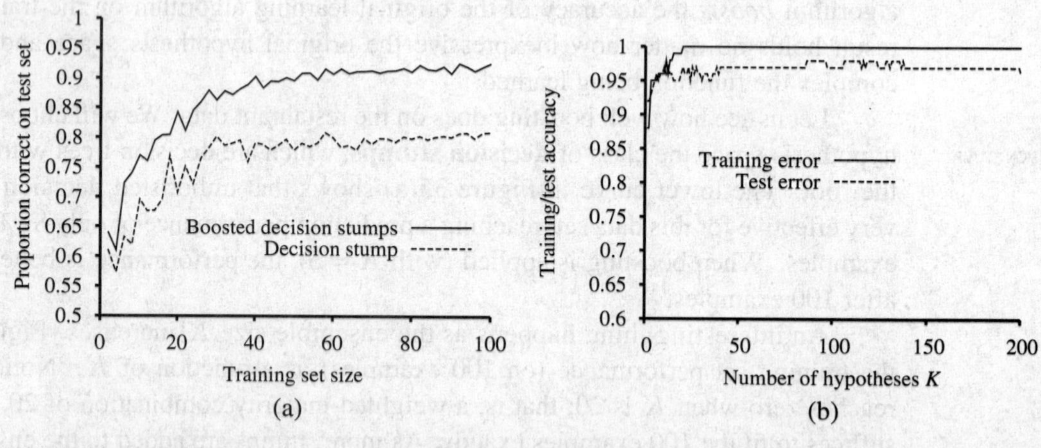

Figure 35 (a) Graph showing the performance of boosted decision stumps with $K = 5$ versus unboosted decision stumps on the restaurant data. (b) The proportion correct on the training set and the test set as a function of K, the number of hypotheses in the ensemble. Notice that the test set accuracy improves slightly even after the training accuracy reaches 1, i.e., after the ensemble fits the data exactly.

complex than necessary, but the graph tells us that the predictions *improve* as the ensemble hypothesis gets more complex! Various explanations have been proposed for this. One view is that boosting approximates **Bayesian learning**, which can be shown to be an optimal learning algorithm, and the approximation improves as more hypotheses are added. Another possible explanation is that the addition of further hypotheses enables the ensemble to be *more definite* in its distinction between positive and negative examples, which helps it when it comes to classifying new examples.

10.1 Online Learning

So far, everything we have done in this chapter has relied on the assumption that the data are i.i.d. (independent and identically distributed). On the one hand, that is a sensible assumption: if the future bears no resemblance to the past, then how can we predict anything? On the other hand, it is too strong an assumption: it is rare that our inputs have captured all the information that would make the future truly independent of the past.

In this section we examine what to do when the data are not i.i.d.; when they can change over time. In this case, it matters *when* we make a prediction, so we will adopt the perspective called **online learning**: an agent receives an input x_j from nature, predicts the corresponding y_j, and then is told the correct answer. Then the process repeats with x_{j+1}, and so on. One might think this task is hopeless—if nature is adversarial, all the predictions may be wrong. It turns out that there are some guarantees we can make.

ONLINE LEARNING

Let us consider the situation where our input consists of predictions from a panel of experts. For example, each day a set of K pundits predicts whether the stock market will go up or down, and our task is to pool those predictions and make our own. One way to do this is to keep track of how well each expert performs, and choose to believe them in proportion to their past performance. This is called the **randomized weighted majority algorithm**. We can described it more formally:

RANDOMIZED WEIGHTED MAJORITY ALGORITHM

1. Initialize a set of weights $\{w_1, \ldots, w_K\}$ all to 1.
2. Receive the predictions $\{\hat{y}_1, \ldots, \hat{y}_K\}$ from the experts.
3. Randomly choose an expert k^*, in proportion to its weight: $P(k) = w_k/(\sum_{k'} w_{k'})$.
4. Predict $\hat{y}_{k^*}$.
5. Receive the correct answer y.
6. For each expert k such that $\hat{y}_k \neq y$, update $w_k \leftarrow \beta w_k$

Here β is a number, $0 < \beta < 1$, that tells how much to penalize an expert for each mistake.

REGRET

We measure the success of this algorithm in terms of **regret**, which is defined as the number of additional mistakes we make compared to the expert who, in hindsight, had the best prediction record. Let M^* be the number of mistakes made by the best expert. Then the number of mistakes, M, made by the random weighted majority algorithm, is bounded by[14]

$$M < \frac{M^* \ln(1/\beta) + \ln K}{1 - \beta} .$$

[14] See (Blum, 1996) for the proof.

This bound holds for *any* sequence of examples, even ones chosen by adversaries trying to do their worst. To be specific, when there are $K=10$ experts, if we choose $\beta=1/2$ then our number of mistakes is bounded by $1.39M^* + 4.6$, and if $\beta=3/4$ by $1.15M^* + 9.2$. In general, if β is close to 1 then we are responsive to change over the long run; if the best expert changes, we will pick up on it before too long. However, we pay a penalty at the beginning, when we start with all experts trusted equally; we may accept the advice of the bad experts for too long. When β is closer to 0, these two factors are reversed. Note that we can choose β to get asymptotically close to M^* in the long run; this is called **no-regret learning** (because the average amount of regret per trial tends to 0 as the number of trials increases).

NO-REGRET LEARNING

Online learning is helpful when the data may be changing rapidly over time. It is also useful for applications that involve a large collection of data that is constantly growing, even if changes are gradual. For example, with a database of millions of Web images, you wouldn't want to train, say, a linear regression model on all the data, and then retrain from scratch every time a new image is added. It would be more practical to have an online algorithm that allows images to be added incrementally. For most learning algorithms based on minimizing loss, there is an online version based on minimizing regret. It is a bonus that many of these online algorithms come with guaranteed bounds on regret.

To some observers, it is surprising that there are such tight bounds on how well we can do compared to a panel of experts. To others, the really surprising thing is that when panels of human experts congregate—predicting stock market prices, sports outcomes, or political contests—the viewing public is so willing to listen to them pontificate and so unwilling to quantify their error rates.

11 PRACTICAL MACHINE LEARNING

We have introduced a wide range of machine learning techniques, each illustrated with simple learning tasks. In this section, we consider two aspects of practical machine learning. The first involves finding algorithms capable of learning to recognize handwritten digits and squeezing every last drop of predictive performance out of them. The second involves anything but—pointing out that obtaining, cleaning, and representing the data can be at least as important as algorithm engineering.

11.1 Case study: Handwritten digit recognition

Recognizing handwritten digits is an important problem with many applications, including automated sorting of mail by postal code, automated reading of checks and tax returns, and data entry for hand-held computers. It is an area where rapid progress has been made, in part because of better learning algorithms and in part because of the availability of better training sets. The United States National Institute of Science and Technology (**NIST**) has archived a database of 60,000 labeled digits, each $20 \times 20 = 400$ pixels with 8-bit grayscale values. It has become one of the standard benchmark problems for comparing new learning algorithms. Some example digits are shown in Figure 36.

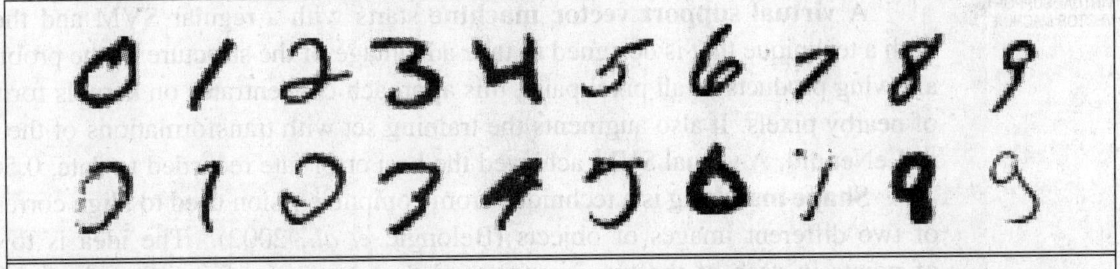

Figure 36 Examples from the NIST database of handwritten digits. Top row: examples of digits 0–9 that are easy to identify. Bottom row: more difficult examples of the same digits.

Many different learning approaches have been tried. One of the first, and probably the simplest, is the **3-nearest-neighbor** classifier, which also has the advantage of requiring no training time. As a memory-based algorithm, however, it must store all 60,000 images, and its run time performance is slow. It achieved a test error rate of 2.4%.

A **single-hidden-layer neural network** was designed for this problem with 400 input units (one per pixel) and 10 output units (one per class). Using cross-validation, it was found that roughly 300 hidden units gave the best performance. With full interconnections between layers, there were a total of 123,300 weights. This network achieved a 1.6% error rate.

A series of **specialized neural networks** called LeNet were devised to take advantage of the structure of the problem—that the input consists of pixels in a two–dimensional array, and that small changes in the position or slant of an image are unimportant. Each network had an input layer of 32×32 units, onto which the 20×20 pixels were centered so that each input unit is presented with a local neighborhood of pixels. This was followed by three layers of hidden units. Each layer consisted of several planes of $n \times n$ arrays, where n is smaller than the previous layer so that the network is down-sampling the input, and where the weights of every unit in a plane are constrained to be identical, so that the plane is acting as a feature detector: it can pick out a feature such as a long vertical line or a short semi-circular arc. The output layer had 10 units. Many versions of this architecture were tried; a representative one had hidden layers with 768, 192, and 30 units, respectively. The training set was augmented by applying affine transformations to the actual inputs: shifting, slightly rotating, and scaling the images. (Of course, the transformations have to be small, or else a 6 will be transformed into a 9!) The best error rate achieved by LeNet was 0.9%.

A **boosted neural network** combined three copies of the LeNet architecture, with the second one trained on a mix of patterns that the first one got 50% wrong, and the third one trained on patterns for which the first two disagreed. During testing, the three nets voted with the majority ruling. The test error rate was 0.7%.

A **support vector machine** (see Section 9) with 25,000 support vectors achieved an error rate of 1.1%. This is remarkable because the SVM technique, like the simple nearest-neighbor approach, required almost no thought or iterated experimentation on the part of the developer, yet it still came close to the performance of LeNet, which had had years of development. Indeed, the support vector machine makes no use of the structure of the problem, and would perform just as well if the pixels were presented in a permuted order.

VIRTUAL SUPPORT VECTOR MACHINE

A **virtual support vector machine** starts with a regular SVM and then improves it with a technique that is designed to take advantage of the structure of the problem. Instead of allowing products of all pixel pairs, this approach concentrates on kernels formed from pairs of nearby pixels. It also augments the training set with transformations of the examples, just as LeNet did. A virtual SVM achieved the best error rate recorded to date, 0.56%.

Shape matching is a technique from computer vision used to align corresponding parts of two different images of objects (Belongie *et al.*, 2002). The idea is to pick out a set of points in each of the two images, and then compute, for each point in the first image, which point in the second image it corresponds to. From this alignment, we then compute a transformation between the images. The transformation gives us a measure of the distance between the images. This distance measure is better motivated than just counting the number of differing pixels, and it turns out that a 3–nearest neighbor algorithm using this distance measure performs very well. Training on only 20,000 of the 60,000 digits, and using 100 sample points per image extracted from a Canny edge detector, a shape matching classifier achieved 0.63% test error.

Humans are estimated to have an error rate of about 0.2% on this problem. This figure is somewhat suspect because humans have not been tested as extensively as have machine learning algorithms. On a similar data set of digits from the United States Postal Service, human errors were at 2.5%.

The following figure summarizes the error rates, run time performance, memory requirements, and amount of training time for the seven algorithms we have discussed. It also adds another measure, the percentage of digits that must be rejected to achieve 0.5% error. For example, if the SVM is allowed to reject 1.8% of the inputs—that is, pass them on for someone else to make the final judgment—then its error rate on the remaining 98.2% of the inputs is reduced from 1.1% to 0.5%.

The following table summarizes the error rate and some of the other characteristics of the seven techniques we have discussed.

	3 NN	300 Hidden	LeNet	Boosted LeNet	SVM	Virtual SVM	Shape Match
Error rate (pct.)	2.4	1.6	0.9	0.7	1.1	0.56	0.63
Run time (millisec/digit)	1000	10	30	50	2000	200	
Memory requirements (Mbyte)	12	.49	.012	.21	11		
Training time (days)	0	7	14	30	10		
% rejected to reach 0.5% error	8.1	3.2	1.8	0.5	1.8		

11.2 Case study: Word senses and house prices

On paper we need to deal with simple, toy data to get the ideas across: a small data set, usually in two dimensions. But in practical applications of machine learning, the data set is usually large, multidimensional, and messy. The data are not handed to the analyst in a prepackaged set of $(\mathbf{x}, y)$ values; rather the analyst needs to go out and acquire the right data. There is a task to be accomplished, and most of the engineering problem is deciding what data are necessary to accomplish the task; a smaller part is choosing and implementing an

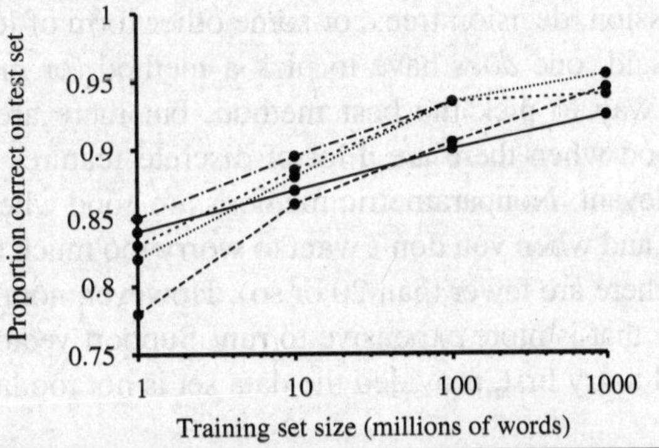

Figure 37 Learning curves for five learning algorithms on a common task. Note that there appears to be more room for improvement in the horizontal direction (more training data) than in the vertical direction (different machine learning algorithm). Adapted from Banko and Brill (2001).

appropriate machine learning method to process the data. Figure 37 shows a typical real-world example, comparing five learning algorithms on the task of word-sense classification (given a sentence such as "The bank folded," classify the word "bank" as "money-bank" or "river-bank"). The point is that machine learning researchers have focused mainly on the vertical direction: Can I invent a new learning algorithm that performs better than previously published algorithms on a standard training set of 1 million words? But the graph shows there is more room for improvement in the horizontal direction: instead of inventing a new algorithm, all I need to do is gather 10 million words of training data; even the *worst* algorithm at 10 million words is performing better than the *best* algorithm at 1 million. As we gather even more data, the curves continue to rise, dwarfing the differences between algorithms.

Consider another problem: the task of estimating the true value of houses that are for sale. In Figure 13 we showed a toy version of this problem, doing linear regression of house size to asking price. You probably noticed many limitations of this model. First, it is measuring the wrong thing: we want to estimate the selling price of a house, not the asking price. To solve this task we'll need data on actual sales. But that doesn't mean we should throw away the data about asking price—we can use it as one of the input features. Besides the size of the house, we'll need more information: the number of rooms, bedrooms and bathrooms; whether the kitchen and bathrooms have been recently remodeled; the age of the house; we'll also need information about the lot, and the neighborhood. But how do we define neighborhood? By zip code? What if part of one zip code is on the "wrong" side of the highway or train tracks, and the other part is desirable? What about the school district? Should the *name* of the school district be a feature, or the *average test scores*? In addition to deciding what features to include, we will have to deal with missing data; different areas have different customs on what data are reported, and individual cases will always be missing some data. If the data you want are not available, perhaps you can set up a social networking site to encourage people to share and correct data. In the end, this process of deciding what features to use, and how to use them, is just as important as choosing between linear regression, decision trees, or some other form of learning.

That said, one *does* have to pick a method (or methods) for a problem. There is no guaranteed way to pick the best method, but there are some rough guidelines. Decision trees are good when there are a lot of discrete features and you believe that many of them may be irrelevant. Nonparametric methods are good when you have a lot of data and no prior knowledge, and when you don't want to worry too much about choosing just the right features (as long as there are fewer than 20 or so). However, nonparametric methods usually give you a function h that is more expensive to run. Support vector machines are often considered the best method to try first, provided the data set is not too large.

12 SUMMARY

This chapter has concentrated on inductive learning of functions from examples. The main points were as follows:

- Learning takes many forms, depending on the nature of the agent, the component to be improved, and the available feedback.
- If the available feedback provides the correct answer for example inputs, then the learning problem is called **supervised learning**. The task is to learn a function $y = h(x)$. Learning a discrete-valued function is called **classification**; learning a continuous function is called **regression**.
- Inductive learning involves finding a hypothesis that agrees well with the examples. **Ockham's razor** suggests choosing the simplest consistent hypothesis. The difficulty of this task depends on the chosen representation.
- **Decision trees** can represent all Boolean functions. The **information-gain** heuristic provides an efficient method for finding a simple, consistent decision tree.
- The performance of a learning algorithm is measured by the **learning curve**, which shows the prediction accuracy on the **test set** as a function of the **training-set** size.
- When there are multiple models to choose from, **cross-validation** can be used to select a model that will generalize well.
- Sometimes not all errors are equal. A **loss function** tells us how bad each error is; the goal is then to minimize loss over a validation set.
- **Computational learning theory** analyzes the sample complexity and computational complexity of inductive learning. There is a tradeoff between the expressiveness of the hypothesis language and the ease of learning.
- **Linear regression** is a widely used model. The optimal parameters of a linear regression model can be found by gradient descent search, or computed exactly.
- A linear classifier with a hard threshold—also known as a **perceptron**—can be trained by a simple weight update rule to fit data that are **linearly separable**. In other cases, the rule fails to converge.

- **Logistic regression** replaces the perceptron's hard threshold with a soft threshold defined by a logistic function. Gradient descent works well even for noisy data that are not linearly separable.
- **Neural networks** represent complex nonlinear functions with a network of linear-threshold units. termMultilayer feed-forward neural networks can represent any function, given enough units. The **back-propagation** algorithm implements a gradient descent in parameter space to minimize the output error.
- **Nonparametric models** use all the data to make each prediction, rather than trying to summarize the data first with a few parameters. Examples include **nearest neighbors** and **locally weighted regression**.
- **Support vector machines** find linear separators with **maximum margin** to improve the generalization performance of the classifier. **Kernel methods** implicitly transform the input data into a high-dimensional space where a linear separator may exist, even if the original data are non-separable.
- Ensemble methods such as **boosting** often perform better than individual methods. In **online learning** we can aggregate the opinions of experts to come arbitrarily close to the best expert's performance, even when the distribution of the data is constantly shifting.

Bibliographical and Historical Notes

William of Ockham[15] (1280–1349), the most influential philosopher of his century and a major contributor to medieval epistemology, logic, and metaphysics, is credited with a statement called "Ockham's Razor"—in Latin, *Entia non sunt multiplicanda praeter necessitatem*, and in English, "Entities are not to be multiplied beyond necessity." Unfortunately, this laudable piece of advice is nowhere to be found in his writings in precisely these words (although he did say "Pluralitas non est ponenda sine necessitate," or "plurality shouldn't be posited without necessity"). A similar sentiment was expressed by Aristotle in 350 B.C. in *Physics* book I, chapter VI: "For the more limited if adequate is always preferable "

The first notable use of decision trees was in EPAM, the "Elementary Perceiver And Memorizer" (Feigenbaum, 1961), which was a simulation of human concept learning. ID3 (Quinlan, 1979) added the crucial idea of choosing the attribute with maximum entropy; it is the basis for the decision tree algorithm in this chapter. Information theory was developed by Claude Shannon to aid in the study of communication (Shannon and Weaver, 1949). (Shannon also contributed one of the earliest examples of machine learning, a mechanical mouse named Theseus that learned to navigate through a maze by trial and error.) The χ^2 method of tree pruning was described by Quinlan (1986). C4.5, an industrial-strength decision tree package, can be found in Quinlan (1993). An independent tradition of decision tree learning exists in the statistical literature. *Classification and Regression Trees* (Breiman *et al.*, 1984), known as the "CART book," is the principal reference.

[15] The name is often misspelled as "Occam," perhaps from the French rendering, "Guillaume d'Occam."

Cross-validation was first introduced by Larson (1931), and in a form close to what we show by Stone (1974) and Golub *et al.* (1979). The regularization procedure is due to Tikhonov (1963). Guyon and Elisseeff (2003) introduce a journal issue devoted to the problem of feature selection. Banko and Brill (2001) and Halevy *et al.* (2009) discuss the advantages of using large amounts of data. It was Robert Mercer, a speech researcher who said in 1985 "There is no data like more data." (Lyman and Varian, 2003) estimate that about 5 exabytes (5×10^{18} bytes) of data was produced in 2002, and that the rate of production is doubling every 3 years.

Theoretical analysis of learning algorithms began with the work of Gold (1967) on **identification in the limit**. This approach was motivated in part by models of scientific discovery from the philosophy of science (Popper, 1962), but has been applied mainly to the problem of learning grammars from example sentences (Osherson *et al.*, 1986).

KOLMOGOROV COMPLEXITY

Whereas the identification-in-the-limit approach concentrates on eventual convergence, the study of **Kolmogorov complexity** or **algorithmic complexity**, developed independently by Solomonoff (1964, 2009) and Kolmogorov (1965), attempts to provide a formal definition for the notion of simplicity used in Ockham's razor. To escape the problem that simplicity depends on the way in which information is represented, it is proposed that simplicity be measured by the length of the shortest program for a universal Turing machine that correctly reproduces the observed data. Although there are many possible universal Turing machines, and hence many possible "shortest" programs, these programs differ in length by at most a constant that is independent of the amount of data. This beautiful insight, which essentially shows that *any* initial representation bias will eventually be overcome by the data itself, is marred only by the undecidability of computing the length of the shortest program. Approximate measures such as the **minimum description length**, or MDL (Rissanen, 1984, 2007) can be used instead and have produced excellent results in practice. The text by Li and Vitanyi (1993) is the best source for Kolmogorov complexity.

MINIMUM DESCRIPTION LENGTH

The theory of PAC-learning was inaugurated by Leslie Valiant (1984). His work stressed the importance of computational and sample complexity. With Michael Kearns (1990), Valiant showed that several concept classes cannot be PAC-learned tractably, even though sufficient information is available in the examples. Some positive results were obtained for classes such as decision lists (Rivest, 1987).

UNIFORM CONVERGENCE THEORY

VC DIMENSION

An independent tradition of sample-complexity analysis has existed in statistics, beginning with the work on **uniform convergence theory** (Vapnik and Chervonenkis, 1971). The so-called **VC dimension** provides a measure roughly analogous to, but more general than, the $\ln |\mathcal{H}|$ measure obtained from PAC analysis. The VC dimension can be applied to continuous function classes, to which standard PAC analysis does not apply. PAC-learning theory and VC theory were first connected by the "four Germans" (none of whom actually is German): Blumer, Ehrenfeucht, Haussler, and Warmuth (1989).

Linear regression with squared error loss goes back to Legendre (1805) and Gauss (1809), who were both working on predicting orbits around the sun. The modern use of multivariate regression for machine learning is covered in texts such as Bishop (2007). Ng (2004) analyzed the differences between L_1 and L_2 regularization.

The term **logistic function** comes from Pierre-François Verhulst (1804–1849), a statistician who used the curve to model population growth with limited resources, a more realistic model than the unconstrained geometric growth proposed by Thomas Malthus. Verhulst called it the *courbe logistique*, because of its relation to the logarithmic curve. The term **regression** is due to Francis Galton, nineteenth century statistician, cousin of Charles Darwin, and initiator of the fields of meteorology, fingerprint analysis, and statistical correlation, who used it in the sense of regression to the mean. The term **curse of dimensionality** comes from Richard Bellman (1961).

Logistic regression can be solved with gradient descent, or with the Newton-Raphson method (Newton, 1671; Raphson, 1690). A variant of the Newton method called L-BFGS is sometimes used for large-dimensional problems; the L stands for "limited memory," meaning that it avoids creating the full matrices all at once, and instead creates parts of them on the fly. BFGS are authors' initials (Byrd *et al.*, 1995).

Nearest-neighbors models date back at least to Fix and Hodges (1951) and have been a standard tool in statistics and pattern recognition ever since. Within AI, they were popularized by Stanfill and Waltz (1986), who investigated methods for adapting the distance metric to the data. Hastie and Tibshirani (1996) developed a way to localize the metric to each point in the space, depending on the distribution of data around that point. Gionis *et al.* (1999) introduced locality-sensitive hashing, which has revolutionized the retrieval of similar objects in high-dimensional spaces, particularly in computer vision. Andoni and Indyk (2006) provide a recent survey of LSH and related methods.

The ideas behind kernel machines come from Aizerman *et al.* (1964) (who also introduced the kernel trick), but the full development of the theory is due to Vapnik and his colleagues (Boser *et al.*, 1992). SVMs were made practical with the introduction of the soft-margin classifier for handling noisy data in a paper that won the 2008 ACM Theory and Practice Award (Cortes and Vapnik, 1995), and of the Sequential Minimal Optimization (SMO) algorithm for efficiently solving SVM problems using quadratic programming (Platt, 1999). SVMs have proven to be very popular and effective for tasks such as text categorization (Joachims, 2001), computational genomics (Cristianini and Hahn, 2007), and natural language processing, such as the handwritten digit recognition of DeCoste and Schölkopf (2002). As part of this process, many new kernels have been designed that work with strings, trees, and other nonnumerical data types. A related technique that also uses the kernel trick to implicitly represent an exponential feature space is the voted perceptron (Freund and Schapire, 1999; Collins and Duffy, 2002). Textbooks on SVMs include Cristianini and Shawe-Taylor (2000) and Schölkopf and Smola (2002). A friendlier exposition appears in the *AI Magazine* article by Cristianini and Schölkopf (2002). Bengio and LeCun (2007) show some of the limitations of SVMs and other local, nonparametric methods for learning functions that have a global structure but do not have local smoothness.

Ensemble learning is an increasingly popular technique for improving the performance of learning algorithms. **Bagging** (Breiman, 1996), the first effective method, combines hypotheses learned from multiple **bootstrap** data sets, each generated by subsampling the original data set. The **boosting** method described in this chapter originated with theoretical work by Schapire (1990). The ADABOOST algorithm was developed by Freund and Schapire

BAGGING

(1996) and analyzed theoretically by Schapire (2003). Friedman *et al.* (2000) explain boosting from a statistician's viewpoint. Online learning is covered in a survey by Blum (1996) and a book by Cesa-Bianchi and Lugosi (2006). Dredze *et al.* (2008) introduce the idea of confidence-weighted online learning for classification: in addition to keeping a weight for each parameter, they also maintain a measure of confidence, so that a new example can have a large effect on features that were rarely seen before (and thus had low confidence) and a small effect on common features that have already been well-estimated.

The literature on neural networks is rather too large (approximately 150,000 papers to date) to cover in detail. Cowan and Sharp (1988b, 1988a) survey the early history, beginning with the work of McCulloch and Pitts (1943). John McCarthy has pointed to the work of Nicolas Rashevsky (1936, 1938) as the earliest mathematical model of neural learning.) Norbert Wiener, a pioneer of cybernetics and control theory (Wiener, 1948), worked with McCulloch and Pitts and influenced a number of young researchers including Marvin Minsky, who may have been the first to develop a working neural network in hardware in 1951 (see Minsky and Papert, 1988, pp. ix–x). Turing (1948) wrote a research report titled *Intelligent Machinery* that begins with the sentence "I propose to investigate the question as to whether it is possible for machinery to show intelligent behaviour" and goes on to describe a recurrent neural network architecture he called "B-type unorganized machines" and an approach to training them. Unfortunately, the report went unpublished until 1969, and was all but ignored until recently.

Frank Rosenblatt (1957) invented the modern "perceptron" and proved the perceptron convergence theorem (1960), although it had been foreshadowed by purely mathematical work outside the context of neural networks (Agmon, 1954; Motzkin and Schoenberg, 1954). Some early work was also done on multilayer networks, including **Gamba perceptrons** (Gamba *et al.*, 1961) and **madalines** (Widrow, 1962). *Learning Machines* (Nilsson, 1965) covers much of this early work and more. The subsequent demise of early perceptron research efforts was hastened (or, the authors later claimed, merely explained) by the book *Perceptrons* (Minsky and Papert, 1969), which lamented the field's lack of mathematical rigor. The book pointed out that single-layer perceptrons could represent only linearly separable concepts and noted the lack of effective learning algorithms for multilayer networks.

The papers in (Hinton and Anderson, 1981), based on a conference in San Diego in 1979, can be regarded as marking a renaissance of connectionism. The two-volume "PDP" (Parallel Distributed Processing) anthology (Rumelhart *et al.*, 1986a) and a short article in *Nature* (Rumelhart *et al.*, 1986b) attracted a great deal of attention—indeed, the number of papers on "neural networks" multiplied by a factor of 200 between 1980–84 and 1990–94. The analysis of neural networks using the physical theory of magnetic spin glasses (Amit *et al.*, 1985) tightened the links between statistical mechanics and neural network theory—providing not only useful mathematical insights but also *respectability*. The back-propagation technique had been invented quite early (Bryson and Ho, 1969) but it was rediscovered several times (Werbos, 1974; Parker, 1985).

The probabilistic interpretation of neural networks has several sources, including Baum and Wilczek (1988) and Bridle (1990). The role of the sigmoid function is discussed by Jordan (1995). Bayesian parameter learning for neural networks was proposed by MacKay

(1992) and is explored further by Neal (1996). The capacity of neural networks to represent functions was investigated by Cybenko (1988, 1989), who showed that two hidden layers are enough to represent any function and a single layer is enough to represent any *continuous* function. The "optimal brain damage" method for removing useless connections is by LeCun et al. (1989), and Sietsma and Dow (1988) show how to remove useless units. The tiling algorithm for growing larger structures is due to Mézard and Nadal (1989). LeCun *et al.* (1995) survey a number of algorithms for handwritten digit recognition. Improved error rates since then were reported by Belongie *et al.* (2002) for shape matching and DeCoste and Schölkopf (2002) for virtual support vectors. At the time of writing, the best test error rate reported is 0.39% by Ranzato *et al.* (2007) using a convolutional neural network.

The complexity of neural network learning has been investigated by researchers in computational learning theory. Early computational results were obtained by Judd (1990), who showed that the general problem of finding a set of weights consistent with a set of examples is NP-complete, even under very restrictive assumptions. Some of the first sample complexity results were obtained by Baum and Haussler (1989), who showed that the number of examples required for effective learning grows as roughly $W \log W$, where W is the number of weights.[16] Since then, a much more sophisticated theory has been developed (Anthony and Bartlett, 1999), including the important result that the representational capacity of a network depends on the *size* of the weights as well as on their number, a result that should not be surprising in the light of our discussion of regularization.

RADIAL BASIS FUNCTION

The most popular kind of neural network that we did not cover is the **radial basis function**, or RBF, network. A radial basis function combines a weighted collection of kernels (usually Gaussians, of course) to do function approximation. RBF networks can be trained in two phases: first, an unsupervised clustering approach is used to train the parameters of the Gaussians—the means and variances—are trained. In the second phase, the relative weights of the Gaussians are determined. This is a system of linear equations, which we know how to solve directly. Thus, both phases of RBF training have a nice benefit: the first phase is unsupervised, and thus does not require labeled training data, and the second phase, although supervised is efficient. See Bishop (1995) for more details.

HOPFIELD NETWORK

Recurrent networks, in which units are linked in cycles, were mentioned in the chapter but not explored in depth. **Hopfield networks** (Hopfield, 1982) are probably the best-understood class of recurrent networks. They use *bidirectional* connections with *symmetric* weights (i.e., $w_{i,j} = w_{j,i}$), all of the units are both input and output units, the activation function g is the sign function, and the activation levels can only be ± 1. A Hopfield network functions as an **associative memory**: after the network trains on a set of examples, a new stimulus will cause it to settle into an activation pattern corresponding to the example in the training set that *most closely resembles* the new stimulus. For example, if the training set consists of a set of photographs, and the new stimulus is a small piece of one of the photographs, then the network activation levels will reproduce the photograph from which the piece was taken. Notice that the original photographs are not stored separately in the network; each

ASSOCIATIVE MEMORY

[16] This approximately confirmed "Uncle Bernie's rule." The rule was named after Bernie Widrow, who recommended using roughly ten times as many examples as weights.

weight is a partial encoding of all the photographs. One of the most interesting theoretical results is that Hopfield networks can reliably store up to $0.138N$ training examples, where N is the number of units in the network.

BOLTZMANN MACHINE

Boltzmann machines (Hinton and Sejnowski, 1983, 1986) also use symmetric weights, but include hidden units. In addition, they use a *stochastic* activation function, such that the probability of the output being 1 is some function of the total weighted input. Boltzmann machines therefore undergo state transitions that resemble a simulated annealing search for the configuration that best approximates the training set. It turns out that Boltzmann machines are very closely related to a special case of Bayesian networks evaluated with a stochastic simulation algorithm.

For neural nets, Bishop (1995), Ripley (1996), and Haykin (2008) are the leading texts. The field of computational neuroscience is covered by Dayan and Abbott (2001).

The approach taken in this chapter was influenced by the excellent course notes of David Cohn, Tom Mitchell, Andrew Moore, and Andrew Ng. There are several top-notch textbooks in Machine Learning (Mitchell, 1997; Bishop, 2007) and in the closely allied and overlapping fields of pattern recognition (Ripley, 1996; Duda *et al.*, 2001), statistics (Wasserman, 2004; Hastie *et al.*, 2001), data mining (Hand *et al.*, 2001; Witten and Frank, 2005), computational learning theory (Kearns and Vazirani, 1994; Vapnik, 1998) and information theory (Shannon and Weaver, 1949; MacKay, 2002; Cover and Thomas, 2006). Other books concentrate on implementations (Segaran, 2007; Marsland, 2009) and comparisons of algorithms (Michie *et al.*, 1994). Current research in machine learning is published in the annual proceedings of the International Conference on Machine Learning (ICML) and the conference on Neural Information Processing Systems (NIPS), in *Machine Learning* and the *Journal of Machine Learning Research*, and in mainstream AI journals.

EXERCISES

1 Consider the problem faced by an infant learning to speak and understand a language. Explain how this process fits into the general learning model. Describe the percepts and actions of the infant, and the types of learning the infant must do. Describe the subfunctions the infant is trying to learn in terms of inputs and outputs, and available example data.

2 Repeat Exercise 1 for the case of learning to play tennis (or some other sport with which you are familiar). Is this supervised learning or reinforcement learning?

3 Suppose we generate a training set from a decision tree and then apply decision-tree learning to that training set. Is it the case that the learning algorithm will eventually return the correct tree as the training-set size goes to infinity? Why or why not?

4 In the recursive construction of decision trees, it sometimes happens that a mixed set of positive and negative examples remains at a leaf node, even after all the attributes have been used. Suppose that we have p positive examples and n negative examples.

a. Show that the solution used by DECISION-TREE-LEARNING, which picks the majority classification, minimizes the absolute error over the set of examples at the leaf.

CLASS PROBABILITY

b. Show that the **class probability** $p/(p+n)$ minimizes the sum of squared errors.

5 Suppose that an attribute splits the set of examples E into subsets E_k and that each subset has p_k positive examples and n_k negative examples. Show that the attribute has strictly positive information gain unless the ratio $p_k/(p_k+n_k)$ is the same for all k.

6 Consider the following data set comprised of three binary input attributes (A_1, A_2, and A_3) and one binary output:

Example	A_1	A_2	A_3	Output y
$\mathbf{x}_1$	1	0	0	0
$\mathbf{x}_2$	1	0	1	0
$\mathbf{x}_3$	0	1	0	0
$\mathbf{x}_4$	1	1	1	1
$\mathbf{x}_5$	1	1	0	1

Use the algorithm in Figure 5 to learn a decision tree for these data. Show the computations made to determine the attribute to split at each node.

7 A decision *graph* is a generalization of a decision tree that allows nodes (i.e., attributes used for splits) to have multiple parents, rather than just a single parent. The resulting graph must still be acyclic. Now, consider the XOR function of *three* binary input attributes, which produces the value 1 if and only if an odd number of the three input attributes has value 1.

a. Draw a minimal-sized decision *tree* for the three-input XOR function.

b. Draw a minimal-sized decision *graph* for the three-input XOR function.

8 This exercise considers χ^2 pruning of decision trees (Section 3.5).

a. Create a data set with two input attributes, such that the information gain at the root of the tree for both attributes is zero, but there is a decision tree of depth 2 that is consistent with all the data. What would χ^2 pruning do on this data set if applied bottom up? If applied top down?

b. Modify DECISION-TREE-LEARNING to include χ^2-pruning. You might wish to consult Quinlan (1986) or Kearns and Mansour (1998) for details.

9 The standard DECISION-TREE-LEARNING algorithm described in the chapter does not handle cases in which some examples have missing attribute values.

a. First, we need to find a way to classify such examples, given a decision tree that includes tests on the attributes for which values can be missing. Suppose that an example $\mathbf{x}$ has a missing value for attribute A and that the decision tree tests for A at a node that $\mathbf{x}$ reaches. One way to handle this case is to pretend that the example has *all* possible values for the attribute, but to weight each value according to its frequency among all of the examples that reach that node in the decision tree. The classification algorithm should follow all branches at any node for which a value is missing and should multiply the weights along each path. Write a modified classification algorithm for decision trees that has this behavior.

b. Now modify the information-gain calculation so that in any given collection of examples C at a given node in the tree during the construction process, the examples with missing values for any of the remaining attributes are given "as-if" values according to the frequencies of those values in the set C.

10 In Section 3.6, we noted that attributes with many different possible values can cause problems with the gain measure. Such attributes tend to split the examples into numerous small classes or even singleton classes, thereby appearing to be highly relevant according to the gain measure. The **gain-ratio** criterion selects attributes according to the ratio between their gain and their intrinsic information content—that is, the amount of information contained in the answer to the question, "What is the value of this attribute?" The gain-ratio criterion therefore tries to measure how efficiently an attribute provides information on the correct classification of an example. Write a mathematical expression for the information content of an attribute, and implement the gain ratio criterion in DECISION-TREE-LEARNING.

11 Suppose you are running a learning experiment on a new algorithm for Boolean classification. You have a data set consisting of 100 positive and 100 negative examples. You plan to use leave-one-out cross-validation and compare your algorithm to a baseline function, a simple majority classifier. (A majority classifier is given a set of training data and then always outputs the class that is in the majority in the training set, regardless of the input.) You expect the majority classifier to score about 50% on leave-one-out cross-validation, but to your surprise, it scores zero every time. Can you explain why?

12 Construct a *decision list* to classify the data below. Select tests to be as small as possible (in terms of attributes), breaking ties among tests with the same number of attributes by selecting the one that classifies the greatest number of examples correctly. If multiple tests have the same number of attributes and classify the same number of examples, then break the tie using attributes with lower index numbers (e.g., select A_1 over A_2).

Example	A_1	A_2	A_3	A_4	y
$\mathbf{x}_1$	1	0	0	0	1
$\mathbf{x}_2$	1	0	1	1	1
$\mathbf{x}_3$	0	1	0	0	1
$\mathbf{x}_4$	0	1	1	0	0
$\mathbf{x}_5$	1	1	0	1	1
$\mathbf{x}_6$	0	1	0	1	0
$\mathbf{x}_7$	0	0	1	1	1
$\mathbf{x}_8$	0	0	1	0	0

13 Prove that a decision list can represent the same function as a decision tree while using at most as many rules as there are leaves in the decision tree for that function. Give an example of a function represented by a decision list using strictly fewer rules than the number of leaves in a minimal-sized decision tree for that same function.

14 This exercise concerns the expressiveness of decision lists (Section 5).

a. Show that decision lists can represent any Boolean function, if the size of the tests is not limited.

b. Show that if the tests can contain at most k literals each, then decision lists can represent any function that can be represented by a decision tree of depth k.

15 Suppose a 7-nearest-neighbors regression search returns $\{7, 6, 8, 4, 7, 11, 100\}$ as the 7 nearest y values for a given x value. What is the value of $\hat{y}$ that minimizes the L_1 loss function on this data? There is a common name in statistics for this value as a function of the y values; what is it? Answer the same two questions for the L_2 loss function.

16 Figure 31 showed how a circle at the origin can be linearly separated by mapping from the features (x_1, x_2) to the two dimensions (x_1^2, x_2^2). But what if the circle is not located at the origin? What if it is an ellipse, not a circle? The general equation for a circle (and hence the decision boundary) is $(x_1 - a)^2 + (x_2 - b)^2 - r^2 = 0$, and the general equation for an ellipse is $c(x_1 - a)^2 + d(x_2 - b)^2 - 1 = 0$.

a. Expand out the equation for the circle and show what the weights w_i would be for the decision boundary in the four-dimensional feature space (x_1, x_2, x_1^2, x_2^2). Explain why this means that any circle is linearly separable in this space.

b. Do the same for ellipses in the five-dimensional feature space $(x_1, x_2, x_1^2, x_2^2, x_1 x_2)$.

17 Construct a support vector machine that computes the XOR function. Use values of +1 and –1 (instead of 1 and 0) for both inputs and outputs, so that an example looks like $([-1, 1], 1)$ or $([-1, -1], -1)$. Map the input $[x_1, x_2]$ into a space consisting of x_1 and $x_1\, x_2$. Draw the four input points in this space, and the maximal margin separator. What is the margin? Now draw the separating line back in the original Euclidean input space.

18 Consider an ensemble learning algorithm that uses simple majority voting among K learned hypotheses. Suppose that each hypothesis has error ϵ and that the errors made by each hypothesis are independent of the others'. Calculate a formula for the error of the ensemble algorithm in terms of K and ϵ, and evaluate it for the cases where $K = 5$, 10, and 20 and $\epsilon = 0.1$, 0.2, and 0.4. If the independence assumption is removed, is it possible for the ensemble error to be *worse* than ϵ?

19 Construct by hand a neural network that computes the XOR function of two inputs. Make sure to specify what sort of units you are using.

20 Recall that there are 2^{2^n} distinct Boolean functions of n inputs. How many of these are representable by a threshold perceptron?

21 Section 6.4 noted that the output of the logistic function could be interpreted as a *probability* p assigned by the model to the proposition that $f(\mathbf{x})=1$; the probability that $f(\mathbf{x}) = 0$ is therefore $1 - p$. Write down the probability p as a function of $\mathbf{x}$ and calculate the derivative of $\log p$ with respect to each weight w_i. Repeat the process for $\log(1-p)$. These calculations give a learning rule for minimizing the negative-log-likelihood loss function for a probabilistic hypothesis. Comment on any resemblance to other learning rules in the chapter.

22 Suppose you had a neural network with linear activation functions. That is, for each unit the output is some constant c times the weighted sum of the inputs.

a. Assume that the network has one hidden layer. For a given assignment to the weights $\mathbf{w}$, write down equations for the value of the units in the output layer as a function of $\mathbf{w}$ and the input layer $\mathbf{x}$, without any explicit mention of the output of the hidden layer. Show that there is a network with no hidden units that computes the same function.

b. Repeat the calculation in part (a), but this time do it for a network with any number of hidden layers.

c. Suppose a network with one hidden layer and linear activation functions has n input and output nodes and h hidden nodes. What effect does the transformation in part (a) to a network with no hidden layers have on the total number of weights? Discuss in particular the case $h \ll n$.

23 Suppose that a training set contains only a single example, repeated 100 times. In 80 of the 100 cases, the single output value is 1; in the other 20, it is 0. What will a back-propagation network predict for this example, assuming that it has been trained and reaches a global optimum? (*Hint:* to find the global optimum, differentiate the error function and set it to zero.)

24 The neural network whose learning performance is measured in Figure 25 has four hidden nodes. This number was chosen somewhat arbitrarily. Use a cross-validation method to find the best number of hidden nodes.

25 Consider the problem of separating N data points into positive and negative examples using a linear separator. Clearly, this can always be done for $N=2$ points on a line of dimension $d=1$, regardless of how the points are labeled or where they are located (unless the points are in the same place).

a. Show that it can always be done for $N=3$ points on a plane of dimension $d=2$, unless they are collinear.

b. Show that it cannot always be done for $N=4$ points on a plane of dimension $d=2$.

c. Show that it can always be done for $N=4$ points in a space of dimension $d=3$, unless they are coplanar.

d. Show that it cannot always be done for $N=5$ points in a space of dimension $d=3$.

e. The ambitious student may wish to prove that N points in general position (but not $N+1$) are linearly separable in a space of dimension $N-1$.

KNOWLEDGE IN LEARNING

KNOWLEDGE IN LEARNING

In which we examine the problem of learning when you know something already.

When approaching learning, in the context of this subject matter, the idea is to construct a function that has the input–output behavior observed in the data. In each case, the learning methods can be understood as searching a hypothesis space to find a suitable function, starting from only a very basic assumption about the form of the function, such as "second-degree polynomial" or "decision tree" and perhaps a preference for simpler hypotheses. Doing this amounts to saying that before you can learn something new, you must first forget (almost) everything you know. In this chapter, we study learning methods that can take advantage of **prior knowledge** about the world. In most cases, the prior knowledge is represented as general first-order logical theories; thus for the first time we bring together the work on knowledge representation and learning.

PRIOR KNOWLEDGE

1 A Logical Formulation of Learning

The "Learning from Examples" chapter defined pure inductive learning as a process of finding a hypothesis that agrees with the observed examples. Here, we specialize this definition to the case where the hypothesis is represented by a set of logical sentences. Example descriptions and classifications will also be logical sentences, and a new example can be classified by inferring a classification sentence from the hypothesis and the example description. This approach allows for incremental construction of hypotheses, one sentence at a time. It also allows for prior knowledge, because sentences that are already known can assist in the classification of new examples. The logical formulation of learning may seem like a lot of extra work at first, but it turns out to clarify many of the issues in learning. It enables us to go well beyond simple learning methods by using the full power of logical inference in the service of learning.

1.1 Examples and hypotheses

Recall from the "Learning from Examples" chapter the restaurant learning problem: learning a rule for deciding whether to wait for a table. Examples were described by **attributes** such as *Alternate, Bar, Fri/Sat*, and so on. In a logical setting, an example is described by a logical sentence; the attributes become unary predicates. Let us generically call the ith example X_i. For instance, thc first example from Figure 3, of the chapter "Learning from Examples", is described by the sentences

$$Alternate(X_1) \land \neg Bar(X_1) \land \neg Fri/Sat(X_1) \land Hungry(X_1) \land \ldots$$

We will use the notation $D_i(X_i)$ to refer to the description of X_i, where D_i can be any logical expression taking a single argument. The classification of the example is given by a literal using the goal predicate, in this case

$$WillWait(X_1) \quad \text{or} \quad \neg WillWait(X_1)\,.$$

The complete training set can thus be expressed as the conjunction of all the example descriptions and goal literals.

The aim of inductive learning in general is to find a hypothesis that classifies the examples well and generalizes well to new examples. Here we are concerned with hypotheses expressed in logic; each hypothesis h_j will have the form

$$\forall x \;\; Goal(x) \Leftrightarrow C_j(x)\,,$$

where *Cj* (*x*) is a candidate definition—some expression involving the attribute predicates. For example, a decision tree can be interpreted as a logical expression of this form. Thus, the tree expresses the following logical definition (which we will call h_r for future reference):

$$\begin{aligned} \forall r \;\; WillWait(r) \Leftrightarrow\; & Patrons(r, Some) \\ \lor\; & Patrons(r, Full) \land Hungry(r) \land Type(r, French) \\ \lor\; & Patrons(r, Full) \land Hungry(r) \land Type(r, Thai) \\ & \quad \land Fri/Sat(r) \\ \lor\; & Patrons(r, Full) \land Hungry(r) \land Type(r, Burger)\,. \end{aligned} \tag{1}$$

EXTENSION

Each hypothesis predicts that a certain set of examples—namely, those that satisfy its candidate definition—will be examples of the goal predicate. This set is called the **extension** of the predicate. Two hypotheses with different extensions are therefore logically inconsistent with each other, because they disagree on their predictions for at least one example. If they have the same extension, they are logically equivalent.

The hypothesis space $\mathcal{H}$ is the set of all hypotheses $\{h_1, \ldots, h_n\}$ that the learning algorithm is designed to entertain. For example, the DECISION-TREE-LEARNING algorithm can entertain any decision tree hypothesis defined in terms of the attributes provided; its hypothesis space therefore consists of all these decision trees. Presumably, the learning algorithm believes that one of the hypotheses is correct; that is, it believes the sentence

$$h_1 \lor h_2 \lor h_3 \lor \ldots \lor h_n\,. \tag{2}$$

As the examples arrive, hypotheses that are not **consistent** with the examples can be ruled out. Let us examine this notion of consistency more carefully. Obviously, if hypothesis h_j is consistent with the entire training set, it has to be consistent with each example in the training set. What would it mean for it to be inconsistent with an example? There are two possible ways that this can happen:

FALSE NEGATIVE

- An example can be a **false negative** for the hypothesis, if the hypothesis says it should be negative but in fact it is positive. For instance, the new example X_{13} described by
$Patrons(X_{13}, Full) \wedge \neg Hungry(X_{13}) \wedge \ldots \wedge WillWait(X_{13})$
would be a false negative for the hypothesis h_r given earlier. From h_r and the example description, we can deduce both $WillWait(X_{13})$, which is what the example says, and $\neg WillWait(X_{13})$, which is what the hypothesis predicts. The hypothesis and the example are therefore logically inconsistent.

FALSE POSITIVE

- An example can be a **false positive** for the hypothesis, if the hypothesis says it should be positive but in fact it is negative.[1]

If an example is a false positive or false negative for a hypothesis, then the example and the hypothesis are logically inconsistent with each other. Assuming that the example is a correct observation of fact, then the hypothesis can be ruled out. Logically, this is exactly analogous to the resolution rule of inference, where the disjunction of hypotheses corresponds to a clause and the example corresponds to a literal that resolves against one of the literals in the clause. An ordinary logical inference system therefore could, in principle, learn from the example by eliminating one or more hypotheses. Suppose, for example, that the example is denoted by the sentence I_1, and the hypothesis space is $h_1 \vee h_2 \vee h_3 \vee h_4$. Then if I_1 is inconsistent with h_2 and h_3, the logical inference system can deduce the new hypothesis space $h_1 \vee h_4$.

We therefore can characterize inductive learning in a logical setting as a process of gradually eliminating hypotheses that are inconsistent with the examples, narrowing down the possibilities. Because the hypothesis space is usually vast (or even infinite in the case of first-order logic), we do not recommend trying to build a learning system using resolution-based theorem proving and a complete enumeration of the hypothesis space. Instead, we will describe two approaches that find logically consistent hypotheses with much less effort.

1.2 Current-best-hypothesis search

CURRENT-BEST-HYPOTHESIS

The idea behind **current-best-hypothesis** search is to maintain a single hypothesis, and to adjust it as new examples arrive in order to maintain consistency. The basic algorithm was described by John Stuart Mill (1843), and may well have appeared even earlier.

Suppose we have some hypothesis such as h_r, of which we have grown quite fond. As long as each new example is consistent, we need do nothing. Then along comes a false negative example, X_{13}. What do we do? Figure 1(a) shows h_r schematically as a region: everything inside the rectangle is part of the extension of h_r. The examples that have actually been seen so far are shown as "+" or "–", and we see that h_r correctly categorizes all the examples as positive or negative examples of $WillWait$. In Figure 1(b), a new example (circled) is a false negative: the hypothesis says it should be negative but it is actually positive.

GENERALIZATION

The extension of the hypothesis must be increased to include it. This is called **generalization**; one possible generalization is shown in Figure 1(c). Then in Figure 1(d), we see a false positive: the hypothesis says the new example (circled) should be positive, but it actually is

[1] The terms "false positive" and "false negative" are used in medicine to describe erroneous results from lab tests. A result is a false positive if it indicates that the patient has the disease when in fact no disease is present.

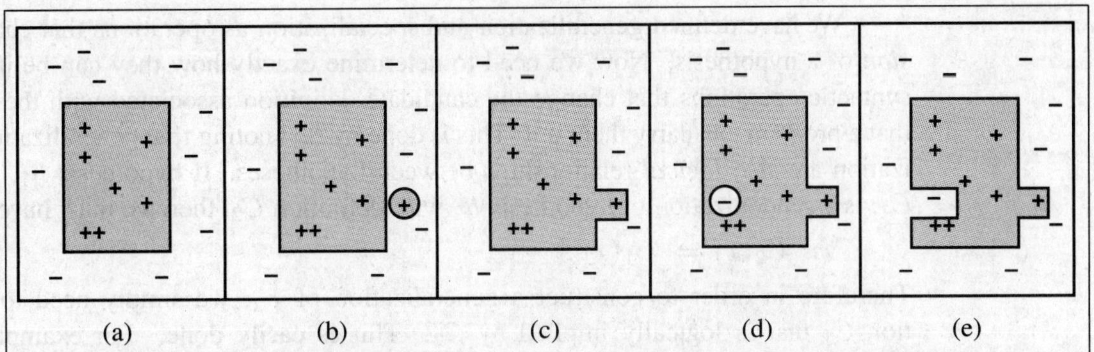

Figure 1 (a) A consistent hypothesis. (b) A false negative. (c) The hypothesis is generalized. (d) A false positive. (e) The hypothesis is specialized.

```
function CURRENT-BEST-LEARNING(examples, h) returns a hypothesis or fail

   if examples is empty then
      return h
   e ← FIRST(examples)
   if e is consistent with h then
      return CURRENT-BEST-LEARNING(REST(examples), h)
   else if e is a false positive for h then
      for each h′ in specializations of h consistent with examples seen so far do
         h″ ← CURRENT-BEST-LEARNING(REST(examples), h′)
         if h″ ≠ fail then return h″
   else if e is a false negative for h then
      for each h′ in generalizations of h consistent with examples seen so far do
         h″ ← CURRENT-BEST-LEARNING(REST(examples), h′)
         if h″ ≠ fail then return h″
   return fail
```

Figure 2 The current-best-hypothesis learning algorithm. It searches for a consistent hypothesis that fits all the examples and backtracks when no consistent specialization/generalization can be found. To start the algorithm, any hypothesis can be passed in; it will be specialized or generalized as needed.

negative. The extension of the hypothesis must be decreased to exclude the example. This is called **specialization**; in Figure 1(e) we see one possible specialization of the hypothesis. The "more general than" and "more specific than" relations between hypotheses provide the logical structure on the hypothesis space that makes efficient search possible.

SPECIALIZATION

We can now specify the CURRENT-BEST-LEARNING algorithm, shown in Figure 2. Notice that each time we consider generalizing or specializing the hypothesis, we must check for consistency with the other examples, because an arbitrary increase/decrease in the extension might include/exclude previously seen negative/positive examples.

We have defined generalization and specialization as operations that change the *extension* of a hypothesis. Now we need to determine exactly how they can be implemented as syntactic operations that change the candidate definition associated with the hypothesis, so that a program can carry them out. This is done by first noting that generalization and specialization are also *logical* relationships between hypotheses. If hypothesis h_1, with definition C_1, is a generalization of hypothesis h_2 with definition C_2, then we must have

$$\forall x \;\; C_2(x) \Rightarrow C_1(x) .$$

Therefore in order to construct a generalization of h_2, we simply need to find a definition C_1 that is logically implied by C_2. This is easily done. For example, if $C_2(x)$ is $Alternate(x) \land Patrons(x, Some)$, then one possible generalization is given by $C_1(x) \equiv Patrons(x, Some)$. This is called **dropping conditions**. Intuitively, it generates a weaker definition and therefore allows a larger set of positive examples. There are a number of other generalization operations, depending on the language being operated on. Similarly, we can specialize a hypothesis by adding extra conditions to its candidate definition or by removing disjuncts from a disjunctive definition. Let us see how this works on the restaurant example, using the data in Figure 3, of the chapter "Learning from Examples".

DROPPING CONDITIONS

- The first example, X_1, is positive. The attribute $Alternate(X_1)$ is true, so let the initial hypothesis be

$$h_1 : \;\; \forall x \;\; WillWait(x) \Leftrightarrow Alternate(x) .$$

- The second example, X_2, is negative. h_1 predicts it to be positive, so it is a false positive. Therefore, we need to specialize h_1. This can be done by adding an extra condition that will rule out X_2, while continuing to classify X_1 as positive. One possibility is

$$h_2 : \;\; \forall x \;\; WillWait(x) \Leftrightarrow Alternate(x) \land Patrons(x, Some) .$$

- The third example, X_3, is positive. h_2 predicts it to be negative, so it is a false negative. Therefore, we need to generalize h_2. We drop the *Alternate* condition, yielding

$$h_3 : \;\; \forall x \;\; WillWait(x) \Leftrightarrow Patrons(x, Some) .$$

- The fourth example, X_4, is positive. h_3 predicts it to be negative, so it is a false negative. We therefore need to generalize h_3. We cannot drop the *Patrons* condition, because that would yield an all-inclusive hypothesis that would be inconsistent with X_2. One possibility is to add a disjunct:

$$h_4 : \;\; \forall x \;\; WillWait(x) \Leftrightarrow Patrons(x, Some) \lor (Patrons(x, Full) \land Fri/Sat(x)) .$$

Already, the hypothesis is starting to look reasonable. Obviously, there are other possibilities consistent with the first four examples; here are two of them:

$$h'_4 : \;\; \forall x \;\; WillWait(x) \Leftrightarrow \neg WaitEstimate(x, 30\text{-}60) .$$

$$h''_4 : \;\; \forall x \;\; WillWait(x) \Leftrightarrow Patrons(x, Some) \lor (Patrons(x, Full) \land WaitEstimate(x, 10\text{-}30)) .$$

The CURRENT-BEST-LEARNING algorithm is described nondeterministically, because at any point, there may be several possible specializations or generalizations that can be applied. The

```
function VERSION-SPACE-LEARNING(examples) returns a version space
   local variables: V, the version space: the set of all hypotheses

   V ← the set of all hypotheses
   for each example e in examples do
       if V is not empty then V ← VERSION-SPACE-UPDATE(V, e)
   return V
```

```
function VERSION-SPACE-UPDATE(V, e) returns an updated version space
   V ← {h ∈ V : h is consistent with e}
```

Figure 3 The version space learning algorithm. It finds a subset of V that is consistent with all the *examples*.

choices that are made will not necessarily lead to the simplest hypothesis, and may lead to an unrecoverable situation where no simple modification of the hypothesis is consistent with all of the data. In such cases, the program must backtrack to a previous choice point.

The CURRENT-BEST-LEARNING algorithm and its variants have been used in many machine learning systems, starting with Patrick Winston's (1970) "arch-learning" program. With a large number of examples and a large space, however, some difficulties arise:

1. Checking all the previous examples over again for each modification is very expensive.
2. The search process may involve a great deal of backtracking, as hypothesis space can be a doubly exponentially large place.

1.3 Least-commitment search

Backtracking arises because the current-best-hypothesis approach has to *choose* a particular hypothesis as its best guess even though it does not have enough data yet to be sure of the choice. What we can do instead is to keep around all and only those hypotheses that are consistent with all the data so far. Each new example will either have no effect or will get rid of some of the hypotheses. Recall that the original hypothesis space can be viewed as a disjunctive sentence

$$h_1 \lor h_2 \lor h_3 \ldots \lor h_n .$$

As various hypotheses are found to be inconsistent with the examples, this disjunction shrinks, retaining only those hypotheses not ruled out. Assuming that the original hypothesis space does in fact contain the right answer, the reduced disjunction must still contain the right answer because only incorrect hypotheses have been removed. The set of hypotheses remaining is called the **version space**, and the learning algorithm (sketched in Figure 3) is called the version space learning algorithm (also the **candidate elimination** algorithm).

VERSION SPACE

CANDIDATE ELIMINATION

One important property of this approach is that it is *incremental*: one never has to go back and reexamine the old examples. All remaining hypotheses are guaranteed to be consistent with them already. But there is an obvious problem. We already said that the

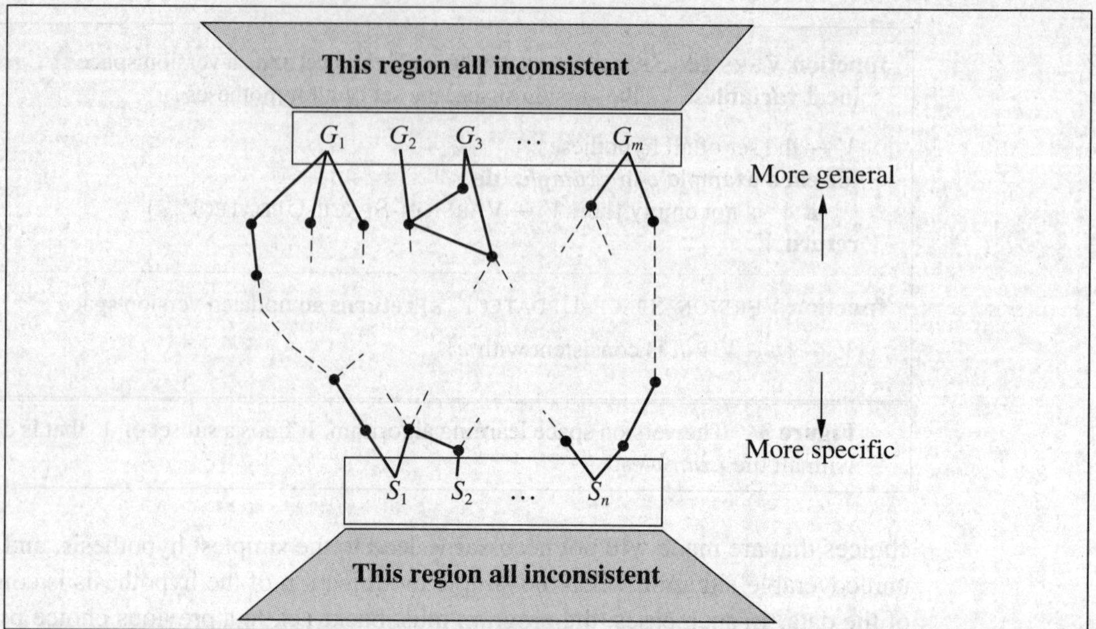

Figure 4 The version space contains all hypotheses consistent with the examples.

hypothesis space is enormous, so how can we possibly write down this enormous disjunction?

The following simple analogy is very helpful. How do you represent all the real numbers between 1 and 2? After all, there are an infinite number of them! The answer is to use an interval representation that just specifies the boundaries of the set: [1,2]. It works because we have an *ordering* on the real numbers.

We also have an ordering on the hypothesis space, namely, generalization/specialization. This is a partial ordering, which means that each boundary will not be a point but rather a set of hypotheses called a **boundary set**. The great thing is that we can represent the entire version space using just two boundary sets: a most general boundary (the **G-set**) and a most specific boundary (the **S-set**). *Everything in between is guaranteed to be consistent with the examples*. Before we prove this, let us recap:

BOUNDARY SET

G-SET

S-SET

- The current version space is the set of hypotheses consistent with all the examples so far. It is represented by the S-set and G-set, each of which is a set of hypotheses.
- Every member of the S-set is consistent with all observations so far, and there are no consistent hypotheses that are more specific.
- Every member of the G-set is consistent with all observations so far, and there are no consistent hypotheses that are more general.

We want the initial version space (before any examples have been seen) to represent all possible hypotheses. We do this by setting the G-set to contain *True* (the hypothesis that contains everything), and the S-set to contain *False* (the hypothesis whose extension is empty).

Figure 4 shows the general structure of the boundary-set representation of the version space. To show that the representation is sufficient, we need the following two properties:

1. Every consistent hypothesis (other than those in the boundary sets) is more specific than some member of the G-set, and more general than some member of the S-set. (That is, there are no "stragglers" left outside.) This follows directly from the definitions of S and G. If there were a straggler h, then it would have to be no more specific than any member of G, in which case it belongs in G; or no more general than any member of S, in which case it belongs in S.
2. Every hypothesis more specific than some member of the G-set and more general than some member of the S-set is a consistent hypothesis. (That is, there are no "holes" between the boundaries.) Any h between S and G must reject all the negative examples rejected by each member of G (because it is more specific), and must accept all the positive examples accepted by any member of S (because it is more general). Thus, h must agree with all the examples, and therefore cannot be inconsistent. Figure 5 shows the situation: there are no known examples outside S but inside G, so any hypothesis in the gap must be consistent.

We have therefore shown that *if* S and G are maintained according to their definitions, then they provide a satisfactory representation of the version space. The only remaining problem is how to *update* S and G for a new example (the job of the VERSION-SPACE-UPDATE function). This may appear rather complicated at first, but from the definitions and with the help of Figure 4, it is not too hard to reconstruct the algorithm.

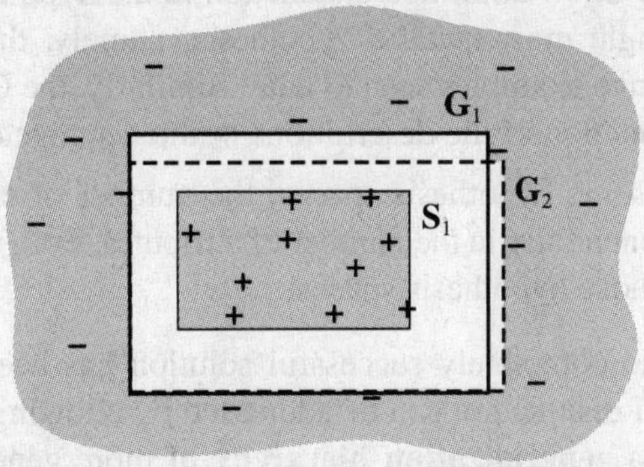

Figure 5 The extensions of the members of G and S. No known examples lie in between the two sets of boundaries.

We need to worry about the members S_i and G_i of the S- and G-sets. For each one, the new example may be a false positive or a false negative.

1. False positive for S_i: This means S_i is too general, but there are no consistent specializations of S_i (by definition), so we throw it out of the S-set.
2. False negative for S_i: This means S_i is too specific, so we replace it by all its immediate generalizations, provided they are more specific than some member of G.
3. False positive for G_i: This means G_i is too general, so we replace it by all its immediate specializations, provided they are more general than some member of S.

4. False negative for G_i: This means G_i is too specific, but there are no consistent generalizations of G_i (by definition) so we throw it out of the G-set.

We continue these operations for each new example until one of three things happens:

1. We have exactly one hypothesis left in the version space, in which case we return it as the unique hypothesis.
2. The version space *collapses*—either S or G becomes empty, indicating that there are no consistent hypotheses for the training set. This is the same case as the failure of the simple version of the decision tree algorithm.
3. We run out of examples and have several hypotheses remaining in the version space. This means the version space represents a disjunction of hypotheses. For any new example, if all the disjuncts agree, then we can return their classification of the example. If they disagree, one possibility is to take the majority vote.

We leave as an exercise the application of the VERSION-SPACE-LEARNING algorithm to the restaurant data.

There are two principal drawbacks to the version-space approach:

- If the domain contains noise or insufficient attributes for exact classification, the version space will always collapse.
- If we allow unlimited disjunction in the hypothesis space, the S-set will always contain a single most-specific hypothesis, namely, the disjunction of the descriptions of the positive examples seen to date. Similarly, the G-set will contain just the negation of the disjunction of the descriptions of the negative examples.
- For some hypothesis spaces, the number of elements in the S-set or G-set may grow exponentially in the number of attributes, even though efficient learning algorithms exist for those hypothesis spaces.

GENERALIZATION HIERARCHY

To date, no completely successful solution has been found for the problem of noise. The problem of disjunction can be addressed by allowing only limited forms of disjunction or by including a **generalization hierarchy** of more general predicates. For example, instead of using the disjunction $WaitEstimate(x, 30\text{-}60) \lor WaitEstimate(x, >60)$, we might use the single literal $LongWait(x)$. The set of generalization and specialization operations can be easily extended to handle this.

The pure version space algorithm was first applied in the Meta-DENDRAL system, which was designed to learn rules for predicting how molecules would break into pieces in a mass spectrometer (Buchanan and Mitchell, 1978). Meta-DENDRAL was able to generate rules that were sufficiently novel to warrant publication in a journal of analytical chemistry—the first real scientific knowledge generated by a computer program. It was also used in the elegant LEX system (Mitchell *et al.*, 1983), which was able to learn to solve symbolic integration problems by studying its own successes and failures. Although version space methods are probably not practical in most real-world learning problems, mainly because of noise, they provide a good deal of insight into the logical structure of hypothesis space.

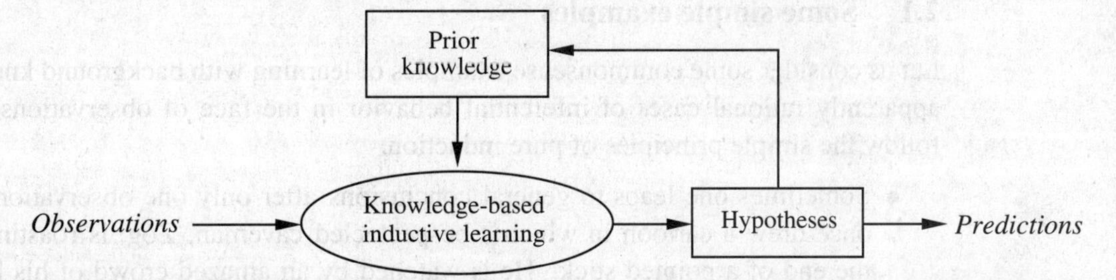

Figure 6 A cumulative learning process uses, and adds to, its stock of background knowledge over time.

2 KNOWLEDGE IN LEARNING

The preceding section described the simplest setting for inductive learning. To understand the role of prior knowledge, we need to talk about the logical relationships among hypotheses, example descriptions, and classifications. Let *Descriptions* denote the conjunction of all the example descriptions in the training set, and let *Classifications* denote the conjunction of all the example classifications. Then a *Hypothesis* that "explains the observations" must satisfy the following property (recall that $\models$ means "logically entails"):

$$Hypothesis \land Descriptions \models Classifications \;. \qquad (3)$$

ENTAILMENT CONSTRAINT

We call this kind of relationship an **entailment constraint**, in which *Hypothesis* is the "unknown." Pure inductive learning means solving this constraint, where *Hypothesis* is drawn from some predefined hypothesis space. For example, if we consider a decision tree as a logical formula (see Equation (1)), then a decision tree that is consistent with all the examples will satisfy Equation (3). If we place *no* restrictions on the logical form of the hypothesis, of course, then $Hypothesis = Classifications$ also satisfies the constraint. Ockham's razor tells us to prefer *small*, consistent hypotheses, so we try to do better than simply memorizing the examples.

This simple knowledge-free picture of inductive learning persisted until the early 1980s. The modern approach is to design agents that *already know something* and are trying to learn some more. This may not sound like a terrifically deep insight, but it makes quite a difference to the way we design agents. It might also have some relevance to our theories about how science itself works. The general idea is shown schematically in Figure 6.

An autonomous learning agent that uses background knowledge must somehow obtain the background knowledge in the first place, in order for it to be used in the new learning episodes. This method must itself be a learning process. The agent's life history will therefore be characterized by *cumulative*, or *incremental*, development. Presumably, the agent could start out with nothing, performing inductions *in vacuo* like a good little pure induction program. But once it has eaten from the Tree of Knowledge, it can no longer pursue such naive speculations and should use its background knowledge to learn more and more effectively. The question is then how to actually do this.

2.1 Some simple examples

Let us consider some commonsense examples of learning with background knowledge. Many apparently rational cases of inferential behavior in the face of observations clearly do not follow the simple principles of pure induction.

- Sometimes one leaps to general conclusions after only one observation. Gary Larson once drew a cartoon in which a bespectacled caveman, Zog, is roasting his lizard on the end of a pointed stick. He is watched by an amazed crowd of his less intellectual contemporaries, who have been using their bare hands to hold their victuals over the fire. This enlightening experience is enough to convince the watchers of a general principle of painless cooking.
- Or consider the case of the traveler to Brazil meeting her first Brazilian. On hearing him speak Portuguese, she immediately concludes that Brazilians speak Portuguese, yet on discovering that his name is Fernando, she does not conclude that all Brazilians are called Fernando. Similar examples appear in science. For example, when a freshman physics student measures the density and conductance of a sample of copper at a particular temperature, she is quite confident in generalizing those values to all pieces of copper. Yet when she measures its mass, she does not even consider the hypothesis that all pieces of copper have that mass. On the other hand, it would be quite reasonable to make such a generalization over all pennies.
- Finally, consider the case of a pharmacologically ignorant but diagnostically sophisticated medical student observing a consulting session between a patient and an expert internist. After a series of questions and answers, the expert tells the patient to take a course of a particular antibiotic. The medical student infers the general rule that that particular antibiotic is effective for a particular type of infection.

These are all cases in which *the use of background knowledge allows much faster learning than one might expect from a pure induction program.*

2.2 Some general schemes

In each of the preceding examples, one can appeal to prior knowledge to try to justify the generalizations chosen. We will now look at what kinds of entailment constraints are operating in each case. The constraints will involve the *Background* knowledge, in addition to the *Hypothesis* and the observed *Descriptions* and *Classifications*.

In the case of lizard toasting, the cavemen generalize by *explaining* the success of the pointed stick: it supports the lizard while keeping the hand away from the fire. From this explanation, they can infer a general rule: that any long, rigid, sharp object can be used to toast small, soft-bodied edibles. This kind of generalization process has been called **explanation-based learning**, or **EBL**. Notice that the general rule *follows logically* from the background knowledge possessed by the cavemen. Hence, the entailment constraints satisfied by EBL are the following:

EXPLANATION-BASED LEARNING

$$Hypothesis \wedge Descriptions \models Classifications$$
$$Background \models Hypothesis \ .$$

Because EBL uses Equation (3), it was initially thought to be a way to learn from examples. But because it requires that the background knowledge be sufficient to explain the *Hypothesis*, which in turn explains the observations, *the agent does not actually learn anything factually new from the example.* The agent *could have* derived the example from what it already knew, although that might have required an unreasonable amount of computation. EBL is now viewed as a method for converting first-principles theories into useful, special-purpose knowledge. We describe algorithms for EBL in Section 3.

The situation of our traveler in Brazil is quite different, for she cannot necessarily explain why Fernando speaks the way he does, unless she knows her papal bulls. Moreover, the same generalization would be forthcoming from a traveler entirely ignorant of colonial history. The relevant prior knowledge in this case is that, within any given country, most people tend to speak the same language; on the other hand, Fernando is not assumed to be the name of all Brazilians because this kind of regularity does not hold for names. Similarly, the freshman physics student also would be hard put to explain the particular values that she discovers for the conductance and density of copper. She does know, however, that the material of which an object is composed and its temperature together determine its conductance.

RELEVANCE

In each case, the prior knowledge *Background* concerns the **relevance** of a set of features to the goal predicate. This knowledge, *together with the observations*, allows the agent to infer a new, general rule that explains the observations:

$$\begin{aligned} &\mathit{Hypothesis} \wedge \mathit{Descriptions} \models \mathit{Classifications}\ , \\ &\mathit{Background} \wedge \mathit{Descriptions} \wedge \mathit{Classifications} \models \mathit{Hypothesis}\ . \end{aligned} \qquad (4)$$

RELEVANCE-BASED LEARNING

We call this kind of generalization **relevance-based learning**, or **RBL** (although the name is not standard). Notice that whereas RBL does make use of the content of the observations, it does not produce hypotheses that go beyond the logical content of the background knowledge and the observations. It is a *deductive* form of learning and cannot by itself account for the creation of new knowledge starting from scratch.

In the case of the medical student watching the expert, we assume that the student's prior knowledge is sufficient to infer the patient's disease D from the symptoms. This is not, however, enough to explain the fact that the doctor prescribes a particular medicine M. The student needs to propose another rule, namely, that M generally is effective against D. Given this rule and the student's prior knowledge, the student can now explain why the expert prescribes M in this particular case. We can generalize this example to come up with the entailment constraint

$$\mathit{Background} \wedge \mathit{Hypothesis} \wedge \mathit{Descriptions} \models \mathit{Classifications}\ . \qquad (5)$$

That is, *the background knowledge and the new hypothesis combine to explain the examples.* As with pure inductive learning, the learning algorithm should propose hypotheses that are as simple as possible, consistent with this constraint. Algorithms that satisfy constraint (5) are called **knowledge-based inductive learning**, or **KBIL**, algorithms.

KNOWLEDGE-BASED INDUCTIVE LEARNING

INDUCTIVE LOGIC PROGRAMMING

KBIL algorithms, which are described in detail in Section 5, have been studied mainly in the field of **inductive logic programming**, or **ILP**. In ILP systems, prior knowledge plays two key roles in reducing the complexity of learning:

1. Because any hypothesis generated must be consistent with the prior knowledge as well as with the new observations, the effective hypothesis space size is reduced to include only those theories that are consistent with what is already known.
2. For any given set of observations, the size of the hypothesis required to construct an explanation for the observations can be much reduced, because the prior knowledge will be available to help out the new rules in explaining the observations. The smaller the hypothesis, the easier it is to find.

In addition to allowing the use of prior knowledge in induction, ILP systems can formulate hypotheses in general first-order logic, rather than restricted attribute-based language. This means that they can learn in environments that cannot be understood by simpler systems.

3 EXPLANATION-BASED LEARNING

Explanation-based learning is a method for extracting general rules from individual observations. As an example, consider the problem of differentiating and simplifying algebraic expressions. If we differentiate an expression such as X^2 with respect to *X*, we obtain 2*X*. (We use a capital letter for the arithmetic unknown *X*, to distinguish it from the logical variable x.) In a logical reasoning system, the goal might be expressed as ASK $(Derivative(X^2, X) = d,\ KB)$, with solution $d = 2X$.

Anyone who knows differential calculus can see this solution "by inspection" as a result of practice in solving such problems. A student encountering such problems for the first time, or a program with no experience, will have a much more difficult job. Application of the standard rules of differentiation eventually yields the expression $1 \times (2 \times (X^{(2-1)}))$, and eventually this simplifies to $2X$. In the authors' logic programming implementation, this takes 136 proof steps, of which 99 are on dead-end branches in the proof. After such an experience, we would like the program to solve the same problem much more quickly the next time it arises.

MEMOIZATION

The technique of **memoization** has long been used in computer science to speed up programs by saving the results of computation. The basic idea of memo functions is to accumulate a database of input–output pairs; when the function is called, it first checks the database to see whether it can avoid solving the problem from scratch. Explanation-based learning takes this a good deal further, by creating *general* rules that cover an entire class of cases. In the case of differentiation, memoization would remember that the derivative of X^2 with respect to X is $2X$, but would leave the agent to calculate the derivative of Z^2 with respect to Z from scratch. We would like to be able to extract the general rule that for any arithmetic unknown u, the derivative of u^2 with respect to u is $2u$. (An even more general rule for u^n can also be produced, but the current example suffices to make the point.) In logical terms, this is expressed by the rule

$$ArithmeticUnknown(u) \Rightarrow Derivative(u^2, u) = 2u\ .$$

If the knowledge base contains such a rule, then any new case that is an instance of this rule can be solved immediately.

This is, of course, merely a trivial example of a very general phenomenon. Once something is understood, it can be generalized and reused in other circumstances. It becomes an "obvious" step and can then be used as a building block in solving problems still more complex. Alfred North Whitehead (1911), co-author with Bertrand Russell of *Principia Mathematica*, wrote *"Civilization advances by extending the number of important operations that we can do without thinking about them,"* perhaps himself applying EBL to his understanding of events such as Zog's discovery. If you have understood the basic idea of the differentiation example, then your brain is already busily trying to extract the general principles of explanation-based learning from it. Notice that you hadn't *already* invented EBL before you saw the example. Like the cavemen watching Zog, you (and we) needed an example before we could generate the basic principles. This is because *explaining why* something is a good idea is much easier than coming up with the idea in the first place.

3.1 Extracting general rules from examples

The basic idea behind EBL is first to construct an explanation of the observation using prior knowledge, and then to establish a definition of the class of cases for which the same explanation structure can be used. This definition provides the basis for a rule covering all of the cases in the class. The "explanation" can be a logical proof, but more generally it can be any reasoning or problem-solving process whose steps are well defined. The key is to be able to identify the necessary conditions for those same steps to apply to another case.

We will use for our reasoning system the simple backward-chaining theorem prover. The proof tree for $Derivative(X^2, X) = 2X$ is too large to use as an example, so we will use a simpler problem to illustrate the generalization method. Suppose our problem is to simplify $1 \times (0 + X)$. The knowledge base includes the following rules:

$$
\begin{aligned}
&Rewrite(u, v) \land Simplify(v, w) \;\Rightarrow\; Simplify(u, w)\,.\\
&Primitive(u) \;\Rightarrow\; Simplify(u, u)\,.\\
&ArithmeticUnknown(u) \;\Rightarrow\; Primitive(u)\,.\\
&Number(u) \;\Rightarrow\; Primitive(u)\,.\\
&Rewrite(1 \times u, u)\,.\\
&Rewrite(0 + u, u)\,.\\
&\qquad\vdots
\end{aligned}
$$

The proof that the answer is X is shown in the top half of Figure 7. The EBL method actually constructs two proof trees simultaneously. The second proof tree uses a *variabilized* goal in which the constants from the original goal are replaced by variables. As the original proof proceeds, the variabilized proof proceeds in step, using *exactly the same rule applications*. This could cause some of the variables to become instantiated. For example, in order to use the rule $Rewrite(1 \times u, u)$, the variable x in the subgoal $Rewrite(x \times (y + z), v)$ must be bound to 1. Similarly, y must be bound to 0 in the subgoal $Rewrite(y + z, v')$ in order to use the rule $Rewrite(0 + u, u)$. Once we have the generalized proof tree, we take the leaves

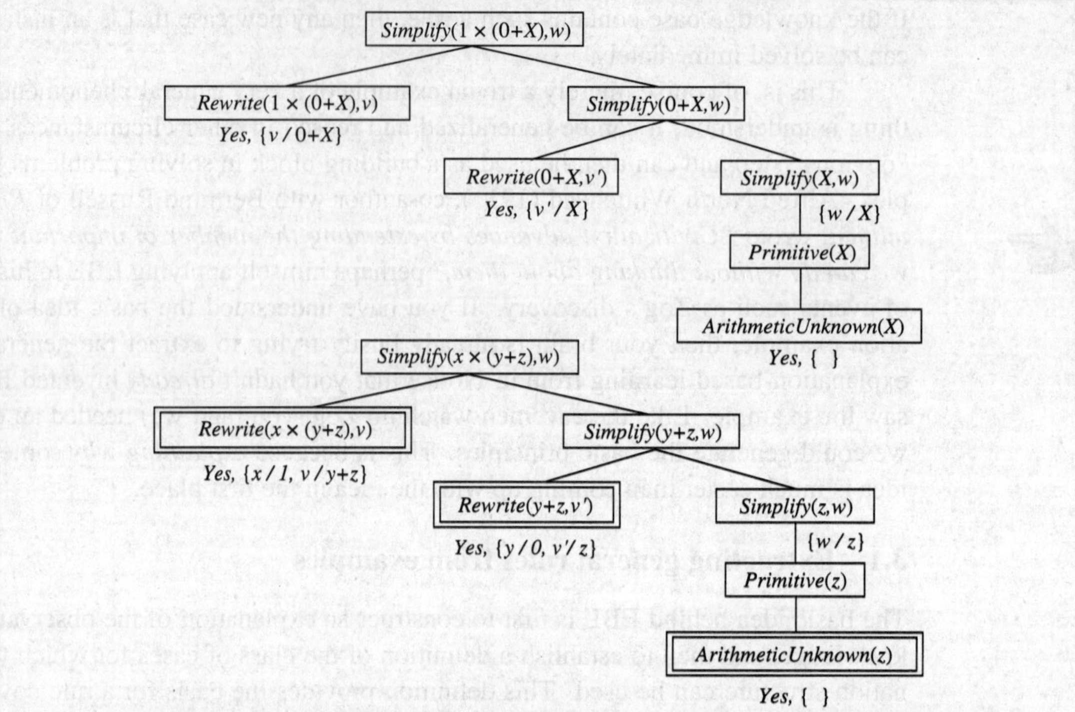

Figure 7 Proof trees for the simplification problem. The first tree shows the proof for the original problem instance, from which we can derive

$$ArithmeticUnknown(z) \Rightarrow Simplify(1 \times (0 + z), z) .$$

The second tree shows the proof for a problem instance with all constants replaced by variables, from which we can derive a variety of other rules.

(with the necessary bindings) and form a general rule for the goal predicate:

$$Rewrite(1 \times (0 + z), 0 + z) \wedge Rewrite(0 + z, z) \wedge ArithmeticUnknown(z)$$
$$\Rightarrow Simplify(1 \times (0 + z), z) .$$

Notice that the first two conditions on the left-hand side are true *regardless of the value of z*. We can therefore drop them from the rule, yielding

$$ArithmeticUnknown(z) \Rightarrow Simplify(1 \times (0 + z), z) .$$

In general, conditions can be dropped from the final rule if they impose no constraints on the variables on the right-hand side of the rule, because the resulting rule will still be true and will be more efficient. Notice that we cannot drop the condition $ArithmeticUnknown(z)$, because not all possible values of z are arithmetic unknowns. Values other than arithmetic unknowns might require different forms of simplification: for example, if z were 2×3, then the correct simplification of $1 \times (0 + (2 \times 3))$ would be 6 and not 2×3.

To recap, the basic EBL process works as follows:

1. Given an example, construct a proof that the goal predicate applies to the example using the available background knowledge.

2. In parallel, construct a generalized proof tree for the variabilized goal using the same inference steps as in the original proof.
3. Construct a new rule whose left-hand side consists of the leaves of the proof tree and whose right-hand side is the variabilized goal (after applying the necessary bindings from the generalized proof).
4. Drop any conditions from the left-hand side that are true regardless of the values of the variables in the goal.

3.2 Improving efficiency

The generalized proof tree in Figure 7 actually yields more than one generalized rule. For example, if we terminate, or **prune**, the growth of the right-hand branch in the proof tree when it reaches the *Primitive* step, we get the rule

$$Primitive(z) \Rightarrow Simplify(1 \times (0 + z), z) .$$

This rule is as valid as, but *more general* than, the rule using $ArithmeticUnknown$, because it covers cases where z is a number. We can extract a still more general rule by pruning after the step $Simplify(y + z, w)$, yielding the rule

$$Simplify(y + z, w) \Rightarrow Simplify(1 \times (y + z), w) .$$

In general, a rule can be extracted from *any partial subtree* of the generalized proof tree. Now we have a problem: which of these rules do we choose?

The choice of which rule to generate comes down to the question of efficiency. There are three factors involved in the analysis of efficiency gains from EBL:

1. Adding large numbers of rules can slow down the reasoning process, because the inference mechanism must still check those rules even in cases where they do not yield a solution. In other words, it increases the **branching factor** in the search space.
2. To compensate for the slowdown in reasoning, the derived rules must offer significant increases in speed for the cases that they do cover. These increases come about mainly because the derived rules avoid dead ends that would otherwise be taken, but also because they shorten the proof itself.
3. Derived rules should be as general as possible, so that they apply to the largest possible set of cases.

A common approach to ensuring that derived rules are efficient is to insist on the **operationality** of each subgoal in the rule. A subgoal is operational if it is "easy" to solve. For example, the subgoal $Primitive(z)$ is easy to solve, requiring at most two steps, whereas the subgoal $Simplify(y + z, w)$ could lead to an arbitrary amount of inference, depending on the values of y and z. If a test for operationality is carried out at each step in the construction of the generalized proof, then we can prune the rest of a branch as soon as an operational subgoal is found, keeping just the operational subgoal as a conjunct of the new rule.

OPERATIONALITY

Unfortunately, there is usually a tradeoff between operationality and generality. More specific subgoals are generally easier to solve but cover fewer cases. Also, operationality is a matter of degree: one or two steps is definitely operational, but what about 10 or 100?

Finally, the cost of solving a given subgoal depends on what other rules are available in the knowledge base. It can go up or down as more rules are added. Thus, EBL systems really face a very complex optimization problem in trying to maximize the efficiency of a given initial knowledge base. It is sometimes possible to derive a mathematical model of the effect on overall efficiency of adding a given rule and to use this model to select the best rule to add. The analysis can become very complicated, however, especially when recursive rules are involved. One promising approach is to address the problem of efficiency empirically, simply by adding several rules and seeing which ones are useful and actually speed things up.

Empirical analysis of efficiency is actually at the heart of EBL. What we have been calling loosely the "efficiency of a given knowledge base" is actually the average-case complexity on a distribution of problems. *By generalizing from past example problems, EBL makes the knowledge base more efficient for the kind of problems that it is reasonable to expect.* This works as long as the distribution of past examples is roughly the same as for future examples. If the EBL system is carefully engineered, it is possible to obtain significant speedups. For example, a very large Prolog-based natural language system designed for speech-to-speech translation between Swedish and English was able to achieve real-time performance only by the application of EBL to the parsing process (Samuelsson and Rayner, 1991).

4 LEARNING USING RELEVANCE INFORMATION

Our traveler in Brazil seems to be able to make a confident generalization concerning the language spoken by other Brazilians. The inference is sanctioned by her background knowledge, namely, that people in a given country (usually) speak the same language. We can express this in first-order logic as follows:[2]

$$Nationality(x,n) \land Nationality(y,n) \land Language(x,l) \;\Rightarrow\; Language(y,l)\,. \quad (6)$$

(Literal translation: "If x and y have the same nationality n and x speaks language l, then y also speaks it.") It is not difficult to show that, from this sentence and the observation that

$$Nationality(Fernando, Brazil) \land Language(Fernando, Portuguese)\,,$$

the following conclusion is entailed (see Exercise 1):

$$Nationality(x, Brazil) \Rightarrow Language(x, Portuguese)\,.$$

FUNCTIONAL DEPENDENCY

DETERMINATION

Sentences such as (6) express a strict form of relevance: given nationality, language is fully determined. (Put another way: language is a function of nationality.) These sentences are called **functional dependencies** or **determinations**. They occur so commonly in certain kinds of applications (e.g., defining database designs) that a special syntax is used to write them. We adopt the notation of Davies (1985):

$$Nationality(x,n) \succ Language(x,l)\,.$$

[2] We assume for the sake of simplicity that a person speaks only one language. Clearly, the rule would have to be amended for countries such as Switzerland and India.

As usual, this is simply a syntactic sugaring, but it makes it clear that the determination is really a relationship between the predicates: nationality determines language. The relevant properties determining conductance and density can be expressed similarly:

$$Material(x,m) \land Temperature(x,t) \succ Conductance(x,\rho) ;$$
$$Material(x,m) \land Temperature(x,t) \succ Density(x,d) .$$

The corresponding generalizations follow logically from the determinations and observations.

4.1 Determining the hypothesis space

Although the determinations sanction general conclusions concerning all Brazilians, or all pieces of copper at a given temperature, they cannot, of course, yield a general predictive theory for *all* nationalities, or for *all* temperatures and materials, from a single example. Their main effect can be seen as limiting the space of hypotheses that the learning agent need consider. In predicting conductance, for example, one need consider only material and temperature and can ignore mass, ownership, day of the week, the current president, and so on. Hypotheses can certainly include terms that are in turn determined by material and temperature, such as molecular structure, thermal energy, or free-electron density. *Determinations specify a sufficient basis vocabulary from which to construct hypotheses concerning the target predicate.* This statement can be proven by showing that a given determination is logically equivalent to a statement that the correct definition of the target predicate is one of the set of all definitions expressible using the predicates on the left-hand side of the determination.

Intuitively, it is clear that a reduction in the hypothesis space size should make it easier to learn the target predicate. Using the basic results of computational learning theory, we can quantify the possible gains. First, recall that for Boolean functions, $\log(|\mathcal{H}|)$ examples are required to converge to a reasonable hypothesis, where $|\mathcal{H}|$ is the size of the hypothesis space. If the learner has n Boolean features with which to construct hypotheses, then, in the absence of further restrictions, $|\mathcal{H}| = O(2^{2^n})$, so the number of examples is $O(2^n)$. If the determination contains d predicates in the left-hand side, the learner will require only $O(2^d)$ examples, a reduction of $O(2^{n-d})$.

4.2 Learning and using relevance information

As we stated in the introduction to this chapter, prior knowledge is useful in learning; but it too has to be learned. In order to provide a complete story of relevance-based learning, we must therefore provide a learning algorithm for determinations. The learning algorithm we now present is based on a straightforward attempt to find the simplest determination consistent with the observations. A determination $P \succ Q$ says that if any examples match on P, then they must also match on Q. A determination is therefore consistent with a set of examples if every pair that matches on the predicates on the left-hand side also matches on the goal predicate. For example, suppose we have the following examples of conductance measurements on material samples:

```
function MINIMAL-CONSISTENT-DET(E, A) returns a set of attributes
  inputs: E, a set of examples
          A, a set of attributes, of size n

  for i = 0 to n do
    for each subset A_i of A of size i do
      if CONSISTENT-DET?(A_i, E) then return A_i
```

```
function CONSISTENT-DET?(A, E) returns a truth value
  inputs: A, a set of attributes
          E, a set of examples
  local variables: H, a hash table

  for each example e in E do
    if some example in H has the same values as e for the attributes A
       but a different classification then return false
    store the class of e in H, indexed by the values for attributes A of the example e
  return true
```

Figure 8 An algorithm for finding a minimal consistent determination.

Sample	Mass	Temperature	Material	Size	Conductance
S1	12	26	Copper	3	0.59
S1	12	100	Copper	3	0.57
S2	24	26	Copper	6	0.59
S3	12	26	Lead	2	0.05
S3	12	100	Lead	2	0.04
S4	24	26	Lead	4	0.05

The minimal consistent determination is $Material \wedge Temperature \succ Conductance$. There is a nonminimal but consistent determination, namely, $Mass \wedge Size \wedge Temperature \succ Conductance$. This is consistent with the examples because mass and size determine density and, in our data set, we do not have two different materials with the same density. As usual, we would need a larger sample set in order to eliminate a nearly correct hypothesis.

There are several possible algorithms for finding minimal consistent determinations. The most obvious approach is to conduct a search through the space of determinations, checking all determinations with one predicate, two predicates, and so on, until a consistent determination is found. We will assume a simple attribute-based representation, like that used for decision tree learning. A determination d will be represented by the set of attributes on the left-hand side, because the target predicate is assumed to be fixed. The basic algorithm is outlined in Figure 8.

The time complexity of this algorithm depends on the size of the smallest consistent determination. Suppose this determination has p attributes out of the n total attributes. Then the algorithm will not find it until searching the subsets of A of size p. There are $\binom{n}{p} = O(n^p)$

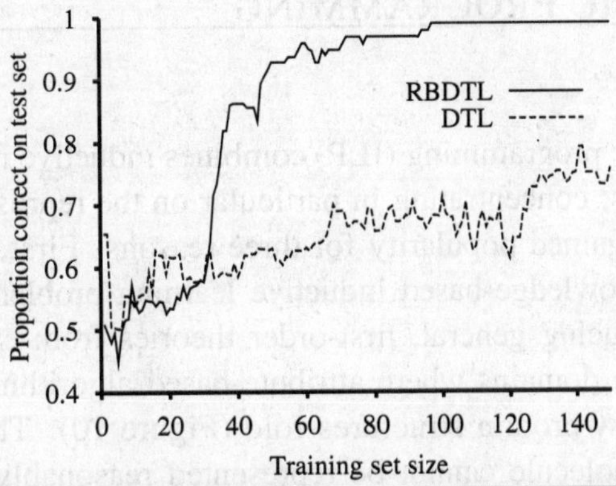

Figure 9 A performance comparison between DECISION-TREE-LEARNING and RBDTL on randomly generated data for a target function that depends on only 5 of 16 attributes.

such subsets; hence the algorithm is exponential in the size of the minimal determination. It turns out that the problem is NP-complete, so we cannot expect to do better in the general case. In most domains, however, there will be sufficient local structure that p will be small.

Given an algorithm for learning determinations, a learning agent has a way to construct a minimal hypothesis within which to learn the target predicate. For example, we can combine MINIMAL-CONSISTENT-DET with the DECISION-TREE-LEARNING algorithm. This yields a relevance-based decision-tree learning algorithm RBDTL that first identifies a minimal set of relevant attributes and then passes this set to the decision tree algorithm for learning. Unlike DECISION-TREE-LEARNING, RBDTL simultaneously learns and uses relevance information in order to minimize its hypothesis space. We expect that RBDTL will learn faster than DECISION-TREE-LEARNING, and this is in fact the case. Figure 9 shows the learning performance for the two algorithms on randomly generated data for a function that depends on only 5 of 16 attributes. Obviously, in cases where all the available attributes are relevant, RBDTL will show no advantage.

DECLARATIVE BIAS

This section has only scratched the surface of the field of **declarative bias**, which aims to understand how prior knowledge can be used to identify the appropriate hypothesis space within which to search for the correct target definition. There are many unanswered questions:

- How can the algorithms be extended to handle noise?
- Can we handle continuous-valued variables?
- How can other kinds of prior knowledge be used, besides determinations?
- How can the algorithms be generalized to cover any first-order theory, rather than just an attribute-based representation?

Some of these questions are addressed in the next section.

5 INDUCTIVE LOGIC PROGRAMMING

Inductive logic programming (ILP) combines inductive methods with the power of first-order representations, concentrating in particular on the representation of hypotheses as logic programs. It has gained popularity for three reasons. First, ILP offers a rigorous approach to the general knowledge-based inductive learning problem. Second, it offers complete algorithms for inducing general, first-order theories from examples, which can therefore learn successfully in domains where attribute-based algorithms are hard to apply. An example is in learning how protein structures fold (Figure 10). The three-dimensional configuration of a protein molecule cannot be represented reasonably by a set of attributes, because the configuration inherently refers to *relationships* between objects, not to attributes of a single object. First-order logic is an appropriate language for describing the relationships. Third, inductive logic programming produces hypotheses that are (relatively) easy for humans to read. For example, the English translation in Figure 10 can be scrutinized and criticized by working biologists. This means that inductive logic programming systems can participate in the scientific cycle of experimentation, hypothesis generation, debate, and refutation. Such participation would not be possible for systems that generate "black-box" classifiers, such as neural networks.

5.1 An example

Recall from Equation (5) that the general knowledge-based induction problem is to "solve" the entailment constraint

$$Background \land Hypothesis \land Descriptions \models Classifications$$

for the unknown *Hypothesis*, given the *Background* knowledge and examples described by *Descriptions* and *Classifications*. To illustrate this, we will use the problem of learning family relationships from examples. The descriptions will consist of an extended family tree, described in terms of *Mother*, *Father*, and *Married* relations and *Male* and *Female* properties. As an example, we will use the family tree, shown here in Figure 11. The corresponding descriptions are as follows:

$$\begin{array}{lll} Father(Philip, Charles) & Father(Philip, Anne) & \ldots \\ Mother(Mum, Margaret) & Mother(Mum, Elizabeth) & \ldots \\ Married(Diana, Charles) & Married(Elizabeth, Philip) & \ldots \\ Male(Philip) & Male(Charles) & \ldots \\ Female(Beatrice) & Female(Margaret) & \ldots \end{array}$$

The sentences in *Classifications* depend on the target concept being learned. We might want to learn *Grandparent*, *BrotherInLaw*, or *Ancestor*, for example. For *Grandparent*, the complete set of *Classifications* contains $20 \times 20 = 400$ conjuncts of the form

$$\begin{array}{lll} Grandparent(Mum, Charles) & Grandparent(Elizabeth, Beatrice) & \ldots \\ \neg Grandparent(Mum, Harry) & \neg Grandparent(Spencer, Peter) & \ldots \end{array}$$

We could of course learn from a subset of this complete set.

The object of an inductive learning program is to come up with a set of sentences for the *Hypothesis* such that the entailment constraint is satisfied. Suppose, for the moment, that the agent has no background knowledge: *Background* is empty. Then one possible solution

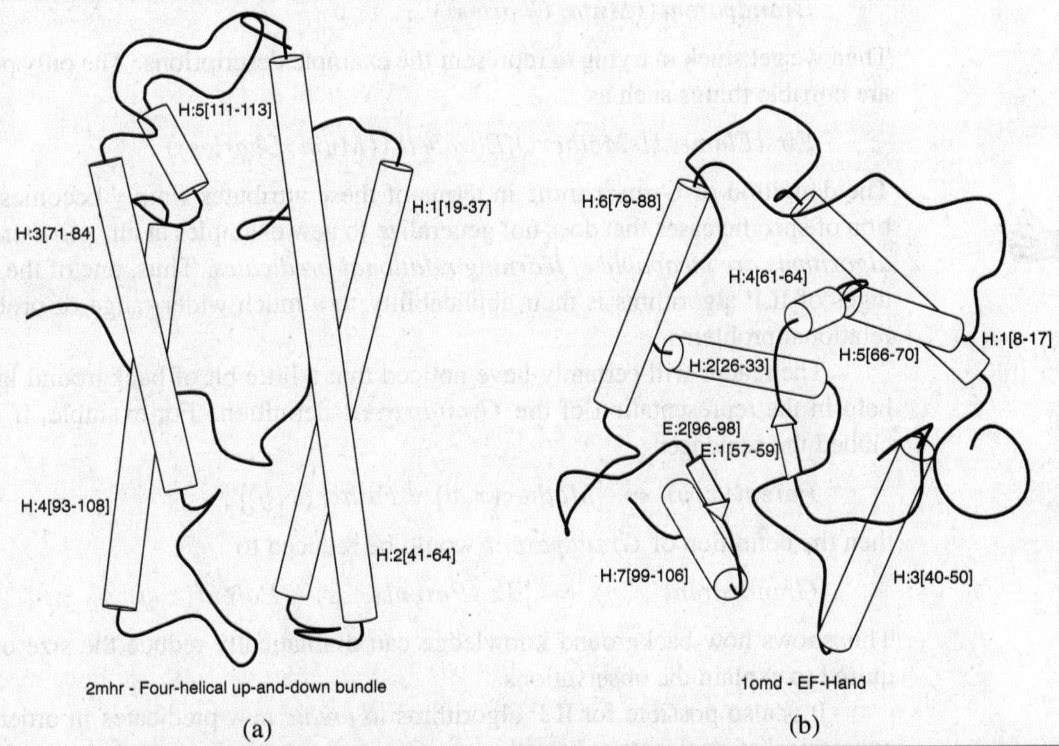

Figure 10 (a) and (b) show positive and negative examples, respectively, of the "four-helical up-and-down bundle" concept in the domain of protein folding. Each example structure is coded into a logical expression of about 100 conjuncts such as $TotalLength(D2mhr, 118) \wedge NumberHelices(D2mhr, 6) \wedge \ldots$. From these descriptions and from classifications such as $Fold(\text{FOUR-HELICAL-UP-AND-DOWN-BUNDLE}, D2mhr)$, the ILP system PROGOL (Muggleton, 1995) learned the following rule:

$$\begin{array}{l} Fold(\text{FOUR-HELICAL-UP-AND-DOWN-BUNDLE}, p) \Leftarrow \\ \quad Helix(p, h_1) \wedge Length(h_1, \text{HIGH}) \wedge Position(p, h_1, n) \\ \quad \wedge (1 \leq n \leq 3) \wedge Adjacent(p, h_1, h_2) \wedge Helix(p, h_2) \,. \end{array}$$

This kind of rule could not be learned, or even represented, by an attribute-based mechanism such as we saw in previous chapters. The rule can be translated into English as " Protein p has fold class "Four-helical up-and-down-bundle" if it contains a long helix h_1 at a secondary structure position between 1 and 3 and h_1 is next to a second helix."

for *Hypothesis* is the following:

$$\begin{aligned} Grandparent(x,y) \;\Leftrightarrow\; & [\exists z \;\; Mother(x,z) \wedge Mother(z,y)] \\ \vee\; & [\exists z \;\; Mother(x,z) \wedge Father(z,y)] \\ \vee\; & [\exists z \;\; Father(x,z) \wedge Mother(z,y)] \\ \vee\; & [\exists z \;\; Father(x,z) \wedge Father(z,y)]\,. \end{aligned}$$

Notice that an attribute-based learning algorithm, such as DECISION-TREE-LEARNING, will get nowhere in solving this problem. In order to express *Grandparent* as an attribute (i.e., a unary predicate), we would need to make *pairs* of people into objects:

$$Grandparent(\langle Mum, Charles\rangle)\ldots$$

Then we get stuck in trying to represent the example descriptions. The only possible attributes are horrible things such as

$$FirstElementIsMotherOfElizabeth(\langle Mum, Charles\rangle)\,.$$

The definition of *Grandparent* in terms of these attributes simply becomes a large disjunction of specific cases that does not generalize to new examples at all. *Attribute-based learning algorithms are incapable of learning relational predicates.* Thus, one of the principal advantages of ILP algorithms is their applicability to a much wider range of problems, including relational problems.

The reader will certainly have noticed that a little bit of background knowledge would help in the representation of the *Grandparent* definition. For example, if *Background* included the sentence

$$Parent(x,y) \;\Leftrightarrow\; [Mother(x,y) \vee Father(x,y)]\,,$$

then the definition of *Grandparent* would be reduced to

$$Grandparent(x,y) \;\Leftrightarrow\; [\exists z \;\; Parent(x,z) \wedge Parent(z,y)]\,.$$

This shows how background knowledge can dramatically reduce the size of hypotheses required to explain the observations.

It is also possible for ILP algorithms to *create* new predicates in order to facilitate the expression of explanatory hypotheses. Given the example data shown earlier, it is entirely reasonable for the ILP program to propose an additional predicate, which we would call

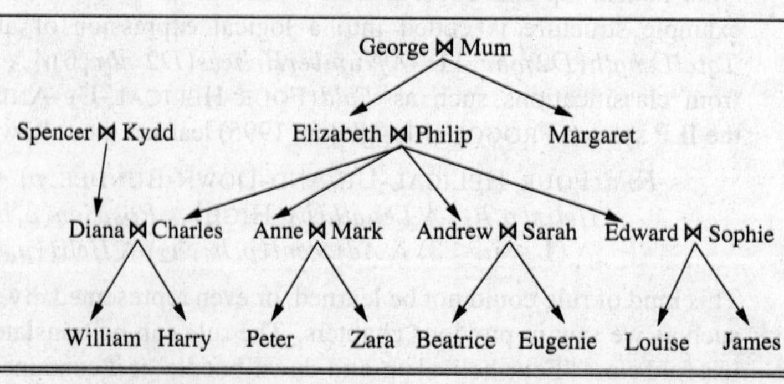

Figure 11 A typical family tree.

CONSTRUCTIVE INDUCTION

"*Parent*," in order to simplify the definitions of the target predicates. Algorithms that can generate new predicates are called **constructive induction** algorithms. Clearly, constructive induction is a necessary part of the picture of cumulative learning. It has been one of the hardest problems in machine learning, but some ILP techniques provide effective mechanisms for achieving it.

In the rest of this chapter, we will study the two principal approaches to ILP. The first uses a generalization of decision tree methods, and the second uses techniques based on inverting a resolution proof.

5.2 Top-down inductive learning methods

The first approach to ILP works by starting with a very general rule and gradually specializing it so that it fits the data. This is essentially what happens in decision-tree learning, where a decision tree is gradually grown until it is consistent with the observations. To do ILP we use first-order literals instead of attributes, and the hypothesis is a set of clauses instead of a decision tree. This section describes FOIL (Quinlan, 1990), one of the first ILP programs.

Suppose we are trying to learn a definition of the $Grandfather(x, y)$ predicate, using the same family data as before. As with decision-tree learning, we can divide the examples into positive and negative examples. Positive examples are

$$\langle George, Anne\rangle,\ \langle Philip, Peter\rangle,\ \langle Spencer, Harry\rangle,\ \ldots$$

and negative examples are

$$\langle George, Elizabeth\rangle,\ \langle Harry, Zara\rangle,\ \langle Charles, Philip\rangle,\ \ldots$$

Notice that each example is a *pair* of objects, because *Grandfather* is a binary predicate. In all, there are 12 positive examples in the family tree and 388 negative examples (all the other pairs of people).

FOIL constructs a set of clauses, each with $Grandfather(x, y)$ as the head. The clauses must classify the 12 positive examples as instances of the $Grandfather(x, y)$ relationship, while ruling out the 388 negative examples. The clauses are Horn clauses, with the extension that negated literals are allowed in the body of a clause and are interpreted using negation as failure, as in Prolog. The initial clause has an empty body:

$$\Rightarrow Grandfather(x, y)\ .$$

This clause classifies every example as positive, so it needs to be specialized. We do this by adding literals one at a time to the left-hand side. Here are three potential additions:

$$Father(x, y) \Rightarrow Grandfather(x, y)\ .$$
$$Parent(x, z) \Rightarrow Grandfather(x, y)\ .$$
$$Father(x, z) \Rightarrow Grandfather(x, y)\ .$$

(Notice that we are assuming that a clause defining *Parent* is already part of the background knowledge.) The first of these three clauses incorrectly classifies all of the 12 positive examples as negative and can thus be ignored. The second and third agree with all of the positive examples, but the second is incorrect on a larger fraction of the negative examples—twice as many, because it allows mothers as well as fathers. Hence, we prefer the third clause.

Now we need to specialize this clause further, to rule out the cases in which x is the father of some z, but z is not a parent of y. Adding the single literal $Parent(z, y)$ gives

$$Father(x, z) \land Parent(z, y) \Rightarrow Grandfather(x, y)\,,$$

which correctly classifies all the examples. FOIL will find and choose this literal, thereby solving the learning task. In general, the solution is a set of Horn clauses, each of which implies the target predicate. For example, if we didn't have the *Parent* predicate in our vocabulary, then the solution might be

$$Father(x, z) \land Father(z, y) \Rightarrow Grandfather(x, y)$$
$$Father(x, z) \land Mother(z, y) \Rightarrow Grandfather(x, y)\,.$$

Note that each of these clauses covers some of the positive examples, that together they cover all the positive examples, and that NEW-CLAUSE is designed in such a way that no clause will incorrectly cover a negative example. In general FOIL will have to search through many unsuccessful clauses before finding a correct solution.

This example is a very simple illustration of how FOIL operates. A sketch of the complete algorithm is shown in Figure 12. Essentially, the algorithm repeatedly constructs a clause, literal by literal, until it agrees with some subset of the positive examples and none of the negative examples. Then the positive examples covered by the clause are removed from the training set, and the process continues until no positive examples remain. The two main subroutines to be explained are NEW-LITERALS, which constructs all possible new literals to add to the clause, and CHOOSE-LITERAL, which selects a literal to add.

NEW-LITERALS takes a clause and constructs all possible "useful" literals that could be added to the clause. Let us use as an example the clause

$$Father(x, z) \Rightarrow Grandfather(x, y)\,.$$

There are three kinds of literals that can be added:

1. *Literals using predicates*: the literal can be negated or unnegated, any existing predicate (including the goal predicate) can be used, and the arguments must all be variables. Any variable can be used for any argument of the predicate, with one restriction: each literal must include *at least one* variable from an earlier literal or from the head of the clause. Literals such as $Mother(z, u)$, $Married(z, z)$, $\neg Male(y)$, and $Grandfather(v, x)$ are allowed, whereas $Married(u, v)$ is not. Notice that the use of the predicate from the head of the clause allows FOIL to learn *recursive* definitions.
2. *Equality and inequality literals*: these relate variables already appearing in the clause. For example, we might add $z \neq x$. These literals can also include user-specified constants. For learning arithmetic we might use 0 and 1, and for learning list functions we might use the empty list [].
3. *Arithmetic comparisons*: when dealing with functions of continuous variables, literals such as $x > y$ and $y \leq z$ can be added. As in decision-tree learning, a constant threshold value can be chosen to maximize the discriminatory power of the test.

The resulting branching factor in this search space is very large (see Exercise 6), but FOIL can also use type information to reduce it. For example, if the domain included numbers as

```
function FOIL(examples, target) returns a set of Horn clauses
  inputs: examples, set of examples
          target, a literal for the goal predicate
  local variables: clauses, set of clauses, initially empty

  while examples contains positive examples do
     clause ← NEW-CLAUSE(examples, target)
     remove positive examples covered by clause from examples
     add clause to clauses
  return clauses
```

```
function NEW-CLAUSE(examples, target) returns a Horn clause
  local variables: clause, a clause with target as head and an empty body
                   l, a literal to be added to the clause
                   extended_examples, a set of examples with values for new variables

  extended_examples ← examples
  while extended_examples contains negative examples do
     l ← CHOOSE-LITERAL(NEW-LITERALS(clause), extended_examples)
     append l to the body of clause
     extended_examples ← set of examples created by applying EXTEND-EXAMPLE
        to each example in extended_examples
  return clause
```

```
function EXTEND-EXAMPLE(example, literal) returns a set of examples
  if example satisfies literal
     then return the set of examples created by extending example with
        each possible constant value for each new variable in literal
  else return the empty set
```

Figure 12 Sketch of the FOIL algorithm for learning sets of first-order Horn clauses from examples. NEW-LITERALS and CHOOSE-LITERAL are explained in the text.

well as people, type restrictions would prevent NEW-LITERALS from generating literals such as $Parent(x, n)$, where x is a person and n is a number.

CHOOSE-LITERAL uses a heuristic somewhat similar to information gain to decide which literal to add. The exact details are not important here, and a number of different variations have been tried. One interesting additional feature of FOIL is the use of Ockham's razor to eliminate some hypotheses. If a clause becomes longer (according to some metric) than the total length of the positive examples that the clause explains, that clause is not considered as a potential hypothesis. This technique provides a way to avoid overcomplex clauses that fit noise in the data.

FOIL and its relatives have been used to learn a wide variety of definitions. One of the most impressive demonstrations (Quinlan and Cameron-Jones, 1993) involved solving a long sequence of exercises on list-processing functions from Bratko's (1986) Prolog textbook. In each case, the program was able to learn a correct definition of the function from a small set of examples, using the previously learned functions as background knowledge.

5.3 Inductive learning with inverse deduction

INVERSE RESOLUTION

The second major approach to ILP involves inverting the normal deductive proof process. **Inverse resolution** is based on the observation that if the example *Classifications* follow from $Background \wedge Hypothesis \wedge Descriptions$, then one must be able to prove this fact by resolution (because resolution is complete). If we can "run the proof backward," then we can find a *Hypothesis* such that the proof goes through. The key, then, is to find a way to invert the resolution process.

We will show a backward proof process for inverse resolution that consists of individual backward steps. Recall that an ordinary resolution step takes two clauses C_1 and C_2 and resolves them to produce the **resolvent** C. An inverse resolution step takes a resolvent C and produces two clauses C_1 and C_2, such that C is the result of resolving C_1 and C_2. Alternatively, it may take a resolvent C and clause C_1 and produce a clause C_2 such that C is the result of resolving C_1 and C_2.

The early steps in an inverse resolution process are shown in Figure 13, where we focus on the positive example $Grandparent(George, Anne)$. The process begins at the end of the proof (shown at the bottom of the figure). We take the resolvent C to be empty clause (i.e. a contradiction) and C_2 to be $\neg Grandparent(George, Anne)$, which is the negation of the goal example. The first inverse step takes C and C_2 and generates the clause $Grandparent(George, Anne)$ for C_1. The next step takes this clause as C and the clause $Parent(Elizabeth, Anne)$ as C_2, and generates the clause

$$\neg Parent(Elizabeth, y) \vee Grandparent(George, y)$$

as C_1. The final step treats this clause as the resolvent. With $Parent(George, Elizabeth)$ as C_2, one possible clause C_1 is the hypothesis

$$Parent(x, z) \wedge Parent(z, y) \Rightarrow Grandparent(x, y)\,.$$

Now we have a resolution proof that the hypothesis, descriptions, and background knowledge entail the classification $Grandparent(George, Anne)$.

Clearly, inverse resolution involves a search. Each inverse resolution step is nondeterministic, because for any C, there can be many or even an infinite number of clauses C_1 and C_2 that resolve to C. For example, instead of choosing $\neg Parent(Elizabeth, y) \vee Grandparent(George, y)$ for C_1 in the last step of Figure 13, the inverse resolution step might have chosen any of the following sentences:

$$\neg Parent(Elizabeth, Anne) \vee Grandparent(George, Anne)\,.$$
$$\neg Parent(z, Anne) \vee Grandparent(George, Anne)\,.$$
$$\neg Parent(z, y) \vee Grandparent(George, y)\,.$$
$$\vdots$$

(See Exercises 4 and 5.) Furthermore, the clauses that participate in each step can be chosen from the *Background* knowledge, from the example *Descriptions*, from the negated

Classifications, or from hypothesized clauses that have already been generated in the inverse resolution tree. The large number of possibilities means a large branching factor (and therefore an inefficient search) without additional controls. A number of approaches to taming the search have been tried in implemented ILP systems:

1. Redundant choices can be eliminated—for example, by generating only the most specific hypotheses possible and by requiring that all the hypothesized clauses be consistent with each other, and with the observations. This last criterion would rule out the clause $\neg Parent(z, y) \lor Grandparent(George, y)$, listed before.
2. The proof strategy can be restricted. Recall that **linear resolution** is a complete, restricted strategy. Linear resolution produces proof trees that have a linear branching structure—the whole tree follows one line, with only single clauses branching off that line (as in Figure 13).
3. The representation language can be restricted, for example by eliminating function symbols or by allowing only Horn clauses. For instance, PROGOL operates with Horn clauses using **inverse entailment**. The idea is to change the entailment constraint

   INVERSE ENTAILMENT

   $$Background \land Hypothesis \land Descriptions \models Classifications$$

   to the logically equivalent form

   $$Background \land Descriptions \land \neg Classifications \models \neg Hypothesis.$$

   From this, one can use a process similar to the normal Prolog Horn-clause deduction, with negation-as-failure to derive *Hypothesis*. Because it is restricted to Horn clauses, this is an incomplete method, but it can be more efficient than full resolution. It is also possible to apply complete inference with inverse entailment (Inoue, 2001).
4. Inference can be done with model checking rather than theorem proving. The PROGOL system (Muggleton, 1995) uses a form of model checking to limit the search. That

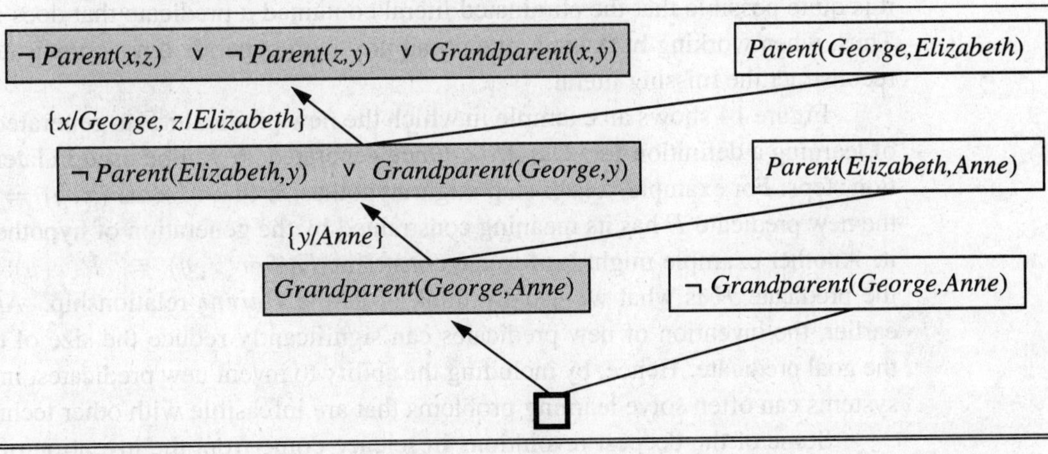

Figure 13 Early steps in an inverse resolution process The shaded clauses are generated by inverse resolution steps from the clause to the right and the clause below. The unshaded clauses are from the *Descriptions* and *Classifications* (including negated *Classifications*).

is, like answer set programming, it generates possible values for logical variables, and checks for consistency.

5. Inference can be done with ground propositional clauses rather than in first-order logic. The LINUS system (Lavrauc and Duzeroski, 1994) works by translating first-order theories into propositional logic, solving them with a propositional learning system, and then translating back. Working with propositional formulas can be more efficient on some problems.

5.4 Making discoveries with inductive logic programming

An inverse resolution procedure that inverts a complete resolution strategy is, in principle, a complete algorithm for learning first-order theories. That is, if some unknown *Hypothesis* generates a set of examples, then an inverse resolution procedure can generate *Hypothesis* from the examples. This observation suggests an interesting possibility: Suppose that the available examples include a variety of trajectories of falling bodies. Would an inverse resolution program be theoretically capable of inferring the law of gravity? The answer is clearly yes, because the law of gravity allows one to explain the examples, given suitable background mathematics. Similarly, one can imagine that electromagnetism, quantum mechanics, and the theory of relativity are also within the scope of ILP programs. Of course, they are also within the scope of a monkey with a typewriter; we still need better heuristics and new ways to structure the search space.

One thing that inverse resolution systems *will* do for you is invent new predicates. This ability is often seen as somewhat magical, because computers are often thought of as "merely working with what they are given." In fact, new predicates fall directly out of the inverse resolution step. The simplest case arises in hypothesizing two new clauses C_1 and C_2, given a clause C. The resolution of C_1 and C_2 eliminates a literal that the two clauses share; hence, it is quite possible that the eliminated literal contained a predicate that does not appear in C. Thus, when working backward, one possibility is to generate a new predicate from which to reconstruct the missing literal.

Figure 14 shows an example in which the new predicate P is generated in the process of learning a definition for $Ancestor$. Once generated, P can be used in later inverse resolution steps. For example, a later step might hypothesize that $Mother(x, y) \Rightarrow P(x, y)$. Thus, the new predicate P has its meaning constrained by the generation of hypotheses that involve it. Another example might lead to the constraint $Father(x, y) \Rightarrow P(x, y)$. In other words, the predicate P is what we usually think of as the $Parent$ relationship. As we mentioned earlier, the invention of new predicates can significantly reduce the size of the definition of the goal predicate. Hence, by including the ability to invent new predicates, inverse resolution systems can often solve learning problems that are infeasible with other techniques.

Some of the deepest revolutions in science come from the invention of new predicates and functions—for example, Galileo's invention of acceleration or Joule's invention of thermal energy. Once these terms are available, the discovery of new laws becomes (relatively) easy. The difficult part lies in realizing that some new entity, with a specific relationship to existing entities, will allow an entire body of observations to be explained with a much

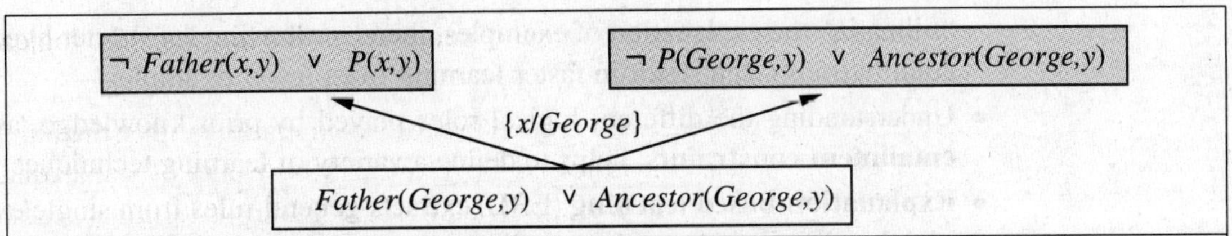

Figure 14 An inverse resolution step that generates a new predicate P.

simpler and more elegant theory than previously existed.

As yet, ILP systems have not made discoveries on the level of Galileo or Joule, but their discoveries have been deemed publishable in the scientific literature. For example, in the *Journal of Molecular Biology*, Turcotte *et al.* (2001) describe the automated discovery of rules for protein folding by the ILP program PROGOL. Many of the rules discovered by PROGOL could have been derived from known principles, but most had not been previously published as part of a standard biological database. (See Figure 10 for an example.). In related work, Srinivasan *et al.* (1994) dealt with the problem of discovering molecular-structure-based rules for the mutagenicity of nitroaromatic compounds. These compounds are found in automobile exhaust fumes. For 80% of the compounds in a standard database, it is possible to identify four important features, and linear regression on these features outperforms ILP. For the remaining 20%, the features alone are not predictive, and ILP identifies relationships that allow it to outperform linear regression, neural nets, and decision trees. Most impressively, King *et al.* (2009) endowed a robot with the ability to perform molecular biology experiments and extended ILP techniques to include experiment design, thereby creating an autonomous scientist that actually discovered new knowledge about the functional genomics of yeast. For all these examples it appears that the ability both to represent relations and to use background knowledge contribute to ILP's high performance. The fact that the rules found by ILP can be interpreted by humans contributes to the acceptance of these techniques in biology journals rather than just computer science journals.

ILP has made contributions to other sciences besides biology. One of the most important is natural language processing, where ILP has been used to extract complex relational information from text.

6 SUMMARY

This chapter has investigated various ways in which prior knowledge can help an agent to learn from new experiences. Because much prior knowledge is expressed in terms of relational models rather than attribute-based models, we have also covered systems that allow learning of relational models. The important points are:

- The use of prior knowledge in learning leads to a picture of **cumulative learning**, in which learning agents improve their learning ability as they acquire more knowledge.
- Prior knowledge helps learning by eliminating otherwise consistent hypotheses and by

"filling in" the explanation of examples, thereby allowing for shorter hypotheses. These contributions often result in faster learning from fewer examples.

- Understanding the different logical roles played by prior knowledge, as expressed by **entailment constraints**, helps to define a variety of learning techniques.
- **Explanation-based learning** (EBL) extracts general rules from single examples by *explaining* the examples and generalizing the explanation. It provides a deductive method for turning first-principles knowledge into useful, efficient, special-purpose expertise.
- **Relevance-based learning** (RBL) uses prior knowledge in the form of determinations to identify the relevant attributes, thereby generating a reduced hypothesis space and speeding up learning. RBL also allows deductive generalizations from single examples.
- **Knowledge-based inductive learning** (KBIL) finds inductive hypotheses that explain sets of observations with the help of background knowledge.
- **Inductive logic programming** (ILP) techniques perform KBIL on knowledge that is expressed in first-order logic. ILP methods can learn relational knowledge that is not expressible in attribute-based systems.
- ILP can be done with a top-down approach of refining a very general rule or through a bottom-up approach of inverting the deductive process.
- ILP methods naturally generate new predicates with which concise new theories can be expressed and show promise as general-purpose scientific theory formation systems.

BIBLIOGRAPHICAL AND HISTORICAL NOTES

Although the use of prior knowledge in learning would seem to be a natural topic for philosophers of science, little formal work was done until quite recently. *Fact, Fiction, and Forecast*, by the philosopher Nelson Goodman (1954), refuted the earlier supposition that induction was simply a matter of seeing enough examples of some universally quantified proposition and then adopting it as a hypothesis. Consider, for example, the hypothesis "All emeralds are grue," where *grue* means "green if observed before time t, but blue if observed thereafter." At any time up to t, we might have observed millions of instances confirming the rule that emeralds are grue, and no disconfirming instances, and yet we are unwilling to adopt the rule. This can be explained only by appeal to the role of relevant prior knowledge in the induction process. Goodman proposes a variety of different kinds of prior knowledge that might be useful, including a version of determinations called **overhypotheses**. Unfortunately, Goodman's ideas were never pursued in machine learning.

The **current-best-hypothesis** approach is an old idea in philosophy (Mill, 1843). Early work in cognitive psychology also suggested that it is a natural form of concept learning in humans (Bruner *et al.*, 1957). In AI, the approach is most closely associated with the work of Patrick Winston, whose Ph.D. thesis (Winston, 1970) addressed the problem of learning descriptions of complex objects. The **version space** method (Mitchell, 1977, 1982) takes a different approach, maintaining the set of *all* consistent hypotheses and eliminating those found to be inconsistent with new examples. The approach was used in the Meta-DENDRAL expert system for chemistry (Buchanan and Mitchell, 1978), and later in Mitchell's (1983) LEX system, which learns to solve calculus problems. A third influential thread was formed by the work of Michalski and colleagues on the AQ series of algorithms, which learned sets of logical rules (Michalski, 1969; Michalski *et al.*, 1986).

EBL had its roots in the techniques used by the STRIPS planner (Fikes *et al.*, 1972). When a plan was constructed, a generalized version of it was saved in a plan library and used in later planning as a **macro-operator**. Similar ideas appeared in Anderson's ACT* architecture, under the heading of **knowledge compilation** (Anderson, 1983), and in the SOAR architecture, as **chunking** (Laird *et al.*, 1986). **Schema acquisition** (DeJong, 1981), **analytical generalization** (Mitchell, 1982), and **constraint-based generalization** (Minton, 1984) were immediate precursors of the rapid growth of interest in EBL stimulated by the papers of Mitchell *et al.* (1986) and DeJong and Mooney (1986). Hirsh (1987) introduced the EBL algorithm described in the text, showing how it could be incorporated directly into a logic programming system. Van Harmelen and Bundy (1988) explain EBL as a variant of the **partial evaluation** method used in program analysis systems (Jones *et al.*, 1993).

Initial enthusiasm for EBL was tempered by Minton's finding (1988) that, without extensive extra work, EBL could easily slow down a program significantly. Formal probabilistic analysis of the expected payoff of EBL can be found in Greiner (1989) and Subramanian and Feldman (1990). An excellent survey of early work on EBL appears in Dietterich (1990).

ANALOGICAL REASONING

Instead of using examples as foci for generalization, one can use them directly to solve new problems, in a process known as **analogical reasoning**. This form of reasoning ranges from a form of plausible reasoning based on degree of similarity (Gentner, 1983), through a form of deductive inference based on determinations but requiring the participation of the example (Davies and Russell, 1987), to a form of "lazy" EBL that tailors the direction of generalization of the old example to fit the needs of the new problem. This latter form of analogical reasoning is found most commonly in **case-based reasoning** (Kolodner, 1993) and **derivational analogy** (Veloso and Carbonell, 1993).

Relevance information in the form of functional dependencies was first developed in the database community, where it is used to structure large sets of attributes into manageable subsets. Functional dependencies were used for analogical reasoning by Carbonell and Collins (1973) and rediscovered and given a full logical analysis by Davies and Russell (Davies, 1985; Davies and Russell, 1987). Their role as prior knowledge in inductive learning was explored by Russell and Grosof (1987). The equivalence of determinations to a restricted-vocabulary hypothesis space was proved in Russell (1988). Learning algorithms for determinations and the improved performance obtained by RBDTL were first shown in the FOCUS algorithm, due to Almuallim and Dietterich (1991). Tadepalli (1993) describes a very ingenious algorithm for learning with determinations that shows large improvements in learning speed.

The idea that inductive learning can be performed by inverse deduction can be traced to W. S. Jevons (1874), who wrote, "The study both of Formal Logic and of the Theory of Probabilities has led me to adopt the opinion that there is no such thing as a distinct method of induction as contrasted with deduction, but that induction is simply an inverse employment of deduction." Computational investigations began with the remarkable Ph.D. thesis by

Gordon Plotkin (1971) at Edinburgh. Although Plotkin developed many of the theorems and methods that are in current use in ILP, he was discouraged by some undecidability results for certain subproblems in induction. MIS (Shapiro, 1981) reintroduced the problem of learning logic programs, but was seen mainly as a contribution to the theory of automated debugging. Work on rule induction, such as the ID3 (Quinlan, 1986) and CN2 (Clark and Niblett, 1989) systems, led to FOIL (Quinlan, 1990), which for the first time allowed practical induction of relational rules. The field of relational learning was reinvigorated by Muggleton and Buntine (1988), whose CIGOL program incorporated a slightly incomplete version of inverse resolution and was capable of generating new predicates. The inverse resolution method also appears in (Russell, 1986), with a simple algorithm given in a footnote. The next major system was GOLEM (Muggleton and Feng, 1990), which uses a covering algorithm based on Plotkin's concept of relative least general generalization. ITOU (Rouveirol and Puget, 1989) and CLINT (De Raedt, 1992) were other systems of that era. More recently, PROGOL (Muggleton, 1995) has taken a hybrid (top-down and bottom-up) approach to inverse entailment and has been applied to a number of practical problems, particularly in biology and natural language processing. Muggleton (2000) describes an extension of PROGOL to handle uncertainty in the form of stochastic logic programs.

A formal analysis of ILP methods appears in Muggleton (1991), a large collection of papers in Muggleton (1992), and a collection of techniques and applications in the book by Lavrauc and Duzeroski (1994). Page and Srinivasan (2002) give a more recent overview of the field's history and challenges for the future. Early complexity results by Haussler (1989) suggested that learning first-order sentences was intractible. However, with better understanding of the importance of syntactic restrictions on clauses, positive results have been obtained even for clauses with recursion (Duzeroski *et al.*, 1992). Learnability results for ILP are surveyed by Kietz and Duzeroski (1994) and Cohen and Page (1995).

DISCOVERY SYSTEM

Although ILP now seems to be the dominant approach to constructive induction, it has not been the only approach taken. So-called **discovery systems** aim to model the process of scientific discovery of new concepts, usually by a direct search in the space of concept definitions. Doug Lenat's Automated Mathematician, or AM (Davis and Lenat, 1982), used discovery heuristics expressed as expert system rules to guide its search for concepts and conjectures in elementary number theory. Unlike most systems designed for mathematical reasoning, AM lacked a concept of proof and could only make conjectures. It rediscovered Goldbach's conjecture and the Unique Prime Factorization theorem. AM's architecture was generalized in the EURISKO system (Lenat, 1983) by adding a mechanism capable of rewriting the system's own discovery heuristics. EURISKO was applied in a number of areas other than mathematical discovery, although with less success than AM. The methodology of AM and EURISKO has been controversial (Ritchie and Hanna, 1984; Lenat and Brown, 1984).

Another class of discovery systems aims to operate with real scientific data to find new laws. The systems DALTON, GLAUBER, and STAHL (Langley *et al.*, 1987) are rule-based systems that look for quantitative relationships in experimental data from physical systems; in each case, the system has been able to recapitulate a well-known discovery from the history of science.

EXERCISES

1 Show, by translating into conjunctive normal form and applying resolution, that the conclusion drawn in section 4 concerning Brazilians is sound.

2 For each of the following determinations, write down the logical representation and explain why the determination is true (if it is):

a. Design and denomination determine the mass of a coin.
b. For a given program, input determines output.
c. Climate, food intake, exercise, and metabolism determine weight gain and loss.
d. Baldness is determined by the baldness (or lack thereof) of one's maternal grandfather.

3 Would a probabilistic version of determinations be useful? Suggest a definition.

4 Fill in the missing values for the clauses C_1 or C_2 (or both) in the following sets of clauses, given that C is the resolvent of C_1 and C_2:

a. $C = \mathit{True} \Rightarrow P(A, B), C_1 = P(x, y) \Rightarrow Q(x, y), C_2 = ??.$
b. $C = \mathit{True} \Rightarrow P(A, B), C_1 = ??, C_2 = ??.$
c. $C = P(x, y) \Rightarrow P(x, f(y)), C_1 = ??, C_2 = ??.$

If there is more than one possible solution, provide one example of each different kind.

5 Suppose one writes a logic program that carries out a resolution inference step. That is, let $\mathit{Resolve}(c_1, c_2, c)$ succeed if c is the result of resolving c_1 and c_2. Normally, *Resolve* would be used as part of a theorem prover by calling it with c_1 and c_2 instantiated to particular clauses, thereby generating the resolvent c. Now suppose instead that we call it with c instantiated and c_1 and c_2 uninstantiated. Will this succeed in generating the appropriate results of an inverse resolution step? Would you need any special modifications to the logic programming system for this to work?

6 Suppose that FOIL is considering adding a literal to a clause using a binary predicate P and that previous literals (including the head of the clause) contain five different variables.

a. How many functionally different literals can be generated? Two literals are functionally identical if they differ only in the names of the *new* variables that they contain.
b. Can you find a general formula for the number of different literals with a predicate of arity r when there are n variables previously used?
c. Why does FOIL not allow literals that contain no previously used variables?

7 Using the data from the family tree in Figure 11, or a subset thereof, apply the FOIL algorithm to learn a definition for the *Ancestor* predicate.

LEARNING PROBABILISTIC MODELS

From Chapter 20 of *Artificial Intelligence: A Modern Approach*, Third Edition. Stuart Russell and Peter Norvig.

LEARNING PROBABILISTIC MODELS

In which we view learning as a form of uncertain reasoning from observations.

There exists a prevalence of uncertainty in real environments. Agents can handle uncertainty by using the methods of probability and decision theory, but first they must learn their probabilistic theories of the world from experience. This chapter explains how they can do that, by formulating the learning task itself as a process of probabilistic inference (Section 1). We will see that a Bayesian view of learning is extremely powerful, providing general solutions to the problems of noise, overfitting, and optimal prediction. It also takes into account the fact that a less-than-omniscient agent can never be certain about which theory of the world is correct, yet must still make decisions by using some theory of the world.

We describe methods for learning probability models—primarily Bayesian networks—in Sections 2 and 3. Some of the material in this chapter is fairly mathematical, although the general lessons can be understood without plunging into the details.

1 STATISTICAL LEARNING

The key concepts in this chapter are **data** and **hypotheses**. Here, the data are **evidence**—that is, instantiations of some or all of the random variables describing the domain. The hypotheses in this chapter are probabilistic theories of how the domain works, including logical theories as a special case.

Consider a simple example. Our favorite Surprise candy comes in two flavors: cherry (yum) and lime (ugh). The manufacturer has a peculiar sense of humor and wraps each piece of candy in the same opaque wrapper, regardless of flavor. The candy is sold in very large bags, of which there are known to be five kinds—again, indistinguishable from the outside:

h_1: 100% cherry,
h_2: 75% cherry + 25% lime,
h_3: 50% cherry + 50% lime,
h_4: 25% cherry + 75% lime,
h_5: 100% lime.

Given a new bag of candy, the random variable H (for *hypothesis*) denotes the type of the bag, with possible values h_1 through h_5. H is not directly observable, of course. As the pieces of candy are opened and inspected, data are revealed—D_1, D_2, ..., D_N, where each D_i is a random variable with possible values *cherry* and *lime*. The basic task faced by the agent is to predict the flavor of the next piece of candy.[1] Despite its apparent triviality, this scenario serves to introduce many of the major issues. The agent really does need to infer a theory of its world, albeit a very simple one.

BAYESIAN LEARNING

Bayesian learning simply calculates the probability of each hypothesis, given the data, and makes predictions on that basis. That is, the predictions are made by using *all* the hypotheses, weighted by their probabilities, rather than by using just a single "best" hypothesis. In this way, learning is reduced to probabilistic inference. Let $\mathbf{D}$ represent all the data, with observed value $\mathbf{d}$; then the probability of each hypothesis is obtained by Bayes' rule:

$$P(h_i \,|\, \mathbf{d}) = \alpha P(\mathbf{d} \,|\, h_i) P(h_i) \,. \tag{1}$$

Now, suppose we want to make a prediction about an unknown quantity X. Then we have

$$\mathbf{P}(X \,|\, \mathbf{d}) = \sum_i \mathbf{P}(X \,|\, \mathbf{d}, h_i) \mathbf{P}(h_i \,|\, \mathbf{d}) = \sum_i \mathbf{P}(X \,|\, h_i) P(h_i \,|\, \mathbf{d}) \,, \tag{2}$$

where we have assumed that each hypothesis determines a probability distribution over X. This equation shows that predictions are weighted averages over the predictions of the individual hypotheses. The hypotheses themselves are essentially "intermediaries" between the raw data and the predictions. The key quantities in the Bayesian approach are the **hypothesis prior**, $P(h_i)$, and the **likelihood** of the data under each hypothesis, $P(\mathbf{d} \,|\, h_i)$.

HYPOTHESIS PRIOR

LIKELIHOOD

For our candy example, we will assume for the time being that the prior distribution over $h_1, \ldots, h_5$ is given by $\langle 0.1, 0.2, 0.4, 0.2, 0.1 \rangle$, as advertised by the manufacturer. The likelihood of the data is calculated under the assumption that the observations are **i.i.d.**, so that

$$P(\mathbf{d} \,|\, h_i) = \prod_j P(d_j \,|\, h_i) \,. \tag{3}$$

For example, suppose the bag is really an all-lime bag (h_5) and the first 10 candies are all lime; then $P(\mathbf{d} \,|\, h_3)$ is 0.5^{10}, because half the candies in an h_3 bag are lime.[2] Figure 1(a) shows how the posterior probabilities of the five hypotheses change as the sequence of 10 lime candies is observed. Notice that the probabilities start out at their prior values, so h_3 is initially the most likely choice and remains so after 1 lime candy is unwrapped. After 2 lime candies are unwrapped, h_4 is most likely; after 3 or more, h_5 (the dreaded all-lime bag) is the most likely. After 10 in a row, we are fairly certain of our fate. Figure 1(b) shows the predicted probability that the next candy is lime, based on Equation (2). As we would expect, it increases monotonically toward 1.

---

[1] Statistically sophisticated readers will recognize this scenario as a variant of the **urn-and-ball** setup. We find urns and balls less compelling than candy; furthermore, candy lends itself to other tasks, such as deciding whether to trade the bag with a friend—see Exercise 2.

[2] We stated earlier that the bags of candy are very large; otherwise, the i.i.d. assumption fails to hold. Technically, it is more correct (but less hygienic) to rewrap each candy after inspection and return it to the bag.

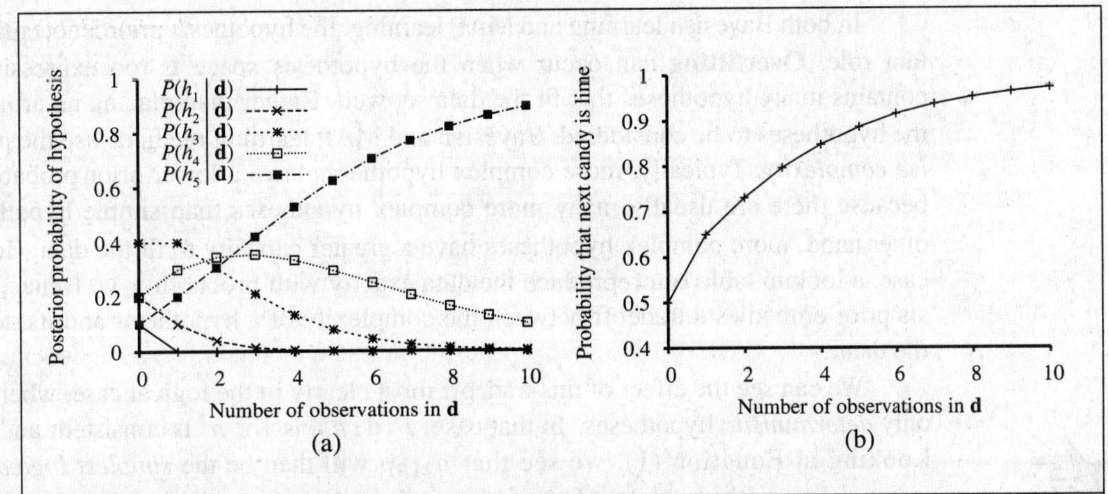

Figure 1 (a) Posterior probabilities $P(h_i \mid d_1, \ldots, d_N)$ from Equation (1). The number of observations N ranges from 1 to 10, and each observation is of a lime candy. (b) Bayesian prediction $P(d_{N+1} = lime \mid d_1, \ldots, d_N)$ from Equation (2).

The example shows that *the Bayesian prediction eventually agrees with the true hypothesis.* This is characteristic of Bayesian learning. For any fixed prior that does not rule out the true hypothesis, the posterior probability of any false hypothesis will, under certain technical conditions, eventually vanish. This happens simply because the probability of generating "uncharacteristic" data indefinitely is vanishingly small. More important, the Bayesian prediction is *optimal*, whether the data set be small or large. Given the hypothesis prior, any other prediction is expected to be correct less often.

The optimality of Bayesian learning comes at a price, of course. For real learning problems, the hypothesis space is usually very large or infinite. In some cases, the summation in Equation (2) (or integration, in the continuous case) can be carried out tractably, but in most cases we must resort to approximate or simplified methods.

MAXIMUM A POSTERIORI

A very common approximation—one that is usually adopted in science—is to make predictions based on a single *most probable* hypothesis—that is, an h_i that maximizes $P(h_i \mid \mathbf{d})$. This is often called a **maximum a posteriori** or MAP (pronounced "em-ay-pee") hypothesis. Predictions made according to an MAP hypothesis h_{MAP} are approximately Bayesian to the extent that $\mathbf{P}(X \mid \mathbf{d}) \approx \mathbf{P}(X \mid h_{\text{MAP}})$. In our candy example, $h_{\text{MAP}} = h_5$ after three lime candies in a row, so the MAP learner then predicts that the fourth candy is lime with probability 1.0—a much more dangerous prediction than the Bayesian prediction of 0.8 shown in Figure 1(b). As more data arrive, the MAP and Bayesian predictions become closer, because the competitors to the MAP hypothesis become less and less probable.

Although our example doesn't show it, finding MAP hypotheses is often much easier than Bayesian learning, because it requires solving an optimization problem instead of a large summation (or integration) problem. We will see example of this later in the chapter.

In both Bayesian learning and MAP learning, the hypothesis prior $P(h_i)$ plays an important role. **Overfitting** can occur when the hypothesis space is too expressive, so that it contains many hypotheses that fit the data set well. Rather than placing an arbitrary limit on the hypotheses to be considered, Bayesian and MAP learning methods use the prior to *penalize complexity*. Typically, more complex hypotheses have a lower prior probability—in part because there are usually many more complex hypotheses than simple hypotheses. On the other hand, more complex hypotheses have a greater capacity to fit the data. (In the extreme case, a lookup table can reproduce the data exactly with probability 1.) Hence, the hypothesis prior embodies a tradeoff between the complexity of a hypothesis and its degree of fit to the data.

We can see the effect of this tradeoff most clearly in the logical case, where H contains only *deterministic* hypotheses. In that case, $P(\mathbf{d} \mid h_i)$ is 1 if h_i is consistent and 0 otherwise. Looking at Equation (1), we see that h_{MAP} will then be the *simplest logical theory that is consistent with the data.* Therefore, maximum *a posteriori* learning provides a natural embodiment of Ockham's razor.

Another insight into the tradeoff between complexity and degree of fit is obtained by taking the logarithm of Equation (1). Choosing h_{MAP} to maximize $P(\mathbf{d} \mid h_i)P(h_i)$ is equivalent to minimizing

$$-\log_2 P(\mathbf{d} \mid h_i) - \log_2 P(h_i)\,.$$

Using the connection between information encoding and probability, we see that the $-\log_2 P(h_i)$ term equals the number of bits required to specify the hypothesis h_i. Furthermore, $-\log_2 P(\mathbf{d} \mid h_i)$ is the additional number of bits required to specify the data, given the hypothesis. (To see this, consider that no bits are required if the hypothesis predicts the data exactly—as with h_5 and the string of lime candies—and $\log_2 1 = 0$.) Hence, MAP learning is choosing the hypothesis that provides maximum *compression* of the data. The same task is addressed more directly by the **minimum description length**, or MDL, learning method. Whereas MAP learning expresses simplicity by assigning higher probabilities to simpler hypotheses, MDL expresses it directly by counting the bits in a binary encoding of the hypotheses and data.

A final simplification is provided by assuming a **uniform** prior over the space of hypotheses. In that case, MAP learning reduces to choosing an h_i that maximizes $P(\mathbf{d} \mid h_i)$.

MAXIMUM-LIKELIHOOD

This is called a **maximum-likelihood** (ML) hypothesis, h_{ML}. Maximum-likelihood learning is very common in statistics, a discipline in which many researchers distrust the subjective nature of hypothesis priors. It is a reasonable approach when there is no reason to prefer one hypothesis over another *a priori*—for example, when all hypotheses are equally complex. It provides a good approximation to Bayesian and MAP learning when the data set is large, because the data swamps the prior distribution over hypotheses, but it has problems (as we shall see) with small data sets.

2 LEARNING WITH COMPLETE DATA

DENSITY ESTIMATION

The general task of learning a probability model, given data that are assumed to be generated from that model, is called **density estimation**. (The term applied originally to probability density functions for continuous variables, but is used now for discrete distributions too.)

COMPLETE DATA

PARAMETER LEARNING

This section covers the simplest case, where we have **complete data**. Data are complete when each data point contains values for every variable in the probability model being learned. We focus on **parameter learning**—finding the numerical parameters for a probability model whose structure is fixed. For example, we might be interested in learning the conditional probabilities in a Bayesian network with a given structure. We will also look briefly at the problem of learning structure and at nonparametric density estimation.

2.1 Maximum-likelihood parameter learning: Discrete models

Suppose we buy a bag of lime and cherry candy from a new manufacturer whose lime–cherry proportions are completely unknown; the fraction could be anywhere between 0 and 1. In that case, we have a continuum of hypotheses. The **parameter** in this case, which we call θ, is the proportion of cherry candies, and the hypothesis is h_θ. (The proportion of limes is just $1 - \theta$.) If we assume that all proportions are equally likely *a priori*, then a maximum-likelihood approach is reasonable. If we model the situation with a Bayesian network, we need just one random variable, *Flavor* (the flavor of a randomly chosen candy from the bag). It has values *cherry* and *lime*, where the probability of *cherry* is θ (see Figure 2(a)). Now suppose we unwrap N candies, of which c are cherries and $\ell = N - c$ are limes. According to Equation (3), the likelihood of this particular data set is

$$P(\mathbf{d} \mid h_\theta) = \prod_{j=1}^{N} P(d_j \mid h_\theta) = \theta^c \cdot (1-\theta)^\ell \, .$$

LOG LIKELIHOOD

The maximum-likelihood hypothesis is given by the value of θ that maximizes this expression. The same value is obtained by maximizing the **log likelihood**,

$$L(\mathbf{d} \mid h_\theta) = \log P(\mathbf{d} \mid h_\theta) = \sum_{j=1}^{N} \log P(d_j \mid h_\theta) = c \log \theta + \ell \log(1-\theta) \, .$$

(By taking logarithms, we reduce the product to a sum over the data, which is usually easier to maximize.) To find the maximum-likelihood value of θ, we differentiate L with respect to θ and set the resulting expression to zero:

$$\frac{dL(\mathbf{d} \mid h_\theta)}{d\theta} = \frac{c}{\theta} - \frac{\ell}{1-\theta} = 0 \qquad \Rightarrow \qquad \theta = \frac{c}{c+\ell} = \frac{c}{N} \, .$$

In English, then, the maximum-likelihood hypothesis h_{ML} asserts that the actual proportion of cherries in the bag is equal to the observed proportion in the candies unwrapped so far!

It appears that we have done a lot of work to discover the obvious. In fact, though, we have laid out one standard method for maximum-likelihood parameter learning, a method with broad applicability:

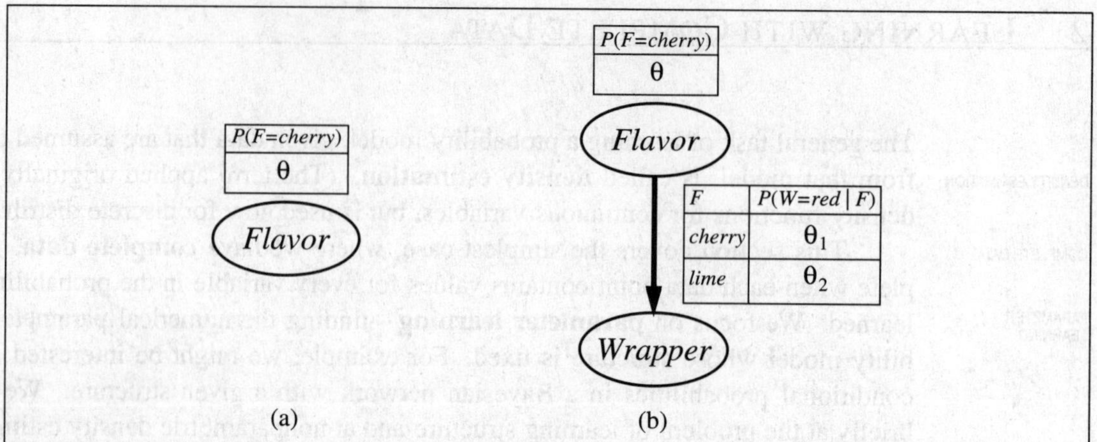

Figure 2 (a) Bayesian network model for the case of candies with an unknown proportion of cherries and limes. (b) Model for the case where the wrapper color depends (probabilistically) on the candy flavor.

1. Write down an expression for the likelihood of the data as a function of the parameter(s).
2. Write down the derivative of the log likelihood with respect to each parameter.
3. Find the parameter values such that the derivatives are zero.

The trickiest step is usually the last. In our example, it was trivial, but we will see that in many cases we need to resort to iterative solution algorithms or other numerical optimization techniques. The example also illustrates a significant problem with maximum-likelihood learning in general: *when the data set is small enough that some events have not yet been observed—for instance, no cherry candies—the maximum-likelihood hypothesis assigns zero probability to those events.* Various tricks are used to avoid this problem, such as initializing the counts for each event to 1 instead of 0.

Let us look at another example. Suppose this new candy manufacturer wants to give a little hint to the consumer and uses candy wrappers colored red and green. The *Wrapper* for each candy is selected *probabilistically*, according to some unknown conditional distribution, depending on the flavor. The corresponding probability model is shown in Figure 2(b). Notice that it has three parameters: θ, θ_1, and θ_2. With these parameters, the likelihood of seeing, say, a cherry candy in a green wrapper can be obtained from the standard semantics for Bayesian networks:

$$\begin{aligned} & P(Flavor = cherry, Wrapper = green \mid h_{\theta,\theta_1,\theta_2}) \\ &= P(Flavor = cherry \mid h_{\theta,\theta_1,\theta_2}) P(Wrapper = green \mid Flavor = cherry, h_{\theta,\theta_1,\theta_2}) \\ &= \theta \cdot (1 - \theta_1) . \end{aligned}$$

Now we unwrap N candies, of which c are cherries and ℓ are limes. The wrapper counts are as follows: r_c of the cherries have red wrappers and g_c have green, while r_ℓ of the limes have red and g_ℓ have green. The likelihood of the data is given by

$$P(\mathbf{d} \mid h_{\theta,\theta_1,\theta_2}) = \theta^c (1-\theta)^\ell \cdot \theta_1^{r_c} (1-\theta_1)^{g_c} \cdot \theta_2^{r_\ell} (1-\theta_2)^{g_\ell} .$$

This looks pretty horrible, but taking logarithms helps:

$$L = [c\log\theta + \ell\log(1-\theta)] + [r_c\log\theta_1 + g_c\log(1-\theta_1)] + [r_\ell\log\theta_2 + g_\ell\log(1-\theta_2)]\,.$$

The benefit of taking logs is clear: the log likelihood is the sum of three terms, each of which contains a single parameter. When we take derivatives with respect to each parameter and set them to zero, we get three independent equations, each containing just one parameter:

$$\begin{aligned}
\frac{\partial L}{\partial\theta} &= \frac{c}{\theta} - \frac{\ell}{1-\theta} = 0 &&\Rightarrow\quad \theta = \frac{c}{c+\ell}\\
\frac{\partial L}{\partial\theta_1} &= \frac{r_c}{\theta_1} - \frac{g_c}{1-\theta_1} = 0 &&\Rightarrow\quad \theta_1 = \frac{r_c}{r_c+g_c}\\
\frac{\partial L}{\partial\theta_2} &= \frac{r_\ell}{\theta_2} - \frac{g_\ell}{1-\theta_2} = 0 &&\Rightarrow\quad \theta_2 = \frac{r_\ell}{r_\ell+g_\ell}\,.
\end{aligned}$$

The solution for θ is the same as before. The solution for θ_1, the probability that a cherry candy has a red wrapper, is the observed fraction of cherry candies with red wrappers, and similarly for θ_2.

These results are very comforting, and it is easy to see that they can be extended to any Bayesian network whose conditional probabilities are represented as tables. The most important point is that, *with complete data, the maximum-likelihood parameter learning problem for a Bayesian network decomposes into separate learning problems, one for each parameter.* (See Exercise 6 for the nontabulated case, where each parameter affects several conditional probabilities.) The second point is that the parameter values for a variable, given its parents, are just the observed frequencies of the variable values for each setting of the parent values. As before, we must be careful to avoid zeroes when the data set is small.

2.2 Naive Bayes models

Probably the most common Bayesian network model used in machine learning is the **naive Bayes** model. In this model, the "class" variable C (which is to be predicted) is the root and the "attribute" variables X_i are the leaves. The model is "naive" because it assumes that the attributes are conditionally independent of each other, given the class. (The model in Figure 2(b) is a naive Bayes model with class *Flavor* and just one attribute, *Wrapper*.) Assuming Boolean variables, the parameters are

$$\theta = P(C = true), \theta_{i1} = P(X_i = true \mid C = true), \theta_{i2} = P(X_i = true \mid C = false).$$

The maximum-likelihood parameter values are found in exactly the same way as for Figure 2(b). Once the model has been trained in this way, it can be used to classify new examples for which the class variable C is unobserved. With observed attribute values $x_1, \ldots, x_n$, the probability of each class is given by

$$\mathbf{P}(C \mid x_1, \ldots, x_n) = \alpha\, \mathbf{P}(C) \prod_i \mathbf{P}(x_i \mid C)\,.$$

A deterministic prediction can be obtained by choosing the most likely class. Figure 3 shows the learning curve for this method when it is applied to a restaurant problem. The method learns fairly well but not as well as decision-tree learning; this is presumably because the true hypothesis—which is a decision tree—is not representable exactly using a naive Bayes model. Naive Bayes learning turns out to do surprisingly well in a wide range of applications; the boosted version (Exercise 4) is one of the most effective general-purpose learning

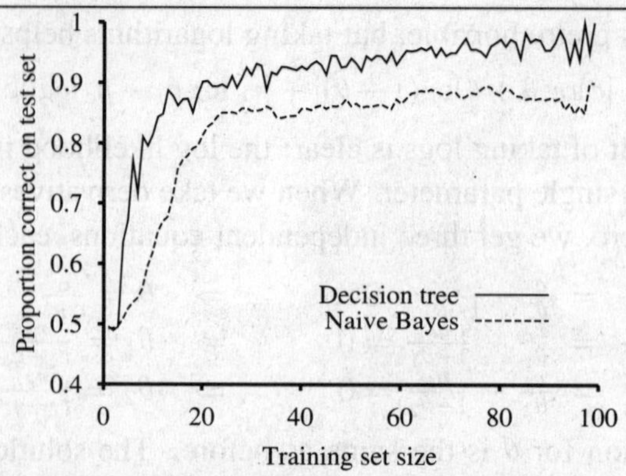

Figure 3 The learning curve for naive Bayes learning applied to the restaurant problem from the chapter "Learning from Examples"; the learning curve for decision-tree learning is shown for comparison.

algorithms. Naive Bayes learning scales well to very large problems: with n Boolean attributes, there are just $2n + 1$ parameters, and *no search is required to find* h_{ML}, *the maximum-likelihood naive Bayes hypothesis*. Finally, naive Bayes learning systems have no difficulty with noisy or missing data and can give probabilistic predictions when appropriate.

2.3 Maximum-likelihood parameter learning: Continuous models

The **linear Gaussian** model is an example of a continuous probability model. Because continuous variables are ubiquitous in real-world applications, it is important to know how to learn the parameters of continuous models from data. The principles for maximum-likelihood learning are identical in the continuous and discrete cases.

Let us begin with a very simple case: learning the parameters of a Gaussian density function on a single variable. That is, the data are generated as follows:

$$P(x) = \frac{1}{\sqrt{2\pi}\sigma} e^{-\frac{(x-\mu)^2}{2\sigma^2}} .$$

The parameters of this model are the mean μ and the standard deviation σ. (Notice that the normalizing "constant" depends on σ, so we cannot ignore it.) Let the observed values be $x_1, \ldots, x_N$. Then the log likelihood is

$$L = \sum_{j=1}^{N} \log \frac{1}{\sqrt{2\pi}\sigma} e^{-\frac{(x_j-\mu)^2}{2\sigma^2}} = N(-\log\sqrt{2\pi} - \log\sigma) - \sum_{j=1}^{N} \frac{(x_j-\mu)^2}{2\sigma^2} .$$

Setting the derivatives to zero as usual, we obtain

$$\begin{aligned} \frac{\partial L}{\partial \mu} &= -\frac{1}{\sigma^2}\textstyle\sum_{j=1}^{N}(x_j-\mu) = 0 & \Rightarrow \quad \mu &= \frac{\sum_j x_j}{N} \\ \frac{\partial L}{\partial \sigma} &= -\frac{N}{\sigma} + \frac{1}{\sigma^3}\textstyle\sum_{j=1}^{N}(x_j-\mu)^2 = 0 & \Rightarrow \quad \sigma &= \sqrt{\frac{\sum_j (x_j-\mu)^2}{N}} . \end{aligned} \tag{4}$$

That is, the maximum-likelihood value of the mean is the sample average and the maximum-likelihood value of the standard deviation is the square root of the sample variance. Again, these are comforting results that confirm "commonsense" practice.

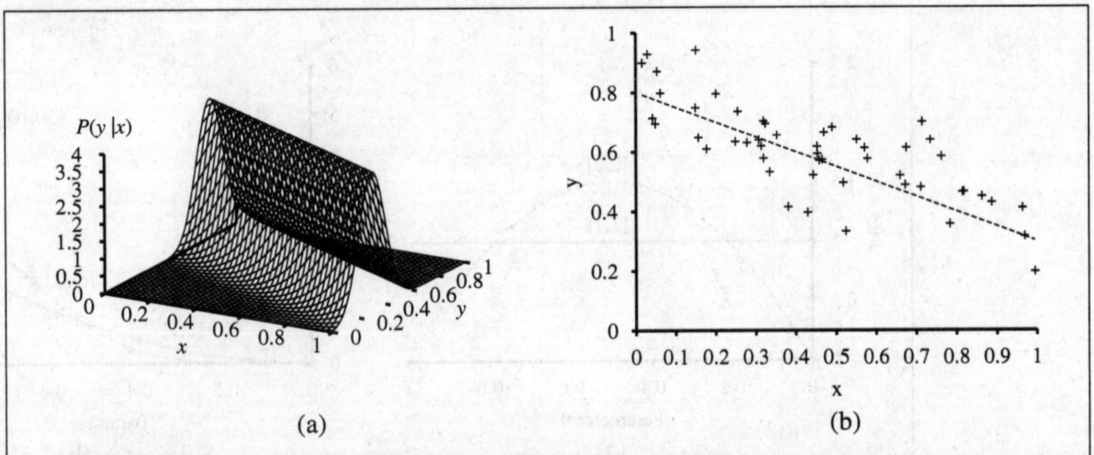

Figure 4 (a) A linear Gaussian model described as $y=\theta_1 x+\theta_2$ plus Gaussian noise with fixed variance. (b) A set of 50 data points generated from this model.

Now consider a linear Gaussian model with one continuous parent X and a continuous child Y. Y has a Gaussian distribution whose mean depends linearly on the value of X and whose standard deviation is fixed. To learn the conditional distribution $P(Y \mid X)$, we can maximize the conditional likelihood

$$P(y \mid x)=\frac{1}{\sqrt{2\pi}\sigma}e^{-\frac{(y-(\theta_1 x+\theta_2))^2}{2\sigma^2}}. \tag{5}$$

Here, the parameters are θ_1, θ_2, and σ. The data are a collection of (x_j, y_j) pairs, as illustrated in Figure 4. Using the usual methods (Exercise 5), we can find the maximum-likelihood values of the parameters. The point here is different. If we consider just the parameters θ_1 and θ_2 that define the linear relationship between x and y, it becomes clear that maximizing the log likelihood with respect to these parameters is the same as *minimizing* the numerator $(y-(\theta_1 x+\theta_2))^2$ in the exponent of Equation (5). This is the L_2 loss, the squared error between the actual value y and the prediction $\theta_1 x+\theta_2$. This is the quantity minimized by the standard **linear regression** procedure. Now we can understand why: minimizing the sum of squared errors gives the maximum-likelihood straight-line model, *provided that the data are generated with Gaussian noise of fixed variance.*

2.4 Bayesian parameter learning

Maximum-likelihood learning gives rise to some very simple procedures, but it has some serious deficiencies with small data sets. For example, after seeing one cherry candy, the maximum-likelihood hypothesis is that the bag is 100% cherry (i.e., $\theta=1.0$). Unless one's hypothesis prior is that bags must be either all cherry or all lime, this is not a reasonable conclusion. It is more likely that the bag is a mixture of lime and cherry. The Bayesian approach to parameter learning starts by defining a prior probability distribution over the possible hypotheses. We call this the **hypothesis prior**. Then, as data arrives, the posterior probability distribution is updated.

HYPOTHESIS PRIOR

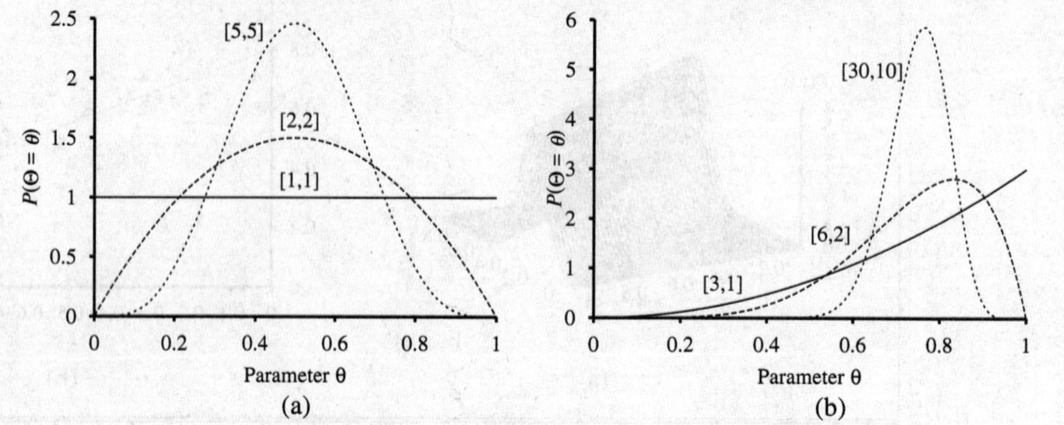

Figure 5 Examples of the beta$[a, b]$ distribution for different values of $[a, b]$.

The candy example in Figure 2(a) has one parameter, θ: the probability that a randomly selected piece of candy is cherry-flavored. In the Bayesian view, θ is the (unknown) value of a random variable Θ that defines the hypothesis space; the hypothesis prior is just the prior distribution $\mathbf{P}(\Theta)$. Thus, $P(\Theta = \theta)$ is the prior probability that the bag has a fraction θ of cherry candies.

If the parameter θ can be any value between 0 and 1, then $\mathbf{P}(\Theta)$ must be a continuous distribution that is nonzero only between 0 and 1 and that integrates to 1. The uniform density $P(\theta) = Uniform[0, 1](\theta)$ is one candidate. It turns out that the uniform density is a member of the family of **beta distributions**. Each beta distribution is defined by two **hyperparameters**[3] a and b such that

BETA DISTRIBUTION

HYPERPARAMETER

$$\text{beta}[a, b](\theta) = \alpha\, \theta^{a-1}(1-\theta)^{b-1}, \tag{6}$$

for θ in the range $[0, 1]$. The normalization constant α, which makes the distribution integrate to 1, depends on a and b. (See Exercise 7.) Figure 5 shows what the distribution looks like for various values of a and b. The mean value of the distribution is $a/(a+b)$, so larger values of a suggest a belief that Θ is closer to 1 than to 0. Larger values of $a + b$ make the distribution more peaked, suggesting greater certainty about the value of Θ. Thus, the beta family provides a useful range of possibilities for the hypothesis prior.

Besides its flexibility, the beta family has another wonderful property: if Θ has a prior beta$[a, b]$, then, after a data point is observed, the posterior distribution for Θ is also a beta distribution. In other words, beta is closed under update. The beta family is called the **conjugate prior** for the family of distributions for a Boolean variable.[4] Let's see how this works. Suppose we observe a cherry candy; then we have

CONJUGATE PRIOR

[3] They are called hyperparameters because they parameterize a distribution over θ, which is itself a parameter.

[4] Other conjugate priors include the **Dirichlet** family for the parameters of a discrete multivalued distribution and the **Normal–Wishart** family for the parameters of a Gaussian distribution. See Bernardo and Smith (1994).

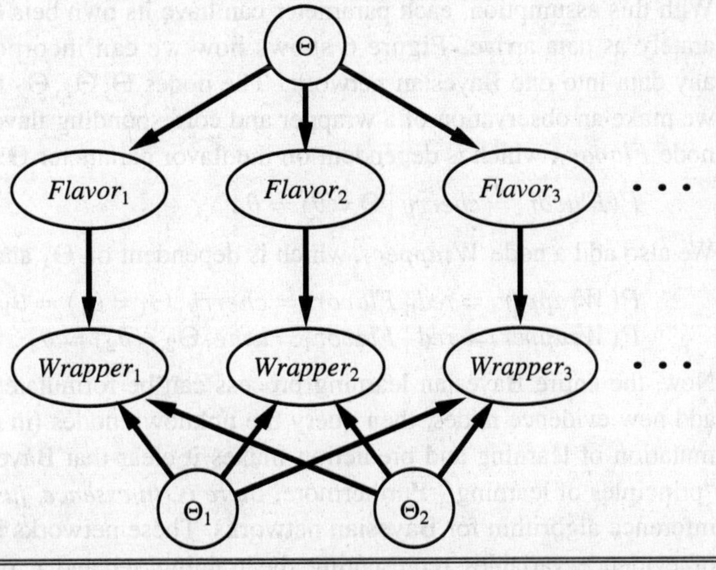

Figure 6 A Bayesian network that corresponds to a Bayesian learning process. Posterior distributions for the parameter variables Θ, Θ_1, and Θ_2 can be inferred from their prior distributions and the evidence in the $Flavor_i$ and $Wrapper_i$ variables.

$$\begin{aligned} P(\theta \mid D_1 = cherry) &= \alpha\, P(D_1 = cherry \mid \theta) P(\theta) \\ &= \alpha'\, \theta \cdot \text{beta}[a,b](\theta) = \alpha'\, \theta \cdot \theta^{a-1}(1-\theta)^{b-1} \\ &= \alpha'\, \theta^{a}(1-\theta)^{b-1} = \text{beta}[a+1,b](\theta)\,. \end{aligned}$$

Thus, after seeing a cherry candy, we simply increment the a parameter to get the posterior; similarly, after seeing a lime candy, we increment the b parameter. Thus, we can view the a and b hyperparameters as **virtual counts**, in the sense that a prior beta$[a, b]$ behaves exactly as if we had started out with a uniform prior beta$[1, 1]$ and seen $a - 1$ actual cherry candies and $b - 1$ actual lime candies.

VIRTUAL COUNTS

By examining a sequence of beta distributions for increasing values of a and b, keeping the proportions fixed, we can see vividly how the posterior distribution over the parameter Θ changes as data arrive. For example, suppose the actual bag of candy is 75% cherry. Figure 5(b) shows the sequence beta$[3, 1]$, beta$[6, 2]$, beta$[30, 10]$. Clearly, the distribution is converging to a narrow peak around the true value of Θ. For large data sets, then, Bayesian learning (at least in this case) converges to the same answer as maximum-likelihood learning.

Now let us consider a more complicated case. The network in Figure 2(b) has three parameters, θ, θ_1, and θ_2, where θ_1 is the probability of a red wrapper on a cherry candy and θ_2 is the probability of a red wrapper on a lime candy. The Bayesian hypothesis prior must cover all three parameters—that is, we need to specify $\mathbf{P}(\Theta, \Theta_1, \Theta_2)$. Usually, we assume **parameter independence**:

PARAMETER INDEPENDENCE

$$\mathbf{P}(\Theta, \Theta_1, \Theta_2) = \mathbf{P}(\Theta)\mathbf{P}(\Theta_1)\mathbf{P}(\Theta_2)\,.$$

With this assumption, each parameter can have its own beta distribution that is updated separately as data arrive. Figure 6 shows how we can incorporate the hypothesis prior and any data into one Bayesian network. The nodes $\Theta, \Theta_1, \Theta_2$ have no parents. But each time we make an observation of a wrapper and corresponding flavor of a piece of candy, we add a node $Flavor_i$, which is dependent on the flavor parameter Θ:

$$P(Flavor_i = cherry \mid \Theta = \theta) = \theta \, .$$

We also add a node $Wrapper_i$, which is dependent on Θ_1 and Θ_2:

$$P(Wrapper_i = red \mid Flavor_i = cherry, \Theta_1 = \theta_1) = \theta_1$$
$$P(Wrapper_i = red \mid Flavor_i = lime, \Theta_2 = \theta_2) = \theta_2 \, .$$

Now, the entire Bayesian learning process can be formulated as an *inference* problem. We add new evidence nodes, then query the unknown nodes (in this case, $\Theta, \Theta_1, \Theta_2$). This formulation of learning and prediction makes it clear that Bayesian learning requires no extra "principles of learning." Furthermore, *there is, in essence, just one learning algorithm* —the inference algorithm for Bayesian networks. These networks have a potentially huge number of evidence variables representing the training set and a prevalence of continuous-valued parameter variables.

2.5 Learning Bayes net structures

So far, we have assumed that the structure of the Bayes net is given and we are just trying to learn the parameters. The structure of the network represents basic causal knowledge about the domain that is often easy for an expert, or even a naive user, to supply. In some cases, however, the causal model may be unavailable or subject to dispute—for example, certain corporations have long claimed that smoking does not cause cancer—so it is important to understand how the structure of a Bayes net can be learned from data. This section gives a brief sketch of the main ideas.

The most obvious approach is to *search* for a good model. We can start with a model containing no links and begin adding parents for each node, fitting the parameters with the methods we have just covered and measuring the accuracy of the resulting model. Alternatively, we can start with an initial guess at the structure and use hill-climbing or simulated annealing search to make modifications, retuning the parameters after each change in the structure. Modifications can include reversing, adding, or deleting links. We must not introduce cycles in the process, so many algorithms assume that an ordering is given for the variables, and that a node can have parents only among those nodes that come earlier in the ordering. For full generality, we also need to search over possible orderings.

There are two alternative methods for deciding when a good structure has been found. The first is to test whether the conditional independence assertions implicit in the structure are actually satisfied in the data. For example, the use of a naive Bayes model for the restaurant problem assumes that

$$\mathbf{P}(Fri/Sat, Bar \mid WillWait) = \mathbf{P}(Fri/Sat \mid WillWait)\mathbf{P}(Bar \mid WillWait)$$

and we can check in the data that the same equation holds between the corresponding conditional frequencies. But even if the structure describes the true causal nature of the domain, statistical fluctuations in the data set mean that the equation will never be satisfied *exactly*, so we need to perform a suitable statistical test to see if there is sufficient evidence that the independence hypothesis is violated. The complexity of the resulting network will depend on the threshold used for this test—the stricter the independence test, the more links will be added and the greater the danger of overfitting.

An approach more consistent with the ideas in this chapter is to assess the degree to which the proposed model explains the data (in a probabilistic sense). We must be careful how we measure this, however. If we just try to find the maximum-likelihood hypothesis, we will end up with a fully connected network, because adding more parents to a node cannot decrease the likelihood (Exercise 8). We are forced to penalize model complexity in some way. The MAP (or MDL) approach simply subtracts a penalty from the likelihood of each structure (after parameter tuning) before comparing different structures. The Bayesian approach places a joint prior over structures and parameters. There are usually far too many structures to sum over (superexponential in the number of variables), so most practitioners use MCMC to sample over structures.

Penalizing complexity (whether by MAP or Bayesian methods) introduces an important connection between the optimal structure and the nature of the representation for the conditional distributions in the network. With tabular distributions, the complexity penalty for a node's distribution grows exponentially with the number of parents, but with, say, noisy-OR distributions, it grows only linearly. This means that learning with noisy-OR (or other compactly parameterized) models tends to produce learned structures with more parents than does learning with tabular distributions.

2.6 Density estimation with nonparametric models

NONPARAMETRIC DENSITY ESTIMATION

It is possible to learn a probability model without making any assumptions about its structure and parameterization by adopting certain nonparametric methods. The task of **nonparametric density estimation** is typically done in continuous domains, such as that shown in Figure 7(a). The figure shows a probability density function on a space defined by two continuous variables. In Figure 7(b) we see a sample of data points from this density function. The question is, can we recover the model from the samples?

First we will consider k-**nearest-neighbors** models. (Here we see nearest-neighbor models for density estimation.) Given a sample of data points, to estimate the unknown probability density at a query point **x** we can simply measure the density of the data points in the neighborhood of **x**. Figure 7(b) shows two query points (small squares). For each query point we have drawn the smallest circle that encloses 10 neighbors—the 10-nearest-neighborhood. We can see that the central circle is large, meaning there is a low density there, and the circle on the right is small, meaning there is a high density there. In Figure 8 we show three plots of density estima-tion using k-nearest-neighbors, for different values of k. It seems clear that (b) is about right, while (a) is too spiky (k is too small) and (c) is too smooth (k is too big).

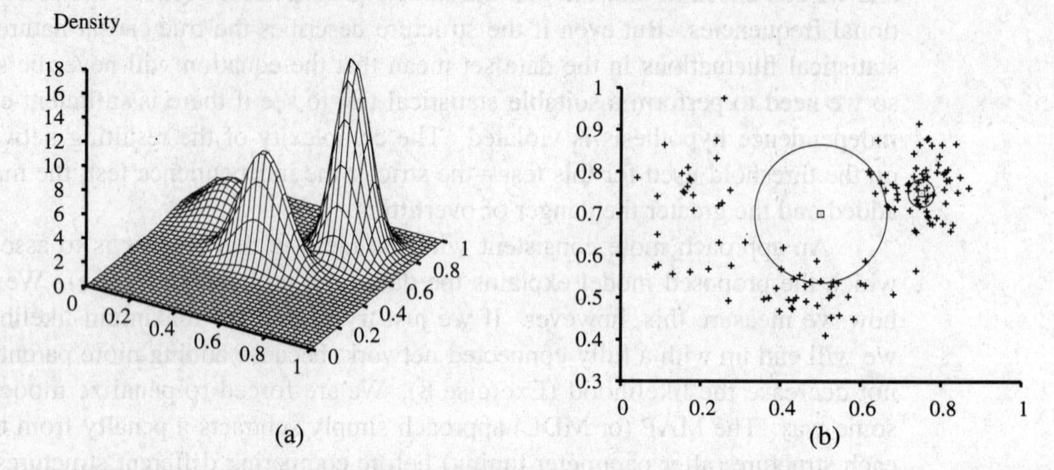

Figure 7 (a) A 3D plot of the mixture of Gaussians from Figure 11(a). (b) A 128-point sample of points from the mixture, together with two query points (small squares) and their 10-nearest-neighborhoods (medium and large circles).

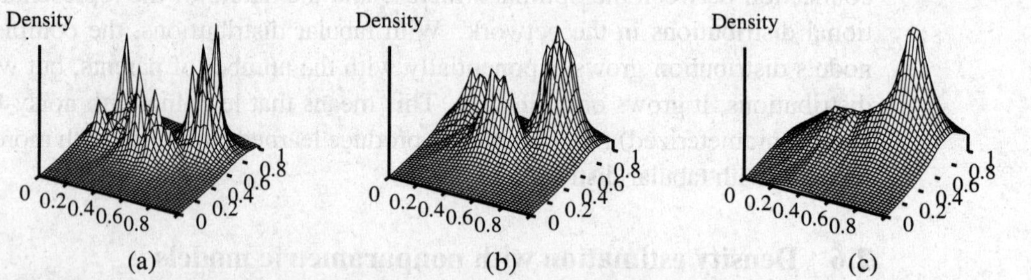

Figure 8 Density estimation using k-nearest-neighbors, applied to the data in Figure 7(b), for $k = 3$, 10, and 40 respectively. $k = 3$ is too spiky, 40 is too smooth, and 10 is just about right. The best value for k can be chosen by cross-validation.

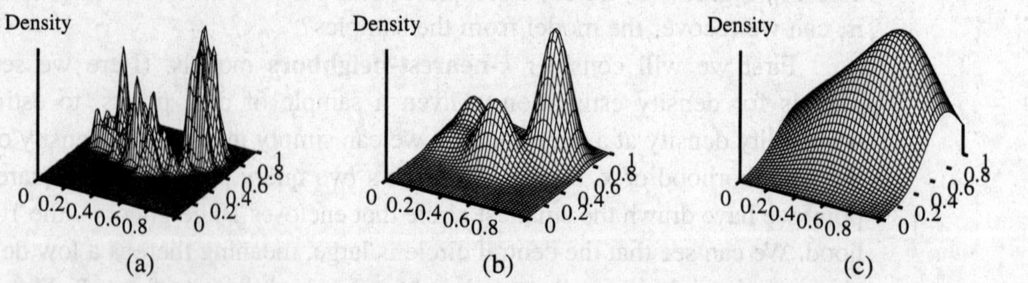

Figure 9 Kernel density estimation for the data in Figure 7(b), using Gaussian kernels with $w = 0.02$, 0.07, and 0.20 respectively. $w = 0.07$ is about right.

Another possibility is to use **kernel functions**, as we did for locally weighted regression. To apply a kernel model to density estimation, assume that each data point generates its own little density function, using a Gaussian kernel. The estimated density at a query point **x** is then the average density as given by each kernel function:

$$P(\mathbf{x}) = \frac{1}{N}\sum_{j=1}^{N} \mathcal{K}(\mathbf{x}, \mathbf{x}_j) .$$

We will assume spherical Gaussians with standard deviation w along each axis:

$$\mathcal{K}(\mathbf{x}, \mathbf{x}_j) = \frac{1}{(w^2\sqrt{2\pi})^d} e^{-\frac{D(\mathbf{x},\mathbf{x}_j)^2}{2w^2}} ,$$

where d is the number of dimensions in **x** and D is the Euclidean distance function. We still have the problem of choosing a suitable value for kernel width w; Figure 9 shows values that are too small, just right, and too large. A good value of w can be chosen by using cross-validation.

3 LEARNING WITH HIDDEN VARIABLES: THE EM ALGORITHM

The preceding section dealt with the fully observable case. Many real-world problems have

LATENT VARIABLE

hidden variables (sometimes called **latent variables**), which are not observable in the data that are available for learning. For example, medical records often include the observed symptoms, the physician's diagnosis, the treatment applied, and perhaps the outcome of the treatment, but they seldom contain a direct observation of the disease itself! (Note that the *diagnosis* is not the *disease*; it is a causal consequence of the observed symptoms, which are in turn caused by the disease.) One might ask, "If the disease is not observed, why not construct a model without it?" The answer appears in Figure 10, which shows a small, fictitious diagnostic model for heart disease. There are three observable predisposing factors and three observable symptoms (which are too depressing to name). Assume that each variable has three possible values (e.g., *none*, *moderate*, and *severe*). Removing the hidden variable from the network in (a) yields the network in (b); the total number of parameters increases from 78 to 708. Thus, *latent variables can dramatically reduce the number of parameters required to specify a Bayesian network.* This, in turn, can dramatically reduce the amount of data needed to learn the parameters.

Hidden variables are important, but they do complicate the learning problem. In Figure 10(a), for example, it is not obvious how to learn the conditional distribution for $HeartDisease$, given its parents, because we do not know the value of $HeartDisease$ in each case; the same problem arises in learning the distributions for the symptoms. This section

EXPECTATION–MAXIMIZATION

describes an algorithm called **expectation–maximization**, or EM, that solves this problem in a very general way. We will show three examples and then provide a general description. The algorithm seems like magic at first, but once the intuition has been developed, one can find applications for EM in a huge range of learning problems.

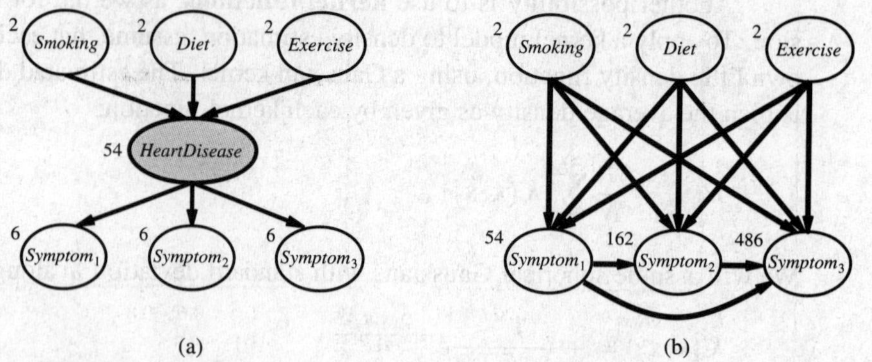

Figure 10 (a) A simple diagnostic network for heart disease, which is assumed to be a hidden variable. Each variable has three possible values and is labeled with the number of independent parameters in its conditional distribution; the total number is 78. (b) The equivalent network with *HeartDisease* removed. Note that the symptom variables are no longer conditionally independent given their parents. This network requires 708 parameters.

3.1 Unsupervised clustering: Learning mixtures of Gaussians

UNSUPERVISED CLUSTERING

Unsupervised clustering is the problem of discerning multiple categories in a collection of objects. The problem is unsupervised because the category labels are not given. For example, suppose we record the spectra of a hundred thousand stars; are there different *types* of stars revealed by the spectra, and, if so, how many types and what are their characteristics? We are all familiar with terms such as "red giant" and "white dwarf," but the stars do not carry these labels on their hats—astronomers had to perform unsupervised clustering to identify these categories. Other examples include the identification of species, genera, orders, and so on in the Linnæan taxonomy and the creation of natural kinds for ordinary objects.

Unsupervised clustering begins with data. Figure 11(b) shows 500 data points, each of which specifies the values of two continuous attributes. The data points might correspond to stars, and the attributes might correspond to spectral intensities at two particular frequencies. Next, we need to understand what kind of probability distribution might have generated the data. Clustering presumes that the data are generated from a **mixture distribution**, P. Such a distribution has k **components**, each of which is a distribution in its own right. A data point is generated by first choosing a component and then generating a sample from that component. Let the random variable C denote the component, with values $1, \ldots, k$; then the mixture distribution is given by

MIXTURE DISTRIBUTION

COMPONENT

$$P(\mathbf{x}) = \sum_{i=1}^{k} P(C=i)\, P(\mathbf{x} \mid C=i)\,,$$

where $\mathbf{x}$ refers to the values of the attributes for a data point. For continuous data, a natural choice for the component distributions is the multivariate Gaussian, which gives the so-called **mixture of Gaussians** family of distributions. The parameters of a mixture of Gaussians are

MIXTURE OF GAUSSIANS

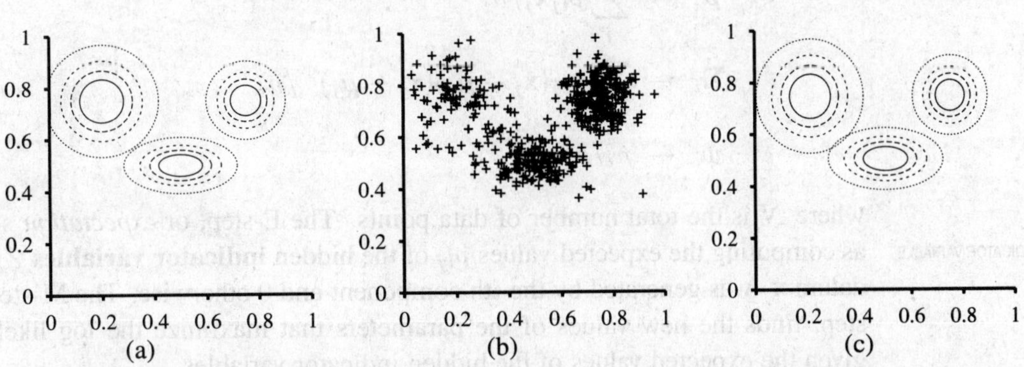

Figure 11 (a) A Gaussian mixture model with three components; the weights (left-to-right) are 0.2, 0.3, and 0.5. (b) 500 data points sampled from the model in (a). (c) The model reconstructed by EM from the data in (b).

$w_i = P(C=i)$ (the weight of each component), $\boldsymbol{\mu}_i$ (the mean of each component), and $\boldsymbol{\Sigma}_i$ (the covariance of each component). Figure 11(a) shows a mixture of three Gaussians; this mixture is in fact the source of the data in (b) as well as being the model shown in Figure 7(a).

The unsupervised clustering problem, then, is to recover a mixture model like the one in Figure 11(a) from raw data like that in Figure 11(b). Clearly, if we *knew* which component generated each data point, then it would be easy to recover the component Gaussians: we could just select all the data points from a given component and then apply (a multivariate version of) Equation (4) for fitting the parameters of a Gaussian to a set of data. On the other hand, if we *knew* the parameters of each component, then we could, at least in a probabilistic sense, assign each data point to a component. The problem is that we know neither the assignments nor the parameters.

The basic idea of EM in this context is to *pretend* that we know the parameters of the model and then to infer the probability that each data point belongs to each component. After that, we refit the components to the data, where each component is fitted to the entire data set with each point weighted by the probability that it belongs to that component. The process iterates until convergence. Essentially, we are "completing" the data by inferring probability distributions over the hidden variables—which component each data point belongs to—based on the current model. For the mixture of Gaussians, we initialize the mixture-model parameters arbitrarily and then iterate the following two steps:

1. **E-step**: Compute the probabilities $p_{ij} = P(C=i \mid \mathbf{x}_j)$, the probability that datum $\mathbf{x}_j$ was generated by component i. By Bayes' rule, we have $p_{ij} = \alpha P(\mathbf{x}_j \mid C=i)P(C=i)$. The term $P(\mathbf{x}_j \mid C=i)$ is just the probability at $\mathbf{x}_j$ of the ith Gaussian, and the term $P(C=i)$ is just the weight parameter for the ith Gaussian. Define $n_i = \sum_j p_{ij}$, the effective number of data points currently assigned to component i.
2. **M-step**: Compute the new mean, covariance, and component weights using the following steps in sequence:

$$\boldsymbol{\mu}_i \leftarrow \sum_j p_{ij}\mathbf{x}_j/n_i$$

$$\boldsymbol{\Sigma}_i \leftarrow \sum_j p_{ij}(\mathbf{x}_j - \boldsymbol{\mu}_i)(\mathbf{x}_j - \boldsymbol{\mu}_i)^\top/n_i$$

$$w_i \leftarrow n_i/N$$

where N is the total number of data points. The E-step, or *expectation* step, can be viewed as computing the expected values p_{ij} of the hidden **indicator variables** Z_{ij}, where Z_{ij} is 1 if datum $\mathbf{x}_j$ was generated by the ith component and 0 otherwise. The M-step, or *maximization* step, finds the new values of the parameters that maximize the log likelihood of the data, given the expected values of the hidden indicator variables.

INDICATOR VARIABLE

The final model that EM learns when it is applied to the data in Figure 11(a) is shown in Figure 11(c); it is virtually indistinguishable from the original model from which the data were generated. Figure 12(a) plots the log likelihood of the data according to the current model as EM progresses.

There are two points to notice. First, the log likelihood for the final learned model slightly *exceeds* that of the original model, from which the data were generated. This might seem surprising, but it simply reflects the fact that the data were generated randomly and might not provide an exact reflection of the underlying model. The second point is that *EM increases the log likelihood of the data at every iteration.* This fact can be proved in general. Furthermore, under certain conditions (that hold in ost cases), EM can be proven to reach a local maximum in likelihood. (In rare cases, it could reach a saddle point or even a local minimum.) In this sense, EM resembles a gradient-based hill-climbing algorithm, but notice that it has no "step size" parameter.

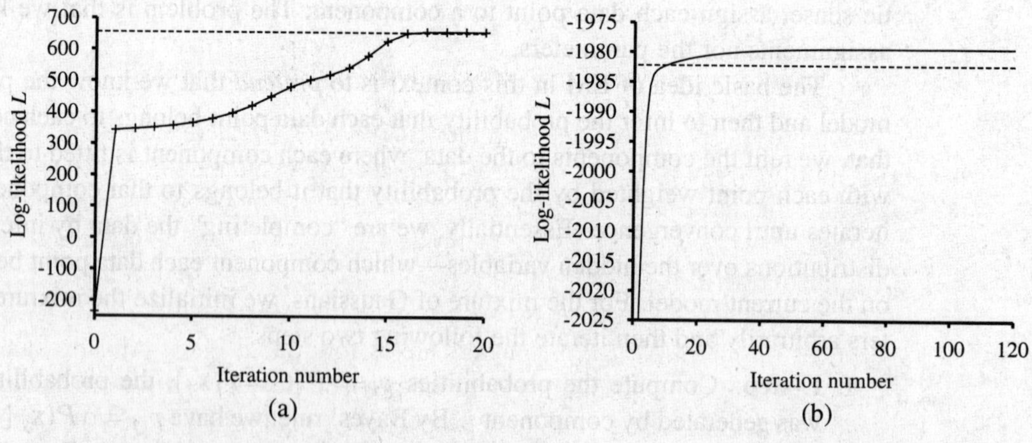

Figure 12 Graphs showing the log likelihood of the data, L, as a function of the EM iteration. The horizontal line shows the log likelihood according to the true model. (a) Graph for the Gaussian mixture model in Figure 11. (b) Graph for the Bayesian network in Figure 13(a).

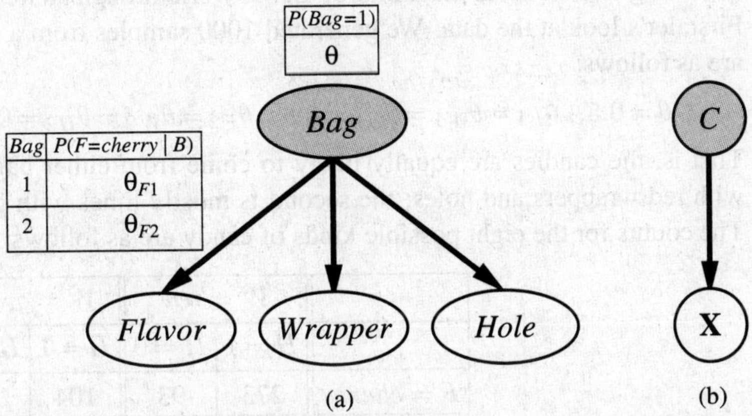

Figure 13 (a) A mixture model for candy. The proportions of different flavors, wrappers, presence of holes depend on the bag, which is not observed. (b) Bayesian network for a Gaussian mixture. The mean and covariance of the observable variables **X** depend on the component C.

Things do not always go as well as Figure 12(a) might suggest. It can happen, for example, that one Gaussian component shrinks so that it covers just a single data point. Then its variance will go to zero and its likelihood will go to infinity! Another problem is that two components can "merge," acquiring identical means and variances and sharing their data points. These kinds of degenerate local maxima are serious problems, especially in high dimensions. One solution is to place priors on the model parameters and to apply the MAP version of EM. Another is to restart a component with new random parameters if it gets too small or too close to another component. Sensible initialization also helps.

3.2 Learning Bayesian networks with hidden variables

To learn a Bayesian network with hidden variables, we apply the same insights that worked for mixtures of Gaussians. Figure 13 represents a situation in which there are two bags of candies that have been mixed together. Candies are described by three features: in addition to the *Flavor* and the *Wrapper*, some candies have a *Hole* in the middle and some do not. The distribution of candies in each bag is described by a **naive Bayes** model: the features are independent, given the bag, but the conditional probability distribution for each feature depends on the bag. The parameters are as follows: θ is the prior probability that a candy comes from Bag 1; θ_{F1} and θ_{F2} are the probabilities that the flavor is cherry, given that the candy comes from Bag 1 or Bag 2 respectively; θ_{W1} and θ_{W2} give the probabilities that the wrapper is red; and θ_{H1} and θ_{H2} give the probabilities that the candy has a hole. Notice that the overall model is a mixture model. (In fact, we can also model the mixture of Gaussians as a Bayesian network, as shown in Figure 13(b).) In the figure, the bag is a hidden variable because, once the candies have been mixed together, we no longer know which bag each candy came from. In such a case, can we recover the descriptions of the two bags by observing candies from the mixture? Let us work through an iteration of EM for this problem. First, let's look at the data. We generated 1000 samples from a model whose true parameters are as follows:

$$\theta = 0.5,\ \ \theta_{F1} = \theta_{W1} = \theta_{H1} = 0.8,\ \ \theta_{F2} = \theta_{W2} = \theta_{H2} = 0.3\ . \tag{7}$$

That is, the candies are equally likely to come from either bag; the first is mostly cherries with red wrappers and holes; the second is mostly limes with green wrappers and no holes. The counts for the eight possible kinds of candy are as follows:

	$W = red$		$W = green$	
	$H = 1$	$H = 0$	$H = 1$	$H = 0$
$F = cherry$	273	93	104	90
$F = lime$	79	100	94	167

We start by initializing the parameters. For numerical simplicity, we arbitrarily choose[5]

$$\theta^{(0)} = 0.6,\ \ \theta^{(0)}_{F1} = \theta^{(0)}_{W1} = \theta^{(0)}_{H1} = 0.6,\ \ \theta^{(0)}_{F2} = \theta^{(0)}_{W2} = \theta^{(0)}_{H2} = 0.4\ . \tag{8}$$

First, let us work on the θ parameter. In the fully observable case, we would estimate this directly from the *observed* counts of candies from bags 1 and 2. Because the bag is a hidden variable, we calculate the *expected* counts instead. The expected count $\hat{N}(Bag = 1)$ is the sum, over all candies, of the probability that the candy came from bag 1:

$$\theta^{(1)} = \hat{N}(Bag = 1)/N = \sum_{j=1}^{N} P(Bag = 1 \mid flavor_j, wrapper_j, holes_j)/N\ .$$

These probabilities can be computed by any inference algorithm for Bayesian networks. For a naive Bayes model such as the one in our example, we can do the inference "by hand," using Bayes' rule and applying conditional independence:

$$\theta^{(1)} = \frac{1}{N} \sum_{j=1}^{N} \frac{P(flavor_j \mid Bag=1) P(wrapper_j \mid Bag=1) P(holes_j \mid Bag=1) P(Bag=1)}{\sum_i P(flavor_j \mid Bag=i) P(wrapper_j \mid Bag=i) P(holes_j \mid Bag=i) P(Bag=i)}\ .$$

Applying this formula to, say, the 273 red-wrapped cherry candies with holes, we get a contribution of

$$\frac{273}{1000} \cdot \frac{\theta^{(0)}_{F1}\theta^{(0)}_{W1}\theta^{(0)}_{H1}\theta^{(0)}}{\theta^{(0)}_{F1}\theta^{(0)}_{W1}\theta^{(0)}_{H1}\theta^{(0)} + \theta^{(0)}_{F2}\theta^{(0)}_{W2}\theta^{(0)}_{H2}(1 - \theta^{(0)})} \approx 0.22797\ .$$

Continuing with the other seven kinds of candy in the table of counts, we obtain $\theta^{(1)} = 0.6124$.

Now let us consider the other parameters, such as θ_{F1}. In the fully observable case, we would estimate this directly from the *observed* counts of cherry and lime candies from bag 1. The *expected* count of cherry candies from bag 1 is given by

$$\sum_{j: Flavor_j = cherry} P(Bag = 1 \mid Flavor_j = cherry, wrapper_j, holes_j)\ .$$

[5] It is better in practice to choose them randomly, to avoid local maxima due to symmetry.

Again, these probabilities can be calculated by any Bayes net algorithm. Completing this process, we obtain the new values of all the parameters:

$$\begin{aligned}&\theta^{(1)}=0.6124,\ \theta_{F1}^{(1)}=0.6684,\ \theta_{W1}^{(1)}=0.6483,\ \theta_{H1}^{(1)}=0.6558,\\&\theta_{F2}^{(1)}=0.3887,\theta_{W2}^{(1)}=0.3817,\ \theta_{H2}^{(1)}=0.3827\ .\end{aligned} \tag{9}$$

The log likelihood of the data increases from about -2044 initially to about -2021 after the first iteration, as shown in Figure 12(b). That is, the update improves the likelihood itself by a factor of about $e^{23} \approx 10^{10}$. By the tenth iteration, the learned model is a better fit than the original model ($L= - 1982.214$). Thereafter, progress becomes very slow. This is not uncommon with EM, and many practical systems combine EM with a gradient-based algorithm such as Newton–Raphson for the last phase of learning.

The general lesson from this example is that *the parameter updates for Bayesian network learning with hidden variables are directly available from the results of inference on each example. Moreover, only* local *posterior probabilities are needed for each parameter.* Here, "local" means that the CPT for each variable X_i can be learned from posterior probabilities involving just X_i and its parents $\mathbf{U}_i$. Defining θ_{ijk} to be the CPT parameter $P(X_i = x_{ij} \mid \mathbf{U}_i = \mathbf{u}_{ik})$, the update is given by the normalized expected counts as follows:

$$\theta_{ijk} \leftarrow \hat{N}(X_i = x_{ij}, \mathbf{U}_i = \mathbf{u}_{ik}) / \hat{N}(\mathbf{U}_i = \mathbf{u}_{ik})\ .$$

The expected counts are obtained by summing over the examples, computing the probabilities $P(X_i = x_{ij}, \mathbf{U}_i = \mathbf{u}_{ik})$ for each by using any Bayes net inference algorithm. For the exact algorithms—including variable elimination—all these probabilities are obtainable directly as a by-product of standard inference, with no need for extra computations specific to learning. Moreover, the information needed for learning is available *locally* for each parameter.

3.3 Learning hidden Markov models

Our final application of EM involves learning the transition probabilities in hidden Markov models (HMMs). A hidden Markov model can be represented by a dynamic Bayes net with a single discrete state variable, as illustrated in Figure 14. Each data point consists of an observation *sequence* of finite length, so the problem is to learn the transition probabilities from a set of observation sequences (or from just one long sequence).

We have already worked out how to learn Bayes nets, but there is one complication: in Bayes nets, each parameter is distinct; in a hidden Markov model, on the other hand, the individual transition probabilities from state i to state j at time t, $\theta_{ijt} = P(X_{t+1} = j \mid X_t = i)$, are *repeated* across time—that is, $\theta_{ijt} = \theta_{ij}$ for all t. To estimate the transition probability from state i to state j, we simply calculate the expected proportion of times that the system undergoes a transition to state j when in state i:

$$\theta_{ij} \leftarrow \sum_t \hat{N}(X_{t+1} = j, X_t = i) / \sum_t \hat{N}(X_t = i)\ .$$

The expected counts are computed by an HMM inference algorithm. The **forward–backward** algorithm can be modified very easily to compute the necessary probabilities. One important point is that the probabilities required are obtained by **smoothing** rather than **filtering**; that is,

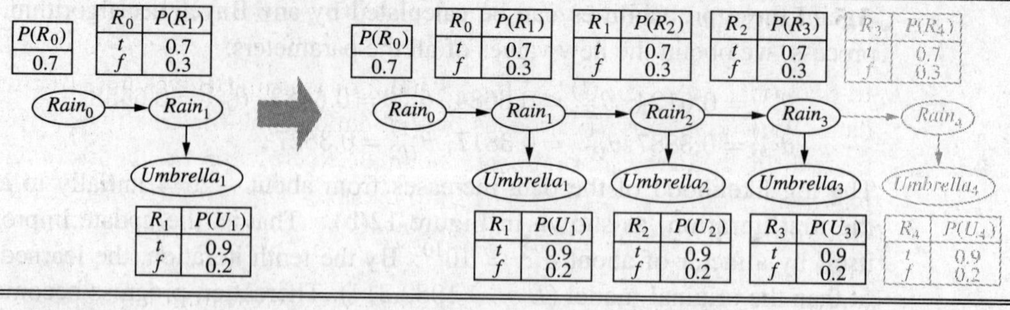

Figure 14 An unrolled dynamic Bayesian network that represents a hidden Markov model.

we need to pay attention to subsequent evidence in estimating the probability that a particular transition occurred. The evidence in a murder case is usually obtained *after* the crime (i.e., the transition from state i to state j) has taken place.

3.4 The general form of the EM algorithm

We have seen several instances of the EM algorithm. Each involves computing expected values of hidden variables for each example and then recomputing the parameters, using the expected values as if they were observed values. Let $\mathbf{x}$ be all the observed values in all the examples, let $\mathbf{Z}$ denote all the hidden variables for all the examples, and let $\boldsymbol{\theta}$ be all the parameters for the probability model. Then the EM algorithm is

$$\boldsymbol{\theta}^{(i+1)} = \operatorname*{argmax}_{\boldsymbol{\theta}} \sum_{\mathbf{z}} P(\mathbf{Z}=\mathbf{z} \mid \mathbf{x}, \boldsymbol{\theta}^{(i)}) L(\mathbf{x}, \mathbf{Z}=\mathbf{z} \mid \boldsymbol{\theta}) .$$

This equation is the EM algorithm in a nutshell. The E-step is the computation of the summation, which is the expectation of the log likelihood of the "completed" data with respect to the distribution $P(\mathbf{Z}=\mathbf{z} \mid \mathbf{x}, \boldsymbol{\theta}^{(i)})$, which is the posterior over the hidden variables, given the data. The M-step is the maximization of this expected log likelihood with respect to the parameters. For mixtures of Gaussians, the hidden variables are the Z_{ij}s, where Z_{ij} is 1 if example j was generated by component i. For Bayes nets, Z_{ij} is the value of unobserved variable X_i in example j. For HMMs, Z_{jt} is the state of the sequence in example j at time t. Starting from the general form, it is possible to derive an EM algorithm for a specific application once the appropriate hidden variables have been identified.

As soon as we understand the general idea of EM, it becomes easy to derive all sorts of variants and improvements. For example, in many cases the E-step—the computation of posteriors over the hidden variables—is intractable, as in large Bayes nets. It turns out that one can use an *approximate* E-step and still obtain an effective learning algorithm. With a sampling algorithm such as MCMC, the learning process is very intuitive: each state (configuration of hidden and observed variables) visited by MCMC is treated exactly as if it were a complete observation. Thus, the parameters can be updated directly after each MCMC transition. Other forms of approximate inference, such as variational and loopy methods, have also proved effective for learning very large networks.

3.5 Learning Bayes net structures with hidden variables

In Section 2.5, we discussed the problem of learning Bayes net structures with complete data. When unobserved variables may be influencing the data that are observed, things get more difficult. In the simplest case, a human expert might tell the learning algorithm that certain hidden variables exist, leaving it to the algorithm to find a place for them in the network structure. For example, an algorithm might try to learn the structure shown in Figure 10(a), given the information that *HeartDisease* (a three-valued variable) should be included in the model. As in the complete-data case, the overall algorithm has an outer loop that searches over structures and an inner loop that fits the network parameters given the structure.

If the learning algorithm is not told which hidden variables exist, then there are two choices: either pretend that the data is really complete—which may force the algorithm to learn a parameter-intensive model such as the one in Figure 10(b)—or *invent* new hidden variables in order to simplify the model. The latter approach can be implemented by including new modification choices in the structure search: in addition to modifying links, the algorithm can add or delete a hidden variable or change its arity. Of course, the algorithm will not know that the new variable it has invented is called *HeartDisease*; nor will it have meaningful names for the values. Fortunately, newly invented hidden variables will usually be connected to preexisting variables, so a human expert can often inspect the local conditional distributions involving the new variable and ascertain its meaning.

As in the complete-data case, pure maximum-likelihood structure learning will result in a completely connected network (moreover, one with no hidden variables), so some form of complexity penalty is required. We can also apply MCMC to sample many possible network structures, thereby approximating Bayesian learning. For example, we can learn mixtures of Gaussians with an unknown number of components by sampling over the number; the approximate posterior distribution for the number of Gaussians is given by the sampling frequencies of the MCMC process.

For the complete-data case, the inner loop to learn the parameters is very fast—just a matter of extracting conditional frequencies from the data set. When there are hidden variables, the inner loop may involve many iterations of EM or a gradient-based algorithm, and each iteration involves the calculation of posteriors in a Bayes net, which is itself an NP-hard problem. To date, this approach has proved impractical for learning complex models. One possible improvement is the so-called **structural EM** algorithm, which operates in much the same way as ordinary (parametric) EM except that the algorithm can update the structure as well as the parameters. Just as ordinary EM uses the current parameters to compute the expected counts in the E-step and then applies those counts in the M-step to choose new parameters, structural EM uses the current structure to compute expected counts and then applies those counts in the M-step to evaluate the likelihood for potential new structures. (This contrasts with the outer-loop/inner-loop method, which computes new expected counts for each potential structure.) In this way, structural EM may make several structural alterations to the network without once recomputing the expected counts, and is capable of learning nontrivial Bayes net structures. Nonetheless, much work remains to be done before we can say that the structure-learning problem is solved.

STRUCTURAL EM

4 SUMMARY

Statistical learning methods range from simple calculation of averages to the construction of complex models such as Bayesian networks. They have applications throughout computer science, engineering, computational biology, neuroscience, psychology, and physics. This chapter has presented some of the basic ideas and given a flavor of the mathematical underpinnings. The main points are as follows:

- **Bayesian learning** methods formulate learning as a form of probabilistic inference, using the observations to update a prior distribution over hypotheses. This approach provides a good way to implement Ockham's razor, but quickly becomes intractable for complex hypothesis spaces.
- **Maximum a posteriori** (MAP) learning selects a single most likely hypothesis given the data. The hypothesis prior is still used and the method is often more tractable than full Bayesian learning.
- **Maximum-likelihood** learning simply selects the hypothesis that maximizes the likelihood of the data; it is equivalent to MAP learning with a uniform prior. In simple cases such as linear regression and fully observable Bayesian networks, maximum-likelihood solutions can be found easily in closed form. **Naive Bayes** learning is a particularly effective technique that scales well.
- When some variables are hidden, local maximum likelihood solutions can be found using the EM algorithm. Applications include clustering using mixtures of Gaussians, learning Bayesian networks, and learning hidden Markov models.
- Learning the structure of Bayesian networks is an example of **model selection**. This usually involves a discrete search in the space of structures. Some method is required for trading off model complexity against degree of fit.
- **Nonparametric models** represent a distribution using the collection of data points. Thus, the number of parameters grows with the training set. Nearest-neighbors methods look at the examples nearest to the point in question, whereas **kernel** methods form a distance-weighted combination of all the examples.

Statistical learning continues to be a very active area of research. Enormous strides have been made in both theory and practice, to the point where it is possible to learn almost any model for which exact or approximate inference is feasible.

BIBLIOGRAPHICAL AND HISTORICAL NOTES

The application of statistical learning techniques in AI was an active area of research in the early years (see Duda and Hart, 1973) but became separated from mainstream AI as the latter field concentrated on symbolic methods. A resurgence of interest occurred shortly after the introduction of Bayesian network models in the late 1980s; at roughly the same time, a statistical view of neural network learning began to emerge. In the late 1990s, there was a noticeable convergence of interests in machine learning, statistics, and neural networks, centered on methods for creating large probabilistic models from data.

The naive Bayes model is one of the oldest and simplest forms of Bayesian network, dating back to the 1950s. Its surprising success is partially explained by Domingos and Pazzani (1997). A boosted form of naive Bayes learning won the first KDD Cup data mining competition (Elkan, 1997). Heckerman (1998) gives an excellent introduction to the general problem of Bayes net learning. Bayesian parameter learning with Dirichlet priors for Bayesian networks was discussed by Spiegelhalter *et al.* (1993). The BUGS software package (Gilks *et al.*, 1994) incorporates many of these ideas and provides a very powerful tool for formulating and learning complex probability models. The first algorithms for learning Bayes net structures used conditional independence tests (Pearl, 1988; Pearl and Verma, 1991). Spirtes *et al.* (1993) developed a comprehensive approach embodied in the TETRAD package for Bayes net learning. Algorithmic improvements since then led to a clear victory in the 2001 KDD Cup data mining competition for a Bayes net learning method (Cheng *et al.*, 2002). (The specific task here was a bioinformatics problem with 139,351 features!) A structure-learning approach based on maximizing likelihood was developed by Cooper and Herskovits (1992) and improved by Heckerman *et al.* (1994). Several algorithmic advances since that time have led to quite respectable performance in the complete-data case (Moore and Wong, 2003; Teyssier and Koller, 2005). One important component is an efficient data structure, the AD-tree, for caching counts over all possible combinations of variables and values (Moore and Lee, 1997). Friedman and Goldszmidt (1996) pointed out the influence of the representation of local conditional distributions on the learned structure.

The general problem of learning probability models with hidden variables and missing data was addressed by Hartley (1958), who described the general idea of what was later called EM and gave several examples. Further impetus came from the Baum–Welch algorithm for HMM learning (Baum and Petrie, 1966), which is a special case of EM. The paper by Dempster, Laird, and Rubin (1977), which presented the EM algorithm in general form and analyzed its convergence, is one of the most cited papers in both computer science and statistics. (Dempster himself views EM as a schema rather than an algorithm, since a good deal of mathematical work may be required before it can be applied to a new family of distributions.) McLachlan and Krishnan (1997) devote an entire book to the algorithm and its properties. The specific problem of learning mixture models, including mixtures of Gaussians, is covered by Titterington *et al.* (1985). Within AI, the first successful system that used EM for mixture modeling was AUTOCLASS (Cheeseman *et al.*, 1988; Cheeseman and Stutz, 1996). AUTOCLASS has been applied to a number of real-world scientific classification tasks, including the discovery of new types of stars from spectral data (Goebel *et al.*, 1989) and new classes of proteins and introns in DNA/protein sequence databases (Hunter and States, 1992).

For maximum-likelihood parameter learning in Bayes nets with hidden variables, EM and gradient-based methods were introduced around the same time by Lauritzen (1995), Russell *et al.* (1995), and Binder *et al.* (1997a). The structural EM algorithm was developed by Friedman (1998) and applied to maximum-likelihood learning of Bayes net structures with latent variables. Friedman and Koller (2003). describe Bayesian structure learning.

The ability to learn the structure of Bayesian networks is closely connected to the issue of recovering *causal* information from data. That is, is it possible to learn Bayes nets in such a way that the recovered network structure indicates real causal influences? For many years, statisticians avoided this question, believing that observational data (as opposed to data generated from experimental trials) could yield only correlational information—after all, any two variables that appear related might in fact be influenced by a third, unknown causal factor rather than influencing each other directly. Pearl (2000) has presented convincing arguments to the contrary, showing that there are in fact many cases where causality can be ascertained and developing the **causal network** formalism to express causes and the effects of intervention as well as ordinary conditional probabilities.

CAUSAL NETWORK

Nonparametric density estimation, also called **Parzen window** density estimation, was investigated initially by Rosenblatt (1956) and Parzen (1962). Since that time, a huge literature has developed investigating the properties of various estimators. Devroye (1987) gives a thorough introduction. There is also a rapidly growing literature on nonparametric Bayesian methods, originating with the seminal work of Ferguson (1973) on the **Dirichlet process**, which can be thought of as a distribution over Dirichlet distributions. These methods are particularly useful for mixtures with unknown numbers of components. Ghahramani (2005) and Jordan (2005) provide useful tutorials on the many applications of these ideas to statistical learning. The text by Rasmussen and Williams (2006) covers the **Gaussian process**, which gives a way of defining prior distributions over the space of continuous functions.

DIRICHLET PROCESS

GAUSSIAN PROCESS

The material in this chapter brings together work from the fields of statistics and pattern recognition, so the story has been told many times in many ways. Good texts on Bayesian statistics include those by DeGroot (1970), Berger (1985), and Gelman *et al.* (1995). Bishop (2007) and Hastie *et al.* (2009) provide an excellent introduction to statistical machine learning. For pattern classification, the classic text for many years has been Duda and Hart (1973), now updated (Duda *et al.*, 2001). The annual NIPS (Neural Information Processing Conference) conference, whose proceedings are published as the series *Advances in Neural Information Processing Systems*, is now dominated by Bayesian papers. Papers on learning Bayesian networks also appear in the *Uncertainty in AI* and *Machine Learning* conferences and in several statistics conferences. Journals specific to neural networks include *Neural Computation*, *Neural Networks*, and the *IEEE Transactions on Neural Networks*. Specifically Bayesian venues include the Valencia International Meetings on Bayesian Statistics and the journal *Bayesian Analysis*.

EXERCISES

1 The data used for Figure 1 can be viewed as being generated by h_5. For each of the other four hypotheses, generate a data set of length 100 and plot the corresponding graphs for $P(h_i \mid d_1, \ldots, d_N)$ and $P(D_{N+1} = lime \mid d_1, \ldots, d_N)$. Comment on your results.

2 Suppose that Ann's utilities for cherry and lime candies are c_A and ℓ_A, whereas Bob's utilities are c_B and ℓ_B. (But once Ann has unwrapped a piece of candy, Bob won't buy it.) Presumably, if Bob likes lime candies much more than Ann, it would be wise for Ann to sell her bag of candies once she is sufficiently sure of its lime content. On the other hand, if Ann unwraps too many candies in the process, the bag will be worth less. Discuss the problem of determining the optimal point at which to sell the bag. Determine the expected utility of the optimal procedure, given the prior distribution from Section 1.

3 Two statisticians go to the doctor and are both given the same prognosis: A 40% chance that the problem is the deadly disease A, and a 60% chance of the fatal disease B. Fortunately, there are anti-A and anti-B drugs that are inexpensive, 100% effective, and free of side-effects. The statisticians have the choice of taking one drug, both, or neither. What will the first statistician (an avid Bayesian) do? How about the second statistician, who always uses the maximum likelihood hypothesis?

The doctor does some research and discovers that disease B actually comes in two versions, dextro-B and levo-B, which are equally likely and equally treatable by the anti-B drug. Now that there are three hypotheses, what will the two statisticians do?

4 Explain how to apply the boosting method of the chapter "Learning from Examples" to naive Bayes learning. Test the performance of the resulting algorithm on the restaurant learning problem.

5 Consider N data points (x_j, y_j), where the y_js are generated from the x_js according to the linear Gaussian model in Equation (5). Find the values of θ_2, θ_1, and σ that maximize the conditional log likelihood of the data.

6 Consider the noisy-OR model for fever described in Section 3 of the chapter "Probabilistic Reasoning". Explain how to apply maximum-likelihood learning to fit the parameters of such a model to a set of complete data. (*Hint*: use the chain rule for partial derivatives.)

7 This exercise investigates properties of the Beta distribution defined in Equation (6).

a. By integrating over the range $[0, 1]$, show that the normalization constant for the distribution beta$[a, b]$ is given by $\alpha = \Gamma(a+b)/\Gamma(a)\Gamma(b)$ where $\Gamma(x)$ is the **Gamma function**, defined by $\Gamma(x+1) = x \cdot \Gamma(x)$ and $\Gamma(1) = 1$. (For integer x, $\Gamma(x+1) = x!$.)

GAMMA FUNCTION

b. Show that the mean is $a/(a+b)$.

c. Find the mode(s) (the most likely value(s) of θ).

d. Describe the distribution beta$[\epsilon, \epsilon]$ for very small ϵ. What happens as such a distribution is updated?

8 Consider an arbitrary Bayesian network, a complete data set for that network, and the likelihood for the data set according to the network. Give a simple proof that the likelihood of the data cannot decrease if we add a new link to the network and recompute the maximum-likelihood parameter values.

9 Consider a single Boolean random variable Y (the "classification"). Let the prior probability $P(Y = true)$ be π. Let's try to find π, given a training set $D = (y_1, \ldots, y_N)$ with N independent samples of Y. Furthermore, suppose p of the N are positive and n of the N are negative.

a. Write down an expression for the likelihood of D (i.e., the probability of seeing this particular sequence of examples, given a fixed value of π) in terms of π, p, and n.

b. By differentiating the log likelihood L, find the value of π that maximizes the likelihood.

c. Now suppose we add in k Boolean random variables $X_1, X_2, \ldots, X_k$ (the "attributes") that describe each sample, and suppose we assume that the attributes are conditionally independent of each other given the goal Y. Draw the Bayes net corresponding to this assumption.

d. Write down the likelihood for the data including the attributes, using the following additional notation:

- α_i is $P(X_i = true|Y = true)$.
- β_i is $P(X_i = true|Y = false)$.
- p_i^+ is the count of samples for which $X_i = true$ and $Y = true$.
- n_i^+ is the count of samples for which $X_i = false$ and $Y = true$.
- p_i^- is the count of samples for which $X_i = true$ and $Y = false$.
- n_i^- is the count of samples for which $X_i = false$ and $Y = false$.

[*Hint*: consider first the probability of seeing a single example with specified values for $X_1, X_2, \ldots, X_k$ and Y.]

e. By differentiating the log likelihood L, find the values of α_i and β_i (in terms of the various counts) that maximize the likelihood and say in words what these values represent.

f. Let $k = 2$, and consider a data set with 4 all four possible examples of theXOR function. Compute the maximum likelihood estimates of π, α_1, α_2, β_1, and β_2.

g. Given these estimates of π, α_1, α_2, β_1, and β_2, what are the posterior probabilities $P(Y = true|x_1, x_2)$ for each example?

10 Consider the application of EM to learn the parameters for the network in Figure 13(a), given the true parameters in Equation (7).

a. Explain why the EM algorithm would not work if there were just two attributes in the model rather than three.

b. Show the calculations for the first iteration of EM starting from Equation (8).

c. What happens if we start with all the parameters set to the same value p? (*Hint*: you may find it helpful to investigate this empirically before deriving the general result.)

d. Write out an expression for the log likelihood of the tabulated candy data in section 3.2 in terms of the parameters, calculate the partial derivatives with respect to each parameter, and investigate the nature of the fixed point reached in part (c).

NATURAL LANGUAGE PROCESSING

From Chapter 22 of *Artificial Intelligence: A Modern Approach*, Third Edition. Stuart Russell and Peter Norvig.

NATURAL LANGUAGE PROCESSING

In which we see how to make use of the copious knowledge that is expressed in natural language.

Homo sapiens is set apart from other species by the capacity for language. Somewhere around 100,000 years ago, humans learned how to speak, and about 7,000 years ago learned to write. Although chimpanzees, dolphins, and other animals have shown vocabularies of hundreds of signs, only humans can reliably communicate an unbounded number of qualitatively different messages on any topic using discrete signs.

Of course, there are other attributes that are uniquely human: no other species wears clothes, creates representational art, or watches three hours of television a day. But when Alan Turing proposed his Test, he based it on language, not art or TV. There are two main reasons why we want our computer agents to be able to process natural languages: first, to communicate with humans, and second, to acquire information from written language, the focus of this chapter.

KNOWLEDGE ACQUISITION

There are over a trillion pages of information on the Web, almost all of it in natural language. An agent that wants to do **knowledge acquisition** needs to understand (at least partially) the ambiguous, messy languages that humans use. We examine the problem from the point of view of specific information-seeking tasks: text classification, information retrieval, and information extraction. One common factor in addressing these tasks is the use of **language models**: models that predict the probability distribution of language expressions.

LANGUAGE MODEL

1 LANGUAGE MODELS

LANGUAGE

GRAMMAR

SEMANTICS

Formal languages, such as the programming languages Java or Python, have precisely defined language models. A **language** can be defined as a set of strings; "`print(2 + 2)`" is a legal program in the language Python, whereas "`2)+(2 print`" is not. Since there are an infinite number of legal programs, they cannot be enumerated; instead they are specified by a set of rules called a **grammar**. Formal languages also have rules that define the meaning or **semantics** of a program; for example, the rules say that the "meaning" of "`2 + 2`" is 4, and the meaning of "`1/0`" is that an error is signaled.

Natural languages, such as English or Spanish, cannot be characterized as a definitive set of sentences. Everyone agrees that "Not to be invited is sad" is a sentence of English, but people disagree on the grammaticality of "To be not invited is sad." Therefore, it is more fruitful to define a natural language model as a probability distribution over sentences rather than a definitive set. That is, rather than asking if a string of *words* is or is not a member of the set defining the language, we instead ask for $P(S = words)$—what is the probability that a random sentence would be *words*.

AMBIGUITY

Natural languages are also **ambiguous**. "He saw her duck" can mean either that he saw a waterfowl belonging to her, or that he saw her move to evade something. Thus, again, we cannot speak of a single meaning for a sentence, but rather of a probability distribution over possible meanings.

Finally, natural languages are difficult to deal with because they are very large, and constantly changing. Thus, our language models are, at best, an approximation. We start with the simplest possible approximations and move up from there.

1.1 *N*-gram character models

CHARACTERS

Ultimately, a written text is composed of **characters**—letters, digits, punctuation, and spaces in English (and more exotic characters in some other languages). Thus, one of the simplest language models is a probability distribution over sequences of characters. We write $P(c_{1:N})$ for the probability of a sequence of N characters, c_1 through c_N. In one Web collection, P("the")=0.027 and P("zgq")=0.000000002. A sequence of written symbols of length n is called an n-gram (from the Greek root for writing or letters), with special case "unigram" for 1-gram, "bigram" for 2-gram, and "trigram" for 3-gram. A model of the probability distribution of n-letter sequences is thus called an **n-gram model**. (But be careful: we can have n-gram models over sequences of words, syllables, or other units; not just over characters.)

N-GRAM MODEL

An n-gram model is defined as a **Markov chain** of order $n-1$. Recall that in a Markov chain the probability of character c_i depends only on the immediately preceding characters, not on any other characters. So in a trigram model (Markov chain of order 2) we have

$$P(c_i \mid c_{1:i-1}) = P(c_i \mid c_{i-2:i-1}) .$$

We can define the probability of a sequence of characters $P(c_{1:N})$ under the trigram model by first factoring with the chain rule and then using the Markov assumption:

$$P(c_{1:N}) = \prod_{i=1}^{N} P(c_i \mid c_{1:i-1}) = \prod_{i=1}^{N} P(c_i \mid c_{i-2:i-1}) .$$

For a trigram character model in a language with 100 characters, $\mathbf{P}(C_i|C_{i-2:i-1})$ has a million entries, and can be accurately estimated by counting character sequences in a body of text of 10 million characters or more. We call a body of text a **corpus** (plural *corpora*), from the Latin word for *body*.

CORPUS

What can we do with n-gram character models? One task for which they are well suited is **language identification**: given a text, determine what natural language it is written in. This is a relatively easy task; even with short texts such as "Hello, world" or "Wie geht es dir," it is easy to identify the first as English and the second as German. Computer systems identify languages with greater than 99% accuracy; occasionally, closely related languages, such as Swedish and Norwegian, are confused.

LANGUAGE IDENTIFICATION

One approach to language identification is to first build a trigram character model of each candidate language, $P(c_i \mid c_{i-2:i-1}, \ell)$, where the variable ℓ ranges over languages. For each ℓ the model is built by counting trigrams in a corpus of that language. (About 100,000 characters of each language are needed.) That gives us a model of $\mathbf{P}(Text \mid Language)$, but we want to select the most probable language given the text, so we apply Bayes' rule followed by the Markov assumption to get the most probable language:

$$\begin{aligned}\ell^* &= \underset{\ell}{\operatorname{argmax}}\; P(\ell \mid c_{1:N}) \\ &= \underset{\ell}{\operatorname{argmax}}\; P(\ell)P(c_{1:N} \mid \ell) \\ &= \underset{\ell}{\operatorname{argmax}}\; P(\ell) \prod_{i=1}^{N} P(c_i \mid c_{i-2:i-1}, \ell)\end{aligned}$$

The trigram model can be learned from a corpus, but what about the prior probability $P(\ell)$? We may have some estimate of these values; for example, if we are selecting a random Web page we know that English is the most likely language and that the probability of Macedonian will be less than 1%. The exact number we select for these priors is not critical because the trigram model usually selects one language that is several orders of magnitude more probable than any other.

Other tasks for character models include spelling correction, genre classification, and named-entity recognition. Genre classification means deciding if a text is a news story, a legal document, a scientific article, etc. While many features help make this classification, counts of punctuation and other character n-gram features go a long way (Kessler *et al.*, 1997). Named-entity recognition is the task of finding names of things in a document and deciding what class they belong to. For example, in the text "Mr. Sopersteen was prescribed aciphex," we should recognize that "Mr. Sopersteen" is the name of a person and "aciphex" is the name of a drug. Character-level models are good for this task because they can associate the character sequence "ex␣" ("ex" followed by a space) with a drug name and "steen␣" with a person name, and thereby identify words that they have never seen before.

1.2 Smoothing *n*-gram models

The major complication of n-gram models is that the training corpus provides only an estimate of the true probability distribution. For common character sequences such as "␣th" any English corpus will give a good estimate: about 1.5% of all trigrams. On the other hand, "␣ht" is very uncommon—no dictionary words start with ht. It is likely that the sequence would have a count of zero in a training corpus of standard English. Does that mean we should assign $P(\text{"␣th"}) = 0$? If we did, then the text "The program issues an http request" would have

an English probability of zero, which seems wrong. We have a problem in generalization: we want our language models to generalize well to texts they haven't seen yet. Just because we have never seen "␣http" before does not mean that our model should claim that it is impossible. Thus, we will adjust our language model so that sequences that have a count of zero in the training corpus will be assigned a small nonzero probability (and the other counts will be adjusted downward slightly so that the probability still sums to 1). The process od adjusting
SMOOTHING the probability of low-frequency counts is called **smoothing**.

The simplest type of smoothing was suggested by Pierre-Simon Laplace in the 18th century: he said that, in the lack of further information, if a random Boolean variable X has been false in all n observations so far then the estimate for $P(X = true)$ should be $1/(n+2)$. That is, he assumes that with two more trials, one might be true and one false. Laplace smoothing (also called add-one smoothing) is a step in the right direction, but performs relatively poorly.
BACKOFF MODEL A better approach is a **backoff model**, in which we start by estimating n-gram counts, but for any particular sequence that has a low (or zero) count, we back off to $(n-1)$-grams. **Linear**
LINEAR INTERPOLATION SMOOTHING **interpolation smoothing** is a backoff model that combines trigram, bigram, and unigram models by linear interpolation. It defines the probability estimate as

$$\widehat{P}(c_i|c_{i-2:i-1}) = \lambda_3 P(c_i|c_{i-2:i-1}) + \lambda_2 P(c_i|c_{i-1}) + \lambda_1 P(c_i)\,,$$

where $\lambda_3 + \lambda_2 + \lambda_1 = 1$. The parameter values λ_i can be fixed, or they can be trained with an expectation–maximization algorithm. It is also possible to have the values of λ_i depend on the counts: if we have a high count of trigrams, then we weigh them relatively more; if only a low count, then we put more weight on the bigram and unigram models. One camp of researchers has developed ever more sophisticated smoothing models, while the other camp suggests gathering a larger corpus so that even simple smoothing models work well. Both are getting at the same goal: reducing the variance in the language model.

One complication: note that the expression $P(c_i \mid c_{i-2:i-1})$ asks for $P(c_1 \mid c_{-1:0})$ when $i = 1$, but there are no characters before c_1. We can introduce artificial characters, for example, defining c_0 to be a space character or a special "begin text" character. Or we can fall back on lower-order Markov models, in effect defining $c_{-1:0}$ to be the empty sequence and thus $P(c_1 \mid c_{-1:0}) = P(c_1)$.

1.3 Model evaluation

With so many possible n-gram models—unigram, bigram, trigram, interpolated smoothing with different values of λ, etc.—how do we know what model to choose? We can evaluate a model with cross-validation. Split the corpus into a training corpus and a validation corpus. Determine the parameters of the model from the training data. Then evaluate the model on the validation corpus.

The evaluation can be a task-specific metric, such as measuring accuracy on language identification. Alternatively we can have a task-independent model of language quality: calculate the probability assigned to the validation corpus by the model; the higher the probability the better. This metric is inconvenient because the probability of a large corpus will be a very small number, and floating-point underflow becomes an issue. A different way of
PERPLEXITY describing the probability of a sequence is with a measure called **perplexity**, defined as

$$Perplexity(c_{1:N}) = P(c_{1:N})^{-\frac{1}{N}}.$$

Perplexity can be thought of as the reciprocal of probability, normalized by sequence length. It can also be thought of as the weighted average branching factor of a model. Suppose there are 100 characters in our language, and our model says they are all equally likely. Then for a sequence of any length, the perplexity will be 100. If some characters are more likely than others, and the model reflects that, then the model will have a perplexity less than 100.

1.4 *N*-gram word models

Now we turn to n-gram models over words rather than characters. All the same mechanism applies equally to word and character models. The main difference is that the **vocabulary**—the set of symbols that make up the corpus and the model—is larger. There are only about 100 characters in most languages, and sometimes we build character models that are even more restrictive, for example by treating "A" and "a" as the same symbol or by treating all punctuation as the same symbol. But with word models we have at least tens of thousands of symbols, and sometimes millions. The wide range is because it is not clear what constitutes a word. In English a sequence of letters surrounded by spaces is a word, but in some languages, like Chinese, words are not separated by spaces, and even in English many decisions must be made to have a clear policy on word boundaries: how many words are in "ne'er-do-well"? Or in "(Tel:1-800-960-5660x123)"?

VOCABULARY

OUT OF VOCABULARY

Word n-gram models need to deal with **out of vocabulary** words. With character models, we didn't have to worry about someone inventing a new letter of the alphabet.[1] But with word models there is always the chance of a new word that was not seen in the training corpus, so we need to model that explicitly in our language model. This can be done by adding just one new word to the vocabulary: `<UNK>`, standing for the unknown word. We can estimate n-gram counts for `<UNK>` by this trick: go through the training corpus, and the first time any individual word appears it is previously unknown, so replace it with the symbol `<UNK>`. All subsequent appearances of the word remain unchanged. Then compute n-gram counts for the corpus as usual, treating `<UNK>` just like any other word. Then when an unknown word appears in a test set, we look up its probability under `<UNK>`. Sometimes multiple unknown-word symbols are used, for different classes. For example, any string of digits might be replaced with `<NUM>`, or any email address with `<EMAIL>`.

To get a feeling for what word models can do, we built unigram, bigram, and trigram models over the words in this text and then randomly sampled sequences of words from the models. The results are

Unigram: logical are as are confusion a may right tries agent goal the was ...
Bigram: systems are very similar computational approach would be represented ...
Trigram: planning and scheduling are integrated the success of naive bayes model is ...

Even with this small sample, it should be clear that the unigram model is a poor approximation of either English or the content of an AI textbook, and that the bigram and trigram models are

[1] With the possible exception of the groundbreaking work of T. Geisel (1955).

much better. The models agree with this assessment: the perplexity was 891 for the unigram model, 142 for the bigram model and 91 for the trigram model.

With the basics of n-gram models—both character- and word-based—established, we can turn now to some language tasks.

2 TEXT CLASSIFICATION

TEXT CLASSIFICATION

We now consider in depth the task of **text classification**, also known as **categorization**: given a text of some kind, decide which of a predefined set of classes it belongs to. Language identification and genre classification are examples of text classification, as is sentiment analysis (classifying a movie or product review as positive or negative) and **spam detection** (classifying an email message as spam or not-spam). Since "not-spam" is awkward, researchers have coined the term **ham** for not-spam. We can treat spam detection as a problem in supervised learning. A training set is readily available: the positive (spam) examples are in my spam folder, the negative (ham) examples are in my inbox. Here is an excerpt:

SPAM DETECTION

Spam: Wholesale Fashion Watches -57% today. Designer watches for cheap ...
Spam: You can buy ViagraFr$1.85 All Medications at unbeatable prices! ...
Spam: WE CAN TREAT ANYTHING YOU SUFFER FROM JUST TRUST US ...
Spam: Sta.rt earn*ing the salary yo,u d-eserve by o'btaining the prope,r crede'ntials!

Ham: The practical significance of hypertree width in identifying more ...
Ham: Abstract: We will motivate the problem of social identity clustering: ...
Ham: Good to see you my friend. Hey Peter, It was good to hear from you. ...
Ham: PDS implies convexity of the resulting optimization problem (Kernel Ridge ...

From this excerpt we can start to get an idea of what might be good features to include in the supervised learning model. Word n-grams such as "for cheap" and "You can buy" seem to be indicators of spam (although they would have a nonzero probability in ham as well). Character-level features also seem important: spam is more likely to be all uppercase and to have punctuation embedded in words. Apparently the spammers thought that the word bigram "you deserve" would be too indicative of spam, and thus wrote "yo,u d-eserve" instead. A character model should detect this. We could either create a full character n-gram model of spam and ham, or we could handcraft features such as "number of punctuation marks embedded in words."

Note that we have two complementary ways of talking about classification. In the language-modeling approach, we define one n-gram language model for $\mathbf{P}(Message \mid spam)$ by training on the spam folder, and one model for $\mathbf{P}(Message \mid ham)$ by training on the inbox. Then we can classify a new message with an application of Bayes' rule:

$$\operatorname*{argmax}_{c \in \{spam, ham\}} P(c \mid message) = \operatorname*{argmax}_{c \in \{spam, ham\}} P(message \mid c)\, P(c) .$$

where $P(c)$ is estimated just by counting the total number of spam and ham messages. This approach works well for spam detection, just as it did for language identification.

In the machine-learning approach we represent the message as a set of feature/value pairs and apply a classification algorithm h to the feature vector $\mathbf{X}$. We can make the language-modeling and machine-learning approaches compatible by thinking of the n-grams as features. This is easiest to see with a unigram model. The features are the words in the vocabulary: "a," "aardvark," ..., and the values are the number of times each word appears in the message. That makes the feature vector large and sparse. If there are 100,000 words in the language model, then the feature vector has length 100,000, but for a short email message almost all the features will have count zero. This unigram representation has been called the

BAG OF WORDS

bag of words model. You can think of the model as putting the words of the training corpus in a bag and then selecting words one at a time. The notion of order of the words is lost; a unigram model gives the same probability to any permutation of a text. Higher-order n-gram models maintain some local notion of word order.

With bigrams and trigrams the number of features is squared or cubed, and we can add in other, non-n-gram features: the time the message was sent, whether a URL or an image is part of the message, an ID number for the sender of the message, the sender's number of previous spam and ham messages, and so on. The choice of features is the most important part of creating a good spam detector—more important than the choice of algorithm for processing the features. In part this is because there is a lot of training data, so if we can propose a feature, the data can accurately determine if it is good or not. It is necessary to constantly update features, because spam detection is an **adversarial task**; the spammers modify their spam in response to the spam detector's changes.

It can be expensive to run algorithms on a very large feature vector, so often a process

FEATURE SELECTION

of **feature selection** is used to keep only the features that best discriminate between spam and ham. For example, the bigram "of the" is frequent in English, and may be equally frequent in spam and ham, so there is no sense in counting it. Often the top hundred or so features do a good job of discriminating between classes.

Once we have chosen a set of features, we can apply any of the supervised learning techniques we have seen; popular ones for text categorization include k-nearest-neighbors, support vector machines, decision trees, naive Bayes, and logistic regression. All of these have been applied to spam detection, usually with accuracy in the 98%–99% range. With a carefully designed feature set, accuracy can exceed 99.9%.

2.1 Classification by data compression

DATA COMPRESSION

Another way to think about classification is as a problem in **data compression**. A lossless compression algorithm takes a sequence of symbols, detects repeated patterns in it, and writes a description of the sequence that is more compact than the original. For example, the text "0.142857142857142857" might be compressed to "0.[142857]*3." Compression algorithms work by building dictionaries of subsequences of the text, and then referring to entries in the dictionary. The example here had only one dictionary entry, "142857."

In effect, compression algorithms are creating a language model. The LZW algorithm in particular directly models a maximum-entropy probability distribution. To do classification by compression, we first lump together all the spam training messages and compress them as a unit. We do the same for the ham. Then when given a new message to classify, we append it to the spam messages and compress the result. We also append it to the ham and compress that. Whichever class compresses better—adds the fewer number of additional bytes for the new message—is the predicted class. The idea is that a spam message will tend to share dictionary entries with other spam messages and thus will compress better when appended to a collection that already contains the spam dictionary.

Experiments with compression-based classification on some of the standard corpora for text classification—the 20-Newsgroups data set, the Reuters-10 Corpora, the Industry Sector corpora—indicate that whereas running off-the-shelf compression algorithms like gzip, RAR, and LZW can be quite slow, their accuracy is comparable to traditional classification algorithms. This is interesting in its own right, and also serves to point out that there is promise for algorithms that use character n-grams directly with no preprocessing of the text or feature selection: they seem to be captiring some real patterns.

3 INFORMATION RETRIEVAL

INFORMATION RETRIEVAL

Information retrieval is the task of finding documents that are relevant to a user's need for information. The best-known examples of information retrieval systems are search engines on the World Wide Web. A Web user can type a query such as [AI book][2] into a search engine and see a list of relevant pages. In this section, we will see how such systems are built. An information retrieval (henceforth **IR**) system can be characterized by

IR

1. **A corpus of documents.** Each system must decide what it wants to treat as a document: a paragraph, a page, or a multipage text.

QUERY LANGUAGE

2. **Queries posed in a query language**. A query specifies what the user wants to know. The query language can be just a list of words, such as [AI book]; or it can specify a phrase of words that must be adjacent, as in ["AI book"]; it can contain Boolean operators as in [AI AND book]; it can include non-Boolean operators such as [AI NEAR book] or [AI book site:www.aaai.org].

RESULT SET

RELEVANT

3. **A result set.** This is the subset of documents that the IR system judges to be **relevant** to the query. By *relevant*, we mean likely to be of use to the person who posed the query, for the particular information need expressed in the query.

PRESENTATION

4. **A presentation of the result set.** This can be as simple as a ranked list of document titles or as complex as a rotating color map of the result set projected onto a three-dimensional space, rendered as a two-dimensional display.

BOOLEAN KEYWORD MODEL

The earliest IR systems worked on a **Boolean keyword model**. Each word in the document collection is treated as a Boolean feature that is true of a document if the word occurs in the document and false if it does not. So the feature "retrieval" is true for the current chapter but false for others. The query language is the language of Boolean expressions over features. A

[2] We denote a search query as [*query*]. Square brackets are used rather than quotation marks so that we can distinguish the query ["two words"] from [two words].

document is relevant only if the expression evaluates to true. For example, the query [information AND retrieval] is true for the current chapter.

This model has the advantage of being simple to explain and implement. However, it has some disadvantages. First, the degree of relevance of a document is a single bit, so there is no guidance as to how to order the relevant documents for presentation. Second, Boolean expressions are unfamiliar to users who are not programmers or logicians. Users find it unintuitive that when they want to know about farming in the states of Kansas *and* Nebraska they need to issue the query [farming (Kansas OR Nebraska)]. Third, it can be hard to formulate an appropriate query, even for a skilled user. Suppose we try [information AND retrieval AND models AND optimization] and get an empty result set. We could try [information OR retrieval OR models OR optimization], but if that returns too many results, it is difficult to know what to try next.

3.1 IR scoring functions

BM25 SCORING FUNCTION

Most IR systems have abandoned the Boolean model and use models based on the statistics of word counts. We describe the **BM25 scoring function**, which comes from the Okapi project of Stephen Robertson and Karen Sparck Jones at London's City College, and has been used in search engines such as the open-source Lucene project.

A scoring function takes a document and a query and returns a numeric score; the most relevant documents have the highest scores. In the BM25 function, the score is a linear weighted combination of scores for each of the words that make up the query. Three factors affect the weight of a query term: First, the frequency with which a query term appears in a document (also known as TF for term frequency). For the query [farming in Kansas], documents that mention "farming" frequently will have higher scores. Second, the inverse document frequency of the term, or IDF. The word "in" appears in almost every document, so it has a high document frequency, and thus a low inverse document frequency, and thus it is not as important to the query as "farming" or "Kansas." Third, the length of the document. A million-word document will probably mention all the query words, but may not actually be about the query. A short document that mentions all the words is a much better candidate.

The BM25 function takes all three of these into account. We assume we have created an index of the N documents in the corpus so that we can look up $TF(q_i, d_j)$, the count of the number of times word q_i appears in document d_j. We also assume a table of document frequency counts, $DF(q_i)$, that gives the number of documents that contain the word q_i. Then, given a document d_j and a query consisting of the words $q_{1:N}$, we have

$$BM25(d_j, q_{1:N}) = \sum_{i=1}^{N} IDF(q_i) \cdot \frac{TF(q_i, d_j) \cdot (k+1)}{TF(q_i, d_j) + k \cdot (1 - b + b \cdot \frac{|d_j|}{L})},$$

where $|d_j|$ is the length of document d_j in words, and L is the average document length in the corpus: $L = \sum_i |d_i|/N$. We have two parameters, k and b, that can be tuned by cross-validation; typical values are $k = 2.0$ and $b = 0.75$. $IDF(q_i)$ is the inverse document frequency of word q_i, given by

$$IDF(q_i) = \log \frac{N - DF(q_i) + 0.5}{DF(q_i) + 0.5} .$$

Of course, it would be impractical to apply the BM25 scoring function to every document in the corpus. Instead, systems create an **index** ahead of time that lists, for each vocabulary word, the documents that contain the word. This is called the **hit list** for the word. Then when given a query, we intersect the hit lists of the query words and only score the documents in the intersection.

INDEX

HIT LIST

3.2 IR system evaluation

How do we know whether an IR system is performing well? We undertake an experiment in which the system is given a set of queries and the result sets are scored with respect to human relevance judgments. Traditionally, there have been two measures used in the scoring: recall and precision. We explain them with the help of an example. Imagine that an IR system has returned a result set for a single query, for which we know which documents are and are not relevant, out of a corpus of 100 documents. The document counts in each category are given in the following table:

	In result set	Not in result set
Relevant	30	20
Not relevant	10	40

PRECISION

Precision measures the proportion of documents in the result set that are actually relevant. In our example, the precision is $30/(30+10) = .75$. The false positive rate is $1 - .75 = .25$.

RECALL

Recall measures the proportion of all the relevant documents in the collection that are in the result set. In our example, recall is $30/(30+20) = .60$. The false negative rate is $1 - .60 = .40$. In a very large document collection, such as the World Wide Web, recall is difficult to compute, because there is no easy way to examine every page on the Web for relevance. All we can do is either estimate recall by sampling or ignore recall completely and just judge precision. In the case of a Web search engine, there may be thousands of documents in the result set, so it makes more sense to measure precision for several different sizes, such as "P@10" (precision in the top 10 results) or "P@50," rather than to estimate precision in the entire result set.

It is possible to trade off precision against recall by varying the size of the result set returned. In the extreme, a system that returns every document in the document collection is guaranteed a recall of 100%, but will have low precision. Alternately, a system could return a single document and have low recall, but a decent chance at 100% precision. A summary of both measures is the F_1 score, a single number that is the harmonic mean of precision and recall, $2PR/(P+R)$.

3.3 IR refinements

There are many possible refinements to the system described here, and indeed Web search engines are continually updating their algorithms as they discover new approaches and as the Web grows and changes.

One common refinement is a better model of the effect of document length on relevance. Singhal *et al.* (1996) observed that simple document length normalization schemes tend to favor short documents too much and long documents not enough. They propose a *pivoted* document length normalization scheme; the idea is that the pivot is the document length at which the old-style normalization is correct; documents shorter than that get a boost and longer ones get a penalty.

The BM25 scoring function uses a word model that treats all words as completely independent, but we know that some words are correlated: "couch" is closely related to both "couches" and "sofa." Many IR systems attempt to account for these correlations.

CASE FOLDING

STEMMING

For example, if the query is [couch], it would be a shame to exclude from the result set those documents that mention "COUCH" or "couches" but not "couch." Most IR systems do **case folding** of "COUCH" to "couch," and some use a **stemming** algorithm to reduce "couches" to the stem form "couch," both in the query and the documents. This typically yields a small increase in recall (on the order of 2% for English). However, it can harm precision. For example, stemming "stocking" to "stock" will tend to decrease precision for queries about either foot coverings or financial instruments, although it could improve recall for queries about warehousing. Stemming algorithms based on rules (e.g., remove "-ing") cannot avoid this problem, but algorithms based on dictionaries (don't remove "-ing" if the word is already listed in the dictionary) can. While stemming has a small effect in English, it is more important in other languages. In German, for example, it is not uncommon to see words like "Lebensversicherungsgesellschaftsangestellter" (life insurance company employee). Languages such as Finnish, Turkish, Inuit, and Yupik have recursive morphological rules that in principle generate words of unbounded length.

SYNONYM

The next step is to recognize **synonyms**, such as "sofa" for "couch." As with stemming, this has the potential for small gains in recall, but can hurt precision. A user who gives the query [Tim Couch] wants to see results about the football player, not sofas. The problem is that "languages abhor absolute synonyms just as nature abhors a vacuum" (Cruse, 1986). That is, anytime there are two words that mean the same thing, speakers of the language conspire to evolve the meanings to remove the confusion. Related words that are not synonyms also play an important role in ranking—terms like "leather", "wooden," or "modern" can serve to confirm that the document really is about "couch." Synonyms and related words can be found in dictionaries or by looking for correlations in documents or in queries—if we find that many users who ask the query [new sofa] follow it up with the query [new couch], we can in the future alter [new sofa] to be [new sofa OR new couch].

METADATA

LINKS

As a final refinement, IR can be improved by considering **metadata**—data outside of the text of the document. Examples include human-supplied keywords and publication data. On the Web, hypertext **links** between documents are a crucial source of information.

3.4 The PageRank algorithm

PAGERANK

PageRank[3] was one of the two original ideas that set Google's search apart from other Web search engines when it was introduced in 1997. (The other innovation was the use of anchor

[3] The name stands both for Web pages and for coinventor Larry Page (Brin and Page, 1998).

```
function HITS(query) returns pages with hub and authority numbers
  pages ← EXPAND-PAGES(RELEVANT-PAGES(query))
  for each p in pages do
    p.AUTHORITY ← 1
    p.HUB ← 1
  repeat until convergence do
    for each p in pages do
      p.AUTHORITY ← Σ_i INLINK_i(p).HUB
      p.HUB ← Σ_i OUTLINK_i(p).AUTHORITY
    NORMALIZE(pages)
  return pages
```

Figure 1 The HITS algorithm for computing hubs and authorities with respect to a query. RELEVANT-PAGES fetches the pages that match the query, and EXPAND-PAGES adds in every page that links to or is linked from one of the relevant pages. NORMALIZE divides each page's score by the sum of the squares of all pages' scores (separately for both the authority and hubs scores).

text—the underlined text in a hyperlink—to index a page, even though the anchor text was on a *different* page than the one being indexed.) PageRank was invented to solve the problem of the tyranny of TF scores: if the query is [IBM], how do we make sure that IBM's home page, `ibm.com`, is the first result, even if another page mentions the term "IBM" more frequently? The idea is that `ibm.com` has many in-links (links to the page), so it should be ranked higher: each in-link is a vote for the quality of the linked-to page. But if we only counted in-links, then it would be possible for a Web spammer to create a network of pages and have them all point to a page of his choosing, increasing the score of that page. Therefore, the PageRank algorithm is designed to weight links from high-quality sites more heavily. What is a high-quality site? One that is linked to by other high-quality sites. The definition is recursive, but we will see that the recursion bottoms out properly. The PageRank for a page p is defined as:

$$PR(p) = \frac{1-d}{N} + d \sum_i \frac{PR(in_i)}{C(in_i)},$$

where $PR(p)$ is the PageRank of page p, N is the total number of pages in the corpus, in_i are the pages that link in to p, and $C(in_i)$ is the count of the total number of out-links on page in_i. The constant d is a damping factor. It can be understood through the **random surfer model**: imagine a Web surfer who starts at some random page and begins exploring. With probability d (we'll assume $d = 0.85$) the surfer clicks on one of the links on the page (choosing uniformly among them), and with probability $1 - d$ she gets bored with the page and restarts on a random page anywhere on the Web. The PageRank of page p is then the probability that the random surfer will be at page p at any point in time. PageRank can be computed by an iterative procedure: start with all pages having $PR(p) = 1$, and iterate the algorithm, updating ranks until they converge.

RANDOM SURFER MODEL

3.5 The HITS algorithm

The Hyperlink-Induced Topic Search algorithm, also known as "Hubs and Authorities" or HITS, is another influential link-analysis algorithm (see Figure 1). HITS differs from PageRank in several ways. First, it is a query-dependent measure: it rates pages with respect to a query. That means that it must be computed anew for each query—a computational burden that most search engines have elected not to take on. Given a query, HITS first finds a set of pages that are relevant to the query. It does that by intersecting hit lists of query words, and then adding pages in the link neighborhood of these pages—pages that link to or are linked from one of the pages in the original relevant set.

AUTHORITY

HUB

Each page in this set is considered an **authority** on the query to the degree that other pages in the relevant set point to it. A page is considered a **hub** to the degree that it points to other authoritative pages in the relevant set. Just as with PageRank, we don't want to merely count the number of links; we want to give more value to the high-quality hubs and authorities. Thus, as with PageRank, we iterate a process that updates the authority score of a page to be the sum of the hub scores of the pages that point to it, and the hub score to be the sum of the authority scores of the pages it points to. If we then normalize the scores and repeat k times, the process will converge.

Both PageRank and HITS played important roles in developing our understanding of Web information retrieval. These algorithms and their extensions are used in ranking billions of queries daily as search engines steadily develop better ways of extracting yet finer signals of search relevance.

3.6 Question answering

QUESTION ANSWERING

Information retrieval is the task of finding documents that are relevant to a query, where the query may be a question, or just a topic area or concept. **Question answering** is a somewhat different task, in which the query really is a question, and the answer is not a ranked list of documents but rather a short response—a sentence, or even just a phrase. There have been question-answering NLP (natural language processing) systems since the 1960s, but only since 2001 have such systems used Web information retrieval to radically increase their breadth of coverage.

The ASKMSR system (Banko *et al.*, 2002) is a typical Web-based question-answering system. It is based on the intuition that most questions will be answered many times on the Web, so question answering should be thought of as a problem in precision, not recall. We don't have to deal with all the different ways that an answer might be phrased—we only have to find one of them. For example, consider the query [Who killed Abraham Lincoln?] Suppose a system had to answer that question with access only to a single encyclopedia, whose entry on Lincoln said

> John Wilkes Booth altered history with a bullet. He will forever be known as the man who ended Abraham Lincoln's life.

To use this passage to answer the question, the system would have to know that ending a life can be a killing, that "He" refers to Booth, and several other linguistic and semantic facts.

AskMSR does not attempt this kind of sophistication—it knows nothing about pronoun reference, or about killing, or any other verb. It does know 15 different kinds of questions, and how they can be rewritten as queries to a search engine. It knows that [Who killed Abraham Lincoln] can be rewritten as the query [* killed Abraham Lincoln] and as [Abraham Lincoln was killed by *]. It issues these rewritten queries and examines the results that come back—not the full Web pages, just the short summaries of text that appear near the query terms. The results are broken into 1-, 2-, and 3-grams and tallied for frequency in the result sets and for weight: an n-gram that came back from a very specific query rewrite (such as the exact phrase match query ["Abraham Lincoln was killed by *"]) would get more weight than one from a general query rewrite, such as [Abraham OR Lincoln OR killed]. We would expect that "John Wilkes Booth" would be among the highly ranked n-grams retrieved, but so would "Abraham Lincoln" and "the assassination of" and "Ford's Theatre."

Once the n-grams are scored, they are filtered by expected type. If the original query starts with "who," then we filter on names of people; for "how many" we filter on numbers, for "when," on a date or time. There is also a filter that says the answer should not be part of the question; together these should allow us to return "John Wilkes Booth" (and not "Abraham Lincoln") as the highest-scoring response.

In some cases the answer will be longer than three words; since the components responses only go up to 3-grams, a longer response would have to be pieced together from shorter pieces. For example, in a system that used only bigrams, the answer "John Wilkes Booth" could be pieced together from high-scoring pieces "John Wilkes" and "Wilkes Booth."

At the Text Retrieval Evaluation Conference (TREC), AskMSR was rated as one of the top systems, beating out competitors with the ability to do far more complex language understanding. AskMSR relies upon the breadth of the content on the Web rather than on its own depth of understanding. It won't be able to handle complex inference patterns like associating "who killed" with "ended the life of." But it knows that the Web is so vast that it can afford to ignore passages like that and wait for a simple passage it can handle.

4 Information Extraction

INFORMATION EXTRACTION

Information extraction is the process of acquiring knowledge by skimming a text and looking for occurrences of a particular class of object and for relationships among objects. A typical task is to extract instances of addresses from Web pages, with database fields for street, city, state, and zip code; or instances of storms from weather reports, with fields for temperature, wind speed, and precipitation. In a limited domain, this can be done with high accuracy. As the domain gets more general, more complex linguistic models and more complex learning techniques are necessary. We can define complex language models of the phrase structure (noun phrases and verb phrases) of English. But so far there are no complete models of this kind, so for the limited needs of information extraction, we define limited models that approximate the full English model, and concentrate on just the parts that are needed for the task at hand. The models we describe in this section are approximations in the same way that the simple 1-CNF logical model is an approximation of the full, wiggly, logical model.

In this section we describe six different approaches to information extraction, in order of increasing complexity on several dimensions: deterministic to stochastic, domain-specific to general, hand-crafted to learned, and small-scale to large-scale.

4.1 Finite-state automata for information extraction

ATTRIBUTE-BASED EXTRACTION

The simplest type of information extraction system is an **attribute-based extraction** system that assumes that the entire text refers to a single object and the task is to extract attributes of that object. For example, the problem of extracting from the text "IBM ThinkBook 970. Our price: $399.00" the set of attributes {Manufacturer=IBM, Model=ThinkBook970, Price=$399.00}. We can address this problem by defining a **template** (also known as a pattern) for each attribute we would like to extract. The template is defined by a finite state automaton, the simplest example of which is the **regular expression**, or regex. Regular expressions are used in Unix commands such as grep, in programming languages such as Perl, and in word processors such as Microsoft Word. The details vary slightly from one tool to another and so are best learned from the appropriate manual, but here we show how to build up a regular expression template for prices in dollars:

TEMPLATE

REGULAR EXPRESSION

`[0-9]`	matches any digit from 0 to 9
`[0-9]+`	matches one or more digits
`[.][0-9][0-9]`	matches a period followed by two digits
`([.][0-9][0-9])?`	matches a period followed by two digits, or nothing
`[$][0-9]+([.][0-9][0-9])?`	matches $249.99 or $1.23 or $1000000 or ...

Templates are often defined with three parts: a prefix regex, a target regex, and a postfix regex. For prices, the target regex is as above, the prefix would look for strings such as "price:" and the postfix could be empty. The idea is that some clues about an attribute come from the attribute value itself and some come from the surrounding text.

If a regular expression for an attribute matches the text exactly once, then we can pull out the portion of the text that is the value of the attribute. If there is no match, all we can do is give a default value or leave the attribute missing; but if there are several matches, we need a process to choose among them. One strategy is to have several templates for each attribute, ordered by priority. So, for example, the top-priority template for price might look for the prefix "our price:"; if that is not found, we look for the prefix "price:" and if that is not found, the empty prefix. Another strategy is to take all the matches and find some way to choose among them. For example, we could take the lowest price that is within 50% of the highest price. That will select $78.00 as the target from the text "List price $99.00, special sale price $78.00, shipping $3.00."

RELATIONAL EXTRACTION

One step up from attribute-based extraction systems are **relational extraction** systems, which deal with multiple objects and the relations among them. Thus, when these systems see the text "$249.99," they need to determine not just that it is a price, but also which object has that price. A typical relational-based extraction system is FASTUS, which handles news stories about corporate mergers and acquisitions. It can read the story

Bridgestone Sports Co. said Friday it has set up a joint venture in Taiwan with a local concern and a Japanese trading house to produce golf clubs to be shipped to Japan.

and extract the relations:

$$e \in JointVentures \land Product(e, \text{“golf clubs”}) \land Date(e, \text{“Friday”})$$
$$\land\, Member(e, \text{“Bridgestone Sports Co”}) \land Member(e, \text{“a local concern”})$$
$$\land\, Member(e, \text{“a Japanese trading house”})\,.$$

CASCADED FINITE-STATE TRANSDUCERS

A relational extraction system can be built as a series of **cascaded finite-state transducers**. That is, the system consists of a series of small, efficient finite-state automata (FSAs), where each automaton receives text as input, transduces the text into a different format, and passes it along to the next automaton. FASTUS consists of five stages:

1. Tokenization
2. Complex-word handling
3. Basic-group handling
4. Complex-phrase handling
5. Structure merging

FASTUS's first stage is **tokenization**, which segments the stream of characters into tokens (words, numbers, and punctuation). For English, tokenization can be fairly simple; just separating characters at white space or punctuation does a fairly good job. Some tokenizers also deal with markup languages such as HTML, SGML, and XML.

The second stage handles **complex words**, including collocations such as “set up” and “joint venture,” as well as proper names such as “Bridgestone Sports Co.” These are recognized by a combination of lexical entries and finite-state grammar rules. For example, a company name might be recognized by the rule

CapitalizedWord+ (“Company” | “Co” | “Inc” | “Ltd”)

The third stage handles **basic groups**, meaning noun groups and verb groups. The idea is to chunk these into units that will be managed by the later stages. Here we have simple rules that only approximate the complexity of English, but have the advantage of being representable by finite state automata. The example sentence would emerge from this stage as the following sequence of tagged groups:

```
1 NG: Bridgestone Sports Co.   10 NG: a local concern
2 VG: said                     11 CJ: and
3 NG: Friday                   12 NG: a Japanese trading house
4 NG: it                       13 VG: to produce
5 VG: had set up               14 NG: golf clubs
6 NG: a joint venture          15 VG: to be shipped
7 PR: in                       16 PR: to
8 NG: Taiwan                   17 NG: Japan
9 PR: with
```

Here NG means noun group, VG is verb group, PR is preposition, and CJ is conjunction.

The fourth stage combines the basic groups into **complex phrases**. Again, the aim is to have rules that are finite-state and thus can be processed quickly, and that result in unambiguous (or nearly unambiguous) output phrases. One type of combination rule deals with domain-specific events. For example, the rule

Company+ SetUp JointVenture ("with" Company+)?

captures one way to describe the formation of a joint venture. This stage is the first one in the cascade where the output is placed into a database template as well as being placed in the output stream. The final stage **merges structures** that were built up in the previous step. If the next sentence says "The joint venture will start production in January," then this step will notice that there are two references to a joint venture, and that they should be merged into one. This is an instance of the **identity uncertainty problem**.

In general, finite-state template-based information extraction works well for a restricted domain in which it is possible to predetermine what subjects will be discussed, and how they will be mentioned. The cascaded transducer model helps modularize the necessary knowledge, easing construction of the system. These systems work especially well when they are reverse-engineering text that has been generated by a program. For example, a shopping site on the Web is generated by a program that takes database entries and formats them into Web pages; a template-based extractor then recovers the original database. Finite-state information extraction is less successful at recovering information in highly variable format, such as text written by humans on a variety of subjects.

4.2 Probabilistic models for information extraction

When information extraction must be attempted from noisy or varied input, simple finite-state approaches fare poorly. It is too hard to get all the rules and their priorities right; it is better to use a probabilistic model rather than a rule-based model. The simplest probabilistic model for sequences with hidden state is the hidden Markov model, or HMM.

Recall that an HMM models a progression through a sequence of hidden states, $\mathbf{x}_t$, with an observation $\mathbf{e}_t$ at each step. To apply HMMs to information extraction, we can either build one big HMM for all the attributes or build a separate HMM for each attribute. We'll do the second. The observations are the words of the text, and the hidden states are whether we are in the target, prefix, or postfix part of the attribute template, or in the background (not part of a template). For example, here is a brief text and the most probable (Viterbi) path for that text for two HMMs, one trained to recognize the speaker in a talk announcement, and one trained to recognize dates. The "-" indicates a background state:

Text:	There	will	be	a	seminar	by	Dr.	Andrew	McCallum	on	Friday
Speaker:	-	-	-	-	PRE	PRE	TARGET	TARGET	TARGET	POST	-
Date:	-	-	-	-	-	-	-	-	-	PRE	TARGET

HMMs have two big advantages over FSAs for extraction. First, HMMs are probabilistic, and thus tolerant to noise. In a regular expression, if a single expected character is missing, the regex fails to match; with HMMs there is graceful degradation with missing characters/words, and we get a probability indicating the degree of match, not just a Boolean match/fail. Second,

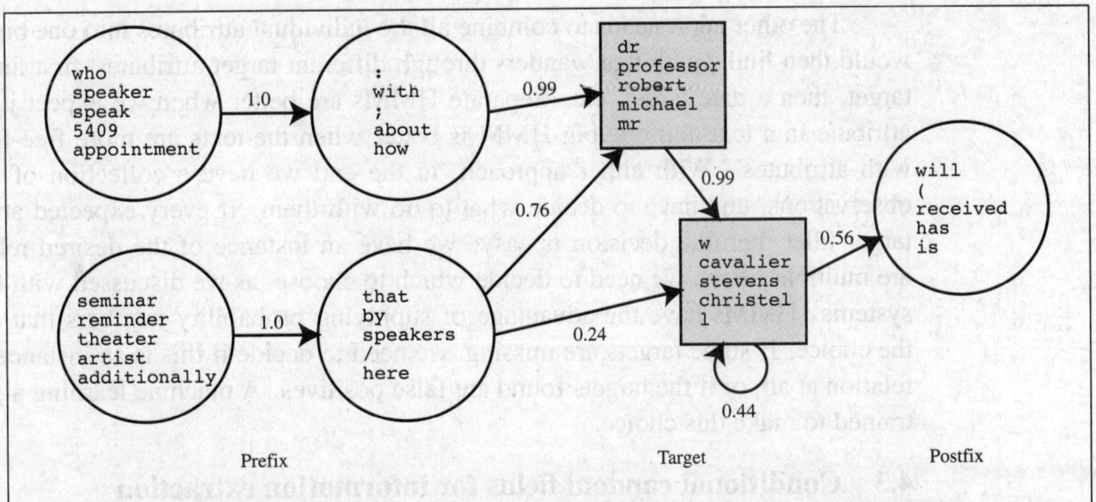

Figure 2 Hidden Markov model for the **speaker** of a talk announcement. The two square states are the target (note the second target state has a self-loop, so the target can match a string of any length), the four circles to the left are the prefix, and the one on the right is the postfix. For each state, only a few of the high-probability words are shown. From Freitag and McCallum (2000).

HMMs can be trained from data; they don't require laborious engineering of templates, and thus they can more easily be kept up to date as text changes over time.

Note that we have assumed a certain level of structure in our HMM templates: they all consist of one or more target states, and any prefix states must precede the targets, postfix states most follow the targets, and other states must be background. This structure makes it easier to learn HMMs from examples. With a partially specified structure, the forward–backward algorithm can be used to learn both the transition probabilities $\mathbf{P}(\mathbf{X}_t \mid \mathbf{X}_{t-1})$ between states and the observation model, $\mathbf{P}(\mathbf{E}_t \mid \mathbf{X}_t)$, which says how likely each word is in each state. For example, the word "Friday" would have high probability in one or more of the target states of the date HMM, and lower probability elsewhere.

With sufficient training data, the HMM automatically learns a structure of dates that we find intuitive: the date HMM might have one target state in which the high-probability words are "Monday," "Tuesday," etc., and which has a high-probability transition to a target state with words "Jan", "January," "Feb," etc. Figure 2 shows the HMM for the speaker of a talk announcement, as learned from data. The prefix covers expressions such as "Speaker:" and "seminar by," and the target has one state that covers titles and first names and another state that covers initials and last names.

Once the HMMs have been learned, we can apply them to a text, using the Viterbi algorithm to find the most likely path through the HMM states. One approach is to apply each attribute HMM separately; in this case you would expect most of the HMMs to spend most of their time in background states. This is appropriate when the extraction is sparse—when the number of extracted words is small compared to the length of the text.

The other approach is to combine all the individual attributes into one big HMM, which would then find a path that wanders through different target attributes, first finding a speaker target, then a date target, etc. Separate HMMs are better when we expect just one of each attribute in a text and one big HMM is better when the texts are more free-form and dense with attributes. With either approach, in the end we have a collection of target attribute observations, and have to decide what to do with them. If every expected attribute has one target filler then the decision is easy: we have an instance of the desired relation. If there are multiple fillers, we need to decide which to choose, as we discussed with template-based systems. HMMs have the advantage of supplying probability numbers that can help make the choice. If some targets are missing, we need to decide if this is an instance of the desired relation at all, or if the targets found are false positives. A machine learning algorithm can be trained to make this choice.

4.3 Conditional random fields for information extraction

One issue with HMMs for the information extraction task is that they model a lot of probabilities that we don't really need. An HMM is a generative model; it models the full joint probability of observations and hidden states, and thus can be used to generate samples. That is, we can use the HMM model not only to parse a text and recover the speaker and date, but also to generate a random instance of a text containing a speaker and a date. Since we're not interested in that task, it is natural to ask whether we might be better off with a model that doesn't bother modeling that possibility. All we need in order to understand a text is a **discriminative model**, one that models the conditional probability of the hidden attributes given the observations (the text). Given a text $\mathbf{e}_{1:N}$, the conditional model finds the hidden state sequence $\mathbf{X}_{1:N}$ that maximizes $P(\mathbf{X}_{1:N} \mid \mathbf{e}_{1:N})$.

Modeling this directly gives us some freedom. We don't need the independence assumptions of the Markov model—we can have an $\mathbf{x}_t$ that is dependent on $\mathbf{x}_1$. A framework for this type of model is the **conditional random field**, or CRF, which models a conditional probability distribution of a set of target variables given a set of observed variables. Like Bayesian networks, CRFs can represent many different structures of dependencies among the variables. One common structure is the **linear-chain conditional random field** for representing Markov dependencies among variables in a temporal sequence. Thus, HMMs are the temporal version of naive Bayes models, and linear-chain CRFs are the temporal version of logistic regression, where the predicted target is an entire state sequence rather than a single binary variable.

CONDITIONAL RANDOM FIELD

LINEAR-CHAIN CONDITIONAL RANDOM FIELD

Let $\mathbf{e}_{1:N}$ be the observations (e.g., words in a document), and $\mathbf{x}_{1:N}$ be the sequence of hidden states (e.g., the prefix, target, and postfix states). A linear-chain conditional random field defines a conditional probability distribution:

$$\mathbf{P}(\mathbf{x}_{1:N}|\mathbf{e}_{1:N}) = \alpha\, e^{\left[\sum_{i=1}^{N} F(\mathbf{x}_{i-1},\mathbf{x}_i,\mathbf{e},i)\right]} ,$$

where α is a normalization factor (to make sure the probabilities sum to 1), and F is a feature function defined as the weighted sum of a collection of k component feature functions:

$$F(\mathbf{x}_{i-1},\mathbf{x}_i,\mathbf{e},i) = \sum_k \lambda_k\, f_k(\mathbf{x}_{i-1},\mathbf{x}_i,\mathbf{e},i) .$$

The λ_k parameter values are learned with a MAP (maximum a posteriori) estimation procedure that maximizes the conditional likelihood of the training data. The feature functions are the key components of a CRF. The function f_k has access to a pair of adjacent states, $\mathbf{x}_{i-1}$ and $\mathbf{x}_i$, but also the entire observation (word) sequence $\mathbf{e}$, and the current position in the temporal sequence, i. This gives us a lot of flexibility in defining features. We can define a simple feature function, for example one that produces a value of 1 if the current word is ANDREW and the current state is SPEAKER:

$$f_1(\mathbf{x}_{i-1}, \mathbf{x}_i, \mathbf{e}, i) = \begin{cases} 1 & \text{if } \mathbf{x}_i = \text{SPEAKER and } \mathbf{e}_i = \text{ANDREW} \\ 0 & \text{otherwise} \end{cases}$$

How are features like these used? It depends on their corresponding weights. If $\lambda_1 > 0$, then whenever f_1 is true, it increases the probability of the hidden state sequence $\mathbf{x}_{1:N}$. This is another way of saying "the CRF model should prefer the target state SPEAKER for the word ANDREW." If on the other hand $\lambda_1 < 0$, the CRF model will try to avoid this association, and if $\lambda_1 = 0$, this feature is ignored. Parameter values can be set manually or can be learned from data. Now consider a second feature function:

$$f_2(\mathbf{x}_{i-1}, \mathbf{x}_i, \mathbf{e}, i) = \begin{cases} 1 & \text{if } \mathbf{x}_i = \text{SPEAKER and } \mathbf{e}_{i+1} = \text{SAID} \\ 0 & \text{otherwise} \end{cases}$$

This feature is true if the current state is SPEAKER and the next word is "said." One would therefore expect a positive λ_2 value to go with the feature. More interestingly, note that both f_1 and f_2 can hold at the same time for a sentence like "Andrew said ...." In this case, the two features overlap each other and both boost the belief in $\mathbf{x}_1 = $ SPEAKER. Because of the independence assumption, HMMs cannot use overlapping features; CRFs can. Furthermore, a feature in a CRF can use any part of the sequence $\mathbf{e}_{1:N}$. Features can also be defined over transitions between states. The features we defined here were binary, but in general, a feature function can be any real-valued function. For domains where we have some knowledge about the types of features we would like to include, the CRF formalism gives us a great deal of flexibility in defining them. This flexibility can lead to accuracies that are higher than with less flexible models such as HMMs.

4.4 Ontology extraction from large corpora

So far we have thought of information extraction as finding a specific set of relations (e.g., speaker, time, location) in a specific text (e.g., a talk announcement). A different application of extraction technology is building a large knowledge base or ontology of facts from a corpus. This is different in three ways: First it is open-ended—we want to acquire facts about all types of domains, not just one specific domain. Second, with a large corpus, this task is dominated by precision, not recall—just as with question answering on the Web (Section 3.6). Third, the results can be statistical aggregates gathered from multiple sources, rather than being extracted from one specific text.

For example, Hearst (1992) looked at the problem of learning an ontology of concept categories and subcategories from a large corpus. (In 1992, a large corpus was a 1000-page encyclopedia; today it would be a 100-million-page Web corpus.) The work concentrated on templates that are very general (not tied to a specific domain) and have high precision (are almost always correct when they match) but low recall (do not always match). Here is one of the most productive templates:

NP **such as** *NP* (**,** *NP*)* (,)? ((**and** | **or**) *NP*)? .

Here the bold words and commas must appear literally in the text, but the parentheses are for grouping, the asterisk means *repetition of zero or more*, and the question mark means *optional al.* *NP* is a variable standing for a noun phrase; for now just assume that we know some words are nouns and other words (such as verbs) that we can reliably assume are not part of a simple noun phrase. This template matches the texts "diseases such as rabies affect your dog" and "supports network protocols such as DNS," concluding that rabies is a disease and DNS is a network protocol. Similar templates can be constructed with the key words "including," "especially," and "or other." Of course these templates will fail to match many relevant passages, like "Rabies is a disease." That is intentional. The "*NP* is a *NP*" template does indeed sometimes denote a subcategory relation, but it often means something else, as in "There is a God" or "She is a little tired." With a large corpus we can afford to be picky; to use only the high-precision templates. We'll miss many statements of a subcategory relationship, but most likely we'll find a paraphrase of the statement somewhere else in the corpus in a form we can use.

4.5 Automated template construction

The *subcategory* relation is so fundamental that is worthwhile to handcraft a few templates to help identify instances of it occurring in natural language text. But what about the thousands of other relations in the world? There aren't enough AI grad students in the world to create and debug templates for all of them. Fortunately, it is possible to *learn* templates from a few examples, then use the templates to learn more examples, from which more templates can be learned, and so on. In one of the first experiments of this kind, Brin (1999) started with a data set of just five examples:

("Isaac Asimov", "The Robots of Dawn")
("David Brin", "Startide Rising")
("James Gleick", "Chaos—Making a New Science")
("Charles Dickens", "Great Expectations")
("William Shakespeare", "The Comedy of Errors")

Clearly these are examples of the author–title relation, but the learning system had no knowledge of authors or titles. The words in these examples were used in a search over a Web corpus, resulting in 199 matches. Each match is defined as a tuple of seven strings,

(*Author, Title, Order, Prefix, Middle, Postfix, URL*) ,

where *Order* is true if the author came first and false if the title came first, *Middle* is the characters between the author and title, *Prefix* is the 10 characters before the match, *Suffix* is the 10 characters after the match, and *URL* is the Web address where the match was made.

Given a set of matches, a simple template-generation scheme can find templates to explain the matches. The language of templates was designed to have a close mapping to the matches themselves, to be amenable to automated learning, and to emphasize high precision (possibly at the risk of lower recall). Each template has the same seven components as a match. The *Author* and *Title* are regexes consisting of any characters (but beginning and ending in letters) and constrained to have a length from half the minimum length of the examples to twice the maximum length. The prefix, middle, and postfix are restricted to literal strings, not regexes. The middle is the easiest to learn: each distinct middle string in the set of matches is a distinct candidate template. For each such candidate, the template's *Prefix* is then defined as the longest common suffix of all the prefixes in the matches, and the *Postfix* is defined as the longest common prefix of all the postfixes in the matches. If either of these is of length zero, then the template is rejected. The *URL* of the template is defined as the longest prefix of the URLs in the matches.

In the experiment run by Brin, the first 199 matches generated three templates. The most productive template was

`<LI><B>` *Title* `</B> by` *Author* `(`
URL: `www.sff.net/locus/c`

The three templates were then used to retrieve 4047 more (author, title) examples. The examples were then used to generate more templates, and so on, eventually yielding over 15,000 titles. Given a good set of templates, the system can collect a good set of examples. Given a good set of examples, the system can build a good set of templates.

The biggest weakness in this approach is the sensitivity to noise. If one of the first few templates is incorrect, errors can propagate quickly. One way to limit this problem is to not accept a new example unless it is verified by multiple templates, and not accept a new template unless it discovers multiple examples that are also found by other templates.

4.6 Machine reading

Automated template construction is a big step up from handcrafted template construction, but it still requires a handful of labeled examples of each relation to get started. To build a large ontology with many thousands of relations, even that amount of work would be onerous; we would like to have an extraction system with *no* human input of any kind—a system that could read on its own and build up its own database. Such a system would be relation-independent; would work for any relation. In practice, these systems work on *all* relations in parallel, because of the I/O demands of large corpora. They behave less like a traditional information-extraction system that is targeted at a few relations and more like a human reader who learns from the text itself; because of this the field has been called **machine reading**.

MACHINE READING

A representative machine-reading system is TEXTRUNNER (Banko and Etzioni, 2008). TEXTRUNNER uses cotraining to boost its performance, but it needs something to bootstrap from. In the case of Hearst (1992), specific patterns (e.g., *such as*) provided the bootstrap, and for Brin (1998), it was a set of five author–title pairs. For TEXTRUNNER, the original inspiration was a taxonomy of eight very general syntactic templates, as shown in Figure 3. It was felt that a small number of templates like this could cover most of the ways that relationships are expressed in English. The actual bootsrapping starts from a set of labelled examples that are extracted from the Penn Treebank, a corpus of parsed sentences. For example, from the parse of the sentence "Einstein received the Nobel Prize in 1921," TEXTRUNNER is able to extract the relation ("Einstein," "received," "Nobel Prize").

Given a set of labeled examples of this type, TEXTRUNNER trains a linear-chain CRF to extract further examples from unlabeled text. The features in the CRF include function words like "to" and "of" and "the," but not nouns and verbs (and not noun phrases or verb phrases). Because TEXTRUNNER is domain-independent, it cannot rely on predefined lists of nouns and verbs.

Type	Template	Example	Frequency
Verb	NP_1 *Verb* NP_2	X established Y	38%
Noun–Prep	NP_1 *NP Prep* NP_2	X settlement with Y	23%
Verb–Prep	NP_1 *Verb Prep* NP_2	X moved to Y	16%
Infinitive	NP_1 **to** *Verb* NP_2	X plans to acquire Y	9%
Modifier	NP_1 *Verb* NP_2 *Noun*	X is Y winner	5%
Noun-Coordinate	NP_1 (, | **and** | - | :) NP_2 *NP*	X-Y deal	2%
Verb-Coordinate	NP_1 (,| **and**) NP_2 *Verb*	X, Y merge	1%
Appositive	NP_1 *NP* (:| ,)? NP_2	X hometown : Y	1%

Figure 3 Eight general templates that cover about 95% of the ways that relations are expressed in English.

TEXTRUNNER achieves a precision of 88% and recall of 45% (F_1 of 60%) on a large Web corpus. TEXTRUNNER has extracted hundreds of millions of facts from a corpus of a half-billion Web pages. For example, even though it has no predefined medical knowledge, it has extracted over 2000 answers to the query [what kills bacteria]; correct answers include antibiotics, ozone, chlorine, Cipro, and broccoli sprouts. Questionable answers include "water," which came from the sentence "Boiling water for at least 10 minutes will kill bacteria." It would be better to attribute this to "boiling water" rather than just "water."

With the techniques outlined in this chapter and continual new inventions, we are starting to get closer to the goal of machine reading.

5 SUMMARY

The main points of this chapter are as follows:

- Probabilistic language models based on n-grams recover a surprising amount of information about a language. They can perform well on such diverse tasks as language identification, spelling correction, genre classification, and named-entity recognition.
- These language models can have millions of features, so feature selection and preprocessing of the data to reduce noise is important.
- **Text classification** can be done with naive Bayes n-gram models or with any of the classification algorithms we have previously discussed. Classification can also be seen as a problem in data compression.

- **Information retrieval** systems use a very simple language model based on bags of words, yet still manage to perform well in terms of **recall** and **precision** on very large corpora of text. On Web corpora, link-analysis algorithms improve performance.
- **Question answering** can be handled by an approach based on information retrieval, for questions that have multiple answers in the corpus. When more answers are available in the corpus, we can use techniques that emphasize precision rather than recall.
- **Information-extraction** systems use a more complex model that includes limited notions of syntax and semantics in the form of templates. They can be built from finite-state automata, HMMs, or conditional random fields, and can be learned from examples.
- In building a statistical language system, it is best to devise a model that can make good use of available **data**, even if the model seems overly simplistic.

BIBLIOGRAPHICAL AND HISTORICAL NOTES

N-gram letter models for language modeling were proposed by Markov (1913). Claude Shannon (Shannon and Weaver, 1949) was the first to generate n-gram word models of English. Chomsky (1956, 1957) pointed out the limitations of finite-state models compared with context-free models, concluding, "Probabilistic models give no particular insight into some of the basic problems of syntactic structure." This is true, but probabilistic models *do* provide insight into some *other* basic problems—problems that context-free models ignore. Chomsky's remarks had the unfortunate effect of scaring many people away from statistical models for two decades, until these models reemerged for use in speech recognition (Jelinek, 1976).

Kessler *et al.* (1997) show how to apply character n-gram models to genre classification, and Klein *et al.* (2003) describe named-entity recognition with character models. Franz and Brants (2006) describe the Google n-gram corpus of 13 million unique words from a trillion words of Web text; it is now publicly available. The **bag of words** model gets its name from a passage from linguist Zellig Harris (1954), "language is not merely a bag of words but a tool with particular properties." Norvig (2009) gives some examples of tasks that can be accomplished with n-gram models.

Add-one smoothing, first suggested by Pierre-Simon Laplace (1816), was formalized by Jeffreys (1948), and interpolation smoothing is due to Jelinek and Mercer (1980), who used it for speech recognition. Other techniques include Witten–Bell smoothing (1991), Good–Turing smoothing (Church and Gale, 1991) and Kneser–Ney smoothing (1995). Chen and Goodman (1996) and Goodman (2001) survey smoothing techniques.

Simple n-gram letter and word models are not the only possible probabilistic models. Blei *et al.* (2001) describe a probabilistic text model called **latent Dirichlet allocation** that views a document as a mixture of topics, each with its own distribution of words. This model can be seen as an extension and rationalization of the **latent semantic indexing** model of (Deerwester *et al.*, 1990) (see also Papadimitriou *et al.* (1998)) and is also related to the multiple-cause mixture model of (Sahami *et al.*, 1996).

Manning and Schütze (1999) and Sebastiani (2002) survey text-classification techniques. Joachims (2001) uses statistical learning theory and support vector machines to give a theoretical analysis of when classification will be successful. Apté *et al.* (1994) report an accuracy of 96% in classifying Reuters news articles into the "Earnings" category. Koller and Sahami (1997) report accuracy up to 95% with a naive Bayes classifier, and up to 98.6% with a Bayes classifier that accounts for some dependencies among features. Lewis (1998) surveys forty years of application of naive Bayes techniques to text classification and retrieval. Schapire and Singer (2000) show that simple linear classifiers can often achieve accuracy almost as good as more complex models and are more efficient to evaluate. Nigam *et al.* (2000) show how to use the EM algorithm to label unlabeled documents, thus learning a better classification model. Witten *et al.* (1999) describe compression algorithms for classification, and show the deep connection between the LZW compression algorithm and maximum-entropy language models.

Many of the n-gram model techniques are also used in bioinformatics problems. Biostatistics and probabilistic NLP are coming closer together, as each deals with long, structured sequences chosen from an alphabet of constituents.

The field of **information retrieval** is experiencing a regrowth in interest, sparked by the wide usage of Internet searching. Robertson (1977) gives an early overview and introduces the probability ranking principle. Croft *et al.* (2009) and Manning *et al.* (2008) are the first textbooks to cover Web-based search as well as traditional IR. Hearst (2009) covers user interfaces for Web search. The TREC conference, organized by the U.S. government's National Institute of Standards and Technology (NIST), hosts an annual competition for IR systems and publishes proceedings with results. In the first seven years of the competition, performance roughly doubled.

The most popular model for IR is the **vector space model** (Salton *et al.*, 1975). Salton's work dominated the early years of the field. There are two alternative probabilistic models, one due to Ponte and Croft (1998) and one by Maron and Kuhns (1960) and Robertson and Sparck Jones (1976). Lafferty and Zhai (2001) show that the models are based on the same joint probability distribution, but that the choice of model has implications for training the parameters. Craswell *et al.* (2005) describe the BM25 scoring function and Svore and Burges (2009) describe how BM25 can be improved with a machine learning approach that incorporates click data—examples of past search queies and the results that were clicked on.

Brin and Page (1998) describe the PageRank algorithm and the implementation of a Web search engine. Kleinberg (1999) describes the HITS algorithm. Silverstein *et al.* (1998) investigate a log of a billion Web searches. The journal *Information Retrieval* and the proceedings of the annual *SIGIR* conference cover recent developments in the field.

Early information extraction programs include GUS (Bobrow *et al.*, 1977) and FRUMP (DeJong, 1982). Recent information extraction has been pushed forward by the annual Message Understand Conferences (MUC), sponsored by the U.S. government. The FASTUS finite-state system was done by Hobbs *et al.* (1997). It was based in part on the idea from Pereira and Wright (1991) of using FSAs as approximations to phrase-structure grammars. Surveys of template-based systems are given by Roche and Schabes (1997), Appelt (1999), and Muslea (1999). Large databases of facts were extracted by Craven *et al.* (2000), Pasca *et al.* (2006), Mitchell (2007), and Durme and Pasca (2008).

Freitag and McCallum (2000) discuss HMMs for Information Extraction. CRFs were introduced by Lafferty *et al.* (2001); an example of their use for information extraction is described in (McCallum, 2003) and a tutorial with practical guidance is given by (Sutton and McCallum, 2007). Sarawagi (2007) gives a comprehensive survey.

Banko *et al.* (2002) present the ASKMSR question-answering system; a similar system is due to Kwok *et al.* (2001). Pasca and Harabagiu (2001) discuss a contest-winning question-answering system. Two early influential approaches to automated knowledge engineering were by Riloff (1993), who showed that an automatically constructed dictionary performed almost as well as a carefully handcrafted domain-specific dictionary, and by Yarowsky (1995), who showed that the task of word sense classification could be accomplished through unsupervised training on a corpus of unlabeled text with accuracy as good as supervised methods.

The idea of simultaneously extracting templates and examples from a handful of labeled examples was developed independently and simultaneously by Blum and Mitchell (1998), who called it **cotraining** and by Brin (1998), who called it DIPRE (Dual Iterative Pattern Relation Extraction). You can see why the term *cotraining* has stuck. Similar early work, under the name of bootstrapping, was done by Jones *et al.* (1999). The method was advanced by the QXTRACT (Agichtein and Gravano, 2003) and KNOWITALL (Etzioni *et al.*, 2005) systems. Machine reading was introduced by Mitchell (2005) and Etzioni *et al.* (2006) and is the focus of the TEXTRUNNER project (Banko *et al.*, 2007; Banko and Etzioni, 2008).

This chapter has focused on natural language text, but it is also possible to do information extraction based on the physical structure or layout of text rather than on the linguistic structure. HTML lists and tables in both HTML and relational databases are home to data that can be extracted and consolidated (Hurst, 2000; Pinto *et al.*, 2003; Cafarella *et al.*, 2008).

The Association for Computational Linguistics (ACL) holds regular conferences and publishes the journal *Computational Linguistics*. There is also an International Conference on Computational Linguistics (COLING). The textbook by Manning and Schütze (1999) covers statistical language processing, while Jurafsky and Martin (2008) give a comprehensive introduction to speech and natural language processing.

EXERCISES

1 This exercise explores the quality of the n-gram model of language. Find or create a monolingual corpus of 100,000 words or more. Segment it into words, and compute the frequency of each word. How many distinct words are there? Also count frequencies of bigrams (two consecutive words) and trigrams (three consecutive words). Now use those frequencies to generate language: from the unigram, bigram, and trigram models, in turn, generate a 100-word text by making random choices according to the frequency counts. Compare the three generated texts with actual language. Finally, calculate the perplexity of each model.

2 Write a program to do **segmentation** of words without spaces. Given a string, such as the URL "thelongestlistofthelongeststuffatthelongestdomainnameatlonglast.com," return a list of component words: ["the," "longest," "list," . . .]. This task is useful for parsing URLs, for spelling correction when words runtogether, and for languages such as Chinese that do not have spaces between words. It can be solved with a unigram or bigram word model and a dynamic programming algorithm similar to the Viterbi algorithm.

3 (Adapted from Jurafsky and Martin (2000).) In this exercise you will develop a classifier for authorship: given a text, the classifier predicts which of two candidate authors wrote the text. Obtain samples of text from two different authors. Separate them into training and test sets. Now train a language model on the training set. You can choose what features to use; n-grams of words or letters are the easiest, but you can add additional features that you think may help. Then compute the probability of the text under each language model and chose the most probable model. Assess the accuracy of this technique. How does accuracy STYLOMETRY change as you alter the set of features? This subfield of linguistics is called **stylometry**; its successes include the identification of the author of the disputed *Federalist Papers* (Mosteller and Wallace, 1964) and some disputed works of Shakespeare (Hope, 1994). Khmelev and Tweedie (2001) produce good results with a simple letter bigram model.

4 This exercise concerns the classification of spam email. Create a corpus of spam email and one of non-spam mail. Examine each corpus and decide what features appear to be useful for classification: unigram words? bigrams? message length, sender, time of arrival? Then train a classification algorithm (decision tree, naive Bayes, SVM, logistic regression, or some other algorithm of your choosing) on a training set and report its accuracy on a test set.

5 Create a test set of ten queries, and pose them to three major Web search engines. Evaluate each one for precision at 1, 3, and 10 documents. Can you explain the differences between engines?

6 Try to ascertain which of the search engines from the previous exercise are using case folding, stemming, synonyms, and spelling correction.

7 Write a regular expression or a short program to extract company names. Test it on a corpus of business news articles. Report your recall and precision.

8 Consider the problem of trying to evaluate the quality of an IR system that returns a ranked list of answers (like most Web search engines). The appropriate measure of quality depends on the presumed model of what the searcher is trying to achieve, and what strategy she employs. For each of the following models, propose a corresponding numeric measure.

a. The searcher will look at the first twenty answers returned, with the objective of getting as much relevant information as possible.

b. The searcher needs only one relevant document, and will go down the list until she finds the first one.

c. The searcher has a fairly narrow query and is able to examine all the answers retrieved. She wants to be sure that she has seen everything in the document collection that is relevant to her query. (E.g., a lawyer wants to be sure that she has found *all* relevant precedents, and is willing to spend considerable resources on that.)

d. The searcher needs just one document relevant to the query, and can afford to pay a research assistant for an hour's work looking through the results. The assistant can look through 100 retrieved documents in an hour. The assistant will charge the searcher for the full hour regardless of whether he finds it immediately or at the end of the hour.

e. The searcher will look through all the answers. Examining a document has cost $\$A$; finding a relevant document has value $\$B$; failing to find a relevant document has cost $\$C$ for each relevant document not found.

f. The searcher wants to collect as many relevant documents as possible, but needs steady encouragement. She looks through the documents in order. If the documents she has looked at so far are mostly good, she will continue; otherwise, she will stop.

REINFORCEMENT LEARNING

REINFORCEMENT LEARNING

In which we examine how an agent can learn from success and failure, from reward and punishment.

1 INTRODUCTION

In this chapter, we will study how agents can learn *what to do* in the absence of labeled examples of what to do.

Consider, for example, the problem of learning to play chess. A supervised learning agent needs to be told the correct move for each position it encounters, but such feedback is seldom available. In the absence of feedback from a teacher, an agent can learn a transition model for its own moves and can perhaps learn to predict the opponent's moves, but *without some feedback about what is good and what is bad, the agent will have no grounds for deciding which move to make.* The agent needs to know that something good has happened when it (accidentally) checkmates the opponent, and that something bad has happened when it is checkmated—or vice versa, if the game is suicide chess. This kind of feedback is called a

REINFORCEMENT

reward, or **reinforcement**. In games like chess, the reinforcement is received only at the end of the game. In other environments, the rewards come more frequently. In ping-pong, each point scored can be considered a reward; when learning to crawl, any forward motion is an achievement. Our framework for agents regards the reward as *part* of the input percept, but the agent must be "hardwired" to recognize that part as a reward rather than as just another sensory input. Thus, animals seem to be hardwired to recognize pain and hunger as negative rewards and pleasure and food intake as positive rewards. Reinforcement has been carefully studied by animal psychologists for over 60 years.

Rewards can serve to define optimal policies in **Markov decision processes** (MDPs). An optimal policy is a policy that maximizes the expected total reward. The task of **reinforcement learning** is to use observed rewards to learn an optimal (or nearly optimal) policy for the environment. Rather than the agent having a complete model of the environment and knowing the reward function, here we assume no prior knowledge of either. Imagine playing a new game whose rules you don't know; after a hundred or so moves, your opponent announces, "You lose." This is reinforcement learning in a nutshell.

In many complex domains, reinforcement learning is the only feasible way to train a program to perform at high levels. For example, in game playing, it is very hard for a human to provide accurate and consistent evaluations of large numbers of positions, which would be needed to train an evaluation function directly from examples. Instead, the program can be told when it has won or lost, and it can use this information to learn an evaluation function that gives reasonably accurate estimates of the probability of winning from any given position. Similarly, it is extremely difficult to program an agent to fly a helicopter; yet given appropriate negative rewards for crashing, wobbling, or deviating from a set course, an agent can learn to fly by itself.

Reinforcement learning might be considered to encompass all of AI: an agent is placed in an environment and must learn to behave successfully therein. To keep the chapter manageable, we will concentrate on simple environments and simple agent designs. For the most part, we will assume a fully observable environment, so that the current state is supplied by each percept. On the other hand, we will assume that the agent does not know how the environment works or what its actions do, and we will allow for probabilistic action outcomes. Thus, the agent faces an unknown Markov decision process. We will consider three of the agent designs:

- A **utility-based agent** learns a utility function on states and uses it to select actions that maximize the expected outcome utility.
- Q-LEARNING Q-FUNCTION A **Q-learning** agent learns an **action-utility function**, or **Q-function**, giving the expected utility of taking a given action in a given state.
- A **reflex agent** learns a policy that maps directly from states to actions.

A utility-based agent must also have a model of the environment in order to make decisions, because it must know the states to which its actions will lead. For example, in order to make use of a backgammon evaluation function, a backgammon program must know what its legal moves are *and how they affect the board position*. Only in this way can it apply the utility function to the outcome states. A Q-learning agent, on the other hand, can compare the expected utilities for its available choices without needing to know their outcomes, so it does not need a model of the environment. On the other hand, because they do not know where their actions lead, Q-learning agents cannot look ahead; this can seriously restrict their ability to learn, as we shall see.

PASSIVE LEARNING ACTIVE LEARNING EXPLORATION We begin in Section 2 with **passive learning**, where the agent's policy is fixed and the task is to learn the utilities of states (or state–action pairs); this could also involve learning a model of the environment. Section 3 covers **active learning**, where the agent must also learn what to do. The principal issue is **exploration**: an agent must experience as much as possible of its environment in order to learn how to behave in it. Section 4 discusses how an agent can use inductive learning to learn much faster from its experiences. Section 5 covers methods for learning direct policy representations in reflex agents. An understanding of Markov decision processes is essential for this chapter.

2 PASSIVE REINFORCEMENT LEARNING

To keep things simple, we start with the case of a passive learning agent using a state-based representation in a fully observable environment. In passive learning, the agent's policy π is fixed: in state s, it always executes the action $\pi(s)$. Its goal is simply to learn how good the policy is—that is, to learn the utility function $U^{\pi}(s)$. We will use as our example the 4×3 world introduced in the chapter, "Making Complex Decisions". Figure 1 shows a policy for that world and the corresponding utilities. Clearly, the passive learning task is similar to the **policy evaluation** task, part of the **policy iteration** algorithm. The main difference is that the passive learning agent does not know the **transition model** $P(s'|s, a)$, which specifies the probability of reaching state s' from state s after doing action a; nor does it know the **reward function** $R(s)$, which specifies the reward for each state.

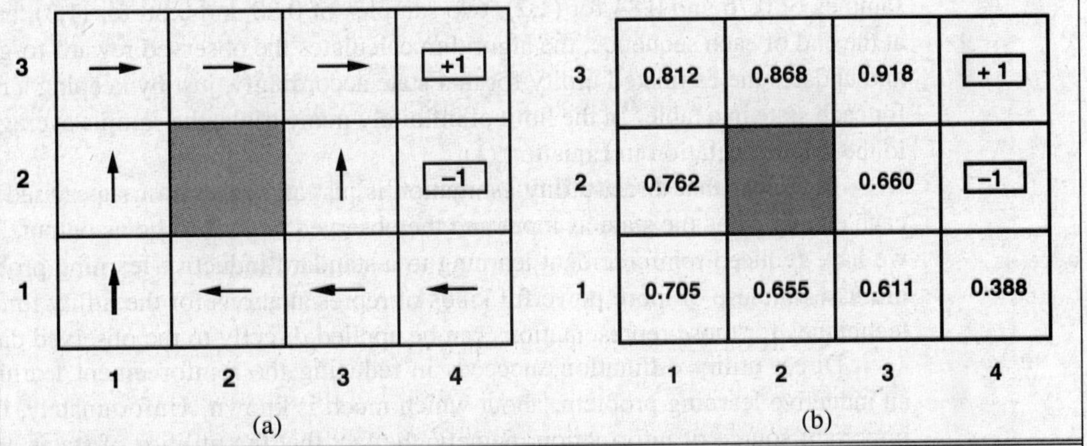

Figure 1 (a) A policy π for the 4×3 world; this policy happens to be optimal with rewards of $R(s) = -0.04$ in the nonterminal states and no discounting. (b) The utilities of the states in the 4×3 world, given policy π.

TRIAL

The agent executes a set of **trials** in the environment using its policy π. In each trial, the agent starts in state (1,1) and experiences a sequence of state transitions until it reaches one of the terminal states, (4,2) or (4,3). Its percepts supply both the current state and the reward received in that state. Typical trials might look like this:

$$(1,1)_{\textbf{-.04}} \rightsquigarrow (1,2)_{\textbf{-.04}} \rightsquigarrow (1,3)_{\textbf{-.04}} \rightsquigarrow (1,2)_{\textbf{-.04}} \rightsquigarrow (1,3)_{\textbf{-.04}} \rightsquigarrow (2,3)_{\textbf{-.04}} \rightsquigarrow (3,3)_{\textbf{-.04}} \rightsquigarrow (4,3)_{\textbf{+1}}$$
$$(1,1)_{\textbf{-.04}} \rightsquigarrow (1,2)_{\textbf{-.04}} \rightsquigarrow (1,3)_{\textbf{-.04}} \rightsquigarrow (2,3)_{\textbf{-.04}} \rightsquigarrow (3,3)_{\textbf{-.04}} \rightsquigarrow (3,2)_{\textbf{-.04}} \rightsquigarrow (3,3)_{\textbf{-.04}} \rightsquigarrow (4,3)_{\textbf{+1}}$$
$$(1,1)_{\textbf{-.04}} \rightsquigarrow (2,1)_{\textbf{-.04}} \rightsquigarrow (3,1)_{\textbf{-.04}} \rightsquigarrow (3,2)_{\textbf{-.04}} \rightsquigarrow (4,2)_{\textbf{-1}} .$$

Note that each state percept is subscripted with the reward received. The object is to use the information about rewards to learn the expected utility $U^{\pi}(s)$ associated with each nonterminal state s. The utility is defined to be the expected sum of (discounted) rewards obtained if policy π is followed. We write

$$U^\pi(s) = E\left[\sum_{t=0}^{\infty} \gamma^t R(S_t)\right] \tag{1}$$

where $R(s)$ is the reward for a state, S_t (a random variable) is the state reached at time t when executing policy π, and $S_0 = s$. We will include a **discount factor** γ in all of our equations, but for the 4×3 world we will set $\gamma = 1$.

2.1 Direct utility estimation

DIRECT UTILITY ESTIMATION
ADAPTIVE CONTROL THEORY
REWARD-TO-GO

A simple method for **direct utility estimation** was invented in the late 1950s in the area of **adaptive control theory** by Widrow and Hoff (1960). The idea is that the utility of a state is the expected total reward from that state onward (called the expected **reward-to-go**), and each trial provides a *sample* of this quantity for each state visited. For example, the first trial in the set of three given earlier provides a sample total reward of 0.72 for state (1,1), two samples of 0.76 and 0.84 for (1,2), two samples of 0.80 and 0.88 for (1,3), and so on. Thus, at the end of each sequence, the algorithm calculates the observed reward-to-go for each state and updates the estimated utility for that state accordingly, just by keeping a running average for each state in a table. In the limit of infinitely many trials, the sample average will converge to the true expectation in Equation (1).

It is clear that direct utility estimation is just an instance of supervised learning where each example has the state as input and the observed reward-to-go as output. This means that we have reduced reinforcement learning to a standard inductive learning problem. Section 4 discusses the use of more powerful kinds of representations for the utility function. Learning techniques for those representations can be applied directly to the observed data.

Direct utility estimation succeeds in reducing the reinforcement learning problem to an inductive learning problem, about which much is known. Unfortunately, it misses a very important source of information, namely, the fact that the utilities of states are not independent! *The utility of each state equals its own reward plus the expected utility of its successor states.* That is, the utility values obey the Bellman equations for a fixed policy:

$$U^\pi(s) = R(s) + \gamma \sum_{s'} P(s' \mid s, \pi(s)) U^\pi(s') . \tag{2}$$

By ignoring the connections between states, direct utility estimation misses opportunities for learning. For example, the second of the three trials given earlier reaches the state (3,2), which has not previously been visited. The next transition reaches (3,3), which is known from the first trial to have a high utility. The Bellman equation suggests immediately that (3,2) is also likely to have a high utility, because it leads to (3,3), but direct utility estimation learns nothing until the end of the trial. More broadly, we can view direct utility estimation as searching for U in a hypothesis space that is much larger than it needs to be, in that it includes many functions that violate the Bellman equations. For this reason, the algorithm often converges very slowly.

```
function PASSIVE-ADP-AGENT(percept) returns an action
  inputs: percept, a percept indicating the current state s' and reward signal r'
  persistent: π, a fixed policy
              mdp, an MDP with model P, rewards R, discount γ
              U, a table of utilities, initially empty
              N_sa, a table of frequencies for state–action pairs, initially zero
              N_s'|sa, a table of outcome frequencies given state–action pairs, initially zero
              s, a, the previous state and action, initially null

  if s' is new then U[s'] ← r'; R[s'] ← r'
  if s is not null then
      increment N_sa[s, a] and N_s'|sa[s', s, a]
      for each t such that N_s'|sa[t, s, a] is nonzero do
          P(t | s, a) ← N_s'|sa[t, s, a] / N_sa[s, a]
  U ← POLICY-EVALUATION(π, U, mdp)
  if s'.TERMINAL? then s, a ← null else s, a ← s', π[s']
  return a
```

Figure 2 A passive reinforcement learning agent based on adaptive dynamic programming. The POLICY-EVALUATION function solves the fixed-policy Bellman equations.

2.2 Adaptive dynamic programming

ADAPTIVE DYNAMIC PROGRAMMING

An **adaptive dynamic programming** (or ADP) agent takes advantage of the constraints among the utilities of states by learning the transition model that connects them and solving the corresponding Markov decision process using a dynamic programming method. For a passive learning agent, this means plugging the learned transition model $P(s' \mid s, \pi(s))$ and the observed rewards $R(s)$ into the Bellman equations (2) to calculate the utilities of the states. These equations are linear (no maximization involved) so they can be solved using any linear algebra package. Alternatively, we can adopt the approach of **modified policy iteration**, using a simplified value iteration process to update the utility estimates after each change to the learned model. Because the model usually changes only slightly with each observation, the value iteration process can use the previous utility estimates as initial values and should converge quite quickly.

The process of learning the model itself is easy, because the environment is fully observable. This means that we have a supervised learning task where the input is a state–action pair and the output is the resulting state. In the simplest case, we can represent the transition model as a table of probabilities. We keep track of how often each action outcome occurs and estimate the transition probability $P(s' \mid s, a)$ from the frequency with which s' is reached when executing a in s . For example, in the three trials given at the beginning of this section, *Right* is executed three times in (1,3) and two out of three times the resulting state is (2,3), so $P((2,3) \mid (1,3), Right)$ is estimated to be 2/3.

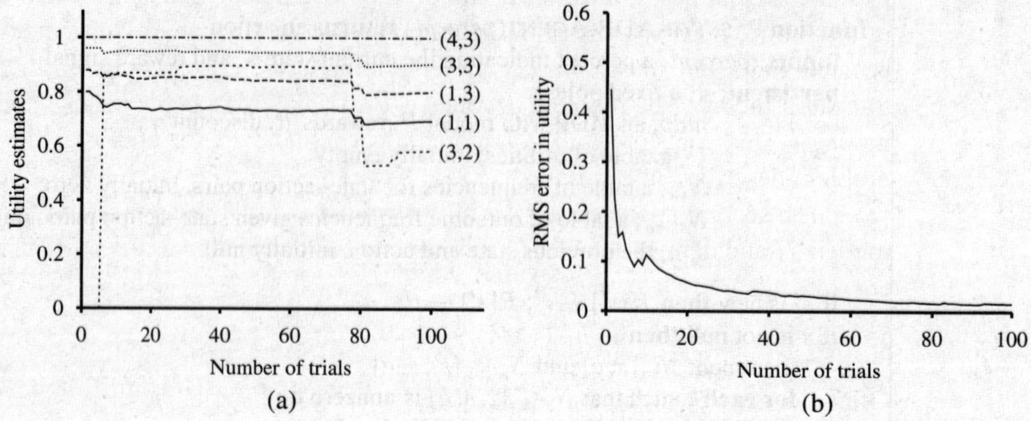

Figure 3 The passive ADP learning curves for the 4×3 world, given the optimal policy shown in Figure 1. (a) The utility estimates for a selected subset of states, as a function of the number of trials. Notice the large changes occurring around the 78th trial—this is the first time that the agent falls into the -1 terminal state at (4,2). (b) The root-mean-square error in the estimate for $U(1,1)$, averaged over 20 runs of 100 trials each.

The full agent program for a passive ADP agent is shown in Figure 2. Its performance on the 4×3 world is shown in Figure 3. In terms of how quickly its value estimates improve, the ADP agent is limited only by its ability to learn the transition model. In this sense, it provides a standard against which to measure other reinforcement learning algorithms. It is, however, intractable for large state spaces. In backgammon, for example, it would involve solving roughly 10^{50} equations in 10^{50} unknowns.

A reader familiar with the Bayesian learning ideas will have noticed that the algorithm in Figure 2 is using maximum-likelihood estimation to learn the transition model; moreover, by choosing a policy based solely on the *estimated* model it is acting *as if* the model were correct. This is not necessarily a good idea! For example, a taxi agent that didn't know about how traffic lights might ignore a red light once or twice without no ill effects and then formulate a policy to ignore red lights from then on. Instead, it might be a good idea to choose a policy that, while not optimal for the model estimated by maximum likelihood, works reasonably well for the whole range of models that have a reasonable chance of being the true model. There are two mathematical approaches that have this flavor.

BAYESIAN REINFORCEMENT LEARNING

The first approach, **Bayesian reinforcement learning**, assumes a prior probability $P(h)$ for each hypothesis h about what the true model is; the posterior probability $P(h \mid \mathbf{e})$ is obtained in the usual way by Bayes' rule given the observations to date. Then, if the agent has decided to stop learning, the optimal policy is the one that gives the highest expected utility. Let u_h^π be the expected utility, averaged over all possible start states, obtained by executing policy π in model h. Then we have

$$\pi^* = \underset{\pi}{\operatorname{argmax}} \sum_h P(h \mid \mathbf{e}) u_h^\pi .$$

In some special cases, this policy can even be computed! If the agent will continue learning in the future, however, then finding an optimal policy becomes considerably more difficult, because the agent must consider the effects of future observations on its beliefs about the transition model. The problem becomes a POMDP whose belief states are distributions over models. This concept provides an analytical foundation for understanding the exploration problem described in Section 3.

ROBUST CONTROL THEORY

The second approach, derived from **robust control theory**, allows for a *set* of possible models $\mathcal{H}$ and defines an optimal robust policy as one that gives the best outcome in the *worst case* over $\mathcal{H}$:

$$\pi^* = \operatorname*{argmax}_{\pi} \min_{h} u_h^{\pi} \; .$$

Often, the set $\mathcal{H}$ will be the set of models that exceed some likelihood threshold on $P(h \mid \mathbf{e})$, so the robust and Bayesian approaches are related. Sometimes, the robust solution can be computed efficiently. There are, moreover, reinforcement learning algorithms that tend to produce robust solutions, although we do not cover them here.

2.3 Temporal-difference learning

Solving the underlying MDP as in the preceding section is not the only way to bring the Bellman equations to bear on the learning problem. Another way is to use the observed transitions to adjust the utilities of the observed states so that they agree with the constraint equations. Consider, for example, the transition from (1,3) to (2,3) in the second trial. Suppose that, as a result of the first trial, the utility estimates are $U^{\pi}(1,3) = 0.84$ and $U^{\pi}(2,3) = 0.92$. Now, if this transition occurred all the time, we would expect the utilities to obey the equation

$$U^{\pi}(1,3) = -0.04 + U^{\pi}(2,3) \; ,$$

so $U^{\pi}(1,3)$ would be 0.88. Thus, its current estimate of 0.84 might be a little low and should be increased. More generally, when a transition occurs from state s to state s', we apply the following update to $U^{\pi}(s)$:

$$U^{\pi}(s) \leftarrow U^{\pi}(s) + \alpha(R(s) + \gamma U^{\pi}(s') - U^{\pi}(s)) \; . \qquad (3)$$

Here, α is the **learning rate** parameter. Because this update rule uses the difference in utilities between successive states, it is often called the **temporal-difference**, or TD, equation.

TEMPORAL-DIFFERENCE

All temporal-difference methods work by adjusting the utility estimates towards the ideal equilibrium that holds locally when the utility estimates are correct. In the case of passive learning, the equilibrium is given by Equation (2). Now Equation (3) does in fact cause the agent to reach the equilibrium given by Equation (2), but there is some subtlety involved. First, notice that the update involves only the observed successor s', whereas the actual equilibrium conditions involve all possible next states. One might think that this causes an improperly large change in $U^{\pi}(s)$ when a very rare transition occurs; but, in fact, because rare transitions occur only rarely, the *average value* of $U^{\pi}(s)$ will converge to the correct value. Furthermore, if we change α from a fixed parameter to a function that decreases as the number of times a state has been visited increases, then $U^{\pi}(s)$ itself will converge to the

```
function PASSIVE-TD-AGENT(percept) returns an action
  inputs: percept, a percept indicating the current state s' and reward signal r'
  persistent: π, a fixed policy
              U, a table of utilities, initially empty
              N_s, a table of frequencies for states, initially zero
              s, a, r, the previous state, action, and reward, initially null

  if s' is new then U[s'] ← r'
  if s is not null then
      increment N_s[s]
      U[s] ← U[s] + α(N_s[s])(r + γ U[s'] − U[s])
  if s'.TERMINAL? then s, a, r ← null else s, a, r ← s', π[s'], r'
  return a
```

Figure 4 A passive reinforcement learning agent that learns utility estimates using temporal differences. The step-size function $\alpha(n)$ is chosen to ensure convergence, as described in the text.

correct value.[1] This gives us the agent program shown in Figure 4. Figure 5 illustrates the performance of the passive TD agent on the 4×3 world. It does not learn quite as fast as the ADP agent and shows much higher variability, but it is much simpler and requires much less computation per observation. Notice that *TD does not need a transition model to perform its updates.* The environment supplies the connection between neighboring states in the form of observed transitions.

The ADP approach and the TD approach are actually closely related. Both try to make local adjustments to the utility estimates in order to make each state "agree" with its successors. One difference is that TD adjusts a state to agree with its *observed* successor (Equation (3)), whereas ADP adjusts the state to agree with *all* of the successors that might occur, weighted by their probabilities (Equation (2)). This difference disappears when the effects of TD adjustments are averaged over a large number of transitions, because the frequency of each successor in the set of transitions is approximately proportional to its probability. A more important difference is that whereas TD makes a single adjustment per observed transition, ADP makes as many as it needs to restore consistency between the utility estimates U and the environment model P. Although the observed transition makes only a local change in P, its effects might need to be propagated throughout U. Thus, TD can be viewed as a crude but efficient first approximation to ADP.

Each adjustment made by ADP could be seen, from the TD point of view, as a result of a "pseudoexperience" generated by simulating the current environment model. It is possible to extend the TD approach to use an environment model to generate several pseudoexperiences—transitions that the TD agent can imagine *might* happen, given its current model. For each observed transition, the TD agent can generate a large number of imaginary

[1] In Figure 5 we have used $\alpha(n) = 60/(59 + n)$, which satisfies the technical conditions.

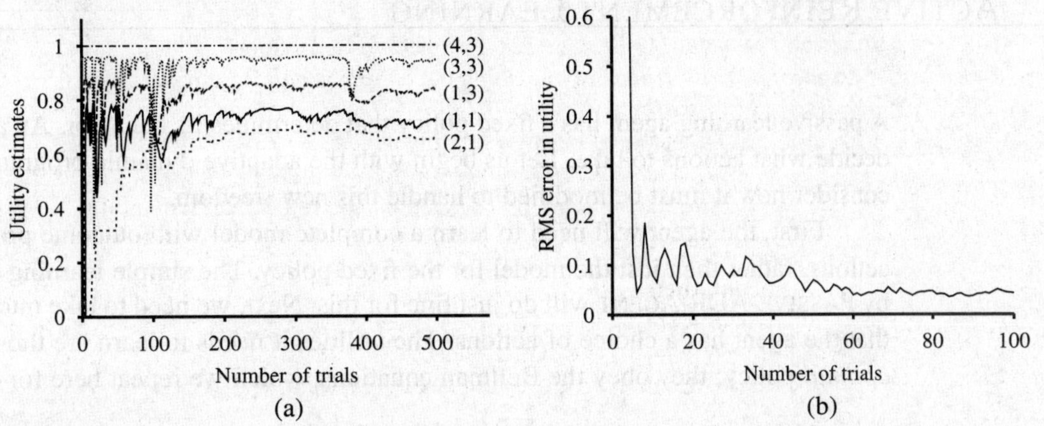

Figure 5 The TD learning curves for the 4×3 world. (a) The utility estimates for a selected subset of states, as a function of the number of trials. (b) The root-mean-square error in the estimate for $U(1,1)$, averaged over 20 runs of 500 trials each. Only the first 100 trials are shown to enable comparison with Figure 3.

transitions. In this way, the resulting utility estimates will approximate more and more closely those of ADP—of course, at the expense of increased computation time.

In a similar vein, we can generate more efficient versions of ADP by directly approximating the algorithms for value iteration or policy iteration. Even though the value iteration algorithm is efficient, it is intractable if we have, say, 10^{100} states. However, many of the necessary adjustments to the state values on each iteration will be extremely tiny. One possible approach to generating reasonably good answers quickly is to bound the number of adjustments made after each observed transition. One can also use a heuristic to rank the possible adjustments so as to carry out only the most significant ones. The **prioritized sweeping** heuristic prefers to make adjustments to states whose *likely* successors have just undergone a *large* adjustment in their own utility estimates. Using heuristics like this, approximate ADP algorithms usually can learn roughly as fast as full ADP, in terms of the number of training sequences, but can be several orders of magnitude more efficient in terms of computation. (See Exercise 3.) This enables them to handle state spaces that are far too large for full ADP. Approximate ADP algorithms have an additional advantage: in the early stages of learning a new environment, the environment model P often will be far from correct, so there is little point in calculating an exact utility function to match it. An approximation algorithm can use a minimum adjustment size that decreases as the environment model becomes more accurate. This eliminates the very long value iterations that can occur early in learning due to large changes in the model.

PRIORITIZED SWEEPING

3 Active Reinforcement Learning

A passive learning agent has a fixed policy that determines its behavior. An active agent must decide what actions to take. Let us begin with the adaptive dynamic programming agent and consider how it must be modified to handle this new freedom.

First, the agent will need to learn a complete model with outcome probabilities for all actions, rather than just the model for the fixed policy. The simple learning mechanism used by PASSIVE-ADP-AGENT will do just fine for this. Next, we need to take into account the fact that the agent has a choice of actions. The utilities it needs to learn are those defined by the *optimal* policy; they obey the Bellman equations, which we repeat here for convenience:

$$U(s) = R(s) + \gamma \max_a \sum_{s'} P(s' \mid s, a) U(s') . \tag{4}$$

These equations can be solved to obtain the utility function U using the value iteration or policy iteration algorithms. The final issue is what to do at each step. Having obtained a utility function U that is optimal for the learned model, the agent can extract an optimal action by one-step look-ahead to maximize the expected utility; alternatively, if it uses policy iteration, the optimal policy is already available, so it should simply execute the action the optimal policy recommends. Or should it?

3.1 Exploration

Figure 6 shows the results of one sequence of trials for an ADP agent that follows the recommendation of the optimal policy for the learned model at each step. The agent *does not* learn the true utilities or the true optimal policy! What happens instead is that, in the 39th trial, it finds a policy that reaches the +1 reward along the lower route via (2,1), (3,1), (3,2), and (3,3). (See Figure 6(b).) After experimenting with minor variations, from the 276th trial onward it sticks to that policy, never learning the utilities of the other states and never finding the optimal route via (1,2), (1,3), and (2,3). We call this agent the **greedy agent**. Repeated experiments show that the greedy agent *very seldom* converges to the optimal policy for this environment and sometimes converges to really horrendous policies.

GREEDY AGENT

How can it be that choosing the optimal action leads to suboptimal results? The answer is that the learned model is not the same as the true environment; what is optimal in the learned model can therefore be suboptimal in the true environment. Unfortunately, the agent does not know what the true environment is, so it cannot compute the optimal action for the true environment. What, then, is to be done?

What the greedy agent has overlooked is that actions do more than provide rewards according to the current learned model; they also contribute to learning the true model by affecting the percepts that are received. By improving the model, the agent will receive greater rewards in the future. An agent therefore must make a tradeoff between **exploitation** to maximize its reward—as reflected in its current utility estimates—and **exploration** to maxi-

EXPLOITATION

EXPLORATION

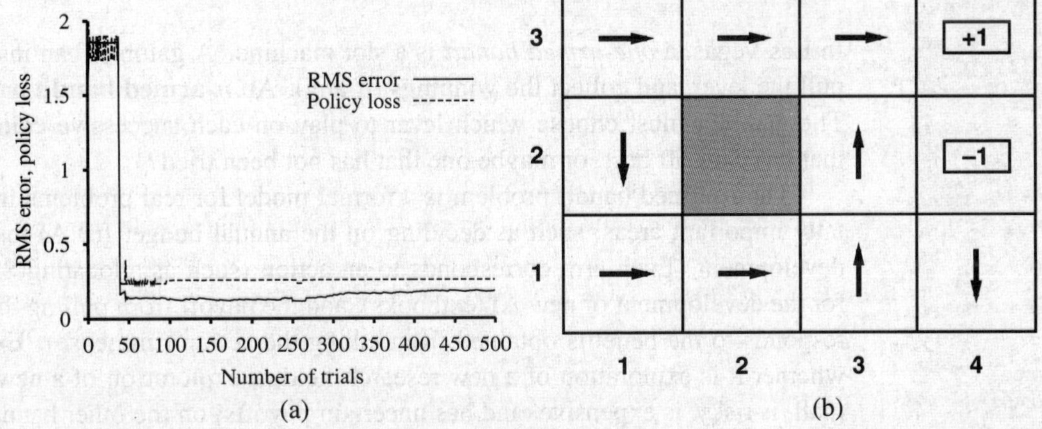

Figure 6 Performance of a greedy ADP agent that executes the action recommended by the optimal policy for the learned model. (a) RMS error in the utility estimates averaged over the nine nonterminal squares. (b) The suboptimal policy to which the greedy agent converges in this particular sequence of trials.

mize its long-term well-being. Pure exploitation risks getting stuck in a rut. Pure exploration to improve one's knowledge is of no use if one never puts that knowledge into practice. In the real world, one constantly has to decide between continuing in a comfortable existence and striking out into the unknown in the hopes of discovering a new and better life. With greater understanding, less exploration is necessary.

Can we be a little more precise than this? Is there an *optimal* exploration policy? This question has been studied in depth in the subfield of statistical decision theory that deals with so-called **bandit problems**. (See sidebar.)

BANDIT PROBLEM

Although bandit problems are extremely difficult to solve exactly to obtain an *optimal* exploration method, it is nonetheless possible to come up with a *reasonable* scheme that will eventually lead to optimal behavior by the agent. Technically, any such scheme needs to be greedy in the limit of infinite exploration, or **GLIE**. A GLIE scheme must try each action in each state an unbounded number of times to avoid having a finite probability that an optimal action is missed because of an unusually bad series of outcomes. An ADP agent using such a scheme will eventually learn the true environment model. A GLIE scheme must also eventually become greedy, so that the agent's actions become optimal with respect to the learned (and hence the true) model.

GLIE

There are several GLIE schemes; one of the simplest is to have the agent choose a random action a fraction $1/t$ of the time and to follow the greedy policy otherwise. While this does eventually converge to an optimal policy, it can be extremely slow. A more sensible approach would give some weight to actions that the agent has not tried very often, while tending to avoid actions that are believed to be of low utility. This can be implemented by altering the constraint equation (4) so that it assigns a higher utility estimate to relatively

EXPLORATION AND BANDITS

In Las Vegas, a *one-armed bandit* is a slot machine. A gambler can insert a coin, pull the lever, and collect the winnings (if any). An n-**armed bandit** has n levers. The gambler must choose which lever to play on each successive coin—the one that has paid off best, or maybe one that has not been tried?

The n-armed bandit problem is a formal model for real problems in many vitally important areas, such as deciding on the annual budget for AI research and development. Each arm corresponds to an action (such as allocating $20 million for the development of new AI textbooks), and the payoff from pulling the arm corresponds to the benefits obtained from taking the action (immense). Exploration, whether it is exploration of a new research field or exploration of a new shopping mall, is risky, is expensive, and has uncertain payoffs; on the other hand, failure to explore at all means that one never discovers *any* actions that are worthwhile.

To formulate a bandit problem properly, one must define exactly what is meant by optimal behavior. Most definitions in the literature assume that the aim is to maximize the expected total reward obtained over the agent's lifetime. These definitions require that the expectation be taken over the possible worlds that the agent could be in, as well as over the possible results of each action sequence in any given world. Here, a "world" is defined by the transition model $P(s' \mid s, a)$. Thus, in order to act optimally, the agent needs a prior distribution over the possible models. The resulting optimization problems are usually wildly intractable.

In some cases—for example, when the payoff of each machine is independent and discounted rewards are used—it is possible to calculate a **Gittins index** for each slot machine (Gittins, 1989). The index is a function only of the number of times the slot machine has been played and how much it has paid off. The index for each machine indicates how worthwhile it is to invest more; generally speaking, the higher the expected return and the higher the uncertainty in the utility of a given choice, the better. Choosing the machine with the highest index value gives an optimal exploration policy. Unfortunately, no way has been found to extend Gittins indices to sequential decision problems.

One can use the theory of n-armed bandits to argue for the reasonableness of the selection strategy in genetic algorithms. If you consider each arm in an n-armed bandit problem to be a possible string of genes, and the investment of a coin in one arm to be the reproduction of those genes, then it can be proven that genetic algorithms allocate coins optimally, given an appropriate set of independence assumptions.

unexplored state–action pairs. Essentially, this amounts to an optimistic prior over the possible environments and causes the agent to behave initially as if there were wonderful rewards scattered all over the place. Let us use $U^+(s)$ to denote the optimistic estimate of the utility (i.e., the expected reward-to-go) of the state s, and let $N(s, a)$ be the number of times action a has been tried in state s. Suppose we are using value iteration in an ADP learning agent; then we need to rewrite the update equation (Equation 6 from the chapter, "Making Complex Decisions") to incorporate the optimistic estimate. The following equation does this:

$$U^+(s) \leftarrow R(s) + \gamma \max_a f\left(\sum_{s'} P(s' \mid s, a) U^+(s'),\ N(s, a)\right). \tag{5}$$

EXPLORATION FUNCTION

Here, $f(u, n)$ is called the **exploration function**. It determines how greed (preference for high values of u) is traded off against curiosity (preference for actions that have not been tried often and have low n). The function $f(u, n)$ should be increasing in u and decreasing in n. Obviously, there are many possible functions that fit these conditions. One particularly simple definition is

$$f(u, n) = \begin{cases} R^+ & \text{if } n < N_e \\ u & \text{otherwise} \end{cases}$$

where R^+ is an optimistic estimate of the best possible reward obtainable in any state and N_e is a fixed parameter. This will have the effect of making the agent try each action–state pair at least N_e times.

The fact that U^+ rather than U appears on the right-hand side of Equation (5) is very important. As exploration proceeds, the states and actions near the start state might well be tried a large number of times. If we used U, the more pessimistic utility estimate, then the agent would soon become disinclined to explore further afield. The use of U^+ means that the benefits of exploration are propagated back from the edges of unexplored regions, so that actions that lead *toward* unexplored regions are weighted more highly, rather than just actions that are themselves unfamiliar. The effect of this exploration policy can be seen clearly in Figure 7, which shows a rapid convergence toward optimal performance, unlike that of the greedy approach. A very nearly optimal policy is found after just 18 trials. Notice that the utility estimates themselves do not converge as quickly. This is because the agent stops exploring the unrewarding parts of the state space fairly soon, visiting them only "by accident" thereafter. However, it makes perfect sense for the agent not to care about the exact utilities of states that it knows are undesirable and can be avoided.

3.2 Learning an action-utility function

Now that we have an active ADP agent, let us consider how to construct an active temporal-difference learning agent. The most obvious change from the passive case is that the agent is no longer equipped with a fixed policy, so, if it learns a utility function U, it will need to learn a model in order to be able to choose an action based on U via one-step look-ahead. The model acquisition problem for the TD agent is identical to that for the ADP agent. What of the TD update rule itself? Perhaps surprisingly, the update rule (3) remains unchanged. This might seem odd, for the following reason: Suppose the agent takes a step that normally

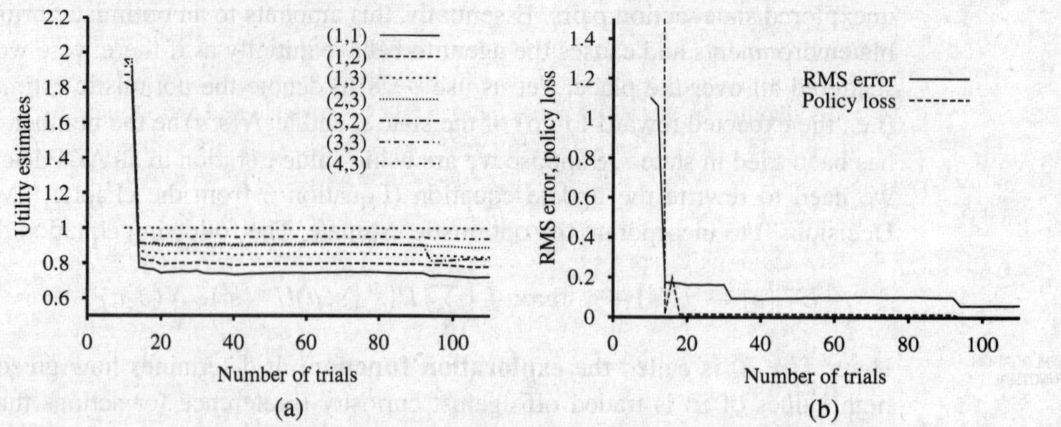

Figure 7 Performance of the exploratory ADP agent. using $R^+ = 2$ and $N_e = 5$. (a) Utility estimates for selected states over time. (b) The RMS error in utility values and the associated policy loss.

leads to a good destination, but because of nondeterminism in the environment the agent ends up in a catastrophic state. The TD update rule will take this as seriously as if the outcome had been the normal result of the action, whereas one might suppose that, because the outcome was a fluke, the agent should not worry about it too much. In fact, of course, the unlikely outcome will occur only infrequently in a large set of training sequences; hence in the long run its effects will be weighted proportionally to its probability, as we would hope. Once again, it can be shown that the TD algorithm will converge to the same values as ADP as the number of training sequences tends to infinity.

There is an alternative TD method, called **Q-learning**, which learns an action-utility representation instead of learning utilities. We will use the notation $Q(s, a)$ to denote the value of doing action a in state s. Q-values are directly related to utility values as follows:

$$U(s) = \max_a Q(s, a) . \tag{6}$$

Q-functions may seem like just another way of storing utility information, but they have a very important property: *a TD agent that learns a Q-function does not need a model of the form $P(s' \mid s, a)$, either for learning or for action selection.* For this reason, Q-learning is called a **model-free** method. As with utilities, we can write a constraint equation that must

MODEL-FREE

hold at equilibrium when the Q-values are correct:

$$Q(s, a) = R(s) + \gamma \sum_{s'} P(s' \mid s, a) \max_{a'} Q(s', a') . \tag{7}$$

As in the ADP learning agent, we can use this equation directly as an update equation for an iteration process that calculates exact Q-values, given an estimated model. This does, however, require that a model also be learned, because the equation uses $P(s' \mid s, a)$. The temporal-difference approach, on the other hand, requires no model of state transitions—all

```
function Q-LEARNING-AGENT(percept) returns an action
  inputs: percept, a percept indicating the current state s′ and reward signal r′
  persistent: Q, a table of action values indexed by state and action, initially zero
              N_sa, a table of frequencies for state–action pairs, initially zero
              s, a, r, the previous state, action, and reward, initially null

  if TERMINAL?(s) then Q[s, None] ← r′
  if s is not null then
      increment N_sa[s, a]
      Q[s, a] ← Q[s, a] + α(N_sa[s, a])(r + γ max_a′ Q[s′, a′] − Q[s, a])
  s, a, r ← s′, argmax_a′ f(Q[s′, a′], N_sa[s′, a′]), r′
  return a
```

Figure 8 An exploratory Q-learning agent. It is an active learner that learns the value $Q(s, a)$ of each action in each situation. It uses the same exploration function f as the exploratory ADP agent, but avoids having to learn the transition model because the Q-value of a state can be related directly to those of its neighbors.

it needs are the Q values. The update equation for TD Q-learning is

$$Q(s,a) \leftarrow Q(s,a) + \alpha(R(s) + \gamma \max_{a'} Q(s',a') - Q(s,a)) , \tag{8}$$

which is calculated whenever action a is executed in state s leading to state s'.

The complete agent design for an exploratory Q-learning agent using TD is shown in Figure 8. Notice that it uses exactly the same exploration function f as that used by the exploratory ADP agent—hence the need to keep statistics on actions taken (the table N). If a simpler exploration policy is used—say, acting randomly on some fraction of steps, where the fraction decreases over time—then we can dispense with the statistics.

SARSA

Q-learning has a close relative called **SARSA** (for State-Action-Reward-State-Action). The update rule for SARSA is very similar to Equation (8):

$$Q(s,a) \leftarrow Q(s,a) + \alpha(R(s) + \gamma\, Q(s',a') - Q(s,a)) , \tag{9}$$

where a' is the action *actually taken* in state s'. The rule is applied at the end of each s, a, r, s', a' quintuplet—hence the name. The difference from Q-learning is quite subtle: whereas Q-learning backs up the *best* Q-value from the state reached in the observed transition, SARSA waits until an action is actually taken and backs up the Q-value for that action. Now, for a greedy agent that always takes the action with best Q-value, the two algorithms are identical. When exploration is happening, however, they differ significantly. Because Q-learning uses the best Q-value, it pays no attention to the actual policy being followed—it is an **off-policy** learning algorithm, whereas SARSA is an **on-policy** algorithm. Q-learning is more flexible than SARSA, in the sense that a Q-learning agent can learn how to behave well even when guided by a random or adversarial exploration policy. On the other hand, SARSA is more realistic: for example, if the overall policy is even partly controlled by other agents, it is better to learn a Q-function for what will actually happen rather than what the agent would like to happen.

OFF-POLICY
ON-POLICY

Both Q-learning and SARSA learn the optimal policy for the 4×3 world, but do so at a much slower rate than the ADP agent. This is because the local updates do not enforce consistency among all the Q-values via the model. The comparison raises a general question: is it better to learn a model and a utility function or to learn an action-utility function with no model? In other words, what is the best way to represent the agent function? This is an issue at the foundations of artificial intelligence. One of the key historical characteristics of much of AI research is its (often unstated) adherence to the **knowledge-based** approach. This amounts to an assumption that the best way to represent the agent function is to build a representation of some aspects of the environment in which the agent is situated.

Some researchers, both inside and outside AI, have claimed that the availability of model-free methods such as Q-learning means that the knowledge-based approach is unnecessary. There is, however, little to go on but intuition. Our intuition, for what it's worth, is that as the environment becomes more complex, the advantages of a knowledge-based approach become more apparent. This is borne out even in games such as chess, checkers (draughts), and backgammon (see next section), where efforts to learn an evaluation function by means of a model have met with more success than Q-learning methods.

4 GENERALIZATION IN REINFORCEMENT LEARNING

So far, we have assumed that the utility functions and Q-functions learned by the agents are represented in tabular form with one output value for each input tuple. Such an approach works reasonably well for small state spaces, but the time to convergence and (for ADP) the time per iteration increase rapidly as the space gets larger. With carefully controlled, approximate ADP methods, it might be possible to handle 10,000 states or more. This suffices for two-dimensional maze-like environments, but more realistic worlds are out of the question. Backgammon and chess are tiny subsets of the real world, yet their state spaces contain on the order of 10^{20} and 10^{40} states, respectively. It would be absurd to suppose that one must visit all these states many times in order to learn how to play the game!

FUNCTION APPROXIMATION

One way to handle such problems is to use **function approximation**, which simply means using any sort of representation for the Q-function other than a lookup table. The representation is viewed as approximate because it might not be the case that the *true* utility function or Q-function can be represented in the chosen form. For example, we can describe an **evaluation function** for chess that is represented as a weighted linear function of a set of **features** (or **basis functions** $f_1, \ldots, f_n$:

BASIS FUNCTION

$$\hat{U}_\theta(s) = \theta_1\, f_1(s) + \theta_2\, f_2(s) + \cdots + \theta_n\, f_n(s)\,.$$

A reinforcement learning algorithm can learn values for the parameters $\theta = \theta_1, \ldots, \theta_n$ such that the evaluation function $\hat{U}_\theta$ approximates the true utility function. Instead of, say, 10^{40} values in a table, this function approximator is characterized by, say, $n = 20$ parameters—an *enormous* compression. Although no one knows the true utility function for chess, no one believes that it can be represented exactly in 20 numbers. If the approximation is good enough, however, the agent might still play excellent chess.[2] Function approximation makes it practical to represent utility functions for very large state spaces, but that is not its principal benefit. *The compression achieved by a function approximator allows the learning agent to generalize from states it has visited to states it has not visited.* That is, the most important aspect of function approximation is not that it requires less space, but that it allows for inductive generalization over input states. To give you some idea of the power of this effect: by examining only one in every 10^{12} of the possible backgammon states, it is possible to learn a utility function that allows a program to play as well as any human (Tesauro, 1992).

On the flip side, of course, there is the problem that there could fail to be any function in the chosen hypothesis space that approximates the true utility function sufficiently well. As in all inductive learning, there is a tradeoff between the size of the hypothesis space and the time it takes to learn the function. A larger hypothesis space increases the likelihood that a good approximation can be found, but also means that convergence is likely to be delayed.

Let us begin with the simplest case, which is direct utility estimation. (See Section 2.) With function approximation, this is an instance of **supervised learning**. For example, suppose we represent the utilities for the 4×3 world using a simple linear function. The features of the squares are just their x and y coordinates, so we have

$$\hat{U}_\theta(x, y) = \theta_0 + \theta_1 x + \theta_2 y . \tag{10}$$

Thus, if $(\theta_0, \theta_1, \theta_2) = (0.5, 0.2, 0.1)$, then $\hat{U}_\theta(1, 1) = 0.8$. Given a collection of trials, we obtain a set of sample values of $\hat{U}_\theta(x, y)$, and we can find the best fit, in the sense of minimizing the squared error, using standard linear regression.

For reinforcement learning, it makes more sense to use an *online* learning algorithm that updates the parameters after each trial. Suppose we run a trial and the total reward obtained starting at (1,1) is 0.4. This suggests that $\hat{U}_\theta(1, 1)$, currently 0.8, is too large and must be reduced. How should the parameters be adjusted to achieve this? As with neural-network learning, we write an error function and compute its gradient with respect to the parameters. If $u_j(s)$ is the observed total reward from state s onward in the jth trial, then the error is defined as (half) the squared difference of the predicted total and the actual total: $E_j(s) = (\hat{U}_\theta(s) - u_j(s))^2/2$. The rate of change of the error with respect to each parameter θ_i is $\partial E_j/\partial \theta_i$, so to move the parameter in the direction of decreasing the error, we want

$$\theta_i \leftarrow \theta_i - \alpha \frac{\partial E_j(s)}{\partial \theta_i} = \theta_i + \alpha\,(u_j(s) - \hat{U}_\theta(s))\frac{\partial \hat{U}_\theta(s)}{\partial \theta_i} . \tag{11}$$

WIDROW–HOFF RULE

DELTA RULE

This is called the **Widrow–Hoff rule**, or the **delta rule**, for online least-squares. For the linear function approximator $\hat{U}_\theta(s)$ in Equation (10), we get three simple update rules:

$$\begin{aligned}
\theta_0 &\leftarrow \theta_0 + \alpha\,(u_j(s) - \hat{U}_\theta(s)) , \\
\theta_1 &\leftarrow \theta_1 + \alpha\,(u_j(s) - \hat{U}_\theta(s))x , \\
\theta_2 &\leftarrow \theta_2 + \alpha\,(u_j(s) - \hat{U}_\theta(s))y .
\end{aligned}$$

[2] We do know that the exact utility function can be represented in a page or two of Lisp, Java, or C++. That is, it can be represented by a program that solves the game exactly every time it is called. We are interested only in function approximators that use a *reasonable* amount of computation. It might in fact be better to learn a very simple function approximator and combine it with a certain amount of look-ahead search. The tradeoffs involved are currently not well understood.

We can apply these rules to the example where $\hat{U}_\theta(1,1)$ is 0.8 and $u_j(1,1)$ is 0.4. θ_0, θ_1, and θ_2 are all decreased by 0.4α, which reduces the error for (1,1). Notice that *changing the parameters θ in response to an observed transition between two states also changes the values of $\hat{U}_\theta$ for every other state!* This is what we mean by saying that function approximation allows a reinforcement learner to generalize from its experiences.

We expect that the agent will learn faster if it uses a function approximator, provided that the hypothesis space is not too large, but includes some functions that are a reasonably good fit to the true utility function. Exercise 5 asks you to evaluate the performance of direct utility estimation, both with and without function approximation. The improvement in the 4×3 world is noticeable but not dramatic, because this is a very small state space to begin with. The improvement is much greater in a 10×10 world with a +1 reward at (10,10). This world is well suited for a linear utility function because the true utility function is smooth and nearly linear. (See Exercise 8.) If we put the +1 reward at (5,5), the true utility is more like a pyramid and the function approximator in Equation (10) will fail miserably. All is not lost, however! Remember that what matters for linear function approximation is that the function be linear in the *parameters*—the features themselves can be arbitrary nonlinear functions of the state variables. Hence, we can include a term such as $\theta_3 f_3(x,y) = \theta_3\sqrt{(x-x_g)^2+(y-y_g)^2}$ that measures the distance to the goal.

We can apply these ideas equally well to temporal-difference learners. All we need do is adjust the parameters to try to reduce the temporal difference between successive states. The new versions of the TD and Q-learning equations (3 and 8) are given by

$$\theta_i \leftarrow \theta_i + \alpha\,[R(s) + \gamma\,\hat{U}_\theta(s') - \hat{U}_\theta(s)]\frac{\partial \hat{U}_\theta(s)}{\partial \theta_i} \tag{12}$$

for utilities and

$$\theta_i \leftarrow \theta_i + \alpha\,[R(s) + \gamma\,\max_{a'} \hat{Q}_\theta(s',a') - \hat{Q}_\theta(s,a)]\frac{\partial Q_\theta(s,a)}{\partial \theta_i} \tag{13}$$

for Q-values. For passive TD learning, the update rule can be shown to converge to the closest possible[3] approximation to the true function when the function approximator is *linear* in the parameters. With active learning and *nonlinear* functions such as neural networks, all bets are off: There are some very simple cases in which the parameters can go off to infinity even though there are good solutions in the hypothesis space. There are more sophisticated algorithms that can avoid these problems, but at present reinforcement learning with general function approximators remains a delicate art.

Function approximation can also be very helpful for learning a model of the environment. Remember that learning a model for an *observable* environment is a *supervised* learning problem, because the next percept gives the outcome state. Supervised learning methods can be used, with suitable adjustments for the fact that we need to predict a complete state description rather than just a Boolean classification or a single real value. For a *partially observable* environment, the learning problem is much more difficult. If we know what the hidden variables are and how they are causally related to each other and to the observable vari-

[3] The definition of distance between utility functions is rather technical; see Tsitsiklis and Van Roy (1997).

ables, then we can fix the structure of a dynamic Bayesian network and use the EM algorithm to learn the parameters. Inventing the hidden variables and learning the model structure are still open problems. Some practical examples are described in Section 6.

5 POLICY SEARCH

POLICY SEARCH

The final approach we will consider for reinforcement learning problems is called **policy search**. In some ways, policy search is the simplest of all the methods in this chapter: the idea is to keep twiddling the policy as long as its performance improves, then stop.

Let us begin with the policies themselves. Remember that a policy π is a function that maps states to actions. We are interested primarily in *parameterized* representations of π that have far fewer parameters than there are states in the state space (just as in the preceding section). For example, we could represent π by a collection of parameterized Q-functions, one for each action, and take the action with the highest predicted value:

$$\pi(s) = \max_a \hat{Q}_\theta(s,a) . \tag{14}$$

Each Q-function could be a linear function of the parameters θ, as in Equation (10), or it could be a nonlinear function such as a neural network. Policy search will then adjust the parameters θ to improve the policy. Notice that if the policy is represented by Q-functions, then policy search results in a process that learns Q-functions. *This process is not the same as Q-learning!* In Q-learning with function approximation, the algorithm finds a value of θ such that $\hat{Q}_\theta$ is "close" to Q^*, the optimal Q-function. Policy search, on the other hand, finds a value of θ that results in good performance; the values found by the two methods may differ very substantially. (For example, the approximate Q-function defined by $\hat{Q}_\theta(s,a) = Q^*(s,a)/10$ gives optimal performance, even though it is not at all close to Q^*.) Another clear instance of the difference is the case where $\pi(s)$ is calculated using, say, depth-10 look-ahead search with an approximate utility function $\hat{U}_\theta$. A value of θ that gives good results may be a long way from making $\hat{U}_\theta$ resemble the true utility function.

One problem with policy representations of the kind given in Equation (14) is that the policy is a *discontinuous* function of the parameters when the actions are discrete. (For a continuous action space, the policy can be a smooth function of the parameters.) That is, there will be values of θ such that an infinitesimal change in θ causes the policy to switch from one action to another. This means that the value of the policy may also change discontinuously, which makes gradient-based search difficult. For this reason, policy search methods often use

STOCHASTIC POLICY

a **stochastic policy** representation $\pi_\theta(s,a)$, which specifies the *probability* of selecting action

SOFTMAX FUNCTION

a in state s. One popular representation is the **softmax function**:

$$\pi_\theta(s,a) = e^{\hat{Q}_\theta(s,a)} / \sum_{a'} e^{\hat{Q}_\theta(s,a')} .$$

Softmax becomes nearly deterministic if one action is much better than the others, but it always gives a differentiable function of θ; hence, the value of the policy (which depends in a continuous fashion on the action selection probabilities) is a differentiable function of θ. Softmax is a generalization of the logistic function to multiple variables.

POLICY VALUE

Now let us look at methods for improving the policy. We start with the simplest case: a deterministic policy and a deterministic environment. Let $\rho(\theta)$ be the **policy value**, i.e., the expected reward-to-go when π_θ is executed. If we can derive an expression for $\rho(\theta)$ in closed form, then we have a standard optimization problem. We can follow the **policy gradient** vector $\nabla_\theta \rho(\theta)$ provided $\rho(\theta)$ is differentiable. Alternatively, if $\rho(\theta)$ is not available in closed form, we can evaluate π_θ simply byexecuting it and observing the accumulated reward. We can follow the **empirical gradient** by hill climbing—i.e., evaluating the change in policy value for small increments in each parameter. With the usual caveats, this process will converge to a local optimum in policy space.

POLICY GRADIENT

When the environment (or the policy) is stochastic, things get more difficult. Suppose we are trying to do hill climbing, which requires comparing $\rho(\theta)$ and $\rho(\theta + \Delta\theta)$ for some small $\Delta\theta$. The problem is that the total reward on each trial may vary widely, so estimates of the policy value from a small number of trials will be quite unreliable; trying to compare two such estimates will be even more unreliable. One solution is simply to run lots of trials, measuring the sample variance and using it to determine that enough trials have been run to get a reliable indication of the direction of improvement for $\rho(\theta)$. Unfortunately, this is impractical for many real problems where each trial may be expensive, time-consuming, and perhaps even dangerous.

For the case of a stochastic policy $\pi_\theta(s, a)$, it is possible to obtain an unbiased estimate of the gradient at θ, $\nabla_\theta \rho(\theta)$, directly from the results of trials executed at θ. For simplicity, we will derive this estimate for the simple case of a nonsequential environment in which the reward $R(a)$ is obtained immediately after doing action a in the start state s_0. In this case, the policy value is just the expected value of the reward, and we have

$$\nabla_\theta \rho(\theta) = \nabla_\theta \sum_a \pi_\theta(s_0, a) R(a) = \sum_a (\nabla_\theta \pi_\theta(s_0, a)) R(a) .$$

Now we perform a simple trick so that this summation can be approximated by samples generated from the probability distribution defined by $\pi_\theta(s_0, a)$. Suppose that we have N trials in all and the action taken on the jth trial is a_j. Then

$$\nabla_\theta \rho(\theta) = \sum_a \pi_\theta(s_0, a) \cdot \frac{(\nabla_\theta \pi_\theta(s_0, a)) R(a)}{\pi_\theta(s_0, a)} \approx \frac{1}{N} \sum_{j=1}^{N} \frac{(\nabla_\theta \pi_\theta(s_0, a_j)) R(a_j)}{\pi_\theta(s_0, a_j)} .$$

Thus, the true gradient of the policy value is approximated by a sum of terms involving the gradient of the action-selection probability in each trial. For the sequential case, this generalizes to

$$\nabla_\theta \rho(\theta) \approx \frac{1}{N} \sum_{j=1}^{N} \frac{(\nabla_\theta \pi_\theta(s, a_j)) R_j(s)}{\pi_\theta(s, a_j)}$$

for each state s visited, where a_j is executed in s on the jth trial and $R_j(s)$ is the total reward received from state s onwards in the jth trial. The resulting algorithm is called REINFORCE (Williams, 1992); it is usually much more effective than hill climbing using lots of trials at each value of θ. It is still much slower than necessary, however.

Consider the following task: given two blackjack[4] programs, determine which is best. One way to do this is to have each play against a standard "dealer" for a certain number of hands and then to measure their respective winnings. The problem with this, as we have seen, is that the winnings of each program fluctuate widely depending on whether it receives good or bad cards. An obvious solution is to generate a certain number of hands in advance and *have each program play the same set of hands.* In this way, we eliminate the measurement error due to differences in the cards received. This idea, called **correlated sampling**, underlies a policy-search algorithm called PEGASUS (Ng and Jordan, 2000). The algorithm is applicable to domains for which a simulator is available so that the "random" outcomes of actions can be repeated. The algorithm works by generating in advance N sequences of random numbers, each of which can be used to run a trial of any policy. Policy search is carried out by evaluating each candidate policy using the *same* set of random sequences to determine the action outcomes. It can be shown that the number of random sequences required to ensure that the value of *every* policy is well estimated depends only on the complexity of the policy space, and not at all on the complexity of the underlying domain.

CORRELATED SAMPLING

6 Applications of Reinforcement Learning

We now turn to examples of large-scale applications of reinforcement learning. We consider applications in game playing, where the transition model is known and the goal is to learn the utility function, and in robotics, where the model is usually unknown.

6.1 Applications to game playing

The first significant application of reinforcement learning was also the first significant learning program of any kind—the checkers program written by Arthur Samuel (1959, 1967). Samuel first used a weighted linear function for the evaluation of positions, using up to 16 terms at any one time. He applied a version of Equation (12) to update the weights. There were some significant differences, however, between his program and current methods. First, he updated the weights using the difference between the current state and the backed-up value generated by full look-ahead in the search tree. This works fine, because it amounts to viewing the state space at a different granularity. A second difference was that the program did *not* use any observed rewards! That is, the values of terminal states reached in self-play were ignored. This means that it is theoretically possible for Samuel's program not to converge, or to converge on a strategy designed to lose rather than to win. He managed to avoid this fate by insisting that the weight for material advantage should always be positive. Remarkably, this was sufficient to direct the program into areas of weight space corresponding to good checkers play.

Gerry Tesauro's backgammon program TD-GAMMON (1992) forcefully illustrates the potential of reinforcement learning techniques. In earlier work (Tesauro and Sejnowski, 1989), Tesauro tried learning a neural network representation of $Q(s, a)$ directly from ex-

[4] Also known as twenty-one or pontoon.

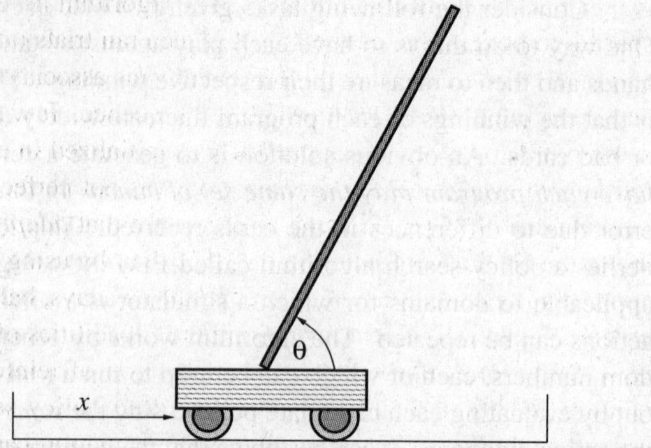

Figure 9 Setup for the problem of balancing a long pole on top of a moving cart. The cart can be jerked left or right by a controller that observes x, θ, $\dot{x}$, and $\dot{\theta}$.

amples of moves labeled with relative values by a human expert. This approach proved extremely tedious for the expert. It resulted in a program, called NEUROGAMMON, that was strong by computer standards, but not competitive with human experts. The TD-GAMMON project was an attempt to learn from self-play alone. The only reward signal was given at the end of each game. The evaluation function was represented by a fully connected neural network with a single hidden layer containing 40 nodes. Simply by repeated application of Equation (12), TD-GAMMON learned to play considerably better than NEUROGAMMON, even though the input representation contained just the raw board position with no computed features. This took about 200,000 training games and two weeks of computer time. Although that may seem like a lot of games, it is only a vanishingly small fraction of the state space. When precomputed features were added to the input representation, a network with 80 hidden nodes was able, after 300,000 training games, to reach a standard of play comparable to that of the top three human players worldwide. Kit Woolsey, a top player and analyst, said that "There is no question in my mind that its positional judgment is far better than mine."

6.2 Application to robot control

CART–POLE
INVERTED PENDULUM

The setup for the famous **cart–pole** balancing problem, also known as the **inverted pendulum**, is shown in Figure 9. The problem is to control the position x of the cart so that the pole stays roughly upright ($\theta \approx \pi/2$), while staying within the limits of the cart track as shown. Several thousand papers in reinforcement learning and control theory have been published on this seemingly simple problem. The cart–pole problem differs from the problems described earlier in that the state variables x, θ, $\dot{x}$, and $\dot{\theta}$ are continuous. The actions are usually discrete: jerk left or jerk right, the so-called **bang-bang control** regime.

BANG-BANG CONTROL

The earliest work on learning for this problem was carried out by Michie and Chambers (1968). Their BOXES algorithm was able to balance the pole for over an hour after only about 30 trials. Moreover, unlike many subsequent systems, BOXES was implemented with a real cart and pole, not a simulation. The algorithm first discretized the four-dimensional state space into boxes—hence the name. It then ran trials until the pole fell over or the cart hit the end of the track. Negative reinforcement was associated with the final action in the final box and then propagated back through the sequencc. It was found that the discretization caused some problems when the apparatus was initialized in a position different from those used in training, suggesting that generalization was not perfect. Improved generalization and faster learning can be obtained using an algorithm that *adaptively* partitions the state space according to the observed variation in the reward, or by using a continuous-state, nonlinear function approximator such as a neural network. Nowadays, balancing a *triple* inverted pendulum is a common exercise—a feat far beyond the capabilities of most humans.

Still more impressive is the application of reinforcement learning to helicopter flight (Figure 10). This work has generally used policy search (Bagnell and Schneider, 2001) as well as the PEGASUS algorithm with simulation based on a learned transition model (Ng *et al.*, 2004).

Figure 10 Superimposed time-lapse images of an autonomous helicopter performing a very difficult "nose-in circle" maneuver. The helicopter is under the control of a policy developed by the PEGASUS policy-search algorithm. A simulator model was developed by observing the effects of various control manipulations on the real helicopter; then the algorithm was run on the simulator model overnight. A variety of controllers were developed for different maneuvers. In all cases, performance far exceeded that of an expert human pilot using remote control. (Image courtesy of Andrew Ng.)

7 Summary

This chapter has examined the reinforcement learning problem: how an agent can become proficient in an unknown environment, given only its percepts and occasional rewards. Reinforcement learning can be viewed as a microcosm for the entire AI problem, but it is studied in a number of simplified settings to facilitate progress. The major points are:

- The overall agent design dictates the kind of information that must be learned. The three main designs we covered were the model-based design, using a model P and a utility function U; the model-free design, using an action-utility function Q; and the reflex design, using a policy π.
- Utilities can be learned using three approaches:
  1. **Direct utility estimation** uses the total observed reward-to-go for a given state as direct evidence for learning its utility.
  2. **Adaptive dynamic programming** (ADP) learns a model and a reward function from observations and then uses value or policy iteration to obtain the utilities or an optimal policy. ADP makes optimal use of the local constraints on utilities of states imposed through the neighborhood structure of the environment.
  3. **Temporal-difference** (TD) methods update utility estimates to match those of successor states. They can be viewed as simple approximations to the ADP approach that can learn without requiring a transition model. Using a learned model to generate pseudoexperiences can, however, result in faster learning.
- Action-utility functions, or Q-functions, can be learned by an ADP approach or a TD approach. With TD, Q-learning requires no model in either the learning or action-selection phase. This simplifies the learning problem but potentially restricts the ability to learn in complex environments, because the agent cannot simulate the results of possible courses of action.
- When the learning agent is responsible for selecting actions while it learns, it must trade off the estimated value of those actions against the potential for learning useful new information. An exact solution of the exploration problem is infeasible, but some simple heuristics do a reasonable job.
- In large state spaces, reinforcement learning algorithms must use an approximate functional representation in order to generalize over states. The temporal-difference signal can be used directly to update parameters in representations such as neural networks.
- Policy-search methods operate directly on a representation of the policy, attempting to improve it based on observed performance. The variation in the performance in a stochastic domain is a serious problem; for simulated domains this can be overcome by fixing the randomness in advance.

Because of its potential for eliminating hand coding of control strategies, reinforcement learning continues to be one of the most active areas of machine learning research. Applications in robotics promise to be particularly valuable; these will require methods for handling continuous, high-dimensional, partially observable environments in which successful behaviors may consist of thousands or even millions of primitive actions.

Bibliographical and Historical Notes

Turing (1948, 1950) proposed the reinforcement-learning approach, although he was not convinced of its effectiveness, writing, "the use of punishments and rewards can at best be a part of the teaching process." Arthur Samuel's work (1959) was probably the earliest successful machine learning research. Although this work was informal and had a number of flaws, it contained most of the modern ideas in reinforcement learning, including temporal differencing and function approximation. Around the same time, researchers in adaptive control theory (Widrow and Hoff, 1960), building on work by Hebb (1949), were training simple networks using the delta rule. (This early connection between neural networks and reinforcement learning may have led to the persistent misperception that the latter is a subfield of the former.) The cart–pole work of Michie and Chambers (1968) can also be seen as a reinforcement learning method with a function approximator. The psychological literature on reinforcement learning is much older; Hilgard and Bower (1975) provide a good survey. Direct evidence for the operation of reinforcement learning in animals has been provided by investigations into the foraging behavior of bees; there is a clear neural correlate of the reward signal in the form of a large neuron mapping from the nectar intake sensors directly to the motor cortex (Montague *et al.*, 1995). Research using single-cell recording suggests that the dopamine system in primate brains implements something resembling value function learning (Schultz *et al.*, 1997). The neuroscience text by Dayan and Abbott (2001) describes possible neural implementations of temporal-difference learning, while Dayan and Niv (2008) survey the latest evidence from neuroscientific and behavioral experiments.

The connection between reinforcement learning and Markov decision processes was first made by Werbos (1977), but the development of reinforcement learning in AI stems from work at the University of Massachusetts in the early 1980s (Barto *et al.*, 1981). The paper by Sutton (1988) provides a good historical overview. Equation (3) in this chapter is a special case for $\lambda = 0$ of Sutton's general TD(λ) algorithm. TD(λ) updates the utility values of all states in a sequence leading up to each transition by an amount that drops off as λ^t for states t steps in the past. TD(1) is identical to the Widrow–Hoff or delta rule. Boyan (2002), building on work by Bradtke and Barto (1996), argues that TD(λ) and related algorithms make inefficient use of experiences; essentially, they are online regression algorithms that converge much more slowly than offline regression. His LSTD (least-squares temporal differencing) algorithm is an online algorithm for passive reinforcement learning that gives the same results as offline regression. Least-squares policy iteration, or LSPI (Lagoudakis and Parr, 2003), combines this idea with the policy iteration algorithm, yielding a robust, statistically efficient, model-free algorithm for learning policies.

The combination of temporal-difference learning with the model-based generation of simulated experiences was proposed in Sutton's DYNA architecture (Sutton, 1990). The idea of prioritized sweeping was introduced independently by Moore and Atkeson (1993) and

Peng and Williams (1993). Q-learning was developed in Watkins's Ph.D. thesis (1989), while SARSA appeared in a technical report by Rummery and Niranjan (1994).

Bandit problems, which model the problem of exploration for nonsequential decisions, are analyzed in depth by Berry and Fristedt (1985). Optimal exploration strategies for several settings are obtainable using the technique called **Gittins indices** (Gittins, 1989). A variety of exploration methods for sequential decision problems are discussed by Barto *et al.* (1995). Kearns and Singh (1998) and Brafman and Tennenholtz (2000) describe algorithms that explore unknown environments and are guaranteed to converge on near-optimal policies in polynomial time. Bayesian reinforcement learning (Dearden *et al.*, 1998, 1999) provides another angle on both model uncertainty and exploration.

Function approximation in reinforcement learning goes back to the work of Samuel, who used both linear and nonlinear evaluation functions and also used feature-selection methods to reduce the feature space. Later methods include the **CMAC** (Cerebellar Model Articulation Controller) (Albus, 1975), which is essentially a sum of overlapping local kernel functions, and the associative neural networks of Barto *et al.* (1983). Neural networks are currently the most popular form of function approximator. The best-known application is TD-Gammon (Tesauro, 1992, 1995), which was discussed in the chapter. One significant problem exhibited by neural-network-based TD learners is that they tend to forget earlier experiences, especially those in parts of the state space that are avoided once competence is achieved. This can result in catastrophic failure if such circumstances reappear. Function approximation based on **instance-based learning** can avoid this problem (Ormoneit and Sen, 2002; Forbes, 2002).

CMAC

The convergence of reinforcement learning algorithms using function approximation is an extremely technical subject. Results for TD learning have been progressively strengthened for the case of linear function approximators (Sutton, 1988; Dayan, 1992; Tsitsiklis and Van Roy, 1997), but several examples of divergence have been presented for nonlinear functions (see Tsitsiklis and Van Roy, 1997, for a discussion). Papavassiliou and Russell (1999) describe a new type of reinforcement learning that converges with any form of function approximator, provided that a best-fit approximation can be found for the observed data.

Policy search methods were brought to the fore by Williams (1992), who developed the REINFORCE family of algorithms. Later work by Marbach and Tsitsiklis (1998), Sutton *et al.* (2000), and Baxter and Bartlett (2000) strengthened and generalized the convergence results for policy search. The method of correlated sampling for comparing different configurations of a system was described formally by Kahn and Marshall (1953), but seems to have been known long before that. Its use in reinforcement learning is due to Van Roy (1998) and Ng and Jordan (2000); the latter paper also introduced the PEGASUS algorithm and proved its formal properties.

As we mentioned in the chapter, the performance of a *stochastic* policy is a continuous function of its parameters, which helps with gradient-based search methods. This is not the only benefit: Jaakkola *et al.* (1995) argue that stochastic policies actually work better than deterministic policies in partially observable environments, if both are limited to acting based on the current percept. (One reason is that the stochastic policy is less likely to get "stuck" because of some unseen hindrance.) Since optimal policies in partially observable MDPs are deterministic functions of the *belief state* rather than the current percept, we would expect still better results by keeping track of the belief state using **filtering** methods. Unfortunately, belief-state space is high-dimensional and continuous, and effective algorithms have not yet been developed for reinforcement learning with belief states.

Real-world environments also exhibit enormous complexity in terms of the number of primitive actions required to achieve significant reward. For example, a robot playing soccer might make a hundred thousand individual leg motions before scoring a goal. One common method, used originally in animal training, is called **reward shaping**. This involves supplying the agent with additional rewards, called **pseudorewards**, for "making progress." For example, in soccer the real reward is for scoring a goal, but pseudorewards might be given for making contact with the ball or for kicking it toward the goal. Such rewards can speed up learning enormously and are simple to provide, but there is a risk that the agent will learn to maximize the pseudorewards rather than the true rewards; for example, standing next to the ball and "vibrating" causes many contacts with the ball. Ng *et al.* (1999) show that the agent will still learn the optimal policy provided that the pseudoreward $F(s, a, s')$ satisfies $F(s, a, s') = \gamma\Phi(s') - \Phi(s)$, where Φ is an arbitrary function of the state. Φ can be constructed to reflect any desirable aspects of the state, such as achievement of subgoals or distance to a goal state.

REWARD SHAPING

PSEUDOREWARD

The generation of complex behaviors can also be facilitated by **hierarchical reinforcement learning** methods, which attempt to solve problems at multiple levels of abstraction—much like **HTN planning** methods. For example, "scoring a goal" can be broken down into "obtain possession," "dribble towards the goal," and "shoot;" and each of these can be broken down further into lower-level motor behaviors. The fundamental result in this area is due to Forestier and Varaiya (1978), who proved that lower-level behaviors of arbitrary complexity can be treated just like primitive actions (albeit ones that can take varying amounts of time) from the point of view of the higher-level behavior that invokes them. Current approaches (Parr and Russell, 1998; Dietterich, 2000; Sutton *et al.*, 2000; Andre and Russell, 2002) build on this result to develop methods for supplying an agent with a **partial program** that constrains the agent's behavior to have a particular hierarchical structure. The partial-programming language for agent programs extends an ordinary programming language by adding primitives for unspecified choices that must be filled in by learning. Reinforcement learning is then applied to learn the best behavior consistent with the partial program. The combination of function approximation, shaping, and hierarchical reinforcement learning has been shown to solve large-scale problems—for example, policies that execute for 10^4 steps in state spaces of 10^{100} states with branching factors of 10^{30} (Marthi *et al.*, 2005). One key result (Dietterich, 2000) is that the hierarchical structure provides a natural *additive decomposition* of the overall utility function into terms that depend on small subsets of the variables defining the state space. This is somewhat analogous to the representation theorems underlying the conciseness of Bayes nets.

HIERARCHICAL REINFORCEMENT LEARNING

PARTIAL PROGRAM

The topic of distributed and multiagent reinforcement learning was not touched upon in the chapter but is of great current interest. In distributed RL, the aim is to devise methods by which multiple, coordinated agents learn to optimize a common utility function. For example,

SUBAGENT can we devise methods whereby separate **subagents** for robot navigation and robot obstacle avoidance could cooperatively achieve a combined control system that is globally optimal? Some basic results in this direction have been obtained (Guestrin *et al.*, 2002; Russell and Zimdars, 2003). The basic idea is that each subagent learns its own Q-function from its own stream of rewards. For example, a robot-navigation component can receive rewards for making progress towards the goal, while the obstacle-avoidance component receives negative rewards for every collision. Each global decision maximizes the sum of Q-functions and the whole process converges to globally optimal solutions.

Multiagent RL is distinguished from distributed RL by the presence of agents who cannot coordinate their actions (except by explicit communicative acts) and who may not share the same utility function. Thus, multiagent RL deals with sequential game-theoretic problems or **Markov games**. The consequent requirement for randomized policies is not a significant complication, as we saw in the section 5. What *does* cause problems is the fact that, while an agent is learning to defeat its opponent's policy, the opponent is changing its policy to defeat the agent. Thus, the environment is **nonstationary** (see page 568). Littman (1994) noted this difficulty when introducing the first RL algorithms for zero-sum Markov games. Hu and Wellman (2003) present a Q-learning algorithm for general-sum games that converges when the Nash equilibrium is unique; when there are multiple equilibria, the notion of convergence is not so easy to define (Shoham *et al.*, 2004).

Sometimes the reward function is not easy to define. Consider the task of driving a car. There are extreme states (such as crashing the car) that clearly should have a large penalty. But beyond that, it is difficult to be precise about the reward function. However, it is easy enough for a human to drive for a while and then tell a robot "do it like that." The robot then has the

APPRENTICESHIP LEARNING task of **apprenticeship learning**; learning from an example of the task done right, without explicit rewards. Ng *et al.* (2004) and Coates *et al.* (2009) show how this technique works for learning to fly a helicopter. Russell (1998) describes the task of **inverse reinforcement**

INVERSE REINFORCEMENT LEARNING **learning**—figuring out what the reward function must be from an example path through that state space. This is useful as a part of apprenticeship learning, or as a part of doing science—we can understand an animal or robot by working backwards from what it does to what its reward function must be.

This chapter has dealt only with atomic states—all the agent knows about a state is the set of available actions and the utilities of the resulting states (or of state-action pairs). But it is also possible to apply reinforcement learning to structured representations rather than

RELATIONAL REINFORCEMENT LEARNING atomic ones; this is called **relational reinforcement learning** (Tadepalli *et al.*, 2004).

The survey by Kaelbling *et al.* (1996) provides a good entry point to the literature. The text by Sutton and Barto (1998), two of the field's pioneers, focuses on architectures and algorithms, showing how reinforcement learning weaves together the ideas of learning, planning, and acting. The somewhat more technical work by Bertsekas and Tsitsiklis (1996) gives a rigorous grounding in the theory of dynamic programming and stochastic convergence. Reinforcement learning papers are published frequently in *Machine Learning*, in the *Journal of Machine Learning Research*, and in the International Conferences on Machine Learning and the Neural Information Processing Systems meetings.

EXERCISES

1 Implement a passive learning agent in a simple environment, such as the 4×3 world. For the case of an initially unknown environment model, compare the learning performance of the direct utility estimation, TD, and ADP algorithms. Do the comparison for the optimal policy and for several random policies. For which do the utility estimates converge faster? What happens when the size of the environment is increased? (Try environments with and without obstacles.)

2 A **proper policy** for is MDP is one that is guaranteed to reach a terminal state. Show that it is possible for a passive ADP agent to learn a transition model for which its policy π is improper even if π is proper for the true MDP; with such models, the POLICY-EVALUATION step may fail if $\gamma = 1$. Show that this problem cannot arise if POLICY-EVALUATION is applied to the learned model only at the end of a trial.

3 Starting with the passive ADP agent, modify it to use an approximate ADP algorithm as discussed in the text. Do this in two steps:

a. Implement a priority queue for adjustments to the utility estimates. Whenever a state is adjusted, all of its predecessors also become candidates for adjustment and should be added to the queue. The queue is initialized with the state from which the most recent transition took place. Allow only a fixed number of adjustments.

b. Experiment with various heuristics for ordering the priority queue, examining their effect on learning rates and computation time.

4 Write out the parameter update equations for TD learning with

$$\hat{U}(x, y) = \theta_0 + \theta_1 x + \theta_2 y + \theta_3 \sqrt{(x - x_g)^2 + (y - y_g)^2} \,.$$

5 Implement an exploring reinforcement learning agent that uses direct utility estimation. Make two versions—one with a tabular representation and one using the function approximator in Equation (10). Compare their performance in three environments:

a. The 4×3 world described in the chapter.

b. A 10×10 world with no obstacles and a +1 reward at (10,10).

c. A 10×10 world with no obstacles and a +1 reward at (5,5).

6 Devise suitable features for reinforcement learning in stochastic grid worlds (generalizations of the 4×3 world) that contain multiple obstacles and multiple terminal states with rewards of $+1$ or -1.

7 Extend the standard game-playing environment from the chapter, "Adversarial Search" to incorporate a reward signal. Put two reinforcement learning agents into the environment (they may, of course, share the agent program) and have them play against each other. Apply the generalized TD update rule (Equation (12)) to update the evaluation function. You might wish to start with a simple linear weighted evaluation function and a simple game, such as tic-tac-toe.

8 Compute the true utility function and the best linear approximation in x and y (as in Equation (10)) for the following environments:

a. A 10×10 world with a single $+1$ terminal state at (10,10).
b. As in (a), but add a -1 terminal state at (10,1).
c. As in (b), but add obstacles in 10 randomly selected squares.
d. As in (b), but place a wall stretching from (5,2) to (5,9).
e. As in (a), but with the terminal state at (5,5).

The actions are deterministic moves in the four directions. In each case, compare the results using three-dimensional plots. For each environment, propose additional features (besides x and y) that would improve the approximation and show the results.

9 Implement the REINFORCE and PEGASUS algorithms and apply them to the 4×3 world, using a policy family of your own choosing. Comment on the results.

10 Is reinforcement learning an appropriate abstract model for evolution? What connection exists, if any, between hardwired reward signals and evolutionary fitness?

NATURAL LANGUAGE FOR COMMUNICATION

NATURAL LANGUAGE FOR COMMUNICATION

In which we see how humans communicate with one another in natural language, and how computer agents might join in the conversation.

COMMUNICATION
SIGN

Communication is the intentional exchange of information brought about by the production and perception of **signs** drawn from a shared system of conventional signs. Most animals use signs to represent important messages: food here, predator nearby, approach, withdraw, let's mate. In a partially observable world, communication can help agents be successful because they can learn information that is observed or inferred by others. Humans are the most chatty of all species, and if computer agents are to be helpful, they'll need to learn to speak the language. In this chapter we look at language models for communication. Models aimed at deep understanding of a conversation necessarily need to be more complex than the simple models aimed at, say, spam classification. We start with grammatical models of the phrase structure of sentences, add semantics to the model, and then apply it to machine translation and speech recognition.

1 PHRASE STRUCTURE GRAMMARS

LEXICAL CATEGORY
SYNTACTIC CATEGORIES
PHRASE STRUCTURE

N-gram language models are based on sequences of words. The big issue for these models is data sparsity—with a vocabulary of, say, 10^5 words, there are 10^{15} trigram probabilities to estimate, and so a corpus of even a trillion words will not be able to supply reliable estimates for all of them. We can address the problem of sparsity through generalization. From the fact that "black dog" is more frequent than "dog black" and similar observations, we can form the generalization that adjectives tend to come before nouns in English (whereas they tend to follow nouns in French: "chien noir" is more frequent). Of course there are always exceptions; "galore" is an adjective that follows the noun it modifies. Despite the exceptions, the notion of a **lexical category** (also known as a **part of speech**) such as *noun* or *adjective* is a useful generalization—useful in its own right, but more so when we string together lexical categories to form **syntactic categories** such as *noun phrase* or *verb phrase*, and combine these syntactic categories into trees representing the **phrase structure** of sentences: nested phrases, each marked with a category.

GENERATIVE CAPACITY

Grammatical formalisms can be classified by their **generative capacity**: the set of languages they can represent. Chomsky (1957) describes four classes of grammatical formalisms that differ only in the form of the rewrite rules. The classes can be arranged in a hierarchy, where each class can be used to describe all the languages that can be described by a less powerful class, as well as some additional languages. Here we list the hierarchy, most powerful class first:

Recursively enumerable grammars use unrestricted rules: both sides of the rewrite rules can have any number of terminal and nonterminal symbols, as in the rule $A\ B\ C \rightarrow D\ E$. These grammars are equivalent to Turing machines in their expressive power.

Context-sensitive grammars are restricted only in that the right-hand side must contain at least as many symbols as the left-hand side. The name "context-sensitive" comes from the fact that a rule such as $A\ X\ B \rightarrow A\ Y\ B$ says that an X can be rewritten as a Y in the context of a preceding A and a following B. Context-sensitive grammars can represent languages such as $a^n b^n c^n$ (a sequence of n copies of a followed by the same number of bs and then cs).

In **context-free grammars** (or **CFG**s), the left-hand side consists of a single nonterminal symbol. Thus, each rule licenses rewriting the nonterminal as the right-hand side in *any* context. CFGs are popular for natural-language and programming-language grammars, although it is now widely accepted that at least some natural languages have constructions that are not context-free (Pullum, 1991). Context-free grammars can represent $a^n b^n$, but not $a^n b^n c^n$.

Regular grammars are the most restricted class. Every rule has a single nonterminal on the left-hand side and a terminal symbol optionally followed by a nonterminal on the right-hand side. Regular grammars are equivalent in power to finite-state machines. They are poorly suited for programming languages, because they cannot represent constructs such as balanced opening and closing parentheses (a variation of the $a^n b^n$ language). The closest they can come is representing $a^* b^*$, a sequence of any number of as followed by any number of bs.

The grammars higher up in the hierarchy have more expressive power, but the algorithms for dealing with them are less efficient. Up to the 1980s, linguists focused on context-free and context-sensitive languages. Since then, there has been renewed interest in regular grammars, brought about by the need to process and learn from gigabytes or terabytes of online text very quickly, even at the cost of a less complete analysis. As Fernando Pereira put it, "The older I get, the further down the Chomsky hierarchy I go." To see what he means, compare Pereira and Warren (1980) with Mohri, Pereira, and Riley (2002) (and note that these three authors all now work on large text corpora at Google).

PROBABILISTIC CONTEXT-FREE GRAMMAR

GRAMMAR

LANGUAGE

There have been many competing language models based on the idea of phrase structure; we will describe a popular model called the **probabilistic context-free grammar**, or PCFG.[1] A **grammar** is a collection of rules that defines a **language** as a set of allowable strings of words. "Context-free" is described in the sidebar, and "probabilistic" means that the grammar assigns a probability to every string. Here is a PCFG rule:

$$\begin{aligned} VP &\rightarrow Verb\ [0.70] \\ &\mid\ VP\ NP\ [0.30]\,. \end{aligned}$$

NON-TERMINAL SYMBOLS

TERMINAL SYMBOL

Here *VP* (*verb phrase*) and *NP* (*noun phrase*) are **non-terminal symbols**. The grammar also refers to actual words, which are called **terminal symbols**. This rule is saying that with probability 0.70 a verb phrase consists solely of a verb, and with probability 0.30 it is a *VP* followed by an *NP*.

We now define a grammar for a tiny fragment of English that is suitable for communication between agents exploring the wumpus world. We call this language $\mathcal{E}_0$. Later sections improve on $\mathcal{E}_0$ to make it slightly closer to real English. We are unlikely ever to devise a complete grammar for English, if only because no two persons would agree entirely on what constitutes valid English.

1.1 The lexicon of $\mathcal{E}_0$

LEXICON

First we define the **lexicon**, or list of allowable words. The words are grouped into the lexical categories familiar to dictionary users: nouns, pronouns, and names to denote things; verbs to denote events; adjectives to modify nouns; adverbs to modify verbs; and function words: articles (such as *the*), prepositions (*in*), and conjunctions (*and*). Figure 1 shows a small lexicon for the language $\mathcal{E}_0$.

OPEN CLASS

CLOSED CLASS

Each of the categories ends in ... to indicate that there are other words in the category. For nouns, names, verbs, adjectives, and adverbs, it is infeasible even in principle to list all the words. Not only are there tens of thousands of members in each class, but new ones–like *iPod* or *biodiesel*—are being added constantly. These five categories are called **open classes**. For the categories of pronoun, relative pronoun, article, preposition, and conjunction we could have listed all the words with a little more work. These are called **closed classes**; they have a small number of words (a dozen or so). Closed classes change over the course of centuries, not months. For example, "thee" and "thou" were commonly used pronouns in the 17th century, were on the decline in the 19th, and are seen today only in poetry and some regional dialects.

1.2 The Grammar of $\mathcal{E}_0$

PARSE TREE

The next step is to combine the words into phrases. Figure 2 shows a grammar for $\mathcal{E}_0$, with rules for each of the six syntactic categories and an example for each rewrite rule.[2] Figure 3 shows a **parse tree** for the sentence "Every wumpus smells." The parse tree

[1] PCFGs are also known as stochastic context-free grammars, or SCFGs.

[2] A relative clause follows and modifies a noun phrase. It consists of a relative pronoun (such as "who" or "that") followed by a verb phrase. An example of a relative clause is *that stinks* in "The wumpus *that stinks* is in 2 2." Another kind of relative clause has no relative pronoun, e.g., *I know* in "the man *I know*."

Noun → **stench** [0.05] | **breeze** [0.10] | **wumpus** [0.15] | **pits** [0.05] | ...
Verb → **is** [0.10] | **feel** [0.10] | **smells** [0.10] | **stinks** [0.05] | ...
Adjective → **right** [0.10] | **dead** [0.05] | **smelly** [0.02] | **breezy** [0.02] ...
Adverb → **here** [0.05] | **ahead** [0.05] | **nearby** [0.02] | ...
Pronoun → **me** [0.10] | **you** [0.03] | **I** [0.10] | **it** [0.10] | ...
RelPro → **that** [0.40] | **which** [0.15] | **who** [0.20] | **whom** [0.02] ∨ ...
Name → **John** [0.01] | **Mary** [0.01] | **Boston** [0.01] | ...
Article → **the** [0.40] | **a** [0.30] | **an** [0.10] | **every** [0.05] | ...
Prep → **to** [0.20] | **in** [0.10] | **on** [0.05] | **near** [0.10] | ...
Conj → **and** [0.50] | **or** [0.10] | **but** [0.20] | **yet** [0.02] ∨ ...
Digit → **0** [0.20] | **1** [0.20] | **2** [0.20] | **3** [0.20] | **4** [0.20] | ...

Figure 1 The lexicon for $\mathcal{E}_0$. *RelPro* is short for relative pronoun, *Prep* for preposition, and *Conj* for conjunction. The sum of the probabilities for each category is 1.

$\mathcal{E}_0$:

S → *NP VP* [0.90] I + feel a breeze
| *S Conj S* [0.10] I feel a breeze + and + It stinks

NP → *Pronoun* [0.30] I
| *Name* [0.10] John
| *Noun* [0.10] pits
| *Article Noun* [0.25] the + wumpus
| *Article Adjs Noun* [0.05] the + smelly dead + wumpus
| *Digit Digit* [0.05] 3 4
| *NP PP* [0.10] the wumpus + in 1 3
| *NP RelClause* [0.05] the wumpus + that is smelly

VP → *Verb* [0.40] stinks
| *VP NP* [0.35] feel + a breeze
| *VP Adjective* [0.05] smells + dead
| *VP PP* [0.10] is + in 1 3
| *VP Adverb* [0.10] go + ahead

Adjs → *Adjective* [0.80] smelly
| *Adjective Adjs* [0.20] smelly + dead
PP → *Prep NP* [1.00] to + the east
RelClause → *RelPro VP* [1.00] that + is smelly

Figure 2 The grammar for $\mathcal{E}_0$, with example phrases for each rule. The syntactic categories are sentence (*S*), noun phrase (*NP*), verb phrase (*VP*), list of adjectives (*Adjs*), prepositional phrase (*PP*), and relative clause (*RelClause*).

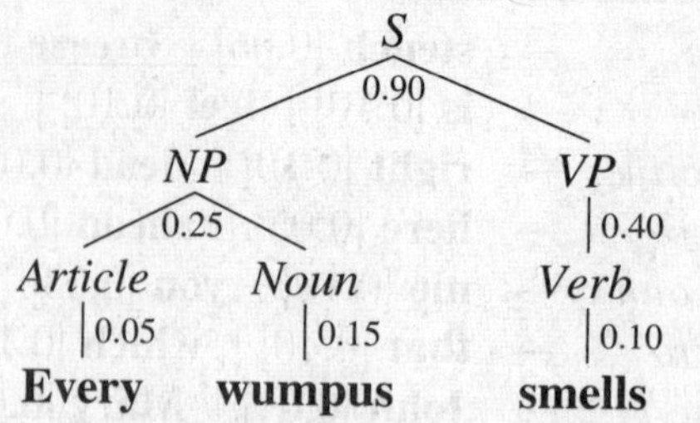

Figure 3 Parse tree for the sentence "Every wumpus smells" according to the grammar $\mathcal{E}_0$. Each interior node of the tree is labeled with its probability. The probability of the tree as a whole is $0.9 \times 0.25 \times 0.05 \times 0.15 \times 0.40 \times 0.10 = 0.0000675$. Since this tree is the only parse of the sentence, that number is also the probability of the sentence. The tree can also be written in linear form as [*S* [*NP* [*Article* **every**] [*Noun* **wumpus**]][*VP* [*Verb* **smells**]]].

gives a constructive proof that the string of words is indeed a sentence according to the rules of $\mathcal{E}_0$. The $\mathcal{E}_0$ grammar generates a wide range of English sentences such as the following:

John is in the pit
The wumpus that stinks is in 2 2
Mary is in Boston and the wumpus is near 3 2

OVERGENERATION UNDERGENERATION

Unfortunately, the grammar **overgenerates**: that is, it generates sentences that are not grammatical, such as "Me go Boston" and "I smell pits wumpus John." It also **undergenerates**: there are many sentences of English that it rejects, such as "I think the wumpus is smelly." We will see how to learn a better grammar later; for now we concentrate on what we can do with the grammar we have.

2 SYNTACTIC ANALYSIS (PARSING)

PARSING

Parsing is the process of analyzing a string of words to uncover its phrase structure, according to the rules of a grammar. Figure 4 shows that we can start with the S symbol and search top down for a tree that has the words as its leaves, or we can start with the words and search bottom up for a tree that culminates in an S. Both top-down and bottom-up parsing can be inefficient, however, because they can end up repeating effort in areas of the search space that lead to dead ends. Consider the following two sentences:

Have the students in section 2 of Computer Science 101 take the exam.
Have the students in section 2 of Computer Science 101 taken the exam?

Even though they share the first 10 words, these sentences have very different parses, because the first is a command and the second is a question. A left-to-right parsing algorithm would have to guess whether the first word is part of a command or a question and will not be able to tell if the guess is correct until at least the eleventh word, *take* or *taken.* If the algorithm guesses wrong, it will have to backtrack all the way to the first word and reanalyze the whole sentence under the other interpretation.

List of items	*Rule*
S	
$NP\ VP$	$S \rightarrow NP\ VP$
$NP\ VP\ Adjective$	$VP \rightarrow VP\ Adjective$
$NP\ Verb\ Adjective$	$VP \rightarrow Verb$
$NP\ Verb$ **dead**	$Adjective \rightarrow$ **dead**
NP **is dead**	$Verb \rightarrow$ **is**
$Article\ Noun$ **is dead**	$NP \rightarrow Article\ Noun$
$Article$ **wumpus is dead**	$Noun \rightarrow$ **wumpus**
the wumpus is dead	$Article \rightarrow$ **the**

Figure 4 Trace of the process of finding a parse for the string "The wumpus is dead" as a sentence, according to the grammar $\mathcal{E}_0$. Viewed as a top-down parse, we start with the list of items being S and, on each step, match an item X with a rule of the form ($X \rightarrow \ldots$) and replace X in the list of items with ($\ldots$). Viewed as a bottom-up parse, we start with the list of items being the words of the sentence, and, on each step, match a string of tokens ($\ldots$) in the list against a rule of the form ($X \rightarrow \ldots$) and replace ($\ldots$) with X.

To avoid this source of inefficiency we can use dynamic programming: *every time we analyze a substring, store the results so we won't have to reanalyze it later.* For example, once we discover that "the students in section 2 of Computer Science 101" is an NP, we can record that result in a data structure known as a **chart**. Algorithms that do this are called **chart parsers**. Because we are dealing with context-free grammars, any phrase that was found in the context of one branch of the search space can work just as well in any other branch of the search space. There are many types of chart parsers; we describe a bottom-up version called the **CYK algorithm**, after its inventors, John Cocke, Daniel Younger, and Tadeo Kasami.

CHART

CYK ALGORITHM

The CYK algorithm is shown in Figure 5. Note that it requires a grammar with all rules in one of two very specific formats: lexical rules of the form $X \rightarrow$ **word**, and syntactic rules of the form $X \rightarrow Y\ Z$. This grammar format, called **Chomsky Normal Form**, may seem restrictive, but it is not: any context-free grammar can be automatically transformed into Chomsky Normal Form. Exercise 8 leads you through the process.

CHOMSKY NORMAL FORM

The CYK algorithm uses space of $O(n^2m)$ for the P table, where n is the number of words in the sentence, and m is the number of nonterminal symbols in the grammar, and takes time $O(n^3m)$. (Since m is constant for a particular grammar, this is commonly described as $O(n^3)$.) No algorithm can do better for general context-free grammars, although there are faster algorithms on more restricted grammars. In fact, it is quite a trick for the algorithm to complete in $O(n^3)$ time, given that it is possible for a sentence to have an exponential number of parse trees. Consider the sentence

Fall leaves fall and spring leaves spring.

It is ambiguous because each word (except "and") can be either a noun or a verb, and "fall" and "spring" can be adjectives as well. (For example, one meaning of "Fall leaves fall" is

```
function CYK-PARSE(words, grammar) returns P, a table of probabilities
  N ← LENGTH(words)
  M ← the number of nonterminal symbols in grammar
  P ← an array of size [M, N, N], initially all 0
  /* Insert lexical rules for each word */
  for i = 1 to N do
    for each rule of form (X → words_i [p]) do
      P[X, i, 1] ← p
  /* Combine first and second parts of right-hand sides of rules, from short to long */
  for length = 2 to N do
    for start = 1 to N − length + 1 do
      for len1 = 1 to N − 1 do
        len2 ← length − len1
        for each rule of the form (X → Y Z [p]) do
          P[X, start, length] ← MAX(P[X, start, length],
                      P[Y, start, len1] × P[Z, start + len1, len2] × p)
  return P
```

Figure 5 The CYK algorithm for parsing. Given a sequence of words, it finds the most probable derivation for the whole sequence and for each subsequence. It returns the whole table, P, in which an entry $P[X, start, len]$ is the probability of the most probable X of length len starting at position $start$. If there is no X of that size at that location, the probability is 0.

equivalent to "Autumn abandons autumn.) With $\mathcal{E}_0$ the sentence has four parses:

[*S* [*S* [*NP* Fall leaves] fall] and [*S* [*NP* spring leaves] spring]
[*S* [*S* [*NP* Fall leaves] fall] and [*S* spring [*VP* leaves spring]]
[*S* [*S* Fall [*VP* leaves fall]] and [*S* [*NP* spring leaves] spring]
[*S* [*S* Fall [*VP* leaves fall]] and [*S* spring [*VP* leaves spring]] .

If we had c two-ways-ambiguous conjoined subsentences, we would have 2^c ways of choosing parses for the subsentences.[3] How does the CYK algorithm process these 2^c parse trees in $O(c^3)$ time? The answer is that it doesn't examine all the parse trees; all it has to do is compute the probability of the most probable tree. The subtrees are all represented in the P table, and with a little work we could enumerate them all (in exponential time), but the beauty of the CYK algorithm is that we don't have to enumerate them unless we want to.

In practice we are usually not interested in all parses; just the best one or best few. Think of the CYK algorithm as defining the complete state space defined by the "apply grammar rule" operator. It is possible to search just part of this space using A^* search. Each state in this space is a list of items (words or categories), as shown in the bottom-up parse table (Figure 4). The start state is a list of words, and a goal state is the single item S. The

[3] There also would be $O(c!)$ ambiguity in the way the components conjoin—for example, (X and (Y and Z)) versus ((X and Y) and Z). But that is another story, one told well by Church and Patil (1982).

```
[ [S [NP-SBJ-2 Her eyes]
     [VP were
         [VP glazed
             [NP *-2]
             [SBAR-ADV as if
                 [S [NP-SBJ she]
                    [VP did n't
                        [VP [VP hear [NP *-1]]
                            or
                            [VP [ADVP even] see [NP *-1]]
                            [NP-1 him]]]]]]]]
  ]
```

Figure 6 Annotated tree for the sentence "Her eyes were glazed as if she didn't hear or even see him." from the Penn Treebank. Note that in this grammar there is a distinction between an object noun phrase (*NP*) and a subject noun phrase (*NP-SBJ*). Note also a grammatical phenomenon we have not covered yet: the movement of a phrase from one part of the tree to another. This tree analyzes the phrase "hear or even see him" as consisting of two constituent *VP*s, [VP hear [NP *-1]] and [VP [ADVP even] see [NP *-1]], both of which have a missing object, denoted *-1, which refers to the *NP* labeled elsewhere in the tree as [NP-1 him].

cost of a state is the inverse of its probability as defined by the rules applied so far, and there are various heuristics to estimate the remaining distance to the goal; the best heuristics come from machine learning applied to a corpus of sentences. With the A^* algorithm we don't have to search the entire state space, and we are guaranteed that the first parse found will be the most probable.

2.1 Learning probabilities for PCFGs

A PCFG has many rules, with a probability for each rule. This suggests that **learning** the grammar from data might be better than a knowledge engineering approach. Learning is easiest if we are given a corpus of correctly parsed sentences, commonly called a **treebank**. The Penn Treebank (Marcus *et al.*, 1993) is the best known; it consists of 3 million words which have been annotated with part of speech and parse-tree structure, using human labor assisted by some automated tools. Figure 6 shows an annotated tree from the Penn Treebank.

TREEBANK

Given a corpus of trees, we can create a PCFG just by counting (and smoothing). In the example above, there are two nodes of the form $[S[NP\ldots][VP\ldots]]$. We would count these, and all the other subtrees with root S in the corpus. If there are 100,000 S nodes of which 60,000 are of this form, then we create the rule:

$$S \rightarrow NP\ VP\ [0.60]\ .$$

What if a treebank is not available, but we have a corpus of raw unlabeled sentences? It is still possible to learn a grammar from such a corpus, but it is more difficult. First of all, we actually have two problems: learning the structure of the grammar rules and learning the probabilities associated with each rule. (We have the same distinction in learning Bayes nets.) We'll assume that we're given the lexical and syntactic category names. (If not, we can just assume categories $X_1, \ldots X_n$ and use cross-validation to pick the best value of n.) We can then assume that the grammar includes every possible ($X \rightarrow Y\ Z$) or ($X \rightarrow$ *word*) rule, although many of these rules will have probability 0 or close to 0.

We can then use an expectation–maximization (EM) approach, just as we did in learning HMMs. The parameters we are trying to learn are the rule probabilities; we start them off at random or uniform values. The hidden variables are the parse trees: we don't know whether a string of words $w_i \ldots w_j$ is or is not generated by a rule ($X \rightarrow \ldots$). The E step estimates the probability that each subsequence is generated by each rule. The M step then estimates the probability of each rule. The whole computation can be done in a dynamic-programming fashion with an algorithm called the **inside–outside algorithm** in analogy to the forward–backward algorithm for HMMs.

INSIDE–OUTSIDE ALGORITHM

The inside–outside algorithm seems magical in that it induces a grammar from unparsed text. But it has several drawbacks. First, the parses that are assigned by the induced grammars are often difficult to understand and unsatisfying to linguists. This makes it hard to combine handcrafted knowledge with automated induction. Second, it is slow: $O(n^3m^3)$, where n is the number of words in a sentence and m is the number of grammar categories. Third, the space of probability assignments is very large, and empirically it seems that getting stuck in local maxima is a severe problem. Alternatives such as simulated annealing can get closer to the global maximum, at a cost of even more computation. Lari and Young (1990) conclude that inside–outside is "computationally intractable for realistic problems."

However, progress can be made if we are willing to step outside the bounds of learning solely from unparsed text. One approach is to learn from **prototypes**: to seed the process with a dozen or two rules, similar to the rules in $\mathcal{E}_1$. From there, more complex rules can be learned more easily, and the resulting grammar parses English with an overall recall and precision for sentences of about 80% (Haghighi and Klein, 2006). Another approach is to use treebanks, but in addition to learning PCFG rules directly from the bracketings, also learning distinctions that are not in the treebank. For example, not that the tree in Figure 6 makes the distinction between NP and $NP - SBJ$. The latter is used for the pronoun "she," the former for the pronoun "her." We will explore this issue in Section 6; for now let us just say that there are many ways in which it would be useful to **split** a category like NP—grammar induction systems that use treebanks but automatically split categories do better than those that stick with the original category set (Petrov and Klein, 2007c). The error rates for automatically learned grammars are still about 50% higher than for hand-constructed grammar, but the gap is decreasing.

2.2 Comparing context-free and Markov models

The problem with PCFGs is that they are context-free. That means that the difference between P("eat a banana") and P("eat a bandanna") depends only on $P(Noun \rightarrow$ "banana") versus $P(Noun \rightarrow$ "bandanna") and not on the relation between "eat" and the respective objects. A Markov model of order two or more, given a sufficiently large corpus, *will* know that "eat a banana" is more probable. We can combine a PCFG and Markov model to get the best of both. The simplest approach is to estimate the probability of a sentence with the geometric mean of the probabilities computed by both models. Then we would know that "eat a banana" is probable from both the grammatical and lexical point of view. But it still wouldn't pick up the relation between "eat" and "banana" in "eat a slightly aging but still palatable banana" because here the relation is more than two words away. Increasing the order of the Markov model won't get at the relation precisely; to do that we can use a **lexicalized** PCFG, as described in the next section.

Another problem with PCFGs is that they tend to have too strong a preference for shorter sentences. In a corpus such as the *Wall Street Journal*, the average length of a sentence is about 25 words. But a PCFG will usually assign fairly high probability to many short sentences, such as "He slept," whereas in the *Journal* we're more likely to see something like "It has been reported by a reliable source that the allegation that he slept is credible." It seems that the phrases in the *Journal* really are not context-free; instead the writers have an idea of the expected sentence length and use that length as a soft global constraint on their sentences. This is hard to reflect in a PCFG.

3 AUGMENTED GRAMMARS AND SEMANTIC INTERPRETATION

In this section we see how to extend context-free grammars—to say that, for example, not every *NP* is independent of context, but rather, certain *NP*s are more likely to appear in one context, and others in another context.

3.1 Lexicalized PCFGs

To get at the relationship between the verb "eat" and the nouns "banana" versus "bandanna," we can use a **lexicalized PCFG**, in which the probabilities for a rule depend on the relationship between words in the parse tree, not just on the adjacency of words in a sentence. Of course, we can't have the probability depend on every word in the tree, because we won't have enough training data to estimate all those probabilities. It is useful to introduce the notion of the **head** of a phrase—the most important word. Thus, "eat" is the head of the VP "eat a banana" and "banana" is the head of the NP "a banana." We use the notation $VP(v)$ to denote a phrase with category VP whose head word is v. We say that the category VP is **augmented** with the head variable v. Here is an **augmented grammar** that describes the verb–object relation:

LEXICALIZED PCFG

HEAD

AUGMENTED GRAMMAR

$$
\begin{array}{lcll}
VP(v) & \rightarrow & Verb(v)\ NP(n) & [P_1(v,n)] \\
VP(v) & \rightarrow & Verb(v) & [P_2(v)] \\
NP(n) & \rightarrow & Article(a)\ Adjs(j)\ Noun(n) & [P_3(n,a)] \\
Noun(\textbf{banana}) & \rightarrow & \textbf{banana} & [p_n] \\
\ldots & & & \ldots
\end{array}
$$

Here the probability $P_1(v,n)$ depends on the head words v and n. We would set this probability to be relatively high when v is "eat" and n is "banana," and low when n is "bandanna."

Note that since we are considering only heads, the distinction between "eat a banana" and "eat a rancid banana" will not be caught by these probabilities. Another issue with this approach is that, in a vocabulary with, say, 20,000 nouns and 5,000 verbs, P_1 needs 100 million probability estimates. Only a few percent of these can come from a corpus; the rest will have to come from smoothing. For example, we can estimate $P_1(v, n)$ for a (v, n) pair that we have not seen often (or at all) by backing off to a model that depends only on v. These objectless probabilities are still very useful; they can capture the distinction between a transitive verb like "eat"—which will have a high value for P_1 and a low value for P_2—and an intransitive verb like "sleep," which will have the reverse. It is quite feasible to learn these probabilities from a treebank.

3.2 Formal definition of augmented grammar rules

Augmented rules are complicated, so we will give them a formal definition by showing how an augmented rule can be translated into a logical sentence. The sentence will have the form of a definite clause, so the result is called a **definite clause grammar**, or DCG. We'll use as an example a version of a rule from the lexicalized grammar for *NP* with one new piece of notation:

DEFINITE CLAUSE GRAMMAR

$$NP(n) \rightarrow Article(a)\ Adjs(j)\ Noun(n)\ \{Compatible(j, n)\}\ .$$

The new aspect here is the notation $\{constraint\}$ to denote a logical constraint on some of the variables; the rule only holds when the constraint is true. Here the predicate $Compatible(j, n)$ is meant to test whether adjective j and noun n are compatible; it would be defined by a series of assertions such as $Compatible(\mathbf{black}, \mathbf{dog})$. We can convert this grammar rule into a definite clause by (1) reversing the order of right- and left-hand sides, (2) making a conjunction of all the constituents and constraints, (3) adding a variable s_i to the list of arguments for each constituent to represent the sequence of words spanned by the constituent, (4) adding a term for the concatenation of words, $Append(s_1, \ldots)$, to the list of arguments for the root of the tree. That gives us

$$\begin{aligned} &Article(a, s_1) \land Adjs(j, s_2) \land Noun(n, s_3) \land Compatible(j, n) \\ &\quad \Rightarrow NP(n, Append(s_1, s_2, s_3))\ . \end{aligned}$$

This definite clause says that if the predicate *Article* is true of a head word a and a string s_1, and *Adjs* is similarly true of a head word j and a string s_2, and *Noun* is true of a head word n and a string s_3, and if j and n are compatible, then the predicate NP is true of the head word n and the result of appending strings s_1, s_2, and s_3.

The DCG translation left out the probabilities, but we could put them back in: just augment each constituent with one more variable representing the probability of the constituent, and augment the root with a variable that is the product of the constituent probabilities times the rule probability.

The translation from grammar rule to definite clause allows us to talk about parsing as logical inference. This makes it possible to reason about languages and strings in many different ways. For example, it means we can do bottom-up parsing using forward chaining or top-down parsing using backward chaining. In fact, parsing natural language with DCGs was one of the first applications of (and motivations for) the Prolog logic programming language. It is sometimes possible to run the process backward and do language generation as well as parsing. For example, skipping ahead to Figure 10, a logic program could be given the semantic form $Loves(John, Mary)$ and apply the definite-clause rules to deduce

LANGUAGE GENERATION

$$S(Loves(John, Mary), [\textbf{John}, \textbf{loves}, \textbf{Mary}]) .$$

This works for toy examples, but serious language-generation systems need more control over the process than is afforded by the DCG rules alone.

$$
\begin{array}{rcl}
\mathcal{E}_1: \quad S & \rightarrow & NP_S\ VP \mid \ldots \\
NP_S & \rightarrow & Pronoun_S \mid Name \mid Noun \mid \ldots \\
NP_O & \rightarrow & Pronoun_O \mid Name \mid Noun \mid \ldots \\
VP & \rightarrow & VP\ NP_O \mid \ldots \\
PP & \rightarrow & Prep\ NP_O \\
Pronoun_S & \rightarrow & \textbf{I} \mid \textbf{you} \mid \textbf{he} \mid \textbf{she} \mid \textbf{it} \mid \ldots \\
Pronoun_O & \rightarrow & \textbf{me} \mid \textbf{you} \mid \textbf{him} \mid \textbf{her} \mid \textbf{it} \mid \ldots \\
 & \ldots &
\end{array}
$$

$$
\begin{array}{rcl}
\mathcal{E}_2: \quad S(head) & \rightarrow & NP(Sbj, pn, h)\ VP(pn, head) \mid \ldots \\
NP(c, pn, head) & \rightarrow & Pronoun(c, pn, head) \mid Noun(c, pn, head) \mid \ldots \\
VP(pn, head) & \rightarrow & VP(pn, head)\ NP(Obj, p, h) \mid \ldots \\
PP(head) & \rightarrow & Prep(head)\ NP(Obj, pn, h) \\
Pronoun(Sbj, 1S, \textbf{I}) & \rightarrow & \textbf{I} \\
Pronoun(Sbj, 1P, \textbf{we}) & \rightarrow & \textbf{we} \\
Pronoun(Obj, 1S, \textbf{me}) & \rightarrow & \textbf{me} \\
Pronoun(Obj, 3P, \textbf{them}) & \rightarrow & \textbf{them} \\
 & \ldots &
\end{array}
$$

Figure 7 Top: part of a grammar for the language $\mathcal{E}_1$, which handles subjective and objective cases in noun phrases and thus does not overgenerate quite as badly as $\mathcal{E}_0$. The portions that are identical to $\mathcal{E}_0$ have been omitted. Bottom: part of an augmented grammar for $\mathcal{E}_2$, with three augmentations: case agreement, subject–verb agreement, and head word. *Sbj, Obj, 1S, 1P* and *3P* are constants, and lowercase names are variables.

3.3 Case agreement and subject–verb agreement

We saw in Section 1 that the simple grammar for $\mathcal{E}_0$ overgenerates, producing nonsentences such as "Me smell a stench." To avoid this problem, our grammar would have to know that "me" is not a valid *NP* when it is the subject of a sentence. Linguists say that the pronoun "I" is in the subjective case, and "me" is in the objective case.[4] We can account for this by

[4] The subjective case is also sometimes called the nominative case and the objective case is sometimes called the accusative case. Many languages also have a dative case for words in the indirect object position.

splitting NP into two categories, NP_S and NP_O, to stand for noun phrases in the subjective and objective case, respectively. We would also need to split the category $Pronoun$ into the two categories $Pronoun_S$ (which includes "I") and $Pronoun_O$ (which includes "me"). The top part of Figure 7 shows the grammar for **case agreement**; we call the resulting language $\mathcal{E}_1$. Notice that all the NP rules must be duplicated, once for NP_S and once for NP_O.

CASE AGREEMENT

SUBJECT–VERB AGREEMENT

Unfortunately, $\mathcal{E}_1$ still overgenerates. English requires **subject–verb agreement** for person and number of the subject and main verb of a sentence. For example, if "I" is the subject, then "I smell" is grammatical, but "I smells" is not. If "it" is the subject, we get the reverse. In English, the agreement distinctions are minimal: most verbs have one form for third-person singular subjects (he, she, or it), and a second form for all other combinations of person and number. There is one exception: the verb "to be" has three forms, "I am / you are / he is." So one distinction (case) splits NP two ways, another distinction (person and number) splits NP three ways, and as we uncover other distinctions we would end up with an exponential number of subscripted NP forms if we took the approach of $\mathcal{E}_1$. Augmentations are a better approach: they can represent an exponential number of forms as a single rule.

In the bottom of Figure 7 we see (part of) an augmented grammar for the language $\mathcal{E}_2$, which handles case agreement, subject–verb agreement, and head words. We have just one NP category, but $NP(c, pn, head)$ has three augmentations: c is a parameter for case, pn is a parameter for person and number, and $head$ is a parameter for the head word of the phrase. The other categories also are augmented with heads and other arguments. Let's consider one rule in detail:

$$S(head) \rightarrow NP(Sbj, pn, h)\ VP(pn, head)\ .$$

This rule is easiest to understand right-to-left: when an *NP* and a *VP* are conjoined they form an *S*, but only if the *NP* has the subjective (*Sbj*) case and the person and number (*pn*) of the *NP* and *VP* are identical. If that holds, then we have an *S* whose head is the same as the head of the *VP*. Note the head of the *NP*, denoted by the dummy variable *h*, is not part of the augmentation of the *S*. The lexical rules for $\mathcal{E}_2$ fill in the values of the parameters and are also best read right-to-left. For example, the rule

$$Pronoun(Sbj, 1S, \mathbf{I}) \rightarrow \mathbf{I}$$

says that "I" can be interpreted as a *Pronoun* in the subjective case, first-person singular, with head "I." For simplicity we have omitted the probabilities for these rules, but augmentation does work with probabilities. Augmentation can also work with automated learning mechanisms. Petrov and Klein (2007c) show how a learning algorithm can automatically split the *NP* category into NP_S and NP_O.

3.4 Semantic interpretation

To show how to add semantics to a grammar, we start with an example that is simpler than English: the semantics of arithmetic expressions. Figure 8 shows a grammar for arithmetic expressions, where each rule is augmented with a variable indicating the semantic interpretation of the phrase. The semantics of a digit such as "3" is the digit itself. The semantics of an expression such as "3 + 4" is the operator "+" applied to the semantics of the phrase "3" and

$$
\begin{aligned}
Exp(x) &\rightarrow Exp(x_1)\ Operator(op)\ Exp(x_2)\ \{x = Apply(op, x_1, x_2)\}\\
Exp(x) &\rightarrow (\ Exp(x)\ )\\
Exp(x) &\rightarrow Number(x)\\
Number(x) &\rightarrow Digit(x)\\
Number(x) &\rightarrow Number(x_1)\ Digit(x_2)\ \{x = 10 \times x_1 + x_2\}\\
Digit(x) &\rightarrow x\ \{0 \leq x \leq 9\}\\
Operator(x) &\rightarrow x\ \{x \in \{+, -, \div, \times\}\}
\end{aligned}
$$

Figure 8 A grammar for arithmetic expressions, augmented with semantics. Each variable x_i represents the semantics of a constituent. Note the use of the $\{test\}$ notation to define logical predicates that must be satisfied, but that are not constituents.

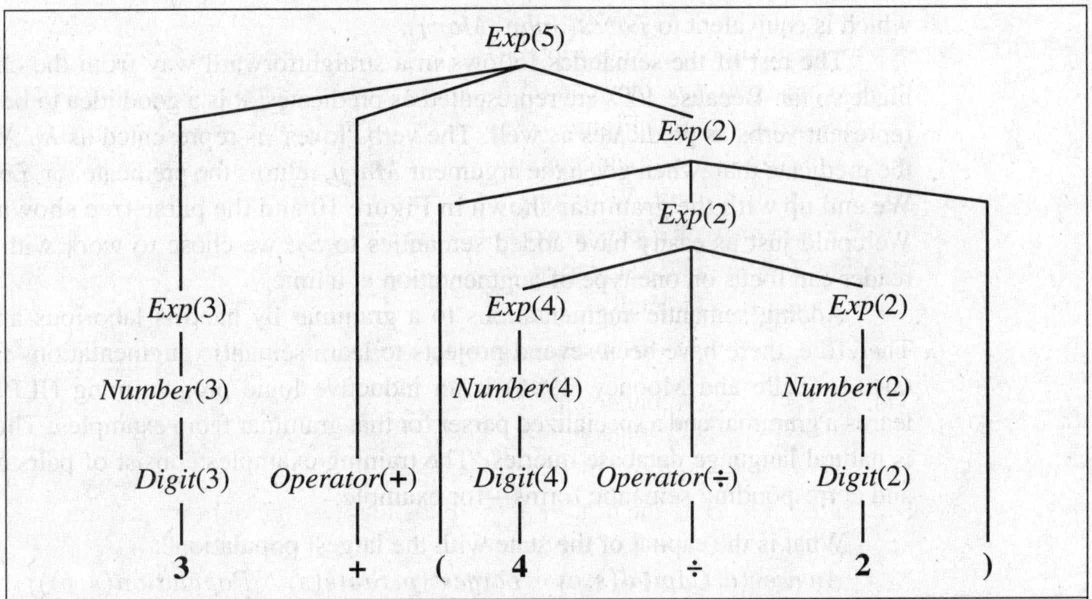

Figure 9 Parse tree with semantic interpretations for the string "$3 + (4 \div 2)$".

COMPOSITIONAL SEMANTICS

the phrase "4." The rules obey the principle of **compositional semantics**—the semantics of a phrase is a function of the semantics of the subphrases. Figure 9 shows the parse tree for $3 + (4 \div 2)$ according to this grammar. The root of the parse tree is $Exp(5)$, an expression whose semantic interpretation is 5.

Now let's move on to the semantics of English, or at least of $\mathcal{E}_0$. We start by determining what semantic representations we want to associate with what phrases. We use the simple example sentence "John loves Mary." The *NP* "John" should have as its semantic interpretation the logical term *John*, and the sentence as a whole should have as its interpretation the logical sentence $Loves(John, Mary)$. That much seems clear. The complicated part is the *VP* "loves Mary." The semantic interpretation of this phrase is neither a logical term nor a complete logical sentence. Intuitively, "loves Mary" is a description that might or might not apply to a particular person. (In this case, it applies to John.) This means that "loves Mary" is a **predicate** that, when combined with a term that represents a person (the person doing the loving), yields a complete logical sentence. Using the λ-notation, we can represent "loves Mary" as the predicate

$$\lambda x \; Loves(x, Mary) \; .$$

Now we need a rule that says "an *NP* with semantics *obj* followed by a *VP* with semantics *pred* yields a sentence whose semantics is the result of applying *pred* to *obj*:"

$$S(pred(obj)) \;\rightarrow\; NP(obj) \; VP(pred) \; .$$

The rule tells us that the semantic interpretation of "John loves Mary" is

$$(\lambda x \; Loves(x, Mary))(John) \; ,$$

which is equivalent to $Loves(John, Mary)$.

The rest of the semantics follows in a straightforward way from the choices we have made so far. Because *VP*s are represented as predicates, it is a good idea to be consistent and represent verbs as predicates as well. The verb "loves" is represented as $\lambda y \; \lambda x \; Loves(x, y)$, the predicate that, when given the argument *Mary*, returns the predicate $\lambda x \; Loves(x, Mary)$. We end up with the grammar shown in Figure 10 and the parse tree shown in Figure 11. We could just as easily have added semantics to $\mathcal{E}_2$; we chose to work with $\mathcal{E}_0$ so that the reader can focus on one type of augmentation at a time.

Adding semantic augmentations to a grammar by hand is laborious and error prone. Therefore, there have been several projects to learn semantic augmentations from examples. CHILL (Zelle and Mooney, 1996) is an inductive logic programming (ILP) program that learns a grammar and a specialized parser for that grammar from examples. The target domain is natural language database queries. The training examples consist of pairs of word strings and corresponding semantic forms—for example;

What is the capital of the state with the largest population?
$Answer(c, Capital(s, c) \wedge Largest(p, State(s) \wedge Population(s, p)))$

CHILL's task is to learn a predicate $Parse(words, semantics)$ that is consistent with the examples and, hopefully, generalizes well to other examples. Applying ILP directly to learn this predicate results in poor performance: the induced parser has only about 20% accuracy. Fortunately, ILP learners can improve by adding knowledge. In this case, most of the *Parse* predicate was defined as a logic program, and CHILL's task was reduced to inducing the control rules that guide the parser to select one parse over another. With this additional background knowledge, CHILL can learn to achieve 70% to 85% accuracy on various database query tasks.

3.5 Complications

The grammar of real English is endlessly complex. We will briefly mention some examples.

TIME AND TENSE

Time and tense: Suppose we want to represent the difference between "John loves Mary" and "John loved Mary." English uses verb tenses (past, present, and future) to indicate

$$S(pred(obj)) \rightarrow NP(obj)\ VP(pred)$$
$$VP(pred(obj)) \rightarrow Verb(pred)\ NP(obj)$$
$$NP(obj) \rightarrow Name(obj)$$

$$Name(John) \rightarrow \textbf{John}$$
$$Name(Mary) \rightarrow \textbf{Mary}$$
$$Verb(\lambda y\ \lambda x\ Loves(x,y)) \rightarrow \textbf{loves}$$

Figure 10 A grammar that can derive a parse tree and semantic interpretation for "John loves Mary" (and three other sentences). Each category is augmented with a single argument representing the semantics.

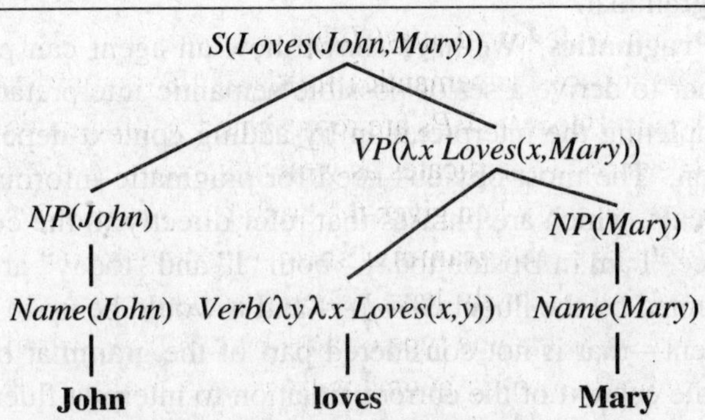

Figure 11 A parse tree with semantic interpretations for the string "John loves Mary".

the relative time of an event. One good choice to represent the time of events is the event calculus notation. In event calculus we have

John loves mary: $E_1 \in Loves(John, Mary) \wedge During(Now, Extent(E_1))$
John loved mary: $E_2 \in Loves(John, Mary) \wedge After(Now, Extent(E_2))$.

This suggests that our two lexical rules for the words "loves" and "loved" should be these:

$$Verb(\lambda y\ \lambda x\ e \in Loves(x,y) \wedge During(Now, e)) \rightarrow \textbf{loves}$$
$$Verb(\lambda y\ \lambda x\ e \in Loves(x,y) \wedge After(Now, e)) \rightarrow \textbf{loved}\ .$$

Other than this change, everything else about the grammar remains the same, which is encouraging news; it suggests we are on the right track if we can so easily add a complication like the tense of verbs (although we have just scratched the surface of a complete grammar for time and tense). It is also encouraging that the distinction between processes and discrete events is actually reflected in language use. We can say "John slept a lot last night," where *Sleeping* is a process category, but it is odd to say "John found a unicorn a lot last night," where *Finding* is a discrete event category. A grammar would reflect that fact by having a low probability for adding the adverbial phrase "a lot" to discrete events.

QUANTIFICATION

Quantification: Consider the sentence "Every agent feels a breeze." The sentence has only one syntactic parse under $\mathcal{E}_0$, but it is actually semantically ambiguous; the preferred meaning is "For every agent there exists a breeze that the agent feels," but an acceptable alternative meaning is "There exists a breeze that every agent feels." [5] The two interpretations can be represented as

$$\begin{array}{l} \forall\, a \;\; a \in Agents \;\Rightarrow \\ \qquad \exists\, b \;\; b \in Breezes \land \exists\, e \;\; e \in Feel(a,b) \land During(Now, e)\ ; \\ \exists\, b \;\; b \in Breezes\ \forall\, a \;\; a \in Agents \;\Rightarrow \\ \qquad \exists\, e \;\; e \in Feel(a,b) \land During(Now, e)\ . \end{array}$$

QUASI-LOGICAL FORM

The standard approach to quantification is for the grammar to define not an actual logical semantic sentence, but rather a **quasi-logical form** that is then turned into a logical sentence by algorithms outside of the parsing process. Those algorithms can have preference rules for preferring one quantifier scope over another—preferences that need not be reflected directly in the grammar.

PRAGMATICS

Pragmatics: We have shown how an agent can perceive a string of words and use a grammar to derive a set of possible semantic interpretations. Now we address the problem of completing the interpretation by adding context-dependent information about the current situation. The most obvious need for pragmatic information is in resolving the meaning of **indexicals**, which are phrases that refer directly to the current situation. For example, in the sentence "I am in Boston today," both "I" and "today" are indexicals. The word "I" would be represented by the fluent *Speaker*, and it would be up to the hearer to resolve the meaning of the fluent—that is not considered part of the grammar but rather an issue of pragmatics; of using the context of the current situation to interpret fluents.

INDEXICAL

SPEECH ACT

Another part of pragmatics is interpreting the speaker's intent. The speaker's action is considered a **speech act**, and it is up to the hearer to decipher what type of action it is—a question, a statement, a promise, a warning, a command, and so on. A command such as "go to 2 2" implicitly refers to the hearer. So far, our grammar for S covers only declarative sentences. We can easily extend it to cover commands. A command can be formed from a VP, where the subject is implicitly the hearer. We need to distinguish commands from statements, so we alter the rules for S to include the type of speech act:

$$\begin{array}{l} S(Statement(Speaker, pred(obj))) \;\rightarrow\; NP(obj)\ VP(pred) \\ S(Command(Speaker, pred(Hearer))) \;\rightarrow\; VP(pred)\ . \end{array}$$

LONG-DISTANCE DEPENDENCIES

Long-distance dependencies: Questions introduce a new grammatical complexity. In "Who did the agent tell you to give the gold to?" the final word "to" should be parsed as [PP to ␣], where the "␣" denotes a gap or **trace** where an NP is missing; the missing NP is licensed by the first word of the sentence, "who." A complex system of augmentations is used to make sure that the missing NPs match up with the licensing words in just the right way, and prohibit gaps in the wrong places. For example, you can't have a gap in one branch of an NP conjunction: "What did he play [NP Dungeons and ␣]?" is ungrammatical. But you can have the same gap in both branches of a VP conjunction: "What did you [VP [VP smell ␣] and [VP shoot an arrow at ␣]]?"

TRACE

AMBIGUITY

Ambiguity: In some cases, hearers are consciously aware of ambiguity in an utterance. Here are some examples taken from newspaper headlines:

[5] If this interpretation seems unlikely, consider "Every Protestant believes in a just God."

Squad helps dog bite victim.
Police begin campaign to run down jaywalkers.
Helicopter powered by human flies.
Once-sagging cloth diaper industry saved by full dumps.
Portable toilet bombed; police have nothing to go on.
Teacher strikes idle kids.
Include your children when baking cookies.
Hospitals are sued by 7 foot doctors.
Milk drinkers are turning to powder.
Safety experts say school bus passengers should be belted.

But most of the time the language we hear seems unambiguous. Thus, when researchers first began to use computers to analyze language in the 1960s, they were quite surprised to learn that *almost every utterance is highly ambiguous, even though the alternative interpretations might not be apparent to a native speaker.* A system with a large grammar and lexicon might find thousands of interpretations for a perfectly ordinary sentence. **Lexical ambiguity**, in which a word has more than one meaning, is quite common; "back" can be an adverb (go back), an adjective (back door), a noun (the back of the room) or a verb (back up your files). "Jack" can be a name, a noun (a playing card, a six-pointed metal game piece, a nautical flag, a fish, a socket, or a device for raising heavy objects), or a verb (to jack up a car, to hunt with a light, or to hit a baseball hard). **Syntactic ambiguity** refers to a phrase that has multiple parses: "I smelled a wumpus in 2,2" has two parses: one where the prepositional phrase "in 2,2" modifies the noun and one where it modifies the verb. The syntactic ambiguity leads to a **semantic ambiguity**, because one parse means that the wumpus is in 2,2 and the other means that a stench is in 2,2. In this case, getting the wrong interpretation could be a deadly mistake for the agent.

LEXICAL AMBIGUITY

SYNTACTIC AMBIGUITY

SEMANTIC AMBIGUITY

Finally, there can be ambiguity between literal and figurative meanings. Figures of speech are important in poetry, but are surprisingly common in everyday speech as well. A **metonymy** is a figure of speech in which one object is used to stand for another. When we hear "Chrysler announced a new model," we do not interpret it as saying that companies can talk; rather we understand that a spokesperson representing the company made the announcement. Metonymy is common and is often interpreted unconsciously by human hearers. Unfortunately, our grammar as it is written is not so facile. To handle the semantics of metonymy properly, we need to introduce a whole new level of ambiguity. We do this by providing *two* objects for the semantic interpretation of every phrase in the sentence: one for the object that the phrase literally refers to (Chrysler) and one for the metonymic reference (the spokesperson). We then have to say that there is a relation between the two. In our current grammar, "Chrysler announced" gets interpreted as

METONYMY

$$x = Chrysler \land e \in Announce(x) \land After(Now, Extent(e)) .$$

We need to change that to

$$x = Chrysler \land e \in Announce(m) \land After(Now, Extent(e)) \\ \land Metonymy(m, x) .$$

This says that there is one entity x that is equal to Chrysler, and another entity m that did the announcing, and that the two are in a metonymy relation. The next step is to define what kinds of metonymy relations can occur. The simplest case is when there is no metonymy at all—the literal object x and the metonymic object m are identical:

$$\forall\, m, x \;\; (m = x) \Rightarrow \; Metonymy(m, x) \,.$$

For the Chrysler example, a reasonable generalization is that an organization can be used to stand for a spokesperson of that organization:

$$\forall\, m, x \;\; x \in Organizations \wedge Spokesperson(m, x) \; \Rightarrow \; Metonymy(m, x) \,.$$

Other metonymies include the author for the works (I read *Shakespeare*) or more generally the producer for the product (I drive a *Honda*) and the part for the whole (The Red Sox need a strong *arm*). Some examples of metonymy, such as "The *ham sandwich* on Table 4 wants another beer," are more novel and are interpreted with respect to a situation.

METAPHOR A **metaphor** is another figure of speech, in which a phrase with one literal meaning is used to suggest a different meaning by way of an analogy. Thus, metaphor can be seen as a kind of metonymy where the relation is one of similarity.

DISAMBIGUATION **Disambiguation** is the process of recovering the most probable intended meaning of an utterance. In one sense we already have a framework for solving this problem: each rule has a probability associated with it, so the probability of an interpretation is the product of the probabilities of the rules that led to the interpretation. Unfortunately, the probabilities reflect how common the phrases are in the corpus from which the grammar was learned, and thus reflect general knowledge, not specific knowledge of the current situation. To do disambiguation properly, we need to combine four models:

1. The **world model**: the likelihood that a proposition occurs in the world. Given what we know about the world, it is more likely that a speaker who says "I'm dead" means "I am in big trouble" rather than "My life ended, and yet I can still talk."
2. The **mental model**: the likelihood that the speaker forms the intention of communicating a certain fact to the hearer. This approach combines models of what the speaker believes, what the speaker believes the hearer believes, and so on. For example, when a politician says, "I am not a crook," the world model might assign a probability of only 50% to the proposition that the politician is not a criminal, and 99.999% to the proposition that he is not a hooked shepherd's staff. Nevertheless, we select the former interpretation because it is a more likely thing to say.
3. The **language model**: the likelihood that a certain string of words will be chosen, given that the speaker has the intention of communicating a certain fact.
4. The **acoustic model**: for spoken communication, the likelihood that a particular sequence of sounds will be generated, given that the speaker has chosen a given string of words. Section 5 covers speech recognition.

4 MACHINE TRANSLATION

Machine translation is the automatic translation of text from one natural language (the source) to another (the target). It was one of the first application areas envisioned for computers (Weaver, 1949), but it is only in the past decade that the technology has seen widespread usage. Here is a passage from page 1 of this text:

> AI is one of the newest fields in science and engineering. Work started in earnest soon after World War II, and the name itself was coined in 1956. Along with molecular biology, AI is regularly cited as the "field I would most like to be in" by scientists in other disciplines.

And here it is translated from English to Danish by an online tool, Google Translate:

> AI er en af de nyeste områder inden for videnskab og teknik. Arbejde startede for alvor lige efter Anden Verdenskrig, og navnet i sig selv var opfundet i 1956. Sammen med molekylær biologi, er AI jævnligt nævnt som "feltet Jeg ville de fleste gerne være i" af forskere i andre discipliner.

For those who don't read Danish, here is the Danish translated back to English. The words that came out different are in italics:

> AI is one of the newest fields *of* science and engineering. Work *began* in earnest *just* after the *Second* World War, and the name itself was *invented* in 1956. *Together* with molecular biology, AI is *frequently mentioned* as ␣ "field I would most like to be in" by *researchers* in other disciplines.

The differences are all reasonable paraphrases, such as *frequently mentioned* for *regularly cited*. The only real error is the omission of the article *the*, denoted by the ␣ symbol. This is typical accuracy: of the two sentences, one has an error that would not be made by a native speaker, yet the meaning is clearly conveyed.

Historically, there have been three main applications of machine translation. *Rough translation*, as provided by free online services, gives the "gist" of a foreign sentence or document, but contains errors. *Pre-edited translation* is used by companies to publish their documentation and sales materials in multiple languages. The original source text is written in a constrained language that is easier to translate automatically, and the results are usually edited by a human to correct any errors. *Restricted-source translation* works fully automatically, but only on highly stereotypical language, such as a weather report.

Translation is difficult because, in the fully general case, it requires in-depth understanding of the text. This is true even for very simple texts—even "texts" of one word. Consider the word "Open" on the door of a store.[6] It communicates the idea that the store is accepting customers at the moment. Now consider the same word "Open" on a large banner outside a newly constructed store. It means that the store is now in daily operation, but readers of this sign would not feel misled if the store closed at night without removing the banner. The two signs use the identical word to convey different meanings. In German the sign on the door would be "Offen" while the banner would read "Neu Eröffnet."

[6] This example is due to Martin Kay.

The problem is that different languages categorize the world differently. For example, the French word "doux" covers a wide range of meanings corresponding approximately to the English words "soft," "sweet," and "gentle." Similarly, the English word "hard" covers virtually all uses of the German word "hart" (physically recalcitrant, cruel) and some uses of the word "schwierig" (difficult). Therefore, representing the meaning of a sentence is more difficult for translation than it is for single-language understanding. An English parsing system could use predicates like $Open(x)$, but for translation, the representation language would have to make more distinctions, perhaps with $Open_1(x)$ representing the "Offen" sense and $Open_2(x)$ representing the "Neu Eröffnet" sense. A representation language that makes all the distinctions necessary for a set of languages is called an **interlingua**.

INTERLINGUA

A translator (human or machine) often needs to understand the actual situation described in the source, not just the individual words. For example, to translate the English word "him," into Korean, a choice must be made between the humble and honorific form, a choice that depends on the social relationship between the speaker and the referent of "him." In Japanese, the honorifics are relative, so the choice depends on the social relationships between the speaker, the referent, and the listener. Translators (both machine and human) sometimes find it difficult to make this choice. As another example, to translate "The baseball hit the window. It broke." into French, we must choose the feminine "elle" or the masculine "il" for "it," so we must decide whether "it" refers to the baseball or the window. To get the translation right, one must understand physics as well as language.

Sometimes there is *no choice* that can yield a completely satisfactory translation. For example, an Italian love poem that uses the masculine "il sole" (sun) and feminine "la luna" (moon) to symbolize two lovers will necessarily be altered when translated into German, where the genders are reversed, and further altered when translated into a language where the genders are the same.[7]

4.1 Machine translation systems

All translation systems must model the source and target languages, but systems vary in the type of models they use. Some systems attempt to analyze the source language text all the way into an interlingua knowledge representation and then generate sentences in the target language from that representation. This is difficult because it involves three unsolved problems: creating a complete knowledge representation of everything; parsing into that representation; and generating sentences from that representation.

TRANSFER MODEL

Other systems are based on a **transfer model**. They keep a database of translation rules (or examples), and whenever the rule (or example) matches, they translate directly. Transfer can occur at the lexical, syntactic, or semantic level. For example, a strictly syntactic rule maps English [*Adjective Noun*] to French [*Noun Adjective*]. A mixed syntactic and lexical rule maps French [S_1 "et puis" S_2] to English [S_1 "and then" S_2]. Figure 12 diagrams the various transfer points.

[7] Warren Weaver (1949) reports that Max Zeldner points out that the great Hebrew poet H. N. Bialik once said that translation "is like kissing the bride through a veil."

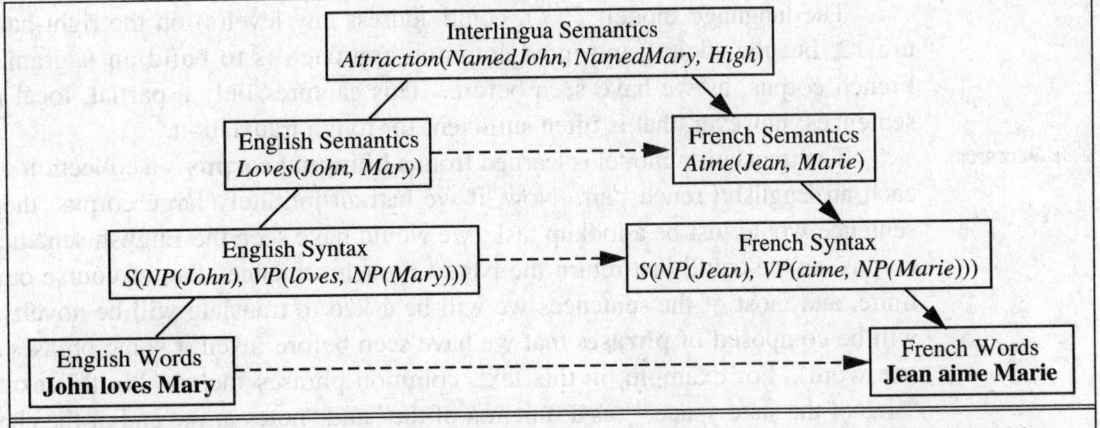

Figure 12 The Vauquois triangle: schematic diagram of the choices for a machine translation system (Vauquois, 1968). We start with English text at the top. An interlingua-based system follows the solid lines, parsing English first into a syntactic form, then into a semantic representation and an interlingua representation, and then through generation to a semantic, syntactic, and lexical form in French. A transfer-based system uses the dashed lines as a shortcut. Different systems make the transfer at different points; some make it at multiple points.

4.2 Statistical machine translation

Now that we have seen how complex the translation task can be, it should come as no surprise that the most successful machine translation systems are built by training a probabilistic model using statistics gathered from a large corpus of text. This approach does not need a complex ontology of interlingua concepts, nor does it need handcrafted grammars of the source and target languages, nor a hand-labeled treebank. All it needs is data—sample translations from which a translation model can be learned. To translate a sentence in, say, English (e) into French (f), we find the string of words f^* that maximizes

$$f^* = \underset{f}{\operatorname{argmax}}\, P(f \mid e) = \operatorname{argmax} P(e \mid f)\, P(f)\,.$$

LANGUAGE MODEL

TRANSLATION MODEL

Here the factor $P(f)$ is the target **language model** for French; it says how probable a given sentence is in French. $P(e|f)$ is the **translation model**; it says how probable an English sentence is as a translation for a given French sentence. Similarly, $P(f \mid e)$ is a translation model from English to French.

Should we work directly on $P(f \mid e)$, or apply Bayes' rule and work on $P(e \mid f)\, P(f)$? In **diagnostic** applications like medicine, it is easier to model the domain in the causal direction: $P(symptoms \mid disease)$ rather than $P(disease \mid symptoms)$. But in translation both directions are equally easy. The earliest work in statistical machine translation did apply Bayes' rule—in part because the researchers had a good language model, $P(f)$, and wanted to make use of it, and in part because they came from a background in speech recognition, which *is* a diagnostic problem. We follow their lead in this chapter, but we note that recent work in statistical machine translation often optimizes $P(f \mid e)$ directly, using a more sophisticated model that takes into account many of the features from the language model.

The language model, $P(f)$, could address any level(s) on the right-hand side of Figure 12, but the easiest and most common approach is to build an n-gram model from a French corpus, as we have seen before. This captures only a partial, local idea of French sentences; however, that is often sufficient for rough translation.[8]

BILINGUAL CORPUS

The translation model is learned from a **bilingual corpus**—a collection of parallel texts, each an English/French pair. Now, if we had an infinitely large corpus, then translating a sentence would just be a lookup task: we would have seen the English sentence before in the corpus, so we could just return the paired French sentence. But of course our resources are finite, and most of the sentences we will be asked to translate will be novel. However, they will be composed of **phrases** that we have seen before (even if some phrases are as short as one word). For example, in this text, common phrases include "in this exercise we will," "size of the state space," "as a function of the" and "notes at the end of the chapter." If asked to translate the novel sentence "In this exercise we will compute the size of the state space as a function of the number of actions." into French, we should be able to break the sentence into phrases, find the phrases in the English corpus (this text), find the corresponding French phrases (from the French translation of the book), and then reassemble the French phrases into an order that makes sense in French. In other words, given a source English sentence, e, finding a French translation f is a matter of three steps:

1. Break the English sentence into phrases $e_1, \ldots, e_n$.
2. For each phrase e_i, choose a corresponding French phrase f_i. We use the notation $P(f_i \mid e_i)$ for the phrasal probability that f_i is a translation of e_i.
3. Choose a permutation of the phrases $f_1, \ldots, f_n$. We will specify this permutation in a way that seems a little complicated, but is designed to have a simple probability distribution: For each f_i, we choose a **distortion** d_i, which is the number of words that phrase f_i has moved with respect to f_{i-1}; positive for moving to the right, negative for moving to the left, and zero if f_i immediately follows f_{i-1}.

DISTORTION

Figure 13 shows an example of the process. At the top, the sentence "There is a smelly wumpus sleeping in 2 2" is broken into five phrases, $e_1, \ldots, e_5$. Each of them is translated into a corresponding phrase f_i, and then these are permuted into the order f_1, f_3, f_4, f_2, f_5. We specify the permutation in terms of the distortions d_i of each French phrase, defined as

$$d_i = \text{START}(f_i) - \text{END}(f_{i-1}) - 1\,,$$

where $\text{START}(f_i)$ is the ordinal number of the first word of phrase f_i in the French sentence, and $\text{END}(f_{i-1})$ is the ordinal number of the last word of phrase f_{i-1}. In Figure 13 we see that f_5, "à 2 2," immediately follows f_4, "qui dort," and thus $d_5 = 0$. Phrase f_2, however, has moved one words to the right of f_1, so $d_2 = 1$. As a special case we have $d_1 = 0$, because f_1 starts at position 1 and $\text{END}(f_0)$ is defined to be 0 (even though f_0 does not exist).

Now that we have defined the distortion, d_i, we can define the probability distribution for distortion, $\mathbf{P}(d_i)$. Note that for sentences bounded by length n we have $|d_i| \leq n$, and

[8] For the finer points of translation, n-grams are clearly not enough. Marcel Proust's 4000-page novel *A la récherche du temps perdu* begins and ends with the same word (*longtemps*), so some translators have decided to do the same, thus basing the translation of the final word on one that appeared roughly 2 million words earlier.

so the full probability distribution $\mathbf{P}(d_i)$ has only $2n + 1$ elements, far fewer numbers to learn than the number of permutations, $n!$. That is why we defined the permutation in this circuitous way. Of course, this is a rather impoverished model of distortion. It doesn't say that adjectives are usually distorted to appear after the noun when we are translating from English to French—that fact is represented in the French language model, $P(f)$. The distortion probability is completely independent of the words in the phrases—it depends only on the integer value d_i. The probability distribution provides a summary of the volatility of the permutations; how likely a distortion of $P(d=2)$ is, compared to $P(d=0)$, for example.

We're ready now to put it all together: we can define $P(f, d \mid e)$, the probability that the sequence of phrases f with distortions d is a translation of the sequence of phrases e. We make the assumption that each phrase translation and each distortion is independent of the others, and thus we can factor the expression as

$$P(f, d \mid e) = \prod_i P(f_i \mid e_i)\, P(d_i)$$

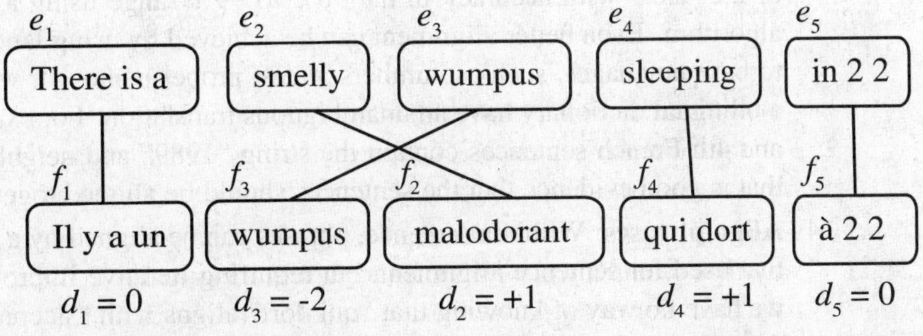

Figure 13 Candidate French phrases for each phrase of an English sentence, with distortion (d) values for each French phrase.

That gives us a way to compute the probability $P(f, d \mid e)$ for a candidate translation f and distortion d. But to find the best f and d we can't just enumerate sentences; with maybe 100 French phrases for each English phrase in the corpus, there are 100^5 different 5-phrase translations, and 5! reorderings for each of those. We will have to search for a good solution. A local beam search with a heuristic that estimates probability has proven effective at finding a nearly-most-probable translation.

All that remains is to learn the phrasal and distortion probabilities. We sketch the procedure; see the notes at the end of the chapter for details.

HANSARD

1. **Find parallel texts**: First, gather a parallel bilingual corpus. For example, a **Hansard**[9] is a record of parliamentary debate. Canada, Hong Kong, and other countries produce bilingual Hansards, the European Union publishes its official documents in 11 languages, and the United Nations publishes multilingual documents. Bilingual text is also available online; some Web sites publish parallel content with parallel URLs, for

[9] Named after William Hansard, who first published the British parliamentary debates in 1811.

example, `/en/` for the English page and `/fr/` for the corresponding French page. The leading statistical translation systems train on hundreds of millions of words of parallel text and billions of words of monolingual text.

2. **Segment into sentences**: The unit of translation is a sentence, so we will have to break the corpus into sentences. Periods are strong indicators of the end of a sentence, but consider "Dr. J. R. Smith of Rodeo Dr. paid $29.99 on 9.9.09."; only the final period ends a sentence. One way to decide if a period ends a sentence is to train a model that takes as features the surrounding words and their parts of speech. This approach achieves about 98% accuracy.
3. **Align sentences**: For each sentence in the English version, determine what sentence(s) it corresponds to in the French version. Usually, the next sentence of English corresponds to the next sentence of French in a 1:1 match, but sometimes there is variation: one sentence in one language will be split into a 2:1 match, or the order of two sentences will be swapped, resulting in a 2:2 match. By looking at the sentence lengths alone (i.e. short sentences should align with short sentences), it is possible to align them (1:1, 1:2, or 2:2, etc.) with accuracy in the 90% to 99% range using a variation on the Viterbi algorithm. Even better alignment can be achieved by using landmarks that are common to both languages, such as numbers, dates, proper names, or words that we know from a bilingual dictionary have an unambiguous translation. For example, if the 3rd English and 4th French sentences contain the string "1989" and neighboring sentences do not, that is good evidence that the sentences should be aligned together.
4. **Align phrases**: Within a sentence, phrases can be aligned by a process that is similar to that used for sentence alignment, but requiring iterative improvement. When we start, we have no way of knowing that "qui dort" aligns with "sleeping," but we can arrive at that alignment by a process of aggregation of evidence. Over all the example sentences we have seen, we notice that "qui dort" and "sleeping" co-occur with high frequency, and that in the pair of aligned sentences, no phrase other than "qui dort" co-occurs so frequently in other sentences with "sleeping." A complete phrase alignment over our corpus gives us the phrasal probabilities (after appropriate smoothing).
5. **Extract distortions**: Once we have an alignment of phrases we can define distortion probabilities. Simply count how often distortion occurs in the corpus for each distance $d = 0, \pm 1, \pm 2, \ldots$, and apply smoothing.
6. **Improve estimates with EM**: Use expectation–maximization to improve the estimates of $P(f \mid e)$ and $P(d)$ values. We compute the best alignments with the current values of these parameters in the E step, then update the estimates in the M step and iterate the process until convergence.

5 SPEECH RECOGNITION

SPEECH RECOGNITION

Speech recognition is the task of identifying a sequence of words uttered by a speaker, given the acoustic signal. It has become one of the mainstream applications of AI—millions of people interact with speech recognition systems every day to navigate voice mail systems, search the Web from mobile phones, and other applications. Speech is an attractive option when hands-free operation is necessary, as when operating machinery.

Speech recognition is difficult because the sounds made by a speaker are ambiguous and, well, noisy. As a well-known example, the phrase "recognize speech" sounds almost the same as "wreck a nice beach" when spoken quickly. Even this short example shows several of the issues that make speech problematic. First, **segmentation**: written words in English have spaces between them, but in fast speech there are no pauses in "wreck a nice" that would distinguish it as a multiword phrase as opposed to the single word "recognize." Second, **coarticulation**: when speaking quickly the "s" sound at the end of "nice" merges with the "b" sound at the beginning of "beach," yielding something that is close to a "sp." Another problem that does not show up in this example is **homophones**—words like "to," "too," and "two" that sound the same but differ in meaning.

SEGMENTATION

COARTICULATION

HOMOPHONES

We can view speech recognition as a problem in most-likely-sequence explanation. This is the problem of computing the most likely sequence of state variables, $\mathbf{x}_{1:t}$, given a sequence of observations $\mathbf{e}_{1:t}$. In this case the state variables are the words, and the observations are sounds. More precisely, an observation is a vector of features extracted from the audio signal. As usual, the most likely sequence can be computed with the help of Bayes' rule to be:

$$\underset{word_{1:t}}{\operatorname{argmax}} P(word_{1:t} \mid sound_{1:t}) = \underset{word_{1:t}}{\operatorname{argmax}} P(sound_{1:t} \mid word_{1:t}) P(word_{1:t}) \,.$$

ACOUSTIC MODEL

Here $P(sound_{1:t}|word_{1:t})$ is the **acoustic model**. It describes the sounds of words—that "ceiling" begins with a soft "c" and sounds the same as "sealing." $P(word_{1:t})$ is known as the **language model**. It specifies the prior probability of each utterance—for example, that "ceiling fan" is about 500 times more likely as a word sequence than "sealing fan."

LANGUAGE MODEL

NOISY CHANNEL MODEL

This approach was named the **noisy channel model** by Claude Shannon (1948). He described a situation in which an original message (the *words* in our example) is transmitted over a noisy channel (such as a telephone line) such that a corrupted message (the *sounds* in our example) are received at the other end. Shannon showed that no matter how noisy the channel, it is possible to recover the original message with arbitrarily small error, if we encode the original message in a redundant enough way. The noisy channel approach has been applied to speech recognition, machine translation, spelling correction, and other tasks.

Once we define the acoustic and language models, we can solve for the most likely sequence of words using the Viterbi algorithm. Most speech recognition systems use a language model that makes the Markov assumption—that the current state $Word_t$ depends only on a fixed number n of previous states—and represent $Word_t$ as a single random variable taking on a definite set of values, which makes it a Hidden Markov Model (HMM). Thus, speech recognition becomes a simple application of the HMM methodology—simple that is, once we define the acoustic and language models. We cover them next.

Vowels		Consonants B–N		Consonants P–Z	
Phone	Example	Phone	Example	Phone	Example
[iy]	b**ea**t	[b]	**b**et	[p]	**p**et
[ih]	b**i**t	[ch]	**Ch**et	[r]	**r**at
[eh]	b**e**t	[d]	**d**ebt	[s]	**s**et
[æ]	b**a**t	[f]	**f**at	[sh]	**sh**oe
[ah]	b**u**t	[g]	**g**et	[t]	**t**en
[ao]	b**ough**t	[hh]	**h**at	[th]	**th**ick
[ow]	b**oa**t	[hv]	**h**igh	[dh]	**th**at
[uh]	b**oo**k	[jh]	**j**et	[dx]	bu**tt**er
[ey]	b**ai**t	[k]	**k**ick	[v]	**v**et
[er]	B**er**t	[l]	**l**et	[w]	**w**et
[ay]	b**uy**	[el]	bott**le**	[wh]	**wh**ich
[oy]	b**oy**	[m]	**m**et	[y]	**y**et
[axr]	din**er**	[em]	bott**om**	[z]	**z**oo
[aw]	d**ow**n	[n]	**n**et	[zh]	mea**s**ure
[ax]	**a**bout	[en]	butt**on**		
[ix]	ros**e**s	[ng]	si**ng**		
[aa]	c**o**t	[eng]	washi**ng**	[-]	*silence*

Figure 14 The ARPA phonetic alphabet, or **ARPAbet**, listing all the phones used in American English. There are several alternative notations, including an International Phonetic Alphabet (IPA), which contains the phones in all known languages.

5.1 Acoustic model

SAMPLING RATE

QUANTIZATION FACTOR

Sound waves are periodic changes in pressure that propagate through the air. When these waves strike the diaphragm of a microphone, the back-and-forth movement generates an electric current. An analog-to-digital converter measures the size of the current—which approximates the amplitude of the sound wave—at discrete intervals called the **sampling rate**. Speech sounds, which are mostly in the range of 100 Hz (100 cycles per second) to 1000 Hz, are typically sampled at a rate of 8 kHz. (CDs and mp3 files are sampled at 44.1 kHz.) The precision of each measurement is determined by the **quantization factor**; speech recognizers typically keep 8 to 12 bits. That means that a low-end system, sampling at 8 kHz with 8-bit quantization, would require nearly half a megabyte per minute of speech.

PHONE

Since we only want to know what words were spoken, not exactly what they sounded like, we don't need to keep all that information. We only need to distinguish between different speech sounds. Linguists have identified about 100 speech sounds, or **phones**, that can be composed to form all the words in all known human languages. Roughly speaking, a phone is the sound that corresponds to a single vowel or consonant, but there are some complications: combinations of letters, such as "th" and "ng" produce single phones, and some letters produce different phones in different contexts (e.g., the "a" in *rat* and *rate*. Figure 14 lists

PHONEME all the phones that are used in English, with an example of each. A **phoneme** is the smallest unit of sound that has a distinct meaning to speakers of a particular language. For example, the "t" in "stick" sounds similar enough to the "t" in "tick" that speakers of English consider them the same phoneme. But the difference is significant in the Thai language, so there they are two phonemes. To represent spoken English we want a representation that can distinguish between different phonemes, but one that need not distinguish the nonphonemic variations in sound: loud or soft, fast or slow, male or female voice, etc.

First, we observe that although the sound frequencies in speech may be several kHz, the *changes* in the content of the signal occur much less often, perhaps at no more than 100 Hz. Therefore, speech systems summarize the properties of the signal over time slices called

FRAME **frames**. A frame length of about 10 milliseconds (i.e., 80 samples at 8 kHz) is short enough to ensure that few short-duration phenomena will be missed. Overlapping frames are used to make sure that we don't miss a signal because it happens to fall on a frame boundary.

FEATURE Each frame is summarized by a vector of **features**. Picking out features from a speech signal is like listening to an orchestra and saying "here the French horns are playing loudly and the violins are playing softly." We'll give a brief overview of the features in a typical system. First, a Fourier transform is used to determine the amount of acoustic energy at about a dozen frequencies. Then we compute a measure called the **mel frequency cepstral**

MEL FREQUENCY CEPSTRAL COEFFICIENT (MFCC) **coefficient (MFCC)** or MFCC for each frequency. We also compute the total energy in the frame. That gives thirteen features; for each one we compute the difference between this frame and the previous frame, and the difference between differences, for a total of 39 features. These are continuous-valued; the easiest way to fit them into the HMM framework is to discretize the values. (It is also possible to extend the HMM model to handle continuous mixtures of Gaussians.) Figure 15 shows the sequence of transformations from the raw sound to a sequence of frames with discrete features.

We have seen how to go from the raw acoustic signal to a series of observations, $\mathbf{e}_t$. Now we have to describe the (unobservable) states of the HMM and define the transition model, $\mathbf{P}(\mathbf{X}_t \mid \mathbf{X}_{t-1})$, and the sensor model, $\mathbf{P}(\mathbf{E}_t \mid \mathbf{X}_t)$. The transition model can be broken

PHONE MODEL into two levels: word and phone. We'll start from the bottom: the **phone model** describes

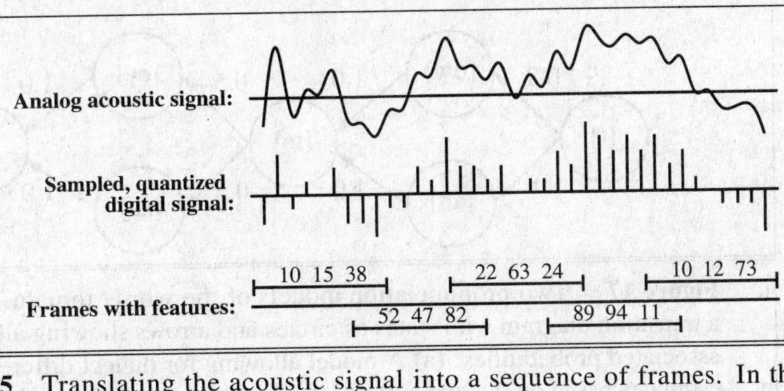

Figure 15 Translating the acoustic signal into a sequence of frames. In this diagram each frame is described by the discretized values of three acoustic features; a real system would have dozens of features.

Phone HMM for [m]:

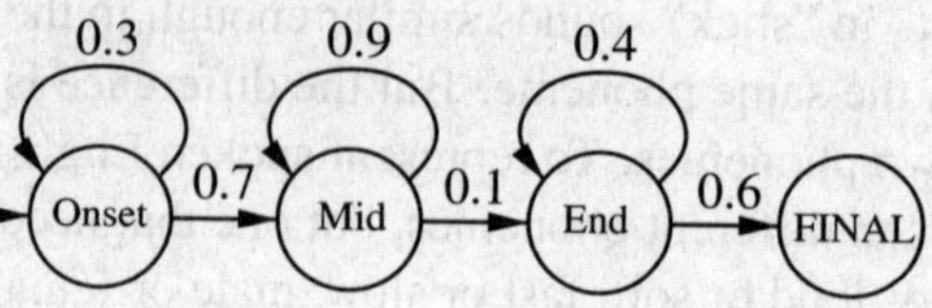

Output probabilities for the phone HMM:

Onset:	Mid:	End:
C_1: 0.5	C_3: 0.2	C_4: 0.1
C_2: 0.2	C_4: 0.7	C_6: 0.5
C_3: 0.3	C_5: 0.1	C_7: 0.4

Figure 16 An HMM for the three-state phone [m]. Each state has several possible outputs, each with its own probability. The MFCC feature labels C_1 through C_7 are arbitrary, standing for some combination of feature values.

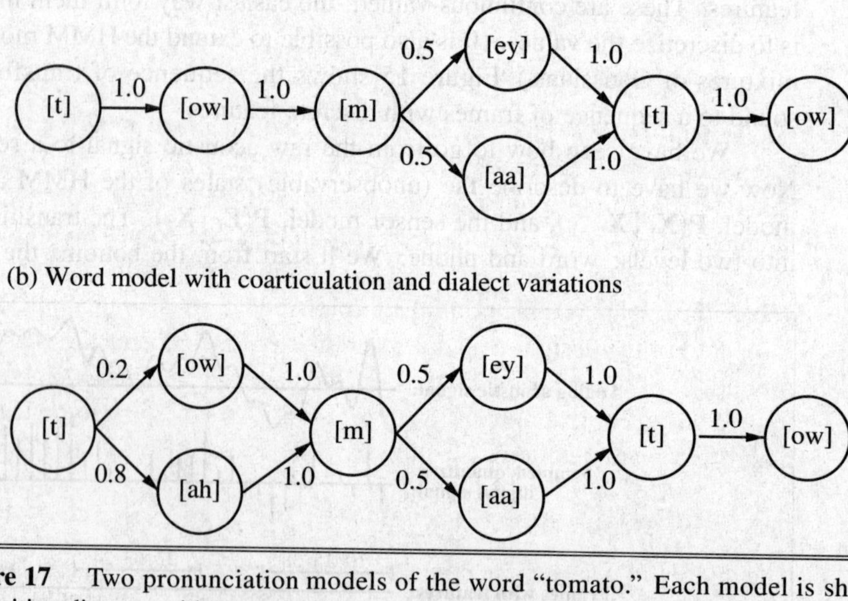

Figure 17 Two pronunciation models of the word "tomato." Each model is shown as a transition diagram with states as circles and arrows showing allowed transitions with their associated probabilities. (a) A model allowing for dialect differences. The 0.5 numbers are estimates based on the two authors' preferred pronunciations. (b) A model with a coarticulation effect on the first vowel, allowing either the [ow] or the [ah] phone.

a phone as three states, the onset, middle, and end. For example, the [t] phone has a silent beginning, a small explosive burst of sound in the middle, and (usually) a hissing at the end. Figure 16 shows an example for the phone [m]. Note that in normal speech, an average phone has a duration of 50–100 milliseconds, or 5–10 frames. The self-loops in each state allows for variation in this duration. By taking many self-loops (especially in the mid state), we can represent a long "mmmmmmmmmmm" sound. Bypassing the self-loops yields a short "m" sound.

PRONUNCIATION MODEL

In Figure 17 the phone models are strung together to form a **pronunciation model** for a word. According to Gershwin (1937), you say [t ow m ey t ow] and I say [t ow m aa t ow]. Figure 17(a) shows a transition model that provides for this dialect variation. Each of the circles in this diagram represents a phone model like the one in Figure 16.

In addition to dialect variation, words can have **coarticulation** variation. For example, the [t] phone is produced with the tongue at the top of the mouth, whereas the [ow] has the tongue near the bottom. When speaking quickly, the tongue doesn't have time to get into position for the [ow], and we end up with [t ah] rather than [t ow]. Figure 17(b) gives a model for "tomato" that takes this coarticulation effect into account. More sophisticated phone models take into account the context of the surrounding phones.

There can be substantial variation in pronunciation for a word. The most common pronunciation of "because" is [b iy k ah z], but that only accounts for about a quarter of uses. Another quarter (approximately) substitutes [ix], [ih] or [ax] for the first vowel, and the remainder substitute [ax] or [aa] for the second vowel, [zh] or [s] for the final [z], or drop "be" entirely, leaving "cuz."

5.2 Language model

For general-purpose speech recognition, the language model can be an n-gram model of text learned from a corpus of written sentences. However, spoken language has different characteristics than written language, so it is better to get a corpus of transcripts of spoken language. For task-specific speech recognition, the corpus should be task-specific: to build your airline reservation system, get transcripts of prior calls. It also helps to have task-specific vocabulary, such as a list of all the airports and cities served, and all the flight numbers.

Part of the design of a voice user interface is to coerce the user into saying things from a limited set of options, so that the speech recognizer will have a tighter probability distribution to deal with. For example, asking "What city do you want to go to?" elicits a response with a highly constrained language model, while asking "How can I help you?" does not.

5.3 Building a speech recognizer

The quality of a speech recognition system depends on the quality of all of its components—the language model, the word-pronunciation models, the phone models, and the signal-processing algorithms used to extract spectral features from the acoustic signal. We have discussed how the language model can be constructed from a corpus of written text, and we leave the details of signal processing to other textbooks. We are left with the pronunciation and phone models. The *structure* of the pronunciation models—such as the tomato models in

Figure 17—is usually developed by hand. Large pronunciation dictionaries are now available for English and other languages, although their accuracy varies greatly. The structure of the three-state phone models is the same for all phones, as shown in Figure 16. That leaves the probabilities themselves.

As usual, we will acquire the probabilities from a corpus, this time a corpus of speech. The most common type of corpus to obtain is one that includes the speech signal for each sentence paired with a transcript of the words. Building a model from this corpus is more difficult than building an n-gram model of text, because we have to build a hidden Markov model—the phone sequence for each word and the phone state for each time frame are hidden variables. In the early days of speech recognition, the hidden variables were provided by laborious hand-labeling of spectrograms. Recent systems use expectation–maximization to automatically supply the missing data. The idea is simple: given an HMM and an observation sequence, we can use smoothing algorithms to compute the probability of each state at each time step and, by a simple extension, the probability of each state–state pair at consecutive time steps. These probabilities can be viewed as uncertain *labels*. From the uncertain labels, we can estimate new transition and sensor probabilities, and the EM procedure repeats. The method is guaranteed to increase the fit between model and data on each iteration, and it generally converges to a much better set of parameter values than those provided by the initial, hand-labeled estimates.

The systems with the highest accuracy work by training a different model for each speaker, thereby capturing differences in dialect as well as male/female and other variations. This training can require several hours of interaction with the speaker, so the systems with the most widespread adoption do not create speaker-specific models.

The accuracy of a system depends on a number of factors. First, the quality of the signal matters: a high-quality directional microphone aimed at a stationary mouth in a padded room will do much better than a cheap microphone transmitting a signal over phone lines from a car in traffic with the radio playing. The vocabulary size matters: when recognizing digit strings with a vocabulary of 11 words (1-9 plus "oh" and "zero"), the word error rate will be below 0.5%, whereas it rises to about 10% on news stories with a 20,000-word vocabulary, and 20% on a corpus with a 64,000-word vocabulary. The task matters too: when the system is trying to accomplish a specific task—book a flight or give directions to a restaurant—the task can often be accomplished perfectly even with a word error rate of 10% or more.

6 Summary

Natural language understanding is one of the most important subfields of AI. Unlike most other areas of AI, natural language understanding requires an empirical investigation of actual human behavior—which turns out to be complex and interesting.

- Formal language theory and **phrase structure** grammars (and in particular, **context-free** grammar) are useful tools for dealing with some aspects of natural language. The probabilistic context-free grammar (PCFG) formalism is widely used.

- Sentences in a context-free language can be parsed in $O(n^3)$ time by a **chart parser** such as the **CYK algorithm**, which requires grammar rules to be in **Chomsky Normal Form**.
- A **treebank** can be used to learn a grammar. It is also possible to learn a grammar from an unparsed corpus of sentences, but this is less successful.
- A **lexicalized PCFG** allows us to represent that some relationships between words are more common than others.
- It is convenient to **augment** a grammar to handle such problems as subject–verb agreement and pronoun case. **Definite clause grammar** (DCG) is a formalism that allows for augmentations. With DCG, parsing and semantic interpretation (and even generation) can be done using logical inference.
- **Semantic interpretation** can also be handled by an augmented grammar.
- **Ambiguity** is a very important problem in natural language understanding; most sentences have many possible interpretations, but usually only one is appropriate. Disambiguation relies on knowledge about the world, about the current situation, and about language use.
- **Machine translation** systems have been implemented using a range of techniques, from full syntactic and semantic analysis to statistical techniques based on phrase frequencies. Currently the statistical models are most popular and most successful.
- **Speech recognition** systems are also primarily based on statistical principles. Speech systems are popular and useful, albeit imperfect.
- Together, machine translation and speech recognition are two of the big successes of natural language technology. One reason that the models perform well is that large corpora are available—both translation and speech are tasks that are performed "in the wild" by people every day. In contrast, tasks like parsing sentences have been less successful, in part because no large corpora of parsed sentences are available "in the wild" and in part because parsing is not useful in and of itself.

Bibliographical and Historical Notes

Like semantic networks, context-free grammars (also known as phrase structure grammars) are a reinvention of a technique first used by ancient Indian grammarians (especially Panini, ca. 350 B.C.) studying Shastric Sanskrit (Ingerman, 1967). They were reinvented by Noam Chomsky (1956) for the analysis of English syntax and independently by John Backus for the analysis of Algol-58 syntax. Peter Naur extended Backus's notation and is now credited (Backus, 1996) with the "N" in BNF, which originally stood for "Backus Normal Form." Knuth (1968) defined a kind of augmented grammar called **attribute grammar** that is useful for programming languages. Definite clause grammars were introduced by Colmerauer (1975) and developed and popularized by Pereira and Shieber (1987).

ATTRIBUTE GRAMMAR

Probabilistic context-free grammars were investigated by Booth (1969) and Salomaa (1969). Other algorithms for PCFGs are presented in the excellent short monograph by

Charniak (1993) and the excellent long textbooks by Manning and Schütze (1999) and Jurafsky and Martin (2008). Baker (1979) introduces the inside–outside algorithm for learning a PCFG, and Lari and Young (1990) describe its uses and limitations. Stolcke and Omohundro (1994) show how to learn grammar rules with Bayesian model merging; Haghighi and Klein (2006) describe a learning system based on prototypes.

Lexicalized PCFGs (Charniak, 1997; Hwa, 1998) combine the best aspects of PCFGs and n-gram models. Collins (1999) describes PCFG parsing that is lexicalized with head features. Petrov and Klein (2007a) show how to get the advantages of lexicalization without actual lexical augmentations by learning specific syntactic categories from a treebank that has general categories; for example, the treebank has the category NP, from which more specific categories such as NP_O and NP_S can be learned.

There have been many attempts to write formal grammars of natural languages, both in "pure" linguistics and in computational linguistics. There are several comprehensive but informal grammars of English (Quirk *et al.*, 1985; McCawley, 1988; Huddleston and Pullum, 2002). Since the mid-1980s, there has been a trend toward putting more information in the lexicon and less in the grammar. Lexical-functional grammar, or LFG (Bresnan, 1982) was the first major grammar formalism to be highly lexicalized. If we carry lexicalization to an extreme, we end up with **categorial grammar** (Clark and Curran, 2004), in which there can be as few as two grammar rules, or with **dependency grammar** (Smith and Eisner, 2008; Kübler *et al.*, 2009) in which there are no syntactic categories, only relations between words. Sleator and Temperley (1993) describe a dependency parser. Paskin (2001) shows that a version of dependency grammar is easier to learn than PCFGs.

The first computerized parsing algorithms were demonstrated by Yngve (1955). Efficient algorithms were developed in the late 1960s, with a few twists since then (Kasami, 1965; Younger, 1967; Earley, 1970; Graham *et al.*, 1980). Maxwell and Kaplan (1993) show how chart parsing with augmentations can be made efficient in the average case. Church and Patil (1982) address the resolution of syntactic ambiguity. Klein and Manning (2003) describe A* parsing, and Pauls and Klein (2009) extend that to *K*-best A* parsing, in which the result is not a single parse but the *K* best.

Leading parsers today include those by Petrov and Klein (2007b), which achieved 90.6% accuracy on the Wall Street Journal corpus, Charniak and Johnson (2005), which achieved 92.0%, and Koo *et al.* (2008), which achieved 93.2% on the Penn treebank. These numbers are not directly comparable, and there is some criticism of the field that it is focusing too narrowly on a few select corpora, and perhaps overfitting on them.

Formal semantic interpretation of natural languages originates within philosophy and formal logic, particularly Alfred Tarski's (1935) work on the semantics of formal languages. Bar-Hillel (1954) was the first to consider the problems of pragmatics and propose that they could be handled by formal logic. For example, he introduced C. S. Peirce's (1902) term *indexical* into linguistics. Richard Montague's essay "English as a formal language" (1970) is a kind of manifesto for the logical analysis of language, but the books by Dowty *et al.* (1991) and Portner and Partee (2002) are more readable.

The first NLP system to solve an actual task was probably the BASEBALL question answering system (Green *et al.*, 1961), which handled questions about a database of baseball statistics. Close after that was Woods's (1973) LUNAR, which answered questions about the rocks brought back from the moon by the Apollo program. Roger Schank and his students built a series of programs (Schank and Abelson, 1977; Schank and Riesbeck, 1981) that all had the task of understanding language. Modern approaches to semantic interpretation usually assume that the mapping from syntax to semantics will be learned from examples (Zelle and Mooney, 1996; Zettlemoyer and Collins, 2005).

Hobbs *et al.* (1993) describes a quantitative nonprobabilistic framework for interpretation. More recent work follows an explicitly probabilistic framework (Charniak and Goldman, 1992; Wu, 1993; Franz, 1996). In linguistics, optimality theory (Kager, 1999) is based on the idea of building soft constraints into the grammar, giving a natural ranking to interpretations (similar to a probability distribution), rather than having the grammar generate all possibilities with equal rank. Norvig (1988) discusses the problems of considering multiple simultaneous interpretations, rather than settling for a single maximum-likelihood interpretation. Literary critics (Empson, 1953; Hobbs, 1990) have been ambiguous about whether ambiguity is something to be resolved or cherished.

Nunberg (1979) outlines a formal model of metonymy. Lakoff and Johnson (1980) give an engaging analysis and catalog of common metaphors in English. Martin (1990) and Gibbs (2006) offer computational models of metaphor interpretation.

The first important result on **grammar induction** was a negative one: Gold (1967) showed that it is not possible to reliably learn a correct context-free grammar, given a set of strings from that grammar. Prominent linguists, such as Chomsky (1957) and Pinker (2003), have used Gold's result to argue that there must be an innate **universal grammar** that all children have from birth. The so-called *Poverty of the Stimulus* argument says that children aren't given enough input to learn a CFG, so they must already "know" the grammar and be merely tuning some of its parameters. While this argument continues to hold sway throughout much of Chomskyan linguistics, it has been dismissed by some other linguists (Pullum, 1996; Elman *et al.*, 1997) and most computer scientists. As early as 1969, Horning showed that it *is* possible to learn, in the sense of PAC learning, a *probabilistic* context-free grammar. Since then, there have been many convincing empirical demonstrations of learning from positive examples alone, such as the ILP work of Mooney (1999) and Muggleton and De Raedt (1994), the sequence learning of Nevill-Manning and Witten (1997), and the remarkable Ph.D. theses of Schütze (1995) and de Marcken (1996). There is an annual International Conference on Grammatical Inference (ICGI). It is possible to learn other grammar formalisms, such as regular languages (Denis, 2001) and finite state automata (Parekh and Honavar, 2001). Abney (2007) is a textbook introduction to semi-supervised learning for language models.

UNIVERSAL GRAMMAR

Wordnet (Fellbaum, 2001) is a publicly available dictionary of about 100,000 words and phrases, categorized into parts of speech and linked by semantic relations such as synonym, antonym, and part-of. The Penn Treebank (Marcus *et al.*, 1993) provides parse trees for a 3-million-word corpus of English. Charniak (1996) and Klein and Manning (2001) discuss parsing with treebank grammars. The British National Corpus (Leech *et al.*, 2001) contains 100 million words, and the World Wide Web contains several trillion words; (Brants *et al.*, 2007) describe n-gram models over a 2-trillion-word Web corpus.

In the 1930s Petr Troyanskii applied for a patent for a "translating machine," but there were no computers available to implement his ideas. In March 1947, the Rockefeller Foundation's Warren Weaver wrote to Norbert Wiener, suggesting that machine translation might be possible. Drawing on work in cryptography and information theory, Weaver wrote, "When I look at an article in Russian, I say: 'This is really written in English, but it has been coded in strange symbols. I will now proceed to decode.'" For the next decade, the community tried to decode in this way. IBM exhibited a rudimentary system in 1954. Bar-Hillel (1960) describes the enthusiasm of this period. However, the U.S. government subsequently reported (ALPAC, 1966) that "there is no immediate or predictable prospect of useful machine translation." However, limited work continued, and starting in the 1980s, computer power had increased to the point where the ALPAC findings were no longer correct.

The basic statistical approach we describe in the chapter is based on early work by the IBM group (Brown *et al.*, 1988, 1993) and the recent work by the ISI and Google research groups (Och and Ney, 2004; Zollmann *et al.*, 2008). A textbook introduction on statistical machine translation is given by Koehn (2009), and a short tutorial by Kevin Knight (1999) has been influential. Early work on sentence segmentation was done by Palmer and Hearst (1994). Och and Ney (2003) and Moore (2005) cover bilingual sentence alignment.

The prehistory of speech recognition began in the 1920s with Radio Rex, a voice-activated toy dog. Rex jumped out of his doghouse in response to the word "Rex!" (or actually almost any sufficiently loud word). Somewhat more serious work began after World War II. At AT&T Bell Labs, a system was built for recognizing isolated digits (Davis *et al.*, 1952) by means of simple pattern matching of acoustic features. Starting in 1971, the Defense Advanced Research Projects Agency (DARPA) of the United States Department of Defense funded four competing five-year projects to develop high-performance speech recognition systems. The winner, and the only system to meet the goal of 90% accuracy with a 1000-word vocabulary, was the HARPY system at CMU (Lowerre and Reddy, 1980). The final version of HARPY was derived from a system called DRAGON built by CMU graduate student James Baker (1975); DRAGON was the first to use HMMs for speech. Almost simultaneously, Jelinek (1976) at IBM had developed another HMM-based system. Recent years have been characterized by steady incremental progress, larger data sets and models, and more rigorous competitions on more realistic speech tasks. In 1997, Bill Gates predicted, "The PC five years from now—you won't recognize it, because speech will come into the interface." That didn't quite happen, but in 2008 he predicted "In five years, Microsoft expects more Internet searches to be done through speech than through typing on a keyboard." History will tell if he is right this time around.

Several good textbooks on speech recognition are available (Rabiner and Juang, 1993; Jelinek, 1997; Gold and Morgan, 2000; Huang *et al.*, 2001). The presentation in this chapter drew on the survey by Kay, Gawron, and Norvig (1994) and on the textbook by Jurafsky and Martin (2008). Speech recognition research is published in *Computer Speech and Language*, *Speech Communications*, and the IEEE *Transactions on Acoustics, Speech, and Signal Processing* and at the DARPA Workshops on Speech and Natural Language Processing and the Eurospeech, ICSLP, and ASRU conferences.

Ken Church (2004) shows that natural language research has cycled between concentrating on the data (empiricism) and concentrating on theories (rationalism). The linguist John Firth (1957) proclaimed "You shall know a word by the company it keeps," and linguistics of the 1940s and early 1950s was based largely on word frequencies, although without the computational power we have available today. Then Noam (Chomsky, 1956) showed the limitations of finite-state models, and sparked an interest in theoretical studies of syntax, disregarding frequency counts. This approach dominated for twenty years, until empiricism made a comeback based on the success of work in statistical speech recognition (Jelinek, 1976). Today, most work accepts the statistical framework, but there is great interest in building statistical models that consider higher-level models, such as syntactic trees and semantic relations, not just sequences of words.

Work on applications of language processing is presented at the biennial Applied Natural Language Processing conference (ANLP), the conference on Empirical Methods in Natural Language Processing (EMNLP), and the journal *Natural Language Engineering*. A broad range of NLP work appears in the journal *Computational Linguistics* and its conference, ACL, and in the Computational Linguistics (COLING) conference.

EXERCISES

1 Read the following text once for understanding, and remember as much of it as you can. There will be a test later.

> The procedure is actually quite simple. First you arrange things into different groups. Of course, one pile may be sufficient depending on how much there is to do. If you have to go somewhere else due to lack of facilities that is the next step, otherwise you are pretty well set. It is important not to overdo things. That is, it is better to do too few things at once than too many. In the short run this may not seem important but complications can easily arise. A mistake is expensive as well. At first the whole procedure will seem complicated. Soon, however, it will become just another facet of life. It is difficult to foresee any end to the necessity for this task in the immediate future, but then one can never tell. After the procedure is completed one arranges the material into different groups again. Then they can be put into their appropriate places. Eventually they will be used once more and the whole cycle will have to be repeated. However, this is part of life.

2 An *HMM grammar* is essentially a standard HMM whose state variable is N (nonterminal, with values such as Det, $Adjective$, $Noun$ and so on) and whose evidence variable is W (word, with values such as is, $duck$, and so on). The HMM model includes a prior $\mathbf{P}(N_0)$, a transition model $\mathbf{P}(N_{t+1}|N_t)$, and a sensor model $\mathbf{P}(W_t|N_t)$. Show that every HMM grammar can be written as a PCFG. [Hint: start by thinking about how the HMM prior can be represented by PCFG rules for the sentence symbol. You may find it helpful to illustrate for the particular HMM with values A, B for N and values x, y for W.]

3 Consider the following PCFG for simple verb phrases:

$0.1 : VP \rightarrow Verb$
$0.2 : VP \rightarrow Copula\ Adjective$
$0.5 : VP \rightarrow Verb\ the\ Noun$
$0.2 : VP \rightarrow VP\ Adverb$
$0.5 : Verb \rightarrow is$
$0.5 : Verb \rightarrow shoots$
$0.8 : Copula \rightarrow is$
$0.2 : Copula \rightarrow seems$
$0.5 : Adjective \rightarrow$ **unwell**
$0.5 : Adjective \rightarrow$ **well**
$0.5 : Adverb \rightarrow$ **well**
$0.5 : Adverb \rightarrow$ **badly**
$0.6 : Noun \rightarrow$ **duck**
$0.4 : Noun \rightarrow$ **well**

a. Which of the following have a nonzero probability as a VP? (i) shoots the duck well well well (ii) seems the well well (iii) shoots the unwell well badly

b. What is the probability of generating "is well well"?

c. What types of ambiguity are exhibited by the phrase in (b)?

d. Given any PCFG, is it possible to calculate the probability that the PCFG generates a string of exactly 10 words?

4 Outline the major differences between Java (or any other computer language with which you are familiar) and English, commenting on the "understanding" problem in each case. Think about such things as grammar, syntax, semantics, pragmatics, compositionality, context-dependence, lexical ambiguity, syntactic ambiguity, reference finding (including pronouns), background knowledge, and what it means to "understand" in the first place.

5 This exercise concerns grammars for very simple languages.

a. Write a context-free grammar for the language $a^n b^n$.

b. Write a context-free grammar for the palindrome language: the set of all strings whose second half is the reverse of the first half.

c. Write a context-sensitive grammar for the duplicate language: the set of all strings whose second half is the same as the first half.

6 Consider the sentence "Someone walked slowly to the supermarket" and a lexicon consisting of the following words:

$Pronoun \rightarrow$ **someone**	$Verb \rightarrow$ **walked**
$Adv \rightarrow$ **slowly**	$Prep \rightarrow$ **to**
$Article \rightarrow$ **the**	$Noun \rightarrow$ **supermarket**

Which of the following three grammars, combined with the lexicon, generates the given sentence? Show the corresponding parse tree(s).

(A):	(B):	(C):
$S \rightarrow NP\ VP$	$S \rightarrow NP\ VP$	$S \rightarrow NP\ VP$
$NP \rightarrow Pronoun$	$NP \rightarrow Pronoun$	$NP \rightarrow Pronoun$
$NP \rightarrow Article\ Noun$	$NP \rightarrow Noun$	$NP \rightarrow Article\ NP$
$VP \rightarrow VP\ PP$	$NP \rightarrow Article\ NP$	$VP \rightarrow Verb\ Adv$
$VP \rightarrow VP\ Adv\ Adv$	$VP \rightarrow Verb\ Vmod$	$Adv \rightarrow Adv\ Adv$
$VP \rightarrow Verb$	$Vmod \rightarrow Adv\ Vmod$	$Adv \rightarrow PP$
$PP \rightarrow Prep\ NP$	$Vmod \rightarrow Adv$	$PP \rightarrow Prep\ NP$
$NP \rightarrow Noun$	$Adv \rightarrow PP$	$NP \rightarrow Noun$
	$PP \rightarrow Prep\ NP$	

For each of the preceding three grammars, write down three sentences of English and three sentences of non-English generated by the grammar. Each sentence should be significantly different, should be at least six words long, and should include some new lexical entries (which you should define). Suggest ways to improve each grammar to avoid generating the non-English sentences.

7 Collect some examples of time expressions, such as "two o'clock," "midnight," and "12:46." Also think up some examples that are ungrammatical, such as "thirteen o'clock" or "half past two fifteen." Write a grammar for the time language.

8 In this exercise you will transform $\mathcal{E}_0$ into Chomsky Normal Form (CNF). There are five steps: (a) Add a new start symbol, (b) Eliminate ϵ rules, (c) Eliminate multiple words on right-hand sides, (d) Eliminate rules of the form $(X \rightarrow Y)$, (e) Convert long right-hand sides into binary rules.

a. The start symbol, S, can occur only on the left-hand side in CNF. Add a new rule of the form $S' \rightarrow S$, using a new symbol S'.

b. The empty string, ϵ cannot appear on the right-hand side in CNF. $\mathcal{E}_0$ does not have any rules with ϵ, so this is not an issue.

c. A word can appear on the right-hand side in a rule only of the form $(X \rightarrow \textit{word})$. Replace each rule of the form $(X \rightarrow \ldots \textit{word} \ldots)$ with $(X \rightarrow \ldots W' \ldots)$ and $(W' \rightarrow \textit{word})$, using a new symbol W'.

d. A rule $(X \rightarrow Y)$ is not allowed in CNF; it must be $(X \rightarrow Y\ Z)$ or $(X \rightarrow \textit{word})$. Replace each rule of the form $(X \rightarrow Y)$ with a set of rules of the form $(X \rightarrow \ldots)$, one for each rule $(Y \rightarrow \ldots)$, where $(\ldots)$ indicates one or more symbols.

e. Replace each rule of the form $(X \rightarrow Y\ Z \ldots)$ with two rules, $(X \rightarrow Y\ Z')$ and $(Z' \rightarrow Z \ldots)$, where Z' is a new symbol.

Show each step of the process and the final set of rules.

9 Using DCG notation, write a grammar for a language that is just like$_1\mathcal{E}$, except that it enforces agreement between the subject and verb of a sentence and thus does not generate ungrammatical sentences such as "I smells the wumpus."

10 Consider the following PCFG:

$S \rightarrow NP\ VP$ [1.0]
$NP \rightarrow Noun$ [0.6] | $Pronoun$ [0.4]
$VP \rightarrow Verb\ NP$ [0.8] | $Modal\ Verb$ [0.2]

$Noun \rightarrow$ **can** [0.1] | **fish** [0.3] | ...
$Pronoun \rightarrow$ **I** [0.4] | ...
$Verb \rightarrow$ **can** [0.01] | **fish** [0.1] | ...
$Modal \rightarrow$ **can** [0.3] | ...

The sentence "I can fish" has two parse trees with this grammar. Show the two trees, their prior probabilities, and their conditional probabilities, given the sentence.

11 An augmented context-free grammar can represent languages that a regular context-free grammar cannot. Show an augmented context-free grammar for the language $a^n b^n c^n$. The allowable values for augmentation variables are 1 and SUCCESSOR(n), where n is a value. The rule for a sentence in this language is

$$S(n) \rightarrow A(n)\ B(n)\ C(n)\ .$$

Show the rule(s) for each of A, B, and C.

12 Augment the $\mathcal{E}_1$ grammar so that it handles article–noun agreement. That is, make sure that "agents" and "an agent" are *NP*s, but "agent" and "an agents" are not.

13 Consider the following sentence (from *The New York Times,* July 28, 2008):

> Banks struggling to recover from multibillion-dollar loans on real estate are curtailing loans to American businesses, depriving even healthy companies of money for expansion and hiring.

a. Which of the words in this sentence are lexically ambiguous?
b. Find two cases of syntactic ambiguity in this sentence (there are more than two.)
c. Give an instance of metaphor in this sentence.
d. Can you find semantic ambiguity?

14 Without looking back at Exercise 1, answer the following questions:

a. What are the four steps that are mentioned?
b. What step is left out?
c. What is "the material" that is mentioned in the text?
d. What kind of mistake would be expensive?
e. Is it better to do too few things or too many? Why?

15 Select five sentences and submit them to an online translation service. Translate them from English to another language and back to English. Rate the resulting sentences for grammaticality and preservation of meaning. Repeat the process; does the second round of iteration give worse results or the same results? Does the choice of intermediate language make a difference to the quality of the results? If you know a foreign language, look at the translation of one paragraph into that language. Count and describe the errors made, and conjecture why these errors were made.

16 The D_i values for the sentence in Figure 13 sum to 0. Will that be true of every translation pair? Prove it or give a counterexample.

17 (Adapted from Knight (1999).) Our translation model assumes that, after the phrase translation model selects phrases and the distortion model permutes them, the language model can unscramble the permutation. This exercise investigates how sensible that assumption is. Try to unscramble these proposed lists of phrases into the correct order:

a. have, programming, a, seen, never, I, language, better

b. loves, john, mary

c. is the, communication, exchange of, intentional, information brought, by, about, the production, perception of, and signs, from, drawn, a, of, system, signs, conventional, shared

d. created, that, we hold these, to be, all men, truths, are, equal, self-evident

Which ones could you do? What type of knowledge did you draw upon? Train a bigram model from a training corpus, and use it to find the highest-probability permutation of some sentences from a test corpus. Report on the accuracy of this model.

18 Calculate the most probable path through the HMM in Figure 16 for the output sequence $[C_1, C_2, C_3, C_4, C_4, C_6, C_7]$. Also give its probability.

19 We forgot to mention that the text in Exercise 1 is entitled "Washing Clothes." Reread Reread the text and answer the questions in Exercise 14. Did you do better this time? Bransford and Johnson (1973) used this text in a controlled experiment and found that the title helped significantly. What does this tell you about how language and memory works?

PERCEPTION

PERCEPTION

In which we connect the computer to the raw, unwashed world.

PERCEPTION

SENSOR

Perception provides agents with information about the world they inhabit by interpreting the response of **sensors**. A sensor measures some aspect of the environment in a form that can be used as input by an agent program. The sensor could be as simple as a switch, which gives one bit telling whether it is on or off, or as complex as the eye. A variety of sensory modalities are available to artificial agents. Those they share with humans include vision, hearing, and touch. Modalities that are not available to the unaided human include radio, infrared, GPS, and wireless signals. Some robots do **active sensing**, meaning they send out a signal, such as radar or ultrasound, and sense the reflection of this signal off of the environment. Rather than trying to cover all of these, this chapter will cover one modality in depth: vision.

A model-based decision-theoretic agent in a partially observable environment has a **sensor model**—a probability distribution $\mathbf{P}(E \mid S)$ over the evidence that its sensors provide, given a state of the world. Bayes' rule can then be used to update the estimation of the state.

OBJECT MODEL

For vision, the sensor model can be broken into two components: An **object model** describes the objects that inhabit the visual world—people, buildings, trees, cars, etc. The object model could include a precise 3D geometric model taken from a computer-aided design (CAD) system, or it could be vague constraints, such as the fact that human eyes are usually 5 to 7 cm apart. A **rendering model** describes the physical, geometric, and statistical processes that produce the stimulus from the world. Rendering models are quite accurate, but they are ambiguous. For example, a white object under low light may appear as the same color as a black object under intense light. A small nearby object may look the same as a large distant object. Without additional evidence, we cannot tell if the image that fills the frame is a toy Godzilla or a real monster.

RENDERING MODEL

Ambiguity can be managed with prior knowledge—we know Godzilla is not real, so the image must be a toy—or by selectively choosing to ignore the ambiguity. For example, the vision system for an autonomous car may not be able to interpret objects that are far in the distance, but the agent can choose to ignore the problem, because it is unlikely to crash into an object that is miles away.

A decision-theoretic agent is not the only architecture that can make use of vision sensors. For example, fruit flies (*Drosophila*) are in part reflex agents: they have cervical giant fibers that form a direct pathway from their visual system to the wing muscles that initiate an escape response—an immediate reaction, without deliberation. Flies and many other flying animals make use of a closed-loop control architecture to land on an object. The visual system extracts an estimate of the distance to the object, and the control system adjusts the wing muscles accordingly, allowing very fast changes of direction, with no need for a detailed model of the object.

Compared to the data from other sensors (such as the single bit that tells the vacuum robot that it has bumped into a wall), visual observations are extraordinarily rich, both in the detail they can reveal and in the sheer amount of data they produce. A video camera for robotic applications might produce a million 24-bit pixels at 60 Hz; a rate of 10 GB per minute. The problem for a vision-capable agent then is: *Which aspects of the rich visual stimulus should be considered to help the agent make good action choices, and which aspects should be ignored?* Vision—and all perception—serves to further the agent's goals, not as an end to itself.

FEATURE EXTRACTION

We can characterize three broad approaches to the problem. The **feature extraction** approach, as exhibited by *Drosophila*, emphasizes simple computations applied directly to the sensor observations. In the **recognition** approach an agent draws distinctions among the objects it encounters based on visual and other information. Recognition could mean labeling each image with a yes or no as to whether it contains food that we should forage, or contains Grandma's face. Finally, in the **reconstruction** approach an agent builds a geometric model of the world from an image or a set of images.

RECOGNITION

RECONSTRUCTION

The last thirty years of research have produced powerful tools and methods for addressing these approaches. Understanding these methods requires an understanding of the processes by which images are formed. Therefore, we now cover the physical and statistical phenomena that occur in the production of an image.

1 IMAGE FORMATION

Imaging distorts the appearance of objects. For example, a picture taken looking down a long straight set of railway tracks will suggest that the rails converge and meet. As another example, if you hold your hand in front of your eye, you can block out the moon, which is not smaller than your hand. As you move your hand back and forth or tilt it, your hand will seem to shrink and grow *in the image*, but it is not doing so in reality (Figure 1). Models of these effects are essential for both recognition and reconstruction.

1.1 Images without lenses: The pinhole camera

SCENE

IMAGE

Image sensors gather light scattered from objects in a **scene** and create a two-dimensional **image**. In the eye, the image is formed on the retina, which consists of two types of cells: about 100 million rods, which are sensitive to light at a wide range of wavelengths, and 5

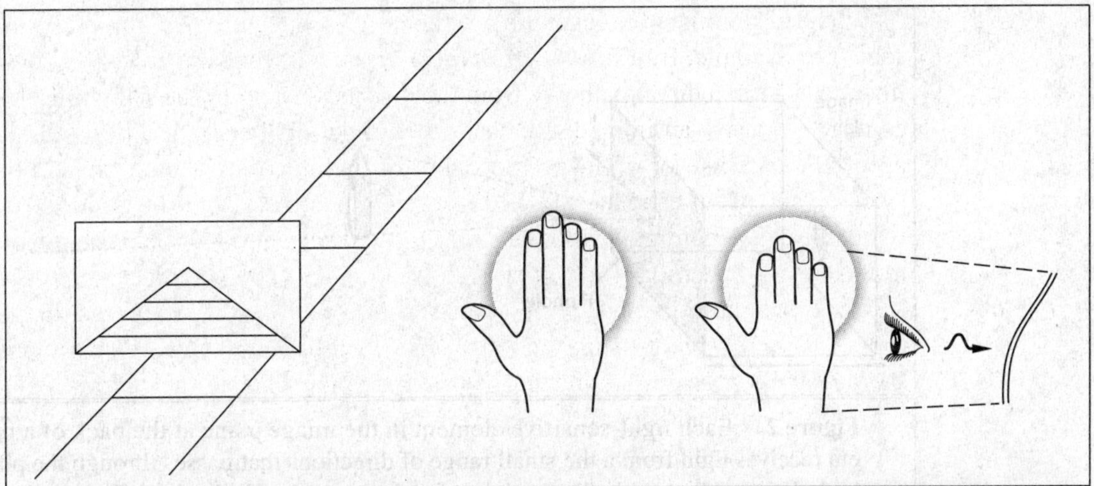

Figure 1 Imaging distorts geometry. Parallel lines appear to meet in the distance, as in the image of the railway tracks on the left. In the center, a small hand blocks out most of a large moon. On the right is a foreshortening effect: the hand is tilted away from the eye, making it appear shorter than in the center figure.

million cones. Cones, which are essential for color vision, are of three main types, each of which is sensitive to a different set of wavelengths. In cameras, the image is formed on an image plane, which can be a piece of film coated with silver halides or a rectangular grid of a few million photosensitive **pixels**, each a complementary metal-oxide semiconductor (CMOS) or charge-coupled device (CCD). Each photon arriving at the sensor produces an effect, whose strength depends on the wavelength of the photon. The output of the sensor is the sum of all effects due to photons observed in some time window, meaning that image sensors report a weighted average of the intensity of light arriving at the sensor.

PIXEL

To see a focused image, we must ensure that all the photons from approximately the same spot in the scene arrive at approximately the same point in the image plane. The simplest way to form a focused image is to view stationary objects with a **pinhole camera**, which consists of a pinhole opening, O, at the front of a box, and an image plane at the back of the box (Figure 2). Photons from the scene must pass through the pinhole, so if it is small enough then nearby photons in the scene will be nearby in the image plane, and the image will be in focus.

PINHOLE CAMERA

The geometry of scene and image is easiest to understand with the pinhole camera. We use a three-dimensional coordinate system with the origin at the pinhole, and consider a point P in the scene, with coordinates (X, Y, Z). P gets projected to the point P' in the image plane with coordinates (x, y, z). If f is the distance from the pinhole to the image plane, then by similar triangles, we can derive the following equations:

$$\frac{-x}{f} = \frac{X}{Z}, \frac{-y}{f} = \frac{Y}{Z} \quad \Rightarrow \quad x = \frac{-fX}{Z}, \; y = \frac{-fY}{Z}.$$

These equations define an image-formation process known as **perspective projection**. Note that the Z in the denominator means that the farther away an object is, the smaller its image

PERSPECTIVE PROJECTION

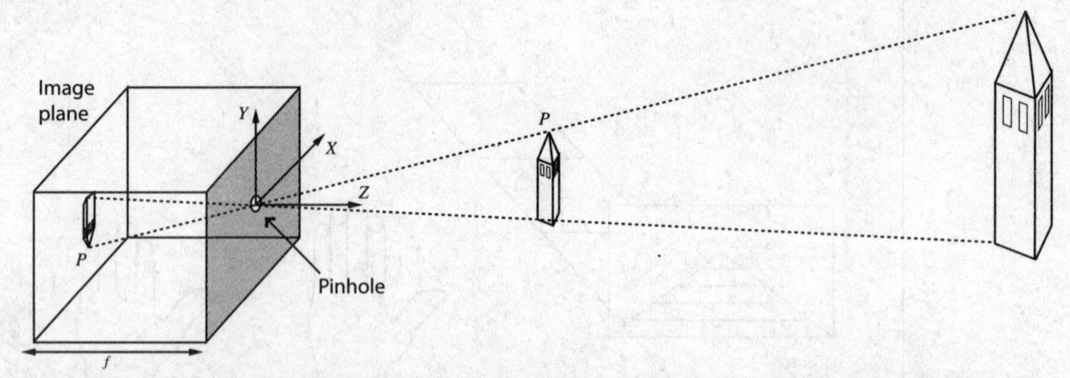

Figure 2 Each light-sensitive element in the image plane at the back of a pinhole camera receives light from a the small range of directions that passes through the pinhole. If the pinhole is small enough, the result is a focused image at the back of the pinhole. The process of projection means that large, distant objects look the same as smaller, nearby objects. Note that the image is projected upside down.

will be. Also, note that the minus signs mean that the image is *inverted*, both left–right and up–down, compared with the scene.

Under perspective projection, distant objects look small. This is what allows you to cover the moon with your hand (Figure 1). An important result of this effect is that parallel lines converge to a point on the horizon. (Think of railway tracks, Figure 1.) A line in the scene in the direction (U, V, W) and passing through the point (X_0, Y_0, Z_0) can be described as the set of points $(X_0 + \lambda U, Y_0 + \lambda V, Z_0 + \lambda W)$, with λ varying between $-\infty$ and $+\infty$. Different choices of (X_0, Y_0, Z_0) yield different lines parallel to one another. The projection of a point P_λ from this line onto the image plane is given by

$$\left(f\frac{X_0 + \lambda U}{Z_0 + \lambda W}, f\frac{Y_0 + \lambda V}{Z_0 + \lambda W} \right).$$

As $\lambda \to \infty$ or $\lambda \to -\infty$, this becomes $p_\infty = (fU/W, fV/W)$ if $W \neq 0$. This means that two parallel lines leaving different points in space will converge in the image—for large λ, the image points are nearly the same, whatever the value of (X_0, Y_0, Z_0) (again, think railway tracks, Figure 1). We call p_∞ the **vanishing point** associated with the family of straight lines with direction (U, V, W). Lines with the same direction share the same vanishing point.

VANISHING POINT

1.2 Lens systems

The drawback of the pinhole camera is that we need a small pinhole to keep the image in focus. But the smaller the pinhole, the fewer photons get through, meaning the image will be dark. We can gather more photons by keeping the pinhole open longer, but then we will get **motion blur**—objects in the scene that move will appear blurred because they send photons to multiple locations on the image plane. If we can't keep the pinhole open longer, we can try to make it bigger. More light will enter, but light from a small patch of object in the scene will now be spread over a patch on the image plane, causing a blurred image.

MOTION BLUR

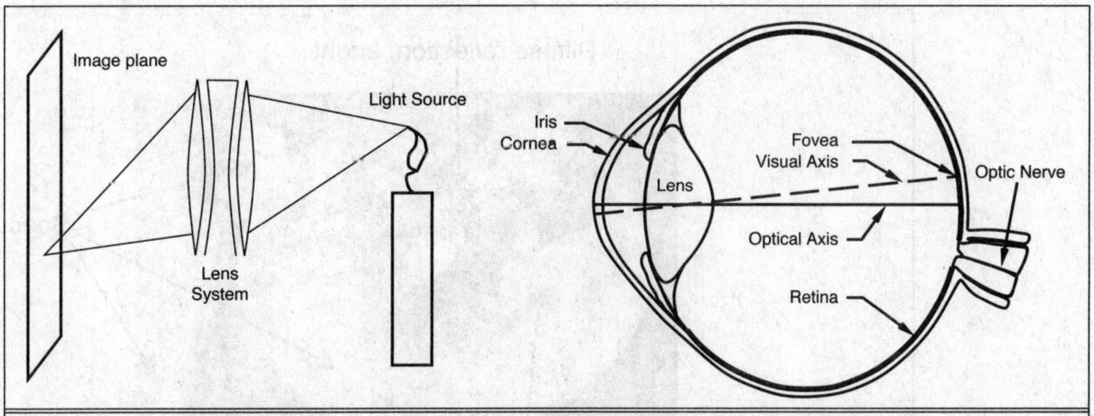

Figure 3 Lenses collect the light leaving a scene point in a range of directions, and steer it all to arrive at a single point on the image plane. Focusing works for points lying close to a focal plane in space; other points will not be focused properly. In cameras, elements of the lens system move to change the focal plane, whereas in the eye, the shape of the lens is changed by specialized muscles.

LENS

Vertebrate eyes and modern cameras use a **lens** system to gather sufficient light while keeping the image in focus. A large opening is covered with a lens that focuses light from nearby object locations down to nearby locations in the image plane. However, lens systems have a limited **depth of field**: they can focus light only from points that lie within a range of depths (centered around a **focal plane**). Objects outside this range will be out of focus in the image. To move the focal plane, the lens in the eye can change shape (Figure 3); in a camera, the lenses move back and forth.

DEPTH OF FIELD

FOCAL PLANE

1.3 Scaled orthographic projection

Perspective effects aren't always pronounced. For example, spots on a distant leopard may look small because the leopard is far away, but two spots that are next to each other will have about the same size. This is because the difference in distance to the spots is small compared to the distance to them, and so we can simplify the projection model. The appropriate model is **scaled orthographic projection**. The idea is as follows: If the depth Z of points on the object varies within some range $Z_0 \pm \Delta Z$, with $\Delta Z \ll Z_0$, then the perspective scaling factor f/Z can be approximated by a constant $s = f/Z_0$. The equations for projection from the scene coordinates (X, Y, Z) to the image plane become $x = sX$ and $y = sY$. Scaled orthographic projection is an approximation that is valid only for those parts of the scene with not much internal depth variation. For example, scaled orthographic projection can be a good model for the features on the front of a distant building.

SCALED ORTHOGRAPHIC PROJECTION

1.4 Light and shading

The brightness of a pixel in the image is a function of the brightness of the surface patch in the scene that projects to the pixel. We will assume a linear model (current cameras have non-linearities at the extremes of light and dark, but are linear in the middle). Image brightness is

Figure 4 A variety of illumination effects. There are specularities on the metal spoon and on the milk. The bright diffuse surface is bright because it faces the light direction. The dark diffuse surface is dark because it is tangential to the illumination direction. The shadows appear at surface points that cannot see the light source. Photo by Mike Linksvayer (mlinksva on flickr).

a strong, if ambiguous, cue to the shape of an object, and from there to its identity. People are usually able to distinguish the three main causes of varying brightness and reverse-engineer the object's properties. The first cause is **overall intensity** of the light. Even though a white object in shadow may be less bright than a black object in direct sunlight, the eye can distinguish relative brightness well, and perceive the white object as white. Second, different points in the scene may **reflect** more or less of the light. Usually, the result is that people perceive these points as lighter or darker, and so see texture or markings on the object. Third, surface patches facing the light are brighter than surface patches tilted away from the light, an effect known as **shading**. Typically, people can tell that this shading comes from the geometry of the object, but sometimes get shading and markings mixed up. For example, a streak of dark makeup under a cheekbone will often look like a shading effect, making the face look thinner.

OVERALL INTENSITY

REFLECT

SHADING

DIFFUSE REFLECTION

Most surfaces reflect light by a process of **diffuse reflection**. Diffuse reflection scatters light evenly across the directions leaving a surface, so the brightness of a diffuse surface doesn't depend on the viewing direction. Most cloth, paints, rough wooden surfaces, vegetation, and rough stone are diffuse. Mirrors are not diffuse, because what you see depends on the direction in which you look at the mirror. The behavior of a perfect mirror is known as **specular reflection**. Some surfaces—such as brushed metal, plastic, or a wet floor—display small patches where specular reflection has occurred, called **specularities**. These are easy to identify, because they are small and bright (Figure 4). For almost all purposes, it is enough to model all surfaces as being diffuse with specularities.

SPECULAR REFLECTION

SPECULARITIES

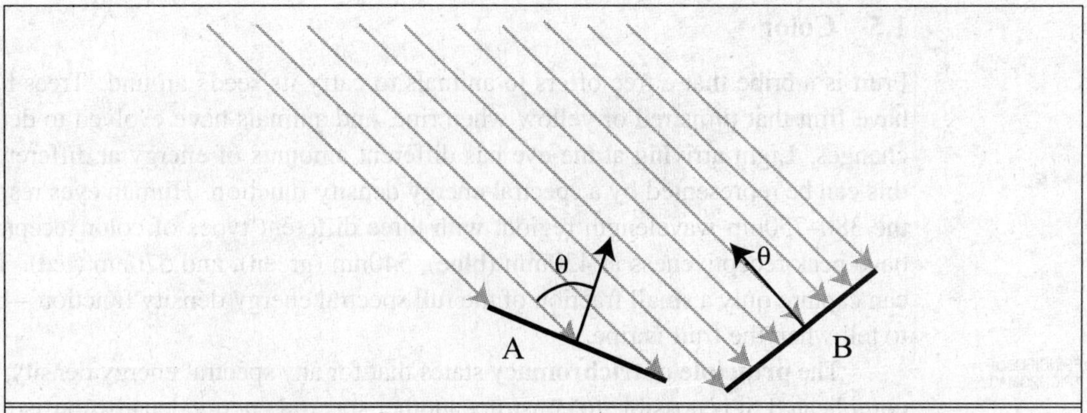

Figure 5 Two surface patches are illuminated by a distant point source, whose rays are shown as gray arrowheads. Patch A is tilted away from the source (θ is close to 90^0) and collects less energy, because it cuts fewer light rays per unit surface area. Patch B, facing the source (θ is close to 0^0), collects more energy.

The main source of illumination outside is the sun, whose rays all travel parallel to one another. We model this behavior as a **distant point light source**. This is the most important model of lighting, and is quite effective for indoor scenes as well as outdoor scenes. The amount of light collected by a surface patch in this model depends on the angle θ between the illumination direction and the normal to the surface.

DISTANT POINT LIGHT SOURCE

A diffuse surface patch illuminated by a distant point light source will reflect some fraction of the light it collects; this fraction is called the **diffuse albedo**. White paper and snow have a high albedo, about 0.90, whereas flat black velvet and charcoal have a low albedo of about 0.05 (which means that 95% of the incoming light is absorbed within the fibers of the velvet or the pores of the charcoal). **Lambert's cosine law** states that the brightness of a diffuse patch is given by

DIFFUSE ALBEDO

LAMBERT'S COSINE LAW

$$I = \rho I_0 \cos\theta ,$$

where ρ is the diffuse albedo, I_0 is the intensity of the light source and θ is the angle between the light source direction and the surface normal (see Figure 5). Lampert's law predicts bright image pixels come from surface patches that face the light directly and dark pixels come from patches that see the light only tangentially, so that the shading on a surface provides some shape information. We explore this cue in Section 4.5. If the surface is not reached by the light source, then it is in **shadow**. Shadows are very seldom a uniform black, because the shadowed surface receives some light from other sources. Outdoors, the most important such source is the sky, which is quite bright. Indoors, light reflected from other surfaces illuminates shadowed patches. These **interreflections** can have a significant effect on the brightness of other surfaces, too. These effects are sometimes modeled by adding a constant **ambient illumination** term to the predicted intensity.

SHADOW

INTERREFLECTIONS

AMBIENT ILLUMINATION

1.5 Color

Fruit is a bribe that a tree offers to animals to carry its seeds around. Trees have evolved to have fruit that turns red or yellow when ripe, and animals have evolved to detect these color changes. Light arriving at the eye has different amounts of energy at different wavelengths; this can be represented by a spectral energy density function. Human eyes respond to light in the 380–750nm wavelength region, with three different types of color receptor cells, which have peak receptiveness at 420mm (blue), 540nm (green), and 570nm (red). The human eye can capture only a small fraction of the full spectral energy density function—but it is enough to tell when the fruit is ripe.

PRINCIPLE OF TRICHROMACY

The **principle of trichromacy** states that for any spectral energy density, no matter how complicated, it is possible to construct another spectral energy density consisting of a mixture of just three colors—usually red, green, and blue—such that a human can't tell the difference between the two. That means that our TVs and computer displays can get by with just the three red/green/blue (or R/G/B) color elements. It makes our computer vision algorithms easier, too. Each surface can be modeled with three different albedos for R/G/B. Similarly, each light source can be modeled with three R/G/B intensities. We then apply Lambert's cosine law to each to get three R/G/B pixel values. This model predicts, correctly, that the same surface will produce different colored image patches under different-colored lights. In fact, human observers are quite good at ignoring the effects of different colored lights and are able to estimate the color of the surface under white light, an effect known as **color constancy**. Quite accurate color constancy algorithms are now available; simple versions show up in the "auto white balance" function of your camera. Note that if we wanted to build a camera for mantis shrimp, we would need 12 different pixel colors, corresponding to the 12 types of color receptors of the crustacean.

COLOR CONSTANCY

2 EARLY IMAGE-PROCESSING OPERATIONS

We have seen how light reflects off objects in the scene to form an image consisting of, say, five million 3-byte pixels. With all sensors there will be noise in the image, and in any case there is a lot of data to deal with. So how do we get started on analyzing this data?

In this section we will study three useful image-processing operations: edge detection, texture analysis, and computation of optical flow. These are called "early" or "low-level" operations because they are the first in a pipeline of operations. Early vision operations are characterized by their local nature (they can be carried out in one part of the image without regard for anything more than a few pixels away) and by their lack of knowledge: we can perform these operations without consideration of the objects that might be present in the scene. This makes the low-level operations good candidates for implementation in parallel hardware—either in a graphics processor unit (GPU) or an eye. We will then look at one mid-level operation: segmenting the image into regions.

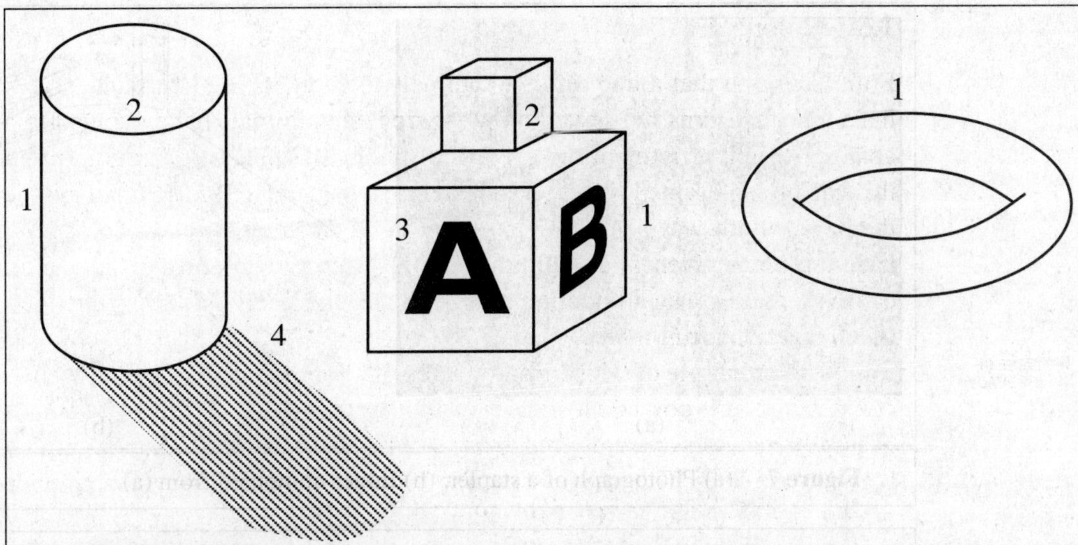

Figure 6 Different kinds of edges: (1) depth discontinuities; (2) surface orientation discontinuities; (3) reflectance discontinuities; (4) illumination discontinuities (shadows).

2.1 Edge detection

EDGE **Edges** are straight lines or curves in the image plane across which there is a "significant" change in image brightness. The goal of edge detection is to abstract away from the messy, multimegabyte image and toward a more compact, abstract representation, as in Figure 6. The motivation is that edge contours in the image correspond to important scene contours. In the figure we have three examples of depth discontinuity, labeled 1; two surface-normal discontinuities, labeled 2; a reflectance discontinuity, labeled 3; and an illumination discontinuity (shadow), labeled 4. Edge detection is concerned only with the image, and thus does not distinguish between these different types of scene discontinuities; later processing will.

Figure 7(a) shows an image of a scene containing a stapler resting on a desk, and (b) shows the output of an edge-detection algorithm on this image. As you can see, there is a difference between the output and an ideal line drawing. There are gaps where no edge appears, and there are "noise" edges that do not correspond to anything of significance in the scene. Later stages of processing will have to correct for these errors.

How do we detect edges in an image? Consider the profile of image brightness along a one-dimensional cross-section perpendicular to an edge—for example, the one between the left edge of the desk and the wall. It looks something like what is shown in Figure 8 (top).

Edges correspond to locations in images where the brightness undergoes a sharp change, so a naive idea would be to differentiate the image and look for places where the magnitude of the derivative $I\ (x)$ is large. That almost works. In Figure 8 (middle), we see that there is indeed a peak at $x = 50$, but there are also subsidiary peaks at other locations (e.g., $x = 75$). These arise because of the presence of noise in the image. If we smooth the image first, the spurious peaks are diminished, as we see in the bottom of the figure.

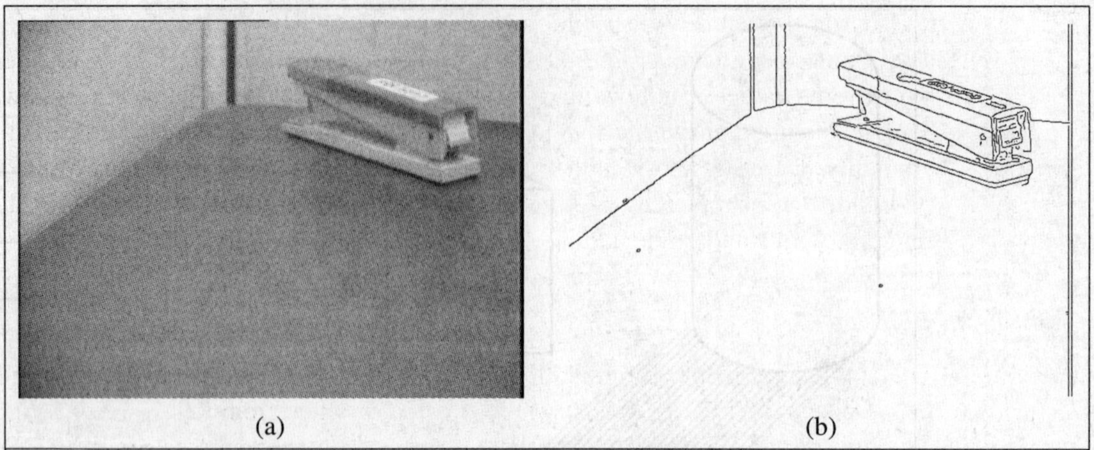

Figure 7 (a) Photograph of a stapler. (b) Edges computed from (a).

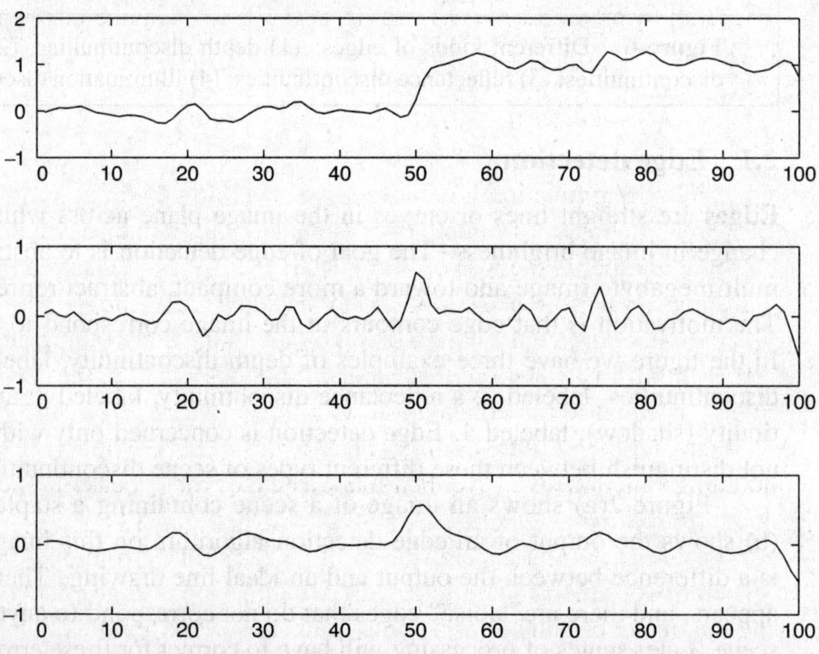

Figure 8 Top: Intensity profile $I(x)$ along a one-dimensional section across an edge at $x = 50$. Middle: The derivative of intensity, $I'(x)$. Large values of this function correspond to edges, but the function is noisy. Bottom: The derivative of a smoothed version of the intensity, $(I * G_\sigma)'$, which can be computed in one step as the convolution $I * G'_\sigma$. The noisy candidate edge at $x = 75$ has disappeared.

The measurement of brightness at a pixel in a CCD camera is based on a physical process involving the absorption of photons and the release of electrons; inevitably there will be statistical fluctuations of the measurement—noise. The noise can be modeled with a Gaussian probability distribution, with each pixel independent of the others. One way to smooth an image is to assign to each pixel the average of its neighbors. This tends to cancel out extreme values. But how many neighbors should we consider—one pixel away, or two, or more? One good answer is a weighted average that weights the nearest pixels the most, then gradually decreases the weight for more distant pixels. The **Gaussian filter** does just that. (Users of Photoshop recognize this as the *Gaussian blur* operation.) Recall that the Gaussian function with standard deviation σ and mean 0 is

GAUSSIAN FILTER

$$N_\sigma(x) = \frac{1}{\sqrt{2\pi}\sigma} e^{-x^2/2\sigma^2} \quad \text{in one dimension, or}$$

$$N_\sigma(x,y) = \frac{1}{2\pi\sigma^2} e^{-(x^2+y^2)/2\sigma^2} \quad \text{in two dimensions.}$$

The application of the Gaussian filter replaces the intensity $I(x_0, y_0)$ with the sum, over all (x, y) pixels, of $I(x, y)\, N_\sigma(d)$, where d is the distance from (x_0, y_0) to (x, y). This kind of weighted sum is so common that there is a special name and notation for it. We say that the function h is the **convolution** of two functions f and g (denoted $f * g$) if we have

CONVOLUTION

$$h(x) = (f * g)(x) = \sum_{u=-\infty}^{+\infty} f(u)\, g(x-u) \qquad \text{in one dimension, or}$$

$$h(x,y) = (f * g)(x,y) = \sum_{u=-\infty}^{+\infty} \sum_{v=-\infty}^{+\infty} f(u,v)\, g(x-u, y-v) \qquad \text{in two.}$$

So the smoothing function is achieved by convolving the image with the Gaussian, $I * N_\sigma$. A σ of 1 pixel is enough to smooth over a small amount of noise, whereas 2 pixels will smooth a larger amount, but at the loss of some detail. Because the Gaussian's influence fades quickly at a distance, we can replace the $\pm\infty$ in the sums with $\pm 3\sigma$.

We can optimize the computation by combining smoothing and edge finding into a single operation. It is a theorem that for any functions f and g, the derivative of the convolution, $(f * g)'$, is equal to the convolution with the derivative, $f * (g')$. So rather than smoothing the image and then differentiating, we can just convolve the image with the derivative of the smoothing function, N'_σ. We then mark as edges those peaks in the response that are above some threshold.

There is a natural generalization of this algorithm from one-dimensional cross sections to general two-dimensional images. In two dimensions edges may be at any angle θ. Considering the image brightness as a scalar function of the variables x, y, its gradient is a vector

$$\nabla I = \begin{pmatrix} \frac{\partial I}{\partial x} \\ \frac{\partial I}{\partial y} \end{pmatrix} = \begin{pmatrix} I_x \\ I_y \end{pmatrix}.$$

Edges correspond to locations in images where the brightness undergoes a sharp change, and so the magnitude of the gradient, $\|\nabla I\|$, should be large at an edge point. Of independent interest is the direction of the gradient

$$\frac{\nabla I}{\|\nabla I\|} = \begin{pmatrix} \cos\theta \\ \sin\theta \end{pmatrix}.$$

ORIENTATION

This gives us a $\theta = \theta(x, y)$ at every pixel, which defines the edge **orientation** at that pixel.

As in one dimension, to form the gradient we don't compute ∇I, but rather $\nabla(I * N_\sigma)$, the gradient after smoothing the image by convolving it with a Gaussian. And again, the shortcut is that this is equivalent to convolving the image with the partial derivatives of a Gaussian. Once we have computed the gradient, we can obtain edges by finding edge points and linking them together. To tell whether a point is an edge point, we must look at other points a small distance forward and back along the direction of the gradient. If the gradient magnitude at one of these points is larger, then we could get a better edge point by shifting the edge curve very slightly. Furthermore, if the gradient magnitude is too small, the point cannot be an edge point. So at an edge point, the gradient magnitude is a local maximum along the direction of the gradient, and the gradient magnitude is above a suitable threshold.

Once we have marked edge pixels by this algorithm, the next stage is to link those pixels that belong to the same edge curves. This can be done by assuming that any two neighboring edge pixels with consistent orientations must belong to the same edge curve.

2.2 Texture

TEXTURE

In everyday language, **texture** is the visual feel of a surface—what you see evokes what the surface might feel like if you touched it ("texture" has the same root as "textile"). In computational vision, texture refers to a spatially repeating pattern on a surface that can be sensed visually. Examples include the pattern of windows on a building, stitches on a sweater, spots on a leopard, blades of grass on a lawn, pebbles on a beach, and people in a stadium. Sometimes the arrangement is quite periodic, as in the stitches on a sweater; in other cases, such as pebbles on a beach, the regularity is only statistical.

Whereas brightness is a property of individual pixels, the concept of texture makes sense only for a multipixel patch. Given such a patch, we could compute the orientation at each pixel, and then characterize the patch by a histogram of orientations. The texture of bricks in a wall would have two peaks in the histogram (one vertical and one horizontal), whereas the texture of spots on a leopard's skin would have a more uniform distribution of orientations.

Figure 9 shows that orientations are largely invariant to changes in illumination. This makes texture an important clue for object recognition, because other clues, such as edges, can yield different results in different lighting conditions.

In images of textured objects, edge detection does not work as well as it does for smooth objects. This is because the most important edges can be lost among the texture elements. Quite literally, we may miss the tiger for the stripes. The solution is to look for differences in texture properties, just the way we look for differences in brightness. A patch on a tiger and a patch on the grassy background will have very different orientation histograms, allowing us to find the boundary curve between them.

2.3 Optical flow

Next, let us consider what happens when we have a video sequence, instead of just a single static image. When an object in the video is moving, or when the camera is moving relative to an object, the resulting apparent motion in the image is called **optical flow**. Optical flow describes the direction and speed of motion of features *in the image*—the optical flow of a

OPTICAL FLOW

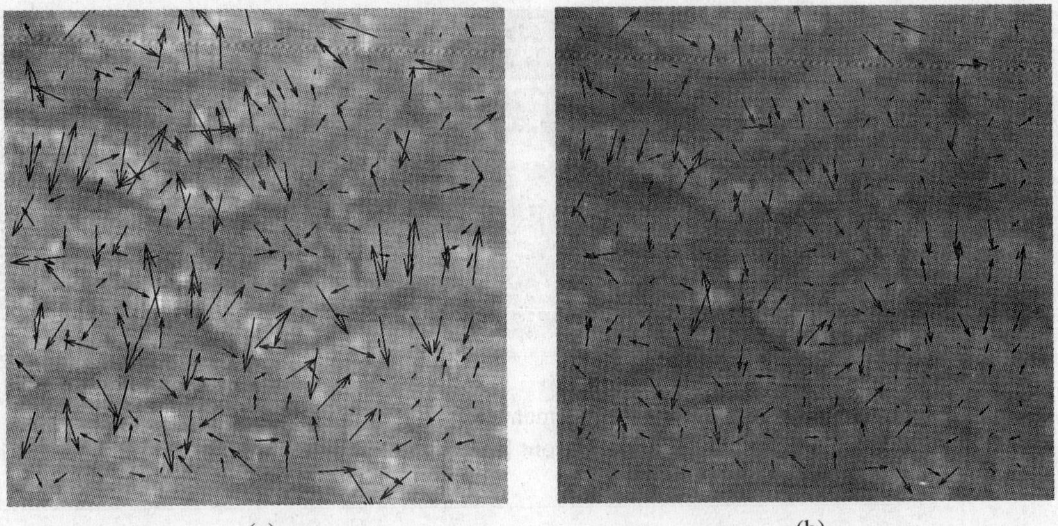

(a) (b)

Figure 9 Two images of the same texture of crumpled rice paper, with different illumination levels. The gradient vector field (at every eighth pixel) is plotted on top of each one. Notice that, as the light gets darker, all the gradient vectors get shorter. The vectors do not rotate, so the gradient orientations do not change.

video of a race car would be measured in pixels per second, not miles per hour. The optical flow encodes useful information about scene structure. For example, in a video of scenery taken from a moving train, distant objects have slower apparent motion than close objects; thus, the rate of apparent motion can tell us something about distance. Optical flow also enables us to recognize actions. In Figure 10(a) and (b), we show two frames from a video of a tennis player. In (c) we display the optical flow vectors computed from these images, showing that the racket and front leg are moving fastest.

The optical flow vector field can be represented at any point (x, y) by its components $v_x(x, y)$ in the x direction and $v_y(x, y)$ in the y direction. To measure optical flow we need to find corresponding points between one time frame and the next. A simple-minded technique is based on the fact that image patches around corresponding points have similar intensity patterns. Consider a block of pixels centered at pixel p, (x_0, y_0), at time t_0. This block of pixels is to be compared with pixel blocks centered at various candidate pixels at $(x_0 + D_x, y_0 + D_y)$ at time $t_0 + D_t$. One possible measure of similarity is the **sum of squared differences** (SSD):

SUM OF SQUARED DIFFERENCES

$$\mathrm{SSD}(D_x, D_y) = \sum_{(x,y)} (I(x, y, t) - I(x + D_x, y + D_y, t + D_t))^2 .$$

Here, (x, y) ranges over pixels in the block centered at (x_0, y_0). We find the (D_x, D_y) that minimizes the SSD. The optical flow at (x_0, y_0) is then $(v_x, v_y) = (D_x/D_t, D_y/D_t)$. Note that for this to work, there needs to be some texture or variation in the scene. If one is looking at a uniform white wall, then the SSD is going to be nearly the same for the different can-

Figure 10 Two frames of a video sequence. On the right is the optical flow field corresponding to the displacement from one frame to the other. Note how the movement of the tennis racket and the front leg is captured by the directions of the arrows. (Courtesy of Thomas Brox.)

didate matches, and the algorithm is reduced to making a blind guess. The best-performing algorithms for measuring optical flow rely on a variety of additional constraints when the scene is only partially textured.

2.4 Segmentation of images

SEGMENTATION

REGIONS

Segmentation is the process of breaking an image into **regions** of similar pixels. Each image pixel can be associated with certain visual properties, such as brightness, color, and texture. Within an object, or a single part of an object, these attributes vary relatively little, whereas across an inter-object boundary there is typically a large change in one or more of these attributes. There are two approaches to segmentation, one focusing on detecting the boundaries of these regions, and the other on detecting the regions themselves (Figure 11).

A boundary curve passing through a pixel (x, y) will have an orientation θ, so one way to formalize the problem of detecting boundary curves is as a machine learning classification problem. Based on features from a local neighborhood, we want to compute the probability $P_b(x, y, \theta)$ that indeed there is a boundary curve at that pixel along that orientation. Consider a circular disk centered at (x, y), subdivided into two half disks by a diameter oriented at θ. If there is a boundary at (x, y, θ) the two half disks might be expected to differ significantly in their brightness, color, and texture. Martin, Fowlkes, and Malik (2004) used features based on differences in histograms of brightness, color, and texture values measured in these two half disks, and then trained a classifier. For this they used a data set of natural images where humans had marked the "ground truth" boundaries, and the goal of the classifier was to mark exactly those boundaries marked by humans and no others.

Boundaries detected by this technique turn out to be significantly better than those found using the simple edge-detection technique described previously. But still there are two limitations. (1) The boundary pixels formed by thresholding $P_b(x, y, \theta)$ are not guaranteed to form closed curves, so this approach doesn't deliver regions, and (2) the decision making exploits only local context and does not use global consistency constraints.

(a) (b) (c) (d)

Figure 11 (a) Original image. (b) Boundary contours, where the higher the P_b value, the darker the contour. (c) Segmentation into regions, corresponding to a fine partition of the image. Regions are rendered in their mean colors. (d) Segmentation into regions, corresponding to a coarser partition of the image, resulting in fewer regions. (Courtesy of Pablo Arbelaez, Michael Maire, Charles Fowlkes, and Jitendra Malik)

The alternative approach is based on trying to "cluster" the pixels into regions based on their brightness, color, and texture. Shi and Malik (2000) set this up as a graph partitioning problem. The nodes of the graph correspond to pixels, and edges to connections between pixels. The weight W_{ij} on the edge connecting a pair of pixels i and j is based on how similar the two pixels are in brightness, color, texture, etc. Partitions that minimize a *normalized cut* criterion are then found. Roughly speaking, the criterion for partitioning the graph is to minimize the sum of weights of connections across the groups of pixels and maximize the sum of weights of connections within the groups.

Segmentation based purely on low-level, local attributes such as brightness and color cannot be expected to deliver the final correct boundaries of all the objects in the scene. To reliably find object boundaries we need high-level knowledge of the likely kinds of objects in the scene. Representing this knowledge is a topic of active research. A popular strategy is to produce an over-segmentation of an image, containing hundreds of homogeneous regions known as **superpixels**. From there, knowledge-based algorithms can take over; they will find it easier to deal with hundreds of superpixels rather than millions of raw pixels. How to exploit high-level knowledge of objects is the subject of the next section.

SUPERPIXELS

3 Object Recognition by Appearance

APPEARANCE

Appearance is shorthand for what an object tends to look like. Some object categories—for example, baseballs—vary rather little in appearance; all of the objects in the category look about the same under most circumstances. In this case, we can compute a set of features describing each class of images likely to contain the object, then test it with a classifier.

Other object categories—for example, houses or ballet dancers—vary greatly. A house can have different size, color, and shape and can look different from different angles. A dancer looks different in each pose, or when the stage lights change colors. A useful abstraction is to say that some objects are made up of local patterns which tend to move around with respect to one another. We can then find the object by looking at local histograms of detector responses, which expose whether some part is present but suppress the details of where it is.

Testing each class of images with a learned classifier is an important general recipe. It works extremely well for faces looking directly at the camera, because at low resolution and under reasonable lighting, all such faces look quite similar. The face is round, and quite bright compared to the eye sockets; these are dark, because they are sunken, and the mouth is a dark slash, as are the eyebrows. Major changes of illumination can cause some variations in this pattern, but the range of variation is quite manageable. That makes it possible to detect face positions in an image that contains faces. Once a computational challenge, this feature is now commonplace in even inexpensive digital cameras.

For the moment, we will consider only faces where the nose is oriented vertically; we will deal with rotated faces below. We sweep a round window of fixed size over the image, compute features for it, and present the features to a classifier. This strategy is sometimes called the **sliding window**. Features need to be robust to shadows and to changes in brightness caused by illumination changes. One strategy is to build features out of gradient orientations. Another is to estimate and correct the illumination in each image window. To find faces of different sizes, repeat the sweep over larger or smaller versions of the image. Finally, we postprocess the responses across scales and locations to produce the final set of detections.

SLIDING WINDOW

Postprocessing is important, because it is unlikely that we have chosen a window size that is exactly the right size for a face (even if we use multiple sizes). Thus, we will likely have several overlapping windows that each report a match for a face. However, if we use a classifier that can report strength of response (for example, logistic regression or a support vector machine) we can combine these partial overlapping matches at nearby locations to yield a single high-quality match. That gives us a face detector that can search over locations and scales. To search rotations as well, we use two steps. We train a regression procedure to estimate the best orientation of any face present in a window. Now, for each window, we estimate the orientation, reorient the window, then test whether a vertical face is present with our classifier. All this yields a system whose architecture is sketched in Figure 12.

Training data is quite easily obtained. There are several data sets of marked-up face images, and rotated face windows are easy to build (just rotate a window from a training data set). One trick that is widely used is to take each example window, then produce new examples by changing the orientation of the window, the center of the window, or the scale very slightly. This is an easy way of getting a bigger data set that reflects real images fairly well; the trick usually improves performance significantly. Face detectors built along these lines now perform very well for frontal faces (side views are harder).

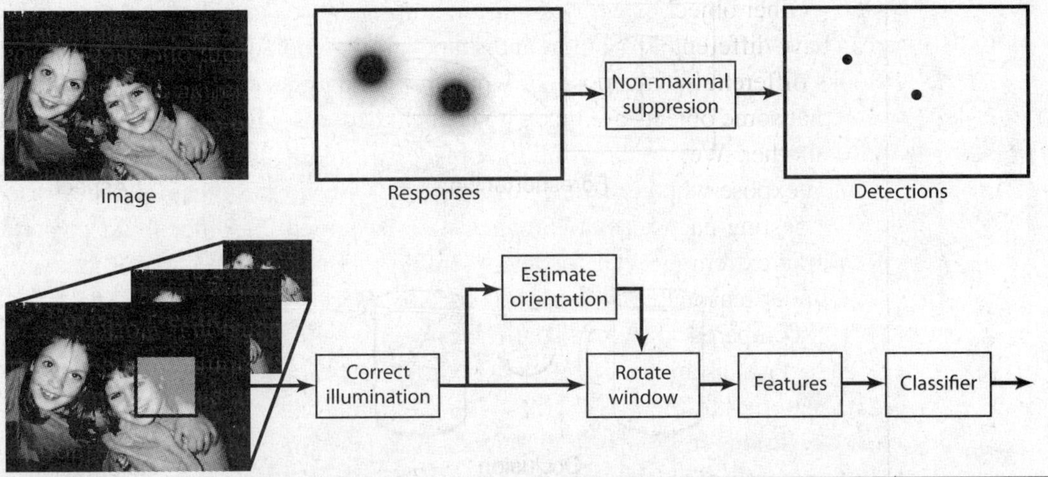

Figure 12 Face finding systems vary, but most follow the architecture illustrated in two parts here. On the top, we go from images to responses, then apply non-maximum suppression to find the strongest local response. The responses are obtained by the process illustrated on the bottom. We sweep a window of fixed size over larger and smaller versions of the image, so as to find smaller or larger faces, respectively. The illumination in the window is corrected, and then a regression engine (quite often, a neural net) predicts the orientation of the face. The window is corrected to this orientation and then presented to a classifier. Classifier outputs are then postprocessed to ensure that only one face is placed at each location in the image.

3.1 Complex appearance and pattern elements

Many objects produce much more complex patterns than faces do. This is because several effects can move features around in an image of the object. Effects include (Figure 13)

- **Foreshortening**, which causes a pattern viewed at a slant to be significantly distorted.
- **Aspect**, which causes objects to look different when seen from different directions. Even as simple an object as a doughnut has several aspects; seen from the side, it looks like a flattened oval, but from above it is an annulus.
- **Occlusion**, where some parts are hidden from some viewing directions. Objects can occlude one another, or parts of an object can occlude other parts, an effect known as self-occlusion.
- **Deformation**, where internal degrees of freedom of the object change its appearance. For example, people can move their arms and legs around, generating a very wide range of different body configurations.

However, our recipe of searching across location and scale can still work. This is because some structure will be present in the images produced by the object. For example, a picture of a car is likely to show some of headlights, doors, wheels, windows, and hubcaps, though they may be in somewhat different arrangements in different pictures. This suggests modeling objects with pattern elements—collections of parts. These pattern elements may move around

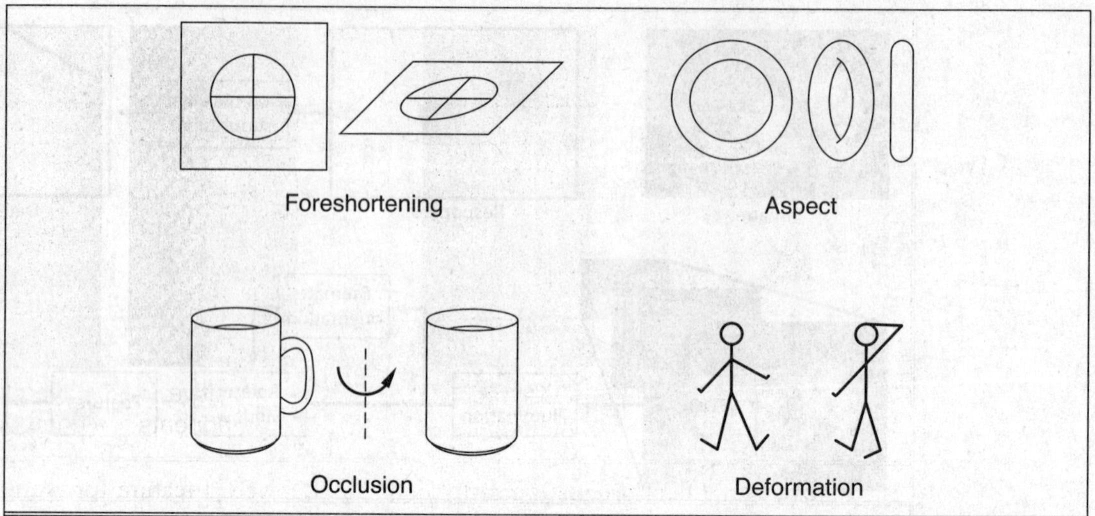

Figure 13 Sources of appearance variation. First, elements can foreshorten, like the circular patch on the top left. This patch is viewed at a slant, and so is elliptical in the image. Second, objects viewed from different directions can change shape quite dramatically, a phenomenon known as aspect. On the top right are three different aspects of a doughnut. Occlusion causes the handle of the mug on the bottom left to disappear when the mug is rotated. In this case, because the body and handle belong to the same mug, we have self-occlusion. Finally, on the bottom right, some objects can deform dramatically.

with respect to one another, but if most of the pattern elements are present in about the right place, then the object is present. An object recognizer is then a collection of features that can tell whether the pattern elements are present, and whether they are in about the right place.

The most obvious approach is to represent the image window with a histogram of the pattern elements that appear there. This approach does not work particularly well, because too many patterns get confused with one another. For example, if the pattern elements are color pixels, the French, UK, and Netherlands flags will get confused because they have approximately the same color histograms, though the colors are arranged in very different ways. Quite simple modifications of histograms yield very useful features. The trick is to preserve some spatial detail in the representation; for example, headlights tend to be at the front of a car and wheels tend to be at the bottom. Histogram-based features have been successful in a wide variety of recognition applications; we will survey pedestrian detection.

3.2 Pedestrian detection with HOG features

The World Bank estimates that each year car accidents kill about 1.2 million people, of whom about two thirds are pedestrians. This means that detecting pedestrians is an important application problem, because cars that can automatically detect and avoid pedestrians might save many lives. Pedestrians wear many different kinds of clothing and appear in many different configurations, but, at relatively low resolution, pedestrians can have a fairly characteristic appearance. The most usual cases are lateral or frontal views of a walk. In these cases,

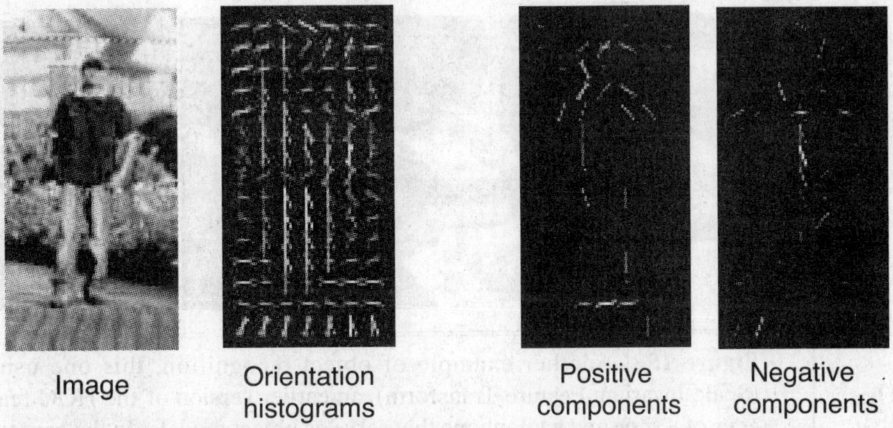

Figure 14 Local orientation histograms are a powerful feature for recognizing even quite complex objects. On the left, an image of a pedestrian. On the center left, local orientation histograms for patches. We then apply a classifier such as a support vector machine to find the weights for each histogram that best separate the positive examples of pedestrians from non-pedestrians. We see that the positively weighted components look like the outline of a person. The negative components are less clear; they represent all the patterns that are not pedestrians. Figure from Dalal and Triggs (2005) © IEEE.

we see either a "lollipop" shape — the torso is wider than the legs, which are together in the stance phase of the walk — or a "scissor" shape — where the legs are swinging in the walk. We expect to see some evidence of arms and legs, and the curve around the shoulders and head also tends to visible and quite distinctive. This means that, with a careful feature construction, we can build a useful moving-window pedestrian detector.

There isn't always a strong contrast between the pedestrian and the background, so it is better to use orientations than edges to represent the image window. Pedestrians can move their arms and legs around, so we should use a histogram to suppress some spatial detail in the feature. We break up the window into cells, which could overlap, and build an orientation histogram in each cell. Doing so will produce a feature that can tell whether the head-and-shoulders curve is at the top of the window or at the bottom, but will not change if the head moves slightly.

One further trick is required to make a good feature. Because orientation features are not affected by illumination brightness, we cannot treat high-contrast edges specially. This means that the distinctive curves on the boundary of a pedestrian are treated in the same way as fine texture detail in clothing or in the background, and so the signal may be submerged in noise. We can recover contrast information by counting gradient orientations with weights that reflect how significant a gradient is compared to other gradients in the same cell. We will write $\| \nabla I_{\mathbf{x}} \|$ for the gradient magnitude at point $\mathbf{x}$ in the image, write $\mathcal{C}$ for the cell whose histogram we wish to compute, and write $w_{\mathbf{x},\mathcal{C}}$ for the weight that we will use for the

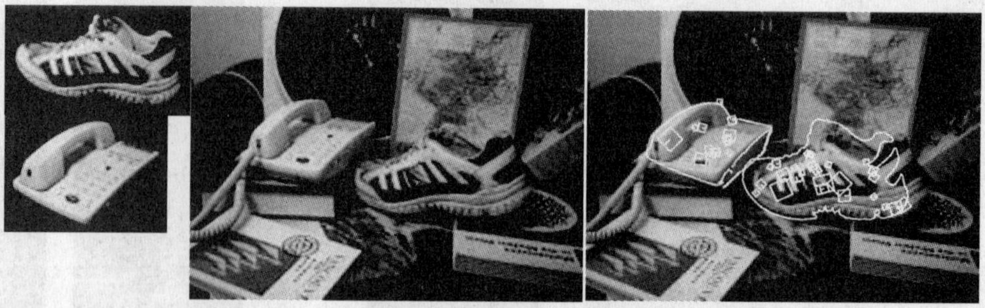

Figure 15 Another example of object recognition, this one using the SIFT feature (Scale Invariant Feature Transform), an earlier version of the HOG feature. On the **left**, images of a shoe and a telephone that serve as object models. In the **center**, a test image. On the **right**, the shoe and the telephone have been detected by: finding points in the image whose SIFT feature descriptions match a model; computing an estimate of pose of the model; and verifying that estimate. A strong match is usually verified with rare false positives. Images from Lowe (1999) © IEEE.

orientation at **x** for this cell. A natural choice of weight is

$$w_{\mathbf{x},\mathcal{C}} = \frac{\|\nabla I_{\mathbf{x}}\|}{\sum_{\mathbf{u}\in\mathcal{C}} \|\nabla I_{\mathbf{u}}\|}.$$

This compares the gradient magnitude to others in the cell, so gradients that are large compared to their neighbors get a large weight. The resulting feature is usually called a **HOG feature** (for Histogram Of Gradient orientations).

HOG FEATURE

This feature construction is the main way in which pedestrian detection differs from face detection. Otherwise, building a pedestrian detector is very like building a face detector. The detector sweeps a window across the image, computes features for that window, then presents it to a classifier. Non-maximum suppression needs to be applied to the output. In most applications, the scale and orientation of typical pedestrians is known. For example, in driving applications in which a camera is fixed to the car, we expect to view mainly vertical pedestrians, and we are interested only in nearby pedestrians. Several pedestrian data sets have been published, and these can be used for training the classifier.

Pedestrians are not the only type of object we can detect. In Figure 15 we see that similar techniques can be used to find a variety of objects in different contexts.

4 Reconstructing the 3D World

In this section we show how to go from the two-dimensional image to a three-dimensional representation of the scene. The fundamental question is this: Given that all points in the scene that fall along a ray to the pinhole are projected to the same point in the image, how do we recover three-dimensional information? Two ideas come to our rescue:

- If we have two (or more) images from different camera positions, then we can triangulate to find the position of a point in the scene.
- We can exploit background knowledge about the physical scene that gave rise to the image. Given an object model $\mathbf{P}(Scene)$ and a rendering model $\mathbf{P}(Image \mid Scene)$, we can compute a posterior distribution $\mathbf{P}(Scene \mid Image)$.

There is as yet no single unified theory for scene reconstruction. We survey eight commonly used visual cues: **motion, binocular stereopsis, multiple views, texture, shading, contour**, and **familiar objects.**

4.1 Motion parallax

If the camera moves relative to the three-dimensional scene, the resulting apparent motion in the image, optical flow, can be a source of information for both the movement of the camera and depth in the scene. To understand this, we state (without proof) an equation that relates the optical flow to the viewer's translational velocity $\mathbf{T}$ and the depth in the scene.

The components of the optical flow field are

$$v_x(x,y) = \frac{-T_x + xT_z}{Z(x,y)}, \qquad v_y(x,y) = \frac{-T_y + yT_z}{Z(x,y)},$$

where $Z(x,y)$ is the z-coordinate of the point in the scene corresponding to the point in the image at (x,y).

FOCUS OF EXPANSION

Note that both components of the optical flow, $v_x(x,y)$ and $v_y(x,y)$, are zero at the point $x = T_x/T_z, y = T_y/T_z$. This point is called the **focus of expansion** of the flow field. Suppose we change the origin in the x–y plane to lie at the focus of expansion; then the expressions for optical flow take on a particularly simple form. Let (x', y') be the new coordinates defined by $x' = x - T_x/T_z$, $y' = y - T_y/T_z$. Then

$$v_x(x',y') = \frac{x'T_z}{Z(x',y')}, \qquad v_y(x',y') = \frac{y'T_z}{Z(x',y')}.$$

Note that there is a scale-factor ambiguity here. If the camera was moving twice as fast, and every object in the scene was twice as big and at twice the distance to the camera, the optical flow field would be exactly the same. But we can still extract quite useful information.

1. Suppose you are a fly trying to land on a wall and you want to know the time-to-contact at the current velocity. This time is given by Z/T_z. Note that although the instantaneous optical flow field cannot provide either the distance Z or the velocity component T_z, it can provide the ratio of the two and can therefore be used to control the landing approach. There is considerable experimental evidence that many different animal species exploit this cue.
2. Consider two points at depths Z_1, Z_2, respectively. We may not know the absolute value of either of these, but by considering the inverse of the ratio of the optical flow magnitudes at these points, we can determine the depth ratio Z_1/Z_2. This is the cue of motion parallax, one we use when we look out of the side window of a moving car or train and infer that the slower moving parts of the landscape are farther away.

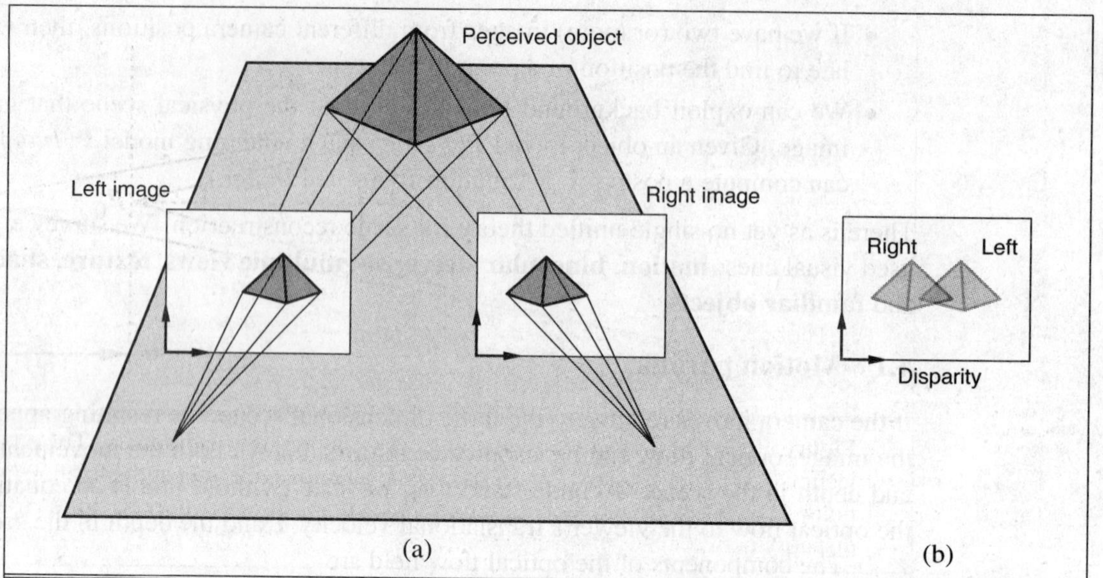

Figure 16 Translating a camera parallel to the image plane causes image features to move in the camera plane. The disparity in positions that results is a cue to depth. If we superimpose left and right image, as in (b), we see the disparity.

4.2 Binocular stereopsis

Most vertebrates have *two* eyes. This is useful for redundancy in case of a lost eye, but it helps in other ways too. Most prey have eyes on the side of the head to enable a wider field of vision. Predators have the eyes in the front, enabling them to use **binocular stereopsis**. The idea is similar to motion parallax, except that instead of using images over time, we use two (or more) images separated in space. Because a given feature in the scene will be in a different place relative to the z-axis of each image plane, if we superpose the two images, there will be a **disparity** in the location of the image feature in the two images. You can see this in Figure 16, where the nearest point of the pyramid is shifted to the left in the right image and to the right in the left image.

BINOCULAR STEREOPSIS

DISPARITY

Note that to measure disparity we need to solve the correspondence problem, that is, determine for a point in the left image, the point in the right image that results from the projection of the same scene point. This is analogous to what one has to do in measuring optical flow, and the most simple-minded approaches are somewhat similar and based on comparing blocks of pixels around corresponding points using the sum of squared differences. In practice, we use much more sophisticated algorithms, which exploit additional constraints.

Assuming that we can measure disparity, how does this yield information about depth in the scene? We will need to work out the geometrical relationship between disparity and depth. First, we will consider the case when both the eyes (or cameras) are looking forward with their optical axes parallel. The relationship of the right camera to the left camera is then just a displacement along the x-axis by an amount b, the baseline. We can use the optical flow equations from the previous section, if we think of this as resulting from a translation

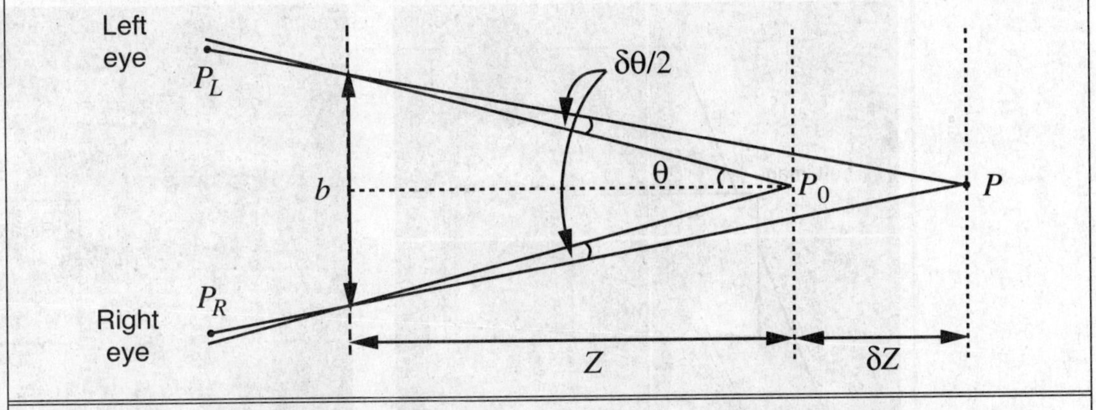

Figure 17 The relation between disparity and depth in stereopsis. The centers of projection of the two eyes are b apart, and the optical axes intersect at the fixation point P_0. The point P in the scene projects to points P_L and P_R in the two eyes. In angular terms, the disparity between these is $\delta\theta$. See text.

vector **T** acting for time δt, with $T_x = b/\delta t$ and $T_y = T_z = 0$. The horizontal and vertical disparity are given by the optical flow components, multiplied by the time step δt, $H = v_x\,\delta t$, $V = v_y\,\delta t$. Carrying out the substitutions, we get the result that $H = b/Z$, $V = 0$. In words, the horizontal disparity is equal to the ratio of the baseline to the depth, and the vertical disparity is zero. Given that we know b, we can measure H and recover the depth Z.

FIXATE

Under normal viewing conditions, humans **fixate**; that is, there is some point in the scene at which the optical axes of the two eyes intersect. Figure 17 shows two eyes fixated at a point P_0, which is at a distance Z from the midpoint of the eyes. For convenience, we will compute the *angular* disparity, measured in radians. The disparity at the point of fixation P_0 is zero. For some other point P in the scene that is δZ farther away, we can compute the angular displacements of the left and right images of P, which we will call P_L and P_R, respectively. If each of these is displaced by an angle $\delta\theta/2$ relative to P_0, then the displacement between P_L and P_R, which is the disparity of P, is just $\delta\theta$. From Figure 17, $\tan\theta = \frac{b/2}{Z}$ and $\tan(\theta - \delta\theta/2) = \frac{b/2}{Z+\delta Z}$, but for small angles, $\tan\theta \approx \theta$, so

$$\delta\theta/2 = \frac{b/2}{Z} - \frac{b/2}{Z+\delta Z} \approx \frac{b\delta Z}{2Z^2}$$

and, since the actual disparity is $\delta\theta$, we have

$$\text{disparity} = \frac{b\delta Z}{Z^2}.$$

BASELINE

In humans, b (the **baseline** distance between the eyes) is about 6 cm. Suppose that Z is about 100 cm. If the smallest detectable $\delta\theta$ (corresponding to the pixel size) is about 5 seconds of arc, this gives a δZ of 0.4 mm. For $Z = 30$ cm, we get the impressively small value $\delta Z = 0.036$ mm. That is, at a distance of 30 cm, humans can discriminate depths that differ by as little as 0.036 mm, enabling us to thread needles and the like.

Figure 18 (a) Four frames from a video sequence in which the camera is moved and rotated relative to the object. (b) The first frame of the sequence, annotated with small boxes highlighting the features found by the feature detector. (Courtesy of Carlo Tomasi.)

4.3 Multiple views

Shape from optical flow or binocular disparity are two instances of a more general framework, that of exploiting multiple views for recovering depth. In computer vision, there is no reason for us to be restricted to differential motion or to only use two cameras converging at a fixation point. Therefore, techniques have been developed that exploit the information available in multiple views, even from hundreds or thousands of cameras. Algorithmically, there are three subproblems that need to be solved:

- The correspondence problem, i.e., identifying features in the different images that are projections of the same feature in the three-dimensional world.
- The relative orientation problem, i.e., determining the transformation (rotation and translation) between the coordinate systems fixed to the different cameras.
- The depth estimation problem, i.e., determining the depths of various points in the world for which image plane projections were available in at least two views

The development of robust matching procedures for the correspondence problem, accompanied by numerically stable algorithms for solving for relative orientations and scene depth, is one of the success stories of computer vision. Results from one such approach due to Tomasi and Kanade (1992) are shown in Figures 18 and 19.

4.4 Texture

Earlier we saw how texture was used for segmenting objects. It can also be used to estimate distances. In Figure 20 we see that a homogeneous texture in the scene results in varying

TEXEL texture elements, or **texels**, in the image. All the paving tiles in (a) are identical in the scene. They appear different in the image for two reasons:

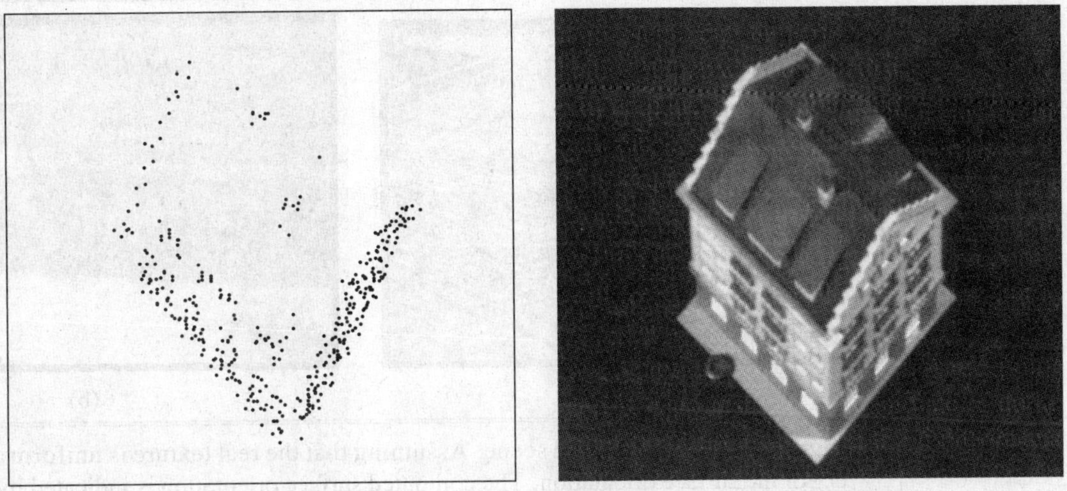

(a) (b)

Figure 19 (a) Three-dimensional reconstruction of the locations of the image features in Figure 18, shown from above. (b) The real house, taken from the same position.

1. *Differences in the distances of the texels from the camera.* Distant objects appear smaller by a scaling factor of $1/Z$.
2. *Differences in the foreshortening of the texels.* If all the texels are in the ground plane then distance ones are viewed at an angle that is farther off the perpendicular, and so are more foreshortened. The magnitude of the foreshortening effect is proportional to $\cos\sigma$, where σ is the slant, the angle between the Z-axis and $\mathbf{n}$, the surface normal to the texel.

Researchers have developed various algorithms that try to exploit the variation in the appearance of the projected texels as a basis for determining surface normals. However, the accuracy and applicability of these algorithms is not anywhere as general as those based on using multiple views.

4.5 Shading

Shading—variation in the intensity of light received from different portions of a surface in a scene—is determined by the geometry of the scene and by the reflectance properties of the surfaces. In computer graphics, the objective is to compute the image brightness $I(x, y)$, given the scene geometry and reflectance properties of the objects in the scene. Computer vision aims to invert the process—that is, to recover the geometry and reflectance properties, given the image brightness $I(x, y)$. This has proved to be difficult to do in anything but the simplest cases.

From the physical model of section 1.4, we know that if a surface normal points toward the light source, the surface is brighter, and if it points away, the surface is darker. We cannot conclude that a dark patch has its normal pointing away from the light; instead, it could have low albedo. Generally, albedo changes quite quickly in images, and shading

(a) (b)

Figure 20 (a) A textured scene. Assuming that the real texture is uniform allows recovery of the surface orientation. The computed surface orientation is indicated by overlaying a black circle and pointer, transformed as if the circle were painted on the surface at that point. (b) Recovery of shape from texture for a curved surface (white circle and pointer this time). Images courtesy of Jitendra Malik and Ruth Rosenholtz (1994).

changes rather slowly, and humans seem to be quite good at using this observation to tell whether low illumination, surface orientation, or albedo caused a surface patch to be dark. To simplify the problem, let us assume that the albedo is known at every surface point. It is still difficult to recover the normal, because the image brightness is one measurement but the normal has two unknown parameters, so we cannot simply solve for the normal. The key to this situation seems to be that nearby normals will be similar, because most surfaces are smooth—they do not have sharp changes.

The real difficulty comes in dealing with interreflections. If we consider a typical indoor scene, such as the objects inside an office, surfaces are illuminated not only by the light sources, but also by the light reflected from other surfaces in the scene that effectively serve as secondary light sources. These mutual illumination effects are quite significant and make it quite difficult to predict the relationship between the normal and the image brightness. Two surface patches with the same normal might have quite different brightnesses, because one receives light reflected from a large white wall and the other faces only a dark bookcase. Despite these difficulties, the problem is important. Humans seem to be able to ignore the effects of interreflections and get a useful perception of shape from shading, but we know frustratingly little about algorithms to do this.

4.6 Contour

When we look at a line drawing, such as Figure 21, we get a vivid perception of three-dimensional shape and layout. How? It is a combination of recognition of familiar objects in the scene and the application of generic constraints such as the following:

- Occluding contours, such as the outlines of the hills. One side of the contour is nearer to the viewer, the other side is farther away. Features such as local convexity and sym-

Figure 21 An evocative line drawing. (Courtesy of Isha Malik.)

FIGURE-GROUND

metry provide cues to solving the **figure-ground** problem—assigning which side of the contour is figure (nearer), and which is ground (farther). At an occluding contour, the line of sight is tangential to the surface in the scene.

- T-junctions. When one object occludes another, the contour of the farther object is interrupted, assuming that the nearer object is opaque. A T-junction results in the image.
- Position on the ground plane. Humans, like many other terrestrial animals, are very often in a scene that contains a **ground plane**, with various objects at different locations on this plane. Because of gravity, typical objects don't float in air but are supported by this ground plane, and we can exploit the very special geometry of this viewing scenario.

GROUND PLANE

Let us work out the projection of objects of different heights and at different locations on the ground plane. Suppose that the eye, or camera, is at a height h_c above the ground plane. Consider an object of height δY resting on the ground plane, whose bottom is at $(X, -h_c, Z)$ and top is at $(X, \delta Y - h_c, Z)$. The bottom projects to the image point $(fX/Z, -fh_c/Z)$ and the top to $(fX/Z, f(\delta Y - h_c)/Z)$. The bottoms of nearer objects (small Z) project to points lower in the image plane; farther objects have bottoms closer to the horizon.

4.7 Objects and the geometric structure of scenes

A typical adult human head is about 9 inches long. This means that for someone who is 43 feet away, the angle subtended by the head at the camera is 1 degree. If we see a person whose head appears to subtend just half a degree, Bayesian inference suggests we are looking at a normal person who is 86 feet away, rather than someone with a half-size head. This line of reasoning supplies us with a method to check the results of a pedestrian detector, as well as a method to estimate the distance to an object. For example, all pedestrians are about the same height, and they tend to stand on a ground plane. If we know where the horizon is in an image, we can rank pedestrians by distance to the camera. This works because we know where their

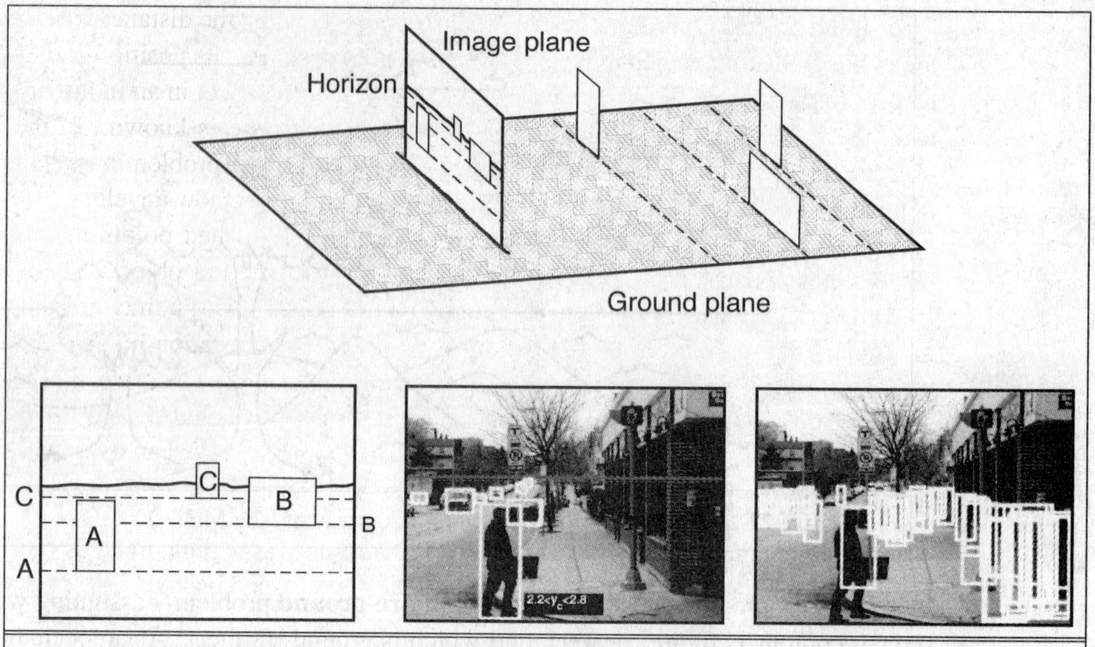

Figure 22 In an image of people standing on a ground plane, the people whose feet are closer to the horizon in the image must be farther away (top drawing). This means they must look smaller in the image (left lower drawing). This means that the size and location of real pedestrians in an image depend upon one another and on the location of the horizon. To exploit this, we need to identify the ground plane, which is done using shape-from-texture methods. From this information, and from some likely pedestrians, we can recover a horizon as shown in the center image. On the right, acceptable pedestrian boxes given this geometric context. Notice that pedestrians who are higher in the scene must be smaller. If they are not, then they are false positives. Images from Hoiem *et al.* (2008) © IEEE.

feet are, and pedestrians whose feet are closer to the horizon in the image are farther away from the camera (Figure 22). Pedestrians who are farther away from the camera must also be smaller in the image. This means we can rule out some detector responses — if a detector finds a pedestrian who is large in the image and whose feet are close to the horizon, it has found an enormous pedestrian; these don't exist, so the detector is wrong. In fact, many or most image windows are not acceptable pedestrian windows, and need not even be presented to the detector.

There are several strategies for finding the horizon, including searching for a roughly horizontal line with a lot of blue above it, and using surface orientation estimates obtained from texture deformation. A more elegant strategy exploits the reverse of our geometric constraints. A reasonably reliable pedestrian detector is capable of producing estimates of the horizon, if there are several pedestrians in the scene at different distances from the camera. This is because the relative scaling of the pedestrians is a cue to where the horizon is. So we can extract a horizon estimate from the detector, then use this estimate to prune the pedestrian detector's mistakes.

If the object is familiar, we can estimate more than just the distance to it, because what it looks like in the image depends very strongly on its pose, i.e., its position and orientation with respect to the viewer. This has many applications. For instance, in an industrial manipulation task, the robot arm cannot pick up an object until the pose is known. In the case of rigid objects, whether three-dimensional or two-dimensional, this problem has a simple and well-defined solution based on the **alignment method**, which we now develop.

ALIGNMENT METHOD

The object is represented by M features or distinguished points $m_1, m_2, \ldots, m_M$ in three-dimensional space—perhaps the vertices of a polyhedral object. These are measured in some coordinate system that is natural for the object. The points are then subjected to an unknown three-dimensional rotation $\mathbf{R}$, followed by translation by an unknown amount $\mathbf{t}$ and then projection to give rise to image feature points $p_1, p_2, \ldots, p_N$ on the image plane. In general, $N \neq M$, because some model points may be occluded, and the feature detector could miss some features (or invent false ones due to noise). We can express this as

$$p_i = \Pi(\mathbf{R}m_i + \mathbf{t}) = Q(m_i)$$

for a three-dimensional model point m_i and the corresponding image point p_i. Here, $\mathbf{R}$ is a rotation matrix, $\mathbf{t}$ is a translation, and Π denotes perspective projection or one of its approximations, such as scaled orthographic projection. The net result is a transformation Q that will bring the model point m_i into alignment with the image point p_i. Although we do not know Q initially, we do know (for rigid objects) that Q must be the *same* for all the model points.

We can solve for Q, given the three-dimensional coordinates of three model points and their two-dimensional projections. The intuition is as follows: we can write down equations relating the coordinates of p_i to those of m_i. In these equations, the unknown quantities correspond to the parameters of the rotation matrix $\mathbf{R}$ and the translation vector $\mathbf{t}$. If we have enough equations, we ought to be able to solve for Q. We will not give a proof here; we merely state the following result:

> Given three noncollinear points m_1, m_2, and m_3 in the model, and their scaled orthographic projections p_1, p_2, and p_3 on the image plane, there exist exactly two transformations from the three-dimensional model coordinate frame to a two-dimensional image coordinate frame.

These transformations are related by a reflection around the image plane and can be computed by a simple closed-form solution. If we could identify the corresponding model features for three features in the image, we could compute Q, the pose of the object.

Let us specify position and orientation in mathematical terms. The position of a point P in the scene is characterized by three numbers, the (X, Y, Z) coordinates of P in a coordinate frame with its origin at the pinhole and the Z-axis along the optical axis (Figure 2). What we have available is the perspective projection (x, y) of the point in the image. This specifies the ray from the pinhole along which P lies; what we do not know is the distance. The term "orientation" could be used in two senses:

1. **The orientation of the object as a whole.** This can be specified in terms of a three-dimensional rotation relating its coordinate frame to that of the camera.

2. **The orientation of the surface of the object at P.** This can be specified by a normal vector, **n**—which is a vector specifying the direction that is perpendicular to the surface. Often we express the surface orientation using the variables **slant** and **tilt**. Slant is the angle between the Z-axis and **n**. Tilt is the angle between the X-axis and the projection of **n** on the image plane.

SLANT

TILT

When the camera moves relative to an object, both the object's distance and its orientation change. What is preserved is the **shape** of the object. If the object is a cube, that fact is not changed when the object moves. Geometers have been attempting to formalize shape for centuries, the basic concept being that shape is what remains unchanged under some group of transformations—for example, combinations of rotations and translations. The difficulty lies in finding a representation of global shape that is general enough to deal with the wide variety of objects in the real world—not just simple forms like cylinders, cones, and spheres—and yet can be recovered easily from the visual input. The problem of characterizing the *local* shape of a surface is much better understood. Essentially, this can be done in terms of curvature: how does the surface normal change as one moves in different directions on the surface? For a plane, there is no change at all. For a cylinder, if one moves parallel to the axis, there is no change, but in the perpendicular direction, the surface normal rotates at a rate inversely proportional to the radius of the cylinder, and so on. All this is studied in the subject called differential geometry.

SHAPE

The shape of an object is relevant for some manipulation tasks (e.g., deciding where to grasp an object), but its most significant role is in object recognition, where geometric shape along with color and texture provide the most significant cues to enable us to identify objects, classify what is in the image as an example of some class one has seen before, and so on.

5 Object Recognition from Structural Information

Putting a box around pedestrians in an image may well be enough to avoid driving into them. We have seen that we can find a box by pooling the evidence provided by orientations, using histogram methods to suppress potentially confusing spatial detail. If we want to know more about what someone is doing, we will need to know where their arms, legs, body, and head lie in the picture. Individual body parts are quite difficult to detect on their own using a moving window method, because their color and texture can vary widely and because they are usually small in images. Often, forearms and shins are as small as two to three pixels wide. Body parts do not usually appear on their own, and representing what is connected to what could be quite powerful, because parts that are easy to find might tell us where to look for parts that are small and hard to detect.

Inferring the layout of human bodies in pictures is an important task in vision, because the layout of the body often reveals what people are doing. A model called a **deformable template** can tell us which configurations are acceptable: the elbow can bend but the head is never joined to the foot. The simplest deformable template model of a person connects lower arms to upper arms, upper arms to the torso, and so on. There are richer models: for example,

DEFORMABLE TEMPLATE

we could represent the fact that left and right upper arms tend to have the same color and texture, as do left and right legs. These richer models remain difficult to work with, however.

5.1 The geometry of bodies: Finding arms and legs

For the moment, we assume that we know what the person's body parts look like (e.g., we know the color and texture of the person's clothing). We can model the geometry of the body as a tree of eleven segments (upper and lower left and right arms and legs respectively, a torso, a face, and hair on top of the face) each of which is rectangular. We assume that the position and orientation (**pose**) of the left lower arm is independent of all other segments given the pose of the left upper arm; that the pose of the left upper arm is independent of all segments given the pose of the torso; and extend these assumptions in the obvious way to include the right arm and the legs, the face, and the hair. Such models are often called "cardboard people" models. The model forms a tree, which is usually rooted at the torso. We will search the image for the best match to this cardboard person using inference methods for a tree-structured Bayes net.

POSE

There are two criteria for evaluating a configuration. First, an image rectangle should look like its segment. For the moment, we will remain vague about precisely what that means, but we assume we have a function ϕ_i that scores how well an image rectangle matches a body segment. For each pair of related segments, we have another function ψ that scores how well relations between a pair of image rectangles match those to be expected from the body segments. The dependencies between segments form a tree, so each segment has only one parent, and we could write $\psi_{i,\mathrm{pa}(i)}$. All the functions will be larger if the match is better, so we can think of them as being like a log probability. The cost of a particular match that allocates image rectangle m_i to body segment i is then

$$\sum_{i \in \text{segments}} \phi_i(m_i) + \sum_{i \in \text{segments}} \psi_{i,\mathrm{pa}(i)}(m_i, m_{\mathrm{pa}(i)}) .$$

Dynamic programming can find the best match, because the relational model is a tree.

It is inconvenient to search a continuous space, and we will discretize the space of image rectangles. We do so by discretizing the location and orientation of rectangles of fixed size (the sizes may be different for different segments). Because ankles and knees are different, we need to distinguish between a rectangle and the same rectangle rotated by 180°. One could visualize the result as a set of very large stacks of small rectangles of image, cut out at different locations and orientations. There is one stack per segment. We must now find the best allocation of rectangles to segments. This will be slow, because there are many image rectangles and, for the model we have given, choosing the right torso will be $O(M^6)$ if there are M image rectangles. However, various speedups are available for an appropriate choice of ψ, and the method is practical (Figure 23). The model is usually known as a **pictorial structure model**.

PICTORIAL STRUCTURE MODEL

Recall our assumption that we know what we need to know about what the person looks like. If we are matching a person in a single image, the most useful feature for scoring segment matches turns out to be color. Texture features don't work well in most cases, because folds on loose clothing produce strong shading patterns that overlay the image texture. These

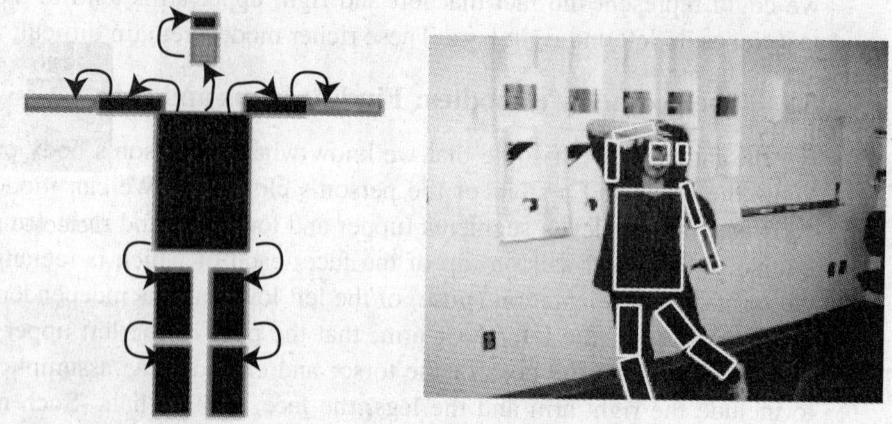

Figure 23 A pictorial structure model evaluates a match between a set of image rectangles and a cardboard person (shown on the left) by scoring the similarity in appearance between body segments and image segments and the spatial relations between the image segments. Generally, a match is better if the image segments have about the right appearance and are in about the right place with respect to one another. The appearance model uses average colors for hair, head, torso, and upper and lower arms and legs. The relevant relations are shown as arrows. On the right, the best match for a particular image, obtained using dynamic programming. The match is a fair estimate of the configuration of the body. Figure from Felzenszwalb and Huttenlocher (2000) © IEEE.

patterns are strong enough to disrupt the true texture of the cloth. In current work, ψ typically reflects the need for the ends of the segments to be reasonably close together, but there are usually no constraints on the angles. Generally, we don't know what a person looks like, and must build a model of segment appearances. We call the description of what a person looks like the **appearance model**. If we must report the configuration of a person in a single image, we can start with a poorly tuned appearance model, estimate configuration with this, then re-estimate appearance, and so on. In video, we have many frames of the same person, and this will reveal their appearance.

APPEARANCE MODEL

5.2 Coherent appearance: Tracking people in video

Tracking people in video is an important practical problem. If we could reliably report the location of arms, legs, torso, and head in video sequences, we could build much improved game interfaces and surveillance systems. Filtering methods have not had much success with this problem, because people can produce large accelerations and move quite fast. This means that for 30 Hz video, the configuration of the body in frame i doesn't constrain the configuration of the body in frame $i+1$ all that strongly. Currently, the most effective methods exploit the fact that appearance changes very slowly from frame to frame. If we can infer an appearance model of an individual from the video, then we can use this information in a pictorial structure model to detect that person in each frame of the video. We can then link these locations across time to make a track.

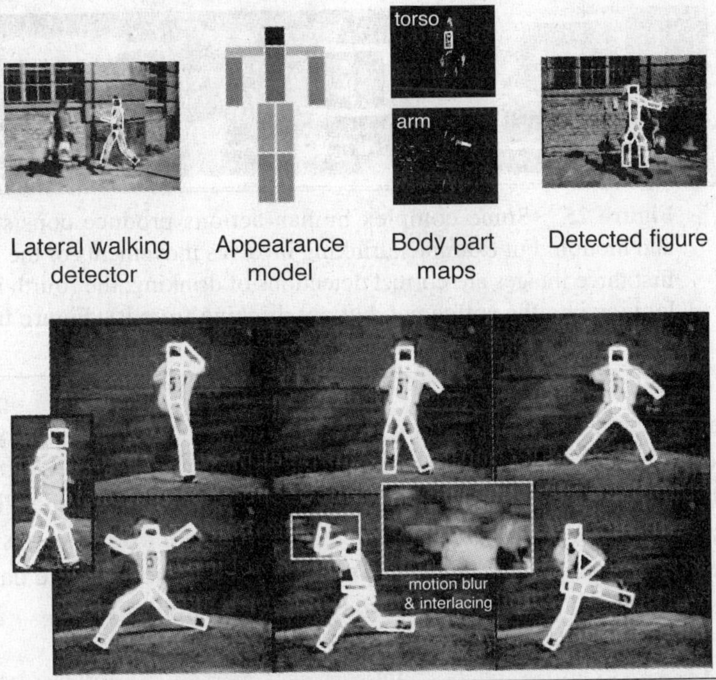

Figure 24 We can track moving people with a pictorial structure model by first obtaining an appearance model, then applying it. To obtain the appearance model, we scan the image to find a lateral walking pose. The detector does not need to be very accurate, but should produce few false positives. From the detector response, we can read off pixels that lie on each body segment, and others that do not lie on that segment. This makes it possible to build a discriminative model of the appearance of each body part, and these are tied together into a pictorial structure model of the person being tracked. Finally, we can reliably track by detecting this model in each frame. As the frames in the lower part of the image suggest, this procedure can track complicated, fast-changing body configurations, despite degradation of the video signal due to motion blur. Figure from Ramanan *et al.* (2007) © IEEE.

There are several ways to infer a good appearance model. We regard the video as a large stack of pictures of the person we wish to track. We can exploit this stack by looking for appearance models that explain many of the pictures. This would work by detecting body segments in each frame, using the fact that segments have roughly parallel edges. Such detectors are not particularly reliable, but the segments we want to find are special. They will appear at least once in most of the frames of video; such segments can be found by clustering the detector responses. It is best to start with the torso, because it is big and because torso detectors tend to be reliable. Once we have a torso appearance model, upper leg segments should appear near the torso, and so on. This reasoning yields an appearance model, but it can be unreliable if people appear against a near-fixed background where the segment detector generates lots of false positives. An alternative is to estimate appearance for many of the frames of video by repeatedly reestimating configuration and appearance; we then see if one appearance model explains many frames. Another alternative, which is quite

Figure 25 Some complex human actions produce consistent patterns of appearance and motion. For example, drinking involves movements of the hand in front of the face. The first three images are correct detections of drinking; the fourth is a false-positive (the cook is looking into the coffee pot, but not drinking from it). Figure from Laptev and Perez (2007) © IEEE.

reliable in practice, is to apply a detector for a fixed body configuration to all of the frames. A good choice of configuration is one that is easy to detect reliably, and where there is a strong chance the person will appear in that configuration even in a short sequence (lateral walking is a good choice). We tune the detector to have a low false positive rate, so we know when it responds that we have found a real person; and because we have localized their torso, arms, legs, and head, we know what these segments look like.

6 Using Vision

If vision systems could analyze video and understood what people are doing, we would be able to: design buildings and public places better by collecting and using data about what people do in public; build more accurate, more secure, and less intrusive surveillance systems; build computer sports commentators; and build human-computer interfaces that watch people and react to their behavior. Applications for reactive interfaces range from computer games that make a player get up and move around to systems that save energy by managing heat and light in a building to match where the occupants are and what they are doing.

Some problems are well understood. If people are relatively small in the video frame, and the background is stable, it is easy to detect the people by subtracting a background image from the current frame. If the absolute value of the difference is large, this **background subtraction** declares the pixel to be a foreground pixel; by linking foreground blobs over time, we obtain a track.

BACKGROUND SUBTRACTION

Structured behaviors like ballet, gymnastics, or tai chi have specific vocabularies of actions. When performed against a simple background, videos of these actions are easy to deal with. Background subtraction identifies the major moving regions, and we can build HOG features (keeping track of flow rather than orientation) to present to a classifier. We can detect consistent patterns of action with a variant of our pedestrian detector, where the orientation features are collected into histogram buckets over time as well as space (Figure 25).

More general problems remain open. The big research question is to link observations of the body and the objects nearby to the goals and intentions of the moving people. One source of difficulty is that we lack a simple vocabulary of human behavior. Behavior is a lot like color, in that people tend to think they know a lot of behavior names but can't produce long lists of such words on demand. There is quite a lot of evidence that behaviors combine—you can, for example, drink a milkshake while visiting an ATM—but we don't yet know what the pieces are, how the composition works, or how many composites there might be. A second source of difficulty is that we don't know what features expose what is happening. For example, knowing someone is close to an ATM may be enough to tell that they're visiting the ATM. A third difficulty is that the usual reasoning about the relationship between training and test data is untrustworthy. For example, we cannot argue that a pedestrian detector is safe simply because it performs well on a large data set, because that data set may well omit important, but rare, phenomena (for example, people mounting bicycles). We wouldn't want our automated driver to run over a pedestrian who happened to do something unusual.

6.1 Words and pictures

Many Web sites offer collections of images for viewing. How can we find the images we want? Let's suppose the user enters a text query, such as "bicycle race." Some of the images will have keywords or captions attached, or will come from Web pages that contain text near the image. For these, image retrieval can be like text retrieval: ignore the images and match the image's text against the query.

However, keywords are usually incomplete. For example, a picture of a cat playing in the street might be tagged with words like "cat" and "street," but it is easy to forget to mention the "garbage can" or the "fish bones." Thus an interesting task is to annotate an image (which may already have a few keywords) with additional appropriate keywords.

In the most straightforward version of this task, we have a set of correctly tagged example images, and we wish to tag some test images. This problem is sometimes known as auto-annotation. The most accurate solutions are obtained using nearest-neighbors methods. One finds the training images that are closest to the test image in a feature space metric that is trained using examples, then reports their tags.

Another version of the problem involves predicting which tags to attach to which regions in a test image. Here we do not know which regions produced which tags for the training data. We can use a version of expectation maximization to guess an initial correspondence between text and regions, and from that estimate a better decomposition into regions, and so on.

6.2 Reconstruction from many views

Binocular stereopsis works because for each point we have four measurements constraining three unknown degrees of freedom. The four measurements are the (x, y) positions of the point in each view, and the unknown degrees of freedom are the (x, y, z) coordinate values of the point in the scene. This rather crude argument suggests, correctly, that there are geometric constraints that prevent most pairs of points from being acceptable matches. Many images of a set of points should reveal their positions unambiguously.

We don't always need a second picture to get a second view of a set of points. If we believe the original set of points comes from a familiar rigid 3D object, then we might have an object model available as a source of information. If this object model consists of a set of 3D points or of a set of pictures of the object, and if we can establish point correspondences, we can determine the parameters of the camera that produced the points in the original image. This is very powerful information. We could use it to evaluate our original hypothesis that the points come from an object model. We do this by using some points to determine the parameters of the camera, then projecting model points in this camera and checking to see whether there are image points nearby.

We have sketched here a technology that is now very highly developed. The technology can be generalized to deal with views that are not orthographic; to deal with points that are observed in only some views; to deal with unknown camera properties like focal length; to exploit various sophisticated searches for appropriate correspondences; and to do reconstruction from very large numbers of points and of views. If the locations of points in the images are known with some accuracy and the viewing directions are reasonable, very high accuracy camera and point information can be obtained. Some applications are

- **Model-building:** For example, one might build a modeling system that takes a video sequence depicting an object and produces a very detailed three-dimensional mesh of textured polygons for use in computer graphics and virtual reality applications. Models like this can now be built from apparently quite unpromising sets of pictures. For example, Figure 26 shows a model of the Statue of Liberty built from pictures found on the Internet.
- **Matching moves:** To place computer graphics characters into real video, we need to know how the camera moved for the real video, so that we can render the character correctly.
- **Path reconstruction:** Mobile robots need to know where they have been. If they are moving in a world of rigid objects, then performing a reconstruction and keeping the camera information is one way to obtain a path.

6.3 Using vision for controlling movement

One of the principal uses of vision is to provide information both for manipulating objects—picking them up, grasping them, twirling them, and so on—and for navigating while avoiding obstacles. The ability to use vision for these purposes is present in the most primitive of animal visual systems. In many cases, the visual system is minimal, in the sense that it extracts from the available light field just the information the animal needs to inform its behavior. Quite probably, modern vision systems evolved from early, primitive organisms that used a photosensitive spot at one end to orient themselves toward (or away from) the light. We saw in Section 4 that flies use a very simple optical flow detection system to land on walls. A classic study, *What the Frog's Eye Tells the Frog's Brain* (Lettvin *et al.*, 1959), observes of a frog that, "He will starve to death surrounded by food if it is not moving. His choice of food is determined only by size and movement."

Let us consider a vision system for an automated vehicle driving on a freeway. The tasks faced by the driver include the following:

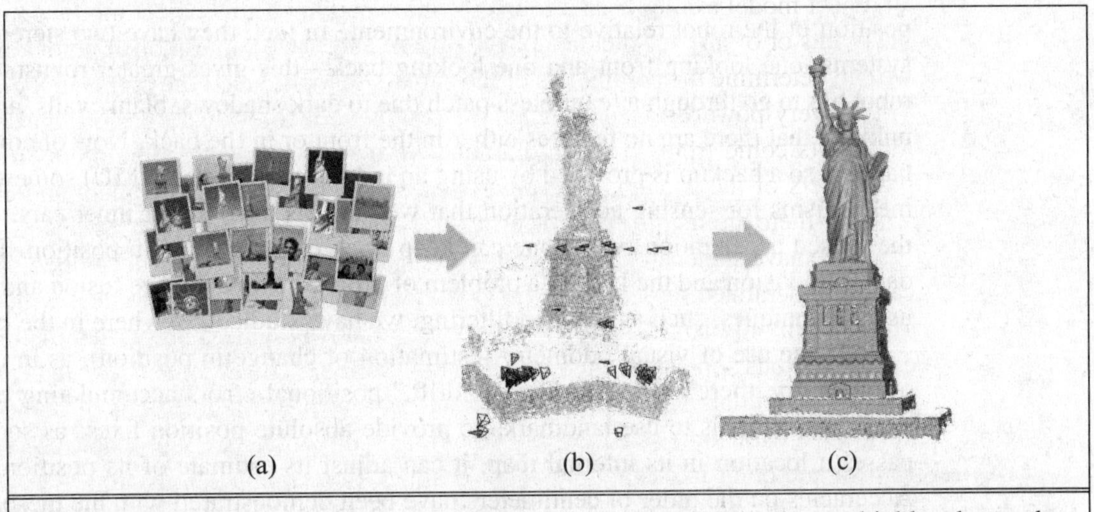

Figure 26 The state of the art in multiple-view reconstruction is now highly advanced. This figure outlines a system built by Michael Goesele and colleagues from the University of Washington, TU Darmstadt, and Microsoft Research. From a collection of pictures of a monument taken by a large community of users and posted on the Internet (a), their system can determine the viewing directions for those pictures, shown by the small black pyramids in (b) and a comprehensive 3D reconstruction shown in (c).

1. Lateral control—ensure that the vehicle remains securely within its lane or changes lanes smoothly when required.
2. Longitudinal control—ensure that there is a safe distance to the vehicle in front.
3. Obstacle avoidance—monitor vehicles in neighboring lanes and be prepared for evasive maneuvers if one of them decides to change lanes.

The problem for the driver is to generate appropriate steering, acceleration, and braking actions to best accomplish these tasks.

For lateral control, one needs to maintain a representation of the position and orientation of the car relative to the lane. We can use edge-detection algorithms to find edges corresponding to the lane-marker segments. We can then fit smooth curves to these edge elements. The parameters of these curves carry information about the lateral position of the car, the direction it is pointing relative to the lane, and the curvature of the lane. This information, along with information about the dynamics of the car, is all that is needed by the steering-control system. If we have good detailed maps of the road, then the vision system serves to confirm our position (and to watch for obstacles that are not on the map).

For longitudinal control, one needs to know distances to the vehicles in front. This can be accomplished with binocular stereopsis or optical flow. Using these techniques, vision-controlled cars can now drive reliably at highway speeds.

The more general case of mobile robots navigating in various indoor and outdoor environments has been studied, too. One particular problem, localizing the robot in its environment, now has pretty good solutions. A group at Sarnoff has developed a system based on two cameras looking forward that track feature points in 3D and use that to reconstruct the position of the robot relative to the environment. In fact, they have two stereoscopic camera systems, one looking front and one looking back—this gives greater robustness in case the robot has to go through a featureless patch due to dark shadows, blank walls, and the like. It is unlikely that there are no features either in the front or in the back. Now of course, that could happen, so a backup is provided by using an inertial motion unit (IMU) somewhat akin to the mechanisms for sensing acceleration that we humans have in our inner ears. By integrating the sensed acceleration twice, one can keep track of the change in position. Combining the data from vision and the IMU is a problem of probabilistic evidence fusion and can be tackled using techniques, such as Kalman filtering, we have studied elsewhere in the book.

In the use of visual odometry (estimation of change in position), as in other problems of odometry, there is the problem of "drift," positional errors accumulating over time. The solution for this is to use landmarks to provide absolute position fixes: as soon as the robot passes a location in its internal map, it can adjust its estimate of its position appropriately. Accuracies on the order of centimeters have been demonstrated with the these techniques.

The driving example makes one point very clear: *for a specific task, one does not need to recover all the information that, in principle, can be recovered from an image.* One does not need to recover the exact shape of every vehicle, solve for shape-from-texture on the grass surface adjacent to the freeway, and so on. Instead, a vision system should compute just what is needed to accomplish the task.

7 SUMMARY

Although perception appears to be an effortless activity for humans, it requires a significant amount of sophisticated computation. The goal of vision is to extract information needed for tasks such as manipulation, navigation, and object recognition.

- The process of **image formation** is well understood in its geometric and physical aspects. Given a description of a three-dimensional scene, we can easily produce a picture of it from some arbitrary camera position (the graphics problem). Inverting the process by going from an image to a description of the scene is more difficult.
- To extract the visual information necessary for the tasks of manipulation, navigation, and recognition, intermediate representations have to be constructed. Early vision **image-processing** algorithms extract primitive features from the image, such as edges and regions.
- There are various cues in the image that enable one to obtain three-dimensional information about the scene: motion, stereopsis, texture, shading, and contour analysis. Each of these cues relies on background assumptions about physical scenes to provide nearly unambiguous interpretations.
- Object recognition in its full generality is a very hard problem. We discussed brightness-based and feature-based approaches. We also presented a simple algorithm for pose estimation. Other possibilities exist.

BIBLIOGRAPHICAL AND HISTORICAL NOTES

The eye developed in the Cambrian explosion (530 million years ago), apparently in a common ancestor. Since then, endless variations have developed in different creatures, but the same gene, Pax-6, regulates the development of the eye in animals as diverse as humans, mice, and *Drosophila*.

Systematic attempts to understand human vision can be traced back to ancient times. Euclid (ca. 300 B.C.) wrote about natural perspective—the mapping that associates, with each point P in the three-dimensional world, the direction of the ray OP joining the center of projection O to the point P. He was well aware of the notion of motion parallax. The use of perspective in art was developed in ancient Roman culture, as evidenced by art found in the ruins of Pompeii (A.D. 79), but was then largely lost for 1300 years. The mathematical understanding of perspective projection, this time in the context of projection onto planar surfaces, had its next significant advance in the 15th-century in Renaissance Italy. Brunelleschi (1413) is usually credited with creating the first paintings based on geometrically correct projection of a three-dimensional scene. In 1435, Alberti codified the rules and inspired generations of artists whose artistic achievements amaze us to this day. Particularly notable in their development of the science of perspective, as it was called in those days, were Leonardo da Vinci and Albrecht Dürer. Leonardo's late 15th century descriptions of the interplay of light and shade (chiaroscuro), umbra and penumbra regions of shadows, and aerial perspective are still worth reading in translation (Kemp, 1989). Stork (2004) analyzes the creation of various pieces of Renaissance art using computer vision techniques.

Although perspective was known to the ancient Greeks, they were curiously confused by the role of the eyes in vision. Aristotle thought of the eyes as devices emitting rays, rather in the manner of modern laser range finders. This mistaken view was laid to rest by the work of Arab scientists, such as Abu Ali Alhazen, in the 10th century. Alhazen also developed the *camera obscura*, a room (*camera* is Latin for "room" or "chamber") with a pinhole that casts an image on the opposite wall. Of course the image was inverted, which caused no end of confusion. If the eye was to be thought of as such an imaging device, how do we see right-side up? This enigma exercised the greatest minds of the era (including Leonardo). Kepler first proposed that the lens of the eye focuses an image on the retina, and Descartes surgically removed an ox eye and demonstrated that Kepler was right. There was still puzzlement as to why we do not see everything upside down; today we realize it is just a question of accessing the retinal data structure in the right way.

In the first half of the 20th century, the most significant research results in vision were obtained by the Gestalt school of psychology, led by Max Wertheimer. They pointed out the importance of perceptual organization: for a human observer, the image is not a collection of pointillist photoreceptor outputs (pixels in computer vision terminology); rather it is organized into coherent groups. One could trace the motivation in computer vision of finding regions and curves back to this insight. The Gestaltists also drew attention to the "figure–ground" phenomenon—a contour separating two image regions that, in the world, are at different depths, appears to belong only to the nearer region, the "figure," and not the farther region, the "ground." The computer vision problem of classifying image curves according to their significance in the scene can be thought of as a generalization of this insight.

The period after World War II was marked by renewed activity. Most significant was the work of J. J. Gibson (1950, 1979), who pointed out the importance of optical flow, as well as texture gradients in the estimation of environmental variables such as surface slant and tilt. He reemphasized the importance of the stimulus and how rich it was. Gibson emphasized the role of the active observer whose self-directed movement facilitates the pickup of information about the external environment.

Computer vision was founded in the 1960s. Roberts's (1963) thesis at MIT was one of the earliest publications in the field, introducing key ideas such as edge detection and model-based matching. There is an urban legend that Marvin Minsky assigned the problem of "solving" computer vision to a graduate student as a summer project. According to Minsky the legend is untrue—it was actually an undergraduate student. But it was an exceptional undergraduate, Gerald Jay Sussman (who is now a professor at MIT) and the task was not to "solve" vision, but to investigate some aspects of it.

In the 1960s and 1970s, progress was slow, hampered considerably by the lack of computational and storage resources. Low-level visual processing received a lot of attention. The widely used Canny edge-detection technique was introduced in Canny (1986). Techniques for finding texture boundaries based on multiscale, multiorientation filtering of images date to work such as Malik and Perona (1990). Combining multiple clues—brightness, texture and color—for finding boundary curves in a learning framework was shown by Martin, Fowlkes and Malik (2004) to considerably improve performance.

The closely related problem of finding regions of coherent brightness, color, and texture, naturally lends itself to formulations in which finding the best partition becomes an optimization problem. Three leading examples are the Markov Random Fields approach of Geman and Geman (1984), the variational formulation of Mumford and Shah (1989), and normalized cuts by Shi and Malik (2000).

Through much of the 1960s, 1970s and 1980s, there were two distinct paradigms in which visual recognition was pursued, dictated by different perspectives on what was perceived to be the primary problem. Computer vision research on object recognition largely focused on issues arising from the projection of three-dimensional objects onto two-dimensional images. The idea of alignment, also first introduced by Roberts, resurfaced in the 1980s in the work of Lowe (1987) and Huttenlocher and Ullman (1990). Also popular was an approach based on describing shapes in terms of volumetric primitives, with **generalized cylinders**, introduced by Tom Binford (1971), proving particularly popular.

GENERALIZED CYLINDER

In contrast, the pattern recognition community viewed the 3D-to-2D aspects of the problem as not significant. Their motivating examples were in domains such as optical character recognition and handwritten zip code recognition where the primary concern is that of learning the typical variations characteristic of a class of objects and separating them from other classes. See LeCun *et al.* (1995) for a comparison of approaches.

In the late 1990s, these two paradigms started to converge, as both sides adopted the probabilistic modeling and learning techniques that were becoming popular throughout AI. Two lines of work contributed significantly. One was research on face detection, such as that of Rowley, Baluja and Kanade (1996), and of Viola and Jones (2002b) which demonstrated the power of pattern recognition techniques on clearly important and useful tasks. The other was the development of point descriptors, which enable one to construct feature vectors from parts of objects. This was pioneered by Schmid and Mohr (1996). Lowe's (2004) SIFT descriptor is widely used. The HOG descriptor is due to Dalal and Triggs (2005).

Ullman (1979) and Longuet-Higgins (1981) are influential early works in reconstruction from multiple images. Concerns about the stability of structure from motion were significantly allayed by the work of Tomasi and Kanade (1992) who showed that with the use of multiple frames shape could be recovered quite accurately. In the 1990s, with great increase in computer speed and storage, motion analysis found many new applications. Building geometrical models of real-world scenes for rendering by computer graphics techniques proved particularly popular, led by reconstruction algorithms such as the one developed by Debevec, Taylor, and Malik (1996). The books by Hartley and Zisserman (2000) and Faugeras *et al.* (2001) provide a comprehensive treatment of the geometry of multiple views.

For single images, inferring shape from shading was first studied by Horn (1970), and Horn and Brooks (1989) present an extensive survey of the main papers from a period when this was a much-studied problem. Gibson (1950) was the first to propose texture gradients as a cue to shape, though a comprehensive analysis for curved surfaces first appears in Garding (1992) and Malik and Rosenholtz (1997). The mathematics of occluding contours, and more generally understanding the visual events in the projection of smooth curved objects, owes much to the work of Koenderink and van Doorn, which finds an extensive treatment in Koenderink's (1990) *Solid Shape*. In recent years, attention has turned to treating the problem of shape and surface recovery from a single image as a probabilistic inference problem, where geometrical cues are not modeled explicitly, but used implicitly in a learning framework. A good representative is the work of Hoiem, Efros, and Hebert (2008).

For the reader interested in human vision, Palmer (1999) provides the best comprehensive treatment; Bruce *et al.* (2003) is a shorter textbook. The books by Hubel (1988) and Rock (1984) are friendly introductions centered on neurophysiology and perception respectively. David Marr's book *Vision* (Marr, 1982) played a historical role in connecting computer vision to psychophysics and neurobiology. While many of his specific models haven't stood the test of time, the theoretical perspective from which each task is analyzed at an informational, computational, and implementation level is still illuminating.

For computer vision, the most comprehensive textbook is Forsyth and Ponce (2002). Trucco and Verri (1998) is a shorter account. Horn (1986) and Faugeras (1993) are two older and still useful textbooks.

The main journals for computer vision are IEEE *Transactions on Pattern Analysis and Machine Intelligence* and *International Journal of Computer Vision*. Computer vision conferences include ICCV (International Conference on Computer Vision), CVPR (Computer Vision and Pattern Recognition), and ECCV (European Conference on Computer Vision). Research with a machine learning component is also published in the NIPS (Neural Information Processing Systems) conference, and work on the interface with computer graphics often appears at the ACM SIGGRAPH (Special Interest Group in Graphics) conference.

Exercises

1 In the shadow of a tree with a dense, leafy canopy, one sees a number of light spots. Surprisingly, they all appear to be circular. Why? After all, the gaps between the leaves through which the sun shines are not likely to be circular.

2 Consider a picture of a white sphere floating in front of a black backdrop. The image curve separating white pixels from black pixels is sometimes called the "outline" of the sphere. Show that the outline of a sphere, viewed in a perspective camera, can be an ellipse. Why do spheres not look like ellipses to you?

3 Consider an infinitely long cylinder of radius r oriented with its axis along the y-axis. The cylinder has a Lambertian surface and is viewed by a camera along the positive z-axis. What will you expect to see in the image if the cylinder is illuminated by a point source at infinity located on the positive x-axis? Draw the contours of constant brightness in the projected image. Are the contours of equal brightness uniformly spaced?

4 Edges in an image can correspond to a variety of events in a scene. Consider Figure 4, and assume that it is a picture of a real three-dimensional scene. Identify ten different brightness edges in the image, and for each, state whether it corresponds to a discontinuity in (a) depth, (b) surface orientation, (c) reflectance, or (d) illumination.

5 A stereoscopic system is being contemplated for terrain mapping. It will consist of two CCD cameras, each having 512×512 pixels on a 10 cm $\times$ 10 cm square sensor. The lenses to be used have a focal length of 16 cm, with the focus fixed at infinity. For corresponding points (u_1, v_1) in the left image and (u_2, v_2) in the right image, $v_1 = v_2$ because the x-axes in the two image planes are parallel to the epipolar lines—the lines from the object to the camera. The optical axes of the two cameras are parallel. The baseline between the cameras is 1 meter.

- **a.** If the nearest distance to be measured is 16 meters, what is the largest disparity that will occur (in pixels)?
- **b.** What is the distance resolution at 16 meters, due to the pixel spacing?
- **c.** What distance corresponds to a disparity of one pixel?

6 Which of the following are true, and which are false?

- **a.** Finding corresponding points in stereo images is the easiest phase of the stereo depth-finding process.
- **b.** Shape-from-texture can be done by projecting a grid of light-stripes onto the scene.
- **c.** Lines with equal lengths in the scene always project to equal lengths in the image.
- **d.** Straight lines in the image necessarily correspond to straight lines in the scene.

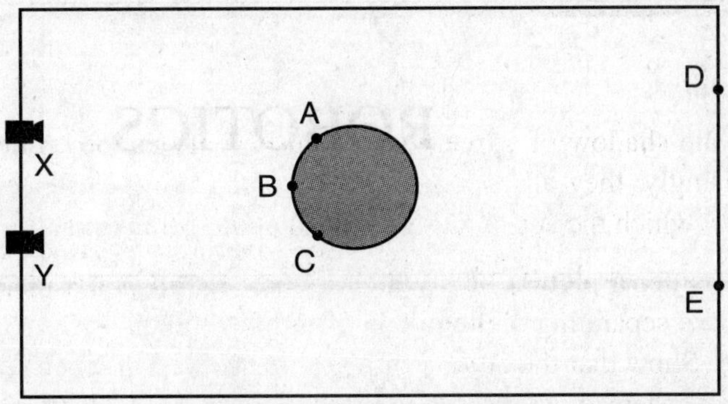

Figure 27 Top view of a two-camera vision system observing a bottle with a wall behind it.

7 (Courtesy of Pietro Perona.) Figure 27 shows two cameras at X and Y observing a scene. Draw the image seen at each camera, assuming that all named points are in the same horizontal plane. What can be concluded from these two images about the relative distances of points A, B, C, D, and E from the camera baseline, and on what basis?

ROBOTICS

In which agents are endowed with physical effectors with which to do mischief.

1 INTRODUCTION

ROBOT
EFFECTOR
SENSOR

Robots are physical agents that perform tasks by manipulating the physical world. To do so, they are equipped with **effectors** such as legs, wheels, joints, and grippers. Effectors have a single purpose: to assert physical forces on the environment.[1] Robots are also equipped with **sensors**, which allow them to perceive their environment. Present day robotics employs a diverse set of sensors, including cameras and lasers to measure the environment, and gyroscopes and accelerometers to measure the robot's own motion.

MANIPULATOR

Most of today's robots fall into one of three primary categories. **Manipulators**, or robot arms (Figure 1(a)), are physically anchored to their workplace, for example in a factory assembly line or on the International Space Station. Manipulator motion usually involves a chain of controllable joints, enabling such robots to place their effectors in any position within the workplace. Manipulators are by far the most common type of industrial robots, with approximately one million units installed worldwide. Some mobile manipulators are used in hospitals to assist surgeons. Few car manufacturers could survive without robotic manipulators, and some manipulators have even been used to generate original artwork.

MOBILE ROBOT
UGV
PLANETARY ROVER
UAV

The second category is the **mobile robot**. Mobile robots move about their environment using wheels, legs, or similar mechanisms. They have been put to use delivering food in hospitals, moving containers at loading docks, and similar tasks. **Unmanned ground vehicles**, or UGVs, drive autonomously on streets, highways, and off-road. The **planetary rover** shown in Figure 2(b) explored Mars for a period of 3 months in 1997. Subsequent NASA robots include the twin Mars Exploration Rovers (one is depicted on the cover of this book), which landed in 2003 and were still operating six years later. Other types of mobile robots include **unmanned air vehicles** (UAVs), commonly used for surveillance, crop-spraying, and

[1] Here we distinguish the effector (the physical device) from the actuator (the control line that communicates a command to the effector).

From Chapter 25 of *Artificial Intelligence: A Modern Approach*, Third Edition. Stuart Russell and Peter Norvig.

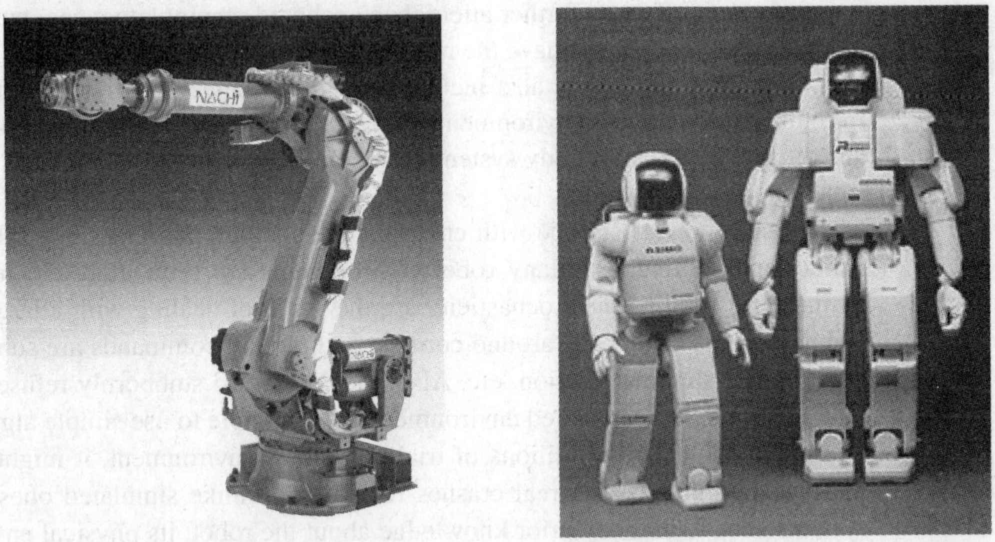

(a) (b)

Figure 1 (a) An industrial robotic manipulator for stacking bags on a pallet. Image courtesy of Nachi Robotic Systems. (b) Honda's P3 and Asimo humanoid robots.

(a) (b)

Figure 2 (a) Predator, an unmanned aerial vehicle (UAV) used by the U.S. Military. Image courtesy of General Atomics Aeronautical Systems. (b) NASA's Sojourner, a mobile robot that explored the surface of Mars in July 1997.

AUV military operations. Figure 2(a) shows a UAV commonly used by the U.S. military. **Autonomous underwater vehicles** (AUVs) are used in deep sea exploration. Mobile robots deliver packages in the workplace and vacuum the floors at home.

MOBILE MANIPULATOR HUMANOID ROBOT The third type of robot combines mobility with manipulation, and is often called a **mobile manipulator**. **Humanoid robots** mimic the human torso. Figure 1(b) shows two early humanoid robots, both manufactured by Honda Corp. in Japan. Mobile manipulators can apply their effectors further afield than anchored manipulators can, but their task is made harder because they don't have the rigidity that the anchor provides.

The field of robotics also includes prosthetic devices (artificial limbs, ears, and eyes for humans), intelligent environments (such as an entire house that is equipped with sensors and effectors), and multibody systems, wherein robotic action is achieved through swarms of small cooperating robots.

Real robots must cope with environments that are partially observable, stochastic, dynamic, and continuous. Many robot environments are sequential and multiagent as well. Partial observability and stochasticity are the result of dealing with a large, complex world. Robot cameras cannot see around corners, and motion commands are subject to uncertainty due to gears slipping, friction, etc. Also, the real world stubbornly refuses to operate faster than real time. In a simulated environment, it is possible to use simple algorithms to learn in a few CPU hours from millions of trials. In a real environment, it might take years to run these trials. Furthermore, real crashes really hurt, unlike simulated ones. Practical robotic systems need to embody prior knowledge about the robot, its physical environment, and the tasks that the robot will perform so that the robot can learn quickly and perform safely.

Robotics brings together many concepts of artificial intelligence, including probabilistic state estimation, perception, planning, unsupervised learning, and reinforcement learning. For some of these concepts robotics serves as a challenging example application. For other concepts this chapter breaks new ground in introducing the continuous version of techniques that we previously saw only in the discrete case.

2 Robot Hardware

Up to this point, you have probably taken the agent architecture—sensors, effectors, and processors— as given, and concentrated on the agent program. The success of real robots depends at least as much on the design of sensors and effectors that are appropriate for the task.

2.1 Sensors

PASSIVE SENSOR

ACTIVE SENSOR

Sensors are the perceptual interface between robot and environment. **Passive sensors**, such as cameras, are true observers of the environment: they capture signals that are generated by other sources in the environment. **Active sensors**, such as sonar, send energy into the environment. They rely on the fact that this energy is reflected back to the sensor. Active sensors tend to provide more information than passive sensors, but at the expense of increased power consumption and with a danger of interference when multiple active sensors are used at the same time. Whether active or passive, sensors can be divided into three types, depending on whether they sense the environment, the robot's location, or the robot's internal configuration.

RANGE FINDER

SONAR SENSORS

Range finders are sensors that measure the distance to nearby objects. In the early days of robotics, robots were commonly equipped with **sonar sensors**. Sonar sensors emit directional sound waves, which are reflected by objects, with some of the sound making it

(a)

(b)

Figure 3 (a) Time of flight camera; image courtesy of Mesa Imaging GmbH. (b) 3D range image obtained with this camera. The range image makes it possible to detect obstacles and objects in a robot's vicinity.

back into the sensor. The time and intensity of the returning signal indicates the distance to nearby objects. Sonar is the technology of choice for autonomous underwater vehicles.

STEREO VISION

Stereo vision relies on multiple cameras to image the environment from slightly different viewpoints, analyzing the resulting parallax in these images to compute the range of surrounding objects. For mobile ground robots, sonar and stereo vision are now rarely used, because they are not reliably accurate.

Most ground robots are now equipped with optical range finders. Just like sonar sensors, optical range sensors emit active signals (light) and measure the time until a reflection of this

TIME OF FLIGHT CAMERA

signal arrives back at the sensor. Figure 3(a) shows a **time of flight camera**. This camera acquires range images like the one shown in Figure 3(b) at up to 60 frames per second. Other range sensors use laser beams and special 1-pixel cameras that can be directed using complex arrangements of mirrors or rotating elements. These sensors are called **scanning**

SCANNING LIDARS

lidars (short for *light detection and ranging*). Scanning lidars tend to provide longer ranges than time of flight cameras, and tend to perform better in bright daylight.

Other common range sensors include radar, which is often the sensor of choice for UAVs. Radar sensors can measure distances of multiple kilometers. On the other extreme

TACTILE SENSORS

end of range sensing are **tactile sensors** such as whiskers, bump panels, and touch-sensitive skin. These sensors measure range based on physical contact, and can be deployed only for sensing objects very close to the robot.

LOCATION SENSORS

A second important class of sensors is **location sensors**. Most location sensors use range sensing as a primary component to determine location. Outdoors, the **Global Position-**

GLOBAL POSITIONING SYSTEM

ing System (GPS) is the most common solution to the localization problem. GPS measures the distance to satellites that emit pulsed signals. At present, there are 31 satellites in orbit, transmitting signals on multiple frequencies. GPS receivers can recover the distance to these satellites by analyzing phase shifts. By triangulating signals from multiple satellites, GPS receivers can determine their absolute location on Earth to within a few meters. **Differential GPS** involves a second ground receiver with known location, providing millimeter accuracy under ideal conditions. Unfortunately, GPS does not work indoors or underwater. Indoors, localization is often achieved by attaching beacons in the environment at known locations. Many indoor environments are full of wireless base stations, which can help robots localize through the analysis of the wireless signal. Underwater, active sonar beacons can provide a sense of location, using sound to inform AUVs of their relative distances to those beacons.

DIFFERENTIAL GPS

PROPRIOCEPTIVE SENSOR

SHAFT DECODER

ODOMETRY

INERTIAL SENSOR

The third important class is **proprioceptive sensors**, which inform the robot of its own motion. To measure the exact configuration of a robotic joint, motors are often equipped with **shaft decoders** that count the revolution of motors in small increments. On robot arms, shaft decoders can provide accurate information over any period of time. On mobile robots, shaft decoders that report wheel revolutions can be used for **odometry**—the measurement of distance traveled. Unfortunately, wheels tend to drift and slip, so odometry is accurate only over short distances. External forces, such as the current for AUVs and the wind for UAVs, increase positional uncertainty. **Inertial sensors**, such as gyroscopes, rely on the resistance of mass to the change of velocity. They can help reduce uncertainty.

FORCE SENSOR

TORQUE SENSOR

Other important aspects of robot state are measured by **force sensors** and **torque sensors**. These are indispensable when robots handle fragile objects or objects whose exact shape and location is unknown. Imagine a one-ton robotic manipulator screwing in a light bulb. It would be all too easy to apply too much force and break the bulb. Force sensors allow the robot to sense how hard it is gripping the bulb, and torque sensors allow it to sense how hard it is turning. Good sensors can measure forces in all three translational and three rotational directions. They do this at a frequency of several hundred times a second, so that a robot can quickly detect unexpected forces and correct its actions before it breaks a light bulb.

2.2 Effectors

DEGREE OF FREEDOM

Effectors are the means by which robots move and change the shape of their bodies. To understand the design of effectors, it will help to talk about motion and shape in the abstract, using the concept of a **degree of freedom** (DOF) We count one degree of freedom for each independent direction in which a robot, or one of its effectors, can move. For example, a rigid mobile robot such as an AUV has six degrees of freedom, three for its (x, y, z) location in space and three for its angular orientation, known as *yaw*, *roll*, and *pitch*. These six degrees define the **kinematic state**[2] or **pose** of the robot. The **dynamic state** of a robot includes these six plus an additional six dimensions for the rate of change of each kinematic dimension, that is, their velocities.

KINEMATIC STATE

POSE

DYNAMIC STATE

For nonrigid bodies, there are additional degrees of freedom within the robot itself. For example, the elbow of a human arm possesses two degree of freedom. It can flex the upper arm towards or away, and can rotate right or left. The wrist has three degrees of freedom. It can move up and down, side to side, and can also rotate. Robot joints also have one, two, or three degrees of freedom each. Six degrees of freedom are required to place an object, such as a hand, at a particular point in a particular orientation. The arm in Figure 4(a)

[2] "Kinematic" is from the Greek word for *motion*, as is "cinema."

REVOLUTE JOINT
PRISMATIC JOINT

has exactly six degrees of freedom, created by five **revolute joints** that generate rotational motion and one **prismatic joint** that generates sliding motion. You can verify that the human arm as a whole has more than six degrees of freedom by a simple experiment: put your hand on the table and notice that you still have the freedom to rotate your elbow without changing the configuration of your hand. Manipulators that have extra degrees of freedom are easier to control than robots with only the minimum number of DOFs. Many industrial manipulators therefore have seven DOFs, not six.

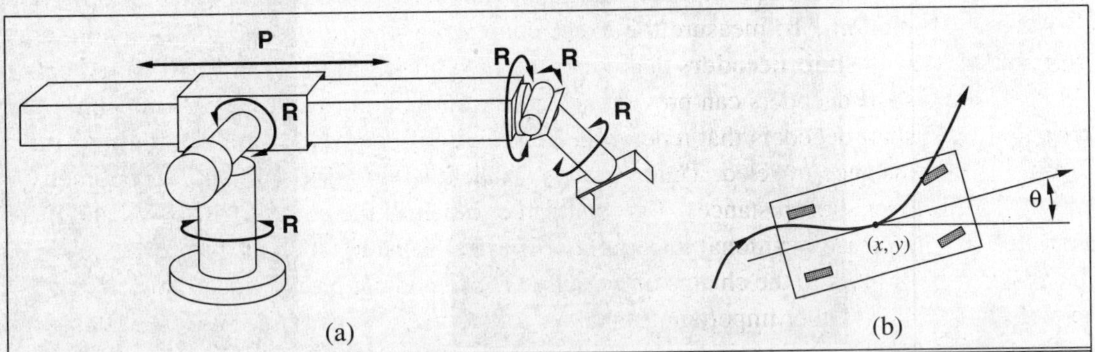

Figure 4 (a) The Stanford Manipulator, an early robot arm with five revolute joints (R) and one prismatic joint (P), for a total of six degrees of freedom. (b) Motion of a nonholonomic four-wheeled vehicle with front-wheel steering.

For mobile robots, the DOFs are not necessarily the same as the number of actuated elements. Consider, for example, your average car: it can move forward or backward, and it can turn, giving it two DOFs. In contrast, a car's kinematic configuration is three-dimensional: on an open flat surface, one can easily maneuver a car to any (x, y) point, in any orientation. (See Figure 4(b).) Thus, the car has three **effective degrees of freedom** but two **controllable degrees of freedom**. We say a robot is **nonholonomic** if it has more effective DOFs than controllable DOFs and **holonomic** if the two numbers are the same. Holonomic robots are easier to control—it would be much easier to park a car that could move sideways as well as forward and backward—but holonomic robots are also mechanically more complex. Most robot arms are holonomic, and most mobile robots are nonholonomic.

EFFECTIVE DOF
CONTROLLABLE DOF
NONHOLONOMIC

Mobile robots have a range of mechanisms for locomotion, including wheels, tracks, and legs. **Differential drive** robots possess two independently actuated wheels (or tracks), one on each side, as on a military tank. If both wheels move at the same velocity, the robot moves on a straight line. If they move in opposite directions, the robot turns on the spot. An alternative is the **synchro drive**, in which each wheel can move and turn around its own axis. To avoid chaos, the wheels are tightly coordinated. When moving straight, for example, all wheels point in the same direction and move at the same speed. Both differential and synchro drives are nonholonomic. Some more expensive robots use holonomic drives, which have three or more wheels that can be oriented and moved independently.

DIFFERENTIAL DRIVE
SYNCHRO DRIVE

Some mobile robots possess arms. Figure 5(a) displays a two-armed robot. This robot's arms use springs to compensate for gravity, and they provide minimal resistance to

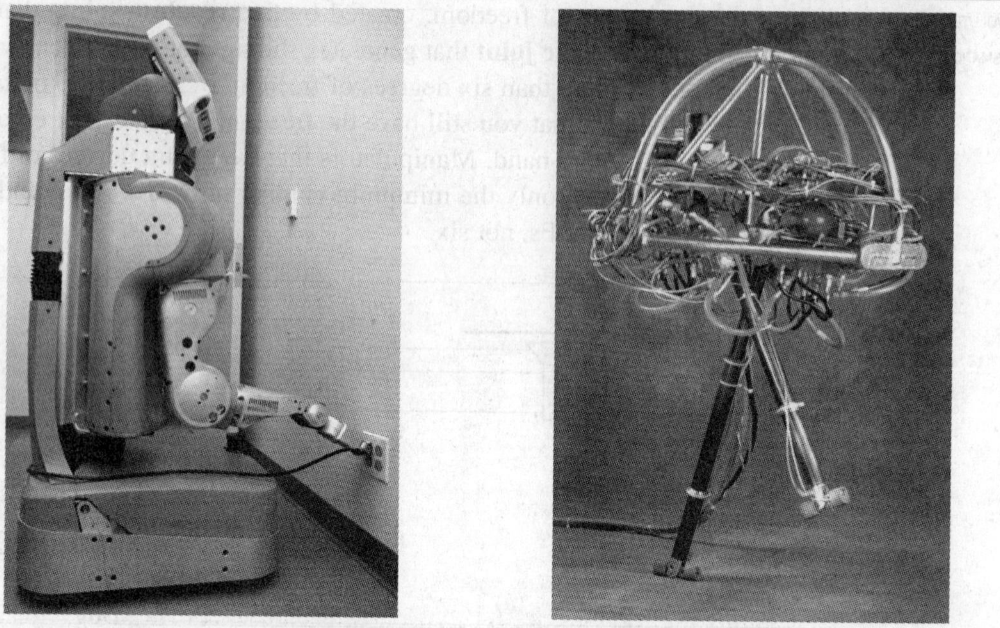

(a) (b)

Figure 5 (a) Mobile manipulator plugging its charge cable into a wall outlet. Image courtesy of Willow Garage, © 2009. (b) One of Marc Raibert's legged robots in motion.

external forces. Such a design minimizes the physical danger to people who might stumble into such a robot. This is a key consideration in deploying robots in domestic environments.

Legs, unlike wheels, can handle rough terrain. However, legs are notoriously slow on flat surfaces, and they are mechanically difficult to build. Robotics researchers have tried designs ranging from one leg up to dozens of legs. Legged robots have been made to walk, run, and even hop—as we see with the legged robot in Figure 5(b). This robot is **dynamically stable**, meaning that it can remain upright while hopping around. A robot that can remain upright without moving its legs is called **statically stable**. A robot is statically stable if its center of gravity is above the polygon spanned by its legs. The quadruped (four-legged) robot shown in Figure 6(a) may appear statically stable. However, it walks by lifting multiple legs at the same time, which renders it dynamically stable. The robot can walk on snow and ice, and it will not fall over even if you kick it (as demonstrated in videos available online). Two-legged robots such as those in Figure 6(b) are dynamically stable.

DYNAMICALLY STABLE

STATICALLY STABLE

Other methods of movement are possible: air vehicles use propellers or turbines; underwater vehicles use propellers or thrusters, similar to those used on submarines. Robotic blimps rely on thermal effects to keep themselves aloft.

Sensors and effectors alone do not make a robot. A complete robot also needs a source of power to drive its effectors. The **electric motor** is the most popular mechanism for both manipulator actuation and locomotion, but **pneumatic actuation** using compressed gas and **hydraulic actuation** using pressurized fluids also have their application niches.

ELECTRIC MOTOR

PNEUMATIC ACTUATION

HYDRAULIC ACTUATION

(a) (b)

Figure 6 (a) Four-legged dynamically-stable robot "Big Dog." Image courtesy Boston Dynamics, © 2009. (b) 2009 RoboCup Standard Platform League competition, showing the winning team, B-Human, from the DFKI center at the University of Bremen. Throughout the match, B-Human outscored their opponents 64:1. Their success was built on probabilistic state estimation using particle filters and Kalman filters; on machine-learning models for gait optimization; and on dynamic kicking moves. Image courtesy DFKI, © 2009.

3 Robotic Perception

Perception is the process by which robots map sensor measurements into internal representations of the environment. Perception is difficult because sensors are noisy, and the environment is partially observable, unpredictable, and often dynamic. In other words, robots have all the problems of **state estimation** (or **filtering**). As a rule of thumb, good internal representations for robots have three properties: they contain enough information for the robot to make good decisions, they are structured so that they can be updated efficiently, and they are natural in the sense that internal variables correspond to natural state variables in the physical world.

Kalman filters, HMMs, and dynamic Bayes nets can represent the transition and sensor models of a partially observable environment, and there exist both exact and approximate algorithms for updating the **belief state**—the posterior probability distribution over the environment state variables. For robotics problems, we include the robot's own past actions as observed variables in the model. Figure 7 shows the notation used in this chapter: $\mathbf{X}_t$ is the state of the environment (including the robot) at time t, $\mathbf{Z}_t$ is the observation received at time t, and A_t is the action taken after the observation is received.

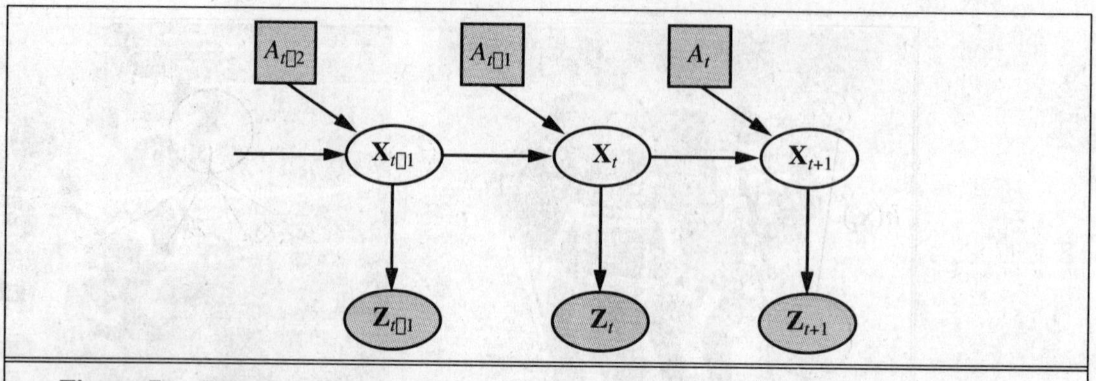

Figure 7 Robot perception can be viewed as temporal inference from sequences of actions and measurements, as illustrated by this dynamic Bayes network.

We would like to compute the new belief state, $\mathbf{P}(\mathbf{X}_{t+1} \mid \mathbf{z}_{1:t+1}, a_{1:t})$, from the current belief state $\mathbf{P}(\mathbf{X}_t \mid \mathbf{z}_{1:t}, a_{1:t-1})$ and the new observation $\mathbf{z}_{t+1}$. We condition explicitly on the actions as well as the observations, and we deal with *continuous* rather than *discrete* variables. Thus, we modify the recursive filtering equation to use integration rather than summation:

$$\mathbf{P}(\mathbf{X}_{t+1} \mid \mathbf{z}_{1:t+1}, a_{1:t}) = \alpha \mathbf{P}(\mathbf{z}_{t+1} \mid \mathbf{X}_{t+1}) \int \mathbf{P}(\mathbf{X}_{t+1} \mid \mathbf{x}_t, a_t)\, P(\mathbf{x}_t \mid \mathbf{z}_{1:t}, a_{1:t-1})\, d\mathbf{x}_t\,. \quad (1)$$

This equation states that the posterior over the state variables $\mathbf{X}$ at time $t+1$ is calculated recursively from the corresponding estimate one time step earlier. This calculation involves the previous action a_t and the current sensor measurement $\mathbf{z}_{t+1}$. For example, if our goal is to develop a soccer-playing robot, $\mathbf{X}_{t+1}$ might be the location of the soccer ball relative to the robot. The posterior $\mathbf{P}(\mathbf{X}_t \mid \mathbf{z}_{1:t}, a_{1:t-1})$ is a probability distribution over all states that captures what we know from past sensor measurements and controls. Equation (1) tells us how to recursively estimate this location, by incrementally folding in sensor measurements (e.g., camera images) and robot motion commands. The probability $\mathbf{P}(\mathbf{X}_{t+1} \mid \mathbf{x}_t, a_t)$ is called the **transition model** or **motion model**, and $\mathbf{P}(\mathbf{z}_{t+1} \mid \mathbf{X}_{t+1})$ is the **sensor model**.

MOTION MODEL

3.1 Localization and mapping

LOCALIZATION

Localization is the problem of finding out where things are—including the robot itself. Knowledge about where things are is at the core of any successful physical interaction with the environment. For example, robot manipulators must know the location of objects they seek to manipulate; navigating robots must know where they are to find their way around.

To keep things simple, let us consider a mobile robot that moves slowly in a flat 2D world. Let us also assume the robot is given an exact map of the environment. (An example of such a map appears in Figure 10.) The pose of such a mobile robot is defined by its two Cartesian coordinates with values x and y and its heading with value θ, as illustrated in Figure 8(a). If we arrange those three values in a vector, then any particular state is given by $\mathbf{X}_t = (x_t, y_t, \theta_t)^\top$. So far so good.

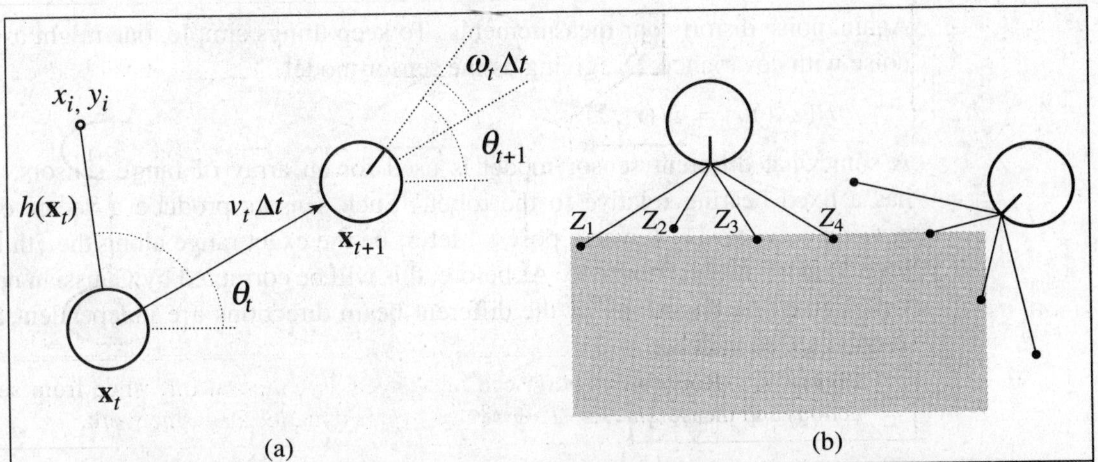

Figure 8 (a) A simplified kinematic model of a mobile robot. The robot is shown as a circle with an interior line marking the forward direction. The state $\mathbf{x}_t$ consists of the (x_t, y_t) position (shown implicitly) and the orientation θ_t. The new state $\mathbf{x}_{t+1}$ is obtained by an update in position of $v_t \Delta_t$ and in orientation of $\omega_t \Delta_t$. Also shown is a landmark at (x_i, y_i) observed at time t. (b) The range-scan sensor model. Two possible robot poses are shown for a given range scan (z_1, z_2, z_3, z_4). It is much more likely that the pose on the left generated the range scan than the pose on the right.

In the kinematic approximation, each action consists of the "instantaneous" specification of two velocities—a translational velocity v_t and a rotational velocity ω_t. For small time intervals Δt, a crude deterministic model of the motion of such robots is given by

$$\hat{\mathbf{X}}_{t+1} = f(\mathbf{X}_t, \underbrace{v_t, \omega_t}_{a_t}) = \mathbf{X}_t + \begin{pmatrix} v_t \Delta t \cos\theta_t \\ v_t \Delta t \sin\theta_t \\ \omega_t \Delta t \end{pmatrix} .$$

The notation $\hat{\mathbf{X}}$ refers to a deterministic state prediction. Of course, physical robots are somewhat unpredictable. This is commonly modeled by a Gaussian distribution with mean $f(\mathbf{X}_t, v_t, \omega_t)$ and covariance $\mathbf{\Sigma}_x$.

$$\mathbf{P}(\mathbf{X}_{t+1} \mid \mathbf{X}_t, v_t, \omega_t) = N(\hat{\mathbf{X}}_{t+1}, \mathbf{\Sigma}_x) .$$

This probability distribution is the robot's motion model. It models the effects of the motion a_t on the location of the robot.

Next, we need a sensor model. We will consider two kinds of sensor model. The first assumes that the sensors detect *stable*, *recognizable* features of the environment called

LANDMARK

landmarks. For each landmark, the range and bearing are reported. Suppose the robot's state is $\mathbf{x}_t = (x_t, y_t, \theta_t)^\top$ and it senses a landmark whose location is known to be $(x_i, y_i)^\top$. Without noise, the range and bearing can be calculated by simple geometry. (See Figure 8(a).) The exact prediction of the observed range and bearing would be

$$\hat{\mathbf{z}}_t = h(\mathbf{x}_t) = \begin{pmatrix} \sqrt{(x_t - x_i)^2 + (y_t - y_i)^2} \\ \arctan \frac{y_i - y_t}{x_i - x_t} - \theta_t \end{pmatrix} .$$

Again, noise distorts our measurements. To keep things simple, one might assume Gaussian noise with covariance $\mathbf{\Sigma}_z$, giving us the sensor model

$$P(\mathbf{z}_t \mid \mathbf{x}_t) = N(\hat{\mathbf{z}}_t, \mathbf{\Sigma}_z) .$$

A somewhat different sensor model is used for an array of range sensors, each of which has a fixed bearing relative to the robot. Such sensors produce a vector of range values $\mathbf{z}_t = (z_1, \ldots, z_M)^\top$. Given a pose $\mathbf{x}_t$, let $\hat{z}_j$ be the exact range along the jth beam direction from $\mathbf{x}_t$ to the nearest obstacle. As before, this will be corrupted by Gaussian noise. Typically, we assume that the errors for the different beam directions are independent and identically distributed, so we have

$$P(\mathbf{z}_t \mid \mathbf{x}_t) = \alpha \prod_{j=1}^{M} e^{-(z_j - \hat{z}_j)/2\sigma^2} .$$

Figure 8(b) shows an example of a four-beam range scan and two possible robot poses, one of which is reasonably likely to have produced the observed scan and one of which is not. Comparing the range-scan model to the landmark model, we see that the range-scan model has the advantage that there is no need to *identify* a landmark before the range scan can be interpreted; indeed, in Figure 8(b), the robot faces a featureless wall. On the other hand, if there *are* visible, identifiable landmarks, they may provide instant localization.

The Kalman filter represents the belief state as a single multivariate Gaussian and the particle filter represents the belief state by a collection of particles that correspond to states. Most modern localization algorithms use one of two representations of the robot's belief $\mathbf{P}(\mathbf{X}_t \mid \mathbf{z}_{1:t}, a_{1:t-1})$.

MONTE CARLO LOCALIZATION

Localization using particle filtering is called **Monte Carlo localization**, or MCL. The MCL algorithm is an instance of the particle-filtering algorithm, which you may be familiar with. All we need to do is supply the appropriate motion model and sensor model. Figure 9 shows one version using the range-scan model. The operation of the algorithm is illustrated in Figure 10 as the robot finds out where it is inside an office building. In the first image, the particles are uniformly distributed based on the prior, indicating global uncertainty about the robot's position. In the second image, the first set of measurements arrives and the particles form clusters in the areas of high posterior belief. In the third, enough measurements are available to push all the particles to a single location.

The Kalman filter is the other major way to localize. A Kalman filter represents the posterior $\mathbf{P}(\mathbf{X}_t \mid \mathbf{z}_{1:t}, a_{1:t-1})$ by a Gaussian. The mean of this Gaussian will be denoted $\boldsymbol{\mu}_t$ and its covariance $\mathbf{\Sigma}_t$. The main problem with Gaussian beliefs is that they are only closed under linear motion models f and linear measurement models h. For nonlinear f or h, the result of updating a filter is in general not Gaussian. Thus, localization algorithms using the Kalman filter **linearize** the motion and sensor models. Linearization is a local approximation of a nonlinear function by a linear function. Figure 11 illustrates the concept of linearization for a (one-dimensional) robot motion model. On the left, it depicts a nonlinear motion model $f(\mathbf{x}_t, a_t)$ (the control a_t is omitted in this graph since it plays no role in the linearization). On the right, this function is approximated by a linear function $\tilde{f}(\mathbf{x}_t, a_t)$. This linear function is tangent to f at the point $\boldsymbol{\mu}_t$, the mean of our state estimate at time t. Such a linearization

LINEARIZATION

```
function MONTE-CARLO-LOCALIZATION(a, z, N, P(X'|X, v, ω), P(z|z*), m) returns
a set of samples for the next time step
  inputs: a, robot velocities v and ω
          z, range scan z_1, ..., z_M
          P(X'|X, v, ω), motion model
          P(z|z*), range sensor noise model
          m, 2D map of the environment
  persistent: S, a vector of samples of size N
  local variables: W, a vector of weights of size N
                   S', a temporary vector of particles of size N
                   W', a vector of weights of size N

  if S is empty then        /* initialization phase */
     for i = 1 to N do
        S[i] ← sample from P(X_0)
     for i = 1 to N do   /* update cycle */
        S'[i] ← sample from P(X'|X = S[i], v, ω)
        W'[i] ← 1
        for j = 1 to M do
           z* ← RAYCAST(j, X = S'[i], m)
           W'[i] ← W'[i] · P(z_j| z*)
     S ← WEIGHTED-SAMPLE-WITH-REPLACEMENT(N,S',W')
  return S
```

Figure 9 A Monte Carlo localization algorithm using a range-scan sensor model with independent noise.

TAYLOR EXPANSION

is called (first degree) **Taylor expansion**. A Kalman filter that linearizes f and h via Taylor expansion is called an **extended Kalman filter** (or EKF). Figure 12 shows a sequence of estimates of a robot running an extended Kalman filter localization algorithm. As the robot moves, the uncertainty in its location estimate increases, as shown by the error ellipses. Its error decreases as it senses the range and bearing to a landmark with known location and increases again as the robot loses sight of the landmark. EKF algorithms work well if landmarks are easily identified. Otherwise, the posterior distribution may be multimodal, as in Figure 10(b). The problem of needing to know the identity of landmarks is an instance of the **data association** problem.

In some situations, no map of the environment is available. Then the robot will have to acquire a map. This is a bit of a chicken-and-egg problem: the navigating robot will have to determine its location relative to a map it doesn't quite know, at the same time building this map while it doesn't quite know its actual location. This problem is important for many robot applications, and it has been studied extensively under the name **simultaneous localization and mapping**, abbreviated as **SLAM**.

SIMULTANEOUS LOCALIZATION AND MAPPING

SLAM problems are solved using many different probabilistic techniques, including the extended Kalman filter discussed above. Using the EKF is straightforward: just augment

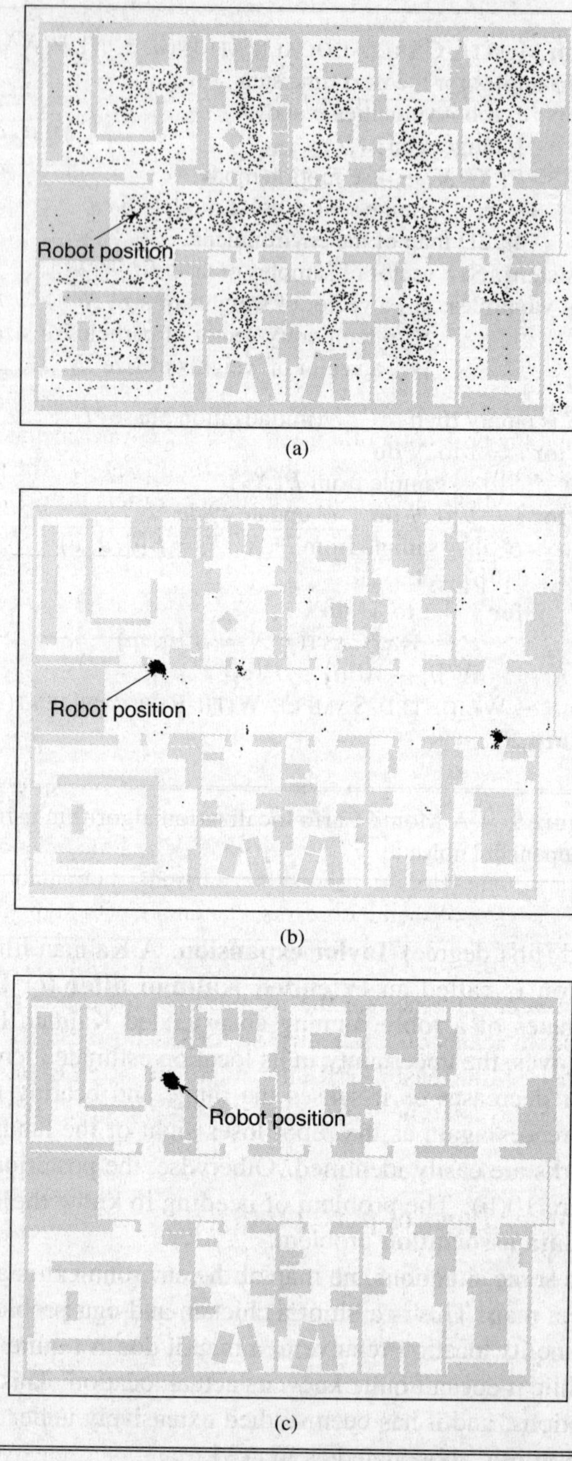

Figure 10 Monte Carlo localization, a particle filtering algorithm for mobile robot localization. (a) Initial, global uncertainty. (b) Approximately bimodal uncertainty after navigating in the (symmetric) corridor. (c) Unimodal uncertainty after entering a room and finding it to be distinctive.

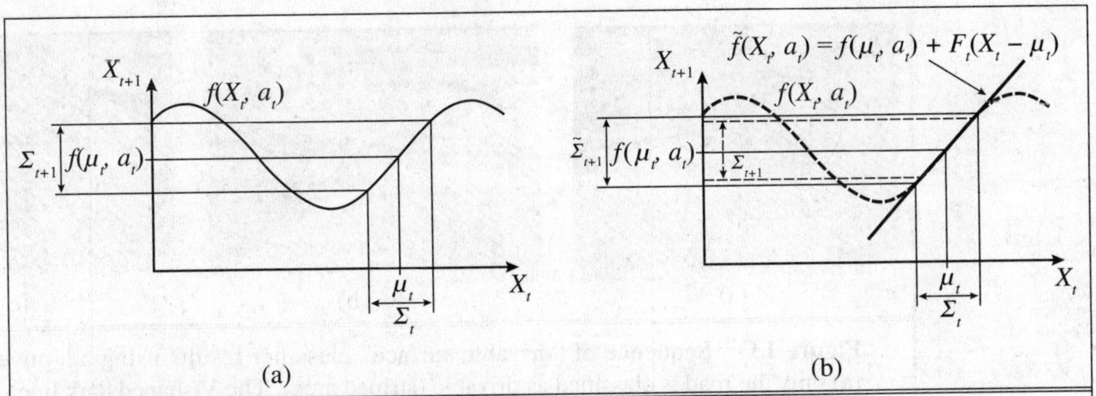

Figure 11 One-dimensional illustration of a linearized motion model: (a) The function f, and the projection of a mean $\boldsymbol{\mu}_t$ and a covariance interval (based on $\boldsymbol{\Sigma}_t$) into time $t+1$. (b) The linearized version is the tangent of f at $\boldsymbol{\mu}_t$. The projection of the mean $\boldsymbol{\mu}_t$ is correct. However, the projected covariance $\tilde{\boldsymbol{\Sigma}}_{t+1}$ differs from $\boldsymbol{\Sigma}_{t+1}$.

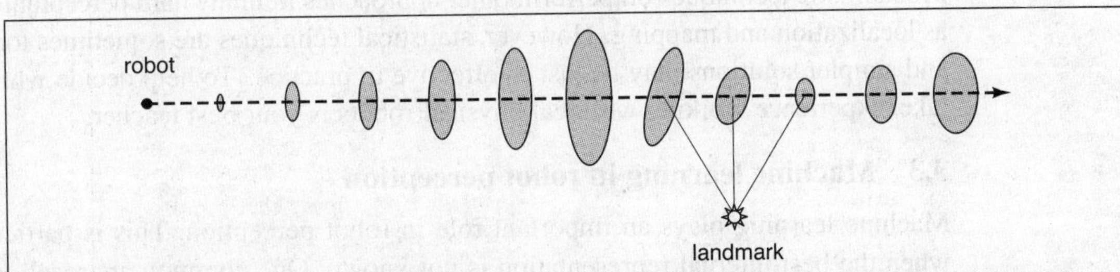

Figure 12 Example of localization using the extended Kalman filter. The robot moves on a straight line. As it progresses, its uncertainty increases gradually, as illustrated by the error ellipses. When it observes a landmark with known position, the uncertainty is reduced.

the state vector to include the locations of the landmarks in the environment. Luckily, the EKF update scales quadratically, so for small maps (e.g., a few hundred landmarks) the computation is quite feasible. Richer maps are often obtained using graph relaxation methods, similar to Bayesian network inference techniques. Expectation maximization is also used for SLAM.

3.2 Other types of perception

Not all of robot perception is about localization or mapping. Robots also perceive the temperature, odors, acoustic signals, and so on. Many of these quantities can be estimated using variants of dynamic Bayes networks. All that is required for such estimators are conditional probability distributions that characterize the evolution of state variables over time, and sensor models that describe the relation of measurements to state variables.

It is also possible to program a robot as a reactive agent, without explicitly reasoning about probability distributions over states. We cover that approach in Section 6.3.

The trend in robotics is clearly towards representations with well-defined semantics.

(a) (b) (c)

Figure 13 Sequence of "drivable surface" classifier results using adaptive vision. In (a) only the road is classified as drivable (striped area). The V-shaped dark line shows where the vehicle is heading. In (b) the vehicle is commanded to drive off the road, onto a grassy surface, and the classifier is beginning to classify some of the grass as drivable. In (c) the vehicle has updated its model of drivable surface to correspond to grass as well as road.

Probabilistic techniques outperform other approaches in many hard perceptual problems such as localization and mapping. However, statistical techniques are sometimes too cumbersome, and simpler solutions may be just as effective in practice. To help decide which approach to take, experience working with real physical robots is your best teacher.

3.3 Machine learning in robot perception

Machine learning plays an important role in robot perception. This is particularly the case when the best internal representation is not known. One common approach is to map high-dimensional sensor streams into lower-dimensional spaces using unsupervised machine learning methods. Such an approach is called **low-dimensional embedding**. Machine learning makes it possible to learn sensor and motion models from data, while simultaneously discovering a suitable internal representations.

LOW-DIMENSIONAL EMBEDDING

Another machine learning technique enables robots to continuously adapt to broad changes in sensor measurements. Picture yourself walking from a sun-lit space into a dark neon-lit room. Clearly things are darker inside. But the change of light source also affects all the colors: Neon light has a stronger component of green light than sunlight. Yet somehow we seem not to notice the change. If we walk together with people into a neon-lit room, we don't think that suddenly their faces turned green. Our perception quickly adapts to the new lighting conditions, and our brain ignores the differences.

Adaptive perception techniques enable robots to adjust to such changes. One example is shown in Figure 13, taken from the autonomous driving domain. Here an unmanned ground vehicle adapts its classifier of the concept "drivable surface." How does this work? The robot uses a laser to provide classification for a small area right in front of the robot. When this area is found to be flat in the laser range scan, it is used as a positive training example for the concept "drivable surface." A mixture-of-Gaussians technique similar to the EM algorithm is then trained to recognize the specific color and texture coefficients of the small sample patch. The images in Figure 13 are the result of applying this classifier to the full image.

SELF-SUPERVISED LEARNING

Methods that make robots collect their own training data (with labels!) are called **self-supervised**. In this instance, the robot uses machine learning to leverage a short-range sensor that works well for terrain classification into a sensor that can see much farther. That allows the robot to drive faster, slowing down only when the sensor model says there is a change in the terrain that needs to be examined more carefully by the short-range sensors.

4 PLANNING TO MOVE

POINT-TO-POINT MOTION

COMPLIANT MOTION

All of a robot's deliberations ultimately come down to deciding how to move effectors. The **point-to-point motion** problem is to deliver the robot or its end effector to a designated target location. A greater challenge is the **compliant motion** problem, in which a robot moves while being in physical contact with an obstacle. An example of compliant motion is a robot manipulator that screws in a light bulb, or a robot that pushes a box across a table top.

PATH PLANNING

We begin by finding a suitable representation in which motion-planning problems can be described and solved. It turns out that the **configuration space**—the space of robot states defined by location, orientation, and joint angles—is a better place to work than the original 3D space. The **path planning** problem is to find a path from one configuration to another in configuration space. We have already encountered various versions of the path-planning problem throughout this book; the complication added by robotics is that path planning involves *continuous* spaces. There are two main approaches: **cell decomposition** and **skeletonization**. Each reduces the continuous path-planning problem to a discrete graph-search problem. In this section, we assume that motion is deterministic and that localization of the robot is exact. Subsequent sections will relax these assumptions.

4.1 Configuration space

WORKSPACE REPRESENTATION

We will start with a simple representation for a simple robot motion problem. Consider the robot arm shown in Figure 14(a). It has two joints that move independently. Moving the joints alters the (x, y) coordinates of the elbow and the gripper. (The arm cannot move in the z direction.) This suggests that the robot's configuration can be described by a four-dimensional coordinate: (x_e, y_e) for the location of the elbow relative to the environment and (x_g, y_g) for the location of the gripper. Clearly, these four coordinates characterize the full state of the robot. They constitute what is known as **workspace representation**, since the coordinates of the robot are specified in the same coordinate system as the objects it seeks to manipulate (or to avoid). Workspace representations are well-suited for collision checking, especially if the robot and all objects are represented by simple polygonal models.

LINKAGE CONSTRAINTS

The problem with the workspace representation is that not all workspace coordinates are actually attainable, even in the absence of obstacles. This is because of the **linkage constraints** on the space of attainable workspace coordinates. For example, the elbow position (x_e, y_e) and the gripper position (x_g, y_g) are always a fixed distance apart, because they are joined by a rigid forearm. A robot motion planner defined over workspace coordinates faces the challenge of generating paths that adhere to these constraints. This is particularly tricky

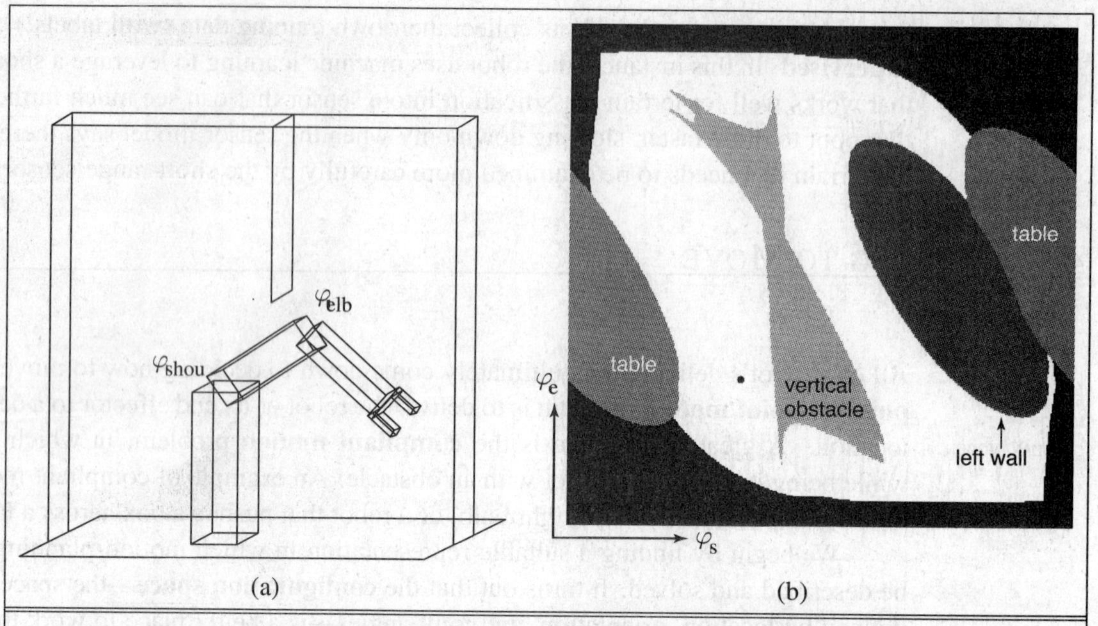

Figure 14 (a) Workspace representation of a robot arm with 2 DOFs. The workspace is a box with a flat obstacle hanging from the ceiling. (b) Configuration space of the same robot. Only white regions in the space are configurations that are free of collisions. The dot in this diagram corresponds to the configuration of the robot shown on the left.

CONFIGURATION SPACE

because the state space is continuous and the constraints are nonlinear. It turns out to be easier to plan with a **configuration space** representation. Instead of representing the state of the robot by the Cartesian coordinates of its elements, we represent the state by a configuration of the robot's joints. Our example robot possesses two joints. Hence, we can represent its state with the two angles φ_s and φ_e for the shoulder joint and elbow joint, respectively. In the absence of any obstacles, a robot could freely take on any value in configuration space. In particular, when planning a path one could simply connect the present configuration and the target configuration by a straight line. In following this path, the robot would then move its joints at a constant velocity, until a target location is reached.

Unfortunately, configuration spaces have their own problems. The task of a robot is usually expressed in workspace coordinates, not in configuration space coordinates. This raises the question of how to map between workspace coordinates and configuration space. Transforming configuration space coordinates into workspace coordinates is simple: it involves a series of straightforward coordinate transformations. These transformations are linear for prismatic joints and trigonometric for revolute joints. This chain of coordinate transformation is known as **kinematics**.

KINEMATICS

INVERSE KINEMATICS

The inverse problem of calculating the configuration of a robot whose effector location is specified in workspace coordinates is known as **inverse kinematics**. Calculating the inverse kinematics is hard, especially for robots with many DOFs. In particular, the solution is seldom unique. Figure 14(a) shows one of two possible configurations that put the gripper in the same location. (The other configuration would have the elbow below the shoulder.)

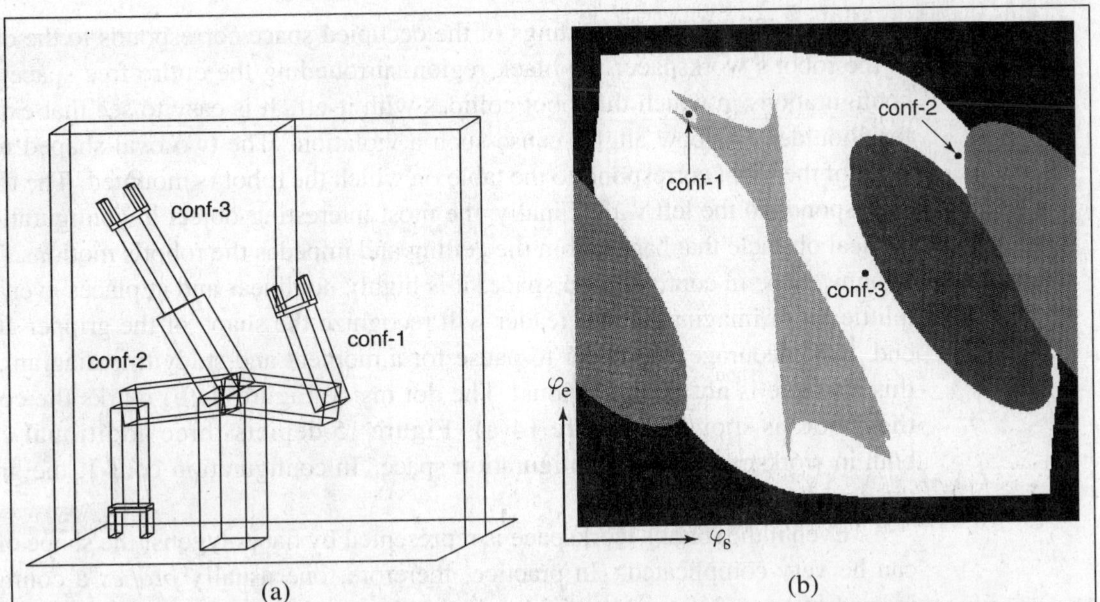

Figure 15 Three robot configurations, shown in workspace and configuration space.

In general, this two-link robot arm has between zero and two inverse kinematic solutions for any set of workspace coordinates. Most industrial robots have sufficient degrees of freedom to find infinitely many solutions to motion problems. To see how this is possible, simply imagine that we added a third revolute joint to our example robot, one whose rotational axis is parallel to the ones of the existing joints. In such a case, we can keep the location (but not the orientation!) of the gripper fixed and still freely rotate its internal joints, for most configurations of the robot. With a few more joints (how many?) we can achieve the same effect while keeping the orientation of the gripper constant as well. We have already seen an example of this in the "experiment" of placing your hand on the desk and moving your elbow. The kinematic constraint of your hand position is insufficient to determine the configuration of your elbow. In other words, the inverse kinematics of your shoulder–arm assembly possesses an infinite number of solutions.

The second problem with configuration space representations arises from the obstacles that may exist in the robot's workspace. Our example in Figure 14(a) shows several such obstacles, including a free-hanging obstacle that protrudes into the center of the robot's workspace. In workspace, such obstacles take on simple geometric forms—especially in most robotics textbooks, which tend to focus on polygonal obstacles. But how do they look in configuration space?

Figure 14(b) shows the configuration space for our example robot, under the specific obstacle configuration shown in Figure 14(a). The configuration space can be decomposed into two subspaces: the space of all configurations that a robot may attain, commonly called FREE SPACE **free space**, and the space of unattainable configurations, called **occupied space**. The white OCCUPIED SPACE area in Figure 14(b) corresponds to the free space. All other regions correspond to occupied space. The different shadings of the occupied space corresponds to the different objects in the robot's workspace; the black region surrounding the entire free space corresponds to configurations in which the robot collides with itself. It is easy to see that extreme values of the shoulder or elbow angles cause such a violation. The two oval-shaped regions on both sides of the robot correspond to the table on which the robot is mounted. The third oval region corresponds to the left wall. Finally, the most interesting object in configuration space is the vertical obstacle that hangs from the ceiling and impedes the robot's motions. This object has a funny shape in configuration space: it is highly nonlinear and at places even concave. With a little bit of imagination the reader will recognize the shape of the gripper at the upper left end. We encourage the reader to pause for a moment and study this diagram. The shape of this obstacle is not at all obvious! The dot inside Figure 14(b) marks the configuration of the robot, as shown in Figure 14(a). Figure 15 depicts three additional configurations, both in workspace and in configuration space. In configuration conf-1, the gripper encloses the vertical obstacle.

Even if the robot's workspace is represented by flat polygons, the shape of the free space can be very complicated. In practice, therefore, one usually *probes* a configuration space instead of constructing it explicitly. A planner may generate a configuration and then test to see if it is in free space by applying the robot kinematics and then checking for collisions in workspace coordinates.

4.2 Cell decomposition methods

CELL DECOMPOSITION

The first approach to path planning uses **cell decomposition**—that is, it decomposes the free space into a finite number of contiguous regions, called cells. These regions have the important property that the path-planning problem within a single region can be solved by simple means (e.g., moving along a straight line). The path-planning problem then becomes a discrete graph-search problem.

The simplest cell decomposition consists of a regularly spaced grid. Figure 16(a) shows a square grid decomposition of the space and a solution path that is optimal for this grid size. Grayscale shading indicates the *value* of each free-space grid cell—i.e., the cost of the shortest path from that cell to the goal. Figure 16(b) shows the corresponding workspace trajectory for the arm. Of course, we can also use the A* algorithm to find a shortest path.

Such a decomposition has the advantage that it is extremely simple to implement, but it also suffers from three limitations. First, it is workable only for low-dimensional configuration spaces, because the number of grid cells increases exponentially with d, the number of dimensions. Sounds familiar? This is the curse!dimensionality@of dimensionality. Second, there is the problem of what to do with cells that are "mixed"—that is, neither entirely within free space nor entirely within occupied space. A solution path that includes such a cell may not be a real solution, because there may be no way to cross the cell in the desired direction in a straight line. This would make the path planner *unsound*. On the other hand, if we insist that only completely free cells may be used, the planner will be *incomplete*, because it might

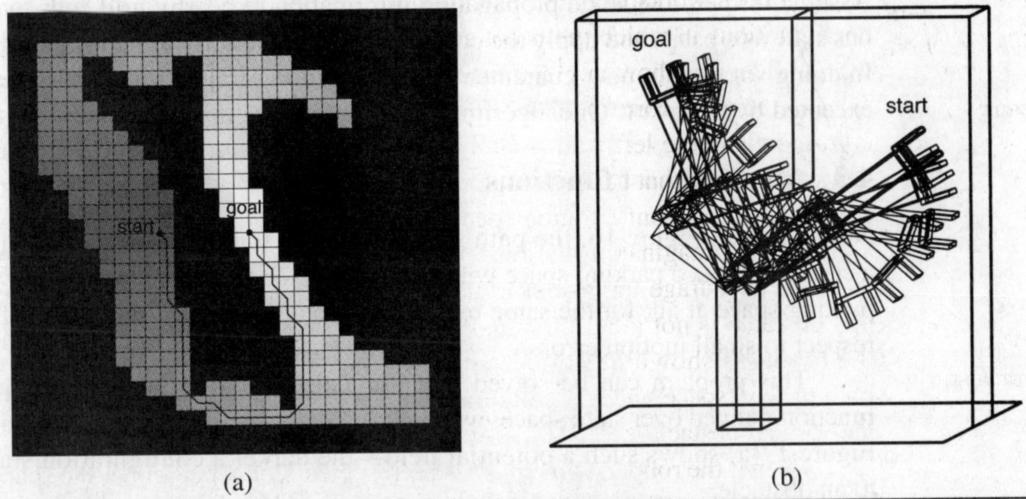

Figure 16 (a) Value function and path found for a discrete grid cell approximation of the configuration space. (b) The same path visualized in workspace coordinates. Notice how the robot bends its elbow to avoid a collision with the vertical obstacle.

be the case that the only paths to the goal go through mixed cells—especially if the cell size is comparable to that of the passageways and clearances in the space. And third, any path through a discretized state space will not be smooth. It is generally difficult to guarantee that a smooth solution exists near the discrete path. So a robot may not be able to execute the solution found through this decomposition.

Cell decomposition methods can be improved in a number of ways, to alleviate some of these problems. The first approach allows *further subdivision* of the mixed cells—perhaps using cells of half the original size. This can be continued recursively until a path is found that lies entirely within free cells. (Of course, the method only works if there is a way to decide if a given cell is a mixed cell, which is easy only if the configuration space boundaries have relatively simple mathematical descriptions.) This method is complete provided there is a bound on the smallest passageway through which a solution must pass. Although it focuses most of the computational effort on the tricky areas within the configuration space, it still fails to scale well to high-dimensional problems because each recursive splitting of a cell creates 2^d smaller cells. A second way to obtain a complete algorithm is to insist on an **exact cell decomposition** of the free space. This method must allow cells to be irregularly shaped where they meet the boundaries of free space, but the shapes must still be "simple" in the sense that it should be easy to compute a traversal of any free cell. This technique requires some quite advanced geometric ideas, so we shall not pursue it further here.

EXACT CELL DECOMPOSITION

Examining the solution path shown in Figure 16(a), we can see an additional difficulty that will have to be resolved. The path contains arbitrarily sharp corners; a robot moving at any finite speed could not execute such a path. This problem is solved by storing certain continuous values for each grid cell. Consider an algorithm which stores, for each grid cell, the exact, continuous state that was attained with the cell was first expanded in the search. Assume further, that when propagating information to nearby grid cells, we use this continuous state as a basis, and apply the continuous robot motion model for jumping to nearby cells. In doing so, we can now guarantee that the resulting trajectory is smooth and can indeed be executed by the robot. One algorithm that implements this is **hybrid A***.

HYBRID A*

4.3 Modified cost functions

Notice that in Figure 16, the path goes very close to the obstacle. Anyone who has driven a car knows that a parking space with one millimeter of clearance on either side is not really a parking space at all; for the same reason, we would prefer solution paths that are robust with respect to small motion errors.

POTENTIAL FIELD

This problem can be solved by introducing a **potential field**. A potential field is a function defined over state space, whose value grows with the distance to the closest obstacle. Figure 17(a) shows such a potential field—the darker a configuration state, the closer it is to an obstacle.

The potential field can be used as an additional cost term in the shortest-path calculation. This induces an interesting tradeoff. On the one hand, the robot seeks to minimize path length to the goal. On the other hand, it tries to stay away from obstacles by virtue of minimizing the potential function. With the appropriate weight balancing the two objectives, a resulting path may look like the one shown in Figure 17(b). This figure also displays the value function derived from the combined cost function, again calculated by value iteration. Clearly, the resulting path is longer, but it is also safer.

There exist many other ways to modify the cost function. For example, it may be desirable to *smooth* the control parameters over time. For example, when driving a car, a smooth path is better than a jerky one. In general, such higher-order constraints are not easy to accommodate in the planning process, unless we make the most recent steering command a part of the state. However, it is often easy to smooth the resulting trajectory after planning, using conjugate gradient methods. Such post-planning smoothing is essential in many real-world applications.

4.4 Skeletonization methods

SKELETONIZATION

The second major family of path-planning algorithms is based on the idea of **skeletonization**. These algorithms reduce the robot's free space to a one-dimensional representation, for which the planning problem is easier. This lower-dimensional representation is called a **skeleton** of the configuration space.

VORONOI GRAPH

Figure 18 shows an example skeletonization: it is a **Voronoi graph** of the free space—the set of all points that are equidistant to two or more obstacles. To do path planning with a Voronoi graph, the robot first changes its present configuration to a point on the Voronoi graph. It is easy to show that this can always be achieved by a straight-line motion in configuration space. Second, the robot follows the Voronoi graph until it reaches the point nearest to the target configuration. Finally, the robot leaves the Voronoi graph and moves to the target. Again, this final step involves straight-line motion in configuration space.

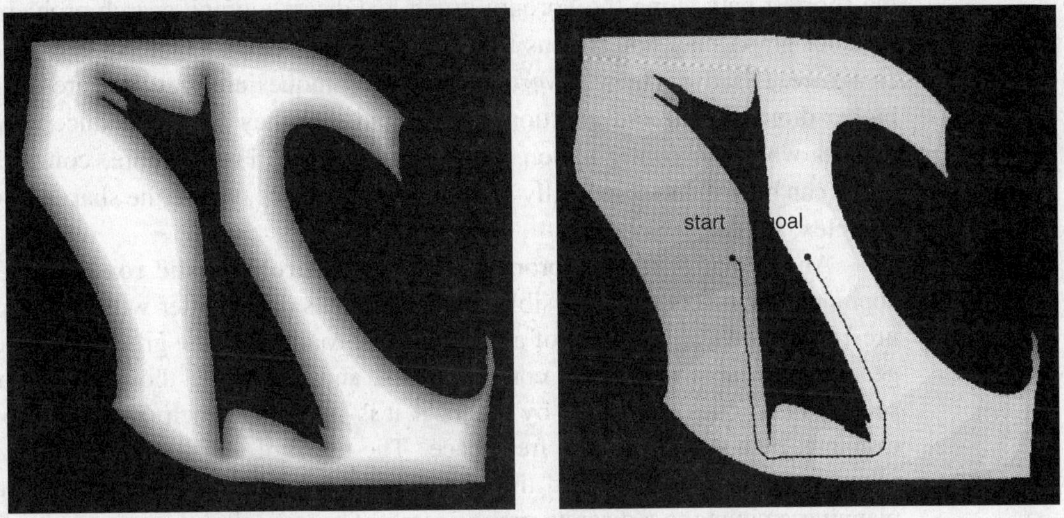

(a) (b)

Figure 17 (a) A repelling potential field pushes the robot away from obstacles. (b) Path found by simultaneously minimizing path length and the potential.

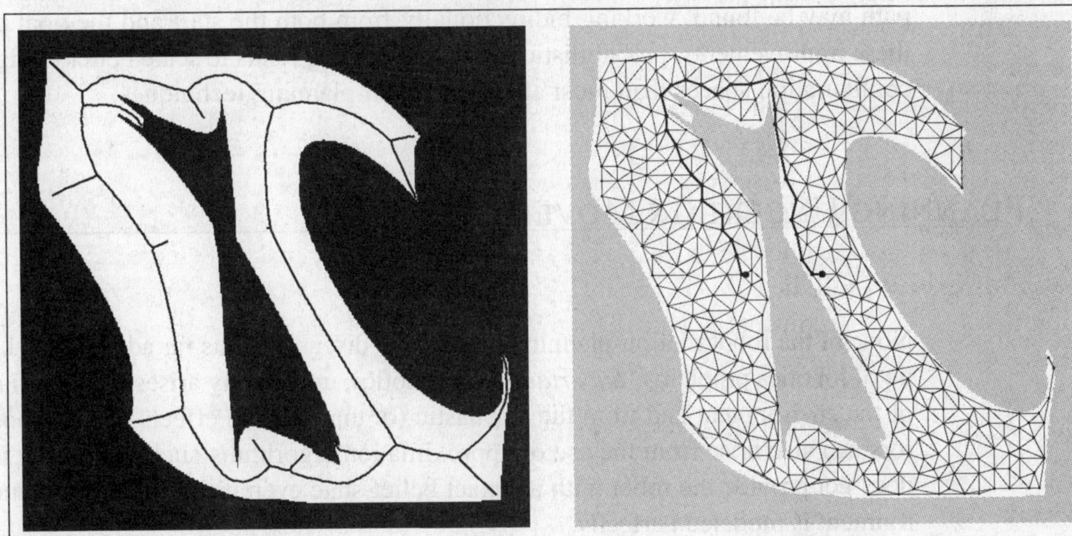

(a) (b)

Figure 18 (a) The Voronoi graph is the set of points equidistant to two or more obstacles in configuration space. (b) A probabilistic roadmap, composed of 400 randomly chosen points in free space.

In this way, the original path-planning problem is reduced to finding a path on the Voronoi graph, which is generally one-dimensional (except in certain nongeneric cases) and has finitely many points where three or more one-dimensional curves intersect. Thus, finding the shortest path along the Voronoi graph is a discrete graph-search problem. Following the Voronoi graph may not give us the shortest path, but the resulting paths tend to maximize clearance. Disadvantages of Voronoi graph techniques are that they are difficult to apply to higher-dimensional configuration spaces, and that they tend to induce unnecessarily large detours when the configuration space is wide open. Furthermore, computing the Voronoi graph can be difficult, especially in configuration space, where the shapes of obstacles can be complex.

PROBABILISTIC ROADMAP

An alternative to the Voronoi graphs is the **probabilistic roadmap**, a skeletonization approach that offers more possible routes, and thus deals better with wide-open spaces. Figure 18(b) shows an example of a probabilistic roadmap. The graph is created by randomly generating a large number of configurations, and discarding those that do not fall into free space. Two nodes are joined by an arc if it is "easy" to reach one node from the other–for example, by a straight line in free space. The result of all this is a randomized graph in the robot's free space. If we add the robot's start and goal configurations to this graph, path planning amounts to a discrete graph search. Theoretically, this approach is incomplete, because a bad choice of random points may leave us without any paths from start to goal. It is possible to bound the probability of failure in terms of the number of points generated and certain geometric properties of the configuration space. It is also possible to direct the generation of sample points towards the areas where a partial search suggests that a good path may be found, working bidirectionally from both the start and the goal positions. With these improvements, probabilistic roadmap planning tends to scale better to high-dimensional configuration spaces than most alternative path-planning techniques.

5 Planning Uncertain Movements

None of the robot motion-planning algorithms discussed thus far addresses a key characteristic of robotics problems: *uncertainty*. In robotics, uncertainty arises from partial observability of the environment and from the stochastic (or unmodeled) effects of the robot's actions. Errors can also arise from the use of approximation algorithms such as particle filtering, which does not provide the robot with an exact belief state even if the stochastic nature of the environment is modeled perfectly.

MOST LIKELY STATE

Most of today's robots use deterministic algorithms for decision making, such as the path-planning algorithms of the previous section. To do so, it is common practice to extract the **most likely state** from the probability distribution produced by the state estimation algorithm. The advantage of this approach is purely computational. Planning paths through configuration space is already a challenging problem; it would be worse if we had to work with a full probability distribution over states. Ignoring uncertainty in this way works when the uncertainty is small. In fact, when the environment model changes over time as the result of incorporating sensor measurements, many robots plan paths online during plan execution. This is the **online replanning** technique.

ONLINE REPLANNING

Unfortunately, ignoring the uncertainty does not always work. In some problems the robot's uncertainty is simply too massive: How can we use a deterministic path planner to control a mobile robot that has no clue where it is? In general, if the robot's true state is not the one identified by the maximum likelihood rule, the resulting control will be suboptimal. Depending on the magnitude of the error this can lead to all sorts of unwanted effects, such as collisions with obstacles.

The field of robotics has adopted a range of techniques for accommodating uncertainty. Some are derived from the algorithms for decision making under uncertainty. If the robot faces uncertainty only in its state transition, but its state is fully observable, the problem is best modeled as a Markov decision process (MDP). The solution of an MDP is an optimal **policy**, which tells the robot what to do in every possible state. In this way, it can handle all sorts of motion errors, whereas a single-path solution from a deterministic planner would be much less robust. In robotics, policies are called **navigation functions**. The value function shown in Figure 16(a) can be converted into such a navigation function simply by following the gradient.

NAVIGATION FUNCTION

Partial observability makes the problem much harder. The resulting robot control problem is a partially observable MDP, or POMDP. In such situations, the robot maintains an internal belief state, like the ones discussed in Section 3. The solution to a POMDP is a policy defined over the robot's belief state. Put differently, the input to the policy is an entire probability distribution. This enables the robot to base its decision not only on what it knows, but also on what it does not know. For example, if it is uncertain about a critical state variable, it can rationally invoke an **information gathering action**. This is impossible in the MDP framework, since MDPs assume full observability. Unfortunately, techniques that solve POMDPs exactly are inapplicable to robotics—there are no known techniques for high-dimensional continuous spaces. Discretization produces POMDPs that are far too large to handle. One remedy is to make the minimization of uncertainty a control objective. For example, the **coastal navigation** heuristic requires the robot to stay near known landmarks to decrease its uncertainty. Another approach applies variants of the probabilistic roadmap planning method to the belief space representation. Such methods tend to scale better to large discrete POMDPs.

INFORMATION GATHERING ACTION

COASTAL NAVIGATION

5.1 Robust methods

ROBUST CONTROL

Uncertainty can also be handled using so-called **robust control** methods rather than probabilistic methods. A robust method is one that assumes a *bounded* amount of uncertainty in each aspect of a problem, but does not assign probabilities to values within the allowed interval. A robust solution is one that works no matter what actual values occur, provided they are within the assumed interval. An extreme form of robust method is the **con-formant planning** approach—it produces plans that work with no state information at all.

FINE-MOTION PLANNING

Here, we look at a robust method that is used for **fine-motion planning** (or FMP) in robotic assembly tasks. Fine-motion planning involves moving a robot arm in very close proximity to a static environment object. The main difficulty with fine-motion planning is

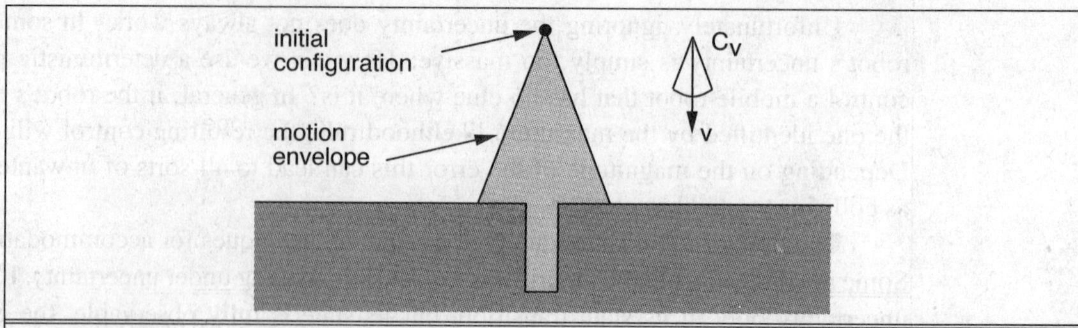

Figure 19 A two-dimensional environment, velocity uncertainty cone, and envelope of possible robot motions. The intended velocity is v, but with uncertainty the actual velocity could be anywhere in C_v, resulting in a final configuration somewhere in the motion envelope, which means we wouldn't know if we hit the hole or not.

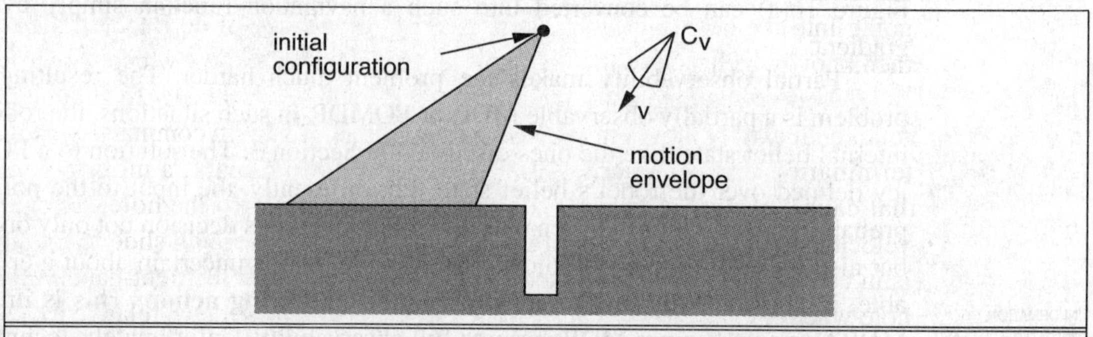

Figure 20 The first motion command and the resulting envelope of possible robot motions. No matter what the error, we know the final configuration will be to the left of the hole.

that the required motions and the relevant features of the environment are very small. At such small scales, the robot is unable to measure or control its position accurately and may also be uncertain of the shape of the environment itself; we will assume that these uncertainties are all bounded. The solutions to FMP problems will typically be conditional plans or policies that make use of sensor feedback during execution and are guaranteed to work in all situations consistent with the assumed uncertainty bounds.

GUARDED MOTION A fine-motion plan consists of a series of **guarded motions**. Each guarded motion consists of (1) a motion command and (2) a termination condition, which is a predicate on the robot's sensor values, and returns true to indicate the end of the guarded move. The motion COMPLIANT MOTION commands are typically **compliant motions** that allow the effector to slide if the motion command would cause collision with an obstacle. As an example, Figure 19 shows a two-dimensional configuration space with a narrow vertical hole. It could be the configuration space for insertion of a rectangular peg into a hole or a car key into the ignition. The motion commands are constant velocities. The termination conditions are contact with a surface. To model uncertainty in control, we assume that instead of moving in the commanded direction, the robot's actual motion lies in the cone C_v about it. The figure shows what would happen

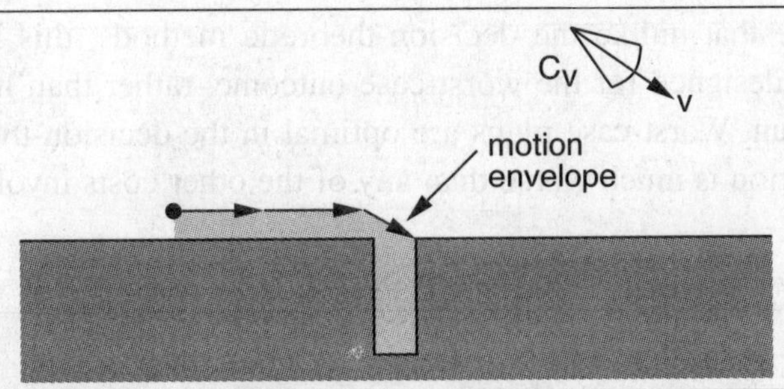

Figure 21 The second motion command and the envelope of possible motions. Even with error, we will eventually get into the hole.

if we commanded a velocity straight down from the initial configuration. Because of the uncertainty in velocity, the robot could move anywhere in the conical envelope, possibly going into the hole, but more likely landing to one side of it. Because the robot would not then know which side of the hole it was on, it would not know which way to move.

A more sensible strategy is shown in Figures 20 and 21. In Figure 20, the and the robot deliberately moves to one side of the hole. The motion command is shown in the figure, termination test is contact with any surface. In Figure 21, a motion command is given that causes the robot to slide along the surface and into the hole. Because all possible velocities in the motion envelope are to the right, the robot will slide to the right whenever it is in contact with a horizontal surface. It will slide down the right-hand vertical edge of the hole when it touches it, because all possible velocities are down relative to a vertical surface. It will keep moving until it reaches the bottom of the hole, because that is its termination condition. In spite of the control uncertainty, all possible trajectories of the robot terminate in contact with the bottom of the hole—that is, unless surface irregularities cause the robot to stick in one place.

As one might imagine, the problem of *constructing* fine-motion plans is not trivial; in fact, it is a good deal harder than planning with exact motions. One can either choose a fixed number of discrete values for each motion or use the environment geometry to choose directions that give qualitatively different behavior. A fine-motion planner takes as input the configuration-space description, the angle of the velocity uncertainty cone, and a specification of what sensing is possible for termination (surface contact in this case). It should produce a multistep conditional plan or policy that is guaranteed to succeed, if such a plan exists.

Our example assumes that the planner has an exact model of the environment, but it is possible to allow for bounded error in this model as follows. If the error can be described in terms of parameters, those parameters can be added as degrees of freedom to the configuration space. In the last example, if the depth and width of the hole were uncertain, we could add them as two degrees of freedom to the configuration space. It is impossible to move the robot in these directions in the configuration space or to sense its position directly. But both those restrictions can be incorporated when describing this problem as an FMP problem by appropriately specifying control and sensor uncertainties. This gives a complex, four-dimensional planning problem, but exactly the same planning techniques can be applied.

Notice that unlike the decision-theoretic methods, this kind of robust approach results in plans designed for the worst-case outcome, rather than maximizing the expected quality of the plan. Worst-case plans are optimal in the decision-theoretic sense only if failure during execution is much worse than any of the other costs involved in execution.

6 MOVING

So far, we have talked about how to *plan* motions, but not about how to *move*. Our plans—particularly those produced by deterministic path planners—assume that the robot can simply follow any path that the algorithm produces. In the real world, of course, this is not the case. Robots have inertia and cannot execute arbitrary paths except at arbitrarily slow speeds. In most cases, the robot gets to exert forces rather than specify positions. This section discusses methods for calculating these forces.

6.1 Dynamics and control

Section 2 introduced the notion of **dynamic state**, which extends the kinematic state of a robot by its velocity. For example, in addition to the angle of a robot joint, the dynamic state also captures the rate of change of the angle, and possibly even its momentary acceleration. The transition model for a dynamic state representation includes the effect of forces on this rate of change. Such models are typically expressed via **differential equations**, which are equations that relate a quantity (e.g., a kinematic state) to the change of the quantity over time (e.g., velocity). In principle, we could have chosen to plan robot motion using dynamic models, instead of our kinematic models. Such a methodology would lead to superior robot performance, if we could generate the plans. However, the dynamic state has higher dimension than the kinematic space, and the curse of dimensionality would render many motion planning algorithms inapplicable for all but the most simple robots. For this reason, practical robot system often rely on simpler kinematic path planners.

DIFFERENTIAL EQUATION

A common technique to compensate for the limitations of kinematic plans is to use a separate mechanism, a **controller**, for keeping the robot on track. Controllers are techniques for generating robot controls in real time using feedback from the environment, so as to achieve a control objective. If the objective is to keep the robot on a preplanned path, it is often referred to as a **reference controller** and the path is called a **reference path**. Controllers that optimize a global cost function are known as **optimal controllers**. Optimal policies for continuous MDPs are, in effect, optimal controllers.

CONTROLLER

REFERENCE CONTROLLER

REFERENCE PATH

OPTIMAL CONTROLLERS

On the surface, the problem of keeping a robot on a prespecified path appears to be relatively straightforward. In practice, however, even this seemingly simple problem has its pitfalls. Figure 22(a) illustrates what can go wrong; it shows the path of a robot that attempts to follow a kinematic path. Whenever a deviation occurs—whether due to noise or to constraints on the forces the robot can apply—the robot provides an opposing force whose magnitude is proportional to this deviation. Intuitively, this might appear plausible, since deviations should be compensated by a counterforce to keep the robot on track. However,

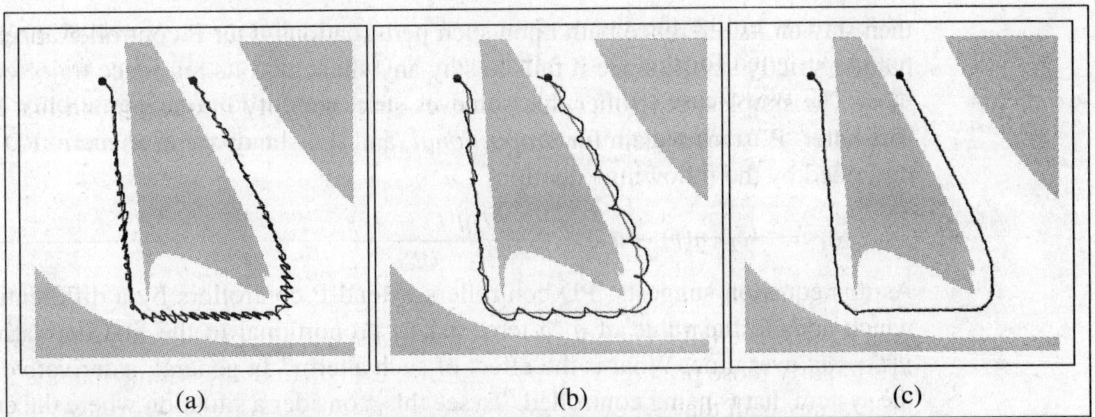

Figure 22 Robot arm control using (a) proportional control with gain factor 1.0, (b) proportional control with gain factor 0.1, and (c) PD (proportional derivative) control with gain factors 0.3 for the proportional component and 0.8 for the differential component. In all cases the robot arm tries to follow the path shown in gray.

as Figure 22(a) illustrates, our controller causes the robot to vibrate rather violently. The vibration is the result of a natural inertia of the robot arm: once driven back to its reference position the robot then overshoots, which induces a symmetric error with opposite sign. Such overshooting may continue along an entire trajectory, and the resulting robot motion is far from desirable.

Before we can define a better controller, let us formally describe what went wrong. Controllers that provide force in negative proportion to the observed error are known as **P controllers**. The letter 'P' stands for *proportional*, indicating that the actual control is proportional to the error of the robot manipulator. More formally, let $y(t)$ be the reference path, parameterized by time index t. The control a_t generated by a P controller has the form:

P CONTROLLER

$$a_t = K_P(y(t) - x_t) .$$

GAIN PARAMETER

Here x_t is the state of the robot at time t and K_P is a constant known as the **gain parameter** of the controller and its value is called the gain factor); K_p regulates how strongly the controller corrects for deviations between the actual state x_t and the desired one $y(t)$. In our example, $K_P = 1$. At first glance, one might think that choosing a smaller value for K_P would remedy the problem. Unfortunately, this is not the case. Figure 22(b) shows a trajectory for $K_P = .1$, still exhibiting oscillatory behavior. Lower values of the gain parameter may simply slow down the oscillation, but do not solve the problem. In fact, in the absence of friction, the P controller is essentially a spring law; so it will oscillate indefinitely around a fixed target location.

Traditionally, problems of this type fall into the realm of **control theory**, a field of increasing importance to researchers in AI. Decades of research in this field have led to a large number of controllers that are superior to the simple control law given above. In particular, a reference controller is said to be **stable** if small perturbations lead to a bounded error between the robot and the reference signal. It is said to be **strictly stable** if it is able to return to and

STABLE

STRICTLY STABLE

then stay on its reference path upon such perturbations. Our P controller appears to be stable but not strictly stable, since it fails to stay anywhere near its reference trajectory.

PD CONTROLLER

The simplest controller that achieves strict stability in our domain is a **PD controller**. The letter 'P' stands again for *proportional*, and 'D' stands for *derivative*. PD controllers are described by the following equation:

$$a_t = K_P(y(t) - x_t) + K_D \frac{\partial(y(t) - x_t)}{\partial t} . \tag{2}$$

As this equation suggests, PD controllers extend P controllers by a differential component, which adds to the value of a_t a term that is proportional to the first derivative of the error $y(t) - x_t$ over time. What is the effect of such a term? In general, a derivative term dampens the system that is being controlled. To see this, consider a situation where the error $(y(t)-x_t)$ is changing rapidly over time, as is the case for our P controller above. The derivative of this error will then counteract the proportional term, which will reduce the overall response to the perturbation. However, if the same error persists and does not change, the derivative will vanish and the proportional term dominates the choice of control.

Figure 22(c) shows the result of applying this PD controller to our robot arm, using as gain parameters $K_P = .3$ and $K_D = .8$. Clearly, the resulting path is much smoother, and does not exhibit any obvious oscillations.

PD controllers do have failure modes, however. In particular, PD controllers may fail to regulate an error down to zero, even in the absence of external perturbations. Often such a situation is the result of a systematic external force that is not part of the model. An autonomous car driving on a banked surface, for example, may find itself systematically pulled to one side. Wear and tear in robot arms cause similar systematic errors. In such situations, an over-proportional feedback is required to drive the error closer to zero. The solution to this problem lies in adding a third term to the control law, based on the integrated error over time:

$$a_t = K_P(y(t) - x_t) + K_I \int (y(t) - x_t)dt + K_D \frac{\partial(y(t) - x_t)}{\partial t} . \tag{3}$$

Here K_I is yet another gain parameter. The term $\int (y(t) - x_t)dt$ calculates the integral of the error over time. The effect of this term is that long-lasting deviations between the reference signal and the actual state are corrected. If, for example, x_t is smaller than $y(t)$ for a long period of time, this integral will grow until the resulting control a_t forces this error to shrink. Integral terms, then, ensure that a controller does not exhibit systematic error, at the expense of increased danger of oscillatory behavior. A controller with all three terms is called a **PID controller** (for proportional integral derivative). PID controllers are widely used in industry, for a variety of control problems.

PID CONTROLLER

6.2 Potential-field control

We introduced potential fields as an additional cost function in robot motion planning, but they can also be used for generating robot motion directly, dispensing with the path planning phase altogether. To achieve this, we have to define an attractive force that pulls the robot towards its goal configuration and a repellent potential field that pushes the robot away from obstacles. Such a potential field is shown in Figure 23. Its single global minimum is

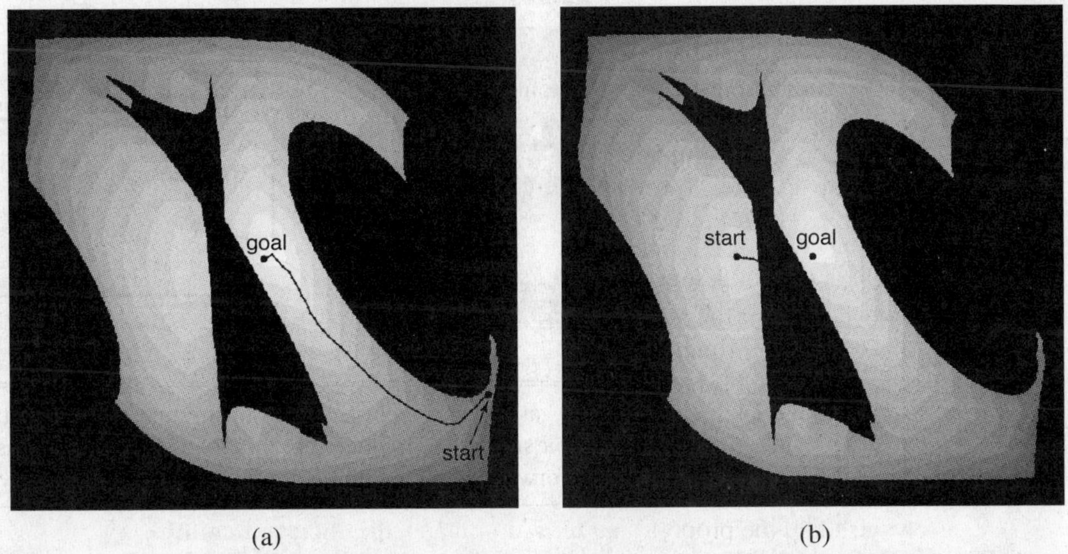

Figure 23 Potential field control. The robot ascends a potential field composed of repelling forces asserted from the obstacles and an attracting force that corresponds to the goal configuration. (a) Successful path. (b) Local optimum.

the goal configuration, and the value is the sum of the distance to this goal configuration and the proximity to obstacles. No planning was involved in generating the potential field shown in the figure. Because of this, potential fields are well suited to real-time control. Figure 23(a) shows a trajectory of a robot that performs hill climbing in the potential field. In many applications, the potential field can be calculated efficiently for any given configuration. Moreover, optimizing the potential amounts to calculating the gradient of the potential for the present robot configuration. These calculations can be extremely efficient, especially when compared to path-planning algorithms, all of which are exponential in the dimensionality of the configuration space (the DOFs) in the worst case.

The fact that the potential field approach manages to find a path to the goal in such an efficient manner, even over long distances in configuration space, raises the question as to whether there is a need for planning in robotics at all. Are potential field techniques sufficient, or were we just lucky in our example? The answer is that we were indeed lucky. Potential fields have many local minima that can trap the robot. In Figure 23(b), the robot approaches the obstacle by simply rotating its shoulder joint, until it gets stuck on the wrong side of the obstacle. The potential field is not rich enough to make the robot bend its elbow so that the arm fits under the obstacle. In other words, potential field control is great for local robot motion but sometimes we still need global planning. Another important drawback with potential fields is that the forces they generate depend only on the obstacle and robot positions, not on the robot's velocity. Thus, potential field control is really a kinematic method and may fail if the robot is moving quickly.

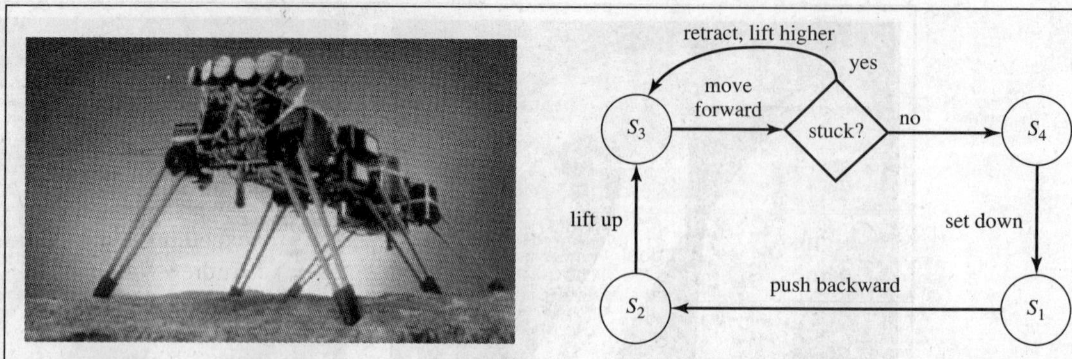

(a) (b)

Figure 24 (a) Genghis, a hexapod robot. (b) An augmented finite state machine (AFSM) for the control of a single leg. Notice that this AFSM reacts to sensor feedback: if a leg is stuck during the forward swinging phase, it will be lifted increasingly higher.

6.3 Reactive control

So far we have considered control decisions that require some model of the environment for constructing either a reference path or a potential field. There are some difficulties with this approach. First, models that are sufficiently accurate are often difficult to obtain, especially in complex or remote environments, such as the surface of Mars, or for robots that have few sensors. Second, even in cases where we can devise a model with sufficient accuracy, computational difficulties and localization error might render these techniques impractical.
REACTIVE CONTROL In some cases, a reflex agent architecture using **reactive control** is more appropriate.

For example, picture a legged robot that attempts to lift a leg over an obstacle. We could give this robot a rule that says lift the leg a small height h and move it forward, and if the leg encounters an obstacle, move it back and start again at a higher height. You could say that h is modeling an aspect of the world, but we can also think of h as an auxiliary variable of the robot controller, devoid of direct physical meaning.

One such example is the six-legged (hexapod) robot, shown in Figure 24(a), designed for walking through rough terrain. The robot's sensors are inadequate to obtain models of the terrain for path planning. Moreover, even if we added sufficiently accurate sensors, the twelve degrees of freedom (two for each leg) would render the resulting path planning problem computationally intractable.

It is possible, nonetheless, to specify a controller directly without an explicit environmental model. (We have already seen this with the PD controller, which was able to keep a complex robot arm on target *without* an explicit model of the robot dynamics; it did, however, require a reference path generated from a kinematic model.) For the hexapod robot we first
GAIT choose a **gait**, or pattern of movement of the limbs. One statically stable gait is to first move the right front, right rear, and left center legs forward (keeping the other three fixed), and then move the other three. This gait works well on flat terrain. On rugged terrain, obstacles may prevent a leg from swinging forward. This problem can be overcome by a remarkably simple control rule: *when a leg's forward motion is blocked, simply retract it, lift it higher,*

Figure 25 Multiple exposures of an RC helicopter executing a flip based on a policy learned with reinforcement learning. Images courtesy of Andrew Ng, Stanford University.

and try again. The resulting controller is shown in Figure 24(b) as a finite state machine; it constitutes a reflex agent with state, where the internal state is represented by the index of the current machine state (s_1 through s_4).

Variants of this simple feedback-driven controller have been found to generate remarkably robust walking patterns, capable of maneuvering the robot over rugged terrain. Clearly, such a controller is model-free, and it does not deliberate or use search for generating controls. Environmental feedback plays a crucial role in the controller's execution. The software alone does not specify what will actually happen when the robot is placed in an environment. Behavior that emerges through the interplay of a (simple) controller and a (complex) environment is often referred to as **emergent behavior**. Strictly speaking, all robots discussed in this chapter exhibit emergent behavior, due to the fact that no model is perfect. Historically, however, the term has been reserved for control techniques that do not utilize explicit environmental models. Emergent behavior is also characteristic of biological organisms.

EMERGENT BEHAVIOR

6.4 Reinforcement learning control

One particularly exciting form of control is based on the **policy search** form of reinforcement learning. This work has been enormously infiuential in recent years, at is has solved challenging robotics problems for which previously no solution existed. An example is acrobatic autonomous helicopter fiight. Figure 25 shows an autonomous flip of a small RC (radio-controlled) helicopter. This maneuver is challenging due to the highly nonlinear nature of the aerodynamics involved. Only the most experienced of human pilots are able to perform it. Yet a policy search method, using only a few minutes of computation, learned a policy that can safely execute a flip every time.

Policy search needs an accurate model of the domain before it can find a policy. The input to this model is the state of the helicopter at time t, the controls at time t, and the resulting state at time $t+\Delta t$. The state of a helicopter can be described by the 3D coordinates of the vehicle, its yaw, pitch, and roll angles, and the rate of change of these six variables. The controls are the manual controls of of the helicopter: throttle, pitch, elevator, aileron, and rudder. All that remains is the resulting state—how are we going to define a model that accurately says how the helicopter responds to each control? The answer is simple: Let an expert human pilot fly the helicopter, and record the controls that the expert transmits over the radio and the state variables of the helicopter. About four minutes of human-controlled flight suffices to build a predictive model that is sufficiently accurate to simulate the vehicle.

What is remarkable about this example is the ease with which this learning approach solves a challenging robotics problem. This is one of the many successes of machine learning in scientific fields previously dominated by careful mathematical analysis and modeling.

7 ROBOTIC SOFTWARE ARCHITECTURES

SOFTWARE ARCHITECTURE

A methodology for structuring algorithms is called a **software architecture**. An architecture includes languages and tools for writing programs, as well as an overall philosophy for how programs can be brought together.

Modern-day software architectures for robotics must decide how to combine reactive control and model-based deliberative planning. In many ways, reactive and deliberate techniques have orthogonal strengths and weaknesses. Reactive control is sensor-driven and appropriate for making low-level decisions in real time. However, it rarely yields a plausible solution at the global level, because global control decisions depend on information that cannot be sensed at the time of decision making. For such problems, deliberate planning is a more appropriate choice.

Consequently, most robot architectures use reactive techniques at the lower levels of control and deliberative techniques at the higher levels. We encountered such a combination in our discussion of PD controllers, where we combined a (reactive) PD controller with a (deliberate) path planner. Architectures that combine reactive and deliberate techniques are called **hybrid architectures**.

HYBRID ARCHITECTURE

7.1 Subsumption architecture

SUBSUMPTION ARCHITECTURE

The **subsumption architecture** (Brooks, 1986) is a framework for assembling reactive controllers out of finite state machines. Nodes in these machines may contain tests for certain sensor variables, in which case the execution trace of a finite state machine is conditioned on the outcome of such a test. Arcs can be tagged with messages that will be generated when traversing them, and that are sent to the robot's motors or to other finite state machines. Additionally, finite state machines possess internal timers (clocks) that control the time it takes to traverse an arc. The resulting machines are refereed to as **augmented finite state machines**, or AFSMs, where the augmentation refers to the use of clocks.

AUGMENTED FINITE STATE MACHINE

An example of a simple AFSM is the four-state machine shown in Figure 24(b), which generates cyclic leg motion for a hexapod walker. This AFSM implements a cyclic controller, whose execution mostly does not rely on environmental feedback. The forward swing phase, however, does rely on sensor feedback. If the leg is stuck, meaning that it has failed to execute the forward swing, the robot retracts the leg, lifts it up a little higher, and attempts to execute the forward swing once again. Thus, the controller is able to *react* to contingencies arising from the interplay of the robot and its environment.

The subsumption architecture offers additional primitives for synchronizing AFSMs, and for combining output values of multiple, possibly conflicting AFSMs. In this way, it enables the programmer to compose increasingly complex controllers in a bottom-up fashion.

In our example, we might begin with AFSMs for individual legs, followed by an AFSM for coordinating multiple legs. On top of this, we might implement higher-level behaviors such as collision avoidance, which might involve backing up and turning.

The idea of composing robot controllers from AFSMs is quite intriguing. Imagine how difficult it would be to generate the same behavior with any of the configuration-space path-planning algorithms described in the previous section. First, we would need an accurate model of the terrain. The configuration space of a robot with six legs, each of which is driven by two independent motors, totals eighteen dimensions (twelve dimensions for the configuration of the legs, and six for the location and orientation of the robot relative to its environment). Even if our computers were fast enough to find paths in such high-dimensional spaces, we would have to worry about nasty effects such as the robot sliding down a slope. Because of such stochastic effects, a single path through configuration space would almost certainly be too brittle, and even a PID controller might not be able to cope with such contingencies. In other words, generating motion behavior deliberately is simply too complex a problem for present-day robot motion planning algorithms.

Unfortunately, the subsumption architecture has its own problems. First, the AFSMs are driven by raw sensor input, an arrangement that works if the sensor data is reliable and contains all necessary information for decision making, but fails if sensor data has to be integrated in nontrivial ways over time. Subsumption-style controllers have therefore mostly been applied to simple tasks, such as following a wall or moving towards visible light sources. Second, the lack of deliberation makes it difficult to change the task of the robot. A subsumptionstyle robot usually does just one task, and it has no notion of how to modify its controls to accommodate different goals. Finally, subsumptionstyle controllers tend to be difficult to understand. In practice, the intricate interplay between dozens of interacting AFSMs (and the environment) is beyond what most human programmers can comprehend. For all these reasons, the subsumption architecture is rarely used in robotics, despite its great historical importance. However, it has had an influence on other architectures, and on individual components of some architectures.

7.2 Three-layer architecture

THREE-LAYER ARCHITECTURE

Hybrid architectures combine reaction with deliberation. The most popular hybrid architecture is the **three-layer architecture**, which consists of a reactive layer, an executive layer, and a deliberative layer.

REACTIVE LAYER

The **reactive layer** provides low-level control to the robot. It is characterized by a tight sensor–action loop. Its decision cycle is often on the order of milliseconds.

EXECUTIVE LAYER

The **executive layer** (or sequencing layer) serves as the glue between the reactive layer and the deliberative layer. It accepts directives by the deliberative layer, and sequences them for the reactive layer. For example, the executive layer might handle a set of via-points generated by a deliberative path planner, and make decisions as to which reactive behavior to invoke. Decision cycles at the executive layer are usually in the order of a second. The executive layer is also responsible for integrating sensor information into an internal state representation. For example, it may host the robot's localization and online mapping routines.

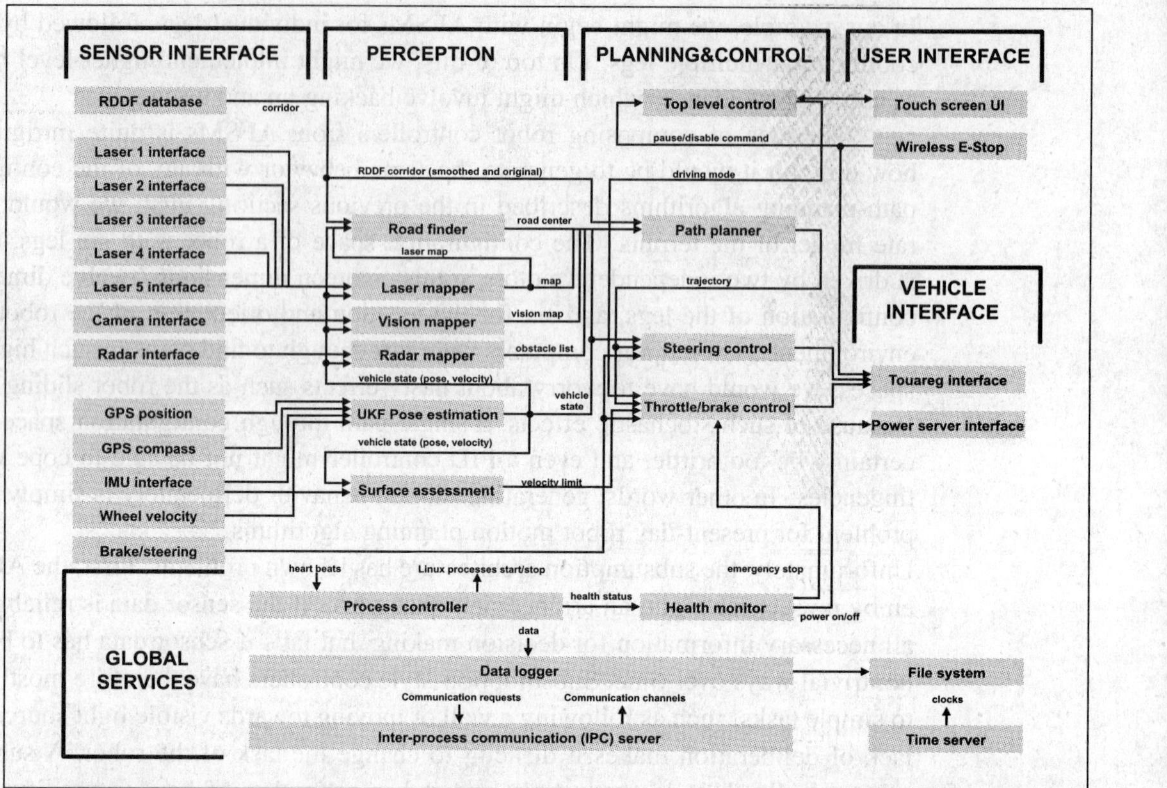

Figure 26 Software architecture of a robot car. This software implements a data pipeline, in which all modules process data simultaneously.

DELIBERATIVE LAYER

The **deliberative layer** generates global solutions to complex tasks using planning. Because of the computational complexity involved in generating such solutions, its decision cycle is often in the order of minutes. The deliberative layer (or planning layer) uses models for decision making. Those models might be either learned from data or supplied and may utilize state information gathered at the executive layer.

Variants of the three-layer architecture can be found in most modern-day robot software systems. The decomposition into three layers is not very strict. Some robot software systems possess additional layers, such as user interface layers that control the interaction with people, or a multiagent level for coordinating a robot's actions with that of other robots operating in the same environment.

7.3 Pipeline architecture

PIPELINE ARCHITECTURE

Another architecture for robots is known as the **pipeline architecture**. Just like the subsumption architecture, the pipeline architecture executes multiple process in parallel. However, the specific modules in this architecture resemble those in the three-layer architecture.

SENSOR INTERFACE LAYER

PERCEPTION LAYER

Figure 26 shows an example pipeline architecture, which is used to control an autonomous car. Data enters this pipeline at the **sensor interface layer**. The **perception layer**

(a) (b)

Figure 27 (a) The Helpmate robot transports food and other medical items in dozens of hospitals worldwide. (b) Kiva robots are part of a material-handling system for moving shelves in fulfillment centers. Image courtesy of Kiva Systems.

then updates the robot's internal models of the environment based on this data. Next, these models are handed to the **planning and control layer**, which adjusts the robot's internal plans turns them into actual controls for the robot. Those are then communicated back to the vehicle through the **vehicle interface layer**.

PLANNING AND CONTROL LAYER

VEHICLE INTERFACE LAYER

The key to the pipeline architecture is that this all happens in parallel. While the perception layer processes the most recent sensor data, the control layer bases its choices on slightly older data. In this way, the pipeline architecture is similar to the human brain. We don't switch off our motion controllers when we digest new sensor data. Instead, we perceive, plan, and act all at the same time. Processes in the pipeline architecture run asynchronously, and all computation is data-driven. The resulting system is robust, and it is fast.

The architecture in Figure 26 also contains other, cross-cutting modules, responsible for establishing communication between the different elements of the pipeline.

8 Application Domains

Here are some of the prime application domains for robotic technology.

Industry and Agriculture. Traditionally, robots have been fielded in areas that require difficult human labor, yet are structured enough to be amenable to robotic automation. The best example is the assembly line, where manipulators routinely perform tasks such as assembly, part placement, material handling, welding, and painting. In many of these tasks, robots have become more cost-effective than human workers. Outdoors, many of the heavy machines that we use to harvest, mine, or excavate earth have been turned into robots. For

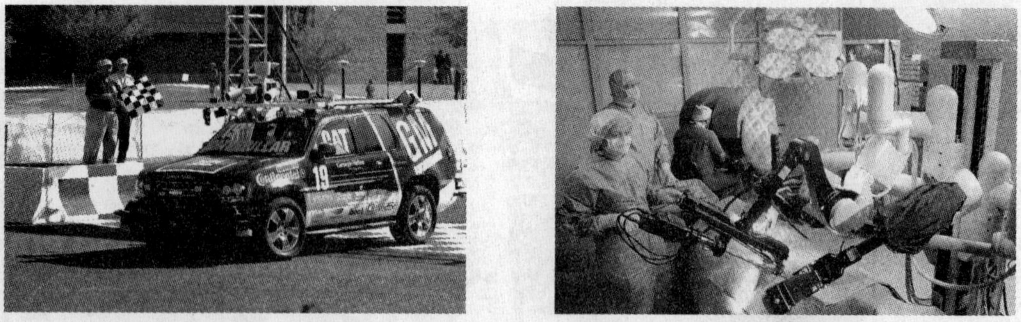

(a) (b)

Figure 28 (a) Robotic car BOSS, which won the DARPA Urban Challenge. Courtesy of Carnegie Mellon University. (b) Surgical robots in the operating room. Image courtesy of da Vinci Surgical Systems.

example, a project at Carnegie Mellon University has demonstrated that robots can strip paint off large ships about 50 times faster than people can, and with a much reduced environmental impact. Prototypes of autonomous mining robots have been found to be faster and more precise than people in transporting ore in underground mines. Robots have been used to generate high-precision maps of abandoned mines and sewer systems. While many of these systems are still in their prototype stages, it is only a matter of time until robots will take over much of the semimechanical work that is presently performed by people.

Transportation. Robotic transportation has many facets: from autonomous helicopters that deliver payloads to hard-to-reach locations, to automatic wheelchairs that transport people who are unable to control wheelchairs by themselves, to autonomous straddle carriers that outperform skilled human drivers when transporting containers from ships to trucks on loading docks. A prime example of indoor transportation robots, or gofers, is the Helpmate robot shown in Figure 27(a). This robot has been deployed in dozens of hospitals to transport food and other items. In factory settings, autonomous vehicles are now routinely deployed to transport goods in warehouses and between production lines. The Kiva system, shown in Figure 27(b), helps workers at fulfillment centers package goods into shipping containers.

Many of these robots require environmental modifications for their operation. The most common modifications are localization aids such as inductive loops in the floor, active beacons, or barcode tags. An open challenge in robotics is the design of robots that can use natural cues, instead of artificial devices, to navigate, particularly in environments such as the deep ocean where GPS is unavailable.

Robotic cars. Most of use cars every day. Many of us make cell phone calls while driving. Some of us even text. The sad result: more than a million people die every year in traffic accidents. Robotic cars like BOSS and STANLEY offer hope: Not only will they make driving much safer, but they will also free us from the need to pay attention to the road during our daily commute.

Progress in robotic cars was stimulated by the DARPA Grand Challenge, a race over 100 miles of unrehearsed desert terrain, which represented a much more challenging task than

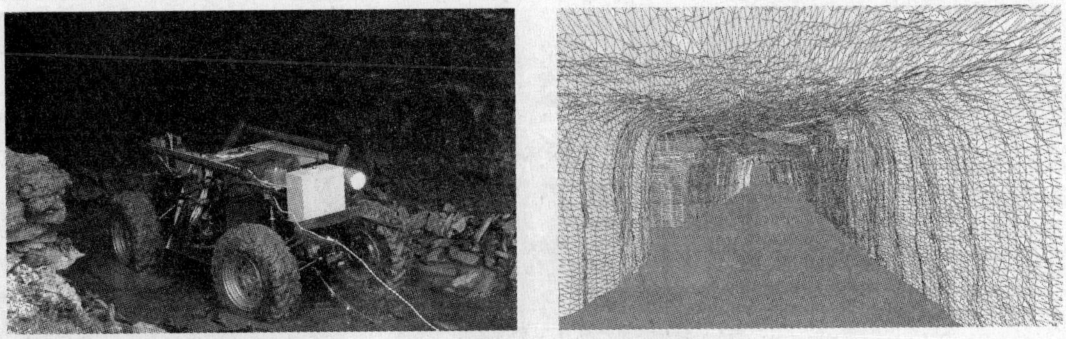

Figure 29 (a) A robot mapping an abandoned coal mine. (b) A 3D map of the mine acquired by the robot.

had ever been accomplished before. Stanford's STANLEY vehicle completed the course in less than seven hours in 2005, winning a $2 million prize and a place in the National Museum of American History. Figure 28(a) depicts BOSS, which in 2007 won the DARPA Urban Challenge, a complicated road race on city streets where robots faced other robots and had to obey traffic rules.

Health care. Robots are increasingly used to assist surgeons with instrument placement when operating on organs as intricate as brains, eyes, and hearts. Figure 28(b) shows such a system. Robots have become indispensable tools in a range of surgical procedures, such as hip replacements, thanks to their high precision. In pilot studies, robotic devices have been found to reduce the danger of lesions when performing colonoscopy. Outside the operating room, researchers have begun to develop robotic aides for elderly and handicapped people, such as intelligent robotic walkers and intelligent toys that provide reminders to take medication and provide comfort. Researchers are also working on robotic devices for rehabilitation that aid people in performing certain exercises.

Hazardous environments. Robots have assisted people in cleaning up nuclear waste, most notably in Chernobyl and Three Mile Island. Robots were present after the collapse of the World Trade Center, where they entered structures deemed too dangerous for human search and rescue crews.

Some countries have used robots to transport ammunition and to defuse bombs—a notoriously dangerous task. A number of research projects are presently developing prototype robots for clearing minefields, on land and at sea. Most existing robots for these tasks are teleoperated—a human operates them by remote control. Providing such robots with autonomy is an important next step.

Exploration. Robots have gone where no one has gone before, including the surface of Mars (see Figure 2(b)). Robotic arms assist astronauts in deploying and retrieving satellites and in building the International Space Station. Robots also help explore under the sea. They are routinely used to acquire maps of sunken ships. Figure 29 shows a robot mapping an abandoned coal mine, along with a 3D model of the mine acquired using range sensors. In

(a) (b)

Figure 30 (a) Roomba, the world's best-selling mobile robot, vacuums floors. Image courtesy of iRobot, © 2009. (b) Robotic hand modeled after human hand. Image courtesy of University of Washington and Carnegie Mellon University.

1996, a team of researches released a legged robot into the crater of an active volcano to acquire data for climate research. Unmanned air vehicles known as **drones** are used in military operations. Robots are becoming very effective tools for gathering information in domains that are difficult (or dangerous) for people to access.

DRONE

Personal Services. Service is an up-and-coming application domain of robotics. Service robots assist individuals in performing daily tasks. Commercially available domestic service robots include autonomous vacuum cleaners, lawn mowers, and golf caddies. The world's most popular mobile robot is a personal service robot: the robotic vacuum cleaner **Roomba**, shown in Figure 30(a). More than three million Roombas have been sold. Roomba can navigate autonomously and perform its tasks without human help.

ROOMBA

Other service robots operate in public places, such as robotic information kiosks that have been deployed in shopping malls and trade fairs, or in museums as tour guides. Service tasks require human interaction, and the ability to cope robustly with unpredictable and dynamic environments.

Entertainment. Robots have begun to conquer the entertainment and toy industry. In Figure 6(b) we see **robotic soccer**, a competitive game very much like human soccer, but played with autonomous mobile robots. Robot soccer provides great opportunities for research in AI, since it raises a range of problems relevant to many other, more serious robot applications. Annual robotic soccer competitions have attracted large numbers of AI researchers and added a lot of excitement to the field of robotics.

ROBOTIC SOCCER

Human augmentation. A final application domain of robotic technology is that of human augmentation. Researchers have developed legged walking machines that can carry people around, very much like a wheelchair. Several research efforts presently focus on the development of devices that make it easier for people to walk or move their arms by providing additional forces through extraskeletal attachments. If such devices are attached permanently, they can be thought of as artificial robotic limbs. Figure 30(b) shows a robotic hand that may serve as a prosthetic device in the future.

Robotic teleoperation, or telepresence, is another form of human augmentation. Teleoperation involves carrying out tasks over long distances with the aid of robotic devices. A popular configuration for robotic teleoperation is the master–slave configuration, where a robot manipulator emulates the motion of a remote human operator, measured through a haptic interface. Underwater vehicles are often teleoperated; the vehicles can go to a depth that would be dangerous for humans but can still be guided by the human operator. All these systems augment people's ability to interact with their environments. Some projects go as far as replicating humans, at least at a very superficial level. Humanoid robots are now available commercially through several companies in Japan.

9 SUMMARY

Robotics concerns itself with intelligent agents that manipulate the physical world. In this chapter, we have learned the following basics of robot hardware and software.

- Robots are equipped with **sensors** for perceiving their environment and effectors with which they can assert physical forces on their environment. Most robots are either manipulators anchored at fixed locations or mobile robots that can move.
- Robotic perception concerns itself with estimating decision-relevant quantities from sensor data. To do so, we need an internal representation and a method for updating this internal representation over time. Common examples of hard perceptual problems include **localization, mapping, and object recognition**.
- **Probabilistic filtering algorithms** such as Kalman filters and particle filters are useful for robot perception. These techniques maintain the belief state, a posterior distribution over state variables.
- The planning of robot motion is usually done in **configuration space**, where each point specifies the location and orientation of the robot and its joint angles.
- Configuration space search algorithms include **cell decomposition** techniques, which decompose the space of all configurations into finitely many cells, and **skeletonization** techniques, which project configuration spaces onto lower-dimensional manifolds. The motion planning problem is then solved using search in these simpler structures.
- A path found by a search algorithm can be executed by using the path as the reference trajectory for a **PID controller**. Controllers are necessary in robotics to accommodate small perturbations; path planning alone is usually insufficient.
- **Potential field** techniques navigate robots by potential functions, defined over the distance to obstacles and the goal location. Potential field techniques may get stuck in local minima, but they can generate motion directly without the need for path planning.
- Sometimes it is easier to specify a robot controller directly, rather than deriving a path from an explicit model of the environment. Such controllers can often be written as simple **finite state machines**.

- There exist different architectures for software design. The **subsumption architecture** enables programmers to compose robot controllers from interconnected finite state machines. **Three-layer architectures** are common frameworks for developing robot software that integrate deliberation, sequencing of subgoals, and control. The related **pipeline architecture** processes data in parallel through a sequence of modules, corresponding to perception, modeling, planning, control, and robot interfaces.

BIBLIOGRAPHICAL AND HISTORICAL NOTES

The word **robot** was popularized by Czech playwright Karel Capek in his 1921 play *R.U.R.* (Rossum's Universal Robots). The robots, which were grown chemically rather than constructed mechanically, end up resenting their masters and decide to take over. It appears (Glanc, 1978) it was Capek's brother, Josef, who first combined the Czech words "robota" (obligatory work) and "robotnik" (serf) to yield "robot" in his 1917 short story *Opilec*.

The term *robotics* was first used by Asimov (1950). Robotics (under other names) has a much longer history, however. In ancient Greek mythology, a mechanical man named Talos was supposedly designed and built by Hephaistos, the Greek god of metallurgy. Wonderful automata were built in the 18th century—Jacques Vaucanson's mechanical duck from 1738 being one early example—but the complex behaviors they exhibited were entirely fixed in advance. Possibly the earliest example of a programmable robot-like device was the Jacquard loom (1805).

UNIMATE

The first commercial robot was a robot arm called **Unimate**, short for *universal automation*, developed by Joseph Engelberger and George Devol. In 1961, the first Unimate robot was sold to General Motors, where it was used for manufacturing TV picture tubes. 1961 was also the year when Devol obtained the first U.S. patent on a robot. Eleven years later, in 1972, Nissan Corp. was among the first to automate an entire assembly line with robots, developed by Kawasaki with robots supplied by Engelberger and Devol's company Unimation. This development initiated a major revolution that took place mostly in Japan and the U.S., and that is still ongoing. Unimation followed up in 1978 with the development of the **PUMA** robot, short for Programmable Universal Machine for Assembly. The PUMA robot, initially developed for General Motors, was the *de facto* standard for robotic manipulation for the two decades that followed. At present, the number of operating robots is estimated at one million worldwide, more than half of which are installed in Japan.

PUMA

The literature on robotics research can be divided roughly into two parts: mobile robots and stationary manipulators. Grey Walter's "turtle," built in 1948, could be considered the first autonomous mobile robot, although its control system was not programmable. The "Hopkins Beast," built in the early 1960s at Johns Hopkins University, was much more sophisticated; it had pattern-recognition hardware and could recognize the cover plate of a standard AC power outlet. It was capable of searching for outlets, plugging itself in, and then recharging its batteries! Still, the Beast had a limited repertoire of skills. The first general-purpose mobile robot was "Shakey," developed at what was then the Stanford Research Institute (now

SRI) in the late 1960s (Fikes and Nilsson, 1971; Nilsson, 1984). Shakey was the first robot to integrate perception, planning, and execution, and much subsequent research in AI was influenced by this remarkable achievement. Shakey appears on the cover of this book with project leader Charlie Rosen (1917–2002). Other influential projects include the Stanford Cart and the CMU Rover (Moravec, 1983). Cox and Wilfong (1990) describes classic work on autonomous vehicles.

The field of robotic mapping has evolved from two distinct origins. The first thread began with work by Smith and Cheeseman (1986), who applied Kalman filters to the simultaneous localization and mapping problem. This algorithm was first implemented by Moutarlier and Chatila (1989), and later extended by Leonard and Durrant-Whyte (1992); see Dissanayake *et al.* (2001) for an overview of early Kalman filter variations. The second thread began with the development of the **occupancy grid** representation for probabilistic mapping, which specifies the probability that each (x, y) location is occupied by an obstacle (Moravec and Elfes, 1985). Kuipers and Levitt (1988) were among the first to propose topological rather than metric mapping, motivated by models of human spatial cognition. A seminal paper by Lu and Milios (1997) recognized the sparseness of the simultaneous localization and mapping problem, which gave rise to the development of nonlinear optimization techniques by Konolige (2004) and Montemerlo and Thrun (2004), as well as hierarchical methods by Bosse *et al.* (2004). Shatkay and Kaelbling (1997) and Thrun *et al.* (1998) introduced the EM algorithm into the field of robotic mapping for data association. An overview of probabilistic mapping methods can be found in (Thrun *et al.*, 2005).

OCCUPANCY GRID

Early mobile robot localization techniques are surveyed by Borenstein *et al.* (1996). Although Kalman filtering was well known as a localization method in control theory for decades, the general probabilistic formulation of the localization problem did not appear in the AI literature until much later, through the work of Tom Dean and colleagues (Dean *et al.*, 1990, 1990) and of Simmons and Koenig (1995). The latter work introduced the term **Markov localization**. The first real-world application of this technique was by Burgard *et al.* (1999), through a series of robots that were deployed in museums. Monte Carlo localization based on particle filters was developed by Fox *et al.* (1999) and is now widely used. The **Rao-Blackwellized particle filter** combines particle filtering for robot localization with exact filtering for map building (Murphy and Russell, 2001; Montemerlo *et al.*, 2002).

MARKOV LOCALIZATION

RAO-BLACKWELLIZED PARTICLE FILTER

HAND–EYE MACHINES

The study of manipulator robots, originally called **hand–eye machines**, has evolved along quite different lines. The first major effort at creating a hand–eye machine was Heinrich Ernst's MH-1, described in his MIT Ph.D. thesis (Ernst, 1961). The Machine Intelligence project at Edinburgh also demonstrated an impressive early system for vision-based assembly called FREDDY (Michie, 1972). After these pioneering efforts, a great deal of work focused on geometric algorithms for deterministic and fully observable motion planning problems. The PSPACE-hardness of robot motion planning was shown in a seminal paper by Reif (1979). The configuration space representation is due to Lozano-Perez (1983). A series of papers by Schwartz and Sharir on what they called **piano movers** problems (Schwartz *et al.*, 1987) was highly influential.

PIANO MOVERS

Recursive cell decomposition for configuration space planning was originated by Brooks and Lozano-Perez (1985) and improved significantly by Zhu and Latombe (1991). The earliest skeletonization algorithms were based on Voronoi diagrams (Rowat, 1979) and **visibility graphs** (Wesley and Lozano-Perez, 1979). Guibas *et al.* (1992) developed efficient techniques for calculating Voronoi diagrams incrementally, and Choset (1996) generalized Voronoi diagrams to broader motion-planning problems. John Canny (1988) established the first singly exponential algorithm for motion planning. The seminal text by Latombe (1991) covers a variety of approaches to motion-planning, as do the texts by Choset *et al.* (2004) and LaValle (2006). Kavraki *et al.* (1996) developed probabilistic roadmaps, which are currently one of the most effective methods. Fine-motion planning with limited sensing was investigated by Lozano-Perez *et al.* (1984) and Canny and Reif (1987). Landmark-based navigation (Lazanas and Latombe, 1992) uses many of the same ideas in the mobile robot arena. Key work applying POMDP methods to motion planning under uncertainty in robotics is due to Pineau *et al.* (2003) and Roy *et al.* (2005).

VISIBILITY GRAPH

The control of robots as dynamical systems—whether for manipulation or navigation—has generated a huge literature that is barely touched on by this chapter. Important works include a trilogy on impedance control by Hogan (1985) and a general study of robot dynamics by Featherstone (1987). Dean and Wellman (1991) were among the first to try to tie together control theory and AI planning systems. Three classic textbooks on the mathematics of robot manipulation are due to Paul (1981), Craig (1989), and Yoshikawa (1990). The area of **grasping** is also important in robotics—the problem of determining a stable grasp is quite difficult (Mason and Salisbury, 1985). Competent grasping requires touch sensing, or **haptic feedback**, to determine contact forces and detect slip (Fearing and Hollerbach, 1985).

GRASPING

HAPTIC FEEDBACK

Potential-field control, which attempts to solve the motion planning and control problems simultaneously, was introduced into the robotics literature by Khatib (1986). In mobile robotics, this idea was viewed as a practical solution to the collision avoidance problem, and was later extended into an algorithm called **vector field histograms** by Borenstein (1991). Navigation functions, the robotics version of a control policy for deterministic MDPs, were introduced by Koditschek (1987). Reinforcement learning in robotics took off with the seminal work by Bagnell and Schneider (2001) and Ng *et al.* (2004), who developed the paradigm in the context of autonomous helicopter control.

VECTOR FIELD HISTOGRAMS

The topic of software architectures for robots engenders much religious debate. The good old-fashioned AI candidate—the three-layer architecture—dates back to the design of Shakey and is reviewed by Gat (1998). The subsumption architecture is due to Brooks (1986), although similar ideas were developed independently by Braitenberg (1984), whose book, *Vehicles*, describes a series of simple robots based on the behavioral approach. The success of Brooks's six-legged walking robot was followed by many other projects. Connell, in his Ph.D. thesis (1989), developed a mobile robot capable of retrieving objects that was entirely reactive. Extensions of the behavior-based paradigm to multirobot systems can be found in (Mataric, 1997) and (Parker, 1996). GRL (Horswill, 2000) and COLBERT (Konolige, 1997) abstract the ideas of concurrent behavior-based robotics into general robot control languages. Arkin (1998) surveys some of the most popular approaches in this field.

Research on mobile robotics has been stimulated over the last decade by several important competitions. The earliest competition, AAAI's annual mobile robot competition, began in 1992. The first competition winner was CARMEL (Congdon *et al.*, 1992). Progress has been steady and impressive: in more recent competitions robots entered the conference complex, found their way to the registration desk, registered for the conference, and even gave a short talk. The **Robocup** competition, launched in 1995 by Kitano and colleagues (1997a), aims to "develop a team of fully autonomous humanoid robots that can win against the human world champion team in soccer" by 2050. Play occurs in leagues for simulated robots, wheeled robots of different sizes, and humanoid robots. In 2009 teams from 43 countries participated and the event was broadcast to millions of viewers. Visser and Burkhard (2007) track the improvements that have been made in perception, team coordination, and low-level skills over the past decade.

ROBOCUP

DARPA GRAND CHALLENGE

The **DARPA Grand Challenge**, organized by DARPA in 2004 and 2005, required autonomous robots to travel more than 100 miles through unrehearsed desert terrain in less than 10 hours (Buehler *et al.*, 2006). In the original event in 2004, no robot traveled more than 8 miles, leading many to believe the prize would never be claimed. In 2005, Stanford's robot STANLEY won the competition in just under 7 hours of travel (Thrun, 2006). DARPA then organized the **Urban Challenge**, a competition in which robots had to navigate 60 miles in an urban environment with other traffic. Carnegie Mellon University's robot BOSS took first place and claimed the $2 million prize (Urmson and Whittaker, 2008). Early pioneers in the development of robotic cars included Dickmanns and Zapp (1987) and Pomerleau (1993).

URBAN CHALLENGE

Two early textbooks, by Dudek and Jenkin (2000) and Murphy (2000), cover robotics generally. A more recent overview is due to Bekey (2008). An excellent book on robot manipulation addresses advanced topics such as compliant motion (Mason, 2001). Robot motion planning is covered in Choset *et al.* (2004) and LaValle (2006). Thrun *et al.* (2005) provide an introduction into probabilistic robotics. The premiere conference for robotics is Robotics: Science and Systems Conference, followed by the IEEE International Conference on Robotics and Automation. Leading robotics journals include *IEEE Robotics and Automation*, the *International Journal of Robotics Research*, and *Robotics and Autonomous Systems*.

EXERCISES

1 Monte Carlo localization is *biased* for any finite sample size—i.e., the expected value of the location computed by the algorithm differs from the true expected value—because of the way particle filtering works. In this question, you are asked to quantify this bias.

To simplify, consider a world with four possible robot locations: $X = \{x_1, x_2, x_3, x_4\}$. Initially, we draw $N \geq 1$ samples uniformly from among those locations. As usual, it is perfectly acceptable if more than one sample is generated for any of the locations X. Let Z be a Boolean sensor variable characterized by the following conditional probabilities:

$$\begin{aligned} P(z \mid x_1) &= 0.8 & \qquad P(\neg z \mid x_1) &= 0.2 \\ P(z \mid x_2) &= 0.4 & \qquad P(\neg z \mid x_2) &= 0.6 \\ P(z \mid x_3) &= 0.1 & \qquad P(\neg z \mid x_3) &= 0.9 \\ P(z \mid x_4) &= 0.1 & \qquad P(\neg z \mid x_4) &= 0.9 . \end{aligned}$$

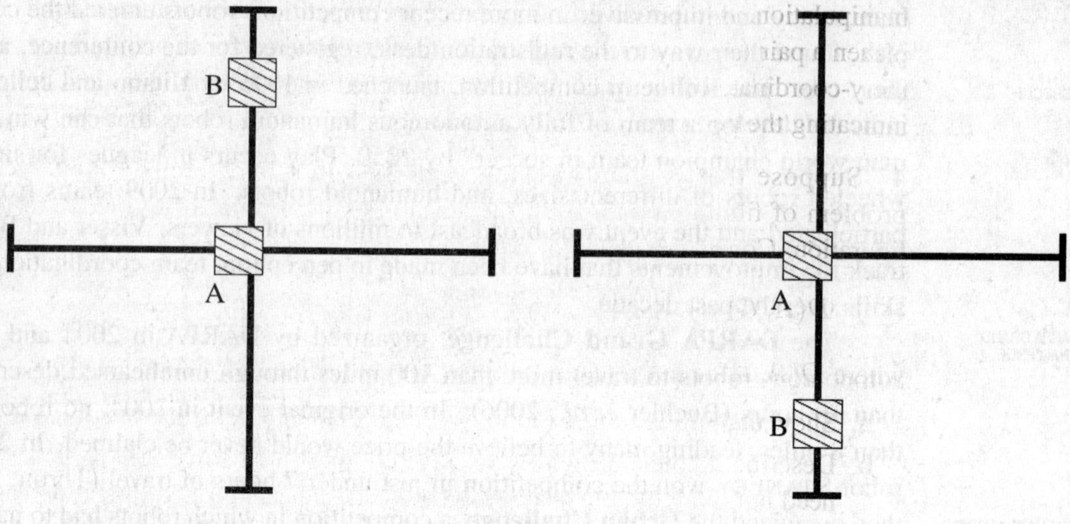

Starting configuration <−0.5, 7> Ending configuration <−0.5, −7>

Figure 31 A Robot manipulator in two of its possible configurations.

MCL uses these probabilities to generate particle weights, which are subsequently normalized and used in the resampling process. For simplicity, let us assume we generate only one new sample in the resampling process, regardless of N. This sample might correspond to any of the four locations in X. Thus, the sampling process defines a probability distribution over X.

a. What is the resulting probability distribution over X for this new sample? Answer this question separately for $N = 1, \ldots, 10$, and for $N = \infty$.

b. The difference between two probability distributions P and Q can be measured by the KL divergence, which is defined as

$$KL(P, Q) = \sum_i P(x_i) \log \frac{P(x_i)}{Q(x_i)} .$$

What are the KL divergences between the distributions in (a) and the true posterior?

c. What modification of the problem formulation (not the algorithm!) would guarantee that the specific estimator above is unbiased even for finite values of N? Provide at least two such modifications (each of which should be sufficient).

2 Implement Monte Carlo localization for a simulated robot with range sensors. A grid map and range data are available from the code repository at `aima.cs.berkeley.edu`. You should demonstrate successful global localization of the robot.

3 Consider a robot with two simple manipulators, as shown in figure 31. Manipulator A is a square block of side 2 which can slide back and on a rod that runs along the x-axis from x=−10 to x=10. Manipulator B is a square block of side 2 which can slide back and on a rod that runs along the y-axis from y=−10 to y=10. The rods lie outside the plane of manipulation, so the rods do not interfere with the movement of the blocks. A configuration is then a pair $\langle x, y\rangle$ where x is the x-coordinate of the center of manipulator A and where y is the y-coordinate of the center of manipulator B. Draw the configuration space for this robot, indicating the permitted and excluded zones.

4 Suppose that you are working with the robot in Exercise 3 and you are given the problem of finding a path from the starting configuration of figure 31 to the ending configuration. Consider a potential function

$$D(A, Goal)^2 + D(B, Goal)^2 + \frac{1}{D(A, B)^2}$$

where $D(A, B)$ is the distance between the closest points of A and B.

a. Show that hill climbing in this potential field will get stuck in a local minimum.

b. Describe a potential field where hill climbing will solve this particular problem. You need not work out the exact numerical coefficients needed, just the general form of the solution. (Hint: Add a term that "rewards" the hill climber for moving A out of B's way, even in a case like this where this does not reduce the distance from A to B in the above sense.)

5 Consider the robot arm shown in Figure 14. Assume that the robot's base element is 60cm long and that its upper arm and forearm are each 40cm long. As argued in section 4.1, the inverse kinematics of a robot is often not unique. State an explicit closed-form solution of the inverse kinematics for this arm. Under what exact conditions is the solution unique?

6 Implement an algorithm for calculating the Voronoi diagram of an arbitrary 2D environment, described by an $n \times n$ Boolean array. Illustrate your algorithm by plotting the Voronoi diagram for 10 interesting maps. What is the complexity of your algorithm?

7 This exercise explores the relationship between workspace and configuration space using the examples shown in Figure 32.

a. Consider the robot configurations shown in Figure 32(a) through (c), ignoring the obstacle shown in each of the diagrams. Draw the corresponding arm configurations in configuration space. (*Hint:* Each arm configuration maps to a single point in configuration space, as illustrated in Figure 14(b).)

b. Draw the configuration space for each of the workspace diagrams in Figure 32(a)–(c). (*Hint:* The configuration spaces share with the one shown in Figure 32(a) the region that corresponds to self-collision, but differences arise from the lack of enclosing obstacles and the different locations of the obstacles in these individual figures.)

c. For each of the black dots in Figure 32(e)–(f), draw the corresponding configurations of the robot arm in workspace. Please ignore the shaded regions in this exercise.

d. The configuration spaces shown in Figure 32(e)–(f) have all been generated by a single workspace obstacle (dark shading), plus the constraints arising from the self-collision constraint (light shading). Draw, for each diagram, the workspace obstacle that corresponds to the darkly shaded area.

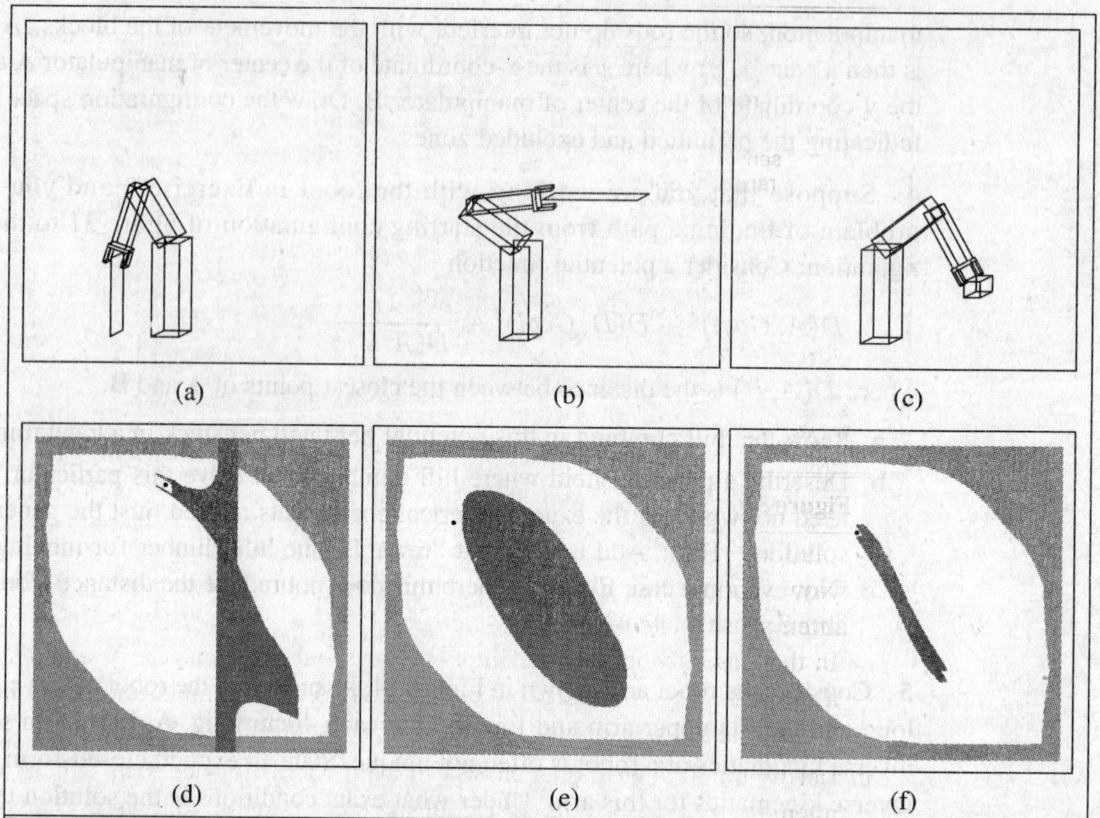

Figure 32 Diagrams for Exercise 7.

e. Figure 32(d) illustrates that a single planar obstacle can decompose the workspace into two disconnected regions. What is the maximum number of disconnected regions that can be created by inserting a planar obstacle into an obstacle-free, connected workspace, for a 2DOF robot? Give an example, and argue why no larger number of disconnected regions can be created. How about a non-planar obstacle?

8 Consider a mobile robot moving on a horizontal surface. Suppose that the robot can execute two kinds of motions:

- Rolling forward a specified distance.
- Rotating in place through a specified angle.

The state of such a robot can be characterized in terms of three parameters $\langle x, y, \phi$, the x-coordinate and y-coordinate of the robot (more precisely, of its center of rotation) and the robot's orientation expressed as the angle from the positive x direction. The action "$Roll(D)$" has the effect of changing state $\langle x, y, \phi$ to $\langle x + D\cos(\phi), y + D\sin(\phi), \phi\rangle$, and the action $Rotate(\theta)$ has the effect of changing state $\langle x, y, \phi\rangle$ to $\langle x, y, \phi + \theta\rangle$.

a. Suppose that the robot is initially at $\langle 0, 0, 0\rangle$ and then executes the actions $Rotate(60°)$, $Roll(1)$, $Rotate(25°)$, $Roll(2)$. What is the final state of the robot?

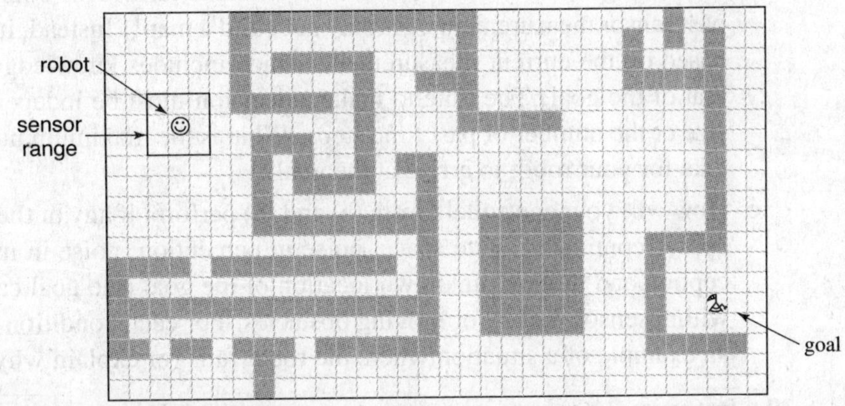

Figure 33 Simplified robot in a maze. See Exercise 9.

b. Now suppose that the robot has imperfect control of its own rotation, and that, if it attempts to rotate by θ, it may actually rotate by any angle between $\theta - 10°$ and $\theta + 10°$. In that case, if the robot attempts to carry out the sequence of actions in (A), there is a range of possible ending states. What are the minimal and maximal values of the x-coordinate, the y-coordinate and the orientation in the final state?

c. Let us modify the model in (B) to a probabilistic model in which, when the robot attempts to rotate by θ, its actual angle of rotation follows a Gaussian distribution with mean θ and standard deviation 10°. Suppose that the robot executes the actions $Rotate(90°)$, $Roll(1)$. Give a simple argument that (a) the expected value of the location at the end is not equal to the result of rotating exactly 90° and then rolling forward 1 unit, and (b) that the distribution of locations at the end does not follow a Gaussian. (Do not attempt to calculate the true mean or the true distribution.)

The point of this exercise is that rotational uncertainty quickly gives rise to a lot of positional uncertainty and that dealing with rotational uncertainty is painful, whether uncertainty is treated in terms of hard intervals or probabilistically, due to the fact that the relation between orientation and position is both non-linear and non-monotonic.

9 Consider the simplified robot shown in Figure 33. Suppose the robot's Cartesian coordinates are known at all times, as are those of its goal location. However, the locations of the obstacles are unknown. The robot can sense obstacles in its immediate proximity, as illustrated in this figure. For simplicity, let us assume the robot's motion is noise-free, and the state space is discrete. Figure 33 is only one example; in this exercise you are required to address all possible grid worlds with a valid path from the start to the goal location.

a. Design a deliberate controller that guarantees that the robot always reaches its goal location if at all possible. The deliberate controller can memorize measurements in the form of a map that is being acquired as the robot moves. Between individual moves, it may spend arbitrary time deliberating.

b. Now design a *reactive* controller for the same task. This controller may not memorize past sensor measurements. (It may not build a map!) Instead, it has to make all decisions based on the current measurement, which includes knowledge of its own location and that of the goal. The time to make a decision must be independent of the environment size or the number of past time steps. What is the maximum number of steps that it may take for your robot to arrive at the goal?

c. How will your controllers from (a) and (b) perform if any of the following six conditions apply: continuous state space, noise in perception, noise in motion, noise in both perception and motion, unknown location of the goal (the goal can be detected only when within sensor range), or moving obstacles. For each condition and each controller, give an example of a situation where the robot fails (or explain why it cannot fail).

10 In Figure 24(b), we encountered an augmented finite state machine for the control of a single leg of a hexapod robot. In this exercise, the aim is to design an AFSM that, when combined with six copies of the individual leg controllers, results in efficient, stable locomotion. For this purpose, you have to augment the individual leg controller to pass messages to your new AFSM and to wait until other messages arrive. Argue why your controller is efficient, in that it does not unnecessarily waste energy (e.g., by sliding legs), and in that it propels the robot at reasonably high speeds. Prove that your controller satisfies the dynamic stability condition given in section 2.2.

11 (This exercise was first devised by Michael Genesereth and Nils Nilsson. It works for first graders through graduate students.) Humans are so adept at basic household tasks that they often forget how complex these tasks are. In this exercise you will discover the complexity and recapitulate the last 30 years of developments in robotics. Consider the task of building an arch out of three blocks. Simulate a robot with four humans as follows:

Brain. The Brain direct the hands in the execution of a plan to achieve the goal. The Brain receives input from the Eyes, but *cannot see the scene directly*. The brain is the only one who knows what the goal is.

Eyes. The Eyes report a brief description of the scene to the Brain: "There is a red box standing on top of a green box, which is on its side" Eyes can also answer questions from the Brain such as, "Is there a gap between the Left Hand and the red box?" If you have a video camera, point it at the scene and allow the eyes to look at the viewfinder of the video camera, but not directly at the scene.

Left hand and **right hand.** One person plays each Hand. The two Hands stand next to each other, each wearing an oven mitt on one hand, Hands execute only simple commands from the Brain—for example, "Left Hand, move two inches forward." They cannot execute commands other than motions; for example, they cannot be commanded to "Pick up the box." The Hands must be *blindfolded*. The only sensory capability they have is the ability to tell when their path is blocked by an immovable obstacle such as a table or the other Hand. In such cases, they can beep to inform the Brain of the difficulty.

MATHEMATICAL BACKGROUND

1 Complexity Analysis and O() Notation

BENCHMARKING

ANALYSIS OF ALGORITHMS

Computer scientists are often faced with the task of comparing algorithms to see how fast they run or how much memory they require. There are two approaches to this task. The first is **benchmarking**—running the algorithms on a computer and measuring speed in seconds and memory consumption in bytes. Ultimately, this is what really matters, but a benchmark can be unsatisfactory because it is so specific: it measures the performance of a particular program written in a particular language, running on a particular computer, with a particular compiler and particular input data. From the single result that the benchmark provides, it can be difficult to predict how well the algorithm would do on a different compiler, computer, or data set. The second approach relies on a mathematical **analysis of algorithms**, independently of the particular implementation and input, as discussed below.

1.1 Asymptotic analysis

We will consider algorithm analysis through the following example, a program to compute the sum of a sequence of numbers:

```
function SUMMATION(sequence) returns a number
  sum ← 0
  for i = 1 to LENGTH(sequence) do
    sum ← sum + sequence[i]
  return sum
```

The first step in the analysis is to abstract over the input, in order to find some parameter or parameters that characterize the size of the input. In this example, the input can be characterized by the length of the sequence, which we will call n. The second step is to abstract over the implementation, to find some measure that reflects the running time of the algorithm but is not tied to a particular compiler or computer. For the SUMMATION program, this could be just the number of lines of code executed, or it could be more detailed, measuring the number of additions, assignments, array references, and branches executed by the algorithm.

Either way gives us a characterization of the total number of steps taken by the algorithm as a function of the size of the input. We will call this characterization $T(n)$. If we count lines of code, we have $T(n) = 2n + 2$ for our example.

If all programs were as simple as SUMMATION, the analysis of algorithms would be a trivial field. But two problems make it more complicated. First, it is rare to find a parameter like n that completely characterizes the number of steps taken by an algorithm. Instead, the best we can usually do is compute the worst case $T_{\text{worst}}(n)$ or the average case $T_{\text{avg}}(n)$. Computing an average means that the analyst must assume some distribution of inputs.

The second problem is that algorithms tend to resist exact analysis. In that case, it is necessary to fall back on an approximation. We say that the SUMMATION algorithm is $O(n)$, meaning that its measure is at most a constant times n, with the possible exception of a few small values of n. More formally,

$$T(n) \text{ is } O(f(n)) \text{ if } T(n) \leq kf(n) \text{ for some } k, \text{ for all } n > n_0 .$$

ASYMPTOTIC ANALYSIS

The $O()$ notation gives us what is called an **asymptotic analysis**. We can say without question that, as n asymptotically approaches infinity, an $O(n)$ algorithm is better than an $O(n^2)$ algorithm. A single benchmark figure could not substantiate such a claim.

The $O()$ notation abstracts over constant factors, which makes it easier to use, but less precise, than the $T()$ notation. For example, an $O(n^2)$ algorithm will always be worse than an $O(n)$ in the long run, but if the two algorithms are $T(n^2 + 1)$ and $T(100n + 1000)$, then the $O(n^2)$ algorithm is actually better for $n < 110$.

Despite this drawback, asymptotic analysis is the most widely used tool for analyzing algorithms. It is precisely because the analysis abstracts over both the exact number of operations (by ignoring the constant factor k) and the exact content of the input (by considering only its size n) that the analysis becomes mathematically feasible. The $O()$ notation is a good compromise between precision and ease of analysis.

1.2 NP and inherently hard problems

COMPLEXITY ANALYSIS

The analysis of algorithms and the $O()$ notation allow us to talk about the efficiency of a particular algorithm. However, they have nothing to say about whether there could be a better algorithm for the problem at hand. The field of **complexity analysis** analyzes problems rather than algorithms. The first gross division is between problems that can be solved in polynomial time and problems that cannot be solved in polynomial time, no matter what algorithm is used. The class of polynomial problems—those which can be solved in time $O(n^k)$ for some k—is called P. These are sometimes called "easy" problems, because the class contains those problems with running times like $O(\log n)$ and $O(n)$. But it also contains those with time $O(n^{1000})$, so the name "easy" should not be taken too literally.

Another important class of problems is NP, the class of nondeterministic polynomial problems. A problem is in this class if there is some algorithm that can guess a solution and then verify whether the guess is correct in polynomial time. The idea is that if you have an arbitrarily large number of processors, so that you can try all the guesses at once, or you are very lucky and always guess right the first time, then the NP problems become P problems. One of the biggest open questions in computer science is whether the class NP is equivalent to the class P when one does not have the luxury of an infinite number of processors or omniscient guessing. Most computer scientists are convinced that $P \neq NP$; that NP problems are inherently hard and have no polynomial-time algorithms. But this has never been proven.

NP-COMPLETE Those who are interested in deciding whether P = NP look at a subclass of NP called the **NP-complete** problems. The word "complete" is used here in the sense of "most extreme" and thus refers to the hardest problems in the class NP. It has been proven that either all the NP-complete problems are in P or none of them is. This makes the class theoretically interesting, but the class is also of practical interest because many important problems are known to be NP-complete. An example is the satisfiability problem: given a sentence of propositional logic, is there an assignment of truth values to the proposition symbols of the sentence that makes it true? Unless a miracle occurs and P = NP, there can be no algorithm that solves *all* satisfiability problems in polynomial time. However, AI is more interested in whether there are algorithms that perform efficiently on *typical* problems drawn from a pre-determined distribution; there are algorithms such as WALKSAT that do quite well on many problems.

CO-NP The class **co-NP** is the complement of NP, in the sense that, for every decision problem in NP, there is a corresponding problem in co-NP with the "yes" and "no" answers reversed. We know that P is a subset of both NP and co-NP, and it is believed that there are problems in co-NP that are not in P. The **co-NP-complete** problems are the hardest problems in co-NP. (CO-NP-COMPLETE)

The class #P (pronounced "sharp P") is the set of counting problems corresponding to the decision problems in NP. Decision problems have a yes-or-no answer: is there a solution to this 3-SAT formula? Counting problems have an integer answer: how many solutions are there to this 3-SAT formula? In some cases, the counting problem is much harder than the decision problem. For example, deciding whether a bipartite graph has a perfect matching can be done in time $O(VE)$ (where the graph has V vertices and E edges), but the counting problem "how many perfect matches does this bipartite graph have" is #P-complete, meaning that it is hard as any problem in #P and thus at least as hard as any NP problem.

Another class is the class of PSPACE problems—those that require a polynomial amount of space, even on a nondeterministic machine. It is believed that PSPACE-hard problems are worse than NP-complete problems, although it could turn out that NP = PSPACE, just as it could turn out that P = NP.

2 VECTORS, MATRICES, AND LINEAR ALGEBRA

VECTOR Mathematicians define a **vector** as a member of a vector space, but we will use a more concrete definition: a vector is an ordered sequence of values. For example, in two-dimensional space, we have vectors such as $\mathbf{x} = \langle 3, 4 \rangle$ and $\mathbf{y} = \langle 0, 2 \rangle$. We follow the convention of boldface characters for vector names, although some authors use arrows or bars over the names: $\vec{x}$ or $\bar{y}$. The elements of a vector can be accessed using subscripts: $\mathbf{z} = \langle z_1, z_2, \ldots, z_n \rangle$. One confusing point: this book is synthesizing work from many subfields, which variously call their sequences vectors, lists, or tuples, and variously use the notations $\langle 1, 2 \rangle$, [1, 2], or (1, 2).

The two fundamental operations on vectors are vector addition and scalar multiplication. The vector addition $\mathbf{x}+\mathbf{y}$ is the elementwise sum: $\mathbf{x}+\mathbf{y}=\langle 3+0, 4+2\rangle = \langle 3, 6\rangle$. Scalar multiplication multiplies each element by a constant: $5\mathbf{x} = \langle 5 \times 3, 5 \times 4\rangle = \langle 15, 20\rangle$.

The length of a vector is denoted $|\mathbf{x}|$ and is computed by taking the square root of the sum of the squares of the elements: $|\mathbf{x}| = \sqrt{(3^2+4^2)} = 5$. The dot product $\mathbf{x}\cdot\mathbf{y}$ (also called scalar product) of two vectors is the sum of the products of corresponding elements, that is, $\mathbf{x}\cdot\mathbf{y} = \sum_i x_i y_i$, or in our particular case, $\mathbf{x}\cdot\mathbf{y} = 3\times 0 + 4\times 2 = 8$.

Vectors are often interpreted as directed line segments (arrows) in an n-dimensional Euclidean space. Vector addition is then equivalent to placing the tail of one vector at the head of the other, and the dot product $\mathbf{x}\cdot\mathbf{y}$ is equal to $|\mathbf{x}|\,|\mathbf{y}|\cos\theta$, where θ is the angle between **x** and **y**.

MATRIX

A **matrix** is a rectangular array of values arranged into rows and columns. Here is a matrix **A** of size 3×4:

$$\begin{pmatrix} \mathbf{A}_{1,1} & \mathbf{A}_{1,2} & \mathbf{A}_{1,3} & \mathbf{A}_{1,4} \\ \mathbf{A}_{2,1} & \mathbf{A}_{2,2} & \mathbf{A}_{2,3} & \mathbf{A}_{2,4} \\ \mathbf{A}_{3,1} & \mathbf{A}_{3,2} & \mathbf{A}_{3,3} & \mathbf{A}_{3,4} \end{pmatrix}$$

The first index of $\mathbf{A}_{i,j}$ specifies the row and the second the column. In programming languages, $\mathbf{A}_{i,j}$ is often written `A[i,j]` or `A[i][j]`.

The sum of two matrices is defined by adding their corresponding elements; for example $(\mathbf{A}+\mathbf{B})_{i,j} = \mathbf{A}_{i,j} + \mathbf{B}_{i,j}$. (The sum is undefined if **A** and **B** have different sizes.) We can also define the multiplication of a matrix by a scalar: $(c\mathbf{A})_{i,j} = c\mathbf{A}_{i,j}$. Matrix multiplication (the product of two matrices) is more complicated. The product **AB** is defined only if **A** is of size $a\times b$ and **B** is of size $b\times c$ (i.e., the second matrix has the same number of rows as the first has columns); the result is a matrix of size $a\times c$. If the matrices are of appropriate size, then the result is

$$(\mathbf{AB})_{i,k} = \sum_j \mathbf{A}_{i,j}\mathbf{B}_{j,k}\,.$$

Matrix multiplication is not commutative, even for square matrices: $\mathbf{AB} \neq \mathbf{BA}$ in general. It is, however, associative: $(\mathbf{AB})\mathbf{C} = \mathbf{A}(\mathbf{BC})$. Note that the dot product can be expressed in terms of a transpose and a matrix multiplication: $\mathbf{x}\cdot\mathbf{y} = \mathbf{x}^\top\mathbf{y}$.

IDENTITY MATRIX

TRANSPOSE

INVERSE

SINGULAR

The **identity matrix I** has elements $\mathbf{I}_{i,j}$ equal to 1 when $i=j$ and equal to 0 otherwise. It has the property that $\mathbf{AI}=\mathbf{A}$ for all **A**. The **transpose** of **A**, written $\mathbf{A}^\top$ is formed by turning rows into columns and vice versa, or, more formally, by $\mathbf{A}^\top{}_{i,j} = \mathbf{A}_{j,i}$. The **inverse** of a square matrix **A** is another square matrix $\mathbf{A}^{-1}$ such that $\mathbf{A}^{-1}\mathbf{A}=\mathbf{I}$. For a **singular** matrix, the inverse does not exist. For a nonsingular matrix, it can be computed in $O(n^3)$ time.

Matrices are used to solve systems of linear equations in $O(n^3)$ time; the time is dominated by inverting a matrix of coefficients. Consider the following set of equations, for which we want a solution in x, y, and z:

$$\begin{aligned} +2x+y-z &= 8 \\ -3x-y+2z &= -11 \\ -2x+y+2z &= -3\,. \end{aligned}$$

We can represent this system as the matrix equation $\mathbf{A}\,\mathbf{x} = \mathbf{b}$, where

$$\mathbf{A} = \begin{pmatrix} 2 & 1 & -1 \\ -3 & -1 & 2 \\ -2 & 1 & 2 \end{pmatrix}, \quad \mathbf{x} = \begin{pmatrix} x \\ y \\ z \end{pmatrix}, \quad \mathbf{b} = \begin{pmatrix} 8 \\ -11 \\ -3 \end{pmatrix}.$$

To solve $\mathbf{A}\,\mathbf{x} = \mathbf{b}$ we multiply both sides by $\mathbf{A}^{-1}$, yielding $\mathbf{A}^{-1}\mathbf{A}\mathbf{x} = \mathbf{A}^{-1}\mathbf{b}$, which simplifies to $\mathbf{x} = \mathbf{A}^{-1}\mathbf{b}$. After inverting $\mathbf{A}$ and multiplying by $\mathbf{b}$, we get the answer

$$\mathbf{x} = \begin{pmatrix} x \\ y \\ z \end{pmatrix} = \begin{pmatrix} 2 \\ 3 \\ -1 \end{pmatrix}.$$

3 PROBABILITY DISTRIBUTIONS

A probability is a measure over a set of events that satisfies three axioms:

1. The measure of each event is between 0 and 1. We write this as $0 \le P(X = x_i) \le 1$, where X is a random variable representing an event and x_i are the possible values of X. In general, random variables are denoted by uppercase letters and their values by lowercase letters.
2. The measure of the whole set is 1; that is, $\sum_{i=1}^{n} P(X = x_i) = 1$.
3. The probability of a union of disjoint events is the sum of the probabilities of the individual events; that is, $P(X = x_1 \vee X = x_2) = P(X = x_1) + P(X = x_2)$, where x_1 and x_2 are disjoint.

A **probabilistic model** consists of a sample space of mutually exclusive possible outcomes, together with a probability measure for each outcome. For example, in a model of the weather tomorrow, the outcomes might be *sunny, cloudy, rainy*, and *snowy*. A subset of these outcomes constitutes an event. For example, the event of precipitation is the subset consisting of $\{$*rainy, snowy*$\}$.

We use $\mathbf{P}(X)$ to denote the vector of values $\langle P(X = x_1), \ldots, P(X = x_n)\rangle$. We also use $P(x_i)$ as an abbreviation for $P(X = x_i)$ and $\sum_x P(x)$ for $\sum_{i=1}^{n} P(X = x_i)$.

The conditional probability $P(B|A)$ is defined as $P(B \cap A)/P(A)$. A and B are conditionally independent if $P(B|A) = P(B)$ (or equivalently, $P(A|B) = P(A)$). For continuous variables, there are an infinite number of values, and unless there are point spikes, the probability of any one value is 0. Therefore, we define a **probability density function**, which we also denote as $P(\cdot)$, but which has a slightly different meaning from the discrete probability function. The density function $P(x)$ for a random variable X, which might be thought of as $P(X = x)$, is intuitively defined as the ratio of the probability that X falls into an interval around x, divided by the width of the interval, as the interval width goes to zero:

PROBABILITY DENSITY FUNCTION

$$P(x) = \lim_{dx \to 0} P(x \le X \le x + dx)/dx\,.$$

The density function must be nonnegative for all x and must have

$$\int_{-\infty}^{\infty} P(x)\, dx = 1\,.$$

CUMULATIVE PROBABILITY DENSITY FUNCTION

We can also define a **cumulative probability density function** $F_X(x)$, which is the probability of a random variable being less than x:

$$F_X(x) = P(X \leq x) = \int_{-\infty}^{x} P(u)\, du\,.$$

Note that the probability density function has units, whereas the discrete probability function is unitless. For example, if values of X are measured in seconds, then the density is measured in Hz (i.e., 1/sec). If values of $\mathbf{X}$ are points in three-dimensional space measured in meters, then density is measured in $1/m^3$.

GAUSSIAN DISTRIBUTION

One of the most important probability distributions is the **Gaussian distribution**, also known as the **normal distribution**. A Gaussian distribution with mean μ and standard deviation σ (and therefore variance σ^2) is defined as

$$P(x) = \frac{1}{\sigma\sqrt{2\pi}} e^{-(x-\mu)^2/(2\sigma^2)}\,,$$

STANDARD NORMAL DISTRIBUTION

MULTIVARIATE GAUSSIAN

where x is a continuous variable ranging from $-\infty$ to $+\infty$. With mean $\mu = 0$ and variance $\sigma^2 = 1$, we get the special case of the **standard normal distribution**. For a distribution over a vector $\mathbf{x}$ in n dimensions, there is the **multivariate Gaussian** distribution:

$$P(\mathbf{x}) = \frac{1}{\sqrt{(2\pi)^n |\boldsymbol{\Sigma}|}} e^{-\frac{1}{2}\left((\mathbf{x}-\boldsymbol{\mu})^\top \boldsymbol{\Sigma}^{-1}(\mathbf{x}-\boldsymbol{\mu})\right)}\,,$$

where $\boldsymbol{\mu}$ is the mean vector and $\boldsymbol{\Sigma}$ is the **covariance matrix** (see below).

CUMULATIVE DISTRIBUTION

In one dimension, we can define the **cumulative distribution** function $F(x)$ as the probability that a random variable will be less than x. For the normal distribution, this is

$$F(x) = \int_{-\infty}^{x} P(z)dz = \frac{1}{2}(1 + \operatorname{erf}(\frac{z-\mu}{\sigma\sqrt{2}}))\,,$$

where $\operatorname{erf}(x)$ is the so-called **error function**, which has no closed-form representation.

CENTRAL LIMIT THEOREM

The **central limit theorem** states that the distribution formed by sampling n independent random variables and taking their mean tends to a normal distribution as n tends to infinity. This holds for almost any collection of random variables, even if they are not strictly independent, unless the variance of any finite subset of variables dominates the others.

EXPECTATION

The **expectation** of a random variable, $E(X)$, is the mean or average value, weighted by the probability of each value. For a discrete variable it is:

$$E(X) = \sum_i x_i P(X = x_i)\,.$$

For a continuous variable, replace the summation with an integral over the probability density function, $P(x)$:

$$E(X) = \int_{-\infty}^{\infty} xP(x)\, dx\,,$$

ROOT MEAN SQUARE The **root mean square**, RMS, of a set of values (often samples of a random variable) is the square root of the mean of the squares of the values,

$$RMS(x_1, \ldots, x_n) = \sqrt{\frac{x_1^2 + \ldots + x_n^2}{n}}.$$

COVARIANCE The **covariance** of two random variables is the expectation of the product of their differences from their means:

$$\text{cov}(X, Y) = E((X - \mu_X)(Y - \mu_Y)).$$

COVARIANCE MATRIX The **covariance matrix**, often denoted $\mathbf{\Sigma}$, is a matrix of covariances between elements of a vector of random variables. Given $\mathbf{X} = \langle X_1, \ldots X_n \rangle^\top$, the entries of the covariance matrix are as follows:

$$\mathbf{\Sigma}_{i,j} = \text{cov}(X_i, X_j) = E((X_i - \mu_i)(X_j - \mu_j)).$$

A few more miscellaneous points: we use $\log(x)$ for the natural logarithm, $\log_e(x)$. We use $\text{argmax}_x\, f(x)$ for the value of x for which $f(x)$ is maximal.

BIBLIOGRAPHICAL AND HISTORICAL NOTES

The $O()$ notation so widely used in computer science today was first introduced in the context of number theory by the German mathematician P. G. H. Bachmann (1894). The concept of NP-completeness was invented by Cook (1971), and the modern method for establishing a reduction from one problem to another is due to Karp (1972). Cook and Karp have both won the Turing award, the highest honor in computer science, for their work.

Classic works on the analysis and design of algorithms include those by Knuth (1973) and Aho, Hopcroft, and Ullman (1974); more recent contributions are by Tarjan (1983) and Cormen, Leiserson, and Rivest (1990). These books place an emphasis on designing and analyzing algorithms to solve tractable problems. For the theory of NP-completeness and other forms of intractability, see Garey and Johnson (1979) or Papadimitriou (1994). Good texts on probability include Chung (1979), Ross (1988), and Bertsekas and Tsitsiklis (2008).

NOTES ON LANGUAGES AND ALGORITHMS

NOTES ON LANGUAGES AND ALGORITHMS

1 DEFINING LANGUAGES WITH BACKUS–NAUR FORM (BNF)

A formal language is defined as a set of strings where each string is a sequence of symbols. The languages we are interested in consist of an infinite set of strings, so we need a concise way to characterize the set. We do that with a **grammar**. The particular type of grammar we use is called a **context-free grammar**, because each expression has the same form in any context. We write our grammars in a formalism called **Backus–Naur form (BNF)**. There are four components to a BNF grammar:

CONTEXT-FREE GRAMMAR
BACKUS–NAUR FORM (BNF)

TERMINAL SYMBOL

- A set of **terminal symbols**. These are the symbols or words that make up the strings of the language. They could be letters (**A, B, C,** . . .) or words (**a, aardvark, abacus,** . . .), or whatever symbols are appropriate for the domain.

NONTERMINAL SYMBOL

- A set of **nonterminal symbols** that categorize subphrases of the language. For example, the nonterminal symbol *NounPhrase* in English denotes an infinite set of strings including "you" and "the big slobbery dog."

START SYMBOL

- A **start symbol**, which is the nonterminal symbol that denotes the complete set of strings of the language. In English, this is *Sentence*; for arithmetic, it might be *Expr*, and for programming languages it is *Program*.
- A set of **rewrite rules**, of the form $LHS \rightarrow RHS$, where LHS is a nonterminal symbol and RHS is a sequence of zero or more symbols. These can be either terminal or nonterminal symbols, or the symbol ϵ, which is used to denote the empty string.

A rewrite rule of the form

$$Sentence \rightarrow NounPhrase\ VerbPhrase$$

means that whenever we have two strings categorized as a *NounPhrase* and a *VerbPhrase*, we can append them together and categorize the result as a *Sentence*. As an abbreviation, the two rules $(S \rightarrow A)$ and $(S \rightarrow B)$ can be written $(S \rightarrow A \mid B)$.

Here is a BNF grammar for simple arithmetic expressions:

$$
\begin{array}{lll}
\textit{Expr} & \rightarrow & \textit{Expr Operator Expr} \mid (\ \textit{Expr}\ ) \mid \textit{Number} \\
\textit{Number} & \rightarrow & \textit{Digit} \mid \textit{Number Digit} \\
\textit{Digit} & \rightarrow & \mathbf{0} \mid \mathbf{1} \mid \mathbf{2} \mid \mathbf{3} \mid \mathbf{4} \mid \mathbf{5} \mid \mathbf{6} \mid \mathbf{7} \mid \mathbf{8} \mid \mathbf{9} \\
\textit{Operator} & \rightarrow & + \mid - \mid \div \mid \times
\end{array}
$$

Be aware that other texts use slightly different notations for BNF; for example, you might see ⟨*Digit*⟩ instead of Digit for a nonterminal, 'word' instead of **word** for a terminal, or **::=** instead of → in a rule.

2 Describing Algorithms with Pseudocode

The algorithms in this book are described in pseudocode. Most of the pseudocode should be familiar to users of languages like Java, C++, or Lisp. In some places we use mathematical formulas or ordinary English to describe parts that would otherwise be more cumbersome. A few idiosyncrasies should be noted.

- **Persistent variables**: We use the keyword **persistent** to say that a variable is given an initial value the first time a function is called and retains that value (or the value given to it by a subsequent assignment statement) on all subsequent calls to the function. Thus, persistent variables are like global variables in that they outlive a single call to their function, but they are accessible only within the function. The agent programs in the book use persistent variables for *memory*. Programs with persistent variables can be implemented as *objects* in object-oriented languages such as C++, Java, Python, and Smalltalk. In functional languages, they can be implemented by *functional closures* over an environment containing the required variables.
- **Functions as values**: Functions and procedures have capitalized names, and variables have lowercase italic names. So most of the time, a function call looks like FN(x). However, we allow the value of a variable to be a function; for example, if the value of the variable f is the square root function, then $f(9)$ returns 3.
- **for each**: The notation "**for each** x **in** c **do**" means that the loop is executed with the variable x bound to successive elements of the collection c.
- **Indentation is significant**: Indentation is used to mark the scope of a loop or conditional, as in the language Python, and unlike Java and C++ (which use braces) or Pascal and Visual Basic (which use **end**).
- **Destructuring assignment**: The notation "$x, y \leftarrow$ *pair*" means that the right-hand side must evaluate to a two-element tuple, and the first element is assigned to x and the second to y. The same idea is used in "**for each** x, y **in** *pairs* **do**" and can be used to swap two variables: "$x, y \leftarrow y, x$"
- **Generators** and **yield**: the notation "**generator** G(x) **yields** numbers" defines G as a generator function. This is best understood by an example. The code fragment shown in

```
generator POWERS-OF-2() yields ints
  i ← 1
  while true do
    yield i
    i ← 2 × i

for p in POWERS-OF-2() do
  PRINT(p)
```

Figure 1 Example of a generator function and its invocation within a loop.

Figure 1 prints the numbers 1, 2, 4, . . . , and never stops. The call to POWERS-OF-2 returns a generator, which in turn yields one value each time the loop code asks for the next element of the collection. Even though the collection is infinite, it is enumerated one element at a time.

- **Lists:** $[x, y, z]$ denotes a list of three elements. $[first|rest]$ denotes a list formed by adding *first* to the list *rest*. In Lisp, this is the `cons` function.
- **Sets:** $\{x, y, z\}$ denotes a set of three elements. $\{x : p(x)\}$ denotes the set of all elements x for which $p(x)$ is true.
- **Arrays start at 1**: Unless stated otherwise, the first index of an array is 1 as in usual mathematical notation, not 0, as in Java and C.

3 ONLINE HELP

Most of the algorithms in the book have been implemented in Java, Lisp, and Python at our online code repository:

`aima.cs.berkeley.edu`

The same Web site includes instructions for sending comments, corrections, or suggestions for improving the book, and for joining discussion lists.

Bibliography

The following abbreviations are used for frequently cited conferences and journals:

AAAI	Proceedings of the AAAI Conference on Artificial Intelligence
AAMAS	Proceedings of the International Conference on Autonomous Agents and Multi-agent Systems
ACL	Proceedings of the Annual Meeting of the Association for Computational Linguistics
AIJ	Artificial Intelligence
AIMag	AI Magazine
AIPS	Proceedings of the International Conference on AI Planning Systems
BBS	Behavioral and Brain Sciences
CACM	Communications of the Association for Computing Machinery
COGSCI	Proceedings of the Annual Conference of the Cognitive Science Society
COLING	Proceedings of the International Conference on Computational Linguistics
COLT	Proceedings of the Annual ACM Workshop on Computational Learning Theory
CP	Proceedings of the International Conference on Principles and Practice of Constraint Programming
CVPR	Proceedings of the IEEE Conference on Computer Vision and Pattern Recognition
EC	Proceedings of the ACM Conference on Electronic Commerce
ECAI	Proceedings of the European Conference on Artificial Intelligence
ECCV	Proceedings of the European Conference on Computer Vision
ECML	Proceedings of the The European Conference on Machine Learning
ECP	Proceedings of the European Conference on Planning
FGCS	Proceedings of the International Conference on Fifth Generation Computer Systems
FOCS	Proceedings of the Annual Symposium on Foundations of Computer Science
ICAPS	Proceedings of the International Conference on Automated Planning and Scheduling
ICASSP	Proceedings of the International Conference on Acoustics, Speech, and Signal Processing
ICCV	Proceedings of the International Conference on Computer Vision
ICLP	Proceedings of the International Conference on Logic Programming
ICML	Proceedings of the International Conference on Machine Learning
ICPR	Proceedings of the International Conference on Pattern Recognition
ICRA	Proceedings of the IEEE International Conference on Robotics and Automation
ICSLP	Proceedings of the International Conference on Speech and Language Processing
IJAR	International Journal of Approximate Reasoning
IJCAI	Proceedings of the International Joint Conference on Artificial Intelligence
IJCNN	Proceedings of the International Joint Conference on Neural Networks
IJCV	International Journal of Computer Vision
ILP	Proceedings of the International Workshop on Inductive Logic Programming
ISMIS	Proceedings of the International Symposium on Methodologies for Intelligent Systems
ISRR	Proceedings of the International Symposium on Robotics Research
JACM	Journal of the Association for Computing Machinery
JAIR	Journal of Artificial Intelligence Research
JAR	Journal of Automated Reasoning
JASA	Journal of the American Statistical Association
JMLR	Journal of Machine Learning Research
JSL	Journal of Symbolic Logic
KDD	Proceedings of the International Conference on Knowledge Discovery and Data Mining
KR	Proceedings of the International Conference on Principles of Knowledge Representation and Reasoning
LICS	Proceedings of the IEEE Symposium on Logic in Computer Science
NIPS	Advances in Neural Information Processing Systems
PAMI	IEEE Transactions on Pattern Analysis and Machine Intelligence
PNAS	Proceedings of the National Academy of Sciences of the United States of America
PODS	Proceedings of the ACM International Symposium on Principles of Database Systems
SIGIR	Proceedings of the Special Interest Group on Information Retrieval
SIGMOD	Proceedings of the ACM SIGMOD International Conference on Management of Data
SODA	Proceedings of the Annual ACM–SIAM Symposium on Discrete Algorithms
STOC	Proceedings of the Annual ACM Symposium on Theory of Computing
TARK	Proceedings of the Conference on Theoretical Aspects of Reasoning about Knowledge
UAI	Proceedings of the Conference on Uncertainty in Artificial Intelligence

Aarup, M., Arentoft, M. M., Parrod, Y., Stader, J., and Stokes, I. (1994). OPTIMUM-AIV: A knowledge-based planning and scheduling system for spacecraft AIV. In Fox, M. and Zweben, M (Eds.), *Knowledge Based Scheduling*. Morgan Kaufmann.

Abney, S. (2007). *Semisupervised Learning for Computational Linguistics*. CRC Press.

Abramson, B. and Yung, M. (1989). Divide and conquer under global constraints: A solution to the N-queens problem. *J. Parallel and Distributed Computing*, *6*(3), 649–662.

Achlioptas, D. (2009). Random satisfiability. In Biere, A., Heule, M., van Maaren, H., and Walsh, T. (Eds.), *Handbook of Satisfiability*. IOS Press.

Achlioptas, D., Beame, P., and Molloy, M. (2004). Exponential bounds for DPLL below the satisfiability threshold. In *SODA-04*.

Achlioptas, D., Naor, A., and Peres, Y. (2007). On the maximum satisfiability of random formulas. *JACM*, *54*(2).

Achlioptas, D. and Peres, Y. (2004). The threshold for random k-SAT is $2k \log 2 - o(k)$. *J. American Mathematical Society*, *17*(4), 947–973.

Ackley, D. H. and Littman, M. L. (1991). Interactions between learning and evolution. In Langton, C., Taylor, C., Farmer, J. D., and Ramussen, S. (Eds.), *Artificial Life II*, pp. 487–509. Addison-Wesley.

Adelson-Velsky, G. M., Arlazarov, V. L., Bitman, A. R., Zhivotovsky, A. A., and Uskov, A. V. (1970). Programming a computer to play chess. *Russian Mathematical Surveys*, *25*, 221–262.

Adida, B. and Birbeck, M. (2008). RDFa primer. Tech. rep., W3C.

Agerbeck, C. and Hansen, M. O. (2008). A multi-agent approach to solving *NP*-complete problems. Master's thesis, Technical Univ. of Denmark.

Aggarwal, G., Goel, A., and Motwani, R. (2006). Truthful auctions for pricing search keywords. In *EC-06*, pp. 1–7.

Agichtein, E. and Gravano, L. (2003). Querying text databases for efficient information extraction. In *Proc. IEEE Conference on Data Engineering*.

Agmon, S. (1954). The relaxation method for linear inequalities. *Canadian Journal of Mathematics*, *6*(3), 382–392.

Agre, P. E. and Chapman, D. (1987). Pengi: an implementation of a theory of activity. In *IJCAI-87*, pp. 268–272.

Aho, A. V., Hopcroft, J., and Ullman, J. D. (1974). *The Design and Analysis of Computer Algorithms*. Addison-Wesley.

Aizerman, M., Braverman, E., and Rozonoer, L. (1964). Theoretical foundations of the potential function method in pattern recognition learning. *Automation and Remote Control*, *25*, 821–837.

Al-Chang, M., Bresina, J., Charest, L., Chase, A., Hsu, J., Jonsson, A., Kanefsky, B., Morris, P., Rajan, K., Yglesias, J., Chafin, B., Dias, W., and Maldague, P. (2004). MAPGEN: Mixed-Initiative planning and scheduling for the Mars Exploration Rover mission. *IEEE Intelligent Systems*, *19*(1), 8–12.

Albus, J. S. (1975). A new approach to manipulator control: The cerebellar model articulation controller (CMAC). *J. Dynamic Systems, Measurement, and Control*, *97*, 270–277.

Aldous, D. and Vazirani, U. (1994). "Go with the winners" algorithms. In *FOCS-94*, pp. 492–501.

Alekhnovich, M., Hirsch, E. A., and Itsykson, D. (2005). Exponential lower bounds for the running time of DPLL algorithms on satisfiable formulas. *JAR*, *35*(1–3), 51–72.

Allais, M. (1953). Le comportment de l'homme rationnel devant la risque: critique des postulats et axiomes de l'école Américaine. *Econometrica*, *21*, 503–546.

Allen, J. F. (1983). Maintaining knowledge about temporal intervals. *CACM*, *26*(11), 832–843.

Allen, J. F. (1984). Towards a general theory of action and time. *AIJ*, *23*, 123–154.

Allen, J. F. (1991). Time and time again: The many ways to represent time. *Int. J. Intelligent Systems*, *6*, 341–355.

Allen, J. F., Hendler, J., and Tate, A. (Eds.). (1990). *Readings in Planning*. Morgan Kaufmann.

Allis, L. (1988). A knowledge-based approach to connect four. The game is solved: White wins. Master's thesis, Vrije Univ., Amsterdam.

Almuallim, H. and Dietterich, T. (1991). Learning with many irrelevant features. In *AAAI-91*, Vol. 2, pp. 547–552.

ALPAC (1966). Language and machines: Computers in translation and linguistics. Tech. rep. 1416, The Automatic Language Processing Advisory Committee of the National Academy of Sciences.

Alterman, R. (1988). Adaptive planning. *Cognitive Science*, *12*, 393–422.

Amarel, S. (1967). An approach to heuristic problem-solving and theorem proving in the propositional calculus. In Hart, J. and Takasu, S. (Eds.), *Systems and Computer Science*. University of Toronto Press.

Amarel, S. (1968). On representations of problems of reasoning about actions. In Michie, D. (Ed.), *Machine Intelligence 3*, Vol. 3, pp. 131–171. Elsevier/North-Holland.

Amir, E. and Russell, S. J. (2003). Logical filtering. In *IJCAI-03*.

Amit, D., Gutfreund, H., and Sompolinsky, H. (1985). Spin-glass models of neural networks. *Physical Review*, *A 32*, 1007–1018.

Andersen, S. K., Olesen, K. G., Jensen, F. V., and Jensen, F. (1989). HUGIN—A shell for building Bayesian belief universes for expert systems. In *IJCAI-89*, Vol. 2, pp. 1080–1085.

Anderson, J. R. (1980). *Cognitive Psychology and Its Implications*. W. H. Freeman.

Anderson, J. R. (1983). *The Architecture of Cognition*. Harvard University Press.

Andoni, A. and Indyk, P. (2006). Near-optimal hashing algorithms for approximate nearest neighbor in high dimensions. In *FOCS-06*.

Andre, D. and Russell, S. J. (2002). State abstraction for programmable reinforcement learning agents. In *AAAI-02*, pp. 119–125.

Anthony, M. and Bartlett, P. (1999). *Neural Network Learning: Theoretical Foundations*. Cambridge University Press.

Aoki, M. (1965). Optimal control of partially observable Markov systems. *J. Franklin Institute*, *280*(5), 367–386.

Appel, K. and Haken, W. (1977). Every planar map is four colorable: Part I: Discharging. *Illinois J. Math.*, *21*, 429–490.

Appelt, D. (1999). Introduction to information extraction. *CACM*, *12*(3), 161–172.

Apt, K. R. (1999). The essence of constraint propagation. *Theoretical Computer Science*, *221*(1–2), 179–210.

Apt, K. R. (2003). *Principles of Constraint Programming*. Cambridge University Press.

Apté, C., Damerau, F., and Weiss, S. (1994). Automated learning of decision rules for text categorization. *ACM Transactions on Information Systems*, *12*, 233–251.

Arbuthnot, J. (1692). *Of the Laws of Chance*. Motte, London. Translation into English, with additions, of Huygens (1657).

Archibald, C., Altman, A., and Shoham, Y. (2009). Analysis of a winning computational billiards player. In *IJCAI-09*.

Ariely, D. (2009). *Predictably Irrational* (Revised edition). Harper.

Arkin, R. (1998). *Behavior-Based Robotics*. MIT Press.

Armando, A., Carbone, R., Compagna, L., Cuellar, J., and Tobarra, L. (2008). Formal analysis of SAML 2.0 web browser single sign-on: Breaking the SAML-based single sign-on for google apps. In *FMSE '08: Proc. 6th ACM workshop on Formal methods in security engineering*, pp. 1–10.

Arnauld, A. (1662). *La logique, ou l'art de penser*. Chez Charles Savreux, au pied de la Tour de Nostre Dame, Paris.

Arora, S. (1998). Polynomial time approximation schemes for Euclidean traveling salesman and other geometric problems. *JACM*, *45*(5), 753–782.

Arunachalam, R. and Sadeh, N. M. (2005). The supply chain trading agent competition. *Electronic Commerce Research and Applications*, *Spring*, 66–84.

Ashby, W. R. (1940). Adaptiveness and equilibrium. *J. Mental Science*, *86*, 478–483.

Ashby, W. R. (1948). Design for a brain. *Electronic Engineering*, *December*, 379–383.

Ashby, W. R. (1952). *Design for a Brain*. Wiley.

Asimov, I. (1942). Runaround. *Astounding Science Fiction*, *March*.

Asimov, I. (1950). *I, Robot*. Doubleday.

Astrom, K. J. (1965). Optimal control of Markov decision processes with incomplete state estimation. *J. Math. Anal. Applic.*, *10*, 174–205.

Audi, R. (Ed.). (1999). *The Cambridge Dictionary of Philosophy*. Cambridge University Press.

Axelrod, R. (1985). *The Evolution of Cooperation*. Basic Books.

Baader, F., Calvanese, D., McGuinness, D., Nardi, D., and Patel-Schneider, P. (2007). *The Description Logic Handbook* (2nd edition). Cambridge University Press.

Baader, F. and Snyder, W. (2001). Unification theory. In Robinson, J. and Voronkov, A. (Eds.), *Handbook of Automated Reasoning*, pp. 447–533. Elsevier.

Bacchus, F. (1990). *Representing and Reasoning with Probabilistic Knowledge*. MIT Press.

Bacchus, F. and Grove, A. (1995). Graphical models for preference and utility. In *UAI-95*, pp. 3–10.

Bacchus, F. and Grove, A. (1996). Utility independence in a qualitative decision theory. In *KR-96*, pp. 542–552.

Bacchus, F., Grove, A., Halpern, J. Y., and Koller, D. (1992). From statistics to beliefs. In *AAAI-92*, pp. 602–608.

Bacchus, F. and van Beek, P. (1998). On the conversion between non-binary and binary constraint satisfaction problems. In *AAAI-98*, pp. 311–318.

Bacchus, F. and van Run, P. (1995). Dynamic variable ordering in CSPs. In *CP-95*, pp. 258–275.

Bachmann, P. G. H. (1894). *Die analytische Zahlentheorie*. B. G. Teubner, Leipzig.

Backus, J. W. (1996). Transcript of question and answer session. In Wexelblat, R. L. (Ed.), *History of Programming Languages*, p. 162. Academic Press.

Bagnell, J. A. and Schneider, J. (2001). Autonomous helicopter control using reinforcement learning policy search methods. In *ICRA-01*.

Baker, J. (1975). The Dragon system—An overview. *IEEE Transactions on Acoustics; Speech; and Signal Processing*, *23*, 24–29.

Baker, J. (1979). Trainable grammars for speech recognition. In *Speech Communication Papers for the 97th Meeting of the Acoustical Society of America*, pp. 547–550.

Baldi, P., Chauvin, Y., Hunkapiller, T., and McClure, M. (1994). Hidden Markov models of biological primary sequence information. *PNAS*, *91*(3), 1059–1063.

Baldwin, J. M. (1896). A new factor in evolution. *American Naturalist*, *30*, 441–451. Continued on pages 536–553.

Ballard, B. W. (1983). The *-minimax search procedure for trees containing chance nodes. *AIJ*, *21*(3), 327–350.

Baluja, S. (1997). Genetic algorithms and explicit search statistics. In Mozer, M. C., Jordan, M. I., and Petsche, T. (Eds.), *NIPS 9*, pp. 319–325. MIT Press.

Bancilhon, F., Maier, D., Sagiv, Y., and Ullman, J. D. (1986). Magic sets and other strange ways to implement logic programs. In *PODS-86*, pp. 1–16.

Banko, M. and Brill, E. (2001). Scaling to very very large corpora for natural language disambiguation. In *ACL-01*, pp. 26–33.

Banko, M., Brill, E., Dumais, S. T., and Lin, J. (2002). Askmsr: Question answering using the worldwide web. In *Proc. AAAI Spring Symposium on Mining Answers from Texts and Knowledge Bases*, pp. 7–9.

Banko, M., Cafarella, M. J., Soderland, S., Broadhead, M., and Etzioni, O. (2007). Open information extraction from the web. In *IJCAI-07*.

Banko, M. and Etzioni, O. (2008). The tradeoffs between open and traditional relation extraction. In *ACL-08*, pp. 28–36.

Bar-Hillel, Y. (1954). Indexical expressions. *Mind*, *63*, 359–379.

Bar-Hillel, Y. (1960). The present status of automatic translation of languages. In Alt, F. L. (Ed.), *Advances in Computers*, Vol. 1, pp. 91–163. Academic Press.

Bar-Shalom, Y. (Ed.). (1992). *Multitarget-multisensor tracking: Advanced applications*. Artech House.

Bar-Shalom, Y. and Fortmann, T. E. (1988). *Tracking and Data Association*. Academic Press.

Bartak, R. (2001). Theory and practice of constraint propagation. In *Proc. Third Workshop on Constraint Programming for Decision and Control (CPDC-01)*, pp. 7–14.

Barto, A. G., Bradtke, S. J., and Singh, S. P. (1995). Learning to act using real-time dynamic programming. *AIJ*, *73*(1), 81–138.

Barto, A. G., Sutton, R. S., and Anderson, C. W. (1983). Neuron-like adaptive elements that can solve difficult learning control problems. *IEEE Transactions on Systems, Man and Cybernetics*, *13*, 834–846.

Barto, A. G., Sutton, R. S., and Brouwer, P. S. (1981). Associative search network: A reinforcement learning associative memory. *Biological Cybernetics*, *40*(3), 201–211.

Barwise, J. and Etchemendy, J. (1993). *The Language of First-Order Logic: Including the Macintosh Program Tarski's World 4.0* (Third Revised and Expanded edition). Center for the Study of Language and Information (CSLI).

Barwise, J. and Etchemendy, J. (2002). *Language, Proof and Logic*. CSLI (Univ. of Chicago Press).

Baum, E., Boneh, D., and Garrett, C. (1995). On genetic algorithms. In *COLT-95*, pp. 230–239.

Baum, E. and Haussler, D. (1989). What size net gives valid generalization? *Neural Computation*, *1*(1), 151–160.

Baum, E. and Smith, W. D. (1997). A Bayesian approach to relevance in game playing. *AIJ*, *97*(1–2), 195–242.

Baum, E. and Wilczek, F. (1988). Supervised learning of probability distributions by neural networks. In Anderson, D. Z. (Ed.), *Neural Information Processing Systems*, pp. 52–61. American Institute of Physics.

Baum, L. E. and Petrie, T. (1966). Statistical inference for probabilistic functions of finite state Markov chains. *Annals of Mathematical Statistics*, *41*.

Baxter, J. and Bartlett, P. (2000). Reinforcement learning in POMDP's via direct gradient ascent. In *ICML-00*, pp. 41–48.

Bayardo, R. J. and Miranker, D. P. (1994). An optimal backtrack algorithm for tree-structured constraint satisfaction problems. *AIJ*, *71*(1), 159–181.

Bayardo, R. J. and Schrag, R. C. (1997). Using CSP look-back techniques to solve real-world SAT instances. In *AAAI-97*, pp. 203–208.

Bayes, T. (1763). An essay towards solving a problem in the doctrine of chances. *Philosophical Transactions of the Royal Society of London*, *53*, 370–418.

Beal, D. F. (1980). An analysis of minimax. In Clarke, M. R. B. (Ed.), *Advances in Computer Chess 2*, pp. 103–109. Edinburgh University Press.

Beal, J. and Winston, P. H. (2009). The new frontier of human-level artificial intelligence. *IEEE Intelligent Systems*, *24*(4), 21–23.

Beckert, B. and Posegga, J. (1995). Leantap: Lean, tableau-based deduction. *JAR*, *15*(3), 339–358.

Beeri, C., Fagin, R., Maier, D., and Yannakakis, M. (1983). On the desirability of acyclic database schemes. *JACM*, *30*(3), 479–513.

Bekey, G. (2008). *Robotics: State Of The Art And Future Challenges*. Imperial College Press.

Bell, C. and Tate, A. (1985). Using temporal constraints to restrict search in a planner. In *Proc. Third Alvey IKBS SIG Workshop*.

Bell, J. L. and Machover, M. (1977). *A Course in Mathematical Logic*. Elsevier/North-Holland.

Bellman, R. E. (1952). On the theory of dynamic programming. *PNAS*, *38*, 716–719.

Bellman, R. E. (1961). *Adaptive Control Processes: A Guided Tour*. Princeton University Press.

Bellman, R. E. (1965). On the application of dynamic programming to the determination of optimal play in chess and checkers. *PNAS*, *53*, 244–246.

Bellman, R. E. (1978). *An Introduction to Artificial Intelligence: Can Computers Think?* Boyd & Fraser Publishing Company.

Bellman, R. E. (1984). *Eye of the Hurricane*. World Scientific.

Bellman, R. E. and Dreyfus, S. E. (1962). *Applied Dynamic Programming*. Princeton University Press.

Bellman, R. E. (1957). *Dynamic Programming*. Princeton University Press.

Belongie, S., Malik, J., and Puzicha, J. (2002). Shape matching and object recognition using shape contexts. *PAMI*, *24*(4), 509–522.

Ben-Tal, A. and Nemirovski, A. (2001). *Lectures on Modern Convex Optimization: Analysis, Algorithms, and Engineering Applications*. SIAM (Society for Industrial and Applied Mathematics).

Bengio, Y. and LeCun, Y. (2007). Scaling learning algorithms towards AI. In Bottou, L., Chapelle, O., DeCoste, D., and Weston, J. (Eds.), *Large-Scale Kernel Machines*. MIT Press.

Bentham, J. (1823). *Principles of Morals and Legislation*. Oxford University Press, Oxford, UK. Original work published in 1789.

Berger, J. O. (1985). *Statistical Decision Theory and Bayesian Analysis*. Springer Verlag.

Berkson, J. (1944). Application of the logistic function to bio-assay. *JASA*, *39*, 357–365.

Berlekamp, E. R., Conway, J. H., and Guy, R. K. (1982). *Winning Ways, For Your Mathematical Plays*. Academic Press.

Berlekamp, E. R. and Wolfe, D. (1994). *Mathematical Go: Chilling Gets the Last Point*. A.K. Peters.

Berleur, J. and Brunnstein, K. (2001). *Ethics of Computing: Codes, Spaces for Discussion and Law*. Chapman and Hall.

Berliner, H. J. (1979). The B* tree search algorithm: A best-first proof procedure. *AIJ*, *12*(1), 23–40.

Berliner, H. J. (1980a). Backgammon computer program beats world champion. *AIJ*, *14*, 205–220.

Berliner, H. J. (1980b). Computer backgammon. *Scientific American*, *249*(6), 64–72.

Bernardo, J. M. and Smith, A. F. M. (1994). *Bayesian Theory*. Wiley.

Berners-Lee, T., Hendler, J., and Lassila, O. (2001). The semantic web. *Scientific American*, *284*(5), 34–43.

Bernoulli, D. (1738). Specimen theoriae novae de mensura sortis. *Proc. St. Petersburg Imperial Academy of Sciences*, *5*, 175–192.

Bernstein, A. and Roberts, M. (1958). Computer vs. chess player. *Scientific American*, *198*(6), 96–105.

Bernstein, P. L. (1996). *Against the Odds: The Remarkable Story of Risk*. Wiley.

Berrou, C., Glavieux, A., and Thitimajshima, P. (1993). Near Shannon limit error control-correcting coding and decoding: Turbo-codes. 1. In *Proc. IEEE International Conference on Communications*, pp. 1064–1070.

Berry, D. A. and Fristedt, B. (1985). *Bandit Problems: Sequential Allocation of Experiments*. Chapman and Hall.

Bertele, U. and Brioschi, F. (1972). *Nonserial dynamic programming*. Academic Press.

Bertoli, P., Cimatti, A., and Roveri, M. (2001a). Heuristic search + symbolic model checking = efficient conformant planning. In *IJCAI-01*, pp. 467–472.

Bertoli, P., Cimatti, A., Roveri, M., and Traverso, P. (2001b). Planning in nondeterministic domains under partial observability via symbolic model checking. In *IJCAI-01*, pp. 473–478.

Bertot, Y., Casteran, P., Huet, G., and Paulin-Mohring, C. (2004). *Interactive Theorem Proving and Program Development*. Springer.

Bertsekas, D. (1987). *Dynamic Programming: Deterministic and Stochastic Models*. Prentice-Hall.

Bertsekas, D. and Tsitsiklis, J. N. (1996). *Neuro-dynamic programming*. Athena Scientific.

Bertsekas, D. and Tsitsiklis, J. N. (2008). *Introduction to Probability* (2nd edition). Athena Scientific.

Bertsekas, D. and Shreve, S. E. (2007). *Stochastic Optimal Control: The Discrete-Time Case*. Athena Scientific.

Bessière, C. (2006). Constraint propagation. In Rossi, F., van Beek, P., and Walsh, T. (Eds.), *Handbook of Constraint Programming*. Elsevier.

Bhar, R. and Hamori, S. (2004). *Hidden Markov Models: Applications to Financial Economics*. Springer.

Bibel, W. (1993). *Deduction: Automated Logic*. Academic Press.

Biere, A., Heule, M., van Maaren, H., and Walsh, T. (Eds.). (2009). *Handbook of Satisfiability*. IOS Press.

Billings, D., Burch, N., Davidson, A., Holte, R., Schaeffer, J., Schauenberg, T., and Szafron, D. (2003). Approximating game-theoretic optimal strategies for full-scale poker. In *IJCAI-03*.

Binder, J., Koller, D., Russell, S. J., and Kanazawa, K. (1997a). Adaptive probabilistic networks with hidden variables. *Machine Learning*, *29*, 213–244.

Binder, J., Murphy, K., and Russell, S. J. (1997b). Space-efficient inference in dynamic probabilistic networks. In *IJCAI-97*, pp. 1292–1296.

Binford, T. O. (1971). Visual perception by computer. Invited paper presented at the IEEE Systems Science and Cybernetics Conference, Miami.

Binmore, K. (1982). *Essays on Foundations of Game Theory*. Pitman.

Bishop, C. M. (1995). *Neural Networks for Pattern Recognition*. Oxford University Press.

Bishop, C. M. (2007). *Pattern Recognition and Machine Learning*. Springer-Verlag.

Bisson, T. (1990). They're made out of meat. *Omni Magazine*.

Bistarelli, S., Montanari, U., and Rossi, F. (1997). Semiring-based constraint satisfaction and optimization. *JACM*, *44*(2), 201–236.

Bitner, J. R. and Reingold, E. M. (1975). Backtrack programming techniques. *CACM*, *18*(11), 651–656.

Bizer, C., Auer, S., Kobilarov, G., Lehmann, J., and Cyganiak, R. (2007). DBPedia – querying wikipedia like a database. In *Developers Track Presentation at the 16th International Conference on World Wide Web*.

Blazewicz, J., Ecker, K., Pesch, E., Schmidt, G., and Weglarz, J. (2007). *Handbook on Scheduling: Models and Methods for Advanced Planning (International Handbooks on Information Systems)*. Springer-Verlag New York, Inc.

Blei, D. M., Ng, A. Y., and Jordan, M. I. (2001). Latent Dirichlet Allocation. In *Neural Information Processing Systems*, Vol. 14.

Blinder, A. S. (1983). Issues in the coordination of monetary and fiscal policies. In *Monetary Policy Issues in the 1980s*. Federal Reserve Bank, Kansas City, Missouri.

Bliss, C. I. (1934). The method of probits. *Science*, *79*(2037), 38–39.

Block, H. D., Knight, B., and Rosenblatt, F. (1962). Analysis of a four-layer series-coupled perceptron. *Rev. Modern Physics*, *34*(1), 275–282.

Blum, A. L. and Furst, M. (1995). Fast planning through planning graph analysis. In *IJCAI-95*, pp. 1636–1642.

Blum, A. L. and Furst, M. (1997). Fast planning through planning graph analysis. *AIJ*, *90*(1–2), 281–300.

Blum, A. L. (1996). On-line algorithms in machine learning. In *Proc. Workshop on On-Line Algorithms, Dagstuhl*, pp. 306–325.

Blum, A. L. and Mitchell, T. M. (1998). Combining labeled and unlabeled data with co-training. In *COLT-98*, pp. 92–100.

Blumer, A., Ehrenfeucht, A., Haussler, D., and Warmuth, M. (1989). Learnability and the Vapnik-Chervonenkis dimension. *JACM*, *36*(4), 929–965.

Bobrow, D. G. (1967). Natural language input for a computer problem solving system. In Minsky, M. L. (Ed.), *Semantic Information Processing*, pp. 133–215. MIT Press.

Bobrow, D. G., Kaplan, R., Kay, M., Norman, D. A., Thompson, H., and Winograd, T. (1977). GUS, a frame driven dialog system. *AIJ*, *8*, 155–173.

Boden, M. A. (1977). *Artificial Intelligence and Natural Man*. Basic Books.

Boden, M. A. (Ed.). (1990). *The Philosophy of Artificial Intelligence*. Oxford University Press.

Bolognesi, A. and Ciancarini, P. (2003). Computer programming of kriegspiel endings: The case of KR vs. k. In *Advances in Computer Games 10*.

Bonet, B. (2002). An epsilon-optimal grid-based algorithm for partially observable Markov decision processes. In *ICML-02*, pp. 51–58.

Bonet, B. and Geffner, H. (1999). Planning as heuristic search: New results. In *ECP-99*, pp. 360–372.

Bonet, B. and Geffner, H. (2000). Planning with incomplete information as heuristic search in belief space. In *ICAPS-00*, pp. 52–61.

Bonet, B. and Geffner, H. (2005). An algorithm better than AO*? In *AAAI-05*.

Boole, G. (1847). *The Mathematical Analysis of Logic: Being an Essay towards a Calculus of Deductive Reasoning*. Macmillan, Barclay, and Macmillan, Cambridge.

Booth, T. L. (1969). Probabilistic representation of formal languages. In *IEEE Conference Record of the 1969 Tenth Annual Symposium on Switching and Automata Theory*, pp. 74–81.

Borel, E. (1921). La théorie du jeu et les équations intégrales à noyau symétrique. *Comptes Rendus Hebdomadaires des Séances de l'Académie des Sciences*, *173*, 1304–1308.

Borenstein, J., Everett, B., and Feng, L. (1996). *Navigating Mobile Robots: Systems and Techniques*. A. K. Peters, Ltd.

Borenstein, J. and Koren., Y. (1991). The vector field histogram—Fast obstacle avoidance for mobile robots. *IEEE Transactions on Robotics and Automation*, *7*(3), 278–288.

Borgida, A., Brachman, R. J., McGuinness, D., and Alperin Resnick, L. (1989). CLASSIC: A structural data model for objects. *SIGMOD Record*, *18*(2), 58–67.

Boroditsky, L. (2003). Linguistic relativity. In Nadel, L. (Ed.), *Encyclopedia of Cognitive Science*, pp. 917–921. Macmillan.

Boser, B., Guyon, I., and Vapnik, V. N. (1992). A training algorithm for optimal margin classifiers. In *COLT-92*.

Bosse, M., Newman, P., Leonard, J., Soika, M., Feiten, W., and Teller, S. (2004). Simultaneous localization and map building in large-scale cyclic environments using the atlas framework. *Int. J. Robotics Research*, *23*(12), 1113–1139.

Bourzutschky, M. (2006). 7-man endgames with pawns. *CCRL Discussion Board*, `kirill-kryukov.com/chess/discussion-board/viewtopic.php?t=805`.

Boutilier, C. and Brafman, R. I. (2001). Partial-order planning with concurrent interacting actions. *JAIR*, *14*, 105–136.

Boutilier, C., Dearden, R., and Goldszmidt, M. (2000). Stochastic dynamic programming with factored representations. *AIJ*, *121*, 49–107.

Boutilier, C., Reiter, R., and Price, B. (2001). Symbolic dynamic programming for first-order MDPs. In *IJCAI-01*, pp. 467–472.

Boutilier, C., Friedman, N., Goldszmidt, M., and Koller, D. (1996). Context-specific independence in Bayesian networks. In *UAI-96*, pp. 115–123.

Bouzy, B. and Cazenave, T. (2001). Computer go: An AI oriented survey. *AIJ*, *132*(1), 39–103.

Bowerman, M. and Levinson, S. (2001). *Language acquisition and conceptual development*. Cambridge University Press.

Bowling, M., Johanson, M., Burch, N., and Szafron, D. (2008). Strategy evaluation in extensive games with importance sampling. In *ICML-08*.

Box, G. E. P. (1957). Evolutionary operation: A method of increasing industrial productivity. *Applied Statistics*, *6*, 81–101.

Box, G. E. P., Jenkins, G., and Reinsel, G. (1994). *Time Series Analysis: Forecasting and Control* (3rd edition). Prentice Hall.

Boyan, J. A. (2002). Technical update: Least-squares temporal difference learning. *Machine Learning*, *49*(2–3), 233–246.

Boyan, J. A. and Moore, A. W. (1998). Learning evaluation functions for global optimization and Boolean satisfiability. In *AAAI-98*.

Boyd, S. and Vandenberghe, L. (2004). *Convex Optimization*. Cambridge University Press.

Boyen, X., Friedman, N., and Koller, D. (1999). Discovering the hidden structure of complex dynamic systems. In *UAI-99*.

Boyer, R. S. and Moore, J. S. (1979). *A Computational Logic*. Academic Press.

Boyer, R. S. and Moore, J. S. (1984). Proof checking the RSA public key encryption algorithm. *American Mathematical Monthly*, *91*(3), 181–189.

Brachman, R. J. (1979). On the epistemological status of semantic networks. In Findler, N. V. (Ed.), *Associative Networks: Representation and Use of Knowledge by Computers*, pp. 3–50. Academic Press.

Brachman, R. J., Fikes, R. E., and Levesque, H. J. (1983). Krypton: A functional approach to knowledge representation. *Computer*, *16*(10), 67–73.

Brachman, R. J. and Levesque, H. J. (Eds.). (1985). *Readings in Knowledge Representation*. Morgan Kaufmann.

Bradtke, S. J. and Barto, A. G. (1996). Linear least-squares algorithms for temporal difference learning. *Machine Learning*, *22*, 33–57.

Brafman, O. and Brafman, R. (2009). *Sway: The Irresistible Pull of Irrational Behavior*. Broadway Business.

Brafman, R. I. and Domshlak, C. (2008). From one to many: Planning for loosely coupled multi-agent systems. In *ICAPS-08*, pp. 28–35.

Brafman, R. I. and Tennenholtz, M. (2000). A near optimal polynomial time algorithm for learning in certain classes of stochastic games. *AIJ*, *121*, 31–47.

Braitenberg, V. (1984). *Vehicles: Experiments in Synthetic Psychology*. MIT Press.

Bransford, J. and Johnson, M. (1973). Consideration of some problems in comprehension. In Chase, W. G. (Ed.), *Visual Information Processing*. Academic Press.

Brants, T., Popat, A. C., Xu, P., Och, F. J., and Dean, J. (2007). Large language models in machine translation. In *EMNLP-CoNLL-2007: Proc. 2007 Joint Conference on Empirical Methods in Natural Language Processing and Computational Natural Language Learning*, pp. 858–867.

Bratko, I. (1986). *Prolog Programming for Artificial Intelligence* (1st edition). Addison-Wesley.

Bratko, I. (2001). *Prolog Programming for Artificial Intelligence* (Third edition). Addison-Wesley.

Bratman, M. E. (1987). *Intention, Plans, and Practical Reason*. Harvard University Press.

Bratman, M. E. (1992). Planning and the stability of intention. *Minds and Machines*, *2*(1), 1–16.

Breese, J. S. (1992). Construction of belief and decision networks. *Computational Intelligence*, *8*(4), 624–647.

Breese, J. S. and Heckerman, D. (1996). Decision-theoretic troubleshooting: A framework for repair and experiment. In *UAI-96*, pp. 124–132.

Breiman, L. (1996). Bagging predictors. *Machine Learning*, *24*(2), 123–140.

Breiman, L., Friedman, J., Olshen, R. A., and Stone, C. J. (1984). *Classification and Regression Trees*. Wadsworth International Group.

Brelaz, D. (1979). New methods to color the vertices of a graph. *CACM*, *22*(4), 251–256.

Brent, R. P. (1973). *Algorithms for minimization without derivatives*. Prentice-Hall.

Bresnan, J. (1982). *The Mental Representation of Grammatical Relations*. MIT Press.

Brewka, G., Dix, J., and Konolige, K. (1997). *Nononotonic Reasoning: An Overview*. CSLI Publications.

Brickley, D. and Guha, R. V. (2004). RDF vocabulary description language 1.0: RDF schema. Tech. rep., W3C.

Bridle, J. S. (1990). Probabilistic interpretation of feedforward classification network outputs, with relationships to statistical pattern recognition. In Fogelman Soulié, F. and Hérault, J. (Eds.), *Neurocomputing: Algorithms, Architectures and Applications*. Springer-Verlag.

Briggs, R. (1985). Knowledge representation in Sanskrit and artificial intelligence. *AIMag*, *6*(1), 32–39.

Brin, D. (1998). *The Transparent Society*. Perseus.

Brin, S. (1999). Extracting patterns and relations from the world wide web. Technical report 1999-65, Stanford InfoLab.

Brin, S. and Page, L. (1998). The anatomy of a large-scale hypertextual web search engine. In *Proc. Seventh World Wide Web Conference*.

Bringsjord, S. (2008). If I were judge. In Epstein, R., Roberts, G., and Beber, G. (Eds.), *Parsing the Turing Test*. Springer.

Broadbent, D. E. (1958). *Perception and Communication*. Pergamon.

Brooks, R. A. (1986). A robust layered control system for a mobile robot. *IEEE Journal of Robotics and Automation*, *2*, 14–23.

Brooks, R. A. (1989). Engineering approach to building complete, intelligent beings. *Proc. SPIE—the International Society for Optical Engineering*, *1002*, 618–625.

Brooks, R. A. (1991). Intelligence without representation. *AIJ*, *47*(1–3), 139–159.

Brooks, R. A. and Lozano-Perez, T. (1985). A subdivision algorithm in configuration space for findpath with rotation. *IEEE Transactions on Systems, Man and Cybernetics*, *15*(2), 224–233.

Brown, C., Finkelstein, L., and Purdom, P. (1988). Backtrack searching in the presence of symmetry. In Mora, T. (Ed.), *Applied Algebra, Algebraic Algorithms and Error-Correcting Codes*, pp. 99–110. Springer-Verlag.

Brown, K. C. (1974). A note on the apparent bias of net revenue estimates. *J. Finance*, *29*, 1215–1216.

Brown, P. F., Cocke, J., Della Pietra, S. A., Della Pietra, V. J., Jelinek, F., Mercer, R. L., and Roossin, P. (1988). A statistical approach to language translation. In *COLING-88*, pp. 71–76.

Brown, P. F., Della Pietra, S. A., Della Pietra, V. J., and Mercer, R. L. (1993). The mathematics of statistical machine translation: Parameter estimation. *Computational Linguistics*, *19*(2), 263–311.

Brownston, L., Farrell, R., Kant, E., and Martin, N. (1985). *Programming expert systems in OPS5: An introduction to rule-based programming*. Addison-Wesley.

Bruce, V., Georgeson, M., and Green, P. (2003). *Visual Perception: Physiology, Psychology and Ecology*. Psychology Press.

Bruner, J. S., Goodnow, J. J., and Austin, G. A. (1957). *A Study of Thinking*. Wiley.

Bryant, B. D. and Miikkulainen, R. (2007). Acquiring visibly intelligent behavior with example-guided neuroevolution. In *AAAI-07*.

Bryce, D. and Kambhampati, S. (2007). A tutorial on planning graph-based reachability heuristics. *AIMag, Spring*, 47–83.

Bryce, D., Kambhampati, S., and Smith, D. E. (2006). Planning graph heuristics for belief space search. *JAIR*, *26*, 35–99.

Bryson, A. E. and Ho, Y.-C. (1969). *Applied Optimal Control*. Blaisdell.

Buchanan, B. G. and Mitchell, T. M. (1978). Model-directed learning of production rules. In Waterman, D. A. and Hayes-Roth, F. (Eds.), *Pattern-Directed Inference Systems*, pp. 297–312. Academic Press.

Buchanan, B. G., Mitchell, T. M., Smith, R. G., and Johnson, C. R. (1978). Models of learning systems. In *Encyclopedia of Computer Science and Technology*, Vol. 11. Dekker.

Buchanan, B. G. and Shortliffe, E. H. (Eds.). (1984). *Rule-Based Expert Systems: The MYCIN Experiments of the Stanford Heuristic Programming Project*. Addison-Wesley.

Buchanan, B. G., Sutherland, G. L., and Feigenbaum, E. A. (1969). Heuristic DENDRAL: A program for generating explanatory hypotheses in organic chemistry. In Meltzer, B., Michie, D., and Swann, M. (Eds.), *Machine Intelligence 4*, pp. 209–254. Edinburgh University Press.

Buehler, M., Iagnemma, K., and Singh, S. (Eds.). (2006). *The 2005 DARPA Grand Challenge: The Great Robot Race*. Springer-Verlag.

Bunt, H. C. (1985). The formal representation of (quasi-) continuous concepts. In Hobbs, J. R. and Moore, R. C. (Eds.), *Formal Theories of the Commonsense World*, chap. 2, pp. 37–70. Ablex.

Burgard, W., Cremers, A. B., Fox, D., Hähnel, D., Lakemeyer, G., Schulz, D., Steiner, W., and Thrun, S. (1999). Experiences with an interactive museum tour-guide robot. *AIJ*, *114*(1–2), 3–55.

Buro, M. (1995). ProbCut: An effective selective extension of the alpha-beta algorithm. *J. International Computer Chess Association*, *18*(2), 71–76.

Buro, M. (2002). Improving heuristic mini-max search by supervised learning. *AIJ*, *134*(1–2), 85–99.

Burstein, J., Leacock, C., and Swartz, R. (2001). Automated evaluation of essays and short answers. In *Fifth International Computer Assisted Assessment (CAA) Conference*.

Burton, R. (2009). *On Being Certain: Believing You Are Right Even When You're Not*. St. Martin's Griffin.

Buss, D. M. (2005). *Handbook of evolutionary psychology*. Wiley.

Butler, S. (1863). Darwin among the machines. *The Press (Christchurch, New Zealand), June 13*.

Bylander, T. (1992). Complexity results for serial decomposability. In *AAAI-92*, pp. 729–734.

Bylander, T. (1994). The computational complexity of propositional STRIPS planning. *AIJ*, *69*, 165–204.

Byrd, R. H., Lu, P., Nocedal, J., and Zhu, C. (1995). A limited memory algorithm for bound constrained optimization. *SIAM Journal on Scientific and Statistical Computing*, *16*(5), 1190–1208.

Cabeza, R. and Nyberg, L. (2001). Imaging cognition II: An empirical review of 275 PET and fMRI studies. *J. Cognitive Neuroscience*, *12*, 1–47.

Cafarella, M. J., Halevy, A., Zhang, Y., Wang, D. Z., and Wu, E. (2008). Webtables: Exploring the power of tables on the web. In *VLDB-2008*.

Calvanese, D., Lenzerini, M., and Nardi, D. (1999). Unifying class-based representation formalisms. *JAIR*, *11*, 199–240.

Campbell, M. S., Hoane, A. J., and Hsu, F.-H. (2002). Deep Blue. *AIJ*, *134*(1–2), 57–83.

Canny, J. and Reif, J. (1987). New lower bound techniques for robot motion planning problems. In *FOCS-87*, pp. 39–48.

Canny, J. (1986). A computational approach to edge detection. *PAMI*, *8*, 679–698.

Canny, J. (1988). *The Complexity of Robot Motion Planning*. MIT Press.

Capen, E., Clapp, R., and Campbell, W. (1971). Competitive bidding in high-risk situations. *J. Petroleum Technology*, *23*, 641–653.

Caprara, A., Fischetti, M., and Toth, P. (1995). A heuristic method for the set covering problem. *Operations Research*, *47*, 730–743.

Carbonell, J. G. (1983). Derivational analogy and its role in problem solving. In *AAAI-83*, pp. 64–69.

Carbonell, J. G., Knoblock, C. A., and Minton, S. (1989). PRODIGY: An integrated architecture for planning and learning. Technical report CMU-CS-89-189, Computer Science Department, Carnegie-Mellon University.

Carbonell, J. R. and Collins, A. M. (1973). Natural semantics in artificial intelligence. In *IJCAI-73*, pp. 344–351.

Cardano, G. (1663). *Liber de ludo aleae*. Lyons.

Carnap, R. (1928). *Der logische Aufbau der Welt*. Weltkreis-verlag. Translated into English as (Carnap, 1967).

Carnap, R. (1948). On the application of inductive logic. *Philosophy and Phenomenological Research*, *8*, 133–148.

Carnap, R. (1950). *Logical Foundations of Probability*. University of Chicago Press.

Carroll, S. (2007). *The Making of the Fittest: DNA and the Ultimate Forensic Record of Evolution*. Norton.

Casati, R. and Varzi, A. (1999). *Parts and places: the structures of spatial representation*. MIT Press.

Cassandra, A. R., Kaelbling, L. P., and Littman, M. L. (1994). Acting optimally in partially observable stochastic domains. In *AAAI-94*, pp. 1023–1028.

Cassandras, C. G. and Lygeros, J. (2006). *Stochastic Hybrid Systems*. CRC Press.

Castro, R., Coates, M., Liang, G., Nowak, R., and Yu, B. (2004). Network tomography: Recent developments. *Statistical Science*, *19*(3), 499–517.

Cesa-Bianchi, N. and Lugosi, G. (2006). *Prediction, learning, and Games*. Cambridge University Press.

Cesta, A., Cortellessa, G., Denis, M., Donati, A., Fratini, S., Oddi, A., Policella, N., Rabenau, E., and Schulster, J. (2007). MEXAR2: AI solves mission planner problems. *IEEE Intelligent Systems*, *22*(4), 12–19.

Chakrabarti, P. P., Ghose, S., Acharya, A., and de Sarkar, S. C. (1989). Heuristic search in restricted memory. *AIJ*, *41*(2), 197–222.

Chandra, A. K. and Harel, D. (1980). Computable queries for relational data bases. *J. Computer and System Sciences*, *21*(2), 156–178.

Chang, C.-L. and Lee, R. C.-T. (1973). *Symbolic Logic and Mechanical Theorem Proving*. Academic Press.

Chapman, D. (1987). Planning for conjunctive goals. *AIJ*, *32*(3), 333–377.

Charniak, E. (1993). *Statistical Language Learning*. MIT Press.

Charniak, E. (1996). Tree-bank grammars. In *AAAI-96*, pp. 1031–1036.

Charniak, E. (1997). Statistical parsing with a context-free grammar and word statistics. In *AAAI-97*, pp. 598–603.

Charniak, E. and Goldman, R. (1992). A Bayesian model of plan recognition. *AIJ*, *64*(1), 53–79.

Charniak, E. and McDermott, D. (1985). *Introduction to Artificial Intelligence*. Addison-Wesley.

Charniak, E., Riesbeck, C., McDermott, D., and Meehan, J. (1987). *Artificial Intelligence Programming* (2nd edition). Lawrence Erlbaum Associates.

Charniak, E. (1991). Bayesian networks without tears. *AIMag*, *12*(4), 50–63.

Charniak, E. and Johnson, M. (2005). Coarse-to-fine n-best parsing and maxent discriminative reranking. In *ACL-05*.

Chater, N. and Oaksford, M. (Eds.). (2008). *The probabilistic mind: Prospects for Bayesian cognitive science*. Oxford University Press.

Chatfield, C. (1989). *The Analysis of Time Series: An Introduction* (4th edition). Chapman and Hall.

Cheeseman, P. (1985). In defense of probability. In *IJCAI-85*, pp. 1002–1009.

Cheeseman, P. (1988). An inquiry into computer understanding. *Computational Intelligence*, *4*(1), 58–66.

Cheeseman, P., Kanefsky, B., and Taylor, W. (1991). Where the really hard problems are. In *IJCAI-91*, pp. 331–337.

Cheeseman, P., Self, M., Kelly, J., and Stutz, J. (1988). Bayesian classification. In *AAAI-88*, Vol. 2, pp. 607–611.

Cheeseman, P. and Stutz, J. (1996). Bayesian classification (AutoClass): Theory and results. In Fayyad, U., Piatesky-Shapiro, G., Smyth, P., and Uthurusamy, R. (Eds.), *Advances in Knowledge Discovery and Data Mining*. AAAI Press/MIT Press.

Chen, S. F. and Goodman, J. (1996). An empirical study of smoothing techniques for language modeling. In *ACL-96*, pp. 310–318.

Cheng, J. and Druzdzel, M. J. (2000). AIS-BN: An adaptive importance sampling algorithm for evidential reasoning in large Bayesian networks. *JAIR*, *13*, 155–188.

Cheng, J., Greiner, R., Kelly, J., Bell, D. A., and Liu, W. (2002). Learning Bayesian networks from data: An information-theory based approach. *AIJ*, *137*, 43–90.

Chklovski, T. and Gil, Y. (2005). Improving the design of intelligent acquisition interfaces for collecting world knowledge from web contributors. In *Proc. Third International Conference on Knowledge Capture (K-CAP)*.

Chomsky, N. (1956). Three models for the description of language. *IRE Transactions on Information Theory*, *2*(3), 113–124.

Chomsky, N. (1957). *Syntactic Structures*. Mouton.

Choset, H. (1996). *Sensor Based Motion Planning: The Hierarchical Generalized Voronoi Graph*. Ph.D. thesis, California Institute of Technology.

Choset, H., Lynch, K., Hutchinson, S., Kantor, G., Burgard, W., Kavraki, L., and Thrun, S. (2004). *Principles of Robotic Motion: Theory, Algorithms, and Implementation*. MIT Press.

Chung, K. L. (1979). *Elementary Probability Theory with Stochastic Processes* (3rd edition). Springer-Verlag.

Church, A. (1936). A note on the Entscheidungsproblem. *JSL*, *1*, 40–41 and 101–102.

Church, A. (1956). *Introduction to Mathematical Logic*. Princeton University Press.

Church, K. and Patil, R. (1982). Coping with syntactic ambiguity or how to put the block in the box on the table. *Computational Linguistics*, *8*(3–4), 139–149.

Church, K. (2004). Speech and language processing: Can we use the past to predict the future. In *Proc. Conference on Text, Speech, and Dialogue*.

Church, K. and Gale, W. A. (1991). A comparison of the enhanced Good–Turing and deleted estimation methods for estimating probabilities of English bigrams. *Computer Speech and Language*, *5*, 19–54.

Churchland, P. M. and Churchland, P. S. (1982). Functionalism, qualia, and intentionality. In Biro, J. I. and Shahan, R. W. (Eds.), *Mind, Brain and Function: Essays in the Philosophy of Mind*, pp. 121–145. University of Oklahoma Press.

Churchland, P. S. (1986). *Neurophilosophy: Toward a Unified Science of the Mind–Brain*. MIT Press.

Ciancarini, P. and Wooldridge, M. (2001). *Agent-Oriented Software Engineering*. Springer-Verlag.

Cimatti, A., Roveri, M., and Traverso, P. (1998). Automatic OBDD-based generation of universal plans in non-deterministic domains. In *AAAI-98*, pp. 875–881.

Clark, A. (1998). *Being There: Putting Brain, Body, and World Together Again*. MIT Press.

Clark, A. (2008). *Supersizing the Mind: Embodiment, Action, and Cognitive Extension*. Oxford University Press.

Clark, K. L. (1978). Negation as failure. In Gallaire, H. and Minker, J. (Eds.), *Logic and Data Bases*, pp. 293–322. Plenum.

Clark, P. and Niblett, T. (1989). The CN2 induction algorithm. *Machine Learning*, *3*, 261–283.

Clark, S. and Curran, J. R. (2004). Parsing the WSJ using CCG and log-linear models. In *ACL-04*, pp. 104–111.

Clarke, A. C. (1968a). *2001: A Space Odyssey*. Signet.

Clarke, A. C. (1968b). The world of 2001. Vogue.

Clarke, E. and Grumberg, O. (1987). Research on automatic verification of finite-state concurrent systems. *Annual Review of Computer Science*, *2*, 269–290.

Clarke, M. R. B. (Ed.). (1977). *Advances in Computer Chess 1*. Edinburgh University Press.

Clearwater, S. H. (Ed.). (1996). *Market-Based Control*. World Scientific.

Clocksin, W. F. and Mellish, C. S. (2003). *Programming in Prolog* (5th edition). Springer-Verlag.

Clocksin, W. F. (2003). *Clause and Effect: Prolog Programming for the Working Programmer*. Springer.

Coarfa, C., Demopoulos, D., Aguirre, A., Subramanian, D., and Yardi, M. (2003). Random 3-SAT: The plot thickens. *Constraints*, *8*(3), 243–261.

Coates, A., Abbeel, P., and Ng, A. Y. (2009). Apprenticeship learning for helicopter control. *JACM*, *52*(7), 97–105.

Cobham, A. (1964). The intrinsic computational difficulty of functions. In *Proc. 1964 International Congress for Logic, Methodology, and Philosophy of Science*, pp. 24–30.

Cohen, P. R. (1995). *Empirical methods for artificial intelligence*. MIT Press.

Cohen, P. R. and Levesque, H. J. (1990). Intention is choice with commitment. *AIJ*, *42*(2–3), 213–261.

Cohen, P. R., Morgan, J., and Pollack, M. E. (1990). *Intentions in Communication*. MIT Press.

Cohen, W. W. and Page, C. D. (1995). Learnability in inductive logic programming: Methods and results. *New Generation Computing*, *13*(3–4), 369–409.

Cohn, A. G., Bennett, B., Gooday, J. M., and Gotts, N. (1997). RCC: A calculus for region based qualitative spatial reasoning. *GeoInformatica*, *1*, 275–316.

Collin, Z., Dechter, R., and Katz, S. (1999). Self-stabilizing distributed constraint satisfaction. *Chicago Journal of Theoretical Computer Science*, *1999*(115).

Collins, F. S., Morgan, M., and Patrinos, A. (2003). The human genome project: Lessons from large-scale biology. *Science*, *300*(5617), 286–290.

Collins, M. (1999). *Head-driven Statistical Models for Natural Language Processing*. Ph.D. thesis, University of Pennsylvania.

Collins, M. and Duffy, K. (2002). New ranking algorithms for parsing and tagging: Kernels over discrete structures, and the voted perceptron. In *ACL-02*.

Colmerauer, A. and Roussel, P. (1993). The birth of Prolog. *SIGPLAN Notices*, *28*(3), 37–52.

Colmerauer, A. (1975). Les grammaires de metamorphose. Tech. rep., Groupe d'Intelligence Artificielle, Université de Marseille-Luminy.

Colmerauer, A., Kanoui, H., Pasero, R., and Roussel, P. (1973). Un systéme de communication homme–machine en Français. Rapport, Groupe d'Intelligence Artificielle, Université d'Aix-Marseille II.

Condon, J. H. and Thompson, K. (1982). Belle chess hardware. In Clarke, M. R. B. (Ed.), *Advances in Computer Chess 3*, pp. 45–54. Pergamon.

Congdon, C. B., Huber, M., Kortenkamp, D., Bidlack, C., Cohen, C., Huffman, S., Koss, F., Raschke, U., and Weymouth, T. (1992). CARMEL versus Flakey: A comparison of two robots. Tech. rep. Papers from the AAAI Robot Competition, RC-92-01, American Association for Artificial Intelligence.

Conlisk, J. (1989). Three variants on the Allais example. *American Economic Review*, *79*(3), 392–407.

Connell, J. (1989). *A Colony Architecture for an Artificial Creature*. Ph.D. thesis, Artificial Intelligence Laboratory, MIT. Also available as AI Technical Report 1151.

Consortium, T. G. O. (2008). The gene ontology project in 2008. *Nucleic Acids Research*, *36*.

Cook, S. A. (1971). The complexity of theorem-proving procedures. In *STOC-71*, pp. 151–158.

Cook, S. A. and Mitchell, D. (1997). Finding hard instances of the satisfiability problem: A survey. In Du, D., Gu, J., and Pardalos, P. (Eds.), *Satisfiability problems: Theory and applications*. American Mathematical Society.

Cooper, G. (1990). The computational complexity of probabilistic inference using Bayesian belief networks. *AIJ*, *42*, 393–405.

Cooper, G. and Herskovits, E. (1992). A Bayesian method for the induction of probabilistic networks from data. *Machine Learning*, *9*, 309–347.

Copeland, J. (1993). *Artificial Intelligence: A Philosophical Introduction*. Blackwell.

Copernicus (1543). *De Revolutionibus Orbium Coelestium*. Apud Ioh. Petreium, Nuremberg.

Cormen, T. H., Leiserson, C. E., and Rivest, R. (1990). *Introduction to Algorithms*. MIT Press.

Cortes, C. and Vapnik, V. N. (1995). Support vector networks. *Machine Learning*, *20*, 273–297.

Cournot, A. (Ed.). (1838). *Recherches sur les principes mathématiques de la théorie des richesses*. L. Hachette, Paris.

Cover, T. and Thomas, J. (2006). *Elements of Information Theory* (2nd edition). Wiley.

Cowan, J. D. and Sharp, D. H. (1988a). Neural nets. *Quarterly Reviews of Biophysics*, *21*, 365–427.

Cowan, J. D. and Sharp, D. H. (1988b). Neural nets and artificial intelligence. *Daedalus*, *117*, 85–121.

Cowell, R., Dawid, A. P., Lauritzen, S., and Spiegelhalter, D. J. (2002). *Probabilistic Networks and Expert Systems*. Springer.

Cox, I. (1993). A review of statistical data association techniques for motion correspondence. *IJCV*, *10*, 53–66.

Cox, I. and Hingorani, S. L. (1994). An efficient implementation and evaluation of Reid's multiple hypothesis tracking algorithm for visual tracking. In *ICPR-94*, Vol. 1, pp. 437–442.

Cox, I. and Wilfong, G. T. (Eds.). (1990). *Autonomous Robot Vehicles*. Springer Verlag.

Cox, R. T. (1946). Probability, frequency, and reasonable expectation. *American Journal of Physics*, *14*(1), 1–13.

Craig, J. (1989). *Introduction to Robotics: Mechanics and Control (2nd edition)*. Addison-Wesley Publishing, Inc.

Craik, K. J. (1943). *The Nature of Explanation*. Cambridge University Press.

Craswell, N., Zaragoza, H., and Robertson, S. E. (2005). Microsoft cambridge at trec-14: Enterprise track. In *Proc. Fourteenth Text REtrieval Conference*.

Crauser, A., Mehlhorn, K., Meyer, U., and Sanders, P. (1998). A parallelization of Dijkstra's shortest path algorithm. In *Proc. 23rd International Symposium on Mathematical Foundations of Computer Science,*, pp. 722–731.

Craven, M., DiPasquo, D., Freitag, D., McCallum, A., Mitchell, T. M., Nigam, K., and Slattery, S. (2000). Learning to construct knowledge bases from the World Wide Web. *AIJ*, *118*(1/2), 69–113.

Crawford, J. M. and Auton, L. D. (1993). Experimental results on the crossover point in satisfiability problems. In *AAAI-93*, pp. 21–27.

Cristianini, N. and Hahn, M. (2007). *Introduction to Computational Genomics: A Case Studies Approach*. Cambridge University Press.

Cristianini, N. and Schölkopf, B. (2002). Support vector machines and kernel methods: The new generation of learning machines. *AIMag*, *23*(3), 31–41.

Cristianini, N. and Shawe-Taylor, J. (2000). *An introduction to support vector machines and other kernel-based learning methods*. Cambridge University Press.

Crockett, L. (1994). *The Turing Test and the Frame Problem: AI's Mistaken Understanding of Intelligence*. Ablex.

Croft, B., Metzler, D., and Stroham, T. (2009). *Search Engines: Information retrieval in Practice*. Addison Wesley.

Cross, S. E. and Walker, E. (1994). DART: Applying knowledge based planning and scheduling to crisis action planning. In Zweben, M. and Fox, M. S. (Eds.), *Intelligent Scheduling*, pp. 711–729. Morgan Kaufmann.

Cruse, D. A. (1986). *Lexical Semantics*. Cambridge University Press.

Culberson, J. and Schaeffer, J. (1996). Searching with pattern databases. In *Advances in Artificial Intelligence (Lecture Notes in Artificial Intelligence 1081)*, pp. 402–416. Springer-Verlag.

Culberson, J. and Schaeffer, J. (1998). Pattern databases. *Computational Intelligence*, *14*(4), 318–334.

Cullingford, R. E. (1981). Integrating knowledge sources for computer "understanding" tasks. *IEEE Transactions on Systems, Man and Cybernetics (SMC)*, *11*.

Cummins, D. and Allen, C. (1998). *The Evolution of Mind*. Oxford University Press.

Cushing, W., Kambhampati, S., Mausam, and Weld, D. S. (2007). When is temporal planning *really* temporal? In *IJCAI-07*.

Cybenko, G. (1988). Continuous valued neural networks with two hidden layers are sufficient. Technical report, Department of Computer Science, Tufts University.

Cybenko, G. (1989). Approximation by superpositions of a sigmoidal function. *Mathematics of Controls, Signals, and Systems*, *2*, 303–314.

Daganzo, C. (1979). *Multinomial probit: The theory and its application to demand forecasting*. Academic Press.

Dagum, P. and Luby, M. (1993). Approximating probabilistic inference in Bayesian belief networks is NP-hard. *AIJ*, *60*(1), 141–153.

Dalal, N. and Triggs, B. (2005). Histograms of oriented gradients for human detection. In *CVPR*, pp. 886–893.

Dantzig, G. B. (1949). Programming of interdependent activities: II. Mathematical model. *Econometrica*, *17*, 200–211.

Darwiche, A. (2001). Recursive conditioning. *AIJ*, *126*, 5–41.

Darwiche, A. and Ginsberg, M. L. (1992). A symbolic generalization of probability theory. In *AAAI-92*, pp. 622–627.

Darwiche, A. (2009). *Modeling and reasoning with Bayesian networks*. Cambridge University Press.

Darwin, C. (1859). *On The Origin of Species by Means of Natural Selection*. J. Murray, London.

Darwin, C. (1871). *Descent of Man*. J. Murray.

Dasgupta, P., Chakrabarti, P. P., and de Sarkar, S. C. (1994). Agent searching in a tree and the optimality of iterative deepening. *AIJ*, *71*, 195–208.

Davidson, D. (1980). *Essays on Actions and Events*. Oxford University Press.

Davies, T. R. (1985). Analogy. Informal note IN-CSLI-85-4, Center for the Study of Language and Information (CSLI).

Davies, T. R. and Russell, S. J. (1987). A logical approach to reasoning by analogy. In *IJCAI-87*, Vol. 1, pp. 264–270.

Davis, E. (1986). *Representing and Acquiring Geographic Knowledge*. Pitman and Morgan Kaufmann.

Davis, E. (1990). *Representations of Commonsense Knowledge*. Morgan Kaufmann.

Davis, E. (2005). Knowledge and communication: A first-order theory. *AIJ*, *166*, 81–140.

Davis, E. (2006). The expressivity of quantifying over regions. *J. Logic and Computation*, *16*, 891–916.

Davis, E. (2007). Physical reasoning. In van Harmelan, F., Lifschitz, V., and Porter, B. (Eds.), *The Handbook of Knowledge Representation*, pp. 597–620. Elsevier.

Davis, E. (2008). Pouring liquids: A study in commonsense physical reasoning. *AIJ*, *172*(1540–1578).

Davis, E. and Morgenstern, L. (2004). Introduction: Progress in formal commonsense reasoning. *AIJ*, *153*, 1–12.

Davis, E. and Morgenstern, L. (2005). A first-order theory of communication and multi-agent plans. *J. Logic and Computation*, *15*(5), 701–749.

Davis, K. H., Biddulph, R., and Balashek, S. (1952). Automatic recognition of spoken digits. *J. Acoustical Society of America*, *24*(6), 637–642.

Davis, M. (1957). A computer program for Presburger's algorithm. In *Proving Theorems (as Done by Man, Logician, or Machine)*, pp. 215–233. Proc. Summer Institute for Symbolic Logic. Second edition; publication date is 1960.

Davis, M., Logemann, G., and Loveland, D. (1962). A machine program for theorem-proving. *CACM*, *5*, 394–397.

Davis, M. and Putnam, H. (1960). A computing procedure for quantification theory. *JACM*, *7*(3), 201–215.

Davis, R. and Lenat, D. B. (1982). *Knowledge-Based Systems in Artificial Intelligence*. McGraw-Hill.

Dayan, P. (1992). The convergence of TD(λ) for general λ. *Machine Learning*, *8*(3–4), 341–362.

Dayan, P. and Abbott, L. F. (2001). *Theoretical Neuroscience: Computational and Mathematical Modeling of Neural Systems*. MIT Press.

Dayan, P. and Niv, Y. (2008). Reinforcement learning and the brain: The good, the bad and the ugly. *Current Opinion in Neurobiology*, *18*(2), 185–196.

de Dombal, F. T., Leaper, D. J., Horrocks, J. C., and Staniland, J. R. (1974). Human and computer-aided diagnosis of abdominal pain: Further report with emphasis on performance of clinicians. *British Medical Journal*, *1*, 376–380.

de Dombal, F. T., Staniland, J. R., and Clamp, S. E. (1981). Geographical variation in disease presentation. *Medical Decision Making*, *1*, 59–69.

de Finetti, B. (1937). Le prévision: ses lois logiques, ses sources subjectives. *Ann. Inst. Poincaré*, *7*, 1–68.

de Finetti, B. (1993). On the subjective meaning of probability. In Monari, P. and Cocchi, D. (Eds.), *Probabilita e Induzione*, pp. 291–321. Clueb.

de Freitas, J. F. G., Niranjan, M., and Gee, A. H. (2000). Sequential Monte Carlo methods to train neural network models. *Neural Computation*, *12*(4), 933–953.

de Kleer, J. (1975). Qualitative and quantitative knowledge in classical mechanics. Tech. rep. AI-TR-352, MIT Artificial Intelligence Laboratory.

de Kleer, J. (1989). A comparison of ATMS and CSP techniques. In *IJCAI-89*, Vol. 1, pp. 290–296.

de Kleer, J. and Brown, J. S. (1985). A qualitative physics based on confluences. In Hobbs, J. R. and Moore, R. C. (Eds.), *Formal Theories of the Commonsense World*, chap. 4, pp. 109–183. Ablex.

de Marcken, C. (1996). *Unsupervised Language Acquisition*. Ph.D. thesis, MIT.

De Morgan, A. (1864). On the syllogism, No. IV, and on the logic of relations. *Transaction of the Cambridge Philosophical Society*, *X*, 331–358.

De Raedt, L. (1992). *Interactive Theory Revision: An Inductive Logic Programming Approach*. Academic Press.

de Salvo Braz, R., Amir, E., and Roth, D. (2007). Lifted first-order probabilistic inference. In Getoor, L. and Taskar, B. (Eds.), *Introduction to Statistical Relational Learning*. MIT Press.

Deacon, T. W. (1997). *The symbolic species: The co-evolution of language and the brain*. W. W. Norton.

Deale, M., Yvanovich, M., Schnitzius, D., Kautz, D., Carpenter, M., Zweben, M., Davis, G., and Daun, B. (1994). The space shuttle ground processing scheduling system. In Zweben, M. and Fox, M. (Eds.), *Intelligent Scheduling*, pp. 423–449. Morgan Kaufmann.

Dean, T., Basye, K., Chekaluk, R., and Hyun, S. (1990). Coping with uncertainty in a control system for navigation and exploration. In *AAAI-90*, Vol. 2, pp. 1010–1015.

Dean, T. and Boddy, M. (1988). An analysis of time-dependent planning. In *AAAI-88*, pp. 49–54.

Dean, T., Firby, R. J., and Miller, D. (1990). Hierarchical planning involving deadlines, travel time, and resources. *Computational Intelligence*, *6*(1), 381–398.

Dean, T., Kaelbling, L. P., Kirman, J., and Nicholson, A. (1993). Planning with deadlines in stochastic domains. In *AAAI-93*, pp. 574–579.

Dean, T. and Kanazawa, K. (1989a). A model for projection and action. In *IJCAI-89*, pp. 985–990.

Dean, T. and Kanazawa, K. (1989b). A model for reasoning about persistence and causation. *Computational Intelligence*, *5*(3), 142–150.

Dean, T., Kanazawa, K., and Shewchuk, J. (1990). Prediction, observation and estimation in planning and control. In *5th IEEE International Symposium on Intelligent Control*, Vol. 2, pp. 645–650.

Dean, T. and Wellman, M. P. (1991). *Planning and Control*. Morgan Kaufmann.

Dearden, R., Friedman, N., and Andre, D. (1999). Model-based Bayesian exploration. In *UAI-99*.

Dearden, R., Friedman, N., and Russell, S. J. (1998). Bayesian q-learning. In *AAAI-98*.

Debevec, P., Taylor, C., and Malik, J. (1996). Modeling and rendering architecture from photographs: A hybrid geometry- and image-based approach. In *Proc. 23rd Annual Conference on Computer Graphics (SIGGRAPH)*, pp. 11–20.

Debreu, G. (1960). Topological methods in cardinal utility theory. In Arrow, K. J., Karlin, S., and Suppes, P. (Eds.), *Mathematical Methods in the Social Sciences, 1959*. Stanford University Press.

Dechter, R. (1990a). Enhancement schemes for constraint processing: Backjumping, learning and cutset decomposition. *AIJ*, *41*, 273–312.

Dechter, R. (1990b). On the expressiveness of networks with hidden variables. In *AAAI-90*, pp. 379–385.

Dechter, R. (1992). Constraint networks. In Shapiro, S. (Ed.), *Encyclopedia of Artificial Intelligence* (2nd edition)., pp. 276–285. Wiley and Sons.

Dechter, R. (1999). Bucket elimination: A unifying framework for reasoning. *AIJ*, *113*, 41–85.

Dechter, R. and Pearl, J. (1985). Generalized best-first search strategies and the optimality of A*. *JACM*, *32*(3), 505–536.

Dechter, R. and Pearl, J. (1987). Network-based heuristics for constraint-satisfaction problems. *AIJ*, *34*(1), 1–38.

Dechter, R. and Pearl, J. (1989). Tree clustering for constraint networks. *AIJ*, *38*(3), 353–366.

Dechter, R. (2003). *Constraint Processing*. Morgan Kaufmann.

Dechter, R. and Frost, D. (2002). Backjump-based backtracking for constraint satisfaction problems. *AIJ*, *136*(2), 147–188.

Dechter, R. and Mateescu, R. (2007). AND/OR search spaces for graphical models. *AIJ*, *171*(2–3), 73–106.

DeCoste, D. and Schölkopf, B. (2002). Training invariant support vector machines. *Machine Learning*, *46*(1), 161–190.

Dedekind, R. (1888). *Was sind und was sollen die Zahlen*. Braunschweig, Germany.

Deerwester, S. C., Dumais, S. T., Landauer, T. K., Furnas, G. W., and Harshman, R. A. (1990). Indexing by latent semantic analysis. *J. American Society for Information Science*, *41*(6), 391–407.

DeGroot, M. H. (1970). *Optimal Statistical Decisions*. McGraw-Hill.

DeGroot, M. H. and Schervish, M. J. (2001). *Probability and Statistics* (3rd edition). Addison Wesley.

DeJong, G. (1981). Generalizations based on explanations. In *IJCAI-81*, pp. 67–69.

DeJong, G. (1982). An overview of the FRUMP system. In Lehnert, W. and Ringle, M. (Eds.), *Strategies for Natural Language Processing*, pp. 149–176. Lawrence Erlbaum.

DeJong, G. and Mooney, R. (1986). Explanation-based learning: An alternative view. *Machine Learning*, *1*, 145–176.

Del Moral, P., Doucet, A., and Jasra, A. (2006). Sequential Monte Carlo samplers. *J. Royal Statistical Society, Series B*, *68*(3), 411–436.

Del Moral, P. (2004). *Feynman–Kac Formulae, Genealogical and Interacting Particle Systems with Applications*. Springer-Verlag.

Delgrande, J. and Schaub, T. (2003). On the relation between Reiter's default logic and its (major) variants. In *Seventh European Conference on Symbolic and Quantitative Approaches to Reasoning with Uncertainty*, pp. 452–463.

Dempster, A. P. (1968). A generalization of Bayesian inference. *J. Royal Statistical Society*, *30 (Series B)*, 205–247.

Dempster, A. P., Laird, N., and Rubin, D. (1977). Maximum likelihood from incomplete data via the EM algorithm. *J. Royal Statistical Society*, *39 (Series B)*, 1–38.

Deng, X. and Papadimitriou, C. H. (1990). Exploring an unknown graph. In *FOCS-90*, pp. 355–361.

Denis, F. (2001). Learning regular languages from simple positive examples. *Machine Learning*, *44*(1/2), 37–66.

Dennett, D. C. (1984). Cognitive wheels: the frame problem of AI. In Hookway, C. (Ed.), *Minds, Machines, and Evolution: Philosophical Studies*, pp. 129–151. Cambridge University Press.

Dennett, D. C. (1991). *Consciousness Explained*. Penguin Press.

Denney, E., Fischer, B., and Schumann, J. (2006). An empirical evaluation of automated theorem provers in software certification. *Int. J. AI Tools*, *15*(1), 81–107.

Descartes, R. (1637). Discourse on method. In Cottingham, J., Stoothoff, R., and Murdoch, D. (Eds.), *The Philosophical Writings of Descartes*, Vol. I. Cambridge University Press, Cambridge, UK.

Descartes, R. (1641). Meditations on first philosophy. In Cottingham, J., Stoothoff, R., and Murdoch, D. (Eds.), *The Philosophical Writings of Descartes*, Vol. II. Cambridge University Press, Cambridge, UK.

Descotte, Y. and Latombe, J.-C. (1985). Making compromises among antagonist constraints in a planner. *AIJ*, *27*, 183–217.

Detwarasiti, A. and Shachter, R. D. (2005). Influence diagrams for team decision analysis. *Decision Analysis*, *2*(4), 207–228.

Devroye, L. (1987). *A course in density estimation*. Birkhauser.

Dickmanns, E. D. and Zapp, A. (1987). Autonomous high speed road vehicle guidance by computer vision. In *Automatic Control—World Congress, 1987: Selected Papers from the 10th Triennial World Congress of the International Federation of Automatic Control*, pp. 221–226.

Dietterich, T. (1990). Machine learning. *Annual Review of Computer Science*, *4*, 255–306.

Dietterich, T. (2000). Hierarchical reinforcement learning with the MAXQ value function decomposition. *JAIR*, *13*, 227–303.

Dijkstra, E. W. (1959). A note on two problems in connexion with graphs. *Numerische Mathematik*, *1*, 269–271.

Dijkstra, E. W. (1984). The threats to computing science. In *ACM South Central Regional Conference*.

Dillenburg, J. F. and Nelson, P. C. (1994). Perimeter search. *AIJ*, *65*(1), 165–178.

Dinh, H., Russell, A., and Su, Y. (2007). On the value of good advice: The complexity of A* with accurate heuristics. In *AAAI-07*.

Dissanayake, G., Newman, P., Clark, S., Durrant-Whyte, H., and Csorba, M. (2001). A solution to the simultaneous localisation and map building (SLAM) problem. *IEEE Transactions on Robotics and Automation*, *17*(3), 229–241.

Do, M. B. and Kambhampati, S. (2001). Sapa: A domain-independent heuristic metric temporal planner. In *ECP-01*.

Do, M. B. and Kambhampati, S. (2003). Planning as constraint satisfaction: solving the planning graph by compiling it into CSP. *AIJ*, *132*(2), 151–182.

Doctorow, C. (2001). Metacrap: Putting the torch to seven straw-men of the meta-utopia. `www.well.com/~doctorow/metacrap.htm`.

Domingos, P. and Pazzani, M. (1997). On the optimality of the simple Bayesian classifier under zero–one loss. *Machine Learning*, *29*, 103–30.

Domingos, P. and Richardson, M. (2004). Markov logic: A unifying framework for statistical relational learning. In *Proc. ICML-04 Workshop on Statistical Relational Learning*.

Donninger, C. and Lorenz, U. (2004). The chess monster hydra. In *Proc. 14th International Conference on Field-Programmable Logic and Applications*, pp. 927–932.

Doorenbos, R. (1994). Combining left and right unlinking for matching a large number of learned rules. In *AAAI-94*.

Doran, J. and Michie, D. (1966). Experiments with the graph traverser program. *Proc. Royal Society of London*, *294, Series A*, 235–259.

Dorf, R. C. and Bishop, R. H. (2004). *Modern Control Systems* (10th edition). Prentice-Hall.

Doucet, A. (1997). *Monte Carlo methods for Bayesian estimation of hidden Markov models: Application to radiation signals*. Ph.D. thesis, Université de Paris-Sud.

Doucet, A., de Freitas, N., and Gordon, N. (2001). *Sequential Monte Carlo Methods in Practice*. Springer-Verlag.

Doucet, A., de Freitas, N., Murphy, K., and Russell, S. J. (2000). Rao-blackwellised particle filtering for dynamic bayesian networks. In *UAI-00*.

Dowling, W. F. and Gallier, J. H. (1984). Linear-time algorithms for testing the satisfiability of propositional Horn formulas. *J. Logic Programming*, *1*, 267–284.

Dowty, D., Wall, R., and Peters, S. (1991). *Introduction to Montague Semantics*. D. Reidel.

Doyle, J. (1979). A truth maintenance system. *AIJ*, *12*(3), 231–272.

Doyle, J. (1983). What is rational psychology? Toward a modern mental philosophy. *AIMag*, *4*(3), 50–53.

Doyle, J. and Patil, R. (1991). Two theses of knowledge representation: Language restrictions, taxonomic classification, and the utility of representation services. *AIJ*, *48*(3), 261–297.

Drabble, B. (1990). Mission scheduling for spacecraft: Diaries of T-SCHED. In *Expert Planning Systems*, pp. 76–81. Institute of Electrical Engineers.

Dredze, M., Crammer, K., and Pereira, F. (2008). Confidence-weighted linear classification. In *ICML-08*, pp. 264–271.

Dreyfus, H. L. (1972). *What Computers Can't Do: A Critique of Artificial Reason*. Harper and Row.

Dreyfus, H. L. (1992). *What Computers Still Can't Do: A Critique of Artificial Reason*. MIT Press.

Dreyfus, H. L. and Dreyfus, S. E. (1986). *Mind over Machine: The Power of Human Intuition and Expertise in the Era of the Computer*. Blackwell.

Dreyfus, S. E. (1969). An appraisal of some shortest-paths algorithms. *Operations Research*, *17*, 395–412.

Dubois, D. and Prade, H. (1994). A survey of belief revision and updating rules in various uncertainty models. *Int. J. Intelligent Systems*, *9*(1), 61–100.

Duda, R. O., Gaschnig, J., and Hart, P. E. (1979). Model design in the Prospector consultant system for mineral exploration. In Michie, D. (Ed.), *Expert Systems in the Microelectronic Age*, pp. 153–167. Edinburgh University Press.

Duda, R. O. and Hart, P. E. (1973). *Pattern classification and scene analysis*. Wiley.

Duda, R. O., Hart, P. E., and Stork, D. G. (2001). *Pattern Classification* (2nd edition). Wiley.

Dudek, G. and Jenkin, M. (2000). *Computational Principles of Mobile Robotics*. Cambridge University Press.

Duffy, D. (1991). *Principles of Automated Theorem Proving*. John Wiley & Sons.

Dunn, H. L. (1946). Record linkage". *Am. J. Public Health*, *36*(12), 1412–1416.

Durfee, E. H. and Lesser, V. R. (1989). Negotiating task decomposition and allocation using partial global planning. In Huhns, M. and Gasser, L. (Eds.), *Distributed AI*, Vol. 2. Morgan Kaufmann.

Durme, B. V. and Pasca, M. (2008). Finding cars, goddesses and enzymes: Parametrizable acquisition of labeled instances for open-domain information extraction. In *AAAI-08*, pp. 1243–1248.

Dyer, M. (1983). *In-Depth Understanding*. MIT Press.

Dyson, G. (1998). *Darwin among the machines : the evolution of global intelligence*. Perseus Books.

Duzeroski, S., Muggleton, S. H., and Russell, S. J. (1992). PAC-learnability of determinate logic programs. In *COLT-92*, pp. 128–135.

Earley, J. (1970). An efficient context-free parsing algorithm. *CACM*, *13*(2), 94–102.

Edelkamp, S. (2009). Scaling search with symbolic pattern databases. In *Model Checking and Artificial Intelligence (MOCHART)*, pp. 49–65.

Edmonds, J. (1965). Paths, trees, and flowers. *Canadian Journal of Mathematics*, *17*, 449–467.

Edwards, P. (Ed.). (1967). *The Encyclopedia of Philosophy*. Macmillan.

Een, N. and Sörensson, N. (2003). An extensible SAT-solver. In Giunchiglia, E. and Tacchella, A. (Eds.), *Theory and Applications of Satisfiability Testing: 6th International Conference (SAT 2003)*. Springer-Verlag.

Eiter, T., Leone, N., Mateis, C., Pfeifer, G., and Scarcello, F. (1998). The KR system dlv: Progress report, comparisons and benchmarks. In *KR-98*, pp. 406–417.

Elio, R. (Ed.). (2002). *Common Sense, Reasoning, and Rationality*. Oxford University Press.

Elkan, C. (1993). The paradoxical success of fuzzy logic. In *AAAI-93*, pp. 698–703.

Elkan, C. (1997). Boosting and naive Bayesian learning. Tech. rep., Department of Computer Science and Engineering, University of California, San Diego.

Ellsberg, D. (1962). *Risk, Ambiguity, and Decision*. Ph.D. thesis, Harvard University.

Elman, J., Bates, E., Johnson, M., Karmiloff-Smith, A., Parisi, D., and Plunkett, K. (1997). *Rethinking Innateness*. MIT Press.

Empson, W. (1953). *Seven Types of Ambiguity*. New Directions.

Enderton, H. B. (1972). *A Mathematical Introduction to Logic*. Academic Press.

Epstein, R., Roberts, G., and Beber, G. (Eds.). (2008). *Parsing the Turing Test*. Springer.

Erdmann, M. A. and Mason, M. (1988). An exploration of sensorless manipulation. *IEEE Journal of Robotics and Automation*, *4*(4), 369–379.

Ernst, H. A. (1961). *MH-1, a Computer-Operated Mechanical Hand*. Ph.D. thesis, Massachusetts Institute of Technology.

Ernst, M., Millstein, T., and Weld, D. S. (1997). Automatic SAT-compilation of planning problems. In *IJCAI-97*, pp. 1169–1176.

Erol, K., Hendler, J., and Nau, D. S. (1994). HTN planning: Complexity and expressivity. In *AAAI-94*, pp. 1123–1128.

Erol, K., Hendler, J., and Nau, D. S. (1996). Complexity results for HTN planning. *AIJ*, *18*(1), 69–93.

Etzioni, A. (2004). *From Empire to Community: A New Approach to International Relation*. Palgrave Macmillan.

Etzioni, O. (1989). Tractable decision-analytic control. In *Proc. First International Conference on Knowledge Representation and Reasoning*, pp. 114–125.

Etzioni, O., Banko, M., Soderland, S., and Weld, D. S. (2008). Open information extraction from the web. *CACM*, *51*(12).

Etzioni, O., Hanks, S., Weld, D. S., Draper, D., Lesh, N., and Williamson, M. (1992). An approach to planning with incomplete information. In *KR-92*.

Etzioni, O. and Weld, D. S. (1994). A softbot-based interface to the Internet. *CACM*, *37*(7), 72–76.

Etzioni, O., Banko, M., and Cafarella, M. J. (2006). Machine reading. In *AAAI-06*.

Etzioni, O., Cafarella, M. J., Downey, D., Popescu, A.-M., Shaked, T., Soderland, S., Weld, D. S., and Yates, A. (2005). Unsupervised named-entity extraction from the web: An experimental study. *AIJ*, *165*(1), 91–134.

Evans, T. G. (1968). A program for the solution of a class of geometric-analogy intelligence-test questions. In Minsky, M. L. (Ed.), *Semantic Information Processing*, pp. 271–353. MIT Press.

Fagin, R., Halpern, J. Y., Moses, Y., and Vardi, M. Y. (1995). *Reasoning about Knowledge*. MIT Press.

Fahlman, S. E. (1974). A planning system for robot construction tasks. *AIJ*, *5*(1), 1–49.

Faugeras, O. (1993). *Three-Dimensional Computer Vision: A Geometric Viewpoint*. MIT Press.

Faugeras, O., Luong, Q.-T., and Papadopoulo, T. (2001). *The Geometry of Multiple Images*. MIT Press.

Fearing, R. S. and Hollerbach, J. M. (1985). Basic solid mechanics for tactile sensing. *Int. J. Robotics Research*, *4*(3), 40–54.

Featherstone, R. (1987). *Robot Dynamics Algorithms*. Kluwer Academic Publishers.

Feigenbaum, E. A. (1961). The simulation of verbal learning behavior. *Proc. Western Joint Computer Conference*, *19*, 121–131.

Feigenbaum, E. A., Buchanan, B. G., and Lederberg, J. (1971). On generality and problem solving: A case study using the DENDRAL program. In Meltzer, B. and Michie, D. (Eds.), *Machine Intelligence 6*, pp. 165–190. Edinburgh University Press.

Feldman, J. and Sproull, R. F. (1977). Decision theory and artificial intelligence II: The hungry monkey. Technical report, Computer Science Department, University of Rochester.

Feldman, J. and Yakimovsky, Y. (1974). Decision theory and artificial intelligence I: Semantics-based region analyzer. *AIJ*, *5*(4), 349–371.

Fellbaum, C. (2001). *Wordnet: An Electronic Lexical Database*. MIT Press.

Fellegi, I. and Sunter, A. (1969). A theory for record linkage". *JASA*, *64*, 1183–1210.

Felner, A., Korf, R. E., and Hanan, S. (2004). Additive pattern database heuristics. *JAIR*, *22*, 279–318.

Felner, A., Korf, R. E., Meshulam, R., and Holte, R. (2007). Compressed pattern databases. *JAIR*, *30*, 213–247.

Felzenszwalb, P. and Huttenlocher, D. (2000). Efficient matching of pictorial structures. In *CVPR*.

Felzenszwalb, P. and McAllester, D. A. (2007). The generalized A* architecture. *JAIR*.

Ferguson, T. (1992). Mate with knight and bishop in kriegspiel. *Theoretical Computer Science*, *96*(2), 389–403.

Ferguson, T. (1995). Mate with the two bishops in kriegspiel. www.math.ucla.edu/~tom/papers.

Ferguson, T. (1973). Bayesian analysis of some nonparametric problems. *Annals of Statistics*, *1*(2), 209–230.

Ferraris, P. and Giunchiglia, E. (2000). Planning as satisability in nondeterministic domains. In *AAAI-00*, pp. 748–753.

Ferriss, T. (2007). *The 4-Hour Workweek*. Crown.

Fikes, R. E., Hart, P. E., and Nilsson, N. J. (1972). Learning and executing generalized robot plans. *AIJ*, *3*(4), 251–288.

Fikes, R. E. and Nilsson, N. J. (1971). STRIPS: A new approach to the application of theorem proving to problem solving. *AIJ*, *2*(3–4), 189–208.

Fikes, R. E. and Nilsson, N. J. (1993). STRIPS, a retrospective. *AIJ*, *59*(1–2), 227–232.

Fine, S., Singer, Y., and Tishby, N. (1998). The hierarchical hidden markov model: Analysis and applications. *Machine Learning*, *32*(41–62).

Finney, D. J. (1947). *Probit analysis: A statistical treatment of the sigmoid response curve*. Cambridge University Press.

Firth, J. (1957). *Papers in Linguistics*. Oxford University Press.

Fisher, R. A. (1922). On the mathematical foundations of theoretical statistics. *Philosophical Transactions of the Royal Society of London, Series A 222*, 309–368.

Fix, E. and Hodges, J. L. (1951). Discriminatory analysis—Nonparametric discrimination: Consistency properties. Tech. rep. 21-49-004, USAF School of Aviation Medicine.

Floreano, D., Zufferey, J. C., Srinivasan, M. V., and Ellington, C. (2009). *Flying Insects and Robots*. Springer.

Fogel, D. B. (2000). *Evolutionary Computation: Toward a New Philosophy of Machine Intelligence*. IEEE Press.

Fogel, L. J., Owens, A. J., and Walsh, M. J. (1966). *Artificial Intelligence through Simulated Evolution*. Wiley.

Foo, N. (2001). Why engineering models do not have a frame problem. In *Discrete event modeling and simulation technologies: a tapestry of systems and AI-based theories and methodologies*. Springer.

Forbes, J. (2002). *Learning Optimal Control for Autonomous Vehicles*. Ph.D. thesis, University of California.

Forbus, K. D. (1985). Qualitative process theory. In Bobrow, D. (Ed.), *Qualitative Reasoning About Physical Systems*, pp. 85–186. MIT Press.

Forbus, K. D. and de Kleer, J. (1993). *Building Problem Solvers*. MIT Press.

Ford, K. M. and Hayes, P. J. (1995). Turing Test considered harmful. In *IJCAI-95*, pp. 972–977.

Forestier, J.-P. and Varaiya, P. (1978). Multilayer control of large Markov chains. *IEEE Transactions on Automatic Control*, *23*(2), 298–304.

Forgy, C. (1981). OPS5 user's manual. Technical report CMU-CS-81-135, Computer Science Department, Carnegie-Mellon University.

Forgy, C. (1982). A fast algorithm for the many patterns/many objects match problem. *AIJ*, *19*(1), 17–37.

Forsyth, D. and Ponce, J. (2002). *Computer Vision: A Modern Approach*. Prentice Hall.

Fourier, J. (1827). Analyse des travaux de l'Académie Royale des Sciences, pendant l'année 1824; partie mathématique. *Histoire de l'Académie Royale des Sciences de France*, *7*, xlvii–lv.

Fox, C. and Tversky, A. (1995). Ambiguity aversion and comparative ignorance. *Quarterly Journal of Economics*, *110*(3), 585–603.

Fox, D., Burgard, W., Dellaert, F., and Thrun, S. (1999). Monte carlo localization: Efficient position estimation for mobile robots. In *AAAI-99*.

Fox, M. S. (1990). Constraint-guided scheduling: A short history of research at CMU. *Computers in Industry*, *14*(1–3), 79–88.

Fox, M. S., Allen, B., and Strohm, G. (1982). Job shop scheduling: An investigation in constraint-directed reasoning. In *AAAI-82*, pp. 155–158.

Fox, M. S. and Long, D. (1998). The automatic inference of state invariants in TIM. *JAIR*, *9*, 367–421.

Franco, J. and Paull, M. (1983). Probabilistic analysis of the Davis Putnam procedure for solving the satisfiability problem. *Discrete Applied Mathematics*, *5*, 77–87.

Frank, I., Basin, D. A., and Matsubara, H. (1998). Finding optimal strategies for imperfect information games. In *AAAI-98*, pp. 500–507.

Frank, R. H. and Cook, P. J. (1996). *The Winner-Take-All Society*. Penguin.

Franz, A. (1996). *Automatic Ambiguity resolution in Natural Language Processing: An Empirical Approach*. Springer.

Franz, A. and Brants, T. (2006). All our n-gram are belong to you. Blog posting.

Frege, G. (1879). *Begriffsschrift, eine der arithmetischen nachgebildete Formelsprache des reinen Denkens*. Halle, Berlin. English translation appears in van Heijenoort (1967).

Freitag, D. and McCallum, A. (2000). Information extraction with hmm structures learned by stochastic optimization. In *AAAI-00*.

Freuder, E. C. (1978). Synthesizing constraint expressions. *CACM*, *21*(11), 958–966.

Freuder, E. C. (1982). A sufficient condition for backtrack-free search. *JACM*, *29*(1), 24–32.

Freuder, E. C. (1985). A sufficient condition for backtrack-bounded search. *JACM*, *32*(4), 755–761.

Freuder, E. C. and Mackworth, A. K. (Eds.). (1994). *Constraint-based reasoning*. MIT Press.

Freund, Y. and Schapire, R. E. (1996). Experiments with a new boosting algorithm. In *ICML-96*.

Freund, Y. and Schapire, R. E. (1999). Large margin classification using the perceptron algorithm. *Machine Learning*, *37*(3), 277–296.

Friedberg, R. M. (1958). A learning machine: Part I. *IBM Journal of Research and Development*, *2*, 2–13.

Friedberg, R. M., Dunham, B., and North, T. (1959). A learning machine: Part II. *IBM Journal of Research and Development*, *3*(3), 282–287.

Friedgut, E. (1999). Necessary and sufficient conditions for sharp thresholds of graph properties, and the k-SAT problem. *J. American Mathematical Society*, *12*, 1017–1054.

Friedman, G. J. (1959). Digital simulation of an evolutionary process. *General Systems Yearbook*, *4*, 171–184.

Friedman, J., Hastie, T., and Tibshirani, R. (2000). Additive logistic regression: A statistical view of boosting. *Annals of Statistics*, *28*(2), 337–374.

Friedman, N. (1998). The Bayesian structural EM algorithm. In *UAI-98*.

Friedman, N. and Goldszmidt, M. (1996). Learning Bayesian networks with local structure. In *UAI-96*, pp. 252–262.

Friedman, N. and Koller, D. (2003). Being Bayesian about Bayesian network structure: A Bayesian approach to structure discovery in Bayesian networks. *Machine Learning*, *50*, 95–125.

Friedman, N., Murphy, K., and Russell, S. J. (1998). Learning the structure of dynamic probabilistic networks. In *UAI-98*.

Friedman, N. (2004). Inferring cellular networks using probabilistic graphical models. *Science*, *303*(5659), 799–805.

Fruhwirth, T. and Abdennadher, S. (2003). *Essentials of constraint programming*. Cambridge University Press.

Fuchs, J. J., Gasquet, A., Olalainty, B., and Currie, K. W. (1990). PlanERS-1: An expert planning system for generating spacecraft mission plans. In *First International Conference on Expert Planning Systems*, pp. 70–75. Institute of Electrical Engineers.

Fudenberg, D. and Tirole, J. (1991). *Game theory*. MIT Press.

Fukunaga, A. S., Rabideau, G., Chien, S., and Yan, D. (1997). ASPEN: A framework for automated planning and scheduling of spacecraft control and operations. In *Proc. International Symposium on AI, Robotics and Automation in Space*, pp. 181–187.

Fung, R. and Chang, K. C. (1989). Weighting and integrating evidence for stochastic simulation in Bayesian networks. In *UAI-98*, pp. 209–220.

Gaddum, J. H. (1933). Reports on biological standard III: Methods of biological assay depending on a quantal response. Special report series of the medical research council 183, Medical Research Council.

Gaifman, H. (1964). Concerning measures in first order calculi. *Israel Journal of Mathematics*, *2*, 1–18.

Gallaire, H. and Minker, J. (Eds.). (1978). *Logic and Databases*. Plenum.

Gallier, J. H. (1986). *Logic for Computer Science: Foundations of Automatic Theorem Proving*. Harper and Row.

Gamba, A., Gamberini, L., Palmieri, G., and Sanna, R. (1961). Further experiments with PAPA. *Nuovo Cimento Supplemento*, *20*(2), 221–231.

Garding, J. (1992). Shape from texture for smooth curved surfaces in perspective projection. *J. Mathematical Imaging and Vision*, *2*(4), 327–350.

Gardner, M. (1968). *Logic Machines, Diagrams and Boolean Algebra*. Dover.

Garey, M. R. and Johnson, D. S. (1979). *Computers and Intractability*. W. H. Freeman.

Gaschnig, J. (1977). A general backtrack algorithm that eliminates most redundant tests. In *IJCAI-77*, p. 457.

Gaschnig, J. (1979). Performance measurement and analysis of certain search algorithms. Technical report CMU-CS-79-124, Computer Science Department, Carnegie-Mellon University.

Gasser, R. (1995). *Efficiently harnessing computational resources for exhaustive search*. Ph.D. thesis, ETH Zürich.

Gasser, R. (1998). Solving nine men's morris. In Nowakowski, R. (Ed.), *Games of No Chance*. Cambridge University Press.

Gat, E. (1998). Three-layered architectures. In Kortenkamp, D., Bonasso, R. P., and Murphy, R. (Eds.), *AI-based Mobile Robots: Case Studies of Successful Robot Systems*, pp. 195–210. MIT Press.

Gauss, C. F. (1809). *Theoria Motus Corporum Coelestium in Sectionibus Conicis Solem Ambientium*. Sumtibus F. Perthes et I. H. Besser, Hamburg.

Gauss, C. F. (1829). Beiträge zur theorie der algebraischen gleichungen. Collected in *Werke, Vol. 3*, pages 71–102. K. Gesellschaft Wissenschaft, Göttingen, Germany, 1876.

Gawande, A. (2002). *Complications: A Surgeon's Notes on an Imperfect Science*. Metropolitan Books.

Geiger, D., Verma, T., and Pearl, J. (1990). Identifying independence in Bayesian networks. *Networks*, *20*(5), 507–534.

Geisel, T. (1955). *On Beyond Zebra*. Random House.

Gelb, A. (1974). *Applied Optimal Estimation*. MIT Press.

Gelernter, H. (1959). Realization of a geometry-theorem proving machine. In *Proc. an International Conference on Information Processing*, pp. 273–282. UNESCO House.

Gelfond, M. and Lifschitz, V. (1988). Compiling circumscriptive theories into logic programs. In *Non-Monotonic Reasoning: 2nd International Workshop Proceedings*, pp. 74–99.

Gelfond, M. (2008). Answer sets. In van Harmelan, F., Lifschitz, V., and Porter, B. (Eds.), *Handbook of Knowledge Representation*, pp. 285–316. Elsevier.

Gelly, S. and Silver, D. (2008). Achieving master level play in 9 x 9 computer go. In *AAAI-08*, pp. 1537–1540.

Gelman, A., Carlin, J. B., Stern, H. S., and Rubin, D. (1995). *Bayesian Data Analysis*. Chapman & Hall.

Geman, S. and Geman, D. (1984). Stochastic relaxation, Gibbs distributions, and Bayesian restoration of images. *PAMI*, *6*(6), 721–741.

Genesereth, M. R. (1984). The use of design descriptions in automated diagnosis. *AIJ*, *24*(1–3), 411–436.

Genesereth, M. R. and Nilsson, N. J. (1987). *Logical Foundations of Artificial Intelligence*. Morgan Kaufmann.

Genesereth, M. R. and Nourbakhsh, I. (1993). Time-saving tips for problem solving with incomplete information. In *AAAI-93*, pp. 724–730.

Genesereth, M. R. and Smith, D. E. (1981). Meta-level architecture. Memo HPP-81-6, Computer Science Department, Stanford University.

Gent, I., Petrie, K., and Puget, J.-F. (2006). Symmetry in constraint programming. In Rossi, F., van Beek, P., and Walsh, T. (Eds.), *Handbook of Constraint Programming*. Elsevier.

Gentner, D. (1983). Structure mapping: A theoretical framework for analogy. *Cognitive Science*, *7*, 155–170.

Gentner, D. and Goldin-Meadow, S. (Eds.). (2003). *Language in mind: Advances in the study of language and though*. MIT Press.

Gerevini, A. and Long, D. (2005). Plan constraints and preferences in PDDL3. Tech. rep., Dept. of Electronics for Automation, University of Brescia, Italy.

Gerevini, A. and Serina, I. (2002). LPG: A planner based on planning graphs with action costs. In *ICAPS-02*, pp. 281–290.

Gerevini, A. and Serina, I. (2003). Planning as propositional CSP: from walksat to local search for action graphs. *Constraints*, *8*, 389–413.

Gershwin, G. (1937). Let's call the whole thing off. Song.

Getoor, L. and Taskar, B. (Eds.). (2007). *Introduction to Statistical Relational Learning*. MIT Press.

Ghahramani, Z. and Jordan, M. I. (1997). Factorial hidden Markov models. *Machine Learning*, *29*, 245–274.

Ghahramani, Z. (1998). Learning dynamic bayesian networks. In *Adaptive Processing of Sequences and Data Structures*, pp. 168–197.

Ghahramani, Z. (2005). Tutorial on nonparametric Bayesian methods. Tutorial presentation at the UAI Conference.

Ghallab, M., Howe, A., Knoblock, C. A., and McDermott, D. (1998). PDDL—The planning domain definition language. Tech. rep. DCS TR-1165, Yale Center for Computational Vision and Control.

Ghallab, M. and Laruelle, H. (1994). Representation and control in IxTeT, a temporal planner. In *AIPS-94*, pp. 61–67.

Ghallab, M., Nau, D. S., and Traverso, P. (2004). *Automated Planning: Theory and practice*. Morgan Kaufmann.

Gibbs, R. W. (2006). Metaphor interpretation as embodied simulation. *Mind*, *21*(3), 434–458.

Gibson, J. J. (1950). *The Perception of the Visual World*. Houghton Mifflin.

Gibson, J. J. (1979). *The Ecological Approach to Visual Perception*. Houghton Mifflin.

Gilks, W. R., Richardson, S., and Spiegelhalter, D. J. (Eds.). (1996). *Markov chain Monte Carlo in practice*. Chapman and Hall.

Gilks, W. R., Thomas, A., and Spiegelhalter, D. J. (1994). A language and program for complex Bayesian modelling. *The Statistician*, *43*, 169–178.

Gilmore, P. C. (1960). A proof method for quantification theory: Its justification and realization. *IBM Journal of Research and Development*, *4*, 28–35.

Ginsberg, M. L. (1993). *Essentials of Artificial Intelligence*. Morgan Kaufmann.

Ginsberg, M. L. (1999). GIB: Steps toward an expert-level bridge-playing program. In *IJCAI-99*, pp. 584–589.

Ginsberg, M. L., Frank, M., Halpin, M. P., and Torrance, M. C. (1990). Search lessons learned from crossword puzzles. In *AAAI-90*, Vol. 1, pp. 210–215.

Ginsberg, M. L. (2001). GIB: Imperfect infoormation in a computationally challenging game. *JAIR*, *14*, 303–358.

Gionis, A., Indyk, P., and Motwani, R. (1999). Similarity search in high dimensions vis hashing. In *Proc. 25th Very Large Database (VLDB) Conference*.

Gittins, J. C. (1989). *Multi-Armed Bandit Allocation Indices*. Wiley.

Glanc, A. (1978). On the etymology of the word "robot". *SIGART Newsletter*, *67*, 12.

Glover, F. and Laguna, M. (Eds.). (1997). *Tabu search*. Kluwer.

Gödel, K. (1930). *Über die Vollständigkeit des Logikkalküls*. Ph.D. thesis, University of Vienna.

Gödel, K. (1931). Über formal unentscheidbare Sätze der Principia mathematica und verwandter Systeme I. *Monatshefte für Mathematik und Physik*, *38*, 173–198.

Goebel, J., Volk, K., Walker, H., and Gerbault, F. (1989). Automatic classification of spectra from the infrared astronomical satellite (IRAS). *Astronomy and Astrophysics*, *222*, L5–L8.

Goertzel, B. and Pennachin, C. (2007). *Artificial General Intelligence*. Springer.

Gold, B. and Morgan, N. (2000). *Speech and Audio Signal Processing*. Wiley.

Gold, E. M. (1967). Language identification in the limit. *Information and Control*, *10*, 447–474.

Goldberg, A. V., Kaplan, H., and Werneck, R. F. (2006). Reach for a*: Efficient point-to-point shortest path algorithms. In *Workshop on algorithm engineering and experiments*, pp. 129–143.

Goldman, R. and Boddy, M. (1996). Expressive planning and explicit knowledge. In *AIPS-96*, pp. 110–117.

Goldszmidt, M. and Pearl, J. (1996). Qualitative probabilities for default reasoning, belief revision, and causal modeling. *AIJ*, *84*(1–2), 57–112.

Golomb, S. and Baumert, L. (1965). Backtrack programming. *JACM*, *14*, 516–524.

Golub, G., Heath, M., and Wahba, G. (1979). Generalized cross-validation as a method for choosing a good ridge parameter. *Technometrics*, *21*(2).

Gomes, C., Selman, B., Crato, N., and Kautz, H. (2000). Heavy-tailed phenomena in satisfiability and constrain processing. *JAR*, *24*, 67–100.

Gomes, C., Kautz, H., Sabharwal, A., and Selman, B. (2008). Satisfiability solvers. In van Harmelen, F., Lifschitz, V., and Porter, B. (Eds.), *Handbook of Knowledge Representation*. Elsevier.

Gomes, C. and Selman, B. (2001). Algorithm portfolios. *AIJ*, *126*, 43–62.

Gomes, C., Selman, B., and Kautz, H. (1998). Boosting combinatorial search through randomization. In *AAAI-98*, pp. 431–437.

Gonthier, G. (2008). Formal proof–The four-color theorem. *Notices of the AMS*, *55*(11), 1382–1393.

Good, I. J. (1961). A causal calculus. *British Journal of the Philosophy of Science*, *11*, 305–318.

Good, I. J. (1965). Speculations concerning the first ultraintelligent machine. In Alt, F. L. and Rubinoff, M. (Eds.), *Advances in Computers*, Vol. 6, pp. 31–88. Academic Press.

Good, I. J. (1983). *Good Thinking: The Foundations of Probability and Its Applications*. University of Minnesota Press.

Goodman, D. and Keene, R. (1997). *Man versus Machine: Kasparov versus Deep Blue*. H3 Publications.

Goodman, J. (2001). A bit of progress in language modeling. Tech. rep. MSR-TR-2001-72, Microsoft Research.

Goodman, J. and Heckerman, D. (2004). Fighting spam with statistics. *Significance, the Magazine of the Royal Statistical Society*, *1*, 69–72.

Goodman, N. (1954). *Fact, Fiction and Forecast*. University of London Press.

Goodman, N. (1977). *The Structure of Appearance* (3rd edition). D. Reidel.

Gopnik, A. and Glymour, C. (2002). Causal maps and bayes nets: A cognitive and computational account of theory-formation. In Caruthers, P., Stich, S., and Siegal, M. (Eds.), *The Cognitive Basis of Science*. Cambridge University Press.

Gordon, D. M. (2000). *Ants at Work*. Norton.

Gordon, D. M. (2007). Control without hierarchy. *Nature*, *446*(8), 143.

Gordon, M. J., Milner, A. J., and Wadsworth, C. P. (1979). *Edinburgh LCF*. Springer-Verlag.

Gordon, N. (1994). *Bayesian methods for tracking*. Ph.D. thesis, Imperial College.

Gordon, N., Salmond, D. J., and Smith, A. F. M. (1993). Novel approach to nonlinear/non-Gaussian Bayesian state estimation. *IEE Proceedings F (Radar and Signal Processing)*, *140*(2), 107–113.

Gorry, G. A. (1968). Strategies for computer-aided diagnosis. *Mathematical Biosciences*, *2*(3–4), 293–318.

Gorry, G. A., Kassirer, J. P., Essig, A., and Schwartz, W. B. (1973). Decision analysis as the basis for computer-aided management of acute renal failure. *American Journal of Medicine*, *55*, 473–484.

Gottlob, G., Leone, N., and Scarcello, F. (1999a). A comparison of structural CSP decomposition methods. In *IJCAI-99*, pp. 394–399.

Gottlob, G., Leone, N., and Scarcello, F. (1999b). Hypertree decompositions and tractable queries. In *PODS-99*, pp. 21–32.

Graham, S. L., Harrison, M. A., and Ruzzo, W. L. (1980). An improved context-free recognizer. *ACM Transactions on Programming Languages and Systems*, *2*(3), 415–462.

Grama, A. and Kumar, V. (1995). A survey of parallel search algorithms for discrete optimization problems. *ORSA Journal of Computing*, *7*(4), 365–385.

Grassmann, H. (1861). *Lehrbuch der Arithmetik*. Th. Chr. Fr. Enslin, Berlin.

Grayson, C. J. (1960). Decisions under uncertainty: Drilling decisions by oil and gas operators. Tech. rep., Division of Research, Harvard Business School.

Green, B., Wolf, A., Chomsky, C., and Laugherty, K. (1961). BASEBALL: An automatic question answerer. In *Proc. Western Joint Computer Conference*, pp. 219–224.

Green, C. (1969a). Application of theorem proving to problem solving. In *IJCAI-69*, pp. 219–239.

Green, C. (1969b). Theorem-proving by resolution as a basis for question-answering systems. In Meltzer, B., Michie, D., and Swann, M. (Eds.), *Machine Intelligence 4*, pp. 183–205. Edinburgh University Press.

Green, C. and Raphael, B. (1968). The use of theorem-proving techniques in question-answering systems. In *Proc. 23rd ACM National Conference*.

Greenblatt, R. D., Eastlake, D. E., and Crocker, S. D. (1967). The Greenblatt chess program. In *Proc. Fall Joint Computer Conference*, pp. 801–810.

Greiner, R. (1989). Towards a formal analysis of EBL. In *ICML-89*, pp. 450–453.

Grinstead, C. and Snell, J. (1997). *Introduction to Probability*. AMS.

Grove, W. and Meehl, P. (1996). Comparative efficiency of informal (subjective, impressionistic) and formal (mechanical, algorithmic) prediction procedures: The clinical statistical controversy. *Psychology, Public Policy, and Law*, *2*, 293–323.

Gruber, T. (2004). Interview of Tom Gruber. *AIS SIGSEMIS Bulletin*, *1*(3).

Gu, J. (1989). *Parallel Algorithms and Architectures for Very Fast AI Search*. Ph.D. thesis, University of Utah.

Guard, J., Oglesby, F., Bennett, J., and Settle, L. (1969). Semi-automated mathematics. *JACM*, *16*, 49–62.

Guestrin, C., Koller, D., Gearhart, C., and Kanodia, N. (2003a). Generalizing plans to new environments in relational MDPs. In *IJCAI-03*.

Guestrin, C., Koller, D., Parr, R., and Venkataraman, S. (2003b). Efficient solution algorithms for factored MDPs. *JAIR*, *19*, 399–468.

Guestrin, C., Lagoudakis, M. G., and Parr, R. (2002). Coordinated reinforcement learning. In *ICML-02*, pp. 227–234.

Guibas, L. J., Knuth, D. E., and Sharir, M. (1992). Randomized incremental construction of Delaunay and Voronoi diagrams. *Algorithmica*, *7*, 381–413. See also *17th Int. Coll. on Automata, Languages and Programming*, 1990, pp. 414–431.

Gumperz, J. and Levinson, S. (1996). *Rethinking Linguistic Relativity*. Cambridge University Press.

Guyon, I. and Elisseeff, A. (2003). An introduction to variable and feature selection. *JMLR*, pp. 1157–1182.

Hacking, I. (1975). *The Emergence of Probability*. Cambridge University Press.

Haghighi, A. and Klein, D. (2006). Prototype-driven grammar induction. In *COLING-06*.

Hald, A. (1990). *A History of Probability and Statistics and Their Applications before 1750*. Wiley.

Halevy, A. (2007). Dataspaces: A new paradigm for data integration. In *Brazilian Symposium on Databases*.

Halevy, A., Norvig, P., and Pereira, F. (2009). The unreasonable effectiveness of data. *IEEE Intelligent Systems, March/April*, 8–12.

Halpern, J. Y. (1990). An analysis of first-order logics of probability. *AIJ*, *46*(3), 311–350.

Halpern, J. Y. (1999). Technical addendum, Cox's theorem revisited. *JAIR*, *11*, 429–435.

Halpern, J. Y. and Weissman, V. (2008). Using first-order logic to reason about policies. *ACM Transactions on Information and System Security*, *11*(4).

Hamming, R. W. (1991). *The Art of Probability for Scientists and Engineers*. Addison-Wesley.

Hammond, K. (1989). *Case-Based Planning: Viewing Planning as a Memory Task*. Academic Press.

Hamscher, W., Console, L., and Kleer, J. D. (1992). *Readings in Model-based Diagnosis*. Morgan Kaufmann.

Han, X. and Boyden, E. (2007). Multiple-color optical activation, silencing, and desynchronization of neural activity, with single-spike temporal resolution. *PLoS One*, *e299*.

Hand, D., Mannila, H., and Smyth, P. (2001). *Principles of Data Mining*. MIT Press.

Handschin, J. E. and Mayne, D. Q. (1969). Monte Carlo techniques to estimate the conditional expectation in multi-stage nonlinear filtering. *Int. J. Control*, *9*(5), 547–559.

Hansen, E. (1998). Solving POMDPs by searching in policy space. In *UAI-98*, pp. 211–219.

Hansen, E. and Zilberstein, S. (2001). LAO*: a heuristic search algorithm that finds solutions with loops. *AIJ*, *129*(1–2), 35–62.

Hansen, P. and Jaumard, B. (1990). Algorithms for the maximum satisfiability problem. *Computing*, *44*(4), 279–303.

Hanski, I. and Cambefort, Y. (Eds.). (1991). *Dung Beetle Ecology*. Princeton University Press.

Hansson, O. and Mayer, A. (1989). Heuristic search as evidential reasoning. In *UAI 5*.

Hansson, O., Mayer, A., and Yung, M. (1992). Criticizing solutions to relaxed models yields powerful admissible heuristics. *Information Sciences*, *63*(3), 207–227.

Haralick, R. M. and Elliot, G. L. (1980). Increasing tree search efficiency for constraint satisfaction problems. *AIJ*, *14*(3), 263–313.

Hardin, G. (1968). The tragedy of the commons. *Science*, *162*, 1243–1248.

Hardy, G. H. (1940). *A Mathematician's Apology*. Cambridge University Press.

Harman, G. H. (1983). *Change in View: Principles of Reasoning*. MIT Press.

Harris, Z. (1954). Distributional structure. *Word*, *10(2/3)*.

Harrison, J. R. and March, J. G. (1984). Decision making and postdecision surprises. *Administrative Science Quarterly*, *29*, 26–42.

Harsanyi, J. (1967). Games with incomplete information played by Bayesian players. *Management Science*, *14*, 159–182.

Hart, P. E., Nilsson, N. J., and Raphael, B. (1968). A formal basis for the heuristic determination of minimum cost paths. *IEEE Transactions on Systems Science and Cybernetics*, *SSC-4(2)*, 100–107.

Hart, P. E., Nilsson, N. J., and Raphael, B. (1972). Correction to "A formal basis for the heuristic determination of minimum cost paths". *SIGART Newsletter*, *37*, 28–29.

Hart, T. P. and Edwards, D. J. (1961). The tree prune (TP) algorithm. Artificial intelligence project memo 30, Massachusetts Institute of Technology.

Hartley, H. (1958). Maximum likelihood estimation from incomplete data. *Biometrics*, *14*, 174–194.

Hartley, R. and Zisserman, A. (2000). *Multiple view geometry in computer vision*. Cambridge University Press.

Haslum, P., Botea, A., Helmert, M., Bonet, B., and Koenig, S. (2007). Domain-independent construction of pattern database heuristics for cost-optimal planning. In *AAAI-07*, pp. 1007–1012.

Haslum, P. and Geffner, H. (2001). Heuristic planning with time and resources. In *Proc. IJCAI-01 Workshop on Planning with Resources*.

Haslum, P. (2006). Improving heuristics through relaxed search – An analysis of TP4 and HSP*a in the 2004 planning competition. *JAIR*, *25*, 233–267.

Haslum, P., Bonet, B., and Geffner, H. (2005). New admissible heuristics for domain-independent planning. In *AAAI-05*.

Hastie, T. and Tibshirani, R. (1996). Discriminant adaptive nearest neighbor classification and regression. In Touretzky, D. S., Mozer, M. C., and Hasselmo, M. E. (Eds.), *NIPS 8*, pp. 409–15. MIT Press.

Hastie, T., Tibshirani, R., and Friedman, J. (2001). *The Elements of Statistical Learning: Data Mining, Inference and Prediction* (2nd edition). Springer-Verlag.

Hastie, T., Tibshirani, R., and Friedman, J. (2009). *The Elements of Statistical Learning: Data Mining, Inference and Prediction* (2nd edition). Springer-Verlag.

Haugeland, J. (Ed.). (1985). *Artificial Intelligence: The Very Idea*. MIT Press.

Hauk, T. (2004). *Search in Trees with Chance Nodes*. Ph.D. thesis, Univ. of Alberta.

Haussler, D. (1989). Learning conjunctive concepts in structural domains. *Machine Learning*, *4*(1), 7–40.

Havelund, K., Lowry, M., Park, S., Pecheur, C., Penix, J., Visser, W., and White, J. L. (2000). Formal analysis of the remote agent before and after flight. In *Proc. 5th NASA Langley Formal Methods Workshop*.

Havenstein, H. (2005). Spring comes to AI winter. *Computer World*.

Hawkins, J. and Blakeslee, S. (2004). *On Intelligence*. Henry Holt and Co.

Hayes, P. J. (1978). The naive physics manifesto. In Michie, D. (Ed.), *Expert Systems in the Microelectronic Age*. Edinburgh University Press.

Hayes, P. J. (1979). The logic of frames, In Metzing, D. (Ed.), *Frame Conceptions and Text Understanding*, pp. 46–61. de Gruyter.

Hayes, P. J. (1985a). Naive physics I: Ontology for liquids. In Hobbs, J. R. and Moore, R. C. (Eds.), *Formal Theories of the Commonsense World*, chap. 3, pp. 71–107. Ablex.

Hayes, P. J. (1985b). The second naive physics manifesto. In Hobbs, J. R. and Moore, R. C. (Eds.), *Formal Theories of the Commonsense World*, chap. 1, pp. 1–36. Ablex.

Haykin, S. (2008). *Neural Networks: A Comprehensive Foundation*. Prentice Hall.

Hays, J. and Efros, A. A. (2007). Scene completion Using millions of photographs. *ACM Transactions on Graphics (SIGGRAPH)*, *26*(3).

Hearst, M. A. (1992). Automatic acquisition of hyponyms from large text corpora. In *COLING-92*.

Hearst, M. A. (2009). *Search User Interfaces*. Cambridge University Press.

Hebb, D. O. (1949). *The Organization of Behavior*. Wiley.

Heckerman, D. (1986). Probabilistic interpretation for MYCIN's certainty factors. In Kanal, L. N. and Lemmer, J. F. (Eds.), *UAI 2*, pp. 167–196. Elsevier/North-Holland.

Heckerman, D. (1991). *Probabilistic Similarity Networks*. MIT Press.

Heckerman, D. (1998). A tutorial on learning with Bayesian networks. In Jordan, M. I. (Ed.), *Learning in graphical models*. Kluwer.

Heckerman, D., Geiger, D., and Chickering, D. M. (1994). Learning Bayesian networks: The combination of knowledge and statistical data. Technical report MSR-TR-94-09, Microsoft Research.

Heidegger, M. (1927). *Being and Time*. SCM Press.

Heinz, E. A. (2000). *Scalable search in computer chess*. Vieweg.

Held, M. and Karp, R. M. (1970). The traveling salesman problem and minimum spanning trees. *Operations Research*, *18*, 1138–1162.

Helmert, M. (2001). On the complexity of planning in transportation domains. In *ECP-01*.

Helmert, M. (2003). Complexity results for standard benchmark domains in planning. *AIJ*, *143*(2), 219–262.

Helmert, M. (2006). The fast downward planning system. *JAIR*, *26*, 191–246.

Helmert, M. and Richter, S. (2004). Fast downward – Making use of causal dependencies in the problem representation. In *Proc. International Planning Competition at ICAPS*, pp. 41–43.

Helmert, M. and Röger, G. (2008). How good is almost perfect? In *AAAI-08*.

Hendler, J., Carbonell, J. G., Lenat, D. B., Mizoguchi, R., and Rosenbloom, P. S. (1995). VERY large knowledge bases – Architecture vs engineering. In *IJCAI-95*, pp. 2033–2036.

Henrion, M. (1988). Propagation of uncertainty in Bayesian networks by probabilistic logic sampling. In Lemmer, J. F. and Kanal, L. N. (Eds.), *UAI 2*, pp. 149–163. Elsevier/North-Holland.

Henzinger, T. A. and Sastry, S. (Eds.). (1998). *Hybrid systems: Computation and control*. Springer-Verlag.

Herbrand, J. (1930). *Recherches sur la Théorie de la Démonstration*. Ph.D. thesis, University of Paris.

Hewitt, C. (1969). PLANNER: a language for proving theorems in robots. In *IJCAI-69*, pp. 295–301.

Hierholzer, C. (1873). Über die Möglichkeit, einen Linienzug ohne Wiederholung und ohne Unterbrechung zu umfahren. *Mathematische Annalen*, *6*, 30–32.

Hilgard, E. R. and Bower, G. H. (1975). *Theories of Learning* (4th edition). Prentice-Hall.

Hintikka, J. (1962). *Knowledge and Belief*. Cornell University Press.

Hinton, G. E. and Anderson, J. A. (1981). *Parallel Models of Associative Memory*. Lawrence Erlbaum Associates.

Hinton, G. E. and Nowlan, S. J. (1987). How learning can guide evolution. *Complex Systems*, *1*(3), 495–502.

Hinton, G. E., Osindero, S., and Teh, Y. W. (2006). A fast learning algorithm for deep belief nets. *Neural Computation*, *18*, 1527–15554.

Hinton, G. E. and Sejnowski, T. (1983). Optimal perceptual inference. In *CVPR*, pp. 448–453.

Hinton, G. E. and Sejnowski, T. (1986). Learning and relearning in Boltzmann machines. In Rumelhart, D. E. and McClelland, J. L. (Eds.), *Parallel Distributed Processing*, chap. 7, pp. 282–317. MIT Press.

Hirsh, H. (1987). Explanation-based generalization in a logic programming environment. In *IJCAI-87*.

Hobbs, J. R. (1990). *Literature and Cognition*. CSLI Press.

Hobbs, J. R., Appelt, D., Bear, J., Israel, D., Kameyama, M., Stickel, M. E., and Tyson, M. (1997). FASTUS: A cascaded finite-state transducer for extracting information from natural-language text. In Roche, E. and Schabes, Y. (Eds.), *Finite-State Devices for Natural Language Processing*, pp. 383–406. MIT Press.

Hobbs, J. R. and Moore, R. C. (Eds.). (1985). *Formal Theories of the Commonsense World*. Ablex.

Hobbs, J. R., Stickel, M. E., Appelt, D., and Martin, P. (1993). Interpretation as abduction. *AIJ*, *63*(1–2), 69–142.

Hoffmann, J. (2001). FF: The fast-forward planning system. *AIMag*, *22*(3), 57–62.

Hoffmann, J. and Brafman, R. I. (2006). Conformant planning via heuristic forward search: A new approach. *AIJ*, *170*(6–7), 507–541.

Hoffmann, J. and Brafman, R. I. (2005). Contingent planning via heuristic forward search with implicit belief states. In *ICAPS-05*.

Hoffmann, J. (2005). Where "ignoring delete lists" works: Local search topology in planning benchmarks. *JAIR*, *24*, 685–758.

Hoffmann, J. and Nebel, B. (2001). The FF planning system: Fast plan generation through heuristic search. *JAIR*, *14*, 253–302.

Hoffmann, J., Sabharwal, A., and Domshlak, C. (2006). Friends or foes? An AI planning perspective on abstraction and search. In *ICAPS-06*, pp. 294–303.

Hogan, N. (1985). Impedance control: An approach to manipulation. Parts I, II, and III. *J. Dynamic Systems, Measurement, and Control*, *107*(3), 1–24.

Hoiem, D., Efros, A. A., and Hebert, M. (2008). Putting objects in perspective. *IJCV*, *80*(1).

Holland, J. H. (1975). *Adaption in Natural and Artificial Systems*. University of Michigan Press.

Holland, J. H. (1995). *Hidden Order: How Adaptation Builds Complexity*. Addison-Wesley.

Holte, R. and Hernadvolgyi, I. (2001). Steps towards the automatic creation of search heuristics. Tech. rep. TR04-02, CS Dept., Univ. of Alberta.

Holzmann, G. J. (1997). The Spin model checker. *IEEE Transactions on Software Engineering*, *23*(5), 279–295.

Hood, A. (1824). Case 4th—28 July 1824 (Mr. Hood's cases of injuries of the brain). *Phrenological Journal and Miscellany*, *2*, 82–94.

Hooker, J. (1995). Testing heuristics: We have it all wrong. *J. Heuristics*, *1*, 33–42.

Hoos, H. and Tsang, E. (2006). Local search methods. In Rossi, F., van Beek, P., and Walsh, T. (Eds.), *Handbook of Constraint Processing*, pp. 135–168. Elsevier.

Hope, J. (1994). *The Authorship of Shakespeare's Plays*. Cambridge University Press.

Hopfield, J. J. (1982). Neurons with graded response have collective computational properties like those of two-state neurons. *PNAS*, *79*, 2554–2558.

Horn, A. (1951). On sentences which are true of direct unions of algebras. *JSL*, *16*, 14–21.

Horn, B. K. P. (1970). Shape from shading: A method for obtaining the shape of a smooth opaque object from one view. Technical report 232, MIT Artificial Intelligence Laboratory.

Horn, B. K. P. (1986). *Robot Vision*. MIT Press.

Horn, B. K. P. and Brooks, M. J. (1989). *Shape from Shading*. MIT Press.

Horn, K. V. (2003). Constructing a logic of plausible inference: A guide to cox's theorem. *IJAR*, *34*, 3–24.

Horning, J. J. (1969). *A study of grammatical inference*. Ph.D. thesis, Stanford University.

Horowitz, E. and Sahni, S. (1978). *Fundamentals of Computer Algorithms*. Computer Science Press.

Horswill, I. (2000). Functional programming of behavior-based systems. *Autonomous Robots*, *9*, 83–93.

Horvitz, E. J. (1987). Problem-solving design: Reasoning about computational value, trade-offs, and resources. In *Proc. Second Annual NASA Research Forum*, pp. 26–43.

Horvitz, E. J. (1989). Rational metareasoning and compilation for optimizing decisions under bounded resources. In *Proc. Computational Intelligence 89*. Association for Computing Machinery.

Horvitz, E. J. and Barry, M. (1995). Display of information for time-critical decision making. In *UAI-95*, pp. 296–305.

Horvitz, E. J., Breese, J. S., Heckerman, D., and Hovel, D. (1998). The Lumiere project: Bayesian user modeling for inferring the goals and needs of software users. In *UAI-98*, pp. 256–265.

Horvitz, E. J., Breese, J. S., and Henrion, M. (1988). Decision theory in expert systems and artificial intelligence. *IJAR*, *2*, 247–302.

Horvitz, E. J. and Breese, J. S. (1996). Ideal partition of resources for metareasoning. In *AAAI-96*, pp. 1229–1234.

Horvitz, E. J. and Heckerman, D. (1986). The inconsistent use of measures of certainty in artificial intelligence research. In Kanal, L. N. and Lemmer, J. F. (Eds.), *UAI 2*, pp. 137–151. Elsevier/North-Holland.

Horvitz, E. J., Heckerman, D., and Langlotz, C. P. (1986). A framework for comparing alternative formalisms for plausible reasoning. In *AAAI-86*, Vol. 1, pp. 210–214.

Howard, R. A. (1960). *Dynamic Programming and Markov Processes*. MIT Press.

Howard, R. A. (1966). Information value theory. *IEEE Transactions on Systems Science and Cybernetics*, *SSC-2*, 22–26.

Howard, R. A. (1977). Risk preference. In Howard, R. A. and Matheson, J. E. (Eds.), *Readings in Decision Analysis*, pp. 429–465. Decision Analysis Group, SRI International.

Howard, R. A. (1989). Microrisks for medical decision analysis. *Int. J. Technology Assessment in Health Care*, *5*, 357–370.

Howard, R. A. and Matheson, J. E. (1984). Influence diagrams. In Howard, R. A. and Matheson, J. E. (Eds.), *Readings on the Principles and Applications of Decision Analysis*, pp. 721–762. Strategic Decisions Group.

Howe, D. (1987). The computational behaviour of girard's paradox. In *LICS-87*, pp. 205–214.

Hsu, F.-H. (2004). *Behind Deep Blue: Building the Computer that Defeated the World Chess Champion*. Princeton University Press.

Hsu, F.-H., Anantharaman, T. S., Campbell, M. S., and Nowatzyk, A. (1990). A grandmaster chess machine. *Scientific American*, *263*(4), 44–50.

Hu, J. and Wellman, M. P. (1998). Multiagent reinforcement learning: Theoretical framework and an algorithm. In *ICML-98*, pp. 242–250.

Hu, J. and Wellman, M. P. (2003). Nash q-learning for general-sum stochastic games. *JMLR*, *4*, 1039–1069.

Huang, T., Koller, D., Malik, J., Ogasawara, G., Rao, B., Russell, S. J., and Weber, J. (1994). Automatic symbolic traffic scene analysis using belief networks. In *AAAI-94*, pp. 966–972.

Huang, T. and Russell, S. J. (1998). Object identification: A Bayesian analysis with application to traffic surveillance. *AIJ*, *103*, 1–17.

Huang, X. D., Acero, A., and Hon, H. (2001). *Spoken Language Processing*. Prentice Hall.

Hubel, D. H. (1988). *Eye, Brain, and Vision*. W. H. Freeman.

Huddleston, R. D. and Pullum, G. K. (2002). *The Cambridge Grammar of the English Language*. Cambridge University Press.

Huffman, D. A. (1971). Impossible objects as nonsense sentences. In Meltzer, B. and Michie, D. (Eds.), *Machine Intelligence 6*, pp. 295–324. Edinburgh University Press.

Hughes, B. D. (1995). *Random Walks and Random Environments, Vol. 1: Random Walks*. Oxford University Press.

Hughes, G. E. and Cresswell, M. J. (1996). *A New Introduction to Modal Logic*. Routledge.

Huhns, M. N. and Singh, M. P. (Eds.). (1998). *Readings in Agents*. Morgan Kaufmann.

Hume, D. (1739). *A Treatise of Human Nature* (2nd edition). Republished by Oxford University Press, 1978, Oxford, UK.

Humphrys, M. (2008). How my program passed the turing test. In Epstein, R., Roberts, G., and Beber, G. (Eds.), *Parsing the Turing Test*. Springer.

Hunsberger, L. and Grosz, B. J. (2000). A combinatorial auction for collaborative planning. In *Int. Conference on Multi-Agent Systems (ICMAS-2000)*.

Hunt, W. and Brock, B. (1992). A formal HDL and its use in the FM9001 verification. *Philosophical Transactions of the Royal Society of London*, *339*.

Hunter, L. and States, D. J. (1992). Bayesian classification of protein structure. *IEEE Expert*, *7*(4), 67–75.

Hurst, M. (2000). *The Interpretation of Text in Tables*. Ph.D. thesis, Edinburgh.

Hurwicz, L. (1973). The design of mechanisms for resource allocation. *American Economic Review Papers and Proceedings*, *63*(1), 1–30.

Husmeier, D. (2003). Sensitivity and specificity of inferring genetic regulatory interactions from microarray experiments with dynamic bayesian networks. *Bioinformatics*, *19*(17), 2271–2282.

Huth, M. and Ryan, M. (2004). *Logic in computer science: modelling and reasoning about systems* (2nd edition). Cambridge University Press.

Huttenlocher, D. and Ullman, S. (1990). Recognizing solid objects by alignment with an image. *IJCV*, *5*(2), 195–212.

Huygens, C. (1657). De ratiociniis in ludo aleae. In van Schooten, F. (Ed.), *Exercitionum Mathematicorum*. Elsevirii, Amsterdam. Translated into English by John Arbuthnot (1692).

Huyn, N., Dechter, R., and Pearl, J. (1980). Probabilistic analysis of the complexity of A*. *AIJ*, *15*(3), 241–254.

Hwa, R. (1998). An empirical evaluation of probabilistic lexicalized tree insertion grammars. In *ACL-98*, pp. 557–563.

Hwang, C. H. and Schubert, L. K. (1993). EL: A formal, yet natural, comprehensive knowledge representation. In *AAAI-93*, pp. 676–682.

Ingerman, P. Z. (1967). Panini–Backus form suggested. *CACM*, *10*(3), 137.

Inoue, K. (2001). Inverse entailment for full clausal theories. In *LICS-2001 Workshop on Logic and Learning*.

Intille, S. and Bobick, A. (1999). A framework for recognizing multi-agent action from visual evidence. In *AAAI-99*, pp. 518–525.

Isard, M. and Blake, A. (1996). Contour tracking by stochastic propagation of conditional density. In *ECCV*, pp. 343–356.

Iwama, K. and Tamaki, S. (2004). Improved upper bounds for 3-SAT. In *SODA-04*.

Jaakkola, T. and Jordan, M. I. (1996). Computing upper and lower bounds on likelihoods in intractable networks. In *UAI-96*, pp. 340–348. Morgan Kaufmann.

Jaakkola, T., Singh, S. P., and Jordan, M. I. (1995). Reinforcement learning algorithm for partially observable Markov decision problems. In *NIPS 7*, pp. 345–352.

Jackson, F. (1982). Epiphenomenal qualia. *Philosophical Quarterly*, *32*, 127–136.

Jaffar, J. and Lassez, J.-L. (1987). Constraint logic programming. In *Proc. Fourteenth ACM Conference on Principles of Programming Languages*, pp. 111–119. Association for Computing Machinery.

Jaffar, J., Michaylov, S., Stuckey, P. J., and Yap, R. H. C. (1992). The CLP(R) language and system. *ACM Transactions on Programming Languages and Systems*, *14*(3), 339–395.

Jaynes, E. T. (2003). *Probability Theory: The Logic of Science*. Cambridge Univ. Press.

Jefferson, G. (1949). The mind of mechanical man: The Lister Oration delivered at the Royal College of Surgeons in England. *British Medical Journal*, *1*(25), 1105–1121.

Jeffrey, R. C. (1983). *The Logic of Decision* (2nd edition). University of Chicago Press.

Jeffreys, H. (1948). *Theory of Probability*. Oxford.

Jelinek, F. (1976). Continuous speech recognition by statistical methods. *Proc. IEEE*, *64*(4), 532–556.

Jelinek, F. (1997). *Statistical Methods for Speech Recognition*. MIT Press.

Jelinek, F. and Mercer, R. L. (1980). Interpolated estimation of Markov source parameters from sparse data. In *Proc. Workshop on Pattern Recognition in Practice*, pp. 381–397.

Jennings, H. S. (1906). *Behavior of the Lower Organisms*. Columbia University Press.

Jenniskens, P., Betlem, H., Betlem, J., and Barifaijo, E. (1994). The Mbale meteorite shower. *Meteoritics*, *29*(2), 246–254.

Jensen, F. V. (2001). *Bayesian Networks and Decision Graphs*. Springer-Verlag.

Jensen, F. V. (2007). *Bayesian Networks and Decision Graphs*. Springer-Verlag.

Jevons, W. S. (1874). *The Principles of Science*. Routledge/Thoemmes Press, London.

Ji, S., Parr, R., Li, H., Liao, X., and Carin, L. (2007). Point-based policy iteration. In *AAAI-07*.

Jimenez, P. and Torras, C. (2000). An efficient algorithm for searching implicit AND/OR graphs with cycles. *AIJ*, *124*(1), 1–30.

Joachims, T. (2001). A statistical learning model of text classification with support vector machines. In *SIGIR-01*, pp. 128–136.

Johnson, W. W. and Story, W. E. (1879). Notes on the "15" puzzle. *American Journal of Mathematics*, *2*, 397–404.

Johnston, M. D. and Adorf, H.-M. (1992). Scheduling with neural networks: The case of the Hubble space telescope. *Computers and Operations Research*, *19*(3–4), 209–240.

Jones, N. D., Gomard, C. K., and Sestoft, P. (1993). *Partial Evaluation and Automatic Program Generation*. Prentice-Hall.

Jones, R., Laird, J., and Nielsen, P. E. (1998). Automated intelligent pilots for combat flight simulation. In *AAAI-98*, pp. 1047–54.

Jones, R., McCallum, A., Nigam, K., and Riloff, E. (1999). Bootstrapping for text learning tasks. In *Proc. IJCAI-99 Workshop on Text Mining: Foundations, Techniques, and Applications*, pp. 52–63.

Jones, T. (2007). *Artificial Intelligence: A Systems Approach*. Infinity Science Press.

Jonsson, A., Morris, P., Muscettola, N., Rajan, K., and Smith, B. (2000). Planning in interplanetary space: Theory and practice. In *AIPS-00*, pp. 177–186.

Jordan, M. I. (1995). Why the logistic function? a tutorial discussion on probabilities and neural networks. Computational cognitive science technical report 9503, Massachusetts Institute of Technology.

Jordan, M. I. (2005). Dirichlet processes, Chinese restaurant processes and all that. Tutorial presentation at the NIPS Conference.

Jordan, M. I., Ghahramani, Z., Jaakkola, T., and Saul, L. K. (1998). An introduction to variational methods for graphical models. In Jordan, M. I. (Ed.), *Learning in Graphical Models*. Kluwer.

Jouannaud, J.-P. and Kirchner, C. (1991). Solving equations in abstract algebras: A rule-based survey of unification. In Lassez, J.-L. and Plotkin, G. (Eds.), *Computational Logic*, pp. 257–321. MIT Press.

Judd, J. S. (1990). *Neural Network Design and the Complexity of Learning*. MIT Press.

Juels, A. and Wattenberg, M. (1996). Stochastic hillclimbing as a baseline method for evaluating genetic algorithms. In Touretzky, D. S., Mozer, M. C., and Hasselmo, M. E. (Eds.), *NIPS 8*, pp. 430–6. MIT Press.

Junker, U. (2003). The logic of ilog (j)configurator: Combining constraint programming with a description logic. In *Proc. IJCAI-03 Configuration Workshop*, pp. 13–20.

Jurafsky, D. and Martin, J. H. (2000). *Speech and Language Processing: An Introduction to Natural Language Processing, Computational Linguistics, and Speech Recognition*. Prentice-Hall.

Jurafsky, D. and Martin, J. H. (2008). *Speech and Language Processing: An Introduction to Natural Language Processing, Computational Linguistics, and Speech Recognition* (2nd edition). Prentice-Hall.

Kadane, J. B. and Simon, H. A. (1977). Optimal strategies for a class of constrained sequential problems. *Annals of Statistics*, *5*, 237–255.

Kadane, J. B. and Larkey, P. D. (1982). Subjective probability and the theory of games. *Management Science*, *28*(2), 113–120.

Kaelbling, L. P., Littman, M. L., and Cassandra, A. R. (1998). Planning and actiong in partially observable stochastic domains. *AIJ*, *101*, 99–134.

Kaelbling, L. P., Littman, M. L., and Moore, A. W. (1996). Reinforcement learning: A survey. *JAIR*, *4*, 237–285.

Kaelbling, L. P. and Rosenschein, S. J. (1990). Action and planning in embedded agents. *Robotics and Autonomous Systems*, *6*(1–2), 35–48.

Kager, R. (1999). *Optimality Theory*. Cambridge University Press.

Kahn, H. and Marshall, A. W. (1953). Methods of reducing sample size in Monte Carlo computations. *Operations Research*, *1*(5), 263–278.

Kahneman, D., Slovic, P., and Tversky, A. (Eds.). (1982). *Judgment under Uncertainty: Heuristics and Biases*. Cambridge University Press.

Kahneman, D. and Tversky, A. (1979). Prospect theory: An analysis of decision under risk. *Econometrica*, pp. 263–291.

Kaindl, H. and Khorsand, A. (1994). Memory-bounded bidirectional search. In *AAAI-94*, pp. 1359–1364.

Kalman, R. (1960). A new approach to linear filtering and prediction problems. *J. Basic Engineering*, *82*, 35–46.

Kambhampati, S. (1994). Exploiting causal structure to control retrieval and refitting during plan reuse. *Computational Intelligence*, *10*, 213–244.

Kambhampati, S., Mali, A. D., and Srivastava, B. (1998). Hybrid planning for partially hierarchical domains. In *AAAI-98*, pp. 882–888.

Kanal, L. N. and Kumar, V. (1988). *Search in Artificial Intelligence*. Springer-Verlag.

Kanazawa, K., Koller, D., and Russell, S. J. (1995). Stochastic simulation algorithms for dynamic probabilistic networks. In *UAI-95*, pp. 346–351.

Kantorovich, L. V. (1939). Mathematical methods of organizing and planning production. Publishd in translation in *Management Science*, *6*(4), 366–422, July 1960.

Kaplan, D. and Montague, R. (1960). A paradox regained. *Notre Dame Journal of Formal Logic*, *1*(3), 79–90.

Karmarkar, N. (1984). A new polynomial-time algorithm for linear programming. *Combinatorica*, *4*, 373–395.

Karp, R. M. (1972). Reducibility among combinatorial problems. In Miller, R. E. and Thatcher, J. W. (Eds.), *Complexity of Computer Computations*, pp. 85–103. Plenum.

Kartam, N. A. and Levitt, R. E. (1990). A constraint-based approach to construction planning of multi-story buildings. In *Expert Planning Systems*, pp. 245–250. Institute of Electrical Engineers.

Kasami, T. (1965). An efficient recognition and syntax analysis algorithm for context-free languages. Tech. rep. AFCRL-65-758, Air Force Cambridge Research Laboratory.

Kasparov, G. (1997). IBM owes me a rematch. *Time*, *149*(21), 66–67.

Kaufmann, M., Manolios, P., and Moore, J. S. (2000). *Computer-Aided Reasoning: An Approach*. Kluwer.

Kautz, H. (2006). Deconstructing planning as satisfiability. In *AAAI-06*.

Kautz, H., McAllester, D. A., and Selman, B. (1996). Encoding plans in propositional logic. In *KR-96*, pp. 374–384.

Kautz, H. and Selman, B. (1992). Planning as satisfiability. In *ECAI-92*, pp. 359–363.

Kautz, H. and Selman, B. (1998). BLACKBOX: A new approach to the application of theorem proving to problem solving. Working Notes of the AIPS-98 Workshop on Planning as Combinatorial Search.

Kavraki, L., Svestka, P., Latombe, J.-C., and Overmars, M. (1996). Probabilistic roadmaps for path planning in high-dimensional configuration spaces. *IEEE Transactions on Robotics and Automation*, *12*(4), 566–580.

Kay, M., Gawron, J. M., and Norvig, P. (1994). *Verbmobil: A Translation System for Face-To-Face Dialog*. CSLI Press.

Kearns, M. (1990). *The Computational Complexity of Machine Learning*. MIT Press.

Kearns, M., Mansour, Y., and Ng, A. Y. (2000). Approximate planning in large POMDPs via reusable trajectories. In Solla, S. A., Leen, T. K., and Müller, K.-R. (Eds.), *NIPS 12*. MIT Press.

Kearns, M. and Singh, S. P. (1998). Near-optimal reinforcement learning in polynomial time. In *ICML-98*, pp. 260–268.

Kearns, M. and Vazirani, U. (1994). *An Introduction to Computational Learning Theory*. MIT Press.

Kearns, M. and Mansour, Y. (1998). A fast, bottom-up decision tree pruning algorithm with near-optimal generalization. In *ICML-98*, pp. 269–277.

Kebeasy, R. M., Hussein, A. I., and Dahy, S. A. (1998). Discrimination between natural earthquakes and nuclear explosions using the Aswan Seismic Network. *Annali di Geofisica*, *41*(2), 127–140.

Keeney, R. L. (1974). Multiplicative utility functions. *Operations Research*, *22*, 22–34.

Keeney, R. L. and Raiffa, H. (1976). *Decisions with Multiple Objectives: Preferences and Value Tradeoffs*. Wiley.

Kemp, M. (Ed.). (1989). *Leonardo on Painting: An Anthology of Writings*. Yale University Press.

Kephart, J. O. and Chess, D. M. (2003). The vision of autonomic computing. *IEEE Computer*, *36*(1), 41–50.

Kersting, K., Raedt, L. D., and Kramer, S. (2000). Interpreting bayesian logic programs. In *Proc. AAAI-2000 Workshop on Learning Statistical Models from Relational Data*.

Kessler, B., Nunberg, G., and Schütze, H. (1997). Automatic detection of text genre. *CoRR*, *cmp-lg/9707002*.

Keynes, J. M. (1921). *A Treatise on Probability*. Macmillan.

Khare, R. (2006). Microformats: The next (small) thing on the semantic web. *IEEE Internet Computing*, *10*(1), 68–75.

Khatib, O. (1986). Real-time obstacle avoidance for robot manipulator and mobile robots. *Int. J. Robotics Research*, *5*(1), 90–98.

Khmelev, D. V. and Tweedie, F. J. (2001). Using Markov chains for identification of writer. *Literary and Linguistic Computing*, *16*(3), 299–307.

Kietz, J.-U. and Duzeroski, S. (1994). Inductive logic programming and learnability. *SIGART Bulletin*, *5*(1), 22–32.

Kilgarriff, A. and Grefenstette, G. (2006). Introduction to the special issue on the web as corpus. *Computational Linguistics*, *29*(3), 333–347.

Kim, J. H. (1983). *CONVINCE: A Conversational Inference Consolidation Engine*. Ph.D. thesis, Department of Computer Science, University of California at Los Angeles.

Kim, J. H. and Pearl, J. (1983). A computational model for combined causal and diagnostic reasoning in inference systems. In *IJCAI-83*, pp. 190–193.

Kim, J.-H., Lee, C.-H., Lee, K.-H., and Kuppuswamy, N. (2007). Evolving personality of a genetic robot in ubiquitous environment. In *The 16th IEEE International Symposium on Robot and Human interactive Communication*, pp. 848–853.

King, R. D., Rowland, J., Oliver, S. G., and Young, M. (2009). The automation of science. *Science*, *324*(5923), 85–89.

Kirk, D. E. (2004). *Optimal Control Theory: An Introduction*. Dover.

Kirkpatrick, S., Gelatt, C. D., and Vecchi, M. P. (1983). Optimization by simulated annealing. *Science*, *220*, 671–680.

Kister, J., Stein, P., Ulam, S., Walden, W., and Wells, M. (1957). Experiments in chess. *JACM*, *4*, 174–177.

Kisynski, J. and Poole, D. (2009). Lifted aggregation in directed first-order probabilistic models. In *IJCAI-09*.

Kitano, H., Asada, M., Kuniyoshi, Y., Noda, I., and Osawa, E. (1997a). RoboCup: The robot world cup initiative. In *Proc. First International Conference on Autonomous Agents*, pp. 340–347.

Kitano, H., Asada, M., Kuniyoshi, Y., Noda, I., Osawa, E., and Matsubara, H. (1997b). RoboCup: A challenge problem for AI. *AIMag*, *18*(1), 73–85.

Kjaerulff, U. (1992). A computational scheme for reasoning in dynamic probabilistic networks. In *UAI-92*, pp. 121–129.

Klein, D. and Manning, C. (2001). Parsing with treebank grammars: Empirical bounds, theoretical models, and the structure of the Penn treebank. In *ACL-01*.

Klein, D. and Manning, C. (2003). A* parsing: Fast exact Viterbi parse selection. In *HLT-NAACL-03*, pp. 119–126.

Klein, D., Smarr, J., Nguyen, H., and Manning, C. (2003). Named entity recognition with character-level models. In *Conference on Natural Language Learning (CoNLL)*.

Kleinberg, J. M. (1999). Authoritative sources in a hyperlinked environment. *JACM*, *46*(5), 604–632.

Klemperer, P. (2002). What really matters in auction design. *J. Economic Perspectives*, *16*(1).

Kneser, R. and Ney, H. (1995). Improved backing-off for M-gram language modeling. In *ICASSP-95*, pp. 181–184.

Knight, K. (1999). A statistical MT tutorial workbook. Prepared in connection with the Johns Hopkins University summer workshop.

Knuth, D. E. (1964). Representing numbers using only one 4. *Mathematics Magazine*, *37*(Nov/Dec), 308–310.

Knuth, D. E. (1968). Semantics for context-free languages. *Mathematical Systems Theory*, *2*(2), 127–145.

Knuth, D. E. (1973). *The Art of Computer Programming* (second edition)., Vol. 2: Fundamental Algorithms. Addison-Wesley.

Knuth, D. E. (1975). An analysis of alpha–beta pruning. *AIJ*, *6*(4), 293–326.

Knuth, D. E. and Bendix, P. B. (1970). Simple word problems in universal algebras. In Leech, J. (Ed.), *Computational Problems in Abstract Algebra*, pp. 263–267. Pergamon.

Kocsis, L. and Szepesvari, C. (2006). Bandit-based Monte-Carlo planning. In *ECML-06*.

Koditschek, D. (1987). Exact robot navigation by means of potential functions: some topological considerations. In *ICRA-87*, Vol. 1, pp. 1–6.

Koehler, J., Nebel, B., Hoffmann, J., and Dimopoulos, Y. (1997). Extending planning graphs to an ADL subset. In *ECP-97*, pp. 273–285.

Koehn, P. (2009). *Statistical Machine Translation*. Cambridge University Press.

Koenderink, J. J. (1990). *Solid Shape*. MIT Press.

Koenig, S. (1991). Optimal probabilistic and decision-theoretic planning using Markovian decision theory. Master's report, Computer Science Division, University of California.

Koenig, S. (2000). Exploring unknown environments with real-time search or reinforcement learning. In Solla, S. A., Leen, T. K., and Müller, K.-R. (Eds.), *NIPS 12*. MIT Press.

Koenig, S. (2001). Agent-centered search. *AIMag*, *22*(4), 109–131.

Koller, D., Meggido, N., and von Stengel, B. (1996). Efficient computation of equilibria for extensive two-person games. *Games and Economic Behaviour*, *14*(2), 247–259.

Koller, D. and Pfeffer, A. (1997). Representations and solutions for game-theoretic problems. *AIJ*, *94*(1–2), 167–215.

Koller, D. and Pfeffer, A. (1998). Probabilistic frame-based systems. In *AAAI-98*, pp. 580–587.

Koller, D. and Friedman, N. (2009). *Probabilistic Graphical Models: Principles and Techniques*. MIT Press.

Koller, D. and Milch, B. (2003). Multi-agent influence diagrams for representing and solving games. *Games and Economic Behavior*, *45*, 181–221.

Koller, D. and Parr, R. (2000). Policy iteration for factored MDPs. In *UAI-00*, pp. 326–334.

Koller, D. and Sahami, M. (1997). Hierarchically classifying documents using very few words. In *ICML-97*, pp. 170–178.

Kolmogorov, A. N. (1941). Interpolation und extrapolation von stationaren zufalligen folgen. *Bulletin of the Academy of Sciences of the USSR, Ser. Math. 5*, 3–14.

Kolmogorov, A. N. (1950). *Foundations of the Theory of Probability*. Chelsea.

Kolmogorov, A. N. (1963). On tables of random numbers. *Sankhya, the Indian Journal of Statistics, Series A 25*.

Kolmogorov, A. N. (1965). Three approaches to the quantitative definition of information. *Problems in Information Transmission*, *1*(1), 1–7.

Kolodner, J. (1983). Reconstructive memory: A computer model. *Cognitive Science*, *7*, 281–328.

Kolodner, J. (1993). *Case-Based Reasoning*. Morgan Kaufmann.

Kondrak, G. and van Beek, P. (1997). A theoretical evaluation of selected backtracking algorithms. *AIJ*, *89*, 365–387.

Konolige, K. (1997). COLBERT: A language for reactive control in Saphira. In *Künstliche Intelligenz: Advances in Artificial Intelligence*, LNAI, pp. 31–52.

Konolige, K. (2004). Large-scale map-making. In *AAAI-04*, pp. 457–463.

Konolige, K. (1982). A first order formalization of knowledge and action for a multi-agent planning system. In Hayes, J. E., Michie, D., and Pao, Y.-H. (Eds.), *Machine Intelligence 10*. Ellis Horwood.

Konolige, K. (1994). Easy to be hard: Difficult problems for greedy algorithms. In *KR-94*, pp. 374–378.

Koo, T., Carreras, X., and Collins, M. (2008). Simple semi-supervised dependency parsing. In *ACL-08*.

Koopmans, T. C. (1972). Representation of preference orderings over time. In McGuire, C. B. and Radner, R. (Eds.), *Decision and Organization*. Elsevier/North-Holland.

Korb, K. B. and Nicholson, A. (2003). *Bayesian Artificial Intelligence*. Chapman and Hall.

Korb, K. B., Nicholson, A., and Jitnah, N. (1999). Bayesian poker. In *UAI-99*.

Korf, R. E. (1985a). Depth-first iterative-deepening: an optimal admissible tree search. *AIJ*, *27(1)*, 97–109.

Korf, R. E. (1985b). Iterative-deepening A*: An optimal admissible tree search. In *IJCAI-85*, pp. 1034–1036.

Korf, R. E. (1987). Planning as search: A quantitative approach. *AIJ*, *33(1)*, 65–88.

Korf, R. E. (1990). Real-time heuristic search. *AIJ*, *42*(3), 189–212.

Korf, R. E. (1993). Linear-space best-first search. *AIJ*, *62*(1), 41–78.

Korf, R. E. (1995). Space-efficient search algorithms. *ACM Computing Surveys*, *27*(3), 337–339.

Korf, R. E. and Chickering, D. M. (1996). Best-first minimax search. *AIJ*, *84*(1–2), 299–337.

Korf, R. E. and Felner, A. (2002). Disjoint pattern database heuristics. *AIJ*, *134*(1–2), 9–22.

Korf, R. E., Reid, M., and Edelkamp, S. (2001). Time complexity of iterative-deepening-A*. *AIJ*, *129*, 199–218.

Korf, R. E. and Zhang, W. (2000). Divide-and-conquer frontier search applied to optimal sequence alignment. In *American Association for Artificial Intelligence*, pp. 910–916.

Korf, R. E. (2008). Linear-time disk-based implicit graph search. *JACM*, *55*(6).

Korf, R. E. and Schultze, P. (2005). Large-scale parallel breadth-first search. In *AAAI-05*, pp. 1380–1385.

Kotok, A. (1962). A chess playing program for the IBM 7090. AI project memo 41, MIT Computation Center.

Koutsoupias, E. and Papadimitriou, C. H. (1992). On the greedy algorithm for satisfiability. *Information Processing Letters*, *43*(1), 53–55.

Kowalski, R. (1974). Predicate logic as a programming language. In *Proc. IFIP Congress*, pp. 569–574.

Kowalski, R. (1979). *Logic for Problem Solving*. Elsevier/North-Holland.

Kowalski, R. (1988). The early years of logic programming. *CACM*, *31*, 38–43.

Kowalski, R. and Sergot, M. (1986). A logic-based calculus of events. *New Generation Computing*, *4*(1), 67–95.

Koza, J. R. (1992). *Genetic Programming: On the Programming of Computers by Means of Natural Selection*. MIT Press.

Koza, J. R. (1994). *Genetic Programming II: Automatic discovery of reusable programs*. MIT Press.

Koza, J. R., Bennett, F. H., Andre, D., and Keane, M. A. (1999). *Genetic Programming III: Darwinian invention and problem solving*. Morgan Kaufmann.

Kraus, S., Ephrati, E., and Lehmann, D. (1991). Negotiation in a non-cooperative environment. *AIJ*, *3*(4), 255–281.

Krause, A. and Guestrin, C. (2009). Optimal value of information in graphical models. *JAIR*, *35*, 557–591.

Krause, A., McMahan, B., Guestrin, C., and Gupta, A. (2008). Robust submodular observation selection. *JMLR*, *9*, 2761–2801.

Kripke, S. A. (1963). Semantical considerations on modal logic. *Acta Philosophica Fennica*, *16*, 83–94.

Krogh, A., Brown, M., Mian, I. S., Sjolander, K., and Haussler, D. (1994). Hidden Markov models in computational biology: Applications to protein modeling. *J. Molecular Biology*, *235*, 1501–1531.

Kübler, S., McDonald, R., and Nivre, J. (2009). *Dependency Parsing*. Morgan Claypool.

Kuhn, H. W. (1953). Extensive games and the problem of information. In Kuhn, H. W. and Tucker, A. W. (Eds.), *Contributions to the Theory of Games II*. Princeton University Press.

Kuhn, H. W. (1955). The Hungarian method for the assignment problem. *Naval Research Logistics Quarterly*, *2*, 83–97.

Kuipers, B. J. (1985). Qualitative simulation. In Bobrow, D. (Ed.), *Qualitative Reasoning About Physical Systems*, pp. 169–203. MIT Press.

Kuipers, B. J. and Levitt, T. S. (1988). Navigation and mapping in large-scale space. *AIMag*, *9*(2), 25–43.

Kuipers, B. J. (2001). Qualitative simulation. In Meyers, R. A. (Ed.), *Encyclopeida of Physical Science and Technology*. Academic Press.

Kumar, P. R. and Varaiya, P. (1986). *Stochastic Systems: Estimation, Identification, and Adaptive Control*. Prentice-Hall.

Kumar, V. (1992). Algorithms for constraint satisfaction problems: A survey. *AIMag*, *13*(1), 32–44.

Kumar, V. and Kanal, L. N. (1983). A general branch and bound formulation for understanding and synthesizing and/or tree search procedures. *AIJ*, *21*, 179–198.

Kumar, V. and Kanal, L. N. (1988). The CDP: A unifying formulation for heuristic search, dynamic programming, and branch-and-bound. In Kanal, L. N. and Kumar, V. (Eds.), *Search in Artificial Intelligence*, chap. 1, pp. 1–27. Springer-Verlag.

Kumar, V., Nau, D. S., and Kanal, L. N. (1988). A general branch-and-bound formulation for AND/OR graph and game tree search. In Kanal, L. N. and Kumar, V. (Eds.), *Search in Artificial Intelligence*, chap. 3, pp. 91–130. Springer-Verlag.

Kurien, J., Nayak, P., and Smith, D. E. (2002). Fragment-based conformant planning. In *AIPS-02*.

Kurzweil, R. (1990). *The Age of Intelligent Machines*. MIT Press.

Kurzweil, R. (2005). *The Singularity is Near*. Viking.

Kwok, C., Etzioni, O., and Weld, D. S. (2001). Scaling question answering to the web. In *Proc. 10th International Conference on the World Wide Web*.

Kyburg, H. E. and Teng, C.-M. (2006). Nonmonotonic logic and statistical inference. *Computational Intelligence*, *22*(1), 26–51.

Kyburg, H. E. (1977). Randomness and the right reference class. *J. Philosophy*, *74*(9), 501–521.

Kyburg, H. E. (1983). The reference class. *Philosophy of Science*, *50*, 374–397.

La Mettrie, J. O. (1748). *L'homme machine*. E. Luzac, Leyde, France.

La Mura, P. and Shoham, Y. (1999). Expected utility networks. In *UAI-99*, pp. 366–373.

Laborie, P. (2003). Algorithms for propagating resource constraints in AI planning and scheduling. *AIJ*, *143*(2), 151–188.

Ladkin, P. (1986a). Primitives and units for time specification. In *AAAI-86*, Vol. 1, pp. 354–359.

Ladkin, P. (1986b). Time representation: a taxonomy of interval relations. In *AAAI-86*, Vol. 1, pp. 360–366.

Lafferty, J., McCallum, A., and Pereira, F. (2001). Conditional random fields: Probabilistic models for segmenting and labeling sequence data. In *ICML-01*.

Lafferty, J. and Zhai, C. (2001). Probabilistic relevance models based on document and query generation. In *Proc. Workshop on Language Modeling and Information Retrieval*.

Lagoudakis, M. G. and Parr, R. (2003). Least-squares policy iteration. *JMLR*, *4*, 1107–1149.

Laird, J., Newell, A., and Rosenbloom, P. S. (1987). SOAR: An architecture for general intelligence. *AIJ*, *33*(1), 1–64.

Laird, J., Rosenbloom, P. S., and Newell, A. (1986). Chunking in Soar: The anatomy of a general learning mechanism. *Machine Learning*, *1*, 11–46.

Laird, J. (2008). Extending the Soar cognitive architecture. In *Artificial General Intelligence Conference*.

Lakoff, G. (1987). *Women, Fire, and Dangerous Things: What Categories Reveal About the Mind*. University of Chicago Press.

Lakoff, G. and Johnson, M. (1980). *Metaphors We Live By*. University of Chicago Press.

Lakoff, G. and Johnson, M. (1999). *Philosophy in the Flesh : The Embodied Mind and Its Challenge to Western Thought*. Basic Books.

Lam, J. and Greenspan, M. (2008). Eye-in-hand visual servoing for accurate shooting in pool robotics. In *5th Canadian Conference on Computer and Robot Vision*.

Lamarck, J. B. (1809). *Philosophie zoologique*. Chez Dentu et L'Auteur, Paris.

Landhuis, E. (2004). Lifelong debunker takes on arbiter of neutral choices: Magician-turned-mathematician uncovers bias in a flip of a coin. *Stanford Report*.

Langdon, W. and Poli, R. (2002). *Foundations of Genetic Programming*. Springer.

Langley, P., Simon, H. A., Bradshaw, G. L., and Zytkow, J. M. (1987). *Scientific Discovery: Computational Explorations of the Creative Processes*. MIT Press.

Langton, C. (Ed.). (1995). *Artificial Life*. MIT Press.

Laplace, P. (1816). *Essai philosophique sur les probabilités* (3rd edition). Courcier Imprimeur, Paris.

Laptev, I. and Perez, P. (2007). Retrieving actions in movies. In *ICCV*, pp. 1–8.

Lari, K. and Young, S. J. (1990). The estimation of stochastic context-free grammars using the inside-outside algorithm. *Computer Speech and Language*, *4*, 35–56.

Larrañaga, P., Kuijpers, C., Murga, R., Inza, I., and Dizdarevic, S. (1999). Genetic algorithms for the travelling salesman problem: A review of representations and operators. *Artificial Intelligence Review*, *13*, 129–170.

Larson, S. C. (1931). The shrinkage of the coefficient of multiple correlation. *J. Educational Psychology*, *22*, 45–55.

Laskey, K. B. (2008). MEBN: A language for first-order bayesian knowledge bases. *AIJ*, *172*, 140–178.

Latombe, J.-C. (1991). *Robot Motion Planning*. Kluwer.

Lauritzen, S. (1995). The EM algorithm for graphical association models with missing data. *Computational Statistics and Data Analysis*, *19*, 191–201.

Lauritzen, S. (1996). *Graphical models*. Oxford University Press.

Lauritzen, S., Dawid, A. P., Larsen, B., and Leimer, H. (1990). Independence properties of directed Markov fields. *Networks*, *20*(5), 491–505.

Lauritzen, S. and Spiegelhalter, D. J. (1988). Local computations with probabilities on graphical structures and their application to expert systems. *J. Royal Statistical Society*, *B 50*(2), 157–224.

Lauritzen, S. and Wermuth, N. (1989). Graphical models for associations between variables, some of which are qualitative and some quantitative. *Annals of Statistics*, *17*, 31–57.

LaValle, S. (2006). *Planning Algorithms*. Cambridge University Press.

Lavrauc, N. and Duzeroski, S. (1994). *Inductive Logic Programming: Techniques and Applications*. Ellis Horwood.

Lawler, E. L., Lenstra, J. K., Kan, A., and Shmoys, D. B. (1992). *The Travelling Salesman Problem*. Wiley Interscience.

Lawler, E. L., Lenstra, J. K., Kan, A., and Shmoys, D. B. (1993). Sequencing and scheduling: Algorithms and complexity. In Graves, S. C., Zipkin, P. H., and Kan, A. H. G. R. (Eds.), *Logistics of Production and Inventory: Handbooks in Operations Research and Management Science, Volume 4*, pp. 445–522. North-Holland.

Lawler, E. L. and Wood, D. E. (1966). Branch-and-bound methods: A survey. *Operations Research*, *14(4)*, 699–719.

Lazanas, A. and Latombe, J.-C. (1992). Landmark-based robot navigation. In *AAAI-92*, pp. 816–822.

LeCun, Y., Jackel, L., Boser, B., and Denker, J. (1989). Handwritten digit recognition: Applications of neural network chips and automatic learning. *IEEE Communications Magazine*, *27*(11), 41–46.

LeCun, Y., Jackel, L., Bottou, L., Brunot, A., Cortes, C., Denker, J., Drucker, H., Guyon, I., Muller, U., Sackinger, E., Simard, P., and Vapnik, V. N. (1995). Comparison of learning algorithms for handwritten digit recognition. In *Int. Conference on Artificial Neural Networks*, pp. 53–60.

Leech, G., Rayson, P., and Wilson, A. (2001). *Word Frequencies in Written and Spoken English: Based on the British National Corpus*. Longman.

Legendre, A. M. (1805). *Nouvelles méthodes pour la détermination des orbites des comètes*. .

Lehrer, J. (2009). *How We Decide*. Houghton Mifflin.

Lenat, D. B. (1983). EURISKO: A program that learns new heuristics and domain concepts: The nature of heuristics, III: Program design and results. *AIJ*, *21*(1–2), 61–98.

Lenat, D. B. and Brown, J. S. (1984). Why AM and EURISKO appear to work. *AIJ*, *23*(3), 269–294.

Lenat, D. B. and Guha, R. V. (1990). *Building Large Knowledge-Based Systems: Representation and Inference in the CYC Project*. Addison-Wesley.

Leonard, H. S. and Goodman, N. (1940). The calculus of individuals and its uses. *JSL*, *5*(2), 45–55.

Leonard, J. and Durrant-Whyte, H. (1992). *Directed sonar sensing for mobile robot navigation*. Kluwer.

Leśniewski, S. (1916). Podstawy ogólnej teorii mnogości. Moscow.

Lettvin, J. Y., Maturana, H. R., McCulloch, W. S., and Pitts, W. (1959). What the frog's eye tells the frog's brain. *Proc. IRE*, *47*(11), 1940–1951.

Letz, R., Schumann, J., Bayerl, S., and Bibel, W. (1992). SETHEO: A high-performance theorem prover. *JAR*, *8*(2), 183–212.

Levesque, H. J. and Brachman, R. J. (1987). Expressiveness and tractability in knowledge representation and reasoning. *Computational Intelligence*, *3*(2), 78–93.

Levin, D. A., Peres, Y., and Wilmer, E. L. (2008). *Markov Chains and Mixing Times*. American Mathematical Society.

Levitt, G. M. (2000). *The Turk, Chess Automaton*. McFarland and Company.

Levy, D. (Ed.). (1988a). *Computer Chess Compendium*. Springer-Verlag.

Levy, D. (Ed.). (1988b). *Computer Games*. Springer-Verlag.

Levy, D. (1989). The million pound bridge program. In Levy, D. and Beal, D. (Eds.), *Heuristic Programming in Artificial Intelligence*. Ellis Horwood.

Levy, D. (2007). *Love and Sex with Robots*. Harper.

Lewis, D. D. (1998). Naive Bayes at forty: The independence assumption in information retrieval. In *ECML-98*, pp. 4–15.

Lewis, D. K. (1966). An argument for the identity theory. *J. Philosophy*, *63*(1), 17–25.

Lewis, D. K. (1980). Mad pain and Martian pain. In Block, N. (Ed.), *Readings in Philosophy of Psychology*, Vol. 1, pp. 216–222. Harvard University Press.

Leyton-Brown, K. and Shoham, Y. (2008). *Essentials of Game Theory: A Concise, Multidisciplinary Introduction*. Morgan Claypool.

Li, C. M. and Anbulagan (1997). Heuristics based on unit propagation for satisfiability problems. In *IJCAI-97*, pp. 366–371.

Li, M. and Vitanyi, P. M. B. (1993). *An Introduction to Kolmogorov Complexity and Its Applications*. Springer-Verlag.

Liberatore, P. (1997). The complexity of the language **A**. *Electronic Transactions on Artificial Intelligence*, *1*, 13–38.

Lifschitz, V. (2001). Answer set programming and plan generation. *AIJ*, *138*(1–2), 39–54.

Lighthill, J. (1973). Artificial intelligence: A general survey. In Lighthill, J., Sutherland, N. S., Needham, R. M., Longuet-Higgins, H. C., and Michie, D. (Eds.), *Artificial Intelligence: A Paper Symposium*. Science Research Council of Great Britain.

Lin, S. (1965). Computer solutions of the travelling salesman problem. *Bell Systems Technical Journal*, *44(10)*, 2245–2269.

Lin, S. and Kernighan, B. W. (1973). An effective heuristic algorithm for the travelling-salesman problem. *Operations Research*, *21*(2), 498–516.

Lindley, D. V. (1956). On a measure of the information provided by an experiment. *Annals of Mathematical Statistics*, *27*(4), 986–1005.

Lindsay, R. K., Buchanan, B. G., Feigenbaum, E. A., and Lederberg, J. (1980). *Applications of Artificial Intelligence for Organic Chemistry: The DENDRAL Project*. McGraw-Hill.

Littman, M. L. (1994). Markov games as a framework for multi-agent reinforcement learning. In *ICML-94*, pp. 157–163.

Littman, M. L., Keim, G. A., and Shazeer, N. M. (1999). Solving crosswords with PROVERB. In *AAAI-99*, pp. 914–915.

Liu, J. S. and Chen, R. (1998). Sequential Monte Carlo methods for dynamic systems. *JASA*, *93*, 1022–1031.

Livescu, K., Glass, J., and Bilmes, J. (2003). Hidden feature modeling for speech recognition using dynamic Bayesian networks. In *EUROSPEECH-2003*, pp. 2529–2532.

Livnat, A. and Pippenger, N. (2006). An optimal brain can be composed of conflicting agents. *PNAS*, *103*(9), 3198–3202.

Locke, J. (1690). *An Essay Concerning Human Understanding*. William Tegg.

Lodge, D. (1984). *Small World*. Penguin Books.

Loftus, E. and Palmer, J. (1974). Reconstruction of automobile destruction: An example of the interaction between language and memory. *J. Verbal Learning and Verbal Behavior*, *13*, 585–589.

Lohn, J. D., Kraus, W. F., and Colombano, S. P. (2001). Evolutionary optimization of yagi-uda antennas. In *Proc. Fourth International Conference on Evolvable Systems*, pp. 236–243.

Longley, N. and Sankaran, S. (2005). The NHL's overtime-loss rule: Empirically analyzing the unintended effects. *Atlantic Economic Journal*.

Longuet-Higgins, H. C. (1981). A computer algorithm for reconstructing a scene from two projections. *Nature*, *293*, 133–135.

Loo, B. T., Condie, T., Garofalakis, M., Gay, D. E., Hellerstein, J. M., Maniatis, P., Ramakrishnan, R., Roscoe, T., and Stoica, I. (2006). Declarative networking: Language, execution and optimization. In *SIGMOD-06*.

Love, N., Hinrichs, T., and Genesereth, M. R. (2006). General game playing: Game description language specification. Tech. rep. LG-2006-01, Stanford University Computer Science Dept.

Lovejoy, W. S. (1991). A survey of algorithmic methods for partially observed Markov decision processes. *Annals of Operations Research*, *28*(1–4), 47–66.

Loveland, D. (1970). A linear format for resolution. In *Proc. IRIA Symposium on Automatic Demonstration*, pp. 147–162.

Lowe, D. (1987). Three-dimensional object recognition from single two-dimensional images. *AIJ*, *31*, 355–395.

Lowe, D. (1999). Object recognition using local scale invariant feature. In *ICCV*.

Lowe, D. (2004). Distinctive image features from scale-invariant keypoints. *IJCV*, *60*(2), 91–110.

Löwenheim, L. (1915). Über möglichkeiten im Relativkalkül. *Mathematische Annalen*, *76*, 447–470.

Lowerre, B. T. (1976). *The* HARPY *Speech Recognition System*. Ph.D. thesis, Computer Science Department, Carnegie-Mellon University.

Lowerre, B. T. and Reddy, R. (1980). The HARPY speech recognition system. In Lea, W. A. (Ed.), *Trends in Speech Recognition*, chap. 15. Prentice-Hall.

Lowry, M. (2008). Intelligent software engineering tools for NASA's crew exploration vehicle. In *Proc. ISMIS*.

Loyd, S. (1959). *Mathematical Puzzles of Sam Loyd: Selected and Edited by Martin Gardner*. Dover.

Lozano-Perez, T. (1983). Spatial planning: A configuration space approach. *IEEE Transactions on Computers*, *C-32*(2), 108–120.

Lozano-Perez, T., Mason, M., and Taylor, R. (1984). Automatic synthesis of fine-motion strategies for robots. *Int. J. Robotics Research*, *3*(1), 3–24.

Lu, F. and Milios, E. (1997). Globally consistent range scan alignment for environment mapping. *Autonomous Robots*, *4*, 333–349.

Luby, M., Sinclair, A., and Zuckerman, D. (1993). Optimal speedup of Las Vegas algorithms. *Information Processing Letters*, *47*, 173–180.

Lucas, J. R. (1961). Minds, machines, and Gödel. *Philosophy*, *36*.

Lucas, J. R. (1976). This Gödel is killing me: A rejoinder. *Philosophia*, *6*(1), 145–148.

Lucas, P. (1996). Knowledge acquisition for decision-theoretic expert systems. *AISB Quarterly*, *94*, 23–33.

Lucas, P., van der Gaag, L., and Abu-Hanna, A. (2004). Bayesian networks in biomedicine and health-care. *Artificial Intelligence in Medicine*.

Luce, D. R. and Raiffa, H. (1957). *Games and Decisions*. Wiley.

Ludlow, P., Nagasawa, Y., and Stoljar, D. (2004). *There's Something About Mary*. MIT Press.

Luger, G. F. (Ed.). (1995). *Computation and intelligence: Collected readings*. AAAI Press.

Lyman, P. and Varian, H. R. (2003). How much information? `www.sims.berkeley.edu/how-much-info-2003`.

Machina, M. (2005). Choice under uncertainty. In *Encyclopedia of Cognitive Science*, pp. 505–514. Wiley.

MacKay, D. J. C. (1992). A practical Bayesian framework for back-propagation networks. *Neural Computation*, *4*(3), 448–472.

MacKay, D. J. C. (2002). *Information Theory, Inference and Learning Algorithms*. Cambridge University Press.

MacKenzie, D. (2004). *Mechanizing Proof*. MIT Press.

Mackworth, A. K. (1977). Consistency in networks of relations. *AIJ*, *8*(1), 99–118.

Mackworth, A. K. (1992). Constraint satisfaction. In Shapiro, S. (Ed.), *Encyclopedia of Artificial Intelligence* (second edition)., Vol. 1, pp. 285–293. Wiley.

Mahanti, A. and Daniels, C. J. (1993). A SIMD approach to parallel heuristic search. *AIJ*, *60*(2), 243–282.

Mailath, G. and Samuelson, L. (2006). *Repeated Games and Reputations: Long-Run Relationships*. Oxford University Press.

Majercik, S. M. and Littman, M. L. (2003). Contingent planning under uncertainty via stochastic satisfiability. *AIJ*, pp. 119–162.

Malik, J. and Perona, P. (1990). Preattentive texture discrimination with early vision mechanisms. *J. Opt. Soc. Am. A*, *7*(5), 923–932.

Malik, J. and Rosenholtz, R. (1994). Recovering surface curvature and orientation from texture distortion: A least squares algorithm and sensitivity analysis. In *ECCV*, pp. 353–364.

Malik, J. and Rosenholtz, R. (1997). Computing local surface orientation and shape from texture for curved surfaces. *IJCV*, *23*(2), 149–168.

Maneva, E., Mossel, E., and Wainwright, M. J. (2007). A new look at survey propagation and its generalizations. *JACM*, *54*(4).

Manna, Z. and Waldinger, R. (1971). Toward automatic program synthesis. *CACM*, *14*(3), 151–165.

Manna, Z. and Waldinger, R. (1985). *The Logical Basis for Computer Programming: Volume 1: Deductive Reasoning*. Addison-Wesley.

Manning, C. and Schütze, H. (1999). *Foundations of Statistical Natural Language Processing*. MIT Press.

Manning, C., Raghavan, P., and Schütze, H. (2008). *Introduction to Information Retrieval*. Cambridge University Press.

Mannion, M. (2002). Using first-order logic for product line model validation. In *Software Product Lines: Second International Conference*. Springer.

Manzini, G. (1995). BIDA*: An improved perimeter search algorithm. *AIJ*, *72*(2), 347–360.

Marbach, P. and Tsitsiklis, J. N. (1998). Simulation-based optimization of Markov reward processes. Technical report LIDS-P-2411, Laboratory for Information and Decision Systems, Massachusetts Institute of Technology.

Marcus, G. (2009). *Kluge: The Haphazard Evolution of the Human Mind*. Mariner Books.

Marcus, M. P., Santorini, B., and Marcinkiewicz, M. A. (1993). Building a large annotated corpus of english: The penn treebank. *Computational Linguistics*, *19*(2), 313–330.

Markov, A. A. (1913). An example of statistical investigation in the text of "Eugene Onegin" illustrating coupling of "tests" in chains. *Proc. Academy of Sciences of St. Petersburg*, *7*.

Maron, M. E. (1961). Automatic indexing: An experimental inquiry. *JACM*, *8*(3), 404–417.

Maron, M. E. and Kuhns, J.-L. (1960). On relevance, probabilistic indexing and information retrieval. *CACM*, *7*, 219–244.

Marr, D. (1982). *Vision: A Computational Investigation into the Human Representation and Processing of Visual Information*. W. H. Freeman.

Marriott, K. and Stuckey, P. J. (1998). *Programming with Constraints: An Introduction*. MIT Press.

Marsland, A. T. and Schaeffer, J. (Eds.). (1990). *Computers, Chess, and Cognition*. Springer-Verlag.

Marsland, S. (2009). *Machine Learning: An Algorithmic Perspective*. CRC Press.

Martelli, A. and Montanari, U. (1973). Additive AND/OR graphs. In *IJCAI-73*, pp. 1–11.

Martelli, A. and Montanari, U. (1978). Optimizing decision trees through heuristically guided search. *CACM*, *21*, 1025–1039.

Martelli, A. (1977). On the complexity of admissible search algorithms. *AIJ*, *8*(1), 1–13.

Marthi, B., Pasula, H., Russell, S. J., and Peres, Y. (2002). Decayed MCMC filtering. In *UAI-02*, pp. 319–326.

Marthi, B., Russell, S. J., Latham, D., and Guestrin, C. (2005). Concurrent hierarchical reinforcement learning. In *IJCAI-05*.

Marthi, B., Russell, S. J., and Wolfe, J. (2007). Angelic semantics for high-level actions. In *ICAPS-07*.

Marthi, B., Russell, S. J., and Wolfe, J. (2008). Angelic hierarchical planning: Optimal and online algorithms. In *ICAPS-08*.

Martin, D., Fowlkes, C., and Malik, J. (2004). Learning to detect natural image boundaries using local brightness, color, and texture cues. *PAMI*, *26*(5), 530–549.

Martin, J. H. (1990). *A Computational Model of Metaphor Interpretation*. Academic Press.

Mason, M. (1993). Kicking the sensing habit. *AIMag*, *14*(1), 58–59.

Mason, M. (2001). *Mechanics of Robotic Manipulation*. MIT Press.

Mason, M. and Salisbury, J. (1985). *Robot hands and the mechanics of manipulation*. MIT Press.

Mataric, M. J. (1997). Reinforcement learning in the multi-robot domain. *Autonomous Robots*, *4*(1), 73–83.

Mates, B. (1953). *Stoic Logic*. University of California Press.

Matuszek, C., Cabral, J., Witbrock, M., and DeOliveira, J. (2006). An introduction to the syntax and semantics of cyc. In *Proc. AAAI Spring Symposium on Formalizing and Compiling Background Knowledge and Its Applications to Knowledge Representation and Question Answering*.

Maxwell, J. and Kaplan, R. (1993). The interface between phrasal and functional constraints. *Computational Linguistics*, *19*(4), 571–590.

McAllester, D. A. (1980). An outlook on truth maintenance. Ai memo 551, MIT AI Laboratory.

McAllester, D. A. (1988). Conspiracy numbers for min-max search. *AIJ*, *35*(3), 287–310.

McAllester, D. A. (1998). What is the most pressing issue facing AI and the AAAI today? Candidate statement, election for Councilor of the American Association for Artificial Intelligence.

McAllester, D. A. and Rosenblitt, D. (1991). Systematic nonlinear planning. In *AAAI-91*, Vol. 2, pp. 634–639.

McCallum, A. (2003). Efficiently inducing features of conditional random fields. In *UAI-03*.

McCarthy, J. (1958). Programs with common sense. In *Proc. Symposium on Mechanisation of Thought Processes*, Vol. 1, pp. 77–84.

McCarthy, J. (1963). Situations, actions, and causal laws. Memo 2, Stanford University Artificial Intelligence Project.

McCarthy, J. (1968). Programs with common sense. In Minsky, M. L. (Ed.), *Semantic Information Processing*, pp. 403–418. MIT Press.

McCarthy, J. (1980). Circumscription: A form of non-monotonic reasoning. *AIJ*, *13*(1–2), 27–39.

McCarthy, J. (2007). From here to human-level AI. *AIJ*, *171*(18), 1174–1182.

McCarthy, J. and Hayes, P. J. (1969). Some philosophical problems from the standpoint of artificial intelligence. In Meltzer, B., Michie, D., and Swann, M. (Eds.), *Machine Intelligence 4*, pp. 463–502. Edinburgh University Press.

McCarthy, J., Minsky, M. L., Rochester, N., and Shannon, C. E. (1955). Proposal for the Dartmouth summer research project on artificial intelligence. Tech. rep., Dartmouth College.

McCawley, J. D. (1988). *The Syntactic Phenomena of English*, Vol. 2 volumes. University of Chicago Press.

McCorduck, P. (2004). *Machines who think: a personal inquiry into the history and prospects of artificial intelligence* (Revised edition). A K Peters.

McCulloch, W. S. and Pitts, W. (1943). A logical calculus of the ideas immanent in nervous activity. *Bulletin of Mathematical Biophysics*, *5*, 115–137.

McCune, W. (1992). Automated discovery of new axiomatizations of the left group and right group calculi. *JAR*, *9*(1), 1–24.

McCune, W. (1997). Solution of the Robbins problem. *JAR*, *19*(3), 263–276.

McDermott, D. (1976). Artificial intelligence meets natural stupidity. *SIGART Newsletter*, *57*, 4–9.

McDermott, D. (1978a). Planning and acting. *Cognitive Science*, *2*(2), 71–109.

McDermott, D. (1978b). Tarskian semantics, or, no notation without denotation! *Cognitive Science*, *2*(3).

McDermott, D. (1985). Reasoning about plans. In Hobbs, J. and Moore, R. (Eds.), *Formal theories of the commonsense world*. Intellect Books.

McDermott, D. (1987). A critique of pure reason. *Computational Intelligence*, *3*(3), 151–237.

McDermott, D. (1996). A heuristic estimator for means-ends analysis in planning. In *ICAPS-96*, pp. 142–149.

McDermott, D. and Doyle, J. (1980). Non-monotonic logic: i. *AIJ*, *13*(1–2), 41–72.

McDermott, J. (1982). R1: A rule-based configurer of computer systems. *AIJ*, *19*(1), 39–88.

McEliece, R. J., MacKay, D. J. C., and Cheng, J.-F. (1998). Turbo decoding as an instance of Pearl's "belief propagation" algorithm. *IEEE Journal on Selected Areas in Communications*, *16*(2), 140–152.

McGregor, J. J. (1979). Relational consistency algorithms and their application in finding subgraph and graph isomorphisms. *Information Sciences*, *19*(3), 229–250.

McIlraith, S. and Zeng, H. (2001). Semantic web services. *IEEE Intelligent Systems*, *16*(2), 46–53.

McLachlan, G. J. and Krishnan, T. (1997). *The EM Algorithm and Extensions*. Wiley.

McMillan, K. L. (1993). *Symbolic Model Checking*. Kluwer.

Meehl, P. (1955). *Clinical vs. Statistical Prediction*. University of Minnesota Press.

Mendel, G. (1866). Versuche über pflanzenhybriden. *Verhandlungen des Naturforschenden Vereins, Abhandlungen, Brünn*, *4*, 3–47. Translated into English by C. T. Druery, published by Bateson (1902).

Mercer, J. (1909). Functions of positive and negative type and their connection with the theory of integral equations. *Philos. Trans. Roy. Soc. London, A*, *209*, 415–446.

Merleau-Ponty, M. (1945). *Phenomenology of Perception*. Routledge.

Metropolis, N., Rosenbluth, A., Rosenbluth, M., Teller, A., and Teller, E. (1953). Equations of state calculations by fast computing machines. *J. Chemical Physics*, *21*, 1087–1091.

Metzinger, T. (2009). *The Ego Tunnel: The Science of the Mind and the Myth of the Self*. Basic Books.

Mézard, M. and Nadal, J.-P. (1989). Learning in feedforward layered networks: The tiling algorithm. *J. Physics*, *22*, 2191–2204.

Michalski, R. S. (1969). On the quasi-minimal solution of the general covering problem. In *Proc. First International Symposium on Information Processing*, pp. 125–128.

Michalski, R. S., Mozetic, I., Hong, J., and Lavrauc, N. (1986). The multi-purpose incremental learning system AQ15 and its testing application to three medical domains. In *AAAI-86*, pp. 1041–1045.

Michie, D. (1966). Game-playing and game-learning automata. In Fox, L. (Ed.), *Advances in Programming and Non-Numerical Computation*, pp. 183–200. Pergamon.

Michie, D. (1972). Machine intelligence at Edinburgh. *Management Informatics*, *2*(1), 7–12.

Michie, D. (1974). Machine intelligence at Edinburgh. In *On Intelligence*, pp. 143–155. Edinburgh University Press.

Michie, D. and Chambers, R. A. (1968). BOXES: An experiment in adaptive control. In Dale, E. and Michie, D. (Eds.), *Machine Intelligence 2*, pp. 125–133. Elsevier/North-Holland.

Michie, D., Spiegelhalter, D. J., and Taylor, C. (Eds.). (1994). *Machine Learning, Neural and Statistical Classification*. Ellis Horwood.

Milch, B., Marthi, B., Sontag, D., Russell, S. J., Ong, D., and Kolobov, A. (2005). BLOG: Probabilistic models with unknown objects. In *IJCAI-05*.

Milch, B., Zettlemoyer, L. S., Kersting, K., Haimes, M., and Kaelbling, L. P. (2008). Lifted probabilistic inference with counting formulas. In *AAAI-08*, pp. 1062–1068.

Milgrom, P. (1997). Putting auction theory to work: The simultaneous ascending auction. Tech. rep. Technical Report 98-0002, Stanford University Department of Economics.

Mill, J. S. (1843). *A System of Logic, Ratiocinative and Inductive: Being a Connected View of the Principles of Evidence, and Methods of Scientific Investigation*. J. W. Parker, London.

Mill, J. S. (1863). *Utilitarianism*. Parker, Son and Bourn, London.

Miller, A. C., Merkhofer, M. M., Howard, R. A., Matheson, J. E., and Rice, T. R. (1976). Development of automated aids for decision analysis. Technical report, SRI International.

Minker, J. (2001). *Logic-Based Artificial Intelligence*. Kluwer.

Minsky, M. L. (1975). A framework for representing knowledge. In Winston, P. H. (Ed.), *The Psychology of Computer Vision*, pp. 211–277. McGraw-Hill. Originally an MIT AI Laboratory memo; the 1975 version is abridged, but is the most widely cited.

Minsky, M. L. (1986). *The society of mind*. Simon and Schuster.

Minsky, M. L. (2007). *The Emotion Machine: Commonsense Thinking, Artificial Intelligence, and the Future of the Human Mind*. Simon and Schuster.

Minsky, M. L. and Papert, S. (1969). *Perceptrons: An Introduction to Computational Geometry* (first edition). MIT Press.

Minsky, M. L. and Papert, S. (1988). *Perceptrons: An Introduction to Computational Geometry* (Expanded edition). MIT Press.

Minsky, M. L., Singh, P., and Sloman, A. (2004). The st. thomas common sense symposium: Designing architectures for human-level intelligence. *AIMag*, *25*(2), 113–124.

Minton, S. (1984). Constraint-based generalization: Learning game-playing plans from single examples. In *AAAI-84*, pp. 251–254.

Minton, S. (1988). Quantitative results concerning the utility of explanation-based learning. In *AAAI-88*, pp. 564–569.

Minton, S., Johnston, M. D., Philips, A. B., and Laird, P. (1992). Minimizing conflicts: A heuristic repair method for constraint satisfaction and scheduling problems. *AIJ*, *58*(1–3), 161–205.

Misak, C. (2004). *The Cambridge Companion to Peirce*. Cambridge University Press.

Mitchell, M. (1996). *An Introduction to Genetic Algorithms*. MIT Press.

Mitchell, M., Holland, J. H., and Forrest, S. (1996). When will a genetic algorithm outperform hill climbing? In Cowan, J., Tesauro, G., and Alspector, J. (Eds.), *NIPS 6*. MIT Press.

Mitchell, T. M. (1977). Version spaces: A candidate elimination approach to rule learning. In *IJCAI-77*, pp. 305–310.

Mitchell, T. M. (1982). Generalization as search. *AIJ*, *18*(2), 203–226.

Mitchell, T. M. (1990). Becoming increasingly reactive (mobile robots). In *AAAI-90*, Vol. 2, pp. 1051–1058.

Mitchell, T. M. (1997). *Machine Learning*. McGraw-Hill.

Mitchell, T. M., Keller, R., and Kedar-Cabelli, S. (1986). Explanation-based generalization: A unifying view. *Machine Learning*, *1*, 47–80.

Mitchell, T. M., Utgoff, P. E., and Banerji, R. (1983). Learning by experimentation: Acquiring and refining problem-solving heuristics. In Michalski, R. S., Carbonell, J. G., and Mitchell, T. M. (Eds.), *Machine Learning: An Artificial Intelligence Approach*, pp. 163–190. Morgan Kaufmann.

Mitchell, T. M. (2005). Reading the web: A breakthrough goal for AI. *AIMag*, *26*(3), 12–16.

Mitchell, T. M. (2007). Learning, information extraction and the web. In *ECML/PKDD*, p. 1.

Mitchell, T. M., Shinkareva, S. V., Carlson, A., Chang, K.-M., Malave, V. L., Mason, R. A., and Just, M. A. (2008). Predicting human brain activity associated with the meanings of nouns. *Science*, *320*, 1191–1195.

Mohr, R. and Henderson, T. C. (1986). Arc and path consistency revisited. *AIJ*, *28*(2), 225–233.

Mohri, M., Pereira, F., and Riley, M. (2002). Weighted finite-state transducers in speech recognition. *Computer Speech and Language*, *16*(1), 69–88.

Montague, P. R., Dayan, P., Person, C., and Sejnowski, T. (1995). Bee foraging in uncertain environments using predictive Hebbian learning. *Nature*, *377*, 725–728.

Montague, R. (1970). English as a formal language. In *Linguaggi nella Società e nella Tecnica*, pp. 189–224. Edizioni di Comunità.

Montague, R. (1973). The proper treatment of quantification in ordinary English. In Hintikka, K. J. J., Moravcsik, J. M. E., and Suppes, P. (Eds.), *Approaches to Natural Language*. D. Reidel.

Montanari, U. (1974). Networks of constraints: Fundamental properties and applications to picture processing. *Information Sciences*, *7*(2), 95–132.

Montemerlo, M. and Thrun, S. (2004). Large-scale robotic 3-D mapping of urban structures. In *Proc. International Symposium on Experimental Robotics*. Springer Tracts in Advanced Robotics (STAR).

Montemerlo, M., Thrun, S., Koller, D., and Wegbreit, B. (2002). FastSLAM: A factored solution to the simultaneous localization and mapping problem. In *AAAI-02*.

Mooney, R. (1999). Learning for semantic interpretation: Scaling up without dumbing down. In *Proc. 1st Workshop on Learning Language in Logic*, pp. 7–15.

Moore, A. and Wong, W.-K. (2003). Optimal reinsertion: A new search operator for accelerated and more accurate Bayesian network structure learning. In *ICML-03*.

Moore, A. W. and Atkeson, C. G. (1993). Prioritized sweeping—Reinforcement learning with less data and less time. *Machine Learning*, *13*, 103–130.

Moore, A. W. and Lee, M. S. (1997). Cached sufficient statistics for efficient machine learning with large datasets. *JAIR*, *8*, 67–91.

Moore, E. F. (1959). The shortest path through a maze. In *Proc. an International Symposium on the Theory of Switching, Part II*, pp. 285–292. Harvard University Press.

Moore, R. C. (1980). Reasoning about knowledge and action. Artificial intelligence center technical note 191, SRI International.

Moore, R. C. (1985). A formal theory of knowledge and action. In Hobbs, J. R. and Moore, R. C. (Eds.), *Formal Theories of the Commonsense World*, pp. 319–358. Ablex.

Moore, R. C. (2005). Association-based bilingual word alignment. In *Proc. ACL-05 Workshop on Building and Using Parallel Texts*, pp. 1–8.

Moravec, H. P. (1983). The stanford cart and the cmu rover. *Proc. IEEE*, *71*(7), 872–884.

Moravec, H. P. and Elfes, A. (1985). High resolution maps from wide angle sonar. In *ICRA-85*, pp. 116–121.

Moravec, H. P. (1988). *Mind Children: The Future of Robot and Human Intelligence*. Harvard University Press.

Moravec, H. P. (2000). *Robot: Mere Machine to Transcendent Mind*. Oxford University Press.

Morgenstern, L. (1998). Inheritance comes of age: Applying nonmonotonic techniques to problems in industry. *AIJ*, *103*, 237–271.

Morjaria, M. A., Rink, F. J., Smith, W. D., Klempner, G., Burns, C., and Stein, J. (1995). Elicitation of probabilities for belief networks: Combining qualitative and quantitative information. In *UAI-95*, pp. 141–148.

Morrison, P. and Morrison, E. (Eds.). (1961). *Charles Babbage and His Calculating Engines: Selected Writings by Charles Babbage and Others*. Dover.

Moskewicz, M. W., Madigan, C. F., Zhao, Y., Zhang, L., and Malik, S. (2001). Chaff: Engineering an efficient SAT solver. In *Proc. 38th Design Automation Conference (DAC 2001)*, pp. 530–535.

Mosteller, F. and Wallace, D. L. (1964). *Inference and Disputed Authorship: The Federalist*. Addison-Wesley.

Mostow, J. and Prieditis, A. E. (1989). Discovering admissible heuristics by abstracting and optimizing: A transformational approach. In *IJCAI-89*, Vol. 1, pp. 701–707.

Motzkin, T. S. and Schoenberg, I. J. (1954). The relaxation method for linear inequalities. *Canadian Journal of Mathematics*, *6*(3), 393–404.

Moutarlier, P. and Chatila, R. (1989). Stochastic multisensory data fusion for mobile robot location and environment modeling. In *ISRR-89*.

Mueller, E. T. (2006). *Commonsense Reasoning*. Morgan Kaufmann.

Muggleton, S. H. (1991). Inductive logic programming. *New Generation Computing*, *8*, 295–318.

Muggleton, S. H. (1992). *Inductive Logic Programming*. Academic Press.

Muggleton, S. H. (1995). Inverse entailment and Progol. *New Generation Computing*, *13*(3-4), 245–286.

Muggleton, S. H. (2000). Learning stochastic logic programs. Proc. AAAI 2000 Workshop on Learning Statistical Models from Relational Data.

Muggleton, S. H. and Buntine, W. (1988). Machine invention of first-order predicates by inverting resolution. In *ICML-88*, pp. 339–352.

Muggleton, S. H. and De Raedt, L. (1994). Inductive logic programming: Theory and methods. *J. Logic Programming*, *19/20*, 629–679.

Muggleton, S. H. and Feng, C. (1990). Efficient induction of logic programs. In *Proc. Workshop on Algorithmic Learning Theory*, pp. 368–381.

Müller, M. (2002). Computer Go. *AIJ*, *134*(1–2), 145–179.

Müller, M. (2003). Conditional combinatorial games, and their application to analyzing capturing races in go. *Information Sciences*, *154*(3–4), 189–202.

Mumford, D. and Shah, J. (1989). Optimal approximations by piece-wise smooth functions and associated variational problems. *Commun. Pure Appl. Math.*, *42*, 577–685.

Murphy, K., Weiss, Y., and Jordan, M. I. (1999). Loopy belief propagation for approximate inference: An empirical study. In *UAI-99*, pp. 467–475.

Murphy, K. (2001). The Bayes net toolbox for MATLAB. *Computing Science and Statistics*, *33*.

Murphy, K. (2002). *Dynamic Bayesian Networks: Representation, Inference and Learning*. Ph.D. thesis, UC Berkeley.

Murphy, K. and Mian, I. S. (1999). Modelling gene expression data using Bayesian networks. `people.cs.ubc.ca/~murphyk/Papers/ismb99.pdf`.

Murphy, K. and Russell, S. J. (2001). Rao-blackwellised particle filtering for dynamic Bayesian networks. In Doucet, A., de Freitas, N., and Gordon, N. J. (Eds.), *Sequential Monte Carlo Methods in Practice*. Springer-Verlag.

Murphy, K. and Weiss, Y. (2001). The factored frontier algorithm for approximate inference in DBNs. In *UAI-01*, pp. 378–385.

Murphy, R. (2000). *Introduction to AI Robotics*. MIT Press.

Murray-Rust, P., Rzepa, H. S., Williamson, J., and Willighagen, E. L. (2003). Chemical markup, XML and the world–wide web. 4. CML schema. *J. Chem. Inf. Comput. Sci.*, *43*, 752–772.

Murthy, C. and Russell, J. R. (1990). A constructive proof of Higman's lemma. In *LICS-90*, pp. 257–269.

Muscettola, N. (2002). Computing the envelope for stepwise-constant resource allocations. In *CP-02*, pp. 139–154.

Muscettola, N., Nayak, P., Pell, B., and Williams, B. (1998). Remote agent: To boldly go where no AI system has gone before. *AIJ*, *103*, 5–48.

Muslea, I. (1999). Extraction patterns for information extraction tasks: A survey. In *Proc. AAAI-99 Workshop on Machine Learning for Information Extraction*.

Myerson, R. (1981). Optimal auction design. *Mathematics of Operations Research*, *6*, 58–73.

Myerson, R. (1986). Multistage games with communication. *Econometrica*, *54*, 323–358.

Myerson, R. (1991). *Game Theory: Analysis of Conflict*. Harvard University Press.

Nagel, T. (1974). What is it like to be a bat? *Philosophical Review*, *83*, 435–450.

Nalwa, V. S. (1993). *A Guided Tour of Computer Vision*. Addison-Wesley.

Nash, J. (1950). Equilibrium points in N-person games. *PNAS*, *36*, 48–49.

Nau, D. S. (1980). Pathology on game trees: A summary of results. In *AAAI-80*, pp. 102–104.

Nau, D. S. (1983). Pathology on game trees revisited, and an alternative to minimaxing. *AIJ*, *21*(1–2), 221–244.

Nau, D. S., Kumar, V., and Kanal, L. N. (1984). General branch and bound, and its relation to A* and AO*. *AIJ*, *23*, 29–58.

Nayak, P. and Williams, B. (1997). Fast context switching in real-time propositional reasoning. In *AAAI-97*, pp. 50–56.

Neal, R. (1996). *Bayesian Learning for Neural Networks*. Springer-Verlag.

Nebel, B. (2000). On the compilability and expressive power of propositional planning formalisms. *JAIR*, *12*, 271–315.

Nefian, A., Liang, L., Pi, X., Liu, X., and Murphy, K. (2002). Dynamic bayesian networks for audio-visual speech recognition. *EURASIP, Journal of Applied Signal Processing*, *11*, 1–15.

Nesterov, Y. and Nemirovski, A. (1994). *Interior-Point Polynomial Methods in Convex Programming*. SIAM (Society for Industrial and Applied Mathematics).

Netto, E. (1901). *Lehrbuch der Combinatorik*. B. G. Teubner.

Nevill-Manning, C. G. and Witten, I. H. (1997). Identifying hierarchical structures in sequences: A linear-time algorithm. *JAIR*, *7*, 67–82.

Newell, A. (1982). The knowledge level. *AIJ*, *18*(1), 82–127.

Newell, A. (1990). *Unified Theories of Cognition*. Harvard University Press.

Newell, A. and Ernst, G. (1965). The search for generality. In *Proc. IFIP Congress*, Vol. 1, pp. 17–24.

Newell, A., Shaw, J. C., and Simon, H. A. (1957). Empirical explorations with the logic theory machine. *Proc. Western Joint Computer Conference*, *15*, 218–239. Reprinted in Feigenbaum and Feldman (1963).

Newell, A., Shaw, J. C., and Simon, H. A. (1958). Chess playing programs and the problem of complexity. *IBM Journal of Research and Development*, *4*(2), 320–335.

Newell, A. and Simon, H. A. (1961). GPS, a program that simulates human thought. In Billing, H. (Ed.), *Lernende Automaten*, pp. 109–124. R. Oldenbourg.

Newell, A. and Simon, H. A. (1972). *Human Problem Solving*. Prentice-Hall.

Newell, A. and Simon, H. A. (1976). Computer science as empirical inquiry: Symbols and search. *CACM*, *19*, 113–126.

Newton, I. (1664–1671). Methodus fluxionum et serierum infinitarum. Unpublished notes.

Ng, A. Y. (2004). Feature selection, l_1 vs. l_2 regularization, and rotational invariance. In *ICML-04*.

Ng, A. Y., Harada, D., and Russell, S. J. (1999). Policy invariance under reward transformations: Theory and application to reward shaping. In *ICML-99*.

Ng, A. Y. and Jordan, M. I. (2000). PEGASUS: A policy search method for large MDPs and POMDPs. In *UAI-00*, pp. 406–415.

Ng, A. Y., Kim, H. J., Jordan, M. I., and Sastry, S. (2004). Autonomous helicopter flight via reinforcement learning. In *NIPS 16*.

Nguyen, X. and Kambhampati, S. (2001). Reviving partial order planning. In *IJCAI-01*, pp. 459–466.

Nguyen, X., Kambhampati, S., and Nigenda, R. S. (2001). Planning graph as the basis for deriving heuristics for plan synthesis by state space and CSP search. Tech. rep., Computer Science and Engineering Department, Arizona State University.

Nicholson, A. and Brady, J. M. (1992). The data association problem when monitoring robot vehicles using dynamic belief networks. In *ECAI-92*, pp. 689–693.

Niemelä, I., Simons, P., and Syrjänen, T. (2000). Smodels: A system for answer set programming. In *Proc. 8th International Workshop on Non-Monotonic Reasoning*.

Nigam, K., McCallum, A., Thrun, S., and Mitchell, T. M. (2000). Text classification from labeled and unlabeled documents using EM. *Machine Learning*, *39*(2–3), 103–134.

Niles, I. and Pease, A. (2001). Towards a standard upper ontology. In *FOIS '01: Proc. international conference on Formal Ontology in Information Systems*, pp. 2–9.

Nilsson, D. and Lauritzen, S. (2000). Evaluating influence diagrams using LIMIDs. In *UAI-00*, pp. 436–445.

Nilsson, N. J. (1965). *Learning Machines: Foundations of Trainable Pattern-Classifying Systems*. McGraw-Hill. Republished in 1990.

Nilsson, N. J. (1971). *Problem-Solving Methods in Artificial Intelligence*. McGraw-Hill.

Nilsson, N. J. (1984). Shakey the robot. Technical note 323, SRI International.

Nilsson, N. J. (1986). Probabilistic logic. *AIJ*, *28*(1), 71–87.

Nilsson, N. J. (1991). Logic and artificial intelligence. *AIJ*, *47*(1–3), 31–56.

Nilsson, N. J. (1995). Eye on the prize. *AIMag*, *16*(2), 9–17.

Nilsson, N. J. (1998). *Artificial Intelligence: A New Synthesis*. Morgan Kaufmann.

Nilsson, N. J. (2005). Human-level artificial intelligence? be serious! *AIMag*, *26*(4), 68–75.

Nilsson, N. J. (2009). *The Quest for Artificial Intelligence: A History of Ideas and Achievements*. Cambridge University Press.

Nisan, N., Roughgarden, T., Tardos, E., and Vazirani, V. (Eds.). (2007). *Algorithmic Game Theory*. Cambridge University Press.

Noe, A. (2009). *Out of Our Heads: Why You Are Not Your Brain, and Other Lessons from the Biology of Consciousness*. Hill and Wang.

Norvig, P. (1988). Multiple simultaneous interpretations of ambiguous sentences. In *COGSCI-88*.

Norvig, P. (1992). *Paradigms of Artificial Intelligence Programming: Case Studies in Common Lisp*. Morgan Kaufmann.

Norvig, P. (2009). Natural language corpus data. In Segaran, T. and Hammerbacher, J. (Eds.), *Beautiful Data*. O'Reilly.

Nowick, S. M., Dean, M. E., Dill, D. L., and Horowitz, M. (1993). The design of a high-performance cache controller: A case study in asynchronous synthesis. *Integration: The VLSI Journal*, *15*(3), 241–262.

Nunberg, G. (1979). The non-uniqueness of semantic solutions: Polysemy. *Language and Philosophy*, *3*(2), 143–184.

Nussbaum, M. C. (1978). *Aristotle's* De Motu Animalium. Princeton University Press.

Oaksford, M. and Chater, N. (Eds.). (1998). *Rational models of cognition*. Oxford University Press.

Och, F. J. and Ney, H. (2003). A systematic comparison of various statistical alignment model. *Computational Linguistics*, *29*(1), 19–51.

Och, F. J. and Ney, H. (2004). The alignment template approach to statistical machine translation. *Computational Linguistics*, *30*, 417–449.

Ogawa, S., Lee, T.-M., Kay, A. R., and Tank, D. W. (1990). Brain magnetic resonance imaging with contrast dependent on blood oxygenation. *PNAS*, *87*, 9868–9872.

Oh, S., Russell, S. J., and Sastry, S. (2009). Markov chain Monte Carlo data association for multi-target tracking. *IEEE Transactions on Automatic Control*, *54*(3), 481–497.

Olesen, K. G. (1993). Causal probabilistic networks with both discrete and continuous variables. *PAMI*, *15*(3), 275–279.

Oliver, N., Garg, A., and Horvitz, E. J. (2004). Layered representations for learning and inferring office activity from multiple sensory channels. *Computer Vision and Image Understanding*, *96*, 163–180.

Oliver, R. M. and Smith, J. Q. (Eds.). (1990). *Influence Diagrams, Belief Nets and Decision Analysis*. Wiley.

Omohundro, S. (2008). The basic AI drives. In *AGI-08 Workshop on the Sociocultural, Ethical and Futurological Implications of Artificial Intelligence*.

O'Reilly, U.-M. and Oppacher, F. (1994). Program search with a hierarchical variable length representation: Genetic programming, simulated annealing and hill climbing. In *Proc. Third Conference on Parallel Problem Solving from Nature*, pp. 397–406.

Ormoneit, D. and Sen, S. (2002). Kernel-based reinforcement learning. *Machine Learning*, *49*(2–3), 161–178.

Osborne, M. J. (2004). *An Introduction to Game Theory*. Oxford University Pres.

Osborne, M. J. and Rubinstein, A. (1994). *A Course in Game Theory*. MIT Press.

Osherson, D. N., Stob, M., and Weinstein, S. (1986). *Systems That Learn: An Introduction to Learning Theory for Cognitive and Computer Scientists*. MIT Press.

Padgham, L. and Winikoff, M. (2004). *Developing Intelligent Agent Systems: A Practical Guide*. Wiley.

Page, C. D. and Srinivasan, A. (2002). ILP: A short look back and a longer look forward. Submitted to Journal of Machine Learning Research.

Palacios, H. and Geffner, H. (2007). From conformant into classical planning: Efficient translations that may be complete too. In *ICAPS-07*.

Palay, A. J. (1985). *Searching with Probabilities*. Pitman.

Palmer, D. A. and Hearst, M. A. (1994). Adaptive sentence boundary disambiguation. In *Proc. Conference on Applied Natural Language Processing*, pp. 78–83.

Palmer, S. (1999). *Vision Science: Photons to Phenomenology*. MIT Press.

Papadimitriou, C. H. (1994). *Computational Complexity*. Addison Wesley.

Papadimitriou, C. H., Tamaki, H., Raghavan, P., and Vempala, S. (1998). Latent semantic indexing: A probabilistic analysis. In *PODS-98*, pp. 159–168.

Papadimitriou, C. H. and Tsitsiklis, J. N. (1987). The complexity of Markov decision processes. *Mathematics of Operations Research*, *12*(3), 441–450.

Papadimitriou, C. H. and Yannakakis, M. (1991). Shortest paths without a map. *Theoretical Computer Science*, *84*(1), 127–150.

Papavassiliou, V. and Russell, S. J. (1999). Convergence of reinforcement learning with general function approximators. In *IJCAI-99*, pp. 748–757.

Parekh, R. and Honavar, V. (2001). DFA learning from simple examples. *Machine Learning*, *44*, 9–35.

Parisi, G. (1988). *Statistical field theory*. Addison-Wesley.

Parisi, M. M. G. and Zecchina, R. (2002). Analytic and algorithmic solution of random satisfiability problems. *Science*, *297*, 812–815.

Parker, A., Nau, D. S., and Subrahmanian, V. S. (2005). Game-tree search with combinatorially large belief states. In *IJCAI-05*, pp. 254–259.

Parker, D. B. (1985). Learning logic. Technical report TR-47, Center for Computational Research in Economics and Management Science, Massachusetts Institute of Technology.

Parker, L. E. (1996). On the design of behavior-based multi-robot teams. *J. Advanced Robotics*, *10*(6).

Parr, R. and Russell, S. J. (1998). Reinforcement learning with hierarchies of machines. In Jordan, M. I., Kearns, M., and Solla, S. A. (Eds.), *NIPS 10*. MIT Press.

Parzen, E. (1962). On estimation of a probability density function and mode. *Annals of Mathematical Statistics*, *33*, 1065–1076.

Pasca, M. and Harabagiu, S. M. (2001). High performance question/answering. In *SIGIR-01*, pp. 366–374.

Pasca, M., Lin, D., Bigham, J., Lifchits, A., and Jain, A. (2006). Organizing and searching the world wide web of facts—Step one: The one-million fact extraction challenge. In *AAAI-06*.

Paskin, M. (2001). Grammatical bigrams. In *NIPS*.

Pasula, H., Marthi, B., Milch, B., Russell, S. J., and Shpitser, I. (2003). Identity uncertainty and citation matching. In *NIPS 15*. MIT Press.

Pasula, H. and Russell, S. J. (2001). Approximate inference for first-order probabilistic languages. In *IJCAI-01*.

Pasula, H., Russell, S. J., Ostland, M., and Ritov, Y. (1999). Tracking many objects with many sensors. In *IJCAI-99*.

Patashnik, O. (1980). Qubic: 4x4x4 tic-tac-toe. *Mathematics Magazine*, *53*(4), 202–216.

Patrick, B. G., Almulla, M., and Newborn, M. (1992). An upper bound on the time complexity of iterative-deepening-A*. *AIJ*, *5*(2–4), 265–278.

Paul, R. P. (1981). *Robot Manipulators: Mathematics, Programming, and Control*. MIT Press.

Pauls, A. and Klein, D. (2009). K-best A* parsing. In *ACL-09*.

Peano, G. (1889). *Arithmetices principia, nova methodo exposita*. Fratres Bocca, Turin.

Pearce, J., Tambe, M., and Maheswaran, R. (2008). Solving multiagent networks using distributed constraint optimization. *AIMag*, *29*(3), 47–62.

Pearl, J. (1982a). Reverend Bayes on inference engines: A distributed hierarchical approach. In *AAAI-82*, pp. 133–136.

Pearl, J. (1982b). The solution for the branching factor of the alpha–beta pruning algorithm and its optimality. *CACM*, *25*(8), 559–564.

Pearl, J. (1984). *Heuristics: Intelligent Search Strategies for Computer Problem Solving*. Addison-Wesley.

Pearl, J. (1986). Fusion, propagation, and structuring in belief networks. *AIJ*, *29*, 241–288.

Pearl, J. (1987). Evidential reasoning using stochastic simulation of causal models. *AIJ*, *32*, 247–257.

Pearl, J. (1988). *Probabilistic Reasoning in Intelligent Systems: Networks of Plausible Inference*. Morgan Kaufmann.

Pearl, J. (2000). *Causality: Models, Reasoning, and Inference*. Cambridge University Press.

Pearl, J. and Verma, T. (1991). A theory of inferred causation. In *KR-91*, pp. 441–452.

Pearson, J. and Jeavons, P. (1997). A survey of tractable constraint satisfaction problems. Technical report CSD-TR-97-15, Royal Holloway College, U. of London.

Pease, A. and Niles, I. (2002). IEEE standard upper ontology: A progress report. *Knowledge Engineering Review*, *17*(1), 65–70.

Pednault, E. P. D. (1986). Formulating multiagent, dynamic-world problems in the classical planning framework. In *Reasoning about Actions and Plans: Proc. 1986 Workshop*, pp. 47–82.

Peirce, C. S. (1870). Description of a notation for the logic of relatives, resulting from an amplification of the conceptions of Boole's calculus of logic. *Memoirs of the American Academy of Arts and Sciences*, *9*, 317–378.

Peirce, C. S. (1883). A theory of probable inference. Note B. The logic of relatives. In *Studies in Logic by Members of the Johns Hopkins University*, pp. 187–203, Boston.

Peirce, C. S. (1902). Logic as semiotic: The theory of signs. Unpublished manuscript; reprinted in (Buchler 1955).

Peirce, C. S. (1909). Existential graphs. Unpublished manuscript; reprinted in (Buchler 1955).

Pelikan, M., Goldberg, D. E., and Cantu-Paz, E. (1999). BOA: The Bayesian optimization algorithm. In *GECCO-99: Proc. Genetic and Evolutionary Computation Conference*, pp. 525–532.

Pemberton, J. C. and Korf, R. E. (1992). Incremental planning on graphs with cycles. In *AIPS-92*, pp. 525–532.

Penberthy, J. S. and Weld, D. S. (1992). UCPOP: A sound, complete, partial order planner for ADL. In *KR-92*, pp. 103–114.

Peng, J. and Williams, R. J. (1993). Efficient learning and planning within the Dyna framework. *Adaptive Behavior*, *2*, 437–454.

Penrose, R. (1989). *The Emperor's New Mind*. Oxford University Press.

Penrose, R. (1994). *Shadows of the Mind*. Oxford University Press.

Peot, M. and Smith, D. E. (1992). Conditional nonlinear planning. In *ICAPS-92*, pp. 189–197.

Pereira, F. and Shieber, S. (1987). *Prolog and Natural-Language Analysis*. Center for the Study of Language and Information (CSLI).

Pereira, F. and Warren, D. H. D. (1980). Definite clause grammars for language analysis: A survey of the formalism and a comparison with augmented transition networks. *AIJ*, *13*, 231–278.

Pereira, F. and Wright, R. N. (1991). Finite-state approximation of phrase structure grammars. In *ACL-91*, pp. 246–255.

Perlis, A. (1982). Epigrams in programming. *SIGPLAN Notices*, *17*(9), 7–13.

Perrin, B. E., Ralaivola, L., and Mazurie, A. (2003). Gene networks inference using dynamic Bayesian networks. *Bioinformatics*, *19*, II 138–II 148.

Peterson, C. and Anderson, J. R. (1987). A mean field theory learning algorithm for neural networks. *Complex Systems*, *1*(5), 995–1019.

Petrik, M. and Zilberstein, S. (2009). Bilinear programming approach for multiagent planning. *JAIR*, *35*, 235–274.

Petrov, S. and Klein, D. (2007a). Discriminative log-linear grammars with latent variables. In *NIPS*.

Petrov, S. and Klein, D. (2007b). Improved inference for unlexicalized parsing. In *ACL-07*.

Petrov, S. and Klein, D. (2007c). Learning and inference for hierarchically split pcfgs. In *AAAI-07*.

Pfeffer, A., Koller, D., Milch, B., and Takusagawa, K. T. (1999). SPOOK: A system for probabilistic object-oriented knowledge representation. In *UAI-99*.

Pfeffer, A. (2000). *Probabilistic Reasoning for Complex Systems*. Ph.D. thesis, Stanford University.

Pfeffer, A. (2007). The design and implementation of IBAL: A general-purpose probabilistic language. In Getoor, L. and Taskar, B. (Eds.), *Introduction to Statistical Relational Learning*. MIT Press.

Pfeifer, R., Bongard, J., Brooks, R. A., and Iwasawa, S. (2006). *How the Body Shapes the Way We Think: A New View of Intelligence*. Bradford.

Pineau, J., Gordon, G., and Thrun, S. (2003). Point-based value iteration: An anytime algorithm for POMDPs. In *IJCAI-03*.

Pinedo, M. (2008). *Scheduling: Theory, Algorithms, and Systems*. Springer Verlag.

Pinkas, G. and Dechter, R. (1995). Improving connectionist energy minimization. *JAIR*, *3*, 223–248.

Pinker, S. (1995). Language acquisition. In Gleitman, L. R., Liberman, M., and Osherson, D. N. (Eds.), *An Invitation to Cognitive Science* (second edition)., Vol. 1. MIT Press.

Pinker, S. (2003). *The Blank Slate: The Modern Denial of Human Nature*. Penguin.

Pinto, D., McCallum, A., Wei, X., and Croft, W. B. (2003). Table extraction using conditional random fields. In *SIGIR-03*.

Pipatsrisawat, K. and Darwiche, A. (2007). RSat 2.0: SAT solver description. Tech. rep. D–153, Automated Reasoning Group, Computer Science Department, University of California, Los Angeles.

Plaat, A., Schaeffer, J., Pijls, W., and de Bruin, A. (1996). Best-first fixed-depth minimax algorithms. *AIJ*, *87*(1–2), 255–293.

Place, U. T. (1956). Is consciousness a brain process? *British Journal of Psychology*, *47*, 44–50.

Platt, J. (1999). Fast training of support vector machines using sequential minimal optimization. In *Advances in Kernel Methods: Support Vector Learning*, pp. 185–208. MIT Press.

Plotkin, G. (1971). *Automatic Methods of Inductive Inference*. Ph.D. thesis, Edinburgh University.

Plotkin, G. (1972). Building-in equational theories. In Meltzer, B. and Michie, D. (Eds.), *Machine Intelligence 7*, pp. 73–90. Edinburgh University Press.

Pohl, I. (1971). Bi-directional search. In Meltzer, B. and Michie, D. (Eds.), *Machine Intelligence 6*, pp. 127–140. Edinburgh University Press.

Pohl, I. (1973). The avoidance of (relative) catastrophe, heuristic competence, genuine dynamic weighting and computational issues in heuristic problem solving. In *IJCAI-73*, pp. 20–23.

Pohl, I. (1977). Practical and theoretical considerations in heuristic search algorithms. In Elcock, E. W. and Michie, D. (Eds.), *Machine Intelligence 8*, pp. 55–72. Ellis Horwood.

Poli, R., Langdon, W., and McPhee, N. (2008). *A Field Guide to Genetic Programming*. Lulu.com.

Pomerleau, D. A. (1993). *Neural Network Perception for Mobile Robot Guidance*. Kluwer.

Ponte, J. and Croft, W. B. (1998). A language modeling approach to information retrieval. In *SIGIR-98*, pp. 275–281.

Poole, D. (1993). Probabilistic Horn abduction and Bayesian networks. *AIJ*, *64*, 81–129.

Poole, D. (2003). First-order probabilistic inference. In *IJCAI-03*, pp. 985–991.

Poole, D., Mackworth, A. K., and Goebel, R. (1998). *Computational intelligence: A logical approach*. Oxford University Press.

Popper, K. R. (1959). *The Logic of Scientific Discovery*. Basic Books.

Popper, K. R. (1962). *Conjectures and Refutations: The Growth of Scientific Knowledge*. Basic Books.

Portner, P. and Partee, B. H. (2002). *Formal Semantics: The Essential Readings*. Wiley-Blackwell.

Post, E. L. (1921). Introduction to a general theory of elementary propositions. *American Journal of Mathematics*, *43*, 163–185.

Poundstone, W. (1993). *Prisoner's Dilemma*. Anchor.

Pourret, O., Naïm, P., and Marcot, B. (2008). *Bayesian Networks: A practical guide to applications*. Wiley.

Prades, J. L. P., Loomes, G., and Brey, R. (2008). Trying to estmate a monetary value for the QALY. Tech. rep. WP Econ 08.09, Univ. Pablo Olavide.

Pradhan, M., Provan, G. M., Middleton, B., and Henrion, M. (1994). Knowledge engineering for large belief networks. In *UAI-94*, pp. 484–490.

Prawitz, D. (1960). An improved proof procedure. *Theoria*, *26*, 102–139.

Press, W. H., Teukolsky, S. A., Vetterling, W. T., and Flannery, B. P. (2007). *Numerical Recipes: The Art of Scientific Computing* (third edition). Cambridge University Press.

Preston, J. and Bishop, M. (2002). *Views into the Chinese Room: New Essays on Searle and Artificial Intelligence*. Oxford University Press.

Prieditis, A. E. (1993). Machine discovery of effective admissible heuristics. *Machine Learning*, *12*(1–3), 117–141.

Prinz, D. G. (1952). Robot chess. *Research*, *5*, 261–266.

Prosser, P. (1993). Hybrid algorithms for constraint satisfaction problems. *Computational Intelligence*, *9*, 268–299.

Pullum, G. K. (1991). *The Great Eskimo Vocabulary Hoax (and Other Irreverent Essays on the Study of Language)*. University of Chicago Press.

Pullum, G. K. (1996). Learnability, hyperlearning, and the poverty of the stimulus. In *22nd Annual Meeting of the Berkeley Linguistics Society*.

Puterman, M. L. (1994). *Markov Decision Processes: Discrete Stochastic Dynamic Programming*. Wiley.

Puterman, M. L. and Shin, M. C. (1978). Modified policy iteration algorithms for discounted Markov decision problems. *Management Science*, *24*(11), 1127–1137.

Putnam, H. (1960). Minds and machines. In Hook, S. (Ed.), *Dimensions of Mind*, pp. 138–164. Macmillan.

Putnam, H. (1963). 'Degree of confirmation' and inductive logic. In Schilpp, P. A. (Ed.), *The Philosophy of Rudolf Carnap*, pp. 270–292. Open Court.

Putnam, H. (1967). The nature of mental states. In Capitan, W. H. and Merrill, D. D. (Eds.), *Art, Mind, and Religion*, pp. 37–48. University of Pittsburgh Press.

Putnam, H. (1975). The meaning of "meaning". In Gunderson, K. (Ed.), *Language, Mind and Knowledge: Minnesota Studies in the Philosophy of Science*. University of Minnesota Press.

Pylyshyn, Z. W. (1974). Minds, machines and phenomenology: Some reflections on Dreyfus' "What Computers Can't Do". *Int. J. Cognitive Psychology*, *3*(1), 57–77.

Pylyshyn, Z. W. (1984). *Computation and Cognition: Toward a Foundation for Cognitive Science*. MIT Press.

Quillian, M. R. (1961). A design for an understanding machine. Paper presented at a colloquium: Semantic Problems in Natural Language, King's College, Cambridge, England.

Quine, W. V. (1953). Two dogmas of empiricism. In *From a Logical Point of View*, pp. 20–46. Harper and Row.

Quine, W. V. (1960). *Word and Object*. MIT Press.

Quine, W. V. (1982). *Methods of Logic* (fourth edition). Harvard University Press.

Quinlan, J. R. (1979). Discovering rules from large collections of examples: A case study. In Michie, D. (Ed.), *Expert Systems in the Microelectronic Age*. Edinburgh University Press.

Quinlan, J. R. (1986). Induction of decision trees. *Machine Learning*, *1*, 81–106.

Quinlan, J. R. (1990). Learning logical definitions from relations. *Machine Learning*, *5*(3), 239–266.

Quinlan, J. R. (1993). *C4.5: Programs for machine learning*. Morgan Kaufmann.

Quinlan, J. R. and Cameron-Jones, R. M. (1993). FOIL: A midterm report. In *ECML-93*, pp. 3–20.

Quirk, R., Greenbaum, S., Leech, G., and Svartvik, J. (1985). *A Comprehensive Grammar of the English Language*. Longman.

Rabani, Y., Rabinovich, Y., and Sinclair, A. (1998). A computational view of population genetics. *Random Structures and Algorithms*, *12*(4), 313–334.

Rabiner, L. R. and Juang, B.-H. (1993). *Fundamentals of Speech Recognition*. Prentice-Hall.

Ralphs, T. K., Ladanyi, L., and Saltzman, M. J. (2004). A library hierarchy for implementing scalable parallel search algorithms. *J. Supercomputing*, *28*(2), 215–234.

Ramanan, D., Forsyth, D., and Zisserman, A. (2007). Tracking people by learning their appearance. *IEEE Pattern Analysis and Machine Intelligence*.

Ramsey, F. P. (1931). Truth and probability. In Braithwaite, R. B. (Ed.), *The Foundations of Mathematics and Other Logical Essays*. Harcourt Brace Jovanovich.

Ranzato, M., Poultney, C., Chopra, S., and LeCun, Y. (2007). Efficient learning of sparse representations with an energy-based model. In *NIPS 19*, pp. 1137–1144.

Raphson, J. (1690). *Analysis aequationum universalis*. Apud Abelem Swalle, London.

Rashevsky, N. (1936). Physico-mathematical aspects of excitation and conduction in nerves. In *Cold Springs Harbor Symposia on Quantitative Biology. IV: Excitation Phenomena*, pp. 90–97.

Rashevsky, N. (1938). *Mathematical Biophysics: Physico-Mathematical Foundations of Biology*. University of Chicago Press.

Rasmussen, C. E. and Williams, C. K. I. (2006). *Gaussian Processes for Machine Learning*. MIT Press.

Rassenti, S., Smith, V., and Bulfin, R. (1982). A combinatorial auction mechanism for airport time slot allocation. *Bell Journal of Economics*, *13*, 402–417.

Ratner, D. and Warmuth, M. (1986). Finding a shortest solution for the $n \times n$ extension of the 15-puzzle is intractable. In *AAAI-86*, Vol. 1, pp. 168–172.

Rauch, H. E., Tung, F., and Striebel, C. T. (1965). Maximum likelihood estimates of linear dynamic systems. *AIAA Journal*, *3*(8), 1445–1450.

Rayward-Smith, V., Osman, I., Reeves, C., and Smith, G. (Eds.). (1996). *Modern Heuristic Search Methods*. Wiley.

Rechenberg, I. (1965). Cybernetic solution path of an experimental problem. Library translation 1122, Royal Aircraft Establishment.

Reeson, C. G., Huang, K.-C., Bayer, K. M., and Choueiry, B. Y. (2007). An interactive constraint-based approach to sudoku. In *AAAI-07*, pp. 1976–1977.

Regin, J. (1994). A filtering algorithm for constraints of difference in CSPs. In *AAAI-94*, pp. 362–367.

Reichenbach, H. (1949). *The Theory of Probability: An Inquiry into the Logical and Mathematical Foundations of the Calculus of Probability* (second edition). University of California Press.

Reid, D. B. (1979). An algorithm for tracking multiple targets. *IEEE Trans. Automatic Control*, *24*(6), 843–854.

Reif, J. (1979). Complexity of the mover's problem and generalizations. In *FOCS-79*, pp. 421–427. IEEE.

Reiter, R. (1980). A logic for default reasoning. *AIJ*, *13*(1–2), 81–132.

Reiter, R. (1991). The frame problem in the situation calculus: A simple solution (sometimes) and a completeness result for goal regression. In Lifschitz, V. (Ed.), *Artificial Intelligence and Mathematical Theory of Computation: Papers in Honor of John McCarthy*, pp. 359–380. Academic Press.

Reiter, R. (2001). *Knowledge in Action: Logical Foundations for Specifying and Implementing Dynamical Systems*. MIT Press.

Renner, G. and Ekart, A. (2003). Genetic algorithms in computer aided design. *Computer Aided Design*, *35*(8), 709–726.

Rényi, A. (1970). *Probability Theory*. Elsevier/North-Holland.

Reynolds, C. W. (1987). Flocks, herds, and schools: A distributed behavioral model. *Computer Graphics*, *21*, 25–34. SIGGRAPH '87 Conference Proceedings.

Riazanov, A. and Voronkov, A. (2002). The design and implementation of VAMPIRE. *AI Communications*, *15*(2–3), 91–110.

Rich, E. and Knight, K. (1991). *Artificial Intelligence* (second edition). McGraw-Hill.

Richards, M. and Amir, E. (2007). Opponent modeling in Scrabble. In *IJCAI-07*.

Richardson, M., Bilmes, J., and Diorio, C. (2000). Hidden-articulator Markov models: Performance improvements and robustness to noise. In *ICASSP-00*.

Richter, S. and Westphal, M. (2008). The LAMA planner. In *Proc. International Planning Competition at ICAPS*.

Ridley, M. (2004). *Evolution*. Oxford Reader.

Rieger, C. (1976). An organization of knowledge for problem solving and language comprehension. *AIJ*, *7*, 89–127.

Riley, J. and Samuelson, W. (1981). Optimal auctions. *American Economic Review*, *71*, 381–392.

Riloff, E. (1993). Automatically constructing a dictionary for information extraction tasks. In *AAAI-93*, pp. 811–816.

Rintanen, J. (1999). Improvements to the evaluation of quantified Boolean formulae. In *IJCAI-99*, pp. 1192–1197.

Rintanen, J. (2007). Asymptotically optimal encodings of conformant planning in QBF. In *AAAI-07*, pp. 1045–1050.

Ripley, B. D. (1996). *Pattern Recognition and Neural Networks*. Cambridge University Press.

Rissanen, J. (1984). Universal coding, information, prediction, and estimation. *IEEE Transactions on Information Theory*, *IT-30*(4), 629–636.

Rissanen, J. (2007). *Information and Complexity in Statistical Modeling*. Springer.

Ritchie, G. D. and Hanna, F. K. (1984). AM: A case study in AI methodology. *AIJ*, *23*(3), 249–268.

Rivest, R. (1987). Learning decision lists. *Machine Learning*, *2*(3), 229–246.

Roberts, L. G. (1963). Machine perception of three-dimensional solids. Technical report 315, MIT Lincoln Laboratory.

Robertson, N. and Seymour, P. D. (1986). Graph minors. II. Algorithmic aspects of tree-width. *J. Algorithms*, *7*(3), 309–322.

Robertson, S. E. (1977). The probability ranking principle in IR. *J. Documentation*, *33*, 294–304.

Robertson, S. E. and Sparck Jones, K. (1976). Relevance weighting of search terms. *J. American Society for Information Science*, *27*, 129–146.

Robinson, A. and Voronkov, A. (2001). *Handbook of Automated Reasoning*. Elsevier.

Robinson, J. A. (1965). A machine-oriented logic based on the resolution principle. *JACM*, *12*, 23–41.

Roche, E. and Schabes, Y. (1997). *Finite-State Language Processing (Language, Speech and Communication)*. Bradford Books.

Rock, I. (1984). *Perception*. W. H. Freeman.

Rosenblatt, F. (1957). The perceptron: A perceiving and recognizing automaton. Report 85-460-1, Project PARA, Cornell Aeronautical Laboratory.

Rosenblatt, F. (1960). On the convergence of reinforcement procedures in simple perceptrons. Report VG-1196-G-4, Cornell Aeronautical Laboratory.

Rosenblatt, F. (1962). *Principles of Neurodynamics: Perceptrons and the Theory of Brain Mechanisms*. Spartan.

Rosenblatt, M. (1956). Remarks on some nonparametric estimates of a density function. *Annals of Mathematical Statistics*, *27*, 832–837.

Rosenblueth, A., Wiener, N., and Bigelow, J. (1943). Behavior, purpose, and teleology. *Philosophy of Science*, *10*, 18–24.

Rosenschein, J. S. and Zlotkin, G. (1994). *Rules of Encounter*. MIT Press.

Rosenschein, S. J. (1985). Formal theories of knowledge in AI and robotics. *New Generation Computing*, *3*(4), 345–357.

Ross, P. E. (2004). Psyching out computer chess players. *IEEE Spectrum*, *41*(2), 14–15.

Ross, S. M. (1988). *A First Course in Probability* (third edition). Macmillan.

Rossi, F., van Beek, P., and Walsh, T. (2006). *Handbook of Constraint Processing*. Elsevier.

Roussel, P. (1975). Prolog: Manual de reference et d'utilization. Tech. rep., Groupe d'Intelligence Artificielle, Université d'Aix-Marseille.

Rouveirol, C. and Puget, J.-F. (1989). A simple and general solution for inverting resolution. In *Proc. European Working Session on Learning*, pp. 201–210.

Rowat, P. F. (1979). *Representing the Spatial Experience and Solving Spatial problems in a Simulated Robot Environment*. Ph.D. thesis, University of British Columbia.

Roweis, S. T. and Ghahramani, Z. (1999). A unifying review of Linear Gaussian Models. *Neural Computation*, *11*(2), 305–345.

Rowley, H., Baluja, S., and Kanade, T. (1996). Neural network-based face detection. In *CVPR*, pp. 203–208.

Roy, N., Gordon, G., and Thrun, S. (2005). Finding approximate POMDP solutions through belief compression. *JAIR*, *23*, 1–40.

Rubin, D. (1988). Using the SIR algorithm to simulate posterior distributions. In Bernardo, J. M., de Groot, M. H., Lindley, D. V., and Smith, A. F. M. (Eds.), *Bayesian Statistics 3*, pp. 395–402. Oxford University Press.

Rumelhart, D. E., Hinton, G. E., and Williams, R. J. (1986a). Learning internal representations by error propagation. In Rumelhart, D. E. and McClelland, J. L. (Eds.), *Parallel Distributed Processing*, Vol. 1, chap. 8, pp. 318–362. MIT Press.

Rumelhart, D. E., Hinton, G. E., and Williams, R. J. (1986b). Learning representations by back-propagating errors. *Nature*, *323*, 533–536.

Rumelhart, D. E. and McClelland, J. L. (Eds.). (1986). *Parallel Distributed Processing*. MIT Press.

Rummery, G. A. and Niranjan, M. (1994). Online *Q*-learning using connectionist systems. Tech. rep. CUED/F-INFENG/TR 166, Cambridge University Engineering Department.

Ruspini, E. H., Lowrance, J. D., and Strat, T. M. (1992). Understanding evidential reasoning. *IJAR*, *6*(3), 401–424.

Russell, J. G. B. (1990). Is screening for abdominal aortic aneurysm worthwhile? *Clinical Radiology*, *41*, 182–184.

Russell, S. J. (1985). The compleat guide to MRS. Report STAN-CS-85-1080, Computer Science Department, Stanford University.

Russell, S. J. (1986). A quantitative analysis of analogy by similarity. In *AAAI-86*, pp. 284–288.

Russell, S. J. (1988). Tree-structured bias. In *AAAI-88*, Vol. 2, pp. 641–645.

Russell, S. J. (1992). Efficient memory-bounded search methods. In *ECAI-92*, pp. 1–5.

Russell, S. J. (1998). Learning agents for uncertain environments (extended abstract). In *COLT-98*, pp. 101–103.

Russell, S. J., Binder, J., Koller, D., and Kanazawa, K. (1995). Local learning in probabilistic networks with hidden variables. In *IJCAI-95*, pp. 1146–52.

Russell, S. J. and Grosof, B. (1987). A declarative approach to bias in concept learning. In *AAAI-87*.

Russell, S. J. and Norvig, P. (2003). *Artificial Intelligence: A Modern Approach* (2nd edition). Prentice-Hall.

Russell, S. J. and Subramanian, D. (1995). Provably bounded-optimal agents. *JAIR*, *3*, 575–609.

Russell, S. J., Subramanian, D., and Parr, R. (1993). Provably bounded optimal agents. In *IJCAI-93*, pp. 338–345.

Russell, S. J. and Wefald, E. H. (1989). On optimal game-tree search using rational meta-reasoning. In *IJCAI-89*, pp. 334–340.

Russell, S. J. and Wefald, E. H. (1991). *Do the Right Thing: Studies in Limited Rationality*. MIT Press.

Russell, S. J. and Wolfe, J. (2005). Efficient belief-state AND-OR search, with applications to Kriegspiel. In *IJCAI-05*, pp. 278–285.

Russell, S. J. and Zimdars, A. (2003). Q-decomposition of reinforcement learning agents. In *ICML-03*.

Rustagi, J. S. (1976). *Variational Methods in Statistics*. Academic Press.

Sabin, D. and Freuder, E. C. (1994). Contradicting conventional wisdom in constraint satisfaction. In *ECAI-94*, pp. 125–129.

Sacerdoti, E. D. (1974). Planning in a hierarchy of abstraction spaces. *AIJ*, *5*(2), 115–135.

Sacerdoti, E. D. (1975). The nonlinear nature of plans. In *IJCAI-75*, pp. 206–214.

Sacerdoti, E. D. (1977). *A Structure for Plans and Behavior*. Elsevier/North-Holland.

Sadri, F. and Kowalski, R. (1995). Variants of the event calculus. In *ICLP-95*, pp. 67–81.

Sahami, M., Dumais, S. T., Heckerman, D., and Horvitz, E. J. (1998). A Bayesian approach to filtering junk E-mail. In *Learning for Text Categorization: Papers from the 1998 Workshop*.

Sahami, M., Hearst, M. A., and Saund, E. (1996). Applying the multiple cause mixture model to text categorization. In *ICML-96*, pp. 435–443.

Sahin, N. T., Pinker, S., Cash, S. S., Schomer, D., and Halgren, E. (2009). Sequential processing of lexical, grammatical, and phonological information within Broca's area. *Science*, *326*(5291), 445–449.

Sakuta, M. and Iida, H. (2002). AND/OR-tree search for solving problems with uncertainty: A case study using screen-shogi problems. *IPSJ Journal*, *43*(01).

Salomaa, A. (1969). Probabilistic and weighted grammars. *Information and Control*, *15*, 529–544.

Salton, G., Wong, A., and Yang, C. S. (1975). A vector space model for automatic indexing. *CACM*, *18*(11), 613–620.

Samuel, A. L. (1959). Some studies in machine learning using the game of checkers. *IBM Journal of Research and Development*, *3*(3), 210–229.

Samuel, A. L. (1967). Some studies in machine learning using the game of checkers II—Recent progress. *IBM Journal of Research and Development*, *11*(6), 601–617.

Samuelsson, C. and Rayner, M. (1991). Quantitative evaluation of explanation-based learning as an optimization tool for a large-scale natural language system. In *IJCAI-91*, pp. 609–615.

Sarawagi, S. (2007). Information extraction. *Foundations and Trends in Databases*, *1*(3), 261–377.

Satia, J. K. and Lave, R. E. (1973). Markovian decision processes with probabilistic observation of states. *Management Science*, *20*(1), 1–13.

Sato, T. and Kameya, Y. (1997). PRISM: A symbolic-statistical modeling language. In *IJCAI-97*, pp. 1330–1335.

Saul, L. K., Jaakkola, T., and Jordan, M. I. (1996). Mean field theory for sigmoid belief networks. *JAIR*, *4*, 61–76.

Savage, L. J. (1954). *The Foundations of Statistics*. Wiley.

Sayre, K. (1993). Three more flaws in the computational model. Paper presented at the APA (Central Division) Annual Conference, Chicago, Illinois.

Schaeffer, J. (2008). *One Jump Ahead: Computer Perfection at Checkers*. Springer-Verlag.

Schaeffer, J., Burch, N., Bjornsson, Y., Kishimoto, A., Müller, M., Lake, R., Lu, P., and Sutphen, S. (2007). Checkers is solved. *Science*, *317*, 1518–1522.

Schank, R. C. and Abelson, R. P. (1977). *Scripts, Plans, Goals, and Understanding*. Lawrence Erlbaum Associates.

Schank, R. C. and Riesbeck, C. (1981). *Inside Computer Understanding: Five Programs Plus Miniatures*. Lawrence Erlbaum Associates.

Schapire, R. E. and Singer, Y. (2000). Boostexter: A boosting-based system for text categorization. *Machine Learning*, *39*(2/3), 135–168.

Schapire, R. E. (1990). The strength of weak learnability. *Machine Learning*, *5*(2), 197–227.

Schapire, R. E. (2003). The boosting approach to machine learning: An overview. In Denison, D. D., Hansen, M. H., Holmes, C., Mallick, B., and Yu, B. (Eds.), *Nonlinear Estimation and Classification*. Springer.

Schmid, C. and Mohr, R. (1996). Combining greyvalue invariants with local constraints for object recognition. In *CVPR*.

Schmolze, J. G. and Lipkis, T. A. (1983). Classification in the KL-ONE representation system. In *IJCAI-83*, pp. 330–332.

Schölkopf, B. and Smola, A. J. (2002). *Learning with Kernels*. MIT Press.

Schöning, T. (1999). A probabilistic algorithm for k-SAT and constraint satisfaction problems. In *FOCS-99*, pp. 410–414.

Schoppers, M. J. (1987). Universal plans for reactive robots in unpredictable environments. In *IJCAI-87*, pp. 1039–1046.

Schoppers, M. J. (1989). In defense of reaction plans as caches. *AIMag*, *10*(4), 51–60.

Schröder, E. (1877). *Der Operationskreis des Logikkalküls*. B. G. Teubner, Leipzig.

Schultz, W., Dayan, P., and Montague, P. R. (1997). A neural substrate of prediction and reward. *Science*, *275*, 1593.

Schulz, D., Burgard, W., Fox, D., and Cremers, A. B. (2003). People tracking with mobile robots using sample-based joint probabilistic data association filters. *Int. J. Robotics Research*, *22*(2), 99–116.

Schulz, S. (2004). System Description: E 0.81. In *Proc. International Joint Conference on Automated Reasoning*, Vol. 3097 of *LNAI*, pp. 223–228.

Schütze, H. (1995). *Ambiguity in Language Learning: Computational and Cognitive Models*. Ph.D. thesis, Stanford University. Also published by CSLI Press, 1997.

Schwartz, J. T., Scharir, M., and Hopcroft, J. (1987). *Planning, Geometry and Complexity of Robot Motion*. Ablex Publishing Corporation.

Schwartz, S. P. (Ed.). (1977). *Naming, Necessity, and Natural Kinds*. Cornell University Press.

Scott, D. and Krauss, P. (1966). Assigning probabilities to logical formulas. In Hintikka, J. and Suppes, P. (Eds.), *Aspects of Inductive Logic*. North-Holland.

Searle, J. R. (1980). Minds, brains, and programs. *BBS*, *3*, 417–457.

Searle, J. R. (1984). *Minds, Brains and Science*. Harvard University Press.

Searle, J. R. (1990). Is the brain's mind a computer program? *Scientific American*, *262*, 26–31.

Searle, J. R. (1992). *The Rediscovery of the Mind*. MIT Press.

Sebastiani, F. (2002). Machine learning in automated text categorization. *ACM Computing Surveys*, *34*(1), 1–47.

Segaran, T. (2007). *Programming Collective Intelligence: Building Smart Web 2.0 Applications*. O'Reilly.

Selman, B., Kautz, H., and Cohen, B. (1996). Local search strategies for satisfiability testing. In *DIMACS Series in Discrete Mathematics and Theoretical Computer Science, Volume 26*, pp. 521–532. American Mathematical Society.

Selman, B. and Levesque, H. J. (1993). The complexity of path-based defeasible inheritance. *AIJ*, *62*(2), 303–339.

Selman, B., Levesque, H. J., and Mitchell, D. (1992). A new method for solving hard satisfiability problems. In *AAAI-92*, pp. 440–446.

Sha, F. and Pereira, F. (2003). Shallow parsing with conditional random fields. Technical report CIS TR MS-CIS-02-35, Univ. of Penn.

Shachter, R. D. (1986). Evaluating influence diagrams. *Operations Research*, *34*, 871–882.

Shachter, R. D. (1998). Bayes-ball: The rational pastime (for determining irrelevance and requisite information in belief networks and influence diagrams). In *UAI-98*, pp. 480–487.

Shachter, R. D., D'Ambrosio, B., and Del Favero, B. A. (1990). Symbolic probabilistic inference in belief networks. In *AAAI-90*, pp. 126–131.

Shachter, R. D. and Kenley, C. R. (1989). Gaussian influence diagrams. *Management Science*, *35*(5), 527–550.

Shachter, R. D. and Peot, M. (1989). Simulation approaches to general probabilistic inference on belief networks. In *UAI-98*.

Shachter, R. D. and Heckerman, D. (1987). Thinking backward for knowledge acquisition. *AIMag*, *3*(Fall).

Shafer, G. (1976). *A Mathematical Theory of Evidence*. Princeton University Press.

Shahookar, K. and Mazumder, P. (1991). VLSI cell placement techniques. *Computing Surveys*, *23*(2), 143–220.

Shanahan, M. (1997). *Solving the Frame Problem*. MIT Press.

Shanahan, M. (1999). The event calculus explained. In Wooldridge, M. J. and Veloso, M. (Eds.), *Artificial Intelligence Today*, pp. 409–430. Springer-Verlag.

Shankar, N. (1986). *Proof-Checking Metamathematics*. Ph.D. thesis, Computer Science Department, University of Texas at Austin.

Shannon, C. E. and Weaver, W. (1949). *The Mathematical Theory of Communication*. University of Illinois Press.

Shannon, C. E. (1948). A mathematical theory of communication. *Bell Systems Technical Journal*, *27*, 379–423, 623–656.

Shannon, C. E. (1950). Programming a computer for playing chess. *Philosophical Magazine*, *41*(4), 256–275.

Shaparau, D., Pistore, M., and Traverso, P. (2008). Fusing procedural and declarative planning goals for nondeterministic domains. In *AAAI-08*.

Shapiro, E. (1981). An algorithm that infers theories from facts. In *IJCAI-81*, p. 1064.

Shapiro, S. C. (Ed.). (1992). *Encyclopedia of Artificial Intelligence* (second edition). Wiley.

Shapley, S. (1953). Stochastic games. In *PNAS*, Vol. 39, pp. 1095–1100.

Shatkay, H. and Kaelbling, L. P. (1997). Learning topological maps with weak local odometric information. In *IJCAI-97*.

Shelley, M. (1818). *Frankenstein: Or, the Modern Prometheus*. Pickering and Chatto.

Sheppard, B. (2002). World-championship-caliber scrabble. *AIJ*, *134*(1–2), 241–275.

Shi, J. and Malik, J. (2000). Normalized cuts and image segmentation. *PAMI*, *22*(8), 888–905.

Shieber, S. (1994). Lessons from a restricted Turing Test. *CACM*, *37*, 70–78.

Shieber, S. (Ed.). (2004). *The Turing Test*. MIT Press.

Shoham, Y. (1993). Agent-oriented programming. *AIJ*, *60*(1), 51–92.

Shoham, Y. (1994). *Artificial Intelligence Techniques in Prolog*. Morgan Kaufmann.

Shoham, Y. and Leyton-Brown, K. (2009). *Multiagent Systems: Algorithmic, Game-Theoretic, and Logical Foundations*. Cambridge Univ. Press.

Shoham, Y., Powers, R., and Grenager, T. (2004). If multi-agent learning is the answer, what is the question? In *Proc. AAAI Fall Symposium on Artificial Multi-Agent Learning*.

Shortliffe, E. H. (1976). *Computer-Based Medical Consultations: MYCIN*. Elsevier/North-Holland.

Sietsma, J. and Dow, R. J. F. (1988). Neural net pruning—Why and how. In *IEEE International Conference on Neural Networks*, pp. 325–333.

Siklossy, L. and Dreussi, J. (1973). An efficient robot planner which generates its own procedures. In *IJCAI-73*, pp. 423–430.

Silverstein, C., Henzinger, M., Marais, H., and Moricz, M. (1998). Analysis of a very large altavista query log. Tech. rep. 1998-014, Digital Systems Research Center.

Simmons, R. and Koenig, S. (1995). Probabilistic robot navigation in partially observable environments. In *IJCAI-95*, pp. 1080–1087. IJCAI, Inc.

Simon, D. (2006). *Optimal State Estimation: Kalman, H Infinity, and Nonlinear Approaches*. Wiley.

Simon, H. A. (1947). *Administrative behavior*. Macmillan.

Simon, H. A. (1957). *Models of Man: Social and Rational*. John Wiley.

Simon, H. A. (1963). Experiments with a heuristic compiler. *JACM*, *10*, 493–506.

Simon, H. A. (1981). *The Sciences of the Artificial* (second edition). MIT Press.

Simon, H. A. (1982). *Models of Bounded Rationality, Volume 1*. The MIT Press.

Simon, H. A. and Newell, A. (1958). Heuristic problem solving: The next advance in operations research. *Operations Research*, *6*, 1–10.

Simon, H. A. and Newell, A. (1961). Computer simulation of human thinking and problem solving. *Datamation, June/July*, 35–37.

Simon, J. C. and Dubois, O. (1989). Number of solutions to satisfiability instances—Applications to knowledge bases. *AIJ*, *3*, 53–65.

Simonis, H. (2005). Sudoku as a constraint problem. In *CP Workshop on Modeling and Reformulating Constraint Satisfaction Problems*, pp. 13–27.

Singer, P. W. (2009). *Wired for War*. Penguin Press.

Singh, P., Lin, T., Mueller, E. T., Lim, G., Perkins, T., and Zhu, W. L. (2002). Open mind common sense: Knowledge acquisition from the general public. In *Proc. First International Conference on Ontologies, Databases, and Applications of Semantics for Large Scale Information Systems*.

Singhal, A., Buckley, C., and Mitra, M. (1996). Pivoted document length normalization. In *SIGIR-96*, pp. 21–29.

Sittler, R. W. (1964). An optimal data association problem in surveillance theory. *IEEE Transactions on Military Electronics*, *8*(2), 125–139.

Skinner, B. F. (1953). *Science and Human Behavior*. Macmillan.

Skolem, T. (1920). Logisch-kombinatorische Untersuchungen über die Erfüllbarkeit oder Beweisbarkeit mathematischer Sätze nebst einem Theoreme über die dichte Mengen. *Videnskapsselskapets skrifter, I. Matematisk-naturvidenskabelig klasse*, *4*.

Skolem, T. (1928). Über die mathematische Logik. *Norsk matematisk tidsskrift*, *10*, 125–142.

Slagle, J. R. (1963). A heuristic program that solves symbolic integration problems in freshman calculus. *JACM*, *10*(4).

Slate, D. J. and Atkin, L. R. (1977). CHESS 4.5—Northwestern University chess program. In Frey, P. W. (Ed.), *Chess Skill in Man and Machine*, pp. 82–118. Springer-Verlag.

Slater, E. (1950). Statistics for the chess computer and the factor of mobility. In *Symposium on Information Theory*, pp. 150–152. Ministry of Supply.

Sleator, D. and Temperley, D. (1993). Parsing English with a link grammar. In *Third Annual Workshop on Parsing technologies*.

Slocum, J. and Sonneveld, D. (2006). *The 15 Puzzle*. Slocum Puzzle Foundation.

Sloman, A. (1978). *The Computer Revolution in Philosophy*. Harvester Press.

Smallwood, R. D. and Sondik, E. J. (1973). The optimal control of partially observable Markov processes over a finite horizon. *Operations Research*, *21*, 1071–1088.

Smart, J. J. C. (1959). Sensations and brain processes. *Philosophical Review*, *68*, 141–156.

Smith, B. (2004). Ontology. In Floridi, L. (Ed.), *The Blackwell Guide to the Philosophy of Computing and Information*, pp. 155–166. Wiley-Blackwell.

Smith, D. E., Genesereth, M. R., and Ginsberg, M. L. (1986). Controlling recursive inference. *AIJ*, *30*(3), 343–389.

Smith, D. A. and Eisner, J. (2008). Dependency parsing by belief propagation. In *EMNLP*, pp. 145–156.

Smith, D. E. and Weld, D. S. (1998). Conformant Graphplan. In *AAAI-98*, pp. 889–896.

Smith, J. Q. (1988). *Decision Analysis*. Chapman and Hall.

Smith, J. E. and Winkler, R. L. (2006). The optimizer's curse: Skepticism and postdecision surprise in decision analysis. *Management Science*, *52*(3), 311–322.

Smith, J. M. (1982). *Evolution and the Theory of Games*. Cambridge University Press.

Smith, J. M. and Szathmáry, E. (1999). *The Origins of Life: From the Birth of Life to the Origin of Language*. Oxford University Press.

Smith, M. K., Welty, C., and McGuinness, D. (2004). OWL web ontology language guide. Tech. rep., W3C.

Smith, R. C. and Cheeseman, P. (1986). On the representation and estimation of spatial uncertainty. *Int. J. Robotics Research*, *5*(4), 56–68.

Smith, S. J. J., Nau, D. S., and Throop, T. A. (1998). Success in spades: Using AI planning techniques to win the world championship of computer bridge. In *AAAI-98*, pp. 1079–1086.

Smolensky, P. (1988). On the proper treatment of connectionism. *BBS*, *2*, 1–74.

Smullyan, R. M. (1995). *First-Order Logic*. Dover.

Smyth, P., Heckerman, D., and Jordan, M. I. (1997). Probabilistic independence networks for hidden Markov probability models. *Neural Computation*, *9*(2), 227–269.

Snell, M. B. (2008). Do you have free will? John Searle reflects on various philosophical questions in light of new research on the brain. *California Alumni Magazine, March/April*.

Soderland, S. and Weld, D. S. (1991). Evaluating nonlinear planning. Technical report TR-91-02-03, University of Washington Department of Computer Science and Engineering.

Solomonoff, R. J. (1964). A formal theory of inductive inference. *Information and Control*, *7*, 1–22, 224–254.

Solomonoff, R. J. (2009). Algorithmic probability–theory and applications. In Emmert-Streib, F. and Dehmer, M. (Eds.), *Information Theory and Statitical Learning*. Springer.

Sondik, E. J. (1971). *The Optimal Control of Partially Observable Markov Decision Processes*. Ph.D. thesis, Stanford University.

Sosic, R. and Gu, J. (1994). Efficient local search with conflict minimization: A case study of the n-queens problem. *IEEE Transactions on Knowledge and Data Engineering*, *6*(5), 661–668.

Sowa, J. (1999). *Knowledge Representation: Logical, Philosophical, and Computational Foundations*. Blackwell.

Spaan, M. T. J. and Vlassis, N. (2005). Perseus: Randomized point-based value iteration for POMDPs. *JAIR*, *24*, 195–220.

Spiegelhalter, D. J., Dawid, A. P., Lauritzen, S., and Cowell, R. (1993). Bayesian analysis in expert systems. *Statistical Science*, *8*, 219–282.

Spielberg, S. (2001). AI. Movie.

Spirtes, P., Glymour, C., and Scheines, R. (1993). *Causation, prediction, and search*. Springer-Verlag.

Srinivasan, A., Muggleton, S. H., King, R. D., and Sternberg, M. J. E. (1994). Mutagenesis: ILP experiments in a non-determinate biological domain. In *ILP-94*, Vol. 237, pp. 217–232.

Srivas, M. and Bickford, M. (1990). Formal verification of a pipelined microprocessor. *IEEE Software*, *7*(5), 52–64.

Staab, S. (2004). *Handbook on Ontologies*. Springer.

Stallman, R. M. and Sussman, G. J. (1977). Forward reasoning and dependency-directed backtracking in a system for computer-aided circuit analysis. *AIJ*, *9*(2), 135–196.

Stanfill, C. and Waltz, D. (1986). Toward memory-based reasoning. *CACM*, *29*(12), 1213–1228.

Stefik, M. (1995). *Introduction to Knowledge Systems*. Morgan Kaufmann.

Stein, L. A. (2002). *Interactive Programming in Java (pre-publication draft)*. Morgan Kaufmann.

Stephenson, T., Bourlard, H., Bengio, S., and Morris, A. (2000). Automatic speech recognition using dynamic bayesian networks with both acoustic and articulatory features. In *ICSLP-00*, pp. 951–954.

Stergiou, K. and Walsh, T. (1999). The difference all-difference makes. In *IJCAI-99*, pp. 414–419.

Stickel, M. E. (1992). A prolog technology theorem prover: a new exposition and implementation in prolog. *Theoretical Computer Science*, *104*, 109–128.

Stiller, L. (1992). KQNKRR. *J. International Computer Chess Association*, *15*(1), 16–18.

Stiller, L. (1996). Multilinear algebra and chess endgames. In Nowakowski, R. J. (Ed.), *Games of No Chance, MSRI, 29, 1996*. Mathematical Sciences Research Institute.

Stockman, G. (1979). A minimax algorithm better than alpha–beta? *AIJ*, *12*(2), 179–196.

Stoffel, K., Taylor, M., and Hendler, J. (1997). Efficient management of very large ontologies. In *Proc. AAAI-97*, pp. 442–447.

Stolcke, A. and Omohundro, S. (1994). Inducing probabilistic grammars by Bayesian model merging. In *Proc. Second International Colloquium on Grammatical Inference and Applications (ICGI-94)*, pp. 106–118.

Stone, M. (1974). Cross-validatory choice and assessment of statostical predictions. *J. Royal Statistical Society*, *36*(111–133).

Stone, P. (2000). *Layered Learning in Multi-Agent Systems: A Winning Approach to Robotic Soccer*. MIT Press.

Stone, P. (2003). Multiagent competitions and research: Lessons from RoboCup and TAC. In Lima, P. U. and Rojas, P. (Eds.), *RoboCup-2002: Robot Soccer World Cup VI*, pp. 224–237. Springer Verlag.

Stone, P., Kaminka, G., and Rosenschein, J. S. (2009). Leading a best-response teammate in an ad hoc team. In *AAMAS Workshop in Agent Mediated Electronic Commerce*.

Stork, D. G. (2004). Optics and realism in rennaissance art. *Scientific American*, pp. 77–83.

Strachey, C. (1952). Logical or non-mathematical programmes. In *Proc. 1952 ACM national meeting (Toronto)*, pp. 46–49.

Stratonovich, R. L. (1959). Optimum nonlinear systems which bring about a separation of a signal with constant parameters from noise. *Radiofizika*, *2*(6), 892–901.

Stratonovich, R. L. (1965). On value of information. *Izvestiya of USSR Academy of Sciences, Technical Cybernetics*, *5*, 3–12.

Subramanian, D. and Feldman, R. (1990). The utility of EBL in recursive domain theories. In *AAAI-90*, Vol. 2, pp. 942–949.

Subramanian, D. and Wang, E. (1994). Constraint-based kinematic synthesis. In *Proc. International Conference on Qualitative Reasoning*, pp. 228–239.

Sussman, G. J. (1975). *A Computer Model of Skill Acquisition*. Elsevier/North-Holland.

Sutcliffe, G. and Suttner, C. (1998). The TPTP Problem Library: CNF Release v1.2.1. *JAR*, *21*(2), 177–203.

Sutcliffe, G., Schulz, S., Claessen, K., and Gelder, A. V. (2006). Using the TPTP language for writing derivations and finite interpretations. In *Proc. International Joint Conference on Automated Reasoning*, pp. 67–81.

Sutherland, I. (1963). Sketchpad: A man-machine graphical communication system. In *Proc. Spring Joint Computer Conference*, pp. 329–346.

Sutton, C. and McCallum, A. (2007). An introduction to conditional random fields for relational learning. In Getoor, L. and Taskar, B. (Eds.), *Introduction to Statistical Relational Learning*. MIT Press.

Sutton, R. S. (1988). Learning to predict by the methods of temporal differences. *Machine Learning*, *3*, 9–44.

Sutton, R. S., McAllester, D. A., Singh, S. P., and Mansour, Y. (2000). Policy gradient methods for reinforcement learning with function approximation. In Solla, S. A., Leen, T. K., and Müller, K.-R. (Eds.), *NIPS 12*, pp. 1057–1063. MIT Press.

Sutton, R. S. (1990). Integrated architectures for learning, planning, and reacting based on approximating dynamic programming. In *ICML-90*, pp. 216–224.

Sutton, R. S. and Barto, A. G. (1998). *Reinforcement Learning: An Introduction*. MIT Press.

Svore, K. and Burges, C. (2009). A machine learning approach for improved bm25 retrieval. In *Proc. Conference on Information Knowledge Management*.

Swade, D. (2000). *Difference Engine: Charles Babbage And The Quest To Build The First Computer*. Diane Publishing Co.

Swerling, P. (1959). First order error propagation in a stagewise smoothing procedure for satellite observations. *J. Astronautical Sciences*, *6*, 46–52.

Swift, T. and Warren, D. S. (1994). Analysis of SLG-WAM evaluation of definite programs. In *Logic Programming. Proc. 1994 International Symposium on Logic programming*, pp. 219–235.

Syrjänen, T. (2000). Lparse 1.0 user's manual. `saturn.tcs.hut.fi/Software/smodels`.

Tadepalli, P. (1993). Learning from queries and examples with tree-structured bias. In *ICML-93*, pp. 322–329.

Tadepalli, P., Givan, R., and Driessens, K. (2004). Relational reinforcement learning: An overview. In *ICML-04*.

Tait, P. G. (1880). Note on the theory of the "15 puzzle". *Proc. Royal Society of Edinburgh*, *10*, 664–665.

Tamaki, H. and Sato, T. (1986). OLD resolution with tabulation. In *ICLP-86*, pp. 84–98.

Tarjan, R. E. (1983). *Data Structures and Network Algorithms*. CBMS-NSF Regional Conference Series in Applied Mathematics. SIAM (Society for Industrial and Applied Mathematics).

Tarski, A. (1935). Die Wahrheitsbegriff in den formalisierten Sprachen. *Studia Philosophica*, *1*, 261–405.

Tarski, A. (1941). *Introduction to Logic and to the Methodology of Deductive Sciences*. Dover.

Tarski, A. (1956). *Logic, Semantics, Metamathematics: Papers from 1923 to 1938*. Oxford University Press.

Tash, J. K. and Russell, S. J. (1994). Control strategies for a stochastic planner. In *AAAI-94*, pp. 1079–1085.

Taskar, B., Abbeel, P., and Koller, D. (2002). Discriminative probabilistic models for relational data. In *UAI-02*.

Tate, A. (1975a). Interacting goals and their use. In *IJCAI-75*, pp. 215–218.

Tate, A. (1975b). *Using Goal Structure to Direct Search in a Problem Solver*. Ph.D. thesis, University of Edinburgh.

Tate, A. (1977). Generating project networks. In *IJCAI-77*, pp. 888–893.

Tate, A. and Whiter, A. M. (1984). Planning with multiple resource constraints and an application to a naval planning problem. In *Proc. First Conference on AI Applications*, pp. 410–416.

Tatman, J. A. and Shachter, R. D. (1990). Dynamic programming and influence diagrams. *IEEE Transactions on Systems, Man and Cybernetics*, *20*(2), 365–379.

Tattersall, C. (1911). *A Thousand End-Games: A Collection of Chess Positions That Can be Won or Drawn by the Best Play*. British Chess Magazine.

Taylor, G., Stensrud, B., Eitelman, S., and Dunham, C. (2007). Towards automating airspace management. In *Proc. Computational Intelligence for Security and Defense Applications (CISDA) Conference*, pp. 1–5.

Tenenbaum, J., Griffiths, T., and Niyogi, S. (2007). Intuitive theories as grammars for causal inference. In Gopnik, A. and Schulz, L. (Eds.), *Causal learning: Psychology, Philosophy, and Computation*. Oxford University Press.

Tesauro, G. (1992). Practical issues in temporal difference learning. *Machine Learning*, *8*(3–4), 257–277.

Tesauro, G. (1995). Temporal difference learning and TD-Gammon. *CACM*, *38*(3), 58–68.

Tesauro, G. and Sejnowski, T. (1989). A parallel network that learns to play backgammon. *AIJ*, *39*(3), 357–390.

Teyssier, M. and Koller, D. (2005). Ordering-based search: A simple and effective algorithm for learning Bayesian networks. In *UAI-05*, pp. 584–590.

Thaler, R. (1992). *The Winner's Curse: Paradoxes and Anomalies of Economic Life*. Princeton University Press.

Thaler, R. and Sunstein, C. (2009). *Nudge: Improving Decisions About Health, Wealth, and Happiness*. Penguin.

Theocharous, G., Murphy, K., and Kaelbling, L. P. (2004). Representing hierarchical POMDPs as DBNs for multi-scale robot localization. In *ICRA-04*.

Thiele, T. (1880). Om anvendelse af mindste kvadraters methode i nogle tilfælde, hvor en komplikation af visse slags uensartede tilfældige fejlkilder giver fejlene en 'systematisk' karakter. *Vidensk. Selsk. Skr. 5. Rk., naturvid. og mat. Afd.*, *12*, 381–408.

Thielscher, M. (1999). From situation calculus to fluent calculus: State update axioms as a solution to the inferential frame problem. *AIJ*, *111*(1–2), 277–299.

Thompson, K. (1986). Retrograde analysis of certain endgames. *J. International Computer Chess Association, May*, 131–139.

Thompson, K. (1996). 6-piece endgames. *J. International Computer Chess Association*, *19*(4), 215–226.

Thrun, S., Burgard, W., and Fox, D. (2005). *Probabilistic Robotics*. MIT Press.

Thrun, S., Fox, D., and Burgard, W. (1998). A probabilistic approach to concurrent mapping and localization for mobile robots. *Machine Learning*, *31*, 29–53.

Thrun, S. (2006). Stanley, the robot that won the DARPA Grand Challenge. *J. Field Robotics*, *23*(9), 661–692.

Tikhonov, A. N. (1963). Solution of incorrectly formulated problems and the regularization method. *Soviet Math. Dokl.*, *5*, 1035–1038.

Titterington, D. M., Smith, A. F. M., and Makov, U. E. (1985). *Statistical analysis of finite mixture distributions*. Wiley.

Toffler, A. (1970). *Future Shock*. Bantam.

Tomasi, C. and Kanade, T. (1992). Shape and motion from image streams under orthography: A factorization method. *IJCV*, *9*, 137–154.

Torralba, A., Fergus, R., and Weiss, Y. (2008). Small codes and large image databases for recognition. In *CVPR*, pp. 1–8.

Trucco, E. and Verri, A. (1998). *Introductory Techniques for 3-D Computer Vision*. Prentice Hall.

Tsitsiklis, J. N. and Van Roy, B. (1997). An analysis of temporal-difference learning with function approximation. *IEEE Transactions on Automatic Control*, *42*(5), 674–690.

Tumer, K. and Wolpert, D. (2000). Collective intelligence and braess' paradox. In *AAAI-00*, pp. 104–109.

Turcotte, M., Muggleton, S. H., and Sternberg, M. J. E. (2001). Automated discovery of structural signatures of protein fold and function. *J. Molecular Biology*, *306*, 591–605.

Turing, A. (1936). On computable numbers, with an application to the Entscheidungsproblem. *Proc. London Mathematical Society, 2nd series*, *42*, 230–265.

Turing, A. (1948). Intelligent machinery. Tech. rep., National Physical Laboratory. reprinted in (Ince, 1992).

Turing, A. (1950). Computing machinery and intelligence. *Mind*, *59*, 433–460.

Turing, A., Strachey, C., Bates, M. A., and Bowden, B. V. (1953). Digital computers applied to games. In Bowden, B. V. (Ed.), *Faster than Thought*, pp. 286–310. Pitman.

Tversky, A. and Kahneman, D. (1982). Causal schemata in judgements under uncertainty. In Kahneman, D., Slovic, P., and Tversky, A. (Eds.), *Judgement Under Uncertainty: Heuristics and Biases*. Cambridge University Press.

Ullman, J. D. (1985). Implementation of logical query languages for databases. *ACM Transactions on Database Systems*, *10*(3), 289–321.

Ullman, S. (1979). *The Interpretation of Visual Motion*. MIT Press.

Urmson, C. and Whittaker, W. (2008). Self-driving cars and the Urban Challenge. *IEEE Intelligent Systems*, *23*(2), 66–68.

Valiant, L. (1984). A theory of the learnable. *CACM*, *27*, 1134–1142.

van Beek, P. (2006). Backtracking search algorithms. In Rossi, F., van Beek, P., and Walsh, T. (Eds.), *Handbook of Constraint Programming*. Elsevier.

van Beek, P. and Chen, X. (1999). CPlan: A constraint programming approach to planning. In *AAAI-99*, pp. 585–590.

van Beek, P. and Manchak, D. (1996). The design and experimental analysis of algorithms for temporal reasoning. *JAIR*, *4*, 1–18.

van Bentham, J. and ter Meulen, A. (1997). *Handbook of Logic and Language*. MIT Press.

Van Emden, M. H. and Kowalski, R. (1976). The semantics of predicate logic as a programming language. *JACM*, *23*(4), 733–742.

van Harmelen, F. and Bundy, A. (1988). Explanation-based generalisation = partial evaluation. *AIJ*, *36*(3), 401–412.

van Harmelen, F., Lifschitz, V., and Porter, B. (2007). *The Handbook of Knowledge Representation*. Elsevier.

van Heijenoort, J. (Ed.). (1967). *From Frege to Gödel: A Source Book in Mathematical Logic, 1879–1931*. Harvard University Press.

Van Hentenryck, P., Saraswat, V., and Deville, Y. (1998). Design, implementation, and evaluation of the constraint language cc(FD). *J. Logic Programming*, *37*(1–3), 139–164.

van Hoeve, W.-J. (2001). The alldifferent constraint: a survey. In *6th Annual Workshop of the ERCIM Working Group on Constraints*.

van Hoeve, W.-J. and Katriel, I. (2006). Global constraints. In Rossi, F., van Beek, P., and Walsh, T. (Eds.), *Handbook of Constraint Processing*, pp. 169–208. Elsevier.

van Lambalgen, M. and Hamm, F. (2005). *The Proper Treatment of Events*. Wiley-Blackwell.

van Nunen, J. A. E. E. (1976). A set of successive approximation methods for discounted Markovian decision problems. *Zeitschrift fur Operations Research, Serie A*, *20*(5), 203–208.

Van Roy, B. (1998). *Learning and value function approximation in complex decision processes*. Ph.D. thesis, Laboratory for Information and Decision Systems, MIT.

Van Roy, P. L. (1990). Can logic programming execute as fast as imperative programming? Report UCB/CSD 90/600, Computer Science Division, University of California, Berkeley, California.

Vapnik, V. N. (1998). *Statistical Learning Theory*. Wiley.

Vapnik, V. N. and Chervonenkis, A. Y. (1971). On the uniform convergence of relative frequencies of events to their probabilities. *Theory of Probability and Its Applications*, *16*, 264–280.

Varian, H. R. (1995). Economic mechanism design for computerized agents. In *USENIX Workshop on Electronic Commerce*, pp. 13–21.

Vauquois, B. (1968). A survey of formal grammars and algorithms for recognition and transformation in mechanical translation. In *Proc. IFIP Congress*, pp. 1114–1122.

Veloso, M. and Carbonell, J. G. (1993). Derivational analogy in PRODIGY: Automating case acquisition, storage, and utilization. *Machine Learning*, *10*, 249–278.

Vere, S. A. (1983). Planning in time: Windows and durations for activities and goals. *PAMI*, *5*, 246–267.

Verma, V., Gordon, G., Simmons, R., and Thrun, S. (2004). Particle filters for rover fault diagnosis. *IEEE Robotics and Automation Magazine, June*.

Vinge, V. (1993). The coming technological singularity: How to survive in the post-human era. In *VISION-21 Symposium*. NASA Lewis Research Center and the Ohio Aerospace Institute.

Viola, P. and Jones, M. (2002a). Fast and robust classification using asymmetric adaboost and a detector cascade. In *NIPS 14*.

Viola, P. and Jones, M. (2002b). Robust real-time object detection. *ICCV*.

Visser, U. and Burkhard, H.-D. (2007). RoboCup 2006: achievements and goals for the future. *AIMag*, *28*(2), 115–130.

Visser, U., Ribeiro, F., Ohashi, T., and Dellaert, F. (Eds.). (2008). *RoboCup 2007: Robot Soccer World Cup XI*. Springer.

Viterbi, A. J. (1967). Error bounds for convolutional codes and an asymptotically optimum decoding algorithm. *IEEE Transactions on Information Theory*, *13*(2), 260–269.

Vlassis, N. (2008). *A Concise Introduction to Multiagent Systems and Distributed Artificial Intelligence*. Morgan and Claypool.

von Mises, R. (1928). *Wahrscheinlichkeit, Statistik und Wahrheit*. J. Springer.

von Neumann, J. (1928). Zur Theorie der Gesellschaftsspiele. *Mathematische Annalen*, *100*(295–320).

von Neumann, J. and Morgenstern, O. (1944). *Theory of Games and Economic Behavior* (first edition). Princeton University Press.

von Winterfeldt, D. and Edwards, W. (1986). *Decision Analysis and Behavioral Research*. Cambridge University Press.

Vossen, T., Ball, M., Lotem, A., and Nau, D. S. (2001). Applying integer programming to AI planning. *Knowledge Engineering Review*, *16*, 85–100.

Wainwright, M. J. and Jordan, M. I. (2008). Graphical models, exponential families, and variational inference. *Machine Learning*, *1*(1–2), 1–305.

Waldinger, R. (1975). Achieving several goals simultaneously. In Elcock, E. W. and Michie, D. (Eds.), *Machine Intelligence 8*, pp. 94–138. Ellis Horwood.

Wallace, A. R. (1858). On the tendency of varieties to depart indefinitely from the original type. *Proc. Linnean Society of London*, *3*, 53–62.

Waltz, D. (1975). Understanding line drawings of scenes with shadows. In Winston, P. H. (Ed.), *The Psychology of Computer Vision*. McGraw-Hill.

Wang, Y. and Gelly, S. (2007). Modifications of UCT and sequence-like simulations for Monte-Carlo Go. In *IEEE Symposium on Computational Intelligence and Games*, pp. 175–182.

Wanner, E. (1974). *On remembering, forgetting and understanding sentences*. Mouton.

Warren, D. H. D. (1974). WARPLAN: A System for Generating Plans. Department of Computational Logic Memo 76, University of Edinburgh.

Warren, D. H. D. (1983). An abstract Prolog instruction set. Technical note 309, SRI International.

Warren, D. H. D., Pereira, L. M., and Pereira, F. (1977). PROLOG: The language and its implementation compared with LISP. *SIGPLAN Notices*, *12*(8), 109–115.

Wasserman, L. (2004). *All of Statistics*. Springer.

Watkins, C. J. (1989). *Models of Delayed Reinforcement Learning*. Ph.D. thesis, Psychology Department, Cambridge University.

Watson, J. D. and Crick, F. H. C. (1953). A structure for deoxyribose nucleic acid. *Nature*, *171*, 737.

Waugh, K., Schnizlein, D., Bowling, M., and Szafron, D. (2009). Abstraction pathologies in extensive games. In *AAMAS-09*.

Weaver, W. (1949). Translation. In Locke, W. N. and Booth, D. (Eds.), *Machine translation of languages: fourteen essays*, pp. 15–23. Wiley.

Webber, B. L. and Nilsson, N. J. (Eds.). (1981). *Readings in Artificial Intelligence*. Morgan Kaufmann.

Weibull, J. (1995). *Evolutionary Game Theory*. MIT Press.

Weidenbach, C. (2001). SPASS: Combining superposition, sorts and splitting. In Robinson, A. and Voronkov, A. (Eds.), *Handbook of Automated Reasoning*. MIT Press.

Weiss, G. (2000a). *Multiagent systems*. MIT Press.

Weiss, Y. (2000b). Correctness of local probability propagation in graphical models with loops. *Neural Computation*, *12*(1), 1–41.

Weiss, Y. and Freeman, W. (2001). Correctness of belief propagation in Gaussian graphical models of arbitrary topology. *Neural Computation*, *13*(10), 2173–2200.

Weizenbaum, J. (1976). *Computer Power and Human Reason*. W. H. Freeman.

Weld, D. S. (1994). An introduction to least commitment planning. *AIMag*, *15*(4), 27–61.

Weld, D. S. (1999). Recent advances in AI planning. *AIMag*, *20*(2), 93–122.

Weld, D. S., Anderson, C. R., and Smith, D. E. (1998). Extending graphplan to handle uncertainty and sensing actions. In *AAAI-98*, pp. 897–904.

Weld, D. S. and de Kleer, J. (1990). *Readings in Qualitative Reasoning about Physical Systems*. Morgan Kaufmann.

Weld, D. S. and Etzioni, O. (1994). The first law of robotics: A call to arms. In *AAAI-94*.

Wellman, M. P. (1985). Reasoning about preference models. Technical report MIT/LCS/TR-340, Laboratory for Computer Science, MIT.

Wellman, M. P. (1988). *Formulation of Tradeoffs in Planning under Uncertainty*. Ph.D. thesis, Massachusetts Institute of Technology.

Wellman, M. P. (1990a). Fundamental concepts of qualitative probabilistic networks. *AIJ*, *44*(3), 257–303.

Wellman, M. P. (1990b). The STRIPS assumption for planning under uncertainty. In *AAAI-90*, pp. 198–203.

Wellman, M. P. (1995). The economic approach to artificial intelligence. *ACM Computing Surveys*, *27*(3), 360–362.

Wellman, M. P., Breese, J. S., and Goldman, R. (1992). From knowledge bases to decision models. *Knowledge Engineering Review*, *7*(1), 35–53.

Wellman, M. P. and Doyle, J. (1992). Modular utility representation for decision-theoretic planning. In *ICAPS-92*, pp. 236–242.

Wellman, M. P., Wurman, P., O'Malley, K., Bangera, R., Lin, S., Reeves, D., and Walsh, W. (2001). A trading agent competition. *IEEE Internet Computing*.

Wells, H. G. (1898). *The War of the Worlds*. William Heinemann.

Werbos, P. (1974). *Beyond Regression: New Tools for Prediction and Analysis in the Behavioral Sciences*. Ph.D. thesis, Harvard University.

Werbos, P. (1977). Advanced forecasting methods for global crisis warning and models of intelligence. *General Systems Yearbook*, *22*, 25–38.

Wesley, M. A. and Lozano-Perez, T. (1979). An algorithm for planning collision-free paths among polyhedral objects. *CACM*, *22*(10), 560–570.

Wexler, Y. and Meek, C. (2009). MAS: A multiplicative approximation scheme for probabilistic inference. In *NIPS 21*.

Whitehead, A. N. (1911). *An Introduction to Mathematics*. Williams and Northgate.

Whitehead, A. N. and Russell, B. (1910). *Principia Mathematica*. Cambridge University Press.

Whorf, B. (1956). *Language, Thought, and Reality*. MIT Press.

Widrow, B. (1962). Generalization and information storage in networks of adaline "neurons". In *Self-Organizing Systems 1962*, pp. 435–461.

Widrow, B. and Hoff, M. E. (1960). Adaptive switching circuits. In *1960 IRE WESCON Convention Record*, pp. 96–104.

Wiedijk, F. (2003). Comparing mathematical provers. In *Mathematical Knowledge Management*, pp. 188–202.

Wiegley, J., Goldberg, K., Peshkin, M., and Brokowski, M. (1996). A complete algorithm for designing passive fences to orient parts. In *ICRA-96*.

Wiener, N. (1942). The extrapolation, interpolation, and smoothing of stationary time series. Osrd 370, Report to the Services 19, Research Project DIC-6037, MIT.

Wiener, N. (1948). *Cybernetics*. Wiley.

Wilensky, R. (1978). *Understanding goal-based stories*. Ph.D. thesis, Yale University.

Wilensky, R. (1983). *Planning and Understanding*. Addison-Wesley.

Wilkins, D. E. (1980). Using patterns and plans in chess. *AIJ*, *14*(2), 165–203.

Wilkins, D. E. (1988). *Practical Planning: Extending the AI Planning Paradigm*. Morgan Kaufmann.

Wilkins, D. E. (1990). Can AI planners solve practical problems? *Computational Intelligence*, *6*(4), 232–246.

Williams, B., Ingham, M., Chung, S., and Elliott, P. (2003). Model-based programming of intelligent embedded systems and robotic space explorers. In *Proc. IEEE: Special Issue on Modeling and Design of Embedded Software*, pp. 212–237.

Williams, R. J. (1992). Simple statistical gradient-following algorithms for connectionist reinforcement learning. *Machine Learning*, *8*, 229–256.

Williams, R. J. and Baird, L. C. I. (1993). Tight performance bounds on greedy policies based on imperfect value functions. Tech. rep. NU-CCS-93-14, College of Computer Science, Northeastern University.

Wilson, R. A. and Keil, F. C. (Eds.). (1999). *The MIT Encyclopedia of the Cognitive Sciences*. MIT Press.

Wilson, R. (2004). *Four Colors Suffice*. Princeton University Press.

Winograd, S. and Cowan, J. D. (1963). *Reliable Computation in the Presence of Noise*. MIT Press.

Winograd, T. (1972). Understanding natural language. *Cognitive Psychology*, *3*(1), 1–191.

Winston, P. H. (1970). Learning structural descriptions from examples. Technical report MAC-TR-76, Department of Electrical Engineering and Computer Science, Massachusetts Institute of Technology.

Winston, P. H. (1992). *Artificial Intelligence* (Third edition). Addison-Wesley.

Wintermute, S., Xu, J., and Laird, J. (2007). SORTS: A human-level approach to real-time strategy AI. In *Proc. Third Artificial Intelligence and Interactive Digital Entertainment Conference (AIIDE-07)*.

Witten, I. H. and Bell, T. C. (1991). The zero-frequency problem: Estimating the probabilities of novel events in adaptive text compression. *IEEE Transactions on Information Theory*, *37*(4), 1085–1094.

Witten, I. H. and Frank, E. (2005). *Data Mining: Practical Machine Learning Tools and Techniques* (2nd edition). Morgan Kaufmann.

Witten, I. H., Moffat, A., and Bell, T. C. (1999). *Managing Gigabytes: Compressing and Indexing Documents and Images* (second edition). Morgan Kaufmann.

Wittgenstein, L. (1922). *Tractatus Logico-Philosophicus* (second edition). Routledge and Kegan Paul. Reprinted 1971, edited by D. F. Pears and B. F. McGuinness. This edition of the English translation also contains Wittgenstein's original German text on facing pages, as well as Bertrand Russell's introduction to the 1922 edition.

Wittgenstein, L. (1953). *Philosophical Investigations*. Macmillan.

Wojciechowski, W. S. and Wojcik, A. S. (1983). Automated design of multiple-valued logic circuits by automated theorem proving techniques. *IEEE Transactions on Computers*, *C-32*(9), 785–798.

Wolfe, J. and Russell, S. J. (2007). Exploiting belief state structure in graph search. In *ICAPS Workshop on Planning in Games*.

Woods, W. A. (1973). Progress in natural language understanding: An application to lunar geology. In *AFIPS Conference Proceedings*, Vol. 42, pp. 441–450.

Woods, W. A. (1975). What's in a link? Foundations for semantic networks. In Bobrow, D. G. and Collins, A. M. (Eds.), *Representation and Understanding: Studies in Cognitive Science*, pp. 35–82. Academic Press.

Wooldridge, M. (2002). *An Introduction to MultiAgent Systems*. Wiley.

Wooldridge, M. and Rao, A. (Eds.). (1999). *Foundations of rational agency*. Kluwer.

Wos, L., Carson, D., and Robinson, G. (1964). The unit preference strategy in theorem proving. In *Proc. Fall Joint Computer Conference*, pp. 615–621.

Wos, L., Carson, D., and Robinson, G. (1965). Efficiency and completeness of the set-of-support strategy in theorem proving. *JACM*, *12*, 536–541.

Wos, L., Overbeek, R., Lusk, E., and Boyle, J. (1992). *Automated Reasoning: Introduction and Applications* (second edition). McGraw-Hill.

Wos, L. and Robinson, G. (1968). Paramodulation and set of support. In *Proc. IRIA Symposium on Automatic Demonstration*, pp. 276–310.

Wos, L., Robinson, G., Carson, D., and Shalla, L. (1967). The concept of demodulation in theorem proving. *JACM*, *14*, 698–704.

Wos, L. and Winker, S. (1983). Open questions solved with the assistance of AURA. In *Automated Theorem Proving: After 25 Years: Proc. Special Session of the 89th Annual Meeting of the American Mathematical Society*, pp. 71–88. American Mathematical Society.

Wos, L. and Pieper, G. (2003). *Automated Reasoning and the Discovery of Missing and Elegant Proofs*. Rinton Press.

Wray, R. E. and Jones, R. M. (2005). An introduction to Soar as an agent architecture. In Sun, R. (Ed.), *Cognition and Multi-agent Interaction: From Cognitive Modeling to Social Simulation*, pp. 53–78. Cambridge University Press.

Wright, S. (1921). Correlation and causation. *J. Agricultural Research*, *20*, 557–585.

Wright, S. (1931). Evolution in Mendelian populations. *Genetics*, *16*, 97–159.

Wright, S. (1934). The method of path coefficients. *Annals of Mathematical Statistics*, *5*, 161–215.

Wu, D. (1993). Estimating probability distributions over hypotheses with variable unification. In *IJCAI-93*, pp. 790–795.

Wu, F. and Weld, D. S. (2008). Automatically refining the wikipedia infobox ontology. In *17th World Wide Web Conference (WWW2008)*.

Yang, F., Culberson, J., Holte, R., Zahavi, U., and Felner, A. (2008). A general theory of additive state space abstractions. *JAIR*, *32*, 631–662.

Yang, Q. (1990). Formalizing planning knowledge for hierarchical planning. *Computational Intelligence*, *6*, 12–24.

Yarowsky, D. (1995). Unsupervised word sense disambiguation rivaling supervised methods. In *ACL-95*, pp. 189–196.

Yedidia, J., Freeman, W., and Weiss, Y. (2005). Constructing free-energy approximations and generalized belief propagation algorithms. *IEEE Transactions on Information Theory*, *51*(7), 2282–2312.

Yip, K. M.-K. (1991). *KAM: A System for Intelligently Guiding Numerical Experimentation by Computer*. MIT Press.

Yngve, V. (1955). A model and an hypothesis for language structure. In Locke, W. N. and Booth, A. D. (Eds.), *Machine Translation of Languages*, pp. 208–226. MIT Press.

Yob, G. (1975). Hunt the wumpus! *Creative Computing, Sep/Oct*.

Yoshikawa, T. (1990). *Foundations of Robotics: Analysis and Control*. MIT Press.

Young, H. P. (2004). *Strategic Learning and Its Limits*. Oxford University Press.

Younger, D. H. (1967). Recognition and parsing of context-free languages in time n^3. *Information and Control*, *10*(2), 189–208.

Yudkowsky, E. (2008). Artificial intelligence as a positive and negative factor in global risk. In Bostrom, N. and Cirkovic, M. (Eds.), *Global Catastrophic Risk*. Oxford University Press.

Zadeh, L. A. (1965). Fuzzy sets. *Information and Control*, *8*, 338–353.

Zadeh, L. A. (1978). Fuzzy sets as a basis for a theory of possibility. *Fuzzy Sets and Systems*, *1*, 3–28.

Zaritskii, V. S., Svetnik, V. B., and Shimelevich, L. I. (1975). Monte-Carlo technique in problems of optimal information processing. *Automation and Remote Control*, *36*, 2015–22.

Zelle, J. and Mooney, R. (1996). Learning to parse database queries using inductive logic programming. In *AAAI-96*, pp. 1050–1055.

Zermelo, E. (1913). Uber Eine Anwendung der Mengenlehre auf die Theorie des Schachspiels. In *Proc. Fifth International Congress of Mathematicians*, Vol. 2, pp. 501–504.

Zermelo, E. (1976). An application of set theory to the theory of chess-playing. *Firbush News*, *6*, 37–42. English translation of (Zermelo 1913).

Zettlemoyer, L. S. and Collins, M. (2005). Learning to map sentences to logical form: Structured classification with probabilistic categorial grammars. In *UAI-05*.

Zhang, H. and Stickel, M. E. (1996). An efficient algorithm for unit-propagation. In *Proc. Fourth International Symposium on Artificial Intelligence and Mathematics*.

Zhang, L., Pavlovic, V., Cantor, C. R., and Kasif, S. (2003). Human-mouse gene identification by comparative evidence integration and evolutionary analysis. *Genome Research*, pp. 1–13.

Zhang, N. L. and Poole, D. (1994). A simple approach to Bayesian network computations. In *Proc. 10th Canadian Conference on Artificial Intelligence*, pp. 171–178.

Zhang, N. L., Qi, R., and Poole, D. (1994). A computational theory of decision networks. *IJAR*, *11*, 83–158.

Zhou, R. and Hansen, E. (2002). Memory-bounded A* graph search. In *Proc. 15th International Flairs Conference*.

Zhou, R. and Hansen, E. (2006). Breadth-first heuristic search. *AIJ*, *170*(4–5), 385–408.

Zhu, D. J. and Latombe, J.-C. (1991). New heuristic algorithms for efficient hierarchical path planning. *IEEE Transactions on Robotics and Automation*, *7*(1), 9–20.

Zimmermann, H.-J. (Ed.). (1999). *Practical applications of fuzzy technologies*. Kluwer.

Zimmermann, H.-J. (2001). *Fuzzy Set Theory—And Its Applications* (Fourth edition). Kluwer.

Zinkevich, M., Johanson, M., Bowling, M., and Piccione, C. (2008). Regret minimization in games with incomplete information. In *NIPS 20*, pp. 1729–1736.

Zollmann, A., Venugopal, A., Och, F. J., and Ponte, J. (2008). A systematic comparison of phrase-based, hierarchical and syntax-augmented statistical MT. In *COLING-08*.

Zweig, G. and Russell, S. J. (1998). Speech recognition with dynamic Bayesian networks. In *AAAI-98*, pp. 173–180.

Index

Page references followed by "f" indicate illustrated figures or photographs; followed by "t" indicates a table.

C

D

E

N

O

P

Q

R

S

T

U

V

W

X

Y

Z